CW01084024

A DICTIONARY OF SCRIPTURE PROPER NAMES

WITH THEIR PRONUNCIATION AND MEANING

TOGETHER WITH

A SUBJECT INDEX

AND

CONCORDANCE

FROM

THE HELPS TO THE STUDY OF THE BIBLE

LONDON
OXFORD · AT THE UNIVERSITY PRESS
NEW YORK TORONTO

New Ruby

Oxford University Press, Walton Street, Oxford OX2 6DP

OXFORD LONDON GLASGOW NEW YORK
TORONTO MELBOURNE WELLINGTON CAPE TOWN
IBADAN NAIROBI DAR ES SALAAM LUSAKA ADDIS ABABA
KUALA LUMPUR SINGAPORE JAKARTA HONG KONG TOKYO
DELHI BOMBAY CALCUTTA MADRAS KARACHI

Printed in Great Britain

DICTIONARY OF
SCRIPTURE PROPER NAMES

TOGETHER WITH COMPENDIOUS REFERENCES TO SOME OF THE PRINCIPAL INCIDENTS CONNECTED WITH THE PERSONS AND PLACES MENTIONED IN HOLY SCRIPTURE

[NOTE.—*The accent (′) shows where the stress of the voice should fall.* (?) *denotes meanings which are conjectural. Modern research has caused some of the older interpretations given in this list to be questioned.*]

AARON, a′ron, light (?). Ex. 4. 14.
BROTHER of MOSES, the FIRST HIGH PRIEST, cometh forth to meet Moses; can speak well.
appointed by God to be Moses' spokesman. Ex. 4. 14, 16, 27.
with Moses appeals to Pharaoh; chided by him. Ex. 5. 1.
his rod becomes a serpent. Ex. 7. 10.
changes the waters into blood. Ex. 7. 20.
causes the plagues of frogs, lice, flies. Ex. 8. 5, 17, 24.
with Moses—the plague of boils. Ex. 9. 10.
with Hur holds up Moses' hands. Ex. 17. 12.
set apart for priest's office. Ex. 28.
makes the golden calf. Ex. 32. 4; God's anger thereat. Ex. 32. 7; Deut. 9. 20.
his excuse to Moses. Ex. 32. 22.
consecration. Ex. 29; Lev. 8.
offers sacrifice. Lev. 9.
his sons (Nadab and Abihu) offer strange fire, and die. Lev. 10. 1; Num. 3. 4.
his sons (Eleazar and Ithamar) censured by Moses. Lev. 10. 16.
not to drink wine when going into the tabernacle. Lev. 10. 8.
speaks against Moses. Num. 12.
rebuked by God. Num. 12. 9.
spoken against by Korah. Num. 16. 3.
makes atonement, and the plague is stayed. Num. 16. 46–48.
his rod buds, and is kept in ark for a token. Num. 17. 8.
for unbelief excluded from the promised land. Num. 20. 12.
dies on mount Hor. Num. 20. 28.
chosen by God. Ps. 105. 26; Heb. 5. 4.
his line. 1 Chr. 6. 49.

AARONITES, a′ron-ites, descendants of Aaron. 1 Chr. 12. 27.

ABADDON, a-bad′don, destruction.
angel of the bottomless pit. Rev. 9. 11.

ABAGTHA, a-bag′thah, given by fortune. Esth. 1. 10.

ABANA, a-ba′nah, stony.
river of Damascus. 2 Kin. 5. 12.

ABARIM, a-ba′rim, regions beyond. Num. 27. 12.
mountains of, including Nebo, Pisgah, Hor. Deut. 32. 49.

ABBA, ab′bah, father. Mark 14. 36; Rom. 8. 15; Gal. 4. 6.

ABDA, ab′dah, servant. 1 Kin. 4. 6.

ABDEEL, ab′de-el, same as ABDIEL. Jer. 36. 26.

ABDI, ab′di, servant of Jehovah. 1 Chr. 6. 44.

ABDIEL, ab′di-el, *s.* of God. 1 Chr. 5. 15.

ABDON, ab′don, servile. A judge. Judg. 12. 13.

ABED-NEGO, a-bed′ne-go, servant or worshipper of Nebo. Dan. 1. 7.
saved in fiery furnace. Dan. 3. *See* Is. 43. 2.

ABEL, a′bel, (1) vanity. Gen. 4. 2. (2) A meadow. 2 Sam. 20. 14.
second son of Adam. Gen. 4. 2.

ABEL—*cont.*
his offering accepted. Gen. 4. 4.
slain by Cain. Gen. 4. 8.
righteous. Matt. 23, 35; 1 John 3. 12.
blood of. Luke 11. 51; Heb. 12. 24.
faith of. Heb. 11. 4.

ABEL-BETH-MAACHAH, a′bel-beth-ma′a-kah, meadow of the house of Maachah. 1 Kin. 15. 20.

ABEL-MAIM, a′bel-ma′im, *m.* of the waters. 2 Chr. 16. 4.

ABEL-MEHOLAH, a′bel-me-ho′lah, *m.* of dancing. Judg. 7. 22; 1 Kin. 4. 12; 19. 16.

ABEL-MIZRAIM, a′bel-miz-ra′im, *m.* of Egypt. Mourning of the Egyptians. Gen. 50. 11.

ABEL-SHITTIM, a′bel-shit′im, *m.* of acacias. Num. 33. 49.

ABEZ, a′bez, whiteness. Josh. 19. 20.

ABI, a′bi, shortened form of ABIAH. 2 Kin. 18. 2.

ABIA, a-bi′ah, Greek form of following. Matt. 1. 7.

ABIAH, a-bi′ah, same as ABIJAH. 2 Kin. 18. 2.

ABI-ALBON, a′bi-al′bon, father of strength. 2 Sam. 23. 31.

ABIASAPH, a-bi′a-saf, *f.* of gathering. Ex. 6. 24.

ABIATHAR, ab-ia′thar, *f.* of plenty. 1 Sam. 22. 20.

ABIB, a′bib, an ear of corn, or green ear. Ex. 13. 4.
the Hebrew passover month. Ex. 23. 15; 34. 18.

ABIDAH, a-bi′dah, father of knowledge. Gen. 25. 4.

ABIDAN, a-bi′dan, *f.* of a judge. Num. 1. 11.

ABIEL, a-bi′el, *f.* of strength. 1 Sam. 9. 1.

ABIEZER, a′bi-e′zer, *f.* of help. Josh. 17. 2.
ancestor of Gideon. Judg. 6.

ABIEZRITE, a′bi-ez′rite, a descendant of ABIEZER. Judg. 6. 11.

ABIGAIL, a-bi-ga′le, father of exultation. 1 Sam. 25. 14.
wife of Nabal, and afterwards of David. 1 Sam. 25. 39.
mother of Chileab, according to 2 Sam. 3. 3, or Daniel, according to 1 Chr. 3. 1.

ABIHAIL, a-bi-ha′le, *f.* of strength. Num. 3. 35.

ABIHU, a-bi′hoo, He (*i.e.* God) is my *f.* Ex. 6. 23.
brother of Nadab, offers strange fire, and dies. Lev. 10. 2.

ABIHUD, a-bi′hood, *f.* of Judah. 1 Chr. 8. 3.

ABIJAH, a-bi′jah, *f.* of Jehovah. 1 Kin. 14. 1.
king of Judah, walked in the sins of his father. 1 Kin. 15. 3.
makes war against Israel. 2 Chr. 13.
—— (son of Jeroboam), his death foretold by Ahijah the prophet. 1 Kin. 14. 12.

ABIJAM, a-bi′jam, another mode of spelling ABIJAH. 1 Kin. 14. 31.

ABILENE, a′bi-le′ne, a grassy place (?). Luke 3. 1.

ABIMAEL, a-bi-ma′el, father of Mael. Gen. 10. 28.

ABIMELECH, a-bi′me-lek, *f.* of the king. Gen. 20. 2.
(king of Gerar) reproved by God about Abraham's wife. Gen. 20. 3.
rebukes Abraham and restores Sarah. Gen. 20. 9, 14.
healed at Abraham's prayer. Gen. 20. 17.

ABIMELECH—*cont.*
—— (another), Isaac rebuked by, for denying his wife. Gen. 26. 10.
covenants with Isaac. Gen. 26. 27.
—— (king at Shechem), son of the judge Gideon. Judg. 8. 31.
murders his brethren. Judg. 9. 5.
his death. Judg. 9. 54.
ABINADAB, a-bi´na-dab, *f.* of nobility. 1 Sam. 7. 1.
receives the ark from Philistines. 2 Sam. 6. 3.
ABINER, ab´ner, same as ABNER. 1 Sam. 14. 50.
ABINOAM, a-bi-no´am, *f.* of pleasantness. Judg. 4. 6.
ABIRAM, a-bi´ram, *f.* of loftiness. Num. 16. 1.
with Korah and Dathan, rebels against Moses. Num. 16.
his punishment. Num. 16. 31; 26. 10.
ABISHAG, a-bi´shag, *f.* of error (?). 1 Kin. 1. 3.
the Shunammite, ministers to David, cause of breach between Solomon and Adonijah. 1 Kin. 2. 22.
ABISHAI, a-bi´shai, *f.* of a gift. 1 Sam. 26. 6.
brother of Joab. 1 Chr. 2. 16.
with David carries off Saul's spear. 1 Sam. 26. 6–9.
slays three hundred men. 2 Sam. 23. 18. *See also* 1 Chr. 11. 20; 18. 12.
ABISHALOM, a-bi´sha-lom´, *f.* of peace. 1 Kin. 15. 2.
ABISHUA, a-bi-sho´o-ah, *f.* of welfare. 1 Chr. 6. 4.
ABISHUR, a-bi´shoor, *f.* of the wall. 1 Chr. 2. 28.
ABITAL, a-bi´tal, *f.* of dew. 2 Sam. 3. 4.
ABITUB, a-bi´toob, *f.* of goodness. 1 Chr. 8. 11.
ABIUD, a-bi´ood, Greek form of ABIHUD. Matt. 1. 13.
ABNER, ab´ner, *f.* of light. 1 Sam. 14. 50.
cousin of Saul, commander of his army. 1 Sam. 14. 50.
reproved by David. 1 Sam. 26. 5, 14.
makes Ish-bosheth king. 2 Sam. 2. 8.
goes over to David. 2 Sam. 3. 8.
slain by Joab. 2 Sam. 3. 27.
mourned by David. 2 Sam. 3. 31.
ABRAM, ab´ram, a high *f.* Gen. 11. 26.
ABRAHAM, a´bra-ham, *f.* of a great multitude. Gen. 17. 5.
—— (Abram) begotten by Terah. Gen. 11. 27.
blessed by God, and sent to Canaan. Gen. 12. 5.
goes down to Egypt. Gen. 12. 10.
causes his wife to pass as his sister. Gen. 12. 13; 20. 2.
strife between him and Lot. Gen. 13. 7.
separates from Lot. Gen. 13. 11.
his seed to be as the dust of the earth. Gen. 13. 16.
delivers Lot from captivity, and refuses the spoil. Gen. 14. 16.
blessed by Melchizedek, king of Salem. Gen. 14. 19; Heb. 7. 4.
his faith counted for righteousness. Gen. 15. 6.
God's covenant with. Gen. 15. 18; Ps. 105. 9.
he and house circumcised. Gen. 17.
entertains angels. Gen. 18.
pleads for Sodom. Gen. 18. 23.
sends away Hagar and Ishmael. Gen. 21. 14.
his faith in offering Isaac. Gen. 22.
buys Machpelah of Ephron the Hittite for a burying-place. Gen. 23.
sends for a wife for his son. Gen. 24.
gives his goods to Isaac. Gen. 25. 5.
dies (in a good old age). Gen. 25. 8.
his faith and works. Is. 41. 8; 51. 2; John 8. 31; Acts 7. 2; Rom. 4; Gal. 3. 6; Heb. 11. 8; James 2. 21.
his posterity. Gen. 25. 1.
ABSALOM, ab´sa-lom, *f.* of peace. 2 Sam. 3. 3.
David's son. 2 Sam. 3. 3.
slays Amnon. 2 Sam. 13. 28.
conspires against David. 2 Sam. 15.
David flies from. 2 Sam. 15. 17.
caught by head in an oak. 2 Sam. 18. 9.
slain by Joab. 2 Sam. 18. 14.
wept by David. 2 Sam. 18. 33; 19. 1.

ACCAD, ak´ad, fortress (?). Gen. 10. 10.
ACCHO, ak´o, sand-heated. Judg. 1. 31.
ACELDAMA, a-kel´da-mah´, field of blood. Matt. 27. 8; Acts 1. 19.
ACHAIA, a-ka´yah, Greece. Acts 18. 12.
Paul in. Acts 18.
contribution for poor by. Rom. 15. 26; 2 Cor. 9. 2. *See* 1 Cor. 16. 15; 2 Cor. 11. 10.
ACHAICUS, a-ka´ik-us, belonging to Achaia. 1 Cor. 16. 17.
ACHAN, or ACHAR, a´kan, a´kar, troubler. Josh. 7. 18.
takes the accursed thing; is stoned. Josh. 7; 22. 20; 1 Chr. 2. 7.
ACHAZ, a´kaz, Greek form of Ahaz. Matt. 1. 9.
ACHBOR, ak´bor, a mouse. Gen. 36. 38.
ACHIM, a´kim, short form of JACHIN (?). Matt. 1. 14.
ACHISH, a´kish, angry (?).
king of Gath, succours David. 1 Sam. 21. 10; 27. 2; 28. 1; 29. 6. *See* 1 Kin. 2. 39.
ACHMETHA, ak´me-thah, fortress (?). Ezra 6. 2.
ACHOR, a´kor, trouble. Josh. 7. 24.
valley of, Achan slain there. Josh. 7. 26. *See* Hos. 2. 15.
ACHSA, ak´sah, same as following. 1 Chr. 2. 49.
ACHSAH, ak´sah, anklet. Josh. 15. 16.
Caleb's daughter, won in marriage by Othniel. Judg. 1. 13.
asks her father's blessing. Judg. 1. 15.
ACHSHAPH, ak´shaf, enchantment. Josh. 11. 1.
ACHZIB, ak´zib, deceit. Josh. 15. 44.
ADADAH, a´d-a-dah, festival (?). Josh. 15. 22.
ADAH, a´dah, ornament. Gen. 4. 19.
ADAIAH, a-da´yah, whom Jehovah adorns. 2 Kin. 22. 1.
ADALIA, a-da´lyah, upright (?). Esth. 9. 8.
ADAM, a´dam, red. Gen. 2. 19.
created. Gen. 1.
called the son of God. Luke 3. 38.
blessed. Gen. 1. 28.
placed in Eden. Gen. 2. 8.
first called Adam. Gen. 2. 19.
creatures named by. Gen. 2. 19.
calls his wife Eve. Gen. 3. 20.
his fall and punishment. Gen. 3.
hides from God. Gen. 3. 8.
ground cursed for his sake. Gen. 3. 17.
his death. Gen. 5. 5.
his transgression. Job 31. 33; Rom. 5. 14.
first Adam. 1 Cor. 15. 45; 1 Tim. 2. 13.
in, all die. 1 Cor. 15. 22.
ADAM, the last. 1 Cor. 15. 45.
ADAMAH, a-dah´mah, red earth. Josh. 19. 36.
ADAMI, a-da´h-mi, human. Josh. 19. 33.
ADAR, a´dar, fire (?). Esth. 3. 7.
ADBEEL, ad´be-el, miracle of God (?). Gen. 25. 13.
ADDAN, a´d-dahn, humble (?).
a city of the captivity. Ezra 2. 59.
ADDAR, a´d-dar, greatness (?). 1 Chr. 8. 3.
ADDI, a´d-di, ornament (?). Luke 3. 28.
ADDON, a´d-don, same as ADDAN. Neh. 7. 61.
ADER, a´der, flock. 1 Chr. 8. 15.
ADIEL, a´di-el, ornament of God. 1 Chr. 4. 36.
ADIN, a´din, slender. Ezra 2. 15.
ADINA, a-di´nah, same as preceding. 1 Chr. 11. 42.
ADINO, a-di´no. 2 Sam. 23. 8.
ADITHAIM, a-di-tha´im, twofold ornament. Josh. 15. 36.
ADLAI, a´d-lai, just (?). 1 Chr. 27. 29.
ADMAH, ad´mah, same as ADAMAH. Gen. 10. 19.
city of the plain. *See* SODOM.
ADMATHA, ad´math-ah. Esth. 1. 14.
ADNA, ad´nah, pleasure. Ezra 10. 30.
ADNAH, same as preceding. 2 Chr. 17. 14.
ADONI-BEZEK, a-do´ni-be´zek, lord of Bezek. Judg. 1. 5.
ADONIJAH, a´do-ni´jah, Jehovah is my Lord. 2 Sam. 3. 4.
fourth son of David, usurps the kingdom. 1 Kin. 1. 5, 11, 25.

ADONIJAH—*cont.*
is pardoned by Solomon. 1 Kin. 1. 53.
seeking to obtain Abishag, is slain. 1 Kin. 2. 17–25.
ADONIKAM, a'-do-ni'-kam, lord of enemies. Ezra 2. 13.
ADONIRAM, a'-do-ni'-ram, lord of height. 1 Kin. 4. 6.
ADONI-ZEDEC, a-do'-ni-ze'-dek, lord of justice.
king of Jerusalem, resists Joshua. Josh. 10. 1.
his death. Josh. 10. 26.
ADORAIM, a-do-ra'-im, two chiefs (?). 2 Chr. 11. 9.
ADORAM, a-do'-ram, contracted from ADONIRAM. 2 Sam. 20. 24.
ADRAMMELECH, ad-ram'-me-lek, magnificence of the king (?), king of fire (?). 2 Kin. 17. 31.
ADRAMYTTIUM, ad'-ra-mit'-ti-um. Acts 27. 2.
ADRIA, a'-dri-ah. Acts 27. 27.
ADRIEL, a'd-ri-el, flock of God. 1 Sam. 18. 19.
ADULLAM, a-dul'-am, justice of the people. Josh. 12. 15.
cave of. 1 Sam. 22. 1; 1 Chr. 11. 15.
ADULLAMITE, a-dul'-am-ite, a native of Adullam. Gen. 38. 1.
ADUMMIM, a-dum'-im, the red (men?). Josh. 15. 7.
ÆNEAS, e'-ne-as, praiseworthy (?).
healing of. Acts 9. 33.
ÆNON, e'-non, springs. John baptizes at. John 3. 23.
AGABUS, ag'-ab-us, probably Greek form of Hagab.
famine and Paul's sufferings foretold by. Acts 11. 28; 21. 10.
AGAG, a'-gag, flaming (?). Num. 24. 7.
king of Amalek, spared by Saul, slain by Samuel. 1 Sam. 15.
spoken of by Balaam. Num. 24.
AGAGITE, a'-gag-ite. Esth. 3. 1.
AGAR, a'-gar, same as HAGAR. Gal. 4. 24.
AGEE, a'-gee, fugitive (?). 2 Sam. 23. 11.
AGRIPPA, a-grip'-ah. Acts 25. 13.
Paul's defence before. Acts 25. 22; 26.
almost persuaded. Acts 26. 28.
AGUR, a'-goor, an assembler.
prophecy. Prov. 30.
AHAB, a'-hab, uncle.
king of Israel. 1 Kin. 16. 29.
marries Jezebel; his idolatry. 1 Kin. 16. 31.
meets Elijah. 1 Kin. 18. 17.
defeats the Syrians. 1 Kin. 20.
punished for sparing Ben-hadad. 1 Kin. 20. 42.
takes Naboth's vineyard. 1 Kin. 21. 17.
his repentance. 1 Kin. 21. 27.
trusts false prophets, and is mortally wounded at Ramoth-gilead. 1 Kin. 22. 6, 34; 2 Chr. 18.
—— (son of Kolaiah), and Zedekiah, lying prophets. Jer. 29. 21.
AHARAH, a'-har-ah, after the brother. 1 Chr. 8. 1.
AHARHEL, a-har'-hel, behind the breastwork. 1 Chr. 4. 8.
AHASAI, a'-ha-zai, probably a corruption of JAHZERAH. Neh. 11. 13.
AHASBAI, a-ha's-bai. 2 Sam. 23. 34.
AHASUERUS, a-haz-u-e'-rus, king (?).
reigns from India to Ethiopia. Esth. 1. 1.
Vashti's disobedience to, and divorce. Esth. 1. 12; 2. 4.
makes Esther queen. Esth. 2. 17.
advances Haman. Esth. 3. 1.
his decree to destroy the Jews. Esth. 3. 12.
rewards Mordecai's loyalty. Esth. 6.
hangs Haman. Esth. 7. 9; 8. 7.
advances Mordecai. Esth. 9. 4; 10.
AHAVA, a'-ha-vah. Ezra 8. 15.
AHAZ, a'-haz, possessor. 2 Kin. 15. 38.
king of Judah. 2 Kin. 16.
spoils the temple. 2 Kin. 16. 17.
his idolatry. 2 Chr. 28. 2.
afflicted by Syrians. 2 Chr. 28. 5.
comforted by Isaiah. Is. 7.
will not ask a sign. Is. 7. 12.
AHAZIAH, a'-haz-i'-ah, whom Jehovah upholds. 1 Kin. 22. 40.

AHAZIAH—*cont.*
king of Judah, his wicked reign. 2 Kin. 8. 25.
goes with Joram to meet Jehu. 2 Kin. 9. 21.
smitten by Jehu. 2 Kin. 9. 27; 2 Chr. 22. 9.
—— king of Israel. 1 Kin. 22. 40, 49.
his sickness and idolatry. 2 Kin. 1.
his judgment by Elijah. 2 Kin. 1.
AHBAN, ah'-ban, brotherly. 1 Chr. 2. 29.
AHER, a'-her, following. 1 Chr. 7. 12.
AHI, a'-hi, brother. 1 Chr. 5. 15.
AHIAH, a-hi'-ah, brother of Jehovah. 1 Sam. 14. 3.
AHIAM, a-hi'-am, *b.* of the father (?). 2 Sam. 23. 33.
AHIAN, a-hi'-an, brotherly. 1 Chr. 7. 19.
AHIEZER, a'-hi-e'-zer, brother of help. Num. 1. 12.
AHIHUD, a-hi'-hood, *b.* of (?). Num. 34. 27.
AHIJAH, a-hi'-jah, same as AHIAH. 1 Kin. 11. 29.
prophesies to Jeroboam against Solomon. 1 Kin. 11. 31; against Jeroboam, and foretells his son's death. 1 Kin. 14. 7.
AHIKAM, a-hi'-kam, *b.* of the enemy. 2 Kin. 22. 12.
protects Jeremiah. Jer. 26. 24.
AHILUD, a-hi'-lood, *b.* of one born. 2 Sam. 8. 16.
AHIMAAZ, a-hi-ma'-az, *b.* of anger.
son of Zadok, serves David. 2 Sam. 15. 27; 17. 17; 18. 19.
AHIMAN, a-hi'-man, *b.* of a gift. Num. 13. 22.
AHIMELECH, a-hi'-me-lek, *b.* of the king. 1 Sam. 21. 1.
slain by Saul's order, for assisting David. 1 Sam. 22. 18.
AHIMOTH, a-hi'-moth, *b.* of death. 1 Chr. 6. 25.
AHINADAB, a-hi'-na-dab, *b.* of a nobleman. 1 Kin. 4. 14.
AHINOAM, a-hi-no'-am, *b.* of grace. 1 Sam. 14. 50.
AHIO, a-hi'-o, brotherly. 2 Sam. 6. 3.
AHIRA, a-hi'-rah, *b.* of a wicked man. Num. 1. 15.
AHIRAM, a-hi'-ram, *b.* of a tall man. Num. 26. 38.
AHIRAMITE, a-hi'-ram-ite, a descendant of Ahiram. Num. 26. 38.
AHISAMACH, a-hi'-sa-mak, *b.* of aid. Ex. 31. 6.
AHISHAHAR, a-hi'-sha-har, *b.* of the dawn. 1 Chr. 7. 10.
AHISHAR, a-hi'-shar, *b.* of the singer. 1 Kin. 4. 6.
AHITHOPHEL, a-hi'-tho-fel, *b.* of impiety. 2 Sam. 15. 12.
his treachery. 2 Sam. 15. 31; 16. 20.
disgrace, and suicide. 2 Sam. 17. 1, 23. *See* Ps. 41. 9; 55. 12; 109.
AHITUB, a-hi'-toob, *b.* of goodness. 1 Sam. 14. 3.
AHLAB, ah'-lab, fertility. Judg. 1. 31.
AHLAI, ah'-lai, sweet (?). 1 Chr. 2. 31.
AHOAH, a-ho'-ah, same as AHIJAH (?). 1 Chr. 8. 4.
AHOHITE, a-hoh'-ite, a descendant of Ahoah. 2 Sam. 23. 9.
AHOLAH, a-ho'-lah, (she has) her own tent.
—— (Samaria), and Aholibah (Jerusalem), their adulteries. Ezek. 23. 4.
AHOLIAB, a'-holi-a'b, father's tent. Ex. 31. 6.
inspired to construct the tabernacle. Ex. 35. 34; 36, &c.
AHOLIBAH, a'-hoii-b'ah, my tent is in her. Ezek. 23. 4.
AHOLIBAMAH, a'-holi-ba'-mah, tent of the high place. Gen. 36. 2.
AHUMAI, a-hoo'-mai, brother of (*i.e.* dweller near) water. 1 Chr. 4. 2.
AHUZAM, a-hooz'-am, their possession. 1 Chr. 4. 6.
AHUZZATH, a-hooz'-ath, possession. Gen. 26. 26.
AI, a'i, a heap of ruins. Josh. 7. 2.
men of, contend with Israel. Josh. 7. 5.
AIAH, ai'-ah, hawk. 2 Sam. 3. 7.
AIJA, ai'-jah, same as AI. Neh. 11. 31.
AJAH, a'-jah, same as AIAH. Gen. 36. 24.
AIATH, ai'-ath, ruins. Is. 10. 28.
AIJALON, ai'-ja-lon, place of gazelles. Josh. 21. 24.
AIJELETH SHAHAR, ai-ye'-leth sha'-har, morning hind. Ps. 22 title.
AIN, a'-in, an eye, or fountain. Num. 34. 11.
AJALON, ad'-jal-on, same as AIJALON. Josh. 19. 42.
AKAN, a'-kan. Gen. 36. 27.
AKKUB, a'k-kub, insidious. 1 Chr. 3. 24.

AKRABBIM, ak-rab´-bim, scorpions. Num. 34. 4.
ALAMETH, a-la´-meth, covering. 1 Chr. 7. 8.
ALAMMELECH, a-la´m-me-lek, king's oak. Josh. 19. 26.
ALAMOTH, a-la-moth´, virgins (?). Ps. 46 title.
ALEMETH, a-le´-meth, same as ALAMETH. 1 Chr. 8. 36.
ALEXANDER, al´-ex-an´-der, defending men. Mark 15. 21.
— a member of the council. Acts 4. 6.
— an Ephesian Jew. Acts 19. 33.
— the coppersmith. 1 Tim. 1. 20; 2 Tim. 4. 14.
ALEXANDRIA, al´-ex-an´-dri-a, the city named after Alexander. Acts 18. 24.
ALIAH, a´l-iah, same as ALVAH. 1 Chr. 1. 51.
ALIAN, a´l-ian, same as ALVAN. 1 Chr. 1. 40.
ALLELUIA, al-el-oo´-ya, praise ye the Lord. Rev. 19. 1.
ALLON, al´-on, an oak. 1 Chr. 4. 37.
ALLON-BACHUTH, al-on-bak´-ooth, oak of weeping. Gen. 35. 8; 1 Kin. 13. 14.
ALMODAD, al-mo´-dad, extension (?). Gen. 10. 26.
ALMON, al´-mon, hidden. Josh. 21. 18.
ALMON-DIBLATHAIM, al´-mon-dib´-lath-a´-im, hiding of the two cakes (?). Num. 33. 46.
ALOTH, a´-loth, yielding milk (?). 1 Kin. 4. 16.
ALPHA, al´-fah, the first letter of the Greek alphabet. Rev. 1. 8; 21. 6; 22. 13.
ALPHÆUS, al-fee´-us, successor. Matt. 10. 3.
AL-TASCHITH, al´-tash-kith´, 'do not destroy.' Ps. 57 title.
ALUSH, a´-loosh. Num. 33. 13.
ALVAH, al´-vah. Gen. 36. 40.
ALVAN, a´l-vahn, tall. Gen. 36. 23.
AMAD, a´m-ad, eternal people (?). Josh. 19. 26.
AMAL, a´-mal, labour, sorrow. 1 Chr. 7. 35.
AMALEK, am´-al-ek. Gen. 36. 12.
fights with Israel in Rephidim, and is defeated. Ex. 17. 8, 13.
perpetual war declared against. Ex. 17. 16; Deut. 25. 17.
smitten by Gideon. Judg. 7. 12.
by Saul. 1 Sam. 14. 48; 15. 8.
by David. 1 Sam. 27. 9; 30. 17.
AMALEKITE, am-al´-ek-ite, self-accused of killing Saul, slain by David. 2 Sam. 1. 10, 15.
AMALEKITES, am-al´-ek-ites, descendants of Amalek. Gen. 14. 7.
AMAM, a´-mam, metropolis (?). Josh. 15. 26.
AMANA, a-ma´-nah, fixed (?). Cant. 4. 8.
AMARIAH, a´-mar-i´-ah, Jehovah has said. 1 Chr. 6. 7.
AMASA, a-ma´-sa, burden.
captain of the host of Absalom. 2 Sam. 17. 25.
slain by Joab. 2 Sam. 20. 9, 10; 1 Kin. 2. 5.
AMASAI, a-ma´-sai, burdensome. 1 Chr. 6. 25.
AMASHAI, a-ma´sh-ai. Neh. 11. 13.
AMASIAH, a´-mas-i´-ah, burden of Jehovah. 2 Chr. 17. 16.
AMAZIAH, a´-maz-i´-ah, Jehovah strengthens.
king of Judah, his good reign. 2 Kin. 14. 1; 2 Chr. 25. 1.
defeats Edom. 2 Chr. 25. 11.
defeated by Joash king of Israel. 2 Chr. 25. 21.
slain at Lachish. 2 Kin. 14. 19.
— priest of Beth-el. Amos 7. 10.
AMI, a´-mi, probably same as AMON. Ezra 2. 57.
AMINADAB, a-mi´-na-dab, same as AMMINADAB. Matt. 1. 4.
AMITTAI, a-mi´t-tai, true. 2 Kin. 14. 25.
AMMAH, am´-ah. 2 Sam. 2. 24.
AMMI, am´-i, my people. Hos. 2. 1.
AMMIEL, am´-i-el, people of God. Num. 13. 12.
AMMIHUD, am-i´-hood, *p.* of praise (?). Num. 1. 10.
AMMINADAB, am-i´-na-dab, *p.* of the prince. Ex. 6. 23.
AMMINADIB, am-i´-na-dib, same as preceding. Cant. 6. 12.
AMMISHADDAI, a´m-i-sha´d-ai, *p.* of the Almighty. Num. 1. 12.
AMMIZABAD, am-i´-za-bad, *p.* of the giver (*i.e.* Jehovah). 1 Chr. 27. 6.

AMMON, am´-on, son of my *p.* (?).
children of. Gen. 19. 38.
not to be meddled with. Deut. 2. 19.
not to enter the congregation. Deut. 23. 3.
make war on Israel, and are conquered by Jephthah. Judg. 11. 4, 33.
slain by Saul. 1 Sam. 11. 11.
outrage David's servants. 2 Sam. 10.
tortured by David. 2 Sam. 12. 26.
prophecies concerning. Jer. 25. 21; 49. 1; Ezek. 21. 28; 25. 2. 3; Amos 1. 13; Zeph. 2. 8.
AMMONITES, am´-on-ites, a tribe descended from Ammon. Deut. 2. 20.
AMMONITESS, am´-on-ite-ess, feminine of preceding. 2 Chr. 12. 13.
AMNON, am´-non, faithful.
son of David. 2 Sam. 3. 2.
outrages Tamar. 2 Sam. 13.
slain by Absalom. 2 Sam. 13. 28.
AMOK, a´-mok, deep. Neh. 12. 7.
AMON, a´-mon. 2 Kin. 21. 18.
king of Judah. 2 Kin. 21. 19; 2 Chr. 33. 20.
his idolatry. 2 Kin. 21. 21; 2 Chr. 33. 23.
killed by his servants. 2 Kin. 21. 23.
AMORITE, am´-or-ite, mountaineer. Gen. 10. 16.
AMORITES, am´-or-ites, their iniquities, Gen. 15. 16; Deut. 20. 17; Josh. 3. 10.
AMOS, a´-mos, burden.
declares God's judgment upon the nations. Amos 1. 1, 2.
and upon Israel. Amos 3. 1, &c.
his call. Amos 7. 14, 15.
foretells Israel's restoration. Amos 9. 11.
AMOZ, a´-moz, strong. Is. 1. 1.
AMPHIPOLIS, am-phi´-pol-is, named from the river Strymon flowing *round the city*. Acts 17. 1.
AMPLIAS, am´-pli-as, short form of Ampliatus, enlarged. Rom. 16. 8.
AMRAM, am´-ram, people of the Highest (*i.e.* God). Ex. 6. 18.
AMRAMITES, am´-ram-ites, the descendants of Amram. Num. 3. 27.
AMRAPHAEL, am´-ra-fel. Gen. 14. 1.
AMZI, am´-zi, strong. 1 Chr. 6. 46.
ANAB, a´-nab, place fertile in grapes. Josh. 11. 21.
ANAH, a´-nah. Gen. 36. 2.
ANAHARATH, a-na´-har-ath. Josh. 19. 19.
ANAIAH, an-ai´-ah, Jehovah has answered. Neh. 8. 4.
ANAK, a´-nak, long-necked (?). Num. 13. 22.
ANAKIM, a´-nak-im, a tribe called after Anak. Deut. 1. 28.
— (giants). Num. 13. 33; Deut. 9. 2.
cut off by Joshua. Josh. 11. 21.
ANAMIM, a´-nam-im. Gen. 10. 13.
ANAMMELECH, a-nam´-me-lek, idol of the king (?), or shepherd and flock (?). 2 Kin. 17. 31.
ANAN, a´-nan, a cloud. Neh. 10. 26.
ANANI, an-a´-ni, shortened form of Ananiah. 1 Chr. 3. 24.
ANANIAH, an-an-i´-ah, whom Jehovah covers. Neh. 3. 23.
ANANIAS, an-an-i´-as, Greek form of HANANIAH.
— (and Sapphira), their lie and death. Acts 5. 1.
— (disciple), sent to Paul at Damascus. Acts 9. 10; 22. 12.
—(high priest), Paul brought before. Acts 22. 30.
Paul smitten by order of. Acts 23. 2.
rebuked by Paul. Acts 23. 3.
ANATH, a´-nath, an answer to prayer. Judg. 3. 31.
ANATHEMA, an-ath´-em-ah, something accursed. 1 Cor. 16. 22.
ANATHOTH, a´-nath-oth, answers to prayer. Josh. 21. 18.
men of, condemned for persecuting Jeremiah. Jer. 11. 21. *See* 1 Kin. 2. 26.
ANDREW, an´-droo. Mark 1. 29.
the APOSTLE. Matt. 4. 18; Mark 13. 3; John 1. 40; 6. 8; 12. 22; Acts 1. 13.
ANDRONICUS, an´-dro-ni´-kus, disciple at Rome. Rom. 16. 7.

ANEM, a´nem, same as EN-GANNIM (?). 1 Chr. 6. 73.
ANER, a´ner, a young man (?). Gen. 14. 13.
ANETHOTHITE, a´n-e-tho-thite, or ANETOTHITE, a´n-e-to-thite, a man of Anathoth. 2 Sam. 23. 27.
ANIAM, a-ni´am. 1 Chr. 7. 19.
ANIM, a´nim, fountains. Josh. 15. 50.
ANNA, an´ah, grace. A prophetess. Luke 2. 36.
ANNAS, an´as, Greek form of HANANIAH.
high priest. Luke 3. 2.
Christ brought to. John 18. 13, 24.
Peter and John before. Acts 4. 6.
ANTICHRIST, an´ti-christ, adversary to Christ. 1 John 2. 18, 22; 2 John 7. *See* 2 Thess. 2. 9; 1 Tim. 4. 1.
ANTIOCH, an´ti-ok, named in honour of Antiochus. Acts 6. 5.
—— (Syria), disciples first called Christians at. Acts 11. 26.
Barnabas and Saul called to apostleship at. Acts 13. 1.
Paul withstands Peter at. Gal. 2. 11.
—— (Pisidia), Paul's first address at. Acts 13. 16.
Paul and Barnabas persecuted at. Acts 13. 50.
ANTIPAS, an´tip-as, contraction of Antipater. Martyr. Rev. 2. 13.
ANTIPATRIS, an´tip-atr´is, from the foregoing. Acts 23. 31.
ANTOTHIJAH, an´to-thi´jah, prayers answered by Jehovah (?). 1 Chr. 8. 24.
ANTOTHITE, an´toth-ite, a man of Anathoth. 1 Chr. 11. 28.
ANUB, a´noob, bound together (?). 1 Chr. 4. 8.
APELLES, a-pel´es. Saluted by Paul. Rom. 16. 10.
APHARSACHITES, a-far´sa-kites. Ezra 5. 6.
APHARSATHCHITES, a-far-sath´kites. Ezra 4. 9.
APHARSITES, a-far´sites. Ezra 4. 9.
APHEK, a´fek, strength. Josh. 12. 18.
defeat of Saul at. 1 Sam. 29. 1. *See* Josh. 13. 4; 1 Sam. 4. 1; 1 Kin. 20. 26.
APHEKAH, a-fe´kah, same as preceding. Josh. 15. 53.
APHIAH, af-i´ah. 1 Sam. 9. 1.
APHIK, a´fik, same as APHEK. Judg. 1. 31.
APHRAH, af´rah, dust. Mic. 1. 10.
APHSES, af´sees, dispersion. 1 Chr. 24. 15.
APOLLONIA, ap´ol-o´ni-ah. Acts 17. 1.
APOLLOS, ap-ol´os, another form of Apollonius or Apollodorus.
eloquent and mighty in the Scriptures. Acts 18. 24; 19. 1; 1 Cor. 1. 12; 3. 4.
APOLLYON, ap-ol´yon, one that exterminates. Rev. 9. 11.
APPAIM, ap-a´im, the nostrils. 1 Chr. 2. 30.
APPHIA, af´yah, the Greek form of Appia. Philem. 2.
APPII FORUM, ap´py-i fo´rum, forum or market-place of Appius. Acts 28. 15.
AQUILA, ak´wil-ah, an eagle.
—— (and Priscilla) go with Paul from Corinth to Ephesus. Acts 18. 2, 19.
their constancy. Rom. 16. 3; 1 Cor. 16. 19.
Apollos instructed by. Acts 18. 26.
AR, city. Num. 21. 15.
ARA, a´ra, lion (?). 1 Chr. 7. 38.
ARAB, a´rab, ambush. Josh. 15. 52.
ARABAH, a-ra´h-bah, a plain. Josh. 18. 18.
ARABIA, a-ra´bi-a. Ps. 72. 10, 15. Gal. 1. 17.
kings of, pay tribute. 2 Chr. 9. 14; 17. 11; 26. 7.
ARABIAN, a-ra´bi-an, a person from Arabia. Neh. 2. 19.
ARABIANS, Is. 13. 20; 21. 13; Jer. 25. 24;—Acts 2. 11.
ARAD, a´rad, wild ass. 1 Chr. 8. 15.
ARAH, a´rah, wandering. 1 Chr. 7. 39.
ARAM, a´ram, height. Gen. 10. 22.
ARAMITESS, a´ram-ite-ess, a female inhabitant of Aram. 1 Chr. 7. 14.
ARAN, a´ran, wild goat. Gen. 36. 28.
ARARAT, a´ra-rat.
ark rested on. Gen. 8. 4. *See* Jer. 51. 27.
ARAUNAH, a-raw´nah, calf (?). 2 Sam. 24. 18.
—— (Ornan), Jebusite, sells to David site for temple.
ARAUNAH (Ornan)—*cont.*
2 Sam. 24. 16; 1 Chr. 21. 15, 18; 22. 1.
ARBA, or ARBAH, ar´bah. Gen. 35. 27.
ARBATHITE, ar´bath-ite. 1 Chr. 11. 32.
ARBEL, *see* BETH-ARBEL.
ARBITE, arb´ite, an inhabitant of Arab. 2 Sam. 23. 35.
ARCHELAUS, ar´ke-la´us, prince, king of Judæa, feared by Joseph. Matt. 2. 22.
ARCHEVITES, ar´kev-ites, the men of ERECH (?), q.v. Ezra 4. 9.
ARCHI, ar´ki, an inhabitant of Erech. Josh. 16. 2.
ARCHIPPUS, ar-kip´us, master of the horse. Col. 4. 17.
ARCHITE, ark´ite, a native of Erech. 2 Sam. 15. 32.
ARCTURUS, ark-tu´rus, probably the constellations known as the Great and Little Bear. Job 9. 9; 38. 32.
ARD, fugitive (?). Gen. 46. 21.
ARDITES, ard´ites, descendants of Ard. Num. 26. 40.
ARDON, ar´don, fugitive. 1 Chr. 2. 18.
ARELI, a-re´li, heroic. Gen. 46. 16.
ARELITES, a´rel-ites, a family descended from Areli. Num. 26. 17.
AREOPAGITE, a´re-op´ag-ite, belonging to the Council held on Areopagus. Acts 17. 34.
AREOPAGUS, a´re-op´ag-us, hill of Mars, at Athens; Paul preaches on. Acts 17. 19.
ARETAS, ar´e-tas, a husbandman (?). 2 Cor. 11. 32.
ARGOB, ar´gobe, a rocky district. Deut. 3. 4.
ARIDAI, a-ri´dai. Esth. 9. 9.
ARIDATHA, ar-ri´dah-thah. Esth. 9. 8.
ARIEH, ar´ieh, lion. 2 Kin. 15. 25.
ARIEL, a´ri-el, lion of God. Ezra 8. 16.
ARIMATHÆA, a´rim-ath-ee´ah, the same as RAMAH. Matt. 27. 57.
ARIOCH, a´ri-ok. Gen. 14. 1.
ARISAI, a-ris´ai. Esth. 9. 9.
ARISTARCHUS, a-ris-tark´us, best ruling.
fellow-prisoner of Paul, Acts 19. 29; 20. 4; 27. 2; Col. 4. 10; Philem. 24.
ARISTOBULUS, a´ris-to-bewl´us, best counsellor.
his household greeted by Paul. Rom. 16. 10.
ARKITE, ark´ite, fugitive (?). Gen. 10. 17.
ARMAGEDDON, ar´ma-ged´on, height of Megiddo. Rev. 16. 16.
ARMENIA, ar-me´ni-a, land of Aram. 2 Kin. 19. 37.
ARMONI, ar-mo´ni, belonging to a palace. 2 Sam. 21. 8.
ARNAN, ar´nan, active. 1 Chr. 3. 21.
ARNON, ar´non, swift. Num. 21. 13.
AROD, a´rod, wild ass. Num. 26. 17.
ARODI, a´rod-i, same as preceding. Gen. 46. 16.
ARODITES, a´rod-ites, descendants of Arod. Num. 26. 17.
AROER, a-ro´er, ruins (?). Deut. 2. 36.
built by children of Gad. Num. 32. 34.
boundary of Reuben. Josh. 13. 16.
AROERITE, ar-o´er-ite, a man of Aroer. 1 Chr. 11. 44.
ARPAD, ar´pad. 2 Kin. 18. 34.
ARPHAD, ar´fad, same as preceding. Is. 36. 19.
ARPHAXAD, ar-fax´ad. Gen. 10. 22.
ARTAXERXES, ar´ta-xerk´ses, honoured king (?). Ezra 4. 8.
(king of Persia), oppresses the Jews. Ezra 4.
—— (Longimanus), permits Ezra to restore the temple, Ezra 7; and Nehemiah to rebuild Jerusalem. Neh. 2.
ARTEMAS, ar´te-mas, shortened form of Artemidorus (?). Tit. 3. 12.
ARUBOTH, a-roob´oth, windows. 1 Kin. 4. 10.
ARUMAH, a-room´ah, elevated. Judg. 9. 41.
ARVAD, ar´vad, wandering. Ezek. 27. 8.
ARVADITES, ar´vad-ites, inhabitants of Arvad. Gen. 10. 18.
ARZA, ar´zah, earth. 1 Kin. 16. 9.
ASA, a´sah, physician.
his good reign. 1 Kin. 15. 8.
wars with Baasha. 1 Kin. 15. 16.
his prayer against the Ethiopians. 2 Chr. 14. 11.
his zeal. 2 Chr. 15.

ASA—*cont.*
seeks aid of the Syrians. 2 Chr. 16.
reproved by Hanani the seer. 2 Chr. 16. 7.
reigns forty years, and dies much honoured. 2 Chr. 16. 10.
ASAHEL, a'sa-hel, whom God made.
his rashness; slain by Abner in self-defence. 2 Sam. 2. 18; 3. 27; 23. 24; 1 Chr. 11. 26.
ASAHIAH, a'sah-i'ah. 2 Kin. 22. 12.
ASAIAH, a-sai'ah. 1 Chr. 4. 36.
ASAPH, a'saf, collector. 2 Kin. 18. 18.
a Levite, musical composer, and leader of David's choir, 1 Chr. 6. 39; 2 Chr. 5. 12; 29. 30; 35. 15; Neh. 12. 46; Psalms 50 and 73 to 83 ascribed to him.
ASAREEL, a-sa'r-eel, whom God has bound. 1 Chr. 4. 16.
ASARELAH, a-sar-e'l-ah, same as JESHARELAH. 1 Chr. 25. 2.
ASENATH, a'se-nath, she who is of Neith (*i.e.* a goddess of the Egyptians) (?). Gen. 41. 45.
wife of Joseph. Gen. 41. 45; 46. 20.
ASER, a'ser, same as ASHER. Luke 2. 36.
ASHAN, a'shan, smoke. Josh. 15. 42.
ASHBEA, ash'be-ah, I conjure. 1 Chr. 4. 21.
ASHBEL, ash'bel, blame (?). Gen. 46. 21.
ASHBELITES, ash'bel-ites, the descendants of Ashbel. Num. 26. 38.
ASHCHENAZ, ash'ken-az, same as ASHKENAZ. 1 Chr. 1. 6.
ASHDOD, ash'dod, a strong place. Josh. 15. 46.
city of Philistines; the ark carried there; men of, smitten. 1 Sam. 5.
reduced by Uzziah. 2 Chr. 26. 6.
predictions concerning. Jer. 25. 20; Amos 1. 8; Zeph. 2. 4; Zech. 9. 6.
ASHDODITES, ash'dod-ites, the inhabitants of Ashdod. Neh. 4. 7.
ASHDOTH-PISGAH, ash'doth-piz'gah, springs of Pisgah. Josh. 12. 3.
ASHDOTHITES, ash'doth-ites, same as ASHDODITES. Josh. 13. 3.
ASHER, ash'er, fortunate, happy.
son of Jacob. Gen. 30. 13.
his descendants. Num. 1. 40; 26. 44; 1 Chr. 7. 30; their inheritance, Josh. 19. 24; Judg. 5. 17. *See* Ezek. 48. 34; Rev. 7. 6.
Anna, prophetess, descended from. Luke 2. 36.
ASHERAH, ash-er'ah, the goddess Ashtoreth. 2 Kin. 17. 10.
ASHERITES, a'sher-ites, descendants of Asher. Judg. 1. 32.
ASHIMA, a-shi'ma. 2 Kin. 17. 30.
ASHKELON, ash'kel-on, migration.
—— (Askelon) taken. Judg. 1. 18; 14. 19; 1 Sam. 6. 17; 2 Sam. 1. 20.
prophecies concerning. Jer. 25. 20; 47. 5; Amos 1. 8; Zeph. 2. 4; Zech. 9. 5.
ASHKENAZ, ash'ken-az. Gen. 10. 3.
ASHNAH, ash'nah, strong. Josh. 15. 33.
ASHPENAZ, ash'pen-az. Dan. 1. 3.
ASHRIEL, ash'ri-el, same as ASRIEL. 1 Chr. 7. 14.
ASHTAROTH, ash'tar-oth, statutes of Ashtoreth. Josh. 9. 10.
idolatrous worship of, by Israel. Judg. 2. 13; 1 Sam. 12. 10; by Solomon, 1 Kin. 11. 5, 33.
ASHTERATHITE, ash-ter'ath-ite, a native of Ashteroth. 1 Chr. 11. 44.
ASHTEROTH KARNAIM, ash'ter-oth kar-na'im, Ashteroth of the two horns. Gen. 14. 5.
ASHTORETH, ash-tor'eth, she who enriches. 1 Kin. 11. 5.
ASHUR, ash'oor. 1 Chr. 2. 24.
ASHURITES, ash'oor-ites. 2 Sam. 2. 9.
ASHVATH, ash'vath. 1 Chr. 7. 33.
ASIA, a'shah. Acts 2. 9.
ASIEL, a'si-el, created by God. 1 Chr. 4. 35.
ASKELON, *see* ASHKELON. Judg. 1. 18.
ASNAH, as'nah, bramble. Ezra 2. 50.
ASNAPPER, as-nap'er, same as ASSUR-BANI-PAL, Assur has formed a son. Ezra 4. 10.
ASPATHA, as-pa'h-thah. Esth. 9. 7.
ASRIEL, as'ri-el, the prohibition of God. Num. 26. 31.
ASRIELITES, as'ri-el-ites, the family of Asriel. Num. 26. 31.
ASSHUR, ash'oor, the gracious One (?). Gen. 10. 22.
ASSHURIM, ash-oor'im. Gen. 25. 3.
ASSIR, as'eer, captive. Ex. 6. 24.
ASSOS, as'os. Acts 20. 13.
ASSYRIA, as-ir'ya, the land so named from ASSHUR. Gen. 2. 14.
Israel carried captive to. 2 Kin. 15. 29; 17.
army of, miraculously destroyed. 2 Kin. 19. 35; Is. 37. 36.
prophecies concerning. Is. 8; 10. 5; 14. 24; 30. 31; 31. 8; Mic. 5. 6; Zeph. 2. 13.
its glory. Ezek. 31. 3.
ASSYRIANS, as-ir'yans, inhabitants of Assyria. Is. 10. 5.
ASTAROTH, as'tar-oth, same as ASHTORETH. Deut. 1. 4.
ASUPPIM, a-soop'im. 1 Chr. 26. 15.
ASYNCRITUS, a-sin'krit-us, incomparable, disciple. Rom. 16. 14.
ATAD, a'tad, buckthorn. Gen. 50. 10.
ATARAH, a-ta'h-rah, a crown. 1 Chr. 2. 26.
ATAROTH, a-ta'h-roth, crowns. Num. 32. 3.
ATER, a'ter, bound, shut up. Ezra 2. 16.
ATHACH, a'thak, lodging-place. 1 Sam. 30. 30.
ATHAIAH, a-thai'ah, whom Jehovah made (?). Neh. 11. 4.
ATHALIAH, ath'al-i'ah, whom Jehovah has afflicted.
daughter of Ahab, mother of Ahaziah. 2 Kin. 8. 26.
slays the seed royal, Joash only saved. 2 Kin. 11. 1; 2 Chr. 22. 10.
slain by order of Jehoiada. 2 Kin. 11. 16; 2 Chr. 23. 15.
ATHLAI, a'th-lai, shortened form of Athaliah. Ezra 10. 28.
ATHENIANS, ath-e'ni-ans, natives of Athens. Acts 17. 21.
ATHENS, ath'ens.
Paul preaches to the philosophers at. Acts. 17. 15; 1 Thess. 3. 1.
men of, described. Acts 17. 21.
ATROTH, at'roth, same as ATAROTH. Num. 32. 35.
ATTAI, a't-tai, opportune. 1 Chr. 2. 35.
ATTALIA, at'ta-li'a, so called from Attalus, the royal founder of the city, sea-port. Acts 14. 25.
AUGUSTUS, aw-gust'us, venerable. Luke 2. 1.
AVAH, a'vah. 2 Kin. 17. 24.
AVEN, a'ven, nothingness. Ezek. 30. 17.
AVIM, av'im, ruins. Josh. 18. 23.
AVITH, a'vith. Gen. 36. 35.
AZAL, a'zal, root of a mountain. Zech. 14. 5.
AZALIAH, a'zal-i'ah, whom Jehovah has reserved. 2 Kin. 22. 3.
AZANIAH, a'zan-i'ah, whom Jehovah hears. Neh. 10. 9.
AZARAEL, a-zar'eel, whom God helps. Neh. 12. 36.
AZAREEL, a-zar'eel, same as preceding. 1 Chr. 12. 6.
AZARIAH, a'zar-i'ah, whom Jehovah aids. 2 Chr. 22. 6.
—— (Uzziah), king of Judah, his good reign. 2 Kin. 14. 21; 2 Chr. 26.
his wars. 2 Chr. 26.
invades the priest's office. 2 Chr. 26. 16.
struck with leprosy. 2 Kin. 15. 5; 2 Chr. 26. 20.
—— prophet, exhorts Asa. 2 Chr. 15.
AZAZ, a'zaz, strong. 1 Chr. 5. 8.
AZAZIAH, a'zaz-i'ah, whom Jehovah strengthened. 1 Chr. 15. 21.
AZBUK, az'book. Neh. 3. 16.
AZEKAH, a-ze'kah, dug over. Josh. 10. 10.
AZEL, a'zel, noble. 1 Chr. 8. 37.
AZEM, a'zem, strength, bone. Josh. 15. 29.
AZGAD, az'gad, strong in fortune. Ezra 2. 12.
AZIEL, az'i-el, whom God strengthens. 1 Chr. 15. 20.
AZIZA, a-zi'zah, strong. Ezra 10. 27.
AZMAVETH, az-ma'veth, strength (?). 2 Sam. 23. 31.

AZMON, az´mon, robust. Num. 34. 4.
AZNOTH-TABOR, az´noth-ta´bor, ears (*i.e.* summits) of Tabor. Josh. 19. 34.
AZOR, a´zor, helper. Matt. 1. 13.
AZOTUS, a-zo´tus, the Greek form of ASHDOD. Acts 8. 40.
AZRIEL, az´ri-el, help of God. 1 Chr. 5. 24.
AZRIKAM, az-ri´kam, help against an enemy. 1 Chr. 3. 23.
AZUBAH, a-zoob´ah, forsaken. 1 Kin. 22. 42.
AZUR, a´zoor, same as AZOR. Jer. 28. 1.
AZZAH, az´ah, strong, fortified. Deut. 2. 23.
AZZAN, az´an, strong. Num. 34. 26.
AZZUR, az´oor, same as AZOR. Neh. 10. 17.

BAAL, ba´al, lord, master, possessor, owner.
worshipped. Num. 22. 41; Judg. 2. 13; 8. 33; 1 Kin. 16. 32; 18. 26; 2 Kin. 17. 16; 19. 18; 21. 3; Jer. 2. 8; 7. 9; 12. 16; 19. 5; 23. 13; Hos. 2. 8; 13. 1, &c.
his altars and priests destroyed by Gideon. Judg. 6. 25; by Elijah. 1 Kin. 18. 40; by Jehu. 2 Kin. 10. 18; by Jehoiada. 2 Kin. 11. 18; by Josiah. 2 Kin. 23. 4; 2 Chr. 34. 4.
BAALAH, ba´al-ah, mistress. Josh. 15. 10.
BAALATH, ba´al-ath, same as preceding. Josh. 19. 44.
BAALATH-BEER, ba´al-ath-be´er, having a well. Josh. 19. 8.
BAAL-BERITH, ba´al-be-ri´th, lord of covenant. Judg. 8. 33.
BAALE, ba´al-ay, plural of Baal. 2 Sam. 6. 2.
BAAL-GAD, ba´al-gad´, lord of fortune. Josh. 11. 17.
BAAL-HAMON, ba´al-ha´mon, place of a multitude. Cant. 8. 11.
BAAL-HANAN, ba´al-ha´nan, lord of benignity. Gen. 36. 38.
BAAL-HAZOR, ba´al-ha´zor, having a village. 2 Sam. 13. 23.
BAAL-HERMON, ba´al-her´mon, place of Hermon. Judg. 3. 3.
BAALI, ba´al-i, my lord. Hos. 2. 16.
BAALIM, ba´al-im, lords. Judg. 2. 11; 2 Chr. 28. 2.
BAALIS, ba´al-is. Jer. 40. 14.
BAAL-MEON, ba´al-me´on, place of habitation. Num. 32. 38.
BAAL-PEOR, ba´al-pe´or, lord of the opening. Num. 25. 3.
the trespass of Israel concerning. Num. 25; Deut. 4. 3; Ps. 106. 28; Hos. 9. 10.
BAAL-PERAZIM, ba´al-pe-raz´im, place of breaches. David's victory over Philistines at. 2 Sam. 5. 20.
BAAL-SHALISHA, ba´al-sha-lish´ah, lord (or place) of Shalisha. 2 Kin. 4. 42.
BAAL-TAMAR, ba´al-ta´mar, place of palm trees. Judg. 20. 33.
BAAL-ZEBUB, ba´al-ze-bo´ob, lord of flies.
false god of Ekron, Ahaziah rebuked for sending to enquire of. 2 Kin. 1. 2.
BAAL-ZEPHON, ba´al-ze-pho´n, place of Zephon, or sacred to Zephon. Ex. 14. 2.
BAANA, ba´a-nah. 1 Kin. 4. 12.
BAANAH, ba´a-nah.
and Rechab, for murdering Ish-bosheth, slain by David. 2 Sam. 4. 2.
BAARA, ba´a-rah, foolish. 1 Chr. 8. 8.
BAASEIAH, ba´as-i´ah, work of Jehovah. 1 Chr. 6. 40.
BAASHA, ba´ash-ah, wicked (?).
king of Israel, destroys the house of Jeroboam. 1 Kin. 15. 16, 27; Jehu's prophecy concerning him. 1 Kin. 16. 1.
BABEL, ba´bel, confusion.
Nimrod king of. Gen. 10. 10.
confusion of tongues at the building of. Gen. 11. 9.
BABYLON, bab´il-on, Greek form of Bab-ilu, the gate of God. Gen. 10. 10; 2 Kin. 17. 30; 20. 12.
ambassadors from, to Hezekiah. 2 Kin. 20. 12; 2 Chr. 32. 31; Is. 39.
Jewish captivity there. 2 Kin. 25; 2 Chr. 36; Jer. 39; 52.
return from. Ezra 1; Neh. 2.

BABYLON—*cont.*
greatness of. Dan. 4. 30.
taken by the Medes. Dan. 5. 30.
fall of. Is. 13. 14; 21. 2; 47; 48; Jer. 25. 12; 50; 51.
church in. 1 Pet. 5. 13.
—— the Great. Rev. 14. 8; 17; 18.
BABYLONISH, bab´il-one-ish, of, or belonging to, Babylon. Josh. 7. 21.
BACA, ba´kah, weeping.
valley of misery. Ps. 84. 6.
BACHRITES, bak´rites, the family of Becher. Num. 26. 35.
BAHARUMITE, ba-ha-r´um-ite, an inhabitant of Bahurim. 1 Chr. 11. 33.
BAHURIM, ba-hoor´im, (town of) young men. 2 Sam. 16. 5.
BAJITH, ba´yith (same as BETH), house. Is. 15. 2.
BAKBAKKAR, bak-bak´ar. 1 Chr. 9. 15.
BAKBUK, bak´book, a bottle. Ezra 2. 51.
BAKBUKIAH, bak´book-i´ah, emptying (*i.e.* wasting) of Jehovah. Neh. 11. 17.
BALAAM, ba´la-am, destruction (?). Num. 22. 5.
requested by Balak to curse Israel, is forbidden. Num. 22. 13.
his anger. Num. 22. 27.
blesses Israel. Num. 23. 19; 24.
his prophecies. Num. 23. 9, 24; 24. 17.
his wicked counsel. Num. 31. 16; Deut. 23. 4. *See* Josh. 24. 9; Judg. 11. 25; Mic. 6. 5; 2 Pet. 2. 15; Jude 11; Rev. 2. 14.
slain. Num. 31. 8; Josh. 13. 22.
BALAC, ba´lac, same as BALAK. Rev. 2. 14.
BALADAN, ba´la-dan, He has given a son. 2 Kin. 20. 12.
BALAH, ba´lah. Josh. 19. 3.
BALAK, ba´lak, to make empty. Num. 22. 2.
BAMAH, ba´mah, high place. Ezek. 20. 29.
BAMOTH, ba´moth, high places. Num. 21. 19.
BAMOTH-BAAL, ba´moth-ba´al, *h.p.* of Baal. Josh. 13. 17.
BANI, ba´ni, built. 2 Sam. 23. 36.
BARABBAS, bar-a´b-as, son of Abba or father. Mark 15. 7.
a robber, released instead of Jesus. Matt. 27. 16; Mark 15. 6; Luke 23. 18; John 18. 40.
BARACHEL, ba´rak-el, whom God blessed. Job 32. 6.
BARACHIAS, ba-rak-i´as, whom Jehovah blesses. Matt. 23. 35.
BARAK, ba´rak, thunderbolt, lightning. Judg. 4. 6.
delivers Israel from Sisera. Judg. 4. 5; Heb. 11. 32.
BARHUMITE, bar´hoom-ite, same as BAHARUMITE. 2 Sam. 23. 31.
BARIAH, ba-ri´ah, a fugitive. 1 Chr. 3. 22.
BAR-JESUS, bar-je´sus, son of JESUS.
(Elymas) smitten with blindness by Paul. Acts 13. 6.
BAR-JONA, bar-jo´nah, son of Jona (Simon). Matt. 16. 17.
BARKOS, bar´kos, painter (?). Ezra 2. 53.
BARNABAS, bar´na-bas, son of exhortation.
Levite of Cyprus, sells his lands. Acts 4. 36.
preaches at Antioch. Acts 11. 22.
accompanies Paul. Acts 11. 30; 12. 25; 13; 14; 15; 1 Cor. 9. 6.
his contention. Acts 15. 36.
his error. Gal. 2. 13.
BARSABAS, bar´sa-bas, *s.* of Seba. Acts 1. 23.
BARTHOLOMEW, bar-thol´o-mew, *s.* of Talmai.
the apostle. Matt. 10. 3; Mark 3. 18; Luke 6. 14; Acts 1. 13.
BARTIMÆUS, bar´ti-me´us, *s.* of Timai.
blindness cured near Jericho. Mark 10. 46.
BARUCH, ba´rook, blessed. Jer. 32. 12.
receives Jeremiah's evidence. Jer. 32. 13; 36.
discredited by Azariah, and carried into Egypt. Jer. 43. 6.
God's message to. Jer. 45.
BARZILLAI, bar-zi´l-ai, of iron.
loyalty to David. 2 Sam. 17. 27.

BARZILLAI—*cont.*
David's recognition of. 2 Sam. 19. 31; 1 Kin. 2. 7.
BASHAN, ba'shan, soft rich soil.
conquered. Num. 21. 33; Deut. 3. 1; Ps. 68. 15, 22; 135. 10; 136. 20.
BASHAN-HAVOTH-JAIR, ba'shan-hav'oth-ja'yir, Bashan of the villages of Jair. Deut. 3. 14.
BASHEMATH, ba'shem-ath, sweet-smelling. Gen. 26. 34.
BASMATH, same as BASHEMATH. 1 Kin. 4. 15.
BATH-RABBIM, bath-rab'im, daughter of many. Cant. 7. 4.
BATH-SHEBA, bath'she-bah, *d.* of the oath. 2 Sam. 11. 3.
wife of Uriah, taken by David. 2 Sam. 11; 12.
appeals to David for Solomon against Adonijah. 1 Kin. 1. 15.
intercedes with Solomon for Adonijah. 1 Kin. 2. 19.
BATH-SHUA, bath'shoo-ah. 1 Chr. 3. 5.
BAVAI, ba'vai. Neh. 3. 18.
BAZLITH, baz'lith, a making naked (?). Neh. 7. 54.
BAZLUTH, baz'looth, same as BAZLITH. Ezra 2. 52.
BEALIAH, be'al-i'ah, whom Jehovah rules. 1 Chr. 12. 5.
BEALOTH, be-a'h-loth, citizens (?), plural of BAALAH. Josh. 15. 24.
BEBAI, be'bai. Ezra 8. 11.
BECHER, be'ker, a young camel. Gen. 46. 21.
BECHORATH, be-kor'ath, offspring of the first birth. 1 Sam. 9. 1.
BEDAD, be'dad, separation, part. Gen. 36. 35.
BEDAN, be'dan, son of Dan (?). 1 Sam. 12. 11.
BEDEIAH, be-di'ah. Ezra 10. 35.
BEELIADA, be-el'ya-dah', whom Baal has known. 1 Chr. 14. 7.
BEELZEBUB, be-el'ze-bub', same as BAALZEBUB. Matt. 10. 25.
prince of devils. Matt. 12. 24; Mark 3. 22; Luke 11. 15.
Christ's miracles ascribed to. Matt. 12. 24, &c.
BEER, be'er, a well. Num. 21. 16.
BEERA, be-er'ah, same as BEER. 1 Chr. 7. 37.
BEERAH, be-er'ah, same as BEER. 1 Chr. 5. 6.
BEER-ELIM, be'er-el'im, well of heroes. Is. 15. 8.
BEERI, be'er-i, man of the *w.* Gen. 26. 34.
BEER-LAHAI-ROI, be'er-la-hai'ro'i, *w.* of vision (of God) to the living. Gen. 16. 14.
BEEROTH, be-er'oth, wells. Josh. 9. 17.
BEEROTHITE, be-er'oth-ite, a native of Beeroth. 2 Sam. 23. 37.
BEER-SHEBA, be'er-she'bah, well of the oath.
Abraham dwells at. Gen. 21. 31; 22. 19; 28. 10.
Hagar relieved at. Gen. 21. 14.
Jacob comforted at. Gen. 46. 1.
Elijah flees to. 1 Kin. 19. 3.
BEESH-TERAH, be-esh'te-rah, house or temple of Astarte (?). Josh. 21. 27.
BEHEMOTH, be-he'moth, the water-ox. Job 40. 15.
BEKAH, be'kah, part, half. Ex. 38. 26.
BEL, bel, another form of BAAL, an idol. Is. 46. 1; Jer. 50. 2.
BELA, be'lah, destruction. Gen. 14. 2.
BELAH, be'lah, same as BELA. Gen. 46. 21.
BELAITES, be'la-ites, descendants of BELA. Num. 26. 38.
BELIAL, be'li-al, worthless.
men of, wicked men so called. Deut. 13. 13; Judg. 19. 22.
sons of. 1 Sam. 10. 27.
BELSHAZZAR, bel-shaz'ar, Bel protect the king. Dan. 5. 1.
his profane feast, warning, and death. Dan. 5.
BELTESHAZZAR, bel'te-shaz'ar, preserve his life.
Daniel so named. Dan. 1. 7; 4. 8, &c.
BEN, ben, son. 1 Chr. 15. 18.
BENAIAH, ben-ai'ah, whom Jehovah has built. 2 Sam. 8. 18.
valiant acts of. 2 Sam. 23. 20; 1 Chr. 11. 22; 27. 5.
proclaims Solomon king. 1 Kin. 1. 32.

BENAIAH—*cont.*
slays Adonijah, Joab, and Shimei. 1 Kin. 2. 25–46.
BEN-AMMI, ben'am'i, son of my own kindred. Gen. 19. 38.
BENE-BERAK, be-ne'be-rak', sons of Barak, or of lightning. Josh. 19. 45.
BENE-JAAKAN, be-ne-ja'ak-an, *s.* of Jaakan. Num. 33. 31.
BEN-HADAD, ben-ha'dad, *s.* of Hadad.
king of Syria, his league with Asa against Baasha. 1 Kin. 15. 18.
—— wars with Ahab. 1 Kin. 20.
baffled by Elisha. 2 Kin. 6. 8.
besieges Samaria. 2 Kin. 6. 24; 7.
slain by Hazael. 2 Kin. 8. 7.
—— son of Hazael, wars with Israel. 2 Kin. 13. 3, 25. *See* Jer. 49. 27; Amos 1. 4.
BEN-HAIL, ben-ha'yil, son of the host. 2 Chr. 17. 7.
BEN-HANAN, ben-ha'nan, *s.* of one who is gracious. 1 Chr. 4. 20.
BENINU, be-ni'noo, our *s.* Neh. 10. 13.
BENJAMIN, ben'ja-min, *s.* of the right hand, *i.e.* fortunate. Gen. 35. 18.
(first named Ben-oni, 'son of my sorrow'), Patriarch, youngest son of Jacob, his birth at Bethlehem. Gen. 35. 16.
goes into Egypt. Gen. 43. 15.
Joseph's stratagem to detain. Gen. 44.
Jacob's prophecy concerning. Gen. 49. 27.
HIS DESCENDANTS. Gen. 46. 21; 1 Chr. 7. 6.
twice numbered. Num. 1. 36; 26. 38.
blessed by Moses. Deut. 33. 12.
their inheritance. Josh. 18. 11.
their wickedness chastised. Judg. 20; 21.
the first king chosen from. 1 Sam. 9; 10.
support the house of Saul. 2 Sam. 2.
afterwards adhere to that of David. 1 Kin. 12. 21; 1 Chr. 11.
the tribe of Paul. Phil. 3. 5. *See* Ps. 68. 27; Ezek. 48. 32; Rev. 7. 8.
BENJAMITE, ben'jam-ite, a man of the tribe of Benjamin. Judg. 20. 35.
BENO, ben-o', his son. 1 Chr. 24. 26.
BEN-ONI be'n-o'ni, *s.* of my sorrow. Gen. 35. 18.
BEN-ZOHETH, ben-zo'heth, *s.* of Zoheth. 1 Chr. 4. 20.
BEON, be'on, contracted from BAAL-MEON. Num. 32. 3.
BEOR, be'or. Gen. 36. 32.
BERA, be'rah. Gen. 14. 2.
BERACHAH, be'rak-ah, blessing. 1 Chr. 12. 3.
valley of, why so named. 2 Chr. 20. 26.
BERACHIAH, be'rak-i'ah, whom Jehovah hath blessed. 1 Chr. 6. 39.
BERAIAH, be-rai'ah, whom Jehovah created. 1 Chr. 8. 21.
BEREA, be-re'ah.
city of Macedonia, Paul preaches at. Acts 17. 10.
people 'more noble'. Acts 17. 11.
BERECHIAH, be'rek-i'ah, same as BERACHIAH. 1 Chr. 3. 20.
BERED, be'red, hail. Gen. 16. 14.
BERI, be'ri, man of the well. 1 Chr. 7. 36.
BERIAH, be-ri'ah, in evil (?). Gen. 46. 17.
BERIITES, be-ri'ites, descendants of Beriah. Num. 26. 44.
BERITES, ber'ites. 2 Sam. 20. 14.
BERITH, be'rith, a covenant. Judg. 9. 46.
BERNICE, ber-ni'see, Victoria. Acts 25. 13.
BERODACH-BALADAN, be'ro-dak-bal'a-dan, Berodach (same as MERODACH) has given a son. 2 Kin. 20. 12.
BEROTHAH, be-ro'thah, wells. Ezek. 47. 16.
BEROTHAI, be-ro'thai, my wells. 2 Sam. 8. 8.
BEROTHITE, be-ro'thite, same as BEEROTHITE. 1 Chr. 11. 39.
BESAI, be'sai, sword (?), or victory (?). Ezra 2. 49.
BESODEIAH, be'sod-i'ah, in the secret of Jehovah. Neh. 3. 6.
BESOR, be'sor, cool. 1 Sam. 30. 9.
BETAH, be'tah, confidence. 2 Sam. 8. 8.

BETEN, be'ten. Josh. 19. 25.
BETHABARA, beth-ab'ar-ah, house of passage.
place where John baptized. John 1. 28.
BETH-ANATH, beth'an-ath, echo. Josh. 19. 38
BETH-ANOTH, beth'an-oth. Josh. 15. 59.
BETHANY, beth'an-y, house of dates.
visited by Christ, Matt. 21. 17; 26. 6; Mark 11. 1; Luke 19. 29; John 12. 1.
raising of Lazarus at, John 11. 18.
ascension of Christ at. Luke 24. 50.
BETH-ARABAH, beth-a-ra'h-bah, *h.* of the desert. Josh. 15. 6.
BETH-ARAM, beth-a'ram, *h.* of the height. Josh. 13. 27.
BETH-ARBEL, beth-arb'el, *h.* of the ambush of God. Hos. 10. 14.
BETH-AVEN, beth-a'ven, *h.* of vanity (*i.e.* of idols). Josh. 7. 2.
BETH-AZMAVETH, beth'az-ma'veth, *h.* of strength. Neh. 7. 28.
BETH-BAAL-MEON, beth'ba'al-me-on', *h.* of Baal-meon. Josh. 13. 17.
BETH-BARAH, beth-ba'rah, same as BETHABARA. Judg. 7. 24.
BETH-BIREI, beth-bir'i, house of my creation. 1 Chr. 4. 31.
BETH-CAR, beth'kar, *h.* of pasture. 1 Sam. 7. 11.
BETH-DAGON, beth-da'gon, *h.* of Dagon. Josh. 15. 41.
BETH-DIBLATHAIM, beth'dib-la-tha'im, *h.* of the two cakes. Jer. 48. 22.
BETH-EL, beth'el, *h.* of God. Gen. 12. 8.
(Luz), city of Palestine, named Beth-el by Jacob. Gen. 28. 19; 31. 13.
altar built by Jacob at. Gen. 35. 1.
occupied by the house of Joseph. Judg. 1. 22.
sons of prophets resident there. 2 Kin. 2. 2, 3; 17. 28.
the king's chapel. Amos 7. 13.
idolatry of Jeroboam at. 1 Kin. 12. 28; 13. 1.
reformation by Josiah at. 2 Kin. 23. 15.
BETHELITE, beth'el-ite, a native of Bethel. 1 Kin. 16. 34.
BETH-EMEK, beth-e'mek, house of the valley. Josh. 19. 27.
BETHER, be'ther, separation. Cant. 2. 17.
BETHESDA, beth-esd'ah, house of mercy.
pool of, at Jerusalem, miracles wrought at. John 5. 2.
BETH-EZEL, beth-e'zel, house of firmness (?). Mic. 1. 11.
BETH-GADER, beth-ga'der, *h.* of the wall. 1 Chr. 2. 51.
BETH-GAMUL, beth-ga'mool, *h.* of the weaned. Jer. 48. 23.
BETH-HACCEREM, beth'hak-er'em, *h.* of the vine-yard. Neh. 3. 14.
BETH-HARAN, beth-ha'ran. Num. 32. 36.
BETH-HOGLAH, beth-hog'lah, *h.* of the partridge. Josh. 15. 6.
BETH-HORON, beth-ho'ron, *h.* of the hollow. Josh. 10. 10.
BETH-JESIMOTH, beth-je-shim'oth, *h.* of the deserts. Num. 33. 49.
BETH-LEBAOTH, beth'le-ba'oth, *h.* of lionesses. Josh. 19. 6.
BETH-LEHEM, beth'le-hem, *h.* of bread. Gen. 35. 19.
BETH-LEHEM EPHRATAH, beth'le-hem ef'ra-tah, B. the fruitful (?).
(originally Ephratah), Naomi and Ruth return to. Ruth 1—4.
David anointed at. 1 Sam. 16. 13; 20. 6.
well of. 2 Sam. 23. 15; 1 Chr. 11. 17.
Christ's birth at. Matt. 2. 1; Luke 2. 4; John 7. 42; predicted. Mic. 5. 2 (Ps. 132. 5, 6).
babes of, slain. Matt. 2. 16.
BETH-LEHEMITE, beth'le-hem-ite, a man of Beth-lehem. 1 Sam. 16. 1.
BETH-LEHEM-JUDAH, beth'le-hem-joo'dah, B. of Judah. Judg. 17. 7.
BETH-MAACHAH, beth'ma'ak-ah, house of Maa-chah. 2 Sam. 20. 14.
BETH-MARCABOTH, beth'mar'kab-oth, *h.* of cha-riots. Josh. 19. 5.
BETH-MEON, be'th-me-o'n, *h.* of habitation. Jer. 48. 23.
BETH-NIMRAH, beth'nim'rah, *h.* of sweet water. Num. 32. 36.
BETH-PALET, beth'pa'let, *h.* of escape, or of Pelet. Josh. 15. 27.
BETH-PAZZEZ, beth'paz'ez, *h.* of dispersion. Josh. 19. 21.
BETH-PEOR, beth'pe'or, temple of Peor. Deut. 3. 29.
BETHPHAGE, be'th-fa-gee, house of unripe figs. Matt. 21. 1.
BETH-PHELET, beth'fe'let, same as BETH-PALET. Neh. 11. 26.
BETH-RAPHA, beth'ra'fah, house of Rapha. 1 Chr. 4. 12.
BETH-REHOB, beth're'hob, *h.* of Rehob. Judg. 18. 28.
BETHSAIDA, beth'sai'dah, *h.* of fishing.
of Galilee, native place of Philip, Peter, and Andrew. Mark 6. 45; John 1. 44; 12. 21.
blind man cured at. Mark 8. 22.
condemned for unbelief. Matt. 11. 21.
Christ feeds the five thousand at. Luke 9. 10–17.
BETH-SHAN, beth'shan', *h.* of rest. 1 Sam. 31. 10.
BETH-SHEAN, beth'she'an, same as BETH-SHAN. Josh. 17. 11.
BETH-SHEMESH, beth'she'mesh, house of the sun. Josh. 15. 10.
men of, punished for looking into the ark. 1 Sam. 6. 19.
great battle at. 2 Kin. 14. 11.
BETHSHEMITE, beth'shem'ite, a native of Beth-shemesh. 1 Sam. 6. 14.
BETH-SHITTAH, beth'shit'ah, house of acacias. Judg. 7. 22.
BETH-TAPPUAH, beth'tap-oo'ah, *h.* of apples. Josh. 15. 53.
BETHUEL, beth'oo-el, house of God. Gen. 22. 22.
BETHUL, beth-ool', same as BETHEL (?). Josh. 19. 4.
BETH-ZUR, beth'zoor', house of the rock. Josh. 15. 58.
BETONIM, be-to'nim, pistachio nuts. Josh. 13. 26.
BEULAH, be-ool'ah, married. Is. 62. 4.
BEZAI, be'zai. Ezra 2. 17.
BEZALEEL, be-zal'e-el, in the shadow of God (?).
constructs the tabernacle. Ex. 31. 2; 35. 30; 36—38.
BEZEK, be'zek, lightning (?). Judg. 1. 4.
BEZER, be'zer, ore of precious metal. Deut. 4. 43.
BICHRI, bik'ri, young. 2 Sam. 20. 1.
BIDKAR, bid'kar, cleaver (?). 2 Kin. 9. 25.
BIGTHA, big'thah. Esth. 1. 10.
BIGTHAN, big'than, given by God.
and Teresh, their conspiracy against Ahasuerus. Esth. 2. 21.
BIGTHANA, big-thah'nah, same as BIGTHAN. Esth. 6. 2.
BIGVAI, big'vai. Ezra 2. 2.
BILDAD, bil'dad, son of contention (?). Job 2. 11.
his answers to Job. Job 8; 18; 25.
BILEAM, bil'e-am, same as BALAAM (?), or IBLEAM (?). 1 Chr. 6. 70.
BILGAH, bil'gah, cheerfulness. 1 Chr. 24. 14.
BILGAI, bil'gai, same as BILGAH. Neh. 10. 8.
BILHAH, bil'hah, modesty. Gen. 29. 29.
Jacob's children by. Gen. 30. 5.
BILHAN, bil'han, modest. Gen. 36. 27.
BILSHAN, bil'shan, seeker (?). Ezra 2. 2.
BIMHAL, bim'hal. 1 Chr. 7. 33.
BINEA, bi'ne-ah. 1 Chr. 8. 37.
BINNUI, bin'oo-i, a building. Ezra 8. 33.
BIRSHA, bir'shah. Gen. 14. 2.
BIRZAVITH, bir'za-vith, wounds (?). 1 Chr. 7. 31.
BISHLAM, bish'lam. Ezra 4. 7.
BITHIAH, bith'yah, daughter (*i.e.* worshipper) of Jehovah. 1 Chr. 4. 18.
BITHRON, bith'ron, a broken place. 2 Sam. 2. 29.

BITHYNIA, bi-thin′yah. Acts 16. 7.
BIZJOTHJAH, biz-joth′jah, contempt of Jehovah. Josh. 15. 28.
BIZTHA, biz′thah. Esth. 1. 10.
BLASTUS, blast′us, a shoot. Acts 12. 20.
BOANERGES, bo′an-er′jes, sons of thunder.
James and John surnamed by Christ. Mark 3. 17.
BOAZ, bo′az, fleetness. Ruth 2. 1.
his conduct towards Ruth. Ruth 2; 3; 4.
ancestor of David and Christ. Ruth 4. 17, 22; Matt. 1. 5; Luke 3. 23, 32.
—— and Jachin (strength and stability), pillars of the temple. 2 Chr. 3. 17.
BOCHERU, bo′ke-roo, firstborn (?). 1 Chr. 8. 38.
BOCHIM, bo′kim, weepers. Judg. 2. 1.
Israel rebuked by an angel at. Judg. 2. 1–3.
Israel repent at. Judg. 2. 4, 5.
BOHAN, bo′han, thumb (?). Josh. 15. 6.
BOOZ, bo′oz, same as BOAZ. Matt. 1. 5.
BOSCATH, bos′kath, stony, elevated ground. 2 Kin. 22. 1.
BOSOR, bo′sor, Greek and Aramaic form of BEOR. 2 Pet. 2. 15.
BOZEZ, bo′zez, shining. 1 Sam. 14. 4.
BOZKATH, boz′kath, same as BOSCATH. Josh. 15. 39.
BOZRAH, boz′rah, sheepfold. Gen. 36. 33.
prophecies concerning. Is. 34. 6; 63. 1; Jer. 48. 24; 49. 13; Amos 1. 12.
BUKKI, book′i, wasting. Num. 34. 22.
BUKKIAH, book′yah, wasting from Jehovah. 1 Chr. 25. 4.
BUL, bool, rain. 1 Kin. 6. 38.
BUNAH, boon′ah, prudence. 1 Chr. 2. 25.
BUNNI, boon′i, built. Neh. 9. 4.
BUZ, booz, contempt. Gen. 22. 21.
BUZI, booz′i, descended from Buz. Ezek. 1. 3.
BUZITE, booz′ite, a descendant of Buz. Job. 32. 2.

CABBON, kab′on, cake. Josh. 15. 40.
CABUL, cah′bool, displeasing (?). Josh. 19. 27.
CÆSAR, see′zar. Matt. 22. 17.
Augustus. Luke 2. 1.
Tiberius. Luke 3. 1.
Claudius, time of dearth. Acts 11. 28.
Paul appeals to. Acts 25. 11.
household of. Phil. 4. 22.
CÆSAREA, see′zar-e′a, named after Augustus. Cæsar. Acts 8. 40.
CÆSAREA PHILIPPI, see′zar-e′a fil-ip′i, named after Philip the tetrarch.
visited by Christ. Matt. 16. 13; Mark 8. 27.
—— (Stratonis), Peter sent there. Acts 10.
Paul visits. Acts 21. 8.
Paul sent to Felix there. Acts 23. 23.
CAIAPHAS, kai′a-fas, depression (?).
high priest, prophesies concerning Christ. John 11. 49.
his counsel. Matt. 26. 3.
he condemns Him. Matt. 26. 65; Mark 14. 63; Luke 22. 71.
CAIN, kane, possession. Gen. 4. 1. Josh. 15. 57.
his anger. Gen. 4. 5.
murders Abel. Gen. 4. 8; 1 John 3. 12.
his punishment. Gen. 4. 11; Jude 11.
CAINAN, kay′nan, possessor. Gen. 5. 9.
CALAH, ka′lah. Gen. 10. 11.
CALCOL, kal′kol. 1 Chr. 2. 6.
CALEB, ka′leb, a dog.
faith of. Num. 13. 30; 14. 6.
permitted to enter Canaan. Num. 26. 65; 32. 12; Deut. 1. 36.
his request. Josh. 14. 6.
his possessions. Josh. 15. 13.
gives his daughter to Othniel to wife. Judg. 1. 13.
CALEB-EPHRATAH, ka′leb-ef′rat-ah, C. the fruitful. 1 Chr. 2. 24.
CALNEH, kal′nay. Gen. 10. 10.
CALNO, kal′no, same as CALNEH. Is. 10. 9.
CALVARY, kal′va-ry, skull. Luke 23. 33.
CAMON, ka′mon, abounding in stalks. Judg. 10. 5.
CANA, ka′nah.
Christ turns water into wine at. John 2.
nobleman visits Christ at. John 4. 47.
CANAAN, ka′na-an, low region. Gen. 9. 18.
land of. Ex. 23. 31; Josh. 1. 4; Zeph. 2. 5.
promised to Abraham. Gen. 12. 7; 13. 14; 17. 8.
inhabitants of. Ex. 15. 15.
their wickedness at Sodom and Gomorrah. Gen. 13. 13; 19.
Israelites not to walk in the ways of. Lev. 18. 3, 24, 30; 20. 23.
daughters of. Gen. 28. 1, 6, 8.
language of. Is. 19. 18.
kingdoms of. Ps. 135. 11.
king of. Judg. 4. 2, 23, 24; 5. 19.
wars of. Judg. 3. 1.
dwelling of Abraham in. Gen. 12. 6. Isaac and Jacob. Gen. 28. Esau. Gen. 36. Joseph. Gen. 37.
allotted to children of Israel. Josh. 14.
the spies visit, and their report. Num. 13.
Moses sees, from Pisgah. Num. 27. 12; Deut. 3. 27; 34. 1.
—— a son of Ham, grandson of Noah, cursed on account of his father's mockery of Noah. Gen. 9. 25.
CANAANITE, ka′na-an-ite, a zealot. Mark 3. 18.
CANAANITES, ka′na-an-ites, inhabitants of Canaan. Judg. 1. 1.
CANAANITESS, ka′na-an-ite-ess, feminine of preceding. 1 Chr. 2. 3.
CANDACE, kan′da-see, Queen of Ethiopia. Acts 8. 27.
CANNEH, kan′ay, probably same as CALNEH. Ezek. 27. 23.
CAPERNAUM, ka-per′na-um, city of consolation (?).
Christ dwells at. Matt. 4. 13; John 2. 12.
preaches at. Matt. 4. 17; Mark 1. 21.
miracles at. Matt. 8. 5; 17. 24; John 4. 46; 6. 17.
parables at. Matt. 13. 18, 24; Mark 4.
condemned for impenitence. Matt. 11. 23; Luke 10. 15.
CAPHTHORIM, kaf′thor-im, same as CAPHTORIM. 1 Chr. 1. 12.
CAPHTOR, kaf′tor. Deut. 2. 23.
CAPHTORIM, kaf′tor-im, inhabitants of Caphtor. Gen. 10. 14.
CAPPADOCIA, kap′ad-o′sha. Acts 2. 9; 1 Pet. 1. 1.
CARCAS, kar′kas. Esth. 1. 10.
CARCHEMISH, kar′kem-ish, fortress of Chemosh. Jer. 46. 2.
CAREAH, ka-re′ah, bald. 2 Kin. 25. 23.
CARMEL, karm′el, park. Josh. 12. 22.
Nabal's conduct to David at. 1 Sam. 25.
mount, Elijah and the prophets of Baal. 1 Kin. 18.
the Shunammite woman goes to Elisha at. 2 Kin. 4. 25.
her child restored to life by Elisha. 2 Kin. 4. 34.
CARMELITE, karm′el-ite, a native of Carmel. 1 Sam. 30. 5.
CARMELITESS, karm′el-ite-ess, feminine of preceding. 1 Sam. 27. 3.
CARMI, karm′i, a vine-dresser. Gen. 46. 9.
CARMITES, karm′ites, descendants of Carmi. Num. 26. 6.
CARPUS, karp′us, fruit (?). 2 Tim. 4. 13.
CARSHENA, kar′shen-ah. Esth. 1. 14.
CASIPHIA, ka-sif′yah, silver (?). Ezra 8. 17.
CASLUHIM, kas′loo-him. Gen. 10. 14.
CASTOR, kas′tor.
and Pollux, Paul's ship. Acts 28. 11.
CEDRON, keed′ron, same as KIDRON. John 18. 1.
CENCHREA, ken′kre-ah, millet, small pulse.
Paul shaves his head at. Acts 18. 18.
seaport of Corinth, church there. Rom. 16. 1.
CEPHAS, kee′fas.
(Peter), a stone. John 1. 42; 1 Cor. 1. 12; 3. 22; 9. 5; 15. 5; Gal. 2. 9. *See* PETER.
CHALCOL, kal′kol, same as CALCOL. 1 Kin. 4. 31.
CHALDEA, kal-de′ah. Jer. 50. 10.
CHALDEANS, kal-de′ans, inhabitants of Chaldea.
afflict Job. Job. 1. 17.
besiege Jerusalem. 2 Kin. 24. 2; 25. 4; Jer. 37—39.

CHALDEANS—*cont.*
wise men of, preserved by Daniel. Dan. 2. 24.
prophecies concerning. Is. 23. 13; 43. 14; 47. 1; 48. 14; Hab. 1. 5.
CHALDEES, kal-dees´, same as preceding. Gen. 11. 28.
CHANAAN, ka´na-an, another form of Canaan. Acts 7. 11.
CHARASHIM, kar´ash-im, craftsmen. 1 Chr. 4. 14.
CHARCHEMISH, same as CARCHEMISH. 2 Chr. 35. 20.
CHARRAN, kar´an, same as HARAN. Acts 7. 2.
CHEBAR, ke´bar, great (?).
the river, Ezekiel's visions at. Ezek. 1; 3. 15; 10. 15.
CHEDORLAOMER, ke-dor´la-o´mer, glory of Laomer (?).
king of Elam, takes Lot prisoner, but subdued by Abram. Gen. 14.
CHELAL, ke´lal, completion. Ezra 10. 30.
CHELLUH, kel´oo. Ezra 10. 35.
CHELUB, kel´oob, bird-trap. 1 Chr. 4. 11.
CHELUBAI, kel-oo´bai, same as CALEB. 1 Chr. 2. 9.
CHEMARIMS, kem-ah´rims, persons dressed in black attire. Zeph. 1. 4.
CHEMOSH, keem´osh, subduer.
god of Moab. Num. 21. 29; Judg. 11. 24; Jer. 48. 7, 13, 46.
worshipped by Solomon. 1 Kin. 11. 7.
CHENAANAH, ke-na´an-ah, probably fem. of Canaan. 1 Kin. 22. 11.
CHENANI, ke´nane´i, probably same as CHENANIAH. Neh. 9. 4.
CHENANIAH, ke´nan-i´ah, whom Jehovah supports. 1 Chr. 15. 22.
CHEPHAR-HAAMMONAI, ke-far´hah-am´on-ai, village of the Ammonites. Josh. 18. 24.
CHEPHIRAH, ke-fi´rah, same as CAPHAR. Josh. 9. 17.
CHERAN, ke´ran. Gen. 36. 26.
CHERETHIMS, ke´reth-ims, Cretans (?). Ezek. 25. 16.
CHERETHITES, ke´reth-ites, probably same as preceding. 2 Sam. 8. 18.
(and Pelethites), David's guard. 2 Sam. 15. 18.
CHERITH, ke´rith, gorge (?). 1 Kin. 17. 3.
CHERUB, cher´ub, blessing (?), strong (?). Ezra 2. 59.
CHERUBIM, cher´oob-im, plural of CHERUB.
in garden of Eden. Gen. 3. 24.
for the mercy seat and the temple. Ex. 25. 18; 37. 7; 1 Kin. 6. 23; 2 Chr. 3. 10; Ps. 80. 1; Ezek. 41. 18.
Ezekiel's visions of. Ezek. 1; 10.
CHESALON, ke-sah´lon, hope. Josh. 15. 10.
CHESED, ke´sed, conqueror (?). Gen. 22. 22.
CHESIL, ke´sil, a fool. Josh. 15. 30.
CHESULLOTH, ke-sool´oth, confidences. Josh. 19. 18.
CHEZIB, ke´zib, false. Gen. 38. 5.
CHIDON, ki´don, javelin. 1 Chr. 13. 9.
CHILEAB, kil´e-ab, probably another form of CALEB. 2 Sam. 3. 3.
CHILION, kil´yon, wasting away. Ruth 1. 2.
CHILMAD, kil´mad. Ezek. 27. 23.
CHIMHAM, kim´ham, longing. 2 Sam. 19. 37.
CHINNERETH, kin´er-eth, a lyre. Josh. 19. 35.
CHINNEROTH, kin´er-oth, plural of CHINNERETH. Josh. 11. 2.
CHIOS, ki´os. Acts 20. 15.
CHISLEU, kis´lew. Neh. 1. 1.
CHISLON, kis´lon, confidence, hope. Num. 34. 21.
CHISLOTH-TABOR, kis´loth-ta´bor, flanks (?) of Tabor. Josh. 19. 12.
CHITTIM, kit´im, probably Cyprus.
prophecies of. Num. 24. 24; Is. 23. 1, 12; Dan. 11. 30.
CHIUN, ki´oon, image. Amos 5. 26.
CHLOE, klo´ee. 1 Cor. 1. 11.
CHOR-ASHAN, kor-ash´an, smoking furnace. 1 Sam. 30. 30.
CHORAZIN, ko-ra´zin. Matt. 11. 21.
CHOZEBA, ko-ze´bah, deceiver. 1 Chr. 4. 22.
CHRIST, the anointed. See *Subject-Index*, p. 197.
CHUB, choob. Ezek. 30. 5.
CHUN, choon, establishment. 1 Chr. 18. 8.
CHUSHAN-RISHATHAIM, koosh´an-rish-a-tha´im. Oppresses Israel. Judg. 3. 8, 9, 10.
CHUZA, koo´zah. Luke 8. 3.
CILICIA, si-lish´ya.
disciples there. Acts 15. 23, 41.
the country of Paul. Acts 21. 39; Gal. 1. 21.
Paul born at Tarsus in. Acts 22. 3.
CINNEROTH, kin´er-oth, same as CHINNEROTH. 1 Kin. 15. 20.
CIS, kis. Acts 13. 21, same as KISH.
CLAUDA, klawd´ah. Acts 27. 16.
CLAUDIA, klawd´yah. 2 Tim. 4. 21.
CLAUDIUS, klawd´yus. Acts 11. 28.
CLAUDIUS LYSIAS, klawd´yus-lis-yas.
chief captain, rescues Paul. Acts 21. 31; 22. 24; 23. 10.
sends him to Felix. Acts 23. 26.
CLEMENT, klem´ent.
fellow labourer of Paul. Phil. 4. 3.
CLEOPAS, kle´op-as, either a shortened form of Cleopatros, or a Greek form of Alphæus.
a disciple. Luke 24. 18. *See* EMMAUS.
CLEOPHAS, kle´of-as, probably same as preceding. John 19. 25.
CNIDUS, kni´dus, nettle (?). Acts 27. 7.
COL-HOZEH, kol-ho´zeh, every one that seeth. Neh. 3. 15.
COLOSSE, ko-los´ee.
brethren at, encouraged and warned. Col. 1; 2.
exhorted to holiness. Col. 3; 4.
COLOSSIANS, ko-los´yans, people of Colosse.
CONANIAH. 2 Chr. 35. 9, same as CONONIAH.
CONIAH, ko-ni´ah, contracted from JECONIAH. Jer. 22. 24.
CONONIAH, kon-on-i´ah, whom Jehovah has set up. 2 Chr. 31. 12.
COOS, ko´os.
Paul sails to. Acts 21. 1.
CORE, ko´re, Greek form of KORAH. Jude 11.
CORINTH, kor´inth.
Paul and Apollos at. Acts 18; 19. 1.
CORINTHIANS, kor-inth´yans, inhabitants of Corinth. Acts 18. 8.
their divisions, &c., censured. 1 Cor. 1; 5; 11. 18.
their faith and graces. 2 Cor. 3.
instructed concerning spiritual gifts. 1 Cor. 14; and the resurrection. 1 Cor. 15.
exhorted to charity, &c. 1 Cor. 13; 14. 1; 2 Cor. 8; 9.
their false teachers exposed. 2 Cor. 11. 3, 4, 13.
Paul commends himself to. 2 Cor. 11; 12.
CORNELIUS, kor-neel´yus. Acts 10. 1.
devout centurion, his prayer answered. Acts 10. 3; sends for Peter, 10, 9; baptized, 10. 48.
COSAM, ko´sam. Luke 3. 28.
COZ, koz, thorn. 1 Chr. 4. 8.
COZBI, kos´bi, deceitful, slain by Phineas. Num. 25. 15.
CRESCENS, kres´ens, growing.
goes to Dalmatia. 2 Tim. 4. 10.
CRETE, kreet.
visited by Paul. Acts 27. 7.
CRETES or CRETIANS, kreet´yans, inhabitants of Crete. Acts 2. 11; Tit. 1. 12.
CRISPUS, krisp´us, curled.
baptized by Paul. Acts 18. 8; 1 Cor. 1. 14.
CUMI, koom´i, arise. Mark 5. 41.
CUSH, koosh, black. Gen. 10. 6.
CUSHAN, koosh´an, same meaning as CUSH. Hab. 3. 7.
CUSHI, koosh´i, same meaning as CUSH.
announces Absalom's death. 2 Sam. 18. 21.
CUTH, kooth. 2 Kin. 17. 30.
CUTHAH, kooth´ah, same as CUTH. 2 Kin. 17. 24.
CYPRUS, si´prus. Acts 4. 36.
disciples there. Acts 11. 19.
Paul and Barnabas preach there. Acts 13. 4.
Barnabas and Mark go there. Acts 15. 39.
CYRENE, si-re´nee. Matt. 27. 32.
disciples of. Acts 11. 20; 13. 1.

CYRENE—*cont.*
Simon of. Mark 15. 21.
CYRENIAN, si-reen´yan, a native of Cyrene. Acts 6. 9.
CYRENIUS, si-reen´yus, Greek form of the Roman name Quirinus.
governor of Syria. Luke 2. 2.
CYRUS, si´rus, the sun. 2 Chr. 36. 22.
king of Persia, prophecies concerning. Is. 44. 28; 45. 1. *See* Dan. 6. 28; 10. 1.
his proclamation for rebuilding the temple. 2 Chr. 36. 22; Ezra 1.

DABAREH, da´bar-ay, pasture. Josh. 21. 28.
DABBASHETH, dab-ash´eth, hump of a camel. Josh. 19. 11.
DABERATH, da´ber-ath. Josh. 19. 12, same as DABAREH.
DAGON, da´gon, fish.
national idol-god of the Philistines, sacrificed to. Judg. 16. 23.
smitten down in temple at Ashdod. 1 Sam. 5. 3, 4.
Saul's head fastened in house of. 1 Chr. 10. 10.
DALAIAH, da-lai´ah, whom Jehovah hath delivered. 1 Chr. 3. 24.
DALMANUTHA, dal´ma-noo´thah. Mark 8. 10.
DALMATIA, dal´ma´shah. 2 Tim. 4. 10.
DALPHON, dal´fon, proud (?). Esth. 9. 7.
DAMARIS, dam´ar-is, calf (?).
cleaves to Paul. Acts 17. 34.
DAMASCENES, dam´as-eens´, people of Damascus. 2 Cor. 11. 32.
DAMASCUS, dam-ask´us, activity (?). Gen. 14. 15.
mentioned. Gen. 15. 2.
subjugated by David. 2 Sam. 8. 6; 1 Chr. 18. 6.
Elisha's prophecy there. 2 Kin. 8. 7.
taken by Tiglath-pileser, king of Assyria. 2 Kin. 16. 9.
restored to Israel by Jeroboam. 2 Kin. 14. 28.
king Ahaz copies an altar there. 2 Kin. 16. 10.
Paul's journey to. Acts 9; 22. 6.
Paul restored to sight, and baptized there. Acts 9. 17, 18.
prophecies concerning. Is. 7. 8; 8. 4; 17. 1; Jer. 49. 23; Amos 1. 3.
DAN, judge.
son of Jacob, by Rachel's handmaid. Gen. 30. 6.
—— TRIBE of, numbered. Num. 1. 38; 26. 42.
their inheritance. Josh. 19. 40.
blessed by Jacob. Gen. 49. 16.
blessed by Moses. Deut. 33. 22.
win Laish, and call it Dan. Judg. 18. 29.
set up idolatry. Judg. 18. 30; 1 Kin. 12. 29.
DAN-JAAN, dan´ja´an, woodland (?) Dan. 2 Sam. 24. 6.
DANIEL, dan´yel, God's judge. Dan. 1. 6.
(Belteshazzar), with other captives, taken from Jerusalem to Babylon. Dan. 1. 3.
taught the learning of the Chaldeans. Dan. 1. 4.
will not take the king's meat or drink. Dan. 1. 8.
has understanding in dreams. Dan. 1. 17.
interprets the royal dreams. Dan. 2; 4; and handwriting on wall. Dan. 5. 17.
made chief president by Darius. Dan. 6. 2.
conspired against by the princes. Dan. 6. 4.
idolatrous decree against, issued. Dan. 6. 9; breach thereof, Dan. 6. 10.
cast into the lions' den. Dan. 6. 16; preservation in, Dan. 6. 22.
his vision of the four beasts. Dan. 7. 12; ram and he-goat. Dan. 8. 3.
his prayer. Dan. 9. 3.
promise of return from captivity. Dan. 9. 20; 10. 10; 12. 13.
name mentioned. Ezek. 14. 14, 20; 28. 3.
DANITES, dan´ites, descendants of Dan. Judg. 13. 2.
DANNAH, dan´ah. Josh. 15. 49.
DARA, da´rah, probably contracted from the next word. 1 Chr. 2. 6.
DARDA, dar´dah, pearl of wisdom (?). 1 Kin. 4. 31.
DARIUS, da-ri´us, governor (?). Ezra 4. 5.

DARIUS—*cont.*
decree concerning the rebuilding of the temple. Ezra 6.
—— (the Median) takes Babylon. Dan. 5. 31; his decree to fear the God of Daniel. Dan. 6. 25.
DARKON, dark´on, scatterer (?). Ezra 2. 56.
DATHAN, da´than. Num. 16. 1.
DAVID, da´vid, beloved.
King, son of Jesse. Ruth 4. 22; 1 Chr. 2; Matt. 1.
anointed by Samuel. 1 Sam. 16. 8.
plays the harp before Saul. 1 Sam. 16. 19.
his zeal and faith. 1 Sam. 17. 26, 34.
kills Goliath of Gath. 1 Sam. 17. 49.
at first honoured by Saul. 1 Sam. 18.
Saul jealous of, tries to kill. 1 Sam. 18. 8, 12.
afterwards persecuted by him. 1 Sam. 19; 20.
loved by Jonathan. 1 Sam. 18. 1; 19. 2; 20; 23. 16; and by Michal. 1 Sam. 18. 28; 19. 11.
overcomes the Philistines. 1 Sam. 18. 27; 19. 8.
flees to Naioth. 1 Sam. 19. 18.
eats of the shewbread. 1 Sam. 21; Ps. 52; Matt. 12. 4.
flees to Gath, and feigns madness. 1 Sam. 21. 10, 13; Ps. 34; 56.
dwells in the cave of Adullam. 1 Sam. 22; Ps. 63; 142.
escapes Saul's pursuit. 1 Sam. 23; Ps. 57.
twice spares Saul's life. 1 Sam. 24. 4; 26. 5.
his wrath against Nabal appeased by Abigail. 1 Sam. 25. 23.
dwells at Ziklag. 1 Sam. 27.
dismissed from the army by Achish. 1 Sam. 29. 9.
chastises the Amalekites, and rescues the captives. 1 Sam. 30. 16.
kills messenger who brings news of Saul's death. 2 Sam. 1. 15.
laments the death of Saul and Jonathan. 2 Sam. 1. 17.
becomes king of Judah. 2 Sam. 2. 4.
forms a league with Abner. 2 Sam. 3. 13.
laments Abner's death. 2 Sam. 3. 31.
avenges the murder of Ish-bosheth. 2 Sam. 4. 9.
becomes king of all Israel. 2 Sam. 5. 3; 1 Chr. 11.
his victories. 2 Sam. 2; 5; 8; 10; 12. 29; 21. 15; 1 Chr. 18—20; Ps. 60.
brings the ark to Zion. 2 Sam. 6; 1 Chr. 13; 15.
his psalms of thanksgiving. 2 Sam. 22; 1 Chr. 16. 7; Ps. 18; 103; 105.
Michal despises him for dancing before the ark. 2 Sam. 6. 20.
reproves her. 2 Sam. 6. 21.
desires to build God a house. 2 Sam. 7. 2; and is forbidden by Nathan. 1 Chr. 17. 4.
God's promises to him. 2 Sam. 7. 11; 1 Chr. 17. 10.
his prayer and thanksgiving. 2 Sam. 7. 18; 1 Chr. 17. 16.
his consideration for Mephibosheth. 2 Sam. 9.
his sin concerning Bath-sheba and Uriah. 2 Sam. 11; 12.
repents at Nathan's parable of the ewe lamb. 2 Sam. 12; Ps. 51.
Absalom conspires against. 2 Sam. 15; Ps. 3.
Ahithophel's treachery against. 1 Sam. 15. 31; 16; 17.
Shimei curses. 2 Sam. 16. 5; Ps. 7.
Barzillai's loyalty. 2 Sam. 17. 27.
grieves over Absalom's death. 2 Sam. 18. 33; 19. 1.
returns to Jerusalem. 2 Sam. 19. 15.
pardons Shimei. 2 Sam. 19. 16.
Sheba's conspiracy against. 2 Sam. 20.
atones for the Gibeonites. 2 Sam. 21.
his mighty men. 2 Sam. 23. 8; 1 Chr. 11. 10.
tempted by Satan, numbers the people. 2 Sam. 24; 1 Chr. 21.
regulates the service of the tabernacle. 1 Chr. 23—26.
exhorts the congregation to fear God. 1 Chr. 28.
appoints Solomon his successor. 1 Kin. 1; Ps. 72.
his charge to Solomon. 1 Kin. 2; 1 Chr. 28. 9; to

DAVID—*cont.*
build a house for the sanctuary. 1 Chr. 22. 6; 28. 10.
his last words. 2 Sam. 23.
his death. 1 Kin. 2; 1 Chr. 29. 26.
the progenitor of Christ. Matt. 1. 1; 9. 27; 21. 9; comp. Ps. 110, with Matt. 22. 41; Luke 1. 32; John 7. 42; Acts 2. 25; 13. 22; 15. 15; Rom. 1. 3; 2 Tim. 2. 8; Rev. 5. 5; 22. 16.
prophecies concerning. Ps. 89; 132; Is. 9. 7; 22. 22; 55. 3; Jer. 30. 9; Hos. 3. 5; Amos 9. 11.
DEBIR, de-bee´r, a recess. Josh. 10. 3.
DEBORAH, deb´or-ah, bee.
the prophetess judges and delivers Israel. Judg. 4.
her song. Judg. 5.
—— Rebekah's nurse, death of. Gen. 35. 8.
DECAPOLIS, de-ka´pol-is, ten cities. Matt. 4. 25.
DEDAN, de´dan. Gen. 10. 7.
DEDANIM, de-dah´nim, inhabitants of Dedan. Is. 21. 13.
DEHAVITES, de´hav-ites. Ezra 4. 9.
DEKAR, de´kar, piercing. 1 Kin. 4. 9.
DELAIAH, de-lai´ah, whom Jehovah has freed. 1 Chr. 24. 18.
DELILAH, de-li´lah, delicate. Judg. 16. 4.
DEMAS, de´mas, probably same as following. Col. 4. 14.
DEMETRIUS, de-me´tri-us, belonging to Demeter.
silversmith. Acts 19. 24.
disciple. 3 John 12.
DERBE, der´bee, juniper (?). Acts 14. 6.
DEUEL, doo´el, the same as REUEL (?). Num. 1. 14.
DEUTERONOMY, a recapitulation of the law.
DIANA, di-an´ah.
of Ephesians, tumult concerning. Acts 19. 24.
DIBLAIM, dib-la´im, two cakes. Hos. 1. 3.
DIBLATHAIM, dib-la-thah´im, same as DIBLAIM. Num. 33. 46.
DIBLATH, dib´lath, supposed to be the same as RIBLAH. Ezek. 6. 14.
DIBON, di´bon, wasting. Num. 21. 30.
DIBON-GAD, di´bon-gad´, wasting of Gad. Num. 33. 45.
DIBRI, dib´ri, eloquent. Lev. 24. 11.
DIDYMUS, did´im-us, twin. John 11. 16.
(Thomas). John 20. 24.
DIKLAH, dik´lah, a palm tree. Gen. 10. 27.
DILEAN, dil´e-an, cucumber field (?). Josh. 15. 38.
DIMNAH, dim´nah, dunghill. Josh. 21. 35.
DIMON, di´mon, same as DIBON. Is. 15. 9.
DIMONAH, di-mo´nah, probably same as preceding. Josh. 15. 22.
DINAH, di´nah, vindicated.
Jacob's daughter. Gen. 30. 21; outraged by Shechem, Gen. 34. 2; avenged by Simeon and Levi, Gen. 34. 25.
DINAITES, di´na-ites. Ezra 4. 9.
DINHABAH, din´hab-ah. Gen. 36. 32.
DIONYSIUS, di´o-nis´yus, belonging to Dionysus.
the Areopagite, believes. Acts 17. 34.
DIOTREPHES, di-ot´ref-ees, nourished by Zeus, loveth preeminence. 3 John 9.
DISHAN, di´shan, antelope (?). Gen. 36. 28.
DISHON, di´shon, same as preceding. Gen. 36. 21.
DIZAHAB, di´za-hab, a place abounding in gold (?). Deut. 1. 1.
DODAI, do´dai, loving. 1 Chr. 27. 4.
DODANIM, do´dah-nim. Gen. 10. 4.
DODAVAH, do´dah-vah, love of Jehovah. 2 Chr. 20. 37.
DODO, do´do, same as DODAI. 2 Sam. 23. 9.
DOEG, do´eg, anxious. 1 Sam. 21. 7.
the Edomite slays the priests. 1 Sam. 22. 9.
DOPHKAH, dof´kah. Num. 33. 12.
DOR, dor, dwelling. Josh. 11. 2.
DORCAS, dor´kas, gazelle. Acts 9. 36.
(Tabitha), raised from death by Peter. Acts 9. 40.
DOTHAN, do´than, two wells or cisterns. Gen. 37. 17.
DRUSILLA, droo-sil´ah. Acts 24. 24.
DUMAH, doom´ah, silence. Gen. 25. 14.
DURA, doo´rah, town.
plain of, golden image set up. Dan. 3. 1.

EBAL, e´bal, stony (?). Gen. 36. 23.
mount, curses delivered from. Deut. 27. 13; Josh. 8. 33.
EBED, e´bed, servant. Judg. 9. 26.
EBED-MELECH, e´bed-me´lek, servant of the king.
Ethiopian eunuch, intercedes with king Zedekiah for Jeremiah. Jer. 38. 7; 39. 16.
EBEN-EZER, e´ben-e´zer, stone of help.
Israelites smitten by Philistines at. 1 Sam. 4. 1.
'hitherto hath the Lord helped us,' (stone raised by Samuel in memory of defeat of the Philistines). 1 Sam. 7. 12.
EBER, e´ber, the region beyond. Gen. 10. 21.
EBIASAPH, e-bi´a-saf, same as ABIASAPH. 1 Chr. 6. 23.
EBRONAH, eb-ro´nah, passage (?). Num. 33. 34.
ECCLESIASTES, ek-lee´zy-ast´ees, preacher.
ED, witness. Josh. 22. 34.
EDAR, e´dar, flock. Gen. 35. 21.
EDEN, e´den, pleasantness. Gen. 2. 8.
Adam driven from. Gen. 3. 24.
mentioned. Is. 51. 3; Ezek. 28. 13; 31. 9; 36. 35; Joel 2. 3.
EDER, e´der, flock, same as EDAR. 1 Chr. 23. 23.
EDOM, e´dom, red. Gen. 25. 30.
—— (Idumea), the land of Esau. Gen. 32. 3; Is. 63. 1.
prophecies concerning. Is. 34; Jer. 25. 21; 49. 7; Ezek. 25. 13; 35; Amos 1. 11; Obad. 1.
EDOMITES, e´dom-ites, inhabitants of Edom. Gen. 36. 9.
the descendants of Esau. Gen. 36.
deny Moses passage through Edom. Num. 20. 18.
their possessions. Deut. 2. 5; Josh. 24. 4.
not to be abhorred. Deut. 23. 7.
subdued by David. 2 Sam. 8. 14.
revolt. 2 Kin. 8. 20; 2 Chr. 21. 8.
subdued by Amaziah. 2 Kin. 14. 7; 2 Chr. 11. 25.
EDREI, ed´re-i, strong. Num. 21. 33.
EGLAH, eg´lah, heifer. 2 Sam. 3. 5.
EGLAIM, eg-la´im, two pools. Is. 15. 8.
EGLON, eg´lon. Judg. 3. 12.
oppresses Israel. Judg. 3. 14; slain by Ehud. Judg. 3. 21.
EGYPT, e´jipt, black.
Abram goes down into. Gen. 12. 10.
Joseph sold into. Gen. 37. 36; his advancement, fall, imprisonment, and restoration there. Gen. 39; 40; 41.
Jacob's sons go to buy corn in. Gen. 42.
Jacob and all his seed go there. Gen. 46. 6.
children of Israel wax mighty there. Ex. 1. 7; afflicted, and build treasure cities. Ex. 1. 11.
plagued on account of Israelites. Ex. 7—11.
children of Israel depart from. Ex. 13. 17.
army of, pursue and perish in the Red sea. Ex. 14.
kings of, harass Judah. 1 Kin. 14. 25; 2 Kin. 23. 29; 2 Chr. 12. 2; 35. 20; 36. 3; Jer. 37. 5.
the 'remnant of Judah' go there. Jer. 43. 7.
Jesus taken to. Matt. 2. 13.
prophecies concerning. Gen. 15. 13; Is. 11. 11; 19; 20; 27. 12; 30. 1; Jer. 9. 26; 25. 19; 43. 8; 44. 28; 46; Ezek. 29—32; Dan. 11. 8; Hos. 9. 3; 11; Joel 3. 19; Zech. 10. 10; 14. 18.
EGYPTIAN, e-jip´shan, a native of Egypt. 1 Sam. 30. 11.
EHI, e´hi, shortened from AHIRAM. Gen. 46. 21.
EHUD, e´hud, joined together (?).
judge, delivers Israel. Judg. 3. 15.
EKER, e´ker, same as ACHAR. 1 Chr. 2. 27.
EKRON, ek´ron, eradication. Josh. 13. 3.
taken. Judg. 1. 18.
men of, smitten with emerods. 1 Sam. 5. 12.
their trespass offering for recovery. 1 Sam. 6. 17.
prophecies concerning. Amos 1. 8; Zeph. 2. 4; Zech. 9. 5.
EKRONITES, ek´ron-ites, inhabitants of Ekron. Josh. 13. 3.

ELADAH, el´a-dah, whom God clothes. 1 Chr. 7. 20.
ELAH, e´lah, terebinth. Gen. 36. 41.
king of Israel. 1 Kin. 16. 8, 10.
—— valley of, Saul sets the battle in array against the Philistines. 1 Sam. 17. 2.
David slays Goliath there. 1 Sam. 17. 49.
ELAM, e´lam.
son of Shem. Gen. 10. 22.
—— Chedorlaomer, king of. Gen. 14.
ELAMITES, e´lam-ites, inhabitants of Elam. Ezra 4. 9; Acts 2. 9.
ELASAH, el´a-sah, whom God made. Ezra 10. 22.
ELATH, e´lath, a grove. Deut. 2. 8.
EL-BETH-EL, el-beth´el, the house of God. Gen. 35. 7.
ELDAAH, el´da-ah, whom God called. Gen. 25. 4.
ELDAD, el´dad, whom God loves. Num. 11. 26.
ELEAD, el´e-ad, whom God praises. 1 Chr. 7. 21.
ELEALEH, el´e-a´lay, whither God ascends. Num. 32. 3.
ELEASAH, e'l-e-a´sah, same as ELASAH. 1 Chr. 2. 39.
ELEAZAR, el´e-a´zar, whom God aids.
son of Aaron, and chief priest. Ex. 6. 23; 28; 29; Lev. 8; Num. 3. 2; 4. 16; 16. 36; 20. 26, 28; 27. 22; 31. 13; 34. 17; Josh. 17. 4; 24. 33.
—— son of Abinadab, keeps the ark. 1 Sam. 7. 1.
—— one of David's captains. 2 Sam. 23. 9; 1 Chr. 11. 12.
EL-ELOHE-ISRAEL, el´el-o´he-iz´ra-el, God, the God of Israel.
the altar erected by Jacob at Shalem. Gen. 33. 20.
ELEPH, e´lef, ox. Josh. 18. 28.
ELHANAN, el´ha´nan, whom God gave.
one of David's warriors. 2 Sam. 21. 19; 23. 24; 1 Chr. 11. 26; 20. 5.
ELI, e´li, my God.
Eli, Eli, lama sabachthani? Matt. 27. 46; Mark 15. 34.
ELI, e´li, height. 1 Sam. 1. 3.
high priest and judge, blesses Hannah, who bears Samuel. 1 Sam. 1. 17, 20.
Samuel brought to. 1 Sam. 1. 25.
wickedness of his sons. 1 Sam. 2. 22.
rebuked by man of God. 1 Sam. 2. 27.
ruin of his house shewed to Samuel by God. 1 Sam. 3. 11.
his sons slain. 1 Sam. 4. 10.
his death. 1 Sam. 4. 18.
ELIAB, el-i´ab, whose father is God. Num. 1. 9.
ELIADA, ELIADAH, el´i´ya-dah, whom God cares for. 2 Sam. 5. 16.
ELIAH, el-i´ah, same name as ELIJAH. 1 Chr. 8. 27.
ELIAHBA, e'l-i-ah´bah, whom God hides. 2 Sam. 23. 32.
ELIAKIM, el-i´a-kim, whom God establishes. 2 Kin. 18. 18.
chief minister of Hezekiah; his conference with Rabshakeh's ambassadors; mission to Isaiah. 2 Kin. 18; 19.
prefigures kingdom of Christ. Is. 22. 20–25.
—— son of Josiah, made king by Pharaoh, and named Jehoiakim. 2 Kin. 23. 34; 2 Chr. 36. 4.
ELIAM, el-i´am, same as AMMIEL. 2 Sam. 11. 3.
ELIAS, el-i´as, same as ELIJAH. Matt. 27. 47, 49; Mark 15. 35, 36; John 1. 21. *See* ELIJAH.
ELIASAPH, el-i´a-saf, whom God added. Num. 1. 14.
ELIASHIB, el-i´a-shib, whom God restores.
high priest, builds the wall. Neh. 3. 1.
allied unto Tobiah. Neh. 13. 4.
ELIATHAH, el-i´a-thah, to whom God comes. 1 Chr. 25. 4.
ELIDAD, el-i´dad, whom God loves. Num. 34. 21.
ELIEL, el-i´el, to whom God is strength. 1 Chr. 5. 24.
ELIENAI, el-i-e´nai, unto Jehovah my eyes are raised (?). 1 Chr. 8. 20.
ELIEZER, el´i-e´zer, my God is help.
Abraham's steward. Gen. 15. 2.
—— son of Moses. Ex. 18. 4; 1 Chr. 23. 15.
—— prophet. 2 Chr. 20. 37.
ELIHOENAI, el´i-ho-e´nai, same as ELIOENAI. Ezra 8. 4.
ELIHOREPH, el´i-ho´ref, to whom God is the reward. 1 Kin. 4. 3.
ELIHU, el-i´hoo, whose God is He. 1 Sam. 1. 1.
reproves Job's friends, Job 32; and Job's impatience, Job 33. 8; and self-righteousness, Job 34. 5.
declares God's justice, Job 33. 12; 34. 10; 35. 13; 36; power, Job 33—37; and mercy, Job 33. 23; 34. 28.
ELIJAH, el-i´jah, my God is Jehovah.
the Tishbite, prophet, predicts great drought. 1 Kin. 17. 1; Luke 4. 25; James 5. 17.
hides at the brook Cherith, and is fed by ravens. 1 Kin. 17. 5 (19. 5).
raises the widow's son. 1 Kin. 17. 21.
his sacrifice at Carmel. 1 Kin. 18. 38.
slays the prophets of Baal at the brook Kishon. 1 Kin. 18. 40.
flees from Jezebel into the wilderness of Beer-sheba. 1 Kin. 19; Rom. 11. 2.
anoints Elisha. 1 Kin. 19. 19.
by God's command denounces Ahab in Naboth's vineyard. 1 Kin. 21. 17.
his prediction fulfilled. 1 Kin. 22. 38; 2 Kin. 9. 36; 10. 10.
condemns Ahaziah for enquiring of Baal-zebub. 2 Kin. 1. 3, 16.
two companies sent to take him burnt with fire from heaven. 2 Kin. 1. 10; Luke 9. 54.
divides Jordan. 2 Kin. 2. 8.
taken up by chariot of fire. 2 Kin. 2. 11.
his mantle taken by Elisha. 2 Kin. 2. 13.
appears at Christ's transfiguration. Matt. 17. 3; Mark 9. 4; Luke 9. 30.
precursor of John the Baptist. Mal. 4. 5; Matt. 11. 14; 16. 14; Luke 1. 17; 9. 8, 19; John 1. 21.
ELIKA, el-i´kah, whom God purifies (?). 2 Sam. 23. 25.
ELIM, eel´im, oaks. Ex. 15. 27.
ELIMELECH, el-i´me-lek, to whom God is king. Ruth 1. 2.
ELIOENAI, el´i-o-e´nai, unto Jehovah my eyes are turned. 1 Chr. 3. 23.
ELIPHAL, el´i-fal, whom God judges. 1 Chr. 11. 35.
ELIPHALET, el-i´fa-let, to whom God is salvation. 2 Sam. 5. 16.
ELIPHAZ, el´i-faz, to whom God is strength. Gen. 36. 4.
reproves Job. Job 4; 5; 15; 22.
God's wrath against him. Job 42. 7; he offers a burnt offering, and Job prays for him. Job 42. 8.
ELIPHELEH, el-i´fe-lay, whom God distinguishes. 1 Chr. 15. 18.
ELIPHELET, el-i´fe-let, same as ELIPHALET. 1 Chr. 3. 8.
ELISABETH, el-iz'-a-beth, same as ELISHEBA.
cousin of Virgin Mary, and mother of John the Baptist. Luke 1. 5.
angel promises her a son. Luke 1. 13.
her salutation to Mary. Luke 1. 42.
ELISEUS, el´i-se´us, Greek form of ELISHA. Luke 4. 27.
ELISHA, el-i´shah, to whom God is salvation.
—— (Eliseus), succeeds Elijah. 1 Kin. 19. 16.
receives his mantle, and divides Jordan. 2 Kin. 2. 13.
heals the waters with salt. 2 Kin. 2. 22.
bears destroy the children who mock him. 2 Kin. 2. 24.
his miracles: water, 2 Kin. 3. 16; oil, 4. 4; Shunammite's son, 4. 32; death in the pot, 4. 40; feeds a hundred men with twenty loaves, 4. 44; Naaman's leprosy, 5. 14; iron swims, 6. 5; Syrians struck blind, 6. 18.
prophesies plenty in Samaria when besieged. 2 Kin. 7. 1.
sends to anoint Jehu. 2 Kin. 9. 1.
his death. 2 Kin. 13. 20.
miracle wrought by his bones. 2 Kin. 13. 21.
ELISHAH, el-i´shah. Gen. 10. 4.

ELISHAMA, el-i´sha-mah, whom God hears. Num. 1. 10.
ELISHAPHAT, el-i´sha-fat, whom God judges. 2 Chr. 23. 1.
ELISHEBA, el-i´she-bah, to whom God is the oath. Ex. 6. 23.
ELISHUA, el-i´shoo´ah, same as ELISHA. 2 Sam. 5. 15.
ELIUD, el-i´ood, God of Judah. Matt. 1. 14.
ELIZAPHAN, el-i´za-fan, whom God protects. Num. 3. 30.
ELIZUR, el-i´zoor, God is a Rock. Num. 1. 5.
ELKANAH, el´ka´nah, whom God possessed. Ex. 6. 24.
 Samuel's father. 1 Sam. 1.
ELKOSHITE, el´kosh-ite, inhabitant of Elkosh. Nah. 1. 1.
ELLASAR, el-ah´sar. Gen. 14. 1.
ELMODAM, el-mo´dam, same as ALMODAD. Luke 3. 28.
ELNAAM, el-na´am, whose pleasure God is. 1 Chr. 11. 46.
ELNATHAN, el-na´than, whom God gave. 2 Kin. 24. 8.
ELOI, el-o´i, my God. Mark 15. 34.
ELON, e´lon, oak. Gen. 26. 34.
 judges Israel. Judg. 12. 11.
ELON-BETH-HANAN, e´lon-beth´ha´nan, oak of the house of grace. 1 Kin. 4. 9.
ELONITES, e´lon-ites, descendants of Elon. Num. 26. 26.
ELOTH, e´loth, same as ELATH. 1 Kin. 9. 26.
ELPAAL, el-pa´al, to whom God is the reward. 1 Chr. 8. 11.
ELPALET, el-pa´let, same as ELIPHALET. 1 Chr. 14. 5.
EL-PARAN, el-par´an, oak of Paran. Gen. 14. 6.
ELTEKEH, el´te-kay, whose fear is God. Josh. 19. 44.
ELTEKON, el´te-kon, whose foundation is God. Josh. 15. 59.
ELTOLAD, el-to´lad, whose posterity is from God. Josh. 15. 30.
ELUL, el´ool. Neh. 6. 15.
ELUZAI, el-oo´zai, God is my praises. 1 Chr. 12. 5.
ELYMAS, el´im-as, a wise man. Acts 13. 8.
 (Bar-jesus). Acts 13. 6.
ELZABAD, el-za´bad, whom God gave. 1 Chr. 12. 12.
ELZAPHAN, el-za´fan, whom God protects. Ex. 6. 22.
EMIMS, eem´ims, terrible men, giants. Gen. 14. 5; Deut. 2. 10.
EMMANUEL, em-an´u-el, same as IMMANUEL.
 God with us. Is. 7. 14; 8. 8; Matt. 1. 23.
EMMAUS, em-a´us, hot springs (?). Luke 24. 13.
 Christ talks with Cleopas and another on the way to. Luke 24. 15.
EMMOR, em´or, same as HAMOR. Acts 7. 16.
ENAM, e´nam, two fountains. Josh. 15. 34.
ENAN, e´nan, having eyes. Num. 1. 15.
EN-DOR, en´-dor, fountain of Dor. Josh. 17. 11.
 witch of. 1 Sam. 28. 7.
ENEAS, e´ne-as. Acts 9. 33, 34.
EN-EGLAIM, en´eg-la´im, *f.* of two calves. Ezek. 47. 10.
EN-GANNIM, en-gan´im, *f.* of gardens. Josh. 15. 34.
EN-GEDI, en´ged-i, *f.* of the kid.
 city of Judah. Josh. 15. 62.
 David dwells there. 1 Sam. 23. 29; 24. 1.
EN-HADDAH, en-had´ah, *f.* of sharpness, *i.e.* swift *f.* Josh. 19. 21.
EN-HAKKORE, en´hak-o´ree, *f.* of him that calleth. Judg. 15. 19.
EN-HAZOR, en-ha´zor, *f.* of the village. Josh. 19. 37.
EN-MISHPAT, en-mish´pat, *f.* of judgment. Gen. 14. 7.
ENOCH, e´nok, experienced (?). Gen. 4. 17.
 his faith, Heb. 11. 5; prophecy, Jude 14; translation, Gen. 5. 24.
ENOS, e´nos, man. Gen. 4. 26.
ENOSH, e´nosh, same as ENOS. 1 Chr. 1. 1.
EN-RIMMON, en´rim´on, fountain of the pomegranate. Neh. 11. 29.
EN-ROGEL, en´ro´gel, *f.* of the fuller.
 fountain. Josh. 15. 7; 18. 16; 2 Sam. 17. 17; 1 Kin. 1. 9.
EN-SHEMESH, en´she´mesh, *f.* of the sun. Josh. 15. 7.
EN-TAPPUAH, en´tap-oo´ah, *f.* of the apple tree. Josh. 17. 7.
EPÆNETUS, e-pe´net-us, laudable. Rom. 16. 5.
EPAPHRAS, ep´af-ras, contracted from the next word (?).
 commended. Col. 1. 7; 4. 12.
EPAPHRODITUS, ep-af´ro-di´tus, handsome.
 Paul's joy at his recovery, Phil. 2. 25; his kindness, Phil. 4. 18.
EPENETUS, same as EPÆNETUS. Rom. 16. 5.
EPHAH, e´fah. Gen. 25. 4.
EPHAI, e´phai, languishing. Jer. 40. 8.
EPHER, e´fer, calf. Gen. 25. 4.
EPHES-DAMMIM, e´fez-dam´im, boundary of blood. 1 Sam. 17. 1.
EPHESIANS, e-fe´zi-ans, inhabitants of Ephesus. Acts 19. 28.
 Paul's epistle to. Eph. 1.
 election. Eph. 1. 4.
 adoption of grace. Eph. 1. 6.
 dead in sin quickened. Eph. 2. 1, 5.
 Gentiles made nigh. Eph. 2. 13.
 unity and kindness enjoined. Eph. 4—6.
EPHESUS, ef´es-us.
 visited by Paul. Acts 18. 19; 19. 1.
 miracles there. Acts 19. 11.
 tumult there. Acts 19. 24.
 Paul's address at Miletus to the elders of. Acts 20. 17.
 Paul fights with beasts there. 1 Cor. 15. 32.
 tarries there. 1 Cor. 16. 8.
EPHLAL, ef´lal, judgment. 1 Chr. 2. 37.
EPHOD, e´fod. Num. 34. 23.
EPHPHATHA, ef´ath-ah, be opened. Mark. 7. 34.
EPHRAIM, ef´ra-im, fruitful (?).
 younger son of Joseph. Gen. 41. 52.
 Jacob blesses Ephraim and Manasseh. Gen. 48. 14.
 his descendants numbered. Num. 1. 10, 32; 2. 18; 26. 35; 1 Chr. 7. 20.
 their possessions. Josh. 16. 5; 17. 14; Judg. 1. 29.
 chastise the Midianites. Judg. 7. 24.
 quarrel with Gideon. Judg. 8. 1; and Jephthah. Judg. 12.
 revolt from the house of David. 1 Kin. 12. 25.
 chastise Ahaz and Judah. 2 Chr. 28. 6, 7.
 release their prisoners. 2 Chr. 28. 12.
 carried into captivity. 2 Kin. 17. 5; Ps. 78. 9, 67; Jer. 7. 15.
 repenting, called God's son. Jer. 31. 20.
 prophecies concerning. Is. 7; 9. 9; 11. 13; 28. 1; Hos. 5—14; Zech. 9. 10; 10. 7.
EPHRAIMITES, ef´ra-im-ites, inhabitants of Ephraim. Judg. 12. 4.
EPHRAIN, ef-ra´in, same as EPHRON. 2 Chr. 13. 19.
EPHRATH, or EPHRATAH, ef´rat-ah, fruitful (?). 1 Chr. 2. 50.
 —— (Beth-lehem). Gen. 35. 16; Ps. 132. 6; Micah 5. 2.
EPHRATHITES, ef´rath-ites, inhabitants of Ephrath. Ruth. 1. 2.
EPHRON, ef´ron, of or belonging to a calf. Gen. 23. 8.
 the Hittite, sells Machpelah to Abraham. Gen. 23. 10.
EPICUREANS, ep´ik-u-re´ans, followers of Epicurus.
 philosophers, encounter Paul at Athens. Acts 17. 18.
ER, watchful. Gen. 38. 3.
ERAN, e´ran. Num. 26. 36.
ERANITES, e´ran-ites, posterity of Eran. Num. 26. 36.
ERASTUS, e-rast´us, beloved.
 ministers to Paul. Acts 19. 22; Rom. 16. 23; 2 Tim. 4. 20.

ERECH, e´rek. Gen. 10. 10.
ERI, e´ri, same as ER. Gen. 46. 16.
ERITES, er´ites, descendants of Eri. Num. 26. 16.
ESAIAS, e´sai-as, same as ISAIAH. Matt. 3. 3.
ESAR-HADDON, e´sar-had´on, Assur giveth a brother.
powerful king of Assyria. 2 Kin. 19. 37; Ezra 4. 2; Is. 37. 38.
ESAU, e´saw, hairy.
son of Isaac. Gen. 25. 25; (Mal. 1. 2; Rom. 9. 13).
sells his birthright. Gen. 25. 29 (Heb. 12. 16).
deprived of the blessing. Gen. 27. 38.
his anger against Jacob. Gen. 27. 41; and reconciliation. Gen. 33.
his riches and descendants. Gen. 36; 1 Chr. 1. 35.
ESEK, e´sek, strife. Gen. 26. 20.
ESH-BAAL, esh-ba´al, man of Baal. 1 Chr. 8. 33.
ESHBAN, esh´ban. Gen. 36. 26.
ESHCOL, esh´kol, cluster. Gen. 14. 13.
grapes of. Num. 13. 23.
ESHEAN, esh´e-an, support (?). Josh. 15. 52.
ESHEK, e´shek, oppression. 1 Chr. 8. 39.
ESHKALONITES, esh´ka-lon-ites, men of Ashkalon. Josh. 13. 3.
ESHTAOL, esh´ta-ol. Josh. 15. 33.
ESHTAULITES, esh-ta´ool-ites, inhabitants of Eshtaol. 1 Chr. 2. 53.
ESHTEMOA, esh´tem-o´ah, obedience. Josh. 21. 14.
ESHTEMOH, esh´te-mo′, same as ESHTEMOA. Josh. 15. 50.
ESHTON, esh´ton, womanly. 1 Chr. 4. 11.
ESLI, es´li, same as AZALIAH (?). Luke 3. 25.
ESROM, es´rom, same as HEZRON. Matt. 1. 3.
ESTHER, es´ter, star. Esth. 2. 7.
(Hadassah), made queen in the place of Vashti. Esth. 2. 17.
pleads for her people. Esth. 7. 3, 4.
ETAM, e´tam, a place of ravenous creatures. Judg. 15. 8.
ETHAM, e´tham, boundary of the sea (?). Ex. 13. 20.
ETHAN, e´than, firmness. 1 Kin. 4. 31.
ETHANIM, e-thah´nim, gifts (?). 1 Kin. 8. 2.
ETHBAAL, eth-ba´al, living with Baal. 1 Kin. 16. 31.
ETHER, e´ther, plenty. Josh. 15. 42.
ETHIOPIA, e´thi-ope´yah, (region of) burnt faces. Gen. 2. 13.
ETHIOPIAN, e´thi-ope´yan, a native of Ethiopia. Jer. 13. 23.
ETHIOPIANS, e´thi-ope´yans, invading Judah, subdued by Asa. 2 Chr. 14. 9. *See* Num. 12. 1; 2 Kin. 19. 19; Esth. 1. 1; Job 28. 19.
prophecies concerning. Ps. 68. 31; 87. 4; Is. 18; 20; 43. 3; 45. 14; Jer. 46. 9; Ezek. 30. 4; 38. 5; Nah. 3. 9; Zeph. 3. 10.
ETHNAN, eth´nan, a gift. 1 Chr. 4. 7.
ETHNI, eth´ni, bountiful. 1 Chr. 6. 41.
EUBULUS, eu-bew´lus, good counsellor. 2 Tim. 4. 21.
EUNICE, eu-ni´see.
commended (Acts 16. 1); 2 Tim. 1. 5.
EUODIAS, eu-ode´yas, success. Phil. 4. 2.
EUPHRATES, eu-fra´tes, the fertile river (?).
river. Gen. 2. 14; 15. 18; Deut. 11. 24; Josh. 1. 4; 2 Sam. 8. 3; Jer. 13. 4; 46. 2; 51. 63.
typical. Rev. 9. 14; 16. 12.
EUROCLYDON, eu-rok´ly-don, storm from the east.
a wind. Acts 27. 14.
EUTYCHUS, eu´tyk-us, fortunate. Acts 20. 9.
restored. Acts 20. 7.
EVE, eve, life. Gen. 3. 20.
created. Gen. 1. 27; 2. 18.
her fall and fate. Gen. 3. *See* ADAM.
EVI, e´vi. Num. 31. 8.
EVIL-MERODACH, e´vil-me´ro-dak, man of Merodach. 2 Kin. 25. 27.
king of Babylon, restores Jehoiachin. 2 Kin. 25. 27; Jer. 52. 31.
EXODUS, ex´od-us, departure.
EZAR, e´zar, treasure. 1 Chr. 1. 38.
EZBAI, ez´bai. 1 Chr. 11. 37.
EZBON, ez´bon. Gen. 46. 16.
EZEKIAS, ez´ek-i´as, same as HEZEKIAH. Matt. 1. 9.
EZEKIEL, ez-e´ki-el, whom God will strengthen. Ezek. 1. 3.
sent to house of Israel. Ezek. 2; 3; 33. 7.
his visions of God's glory. Ezek. 1; 8; 10; 11. 22.
of the Jews' abominations, &c. Ezek. 8. 5.
their punishment. Ezek. 9; 11.
of the resurrection of dry bones. Ezek. 37.
his vision of the measuring of the temple. Ezek. 40.
intercedes for Israel. Ezek. 9. 8; 11. 13.
his dumbness. Ezek. 3. 26; 24. 26; 33. 22.
his parables. Ezek. 15; 16; 17; 19; 23; 24.
exhorts Israel against idols. Ezek. 14. 1; 20. 1; 33. 30.
rehearses Israel's rebellions. Ezek. 20; and the sins of the rulers and people of Jerusalem, 22; 23; 24.
predicts Israel's and the nations' doom. Ezek. 21; 25.
EZEL, e´zel, departure. 1 Sam. 20. 19.
EZEM, e´zem, bone. 1 Chr. 4. 29.
EZER, e´zer, help. 1 Chr. 4. 4.
EZION-GABER, or EZION-GEBER, e´zi-on-ga´ber, the backbone of a giant.
on the Red Sea. Num. 33. 35; 1 Kin. 9. 26.
EZNITE, ez´nite. 2 Sam. 23. 8.
EZRA, ez´rah, help. Ezra 7. 1.
scribe, goes up from Babylon to Jerusalem. Ezra 7. 1; 8. 1.
his commission from Artaxerxes to rebuild the temple. Ezra 7. 11.
fast ordered by. Ezra 8. 21.
reproves the people. Ezra 10. 9.
reads the book of the law. Neh. 8.
reforms corruptions. Ezra 10; Neh. 13.
EZRAHITE, ez´rah-ite, a descendant of Zerah. 1 Kin. 4. 31.
EZRI, ez´ri, the help of Jehovah (?). 1 Chr. 27. 26.

FAIR HAVENS. Acts 27. 8.
FELIX, fe´lix, happy. Acts 23. 24.
governor of Judæa, Paul sent to. Acts 23. 23.
Paul's defence before him. Acts 24. 10.
trembles at Paul's preaching, but leaves him bound. Acts 24. 25.
FESTUS, fest´us, joyful. Acts 24. 27.
governor of Judæa. Acts 24. 27.
Paul brought before him. Acts 25.
Paul's defence before. Acts 25. 8; 26.
acquits Paul. Acts 25. 14; 26. 31.
FORTUNATUS, for´tu-na´tus, prosperous.
succours Paul. 1 Cor. 16. 17.

GAAL, ga´al, loathing. Judg. 9. 26.
GAASH, ga´ash, shaking. Josh. 24. 30.
GABA, ga´bah, hill. Josh. 18. 24.
GABBAI, gab´ai, a collector of tribute. Neh. 11. 8.
GABBATHA, gab´ath-ah, height (pavement). John 19. 13.
GABRIEL, ga´bri-el, man of God.
archangel, appears to Daniel. Dan. 8. 16; 9. 21.
to Zacharias. Luke 1. 19.
to Mary. Luke 1. 26.
GAD, gad, a troop, good fortune.
birth of. Gen. 30. 11.
his descendants. Gen. 46. 16.
blessed by Jacob. Gen. 49. 19.
—— tribe of, blessed by Moses. Deut. 33. 20.
numbered. Num. 1. 24; 26. 15.
their possessions. Num. 32; 34. 14.
divers commands to. Deut. 27. 13; Josh. 4. 12.
commended by Joshua. Josh. 22. 1.
charged with idolatry. Josh. 22. 11.
their defence. Josh. 22. 21.
—— seer, his message to David. 2 Sam. 24. 11; 1 Chr. 21. 9; 2 Chr. 29. 25.
GADARENES, gad´ar-eens′, inhabitants of Gadara.
or Gergesenes, Christ's miracle in the country of, Matt. 8. 28; Mark 5. 1; Luke 8. 26.
GADDI, gad´i, fortunate. Num. 13. 11.
GADDIEL, gad´i-el, fortune sent from God. Num. 13. 10.

GADI, ga´di. 2 Kin. 15. 14.
GADITES, gad´ites, persons belonging to the tribe of Gad. Deut. 3. 12.
GAHAM, ga´ham, sunburnt (?). Gen. 22. 24.
GAHAR, ga´har, hiding-place. Ezra 2. 47.
GAIUS, ga´yus. The Greek form of Caius. Acts 19. 29.
his piety. 3 John.
GALAL, ga´lal, worthy (?). 1 Chr. 9. 15.
GALATIA, ga-la´shah, a place colonised by Gauls. Acts 16. 6.
GALATIANS, ga-la´shans, inhabitants of Galatia. Gal. 3. 1.
Paul visits. Acts 16. 6.
reproved. Gal. 1. 6; 3.
exhorted. Gal. 5; 6.
their love to Paul. Gal. 4. 13.
GALEED, gal´e-ed, witness-heap. Gen. 31. 47.
GALILEANS, gal´il-e´yans, slaughter of. Luke 13. 1.
disciples so called. Acts 1. 11; 2. 7.
GALILEE, gal´il-ee, circuit. Josh. 20. 7.
Isaiah's prophecy concerning. Is. 9. 1; Matt. 4. 15.
work of Christ there. Matt. 2. 22; 15. 29; 26. 32; 27. 55; 28. 7; Mark 1. 9; Luke 4. 14; 23. 5; 24. 6; Acts 10. 37; 13. 31.
GALLIM, gal´im, heaps. 1 Sam. 25. 44.
GALLIO. gal´yo.
dismisses Paul. Acts 18. 12.
GAMALIEL, ga-ma´li-el, benefit of God. Num. 1. 10.
advises the council. Acts 5. 34.
Paul brought up at feet of. Acts 22. 3.
GAMMADIMS, gam-ah´dims, warriors (?). Ezek. 27. 11.
GAMUL, ga´mool, weaned. 1 Chr. 24. 17.
GAREB, ga´reb, scabby. 2 Sam. 23. 38.
GARMITE, garm´ite, bony. 1 Chr. 4. 19.
GASHMU, gash´moo, same as GESHEM. Neh. 6. 6.
GATAM, ga´tam. Gen. 36. 11.
GATH, gath, wine-press. Josh. 11. 22.
Goliath of. 1 Sam. 17. 4.
men of, smitten with emerods. 1 Sam. 5. 8.
David a refugee there. 1 Sam. 27. 4.
taken by David. 1 Chr. 18. 1.
by Hazael. 2 Kin. 12. 17.
Uzziah breaks down the wall of. 2 Chr. 26. 6.
GATH-HEPHER, gath-he´fer, the wine-press of the well. 2 Kin. 14. 25.
GATH-RIMMON, gath-rim´on, wine-press of the pomegranate. Josh. 19. 45.
GAZA, ga´zah, same as AZZAH. Gen. 10. 19.
Samson carries away the gates of. Judg. 16.
destruction of, foretold. Jer. 47; Amos 1. 6; Zeph. 2. 4; Zech. 9. 5.
GAZATHITES, ga´zath-ites, inhabitants of Gaza. Josh. 13. 3.
GAZER, ga´zer, place cut off. 2 Sam. 5. 25.
GAZEZ, ga´zez, shearer. 1 Chr. 2. 46.
GAZITES, ga´zites, inhabitants of Gaza. Judg. 16. 2.
GAZZAM, gaz´am, eating up. Ezra 2. 48.
GEBA, ge´bah, hill. Josh. 21. 17.
GEBAL, ge´bal, mountain. Ps. 83. 7.
GEBER, ge´ber, man. 1 Kin. 4. 13.
GEBIM, ge´bim, trenches. Is. 10. 31.
GEDALIAH, ged´al-i´ah, whom Jehovah has made great.
governor of the remnant of Judah. 2 Kin. 25. 22 (Jer. 40. 5).
treacherously killed by Ishmael. 2 Kin. 25. 25 (Jer. 41).
GEDEON, ged´e-on, Greek form of Gideon. Heb. 11. 32.
GEDER, ged´er, wall. Josh. 12. 13.
GEDERAH, ged-er´ah, enclosure, sheep-fold. Josh. 15. 36.
GEDERATHITE, ged-er´ath-ite, an inhabitant of Gederah. 1 Chr. 12. 4.
GEDERITE, ged´er-ite, native of Geder. 1 Chr. 27. 28.
GEDEROTH, ged-er´oth, sheep-folds. Josh. 15. 41.
GEDEROTHAIM, ged-er´oth-a´im, two sheep-folds. Josh. 15. 36.
GEDOR, ged´or, wall. Josh. 15. 58.

GEDOR—*cont.*
conquered by Simeonites. 1 Chr. 4. 41.
GEHAZI, ge-ha´zi, valley of vision.
servant of Elisha. 2 Kin. 4. 12.
his covetousness. 2 Kin. 5. 20.
GELILOTH, gel-il´oth, regions. Josh. 18. 17.
GEMALLI, ge-mal´i, possessor of camels. Num. 13. 12.
GEMARIAH, gem´ar-i´ah, whom Jehovah has completed. Jer. 29. 3.
GENESIS, jen´es-is, generation, or beginning.
GENNESARET, gen-es´a-ret. Matt. 14. 34.
a lake of Palestine, miracles wrought there. Matt. 17. 27; Luke 5. 1; John 21. 6.
GENTILES, jen´tiles.
origin of. Gen. 10. 5.
their state by nature. Rom. 1. 21; 1 Cor. 12. 2; Eph. 2; 4. 17; 1 Thess. 4. 5.
God's judgments on. Joel 3. 9.
their conversion predicted. Is. 11. 10; 42. 1; 49. 6 (Matt. 12. 18; Luke 2. 32; Acts 13. 47); 62. 2; Jer. 16. 19; Hos. 2. 23; Mal. 1. 11; Matt. 8. 11.
prediction fulfilled. John 10. 16; Acts 8. 37; 10; 14; 15; Eph. 2; 1 Thess. 1. 1.
calling of. Rom. 9. 24. *See* Is. 66. 19.
become fellow-citizens of the saints. Eph. 2. 11.
Christ made known to. Col. 1. 27.
GENUBATH, ge-noob´ath. 1 Kin. 11. 20.
GERA, ge´ra, a grain. Gen. 46. 21.
GERAH, ge´rah. Ex. 30. 13.
GERAR, ge´rar, sojourning. Gen. 10. 19.
herdmen of, strive with Isaac's. Gen. 26. 20.
GERGESENES, ger´ge-seens', inhabitants of Gerasa. Matt. 8. 28.
GERIZIM, ge-rize´im, persons living in a desert.
mount of blessing. Deut. 11. 29; 27. 12; Josh. 8. 33.
GERSHOM, ger´shom, expulsion.
son of Moses. Ex. 2. 22; 18. 3.
(Gershon), son of Levi. Gen. 46. 11; Num. 3. 17.
GERSHONITES, ger´shon-ites, descendants of Gershon. Num. 3. 21.
their duties in the service of the tabernacle. Num. 4; 7; 10. 17.
GESHAM, ge´sham. 1 Chr. 2. 47.
GESHEM, ge´shem, stout (?). Neh. 2. 19.
GESHUR, ge´shoor, bridge. 2 Sam. 3. 3.
Absalom takes refuge there after killing Amnon. 2 Sam. 13. 37; 14. 23 (Josh. 13. 13).
GESHURI, ge-shoor´i, inhabitants of Geshur. Deut. 3. 14.
GESHURITES, ge-shoor´ites, same as preceding. Josh. 12. 5.
GETHER, ge´ther, dregs (?). Gen. 10. 23.
GETHSEMANE, geth-sem´an-e, oil-press.
garden of, our Lord's agony there. Matt. 26. 36; Mark 14. 32; Luke 22. 39; John 18. 1.
GEUEL, goo´el, majesty of God. Num. 13. 15.
GEZER, ge´zer, precipice. Josh. 10. 33.
GEZRITES, gez´rites, dwelling in a desert land. 1 Sam. 27. 8.
GIAH, gi´ah, gushing forth. 2 Sam. 2. 24.
GIBBAR, gib´ar, a hero. Ezra 2. 20.
GIBBETHON, gib´eth-on, a lofty place. Josh. 19. 44.
GIBEA, gib´e-ah, hill. 1 Chr. 2. 49.
GIBEAH, gib´e-ah, hill. Josh. 15. 57.
a city of Benjamin. Judg. 19. 14.
sin of its inhabitants. Judg. 19. 22.
their punishment. Judg. 20.
the city of Saul. 1 Sam. 10. 26; 11. 4; 14. 2; 15. 34; 2 Sam. 21. 6.
GIBEATH, gib´e-ath, hill. Josh. 18. 28.
GIBEON, gib´e-on, pertaining to a hill. Josh. 9. 3.
its inhabitants deceive Joshua. Josh. 9.
delivered by him from the five kings. Josh. 10.
Saul persecutes them. 2 Sam. 21. 1.
David makes atonement. 2 Sam. 21. 3–9.
Solomon's dream at. 1 Kin. 3. 5.
tabernacle of the Lord kept at. 1 Chr. 16. 39; 21. 29.
GIBEONITES, gib´e-on-ites, inhabitants of Gibeon. 2 Sam. 21. 1.

GIBLITES, gib-lites, inhabitants of Gebal. Josh. 13. 5.
GIDDALTI, gid-al-ti, I have increased. 1 Chr. 25. 4.
GIDDEL, gid-el, gigantic. Ezra 2. 47.
GIDEON, gid-e-on, one who cuts down. Judg. 6. 11.
God appoints him to deliver Israel from the Midianites. Judg. 6. 14.
destroys the altar and grove of Baal. Judg. 6. 25, 27.
called Jerubbaal. Judg. 6. 32.
God gives him two signs. Judg. 6. 36–40.
his army reduced, and selected by a test of water. Judg. 7. 2–7.
his stratagem. Judg. 7. 16.
subdues the Midianites. Judg. 7. 19; 8.
makes an ephod of the spoil. Judg. 8. 24.
his death. Judg. 8. 32. *See* Heb. 11. 32.
GIDEONI, gid-e-on-i, cutting down. Num. 1. 11.
GIDOM, gi-dom. Judg. 20. 45.
GIHON, gi-hon, a river. Gen. 2. 13.
GILALAI, gil-a-lai, dungy (?). Neh. 12. 36.
GILBOA, gil-bo-ah, bubbling fountain. 1 Sam. 28. 4.
mount, Saul slain there. 1 Sam. 31; 2 Sam. 1. 21.
GILEAD, gil-e-ad, hill of witness. Gen. 31. 21.
land of, granted to the Reubenites, &c. Num. 32.
invaded by the Ammonites. Judg. 10. 17.
Jephthah made captain of. Judg. 11.
GILEADITE, gil-e-ad-ite, inhabitant of Gilead. Judg. 10. 3.
GILGAL, gil-gal, a circle.
Joshua encamps there. Josh. 4. 19; 9. 6.
Saul made king there. 1 Sam. 10. 8; 11. 14.
Saul sacrifices at. 1 Sam. 13. 8; 15. 12.
GILOH, gi-lo, exile. Josh. 15. 51.
GILONITE, gi-lon-ite, an inhabitant of Giloh. 2 Sam. 15. 12.
GIMZO, gim-zo, a place abounding with sycamores. 2 Chr. 28. 18.
GINATH, gi-nath, garden. 1 Kin. 16. 21.
GINNETHO, gin-eth-o, garden. Neh. 12. 4.
GINNETHON, gin-eth-on, same as preceding. Neh. 10. 6.
GIRGASHITE, gir-gash-ite, dwelling in a clayey soil. 1 Chr. 1. 14.
GIRGASHITES, gir-gash-ites, descendants of Canaan. Gen. 10. 15; 15. 21.
communion with, forbidden. Deut. 7. 1.
driven out. Josh. 3. 10; 24. 11.
GIRGASITE, gir-gas-ite, same as preceding. Gen. 10. 16.
GISPA, gis-pah, flattery. Neh. 11. 21.
GITTAH-HEPHER, git-tah-he-fer, wine-press of the well. Josh. 19. 13.
GITTAIM, git-a-im, two wine-presses. 2 Sam. 4. 3.
GITTITES, git-ites, inhabitants of Gath. Josh. 13. 3.
GITTITH, git-ith, after the manner of Gittites. Ps. 8, title.
GIZONITE, gi-zon-ite. 1 Chr. 11. 34.
GOATH, go-ath, lowing. Jer. 31. 39.
GOB, gobe, pit, cistern. 2 Sam. 21. 18.
GOG. 1 Chr. 5. 4.
GOG and MAGOG. Ezek. 38; 39; Rev. 20. 8.
GOLAN, go-lan, exile. Deut. 4. 43.
GOLGOTHA, gol-goth-ah, place of a skull. Matt. 27. 33; Mark 15. 22; Luke 23. 33; John 19. 17.
GOLIATH, go-li-ath, exile (?). 1 Sam. 17. 4.
of Gath. 1 Sam. 17; 21. 9; 22. 10.
GOMER, go-mer, complete. Gen. 10. 2.
GOMORRAH, go-mor-ah. Gen. 10. 19.
(and Sodom). Gen. 18. 20; 19. 24, 28; Is. 1. 9; Matt. 10. 15; Mark 6. 11.
GOMORRHA, go-mor-ah, same as preceding. Matt. 10. 15.
GOSHEN, go-shen, land of (Egypt), Israelites placed there. Gen. 45. 10; 46. 34; 47. 4.
no plagues there. Ex. 8. 22; 9. 26.
—— (Canaan). Josh. 10. 41; 11. 16.
GOZAN, go-zan. 2 Kin. 17. 6.
GREECE, grees, country of the Greeks. Acts 20. 2.
prophecies of. Dan. 8. 21; 10. 20; 11. 2; Zech. 9. 13.
GREECE—*cont.*
Paul preaches in. Acts 16; 20.
GRECIA, greesh-ah, same as GREECE. Dan. 8. 21.
GRECIAN, greesh-an, a Jew who speaks Greek. Acts 11. 20.
GREEK, the language of Greece. Acts 21. 37.
GREEKS, inhabitants of Greece. Acts 18. 17.
would see Jesus. John 12. 20.
believe in Him. Acts 11. 21; 17. 4.
GUDGODAH, gud-go-dah, thunder (?). Deut. 10. 7.
GUNI, goon-i, painted with colours. Gen. 46. 24.
GUNITES, goon-ites, descendants of Guni. Num. 26. 48.
GUR, goor, a young lion. 2 Kin. 9. 27.
GUR-BAAL, goor-ba-al, Gur of Baal. 2 Chr. 26. 7.

HAAHASHTARI, ha-a-hash-tar-i, the muleteer (?). 1 Chr. 4. 6.
HABAIAH, hab-ai-ah, whom Jehovah hides. Ezra 2. 61.
HABAKKUK, ha-bak-ook, embrace. Hab. 1. 1.
prophet, his burden, complaint to God, his answer, and faith. Hab. 1; 2; 3.
HABAZINIAH, hab-az-in-i-ah, lamp of Jehovah (?). Jer. 35. 3.
HABOR, ha-bor, joining together. 2 Kin. 17. 6.
HACHALIAH, hak-al-i-ah, whom Jehovah disturbs. Neh. 1. 1.
HACHILAH, hak-i-lah, dark. 1 Sam. 23. 19.
HACHMONI, hak-mon-i, wise. 1 Chr. 27. 32.
HACHMONITE, hak-mon-ite, a descendant of Hachmoni. 1 Chr. 11. 11.
HADAD, ha-dad. Gen. 36. 35.
Edomite. 1 Kin. 11. 14.
HADADEZER, had-ad-e-zer, whose help is Hadad. 2 Sam. 8. 3.
—— (Hadarezer), king of Zobah, David's wars with. 2 Sam. 8; 10. 15; 1 Chr. 18.
HADADRIMMON, had-ad-rim-on, named from Hadad and Rimmon. Zech. 12. 11.
HADAR, ha-dar, enclosure. Gen. 25. 15.
HADAREZER, had-ar-e-zer, same as HADADEZER. 1 Chr. 18. 3.
HADASHAH, had-ash-ah, new. Josh. 15. 37.
HADASSAH, had-as-ah, myrtle. Esth. 2. 7.
HADATTAH, had-at-ah, new. Josh. 15. 25.
HADID, ha-did, sharp. Ezra 2. 33.
HADLAI, had-lai, rest. 2 Chr. 28. 12.
HADORAM, had-or-am. Gen. 10. 27.
HADRACH, had-rak. Zech. 9. 1.
HAGAB, ha-gab, locust. Ezra 2. 46.
HAGABA, hag-a-ba, same as HAGAR. Neh. 7. 48.
HAGAR, ha-gar, flight. Gen. 16. 3.
mother of Ishmael. Gen. 16.
fleeing from Sarah is comforted by an angel. Gen. 16. 10, 11.
sent away with her son, Gen. 21. 14; allegory of, Gal. 4. 24.
HAGARENES, hag-ar-e-nes, inhabitants of Hagar. Ps. 83. 6.
HAGARITES, hag-ar-ites, same as preceding. 1 Chr. 5. 10.
HAGERITE, hag-er-ite, same as HAGARENE. 1 Chr. 27. 31.
HAGGAI, hag-ai, festive.
prophet. Ezra 5; 6. 14. *See* Hag. 1; 2.
HAGGI, hag-i, same as preceding. Gen. 46. 16.
HAGGERI, hag-er-i. 1 Chr. 11. 38.
HAGGIAH, hag-i-ah, festival of Jehovah. 1 Chr. 6. 30.
HAGGITES, hag-ites, the posterity of Haggi. Num. 26. 15.
HAGGITH, hag-ith, festive. 2 Sam. 3. 4.
HAI, hai, same as AI. Gen. 12. 8.
HAKKATAN, hak-ah-tan, the small. Ezra 8. 12.
HAKKOZ, hak-oz, the thorn. 1 Chr. 24. 10.
HAKUPHA, ha-koo-fah. Ezra 2. 51.
HALAH, ha-lah, same as CALAH (?). 2 Kin. 17. 6.
HALAK, ha-lak, smooth. Josh. 11. 17.
HALHUL, hal-hool. Josh. 15. 58.
HALI, ha-li, necklace. Josh. 19. 25.

HALLELUIAH, hal-el-oo´ya, praise the Lord. Rev. 19. 1.
HALLELUJAH (Alleluia). Ps. 106; 111; 113; 146; 148; 149; 150; Rev. 19. 1, 3, 4, 6.
HALLOHESH, hal-o´hesh, same as following. Neh. 10. 24.
HALOHESH, hal-o´hesh, the enchanter. Neh. 3. 12.
HAM, ham, warm. Gen. 9. 18.
son of Noah, cursed. Gen. 9. 22.
his descendants. Gen. 10. 6; 1 Chr. 1. 8; Ps. 105. 23; smitten by the Simeonites. 1 Chr. 4. 40.
HAMAN, ha´man. Esth. 3. 1.
HAMAN's advancement. Esth. 3.
anger against Mordecai. Esth. 3. 8.
his fall. Esth. 7.
HAMATH, ha´math, fortress.
—— (Syria). Num. 34. 8; Josh. 13. 5; 2 Kin. 14. 28; 17. 24.
conquered. 2 Kin. 18. 34; Is. 37. 13; Jer. 49. 23.
HAMATHITE, ha´math-ite, a dweller at Hamath. Gen. 10. 18.
HAMATH-ZOBAH, ha´math-zo´bah, fortress of Zobah. 2 Chr. 8. 3.
HAMMATH, ham´ath, warm springs. Josh. 19. 35.
HAMMEDATHA, ham´ed-ah´thah, given by the moon (?). Esth. 3. 1.
HAMMELECH, ham-me´lek, the king. Jer. 36. 26.
HAMMOLEKETH, ham´mo-le´keth, the queen. 1 Chr. 7. 18.
HAMMON, ham´on, warm. Josh. 19. 28.
HAMMOTH-DOR, ham´oth-dor´, warm springs of Dor. Josh. 21. 32.
HAMONAH, ha-mo´nah, multitude. Ezek. 39. 16.
HAMON-GOG, ham´on-gog´, *m.* of Gog. Ezek. 39. 11.
HAMOR, ha´mor, ass. Gen. 33. 19.
father of Shechem. Gen. 34; Acts 7. 16.
HAMUEL, ham´oo-el, heat (wrath) of God. 1 Chr. 4. 26.
HAMUL, ha´mool, who has experienced mercy. Gen. 46. 12.
HAMULITES, ha´mool-ites, the posterity of Hamul. Num. 26. 21.
HAMUTAL, ha-moo´tal, refreshing like dew. 2 Kin. 23. 31.
HANAMEEL, han´am-e´el, probably another form of HANANEEL. Jer. 32. 7.
HANAN, ha´nan, merciful. 1 Chr. 8. 23.
HANANEEL, han´an-e´el, whom God graciously gave. Neh. 3. 1.
HANANI, ha-na´ni, probably same as HANANIAH. 1 Kin. 16. 1.
prophet. 2 Chr. 16. 7.
—— brother of Nehemiah. Neh. 1. 2; 7. 2; 12. 36.
HANANIAH, han´an-i´ah, whom Jehovah graciously gave. 1 Chr. 3. 19.
false prophet. Jer. 28.
his death. Jer. 28. 16.
HANES, ha´nees. Is. 30. 4.
HANIEL, han´i-el, favour of God. 1 Chr. 7. 39.
HANNAH, han´ah, gracious.
her song. 1 Sam. 2.
vow and prayer. 1 Sam. 1. 11; answered. 1 Sam. 1. 19.
HANNATHON, han-a´thon, gracious. Josh. 19. 14.
HANNIEL, han´i-el, same as HANIEL. Num. 34. 23.
HANOCH, ha´nok, same as ENOCH. Gen. 25. 4.
HANOCHITES, ha´nok-ites, descendants of Hanoch. Num. 26. 5.
HANUN, ha´noon, whom (God) pities. 2 Sam. 10. 1.
king of the Ammonites, dishonours David's messengers. 2 Sam. 10. 4.
chastised. 2 Sam. 12. 30.
HAPHRAIM, haf-ra´im, two pits. Josh. 19. 19.
HARA, ha´ra, mountainous. 1 Chr. 5. 26.
HARADAH, har-a´dah, fear. Num. 33. 24.
HARAN, ha´ran, mountaineer. Gen. 11. 27.
son of Terah. Gen. 11. 26.
—— (city of Nahor), Abram comes to. Gen. 11. 31; departs from. Gen. 12. 4.
Jacob flees to Laban at. Gen. 27. 43; 28. 10; 29.
HARARITE, ha´rar-ite, a mountaineer. 2 Sam. 23. 11.

HARBONAH, har-bo´nah. Esth. 7. 9.
HAREPH, ha´ref, plucking. 1 Chr. 2. 51.
HARETH, ha´reth, thicket. 1 Sam. 22. 5.
HARHAIAH, har-hai´ah, dried up (?). Neh. 3. 8.
HARHAS, har´has. 2 Kin. 22. 14.
HARHUR, har´hoor, inflammation. Ezra 2. 51.
HARIM, ha´rim, flat-nosed. 1 Chr. 24. 8.
HARIPH, ha´rif, autumnal showers. Neh. 7. 24.
HARNEPHER, har-ne´fer. 1 Chr. 7. 36.
HAROD, ha´rod, terror. Judg. 7. 1.
HARODITE, har´od-ite, inhabitant of Harod. 2 Sam. 23. 25.
HAROEH, har-ro´eh, the seer. 1 Chr. 2. 52.
HARORITE, har´or-ite, probably another form of HARODITE. 1 Chr. 11. 27.
HAROSHETH, ha-rosh´eth, carving. Judg. 4. 2.
HARSHA, har´shah, enchanter, magician. Ezra 2. 52.
HARUM, ha´room, high (?). 1 Chr. 4. 8.
HARUMAPH, ha-roo´maf, flat-nosed. Neh. 3. 10.
HARUPHITE, ha-roof´ite. 1 Chr. 12. 5.
HARUZ, ha´rooz, active. 2 Kin. 21. 19.
HASADIAH, ha´sad-i´ah, whom Jehovah loves. 1 Chr. 3. 20.
HASENUAH, ha´se-noo´ah, she that is hated. 1 Chr. 9. 7.
HASHABIAH, ha´shab-i´ah, whom Jehovah esteems. 1 Chr. 6. 45.
HASHABNAH, ha-shab´nah, same as preceding (?). Neh. 10. 25.
HASHABNIAH, ha´shab-ni´ah, same as HASHABIAH. Neh. 3. 10.
HASHBADANA, hash´bad-a´na. Neh. 8. 4.
HASHEM, ha´shem, fat. 1 Chr. 11. 34.
HASHMONAH, hash-mo´nah, fatness, fat soil. Num. 33. 29.
HASHUB, hash´oob, thoughtful. Neh. 3. 11.
HASHUBAH, hash-oob´ah, same as preceding. 1 Chr. 3. 20.
HASHUM, hash´oom, rich. Ezra 2. 19.
HASHUPHA, hash-oof´ah, another form of HASUPHA. Neh. 7. 46.
HASRAH, haz´rah, probably same as HARHAS. 2 Chr. 34. 22.
HASSENAAH, has´en-a´ah, the thorny. Neh. 3. 3.
HASSHUB, hash´oob, same as HASHUB. 1 Chr. 9. 14.
HASUPHA, has-oof´ah, one of the Nethinims. Ezra 2. 43.
HATACH, ha´tak. Esth. 4. 5.
HATHATH, ha´thath, terror. 1 Chr. 4. 13.
HATIPHA, ha´tee´fah, seized. Ezra 2. 54.
HATITA, ha-tee´tah, digging. Ezra 2. 42.
HATTIL, hat´il, wavering. Ezra 2. 57.
HATTUSH, hat´oosh, assembled (?). 1 Chr. 3. 22.
HAURAN, how´ran, hollow land. Ezek. 47. 16.
HAVILAH, ha-vil´ah. Gen. 10. 7.
HAVOTH-JAIR, hav´oth-ja´ir, villages of Jair. Num. 32. 41.
HAZAEL, ha´za-el, whom God watches over.
king of Syria. 1 Kin. 19. 15.
Elisha's prediction. 2 Kin. 8. 7.
slays Ben-hadad. 2 Kin. 8. 15.
oppresses Israel. 2 Kin. 9. 14; 10. 32; 12. 17; 13. 22.
HAZAIAH, ha-zai´ah, whom Jehovah watches over. Neh. 11. 5.
HAZAR-ADDAR, ha´zar-ad´ar, Addar-town. Num. 34. 4.
HAZAR-ENAN, ha´zar-e´nan, fountain-town. Num. 34. 9.
HAZAR-GADDAH, ha´zar-gad´ah, luck-town. Josh. 15. 27.
HAZAR-HATTICON, ha´zar-hat´ik-on, middle-town. Ezek. 47. 16.
HAZARMAVETH, ha´zar-ma´veth, death-town. Gen. 10. 26.
HAZAR-SHUAL, ha´zar-shoo´al, jackal-town. Josh. 15. 28.
HAZAR-SUSAH, ha´zar-soo´sah, mare-town. Josh. 19. 5.
HAZAR-SUSIM, ha´zar-soo´sim, horses-town. 1 Chr. 4. 31.

HAZELELPONI, haz-lel-po-ni, the shadow looking on me. 1 Chr. 4. 3.
HAZERIM, haz-e-rim, villages. Deut. 2. 23.
HAZEROTH, haz-e-roth, same as HAZERIM. Num. 11. 35.
HAZEZON-TAMAR, ha-ze-zon-ta-mar, pruning of the palm. Gen. 14. 7.
HAZIEL, ha-zi-el, the vision of God. 1 Chr. 23. 9.
HAZO, ha-zo, vision. Gen. 22. 22.
HAZOR, ha-zor, castle. Josh. 11. 1.
Canaan, burnt. Josh. 11. 10; 15. 25.
HEBER, he-ber. Gen. 10. 21; Luke 3. 35.
—— the Kenite. Judg. 4. 11.
(1) same as EBER. 1 Chr. 5. 13; (2) fellowship. Gen. 46. 17.
HEBERITES, he-ber-ites, descendants of Heber. Num. 26. 45.
HEBREW, he-broo, the (name of Abraham), Gen. 14. 13; the language spoken by the Jews: John 19. 20. Or a Jew: Jer. 34. 9.
HEBREWESS, he-broo-ess', a Jewess. Jer. 34. 9.
HEBREWS, he-broos, descendants of Abraham. Gen. 40. 15; 43. 32; Ex. 2. 6; 2 Cor. 11. 22; Phil. 3. 5.
HEBRON, heb-ron, alliance.
—— (Mamre), in Canaan, Abraham dwells there. Gen. 13. 18; 23. 2.
the spies come to. Num. 13. 22.
taken. Josh. 10. 36.
given to Caleb. Josh. 14. 13; 15. 13.
David reigns there. 2 Sam. 2. 1; 3. 2; 5. 1; 1 Chr. 11; 12. 38; 29. 27.
HEBRONITES, he-bron-ites, the people of Hebron. Num. 3. 27.
HEGAI, or HEGE, he-gai. Esth. 2. 3, 8.
HELAH, he-lah, rust. 1 Chr. 4. 5.
HELAM, he-lam, stronghold. 2 Sam. 10. 16.
HELBAH, hel-bah, fatness. Judg. 1. 31.
HELBON, hel-bon, fertile. Ezek. 27. 18.
HELDAI, hel-dai, terrestrial. 1 Chr. 27. 15.
HELEB, he-leb, fat, fatness. 2 Sam. 23. 29.
HELED, he-led, the world. 1 Chr. 11. 30.
HELEK, he-lek, portion. Num. 26. 30.
HELEKITES, he-lek-ites, descendants of Helek. Num. 26. 30.
HELEM, he-lem, another form of HELDAI. 1 Chr. 7. 35.
HELEPH, he-lef, exchange. Josh. 19. 33.
HELEZ, he-lez, liberation. 2 Sam. 23. 26.
HELI, he-li, the Greek form of ELI. Luke 3. 23.
HELKAI, hel-kai, another form of HILKIAH. Neh. 12. 15.
HELKATH, hel-kath, a portion. Josh. 19. 25.
HELKATH-HAZZURIM, hel-kath-haz-oor-im, the field of swords (?). 2 Sam. 2. 16.
HELON, he-lon, strong. Num. 1. 9.
HEMAM, he-mam, same as HOMAM. Gen. 36. 22.
HEMAN, he-man, faithful. 1 Kin. 4. 31.
HEMATH, he-math; (1) fortress, 1 Chr. 2. 55; (2) same as HAMATH, Amos 6. 14.
HEMDAN, hem-dan, pleasant. Gen. 36. 26.
HEN, hen, favour. Zech. 6. 14.
HENA, he-nah. 2 Kin. 18. 34.
HENADAD, hen-a-dad, favour of Hadad (?). Ezra 3. 9.
HENOCH, he-nok, same as ENOCH. 1 Chr. 1. 3.
HEPHER, he-fer, pit. Josh. 12. 17.
HEPHERITES, he-fer-ites, descendants of Hepher. Num. 26. 32.
HEPHZI-BAH, heph-zi-bah, in whom is my delight. queen of Hezekiah, and mother of Manasseh. 2 Kin. 21. 1.
the restored Jerusalem. Is. 62. 4.
HERES, he-res, the sun. Judg. 1. 35.
HERESH, he-resh, artificer. 1 Chr. 9. 15.
HERMAS and HERMES, her-mas and her-mes, of Rome, saluted by Paul. Rom. 16. 14.
HERMOGENES, her-mog-e-nees. 2 Tim. 1. 15.
HERMON, her-mon, lofty. Deut. 3. 8.
mount. Deut. 4. 48; Josh. 12. 5; 13. 5; Ps. 89. 12; 133. 3.
HERMONITES, her-mon-ites, the summits of Hermon. Ps. 42. 6.
HEROD, her-od (the Great), king of Judæa. Matt. 2. 1.
troubled at Christ's birth. Matt. 2. 3.
slays the babes of Bethlehem. Matt. 2. 16.
—— (Antipas) reproved by John the Baptist, imprisons him, Luke 3. 19; beheads him. Matt. 14; Mark 6. 14.
desires to see Christ. Luke 9. 9.
scourges Him, and is reconciled to Pilate. Luke 23. 7; Acts 4. 27.
—— (Agrippa) persecutes the church. Acts 12. 1.
his pride and miserable death. Acts 12. 23.
HERODIANS, he-ro-di-ans, partisans of Herod, a sect, rebuked by Christ. Matt. 22. 16; Mark 12. 13.
plot against him. Mark 3. 6; 8. 15; 12. 13.
HERODIAS, he-ro-di-as. Matt. 14. 3.
married to Herod Antipas. Mark 6. 17.
plans the death of John the Baptist. Matt. 14; Mark 6. 24.
HERODION, he-ro-di-on. Rom. 16. 11.
Paul's kinsman. Rom. 16. 11.
HESED, he-sed, mercy. 1 Kin. 4. 10.
HESHBON, hesh-bon, counting. Num. 21. 25.
city of Sihon, taken. Num. 21. 26; Deut. 2. 24; Neh. 9. 22; Is. 16. 8.
HESHMON, hesh-mon, fatness. Josh. 15. 27.
HETH, sons of. Gen. 10. 15.
their kindness to Abraham. Gen. 23. 7; 25. 10.
HETHLON, heth-lon, hiding-place. Ezek. 47. 15.
HEZEKI, hez-ek-i, shortened from Hizkiah. 1 Chr. 8. 17.
HEZEKIAH, hez-ek-i-ah, the might of Jehovah. 2 Kin. 18. 1.
king of Judah. 2 Kin. 16. 19 (2 Chr. 28. 27).
abolishes idolatry. 2 Kin. 18.
attacked by the Assyrians, his prayer and deliverance. 2 Kin. 19.
his life lengthened, shadow of dial goes backward, displays his treasure, Isaiah's prediction. 2 Kin. 20 (Is. 38); his passover. 2 Chr. 30. 13.
his piety, and good reign. 2 Chr. 29.
his death. 2 Kin. 20. 20.
HEZION, hez-yon, vision. 1 Kin. 15. 18.
HEZIR, he-zir, swine. 1 Chr. 24. 15.
HEZRAI, hez-rai, enclosed wall. 2 Sam. 23. 35.
HEZRO, hez-ro, same as preceding. 1 Chr. 11. 37.
HEZRON, hez-ron, same as HEZRAI. Gen. 46. 12.
HEZRONITES, hez-ron-ites, descendants of Hezron. Num. 26. 6.
HIDDAI, hid-ai, the rejoicing of Jehovah. 2 Sam. 23. 30.
HIDDEKEL, hid-ek-el. Gen. 2. 14.
HIEL, hi-el, God liveth. 1 Kin. 16. 34.
—— *See* JERICHO.
HIERAPOLIS, hi-e-ra-pol-is, a sacred or holy city. Col. 4. 13.
HIGGAION, hig-a-yon, meditation. Ps. 9. 16.
HILEN, hi-len. 1 Chr. 6. 58.
HILKIAH, hilk-i-ah, portion of Jehovah. 2 Kin. 18. 18.
finds the book of the law. 2 Kin. 22. 8.
HILLEL, hil-el, praising. Judg. 12. 13.
HINNOM, hin-ome, valley of (Josh. 15. 8); 2 Kin. 23. 10; 2 Chr. 28. 3; 33. 6; Jer. 7. 31; 19. 11; 32. 35. *See* TOPHET AND MOLOCH.
HIRAH, hi-rah, nobility. Gen. 38. 1.
HIRAM, hi-ram, noble (?) (Huram), king of Tyre, sends aid to David and Solomon. 2 Sam. 5. 11; 1 Kin. 5; 9. 11; 10. 11; 1 Chr. 14. 1; 2 Chr. 2. 11.
—— principal brass-worker to Solomon. 1 Kin. 7. 13.
HITTITES, hit-ites, descendants of Heth. Gen. 15. 20; Judg. 1. 26; 3. 5.
HIVITES, hive-ites, villagers. Gen. 10. 17; Ex. 3. 8, 17.
deceive Joshua. Josh. 9.
HIZKIAH, hizk-i-ah, might of Jehovah. Zeph. 1. 1.
HIZKIJAH, hizk-i-jah, same as preceding. Neh. 10. 17.
HOBAB, ho-bab, beloved. Num. 10. 29. *See* JETHRO.
HOBAH, ho-bah, a hiding-place. Gen. 14. 15.

HOD, hode, splendour. 1 Chr. 7. 37.
HODAIAH, ho-dai´ah, praise of Jehovah. 1 Chr. 3. 24.
HODAVIAH, ho´dav-i´ah, Jehovah is his praise. 1 Chr. 5. 24.
HODESH, ho´desh, new moon. 1 Chr. 8. 9.
HODEVAH, ho´de-vah, same as HODAVIAH. Neh. 7. 43.
HODIAH, ho-di´ah, same as HODAIAH. 1 Chr. 4. 19.
HODIJAH, ho-di´jah, same as preceding. Neh. 8. 7.
HOGLAH, hog´lah, partridge. Num. 26. 33.
HOHAM, ho´ham. Josh. 10. 3.
HOLON, ho´lon, sandy. Josh. 15. 51.
HOMAM, ho´mam, destruction. 1 Chr. 1. 39.
HOPHNI, hof´ni, pugilist; and PHINEHAS, sons of Eli. 1 Sam. 1. 3.
their sin and death. 1 Sam. 2. 12, 22; 4. 11.
HOPHRA, hof´rah, priest of the sun. Jer. 44. 30.
HOR, mountain. Num. 20. 23.
mount, Aaron dies on. Num. 20. 25.
HORAM, ho´ram. Josh. 10. 33.
HOREB, ho´reb, desert, mount (Sinai). Ex. 3. 1; 17. 6; 33. 6; Deut. 1. 6; 4. 10.
law given. Ex. 19; 20; Deut. 4. 10; 5. 2; 18. 16; 1 Kin. 8. 9; Mal. 4. 4.
Moses twice there for forty days. Ex. 24. 18; 34. 28; Deut. 9. 9.
Elijah there for forty days. 1 Kin. 19. 8.
HOREM, ho´rem. Josh. 19. 38.
HOR-HAGIDGAD, hor´hag-gid´gad, mountain of Gudgodah. Num. 33. 32.
HORI, ho´ri, cave-dweller. Gen. 36. 22.
HORIMS, hor´ims, descendants of Hori. Deut. 2. 12.
HORITES, hor´ites, same as preceding. Gen. 14. 6.
HORMAH, hor´mah, a devoting, a place laid waste. Num. 14. 45.
destruction of. Num. 21. 3; Judg. 1. 17.
HORONAIM, hor´o-na´im, two caverns. Is. 15. 5.
HORONITE, hor´on-ite, native of Beth-horon. Neh. 2. 10.
HOSAH, ho´sah, fleeing to Jehovah for refuge (?). Josh. 19. 29.
HOSANNA, ho-san´nah, save us we pray, children sing, to Christ. Matt. 21. 9, 15; Mark 11. 9; John 12. 13; (Ps. 118. 25, 26).
HOSEA, ho-ze´ah, salvation. Hos. 1. 1.
prophet, declares God's judgment against idolatrous Israel. Hos. 1; 2; 4; and his reconciliation. Hos. 2. 14; 11; 13; 14.
HOSHAIAH, ho-shai´ah, whom Jehovah has set free. Neh. 12. 32.
HOSHAMA, ho´sha-mah. 1 Chr. 3. 18.
HOSHEA, ho-she´ah, same as HOSEA. Deut. 32. 44.
last king of Israel, his wicked reign, defeat by the king of Assyria, and captivity. 2 Kin. 15. 30; 17.
HOTHAM, ho´tham, signet ring. 1 Chr. 7. 32.
HOTHAN, ho´than. 1 Chr. 11. 44.
HOTHIR, ho´thir. 1 Chr. 25. 4.
HUKKOK, hook´oke, decreed. Josh. 19. 34.
HUKOK, hook´oke, same as preceding. 1 Chr. 6. 75.
HUL, hool, circle. Gen. 10. 23.
HULDAH, hool´dah, weasel. 2 Kin. 22. 14.
HUMTAH, hoom´tah, fortress (?). Josh. 15. 54.
HUPHAM, hoo´fam, inhabitant of the shore (?). Num. 26. 39.
HUPHAMITES, hoo´fam-ites, descendants of Hupham. Num. 26. 39.
HUPPAH, hoop´ah, covering. 1 Chr. 24. 13.
HUPPIM, hoop´im, same as HUPHAM (?). Gen. 46. 21.
HUR, hoor, cavern. Ex. 17. 10.
HURAI, hoo´rai, another way of writing Hiddai. 1 Chr. 11. 32.
HURAM, hoo´ram, the older way of spelling Hiram. 2 Chr. 2. 13.
HURI, hoo´ri, linen-worker (?). 1 Chr. 5. 14.
HUSHAH, hoo´shah, haste. 1 Chr. 4. 4.
HUSHAI, hoo´shai, hasting, loyalty. 2 Sam. 15. 32.
defeats Ahithophel's counsel. 2 Sam. 16. 16; 17. 5.
HUSHAM, hoo´sham, haste. Gen. 36. 34.
HUSHATHITE, hoo´shath-ite, inhabitant of Hushah. 2 Sam. 23. 27.
HUSHIM, hoosh´im, those who make haste. Gen. 46. 23.
HUZ. Gen. 22. 21.
HUZZAB, hooz´ab, it is decreed. Nah. 2. 7.
HYMENÆUS, hi´men-e´us, belonging to Hymen. 1 Tim. 1. 20; 2 Tim. 2. 17.

IBHAR, ib´har, whom God chooses. 2 Sam. 5. 15.
IBLEAM, ib´le-am, He destroys the people. Josh. 17. 11.
IBNEIAH, ib-ni´ah, whom Jehovah will build up. 1 Chr. 9. 8.
IBNIJAH, ib-ni´jah, same as preceding. 1 Chr. 9. 8.
IBRI, ib´ri, Hebrew. 1 Chr. 24. 27.
IBZAN, ib´zan, active (?). Judg. 12. 8.
I-CHABOD, i´ka-bod, inglorious. 1 Sam. 4. 21; 14. 3.
ICONIUM, i-kon´yum, gospel preached at. Acts 13. 51; 14. 1; 16. 2.
Paul persecuted at. 2 Tim. 3. 11.
IDALAH, id´al-ah, snares (?). Josh. 19. 15.
IDBASH, id´bash, honeyed. 1 Chr. 4. 3.
IDDO, id´o, (1) loving, 1 Chr. 27. 21; (2) Ezra 8. 17; (3) seasonable, Zech. 1. 1.
IDUMEA, i´du-me´ah, same as EDOM. Is. 34. 5.
IGAL, i´gal, whom God will avenge. Num. 13. 7.
IGDALIAH, ig´dal-i´ah, whom Jehovah shall make great. Jer. 35. 4.
IGEAL, i´ge-al, same as IGAL. 1 Chr. 3. 22.
IIM, i´im, ruins. Num. 33. 45.
IJE-ABARIM, i-je-a-bar´im, ruinous heaps of Abarim. Num. 21. 11.
IJON, i´jon, a ruin. 1 Kin. 15. 20.
IKKESH, ik´esh, perverseness of mouth. 2 Sam. 23. 26.
ILAI, ee´lai, most high. 1 Chr. 11. 29.
ILLYRICUM, il-ir´ik-um, gospel preached there. Rom. 15. 19.
IMLA, im´lah, same as IMLAH. 2 Chr. 18. 7.
IMLAH, im´lah, whom (God) will fill up. 1 Kin. 22. 8.
IMMANUEL, im-an´u-el (*see* EMMANUEL), God with us. Is. 7. 14; Matt. 1. 23.
IMMER, im´er, talkative. 1 Chr. 9. 12.
IMNA, im´nah, whom (God) keeps back. 1 Chr. 7. 35.
IMNAH, im´nah, whom (God) assigns (?). 1 Chr. 7. 30.
IMRAH, im´rah, stubborn. 1 Chr. 7. 36.
IMRI, im´ri, eloquent. 1 Chr. 9. 4.
INDIA, ind´ya. Esth. 1. 1.
IPHEDEIAH, if´ed-i´ah, whom Jehovah frees. 1 Chr. 8. 25.
IR, eer, city. 1 Chr. 7. 12.
IRA, i´rah, watchful. 2 Sam. 20. 26.
IRAD, i´rad. Gen. 4. 18.
IRAM, i´ram, belonging to a city. Gen. 36. 43.
IRI, i´ri, same as IRAM. 1 Chr. 7. 7.
IRIJAH, i-ri´jah, whom Jehovah looks on. Jer. 37. 13.
IR-NAHASH, ir-na´hash, snake-town. 1 Chr. 4. 12.
IRON, i´ron, reverence. Josh. 19. 38.
IRPEEL, ir´pe-el, which God heals. Josh. 18. 27.
IR-SHEMESH, ir´she´mesh, sun-town. Josh. 19. 41.
IRU, i´roo, same as IRAM. 1 Chr. 4. 15.
ISAAC, i´zak, laughter. Gen. 17. 19.
his birth promised. Gen. 15. 4; 17. 16; 18. 10; born. Gen. 21. 2.
offered by Abraham. Gen. 22. 7.
marries Rebekah. Gen. 24. 67.
blesses his sons, Gen. 27. 28; dies, Gen. 35. 29.
ISAIAH, i-zai´ah, salvation of Jehovah (Esaias), prophet. Is. 1. 1; 2. 1.
sent to Ahaz. Is. 7; and Hezekiah. Is. 37. 6; 38. 4; 39. 3.
prophesies concerning various nations. Is. 7; 8; 10; 13—23; 45—47.
referred to in Matt. 3. 3; 4. 14; 8. 17; 12. 17; 13. 14; 15. 7; Mark 1. 3; Luke 3. 4; 4. 17; John 1. 23; 12. 38; Acts 8. 32; 28. 25; Rom. 9. 27; 10. 16; 15. 12.
ISCAH, is´kah. Gen. 11. 29.
ISCARIOT, is-kar´i-ot, man of Kerioth. Judas, Matt. 10. 4; Mark 3. 19.

ISCARIOT—*cont.*
his treachery. Matt. 26. 21; Mark 14. 18; Luke 22. 47; John 18. 3.
death, Matt. 27. 5; Acts 1. 18.

ISHBAH, ish´bah, praising. 1 Chr. 4. 17.

ISHBAK, ish´bak. Gen. 25. 2.

ISHBI-BENOB, ish´bi-ben-ob´e, one who dwells at Nob. 2 Sam. 21. 16.

ISH-BOSHETH, ish-bo´sheth, man of shame. 2 Sam. 2. 8; 3. 7; 4. 5, 8.

ISHI, eesh´i, my husband. Hos. 2. 16.

ISHI, yish´i, salutary. 1 Chr. 2. 31.

ISHIAH, ish-i´ah, whom Jehovah lends. 1 Chr. 7. 3.

ISHIJAH, ish-i´jah, same as ISHIA. Ezra 10. 31.

ISHMA, ish´mah. 1 Chr. 4. 3.

ISHMAEL, ish´ma-el, whom God hears, son of Abram. Gen. 16. 15; 17. 20; 21. 17; 25. 17; his descendants. Gen. 25. 12; 1 Chr. 1. 29.
—— son of Nethaniah, slays Gedaliah. 2 Kin. 25. 25; Jer. 40. 14; 41.

ISHMAELITES, ish´ma-el-ites, descendants of Ishmael. Judg. 8. 24.

ISHMAIAH, ish-mai´ah, whom Jehovah hears. 1 Chr. 27. 19.

ISHMEELITES, ish´me-el-ites, same as ISHMAELITES. Gen. 37. 25.

ISHMERAI, ish´mer-ai, whom Jehovah keeps. 1 Chr. 8. 18.

ISHOD, ish´hode, man of glory. 1 Chr. 7. 18.

ISHPAN, ish´pan, cunning (?). 1 Chr. 8. 22.

ISH-TOB, ish´tobe, men of Tob. 2 Sam. 10. 6.

ISHUAH, ish´oo-ah, level. Gen. 46. 17.

ISHUAI, ish´oo-ai, same as ISUI. 1 Chr. 7. 30.

ISHUI, ish´oo-i, same as ISHUAH. 1 Sam. 14. 49.

ISMACHIAH, is-mak-i´ah, whom Jehovah upholds. 2 Chr. 31. 13.

ISMAIAH, is-mai´ah, same as ISHMAIAH. 1 Chr. 12. 4.

ISPAH, is´pah, bald. 1 Chr. 8. 16.

ISRAEL, iz´ra-el, soldier of God. Jacob so called after wrestling with God. Gen. 32. 28; 35. 10; Hos. 12. 3.

ISRAELITES, iz´ra-el-ites, descendants of Israel. Ex. 9. 7.
in Egypt. Ex. 1—12.
the first passover instituted. Ex. 12.
flight from Egypt. Ex. 12. 31.
pass through the Red Sea. Ex. 14.
their journeys. Ex. 14. 1, 19; Num. 9. 15; Ps. 78. 14.
fed by manna and water in the wilderness. Ex. 16. 4; 17. 1; Num. 11; 20.
God's covenant with at Sinai. Ex. 19; 20; Deut. 29. 10.
their idolatry. Ex. 32. *See also* 2 Kin. 17; Ezra 9; Neh. 9; Ezek. 20; 22; 23; Acts 7. 39; 1 Cor. 10. 1.
their rebellious conduct rehearsed by Moses. Deut. 1; 2; 9.
conquer and divide Canaan under Joshua. Josh. 1; 12; 13.
governed by judges. Judg. 2; by kings. 1 Sam. 10; 2 Sam.; 1 & 2 Kin.; 1 & 2 Chr.
their captivity in Assyria, 2 Kin. 17; in Babylon, 2 Kin. 25; 2 Chr. 36; Jer. 39; 52; their return, Ezra; Neh.; Hag.; Zech.
God's wrath against. Ps. 78; 106; deliverances of. Ps. 105.
their sufferings our examples. 1 Cor. 10. 6.

ISRAELITISH, iz´ra-el-ite-ish, after the fashion of an Israelite. Lev. 24. 10.

ISSACHAR, is´ak-ar, he is hired (?). Gen. 30. 18; 35. 23.
descendants of. Gen. 46. 13; Judg. 5. 15; 1 Chr. 7. 1. *See* Num. 1. 28; 26. 23; Gen. 49. 14; Deut. 33. 18; Josh. 19. 17; Ezek. 48. 33; Rev. 7. 7.

ISSHIAH, ish-hi´ah, same as ISHIAH. 1 Chr. 24. 21.

ISUAH, is´oo-ah, same as ISHUAH. 1 Chr. 7. 30.

ISUI, is´oo-i, same as ISHUI. Gen. 46. 17.

ITALIAN, it-al´yan, belonging to Italy. Acts 10. 1.

ITALY, it´a-ly. Acts 18. 2.

ITHAI, ee´thai, ploughman. 1 Chr. 11. 31.

ITHAMAR, i´tha-mar, island of palms. Ex. 6. 23; Lev. 10. 6; his charge. Num. 4.

ITHIEL, ith´i-el, God is with me. Neh. 11. 7; Prov. 30. 1.

ITHMAH, ith´mah, bereavedness. 1 Chr. 11. 46.

ITHNAN, ith´nan. Josh. 15. 23.

ITHRA, ith´rah, excellence. 2 Sam. 17. 25.

ITHRAN, ith´ran, same as ITHRA. Gen. 36. 26.

ITHREAM, ith´re-am, remainder of the people. 2 Sam. 3. 5.

ITHRITE, ith´rite, descendant of Jether (?). 2 Sam. 23. 38.

ITTAH-KAZIN, it´ah-ka´zin, time of the chief. Josh. 19. 13.

ITTAI, it´tai, same as ITHAI (the Gittite). 2 Sam. 15. 19; 18. 2.

ITURÆA, i´tu-re´ah, a province so named from Jetur. Luke 3. 1.

IVAH, i´vah. 2 Kin. 18. 34.

IZEHAR, iz´e-har, oil. Num. 3. 19.

IZEHARITES, i´ze-har´ites, the descendants of Izehar. Num. 3. 27.

IZHAR, iz´har, same as IZEHAR. Ex. 6. 18.

IZHARITES, iz´har-ites, the same as IZEHARITES. 1 Chr. 26. 23.

IZRAHIAH, iz-rah-i´ah, whom Jehovah brought to light. 1 Chr. 7. 3.

IZRAHITE, iz´rah-ite, probably same as ZARHITE. 1 Chr. 27. 8.

IZRI, iz´ri, a descendant of Jezer. 1 Chr. 25. 11.

JAAKAN, ja´ak-an, one who turns. Deut. 10. 6.

JAAKOBAH, ja´ak-o´bah, same as JACOB. 1 Chr. 4. 36.

JAALA, ja´a-lah, wild she-goat. Neh. 7. 58.

JAALAH, ja´a-lah, same as JAALA. Ezra 2. 56.

JAALAM, ja´a-lam, whom God hides. Gen. 36. 5.

JAANAI, ja´a-nai, whom Jehovah answers. 1 Chr. 5. 12.

JAARE-OREGIM, ja´ar-e-or´eg-im, forests of the weavers. 2 Sam. 21. 19.

JAASAU, ja´a-saw. Ezra 10. 37.

JAASIEL, ja-as´i-el, whom God created. 1 Chr. 27. 21.

JAAZANIAH, ja´az-an-i´ah, whom Jehovah hears. 2 Kin. 25. 23.

JAAZER, ja´a-zer, whom (God) aids. Num. 21. 32.

JAAZIAH, ja´az-i´ah, whom Jehovah strengthens. 1 Chr. 24. 26.

JAAZIEL, ja´az´i-el, whom God strengthens. 1 Chr. 15. 18.

JABAL, ja´bal. Gen. 4. 20.

JABBOK, jab´ok, pouring out, river. Gen. 32. 22; Num. 21. 24; Deut. 3. 16; Josh. 12. 2.

JABESH, ja´besh, dry. 2 Kin. 15. 10.

JABESH-GILEAD, ja´besh-gil´e-ad, Jabesh of Gilead. Judg. 21. 8.
inhabitants smitten by Israel. Judg. 21.
threatened by Ammonites. 1 Sam. 11. 1; delivered by Saul. 1 Sam. 11. 11.

JABEZ, ja´bez, causing pain, prayer of. 1 Chr. 4. 9.

JABIN, ja´bin, whom He (God) considered. Judg. 4. 2.
king of Hazor, conquered by Joshua. Josh. 11.
—— (another), destroyed by Barak. Judg. 4.

JABNEEL, jab´ne-el, may God cause to be built. Josh. 15. 11.

JABNEH, jab´nay, which (God) causes to be built. 2 Chr. 26. 6.

JACHAN, ja´kan, troubled. 1 Chr. 5. 13.

JACHIN, ja´kin, whom (God) strengthens, one of the pillars of the porch of the temple. 1 Kin. 7. 21; 2 Chr. 3. 17.

JACHINITES, ja´kin-ites, descendants of Jachin. Num. 26. 12.

JACOB, ja´kob, supplanter, his birth, Gen. 25. 26; birthright, 25. 33; blessing, 27. 27; sent to Padan-aram, 27. 43; 28. 1; his vision of the ladder, and vow, 28. 10; marriages, 29; sons, 29. 31; 30; dealings with Laban, 31; his vision of God's host, 32. 1; his prayer, 32. 9; wrestles with an angel, 32. 24; Hos. 12. 4; reconciled

JACOB—*cont.*
with Esau. Gen. 33; builds an altar at Beth-el, 35. 1; his grief for Joseph and Benjamin, 37; 42. 38; 43; goes down to Egypt, 46; brought before Pharaoh, 47. 7; blesses his sons, 48; 49. his death, and burial. Gen. 49. 33; 50. *See* Ps. 105. 23; Mal. 1. 2; Rom. 9. 10; Heb. 11. 21.
JACOB'S WELL. John 4. 5.
JADA, ja´dah, wise. 1 Chr. 2. 28.
JADAU, ja´daw. Ezra 10. 43.
JADDUA, jad´oo-ah, skilled. Neh. 10. 21.
JADON, ja´don, a judge. Neh. 3. 7.
JAEL, ja´el, same as JAALA, kills Sisera. Judg. 4. 17; 5. 24.
JAGUR, ja´goor, a lodging. Josh. 15. 21.
JAH, poetic form of JEHOVAH. Ps. 68. 4.
JAHATH, ja´hath. 1 Chr. 6. 20.
JAHAZ, ja´haz, a place trodden down. Num. 21. 23.
JAHAZA, ja´haz-ah, same as JAHAZ. Josh. 13. 18.
JAHAZAH, same as JAHAZA. Josh. 21. 36.
JAHAZIAH, ja´haz-i´ah, whom Jehovah watches over. Ezra 10. 15.
JAHAZIEL, ja-haz´i-el, whom God watches over. 1 Chr. 16. 6.
comforts Jehoshaphat. 2 Chr. 19. 14.
prophecies against Moab and Ammon. 2 Chr. 20. 14.
JAHDAI, jah´dai, whom Jehovah directs. 1 Chr. 2. 47.
JAHDIEL, jah´di-el, whom God makes glad. 1 Chr. 5. 24.
JAHDO, jah´do, union. 1 Chr. 5. 14.
JAHLEEL, jah´le-el, hoping in God. Num. 26. 26.
JAHLEELITES, jah´le-el-ites, descendants of Jahleel. Num. 26. 26.
JAHMAI, jah´mai. 1 Chr. 7. 2.
JAHZAH, ja´zah, same as JAHAZ. 1 Chr. 6. 78.
JAHZEEL, jah´ze-el, whom God allots. Gen. 46. 24.
JAHZEELITES, jah´ze-el-ites, descendants of Jahzeel. Num. 26. 48.
JAHZERAH, jah-ze´rah, may he bring back. 1 Chr. 9. 12.
JAHZIEL, jah´zi-el, same as JAHZEEL. 1 Chr. 7. 13.
JAIR, ja´er, (*i.e.* God) enlightens. Num. 32. 41.
Gileadite, judge. Judg. 10. 3.
JAIRITE, ja´er-ite, a descendant of JAIR. 2 Sam. 20. 26.
JAIRUS, ja-i´rus, Greek form of JAIR, daughter of, raised. Matt. 9. 18; Mark 5. 22; Luke 8. 41.
JAKAN, ja´kan, same as JAAKAN. 1 Chr. 1. 42.
JAKEH, ja´kay, pious (?). Prov. 30. 1.
JAKIM, ja´kim, (God) sets up. 1 Chr. 8. 19.
JALON, ja´lon, passing the night. 1 Chr. 4. 17.
JAMBRES, jam´brees. 2 Tim. 3. 8.
JAMES, the English equivalent for Jacob in the New Testament.
—— (APOSTLE), son of Zebedee, called. Matt. 4. 21; Mark 1. 19; Luke 5. 10.
ordained one of the twelve. Matt. 10. 2; Mark 3. 14; Luke 6. 13.
witnessed Christ's transfiguration. Matt. 17. 1; Mark 9. 2; Luke 9. 28.
present at the passion. Matt. 26. 36; Mark 14. 33.
slain by Herod. Acts 12. 2.
—— (APOSTLE), son of Alphæus. Matt. 10. 3; Mark 3. 18; 6. 3; Luke 6. 15; Acts 1. 13; 12. 17.
his judgment respecting ceremonial. Acts 15. 13–29; *See* 1 Cor. 15. 7; Gal. 1. 19; 2. 9.
his teaching. James 1—5.
mentioned. Acts 21. 18; 1 Cor. 15. 7; Gal. 1. 19; 2. 9.
JAMIN, ja´min, right hand. Gen. 46. 10.
JAMINITES, ja´min-ites, descendants of Jamin. Num. 26. 12.
JAMLECH, jam´lek, He makes to reign. 1 Chr. 4. 34.
JANNA, jan´nah, probably another form of John. Luke 3. 24.
JANNES and JAMBRES, magicians of Egypt. 2 Tim. 3. 8 (Ex. 7. 11).
JANOAH, ja-no´ah, rest. 2 Kin. 15. 29.
JANOHAH, ja-no´hah, same as preceding. Josh. 16. 6.
JANUM, ja´noom, sleep. Josh. 15. 53.
JAPHETH, ja´feth, extension. Gen. 5. 32.
son of Noah, blessed. Gen. 9. 27.
his descendants. Gen. 10. 1; 1 Chr. 1. 4.
JAPHIA, ja-fi´ah, splendid. Josh. 19. 12.
JAPHLET, jaf´let, may he deliver. 1 Chr. 7. 32.
JAPHLETI, jaf-le´ti, the Japhletite, or descendant of Japhlet. Josh. 16. 3.
JAPHO, ja´fo, beauty. Josh. 19. 46.
JARAH, ja´rah, forest. 1 Chr. 9. 42.
JAREB, ja´reb, one who is contentious. Hos. 5. 13.
JARED, ja´red, descent. Gen. 5. 15; Luke 3. 37.
JARESIAH, ja´res-i´ah, whom Jehovah nourishes. 1 Chr. 8. 27.
JARHA, jar´hah. 1 Chr. 2. 34.
JARIB, ja´rib, adversary. 1 Chr. 4. 24.
JARMUTH, jar´mooth, height. Josh. 10. 3.
JAROAH, ja-ro´ah, moon (?). 1 Chr. 5. 14.
JASHEN, ja´shen, sleeping. 2 Sam. 23. 32.
JASHER, ja´sher, upright, book of. Josh. 10. 13; 2 Sam. 1. 18.
JASHOBEAM, ja-shob´e-am, the people returns, valour of. 1 Chr. 11. 11.
JASHUB, ja´shoob, he returns. Num. 26. 24.
JASHUBI-LEHEM, ja-shoob´i-le´hem, giving bread (?). 1 Chr. 4. 22.
JASHUBITES, ja´shoob-ites, descendants of Jashub. Num. 26. 24.
JASIEL, ja-si´el, whom God made. 1 Chr. 11. 47.
JASON, ja´son, Græco-Judæan equivalent of Joshua. persecuted at Thessalonica. Acts 17. 5; Rom. 16. 21.
JATHNIEL, jath´ni-el, God gives. 1 Chr. 26. 2.
JATTIR, jat´yer, excelling. Josh. 15. 48.
JAVAN, ja´van, wine (?), son of Japheth. Gen. 10. 2.
JAZER, ja´zer, same as JAAZER. Num. 32. 1.
JAZIZ, ja´ziz, wanderer (?). 1 Chr. 27. 31.
JEARIM, je-ar´im, forests. Josh. 15. 10.
JEATERAI, je-at´er-ai´. 1 Chr. 6. 21.
JEBERECHIAH, je-ber´ek-i´ah, whom Jehovah blesses. Is. 8. 2.
JEBUS, je´boos, a place trodden down (?). Judg. 19. 10.
JEBUSI, je-boo´si, a Jebusite. Josh. 18. 16.
JEBUSITES, je-boo´sites, the descendants of Jebus, the son of Canaan. Gen. 15. 21; Num. 13. 29; Josh. 15. 63; Judg. 1. 21; 19. 11; 2 Sam. 5. 6.
JECAMIAH, jek´am-i´ah. 1 Chr. 3. 18.
JECHOLIAH, jek´ol-i´ah, Jehovah is strong. 2 Kin. 15. 2.
JECHONIAS, jek´on-i´as, the Greek way of spelling Jeconiah. Matt. 1. 11, 12; 1 Chr. 3. 17.
JECOLIAH, jek´ol-i´ah, same as JECHOLIAH. 2 Chr. 26. 3.
JECONIAH, jek´on-i´ah, Jehovah establishes. 1 Chr. 3. 16.
JEDAIAH, jed-ai´ah, (1) Jehovah—(?). 1 Chr. 4. 37.
(2) Jehovah knoweth. 1 Chr. 24. 7.
JEDIAEL, je-di´a-el, known of God. 1 Chr. 7. 6.
JEDIDAH, jed-i´dah, beloved. 2 Kin. 22. 1.
JEDIDIAH, jed´id-i´ah (beloved of the Lord), a name of Solomon. 2 Sam. 12. 25.
JEDUTHUN, jed-ooth´oon, friendship (?). 1 Chr. 16. 38, 41; 25. 6.
JEEZER, je-e´zer, contracted from ABIEZER. Num. 26. 30.
JEEZERITES, je-ez´er-ites, descendants of Jeezer. Num. 26. 30.
JEGAR-SAHADUTHA, je-gar´sa-ha-doo´thah, the heap of testimony. Gen. 31. 47.
JEHALELEEL, je-hal´el-e´el, he praises God. 1 Chr. 4. 16.
JEHALELEL, je-hal´e-lel, same as preceding. 2 Chr. 29. 12.
JEHDEIAH, jed-i´ah, whom Jehovah makes glad. 1 Chr. 24. 20.
JEHEZEKEL, je-hez´e-kel, same as EZEKIEL. 1 Chr. 24. 16.
JEHIAH, je-hi´ah, Jehovah lives. 1 Chr. 15. 24.
JEHIEL, je-hi´el, God liveth. 1 Chr. 15. 18.

JEHIELI, je-hi´el-i, a Jehielite. 1 Chr. 26. 21.
JEHIZKIAH, je´hizk-i´ah, same as HEZEKIAH. 2 Chr. 28. 12.
JEHOADAH, je-ho´a-dah, whom Jehovah adorns. 1 Chr. 8. 36.
JEHOADDAN, je-ho´ad-an. Jehovah is beauteous (?). 2 Kin. 14. 2.
JEHOAHAZ, je-ho´a-haz, whom Jehovah holds fast. son of Jehu, king of Israel. 2 Kin. 10. 35; 13. 4.
—— (Shallum), king of Judah, his evil reign. 2 Kin. 23. 31; 2 Chr. 36. 1.
JEHOASH, je-ho´ash, Jehovah supports. 2 Kin. 11. 21.
JEHOHANAN, je-ho´han-an, Jehovah is gracious. 1 Chr. 26. 3.
JEHOIACHIN, je-ho´ya-kin, Jehovah has established. king of Judah, his defeat and captivity. 2 Kin. 24. 6; 2 Chr. 36. 8.
JEHOIADA, je-ho´ya-dah, Jehovah knoweth. 2 Sam. 8. 18.
high priest, deposes and slays Athaliah, and restores Jehoash. 2 Kin. 11. 4; 2 Chr. 23; repairs the temple. 2 Kin. 12. 7; 2 Chr. 24. 6.
abolishes idolatry. 2 Chr. 23. 16.
JEHOIAKIM, je-ho´ya-kim, Jehovah has set up.
—— (Eliakim), made king of Judah by Pharaoh-nechoh, his evil reign and captivity. 2 Kin. 23. 34; 24. 1; 2 Chr. 36. 4; Dan. 1. 2. *See* Jer. 22. 18.
JEHOIARIB, je-ho´ya-rib, Jehovah will contend. 1 Chr. 9. 10.
JEHONADAB, je-ho´na-dab, Jehovah is bounteous. 2 Kin. 10. 15.
JEHONATHAN, je-ho´na-than, same as JONATHAN. 1 Chr. 27. 25.
JEHORAM, je-ho´ram, Jehovah is high.
—— (son of Jehoshaphat), king of Judah. 1 Kin. 22. 50; 2 Kin. 8. 16; his cruelty and death, 2 Chr. 21. 4, 18.
—— (Joram), king of Israel, son of Ahab. 2 Kin. 1. 17; 3. 1; his evil reign. 2 Kin. 3. 2; slain by Jehu. 2 Kin. 9. 24.
JEHOSHABEATH, je-ho´shab´e-ath, Jehovah is the oath. 2 Chr. 22. 11.
JEHOSHAPHAT, je-hosh´af-at, whom Jehovah judges. king of Judah, his good reign. 1 Kin. 15. 24; 2 Chr. 17; his death. 1 Kin. 22. 50; 2 Chr. 21. 1.
—— valley of. Joel 3. 2.
JEHOSHEBA, je-ho´she-bah, same as JEHOSHABEATH. 2 Kin. 11. 2; 2 Chr. 22. 11.
JEHOSHUA, je-hosh´oo-ah, same as JOSHUA. Num. 13. 16.
JEHOSHUAH, je-hosh´oo-ah, same as JOSHUA. 1 Chr. 7. 27.
JEHOVAH, je-ho´vah, the Eternal One.
JEHOVAH, (ELOHIM, I AM THAT I AM). Ex. 6. 3; Ps. 83. 18; Is. 12. 2; 26. 4.
JEHOVAH-JIREH, je-ho´vah-ji´ray, Jehovah will provide. Gen. 22. 14.
JEHOVAH-NISSI, je-ho´vah-nis´i, Jehovah my banner. Ex. 17. 15.
JEHOVAH-SHALOM, je-ho´vah-sha´lom, Jehovah send peace. Judg. 6. 24.
— SHAMMAH, je-ho´vah-sham´mah (the LORD is there). Ezek. 48. 35.
— TSIDKENU, je-ho´vah-tsid-ke´nu (the LORD is our righteousness). Jer. 23. 6.
JEHOZABAD, je-ho´za-bad, Jehovah gave. 2 Kin. 12. 21.
JEHOZADAK, je-ho´za-dak, Jehovah is just. 1 Chr. 6. 14.
JEHU, je´hu, Jehovah is He (?), son of Hanani, prophesies against Baasha. 1 Kin. 16. 1.
rebukes Jehoshaphat. 2 Chr. 19. 2; 20. 34.
—— son of Nimshi, to be anointed king of Israel. 1 Kin. 19. 16; 2 Kin. 9. 1.
his reign. 2 Kin. 9. 10.
JEHUBBAH, je-hoob´ah, hidden. 1 Chr. 7. 34.
JEHUCAL, je-hoo´kal, Jehovah is mighty. Jer. 37. 3.
JEHUD, je´hood, praise. Josh. 19. 45.
JEHUDI, je-hood´i, a Jew. Jer. 36. 14.
JEHUDIJAH, je-hood-i´jah, a Jewess. 1 Chr. 4. 18.
JEHUSH, je´hoosh, to whom God hastens. 1 Chr. 8. 39.
JEIEL, ji´el. 1 Chr. 5. 7.
JEKABZEEL, je-kab´ze-el, God gathers. Neh. 11. 25.
JEKAMEAM, je-kam´e-am. 1 Chr. 23. 19.
JEKAMIAH, jek´am-i´ah, same as JECAMIAH. 1 Chr. 2. 41.
JEKUTHIEL, je-koo´thi-el, the fear of God. 1 Chr. 4. 18.
JEMIMA, je-mi´mah, dove. Job 42. 14.
JEMUEL, jem-oo´el, day of God. Gen. 46. 10.
JEPHTHAE, jef´thah, Greek way of writing Jephthah. Heb. 11. 32.
JEPHTHAH, jef´thah, God opens. Judg. 11. 1.
judge, his dealings with the Gileadites. Judg. 11. 4.
defeats the Ammonites. Judg. 11. 14.
his rash vow. Judg. 11. 30, 34.
chastises the Ephraimites. Judg. 12.
JEPHUNNEH, je-foon´eh, for whom it is prepared. Num. 13. 6.
JERAH, je´rah, the moon. Gen. 10. 26.
JERAHMEEL, je-rah´me-el, whom God loves. 1 Chr. 2. 9.
JERAHMEELITES, je-rah´me-el-ites, descendants of Jerahmeel. 1 Sam. 27. 10.
JERED, je´red, descent. 1 Chr. 1. 2.
JEREMAI, jer-e´mai, dwelling in heights. Ezra 10. 33.
JEREMIAH, jer´em-i´ah, whom Jehovah has appointed.
(prophet), his call and visions. Jer. 1.
his mission. Jer. 1. 17; 7.
his complaint. Jer. 20. 14.
his message to Zedekiah. Jer. 21. 3; 34. 1.
foretells the seventy years' captivity. Jer. 25. 8.
arraigned, condemned, but delivered. Jer. 26.
denounces the false prophet Hananiah. Jer. 28. 5.
writes to the captives in Babylon. Jer. 29.
his promises of comfort and redemption to Israel. Jer. 31.
writes a roll of a book. Jer. 36. 4; Baruch reads it. Jer. 36. 8.
imprisoned by Zedekiah. Jer. 32; 37; 38.
released. Jer. 38. 7.
predicts slaughter of innocents. Jer. 31. 15; fulfilled. Matt. 2. 17.
with all the remnant of Judah carried into Egypt. Jer. 43. 4.
various predictions. Jer. 46—51; 51. 59.
mentioned. Matt. 16. 14; 27. 9.
JEREMIAS, jer´em-i´as, Greek form of Jeremiah. Matt. 16. 14.
JEREMOTH, je-re´moth, high places. 1 Chr. 8. 14.
JEREMY, jer´em-y, shortened English form of Jeremiah. Matt. 2. 17.
JERIAH, jer-i´ah, whom Jehovah regards (?). 1 Chr. 23. 19.
JERIBAI, jer-ee´bai, contentious. 1 Chr. 11. 46.
JERICHO, jer´ik-o, a fragrant place. Num. 22. 1.
the spies at. Josh. 2. 1.
capture of. Josh. 6. 20 (Heb. 11. 30).
rebuilt by Hiel. 1 Kin. 16. 34. *See* Josh. 6. 26.
JERIEL, je-ri´el, founded by God. 1 Chr. 7. 2.
JERIJAH, jer-i´jah, same as JERIAH. 1 Chr. 26. 31.
JERIMOTH, jer-ee´moth, same as JEREMOTH. 1 Chr. 7. 7.
JERIOTH, je-ri´oth, curtains. 1 Chr. 2. 18.
JEROBOAM I, jer´ob-o´am, whose people are many. 1 Kin. 11. 26.
promoted by Solomon. 1 Kin. 11. 28.
Ahijah's prophecy to. 1 Kin. 11. 29.
made king. 1 Kin. 12. 20 (2 Chr. 10).
his idolatry, withered hand, denunciation. 1 Kin. 12; 13; 14.
death. 1 Kin. 14. 20.
evil example. 1 Kin. 15. 34.
JEROBOAM II. 2 Kin. 13. 13; 14. 23–29.
JEROHAM, je-ro´ham, who is loved. 1 Sam. 1. 1.
JERUBBAAL, jer-oob-ba´al, let Baal plead. Judg. 6. 32.
JERUBBESHETH, jer-oob-be´sheth, let shame plead, another name for JERUBBAAL. 2 Sam. 11. 21.

JERUEL, je-roo´el, same as JERIEL. 2 Chr. 20. 16.
JERUSALEM, je-roo´sa-lem, founded in peace (?). Josh. 10. 1.
—— Adoni-zedec, king of, slain by Joshua. Josh. 10.
borders of. Josh. 15. 8.
David reigns there. 2 Sam. 5. 6.
the ark brought there. 2 Sam. 6.
saved from the pestilence. 2 Sam. 24. 16.
temple built at. 1 Kin. 5—8; 2 Chr. 1—7.
sufferings from war. 1 Kin. 14. 25; 2 Kin. 14. 14; 25; 2 Chr. 12; 25. 24; 36; Jer. 39; 52.
capture and destruction by Nebuchadrezzar. Jer. 52. 12–15.
captives return: and rebuilding of the temple begun by Cyrus. Ezra 1—3; continued by Artaxerxes. Neh. 2.
wall rebuilt and dedicated by Nehemiah. Neh. 12. 38.
abominations there. Ezek. 16. 2.
presentation of Christ at. Luke 2. 22.
the child Jesus tarries at. Luke 2. 42.
Christ rides into. Matt. 21. 1; Mark 11. 7; Luke 19. 35; John 12. 14.
laments over it. Matt. 23. 37; Luke 13. 34; 19. 41.
foretells its destruction. Matt. 24; Mark 13; Luke 13. 34; 17; 23; 19. 41; 21.
disciples filled with the Holy Ghost at. Acts 2. 4.
which is above. Gal. 4. 26.
the new. Rev. 21. 2.
JERUSHA, je-roo´shah, possession. 2 Kin. 15. 33.
JERUSHAH, je-roo´shah, same as preceding. 2 Chr. 27. 1.
JESAIAH, je-sai´ah, same as ISAIAH. 1 Chr. 3. 21.
JESHAIAH, je-shai´ah, same as preceding. 1 Chr. 25. 3.
JESHANAH, je-shan´ah, old. 2 Chr. 13. 19.
JESHARELAH, jesh´ar-el´ah, right before God (?). 1 Chr. 25. 14.
JESHEBEAB, je-sheb´e-ab, father's seat. 1 Chr. 24. 13.
JESHER, je´sher, uprightness. 1 Chr. 2. 18.
JESHIMON, je-shim´on, the waste. Num. 21. 20.
JESHISHAI, je-shee´shai, like an old man. 1 Chr. 5. 14.
JESHOHAIAH, je-sho-hai´ah, whom Jehovah humbles. 1 Chr. 4. 36.
JESHUA (Joshua), jesh´oo-ah, Jehovah is salvation. Ezra 2. 2; Neh. 8. 17. *See* JOSHUA.
JESHUAH, jesh´oo-ah, help. 1 Chr. 24. 11.
JESHURUN, jesh-oor´oon, righteous, symbolical name of Israel. Deut. 32. 15; 33. 5, 26; Is. 44. 2.
JESIAH, je-si´ah. 1 Chr. 12. 6.
JESIMIEL, je-sim´i-el, whom God founds (?). 1 Chr. 4. 36.
JESSE, jes´sy, gift (?). Ruth 4. 17.
David's father. Ruth 4. 22.
and his sons sanctified by Samuel. 1 Sam. 16. 5.
his son David anointed to be king. 1 Sam. 16. 13. *See* Is. 11. 1.
his posterity. 1 Chr. 2. 13.
JESUI, je-soo´i, same as ISHUA. Num. 26. 44.
JESUITES, je´soo-ites, the posterity of Jesui. Num. 26. 44.
JESURUN, je-soor´oon, wrongly printed for Jeshurun. Is. 44. 2.
JESUS, je´sus, Saviour. Matt. 1. 21. *See* CHRIST, *Subject-Index*, p. 51.
JETHER, je´ther, same as ITHRA. Judg. 8. 20.
JETHETH, je´theth. Gen. 36. 40.
JETHLAH, jeth´lah, lofty. Josh. 19. 42.
JETHRO, jeth´ro, same as ITHRA. Ex. 3. 1.
Moses' father-in-law. Ex. 18. 12.
JETUR, je´toor, an enclosure. Gen. 25. 15.
JEUEL, je-oo´el, same as JEIEL. 1 Chr. 9. 6.
JEUSH, je´oosh, same as JEHUSH. Gen. 36. 5.
JEUZ, je´ooz, counsellor. 1 Chr. 8. 10.
JEW, joo, an Israelite. Esth. 2. 5.
JEWESS, joo´ess, a female Jew. Acts 16. 1.
JEWISH, joo´ish, of or belonging to Jews. Tit. 1. 14.
JEWRY, joo´ry, Old English name for Judea. Dan. 5. 13.
JEWS, joos, inhabitants of Judea (Israelites first so called). 2 Kin. 16. 6.
Christ's mission to. Matt. 15. 24; 21. 37; Acts 3. 26.
Christ's compassion for. Matt. 23. 37; Luke 19. 41.
Christ rejected by. Matt. 11. 20; 13. 15, 58; John 5. 16, 38, 43; Acts 3. 13; 13. 46; 1 Thess. 2. 15.
gospel first preached to, Matt. 10. 6; Luke 24. 47; Acts 1. 8.
St. Paul's teaching rejected by, Acts 13. 46; 28. 24, 26, &c.
JEZANIAH, jez´an-i´ah, Jehovah adorns (?). Jer. 40. 8.
JEZEBEL, jez´e-bel, unmarried.
wife of Ahab. 1 Kin. 16. 31.
kills the prophets, 1 Kin. 18. 4; 19. 2.
causes Naboth to be put to death. 1 Kin. 21.
her violent death. 2 Kin. 9. 30.
JEZER, je´zer, anything made. Gen. 46. 24.
JEZERITES, je´zer-ites, descendants of Jezer. Num. 26. 49.
JEZIAH, jez-i´ah, whom Jehovah assembles. Ezra 10. 25.
JEZIEL, jez-i´el, the assembly of God. 1 Chr. 12. 3.
JEZLIAH, jez-li´ah, deliverance (?). 1 Chr. 8. 18.
JEZOAR, je-zo´ar, splendid. 1 Chr. 4. 7.
JEZRAHIAH, jez´rah-i´ah, Jehovah shines forth. Neh. 12. 42.
JEZREEL, jez´re-el, God scatters. 1 Chr. 4. 3. *See* AHAB.
JEZREELITE, jez´re-el-ite, an inhabitant of Jezreel. 1 Kin. 21. 6.
JEZREELITESS, jez´re-el-ite-ess, feminine of preceding. 1 Sam. 27. 3.
JIBSAM, jib´sam, fragrant. 1 Chr. 7. 2.
JIDLAPH, jid´laf, weeping (?). Gen. 22. 22.
JIMNA, jim´nah, same as IMNA. Num. 26. 44.
JIMNAH, jim´nah, same as IMNAH. Gen. 46. 17.
JIMNITES, jim´nites, descendants of Jimnah. Num. 26. 44.
JIPHTAH, jif´tah, same as JEPHTHAH. Josh. 15. 43.
JIPHTHAH-EL, jif´thah-el, which God opens. Josh. 19. 14.
JOAB, jo´ab, Jehovah is father. 2 Sam. 2. 13.
nephew of David, and captain of the host. 2 Sam. 8. 16.
kills Abner. 2 Sam. 3. 23.
intercedes for Absalom, 2 Sam. 14; slays him in an oak, 2 Sam. 18. 14.
reproves David's grief. 2 Sam. 19. 5.
slays Amasa. 2 Sam. 20. 9.
unwillingly numbers the people. 2 Sam. 24. 3 (1 Chr. 21. 3).
joins Adonijah's usurpation. 1 Kin. 1. 7.
slain by Solomon's command. 1 Kin. 2. 5, 28.
JOAH, jo´ah, Jehovah is brother. 2 Kin. 18. 18; 2 Chr. 34. 8.
JOAHAZ, jo´a-haz, whom Jehovah holds. 2 Chr. 34. 8.
JOANNA, jo-an´ah, Greek way of writing Jehonan. Luke 3. 27; 8. 2, 3; 24. 10.
JOASH, jo´ash, whom Jehovah supports (?). 2 Kin. 11. 2.
(Jehoash), king of Israel. 2 Kin. 13. 10.
visits Elisha sick. 2 Kin. 13. 14.
defeats the Syrians. 2 Kin. 13. 25.
chastises Amaziah. 2 Kin. 14. 8; 2 Chr. 25. 17.
—— king of Judah. 2 Kin. 11. 4; 2 Chr. 23.
repairs the temple. 2 Kin. 12; 2 Chr. 24.
kills Zechariah. 2 Chr. 24. 17.
slain by his servants. 2 Kin. 12. 19; 2 Chr. 24. 23.
JOATHAM, jo´ath-am, Greek form of Jotham. Matt. 1. 9.
JOB, jobe, (1) a desert, Gen. 46. 13; (2) one persecuted.
his character, Job 1. 1, 8; 2. 3 (Ezek. 14. 14, 20).
his afflictions and patience. Job. 1. 13, 20; 2. 7, 10 (James 5. 11).
complains of his life. Job 3.
reproves his friends. Job 6; 7; 9; 10; 12—14; 16; 17; 19; 21; 23; 24; 26—30.
solemnly protests his integrity. Job. 31.

JOB—*cont*
humbles himself. Job 40. 3; 42. 1.
God accepts and doubly blesses. Job 42. 10.
JOBAB, jo′bab, a desert. Gen. 10. 29.
JOCHEBED, jo′ke-bed, Jehovah is glorious (?).
mother of Moses. Ex. 6. 20; Num. 26. 59.
JOED, jo′ed, for whom Jehovah is witness. Neh. 11. 7.
JOEL, jo′el, Jehovah is might.
delivers God's judgments. Joel 1—3.
proclaims a fast, and declares God's mercy. Joel 1. 14; 2. 12; 3.
quoted. Acts 2. 16.
JOELAH, jo′el-ah, He helps (?). 1 Chr. 12. 7.
JOEZER, jo′e-zer, Jehovah is help. 1 Chr. 12. 6.
JOGBEHAH, jog′be-hah, lofty. Num. 32. 35.
JOGLI, jo′gli, an exile. Num. 34. 22.
JOHA, jo′hah, Jehovah lives (?). 1 Chr. 8. 16.
JOHANAN, jo-ha′nan, Jehovah is gracious. 2 Kin. 25. 23; Jer. 40. 8, 15; 41. 11; 42; 43.
JOHN, English way of spelling Johanan. Matt. 3. 1.
the APOSTLE, called, Matt. 4. 21; Mark 1. 19; Luke 5. 10.
ordained. Matt. 10. 2; Mark 3. 17.
enquires of Jesus. Mark 13. 3.
reproved. Matt. 20. 20; Mark 10. 35–40; Luke 9. 50.
sent to prepare the passover. Luke 22. 8.
declares the divinity and humanity of Jesus Christ. John 1; 1 John 1; 4; 5.
Christ's love for. John 13. 23; 19. 26; 21. 7, 20, 24.
his care for Mary the Lord's mother. John 19. 27.
meets for prayer. Acts 1. 13.
accompanies Peter before the council. Acts 3; 4.
exhorts to obedience and warns against false teachers. 1 John 1—5.
sees Christ's glory in heaven. Rev. 1. 13.
writes the Revelation. Rev. 1. 19.
forbidden to worship the angel. Rev. 19. 10; 22. 8.
—— (MARK). Acts 12. 12, 25. *See* MARK.
—— the BAPTIST, his coming foretold. Is. 40. 3; Mal. 4. 5; Luke 1. 17.
his birth and circumcision. Luke 1. 57.
office, preaching, and baptism. Matt. 3; Mark 1; Luke 3; John 1. 6; 3. 26; Acts 1. 5; 13. 24.
baptizes Christ. Matt. 3; Mark 1; Luke 3; John 1. 32; 3. 26.
imprisoned by Herod, Matt. 4. 12; Mark 1. 14; Luke 3. 20; and beheaded, Matt. 14; Mark 6. 14.
sends his disciples to Christ. Matt. 11. 1; Luke 7. 18.
Christ's testimony to. Matt. 11. 11, 14; 17. 12; Mark 9. 11; Luke 7. 27.
his disciples receive the Holy Ghost. Acts 18. 24; 19. 1.
JOIADA, jo′ya-dah, Jehovah knows. Neh. 12. 10.
JOIAKIM, jo′ya-kim, shortened from Jehoiakim. Neh. 12. 10.
JOIARIB, jo′ya-rib, whom Jehovah defends. Ezra 8. 16.
JOKIM, jo′kim, shortened from Jehoiakim. 1 Chr. 4. 22.
JOKDEAM, jok′de-am, burning of the people. Josh. 15. 56.
JOKMEAM, jok′me-am. 1 Chr. 6. 68.
JOKNEAM, jok′ne-am, possessed by the people. Josh. 12. 22.
JOKSHAN, jok′shan, fowler. Gen. 25. 2.
JOKTAN, jok′tan, small. Gen. 10. 25.
JOKTHEEL, jok′the-el, subdued by God. Josh. 15. 38.
JONA, jo′nah, a Greek way of spelling Johanan. John 1. 42.
JONADAB, jo′na-dab, same as JEHONADAB. 2 Sam. 13. 3.
—— (Jehonadab), son of Rechab. 2 Kin. 10. 15.
JONAH, jo′nah, dove.
prophet. 2 Kin. 14. 25.
his disobedience, punishment, prayer, and repentance. Jonah 1—4.
a type of Christ. Matt. 12. 39; Luke 11. 29.
JONAN, jo′nan, contracted from JOHANAN. Luke 3. 30.
JONAS, jo′nas, (1) same as JONA. John 21. 15.
(2) Or JONAH. Matt. 12. 39.
JONATH-ELEM-RECHOKIM, jo′nath-e′lem-re-ko-kim′, the silent dove afar off. Title of Ps. 56.
JONATHAN, jo′na-than, whom Jehovah gave.
son of Saul, smites the Philistines. 1 Sam. 13. 2; 14.
his love for David. 1 Sam. 18. 1; 19; 20; 23. 16.
slain by the Philistines. 1 Sam. 31. 2.
David's lamentation for. 2 Sam. 1. 17.
—— son of Abiathar. 2 Sam. 15. 27; 1 Kin. 1. 42.
—— one of David's nephews, his deeds. 2 Sam. 21. 21; 1 Chr. 20. 7.
—— a Levite, hired by Micah. Judg. 17. 7; 18.
JOPPA, jop′ah, beauty (?).
(Jaffa). 2 Chr. 2. 16; Jonah 1. 3.
Tabitha raised at. Acts 9. 36.
Peter dwells at. Acts 10. 5; 11. 5.
JORAH, jo′rah, watering (?). Ezra 2. 18.
JORAI, jo′rai, archer (?). 1 Chr. 5. 13.
JORAM, jo′ram, same as JEHORAM. 2 Sam. 8. 10.
JORDAN, jor′dan, flowing down. Gen. 13. 10.
river, waters of, divided for the Israelites. Josh. 3; 4; Ps. 114. 3; by Elijah and Elisha. 2 Kin. 2. 8, 13.
Naaman's leprosy cured at. 2 Kin. 5. 10.
John baptizes there. Matt. 3; Mark 1. 5; Luke 3. 3; *See* Job 40. 23; Ps. 42. 6; Jer. 12. 5; 49. 19; Zech. 11. 3.
JORIM, jo′rim, a form of JORAM (?). Luke 3. 29.
JORKOAM, jor′ko-am, spreading of the people (?). 1 Chr. 2. 44.
JOSABAD, jo′sa-bad, same as JEHOZABAD. 1 Chr. 12. 4.
JOSAPHAT, jo′saf-at, Greek form of Jehoshaphat. Matt. 1. 8.
JOSEDECH, jo′se-dek, same as JEHOZADAK. Hag. 1. 1.
JOSEPH, jo′sef, he shall add.
son of Jacob. Gen. 30. 24. *See* Ps. 105. 17; Acts 7. 9; Heb. 11. 22.
his dreams, and the jealousy of his brethren. Gen. 37. 5.
sold to the Ishmeelites. Gen. 37. 28.
slave to Potiphar. Gen. 39.
resists Potiphar's wife. Gen. 39. 7.
interprets the dreams of Pharaoh's servants. Gen. 40; and of Pharaoh, predicting famine. Gen. 41. 25.
made ruler of Egypt. Gen. 41. 39.
prepares for the famine. Gen. 41. 48.
receives his brethren and father. Gen. 42—46.
gives direction concerning his bones. Gen. 50. 25.
his death. Gen. 50. 26.
—— son of Heli, husband of the Virgin. Matt. 1. 19; 2. 13, 19; Luke 1. 27; 2. 4.
—— of Arimathæa. Matt. 27. 57; Mark 15. 42; Luke 23. 50; John 19. 38.
—— (Barsabas), Justus. Acts 1. 23.
JOSES, jo′ses. Matt. 13. 55.
JOSHAH, jo′shah, Jehovah presents (?). 1 Chr. 4. 34.
JOSHAPHAT, jo′sha-fat, shortened from Jehoshaphat. 1 Chr. 11. 43.
JOSHAVIAH, jo′shav-i′ah, same as JOSHAH. 1 Chr. 11. 46.
JOSHBEKASHAH, josh′be-ka′shah, seat of hardship (?). 1 Chr. 25. 4.
JOSHUA, josh′you-ah, Jehovah is salvation. Num. 14. 6.
(Hoshea, Oshea, Jehoshua, Jeshua, and Jesus), son of Nun. 1 Chr. 7. 27; Heb. 4. 8.
discomfits Amalek. Ex. 17. 9.
ministers to Moses. Ex. 24. 13; 32. 17; 33. 11.
spies out Canaan. Num. 13. 16.
ordained to succeed Moses. Num. 27. 18; 34. 17; Deut. 1. 38; 3. 28; 34. 9.
reassured by God. Josh. 1.
harangues his officers. Josh. 1. 10.
crosses river Jordan. Josh. 3.
erects memorial pillars. Josh. 4.
re-enacts circumcision. Josh. 5.

JOSHUA—*cont.*
assaults and destroys Jericho. Josh. 6.
condemns Achan. Josh. 7.
subdues Ai. Josh. 8.
his victories. Josh. 10—12.
apportions the land. Josh. 14—21; Heb. 4. 8.
his charge to the Reubenites. Josh. 22.
exhortation to the people. Josh. 23.
reminds them of God's mercies. Josh. 24.
renews the covenant. Josh. 24. 14.
his death. Josh. 24. 29; Judg. 2. 8.
his curse, Josh. 6. 26; fulfilled, 1 Kin. 16. 34.
JOSIAH, jo-si´ah, whom Jehovah heals. 2 Kin. 21. 24.
prophecy concerning, 1 Kin. 13. 2; fulfilled, 2 Kin. 23. 15.
reigns well. 2 Kin. 22.
repairs the temple. 2 Kin. 22. 3.
hears the words of the book of the law. 2 Kin. 22. 8.
Huldah's message from God to him. 2 Kin. 22. 15.
ordains the reading of the book. 2 Kin. 23.
keeps a signal passover to the Lord. 2 Chr. 35.
slain by Pharaoh-nechoh at Megiddo. 2 Kin. 23. 29.
JOSIAS, jo-si´as, Greek form of Josiah. Matt. 1. 10.
JOSIBIAH, jos´ib-i´ah, to whom God gives a dwelling. 1 Chr. 4. 35.
JOSIPHIAH, jos´if-i´ah, whom Jehovah will increase. Ezra 8. 10.
JOTBAH, jot´bah, pleasantness (?). 2 Kin. 21. 19.
JOTBATH, jot´bath, same as JOTBAH. Deut. 10. 7.
JOTBATHAH, jot-bah´thah, same as JOTBAH. Num. 33. 33.
JOTHAM, jo´tham, Jehovah is upright. Judg. 9. 5.
son of Gideon, his apologue. Judg. 9. 7.
—— king of Judah. 2 Kin. 15. 32; 2 Chr. 27.
JOZABAD, jo´za-bad, same as JEHOZABAD. 1 Chr. 12. 20.
JOZACHAR, jo´za-kar, whom Jehovah has remembered. 2 Kin. 12. 21.
JOZADAK, jo´za-dak, same as JEHOZADAK. Ezra 3. 2.
JUBAL, joo´bal, music (?).
inventor of harp and organ. Gen. 4. 21.
JUCAL, joo´kal, same as JEHUCAL. Jer. 38. 1.
JUDA, joo´dah, same as JUDAH. Luke 3. 30.
JUDAH, joo´dah, praised.
son of Jacob. Gen. 29. 35.
his descendants. Gen. 38; 46. 12; Num. 1. 26; 26. 19; 1 Chr. 2—4.
pledges himself for Benjamin. Gen. 43. 3.
his interview with Joseph. Gen. 44. 18;—46. 28.
blessed by Jacob. Gen. 49. 8.
—— tribe of, their blessing by Moses. Deut. 33. 7.
their inheritance. Josh. 15.
they make David king, 2 Sam. 2. 4; and adhere to his house. 1 Kin. 12; 2 Chr. 10; 11. *See* JEWS.
JUDAS, joo´das, Greek form of Judah. Matt. 10. 4.
(JUDE, Lebbæus, Thaddæus), APOSTLE, brother of James. Matt. 10. 3; Mark 3. 18; Luke 6. 16; Acts 1. 13.
his question to our Lord. John 14. 22.
enjoins perseverance. Jude 3. 20.
denounces false disciples. Jude 4.
—— the Lord's brother. Matt. 13. 55; Mark 6. 3.
—— (Barsabas). Acts 15. 22.
JUDAS ISCARIOT. Matt. 10. 4; Mark 3. 19; Luke 6. 16; John 6. 70.
betrays Jesus. Matt. 26. 14, 47; Mark 14. 10, 43; Luke 22. 3, 47; John 13. 26; 18. 2.
hangs himself. Matt. 27. 5 (Acts 1. 18).
JUDE, jood, abbreviated from Judas. Jude 1.
JUDEA, joo-de´ah (land of Judah). Ezra 5. 8.
JUDITH, joo´dith (probably from the same). Gen. 26. 34.
JULIA, joo´li-ah, *feminine* form of Julius. Rom. 16. 15.
JULIUS, joo´li-us, downy. Acts 27. 1.
JUNIA, joo´ni-ah.
saluted by Paul. Rom. 16. 7.
JUPITER, joo´pit-er.
Barnabas addressed as. Acts 14. 12;—19. 35.
JUSHAB-HESED, joo´shab-he´sed, whose love is returned. 1 Chr. 3. 20.
JUSTUS, just´us, upright. Acts 1. 23.
JUTTAH, joot´ah, extended. Josh. 15. 55.

KABZEEL, kab´ze-el, God has gathered. Josh. 15. 21.
KADESH, ka´desh, consecrated. Gen. 20. 1.
KADESH-BARNEA, ka´desh-bar´ne-ah. Num. 34. 4.
Israelites murmur against Moses and Aaron, threaten to stone Caleb and Joshua, and provoke God's anger. Num. 13; 14; Deut. 1. 19; Josh. 14. 6.
KADMIEL, kad´mi-el, eternity of God (?). Ezra 2. 40.
KADMONITES, kad´mon-ites, Orientals. Gen. 15. 19.
KALLAI, kal´ai, swift. Neh. 12. 20.
KANAH, ka´nah, a place of reeds. Josh. 19. 28.
KAREAH, ka-re´ah, bald. Jer. 40. 8.
KARKAA, kar-ka´ah, floor. Josh. 15. 3.
KARKOR, kar´kor, plain (?). Judg. 8. 10.
KARNAIM, kar-na´im, two horns. Gen. 14. 5.
KARTAH, kar´tah, city. Josh. 21. 34.
KARTAN, kar´tan, double city. Josh. 21. 32.
KATTATH, kat´ath, small (?). Josh. 19. 15.
KEDAR, ke´dar, black-skinned.
son of Ishmael. Gen. 25. 13; 1 Chr. 1. 29; Ps. 120. 5; Cant. 1. 5; Jer. 2. 10; Ezek. 27. 21.
—— tribe of, prophecies concerning. Is. 21. 16; 42. 11; 60. 7; Jer. 49. 28.
KEDEMAH, ke-de´mah, eastward. Gen. 25. 15.
KEDEMOTH, ke-de´moth, eastern parts. Josh. 13. 18.
KEDESH, ke´desh, sanctuary. Josh. 12. 22.
KEDRON (Kidron, Cedron), ke´dron, brook and ravine, near garden of Gethsemane, frequented by our Lord. John 18. 1.
crossed by David. 2 Sam. 15. 23.
idols destroyed there. 1 Kin. 15. 13; 2 Kin. 23. 6; 2 Chr. 29. 16; Jer. 31. 40. *See* KIDRON.
KEHELATHAH, ke-he-lah´thah, assembly. Num. 33. 22.
KEILAH, ke-ee´lah, sling (?). Josh. 15. 44.
David there. 1 Sam. 23. 1, 12.
KELAIAH, ke-lai´ah, contempt (?). Ezra 10. 23.
KELITA, ke-li´tah, dwarf. Neh. 8. 7.
KEMUEL, ke-moo´el, congregation of God. Gen. 22. 21.
KENAN, ke´nan, smith (?). 1 Chr. 1. 2.
KENATH, ke´nath, possession. Num. 32. 42.
KENAZ, ke´naz, hunting. Gen. 36. 11.
KENEZITE, ke´nez-ite, descendant of Kenaz. Num. 32. 12.
KENITES, keen´ites, descendants of an unknown man named Kain. Gen. 15. 19.
their fate foretold. Num. 24. 22.
KENIZZITES, ke´niz-ites, same as KENEZITE. Gen. 15. 19.
KEREN-HAPPUCH, ke´ren-hap´ook, horn of paint.
one of Job's daughters. Job 42. 14.
KERIOTH, ke-ri´oth, cities.
a city of Judah. Josh. 15. 25; Jer. 48. 24, 41; Amos 2. 2.
KEROS, ke´ros, crook (?). Ezra 2. 44.
KETURAH, ke-too´rah, incense.
Abraham's wife, Gen. 25; her children, 1 Chr. 1. 32.
KEZIA, ke-zi´ah, cassia. Job 42. 14.
KEZIZ, ke´ziz, cut off. Josh. 18. 21.
KIBROTH-HATTAAVAH, kib´roth-hat-ta´a-vah, graves of lust. Num. 11. 34.
KIBZAIM, kib-za´im, two heaps. Josh. 21. 22.
KIDRON, kid´ron, turbid. 2 Sam. 15. 23.
KINAH, ki´nah, song of mourning, lamentation. Josh. 15. 22.
KIR, kir, town. 2 Kin. 16. 9; Is. 15. 1; 22. 6; Amos 1. 5; 9. 7.
KIR-HARASETH, kir´ha-ras´eth, brick-town. 2 Kin. 3. 25; Is. 16. 7, 11.
KIR-HARESETH, kir´ha-res´eth, same as preceding. Is. 16. 7.
KIR-HARESH, kir-har´esh, same as preceding. Is. 16. 11.
KIR-HERES, kir-her´es, same as preceding. Jer. 48. 31.
KIRIATHAIM, kir´yath-a´im, same as KIRJATHAIM. Ezek. 25. 9.

KIRIOTH, ki-ri'-oth, cities. Amos 2. 2.
KIRJATH, kir'-jath, city (?). Josh. 18. 28.
KIRJATHAIM, kir'-jath-a'-im, double city. Num. 32. 37.
KIRJATH-ARBA, kir'-jath-ar'-bah, city of Arba. Gen. 23. 2.
KIRJATH-ARIM, kir'-jath-ar'-im, contracted from KIRJATH-JEARIM. Ezra 2. 25.
KIRJATH-BAAL, kir'-jath-ba'-al, city of Baal. Josh. 15. 60.
KIRJATH-HUZOTH, kir'-jath-hooz'-oth, *c.* of streets. Num. 22. 39.
KIRJATH-JEARIM, kir'-jath-je'-ar-im, *c.* of woods. Josh. 9. 17; 18. 14; 1 Chr. 13. 6.
 the ark brought to. 1 Sam. 7. 1.
 ark fetched from. 1 Chr. 13. 5; 2 Chr. 1. 4.
KIRJATH-SANNAH, kir'-jath-san'-ah, *c.* of thorns. Josh. 15. 49.
KIRJATH-SEPHER, kir'-jath-se'-fer, book-city. Josh. 15. 15.
KISH, kish, bow.
 Saul's father. 1 Sam. 9. 1.
KISHI, kish'-i, bow of Jehovah. 1 Chr. 6. 44.
KISHION, kish'-i-on, hardness. Josh. 19. 20.
KISHON, ki'-shon, tortuous.
 waters of Megiddo. Judg. 4. 7; 5. 21; 1 Kin. 18. 40.
KISON, ki'-son, same as KISHON. Ps. 83. 9.
KITHLISH, kith'-lish, fortified. Josh. 15. 40.
KITRON, kit'-ron, burning. Judg. 1. 30.
KITTIM, kit'-im, same as CHITTIM. Gen. 10. 4.
KOA, ko'-ah, prince. Ezek. 23. 23.
KOHATH, ko'-hath, assembly.
 son of Levi. Gen. 46. 11.
 his descendants. Ex. 6. 18; 1 Chr. 6. 2.
 their duties. Num. 4. 15; 10. 21; 2 Chr. 29. 12; 34. 12.
KOHATHITES, ko'-hath-ites, descendants of Kohath. Num. 3. 27.
KOLAIAH, kol-ai'-ah, voice of Jehovah (?). Neh. 11. 7.
KORAH, ko'-rah, bald.
 Dathan, &c., their sedition and punishment. Num. 16; 26. 9; 27. 3.
 (Core), Jude 11.
KORAHITES, ko'-rah-ites, descendants of Korah. 1 Chr. 9. 19.
KORATHITES, ko'-rath-ites, same as preceding. Num. 26. 58.
KORE, ko'-re, partridge. 1 Chr. 9. 19.
KORHITE, kor'-ite, same as KORATHITE. 2 Chr. 20. 19.
KOZ, thorn. Ezra 2. 61.
KUSHAIAH, kush-ai'-ah, longer form of Kishi. 1 Chr. 15. 17.

LAADAH, la'-ad-ah, order (?). 1 Chr. 4. 21.
LAADAN, la'-ad-an, put in order (?). 1 Chr. 7. 26.
LABAN, la'-ban, white.
 hospitality of. Gen. 24. 29.
 gives Jacob his two daughters. Gen. 29.
 envies and oppresses him. Gen. 30. 27; 31. 1.
 his dream. Gen. 31. 24.
 his covenant with Jacob. Gen. 31. 43.
LACHISH, la'-kish, impregnable. Josh. 10. 3.
 conquered. Josh. 10. 31; 12. 11.
 Amaziah slain at. 2 Kin. 14. 19.
LAEL, la'-el, (devoted) to God. Num. 3. 24.
LAHAD, la'-had, oppression. 1 Chr. 4. 2.
LAHAI-ROI, la-hai-ro'-i, to the living is sight. Gen. 24. 62.
LAHMAM, lah'-mam. Josh. 15. 40.
LAHMI, lah'-mi, warrior. 1 Chr. 20. 5.
LAISH, la'-ish, lion. 1 Sam. 25. 44.
 taken. Judg. 18. 14.
LAKUM, la'-koom, fort (?). Josh. 19. 33.
LAMA, lam'-ah, why? Matt. 27. 46.
LAMECH, la'-mek, destroyer.
 descendant of Cain. Gen. 4. 18.
 —— father of Noah. Gen. 5. 25, 29.
LAODICEA, la'-od-i-se'-ah. Col. 2. 1.
LAODICEANS, la'-od-i-se'-ans, inhabitants of Laodicea. Rev. 1. 11; 3. 14.

LAODICEANS—*cont.*
 Paul's epistle to. Col. 4. 16.
LAPIDOTH, la'-pid-oth, torches. Judg. 4. 4.
LASEA, la-se'-ah. Acts 27. 8.
LASHA, la'-shah, fissure. Gen. 10. 19.
LASHARON, la-sha'-ron, of the plain. Josh. 12. 18.
LATIN, lat'-in, the language spoken by Romans. John 19. 20.
LAZARUS, laz'-ar-us, Greek form of Eleazar. Luke 16. 20.
 and the rich man. Luke 16. 19.
LAZARUS, brother of Mary and Martha, raised from the dead. John 11; 12. 1.
LEAH, le'-ah, languid. Gen. 29. 16, 31; 30. 17; 31. 4; 33. 2; 49. 31. *See* Ruth 4. 11.
LEBANAH, le-bah'-nah, white. Ezra 2. 45.
LEBANON, leb'-an-on, the white (mountain). Deut. 1. 7.
 forest and mountain. Deut. 3. 25; Judg. 3. 3; 1 Kin. 5. 14.
 its cedars. 2 Kin. 14. 9; 2 Chr. 2. 8; Ps. 92. 12; Cant. 3. 9; Is. 40. 16; Hos. 14. 5.
LEBAOTH, le-ba'-oth, lionesses. Josh. 15. 32.
LEBBÆUS, leb-e'-us. Matt. 10. 3. *See* JUDE.
LEBONAH, leb-o'-nah, frankincense. Judg. 21. 19.
LECAH, le'-kah, journey (?). 1 Chr. 4. 21.
LEHABIM, le-hah'-bim. Gen. 10. 13.
LEHI, le'-hi, jaw-bone. Judg. 15. 9.
LEMUEL, lem'-oo-el, (devoted) to God (?).
 king, his lesson. Prov. 31. 1.
LESHEM, le'-shem, precious stone. Josh. 19. 47.
LETUSHIM, le-toosh'-im, the hammered. Gen. 25. 3.
LEUMMIM, le-oom'-im, peoples. Gen. 25. 3.
LEVI, le'-vi, associate (?).
 son of Jacob. Gen. 29. 34.
 avenges Dinah. Gen. 34. 25; 49. 5.
 —— *See* MATTHEW.
LEVIATHAN, le-vi'-a-than, a water monster. Ps. 104. 26.
LEVITES, le'-vites, descendants of Levi, mentioned. Ex. 6. 25; 32. 26.
 their service. Ex. 38. 21.
 appointed over the tabernacle. Num. 1. 47.
 their divisions, Gershonites, Kohathites, Merarites. Num. 3.
 duties of. Num. 3. 23; 4; 8. 23; 18.
 their consecration. Num. 8. 5.
 inheritance of. Num. 35; Deut. 18; Josh. 21.
 not to be forsaken. Deut. 12. 19; 14. 27.
 their genealogies. 1 Chr. 6; 9.
 charged with the temple service. 1 Chr. 23—27.
 twenty-four courses, instituted by David, 1 Chr. 23. 6; re-divided by Ezra, Ezra 6. 18.
 their sin censured. Mal. 1. 2; Ezek. 22. 26.
LEVITICUS, le-vit'-ic-us, the book which treats of the affairs of the Levitical law.
LIBERTINES, lib'-ert-ines, freedmen. Acts 6. 9.
LIBNAH, lib'-nah, whiteness. Num. 33. 20.
 subdued. Josh. 10. 29; 21. 13.
 rebels. 2 Kin. 8. 22.
 attacked by Assyrians. 2 Kin. 19. 8; Is. 37. 8.
LIBNI, lib'-ni, white. Ex. 6. 17.
LIBNITES, lib'-nites, descendants of Libni. Num. 3. 21.
LIBYA, lib'-yah. Jer. 46. 9; Ezek. 30. 5; Dan. 11. 43; Acts 2. 10.
LIKHI, lik'-hi, fond of learning (?). 1 Chr. 7. 19.
LINUS, li'-nus, flax. 2 Tim. 4. 21.
LO-AMMI, lo-am'-i, not my people. Hos. 1. 9.
LOD, lode, strife (?). 1 Chr. 8. 12.
LO-DEBAR, lo'-de-bar, without pasture (?). 2 Sam. 9. 4.
LOIS, lo'-is. 2 Tim. 1. 5.
LO-RUHAMAH, lo-ru-hah'-mah, not having obtained mercy. Hos. 1. 6.
LOT, veil. Gen. 11. 27.
 (Abram's nephew), separates from Abram. Gen. 13. 10.
 captured by four kings, and rescued by Abram. Gen. 14.

LOT—*cont.*
entertains angel visitors. Gen. 19. 1.
saved from Sodom. Gen. 19. 16; 2 Pet. 2. 7.
his wife turned into a pillar of salt. Gen. 19. 26; Luke 17. 28, 32.
LOTAN, lo´tan, veiling. Gen. 36. 20.
LUBIMS, loob´ims, same as LEHABIM. 2 Chr. 12. 3.
LUCAS, loo´kas, same as LUKE. Phil. 24.
LUCIFER, loo´sif-er, light-bearer. Is. 14. 12.
LUCIUS, loosh´yus, a noble (?).
of Cyrene, a teacher. Acts 13. 1; Rom. 16. 21.
LUD, lood, strife (?). Gen. 10. 22.
LUDIM, lood´im. Gen. 10. 13.
LUHITH, loo´hith, abounding in boards. Is. 15. 5.
LUKE, of or belonging to Lucania.
the beloved physician, companion of Paul. Col. 4. 14; 2 Tim. 4. 11; Phil. 24 (Acts 16. 12; 20. 5).
LUZ, looz, almond tree. Gen. 28. 19.
LYCAONIA, li´ka-o´ni-ah. Acts 14. 6.
LYCIA, lish´yah. Acts 27. 5.
LYDDA, lid´ah, Greek form of LOD (?).
miracle at. Acts 9. 32.
LYDIA, lid´yah.
of Thyatira, piety of. Acts 16. 14, 40.
LYSANIAS, li-sa´ni-as, ending sorrow. Luke 3. 1.
LYSIAS, lis´yas, a person of Lysia. Acts 23. 26.
LYSTRA, lis´trah. Acts 14. 6.
miracle at. Acts 14. 8.
Paul and Barnabas taken for gods at. Acts 14. 11.
Paul stoned at, by Jews. Acts 14. 19.

MAACAH, ma´ak-ah (same as MAACHAH). 2 Sam. 3. 3.
MAACHAH, ma´ak-ah, royal (?). 1 Kin. 2. 39.
—— queen, her idolatry. 1 Kin. 15. 13; 2 Chr. 15. 16.
MAACHATHI, ma´a-chah´thi, an inhabitant of Maachah. Deut. 3. 14.
MAACHATHITES, ma-ak´ath-ites, plural of preceding. Josh. 12. 5.
MAADAI, ma´a-dai, adorned. Ezra 10. 34.
MAADIAH, ma´ad-i´ah, ornament of Jehovah. Neh. 12. 5.
MAAI, ma´ai, compassionate (?). Neh. 12. 36.
MAALEH-ACRABBIM, ma´al-eh-ak´rab-im, ascent of scorpions. Josh. 15. 3.
MAARATH, ma´ar-ath, a treeless place. Josh. 15. 59.
MAASEIAH, ma´as-i´ah, work of Jehovah. Ezra 10. 18.
MAASIAI, ma´as-i-ai, same as AMASHAI (?). 1 Chr. 9. 12.
MAATH, ma´ath, small (?). Luke 3. 26.
MAAZ, ma´az, wrath. 1 Chr. 2. 27.
MAAZIAH, ma´az-i´ah. 1 Chr. 24. 18.
MACEDONIA, mas´ed-o´ni-ah.
Paul's mission there. Acts 16. 9; 17.
liberality of. 2 Cor. 8; 9; 11. 9; Phil. 4. 15.
its churches. 1 & 2 Thess.
MACHBANAI, mak-ban´ai, cloak. 1 Chr. 12. 13.
MACHBENAH, mak´be-nah´, clad with a cloak (?). 1 Chr. 2. 49.
MACHI, ma´ki. Num. 13. 15.
MACHIR, ma´kir, sold. Gen. 50. 23.
MACHIRITES, ma´kir-ites, the descendants of Machir. Num. 26. 29.
MACHNADEBAI, mak-nad´eb-ai. Ezra 10. 40.
MACHPELAH, mak-pe´lah, a doubling. Gen. 23. 9.
field of. Gen. 23.
patriarchs buried there. Gen. 23. 19; 25. 9; 35. 29; 49. 30; 50. 12.
MADAI, ma´dai. Gen. 10. 2.
MADIAN, ma´di-an, Greek form of MIDIAN. Acts 7. 29.
MADMANNAH, mad-man´ah, dunghill. Josh. 15. 31.
MADMEN, mad´men, dungheap. Jer. 48. 2.
MADMENAH, mad-may´nah, same as MADMEN. Is. 10. 31.
MADON, ma´don, place of contention. Josh. 11. 1.
MAGBISH, mag´bish, congregating. Ezra 2. 30.
MAGDALA, mag´dal-ah, tower. Matt. 15. 39.
MAGDALENE, mag´dal-e´ne, inhabitant of Magdala. Matt. 27. 56.
MAGDIEL, mag´di-el, praise of God. Gen. 36. 43.
MAGOG, ma´gog. Gen. 10. 2.
MAGOR-MISSABIB, ma´gor-mis´a-bib, fear round about. Jer. 20. 3.
MAGPIASH, mag´pi-ash. Neh. 10. 20.
MAHALAH, mah´hai-ah, disease. 1 Chr. 7. 18.
MAHALALEEL, ma´ha-lal´e-el, praise of God. Gen. 5. 12.
MAHALATH, mah´al-ath, a musical instrument. Gen. 28. 9.
MAHALATH LEANNOTH, m. le-an-oth´. Ps. 88, title.
MAHALI, ma´ha-li, weak. Ex. 6. 19.
MAHANAIM, ma´han-a´im, two camps. Gen. 32. 2.
Jacob's vision at. Gen. 32.
Ish-bosheth made king at. 2 Sam. 2. 8.
David takes refuge from Absalom at. 2 Sam. 17. 24.
MAHANEH-DAN, ma´han-e-dan´, camp of Dan. Judg. 18. 12.
MAHARAI, ma´ha-rai, impetuous. 2 Sam. 23. 28.
MAHATH, ma´hath, taking hold (?). 1 Chr. 6. 35.
MAHAVITE, ma´hav-ite. 1 Chr. 11. 46.
MAHAZIOTH, ma-haz´i-oth, visions. 1 Chr. 25. 4.
MAHER-SHALAL-HASH-BAZ, ma´her-sha´lal-hash´baz, the spoil hastens, the prey speeds. Is. 8. 1.
MAHLAH, mah´lah, same as MAHALAH. Num. 26. 33.
MAHLI, mah´li, same as MAHALI. 1 Chr. 6. 19.
MAHLITES, mah´lites, the descendants of Mahli. Num. 3. 33.
MAHLON, mah´lon, a sick person.
and Chilion die in Moab. Ruth 1. 2.
MAHOL, ma´hol, a dance. 1 Kin. 4. 31.
MAKAZ, ma´kaz, end (?). 1 Kin. 4. 9.
MAKHELOTH, mak´hel-oth, assemblies. Num. 33. 25.
MAKKEDAH, mak´ed-ah, place of shepherds (?). Josh. 10. 10.
cave of, five kings hide in. Josh. 10. 16.
MAKTESH, mak´tesh, a mortar. Zeph. 1. 11.
MALACHI, mal´ak-i, the messenger of Jehovah.
deplores and reproves Israel's ingratitude. Mal. 1; 2.
foretells the Messiah and His messenger. Mal. 3; 4.
MALCHAM, mal´kam, their king. 1 Chr. 8. 9.
MALCHIAH, malk-i´ah, Jehovah's king. 1 Chr. 6. 40.
MALCHIEL, malk´i-el, God's king. Gen. 46. 17.
MALCHIELITES, malk´i-el-ites, the descendants of Malchiel. Num. 26. 45.
MALCHIJAH, malk-i´jah, same as MALCHIAH. 1 Chr. 9. 12.
MALCHIRAM, malk-i´ram, king of height (?). 1 Chr. 3. 18.
MALCHI-SHUA, malk´i-shoo´ah, king of aid. 1 Chr. 8. 33.
MALCHUS, mal´kus, Greek form of Malluch. John 18. 10.
wounded by Peter. John 18. 10; Matt. 26. 51; Mark 14. 47.
healed by Jesus. Luke 22. 51.
MALELEEL, ma´le-le-el´, same as MAHALELEEL. Luke 3. 37.
MALLOTHI, mal-o´thi. 1 Chr. 25. 4.
MALLUCH, mal´ook, counsellor. 1 Chr. 6. 44.
MAMMON, mam´on, fulness.
worship of. Matt. 6. 24; Luke 16. 9.
MAMRE, mam´re, fatness.
Abram dwells there. Gen. 13. 18; 14; 18; 23. 17; 35. 27.
MANAEN, ma-na´en, Greek form of Menahem. Acts 13. 1.
MANAHATH, ma-na´hath, rest. Gen. 36. 23.
MANAHETHITES, ma-na´heth-ites, inhabitants of Manahath (?). 1 Chr. 2. 52.
MANASSEH, ma-nas´ay, one who causes to forget.
firstborn son of Joseph. Gen. 41. 51.
his blessing. Gen. 48.
his descendants numbered, &c. Num. 1. 34; 26. 29; Josh. 22. 1; 1 Chr. 5. 23; 7. 14.
their inheritance. Num. 32. 33; 34. 14; Josh. 13. 29; 17.
incline to David's cause. 1 Chr. 9. 3; 12. 19; 2 Chr. 15. 9; 30. 11.

MANASSEH—*cont.*
—— king of Judah, his reign. 2 Kin. 21; 2 Chr. 33.
MANASSES, ma-nas´es, Greek form of Manasseh. Matt. 1. 10.
MANASSITES, ma-nas´ites, members of the tribe of Manasseh. Deut. 4. 43.
MANEH, ma´ne, a weight. Ezek. 45. 12.
MANOAH, ma-no´ah, rest.
(father of Samson). Judg. 13; 16. 31.
MAOCH, ma´ok, oppressed (?). 1 Sam. 27. 2.
MAON, ma´on, habitation. Josh. 15. 55.
MAONITES, ma´on-ites. Judg. 10. 12.
MARA, ma´rah, sad. Ruth 1. 20.
MARAH, ma´rah, bitter.
bitter waters healed there. Ex. 15. 23.
MARALAH, mar´al-ah, trembling. Josh. 19. 11.
MARANATHA, ma´ran-ah´thah, our lord cometh. 1 Cor. 16. 22.
MARCUS, mar´kus. Col. 4. 10.
MARESHAH, ma-resh´ah, capital. Josh. 15. 44.
MARK, English form of Marcus.
EVANGELIST. Acts 12. 12.
goes with Paul and Barnabas. Acts 12. 25; 13. 5.
leaves them at Perga. Acts 13. 13.
contention about him. Acts 15. 37.
approved by Paul. 2 Tim. 4. 11.
MAROTH, mar´oth, bitterness. Mic. 1. 12.
MARS' HILL, English of Areopagus. Acts 17. 22.
MARSENA, mar´se-nah. Esth. 1. 14.
MARTHA, mar´thah, lady.
instructed by Christ. John 11. 5, 21.
reproved by Him. Luke 10. 38.
MARY, Greek form of Miriam. Matt. 1. 16.
the VIRGIN, mother of Jesus, visited by the angel Gabriel. Luke 1. 26.
believes, and magnifies the Lord. Luke 1. 38, 46; John 2. 5.
Christ born of. Matt. 1. 18; Luke 2.
witnesses the miracle at Cana. John 2. 1.
desires to speak with Christ. Matt. 12. 46; Mark 3. 31; Luke 8. 19.
commended to John by Christ at His crucifixion. Matt. 27. 56; John 19. 25.
MARY MAGDALENE. Luke 8. 2.
at the cross. Matt. 27. 56; Mark 15. 40; John 19. 25.
Christ appears first to. Matt. 28. 1; Mark 16. 1; Luke 24. 10; John 20. 1.
—— sister of Lazarus, commended. Luke 10. 42.
Christ's love for. John 11. 5, 33.
anoints Christ's feet, John 12. 3; (head), Matt. 26. 6; Mark 14. 3.
MARYS, THE THREE, at the cross. John 19. 25.
MASCHIL, mas´kil, understanding. Ps. 53, title.
MASH. Gen. 10. 23.
MASHAL, ma´shal, entreaty (?). 1 Chr. 6. 74.
MASREKAH, mas-rek´ah, vineyard. Gen. 36. 36.
MASSA, mas´ah, burden. Gen. 25. 14.
MASSAH, mas´ah, temptation.
the rebellion at. Ex. 17. 7; Deut. 9. 22; 33. 8.
MATHUSALA, ma-thoo´sa-lah, Greek form of Methuselah. Luke 3. 37.
MATRED, ma´tred, pushing forward. Gen. 36. 39.
MATRI, ma´tri, rainy. 1 Sam. 10. 21.
MATTAN, mat´an, a gift.
slain. 2 Kin. 11. 18; 2 Chr. 23. 17.
MATTANAH, mat´an-ah, same as preceding. Num. 21. 18.
MATTANIAH, mat´an-i´ah, gift of Jehovah. 2 Kin. 24. 17.
MATTATHA, mat´ath-ah, a Greek form of above. Luke 3. 31.
MATTATHAH, mat´ath-ah, gift of Jehovah. Ezra 10. 33.
MATTATHIAS, mat´ath-i´as, a Greek form of the preceding. Luke 3. 26.
MATTENAI, mat´en-ai, liberal. Ezra 10. 33.
MATTHAN, mat´than, gift. Matt. 1. 15.
MATTHAT, mat´that, another form of Matthan. Luke 3. 24.
MATTHEW, English way of spelling Mattathiah.

MATTHEW—*cont.*
(Levi), APOSTLE and EVANGELIST, called. Matt. 9. 9; Mark 2. 14; Luke 5. 27.
sent out. Matt. 10. 3; Mark 3. 18; Luke 6. 15;—Acts 1. 13.
MATTHIAS, math-i´as, another Greek form of Mattathias, apostle. Acts 1. 23; 26.
MATTITHIAH, mat-ith-i´ah, another form of Mattathias. 1 Chr. 9. 31.
MAZZAROTH, maz´ar-oth, the signs of the zodiac. Job 38. 32.
MEAH, me´ah, a hundred. Neh. 3. 1.
MEARAH, me-ar´ah, cave. Josh. 13. 4.
MEBUNNAI, me-boon´ai, built (?). 2 Sam. 23. 27.
MECHERATHITE, me-ker´ath-ite, inhabitant of Mecherah (?). 1 Chr. 11. 36.
MEDAD, me´dad.
prophesies. Num. 11. 26.
MEDAN, me´dan, contention. Gen. 25. 2.
MEDEBA, me´deb-ah, flowing water (?). Num. 21. 30.
MEDES, inhabitants of Media. 2 Kin. 17. 6.
capture Babylon (Is. 21. 2). Dan. 5. 28, 31.
MEDIA, me´di-ah, Greek form of Madai. Esth. 1. 3.
Israel taken captive to. 2 Kin. 17. 6; 18. 11; Esth. 2. 6.
Daniel's prophecy of. Dan. 8. 20.
MEGIDDO, me-gid´o, place of troops. Josh. 12. 21; 17. 11; Judg. 1. 27; 5. 19.
Ahaziah and Josiah slain there. 2 Kin. 9. 27; 23. 29; Zech. 12. 11.
MEGIDDON, me-gid´on, same as preceding. Zech. 12. 11.
MEHETABEEL, me-het´ab-e´el, lengthened form of the following. Neh. 6. 10.
MEHETABEL, me-het´ab-el, God makes happy. Gen. 36. 39.
MEHIDA, me-hi´dah. Ezra 2. 52.
MEHIR, me´hir, price. 1 Chr. 4. 11.
MEHOLATHITE, me-ho´lath-ite, native of Meholah. 1 Sam. 18. 19.
MEHUJAEL, me-hoo´ja-el, struck by God. Gen. 4. 18.
MEHUMAN, me-hoo´man. Esth. 1. 10.
MEHUNIM, me-hoon´im. Ezra 2. 50.
MEHUNIMS, me-hoon´ims, the people of Maon (?). 2 Chr. 26. 7.
ME-JARKON, me´jar´kon, waters of yellowness. Josh. 19. 46.
MEKONAH, me-ko´nah, a base. Neh. 11. 28.
MELATIAH, mel´at-i´ah, whom Jehovah freed. Neh. 3. 7.
MELCHI, melk´i, Greek form of Melchiah. Luke 3. 24.
MELCHIAH, melk-i´ah, Jehovah's king. Jer. 21. 1.
MELCHISEDEC, melk-is´ed-ek, Greek form of Melchizedek. Heb. 5. 6.
MELCHI-SHUA, melk´i-shoo´ah, same as MALCHI-SHUA. 1 Sam. 14. 49.
MELCHIZEDEK, melk-iz´ed-ek, king of righteousness.
king of Salem, blesses Abram. Gen. 14. 18.
his priesthood and Aaron's. Ps. 110. 4; Heb. 5. 6, 10; 6. 20; 7. 1.
MELEA, mel´e-ah, fulness (?). Luke 3. 31.
MELECH, mel´ech, king. 1 Chr. 8. 35.
MELICU, me-lee´koo, same as MALLUCH. Neh. 12. 14.
MELITA, mel´it-ah.
Paul shipwrecked near, and lands at, Acts 28. 1; received kindly by the people, Acts 28. 2; shakes off the viper at, Acts 28. 5; heals Publius' father and others at, Acts 28.
MELZAR, mel´zar, steward.
favours Daniel. Dan. 1. 11.
MEMPHIS, mem´fis, in Egypt. Hos. 9. 6.
MEMUCAN, me-moo´kan. Esth. 1. 14.
MENAHEM, me-na´hem, comforter.
king of Israel, his evil rule. 2 Kin. 15. 14, 18.

MENAN, me´nan. Luke 3. 31.
MENE, me´ne, numbered.
MENE, TEKEL, UPHARSIN. Dan. 5. 25–28.
MEONENIM, me-o´nen-im. Judg. 9. 37.
MEONOTHAI, me-o´no-thai', my habitations. 1 Chr. 4. 14.
MEPHAATH, me-fa´ath, beauty. Josh. 13. 18.
MEPHIBOSHETH, mef-ib´osh-eth, destroying shame.
son of Jonathan, his lameness. 2 Sam. 4. 4.
cherished by David. 2 Sam. 9. 1.
slandered by Ziba. 2 Sam. 16. 1; 19. 24.
spared by David. 2 Sam. 21. 7.
MERAB, me´rab, increase.
Saul's daughter. 1 Sam. 14. 49; 18. 17.
her five sons hanged by the Gibeonites. 2 Sam. 21. 8.
MERAIAH, me-rai´ah, contumacy. Neh. 12. 12.
MERAIOTH, me-rai´oth, rebellions. 1 Chr. 6. 6.
MERARI, me-rah´ri, bitter. Gen. 46. 11.
MERARITES, descendants of Levi. Ex. 6. 19; 1 Chr. 6. 1; 23. 21; 24. 26.
their duties and dwellings. Num. 4. 29; 7. 8; 10. 17; Josh. 21. 7; 1 Chr. 6. 63.
MERATHAIM, mer´ath-a´im, rebellions. Jer. 50. 21.
MERCURIUS, mer-ku´ri-us.
Paul so called. Acts 14. 12.
MERED, me´red, rebellion. 1 Chr. 4. 17.
MEREMOTH, mer-e´moth, elevations. Ezra 8. 33.
MERES, me´res, worthy (?). Esth. 1. 14.
MERIBAH, me-ree´bah, water of strife.
Israel rebels there. Ex. 17. 7; Num. 20. 13; 27. 14; Deut. 32. 51; 33. 8; Ps. 81. 7.
MERIB-BAAL, me´rib-ba´al, contender (?) against Baal. 1 Chr. 8. 34.
MERODACH, me´ro-dak. Jer. 50. 2.
MERODACH-BALADAN, me´ro-dak-bal´a-dan, Merodach gives a son.
(or Berodach) BALADAN, sends messengers to Hezekiah. 2 Kin. 20. 12; 2 Chr. 32. 31; Is. 39; —Jer. 50. 2.
MEROM, me´rom, a high place.
waters of. Josh. 11. 5.
MERONOTHITE, me-ro´noth-ite, an inhabitant of Meronoth. 1 Chr. 27. 30.
MEROZ, me´roz, refuge (?).
cursed. Judg. 5. 23.
MESECH, me´sech, same as MESHECH. Ps. 120. 5.
MESHA, me´shah, deliverance. 2 Kin. 3. 4.
MESHACH, me´shak. Dan. 1. 7. *See* SHADRACH.
MESHECH, me´shek, tall (?).
son of Japheth. Gen. 10. 2.
traders of. Ezek. 27. 13; 32. 26; 38. 2; 39. 1.
MESHELEMIAH, me-shel´em-i´ah, Jehovah repays. 1 Chr. 9. 21.
MESHEZABEEL, me-she´zab-eel, God delivers. Neh. 3. 4.
MESHILLEMITH, me-shil´em-ith, recompense. 1 Chr. 9. 12.
MESHILLEMOTH, me-shil´em-oth, retribution. 2 Chr. 28. 12.
MESHOBAB, me-sho´bab, brought back. 1 Chr. 4. 34.
MESHULLAM, me-shool´am, friend. 2 Kin. 22. 3.
MESHULLEMETH, me-shool-e´meth, feminine of preceding. 2 Kin. 21. 19.
MESOBAITE, me-so´ba-ite, inhabitant of Mesoba (?). 1 Chr. 11. 47.
MESOPOTAMIA, mes´o-pot-a´mi-ah, amidst the rivers. (Ur), country of the two rivers.
Abram leaves. Gen. 11. 31; 12. 1; 24. 4, 10. *See* Acts 2. 9; 7. 2.
king of, slain by Othniel. Judg. 3. 8.
MESSIAH, mes-i´ah, anointed (anointed CHRIST).
Prince, prophecy about. Dan. 9. 25.
MESSIAS, mes-i´as, Greek form of the above. John 1. 41; 4. 25. *See* Is. 9. 6.
METHEG-AMMAH, me´theg-am´ah, bridle of Ammah. 2 Sam. 8. 1.
METHUSAEL, me-thoo´sa-el, man of God. Gen. 4. 18.
METHUSELAH, me-thoo´se-lah, man of the dart (?). Gen. 5. 21.
his great age. Gen. 5. 27.

MEUNIM, me-oon´im, same as MEHUNIM. Neh. 7. 52.
MEZAHAB, me´za-hab, water of gold. Gen. 36. 39.
MIAMIN, mi´ya-min, on the right hand. Ezra. 10. 25.
MIBHAR, mib´har, choicest. 1 Chr. 11. 38.
MIBSAM, mib´sam, sweet odour. Gen. 25. 13.
MIBZAR, mib´zar, a fortress. Gen. 36. 42.
MICAH, mi´kah, who (is) like unto Jehovah? Judg. 17. 1.
makes and worships idols. Judg. 17; 18.
—— prophet (Jer. 26. 18); denounces Israel's sin. Mic. 1—3; 6; 7.
predicts the Messiah. Mic. 4; 5; 7.
MICAIAH, mi-kai´ah, fuller form of Micah.
forewarns Ahab. 1 Kin. 22; 2 Chr. 18.
MICHAEL, mi´ka-el, who (is) like unto God? Dan. 10. 13, 21; 12. 1.
Archangel. Jude 9; Rev. 12. 7.
MICHAH, mi´kah, same as MICAH. 1 Chr. 24. 24.
MICHAIAH, mi-kai´ah, same as MICAIAH. Neh. 12. 35.
MICHAL, mi´kal, brook. 1 Sam. 14. 49.
David's wife. 1 Sam. 18. 20.
given to another. 1 Sam. 25. 44.
restored to David. 2 Sam. 3. 13.
mocks his religious dancing, and is rebuked. 2 Sam. 6. 16, 20; 1 Chr. 15. 29.
MICHMAS, mik´mas, later form of Michmash. Ezra 2. 27.
MICHMASH, mik´mash, treasured. 1 Sam. 13. 2.
MICHMETHAH, mik´meth-ah, hiding place (?). Josh. 16. 6.
MICHRI, mik´ri, precious (?). 1 Chr. 9. 8.
MICHTAM, mik´tam, writing (?). Ps. 16, title.
MIDDIN, mid´in, extensions. Josh. 15. 61.
MIDIAN, mid´yan, strife. Gen. 25. 2.
sons of. Gen. 25. 4.
—— land of. Ex. 2. 15. *See* 1 Kin. 11. 18; Is. 60. 6; Hab. 3. 7.
MIDIANITES, mid´yan-ites, people of Midian. Gen. 37. 28.
their cities destroyed by Moses. Num. 31. 1.
subdued by Gideon. Judg. 6—8. *See* Ps. 83. 9; Is. 9. 4; 10. 26.
MIGDAL-EL, mig´dal-el, tower of God. Josh. 19. 38.
MIGDAL-GAD, mig´dal-gad, tower of Gad. Josh. 15. 37.
MIGDOL, mig´dol. Ex. 14. 2.
MIGRON, mig´ron, a precipice. Is. 10. 28.
MIJAMIN, mi´ja-min, same as MIAMIN. 1 Chr. 24. 9.
MIKLOTH, mik´loth, staves, lots. 1 Chr. 8. 32.
MIKNEIAH, mik-ni´ah, possession of Jehovah. 1 Chr. 15. 18.
MILALAI, mil´al-ai, eloquent (?). Neh. 12. 36.
MILCAH, mil´kah, counsel (?). Gen. 11. 29; 22. 20.
MILCOM, mil´kom, same as MOLOCH.
false god. 1 Kin. 11. 5, 33; 2 Kin. 23. 13.
MILETUM, mi-le´tum, improper form of MILETUS. 2 Tim. 4. 20.
MILETUS, mi-le´tus.
Paul takes leave of elders at. Acts 20. 15.
Trophimus left at. 2 Tim. 4. 20.
MILLO, mil´o, a mound.
house of. Judg. 9. 6; 1 Sam. 5. 9.
MINIAMIN, min´ya-min, full form of Miamin. 2 Chr. 31. 15.
MINNI, min´i, Armenia. Jer. 51. 27.
MINNITH, min´ith, allotment. Judg. 11. 33.
MIPHKAD, mif´kad, place of meeting. Neh. 3. 31.
MIRIAM, mir´yam, rebellion (?).
sister of Moses and Aaron. Ex. 15. 20; Num. 26. 59.
song of. Ex. 15. 20, 21.
murmurs against Moses. Num. 12. 1, 2.
is smitten with leprosy, and shut out of the camp. Num. 12. 10, 15.
her death. Num. 20. 1.
MIRMA, mir´mah, fraud. 1 Chr. 8. 10.
MISGAB, mis´gab, height. Jer. 48. 1.
MISHAEL, mish´a-el, who is what God is? Ex. 6. 22.
MISHAL, mi´shal, prayer. Josh. 21. 30.

MISHEAL, mi'she-al, same as MISHAL. Josh. 19. 26.
MISHAM, mi'sham, cleansing. 1 Chr. 8. 12.
MISHMA, mish'mah, report. Gen. 25. 14.
MISHMANNAH, mish-man'ah, fatness. 1 Chr. 12. 10.
MISHRAITES, mish'ra-ites. 1 Chr. 2. 53.
MISPERETH, mis-per'eth, number. Neh. 7. 7.
MISREPHOTH-MAIM, mis're-foth-ma'im, burning of waters. Josh. 11. 8.
MITHCAH, mith'kah, place of sweetness. Num. 33. 28.
MITHNITE, mith'nite. 1 Chr. 11. 43.
MITHREDATH, mith're-dath, given by Mithra. Ezra 1. 8.
MITYLENE, mit'il-e'ne. Acts 20. 14.
MIZAR, mi'zar, smallness. Ps. 42. 6.
MIZPAH, miz'pah (Gilead), a look out.
Jacob and Laban meet at. Gen. 31. 49.
Jephthah at. Judg. 10. 17; 11. 11; 20. 1.
Samuel at. 1 Sam. 7. 5.
—— (Moab). 1 Sam. 22. 3.
MIZPAR, miz'par, number. Ezra 2. 2.
MIZPEH, miz'peh, watch-tower. Josh. 11. 3.
MIZRAIM, miz-ra'im, fortresses. Gen. 10. 6.
MIZZAH, miz'ah. Gen. 36. 13.
MNASON, na'son, an old disciple. Acts 21. 16.
MOAB, mo'ab, progeny of a father. Gen. 19. 37.
his descendants, and territory. Deut. 2. 9, 18; 34. 5.
MOABITES, mo'ab-ites, people of Moab. Deut. 2. 9.
excluded from the congregation. Deut. 23. 3.
conquered by Ehud. Judg. 3. 12; by David. 2 Sam. 8. 2; by Jehoshaphat and Jehoram. 2 Kin. 1. 1; 3.
their overthrow. 2 Chr. 20. 23.
prophecies concerning. Ex. 15. 15; Num. 21. 29; 24. 17; Ps. 60. 8; 83. 6; Is. 11. 14; 15; 16; 25. 10; Jer. 9. 26; 25. 21; 48; Ezek. 25. 8; Amos 2. 1; Zeph. 2. 8.
MOABITESS, mo'ab-ite-ess, a lady of Moab. Ruth 4. 5.
MOADIAH, mo'ad-i'ah, festival of Jehovah. Neh. 12. 17.
MOLADAH, mo-la'dah, birth. Josh. 15. 26.
MOLECH, mo'lek, English form for Moloch. Lev. 18. 21; 20. 2.
worship of. 1 Kin. 11. 7; 2 Kin. 23. 10; Jer. 32. 35; Amos 5. 26; Acts 7. 43.
MOLOCH, mo'lok, king. Amos 5. 26.
MOLID, mo'lid, begetter. 1 Chr. 2. 29.
MORASTHITE, mo'rasth-ite, native of Moresheth. Jer. 26. 18.
MORDECAI, mor'dek-ai, worshipper of Merodach (?). Esth. 2. 5.
reveals conspiracy against king Ahasuerus. Esth. 2. 21.
is hated by Haman. Esth. 3. 5.
honoured by the king. Esth. 6.
advanced. Esth. 8—10 (Ezra 2. 2; Neh. 7. 7).
MOREH, mo'reh, archer. Gen. 12. 6.
MORESHETH-GATH, mo-resh'eth-gath', the possession of Gath. Mic. 1. 14.
MORIAH, mor-i'ah, provided by Jehovah. Gen. 22. 2.
mount. Gen. 22.
David's sacrifice there. 2 Sam. 24. 18; 1 Chr. 21. 18; 22. 1.
temple built on. 2 Chr. 3. 1.
MOSERA, mo-se'rah, bond. Deut. 10. 6.
MOSEROTH, mo-se'roth, bonds. Num. 33. 30.
MOSES, mo'zes, saved from the water.
born, and hidden. Ex. 2 (Acts 7. 20; Heb. 11. 23).
escapes to Midian. Ex. 2. 15.
revelation from God. Ex. 3; confirmed by signs. Ex. 4.
returns to Egypt. Ex. 4. 20.
intercedes with Pharaoh for Israel. Ex. 5—12.
leads Israel forth. Ex. 14.
meets God in mount Sinai. Ex. 19. 3 (24. 18).
brings the law to the people. Ex. 19. 25; 20—23; 34. 10; 35. 1; Lev. 1; Num. 5; 6; 15; 27—30; 36; Deut. 12—26.

MOSES—*cont.*
instructed to build the tabernacle. Ex. 25—31; 35. 40; Num. 4; 8—10; 18; 19.
his grief at Israel's idolatry. Ex. 32. 19.
his intercession. Ex. 32. 11 (33. 12).
again meets God in the mount. Ex. 34. 2.
skin of his face shines. Ex. 34. 29 (2 Cor. 3. 7, 13).
sets apart Aaron. Lev. 8; 9.
numbers the people. Num. 1; 26.
sends out the spies to Canaan. Num. 13.
intercedes for the murmuring people. Num. 14. 13.
Korah's sedition against. Num. 16.
for his unbelief suffered not to enter Canaan. Num. 20. 12; 27. 12; Deut. 1. 35; 3. 23.
his government of Israel in the wilderness. Num. 20; 21.
makes the brazen serpent. Num. 21. 9 (John 3. 14).
recounts Israel's history, and exhorts to obedience. Deut. 1; 3—12; 27—31.
his charge to Joshua. Deut. 3. 28; 31. 7, 23.
his death. Deut. 34. 5; his body, Jude 9.
seen at Christ's transfiguration. Matt. 17. 3; Mark 9. 4; Luke 9. 30.
his meekness, Num. 12. 3; dignity, Deut. 34. 10; faithfulness, Num. 12. 7; Heb. 3. 2.
MOZA, mo'zah, fountain. 1 Chr. 2. 46.
MOZAH, mo'zah, same as MOZA. Josh. 18. 26.
MUPPIM, moop'im, probably written for Shupham. Gen. 46. 21.
MUSHI, moo'shi, withdrawn. Ex. 6. 19.
MUTH-LABBEN, mooth'la-ben', death to the son (?). Ps. 9, title.
MYRA, mi'rah, balsam. Acts 27. 5.
MYSIA, mish'yah. Acts 16. 7.

NAAM, na'am, pleasantness. 1 Chr. 4. 15.
NAAMAH, na'am-ah, pleasant. Gen. 4. 22.
NAAMAN, na'am-an, pleasantness. 2 Kin. 5. 1.
the Syrian, his anger. 2 Kin. 5. 11.
his leprosy healed. 2 Kin. 5. 14.
his request. 2 Kin. 5. 17. *See* Luke 4. 27.
NAAMATHITE, na-am'ath-ite. Job. 2. 11.
NAAMITES, na'am-ites, descendants of Naaman. Num. 26. 40.
NAARAH, na'ar-ah, a girl. 1 Chr. 4. 5.
NAARAI, na'ar-ai, youthful. 1 Chr. 11. 37.
NAARAN, na'ar-an, same as NAARAH. 1 Chr. 7. 28.
NAARATH, na'ar-ath, to Naarah. Josh. 16. 7.
NAASHON, na'ash-on, enchanter. Ex. 6. 23.
NAASSON, na-as'on, Greek form of NAASHON. Matt. 1. 4.
NABAL, na'bal, foolish. 1 Sam. 25. 3.
conduct to David. 1 Sam. 25. 10.
Abigail, intercedes for. 1 Sam. 25. 18.
his death. 1 Sam. 25. 38.
NABOTH, na'both, fruits (?).
slain by Jezebel. 1 Kin. 21.
his murder avenged. 2 Kin. 9. 21.
NACHON, na'kon, prepared. 2 Sam. 6. 6.
NACHOR, na'kor, snorting. Josh. 24. 2.
NADAB, na'dab, liberal. Ex. 6. 23.
son of Aaron, offers strange fire. Lev. 10. 1, 2.
—— king of Israel, slain by Baasha. 1 Kin. 14. 20; 15. 25, 28.
NAGGE, nag'e, Greek form of Nogah. Luke 3. 25.
NAHALAL, na'hal-al, a pasture. Josh. 21. 35.
NAHALIEL, na-hal'i-el, valley of God. Num. 21. 19.
NAHALLAL, na'hal-al, same as NAHALAL. Josh. 19. 15.
NAHALOL, na'hal-ol, same as preceding. Judg. 1. 30.
NAHAM, na'ham, consolation. 1 Chr. 4. 19.
NAHAMANI, na'ham-a'ni, comforter. Neh. 7. 7.
NAHARAI, na'ha-rai, one who snores. 1 Chr. 11. 39.
NAHARI, na'har-i, same as preceding. 2 Sam. 23. 37.
NAHASH, na'hash, serpent.
the Ammonite, invades Jabesh-Gilead. 1 Sam. 11.
NAHATH, na'hath, descent. Gen. 36. 13.

NAHBI, nah´bi, hidden. Num. 13. 14.
NAHOR, na´hor, another way of spelling Nachor. Gen. 11. 22.
Abram's brother. Gen. 11. 26; 22. 20; 24. 10.
NAHSHON, nah´shon, same as NAASHON. Num. 1. 7.
NAHUM, na´hoom, comforter.
vision of. Nah. 1. 1–3.
NAIN, na´in, pasture.
miracle at. Luke 7. 11.
NAIOTH, nai´oth, habitations. 1 Sam. 19. 18.
school of prophets. 1 Sam. 19. 23; 20. 1.
NAOMI, na´om-i, pleasant. Ruth 1. 2.
NAPHISH, na´fish, cheerful. Gen. 25. 15.
NAPHTALI, naf´tal-i, my wrestling.
son of Jacob. Gen. 30. 8; 35. 25; 46. 24; 49. 21; Deut. 33. 23.
—— tribe of, numbered. Num. 1. 42; 10. 27; 13. 14; 26. 48; Judg. 1. 33.
subdue the Canaanites. Judg. 4. 10; 5. 18; 6. 35; 7. 23.
carried captive. 2 Kin. 15. 29. *See* Is. 9. 1; Matt. 4. 13.
NAPHTUHIM, naf´too-him. Gen. 10. 13.
NARCISSUS, nar-sis´us, benumbing.
household of. Rom. 16. 11.
NATHAN, na´than, gift.
the prophet. 2 Sam. 7.
shews David his sin. 2 Sam. 12. 1.
anoints Solomon king. 1 Kin. 1. 34; 1 Chr. 29. 29; 2 Chr. 9. 29.
—— son of David. 2 Sam. 5. 14; Zech. 12. 12; Luke 3. 31.
NATHANAEL, na-than´a-el, gift of God.
'Israelite indeed.' John 1. 45; 21. 2.
NATHAN-MELECH, na´than-me´lek, gift of the king. 2 Kin. 23. 11.
NAUM, na´oom, same as NAHUM. Luke 3. 25.
NAZARENE, naz´ar-een′, a native of Nazareth. Acts 24. 5.
NAZARETH, naz´ar-eth, branch. Luke 1. 26.
Jesus of. Matt. 2. 23; 21. 11; Luke 1. 26; 2. 39, 51; 4. 16; John 1. 45; 18. 5; Acts 2. 22; 3. 6.
NAZARITE, naz´ar-ite, one separated. Num. 6. 2.
NAZARITES, law of the. Num. 6.
NEAH, ne´ah, of a slope. Josh. 19. 13.
NEAPOLIS, ne-a´po-lis, new city. Acts 16. 11.
NEARIAH, ne´ar-i´ah, servant of Jehovah. 1 Chr. 3. 22.
NEBAI, ne´bai, fruitful. Neh. 10. 19.
NEBAIOTH, ne-bai´oth, high places. 1 Chr. 1. 29.
NEBAJOTH, ne-ba´joth, same as NEBAIOTH. Gen. 25. 13.
NEBALLAT, ne-bal´at. Neh. 11. 34.
NEBAT, ne´bat, aspect. 1 Kin. 11. 26.
NEBO, ne´bo, a lofty place. Deut. 32. 49.
NEBUCHADNEZZAR, neb´u-kad-nez´ar, another way of spelling the following. 2 Kin. 24. 1.
king of Babylon. Jer. 20; 21; 25; 27; 28; 32; 34; Ezek. 26. 7; 29. 19.
captures Jerusalem. 2 Kin. 24; 25; 2 Chr. 36; Jer. 37—39; 52; Dan. 1. 1.
his dreams. Dan. 2; 4.
sets up the golden image. Dan. 3.
his madness. Dan. 4. 33.
his restoration and confession. Dan. 4. 34.
NEBUCHADREZZAR, neb´u-kad-rez´ar, Nebo protect the landmark. Jer. 21. 2.
NEBUSHASBAN, neb´u-shas´ban, Nebo will save me. Jer. 39. 13.
NEBUZAR-ADAN, neb´u-zar´a-dan′, Nebo gives posterity. 2 Kin. 25. 8.
his care of Jeremiah. Jer. 39. 11; 40. 1.
NECHO, ne´ko, conqueror (?). Jer. 46. 2.
NECHOH, same as NECHO. 2 Kin. 23. 29.
NEDABIAH, ned´ab-i´ah, Jehovah is bountiful (?). 1 Chr. 3. 18.
NEGINAH, neg-een´ah, a stringed instrument. Ps. 61, title.
NEGINOTH, neg-een´oth, stringed instruments. Ps. 4; 54; 55; 76; 77, title.
NEGO, ne´go, same as NEBO. Dan. 1. 7.
NEHELAMITE, ne-he-lam´ite. Jer. 29. 24.
NEHEMIAH, ne´hem-i´ah, Jehovah comforts.
his grief for Jerusalem. Neh. 1.
his prayer for. Neh. 1. 5.
his visit to. Neh. 2. 5, 9, 17.
his conduct at. Neh. 4—6; 8—10; 13.
NEHILOTH, ne-hil´oth, flutes. Ps. 5, title.
NEHUM, ne´hoom, consolation. Neh. 7. 7.
NEHUSHTA, ne-hoosh´tah, bronze. 2 Kin. 24. 8.
NEHUSHTAN, ne-hoosh´tan, brazen.
the brazen serpent of Moses, idolatrously used by Israelites, so called by Hezekiah, and destroyed by him. 2 Kin. 18. 4.
NEIEL, ni´el, moved by God. Josh. 19. 27.
NEKEB, ne´keb, cavern. Josh. 19. 33.
NEKODA, ne-ko´dah, a herdman. Ezra 2. 48.
NEMUEL, ne-moo´el, same as JEMUEL (?). Num 26. 9.
NEMUELITES, ne-moo´el-ites, descendants of Nemuel. Num. 26. 12.
NEPHEG, ne´feg, sprout. Ex. 6. 21.
NEPHISH, ne´fish, same as NAPHISH. 1 Chr. 5. 19.
NEPHISHESIM, ne-fish´es-im, expansions. Neh. 7. 52.
NEPHTHALIM, nef´tal-im, Greek form of Naphtali. Matt. 4. 13.
NEPHTOAH, nef-to´ah, opened. Josh. 15. 9.
NEPHUSIM, nefoos´im, a better form for Nephishesim. Ezra 2. 50.
NER, light. 1 Sam. 14. 50.
NEREUS, ne´roos, liquid (?). Rom. 16. 15.
NERGAL, ner´gal, lion. 2 Kin. 17. 30.
NERGAL-SHAREZER, ner´gal-shar-e´zer, Nergal protect the king. Jer. 39. 3.
NERI, ne´ri, Greek form of Neriah. Luke 3. 27.
NERIAH, ner-i´ah, lamp of Jehovah. Jer. 32. 12.
NETHANEEL, neth-an´e-el, same as NATHANAEL. Num. 1. 8.
NETHANIAH, neth´an-i´ah, whom Jehovah gave. 2 Kin. 25. 23.
NETHINIMS, neth´in-ims, the appointed. 1 Chr. 9. 2; Ezra 2. 43; 7. 7, 24; 8. 17; Neh. 10. 28.
NETOPHAH, ne-to´phah, dropping. Ezra 2. 22.
NETOPHATHI, net-of´ath-i, an inhabitant of Netophah. Neh. 12. 28.
NETOPHATHITE, net-of´ath-ite, same as the preceding. 2 Sam. 23. 28.
NEZIAH, ne-zi´ah, illustrious. Ezra 2. 54.
NEZIB, ne´zib, garrison. Josh. 15. 43.
NIBHAZ, nib´haz. 2 Kin. 17. 31.
NIBSHAN, nib´shan, level (?). Josh. 15. 62.
NICANOR, ni-ka´nor, one of the seven deacons. Acts 6. 5.
NICODEMUS, nik´o-de´mus, Pharisee and ruler.
goes to Jesus by night. John 3. 1.
takes His part. John 7. 50.
assists at Christ's burial. John 19. 39.
NICOLAITANES, nik´o-la´it-ans, named after Nicolas. Rev. 2. 6.
NICOLAS, nik´o-las. Acts 6. 5.
NICOPOLIS, nik-o´pol-is, city of victory. Tit. 3. 12.
NIGER, ni´ger, black. Acts 13. 1.
NIMRAH, nim´rah, limpid (water). Num. 32. 3.
NIMRIM, nim´rim, clear waters. Is. 15. 6.
NIMROD, nim´rod, an inhabitant of Marad (?). Gen. 10. 8.
mighty hunter. Gen. 10. 9.
NIMSHI, nim´shi, discloser (?). 1 Kin. 19. 16.
NINEVEH, nin´ev-ay, dwelling (?). Gen. 10. 11.
Jonah's mission to. Jonah 1. 1; 3. 2.
denounced by Jonah. Jonah 3. 4.
repenting, is spared by God. Jonah 3. 5–10 (Matt. 12. 41; Luke 11. 32).
the burden of. Nah. 1. 1; 2; 3.
NINEVITES, nin´ev-ites, inhabitants of Nineveh. Luke 11. 30.
NISAN, ni´san, month. Neh. 2. 1; Esth. 3. 7.
NISROCH, nis´rok, eagle (?). 2 Kin. 19. 37; Is. 37. 38.
NO, abode (?). Nah. 3. 8.
multitude of, threatened. Jer. 46. 25; Ezek. 30. 14.
NO AMON, no a´mon, abode of Amon. Jer. 46. 25.

NOADIAH, no´ad-i´ah, whom Jehovah meets. Neh. 6. 14.
NOAH, no´ah, (1) rest. Gen. 5. 29. (2) wandering. Num. 26. 33.
son of Lamech. Gen. 5. 29.
finds grace with God. Gen. 6. 8.
ordered to build the ark. Gen. 6. 14.
with his family and living creatures enters into the ark. Gen. 7.
flood assuaging, goes forth. Gen. 8. 18.
God blesses and makes a covenant with. Gen. 9. 1, 8.
is drunken, and mocked of Ham. Gen. 9. 22.
his death. Gen. 9. 29.
NOB, nobe, high place.
city of, David comes to, and eats hallowed bread at. 1 Sam. 21. 1.
smitten by Saul. 1 Sam. 22. 19.
NOBAH, no´bah, a barking. Num. 32. 42.
NOD, node, flight, wandering. Gen. 4. 16.
NODAB, no´dab, nobility. 1 Chr. 5. 19.
NOE, no´e, Greek form of Noah. Matt. 24. 37.
NOGAH, no´gah, brightness. 1 Chr. 3. 7.
NOHAH, no´hah, rest. 1 Chr. 8. 2.
NON, none, same as NUN. 1 Chr. 7. 27.
NOPH, nofe, same as MEMPHIS.
city, warned. Is. 19. 13; Jer. 2. 16; 46. 14; Ezek. 30. 13.
NOPHAH, no´fah, windy. Num. 21. 30.
NUN, noon, fish. Ex. 33. 11.
NYMPHAS, nim´fas, shortened form of Nymphodorus. Col. 4. 15.

OBADIAH, ob´ad-i´ah, worshipper of Jehovah. Obad. 1.
prophet, his prediction. Obad. 17.
—— Levite, porter in the temple. Neh. 12. 25.
—— sent by Ahab to find water. 1 Kin. 18. 3.
meets Elijah. 1 Kin. 18. 7.
how he hid a hundred prophets, 1 Kin. 18. 4, 13.
OBAL, o´bal, hill (?). Gen. 10. 28.
OBED, o´bed, worshipping (God). Ruth 4. 17.
OBED-EDOM, o´bed-e´dom, serving Edom.
prospered while taking charge of the ark. 2 Sam. 6. 10; 1 Chr. 13. 14; 15. 18, 24; 16. 5.
his sons. 1 Chr. 26. 4, 5.
OBIL, o´bil, camel keeper. 1 Chr. 27. 30.
OBOTH, o´both, bottles (of skin). Num. 21. 10.
OCRAN, ok´ran, troublesome. Num. 1. 13.
ODED, o´ded, setting up (?).
prophet. 2 Chr. 15. 1; 28. 9.
OG, circle (?).
king of Bashan. Num. 21. 33; Deut. 3. 1; Ps. 135. 11; 136. 20.
OHAD, o´had, might. Gen. 46. 10.
OHEL, o´hel, tent. 1 Chr. 3. 20.
OLIVET, ol´iv-et, place of olives.
(Olives) mount. 2 Sam. 15. 30; Matt. 21. 1; 24. 3; Mark 11. 1; 13. 3; Luke 21. 37; John 8. 1; Acts 1. 12.
OLYMPAS, o-limp´as, bright (?). Rom. 16. 15.
OMAR, o´mar, talkative. Gen. 36. 11.
OMEGA, o´meg-ah, great O. Rev. 1. 8, 11; 21. 6; 22. 13.
OMRI, om´ri, like a sheaf (?).
king of Israel. 1 Kin. 16. 16, &c.; Mic. 6. 16.
ON, the sun. Gen. 41. 45.
ONAM, o´nam, wealthy. Gen. 36. 23.
ONAN, o´nan, strong. Gen. 38. 4.
ONESIMUS, o-ne´sim-us, profitable. Col. 4. 9; Philem. 10.
ONESIPHORUS, o´nes-if´or-us, bringing profit. 2 Tim. 1. 16.
ONO, o´no, strong. 1 Chr. 8. 12.
OPHEL, o´fel, a hill. 2 Chr. 27. 3.
OPHIR, o´feer.
gold of. Gen. 10. 29; 1 Kin. 9. 28; 10. 11; 22. 48; 1 Chr. 29. 4; 2 Chr. 8. 18; Job 22. 24; Ps. 45. 9; Is. 13. 12.
OPHNI, of´ni, man of the hill. Josh. 18. 24.
OPHRAH, of´rah, fawn. 1 Chr. 4. 14.
OREB, o´reb, raven. Judg. 7. 25.
OREN, o´ren, pine tree. 1 Chr. 2. 25.
ORION, o-ri´on. Job 9. 9.
ORNAN, or´nan (Araunah). 2 Sam. 24. 16; 1 Chr. 21. 15.
ORPAH, orp´ah, hind (?). Ruth. 1. 4.
OSEE, o´zee, same as HOSEA. Rom. 9. 25.
OSHEA, o-she´ah, same as JOSHUA. Num. 13. 8.
OTHNI, oth´ni, powerful (?). 1 Chr. 26. 7.
OTHNIEL, oth´ni-el, powerful man of God. Josh. 15. 17; Judg. 1. 13; 3. 9.
OZEM, o´zem, strength. 1 Chr. 2. 15.
OZIAS, o-zi´as, Greek form of Uzziah. Matt. 1. 8.
OZNI, oz´ni, hearing. Num. 26. 16.
OZNITES, oz´nites, descendants of Ozni. Num. 26. 16.

PAARAI, pah´a-rai, devoted to Peor (?). 2 Sam. 23. 35.
PADAN-ARAM, pa´dan-a´ram, the plain of Syria. Gen. 25. 20; 28. 2.
PADON, pa´don, redemption. Ezra 2. 44.
PAGIEL, pag´i-el, intervention of God. Num. 1. 13.
PAHATH-MOAB, pa´hath-mo´ab, governor of Moab. Ezra 2. 6.
PAI, pa´i, bleating. 1 Chr. 1. 50.
PALAL, pa´lal, judge. Neh. 3. 25.
PALESTINA, pal´es-ti´nah, land of strangers (?).
predictions about. Ex. 15. 14; Is. 14. 29, 31.
PALLU, pal´oo, distinguished. Ex. 6. 14.
PALLUITES, pal´oo-ites, descendants of Pallu. Num. 26. 5.
PALTI, pal´ti, deliverance of Jehovah. Num. 13. 9.
PALTIEL, pal´ti-el, deliverance of God. Num. 34. 26.
PALTITE, palt´ite, a descendant of Palti. 2 Sam. 23. 26.
PAMPHYLIA, pam-fil´yah.
Paul preaches there. Acts 13. 13; 14. 24; 27. 5.
PAPHOS, pa´fos.
Paul at. Acts 13. 6.
Elymas the sorcerer at. Acts 13. 8.
PARAH, pa´rah, heifer. Josh. 18. 23.
PARAN, pa´ran, cavernous.
mount. Gen. 21. 21; Num. 10. 12; 12. 16; 13. 26; Deut. 33. 2; Hab. 3. 3.
PARBAR, par´bar, open apartment. 1 Chr. 26. 18.
PARMASHTA, par-mash´tah, superior (?). Esth. 9. 9.
PARMENAS, par´men-as, standing firm. Acts 6. 5.
PARNACH, par´nak. Num. 34. 25.
PAROSH, pa´rosh, flea. Ezra 2. 3.
PARSHANDATHA, par´shan-da´thah, given to Persia (?). Esth. 9. 7.
PARTHIANS, parth´yans. Acts 2. 9.
PARUAH, par-oo´ah, flourishing. 1 Kin. 4. 17.
PARVAIM, parv-a´im, oriental regions (?). 2 Chr. 3. 6.
PASACH, pa´sak, divider. 1 Chr. 7. 33.
PAS-DAMMIM, pas-dam´im, shortened from Ephes-dammim. 1 Chr. 11. 13.
PASEAH, pa-se´ah, lame. 1 Chr. 4. 12.
PASHUR, pash´oor, prosperity round about.
his cruelty to Jeremiah. Jer. 20.
PATARA, pat´ar-ah. Acts 21. 1.
PATHROS, path´ros.
in Egypt. Is. 11. 11; Jer. 44. 1, 15; Ezek. 29. 14; 30. 14.
PATHRUSIM, path-roos´im, people of Pathros. Gen. 10. 14.
PATMOS, pat´mos.
place of St. John's exile. Rev. 1. 9.
PATROBAS, pat´ro-bas. Rom. 16. 14.
PAU, pa´oo, older form of Pai. Gen. 36. 39.
PAUL, or PAULUS, little. Acts 13. 9.
as a persecutor. Acts 7. 58; 8. 1; 9. 1; 22. 4; 26. 9; 1 Cor. 15. 9; Gal. 1. 13; Phil. 3. 6; 1 Tim. 1. 13.
as a convert to the Gospel. Acts 9. 3; 22. 6; 26. 12.
as a preacher. Acts 9. 19, 29; 13. 1, 4, 14; 17. 18 (2 Cor. 11. 32; Gal. 1. 17).
stoned at Lystra. Acts 14. 8, 19.
contends with Barnabas. Acts 15. 36.
is persecuted at Philippi. Acts 16.
the Holy Ghost given by his hands to John's disciples at Ephesus. Acts 19. 6.

PAUL—*cont.*
restores Eutychus. Acts 20. 10.
his charge to the elders of Ephesus, at Miletus. Acts 20. 17.
his return to Jerusalem, and persecution there. Acts 21.
his defence before the people and the council. Acts 22; 23.
before Felix, Acts 24; Festus, Acts 25; and Agrippa, Acts 26.
appeals to Cæsar at Rome. Acts 25.
his voyage and shipwreck. Acts 27.
miracles by, at Melita. Acts 28. 3, 8.
at Rome, reasons with the Jews. Acts 28. 17.
his love to the churches. Rom. 1. 8; 15; 1 Cor. 1. 4; 4. 14; 2 Cor. 1; 2; 6; 7; Phil. 1; Col. 1; 1 & 2 Thess.
his sufferings. 1 Cor. 4. 9; 2 Cor. 11. 23; 12. 7; Phil. 1. 12; 2 Tim. 3. 11.
divine revelations to. 2 Cor. 12. 1.
defends his apostleship. 1 Cor. 9; 2 Cor. 11; 12; 2 Tim. 3. 10.
commends Timothy, &c. 1 Cor. 16. 10; Phil. 2. 19; 1 Thess. 3. 2.
commends Titus. 2 Cor. 7. 13; 8. 23.
blames Peter. Gal. 2. 14.
pleads for Onesimus. Philem.
his epistles mentioned by St. Peter. 2 Pet. 3. 15.

PEDAHEL, pe-dah´el, God redeemed. Num. 34. 28.
PEDAHZUR, pe-dah´zoor, the Rock redeemed. Num. 1. 10.
PEDAIAH, pe-dah-i´ah, whom Jehovah redeemed. 1 Chr. 27. 20.
PEKAH, pe´kah, open-eyed.
king of Israel. 2 Kin. 15. 25.
his victory over Judah. 2 Chr. 28. 6.
denounced in prophecy. Is. 7. 1.
PEKAHIAH, pe´kah-i´ah, whose eyes Jehovah opened.
king of Israel. 2 Kin. 15. 22.
PEKOD, pe´kod, visitation. Jer. 50. 21.
PELAIAH, pe-la´yah, whom Jehovah made distinguished. 1 Chr. 3. 24.
PELALIAH, pe-lal-i´ah, whom Jehovah judged. Neh. 11. 12.
PELATIAH, pe´lat-i´ah, whom Jehovah delivered. Ezek. 11. 1.
PELEG, pe´leg, division. Gen. 10. 25.
PELET, pe´let, liberation. 1 Chr. 2. 47.
PELETH, pe´leth, swiftness. Num. 16. 1.
PELETHITES, pel´eth-ites, runners. 2 Sam. 8. 18.
PELONITE, pel´on-ite. 1 Chr. 11. 27.
PENIEL, pe-nee´el, the face of God.
scene of Jacob's wrestling with an angel. Gen. 32. 30.
Gideon's vengeance upon. Judg. 8. 17.
PENINNAH, pe-nin´ah, coral. 1 Sam. 1. 2. *See* HANNAH.
PENTECOST, pen´te-kost, fiftieth.
(feast of weeks), how observed. Lev. 23. 15; Deut. 16. 9.
Holy Spirit given at. Acts 2.
PENUEL, pe-noo´el, old form of Peniel. Gen. 32. 31.
PEOR, pe´or, point.
(Baal), Num. 23. 28; 25. 3, 18; Josh. 22. 17.
PERAZIM, pe-raz´im, breaches. Is. 28. 21.
PERES, pe´res, divided. Dan. 5. 28.
PERESH, pe´resh, distinction. 1 Chr. 7. 16.
PEREZ, pe´rez, breach. 1 Chr. 27. 3.
PEREZ-UZZA, pe´rez-uz´ah, same as following. 1 Chr. 13. 11.
PEREZ-UZZAH, pe´rez-uz´ah, breach of Uzzah. 2 Sam. 6. 8.
PERGA, per´gah.
visited by Paul. Acts 13. 13; 14. 25.
PERGAMOS, per´ga-mos, citadel (?).
epistle to. Rev. 1. 11; 2. 12.
PERIDA, pe-ree´dah, a recluse. Neh. 7. 57.
PERIZZITES, per´iz-ites, belonging to a village. Gen. 13. 7; 15. 20; 34. 30; Judg. 1. 4; 2 Chr. 8. 7.
PERSIA, per´shah.

PERSIA—*cont.*
kingdom of. 2 Chr. 36. 20; Esth. 1. 3; Ezek. 27. 10; 38. 5; Dan. 6.
prophecies concerning. Is. 21. 2; Dan. 5. 28; 8. 20; 10. 13; 11. 2.
PERSIAN, per´shan, belonging to Persia. Dan. 6. 28.
PERSIS, per´sis, a Persian woman.
the beloved. Rom. 16. 12.
PERUDA, pe-roo´dah, same as PERIDA. Ezra 2. 55.
PETER, pe´ter, a stone. Matt. 16. 18.
APOSTLE, called. Matt. 4. 18; Mark 1. 16; Luke 5; John 1. 35.
sent forth. Matt. 10. 2; Mark 3. 16; Luke 6. 14.
tries to walk to Jesus on the sea. Matt. 14. 29.
confesses Jesus to be the Christ. Matt. 16. 16; Mark 8. 29; Luke 9. 20.
witnesses the transfiguration. Matt. 17; Mark 9; Luke 9. 28; 2 Pet. 1. 16.
his self-confidence reproved. Luke 22. 31; John 13. 36.
thrice denies Christ. Matt. 26. 69; Mark 14. 66; Luke 22. 57; John 18. 17.
his repentance. Matt. 26. 75; Mark 14. 72; Luke 22. 62.
the assembled disciples addressed by. Acts 1. 15.
the Jews preached to by. Acts 2. 14; 3. 12.
brought before the council. Acts 4.
condemns Ananias and Sapphira. Acts 5.
denounces Simon the sorcerer. Acts 8. 18.
restores Æneas and Tabitha. Acts 9. 32, 40.
sent for by Cornelius. Acts 10.
instructed by a vision not to despise the Gentiles. Acts 10. 9.
imprisoned, and liberated by an angel. Acts 12.
his decision about circumcision. Acts 15. 7.
rebuked by Paul. Gal. 2. 14.
bears witness to Paul's teaching. 2 Pet. 3. 15.
comforts the church, and exhorts to holy living by his epistles. 1 & 2 Pet.
his martyrdom foretold by Christ. John 21. 18; 2 Pet. 1. 14.
PETHAHIAH, pe´thah-i´ah, whom Jehovah looses. 1 Chr. 24. 16.
PETHOR, pe´thor. Num. 22. 5.
PETHUEL, pe-thoo´el, God's opening (?). Joel. 1. 1.
PEULTHAI, pe-ool´thai, deed of Jehovah. 1 Chr. 26. 5.
PHALEC, fa´lek, Greek form of Peleg. Luke 3. 35.
PHALLU, fal´oo, an English way of spelling Pallu. Gen. 46. 9.
PHALTI, fal´ti, deliverance of Jehovah. 1 Sam. 25. 44.
PHALTIEL, fal´ti-el, deliverance of God. 2 Sam. 3. 15.
PHANUEL, fan-oo´el, Greek form of Penuel. Luke 2. 36.
PHARAOH, fa´roh, the sun (title of rulers of Egypt). Gen. 12. 14; Ezek. 29. 3.
Abram's wife taken into house of. Gen. 12. 15.
Pharaoh plagued because of her. Gen. 12. 17.
—— (patron of Joseph), his dreams, &c. Gen. 40.
his hospitality to Joseph's father and brethren. Gen. 47.
—— (oppressor of the Israelites). Ex. 1. 8.
daughter preserves Moses. Ex. 2. 5, 10; Acts 7. 21.
miracles performed before, and plagues sent. Ex. 7—10.
grants Moses' request. Ex. 12. 31.
repenting, pursues Israel, and perishes in the Red sea. Ex. 14 (Neh. 9. 10; Ps. 135. 9; 136. 15; Rom. 9. 17).
—— (father-in-law of Solomon). 1 Kin. 3. 1.
shelters Hadad, Solomon's adversary. 1 Kin. 11. 19.
PHARAOH-HOPHRA, fa´roh-hof´rah, Pharaoh the priest of the sun.
his fate predicted. Jer. 44. 30. *See* Ezek. 30—32.
compared to a dragon. Ezek. 29. 3.
PHARAOH-NECHO, fa´roh-ne´ko, Pharaoh the lame.
slays Josiah. 2 Kin. 23. 29; 2 Chr. 35. 20.
his wars with Israel. 2 Kin. 23. 33; 2 Chr. 36. 3.
PHARES, fa´res, Greek form of Pharez. Luke 3. 33.

PHAREZ, fa´rez, breach. Gen. 38. 29; Ruth 4. 18.
PHARISEES, far´is-ees, the separated.
celebrated ones: Nicodemus, John 3. 1; Simon, Luke 7; Gamaliel, Acts 5. 34; Saul of Tarsus, Acts 23. 6; 26. 5; Phil. 3. 5.
Christ entertained by. Luke 7. 36; 11. 37; 14. 1.
Christ utters woes against. Matt. 23. 13; Luke 11. 42.
Christ questioned by, about divorce, Matt. 19. 3; eating, Matt. 9. 11; 15. 1; Mark 2. 16; Luke 5. 30; forgiveness of sin, Luke 5. 21; sabbath, Matt. 12. 2, 10; fasting, Mark 2. 18; tribute, Matt. 22. 17.
deride Christ. Luke 16. 14.
murmur against Christ. Matt. 9. 34; Luke 15. 2.
denounced by Christ. Matt. 5. 20; 16. 6; 21. 43; 23. 2; Luke 11. 39.
people cautioned against. Mark 8. 15; Luke 12. 1.
seek a sign from Christ. Matt. 12. 38; 16. 1.
take counsel against Christ. Matt. 12. 14; Mark 3. 6.
Nicodemus remonstrates with. John 7. 51.
cast out the man cured of blindness. John 9. 13.
dissensions about. John 9. 16.
send officers to take Christ. John 7. 32.
contend about circumcision. Acts 15. 5.
their belief in the resurrection, &c. Acts 23. 8.
and publican. Luke 18.
PHAROSH, fa´rosh, same as PAROSH. Ezra 8. 3.
PHARPAR, far´par, swift. 2 Kin. 5. 12.
PHARZITES, farz´ites, descendants of Pharez. Num. 26. 20.
PHASEAH, fa-se´ah, same as PASEAH. Neh. 7. 51.
PHEBE, fe´be, moon. Rom. 16. 1.
PHENICE, fe-ni´see, palm tree. Acts 11. 19; 15. 3; 27. 12.
PHENICIA, fe-nish´yah, land of palms. Acts 21. 2.
PHICHOL, fi´kol, attentive (?). Gen. 21. 22.
PHILADELPHIA, fil´a-delf´yah, brotherly love.
church of, commended. Rev. 1. 11; 3. 7.
PHILEMON, fil-e´mon, affectionate.
Paul's letter to, concerning Onesimus. Philem.
PHILETUS, fil-e´tus, beloved. 2 Tim. 2. 17.
PHILIP, fil´ip, lover of horses.
APOSTLE, called. John 1. 43.
sent forth. Matt. 10. 3; Mark 3. 18; Luke 6. 14; John 12. 22; Acts 1. 13.
remonstrated with by Christ. John 14. 8.
— deacon, elected. Acts 6. 5.
preaches in Samaria. Acts 8. 5.
baptizes the eunuch. Acts 8. 27.
his four virgin daughters prophesy. Acts 21. 8.
—— (brother of Herod). Matt. 14. 3; Mark 6. 17; Luke 3. 1, 19.
PHILIPPI, fil-ip´i, a town so called after Philip of Macedon.
Paul persecuted at. Acts 16. 12.
church at, commended and exhorted. Phil. 1–4.
PHILIPPIANS, fil-ip´yans, the people of Philippi. Phil. 4. 15.
PHILISTIA, fil-ist´yah, the land of the Philistines. Gen. 21. 34; Ex. 13. 17; Josh. 13. 2; 2 Kin. 8. 2; Ps. 60. 8.
PHILISTIM, fil´ist-im, wanderers. Gen. 10. 14.
PHILISTINES, fil´ist-ines, same as PHILISTIM. Gen. 21. 34.
origin of. Gen. 10. 14; 1 Chr. 1. 12.
fill up Isaac's wells. Gen. 26. 15.
contend with Joshua. Josh. 13; Shamgar, Judg. 3. 31; Samson, Judg. 14—16; Samuel, 1 Sam. 4; 7; Jonathan, 1 Sam. 14; Saul, 1 Sam. 17; David, 1 Sam. 18.
their wars with Israel. 1 Sam. 4. 1; 28; 29; 31; 2 Chr. 21. 16.
mentioned. Ps. 60. 8; 83. 7; 87. 4; 108. 9; Is. 2. 6; 9. 12; 11. 14; Jer. 25. 20.
their destruction predicted. Jer. 47; Ezek. 25. 15; Amos 1. 8; Obad. 19; Zeph. 2. 5; Zech. 9. 6.
PHILOLOGUS, fil-o´log-us, talkative.
Julia, and all saints with them. Rom. 16. 15.
PHINEHAS, fin´e-as, serpent's mouth. Ex. 6. 25.

PHINEHAS—*cont.*
slays Zimri and Cozbi. Num. 25. 7, 11; Ps. 106. 30.
sent against the Midianites, Reubenites, and Benjamites. Num. 31. 6; Josh. 22. 13; Judg. 20. 28.
—— son of Eli, his sin and death. 1 Sam. 1. 3; 2. 22; 4. 11.
PHLEGON, fleg´on, zealous, burning. Rom. 16. 14.
PHRYGIA, frij´yah. Acts 2. 10; 16. 6; 18. 23.
PHURAH, foor´ah, branch (?). Judg. 7. 10.
PHUT, foot. Gen. 10. 6.
PHUVAH, foo´vah, mouth. Gen. 46. 13.
PHYGELLUS, fi-gel´us, little fugitive.
and Hermogenes turned away from Paul. 2 Tim. 1. 15.
PI-BESETH, pi-be´seth, the city of Bast. Ezek. 30. 17.
PI-HAHIROTH, pi´ha-hi´roth, where sedge grows. Ex. 14. 2.
PILATE, pi´lat, armed with a javelin (?). Matt. 27. 2.
Pontius, governor of Judæa during our Lord's ministry, sufferings, and death. Luke 3. 1.
Christ delivered to, admonished by his wife, examines Jesus, washes his hands, but delivers Him to be crucified. Matt. 27; Mark 15; Luke 23; John 18; 19.
grants request of Joseph of Arimathæa. Matt. 27. 57; Mark 15. 42; Luke 23. 50; John 19. 38.
See Acts 3. 13; 4. 27; 13. 28; 1 Tim. 6. 13.
PILDASH, pil´dash, steel (?). Gen. 22. 22.
PILEHA, pi´le-hah, ploughman (?). Neh. 10. 24.
PILTAI, pil´tai, whom Jehovah delivers. Neh. 12. 17.
PINON, pi´non, darkness. Gen. 36. 41.
PIRAM, pi´ram, like a wild ass. Josh. 10. 3.
PIRATHON, pir-ah´thon, leader. Judg. 12. 15.
PIRATHONITE, pir-ah´thon-ite, an inhabitant of Pirathon. Judg. 12. 13.
PISGAH, piz´gah, a part, boundary.
mount. Num. 21. 20; 23. 14; Deut. 3. 27; 34. 1.
PISIDIA, pi-sid´yah. Acts 13. 14; 14. 24.
PISON, pi´son, flowing stream (?), a river in Eden. Gen. 2. 11.
PISPAH, pis´pah, expansion. 1 Chr. 7. 38.
PITHOM, pi´thom.
(and Raamses), cities built by Israelites in Egypt. Ex. 1. 11.
PITHON, pi´thon, simple (?). 1 Chr. 8. 35.
PLEIADES, pli´ad-ees, (coming at) the sailing season (?). Job 9. 9; 38. 31; Amos 5. 8.
POCHERETH OF ZEBAIM, po-ke´reth of Ze-ba´im, offspring of gazelles (?). Ezra 2. 57.
POLLUX, pol´ux. Acts 28. 11.
PONTIUS, pon´shus, belonging to the sea. Matt. 27. 2. *See* PILATE.
PONTUS, pont´us, sea. Acts 2. 9.
PORATHA, po-rah´thah, having many chariots (?). Esth. 9. 8.
PORCIUS FESTUS, por´shus fest´us. Acts 24. 27.
POTIPHAR, pot´i-far, belonging to the sun. Gen. 37. 36.
Joseph's master. Gen. 39.
POTI-PHERAH, pot´i-fer´ah, same as POTIPHAR. Gen. 41. 45.
PRISCA, pris´kah, ancient. 2 Tim. 4. 19.
PRISCILLA, pris-il´ah, diminutive of PRISCA. Acts 18. 2.
(and AQUILA). Acts 18; Rom. 16. 3; 1 Cor. 16. 19.
PROCHORUS, prok´or-us, he that presides over the choir. Acts 6. 5.
PTOLEMAIS, tol´em-a´is, city of Ptolemy.
Paul at. Acts 21. 7.
PUA, poo´ah, same as PHUVAH. Num. 26. 23.
PUAH, poo´ah, splendour. Ex. 1. 15.
PUBLIUS, pub´li-us.
entertains Paul. Acts 28. 7.
PUDENS, pu´dens, shamefaced. 2 Tim. 4. 21.
PUHITES, poo´hites. 1 Chr. 2. 53.
PUL, pool, (1) a short name for Tiglath-Pileser (?). 2 Kin. 15. 19. (2) son (?). Is. 66. 19.
king of Assyria. 1 Chr. 5. 26.
PUNITES, poon´ites, descendants of Pua. Num. 26. 23.
PUNON, poon´on, same as PINON. Num. 33. 42.

Pur, poor, a lot. Esth. 3. 7.

Purim, poor´im, lots. Esth. 9. 26.
feast of. Esth. 9. 20.

Put, poot, same as Phut. 1 Chr. 1. 8.

Puteoli, poo-te´o-li, wells.
(Pozzuoli), seaport of Italy. Acts 28. 13.

Putiel, poot´i-el. Ex. 6. 25.

Quartus, kwart´us, the fourth. Rom. 16. 23.

Raamah, ra´am-ah, trembling. Gen. 10. 7.

Raamiah, ra´am-i´ah, trembling of Jehovah. Neh. 7. 7.

Raamses, ra-am´ses, son of the sun. Ex. 1. 11.

Rabbah, rab´ah, capital city. Josh. 13. 25.
city. 2 Sam. 11; 12. 26; Jer. 49. 2; Ezek. 21. 20; 25. 5; Amos 1. 14.

Rabbath, rab´ath, same as Rabbah. Deut. 3. 11.

Rabbi, rab´i, master. Matt. 23. 7, 8; John 1. 38; 3. 2.

Rabbith, rab´ith, populous. Josh. 19. 20.

Rabboni, rab-o´ni, my master.
title addressed to Christ by Mary. John 20. 16.

Rab-mag, rab´mag, most exalted. Jer. 39. 3.

Rab-saris, rab´sar-is, chief eunuch. 2 Kin. 18. 17.

Rab-shakeh, rab´sha-kay, chief of the cupbearers. 2 Kin. 18. 17.
reviles Hezekiah. 2 Kin. 18. 19; 19. 1; Is. 36. 4.

Rachab, ra´kab, Greek form of Rahab. Matt. 1. 5.

Rachal, ra´kal, traffic. 1 Sam. 30. 29.

Rachel, ra´chel, ewe. Gen. 29. 6.
(Rahel) and Jacob. Gen. 29. 10, 28; 30; 31. 4, 19, 34; 35. 16.

Raddai, rad´ai, subduing. 1 Chr. 2. 14.

Ragau, ra´gaw, Greek form of Reu. Luke 3. 35.

Raguel, ra-goo´el, friend of God. Num. 10. 29.

Rahab, ra´hab, (1) broad. Josh. 2. 1. (2) violence. Ps. 87. 4.
the harlot. Josh. 2; 6. 22. *See* Matt. 1. 5; Heb. 11. 31; James 2. 25.
—— (Egypt). Ps. 87. 4; 89. 10; Is. 51. 9.

Raham, ra´ham. 1 Chr. 2. 44.

Rahel, ra´hel, same as Rachel. Jer. 31. 15.

Rakem, ra´kem, variegated. 1 Chr. 7. 16.

Rakkath, rak´ath, shore. Josh. 19. 35.

Rakkon, rak´on, same as Rakkath. Josh. 19. 46.

Ram, high. Ruth 4. 19.

Rama, ra´mah, Greek form of Ramah. Matt. 2. 18.

Ramah, ra´mah, high place. Josh. 18. 25; Judg. 4. 5; 1 Sam. 1. 19; 7. 17; 8. 4; 19. 18; 25. 1; Jer. 31. 15.

Ramath, ra´math, same as preceding. Josh. 19. 8.

Ramathaim, ra´math-a´im, double high place. 1 Sam. 1. 1.

Ramathite, ra´math-ite, a native of Ramah. 1 Chr. 27. 27.

Ramath-lehi, ra´math-le´hi, height of Lehi. Judg. 15. 17.

Ramath-mizpeh, ra´math-miz´peh, height of Mizpeh. Josh. 13. 26.

Rameses, ra´me-sees, same as Raamses. Gen. 47. 11.

Ramiah, ram-i´ah, Jehovah is high. Ezra 10. 25.

Ramoth, ra´moth, plural of Ramah. 1 Chr. 6. 73.

Ramoth-gilead, ra´moth gil´yad, heights of Gilead. Deut. 4. 43; 1 Kin. 4. 13, 22; 2 Kin. 8. 28; 9. 1; 2 Chr. 18; 22. 5.

Rapha, ra´fah, giant (?). 1 Chr. 8. 37.

Raphu, ra´foo, healed. Num. 13. 9.

Reaia, re-ai´ah, Jehovah has seen. 1 Chr. 5. 5.

Reaiah, correct form of Reaia. 1 Chr. 4. 2.

Reba, re´bah, a fourth part. Num. 31. 8.

Rebecca, Greek form of Rebekah. Rom. 9. 10.

Rebekah, re-bek´ah, a noose.
history of. Gen. 22; 24. 15, 67; 27. 6, 43; 49. 31; Rom. 9. 10.

Rechab, re´kab, horseman. 2 Kin. 10. 15.

Rechabites, re´kab-ites, descendants of Rechab. Jer. 35. 2.

Rechah, re´kah, side (?). 1 Chr. 4. 12.

Reelaiah, re´el-ai´ah, trembling caused by Jehovah. Ezra 2. 2.

Regem, re´gem, friend. 1 Chr. 2. 47.

Regem-melech, re´gem-me´lek, friend of the king. Zech. 7. 2.

Rehabiah, re´hab-i´ah, Jehovah enlarges. 1 Chr. 23. 17.

Rehob, re´hob, street. 2 Sam. 8. 3.

Rehoboam, re´hob-o´am, who enlarges the people. 1 Kin. 11. 43.
king of Judah. 1 Kin. 11; 12; 14; 2 Chr. 9—12.

Rehoboth, re-ho´both, roominess. Gen. 10. 11; 26. 22.

Rehum, re´hoom, merciful. Ezra 4. 8.

Rei, re´i, friendly. 1 Kin. 1. 8.

Rekem, re´kem, same as Rakem. Num. 31. 8.

Remaliah, rem´al-i´ah, whom Jehovah adorned. 2 Kin. 15. 25.

Remeth, re´meth, a high place. Josh. 19. 21.

Remmon, rem´on, more correctly spelt Rimmon. Josh. 19. 7.

Remmon-methoar, rem´on-me-tho´ar, R. stretching (to Neah). Josh. 19. 13.

Remphan, rem´fan. Acts 7. 43.

Rephael, re´fa-el, whom God healed. 1 Chr. 26. 7.

Rephah, re´fah, riches. 1 Chr. 7. 25.

Rephaiah, ref-ai´ah, whom Jehovah healed. 1 Chr. 3. 21.

Rephaim, re-fa´im, giants. 2 Sam. 5. 18.

Rephaims, re-fa´ims, same as Rephaim. Gen. 14. 5.

Rephidim, re-fee´dim, supports.
Amalek subdued there by Joshua. Ex. 17.

Resen, re´sen, bridle. Gen. 10. 12.

Resheph, re´shef, flame. 1 Chr. 7. 25.

Reu, re-oo´, same as Raguel. Gen. 11. 18.

Reuben, roo´ben, behold a son (?).
son of Jacob. Gen. 29; 30; 35; 37; 42; 49; 1 Chr. 5. 1.

Reubenites, roo´ben-ites, descendants of Reuben.
their number and possessions. Num. 1; 2; 26; 32; Deut. 3. 12; Josh. 13. 15; 1 Chr. 5. 18.
dealings of Moses and Joshua with. Num. 32; Deut. 33; Josh. 1; 22.
go into captivity. 1 Chr. 5. 26 (Rev. 7. 5).

Reuel, roo´el, friend of God. 1 Chr. 9. 8.

Reumah, room´ah, exalted. Gen. 22. 24.

Rezeph, re´zef, a stone. 2 Kin. 19. 12.

Rezia, rez´yah, delight. 1 Chr. 7. 39.

Rezin, re´zin, firm.
king of Syria. 2 Kin. 15. 37; 16. 5, 9; Is. 7. 1.

Rezon, re´zon, lean.
of Damascus. 1 Kin. 11. 23.

Rhegium, re´ji-um. Acts 28. 13.

Rhesa, re´sah, chieftain (?). Luke 3. 27.

Rhoda, ro´dah, a rose. Acts 12. 13.

Rhodes, rodes.
island of. Acts 21. 1.

Ribai, rib´ai, contentious. 2 Sam. 23. 29.

Riblah, rib´lah, fertility. Num. 34. 11.
in Syria. 2 Kin. 23. 33; 25. 6; Jer. 39. 5; 52. 9.

Rimmon, rim´on, (1) pomegranate, 2 Sam. 4. 2; (2) idol, 2 Kin. 5. 18.

Rimmon-parez, rim´on-pa´rez, pomegranate of the breach. Num. 33. 19.

Rinnah, rin´ah, shout. 1 Chr. 4. 20.

Riphath, ri´fath. Gen. 10. 3.

Rissah, ris´ah, ruin. Num. 33. 21.

Rithmah, rith´mah, broom. Num. 33. 18.

Rizpah, riz´pah, hot coal. 2 Sam. 3. 7.

Roboam, rob-o´am, Greek form of Rehoboam. Matt. 1. 7.

Rogelim, ro´gel-im, fullers. 2 Sam. 17. 27.

Rohgah, ro´gah, outcry. 1 Chr. 7. 34.

Romamti-ezer, ro-mam´ti-e´zer, I have exalted help. 1 Chr. 25. 4.

Romans, ro´mans, men of Rome. John 11. 48.
St. Paul's teaching to. *See* Epistle to Romans, *also* Faith, Works, Righteousness.

Rome, strength (?).
strangers of, at Pentecost. Acts 2. 10.
Jews ordered to depart from. Acts 18. 2.
Paul preaches there. Acts 28.

Rosh, head. Gen. 46. 21.

Rufus, roo´fus, red. Mark 15. 21.

Rufus—*cont.*
(chosen in the Lord). Rom. 16. 13.
Ruhamah, roo-hah′mah, compassionated. Hos. 2. 1.
Rumah, roo′mah, height. 2 Kin. 23. 36.
Ruth, rooth, friendship (?). Ruth 1. 4.
story of. Ruth 1—4.
Christ descended from, Matt. 1. 5.

Sabachthani, sa-bac-thah′ni, thou hast forsaken me. Mark 15. 34.
Sabaoth, sab-a′oth (Hosts), the Lord of. Rom. 9. 29; James 5. 4.
Sabeans, sab-e′ans, people of Seba. Job 1. 15; Is. 45. 14.
Sabtah, sab′tah, rest (?). Gen. 10. 7.
Sabtecha, sab′te-kah. 1 Chr. 1. 9.
Sabtechah, sab′te-kah. Gen. 10. 7.
Sacar, sa′kar, hire, reward. 1 Chr. 11. 35.
Sadducees, sad′u-sees (named from Zadok, founder of the sect).
their controversies with Christ, Matt. 16. 1; 22. 23; Mark 12. 18; Luke 20. 27; with the apostles, Acts 4. 1; with Paul, Acts 23. 6.
their doctrines. Matt. 22. 23; Mark 12. 18; Acts 23. 8.
Sadoc, sa′dok, Greek form of Zadok. Matt. 1. 14.
Sala, sa′lah, Greek form of Salah. Luke 3. 35.
Salah, sa′lah, sprout (?). Gen. 10. 24.
Salamis, sal′am-is. Acts 13. 5.
Salathiel, sa-la′thi-el, Greek form of Shealtiel. 1 Chr. 3. 17.
Salcah, or Salchah, sal′kah, road. Deut. 3. 10.
Salem, sa′lem, perfect. Gen. 14. 18; Heb. 7. 1.
Salim, sa′lim, Greek form of Salem. John 3. 23.
Sallai, sal′ai, exaltation. Neh. 11. 8.
Sallu, sal′oo, same as Sallai. 1 Chr. 9. 7.
Salma, sal′mah, garment. 1 Chr. 2. 11.
Salmon, sal′mon, shady. Ps. 68. 14.
Salmone, sal-mo′ne. Acts 27. 7.
Salome, sal-o′me, perfect. Mark 15. 40; 16. 1.
Salu, sa′loo, same as Sallu. Num. 25. 14.
Samaria, sa-ma′ri-ah, Greek equivalent of Shomron which means guard.
(city of). 1 Kin. 16. 24; 20. 1; 2 Kin. 6. 24.
—— (region of), visited by Christ. Luke 17. 11; John 4.
gospel preached there. Acts 8.
Samaritan, sa-mar′it-an.
parable of the good. Luke 10. 33.
miracle performed on. Luke 17. 16.
Samaritans, sa-mar′it-ans, inhabitants of Samaria. 2 Kin. 17. 29.
Samgar-nebo, sam-gar′ne-bo, Be gracious, Nebo. Jer. 39. 3.
Samlah, sam′lah, garment. Gen. 36. 36.
Samos, sa′mos, a height (?). Acts 20. 15.
Samothracia, sa′mo-thra′shah. Acts 16. 11.
Samson, sam′son, like the sun. Judg. 13—16.
delivered up to Philistines. Judg. 16. 21.
his death. Judg. 16. 30.
Samuel, sam′u-el, name of God, or, heard of God. 1 Sam. 1. 20.
born, and presented to the Lord. 1 Sam. 1. 19, 26.
ministers to the Lord. 1 Sam. 3.
the Lord speaks to. 1 Sam. 3. 11.
judges Israel. 1 Sam. 7; 8. 1; Acts 13. 20.
anoints Saul king. 1 Sam. 10. 1.
rebukes Saul for sin. 1 Sam. 13. 13; 15. 16.
anoints David. 1 Sam. 16; 19. 18.
his death. 1 Sam. 25. 1; 28. 3.
his spirit consulted by Saul. 1 Sam. 28. 12.
as a prophet. Ps. 99. 6; Acts 3. 24; Heb. 11. 32.
Sanballat, san-bal′at, Sin (the moon) giveth life (?). Neh. 2. 10; 4; 6. 2; 13. 28.
Sansannah, san-san′ah, palm branch. Josh. 15. 31.
Saph, threshold. 2 Sam. 21. 18.
Saphir, saf′ir, beautiful. Mic. 1. 11.
Sapphira, saf-i′rah, Greek form of the above (feminine). Acts 5. 1.
Sara, sa′rah, Greek form of Sarah. Heb. 11. 11.
Sarah, sa′rah, princess. Gen. 17. 15.
(Sarai). Gen. 11; 12; 20. 2. *See* Abraham.
her death and burial. Gen. 23 (Heb. 11. 11; 1 Pet. 3. 6).
Sarai, sa′rai, contentious (?). Gen. 11. 29.
Saraph, sa′raf, burning. 1 Chr. 4. 22.
Sardis, sard′is.
church of. Rev. 1. 11; 3. 1.
Sardites, sard′ites, descendants of Sered. Num. 26. 26.
Sarepta, sa-rep′tah, Greek form of Zarephath. Luke 4. 26.
Sargon, sar′gon, [God] appoints the king. Is. 20. 1.
Sarid, sa′rid, survivor. Josh. 19. 10.
Saron, sa′ron, Greek form of Sharon. Acts 9. 35.
Sarsechim, sar′se-kim. Jer. 39. 3.
Saruch, sa′rook, Greek form of Serug. Luke 3. 35.
Satan, sa′tan, adversary. 1 Chr. 21. 1. *See* Devil, *Subject-Index*, p. 57.
Saul, asked for. 1 Sam. 9. 2.
king of Israel, his parentage, anointing by Samuel, prophesying, and acknowledgment as king. 1 Sam. 9; 10.
his disobedience, and rejection by God. 1 Sam. 14. 31; 15.
possessed by an evil spirit, quieted by David. 1 Sam. 16. 14, 15, 23.
favours David, 1 Sam. 18. 5; seeks to kill him, 1 Sam. 18. 10; pursues him, 1 Sam. 20; 23; 24; 26.
slays priests for succouring David. 1 Sam. 22. 9.
enquires of the witch of En-dor. 1 Sam. 28. 7.
his ruin and suicide. 1 Sam. 28. 15; 31; 1 Chr. 10.
his posterity. 1 Chr. 8. 33.
—— of Tarsus. *See* Paul.
Sceva, se′vah, left-handed. Acts 19. 14.
Scythian, sith′yan. Col. 3. 11.
Seba, se′bah, man (?). Gen. 10. 7.
Sebat, se′bat, rest (?). Zech. 1. 7.
Secacah, se-kah′kah, enclosure. Josh. 15. 61.
Sechu, se′koo, watch-tower. 1 Sam. 19. 22.
Secundus, se-cun′dus, second. Acts 20. 4.
Segub, se′goob, elevated. 1 Kin. 16. 34.
Seir, se′ir, hairy.
mount, Edom, land of Esau. Gen. 14. 6; 32. 3; 36. 8, 20; Deut. 33. 2; Josh. 24. 4; Is. 21. 11; Ezek. 25. 8.
predictions about. Num. 24. 18; Ezek. 35. 2.
Seirath, se-ir′ath, well wooded. Judg. 3. 26.
Sela, se′lah, rock. Is. 16. 1.
Sela-hammahlekoth, se′lah-ham-ah′lek-oth, rock of escapes. 1 Sam. 23. 28.
Selah, se′lah, forte (?), a musical direction, pause. Ps. 3. 2; 4. 2; 24. 6; 39. 5, 11; 46. 3; 48. 8; 50. 6; Hab. 3. 3, 9, 12, &c.
Seled, se′led, exultation, or burning. 1 Chr. 2. 30.
Seleucia, se-loo′shah, called after Seleucus.
apostles at. Acts 13. 4.
Sem, Greek form of Shem. Luke 3. 36.
Semachiah, sem′ak-i′ah, whom Jehovah sustains. 1 Chr. 26. 7.
Semei, sem′e-i, Greek form of Shimei. Luke 3. 26.
Senaah, sen-a′ah, perhaps thorny. Ezra 2. 35.
Seneh, se′nay, crag, thorn. 1 Sam. 14. 4.
Senir, se′nir, coat of mail. 1 Chr. 5. 23.
Sennacherib, sen-ak′er-ib, Sin (the moon) multiplies brethren. 2 Kin. 18. 13; 2 Chr. 32; Is. 36. 37.
Senuah, se-noo′ah, bristling (?). Neh. 11. 9.
Seorim, se-or′im, barley. 1 Chr. 24. 8.
Sephar, se′far, a numbering. Gen. 10. 30.
Sepharad, se-far′ad. Obad. 20.
Sepharvaim, se′far-va′im. 2 Kin. 17. 24; 18. 34; 19. 13.
Serah, se′rah, abundance. Gen. 46. 17.
Seraiah, ser-ai′ah, soldier of Jehovah (?). 2 Sam. 8. 17.
Seraphims, ser′af-ims, burning ones. Is. 6. 2.
Sered, se′red, fear. Gen. 46. 14.
Sergius, ser′ji-us. Acts 13. 7.
Serug, se′roog, shoot. Gen. 11. 20.
Seth, substitute.

SETH—*cont.*
son of Adam. Gen. 4. 25; 5. 3.
SETHUR, se´thoor, hidden. Num. 13. 13.
SHAALABBIN, sha´al-ab´in, earths of foxes. Josh. 19. 42.
SHAALBIM, sha-alb´im, same as preceding. Judg. 1. 35.
SHAALBONITE, sha-alb´on-ite, inhabitant of Shaalbim. 2 Sam. 23. 32.
SHAAPH, sha´af, anger (?). 1 Chr. 2. 47.
SHAARAIM, sha´ar-a´im, two gates. 1 Sam. 17. 52.
SHAASHGAZ, sha-ash´gaz, beauty's servant (?). Esth. 2. 14.
SHABBETHAI, shab´e-thai, born on the sabbath. Ezra 10. 15.
SHACHIA, sha´ki-ah, lustful. 1 Chr. 8. 10.
SHADDAI, shad´ai, Almighty. Num. 1. 6.
SHADRACH, shad´rak. Dan. 1. 7.
Meshach, and Abed-nego, their faith and sufferings, and deliverance. Dan. 1; 3.
SHAGE, sha´ge, wanderer. 1 Chr. 11. 34.
SHAHARAIM, sha´har-a´im, two dawns. 1 Chr. 8. 8.
SHAHAZIMAH, sha-ha-zee´mah, lofty places. Josh. 19. 22.
SHALEM, sha´lem, safe, perfect. Gen. 33. 18.
SHALIM, sha´lim, foxes. 1 Sam. 9. 4.
SHALISHA, sha-lish´ah, a third part. 1 Sam. 9. 4.
SHALLECHETH, shal-e´keth, felling. 1 Chr. 26. 16.
SHALLUM, shal´oom, retribution. 2 Kin. 15. 10; 22. 14; 2 Chr. 34. 22; Jer. 22. 11.
SHALLUN, shal´oon, spoliation. Neh. 3. 15.
SHALMAI, shal´mai, peaceful (?). Ezra 2. 46.
SHALMAN, shal´man, shortened form of following. Hos. 10. 14.
SHALMANESER, shal´man-e´zer, Shalman be propitious. 2 Kin. 17. 3.
carries ten tribes captive. 2 Kin. 17; 18. 9.
SHAMA, sha´mah, obedient. 1 Chr. 11. 44.
SHAMARIAH, sha´mar-i´ah, whom Jehovah guards. 2 Chr. 11. 19.
SHAMED, sha´med, destroyer. 1 Chr. 8. 12.
SHAMER, sha´mer, keeper. 1 Chr. 6. 46.
SHAMGAR, sham´gar, destroyer (?).
judges Israel. Judg. 3. 31; 5. 6.
SHAMHUTH, sham´hooth, notoriety (?). 1 Chr. 27. 8.
SHAMIR, sha´mir, a thorn. 1 Chr. 24. 24.
SHAMMA, sham´ah, desert. 1 Chr. 7. 37.
SHAMMAH, sham´ah, same as SHAMMA. Gen. 36. 13.
his valour. 2 Sam. 23. 11.
SHAMMAI, sham´ai, wasted. 1 Chr. 2. 28.
SHAMMOTH, sham´oth, deserts. 1 Chr. 11. 27.
SHAMMUA, sham´oo-ah, famous. Num. 13. 4.
SHAMMUAH, same as preceding. 2 Sam. 5. 14.
SHAMSHERAI, sham´sher-ai. 1 Chr. 8. 26.
SHAPHAM, sha´fam, bald. 1 Chr. 5. 12.
SHAPHAN, sha´fan, coney.
repairs the temple. 2 Kin. 22. 3; 2 Chr. 34. 8.
SHAPHAT, sha´fat, judge. Num. 13. 5.
SHAPHER, sha´fer, pleasantness. Num. 33. 23.
SHARAI, shar´ai, free. Ezra 10. 40.
SHARAIM, shar-a´im, same as SHAARAIM. Josh. 15. 36.
SHARAR, shar´ar, firm. 2 Sam. 23. 33.
SHAREZER, shar-e´zer, [God] protect the king. 2 Kin. 19. 37.
SHARON, sha´ron, plain. 1 Chr. 27. 29.
rose of. Cant. 2. 1.
SHARONITE, sha´ron-ite, one who lives in Sharon. 1 Chr. 27. 29.
SHARUHEN, sha-roo´hen. Josh. 19. 6.
SHASHAI, shash´ai, pale. Ezra 10. 40.
SHASHAK, sha´shak, activity (?). 1 Chr. 8. 14.
SHAUL, sha´ool, same as SAUL. Gen. 46. 10.
SHAULITES, sha´ool-ites, the family of Shaul. Num. 26. 13.
SHAVEH, sha´vay, plain. Gen. 14. 17.
SHAVEH KIRIATHAIM, sha´vay kir-iath-a´im, plain of Kiriathaim. Gen. 14. 5.
SHAVSHA, shav´shah, another name of Seraiah. 1 Chr. 18. 16.
SHEAL, she´al, prayer. Ezra 10. 29.
SHEALTIEL, she-al´ti-el, I asked from God. Ezra 3. 2.
SHEARIAH, she´ar-i´ah, gate of Jehovah. 1 Chr. 8. 38.
SHEAR-JASHUB, she´ar-ja´shoob, the remnant shall return. Is. 7. 3.
SHEBA, she´bah, an oath. Gen. 25. 3; 2 Sam. 20. 1; Job 6. 19; Ps. 72. 10; Jer. 6. 20; Ezek. 27. 22; 38. 13.
queen of. 1 Kin. 10; 2 Chr. 9; Matt. 12. 42.
—— (Benjamite) revolts. 2 Sam. 20.
SHEBAH, seven. Gen. 26. 33.
SHEBAM, she´bam, fragrance. Num. 32. 3.
SHEBANIAH, she´ban-i´ah, whom Jehovah hides. 1 Chr. 15. 24.
SHEBARIM, she-bar´im, breaches. Josh. 7. 5.
SHEBER, she´ber, breaking. 1 Chr. 2. 48.
SHEBNA, sheb´nah, youth (?).
the scribe. 2 Kin. 18. 18; 19. 2; Is. 22. 15; 36. 3; 37. 2.
SHEBUEL, she-boo´el, captive of God. 1 Chr. 23. 16.
SHECANIAH, she´kan-i´ah, same as following. 1 Chr. 24. 11.
SHECHANIAH, she´kan-i´ah, Jehovah dwells. 1 Chr. 3. 21.
SHECHEM, she´kem, back, shoulder. Gen. 34. 2.
the Hivite. Gen. 34.
—— city of. Josh. 17. 7; Ps. 60. 6.
charge of Joshua at. Josh. 24.
its treachery and penalty. Judg. 9. 1, 41.
SHECHEMITES, she´kem-ites, people of Shechem. Num. 26. 31.
SHEDEUR, she´de-oor, giving forth of light. Num. 1. 5.
SHEHARIAH, she´har-i´ah, Jehovah seeks. 1 Chr. 8. 26.
SHELAH, she´lah, petition.
son of Judah. Gen. 38. 5.
SHELANITES, she´lan-ites, descendants of Shelah. Num. 26. 20.
SHELEMIAH, she´lem-i´ah, whom Jehovah repays. 1 Chr. 26. 14.
SHELEPH, she´lef, drawing out. Gen. 10. 26.
SHELESH, she´lesh, triad. 1 Chr. 7. 35.
SHELOMI, she-lo´mi, peaceful. Num. 34. 27.
SHELOMITH, she-lo´mith, peacefulness. Lev. 24. 11.
SHELOMOTH, she-lo´moth, same as Shelomith. 1 Chr. 24. 22.
SHELUMIEL, she-loom´i-el, friend of God. Num. 1. 6.
SHEM, name. Gen. 5. 32; 9. 26; 10. 21; 11. 10; 1 Chr. 1. 17.
SHEMA, she´mah, (1) echo (?), Josh. 15. 26; (2) fame, 1 Chr. 2. 43.
SHEMAAH, she-ma´ah, fame. 1 Chr. 12. 3.
SHEMAIAH, she-mai´ah, Jehovah has heard.
prophet. 1 Kin. 12. 22; 2 Chr. 11. 2; 12. 5 (Jer. 29. 24).
SHEMARIAH, she´mar-i´ah, Jehovah guards. 1 Chr. 12. 5.
SHEMEBER, shem-e´ber, soaring on high (?). Gen. 14. 2.
SHEMER, she´mer, guardian. 1 Kin. 16. 24.
SHEMIDA, shem-i´dah, fame of wisdom. Num. 26. 32.
SHEMIDAH, shem-i´dah, same as preceding. 1 Chr. 7. 19.
SHEMIDAITES, shem-id´a-ites, descendants of Shemida. Num. 26. 32.
SHEMINITH, she-mi´nith, eighth. 1 Chr. 15. 21.
SHEMIRAMOTH, she-mi´ram-oth, most high name. 1 Chr. 15. 18.
SHEMUEL, she´moo-el, same as SAMUEL. Num. 34. 20.
SHEN, tooth. 1 Sam. 7. 12.
SHENAZAR, she-na´zar. 1 Chr. 3. 18.
SHENIR, she´nir, same as SENIR. Deut. 3. 9.
SHEPHAM, she´fam, nakedness. Num. 34. 10.
SHEPHATHIAH, she´fat-i´ah, an incorrect way of spelling the next word. 1 Chr. 9. 8.
SHEPHATIAH, she´fat-i´ah, whom Jehovah defends. 2 Sam. 3. 4.

SHEPHI, she´fi, baldness. 1 Chr. 1. 40.
SHEPHO, she´fo, same as SHEPHI. Gen. 36. 23.
SHEPHUPHAN, she´foof-an, serpent (?). 1 Chr. 8. 5.
SHERAH, she´rah, consanguinity. 1 Chr. 7. 24.
SHEREBIAH, she´reb-i´ah, heat of Jehovah. Ezra 8. 18.
SHERESH, she´resh, root. 1 Chr. 7. 16.
SHEREZER, sher-e´zer, same as SHAREZER (?). Zech. 7. 2.
SHESHACH, she´shak, a name for Babel. Jer. 25. 26; 51. 41.
SHESHAI, shesh´ai, clothed in white (?). Num. 13. 22.
SHESHAN, she´shan, lily (?). 1 Chr. 2. 31.
SHESHBAZZAR, shesh-baz´ar. Ezra 1. 8; 5. 14.
SHETH, shayth, tumult. Num. 24. 17.
SHETHAR, she´thar, star. Esth. 1. 14.
SHETHAR-BOZNAI, she´thar-boz´nai, bright star. Ezra 5. 3.
and Tatnai oppose rebuilding of temple. Ezra 5. 6.
SHEVA, she´vah, vanity. 2 Sam. 20. 25.
SHIBBOLETH, shib´ol-eth, an ear of corn, or a flood. Judg. 12. 6.
SHIBMAH, shib´mah, fragrant. Num. 32. 38.
SHICRON, shik´ron, drunkenness. Josh. 15. 11.
SHIGGAION, shig-ai´on, irregular. Ps. 7, title.
SHIGIONOTH, shig´i-o´noth. Hab. 3. 1.
SHIHON, shi´hon, ruin. Josh. 19. 19.
SHIHOR, shi´hor, black. 1 Chr. 13. 5.
SHIHOR-LIBNATH, shi´hor-lib´nath. Josh. 19. 26.
SHILHI, shil´hi, darter. 1 Kin. 22. 42.
SHILHIM, shil´him, aqueducts. Josh. 15. 32.
SHILLEM, shil´em, requital. Gen. 46. 24.
SHILOAH, shi-lo´ah, outlet of water. Is. 8. 6.
SHILOH, shi´lo, rest, Messiah. Gen. 49. 10.
—— site of tabernacle. Josh. 18. 1; Judg. 21. 19; 1 Sam. 1. 3; 2. 14; 3. 21; Ps. 78. 60; Jer. 7. 12; 26. 6.
SHILONI, shi´lo-ni, native of Shiloh. Neh. 11. 5.
SHILONITE, shi´lo-nite, same as preceding. 1 Kin. 11. 29.
SHILSHAH, shil´shah, triad. 1 Chr. 7. 37.
SHIMEA, shim´e-ah, famous. 1 Chr. 3. 5.
SHIMEAH, shim´e-ah, same as SHEMAAH. 2 Sam. 21. 21.
SHIMEAM, shim´e-am, same as preceding. 1 Chr. 9. 38.
SHIMEATH, shim´e-ath, fame. 2 Kin. 12. 21.
SHIMEATHITE, shi´me-ath-ite. 1 Chr. 2. 55.
SHIMEI, shim´e-i, my fame. Num. 3. 18.
curses David. 2 Sam. 16. 5.
slain by Solomon. 1 Kin. 2. 36.
SHIMEON, shim´e-on, a hearkening. Ezra 10. 31.
SHIMHI, shim´hi, same as SHIMEI. 1 Chr. 8. 21.
SHIMI, shim´i, same as preceding. Ex. 6. 17.
SHIMITES, shim´ites, descendants of Shimei. Num. 3. 21.
SHIMMA, shim´ah, rumour. 1 Chr. 2. 13.
SHIMON, shi´mon. 1 Chr. 4. 20.
SHIMRATH, shim´rath, watchfulness. 1 Chr. 8. 21.
SHIMRI, shim´ri, watchful. 1 Chr. 4. 37.
SHIMRITH, shim´rith, vigilant. 2 Chr. 24. 26.
SHIMROM, shim´rome, watch-post. 1 Chr. 7. 1.
SHIMRON, shim´rone, watchful. Josh. 11. 1.
SHIMRONITES, shim´ron-ites, descendants of Shimron. Num. 26. 24.
SHIMRON-MERON, shim´ron-me´ron. Josh. 12. 20.
SHIMSHAI, shim´shai, sunny. Ezra. 4. 8.
SHINAB, shi´nab, hostile (?). Gen. 14. 2.
SHINAR, shi´nar. Gen. 10. 10.
SHIPHI, shi´fi, abundant. 1 Chr. 4. 37.
SHIPHMITE, shif´mite, a native of Shephan. 1 Chr. 27. 27.
SHIPHRAH, shif´rah, beauty. Ex. 1. 15.
SHIPHTAN, shif´tan, judicial. Num. 34. 24.
SHISHA, shi´shah, brightness. 1 Kin. 4. 3.
SHISHAK, shi´shak, illustrious. 1 Kin. 11. 40.
invades and spoils Jerusalem. 1 Kin. 14. 25; 2 Chr. 12.
SHITRAI, shit´rai, official. 1 Chr. 27. 29.
SHITTIM, shit´im, acacias. Num. 25. 1.
SHIZA, shi´zah, cheerful (?). 1 Chr. 11. 42.
SHOA, sho´ah, opulent. Ezek. 23. 23.
SHOBAB, sho´bab, apostate. 2 Sam. 5. 14.
SHOBACH, sho´bak, pouring. 2 Sam. 10. 16.
SHOBAI, sho´bai, bright (?). Ezra 2. 42.
SHOBAL, sho´bal, stream. Gen. 36. 20.
SHOBEK, sho´bek, forsaker. Neh. 10. 24.
SHOBI, sho´bi, taking captive. 2 Sam. 17. 27.
SHOCHO, sho´ko, same as the next word. 2 Chr. 28. 18.
SHOCHOH, sho´ko, a hedge. 1 Sam. 17. 1.
SHOCO, sho´ko, same as the preceding. 2 Chr. 11. 7.
SHOHAM, sho´ham, onyx. 1 Chr. 24. 27.
SHOMER, sho´mer, watchman. 2 Kin. 12. 21.
SHOPHACH, sho´fak, same as SHOBAK. 1 Chr. 19. 16.
SHOPHAN, sho´fan, baldness. Num. 32. 35.
SHOSHANNIM, sho-shan´im, lilies. Ps. 45, title.
SHOSHANNIM-EDUTH, sh.-e´dooth, lilies a testimony. Ps. 80, title.
SHUA, shoo´ah, wealth. 1 Chr. 2. 3.
SHUAH, shoo´ah, depression. Gen. 25. 2.
SHUAL, shoo´al, jackal. 1 Chr. 7. 36.
SHUBAEL, shoo´ba-el, same as SHEBUEL (?). 1 Chr. 24. 20.
SHUHAM, shoo´ham, pitman (?). Num. 26. 42.
SHUHAMITES, shoo´ham-ites, the descendants of Shuham. Num. 26. 42.
SHUHITE, shoo´hite, a descendant of Shua. Job 8. 1.
SHULAMITE, shoo´lam-ite, same as SHELOMITH. Cant. 6. 13.
SHUMATHITES, shoo´math-ites, people of Shumah. 1 Chr. 2. 53.
SHUNAMMITE, shoon´am-ite, an inhabitant of Shunem. 1 Kin. 1. 3.
SHUNEM, shoon´em, two resting-places. Josh. 19. 18; 1 Sam. 28. 4; 2 Kin. 4. 8.
SHUNI, shoon´i, quiet. Gen. 46. 16.
SHUNITES, shoon´ites, descendants of Shuni. Num. 26. 15.
SHUPHAM, shoo´fam, serpent. Num. 26. 39.
SHUPHAMITES, shoo´fam-ites, the descendants of Shupham. Num. 26. 39.
SHUPPIM, shoop´im. 1 Chr. 7. 12.
SHUR, shoor, a fort. Gen. 16. 7.
SHUSHAN, shoo´shan.
city, Artaxerxes at. Neh. 1. 1; Esth. 2. 8; 3. 15.
SHUSHAN-EDUTH, sh.-e´dooth, lily of the testimony. Ps. 60, title.
SHUTHALHITES, shoo´thal-ites, the descendants of Shuthelah. Num. 26. 35.
SHUTHELAH, shoo-theel´ah, plantation (?). Num. 26. 35.
SIA, si´ah, assembly. Neh. 7. 47.
SIAHA, si´a-hah, council. Ezra 2. 44.
SIBBECAI, sib´e-kai, entangling. 1 Chr. 11. 29.
SIBBECHAI, same as preceding. 2 Sam. 21. 18.
SIBBOLETH, sib´o-leth, same as SHIBBOLETH. Judg. 12. 6.
SIBMAH, sib´mah, same as SHIBMAH. Josh. 13. 19.
SIBRAIM, sib-ra´im, two hills (?). Ezek. 47. 16.
SICHEM, si´kem, the shoulder-blade. Gen. 12. 6.
SIDDIM, sid´im, the plains. Gen. 14. 3.
SIDON, si´don, fishing.
son of Canaan. Gen. 10. 15.
—— (Zidon), city of. Josh. 19. 28; 1 Kin. 5. 6; Acts 27. 3.
SIDONIANS, si-do´ni-ans, persons living in Sidon. Deut. 3. 9.
SIHON, si´hon, brush.
king of the Amorites. Num. 21. 21; Deut. 1. 4; 2. 26; Ps. 135. 11; 136. 19.
SIHOR, si´hor, same as SHICHOR. Josh. 13. 3.
SILAS, si´las, shortened form of Silvanus. Acts 15. 22; 16. 19; 17. 4. *See* 2 Cor. 1. 19; 1 Thess. 1. 1; 1 Pet. 5. 12.
SILLA, sil´ah, way, highway (?). 2 Kin. 12. 20.
SILOAM, si-lo´am, same as SHILOAH. John 9. 7.
SILVANUS, sil-vane´us, of the forest. 2 Cor. 1. 19.

SIMEON, sim´e-on, same as SHIMEON.
son of Jacob. Gen. 29. 33; 34. 7, 25; 42. 24.
his descendants. Gen. 46. 10; Ex. 6. 15; Num. 1. 22; 26. 12; 1 Chr. 4. 24; 12. 25.
prophecy concerning. Gen. 49. 5.
—— blesses Christ. Luke 2. 25.
SIMON, si´mon, same as preceding.
brother of Christ. Matt. 13. 55; Mark 6. 3.
—— (Zelotes), APOSTLE. Matt. 10. 4; Mark 3. 18; Luke 6. 15.
—— (Pharisee), reproved. Luke 7. 36.
—— (leper). Matt. 26. 6; Mark 14. 3.
—— (of Cyrene), bears the cross of Jesus. Matt. 27. 32; Mark 15. 21; Luke 23. 26.
—— (a tanner), Peter's vision in his house. Acts 9. 43; 10. 6.
—— (a sorcerer), baptized. Acts 8. 9; rebuked by Peter. Acts 8. 18.
—— PETER. *See* PETER.
SIMRI, sim´ri, same as SHIMRI. 1 Chr. 26. 10.
SIN, clay. Ex. 16. 1.
(Zin), wilderness of. Ex. 16; Num. 13. 21; 20; 27. 14.
SINA, si´nah, Greek form of Sinai. Acts 7. 30.
SINAI, si´nai, pointed. Ex. 19. 1.
mount. Deut. 33. 2; Judg. 5. 5; Ps. 68. 8, 17; Gal. 4. 24.
SINIM, sin´im. Chinese (?). Is. 49. 12.
SINITE, sin´ite. Gen. 10. 17.
SION, si´on, (1) lifted up, Deut. 4. 48; (2) Greek name for Mount Zion, Matt. 21. 5.
SIPHMOTH, sif´moth, bare places (?). 1 Sam. 30. 28.
SIPPAI, sip´ai, belonging to the doorstep (?). 1 Chr. 20. 4.
SIRAH, si´rah, withdrawing. 2 Sam. 3. 26.
SIRION, sir´i-on, a coat of mail.
mount. Deut. 8. 9; Ps. 29. 6.
SISAMAI, sis´a-mai, fragrant (?). 1 Chr. 2. 40.
SISERA, si´ser-ah, binding in chains (?). Judg. 4. 2, 21; 5. 24; 1 Sam. 12. 9; Ps. 83. 9.
SITNAH, sit´nah, contention. Gen. 26. 21.
SIVAN, si´van, bright. Esth. 8. 9.
SMYRNA, smir´nah, myrrh. Rev. 1. 11.
So, Hebrew form of Egyptian word Sevech. 2 Kin. 17. 4.
SOCHO, so´ko, same as SHOCHO. 1 Chr. 4. 18.
SOCHOH, same as SHOCHOH. 1 Kin. 4. 10.
SOCOH, same as SHOCO. Josh. 15. 35.
SODI, so´di, an acquaintance. Num. 13. 10.
SODOM, sod´om, burning. Gen. 10. 19.
its iniquity and destruction. Gen. 13. 13; 18. 20; 19. 4–24; Deut. 23. 17; 1 Kin. 14. 24.
Lot's deliverance from. Gen. 19.
a warning. Deut. 29. 23; 32. 32; Is. 1. 9; 13. 19; Lam. 4. 6; Matt. 10. 15; Luke 17. 29; Jude 7; Rev. 11. 8.
SODOMA, sod´om-ah, Greek form of the preceding. Rom. 9. 29.
SODOMITES, sod´om-ites, persons who were as wicked as the men of Sodom. 1 Kin. 15. 12.
SOLOMON, sol´om-on, peaceable. 2 Sam. 5. 14.
king of Israel. 2 Sam. 12. 24; 1 Kin. 1; 2. 24; 1 Chr. 28. 9; 29.
asks of God wisdom. 1 Kin. 3. 5 (4. 29); 2 Chr. 1. 7.
the wise judgment of. 1 Kin. 3. 16.
his league with Hiram for building the temple. 1 Kin. 5; 2 Chr. 2.
builds the temple (2 Sam. 7. 12; 1 Chr. 17. 11); 1 Kin. 6; 7; 2 Chr. 3—5; the dedication, 1 Kin. 8; 2 Chr. 6.
God's covenant with. 1 Kin. 9; 2 Chr. 7. 12.
the queen of Sheba visits. 1 Kin. 10; 2 Chr. 9; Matt. 6. 29; 12. 42.
David's prayer for. Ps. 72.
his idolatry, rebuke, and death. 1 Kin. 11. 1, 9, 14, 31, 41; 2 Chr. 9. 29; Neh. 13. 26.
his Proverbs and Canticles. Prov. 1. 1; Eccles. 1. 1; Cant. 1. 1.
SON of GOD. *See* CHRIST.
—— of MAN. *See* CHRIST.
SOPATER, so´pa-ter. Acts 20. 4.
SOPHERETH, so-fer´eth, scribe. Ezra 2. 55.
SOREK, so´rek, choice vine. Judg. 16. 4.
SOSIPATER, so-si´pat-er. Rom. 16. 21.
SOSTHENES, sos´then-ees. Acts 18. 17.
SOTAI, so´tai, deviator. Ezra 2. 55.
SPAIN. Rom. 15. 24.
STACHYS, sta´kis, an ear of corn. Rom. 16. 9.'
STEPHANAS, ste´fan-as, crowned. 1 Cor. 1. 16.
STEPHEN, ste´ven, English form of Stephanas.
deacon and protomartyr. Acts 6. 5, 8; 7. 58.
STOICKS, sto´ics, philosophers whose founder taught in a famous porch or Stoa. Acts 17. 18.
SUAH, soo´ah, sweepings. 1 Chr. 7. 36.
SUCCOTH, sook´oth, booths.
(Canaan). Gen. 33. 17; Josh. 13. 27; 1 Kin. 7. 46; Ps. 60. 6.
punished by Gideon. Judg. 8. 5, 16.
—— (in Egypt). Ex. 12. 37; 13. 20.
SUCCOTH-BENOTH, suc-coth´be-noth. 2 Kin. 17. 30.
SUCHATHITES, sook´ath-ites. 1 Chr. 2. 55.
SUKKIIMS, sook´i-ims, nomads. 2 Chr. 12. 3.
SUR, soor. 2 Kin. 11. 6.
SUSANCHITES, soo´sank-ites, inhabitants of Susa or Susinak. Ezra. 4. 9.
SUSANNA, su-san´ah, lily. Luke 8. 3.
SUSI, soo´si, horseman. Num. 13. 11.
SYCHAR, si´kar, drunken (?). John 4. 5.
SYCHEM, si´kem, Greek form of Shechem. Acts 7. 16.
SYENE, si-e´ne, opening. Ezek. 29. 10.
SYNTYCHE, sin´ty-kee, fortunate. Phil. 4. 2.
SYRACUSE, si´ra-kuse. Acts 28. 12.
SYRIA, sir´yah. Judg. 10. 6.
SYRIAN, sir´yan, inhabitant of Syria. Gen. 25. 20.
SYRIANS, sir´yans. Gen. 25. 20; Deut. 26. 5.
subdued by David. 2 Sam. 8; 10.
contend with Israel. 1 Kin. 10. 29; 11. 25; 20; 22; 2 Kin. 6. 24; 7; 8. 13; 13. 7; 16. 6; 2 Chr. 18.
employed to punish Joash. 2 Chr. 24. 23. *See* 2 Chr. 28. 23; Is. 7. 2; Ezek. 27. 16; Hos. 12. 12; Amos 1. 5.
gospel preached to. Matt. 4. 24; Acts 15. 23; 18. 18; Gal. 1. 21.
SYROPHENICIAN, si´ro-fee-nish´yan, Phenician living in Syria. Mark 7. 26.

TAANACH, ta´a-nak, castle (?). Josh. 12. 21.
TAANATH-SHILOH, ta´a-nath-shi´lo, fig-tree of Shiloh (?). Josh. 16. 6.
TABBAOTH, tab´a-oth, rings. Ezra 2. 43.
TABBATH, tab´ath, pleasantness. Judg. 7. 22.
TABEAL, tab´e-al, God is good. Is. 7. 6.
TABEEL, tab´e-el, another way of writing Tabeal. Ezra 4. 7.
TABERAH, tab-er´ah, burning. Num. 11. 3.
TABITHA, tab´ith-ah, gazelle. Acts 9. 36.
TABOR, ta´bor, height. Josh. 19. 22.
(mount). Judg. 4. 14. *See* Judg. 8. 18; 1 Sam. 10. 3; Ps. 89. 12; Jer. 46. 18; Hos. 5. 1.
TABRIMON, tab´rim-on, Rimmon is good. 1 Kin. 15. 18.
TACHMONITE, tak´mon-ite, same as HACHMONITE (?). 2 Sam. 23. 8.
TADMOR, tad´mor, city of palms (?).
(Palmyra), built by Solomon. 1 Kin. 9. 18.
TAHAN, ta´han, camp. Num. 26. 35.
TAHANITES, ta´han-ites, descendants of Tahan. Num. 26. 35.
TAHAPANES, ta´ha-pan´es, head of the land. Jer. 2. 16.
TAHPANHES, same as preceding. Jer. 43. 7.
TAHPENES, tah´pen-es. 1 Kin. 11. 19.
TAHATH, ta´hath, substitute. 1 Chr. 6. 24.
TAHREA, tah-re´ah, cunning (?). 1 Chr. 9. 41.
TAHTIM-HODSHI, tah´tim-hod´shi, nether land newly inhabited (?). 2 Sam. 24. 6.
TALITHA, ta-li´tha, girl. Mark 5. 41.
TALMAI, tal´mai, abounding in furrows. Num. 13. 22.
TALMON, tal´mon, oppressed. 1 Chr. 9. 17.

TAMAH, ta´mah, joy. Neh. 7. 55.
TAMAR, ta´mar, a palm tree. Gen. 38. 6.
TAMMUZ, tam´ooz, son of life (?).
 women weeping for. Ezek. 8. 14.
TANACH, ta´nak, same as TAANACH. Josh. 21. 25.
TANHUMETH, tan-hoom´eth, consolation. 2 Kin. 25. 23.
TAPHATH, ta´fath, a drop (?). 1 Kin. 4. 11.
TAPPUAH, tap-oo´ah, apple. 1 Chr. 2. 43.
TARAH, ta´rah, station. Num. 33. 27.
TARALAH, ta´ra-lah, reeling (?). Josh. 18. 27.
TAREA, ta-re´ah, same as TAHREA. 1 Chr. 8. 35.
TARPELITES, tar´pel-ites, people of Tarpel. Ezra 4. 9.
TARSHISH, tar´shish. Gen. 10. 4; 1 Kin. 10. 22; 2 Chr. 9. 21; 20. 36; Jer. 10. 9; Ezek. 27. 12; 38. 13.
 Jonah going there. Jonah 1. 3.
 prophecies concerning. Ps. 48. 7; 72. 10; Is. 2. 16; 23; 60. 9; 66. 19.
TARSUS, tar´sus, city of the apostle Paul. Acts 9. 11; 11. 25; 21. 39.
TARTAK, tar´tak. 2 Kin. 17. 31.
TARTAN, tar´tan, military chief. 2 Kin. 18. 17.
TATNAI, tat´nai, gift (?).
 and Shethar-boznai hinder the rebuilding of the temple. Ezra 5. 3; 6. 13.
TEBAH, te´bah, slaughter. Gen. 22. 24.
TEBALIAH, te-bal-i´ah, whom Jehovah has immersed. 1 Chr. 26. 11.
TEBETH, te´beth. Esth. 2. 16.
TEHAPHNEHES, te-haph´ne-hes, same as TAHAPANES. Ezek. 30. 18.
TEHINNAH, te-hin´ah, cry for mercy. 1 Chr. 4. 12.
TEKEL, te´kel, weighed. Dan. 5. 25.
TEKOA, te-ko´ah, sound of trumpet (1 Chr. 2. 24; 4. 5).
 widow of. 2 Sam. 14 (Jer. 6. 1).
TEKOAH, te-ko´ah, same as TEKOA. 2 Sam. 14. 2.
TEKOITE, te-ko´ite, inhabitant of Tekoah. 2 Sam. 23. 26.
TEL-ABIB, tel-a´bib, hill of ears of corn. Ezek. 3. 15.
TELAH, te´lah. 1 Chr. 7. 25.
TELAIM, te-la´im, lambs. 1 Sam. 15. 4.
TELASSAR, tel´as´ar, Assyrian hill. Is. 37. 12.
TELEM, te´lem, oppression. Ezra 10. 24.
TEL-HARESHA, tel-har´e-shah, forest-hill. Neh. 7. 61.
TEL-HARSA, tel-har´sah, same as preceding. Ezra 2. 59.
TEL-MELAH, tel-me´lah, salt-hill. Ezra 2. 59.
TEMA, te´mah, a desert. Gen. 25. 15; Job 6. 19; Is. 21. 14; Jer. 25. 23.
TEMAN, te´man, on the right hand. Gen. 36. 11; Jer. 49. 7, 20; Ezek. 25. 13; Amos 1. 12; Obad. 9; Hab. 3. 3.
TEMANI, te´man-i, descendants of Teman. Gen. 36. 34.
TEMANITE, te´man-ite, same as preceding. Job 2. 11.
TEMENI, te´men-i, same as TEMANI. 1 Chr. 4. 6.
TERAH, te´rah, a station (?). Gen. 11. 24.
TERAPHIM, ter´af-im, nourishers.
 of Laban. Gen. 31. 34.
 of Micah. Judg. 17. 5; 18. 14.
 of Michal. 1 Sam. 19. 13.
TERESH, te´resh, severe (?). Esth. 2. 21.
TERTIUS, ter´shus, the third. Rom. 16. 22.
TERTULLUS, ter-tul´us (*dim.* of TERTIUS). Acts 24. 1.
TETRARCH, tet´rark, ruler of a fourth part of a country. Matt. 14. 1.
THADDÆUS, thad-e´us, Greek form of Theudas. Matt. 10. 3.
THAHASH, tha´hash, seal (?). Gen. 22. 24.
THAMAH, tha´mah, laughter. Ezra 2. 53.
THAMAR, tha´mar, Greek equivalent of Tamar. Matt. 1. 3.
THARA, tha´rah, Greek form of Terah. Luke 3. 34.
THARSHISH, thar´shish, same as TARSHISH. 1 Kin. 10. 22.
THEBEZ, the´bez, brightness.
 Abimelech wounded at. Judg. 9. 50.
THELASAR, thel´as´ar, same as TELASSAR. 2 Kin. 19. 12.
THEOPHILUS, the-o´fil-us, loved of God. Luke 1. 3.
THESSALONICA, thes´al-on-i´kah.
 Paul at. Acts 17.
 church there instructed. 1 & 2 Thess.
THEUDAS, thoo´das, praise (?). Acts 5. 36.
THIMNATHAH, thim-nah´thah, portion. Josh. 19. 43.
THOMAS, tom´as, a twin.
 APOSTLE. Matt. 10. 3; Mark 3. 18; Luke 6. 15; Acts 1. 13.
 his zeal. John 11. 16.
 his unbelief and confession. John 20. 24.
THUMMIM, thoom´im, truth (?).
 on high priest's breastplate. Ex. 28. 30; Lev. 8. 8; Deut. 33. 8; Ezra 2. 63; Neh. 7. 65.
THYATIRA, thi´at-i´rah (Acts 16. 14).
 angel of. Rev. 1. 11; 2. 18.
TIBERIAS, ti-be´ri-as, a place named after Tiberius. John 6. 1.
TIBERIUS, ti-be´ri-us. Luke 3. 1.
TIBHATH, tib´hath, butchery. 1 Chr. 18. 8.
TIBNI, tib´ni, made of straw (?). 1 Kin. 16. 21.
TIDAL, ti´dal, dread. Gen. 14. 1.
TIGLATH-PILESER, tig´lath-pil-e´zer, the son of the temple of Sarra is a ground of confidence (?). (Tilgath-pilneser, 1 Chr. 5. 6, 26), 2 Kin. 15. 29; 16. 7; 2 Chr. 28. 20.
TIKVAH, tik´vah, expectation. 2 Kin. 22. 14.
TIKVATH, tik´vath, same as TIKVAH. 2 Chr. 34. 22.
TILGATH-PILNESER, til´gath-pil-ne´ser, same as TIGLATH-PILESER. 1 Chr. 5. 6.
TILON, ti´lon, gift (?). 1 Chr. 4. 20.
TIMÆUS, ti-me´us, polluted (?). Mark 10. 46.
TIMNA, tim´nah, unapproachable. Gen. 36. 12.
TIMNAH, tim´nah, a portion. Josh. 15. 10.
TIMNATH, tim´nath, same as TIMNAH. Gen. 38. 12.
TIMNATH-HERES, tim´nath-he´res, portion of the sun. Judg. 2. 9.
TIMNATH-SERAH, tim´nath-se´rah, portion of the remainder. Josh. 19. 50.
 Joshua buried there. Josh. 24. 30.
TIMNITE, tim´nite, a man of Timna. Judg. 15. 6.
TIMON, ti´mon. Acts 6. 5.
TIMOTHEUS, ti-mo´the-us, honouring God. Acts 16. 1.
TIMOTHY, tim´oth-y, English form of the above.
 accompanies Paul. Acts 16. 3; 17. 14, 15; Rom. 16. 21; 2 Cor. 1. 1, 19.
 commended. 1 Cor. 16. 10; Phil. 2. 19.
 instructed in letters by Paul. 1 & 2 Tim.
TIPHSAH, tif´sah, passage. 1 Kin. 4. 24.
TIRAS, ti´ras, crushing (?). Gen. 10. 2.
TIRATHITES, ti´rath-ites. 1 Chr. 2. 55.
TIRHAKAH, tir-hah´kah, distance (?).
 Sennacherib's war with. 2 Kin. 19. 9.
TIRHANAH, tir´han-ah, murmuring (?). 1 Chr. 2. 48.
TIRIA, tir´i-ah, fear. 1 Chr. 4. 16.
TIRSHATHA, tir-sha´thah, the feared (?). Ezra 2. 63; Neh. 7. 70.
TIRZAH, tir´zah, pleasantness. Num. 26. 33; 1 Kin. 14. 17; 15. 21; 16. 8, 15; 2 Kin. 15. 16; Cant. 6. 4 (Josh. 12. 24).
TISHBITE, tish´bite, inhabitant of Tishbe. 1 Kin. 17. 1.
TITUS, ti´tus, protected. Gal. 2. 3.
 Paul's love for. 2 Cor. 2. 13; 7. 6, 13.
 instructed by Paul. Tit. 1—3.
TIZITE, ti´zite. 1 Chr. 11. 45.
TOAH, to´ah, low. 1 Chr. 6. 34.
TOB, tobe, good. Judg. 11. 3.
TOB-ADONIJAH, tob´a-do-ni´jah, good is my lord Jehovah. 2 Chr. 17. 8.
TOBIAH, tob-i´ah, Jehovah is good. Ezra 2. 60.
 the Ammonite, vexes the Jews. Neh. 4. 3; 6. 1, 12, 14; 13. 4.
TOBIJAH, tob-i´jah, same as TOBIAH. 2 Chr. 17. 8.
TOCHEN, to´ken, a measure. 1 Chr. 4. 32.
TOGARMAH, to-gar´mah, rugged. Gen. 10. 3.
TOHU, to´hoo, same as TOAH. 1 Sam. 1. 1.
TOI, to´i, wanderer. 2 Sam. 8. 9.

TOLA, to-lah, worm. Gen. 46. 13.
TOLAD, to-lad, birth. 1 Chr. 4. 20.
TOLAITES, to-la-ites, descendants of Tola. Num. 26. 23.
TOPHEL, to-fel, lime. Deut. 1. 1.
TOPHET, to-fet, burning. Is. 30. 33.
TOPHETH, to-feth, same as TOPHET. 2 Kin. 23. 10. *See* MOLOCH.
TORMAH, torm-ah, privily. Judg. 9. 31.
TOU, to-oo, older form of Toi. 1 Chr. 18. 9.
TRACHONITIS, tra-ko-ni-tis, rugged. Luke 3. 1.
TROAS, tro-as, so called from Tros.
visited by Paul. Acts 16. 8; 20. 5; 2 Cor. 2. 12; 2 Tim. 4. 13.
TROGYLLIUM, tro-gil-yum. Acts 20. 15.
TROPHIMUS, trof-im-us, master of the house (?).
companion of Paul. Acts 20. 4; 21. 29; 2 Tim. 4. 20.
TRYPHENA, tri-fe-nah, delicate. Rom. 16. 12.
TRYPHOSA, tri-fo-sah, delicate. Rom. 16. 12.
TUBAL, too-bal, production (?). Gen. 10. 2; Is. 66. 19; Ezek. 27. 13; 32. 26; 38; 39.
TUBAL-CAIN, too-bal-kane', producer of weapons (?). Gen. 4. 22.
TYCHICUS, tik-ik-us, fortuitous.
companion of Paul. Acts 20. 4; 2 Tim. 4. 12; Tit. 3. 12.
commended. Eph. 6. 21; Col. 4. 7.
TYRANNUS, ti-ran-us, tyrant. Acts 19. 9.
TYRE, tire, rock. Josh. 19. 29.
its wealth. Ezek. 27.
fall. Ezek. 26. 7.
Christ visits coasts of. Matt. 15. 21.
Paul lands at. Acts 21. 3.
TYRUS, ti-rus, Latin name of Tyre. Jer. 25. 22.

UCAL, oo-kal, I shall prevail. Prov. 30. 1.
UEL, oo-el, will of God (?). Ezra 10. 34.
ULAI, oo-lai. Dan. 8. 2.
ULAM, oo-lam, foremost. 1 Chr. 7. 16.
ULLA, ool-ah, yoke. 1 Chr. 7. 39.
UMMAH, oom-ah, community. Josh. 19. 30.
UNNI, oon-i, depressed. 1 Chr. 15. 18.
UPHARSIN, oo-far-sin, and dividers. Dan. 5. 25.
UPHAZ, oo-faz, gold of. Jer. 10. 9; Dan. 10. 5.
UR, oor, light.
land of. Gen. 11. 28; 15. 7.
URBANE, ur-ban, pleasant. Rom. 16. 9.
URI, oo-ri, fiery. Ex. 31. 2.
URIAH, oo-ri-ah, light of Jehovah.
the HITTITE. 2 Sam. 11; 1 Kin. 15. 5; Matt. 1. 6.
URIAS, oo-ri-as, Greek form of Uriah. Matt. 1. 6.
URIEL, oo-ri-el, light of God. 1 Chr. 6. 24.
URIJAH, oo-ri-jah, same as URIAH.
(priest). 2 Kin. 16. 10, 16.
—— (prophet). Jer. 26. 20.
URIM, oo-rim, light. Ex. 28. 30. *See* THUMMIM.
UTHAI, oo-thai, helpful. 1 Chr. 9. 4.
UZ, fertile. Gen. 10. 23.
UZAI, oo-zai, hoped for (?). Neh. 3. 25.
UZAL, ooz-al, wanderer. Gen. 10. 27.
UZZA, ooz-ah, strength. 2 Kin. 21. 18.
UZZAH, another form of Uzza.
his trespass. 2 Sam. 6. 3.
his death. 1 Chr. 13. 7.
UZZEN-SHERAH, ooz-en-she-rah. 1 Chr. 7. 24.
UZZI, ooz-i, shortened form of Uzziah. 1 Chr. 6. 5.
UZZIA, ooz-i-ah, another form of Uzziah. 1 Chr. 11. 44.
UZZIAH, ooz-i-ah, might of Jehovah. 2 Kin. 15. 13. *See* AZARIAH.
UZZIEL, ooz-i-el, power of God. Ex. 6. 18.
UZZIELITES, ooz-i-el-ites, descendants of Uzziel. Num. 3. 27.

VAJEZATHA, va-je-za-thah, strong as the wind (?). Esth. 9. 9.
VANIAH, va-ni-ah, distress (?). Ezra 10. 36.
VASHNI, vash-ni, strong (?); but perhaps not a proper name. 1 Chr. 6. 28.
VASHTI, vash-ti, beautiful. Esth. 1. 9.
VOPHSI, vof-si, expansion (?). Num. 13. 14.

ZAANAIM, za-an-a-im, wanderings (?). Judg. 4. 11.
ZAANAN, za-a-nan, place of flocks. Mic. 1. 11.
ZAANANNIM, za-a-nan-im, same as ZAANAIM. Josh. 19. 33.
ZAAVAN, za-av-an, disturbed. Gen. 36. 27.
ZABAD, za-bad, gift. 1 Chr. 2. 36.
ZABBAI, zab-ai. Ezra 10. 28.
ZABBUD, zab-ood, given. Ezra 8. 14.
ZABDI, zab-di, the gift of Jehovah. Josh. 7. 1.
ZABDIEL, zab-di-el, the gift of God. 1 Chr. 27. 2.
ZABUD, za-bood, same as ZABBUD. 1 Kin. 4. 5.
ZABULON, Greek form of Zebulun. Matt. 4. 13.
ZACCAI, zak-ai, pure. Ezra 2. 9.
ZACCHÆUS, zak-e-us, Greek form of Zaccai. Luke 19. 2.
ZACCHUR, zak-oor, mindful. 1 Chr. 4. 26.
ZACCUR, zak-oor, same as preceding. Num. 13. 4.
ZACHARIAH, zak-ar-i-ah, whom Jehovah remembers.
last king of Israel of Jehu's race, as foretold by the word of the Lord, begins to reign. 2 Kin. 14. 29.
smitten by Shallum, who succeeds him. 2 Kin. 15. 10.
ZACHARIAS, zak-ar-i-as, Greek form of preceding.
father of John the Baptist, with Elisabeth his wife, accounted righteous before God. Luke 1. 6.
is promised a son. Luke 1. 13.
doubting, is stricken with dumbness. Luke 1. 18, 22.
his recovery and song. Luke 1. 64, 68.
—— 'son of Barachias', slain 'between the temple and the altar'. Matt. 23. 35; Luke 11. 51. *See* ZECHARIAH.
ZACHER, za-ker, memorial. 1 Chr. 8. 31.
ZADOK, za-dok, just.
priest. 2 Sam. 8. 17; 15. 24; 20. 25.
anoints Solomon king. 1 Kin. 1. 39.
ZAHAM, za-ham, loathing. 2 Chr. 11. 19.
ZAIR, za-ir, small. 2 Kin. 8. 21.
ZALAPH, za-laf, wound (?). Neh. 3. 30.
ZALMON, zal-mon, shady. 2 Sam. 23. 28.
ZALMONAH, zal-mo-nah, same as preceding. Num. 33. 41.
ZALMUNNA, zal-moon-ah, shelter denied. Judg. 8. 5.
ZAMZUMMIMS, zam-zoom-ims, giant race, destroyed by the Ammonites. Deut. 2. 20, 21.
ZANOAH, za-no-ah, marsh. Josh. 15. 34.
ZAPHNATH-PAANEAH, zaf-nath-pa-a-ne-ah, prince of the life of the age. Gen. 41. 45.
ZAPHON, za-fon, north. Josh. 13. 27.
ZARA, za-rah, Greek form of Zarah. Matt. 1. 3.
ZARAH, za-rah, sunrise (?). Gen. 38. 30.
ZAREAH, za-re-ah, hornet. Neh. 11. 29.
ZAREATHITES, za-re-ath-ites, inhabitants of Zareah. 1 Chr. 2. 53.
ZARED, za-red, exuberant growth. Num. 21. 12.
ZAREPHATH, zar-ef-ath, workshop for refining metals.
(Sarepta), Elijah there. 1 Kin. 17. 10. *See* ELIJAH.
ZARETAN, za-ret-an, same as ZARTHAN. Josh. 3. 16.
ZARETH-SHAHAR, za-reth-sha-har, the splendour of the morning. Josh. 13. 19.
ZARHITES, zar-hites, persons descended from Zerah. Num. 26. 13.
ZARTANAH, zar-tah-nah. 1 Kin. 4. 12.
ZARTHAN, zar-than, same as ZARETAN. 1 Kin. 7. 46.
ZATTHU, zat-thoo, same as ZATTU. Neh. 10. 14.
ZATTU, zat-oo, irascible (?). Ezra 2. 8.
ZAVAN, za-van, same as ZAAVAN. 1 Chr. 1. 42.
ZAZA, za-zah. 1 Chr. 2. 33.
ZEBADIAH, zeb-ad-i-ah, full form of ZABDI. 1 Chr. 8. 15.
ZEBAH, ze-bah, sacrifice.
and Zalmunna. Judg. 8. 5, 21; Ps. 83. 11.
ZEBAIM, ze-ba-im, same as ZEBOIM. Ezra 2. 57.
ZEBEDEE, zeb-ed-ee, Greek form of Zebadiah. Matt. 4. 21; Mark 1. 20.

ZEBINA, ze-bi'-nah, bought. Ezra 10. 43.
ZEBOIM, ze-bo'-im, gazelles. Gen. 10. 19; 14. 2; 19. 25; Deut. 29. 23; Hos. 11. 8.
ZEBUDAH, ze-boo'-dah, given. 2 Kin. 23. 36.
ZEBUL, ze'-bool, habitation. Judg. 9. 28.
ZEBULONITE, ze-bool'-on-ite, a member of the tribe of Zebulun. Judg. 12. 11.
ZEBULUN, ze-bool'-un. Gen. 30. 20; 35. 23; 49. 13; Num. 1. 30; 26. 26; Deut. 33. 13; Josh. 19. 10; Judg. 4. 6; 5. 14, 18; 6. 35; 2 Chr. 30. 11, 18; Ps. 68. 27; Ezek. 48. 26; Rev. 7. 8.
Christ preaches in the land of (Is. 9. 1); Matt. 4. 13.
ZEBULUNITES, ze-bool'-un-ites, a less correct way of spelling Zebulonites. Num. 26. 27.
ZECHARIAH, zek'-ar-i'-ah, a better way of spelling Zachariah.
son of Jehoiada, stoned in the court of the Lord's house. 2 Chr. 24. 20, 21.
—— son of Jeberechiah. Is. 8. 2.
—— the prophet, his exhortations to repentance, his visions and predictions. Zech. 1—14.
ZEDAD, ze'-dad, hunting (?). Num. 34. 8.
ZEDEKIAH, zed'-ek-i'-ah, justice of Jehovah.
false prophet. 1 Kin. 22. 11; 2 Chr. 18. 10, 23.
—— another. Jer. 29. 22.
—— (Mattaniah), king of Judah. 2 Kin. 24. 17; 25; 2 Chr. 36. 10, 11; Jer. 37; 38; 39; 52.
ZEEB, ze'-eb, wolf. Judg. 7. 25.
ZELAH, ze'-lah, side. Josh. 18. 28.
ZELEK, ze'-lek, fissure. 2 Sam. 23. 37.
ZELOPHEHAD, ze-lo'-fe-had, fracture. Num. 26. 33.
ZELOTES, ze-lo'-tees, Greek equivalent of Canaanite, an emulator. Luke 6. 15.
ZELZAH, zel'-zah, shade in the heat. 1 Sam. 10. 2.
ZEMARAIM, zem'-ar-a'-im, two fleeces. Josh. 18. 22.
ZEMARITE, zem'-ar-ite. Gen. 10. 18.
ZEMIRA, ze-mi'-rah. 1 Chr. 7. 8.
ZENAN, ze'-nan, same as ZAANAN. Josh. 15. 37.
ZENAS, ze'-nas, contraction of Zenodorus. Tit. 3. 13.
ZEPHANIAH, zef'-an-i'-ah, whom Jehovah hid. 2 Kin. 25. 18.
priest. Jer. 29. 25; 37. 3.
—— prophet. Zeph. 1; 2; 3.
ZEPHATH, ze'-fath, watch-tower (?). Judg. 1. 17.
ZEPHATHAH, ze'-fath-ah. 2 Chr. 14. 10.
ZEPHI, ze'-fi, same as ZEPHATH. 1 Chr. 1. 36.
ZEPHO, ze'-fo, older form of Zephi. Gen. 36. 11.
ZEPHON, ze'-fon, a looking out. Num. 26. 15.
ZEPHONITES, ze'-fon-ites, descendants of Zephon. Num. 26. 15.
ZER, flint (?). Josh. 19. 35.
ZERAH, ze'-rah, dawn. 2 Chr. 14. 9; 16. 8.
ZERAHIAH, zer'-ah-i'-ah, whom Jehovah caused to rise. 1 Chr. 6. 6.
ZERED, ze'-red, same as ZARED. Deut. 2. 13.
ZEREDA, ze-re'-dah, cool. 1 Kin. 11. 26.
ZEREDATHAH, ze-re-dah'-thah, same as preceding. 2 Chr. 4. 17.
ZERERATH, ze-re'-rath. Judg. 7. 22.
ZERESH, ze'-resh, gold. Esth. 5. 10.
ZERETH, ze'-reth, gold (?). 1 Chr. 4. 7.
ZERI, ze'-ri, same as IZRI. 1 Chr. 25. 3.
ZEROR, ze'-ror, bundle. 1 Sam. 9. 1.
ZERUAH, ze-roo'-ah, leprous. 1 Kin. 11. 26.
ZERUBBABEL, ze-roob'-ab-el, scattered in Babylon. (Zorobabel), prince of Judah. Ezra 2. 2.
restores the worship of God. Ezra 3. 1; Neh. 12. 47; Hag. 1. 1, 14; 2. 1; Zech. 4. 6.
ZERUIAH, ze-roo'-yah. 1 Sam. 26. 6.
ZETHAM, ze'-tham, olive. 1 Chr. 23. 8.
ZETHAN, ze'-than, same as ZETHAM. 1 Chr. 7. 10.
ZETHAR, ze'-thar. Esth. 1. 10.
ZIA, zi'-ah, motion. 1 Chr. 5. 13.
ZIBA, zi'-bah, planter. 2 Sam. 9. 2.
ZIBEON, zib'-e-on, dyed. Gen. 36. 2.
ZIBIA, zib'-i-ah, gazelle (?). 1 Chr. 8. 9.
ZIBIAH, zib'-i-ah, same as ZIBIA. 2 Kin. 12. 1.
ZICHRI, zik'-ri, famous. 2 Chr. 23. 1; 28.
ZIDDIM, zid'-im, sides. Josh. 19. 35.
ZIDKIJAH, zid-ki'-jah, justice of Jehovah. Neh. 10. 1.
ZIDON, zi'-don, fishing. Gen. 49. 13; Josh. 11. 8; Judg. 10. 6; 18. 7; 1 Kin. 11. 1; Ezra 3. 7; Luke 4. 26; Acts 12. 20.
prophecies concerning. Is. 23; Jer. 25. 22; 27. 3; 47. 4; Ezek. 27. 8; 28. 21; 32. 30; Joel 3. 4; Zech. 9. 2.
ZIDONIANS, zi-done'-yans, inhabitants of Zidon. Judg. 10. 12; 18. 7; 1 Kin. 11. 1.
ZIF, blossom. 1 Kin. 6. 1.
ZIHA, zi'-hah, drought. Ezra 2. 43.
ZIKLAG, zik'-lag. Josh. 15. 31; 1 Sam. 27. 6; 30. 1; 2 Sam. 1. 1; 1 Chr. 12. 1.
ZILLAH, zil'-ah, shade. Gen. 4. 19.
ZILPAH, zil'-pah, dropping. Gen. 29. 24.
ZILTHAI, zil'-thai, shady. 1 Chr. 8. 20.
ZIMMAH, zim'-ah, planning. 1 Chr. 6. 20.
ZIMRAN, zim'-ran, celebrated. Gen. 25. 2.
ZIMRI, zim'-ri, same as ZIMRAN. 1 Kin. 16. 9.
ZIN, thorn.
wilderness of. Num. 13. 21; Josh. 15. 1.
ZINA, zi'-nah, abundance (?). 1 Chr. 23. 10.
ZION, zi'-on, sunny.
(mount). 2 Sam. 5. 7; 1 Kin. 8. 1; Rom. 11. 26; Heb. 12. 22; Rev. 14. 1.
ZIOR, zi'-or, smallness. Josh. 15. 54.
ZIPH, zif, flowing. 1 Chr. 4. 16.
ZIPHAH, zi'-fah, feminine of ZIPH. 1 Chr. 4. 16.
ZIPHIMS, zif'-ims, inhabitants of Ziph. Ps. 54, title.
ZIPHITES, zif'-ites, same as ZIPHIMS. 1 Sam. 23. 19.
ZIPHION, zif'-yon, same as ZEPHON. Gen. 46. 16.
ZIPHRON, zif'-ron, sweet smell. Num. 34. 9.
ZIPPOR, zip'-or, bird. Num. 22. 2.
ZIPPORAH, zip-or'-ah, *fem.* of ZIPPOR. Ex. 2. 21; 4. 20.
ZITHRI, zith'-ri, protection of Jehovah (?). Ex. 6. 22.
ZIZ, a flower. 2 Chr. 20. 16.
ZIZA, zi'-zah, abundance. 1 Chr. 4. 37.
ZIZAH, fulness. 1 Chr. 23. 11.
ZOAN, zo'-an, low region. Num. 13. 22; Ps. 78. 12.
ZOAR, zo'-ar, smallness. Gen. 13. 10; 14. 2; 19. 22 (Is. 15. 5); Deut. 34. 3; Jer. 48. 34.
ZOBA, zo'-bah, a plantation. 2 Sam. 10. 6.
ZOBAH, same as preceding.
kings of, subdued. 1 Sam. 14. 47; 2 Sam. 8. 3; 1 Kin. 11. 23.
ZOBEBAH, zo-be'-bah, walking slowly. 1 Chr. 4. 8.
ZOHAR, zo'-har, light. Gen. 23. 8.
ZOHELETH, zo-he'-leth, serpent stone. 1 Kin. 1. 9.
ZOHETH, zo'-heth, strong (?). 1 Chr. 4. 20.
ZOPHAH, zo'-fah, a cruse (?). 1 Chr. 7. 35.
ZOPHAI, zo'-phai, honeycomb. 1 Chr. 6. 26.
ZOPHAR, zo'-far, chatterer. Job. 2. 11; 11; 20; 42. 9.
ZOPHIM, zo'-fim, watchers. Num. 23. 14.
ZORAH, zo'-rah, a place of hornets.
city of Samson. Josh. 19. 41; Judg. 13. 2, 25; 16. 31.
ZORATHITES, zo'-rath-ites, people of Zorah. 1 Chr. 4. 2.
ZOREAH, zo'-re-ah, same as ZORAH. Josh. 15. 33.
ZORITES, zor'-ites, same as ZORATHITES. 1 Chr. 2. 54.
ZOROBABEL, zo-rob'-ab-el, Greek form of Zerubbabel. Matt. 1. 12.
ZUAR, zoo'-ar, same as ZOAR. Num. 1. 8.
ZUPH, zoof, flag, sedge. 1 Sam. 1. 1.
ZUR, zoor, rock. Num. 25. 15.
ZURIEL, zoor'-i-el, God is the Rock. Num. 3. 35.
ZURISHADDAI, zoor'-i-shad'-ai, whose Almighty is the Rock. Num. 1. 6.
ZUZIMS, zooz'-ims, giants. Gen. 14. 5.

OMEGA, the end. Rev. 1. 8, 11; 21. 6; 22. 13.

SUBJECT-INDEX
TO THE HOLY SCRIPTURES

CHRIST (HIS TEACHING)—*cont.*
prophesies destruction of Jerusalem, and the last times, Matt. 24; Mark 13; Luke 13. 34; 17. 20; 19. 41; 21.
preaches daily in the temple, Luke 19. 47.
His invitation to the weary and heavy laden, Matt. 11. 23.
His discourses on suffering for the Gospel's sake, Luke 14. 26 (Matt. 10. 37).
on marriage, Matt. 19; Mark 10.
riches, Matt. 19. 16; Mark 10. 17; Luke 12. 13; 18. 18.
on paying tribute, Matt. 22. 15; Mark 12. 13; Luke 20. 20.
the resurrection, Matt. 22. 23; Mark 12. 18.
the two great commandments, Matt. 22. 35; Mark 12. 28.
the Son of David, Matt. 22. 41; Mark 12. 35; Luke 20. 41.
the widow's mite, Mark 12. 41; Luke 21. 1.
watchfulness, Matt. 24. 42; Mark 13. 33; Luke 21. 34; 12. 35.
the last judgment, Matt. 25. 31.
SERMON ON THE MOUNT:—who are the blessed, Matt. 5. 1; salt of the earth, 5. 13; light of the world, 5. 14; the righteousness of scribes and Pharisees, 5. 20; anger with a brother (Raca), 5. 22; thou fool, 5. 22; reconciliation, 5. 24; adultery, 5. 27; right hand and right eye, 5. 29, 30; divorce, 5. 32, 33; oaths, 5. 33; eye for an eye, 5. 38; love to neighbour and enemy, 5. 43; be perfect, 5. 48; almsgiving, 6. 1; prayer, 6. 5; no vain repetitions, 6. 7; Lord's Prayer, 6. 9; Luke 11. 2; fasting, Matt. 6. 16; treasure upon earth, 6. 19; evil eye, 6. 23; two masters, 6. 24; God and mammon, 6. 24; no thought for life, 6. 25; fowls of the air, 6. 26; taking thought, raiment, lilies of the field, 6. 27; seek kingdom of God, 6. 33; judge not, 7. 1; beam in eye, 7. 3; holy things not to be cast to dogs, 7. 6; ask, seek, find, 7. 7; Luke 11. 9; bread, stone, fish, serpent, Matt. 7. 9, 10; Luke 11. 11; strait gate, Matt. 7. 13; false prophets, 7. 15; grapes, thorns, figs, thistles, 7. 16; the good and corrupt tree, 7. 17; not to be hearers but doers, 7. 23, 24; house on rock, 7. 24; on sand, 7. 27; taught as having authority, 7. 29.
[1] Sermon to disciples and multitudes on the plain:— the blessed, Luke 6. 20, 21, 22; woe to the rich, 6. 24; to the full, 6. 25; to those men speak well of, 6. 26; love to enemies, 6. 27, 35; submission under injury, 6. 29; giving, 6. 30, 38; doing as we would be done to, 6. 31; be merciful, 6. 36; judge not, 6. 37; hearers and doers, 6. 46.
epistles to the seven churches in Asia, Rev. 1; 2; 3.
DISCOURSES:—
on faith, the centurion's, Matt. 8. 8.
to those who would follow Him, Luke 9. 23, 57.
on fasting, Matt. 9. 14; Mark 2. 18; Luke 5. 33.
on blasphemy, Matt. 12. 31; Mark 3. 28; Luke 11. 15.
who are His brethren, Matt. 12. 46; Mark 3. 31; Luke 8. 19.

—— CHARACTER OF:—
holy, Luke 1. 35; Acts 4. 27; Rev. 3. 7.
righteous, Is. 53. 11; Heb. 1. 9.
good, Matt. 19. 16.
faithful, Is. 11. 5; 1 Thess. 5. 24.
true, John 1. 14; 7. 18; 1 John 5. 20.
just, Zech. 9. 9; John 5. 30; Acts 22. 14.
guileless, Is. 53. 9; 1 Pet. 2. 22.
sinless, John 8. 46; 2 Cor. 5. 21.
spotless, 1 Pet. 1. 19.
innocent, Matt. 27. 4.
harmless, Heb. 7. 26.
resisting temptation, Matt. 4. 1–10.

[1] It is the opinion of some eminent commentators that the sermons on the mount and on the plain were one and the same.

CHRIST (CHARACTER OF)—*cont.*
obedient to God the Father, Ps. 40. 8; John 4. 34; 15. 10.
subject to His parents, Luke 2. 51.
zealous, Luke 2. 49; John 2. 17; 8. 29.
meek, Is. 53. 7; Zech. 9. 9; Matt. 11. 29.
lowly in heart, Matt. 11. 29.
merciful, Heb. 2. 17.
patient, Is. 53. 7; Matt. 27. 14.
long-suffering, 1 Tim. 1. 16.
compassionate, Is. 40. 11; Matt. 15. 32; Luke 7. 13; 19. 41.
benevolent, Matt. 4. 23, 24; 9. 35; Acts 10. 38.
loving, John 13. 1; 15. 13.
self-denying, Matt. 8. 20; 2 Cor. 8. 9.
humble, Luke 22. 27; Phil. 2. 8.
resigned, Luke 22. 42.
forgiving, Luke 23. 34.
saints to be conformed to, Rom. 8. 29.

—— COMPASSION OF:—
necessary to His priestly office, Heb. 5. 2, with verse 7.
MANIFESTED FOR THE
weary and heavy-laden, Matt. 11. 28–30.
weak in faith, Is. 40. 11; 42. 3, with Matt. 12. 20.
tempted, Heb. 2. 18.
afflicted, Luke 7. 13; John 11. 33.
diseased, Matt. 14. 14; Mark 1. 41.
poor, Mark 8. 2.
perishing sinners, Matt. 9. 36; Luke 19. 41; John 3. 16.
an encouragement to prayer, Heb. 4. 15.

—— GLORY OF:—
as divine, John 1. 1–5; Phil. 2. 6, 9, 10.
God the Son, Matt. 3. 17; Heb. 1. 6, 8.
equal to the Father, John 10. 30, 38.
the Firstborn, Col. 1. 5, 18.
the Firstbegotten, Heb. 1. 6.
Lord of lords, &c., Rev. 17. 14.
the image of God, Col. 1. 15; Heb. 1. 3.
Creator, John 1. 3; Col. 1. 16; Heb. 1. 2.
the Blessed of God, Ps. 45. 2.
Mediator, 1 Tim. 2. 5; Heb. 8. 6.
Prophet, Deut. 18. 15, 16, with Acts 3. 22.
Priest, Ps. 110. 4; Heb. 4. 15.
King, Is. 6. 1–5, with John 12. 41.
Judge, Matt. 16. 27; 25. 31, 33.
Shepherd, Is. 40. 10, 11; Ezek. 34; John 10; 11; 14.
Head of the Church, Eph. 1. 22.
the true Light, Luke 1. 78, 79; John 1. 4, 9.
the foundation of the Church, Is. 28. 16.
the Way, John 14. 6; Heb. 10. 19, 20.
the Truth, 1 John 5. 20; Rev. 3. 7.
the Life, John 11. 25; Col. 3. 4; 1 John 5. 11.
Incarnate, John 1. 14.
in His words, Luke 4. 22; John 7. 46.
His works, Matt. 13. 54; John 2. 11.
His sinless perfection, Heb. 7. 26–28.
the fulness of His grace and truth, Ps. 45. 2, with John 1. 14.
His transfiguration, Matt. 17. 2, with 2 Pet. 1. 16–18.
His exaltation, Acts 7. 55, 56; Eph. 1. 21.
celebrated by the redeemed, Rev. 5. 8–14; 7. 9–12.
revealed in the gospel, Is. 40. 5.
saints shall rejoice at the revelation of, 1 Pet. 4. 13.
saints shall behold, in heaven, John 17. 24.

—— DIVINE NATURE OF:—
as Jehovah, Col. 1. 16; Is. 6. 1–3, with John 12. 41; Is. 8. 13, 14, with 1 Pet. 2. 8; Is. 40. 3, with Matt. 3. 3; Is. 40. 11; 44. 6, with Rev. 1. 17; Is. 48. 12–16, with Rev. 22. 13; Jer. 23. 5, 6, with 1 Cor. 1. 30; Joel 2. 32, with Acts 2. 21, and 1 Cor. 1. 2; Mal. 3. 1, with Mark 1. 2, and Luke 2. 27; Heb. 13. 20; James 2. 1.
the Eternal God and Creator, Judge and Saviour, Ps. 45. 6, 7; 102. 24–27, with Heb. 1. 8, 10–12; Is. 9. 6; Eccles. 12. 14, with 1 Cor. 4. 5; Jer. 10. 10, with John 15. 20; Hos. 1. 7, with Tit. 2. 13; John 1. 1; Rom.

COUNSEL—*cont.*
danger of rejecting, 2 Chr. 25. 16; Prov. 1. 25, 26; Jer. 23. 18–22; Luke 7. 30.
of the wicked, condemned, Job. 5. 13; 10. 3; 21. 16; Ps. 1. 1: 5. 10; 33. 10; 64. 2–7; 81. 12; 106. 43; Is. 7. 5; Hos. 11. 6; Mic. 6. 16.
COURAGE, exhortations to, Num. 13. 20; Deut. 31. 6; Josh. 1. 6; 10. 25; 2 Sam. 10. 12; 2 Chr. 19. 11; Ezra 10. 4; Ps. 27. 14; 31. 24; Is. 41. 6; 1 Cor. 16. 13; Eph. 6. 10.
through faith: Abraham, Heb. 11. 8, 17. Moses, Heb. 11. 25. Israelites, Heb. 11. 29. Barak, Judg. 4. 16. Gideon, Judg. 7. 1. Jephthah, Judg. 11. 29. Samson, Judg. 16. 28. Jonathan, 1 Sam. 14. 6. Daniel, Dan. 6. 10, 23. Jonah, Jonah 3. 3. *See* BOLDNESS, CONFIDENCE.
COURSES of the Levites established by David, 1 Chr. 23; 24. *See* Luke 1. 5.
of the singers, 1 Chr. 25.
of the porters, 1 Chr. 26.
of the captains, 1 Chr. 27.
COURTESY, exhortation to, Col. 4. 6; James 3. 17; 1 Pet. 3. 8.
examples of, Acts 27. 3; 28. 7.
COVENANT of GOD:—
with Noah, Gen. 6. 18; 9. 8.
with Abraham, Gen. 15. 7, 18; 17. 2 (Luke 1. 72; Acts 3. 25; Gal. 3. 16, 17).
with Isaac, Gen. 17. 19; 26. 3.
with Jacob, Gen. 28. 13 (Ex. 2. 24; 6. 4; 1 Chr. 16. 16).
with the Israelites, Ex. 6. 4; 19. 5; 24; 34. 27; Lev. 26. 9; Deut. 5. 2; 9. 9; 26. 16; 29; Judg. 2. 1; Jer. 11; 31. 33; Acts 3. 25.
with Phinehas, Num. 25. 13.
with David, 2 Sam. 23. 5; Ps. 89. 3, 28, 34. *See* Ps. 25. 14.
God mindful of, Deut. 7. 9; 1 Kin. 8. 23; Ps. 105. 8; 111. 5, &c.
danger of despising, Deut. 28. 15; Jer. 11. 2; Heb. 10. 29.
COVENANT, signs of:—salt, Lev. 2. 13; Num. 18. 19; 2 Chr. 13. 5; the sabbath, Ex. 31. 12.
book of the, Ex. 24. 7; 2 Kin. 23. 2; Heb. 9. 19.
—— between Abraham and Abimelech, Gen. 21. 27.
Joshua and Israelites, Josh. 24. 25.
David and Jonathan, 1 Sam. 18. 3; 20. 16; 23. 18.
NEW COVENANT, Jer. 31. 31; Rom. 11. 27; Heb. 8. 8.
ratified by Christ (Mal. 3. 1), Luke 1. 68–80; Gal. 3. 17; Heb. 8. 6; 9. 15; 12. 24.
a covenant of peace, Is. 54. 10; Ezek. 34. 25; 37. 26.
unchangeable, Ps. 89. 34; Is. 54. 10; 59. 21.
everlasting, Gen. 9. 16; 17. 13; Lev. 24. 8; Is. 55. 3; 61. 8; Ezek. 16. 60, 62; 37. 26; Heb. 13. 20.
COVETOUSNESS described, Ps. 10. 3; Prov. 21. 26; Eccles. 4. 8; 5. 10; Ezek. 33. 31; Hab. 2; Mark 7. 22; Eph. 5. 5; 1 Tim. 6. 10; 2 Pet. 2. 14.
forbidden, Ex. 20. 17; Luke 12. 15; Rom. 13. 9.
its evil consequences, Prov. 1. 18; 15. 27; 28. 20; Ezek. 22. 13; 1 Tim. 6. 9.
its punishment, Job 20. 15; Is. 5. 8; 57. 17; Jer. 6. 12; 22. 17; Mic. 2. 1; Hab. 2. 9; 1 Cor. 5. 10; 6. 10; Eph. 5. 5; Col. 3. 5.
of Laban, Gen. 31. 41.
of Balaam, Num. 22. 21 (2 Pet. 2. 15; Jude 11).
of Achan, Josh. 7. 21.
of Saul, 1 Sam. 15. 9.
of Ahab, 1 Kin. 21.
of Gehazi, 2. Kin. 5. 20.
of Judas, Matt. 26. 14.
of Ananias and Sapphira, Acts 5.
of Felix, Acts 24. 26.
CROSS, Christ dies upon the, Matt. 27. 32; Phil. 2. 8; Heb. 12. 2.
preaching of, 1 Cor. 1. 18.
to be taken up, self-denial, Matt. 10. 38; 16. 24; offence of the, Gal. 5. 11; persecution for, Gal. 6. 12.
CROWN (and mitre), high priest's, Ex. 29. 6; 39. 30; Lev. 8. 9.

CROWN—*cont.*
of thorns, John 19. 5.
of righteousness, 2 Tim. 4. 8.
of life, James 1. 12; Rev. 2. 10.
of glory, 1 Pet. 5. 4.
incorruptible, 1 Cor. 9. 25. *See* Rev. 4. 4; 9. 7; 12. 3; 13. 1; 19. 12.
CRUELTY condemned, Ex. 23. 5; Ps. 27. 12; Prov. 11. 17; 12. 10; Ezek. 18. 18.
of Simeon and Levi, Gen. 34. 25; 49. 5.
of Pharaoh, Ex. 1. 8.
of Adoni-bezek, Judg. 1. 7.
of Herod, Matt. 2. 16 (Judg. 9. 5; 2 Kin. 3. 27; 10; 15, 16).
CURSE upon the earth in consequence of the fall, Gen. 3. 17.
upon Cain, Gen. 4. 11.
on Canaan, Gen. 9. 25.
by Job on his birth, Job 3. 1; also by Jeremiah, Jer. 20. 14.
upon the breakers of the law, Lev. 26. 14; Deut. 11. 26; 27. 13; 28. 15; 29. 19; Josh. 8. 34; Prov. 3. 33.
Christ redeems from, Rom. 3; Gal. 3. 1.
CURSED, who so called, Deut. 27. 15; Prov. 11. 26; 27. 14; Jer. 11. 3; 17. 5; Lam. 3. 65; Zech. 5. 3; Mal. 1. 14; Matt. 25. 41; Gal. 3. 10; 2 Pet. 2. 14.
of God to be cut off, Ps. 37. 22.
CURSING forbidden, Ex. 21. 17; Ps. 109. 17; Prov. 30. 11; James 3. 10.
to return blessing for, Matt. 5. 44; Rom. 12. 14.
CUTTING the flesh forbidden, Lev. 19. 28; Deut. 14. 1; practised by prophets of Baal, 1 Kin. 18. 28.

DAMNATION, Matt. 23. 14; Mark 16. 16; John 5. 29; Rom. 3. 8; 13. 2; 2 Thess. 2. 12; 1 Tim. 5. 12; 2 Pet. 2. 3.
DANCING as a mark of rejoicing, Ex. 15. 20; 32. 19; Judg. 11. 34; 1 Sam. 21. 11; 2 Sam. 6. 14; Eccles. 3. 4.
of Herodias's daughter pleases Herod, Matt. 14. 6; Mark 6. 22.
DARKNESS divided from light, Gen. 1. 18.
created by God, Is. 45. 7.
supernatural, Gen. 15. 12; Ex. 10. 21; 14. 20; Josh. 24. 7; Rev. 8. 12; 9. 2; 16. 10.
at the crucifixion, Matt. 27. 45; Mark 15. 33; Luke 23. 44.
figurative of punishment, Matt. 8. 12; 22. 13; 2 Pet. 2. 4, 17; Jude 6.
of the mind, Job 37. 19; Prov. 2. 13; Eccles. 2. 14; Is. 9. 2; 42. 7; John 1. 5; 3. 19; 8. 12; 12. 35; Rom. 13. 12; 1 Cor. 4. 5; 2 Cor. 4. 6; 6. 14; Eph. 5. 8; 1 Thess. 5. 4; 1 Pet. 2. 9; 1 John 1. 5; 2. 9.
powers of, Luke 22. 53; Eph. 6. 12; Col. 1. 13.
DAUGHTERS, their inheritance determined, Num. 27. 6; 36.
DEACONS appointed, Acts 6; Phil. 1. 1.
their qualifications, Acts 6. 3; 1 Tim. 3. 8.
DEAD, the, Job 3. 18; 14. 12; Ps. 6. 5; 88. 10; 115. 17; 146. 4; Eccles. 9. 5; 12. 7; Is. 38. 18.
resurrection of, Job 19. 26; Ps. 49. 15; Is. 26. 19; Dan. 12. 2, 13; John 5. 25; 1 Cor. 15. 12.
raised by Elijah, 1 Kin. 17. 17; by Elisha, 2 Kin. 4. 32; 13. 21; by CHRIST, Matt. 9. 24; Mark 5. 41; Luke 7. 12; 8. 54; John 11; by Peter, Acts 9. 40; by Paul, Acts 20. 10.
sleep in Jesus, 1 Thess. 4. 13.
DEATH the consequence of Adam's sin, Gen. 2. 17; 3. 19; Rom. 5. 12; 6. 23; 1 Cor. 15. 21.
universal, Job 1. 21; 3. 17; 14. 1; 21. 13; Ps. 49. 19; 89. 48; Eccles. 5. 15; 8. 8; 9. 5, 10; 11. 8; Heb. 9. 27.
threatened, Rom. 1. 32.
characterized, Gen. 3. 19; Deut. 31. 16 (John 11. 11); Job 1. 21; 3. 13; 10. 21; 12. 22; 14. 2; 16. 22; 24. 17; Ps. 16. 10; 23. 4; 104. 29; Eccles. 9. 10; Hab. 2. 5; Luke 12. 20; 2 Cor. 5. 1, 8; Phil. 1. 23; 1 Tim. 6. 7; 2 Pet. 1. 14.

DEVIL—*cont.*
CHARACTER OF:—
malignant, Job. 1. 9; 2. 4.
subtle, Gen. 3. 1, with 2 Cor. 11. 3.
deceitful, 2 Cor. 11. 14; Eph. 6. 11.
fierce and cruel, Luke 8. 29; 9. 39, 42; 1 Pet. 5. 8.
Apostasy is of the, 2 Thess. 2. 9; 1 Tim. 4. 1.
shall be condemned at the judgment, Jude 6; Rev. 20. 10.
everlasting fire is prepared for, Matt. 25. 41.
COMPARED TO: *a fowler*, Ps. 91. 3; *fowls*, Matt. 13. 4; *a sower of tares*, Matt. 13. 25, 28; *a wolf*, John 10. 12; *a roaring lion*, 1 Pet. 5. 8; *a serpent*, Rev. 12. 9; 20. 2.
THE WICKED:—
are the children of, Matt. 13. 38; Acts 13. 10; 1 John 3. 10.
turn aside after, 1 Tim. 5. 15.
do the lusts of, John 8. 44.
are possessed by, Luke 22. 3; Acts 5. 3; Eph. 2. 2.
blinded by, 2 Cor. 4. 4.
deceived by, 1 Kin. 22. 21, 22; Rev. 20. 7, 8.
ensnared by, 1 Tim. 3. 7; 2 Tim. 2. 26.
troubled by, 1 Sam. 16. 14.
punished together with, Matt. 25. 41.
DILIGENCE, exhortations to, in the service of God, &c., Ex. 15. 26; Deut. 4. 9; 6. 7; 13. 14; 24. 8; Josh. 1. 7; Ezra 7. 23; Ps. 37. 10; 112. 1; Prov. 2; 3; 4; 7; 8; Is. 55. 2; Jer. 12. 16; Zech. 6. 15; Luke 12. 58; Rom. 12. 8; 2 Cor. 8. 7; 1 Tim. 5. 10; Heb. 6. 11; 11. 6; 12. 15; 1 Pet. 1. 10; 2 Pet. 3. 14.
in worldly business, Prov. 10. 4; 12. 24; 13. 4; 21. 5; 22. 29; 27. 23; Rom. 12. 11; 2 Thess. 3. 11.
DISCIPLES of CHRIST:—
the seventy sent out to work miracles and preach, Luke 10.
their names written in heaven, Luke 10. 20.
three thousand added to the church, Acts 2. 41.
five thousand believers, Acts 4. 4.
called Christians at Antioch, Acts 11. 26.
of JOHN enquire of Christ, Matt. 9. 14; 11. 2.
follow Christ, John 1. 37.
dispute about purifying, John 3. 25.
baptized by Paul, and receive the Holy Ghost, Acts 19. 1.
DISCORD censured, Prov. 6. 14, 19; 16. 29; 17. 9; 18. 8; 26. 20; Rom. 1. 29; 2 Cor. 12. 20.
DISCRETION commended, Ps. 34. 12; Prov. 1. 4; 2. 11; 3. 21; 5. 2; 19. 11.
DISEASES sent by God, Ex. 9; 15. 26; Num. 12. 10; Deut. 28. 60; 2 Kin. 1. 4; 5. 27; 2 Chr. 21. 18; 26. 21; Job 2. 6, 7.
cured by Christ, Matt. 4. 23; 9. 20; John 5. 8.
power given to His disciples to cure, Luke 9. 1; Acts 28. 8; exercised, Acts 3. 1; 9. 34; 28. 8.
DISGUISES resorted to, 1 Sam. 28. 8; 1 Kin. 14. 2; 20. 38; 22. 30; 2 Chr. 18. 29; 35. 22.
disfiguring of face for the dead forbidden, Lev. 19. 28; Deut. 14. 1.
DISOBEDIENCE, and its results, Lev. 26. 14; Deut. 8. 11; 27; 28. 15; Josh. 5. 6; 1 Sam. 2. 30; 12. 15; Ps. 78. 10; Is. 3. 8; 42. 24; Jer. 9. 13; 18. 10; 22. 21; 35. 14; Eph. 5. 6; Tit. 1. 16; 3. 3; Heb. 2. 2. *See* Adam and Eve, Gen. 3. Pharaoh, Ex. 5. 2. Achan, Josh. 7. Saul, 1 Sam. 13. 9; 15. Man of God, 1 Kin. 13. 21. Jonah, Jonah 1; 2.
DISPUTING, with God, forbidden, Rom. 9. 20; 1 Cor. 1. 20.
with men, Mark 9. 33; Rom. 14. 1; Phil. 2. 14; 1 Tim. 1. 4; 4. 7; 6. 20; 2 Tim. 2. 14; Tit. 3. 9.
DIVORCE, when permitted, Deut. 24. 1; Matt. 5. 32.
condemned by Christ, Mark 10. 4.
DOCTRINE of CHRIST, Matt. 7. 28, 29; Mark 4. 2; John 7. 16; Acts 2. 42; 1 Tim. 4. 16; 6. 3; 2 Tim. 3. 16; Tit. 1. 1; 2. 1; Heb. 6. 1; 2 John 9.
obedience to, Rom. 6. 17.
not to be blasphemed, 1 Tim. 6. 1, 3; Tit. 2. 7, 10; 2 John 10.

DOCTRINE—*cont.*
no other to be taught, 1 Tim. 1. 3; 4. 6, 13.
DOCTRINES, false, Jer. 10. 8; Matt. 15. 9; 16. 12; Eph. 4. 14; 2 Thess. 2. 11; 1 Tim. 4. 1; 2 Tim. 4. 3; Heb. 13. 9; Rev. 2. 14.
to be avoided, Jer. 23. 16; 29. 8; Col. 2. 8; 1 Tim. 1. 4; 6. 20.
DOVE, Noah's, Gen. 8. 8.
sacrificial, Gen. 15. 9; Lev. 12. 6; 14. 22.
figurative, Ps. 68. 13; 74. 19; Cant. 1. 15; 2. 14.
Holy Spirit in form of, Matt. 3. 16; Mark 1. 10; Luke 3. 22; John 1. 32.
DREAMS, vanity of, Job 20. 8; Ps. 73. 20; Is. 29. 8; Jer. 23. 28; 27. 9; Zech. 10. 2.
from God, Job 33. 15; Joel 2. 28.
of Abimelech, Gen. 20. 3. Jacob, Gen. 28. 12; 31. 10. Laban, Gen. 31. 24. Joseph, Gen. 37. 5. Pharaoh's servants, Gen. 40. 5. Pharaoh, Gen. 41. Midianite, Judg. 7. 13. Solomon, 1 Kin. 3. 5. Nebuchadnezzar, Dan. 2; 4. Joseph, Matt. 1. 20; 2. 13. Wise men, Matt. 2. 12. Pilate's wife, Matt. 27. 19.
DRINK OFFERINGS, Ex. 29. 40; Lev. 23. 13; Num. 6. 17; 15. 5 (Gen. 35. 14).
to idols, Is. 57. 6; Jer. 7. 18; 44. 17; Ezek. 20. 28.
DRUNKARDS, woe to, Is. 5. 11; 28. 1; Joel 1. 5; Luke 21. 34; Rom. 13. 13; 1 Cor. 5. 11; Gal. 5. 21. *See also* 1 Thess. 5. 7; 1 Pet. 4. 3. *See* WINE.
punished, Deut. 21. 20; Amos 6. 7; Nah. 1. 10; Matt. 24. 49; Luke 12. 45; 1 Cor. 6. 10; Gal. 5. 21.
DRUNKENNESS of Noah, Gen. 9. 21. Lot, Gen. 19. 33. Nabal, 1 Sam. 25. 36. Elah, 1 Kin. 16. 9. Benhadad, 1 Kin. 20. 16. Belshazzar, Dan. 5. 4. The Corinthians, 1 Cor. 11. 21.
DWARFS not to minister, Lev. 21. 20.

EARS, he that hath, to hear, Matt. 11. 15; 13. 16; Mark 4. 9, 23; 7. 16.
have, but hear not, Ps. 115. 6; Is. 42. 20; Ezek. 12. 2; Matt. 13. 12; Mark 8. 18; Rom. 11. 8.
the Lord's, open to prayer, 2 Sam. 22. 7; Ps. 18. 6; 34. 15; James 5. 4; 1 Pet. 3. 12.
opened by God, Job 33. 16; 36. 15; Ps. 40. 6; Mark 7. 35.
EARLY RISING, Gen. 19. 27; 26. 31; 28. 18; Josh. 3. 1; Judg. 6. 38; 1 Sam. 9. 26; 15. 12; 17. 20; Mark 1. 35; 16. 2; John 8. 2; 20. 1; Acts 5. 21.
ELDERS, seventy, Ex. 24. 1; Num. 11. 16.
of ISRAEL, Lev. 4. 15; Deut. 21. 19; 1 Sam. 16. 4; Ezra 5. 5; Ps. 107. 32; Ezek. 8. 1.
of EGYPT, Gen. 50. 7.
of the CHURCH, Acts 14. 23; 15. 4, 6, 23; 16. 4; 20. 17; Tit. 1. 5; James 5. 14; 1 Pet. 5. 1.
Paul's charge to, Acts 20. 17.
Peter's charge to, 1 Pet. 5.
the TWENTY-FOUR, Rev. 4. 4; 7. 11; 14. 3.
ELECTION, of God, 1 Thess. 1. 4.
its privileges and duties, Mark 13. 20; Luke 18. 7; Rom. 8. 29; 1 Cor. 1. 27; 2 Pet. 1. 10.
ENCHANTMENTS forbidden, Lev. 19. 26; Deut. 18. 9; Is. 47. 9.
ENEMIES, treatment of, Ex. 23. 4; 1 Sam. 24. 10; Job 31. 29; Prov. 24. 17; 25. 21; Matt. 5. 44; Luke 6. 35.
David and Saul, 1 Sam. 24. 10; 26. 9.
God delivers out of the hand of, 1 Sam. 12. 11; Ezra 8. 31; Ps. 18. 48; 59; 61. 3.
of God, their punishment, Ex. 15. 6; Deut. 32. 41; Judg. 5. 31; Esth. 7; 8; Ps. 68. 1; 92. 9; Is. 1. 24; 37. 36; 2 Thess. 1. 8; Rev. 21. 8.
ENTICERS to idolatry to be stoned, Deut. 13. 10.
ENVY, Prov. 14. 30; 27. 4; Eccles. 4. 4; Matt. 27. 18; Acts 7. 9; Rom. 1. 29; 1 Cor. 3. 3; 2 Cor. 12. 20; Gal. 5. 21; 1 Tim. 6. 4; Tit. 3. 3; James 4. 5.
forbidden, Ps. 37. 1; Prov. 3. 31; 24. 1, 19; Rom. 13. 13; 1 Pet. 2. 1.
its evil consequences, Job 5. 2; Prov. 14. 30; Is. 26. 11; James 3. 16.
Joseph sold for, Acts 7. 9.
EXACTION (usury, &c.), forbidden, Lev. 25. 35;

PRICE—*cont.*
of virtue, Prov. 31. 10; of wisdom, Job 28. 13.
of redemption, 1 Cor. 6. 20; 7. 23.
pearl of great, Matt. 13. 46; ornament of, 1 Pet. 3. 4.
PRIDE, 1 Sam. 2. 3; Prov. 6. 16; 8. 13; 16. 5; 21. 4; Dan. 5. 20; Mark 7. 20; Rom. 12. 3, 16.
origin of, 2 Kin. 20. 13; Zeph. 3. 11; Luke 18. 11; 1 Cor. 8. 1; 1 Tim. 3. 6.
evil results of, Ps. 10. 2; Prov. 13. 10; 21. 24; 28. 25; Jer. 43. 2; 49. 16; Obad. 3.
followed by shame and destruction, Prov. 11. 2; 16. 18; 18. 12; 29. 23; Is. 28. 3.
exhortations against, Is. 28.1; Jer. 13. 15.
PRIEST, HIGH, Ex. 28; 39; Lev. 8; 16.
PRIESTHOOD of Christ, Aaron, and Melchizedec, Rom. 8. 34; Heb. 2. 17; 3; 5; 7; 1 John 2. 1.
PRIESTS, Levitical, Ex. 28. 1; Lev. 8; their duties, offerings, rites, Lev. 1; 9; 21; 22; Num. 3; Deut. 31. 9; Josh. 3; 4; 1 Kin. 8. 3.
fourscore and five slain by command of Saul, 1 Sam. 22. 17.
divided by lot by David, 1 Chr. 24.
denounced for unfaithfulness, Jer. 1. 18; 5. 31; Hos. 5; 6; Mic. 3. 11; Zeph. 3. 4; Mal. 2.
—— of Baal, slain, 1 Kin. 18. 40; 2 Kin. 10. 19; 11. 18.
—— Christians called, 1 Pet. 2. 5; Rev. 1. 6; 5. 10; 20. 6.
PRINCE of peace, Is. 9. 6; of life, Acts 3. 15.
—— of this world, John 12. 31; 14. 30; 16. 11; of the power of the air, Eph. 2. 2.
—— of devils, Christ's miracles ascribed to, Matt. 9. 34; 12. 24; Mark 3. 22; Luke 11. 15.
PRINCES of the tribes, Num. 1. 5.
their offerings, Num. 7.
PRINCIPALITIES and powers, Eph. 6. 12; Col. 2. 15.
Christ the head of all, Eph. 1. 21; Col. 1. 16; 2. 10.
PRODIGAL SON, parable of, Luke 15. 11.
PROFANITY, Lev. 18. 21; 19. 12; Neh. 13. 18; Ezek. 22. 8; Mal. 1. 12.
PROFESSION of Christ, to hold fast, 1 Tim. 6. 12; Heb. 3. 1; 4. 14; 10. 23.
PROMISES of God, Ps. 89. 3; Rom. 1. 2; Eph. 3. 6; 2 Tim. 1. 1; Heb. 6. 17; 8. 6.
inviolable and precious, Num. 23. 19; Deut. 7. 9; Josh. 23. 14; 1 Kin. 8. 56; Ps. 77. 8; 89. 3; 105. 42; 2 Cor. 1. 20; Gal. 3. 21; Heb. 6. 17; 2 Pet. 1. 4.
God faithful to His, Ps. 105. 42; Luke 1. 54; Tit. 1. 2; Heb. 10. 23.
pleaded in prayer, Gen. 32. 9, 12; 1 Chr. 17. 23; Is. 43. 26.
to the repentant and returning, Ex. 34. 7; Ps. 65. 3; 103. 9, 13; 130. 4; Is. 1. 18; 27. 5; 43. 25; 44. 22; 45. 25; 46. 13; 53; 55; Jer. 31. 34; 33. 8; Ezek. 33. 16; 36. 25; Mic. 7. 18; Rom. 4; 5; 2 Cor. 6. 18; 7. 1; Eph. 2. 13.
to uphold and perfect, Ps. 23; 37. 17; 42. 8; 73. 26; 84. 11; 94. 14; 103. 13; Is. 25. 8; 30. 18; 40. 29; 41. 10; 43. 4; 46. 3; 49. 14; 63. 9; Jer. 31. 3; Hos. 13. 10; 14. 4; Zeph. 3. 17; Zech. 2. 8; 10; Rom. 16. 20; 1 Cor. 10. 13; 15. 57; 2 Cor. 6. 18; 12. 9; Eph. 1. 3; 1 Pet. 1. 3; 5. 7.
to Adam, Gen. 3. 15; to Noah, Gen. 8. 21; 9. 9; to Abraham, Gen. 12. 7; 13. 14; 15; 17; 18. 10; 22. 15; to Hagar, Gen. 16. 10; 21. 17; to Isaac, Gen. 26. 2; to Jacob, Gen. 28. 13; 31. 3; 32. 12; 35. 11; 46. 3; to David, 2 Sam. 7. 11; 1 Chr. 17. 10; to Solomon, 1 Kin. 9; 2 Chr. 1. 7; 7. 12.
of Christ to His disciples, Matt. 6. 4, 33; 7. 7; 10; 11. 28; 12. 50; 16. 18, 24; 17. 20; 19. 28; 28. 20; Luke 9—12; 12. 32; 22. 29; John 14—16; 20. 21.
Gentiles partakers of, Eph. 3.
fulfilled in Christ, 2 Sam. 7. 12 (with Acts 13. 23); Luke 1. 69–73.
to the poor, fatherless, &c., Deut. 10. 18; Ps. 9. 8; 10. 14; 12. 5; 68. 5; 69. 33; 72. 12; 102. 17; 107. 41; 109. 31; 113. 7; 146. 9; Prov. 15. 25; 23. 10; Jer. 49. 11; Hos. 14. 3.

PROMISES—*cont.*
of temporal blessings, Ex. 23. 25; Lev. 26. 6; Ps. 34. 9; 37. 3; 91; 102. 28; 112; 121. 3; 128; Prov. 3. 10; Is. 32. 18; 33. 16; Matt. 6. 25; Phil. 4. 19; 1 Tim. 4. 8.
exhortation concerning, Heb. 4. 1.
PROPHECIES respecting Christ, and their fulfilment:—Prophecy, Ps. 2. 7; fulfilled, Luke 1. 32, 35. Gen. 3. 15—(Gal. 4. 4). Gen. 17. 7; 22. 18—(Gal. 3. 16). Gen. 21. 12—(Heb. 11. 17–19). Ps. 132. 11; Jer. 23. 5—(Acts 13. 23; Rom. 1. 3). Gen. 49. 10; Dan. 9. 24, 25—(Luke 2. 1). Is. 7. 14—(Matt. 1. 18; Luke 2. 7). Is. 7. 14—(Matt. 1. 22, 23). Mic. 5. 2—(Matt. 2. 1; Luke 2. 4–6). Ps. 72. 10—(Matt. 2. 1–11). Jer. 31. 15—(Matt. 2. 16–18). Hos. 11. 1—(Matt. 2. 15). Is. 40. 3; Mal. 3. 1—(Matt. 3. 1, 3; Luke 1. 17). Ps. 45. 7; Is. 11. 2; 61. 1—(Matt. 3. 16; John 3. 34; Acts 10. 38). Deut. 18. 15–18—(Acts 3. 20–22). Ps. 110. 4—(Heb. 5. 5, 6). Is. 61. 1, 2—(Luke 4. 16–21, 43). Is. 9. 1, 2—(Matt. 4. 12–16, 23). Zech. 9. 9—(Matt. 21. 1–5). Hag. 2. 7, 9; Mal. 3. 1—(Matt. 21. 12; Luke 2. 27—32; John 2. 13–16). Is. 53. 2—(Mark 6. 3; Luke 9. 58). Is. 42. 2—(Matt. 12. 15, 16, 19). Is. 40. 11; 42. 3—(Matt. 12. 15, 20; Heb. 4. 15). Is. 53. 9—(1 Pet. 2. 22). Ps. 69. 9—(John 2. 17). Ps. 78. 2—(Matt. 13. 34, 35). Is. 35. 5, 6—(Matt. 11. 4–6; John 11. 47). Ps. 22. 6; 69. 7, 9, 20—(Rom. 15. 3). Ps. 69. 8; Is. 63. 3—(John 1. 11; 7. 3). Is. 8. 14—(Rom. 9. 32; 1 Pet. 2. 8). Ps. 69. 4; Is. 49. 7—(John 15. 24, 25). Ps. 118. 22—(Matt. 21. 42; John 7. 48). Ps. 2. 1, 2—(Luke 23. 12; Acts 4. 27). Ps. 41. 9; 55. 12–14—(John 13. 18, 21). Zech. 13. 7—(Matt. 26. 31, 56). Zech. 11. 12—(Matt. 26. 15). Zech. 11. 13—(Matt. 27. 7). Ps. 22. 14, 15—(Luke 22. 42, 44). Is. 53. 4—6, 12; Dan. 9. 26—(Matt. 20. 28). Is. 53. 7—(Matt. 26. 63; 27. 12–14). Mic. 5. 1—(Matt. 27. 30). Is. 52. 14; 53. 3—(John 19. 5). Is. 50. 6—(Mark 14. 65; John 19. 1). Ps. 22. 16—(John 19. 18; 20. 25). Ps. 22. 1—(Matt. 27. 46). Ps. 22. 7, 8—(Matt. 27. 39–44). Ps. 69. 21—(Matt. 27. 34). Ps. 22. 18—(Matt. 27. 35). Is. 53. 12—(Mark 15. 28). Is. 53. 12—(Luke 23. 34). Is. 53. 12—(Matt. 27. 50). Ex. 12. 46; Ps. 34. 20—(John 19. 33, 36). Zech. 12. 10—(John 19. 34, 37). Is. 53. 9—(Matt. 27. 57–60). Ps. 16. 10—(Acts 2. 31). Ps. 16. 10; Is. 26. 19—(Luke 24. 6, 31, 34). Ps. 68. 18—(Luke 24. 51; Acts 1. 9). Ps. 110. 1—(Heb. 1. 3). Zech. 6. 13—(Rom. 8. 34). Is. 28. 16—(1 Pet. 2. 6, 7). Ps. 2. 6—(Luke 1. 32; John 18. 33–37). Is. 11. 10; 42. 1—Matt. 1. 17, 21; John 10. 16; Acts 10. 45, 47). Ps. 45. 6, 7—(John 5. 30; Rev. 19. 11). Ps. 72. 8; Dan. 7. 14—(Phil. 2. 9, 11). Is. 9. 7; Dan. 7. 14—(Luke 1. 32, 33).
PROPHECY, God author of, Is. 44. 7; 45. 21; Luke 1. 70; 2 Pet. 1. 19, 21; Rev. 1. 1.
gift of Christ, Eph. 4. 11; Rev. 11. 3.
of Holy Ghost, 1 Cor. 12. 10.
Christ the great subject of, Luke 24. 44; Acts 3. 22–24; 10. 43; 1 Pet. 1. 10, 11.
to be received with faith and reverence, 2 Chr. 20. 20; Luke 24. 25; 1 Thess. 5. 20; 2 Pet. 1. 19.
pretended, guilt of, Jer. 14. 14; 23. 13; Ezek. 13. 3.
how tested, Deut. 13. 1; 18. 20; Jer. 14. 15; 23. 16.
PROPHETS sent by God, Is. 58. 1; Jer. 1. 4; 23. 28; 25. 4; Ezek. 2. 3.
Christ predicted as a Prophet, Deut. 18. 15; called one, Matt. 21. 11; Luke 7. 16; mocked at as, Luke 22. 64.
persons so called:—Aaron, Ex. 7. 1; Abraham, Gen. 20. 7; Agabus, Acts 21. 10; Ahijah, 1 Kin. 11. 29; Amos, Amos 7. 14; Balaam, Num. 24. 2; Daniel, Dan. 10; Matt. 24. 15; David, Matt. 13. 35; Acts 2. 30; Eldad, Num. 11. 26; Elijah, 1 Kin. 18. 36; Elisha, 2 Kin. 6. 12; Ezekiel, Ezek. 1. 3; Gad, 1. Sam. 22. 5; Habakkuk, Hab. 1. 1; Haggai, Ezra 5. 1; 6. 14; Hag. 1. 1; Hana-

CONCORDANCE

TO THE HOLY SCRIPTURES

ABASE. Ezek. 21. 26, and *a.* him that is high.
Dan. 4. 37, walk in pride, he is able to *a.*
Mat. 23. 12; Lu. 14. 11; 18. 14, whosoever exalteth himself shall be *a.*
Phil. 4. 12, I know how to be *a.*
See Job 40. 11; Isa. 31. 4; 2 Cor. 11. 7.
ABATED. Gen. 8. 3; Lev. 27. 18; Deut. 34. 7; Judg. 8. 3.
ABHOR. Ex. 5. 21, made our savour to be *a.*
Job 19. 19, my inward friends *a.*
Ps. 78. 59, Lord wroth, and *a.* Israel.
89. 38, thou hast cast off and *a.*
107. 18, soul *a.* all manner of meat.
119. 163, I hate and *a.* lying.
Prov. 22. 14, *a.* of the Lord shall fall there.
Isa. 7. 16, land thou *a.* shall be forsaken.
66. 24, they shall be an *a.* unto all flesh.
Ezek. 16. 25, made thy beauty to be *a.*
Amos 6. 8, I *a.* the excellency of Jacob.
See Lev. 26. 11; Job 42. 6; Rom. 12. 9.
ABIDE. Gen. 44. 33, let servant *a.* instead of lad.
Ex. 16. 29, *a.* every man in his place.
Num. 24. 2, he saw Israel *a.* in tents.
31. 19, *a.* without camp seven days.
1 Sam. 5. 7, ark of God not *a.* with us.
Job 24. 13, nor *a.* in the paths thereof.
Ps. 15. 1, Lord, who shall *a.* in thy tabernacle.
91. 1, shall *a.* under the shadow.
Prov. 15. 31, reproof *a.* among wise.
Eccl. 1. 4, the earth *a.* for ever.
Jer. 42. 10, if ye will still *a.* in this land.
49. 18, 33; 50. 40, there shall no man *a.*
Hos. 3. 3, thou shalt *a.* many days.
Joel 2. 11, day very terrible, who can *a.* it.
Mat. 10. 11; Mk. 6. 10; Lu. 9. 4, there *a.* till ye go.
Lu. 2. 8, shepherds *a.* in field.
19. 5, to-day I must *a.* at thy house.
24. 29, *a.* with us, it is toward evening.
John 3. 36, wrath of God *a.* on him.
5. 38, not his word *a.* in you.
14. 16, another Comforter that he may *a.*
15. 4, *a.* in me.
5, he that *a.* in me bringeth.
10, *a.* in my love.
Acts 16. 15, come to my house and *a.*
1 Cor. 3. 14, if any man's work *a.*
13. 13, now *a.* faith, hope, charity.
2 Tim. 2. 13, if we believe not he *a.*
See Gen. 29. 19; Num. 35. 25; Eccl. 8. 15.
ABILITY. Ezra 2. 69, they gave after their *a.*
Dan. 1. 4, had *a.* to stand in the palace.
Mat. 25. 15, to teach according to *a.*
1 Pet. 4. 11, as of the *a.* God giveth.
See Lev. 27. 8; Neh. 5. 8; Acts 11. 29.
ABJECTS. Ps. 35. 15, the *a.* gathered themselves together.
ABLE. Deut. 16. 17, every man give as he is *a.*
Josh. 23. 9, no man *a.* to stand before you.
1 Sam. 6. 20, who is *a.* to stand before God.
1 Kings 3. 9, who is *a.* to judge.
2 Chron. 2. 6, who is *a.* to build.
Prov. 27. 4, who is *a.* to stand before envy.
Amos 7. 10, land not *a.* to bear his words.
Mat. 3. 9, God is *a.* of these stones.
9. 28, believe ye that I am *a.*
20. 22, are ye *a.* to drink of cup.
Lu. 12. 26, not *a.* to do least.
Acts 6. 10, not *a.* to resist wisdom.
Rom. 4. 21, what he had promised he was *a.*
8. 39, *a.* to separate us from love of God.
1 Cor. 10. 13, tempted above that ye are *a.*
2 Cor. 3. 6, *a.* ministers of new testament.
Eph. 3. 18, *a.* to comprehend with all saints.
Phil. 3. 21, *a.* to subdue all things.
Heb. 2. 18, *a.* to succour tempted.
Jas. 4. 12, *a.* to save and destroy.
Jude 24, *a.* to keep you from falling.
Rev. 5. 3, no man *a.* to open book.
6. 17, who shall be *a.* to stand.
See Ex. 18. 21.
ABOARD. Acts 21. 2.
ABODE (*n.*). John 14. 23, we will come and make our *a.*
See 2 Kings 19. 27; Isa. 37. 28.
ABODE (*v.*). Gen. 49. 24, his bow *a.* in strength.
Ex. 24. 16, glory of the Lord *a.* on Sinai.
Judg. 21. 2, the people *a.* there before God.
Lu. 1. 56, Mary *a.* with her three months.
John 1. 32, the Spirit, and it *a.* on him.
39, they came and *a.* with him.
8. 44, a murderer, and *a.* not in truth.
Acts 14. 3, long time *a.*, speaking boldly.
18. 3, Paul *a.* with them and wrought.
See 1 Sam. 7. 2; Ezra 8. 15.
ABOLISH. 2 Cor. 3. 13, the end of that which is *a.*
Eph. 2. 15, *a.* in his flesh the enmity.
2 Tim. 1. 10, Christ, who hath *a.* death.
See Isa. 2. 18; 51. 6; Ezek. 6. 6.
ABOMINABLE. 1 Kings 21. 26, Ahab *a.* in following idols.
Job 15. 16, how much more *a.* is man.
Ps. 14. 1; 53. 1, they have done *a.* works.
Isa. 14. 19, cast out like *a.* branch.
65. 4; Jer. 16. 18, broth of *a.* things.
Jer. 44. 4, this *a.* thing that I hate.
Tit. 1. 16, in works they deny him, being *a.*
1 Pet. 4. 3, walked in *a.* idolatries.
See Lev. 11. 43; Deut. 14. 3; Rev. 21. 8.
ABOMINATION. Gen. 43. 32; 46. 34, *a.* to Egyptians.
Lev. 18. 26, shall not commit any *a.*
Deut. 7. 26, nor bring *a.* into house.
18. 9, after the *a.* of nations.
12, because of *a.* the Lord doth drive.
25. 16, do unrighteously are *a.* to God.
1 Sam. 13. 4, Israel had in *a.* with Philistines.
Prov. 3. 32; 11. 20, froward *a.* to the Lord.
8. 7, wickedness an *a.* to my lips.
15, 8, 9, 26; 21. 27, sacrifice, etc. of wicked are *a.*
28. 9, even his prayer shall be *a.*
Isa. 44. 19, residue thereof an *a.*
Jer. 4. 1, put away thine *a.* out of sight.
6. 15; 8. 12, ashamed when committed *a.*
Ezek. 5. 9, the like, because of all thine *a.*
33. 29, land desolate because of *a.*
Dan. 11. 31; Mat. 24. 15; Mk. 13. 14, *a.* of desolation.
Lu. 16. 15, esteemed among men *a.* with God.
Rev. 21. 27, in no wise enter that worketh *a.*
See Lev. 7. 18; 11. 41; Mal. 2. 11; Rev. 17. 4.
ABOUND. Prov. 28. 20, faithful shall *a.* with blessings.
Rom. 15. 12, that ye may *a.* in hope.
1 Cor. 15. 58, always *a.* in work.
2 Cor. 1. 5, as sufferings *a.* so consolation *a.*
See Rom. 3. 7; 5. 15; Phil. 4. 12.
ABOVE. Deut. 28. 13, *a.* only and not beneath.
Job 31. 2, portion of God from *a.*
Prov. 15. 24, way of life *a.* to wise.
Mat. 10. 24; Lu. 6. 40, disciple not *a.* master.
John 3. 31, cometh from *a.* is *a.* all.
8. 23, I am from *a.*
Rom. 14. 5, one day *a.* another.
1 Cor. 4. 6, *a.* that which is written.

Gal. 4. 26, Jerusalem *a.* is free.
See Gen. 48. 22; Ps. 138. 2; Jas. 1. 17.
ABSENT. 1 Cor. 5. 3; Col. 2. 5, *a.* in body.
2 Cor. 5. 6, *a.* from Lord.
See Gen. 31. 49; 2 Cor. 10. 1.
ABSTAIN. Acts 15. 20, 29, *a.* from pollutions of idols.
1 Thess. 5. 22, *a.* from all appearance of evil.
1 Pet. 2. 11, *a.* from fleshly lusts.
See 1 Thess. 4. 3; 1 Tim. 4. 3.
ABSTINENCE. Acts 27. 21, after long *a.* Paul stood forth.
ABUNDANCE. 1 Sam. 1. 16, out of *a.* of my complaint.
1 Kings 18. 41, sound of *a.* of rain.
1 Chron. 29. 21, offered sacrifices in *a.*
Ps. 52. 7, trusted in *a.* of riches.
72. 7; Jer. 33. 6, *a.* of peace.
Eccl. 5. 10, loveth *a.* with increase.
12, *a.* of rich not suffer to sleep.
Mat. 12. 34; Lu. 6. 45, out of *a.* of heart.
13. 12; 25. 29, he shall have more *a.*
Lu. 12. 15, life consisteth not in *a.*
2 Cor. 8. 2, of affliction the *a.* of their joy.
12. 7, through *a.* of revelations.
See Job 36. 31; Rom. 5. 17; Rev. 18. 3.
ABUNDANT. Job 36. 28, clouds drop and distil *a.*
Ps. 145. 7, *a.* utter the memory.
Isa. 56, 12, as this day and more *a.*
1 Cor. 15. 10; 2 Cor. 11. 23, laboured more *a.* than all.
1 Tim. 1. 14, grace was exceeding *a.*
Tit. 3. 6, shed *a.* through Jesus Christ.
2 Pet. 1. 11, entrance administered *a.*
See Ex. 31. 6; Isa. 55. 7; 1 Pet. 1. 3.
ABUSE. 1 Cor. 7. 31, use world as not *a.*
9. 18, that I *a.* not my power.
See 1 Sam. 31. 4; 1 Chron. 10. 4.
ACCEPT. Gen. 4. 7, shalt thou not be *a.*
Ex. 28. 38; Lev. 10. 19, *a.* before the Lord.
Deut. 33. 11, *a.* the work of his hands.
1 Sam. 18. 5, *a.* in sight of all people.
2 Sam. 24. 23, the Lord thy God *a.* thee.
Esth. 10. 3, *a.* of his brethren.
Job 13. 8; 32. 21, will ye *a.* his person.
42. 8, 9, him will I *a.*
Prov. 18. 5, not good to *a.* wicked.
Jer. 14. 12; Amos 5. 22, I will not *a.* them
37. 20; 42. 2, supplication be *a.*
Ezek. 20. 40; 43. 27, I will *a.*
Mal. 1. 13, should I *a.* this.
Lu. 4. 24, no prophet is *a.*
Acts 10. 35, he that worketh righteousness is *a.*
Rom. 15. 31, service *a.* of saints.
2 Cor. 5. 9, present or absent we may be *a.*
See Ps. 119. 108; Eccl. 12. 10; Mal. 1. 8.
ACCESS. Rom. 5. 2; Eph. 2. 18; 3. 12.
ACCOMPLISH. Job 14. 6, *a.* as an hireling.
Ps. 64. 6, they *a.* diligent search.
Prov. 13. 19, desire *a.* is sweet.
Isa. 40. 2, her warfare is *a.*
Lu. 12. 50, straitened till it be *a.*
1 Pet. 5. 9, afflictions are *a.* in brethren.
See Isa. 55. 11; Lu. 18. 31; 22. 37.
ACCORD. Acts 1. 14; 4. 24; 8. 6; Phil. 2. 2.
ACCORDING. Ex. 12. 25, *a.* as he hath promised.
Deut. 16. 10, *a.* as God hath blessed thee.
Job 34. 11; Jer. 17. 10; 25. 14; 32. 19, *a.* to ways.
Mat. 16. 27; Rom. 2. 6; 2 Tim. 4. 14, *a.* to works.
John 7. 24, *a.* to the appearance.
Rom. 8. 28, called *a.* to his purpose.
12. 6, gifts differing *a.* to grace.
2 Cor. 8. 12, *a.* to that a man hath.
See Mat. 9. 29; Tit. 3. 5.
ACCOUNT. Mat. 12. 36, give *a.* in day of judgment.
Lu. 16. 2, give *a.* of stewardship.
20. 35, *a.* worthy to obtain.
Rom. 14. 12, every one give *a.* to God.
Gal. 3. 6, *a.* to him for righteousness.
Heb. 13. 17, watch as they that give *a.*
See Job 33. 13; Ps. 144. 3; 1 Pet. 4. 5.
ACCURSED. Josh. 6. 18; 7. 1; 22. 20; 1 Chron. 2. 7, *a.* thing.
Rom. 9. 3, wish myself *a.* from Christ.
1 Cor. 12. 3, no man calleth Jesus *a.*
Gal. 1. 8, 9, preach other gospel, let him be *a.*
See Deut. 21. 23; Josh. 6. 17; Isa. 65. 20.
ACCUSATION. Lu. 19. 8, anything by false *a.*
1 Tim. 5. 19, against elder receive not *a.*
2 Pet. 2. 11; Jude 9, railing *a.*
See Mat. 27. 37; Mk. 15. 26; Lu. 6. 7.
ACCUSE. Prov. 30. 10, *a.* not servant to his master.
Mat. 27. 12, when *a.* he answered nothing.
Lu. 16. 1, was *a.* that he had wasted.
John 5. 45, I will *a.* you to the Father.
Tit. 1. 6, not *a.* of riot or unruly.
See Mat. 12. 10; Mk. 3. 2; Lu. 11. 54; Rev. 12. 10.
ACKNOWLEDGE. Ps. 32. 5; 51. 3, I *a.* my sin.
Prov. 3. 6, in all thy ways *a.* him.
Isa. 63. 16, though Israel *a.* us not.
1 John 2. 23, he that *a.* the Son.
See Dan. 11. 39; Hos. 5. 15.
ACQUAINT. Job 22. 21; Ps. 139. 3; Eccl. 2. 3; Isa. 53. 3.
ACQUAINTANCE. Job. 19. 13; Ps. 31. 11; 55. 13.
ACQUIT. Job 10. 14; Nah. 1. 3.
ACTIONS. 1 Sam. 2. 3.
ACTIVITY. Gen. 47. 6.
ADDER. Gen. 49. 17; Ps. 58. 4; 91. 13; 140. 3; Prov. 23. 32.
ADDICTED. 1 Cor. 16. 15.
ADDITION. 1 Kings 7. 29, 30, 36.
ADJURE. Josh. 6. 26; 1 Sam. 14. 24; 1 Kings 22. 16; 2 Chron. 18. 15; Mat. 26. 63; Mk. 5. 7; Acts 19. 13.
ADMINISTER. 1 Cor. 12. 5; 2 Cor. 8. 19, 20; 9. 12.
ADMIRE. 2 Thess. 1. 10; Jude 16; Rev. 17. 6.
ADMONISH. Acts 27. 9, Paul *a.* them.
Rom. 15. 14; Col. 3. 16, *a.* one another.
1 Thess. 5. 12, over you in Lord, and *a.* you.
2 Thess. 3. 15, *a.* him as a brother.
Heb. 8. 5, Moses was *a.* of God.
See Eccl. 4. 13; 12. 12; Jer. 42. 19.
ADMONITION. 1 Cor. 10. 11; Eph. 6. 4; Tit. 3. 10.
ADO. Mk. 5. 39.
ADOPTION. Rom. 8. 15, 23; 9. 4; Gal. 4. 5; Eph. 1. 5.
ADORN. Isa. 61. 10; Rev. 21. 2, bride *a.* herself.
1 Tim. 2. 9; 1 Pet. 3. 3, 5, women *a.*
Tit. 2. 10, *a.* doctrine of God.
See Jer. 31. 4; Lu. 21. 5.
ADVANCED. 1 Sam. 12. 6; Esth. 3. 1; 5. 11; 10. 2.
ADVANTAGE. Lu. 9. 25, what is a man *a.*
Rom. 3. 1; 1 Cor. 15. 32, what *a.*?
2 Cor. 2. 11, lest Satan get *a.*
See Job 35. 3; Jude 16.
ADVENTURE. Deut. 28. 56; Judg. 9. 17; Acts 19. 31.
ADVERSARY. Deut. 32. 43; Ps. 89. 42; Isa. 59. 18; Jer. 46. 10; Nah. 1. 2; Lu. 13. 17, his *a.*
Ex. 23. 22, I will be *a.* to thy *a.*
Num. 22. 22, angel stood for *a.*
1 Kings 5. 4, neither *a.* nor evil.
11. 14, 23, Lord stirred up *a.*
Job 31. 35, that mine *a.* had written.
Ps. 38. 20; 69. 19; 109. 4, 20, 29; Isa. 1. 24, my *a.*
74. 10, how long shall *a.* reproach.
Isa. 50. 8, who is mine *a.*
64. 2; Jer. 30. 16; Mic. 5. 9, thy *a.*
Amos 3. 11, *a.* shall be round the land.
Mat. 5. 25, agree with thine *a.*
Lu. 12. 58, when thou goest with thine *a.*
1 Cor. 16. 9, there are many *a.*
Phil. 1. 28, terrified by your *a.*
1 Tim. 5. 14, give no occasion to *a.*

Heb. 10. 27, indignation shall devour *a*.
1 Pet. 5. 8, 9, because your *a*. the devil.
See 1 Sam. 2. 10; Isa. 9. 11; 11. 13.
ADVERSITY. 1 Sam. 10. 19; 2 Sam. 4. 9; 2 Chron. 15. 6, all *a*.
Ps. 10. 6, I shall never be in *a*.
94. 13; Prov. 24. 10; Eccl. 7. 14, day of *a*.
Prov. 17. 17, brother is born for *a*.
Isa. 30. 20, bread of *a*.
Heb. 13. 3, remember them which suffer *a*.
See Ps. 31. 7; 35. 15.
ADVERTISE. Num. 24. 14; Ruth 4. 4.
ADVICE. 1 Sam. 25. 33, blessed be thy *a*.
2 Sam. 19. 43, that our *a*. should not be first.
2 Chron. 10. 9, 14, what *a*. give ye.
Prov. 20. 18, with good *a*. make war.
2 Cor. 8. 10, herein I give my *a*.
See Judg. 19. 30; 20. 7; 2 Chron. 25. 17.
ADVISE. Prov. 13. 10, with the well *a*. is wisdom.
Acts 27. 12, the more part *a*. to depart.
See 2 Sam. 24. 13; 1 Kings 12. 6; 1 Chron. 21. 12.
ADVISEMENT. 1 Chron. 12. 19.
ADVOCATE. 1 John 2. 1, an *a*. with the Father.
AFAR-OFF. Jer. 23. 23, a God *a*.
30. 10; 46. 27, I will save them from *a*.
Mat. 26. 58; Mk. 14. 54; Lu. 22. 54, followed *a*.
Acts 2. 39, promise to all *a*.
Eph. 2. 17, preached to you *a*.
Heb. 11. 13, seen the promises *a*.
See Gen. 22. 4; Ezra 3. 13.
AFFAIRS. 1 Chron. 26. 32, pertaining to God and *a*. of king.
2 Tim. 2. 4, entangleth himself with *a*.
See Dan. 2. 49; 3. 12; Eph. 6. 21, 22.
AFFECTED. Acts 14. 2, minds evil *a*. against brethren.
Gal. 4. 17, 18 zealously *a*.
See Lam. 3. 51.
AFFECTION. 1 Chron. 29. 3, have set *a*. to house of God.
Rom. 1. 26, vile *a*.
31; 2 Tim. 3. 3, without natural *a*.
12. 10, be kindly *a*. one to another.
Gal. 5. 24, crucified with *a*.
Col. 3. 2, set your *a*. on things above.
5, inordinate *a*.
See 2 Cor. 7. 15.
AFFINITY. 1 Kings 3. 1; 2 Chron. 18. 1; Ezra 9. 14.
AFFIRM. Acts 25. 19, Jesus, whom Paul *a*. to be alive.
See Rom. 3. 8; 1 Tim. 1. 7; Tit. 3. 8.
AFFLICT. Lev. 16. 29, 31; Num. 29. 7; Isa. 58. 3, 5, *a*. your souls.
Num. 11. 11, wherefore hast thou *a*.
Ruth 1. 21, Almighty hath *a*. me.
1 Kings 11. 39, I will *a*. seed of David.
2 Chron. 6. 26; 1 Kings 8. 35, turn when thou dost *a*.
Job 6. 14, to *a*. pity should be showed.
Ps. 44. 2, how thou didst *a*. people.
55. 19, God shall hear and *a*.
82. 3, do justice to the *a*.
90. 15, the days wherein thou hast *a*.
119. 67, before I was *a*.
140. 12, maintain cause of *a*.
Prov. 15. 15, days of the *a*. evil.
22. 22, neither oppress the *a*.
31. 5, pervert judgment of *a*.
Isa. 51. 21, hear thou *a*. and drunken.
53. 4, 7, smitten of God and *a*.
54. 11, thou *a*. tossed with tempest.
63. 9, in all their *a*. he was *a*.
Lam. 1. 5, 12, the Lord hath *a*.
Nah. 1. 12, I will *a*. no more.
Zeph. 3. 12, I will leave an *a*. people.
2 Cor. 1. 6, *a*. it is for consolation.
1 Tim. 5. 10, if she have relieved the *a*.
Heb. 11. 37, destitute, *a*., tormented.
Jas. 4. 9, be *a*. and mourn and weep.
5. 13, is any *a*., let him pray.
See Ex. 1. 11, 12; 22. 22, 23.
AFFLICTION. Gen. 29. 32; Deut. 26. 7; Ps. 25. 18, looked on *a*.
Ex. 3. 7; Acts 7. 10, 11, 34, have seen *a*. of people.
Deut. 16. 3; 1 Kings 22. 27; 2 Chron. 18. 26, bread of *a*.
2 Chron. 20. 9, cry to thee in *a*.
33. 12, in *a*. besought the Lord.
Job 5. 6, *a*. cometh not forth of the dust.
30. 16. 27, days of *a*.
36. 8, cords of *a*.
Ps. 34. 19, many are *a*. of righteous.
119. 50, this my comfort in *a*.
132. 1, remember David and all his *a*
Isa. 30. 20, water of *a*.
48. 10, furnace of *a*.
Jer. 16. 19, refuge in day of *a*.
Lam. 3. 1, man that hath seen *a*.
Hos. 5. 15, in their *a*. they will seek.
Mk. 4. 17, *a*. ariseth for the word's sake.
Acts 20. 23, bonds and *a* abide me.
2 Cor. 2. 4, out of much *a*. I wrote.
4. 17, light *a*. for moment.
8. 2, great trial of *a*.
Phil. 1. 16, add *a*. to bonds.
Heb. 10. 32, great fight of *a*.
11. 25, suffer *a*. with people.
Jas. 1. 27, visit fatherless in *a*.
See 2 Kings 14. 26; Col. 1. 24.
AFFRIGHT. Isa. 21. 4, fearfulness *a*. me.
Mk. 16. 5; Lu. 24. 37, they were *a*.
Mk. 16. 6, be not *a*. ye seek Jesus.
See Deut. 7. 21; 2 Chron. 32. 18; Jer. 51. 32.
AFOOT. Mk. 6. 33; Acts 20. 13.
AFORETIME. Dan. 6. 10, prayed as *a*.
Rom. 15. 4, things were written *a*.
See Isa. 52. 4; Jer. 30. 20.
AFRAID. Mat. 14. 27; Mk. 5. 36; 6. 50; John 6. 20, be not *a*.
Gen. 20. 8; Ex. 14. 10; Mk. 9. 6; Lu. 2. 9, sore *a*.
Lev. 26. 6; Job 11. 19; Isa. 17. 2; Ezek. 34. 28; Mic. 4. 4; Zeph. 3. 13, none make *a*.
Judg. 7. 3, whosoever is fearful and *a*.
1 Sam. 18. 29, Saul yet the more *a*.
Neh. 6. 9, they all made us *a*.
Job 3. 25, that I was *a*. of is come.
9. 28, I am *a*. of sorrows.
Ps. 27. 1, of whom shall I be *a*.
56. 3, 11, what time I am *a*.
65. 8, *a*. at thy tokens.
91. 5, *a* for terror by night.
112. 7, *a*. of evil tidings.
Isa. 51. 12, be *a*. of a man that shall die.
Mk. 9. 32; 10. 32, *a*. to ask him.
John 19. 8, Pilate was more *a*.
Gal. 4. 11, I am *a*. of you.
Heb. 11. 23, not *a*. of commandment.
See Deut. 1. 17; Ps. 3. 6.
AFRESH. Heb. 6. 6.
AFTERNOON. Judg. 19. 8.
AFTERWARDS. 1 Sam 24. 5, *a*. David's heart smote him.
Ps. 73. 24, *a* receive me to glory.
Prov. 20. 17, deceit sweet, but *a*.
24. 27, prepare work and *a*. build.
29. 11, wise man keepeth till *a*.
John 13. 36, thou shalt follow me *a*.
1 Cor. 15. 23, *a*. they that are Christ's.
See Ex. 11. 1; Mat. 21. 32; Gal. 3. 23.
AGAINST. Lu. 2. 34; Acts 19. 36; 28. 22, spoken *a*.
See Gen. 16. 12; Mat. 12. 30; Lu. 11. 23.
AGATE. Ex. 28. 19; 39. 12, an *a*.
Isa. 54. 12, make thy windows of *a*.
Ezek. 27. 16, and *a*.
AGED. 2 Sam. 19. 32; Job 15. 10; Tit. 2. 2, *a*. men.
Philem. 9, Paul the *a*.
See Job 12. 20; 29. 8; 32. 9.
AGES. Eph. 2. 7; 3. 5, 21; Col. 1. 26.
AGONE. 1 Sam. 30. 13.
AGONY. Lu. 22. 44.

AGREE. Amos 3. 3, except they be *a.*
Mat. 5. 25, *a.* with adversary.
18. 19, two of you shall *a.*
Mk. 14. 56, 59, witness *a.* not.
Acts 15. 15, to this *a.* words of the prophets.
1 John 5. 8, these three *a.* in one.
See Mat. 20. 2; Lu. 5. 36; Acts 5. 9; Rev. 17. 17.
AGREEMENT. Isa. 28. 15; 2 Cor. 6. 16.
AGROUND. Acts 27. 41.
AHA. Ps. 35. 21; 40. 15; 70. 3; Isa. 44. 16; Ezek. 25. 3; 26. 2; 36. 2.
AILETH. Gen. 21. 17; Judg. 18. 23; 1 Sam. 11. 5; 2 Sam. 14. 5; Ps. 114. 5; Isa. 22. 1.
AIR. Job 41. 16, no *a.* can come between.
1 Cor. 9. 26, as one that beateth the *a.*
14. 9, ye shall speak into *a.*
1 Thess. 4. 17, meet Lord in *a.*
See 2 Sam. 21. 10; Eccl. 10. 20; Acts 22. 23; Rev. 9. 2.
ALARM (how sounded). Num. 10. 5, when ye blow an *a.*
Jer. 4. 19; 49. 2, *a.* of war.
Joel 2. 1, sound *a.* in holy mountain.
See 2 Chron. 13. 12; Zeph. 1. 16.
ALAS. 2 Kings 6. 5, 15, *a.* my master.
Ezek. 6. 11, stamp and say *a.*
See Num. 24. 23; Jer. 30. 7; Rev. 18. 10.
ALBEIT. Ezek. 13. 7; Philem. 19.
ALIEN. Deut. 14. 21, sell it to an *a.*
Ps. 69. 8, an *a.* unto my mother's children.
Eph. 2. 12, *a.* from commonwealth.
Heb. 11. 34, armies of the *a.*
See Ex. 18. 3; Job 19. 15; Isa. 61. 5; Lam. 5. 2.
ALIENATED. Ezek. 23. 17; Eph. 4. 18; Col. 1. 21.
ALIKE. Job 21. 26, lie down *a.* in dust.
Ps. 33. 15, fashioneth hearts *a.*
Eccl. 9. 2, things cometh *a.* to all.
See Ps. 139. 12; Eccl. 11. 6; Rom. 14. 5.
ALIVE. Lev. 16. 10, scapegoat presented *a.*
Num. 16. 33, went down *a.* into pit.
Deut. 4. 4, are *a.* every one of you.
32. 39; 1 Sam. 2. 6, I kill and I make *a.*
Ezek. 13. 18; 18. 27, save soul *a.*
Mk. 16. 11, heard that he was *a.*
Lu. 15. 24, 32, son was dead and is *a.*
24. 23, angels who said he was *a.*
Acts 1. 3, showed himself *a.*
Rom. 6. 11, 13 *a.* to God.
1 Cor. 15. 22, all be made *a.*
1 Thess. 4. 15, we who are *a.* and remain.
Rev. 1. 18, I am *a.* for evermore.
See 2 Kings 5. 7; Dan. 5. 19; Rev. 2. 8; 19. 20.
ALLEGING. Acts 17. 3.
ALLEGORY. Gal. 4. 24, which things are an *a.*
ALLOW. Lu. 11. 48; Acts 24. 25; Rom. 7. 15; 14. 22.
ALLOWANCE. 2 Kings 25. 30.
ALL THINGS. 1 Cor. 6. 12, *a.* are lawful, but not expedient.
ALLURE. Hos. 2. 14; 2 Pet. 2. 18.
ALMIGHTY. Ex. 6. 3, by the name of God *A.*
Job 11. 7, canst thou find out the *A.*
29. 5, when *A.* was yet with me.
Ezek. 1. 24; 10. 5, I heard as voice of *A.*
Rev. 1. 8; 4. 8; 11. 17, *A.* who was, and is.
See Gen. 17. 1; Job 21. 15; Ps. 91. 1.
ALMS. Mat. 6. 1; Lu. 11. 41; 12. 33; Acts 10. 2.
ALMOND. Num. 17. 8, and yielded *a.*
Jer. 1. 11, a rod of an *a.* tree.
Eccl. 12. 5, *a.* tree shall flower.
ALOES. Ps. 45. 8, smell of . . . . and *a.*
Cant. 4. 14, *a.*, with all the chief spices.
John 19. 39, a mixture of myrrh and *a.*
ALONE. Num. 11. 14; Deut. 1. 9, bear all these people *a.*
1 Kings 11. 29, they two *a.* in field.
Job 1. 15, escaped *a.* to tell.
Ps. 136. 4, *a.* doeth great wonders.
Mat. 4. 4; Lu. 4. 4, not live by bread *a.*
Lu. 9. 18, 36; John 6. 15, Jesus was *a.*
13. 8, let *a.* this year also.
See Gen. 2. 18; Mat. 18. 15; Jas. 2. 17.
ALREADY. Eccl. 1. 10; Mal. 2. 2; John 3. 18; Phil. 3. 16.
ALTAR. Mat. 5. 23, bring gift to *a.*
23. 18, swear by *a.*
1 Cor. 9. 13; 10. 18, wait at *a.*
Heb. 13. 10, we have an *a.*
See 1 Kings 13. 2; Isa. 19. 19; Acts 17. 23.
ALTER. Ps. 89. 34, nor *a.* thing gone out of my lips.
Lu. 9. 29, fashion of countenance *a.*
See Lev. 27. 10; Dan. 6. 8.
ALTOGETHER. Ps. 14. 3; 53. 3, *a.* become filthy.
50. 21, *a.* such an one as thyself.
Cant. 5. 16, he is *a.* lovely.
See Ps. 19. 9; 39. 5; 139. 4.
ALWAYS. Job 7. 16, I would not live *a.*
Ps. 103. 9, not *a.* chide.
Mat. 28. 20, I am with you *a.*
Mk. 14. 7; John 12. 8, me ye have not *a.*
Phil. 4. 4, rejoice in Lord *a.*
See Ps. 16. 8; Isa. 57. 16; John 11. 42.
AMAZED. Mat. 19. 25, disciples exceedingly *a.*
Mk. 2. 12; Lu. 5. 26, *a.*, and glorified God.
14. 33, he began to be sore *a.*
Lu. 9. 43, *a.* at mighty power of God.
See Ezek. 32. 10; Acts 3. 10; 1 Pet. 3. 6.
AMBASSADORS. 2 Chron. 32. 31, the business of the *a.*
2 Cor. 5. 20, we are *a.* for Christ.
See Prov. 13. 17; Isa. 18. 2; 33. 7; Jer. 49. 14; Obad. 1; Eph. 6. 20.
AMBER. Ezek. 1. 4, 27; 8. 2, as the colour of *a.*
AMEN (tantamount to an oath). Num. 5. 22, the woman shall say, *A.*
Deut. 27. 15–26, the people shall say, *A.*
Ps. 41. 13; 72. 19; 89. 52, *A.* and *A.*
106. 48, let all the people say, *A.*
Mat. 6. 13, and the glory for ever, *A.*
1 Cor. 14. 16, of the unlearned say, *A.*
2 Cor. 1. 20, and in him, *A.*
Rev. 3. 14, These things saith the *A.*
See Rev. 22. 20.
AMEND. Jer. 7. 3; 26. 13; 35. 15; John 4. 52.
AMIABLE. Ps. 84. 1.
AMISS. 2 Chron. 6. 37; Dan. 3. 29; Lu. 23. 41; Jas. 4. 3.
ANCHOR. Heb. 6. 19, have as an *a.* of the soul.
ANCIENT OF DAYS. Dan. 7. 22, until the *a.* came.
ANGEL. Gen. 48. 16, the *A.* who redeemed me.
Ps. 34. 7, *a.* of Lord encampeth.
78. 25, man did eat *a.* food.
Eccl. 5. 6, nor say before *a.* it was error.
Isa. 63. 9, *a.* of his presence saved them.
Hos. 12. 4, he had power over *a.*
Mat. 13. 39, reapers are the *a.*
Mk. 12. 25; Lu. 20. 36, are as *a.* in heaven.
Lu. 22. 43, an *a.* strengthening him.
John 5. 4, *a.* went down at a certain season.
Acts 12. 15, it is his *a.*
1 Cor. 6. 3, we shall judge *a.*
2 Cor. 11. 14, transformed into *a.* of light.
Heb. 2. 2, word spoken by *a.*
16, not nature of *a.*
13. 2, entertained *a.* unawares.
1 Pet. 1. 12, *a.* desire to look into.
See Gen. 19. 1; Ps. 8. 5; Mat. 25. 41; Heb. 2. 7.
ANGER. Gen. 49. 7, cursed be their *a.*
Neh. 9. 17, slow to *a.*
Ps. 6. 1; Jer. 10. 24, rebuke me not in *a.*
30. 5, *a.* endureth but a moment.
Prov. 15. 1, grievous words stir up *a.*
19. 11, discretion deferreth *a.*
Eccl. 7. 9, *a.* resteth in bosom of fools.
Mk. 3. 5, he looked on them with *a.*
Col. 3. 8, put off *a.*, wrath, malice.
See Ps. 37. 8; 85. 3; 90. 7; Prov. 16. 32.
ANGRY. Ps. 7. 11, God is *a.* with the wicked.
Prov. 14. 17, he that is soon *a.*
22. 24, make no friendship with *a.* man.
25. 23, so doth an *a.* countenance.

Jon. 4. 4, doest thou well to be *a.*
Mat. 5. 22, whosoever is *a.* with brother.
John 7. 23, are ye *a.* at me.
Eph. 4. 26, be *a.* and sin not.
Tit. 1. 7, bishop not soon *a.*
See Gen. 18. 30; Prov. 21. 19; Eccl. 5. 6; 7. 9.
ANGUISH. Ex. 6. 9, hearkened not for *a.*
Job 7. 11, I will speak in *a.* of spirit.
Rom. 2. 9, tribulation and *a.* on every soul.
2 Cor. 2. 4, out of much *a.* of heart.
See Gen. 42. 21; Isa. 8. 22; John 16. 21.
ANOINT. Deut. 28. 40; 2 Sam. 14. 2, *a.* not thyself.
Isa. 21. 5, arise and *a.* shield.
61. 1; Lu. 4. 18, *a.* to preach.
Mk. 14. 8, *a.* my body to burying.
Lu. 7. 46, my head thou didst not *a.*
John 9. 6, *a.* eyes of blind man.
12. 3, Mary *a.* feet of Jesus.
2 Cor. 1. 21, he which *a.* us is God.
1 John 2. 27, the same *a.* teacheth.
Rev. 3. 18, *a.* thine eyes with eyesalve.
See Judg. 9. 8; Ps. 2. 2; 84. 9; Jas. 5. 14.
ANOINTED. 1 Sam. 26. 9.
ANOINTING OIL. Ex. 30. 25, it shall be an holy *a.*
37. 29, he made the holy *a.*
ANON. Mat. 13. 20; Mk. 1. 30.
ANOTHER. Prov. 27. 2, let *a.* praise thee.
2 Cor. 11. 4; Gal. 1. 6, 7, *a.* gospel.
Jas. 5. 16, pray one for *a.*
See 1 Sam. 10. 6; Job 19. 27; Isa. 42. 8; 48. 11.
ANSWER (*n.*). Job 19. 16; 32. 3; Cant. 5. 6; Mic. 3. 7; John 19. 9, no *a.*
Prov. 15. 1, a soft *a.* turneth.
16. 1, *a.* of tongue from the Lord.
1 Pet. 3. 15, be ready to give *a.*
21, *a.* of good conscience.
See Job 35. 12; Lu. 2. 47; 2 Tim. 4. 16.
ANSWER (*v*). Job 11. 2, multitude of words be *a.*
Ps. 65. 5, by terrible things wilt thou *a.*
Prov. 1. 28, I will not *a.*
18. 13, *a.* a matter before he heareth.
26. 4, 5, *a.* not a fool.
Eccl. 10. 19, money *a.* all things.
Lu. 21. 14, meditate not what to *a.*
2 Cor. 5. 12, somewhat to *a.*
Col. 4. 6, how ye ought to *a.*
Tit. 2. 9, not *a.* again.
See 1 Kings 18. 29; Ps. 138. 3; Isa. 65. 12, 24.
ANTIQUITY. Isa. 23. 7.
APART. Mat. 14. 13, desert place *a.*
23; 17. 1; Lu. 9. 28, mountain *a.*
Mk. 6. 31, come ye yourselves *a.*
See Ps. 4. 3; Zech. 12. 12; Jas. 1. 21.
APPARENTLY. Num. 12. 8.
APPEAR. Col. 3. 4; 1 Tim. 6. 14; 2 Tim. 1. 10; 4. 8; Tit. 2. 13; Heb. 9. 28; 1 Pet. 1. 7, *a.* of Christ.
1 Sam. 16. 7, man looketh on the outward *a.*
Ps. 42. 2, when shall I *a.* before God.
90. 16, let thy work *a.*
Cant. 2. 12, flowers *a.* on earth.
Mat. 6. 16, *a.* to men to fast.
23. 28, outwardly *a.* righteous.
Rom. 7. 13, that it might *a.* sin.
2 Cor. 5. 10, we must all *a.*
12, glory in *a.*
1 Thess. 5. 22, *a.* of evil.
1 Tim. 4. 15, profiting may *a.*
See Ex. 23. 15; Mat. 24. 30; Lu. 19. 11.
APPEASE. Gen. 32. 20; Prov. 15. 18; Acts 19. 35.
APPERTAIN. Num. 16. 30; Jer. 10. 7; Rom. 4. 1.
APPETITE. Job 38. 39; Prov. 23. 2; Eccl. 6. 7; Isa. 29. 8.
APPLY. Ps. 90. 12; Prov. 2. 2; 22. 17; 23. 12; Eccl. 7. 25.
APPOINT. Job 7. 3, wearisome nights are *a.*
14. 5, thou hast *a.* bounds.
30. 23, house *a.* for all living.
Ps. 79. 11; 102. 20, preserve those *a.* to die.
Mat. 24. 51; Lu. 12. 46, *a.* him his portion.
Acts 6. 3, seven men whom we may *a.*
1 Thess. 5. 9, not *a.* to wrath.
See Job 14. 13; Ps. 104. 19; Acts 17. 31.
APPREHEND. Acts 12. 4; 2 Cor. 11. 32; Phil. 3. 12.
APPROACH. Isa. 58. 2, take delight in *a.* God.
Lu. 12. 33, where no thief *a.*
1 Tim. 6. 16, light no man can *a.*
Heb. 10. 25, as ye see the day *a.*
See Deut. 31. 14; Job 40. 19; Ps. 65. 4.
APPROVE. Acts 2. 22, a man *a.* of God.
Rom. 16. 10, *a.* in Christ.
Phil. 1. 10, *a.* things that are excellent.
2 Tim. 2. 15, show thyself *a.*
See Ps. 49. 13; 1 Cor. 11. 19; Phil. 1. 10.
APT. 2 Kings 24. 16; 1 Tim. 3. 2; 2 Tim. 2. 24.
ARCHANGEL. 1 Thess. 4. 16, voice of *a.*
Jude 9, Michael the *a.* contending.
ARCHERS. Gen. 21. 20, and became an *a.*
49. 23, the *a.* have sorely grieved him.
1 Sam. 31. 3, and the *a.* hit him.
2 Chron. 35. 23, and the *a.* shot at king Josiah.
Job 16. 13, his *a.* compass me.
See 1 Kings 22. 34.
ARGUING. Job 6. 25.
ARGUMENTS. Job 23. 4.
ARIGHT. Ps. 50. 23; 78. 8; Prov. 15. 2; 23. 31.
ARISE. 1 Kings 18. 44, there *a.* a little cloud.
Neh. 2. 20, *a.* and build.
Ps. 68. 1, let God *a.*
88. 10, dead *a.* and praise thee.
112. 4, to upright *a.* light.
Mal. 4. 2, Sun of righteousness *a.*
Mk. 2. 11; Lu. 7. 14; 8. 54; Acts 9. 40, I say *a.*
Lu. 15. 18, I will *a.* and go.
Eph. 5. 14, *a.* from the dead.
2 Pet. 1. 19, till daystar *a.*
See Isa. 26. 19; Jer. 2. 27.
ARMOUR (Goliath's). 1 Sam. 17. 54, but he put his *a.* in his tent.
1 Kings 22, 38, and they washed his *a.*
Isa. 22. 8, didst look in that day to *a.*
Lu. 11. 22, his *a.* wherein he trusted.
Rom. 13. 12, let us put on *a.* of light.
2 Cor. 6. 7, approving by *a.* of righteousness.
Eph. 6. 11, 13, put on the *a.* of God.
See 2 Cor. 10. 3; 1 Thess. 5. 8.
ARMS. Deut. 33. 27, underneath are the everlasting *a.*
See Gen. 49. 24; Job 22. 9; Ps. 37. 17; Mk. 10. 16.
ARMY. 1 Sam. 17. 10, I defy the *a.* of Israel.
Job 25. 3, is there any number of his *a.*
Lu. 21. 20, Jerusalem compassed with *a.*
Acts 23. 27, then came I with an *a.*
Heb. 11. 34, *a.* of the aliens.
See Cant. 6. 4; Ezek. 37. 10.
ARRAY. Jer. 43. 12, shall *a.* himself with land.
Mat. 6. 29; Lu. 12. 27, *a.* like one of these.
1 Tim. 2. 9, not with costly *a.*
Rev. 7. 13, *a.* in white robes.
See Job 40. 10; Rev. 17. 4; 19. 8.
ARRIVED. Lu. 8. 26; Acts 20. 15.
ARROGANCY. 1 Sam. 2. 3; Prov. 8. 13; Isa. 13. 11; Jer. 48. 29.
ARROW. Num. 24. 8, pierce through with *a.*
Ps. 38. 2, thine *a.* stick fast.
76. 3, brake the *a.* of the bow.
91. 5, *a.* that flieth by day.
Prov. 25. 18, false witness sharp *a.*
26. 18, casteth *a.* and death.
Ezek. 5. 16, evil *a.* of famine.
See Deut. 32. 23; 2 Sam. 22. 15; Job 6. 4; 41. 28.
ARTIFICER. Gen. 4. 22; 1 Chron. 29. 5; 2 Chron. 34. 11; Isa. 3. 3.
ARTILLERY. 1 Sam. 20. 40.
ASCEND. Ps. 68. 18; Rom. 10. 6; Eph. 4. 8, *a.* on high.
John 1. 51, angels of God *a.*
3. 13, no man hath *a.* to heaven.
20. 17, I am not yet *a.*

Rev. 8. 4, smoke of incense *a.*
11. 12, they *a.* up to heaven.
See Ps. 24. 3; 139. 8.
ASCRIBE. Deut. 32. 3; Job 36. 3; Ps. 68. 34.
ASHAMED. Job 11. 3, shall no man make *a.*
Ps. 25. 3, let none that wait be *a.*
31. 1, let me never be *a.*
34. 5, their faces were not *a.*
Isa. 45. 17, not *a.* world without end.
65. 13, ye shall be *a.*
Jer. 2. 26, as a thief is *a.*
6. 15; 8. 12, were they *a.*
12. 13, *a.* of your revenues.
14. 4, plowmen were *a.*
Lu. 16. 3, to beg I am *a.*
Rom. 1. 16, not *a.* of Gospel.
5. 5, hope maketh not *a.*
9. 33; 10. 11, believeth shall not be *a.*
2 Tim. 1. 8, not *a.* of testimony.
2. 15, workman that needeth not to be *a.*
Heb. 2. 11, not *a.* to call them brethren.
11. 16, not *a.* to be called their God.
1 Pet. 4. 16, suffer as Christian, not be *a.*
See Gen. 2. 25; 2 Tim. 1. 12.
ASHES. Gen. 18. 27, which am but dust and *a.*
Job. 2. 8, and he sat down among the *a.*
13. 12, remembrances are like unto *a.*
30. 19, and become like dust and *a.*
42. 6, and repent in dust and *a.*
Ps. 102. 9, I have eaten *a.* like bread.
Isa. 44. 20, he feedeth on *a.*
Jon. 3. 6, king sat in *a.*
Heb. 9. 13, if the *a.* of an heifer.
See 2 Sam. 13. 19; Esth. 4. 1; Isa. 58. 5; Mat. 11. 21.
ASIDE. 2 Kings 4. 4; Mk. 7. 33; Heb. 12. 1.
ASK. Ps. 2. 8; Isa. 45. 11, *a.* of me.
Isa. 65. 1, sought of them that *a.* not.
Mat. 7. 7; Lu. 11. 9, *a.* and it shall be given.
21. 22, whatsoever ye *a.*
Mk. 6. 22, *a.* what thou wilt.
John 14. 13; 15. 16, *a.* in my name.
Jas. 1. 5, let him *a.* of God.
1 Pet. 3. 15, *a.* reason of hope.
1 John 3. 22; 5. 14, whatsoever we *a.*
See Deut. 32. 7; John 4. 9, 10; 1 Cor. 14. 35.
ASLEEP. Mat. 8. 24; Mk. 4. 38, but he was *a.*
26. 40; Mk. 14. 40, disciples *a.*
1 Cor. 15. 6, some are fallen *a.*
1 Thess. 4. 13, 15, them that are *a.*
2 Pet. 3. 4, since fathers fell *a.*
See Cant. 7. 9.
ASP. Deut. 32. 33, the cruel venom of *a.*
Job 20. 14, 16, it is the gall of *a.*
Isa. 11. 8, play on the hole of the *a.*
Rom. 3. 13, the poison of *a.*
ASS. Num. 22. 30, am not I thine *a.*
Prov. 26. 3, bridle for *a.*
Isa. 1. 3, *a.* his master's crib.
Jer. 22. 19, burial of an *a.*
Zech. 9. 9; Mat. 21. 5, riding on *a.*
Lu. 14. 5, *a.* fallen into pit.
2 Pet. 2. 16, dumb *a.* speaking.
See Gen. 49. 14; Ex. 23. 4; Deut. 22. 10.
ASSAULT. Esth. 8. 11; Acts 14. 5; 17. 5.
ASSAY. Acts 9. 26, Saul *a.* to join disciples.
16. 7, they *a.* to go to Bithynia.
Heb. 11. 29, Egyptians *a.* to do.
See Deut. 4. 34; 1 Sam. 17. 39; Job 4. 2.
ASSENT. 2 Chron. 18. 12; Acts 24. 9.
ASSIGNED. Gen. 47. 22; Josh. 20. 8; 2 Sam. 11. 16.
ASSIST. Rom. 16. 2.
ASSOCIATE. Isa. 8. 9.
ASSURANCE. Isa. 32. 17, effect of righteousness *a.*
Col. 2. 2, full *a.* of understanding.
1 Thess. 1. 5, gospel came in much *a.*
Heb. 6. 11; 10. 22, full *a.* of hope.
See Deut. 28. 66; Acts 17. 31.
ASSURE. 2 Tim. 3. 14; 1 John 3. 19.
ASSWAGE. Gen. 8. 1; Job 16. 5.
ASTONIED. Ezra 9. 3; Job 17. 8; Dan. 3. 24; 4. 19.
ASTONISHED. Mat. 7. 28; 22. 33; Mk. 1. 22; 6. 2; 11. 18; Lu. 4. 32, *a.* at his doctrine.
Lu. 2. 47, *a.* at his understanding.
5. 9, *a.* at draught of fishes.
24. 22, women made us *a.*
Acts 9. 6, Saul trembling and *a.*
12. 16, saw Peter, they were *a.*
13. 12, deputy believed, being *a.*
See Job 26. 11; Jer. 2. 12.
ASTONISHMENT. 2 Chron. 29. 8; Jer. 25. 9, *a.* and hissing.
Ps. 60. 3, made us drink wine of *a.*
Jer. 8. 21, *a.* hath taken hold.
See Deut. 28. 28, 37; Ezek. 5. 15.
ASTROLOGERS. Isa. 47. 13, let now the *a.*
Dan. 2. 2; 4. 7; 5. 7, the *a.*
ATHIRST. Mat. 25. 44; Rev. 21. 6; 22. 17.
ATONEMENT. Lev. 23. 28; 25. 9, a day of *a.*
2 Sam. 21. 3, wherewith shall I make *a.*
Rom. 5. 11, by whom we received *a.*
See Lev. 4. 20; 16. 17; Num. 8. 21.
ATTAIN. Ps. 139. 6, I cannot *a.* to it.
2 Sam. 23. 19; 1 Chron. 11. 26, he *a.* not to first three.
Rom. 9. 30, Gentiles *a.* to righteousness.
Phil. 3. 11, 12, 16, that I might *a.*
See Gen. 47. 9; Prov. 1. 5; Ezek. 46. 7; 1 Tim. 4. 6.
ATTEND. Ps. 17. 1; 61. 1; 142. 6, *a.* to my cry.
Prov. 4. 20, my son *a.* to my words.
See Ps. 55. 2; 86. 6.
ATTENDANCE. 1 Tim. 4. 13; Heb. 7. 13.
ATTENT. 2 Chron. 6. 40; 7. 15.
ATTENTIVE. Neh. 1. 6; Job 37. 2; Ps. 130. 2; Lu. 19. 48.
ATTIRE. Jer. 2. 32; Ezek. 23. 15.
AUDIENCE. 1 Chron. 28. 8, in *a.* of our God.
Lu. 7. 1; 20. 45, in *a.* of people.
Acts 13. 16, ye that fear God give *a.*
See Ex. 24. 7; Acts 15. 12.
AUGMENT. Num. 32. 14.
AUSTERE. Lu. 19. 21.
AUTHOR. 1 Cor. 14. 33; Heb. 5. 9; 12. 2.
AUTHORITY. Mat. 7. 29; Mk. 1. 22, as one having *a.*
8. 9; Lu. 7. 8, I am a man under *a.*
21. 23; Lu. 4. 36, by what *a.*
Lu. 9. 1, power and *a.* over devils.
19. 17, have *a.* over ten cities.
John 5. 27, *a.* to execute judgment.
1 Cor. 15. 24, put down all *a.*
1 Tim. 2. 2, kings and all in *a.*
12, suffer not a woman to usurp *a.*
Tit. 2. 15, rebuke with all *a.*
1 Pet. 3. 22, angels and *a.* subject.
See Prov. 29. 2; 2 Cor. 10. 8; Rev. 13. 2.
AVAILETH. Esth. 5. 13; Gal. 5. 6; Jas. 5. 16.
AVENGE. Deut. 32. 43, he will *a.* blood.
Josh. 10. 13, sun stayed till people *a.*
1 Sam. 24. 12, the Lord judge and *a.*
2 Sam. 22. 48; Ps. 18. 47, it is God that *a.* me.
Esth. 8. 13, Jews *a.* themselves.
Isa. 1. 24, I will *a.* me of mine enemies.
Lu. 18. 3, *a.* me of my adversary.
See Gen. 4. 24; Lev. 19. 18; Jer. 5. 9; 9. 9.
AVENGER. Ps. 8. 2; 44. 16, enemy and *a.*
1 Thess. 4. 6, the Lord is the *a.*
See Num. 35. 12; Deut. 19. 6; Josh. 20. 5.
AVERSE. Mic. 2. 8.
AVOID. Prov. 4. 15, *a.* it, pass not by it.
1 Tim. 6. 20; 2 Tim. 2. 23; Tit. 3. 9, *a.* babblings.
See Rom. 16. 17; 2 Cor. 8. 20.
AVOUCHED. Deut. 26. 17, 18.
AWAKE. Ps. 17. 15, when I *a.*, with thy likeness.
73. 20, as a dream when one *a.*
Prov. 23. 35, *a.* I will seek it again.
Isa. 51. 9, *a.*, *a.*, put on strength.
Joel 1. 5, *a.* ye drunkards.

Zech. 13. 7, *a.* O sword.
Lu. 9. 32, when *a.* they saw his glory.
Rom. 13. 11, high time to *a.*
1 Cor. 15. 34, *a.* to righteousness.
Eph. 5. 14, *a.* thou that sleepest.
See Jer. 51. 57; John 11. 11.
AWARE. Cant. 6. 12; Jer. 50. 24; Lu. 11. 44.
AWE. Ps. 4. 4; 33. 8; 119. 161.
AWL. Ex. 21. 6; Deut. 15. 17.
AXE. Ps. 74. 5, famous as he had lifted up *a.*
Isa. 10. 15, shall the *a.* boast.
Mat. 3. 10; Lu. 3. 9, the *a.* is laid to root.
See 1 Sam. 13. 20; 1 Kings 6. 7; 2 Kings 6. 5.

B

BABBLER. Eccl. 10. 11; Acts 17. 18.
BABBLING. Prov. 23. 29; 1 Tim. 6. 20; 2 Tim. 2. 16.
BABE. Ps. 8. 2; Mat. 21. 16, out of mouth of *b.*
17. 14, leave their substance to *b.*
Isa. 3. 4, *b.* shall rule over them.
Mat. 11. 25; Lu. 10. 21, revealed to *b.*
Rom. 2. 20, teacher of *b.*
1 Cor. 3. 1, *b.* in Christ.
1 Pet. 2. 2, newborn *b.*
See Ex. 2. 6; Lu. 2. 12, 16; Heb. 5. 13.
BACK. Josh. 8. 26, drew not his hand *b.*
1 Sam. 10. 9, he turned his *b.*
Neh. 9. 26, cast law behind *b.*
Ps. 129. 3, plowers plowed upon my *b.*
Prov. 10. 13; 19. 29; 26. 3, rod for *b.*
Isa. 38. 17, cast sins behind *b.*
50. 6, gave *b.* to smiters.
See Num. 24. 11; 2 Sam. 19. 10; Job 26. 9.
BACKBITERS. Rom. 1. 30.
BACKBITING. Ps. 15. 3; Prov. 25. 23; 2 Cor. 12. 20.
BACKSLIDER. Prov. 14. 14, *b.* in heart filled with his own ways.
Jer. 3. 6, 8, 11, 12, *b.* Israel.
8. 5, perpetual *b.*
14. 7, our *b.* are many.
Hos. 4. 16, as a *b.* heifer.
11. 7, bent to *b.* from me.
14. 4, will heal their *b.*
See Jer. 2. 19; 5. 6; 31. 22; 49. 4.
BACKWARD. 2 Kings 20. 10; Isa. 38. 8, let shadow return *b.*
Job 23. 8, *b.*, but I cannot perceive.
Ps. 40. 14; 70. 2, driven *b.*
Isa. 59. 14, judgment is turned *b.*
Jer. 7. 24, they went *b.* and not forward.
See Gen. 9. 23; 49. 17; John 18. 6.
BAD. Gen. 24. 50; 31. 24, 29; Lev. 27. 12, 14, 33; Num. 13. 19; 24. 13; 2 Sam. 13. 22; 14. 17; 1 Kings 3. 9; Mat. 22. 10; 2 Cor. 5. 10, good or *b.*
See Lev. 27. 10; Ezra 4. 12; Jer. 24. 2; Mat. 31. 48.
BADGERS' SKINS. Ex. 25. 5, and *b.*
26. 14, a covering above of *b.*
BADNESS. Gen. 41. 19.
BAG. Deut. 25. 13; Prov. 16. 11; Mic. 6. 11, *b.* of weights.
Job 14. 17, transgression sealed in *b.*
Isa. 46. 6, lavish gold out of *b.*
Hag. 1. 6, *b.* with holes.
Lu. 12. 33, *b.* that wax not old.
John 12. 6; 13. 29, a thief, and had the *b.*
See 1 Sam. 17. 40; 2 Kings 5. 23; Prov. 7. 20.
BAKE. Gen. 19. 3; Lev. 26. 26; 1 Sam. 28. 24; Isa. 44. 15, *b.* bread.
Ex. 12. 39; Lev. 24. 5, *b.* cakes.
See Gen. 40. 17; Ex. 16. 23; Lev. 2. 4; Num. 11. 8.
BAKER. Gen. 40. 1; 41. 10; 1 Sam. 8. 13; Jer. 37. 21; Hos. 7. 4.
BALANCE. Lev. 19. 36; Prov. 16. 11; Ezek. 45. 10, just *b.*
Job 37. 16, the *b.* of clouds.
Ps. 62. 9, laid in *b.*, lighter than vanity.
Prov. 11. 1; 20. 23; Hos. 12. 7; Amos 8. 5; Mic. 6. 11, false *b.*
Isa. 40. 12, 15, weighed hills in *b.*
46. 6, weigh silver in the *b.*
Rev. 6. 5, a pair of *b.*
See Job 6. 2; 31. 6; Jer. 32. 10.
BALD. 2 Kings 2. 23, go up, thou *b.* head.
Jer. 48. 37; Ezek. 29. 18, every head *b.*
See Lev. 13. 40; Jer. 16. 6; Ezek. 27. 31.
BALDNESS. Isa. 3. 24, instead of well set hair *b.*
22. 12, call to weeping and *b.*
Mic. 1. 16, enlarge thy *b.* as eagle.
See Lev. 21. 5; Deut. 14. 1; Ezek. 7. 18; Amos 8. 10.
BALL. Isa. 22. 18.
BALM. Jer. 8. 22; 46. 11, *b.* in Gilead.
See Gen. 37. 25; 43. 11; Jer. 51. 8; Ezek. 27. 17.
BANDS. Ps. 2. 3; 107. 14, break their *b.* asunder.
73. 4, there are no *b.* in their death.
Hos. 11. 4, drew them with *b.* of love.
Zech. 11. 7, two staves, Beauty and *B.*
Mat. 27. 27; Mk. 15. 16, gathered to him whole *b.*
See Job 38. 31; Eccl. 7. 26; Lu. 8. 29; Col. 2. 19.
BANISHED. 2 Sam. 14. 13; Ezra 7. 26; Lam. 2. 14.
BANK. Lu. 19. 23, gavest not money into *b.*
See Gen. 41. 17; 2 Sam. 20. 15; Ezek. 47. 7.
BANNER. Ps. 20. 5, in name of God set up *b.*
See Ps. 60. 4; Cant. 2. 4; 6. 4; Isa. 13. 2.
BANQUET. Esth. 5. 4; Job 41. 6; Cant. 2. 4; Dan. 5; Amos 6. 7.
BAPTISM. Mat. 20. 22; Mk. 10. 38; Lu. 12. 50, to be baptized with *b.*
21. 25; Mk. 11. 30; Lu. 7. 29; 20. 4; Acts 1. 22; 18. 25; 19. 3, *b.* of John.
Mk. 1. 4; Lu. 3. 3; Acts 13. 24; 19. 4, *b.* of repentance.
Rom. 6. 4; Col. 2. 12, buried with him by *b.*
Eph. 4. 5, one Lord, one faith, one *b.*
Heb. 6. 2, doctrine of *b.*
See Mat. 3. 7; 1 Pet. 3. 21.
BAPTIZE. Mat. 3. 11; Mk. 1. 8; Lu. 3. 16; John 1. 26, *b.* with Holy Ghost.
14, I have need to be *b.*
16, Jesus when *b.* went up.
Mk. 16. 16, he that believeth and is *b.*
Lu. 3. 7, multitude came to be *b.*
12; 7. 29, publicans to be *b.*
21, Jesus being *b.*, and praying.
7. 30, Pharisees and lawyers being not *b.*
John 1. 33, he that sent me to *b.*
3. 22, 23, tarried with them and *b.*
4. 1, 2, Jesus made and *b.* more.
Acts 2. 38, repent and be *b.*
41, gladly received word were *b.*
8. 12, *b.* both men and women.
16, *b.* in name of Jesus.
36, what doth hinder to be *b.*
9. 18, Saul arose and was *b.*
10. 47, can any forbid *b.*
16. 15, 33, *b.* and household.
18. 8, many believed and were *b.*
22. 16, be *b.* and wash away thy sins.
Rom. 6. 3; Gal. 3. 27, were *b.* into Jesus.
1 Cor. 1. 13, were ye *b.* in name of Paul.
10. 2, were all *b.* in cloud.
12. 13, all *b.* into one body.
15. 29, *b.* for the dead.
See Mat. 28. 19; John 1. 25, 28, 31.
BARBARIANS. Acts 28. 4; Rom. 1. 14; 1 Cor. 14. 11.
BARBAROUS. Acts 28. 2.
BARBED. Job 41. 7.
BARBER. Ezek. 5. 1.
BARE (*v.*). Ex. 19. 4; Deut. 1. 31; Isa. 53. 12; 63. 9; Mat. 8. 17; 1 Pet. 2. 24.
BARE (*ad.*). Isa. 52. 10; 1 Cor. 15. 37.
BARLEY. Ex. 9. 31, *b.* was in the ear.
Deut. 8. 8, a land of wheat and *b.*
Ruth 1. 22, beginning of *b.* harvest.
John 6. 9, five *b.* loaves.

Rev. 6. 6, three measures of *b*.
BARKED. Joel 1. 7.
BARN. Job 39. 12, gather thy seed into *b*.
Mat. 6. 26; Lu. 12. 24, nor gather into *b*.
13. 30, gather wheat into *b*.
Lu. 12. 18, pull down my *b*.
See 2 Kings 6. 27; Joel 1. 17; Hag. 2. 19.
BARREL. 1 Kings 17. 12, 14; 18. 33.
BARREN. 2 Kings 2. 19, water naught and ground *b*.
Ps. 107. 34, turneth fruitful land into *b*.
Isa. 54. 1, sing, O *b*., thou that didst not bear.
2 Pet. 1. 8, neither *b*. nor unfruitful.
See Ex. 23. 26; Job 24. 21; Lu. 23. 29.
BARS. Job 17. 16, down to the *b*. of the pit.
Ezek. 38. 11, having neither *b*. nor gates.
See 1 Sam. 23. 7; Job 38. 10; Ps. 107. 16; Isa. 45. 2.
BASE. Job 30. 8, children of *b*. men.
Mal. 2. 9, I have made you *b*.
Acts 17. 5, fellows of *b*. sort.
1 Cor. 1. 28, *b*. things of the world.
2 Cor. 10. 1, in presence am *b*.
See 2 Sam. 6. 22; Isa. 3. 5; Ezek. 17. 14; Dan. 4. 17.
BASKET. Deut. 28. 5, 17, blessed be thy *b*.
Amos 8. 1, *b*. of summer fruit.
Mat. 14. 20; Mk. 6. 43; Lu. 9. 17; John 6. 13, twelve *b*.
15. 37; Mk. 8. 8, seven *b*.
16. 9; Mk. 8. 19, how many *b*.
See Gen. 40. 16; Ex. 29. 23; Judg. 6. 19; Jer. 24. 2.
BASON. John 13. 5, poureth water into a *b*.
See Ex. 12. 22; 24. 6; 1 Chron. 28. 17; Jer. 52. 19.
BASTARD. Deut. 23. 2, a *b*. shall not enter.
Zech. 9. 6, *b*. shall dwell in Ashdod.
Heb. 12. 8, *b*. and not sons.
BATH (a measure). 1 Kings 7. 26, it contained two thousand *b*.
2 Chron. 2. 10, twenty thousand *b*. of wine.
Ezra 7. 22, an hundred *b*. of wine.
Isa. 5. 10, shall yield one *b*.
BATHE. Lev. 15. 5; 17. 16; Num. 19. 7; Isa. 34. 5.
BATS. Lev. 11. 19; Deut. 14. 18; Isa. 2. 20.
BATTLE. 1 Sam. 17. 20, host shouted for *b*.
47; 2 Chron. 20. 15, the *b*. is the Lord's.
1 Chron. 5. 20, they cried to God in *b*.
Ps. 18. 39, strength to *b*.
55. 18, delivered my soul from *b*.
Eccl. 9. 11, nor *b*. to strong.
Jer. 50. 22, sound of *b*. in land.
See Job 39. 25; 41. 8; Ps. 76. 3; 140. 7.
BATTLEMENTS. Deut. 22. 8; Jer. 5. 10.
BAY TREE. Ps. 37. 35.
BEACON. Isa. 30. 17.
BEAM. Ps. 104. 3, who layeth *b*. in waters.
Mat. 7. 5; Lu. 6. 42, cast out *b*.
See Judg. 16. 14; 2 Kings 6. 2; Hab. 2. 11.
BEAR (*v*.). Gen. 4. 13, greater than I can *b*.
13. 6; 36. 7, land not able to *b*.
43. 9; 44. 32, let me *b*. blame.
Ex. 20. 16; 1 Kings 21. 10; Lu. 11. 48; John 1. 7; 5. 31; 8. 18; 15. 27; Acts 23. 11; Rom. 8. 16; 1 John 1. 2; 5. 8, *b*. witness.
28. 12, Aaron *b*. names before Lord.
Lev. 24. 15; Ezek. 23. 49; Heb. 9. 28, *b*. sin.
Num. 11. 14; Deut. 1. 9, not able to *b*. people.
Esth. 1. 22; Jer. 5. 31; Dan. 2. 39, *b*. rule.
Ps. 91. 12; Mat. 4. 6; Lu. 4. 11, they shall *b*. thee up.
Prov. 18. 14, wounded spirit who can *b*.
Isa. 52. 11, clean that *b*. vessels.
Jer. 31. 19, *b*. reproach of youth.
Lam. 3. 27, good to *b*. yoke in youth.
Mat. 3. 11, not worthy to *b*.
27. 32; Mk. 15. 21; Lu. 23. 26, *b*. cross.
John 16. 12, cannot *b*. them now.
Rom. 13. 4, *b*. not sword in vain.
15. 1, *b*. infirmities of the weak.
1 Cor. 13. 7, charity *b*. all things.
1 Cor. 15. 49, *b*. image of the heavenly.
Gal. 6. 2, 5, *b*. burdens.
17, *b*. in my body.
See Ex. 28. 38; Deut. 1. 31; Prov. 12. 24.
BEAR (*n*.). Isa. 11. 7, cow and *b*. shall feed.
59. 11, roar like *b*.
Hos. 13. 8, as a *b*. bereaved.
Amos 5. 19, as if a man did flee from *b*.
See 1 Sam. 17. 34; 2 Sam. 17. 8; Prov. 17. 12.
BEARD. 2 Sam. 10. 5; 1 Chron. 19. 5, till *b*. be grown.
Ps. 133. 2, even Aaron's *b*.
Ezek. 5. 1, cause razor to pass on *b*.
See Lev. 13. 29; 1 Sam. 21. 13; 2 Sam. 20. 9.
BEARING. Ps. 126. 6, *b*. precious seed.
John 19. 17, *b*. cross.
Rom. 2. 15; 9. 1, conscience *b*. witness.
2 Cor. 4. 10, *b*. about in body dying of Jesus.
Heb. 13. 13, *b*. his reproach.
See Gen. 1. 29; Num. 10. 17; Mk. 14. 13.
BEAST. Job 12. 7, ask *b*., they shall teach.
Job 18. 3, counted as *b*.
Ps. 49. 12, like *b*. that perish.
73. 22, as *b*. before thee.
Prov. 12. 10, regardeth life of *b*.
Eccl. 3. 19, no pre-eminence above *b*.
1 Cor. 15. 32, fought with *b*.
Jas. 3. 7, every kind of *b*. is tamed.
2 Pet. 2. 12, as natural brute *b*.
See Lev. 11. 47; Ps. 50. 10; 147. 9; Rom. 1. 23.
BEAT. Isa. 2. 4; Joel 3. 10; Mic. 4. 3, *b*. swords.
Lu. 12. 47, *b*. with many stripes.
1 Cor. 9. 26, as one that *b*. the air.
See Prov. 23. 14; Mic. 4. 13; Mk. 12. 5; 13. 9.
BEAUTIFUL. Ps. 48. 2, *b*. for situation is Zion.
Eccl. 3. 11, everything *b*. in his time.
Cant. 6. 4, thou art *b*., O my love..
Isa. 4. 2, the branch of the Lord be *b*.
52. 1, O Zion, put on thy *b*. garments.
7; Rom. 10. 15, how *b*. are the feet.
64. 11, *b*. house is burnt up.
Jer. 13. 20, where is thy *b*. flock?
Mat. 23. 27, sepulchres which appear *b*.
Acts 3. 2, 10, at the gate called *B*.
BEAUTY. 1 Chron. 16. 29; 2 Chron. 20. 21; Ps. 29. 2; 96. 9; 110. 3, *b*. of holiness.
Ezra 7. 27, to *b*. the Lord's house.
Ps. 27. 4, behold *b*. of the Lord.
39. 11, *b*. to consume away.
50. 2, perfection of *b*.
Prov. 31. 30, *b*. is vain.
See 2 Sam. 1. 19; Ps. 90. 17; Zech. 9. 17.
BEAUTY AND BANDS. Zech. 11. 7, two staves, *B*.
BECKON. Lu. 1. 22; John 13. 24; Acts 12. 17; 21. 40.
BECOMETH. Ps. 93. 5, holiness *b*. thy house.
Rom. 16. 2; Eph. 5. 3, as *b*. saints.
Phil. 1. 27; 1 Tim. 2. 10; Tit. 2. 3, as *b*. gospel.
See Prov. 17. 7; Mat. 3. 15.
BED. Job 7. 13, when I say my *b*. shall comfort.
33. 15, in slumberings upon *b*.
Ps. 63. 6, when I remember thee upon my *b*.
Mat. 9. 6; Mk. 2. 9; John 5. 11, take up *b*.
See 2 Kings 4. 10; Isa. 28. 20; Mk. 4. 21; Lu. 8. 16.
BEDSTEAD. Deut. 3. 11, was a *b*. of iron.
BEES. Deut. 1. 44; Judg. 14. 8; Ps. 118. 12; Isa. 7. 18.
BEEVES. Lev. 22. 19; Num. 31. 28, 38.
BEFALL. Gen. 42. 4; 44. 29, mischief *b*. him.
49. 1; Deut. 31. 29; Dan. 10. 14, *b*. in last days.
Judg. 6. 13, why is all this *b*. us?
Ps. 91. 10, no evil *b*. thee.
Eccl. 3. 19, *b*. men, *b*. beasts, one thing *b*.
See Lev. 10. 19; Deut. 31. 17; Acts 20. 19.
BEG. Ps. 37. 25; 109. 10; Prov. 20. 4; Lu. 16. 3.
BEGGARLY. Gal. 4. 9.
BEGIN. Ezek. 9. 6, *b*. at my sanctuary.
1 Pet. 4. 17, judgment *b*. at house of God.
See 1 Sam. 3. 12; 2 Cor. 3. 1.
BEGINNING. Gen. 1. 1, in the *b*. God created heaven.

Job 8. 7, though thy *b.* was small.
Ps. 111. 10; Prov. 1. 7; 9. 10, *b.* of wisdom.
119. 160, word true from *b.*
Eccl. 7. 8, better end than *b.*
Mat. 19. 8, from *b.* not so.
Lu. 24. 47, *b.* at Jerusalem.
John 1. 1, in the *b.* was the Word.
2. 11, this *b.* of miracles.
Heb. 3. 14, hold *b.* of confidence.
Rev. 1. 8; 21. 6; 22, 13, I am the *b.*
See 1 Chron. 17. 9; Prov. 8. 22. 23; Col. 1. 18.
BEGOTTEN. Ps. 2. 7; Acts 13. 33; Heb. 1. 5; 5. 5, this day have I *b.* thee.
1 Pet. 1. 3, *b.* to a lively hope.
See Job 38. 28; 1 Cor. 4. 15; Philem. 10.
BEGUILE. Gen. 29. 25; Josh. 9. 22, wherefore hast thou *b.* me.
2 Pet. 2. 14, *b.* unstable souls.
See Num. 25. 18; 2 Cor. 11. 3.
BEGUN. Gal. 3. 3, having *b.* in Spirit.
Phil. 1. 6, hath *b.* good work.
See Deut. 3. 24; 2 Cor. 8. 16; 1 Tim. 5. 11.
BEHALF. Job 36. 2, speak on God's *b.*
Phil. 1. 29, in *b.* of Christ.
See 2 Chron. 16. 9; 2 Cor. 1. 11; 5. 12.
BEHAVE. 1 Sam. 18. 5, 14, 15, 30, David *b.* wisely.
1 Chron. 19. 13, *b.* ourselves valiantly.
Ps. 101. 2, I will *b.* wisely.
Isa. 3. 5, child shall *b.* proudly.
1 Thess. 2. 10, how unblameably we *b.*
1 Tim. 3. 2, bishop of good *b.*
See Ps. 131. 2; 1 Cor. 13. 5; Tit. 2. 3.
BEHEADED. Mat. 14. 10; Mk. 6. 16; Lu. 9. 9; Rev. 20. 4.
BEHIND. Ex. 10. 26, not hoof be left *b.*
Phil. 3. 13, things which are *b.*
Col. 1. 24, fill up what is *b.*
See 1 Kings 14. 9; Neh. 9. 26; 2 Cor. 11. 5.
BEHOLD. Ps. 37. 37, *b.* the upright.
Mat. 18. 10, their angels always *b.*
John 17. 24, that they may *b.* glory.
2 Cor. 3. 18, *b.* as in a glass.
See Num. 24. 17; Ps. 91. 8; 119. 37.
BEHOVED. Lu. 24. 46; Heb. 2. 17.
BELIEF. 2 Thess. 2. 13.
BELIEVE. Num. 14. 11, how long ere they *b.* me.
2 Chron. 20. 20, *b.* Lord, *b.* prophets.
Ps. 78. 22, they *b.* not in God.
Prov. 14. 15, simple *b.* every word.
Mat. 8. 13, as thou hast *b.* so be it.
9. 28, *b.* ye that I am able.
21. 25; Mk. 11. 31, why then did ye not *b.*
27. 42, come down and we will *b.*
Mk. 5. 36; Lu. 8. 50, only *b.*
9. 23, canst *b.* all things possible.
11. 24, *b.* that ye receive.
16. 13, neither *b.* they them.
Lu. 1. 1, things most surely *b.*
8. 13, which for a while *b.*
24. 25, slow of heart to *b.*
41, *b.* not for joy.
John 1. 7, all through him might *b.*
2. 22, they *b.* the scripture.
3. 12, *b.* heavenly things.
5. 44, how can ye *b.* which receive honour.
47, how shall ye *b.* my words.
6. 36, seen me and *b.* not.
7. 5, neither did his brethren *b.*
48, have any of the rulers *b.*?
10. 38, *b.* the works.
11. 15, to intent ye may *b.*
26, never die, *b.* thou this?
48, all men will *b.*
12. 36, *b.* in the light.
17. 21, the world may *b.*
20. 25, I will not *b.*
29, have not seen yet have *b.*
Acts 4. 32, multitude of them that *b.*
13. 39, all that *b.* are justified.
48, ordained to eternal life *b.*
16. 34, *b.* with all his house.
Rom. 4. 11, father of all that *b.*
18, against hope *b.* in hope.
9. 33, *b.* not ashamed.
10. 14, how shall they *b.*
1 Cor. 7. 12, wife that *b.* not.
2 Cor. 4. 13, we *b.* and therefore speak.
Gal. 3. 22, promise to them that *b.*
2 Thess. 1. 10, admired in all that *b.*
Heb. 10. 39, *b.* to saving of soul.
11. 6, must *b.* that he is.
Jas. 2. 19, devils *b.* and tremble.
1 Pet. 2. 6, he that *b.* shall not be confounded.
See Ex. 4. 5; 19. 9; Isa. 43. 10; Mat. 21. 22; John 8. 24; 10. 37; Acts 9. 26.
BELLY. Gen. 3. 14; Job 15. 2; Mat. 15. 17; Mk. 7. 19; John 7. 38; Rom. 16. 18; Phil. 3. 19; Tit. 1. 12.
BELONGETH. Deut. 32. 35; Ps. 94. 1; Heb. 10. 30.
BELOVED. Deut. 33. 12, *b.* dwell in safety.
Ps. 127. 2, giveth his *b.* sleep.
Dan. 9. 23; 10. 11, 19, greatly *b.*
Mat. 3. 17; 17. 5; Mk. 1. 11; 9. 7; Lu. 3. 22; 9. 35; 2 Pet. 1. 17, *b.* son.
Rom. 11. 28, *b.* for fathers' sakes.
Eph. 1. 6, accepted in the *b.*
Col. 4. 9; Philem. 16, *b.* brother.
See Neh. 13. 26; Cant. 2. 16; Rom. 16. 9.
BEMOAN. Job 42. 11; Jer. 15. 5; Nah. 3. 7.
BEND. Ps. 11. 2; Isa. 60. 14; Ezek. 17. 7.
BENEATH. Prov. 15. 24, depart from hell *b.*
Isa. 14. 9, hell from *b.* is moved.
John 8. 23, ye are from *b.*
See Deut. 4. 39; Jer. 31. 37.
BENEFACTORS. Lu. 22. 25.
BENEFIT. Ps. 68. 19, loadeth us with *b.*
1 Tim. 6. 2, partakers of the *b.*
See 2 Chron. 32. 25; Ps. 103. 2; 2 Cor. 1. 15; Philem. 14.
BENEVOLENCE. 1 Cor. 7. 3.
BEREAVE. Gen. 42. 36; 43. 14, *b.* of children.
Eccl. 4. 8, *b.* my soul of God.
Jer. 15. 7; 18. 21, I will *b.* thee.
See Ezek. 5. 17; 36. 12; Hos. 13. 8.
BESEECH. Job 42. 4, hear I *b.* thee.
Mat. 8. 5; Lu. 7. 3, centurion *b.* him.
Lu. 9. 38, I *b.* thee, look on my son.
2 Cor. 5. 20, as though God did *b.* you.
Eph. 4. 1, *b.* you to walk.
Philem. 9, for love's sake *b.* thee.
See Ex. 33. 18; Jon. 1. 14; Rom. 12. 1.
BESET. Ps. 22. 12; 139. 5; Hos. 7. 2; Heb. 12. 1.
BESIDE. Mk. 3. 21; Acts 26. 24; 2 Cor. 5. 13.
BESIEGE. Deut. 28. 52; Eccl. 9. 14; Isa. 1. 8.
BESOUGHT. Ex. 32. 11; Deut. 3. 23; 1 Kings 13. 6; 2 Chron. 33. 12; Jer. 26. 19, *b.* the Lord.
Mat. 8. 31; Mk. 5. 10; Lu. 8. 31, devils *b.* him.
34; Lu. 8. 37, *b.* him to depart.
John 4. 40, *b.* that he would tarry.
2 Cor. 12. 8, I *b.* the Lord thrice.
See Gen. 42. 21; Esth. 8. 3.
BEST. 1 Sam. 15. 9, 15, spared *b.* of sheep.
Ps. 39. 5, at *b.* state vanity.
Lu. 15. 22, *b.* robe.
1 Cor. 12. 31, *b.* gifts.
See Gen. 43. 11; Deut. 23. 16; 2 Sam. 18. 4.
BESTEAD. Isa. 8. 21.
BESTIR. 2 Sam. 5. 24.
BESTOW. Lu. 12. 17, no room to *b.* my fruits.
1 Cor. 15. 10, grace *b.* on us not in vain.
Gal. 4. 11, lest I have *b.* labour in vain.
1 John 3. 1, manner of love Father *b.*
See 1 Chron. 29. 25; Isa. 63. 7; John 4. 38.
BETHINK. 1 Kings 8. 47; 2 Chron. 6. 37.
BETIMES. Gen. 26. 31; 2 Chron. 36. 15; Job 8. 5; Prov. 13. 24.
BETRAY. Mat. 26. 16; Mk. 14. 11; Lu. 22. 21, 22, opportunity to *b.*
27. 4, I *b.* innocent blood.
1 Cor. 11. 23, same night he was *b.*
See Mat. 24. 10; Mk. 14. 18; John 6. 64; 21. 20.

BETROTH. Hos. 2. 19, 20.
BETTER. 1 Sam. 15. 22, to obey *b.* than sacrifice.
1 Kings 19. 4, I am not *b.* than my fathers.
Ps. 63. 3, lovingkindness *b.* than life.
Eccl. 4. 9, two are *b.* than one.
7. 10, former days *b.* than these.
Mat. 12. 12, man *b.* than a sheep.
Lu. 5. 39, he saith, the old is *b.*
Phil. 2. 3, each esteem other *b.* than himself.
Heb. 1. 4, much *b.* than angels.
11. 16, a *b.* country.
2 Pet. 2. 21, *b.* not have known the way.
See Eccl. 2. 24; Cant. 1. 2; Jon. 4. 3.
BEWAIL. Lu. 8. 52, all wept and *b.* her.
Lu. 23. 27, of women which also *b.*
2 Cor. 12. 21, *b.* many who have sinned.
See Deut. 21. 13; Judg. 11. 37; Rev. 18. 9.
BEWARE. Judg. 13. 4, *b.* and drink not wine.
Job 36. 18, *b.* lest he take thee away.
Mat. 16. 6; Mk. 8. 15; Lu. 12. 1, *b.* of leaven.
Mk. 12. 38; Lu. 20. 46, *b.* of scribes.
Lu. 12. 15, *b.* of covetousness.
Phil. 3. 2, *b.* of dogs, *b.* of evil workers.
See Deut. 6. 12; 8. 11; 15. 9.
BEWITCHED. Acts 8. 9; Gal. 3. 1.
BEWRAY. Isa. 16. 3; Prov. 27. 16; 29. 24; Mat. 26. 73.
BEYOND. Num. 22. 18; 2 Cor. 8. 3; Gal. 1. 13; 1 Thess. 4. 6.
BIER. 2 Sam. 3. 31; Lu. 7. 14.
BILLOWS. Ps. 42. 7; Jon. 2. 3.
BIND. Prov. 6. 21, *b.* them continually upon heart.
Isa. 61. 1, *b.* up brokenhearted.
Mat. 12. 29; Mk. 3. 27, *b.* strong man.
16. 19; 18. 18, *b.* on earth.
See Num. 30. 2; Job 26. 8; 38. 31.
BIRD. 2 Sam. 21. 10, suffered not *b.* to rest.
Cant. 2. 12, time of the singing of *b.*
Jer. 12. 9, heritage like a speckled *b.*
Mat. 8. 20; Lu. 9. 58, *b.* of the air have nests.
See Ps. 11. 1; 124. 7; Prov. 1. 17; Eccl. 10. 20.
BIRTH. John 9. 1, blind from *b.*
Gal. 4. 19, of whom I travail in *b.*
See Eccl. 7. 1; Isa. 66. 9; Lu. 1. 14.
BIRTHDAY. Gen. 40. 20, which was Pharaoh's *b.*
Mat. 14. 6; Mk. 6. 21, when Herod's *b.* was kept.
BIRTHRIGHT. Gen. 25. 31; 27. 36; Heb. 12. 16.
BISHOP (qualifications of). 1 Tim. 3. 1, if a man desire office of *b.*
Tit. 1. 7, *b.* must be blameless.
1 Pet. 2. 25, Shepherd and *B.* of your souls.
See Acts 1. 20; Phil. 1. 1.
BIT. Ps. 32. 9; Jas. 3. 3.
BITE. Prov. 23. 32, at last it *b.* like serpent.
Mic. 3. 5, prophets that *b.* with teeth.
Gal. 5. 15, if ye *b.* and devour one another.
See Eccl. 10. 8; Amos 5. 19; 9. 3.
BITTER. Ex. 12. 8; Num. 9. 11, with *b.* herbs.
Deut. 32. 24, devoured with *b.* destruction.
Job. 13. 26, writest *b.* things.
Isa. 5. 20, that put *b.* for sweet.
24. 9, drink *b.* to them that drink it.
Jer. 2. 19, an evil thing and *b.*
Mat. 26. 75; Lu. 22. 62, Peter wept *b.*
Col. 3. 19, be not *b.* against them.
See Ex. 1. 14; 15. 23; 2 Kings 14. 26.
BITTERNESS. Job 10. 1; 21. 25; Isa. 38. 15, in *b.* of soul.
Prov. 14. 10, heart knoweth own *b.*
Acts 8. 23, in the gall of *b.*
Eph. 4. 31, let all *b.* be put away.
Heb. 12. 15, lest any root of *b.*
See 1 Sam. 15. 32; Prov. 17. 25; Rom. 3. 14.
BLACK. Mat. 5. 36; Jude 13; Rev. 6. 5.
BLADE. Judg. 3. 22; Mat. 13. 26; Mk. 4. 28.
BLAME. 2 Cor. 6. 3; 8. 20; Gal. 2. 11; Eph. 1. 4.
BLAMELESS. 1 Cor. 1. 8, be *b.* in day of the Lord.
Phil. 2. 15, that ye may be *b.*
See Mat. 12. 5; Phil. 3. 6; Tit. 1. 6, 7.
BLASPHEME. 2 Sam. 12. 14, occasion to enemies to *b.*
Isa. 52. 5, my name continually is *b.*
Mat. 9. 3, scribes said, this man *b.*
Mk. 3. 29, *b.* against Holy Ghost.
Acts 26. 11, I compelled them to *b.*
Rom. 2. 24, name of God is *b.* through you.
Jas. 2. 7, *b.* that worthy name.
See 1 Kings 21. 10; Ps. 74. 10, 18; 1 Tim. 1. 20.
BLASPHEMY. Mat. 12. 31, all manner of *b.*
26. 65; Mk. 14. 64, he hath spoken *b.*
Lu. 5. 21, who is this which speaketh *b.*?
See 2 Kings 19. 3; Ezek. 35. 12; Mat. 15. 19.
BLAST. Gen. 41. 6; Deut. 28. 22; 1 Kings 8. 37.
BLAZE. Mk. 1. 45.
BLEATING. Judg. 5. 16; 1 Sam. 15. 14.
BLEMISH. Dan. 1. 4, children in whom was no *b.*
Eph. 5. 27, holy and without *b.*
1 Pet. 1. 19, a lamb without *b.* and spot.
See Lev. 21. 17; Deut. 15. 21; 2 Sam. 14. 25.
BLESS. Deut. 28. 3, *b.* in city, *b.* in field.
1 Chron. 4. 10, Oh that thou wouldest *b.* me.
Prov. 10. 7, memory of just is *b.*
Isa. 32. 20, *b.* are ye that sow.
65. 16, *b.* himself in God of truth.
Mat. 5. 44; Lu. 6. 28; Rom. 12. 14, *b.* them that curse.
Acts 20. 35, more *b.* to give than receive.
2 Cor. 11. 32, *b.* for evermore.
Tit. 2. 13, looking for that *b.* hope.
Rev. 14. 13, *b.* are dead that die in Lord.
See Gen. 22. 17; Hag. 2. 19; Jas. 3. 9, 10.
BLESSING. Deut. 23. 5; Neh. 13. 2, turned curse into *b.*
Job 29. 13, *b.* of him that was ready to perish.
Prov. 10. 22, *b.* of Lord maketh rich.
28. 20, faithful man shall abound with *b.*
Isa. 65. 8, destroy it not, a *b.* is in it.
Mal. 2. 2, I will curse your *b.*
3. 10, pour you out a *b.*
Rom. 15. 29, fulness of *b.* of Gospel.
1 Cor. 10. 16, cup of *b.* which we bless.
Jas. 3. 10, proceed *b.* and cursing.
Rev. 5. 12, worthy to receive honour and *b.*
See Gen. 27. 35; 39. 5; Deut. 11. 26, 29.
BLIND (*v.*). Ex. 23. 8, the gift *b.* the wise.
2 Cor. 3. 14; 4. 4, their minds were *b.*
1 John 2. 11, darkness hath *b.*
See Deut. 16. 19; 1 Sam. 12. 3.
BLINDNESS. Eph. 4. 18, because of *b.* of their heart.
See Deut. 28. 28; 2 Kings 6. 18; Zech. 12. 4.
BLOOD. Gen. 9. 6, whoso sheddeth man's *b.*
Josh. 2. 19; 1 Kings 2. 32, *b.* on head.
Ps. 51. 14, deliver me from *b.*-guiltiness.
72. 14, precious shall *b.* be in his sight.
Prov. 29. 10, the *b.*-thirsty hate upright.
Isa. 9. 5, garments rolled in *b.*
Jer. 2. 34, the *b.* of poor innocents.
Ezek. 9. 9, land is full of *b.*
18. 13; 33. 5, his *b.* be upon him.
Hab. 2. 12, buildeth a town with *b.*
Mat. 9. 20; Mk. 5. 25; Lu. 8. 43, issue of *b.*
16. 17, flesh and *b.* hath not revealed.
27. 4, I have betrayed innocent *b.*
25, his *b.* be on us and our children.
Mk. 14. 24; Lu. 22. 20, my *b.* shed.
Lu. 22. 20; 1 Cor. 11. 25, new testament in my *b.*
44, sweat as drops of *b.* falling.
John 1. 13, born not of *b.*
6. 54, 55, 56, drinketh my *b.*
Acts 15. 20; 21. 25, abstain from *b.*
17. 26, made of one *b.*
20. 28, church purchased with his *b.*
Rom. 3. 25, through faith in his *b.*
5. 9, justified by his *b.*
1 Cor. 10. 16. communion of *b.* of Christ.
11. 27, guilty of body and *b.* of the Lord.
15. 50, flesh and *b.* cannot inherit.

Eph. 1. 7; Col. 1. 14, redemption through his *b*.
Heb. 9. 22, without shedding of *b*.
10. 29; 13. 20, *b*. of the covenant.
1 Pet. 1. 19, with precious *b*. of Christ.
Rev. 7. 14; 12. 11, in the *b*. of the Lamb.
See Gen. 9. 4; Ex. 4. 9; 12. 13; Lev. 3. 17; Ps. 55. 23; Rev. 16. 6; 17. 6.

BLOSSOM. Isa. 35. 1, desert shall *b*. as the rose.
Hab. 3. 17, fig tree shall not *b*.
See Gen. 40. 10; Num. 17. 5; Isa. 27. 6.

BLOT. Ex. 32. 32; Ps. 69. 28; Rev. 3. 5, *b*. out of book.
Isa. 44. 22, *b*. out as thick cloud.
Acts 3. 19, repent that sins may be *b*. out.
Col. 2. 14, *b*. out handwriting.
See Deut. 9. 14; 2 Kings 14. 27; Jer. 18. 23.

BLUSH. Ezra 9. 6; Jer. 6. 15; 8. 12.

BOAST (*n*.). Ps. 34. 2; Rom. 2. 17, 23; 3. 27.

BOAST (*v*.). 1 Kings 20. 11, not *b*. as he that putteth it off.
Ps. 49. 6; 94. 4, *b*. themselves.
Prov. 27. 1, *b*. not of to-morrow.
2 Cor. 11. 16, that I may *b*. myself a little.
Eph. 2. 9, lest any man should *b*.
Jas. 3. 5, tongue *b*. great things.
See 2 Chron. 25. 19; Prov. 20. 14; Jas. 4. 16.

BOATS. John 6. 22; Acts 27. 16, 30.

BODY. Job 19. 26, worms destroy this *b*.
Prov. 5. 11, when thy flesh and *b*. are consumed.
Mat. 5. 29, *b*. cast into hell.
6. 22; Lu. 11. 34, *b*. full of light.
25; Lu. 12. 22, take no thought for *b*.
Mk. 5. 29, felt in *b*. that she was healed.
Lu. 17. 37, wheresoever the *b*. is.
John 2. 21, the temple of his *b*.
Acts 19. 12, from his *b*. were brought.
Rom. 6. 6, *b*. of sin destroyed.
7. 24, *b*. of this death.
12. 1, present your *b*. a living sacrifice.
4; 1 Cor. 12. 14, many members, one *b*.
1 Cor. 9. 27, I keep under my *b*.
13. 3, though I give my *b*. to be burned.
2 Cor. 5. 8, absent from the *b*.
12. 2, whether in *b*. or out of the *b*.
Gal. 6. 17, I bear in *b*. marks.
Phil. 3. 21, like to his glorious *b*.
1 Pet. 2. 24, in his own *b*. on tree.
See Gen. 47. 18; Deut. 28. 4; Rom. 12. 5.

BODILY. Lu. 3. 22; 2 Cor. 10. 10; Col. 2. 9; 1 Tim. 4. 8.

BOLD. Eccl. 8. 1, the *b*. of face changed.
John 7. 26, he speaketh *b*.
2 Cor. 10. 2, I may not be *b*.
Eph. 3. 12, we have *b*. and access.
Heb. 4. 16, let us come *b*. to throne.
1 John 4. 17, have *b*. in day of judgment.
See Prov. 28. 1; Acts 13. 46; Rom. 10. 20.

BOND. Acts 8. 23, in *b*. of iniquity.
Eph. 4. 3, *b*. of peace.
Col. 3. 14, *b*. of perfectness.
See Num. 30. 2; Ezek. 20. 37; Lu. 13. 16.

BONDAGE. John 8. 33, never in *b*. to any man.
See Rom. 8. 15; Gal. 5. 1; Heb. 2. 15.

BONDMAID. Lev. 19. 20, a woman that is a *b*.
25. 44, and thy *b*.

BONDMAN. Deut. 15. 15; 16. 12; 24. 18.

BONDMEN. Lev. 25. 39, both thy *b*.

BONDWOMAN. Gen. 21. 10; Gal. 4. 30.

BONE. Ex. 12. 46; Num. 9. 12, neither shall ye break a *b*. thereof.
Job 20. 11, *b*. full of sin.
40. 18, *b*. as pieces of brass.
Ps. 51. 8, the *b*. broken may rejoice.
Prov. 12. 4, as rottenness in his *b*.
Mat. 23. 27, full of dead men's *b*.
Lu. 24. 39, spirit hath not flesh and *b*.
See Gen. 2. 23; Ezek. 37. 7; John 19. 36.

BOOK. Job 19. 23, printed in a *b*.
31. 35, adversary had written a *b*.
Isa. 34. 16, seek out of the *b*. of the Lord.
Mal. 3. 16, *b*. of remembrance.
Lu. 4. 17, when he had opened *b*.
John 21. 25, world could not contain *b*.
Phil. 4. 3; Rev. 3. 5; 13. 8; 17. 8; 20. 12; 21. 27; 22. 19, *b*. of life.
Rev. 22. 19, take away from words of *b*.
See Ex. 17. 14; Ezra 4. 15; Acts 19. 19; 2 Tim. 4. 13.

BOOTH. Job 27. 18; Jon. 4. 5.

BOOTHS. Lev. 23. 42, ye shall dwell in *b*.
Neh. 8. 14, Israel shall dwell in *b*.

BOOTY. Num. 31. 32; Jer. 49. 32; Hab. 2. 7; Zeph. 1. 13.

BORN. Job 5. 7, man *b*. to trouble.
14. 1; 15. 14; 25. 4; Mat. 11. 11, *b*. of a woman.
Ps. 87. 4, this man was *b*. there.
Isa. 9. 6, unto us a child is *b*.
66. 8, shall a nation be *b*. at once.
John 1. 13; 1 John 4. 7; 5. 1, 4, 18, *b*. of God.
3. 3; 1 Pet. 1. 23, *b*. again.
6. 8, *b*. of Spirit.
1 Cor. 15 8, as one *b*. out of due time.
1 Pet. 2. 2, as new-*b*. babes.
See Job 3. 3; Prov. 17. 17; Eccl. 3. 2.

BORNE. Ps. 55. 12, an enemy, then I could have *b*. it.
Isa. 53. 4, *b*. our griefs, carried our sorrows.
Mat. 23. 4; Lu. 11. 46, grievous to be *b*.
See Job 34. 31; Lam. 5. 7; Mat. 20. 12.

BORROW. Deut. 15. 6; 28. 12, lend but not *b*.
Ps. 37. 21, wicked *b*. and payeth not.
Prov. 22. 7, the *b*. is servant.
Mat. 5. 42, him that would *b*. of thee.
See Ex. 3. 22; 11. 2; 22. 14; 2 Kings 4. 3.

BOSOM. Ps. 35. 13, prayer returned into own *b*.
Prov. 6. 27, take fire in his *b*.
Isa. 40. 11, carry lambs in *b*.
Lu. 16. 22, carried into Abraham's *b*.
John 1. 18, in the *b*. of the Father.
13. 23, leaning on Jesus' *b*.
See Ex. 4. 6; Deut. 13. 6; Job 31. 33.

BOSSES. Job 15. 26.

BOTCH. Deut. 28. 27, 35.

BOTTLE. Judg. 4. 19, a *b*. of milk.
1 Sam. 1. 24; 10. 3; 16. 20; 2 Sam. 16. 1, a *b*. of wine.
Ps. 56. 8, put thou my tears into thy *b*.
119. 83, like a *b*. in the smoke.
See Gen. 21. 14, 15; Hab. 2. 15.

BOTTLES. Josh. 9. 13, these *b*. of wine.
1 Sam. 25. 18, and two *b*. of wine.
Job 32. 19, ready to burst like new *b*.
Hos. 7. 5, sick with *b*. of wine.
Mat. 9. 17; Mk. 2. 22; Lu. 5. 37, new wine in old *b*.

BOTTOMLESS. Rev. 9. 1; 11. 7; 17. 8; 20. 1, 2, the *b*. pit.

BOUGH. Gen. 49. 22; Judg. 9. 48; Deut. 24. 20; Job 14. 9; Ps. 80. 10; Ezek. 31. 30.

BOUGHT. Lu. 14. 18; 1 Cor. 6. 20; 7. 23; 2 Pet. 2. 1.

BOUND. Ps. 107. 10, being *b*. in affliction.
Prov. 22. 15, foolishness *b*. in heart of child.
Acts 20. 22, *b*. in spirit to Jerusalem.
1 Cor. 7. 27, art thou *b*. to a wife.
2 Tim. 2. 9, word of God is not *b*.
Heb. 13. 3, in bonds as *b*. with them.
See Gen. 44. 30; Mat. 16. 19; Mk. 5. 4.

BOUNTY. 1 Kings 10. 13; 2 Cor. 9. 5.

BOUNTIFUL. Prov. 22. 9, a *b*. eye shall be blessed.
Isa. 32. 5, nor churl said to be *b*.
See Ps. 13. 6; 116. 7; 119. 17; 2 Cor. 9. 6.

BOWELS. Gen. 43. 30, his *b*. did yearn.
Isa. 63. 15, where is sounding of thy *b*.
2 Cor. 6. 12, straitened in *b*.
Col. 3. 12, *b*. of mercies.
Phil. 1. 8, after you in *b*. of Christ.
2. 1, if there be any *b*.
1 John 3. 17, *b*. of compassion.
See Acts 1. 18; Philem. 12.

BOWLS. Num. 7. 25, one silver *b.*
Eccl. 12. 6, golden *b.* be broken.
Amos 6. 6, that drink wine in *b.*
Zech. 4. 2, with a *b.* upon the top of it.
BRACELET. Gen. 24. 30; Ex. 35. 22; Isa. 3. 19.
BRAKE. 2 Kings 23. 14; 2 Chron. 34. 4, Josiah *b.* images.
Mat. 14. 19; 15. 36; 26. 26; Mk. 6. 41; 8. 6; 14. 22; Lu. 9. 16; 22. 19; 24. 30; 1 Cor. 11. 24, blessed and *b.*
See Ex. 32. 19; 1 Sam. 4. 18; Lu. 5. 6; John 19. 32.
BRAMBLE. Judg. 9. 14; Isa. 34. 13; Lu. 6. 44.
BRANCH. Job 14. 7, tender *b.* not cease.
Prov. 11. 28, righteous flourish as *b.*
Jer. 23. 5, will raise a righteous *b.*
Mat. 13. 32; Lu. 13. 19, birds lodge in *b.*
21. 8; Mk. 11. 8; John 12. 13, cut down *b.*
See Zech. 3. 8; 6. 12; John 15. 2, 4, 5, 6; Rom. 11. 16.
BRAND. Judg. 15. 5, set the *b.* on fire.
Zech. 3. 2, as a fire *b.* plucked out.
BRASS. Deut. 8. 9; 28. 23; 1 Cor. 13. 1.
BRAVERY. Isa. 3. 18.
BRAWLER. Prov. 25. 24; 1 Tim. 3. 3; Tit. 3. 2.
BRAY. Job 6. 5; 30. 7; Prov. 27. 22.
BREACH. Isa. 58. 12, the repairer of the *b.*
Lam. 2. 13, thy *b.* is great like the sea.
See Lev. 24. 20; Ps. 106. 23; Amos 4. 3; 6. 11.
BREAD. Deut. 8. 3; Mat. 4. 4; Lu. 4. 4, not live by *b.* alone.
Ruth 1. 6, visited people in giving them *b.*
1 Kings 17. 6, ravens brought *b.* and flesh.
Job 22. 7, withholden *b.* from hungry.
33. 20, soul abhorreth *b.*
Ps. 132. 15, satisfy poor with *b.*
Prov. 9. 17, *b.* eaten in secret.
12. 11; 20. 13; 28. 19, satisfied with *b.*
31. 27, eateth not *b.* of idleness.
Eccl. 11. 1, cast *b.* on waters.
Isa. 33. 16, *b.* given and waters sure.
55. 2, money for that which is not *b.*
10, seed to sower, *b.* to eater.
Mat. 4. 3; Lu. 4. 3, stones made *b.*
6. 11; Lu. 11. 11, give us daily *b.*
15. 26; Mk. 7. 27, take children's *b.*
Lu. 24. 35, known in breaking *b.*
Acts 2. 42; 20. 7; 27. 35, breaking *b.*
2 Thess. 3. 8, eat any man's *b.* for nought.
See Ex. 16. 4; 23. 25; Josh. 9. 5; Judg. 7. 13.
BREAK. Cant. 2. 17; 4. 6, day *b.* and shadows flee.
Isa. 42. 3; Mat. 12. 20, bruised reed shall he not *b.*
Jer. 4. 3; Hos. 10. 12, *b.* up fallow ground.
Acts 21. 13, to weep and *b.* my heart.
See Ps. 2. 3; Mat. 5. 19; 9. 17; 1 Cor. 10. 16.
BREATH. Gen. 2. 7; 6. 17; 7. 15, *b.* of life.
Isa. 2. 22, cease from man whose *b.*
Ezek. 37. 5, 10, I will cause *b.* to enter.
Acts 17. 25, he giveth to all life and *b.*
See Job 12. 10; 33. 4; Ps. 146. 4; 150. 6.
BREATHE. Ps. 27. 12; Ezek. 37. 9; John 20. 22.
BREECHES. Ex. 28. 42; Lev. 6. 10; 16. 4; Ezek. 44. 18.
BRETHREN. Mat. 23. 8, all ye are *b.*
Mk. 10. 29; Lu. 18. 29, no man left house or *b.*
Col. 1. 2, faithful *b.* in Christ.
1 John 3. 14, because we love the *b.*
See Gen. 42. 8; Prov. 19. 7; John 7. 5.
BRIBE. 1 Sam. 12. 3, have I received any *b.*
Ps. 26. 10, right hand is full of *b.*
See 1 Sam. 8. 3; Isa. 33. 15; Job 15. 34.
BRICK. Gen. 11. 3; Ex. 1. 14; 5. 7; Isa. 9. 10; 65. 3.
BRIDE. Isa. 61. 10; Jer. 2. 32; Rev. 21. 2; 22. 17.
BRIDEGROOM. Mat. 25. 1, to meet the *b.*
John 3. 29, because of *b.* voice.
See Ps. 19. 5; Isa. 62. 5; Mat. 9. 15.
BRIDLE. Prov. 26. 3, a *b.* for the ass.
Jas. 1. 26, *b.* not his tongue.
3. 2, able to *b.* whole body.
See 2 Kings 19. 28; Ps. 39. 1; Isa. 37. 29.
BRIGANDINE. Jer. 46. 4; 51. 3.
BRIGHT. Job 37. 21, *b.* light in the clouds.
Isa. 60. 3, to *b.* of thy rising.
62. 1, righteousness go forth as *b.*
Mat. 17. 5, *b.* cloud overshadowed.
2 Thess. 2. 8, *b.* of his coming.
Heb. 1. 3, the *b.* of his glory.
Rev. 22. 16, the *b.* and morning star.
See Lev. 13. 2; Jer. 51. 11; Zech. 10. 1.
BRIMSTONE. Gen. 19. 24, rained upon Sodom and Gomorrah *b.*
Isa. 30. 33, like a stream of *b.*
Rev. 9. 17, issued fire and *b.*
14. 10, tormented with fire and *b.*
19. 20, a lake of fire and *b.*
BRINK. Gen. 41. 3; Ex. 2. 3; 7. 15; Josh. 3. 8.
BROAD. Ps. 119. 96; Mat. 7. 13; 23. 5.
BROIDERED. Ezek. 16. 10, 13; 27. 7, 16, 24, *b.* work.
See Ex. 28. 4; 1 Tim. 2. 9.
BROILED. Lu. 24. 42.
BROKEN. Ps. 34. 18; 51. 17; 69. 20, *b.* heart.
John 10. 35, scripture cannot be *b.*
19. 36, bone shall not be *b.*
Eph. 2. 14, *b.* down middle wall.
See Job 17. 11; Prov. 25. 19; Jer. 2. 13.
BROOD. Lu. 13. 34.
BROOK. 1 Sam. 17. 40; Ps. 42. 1; 110. 7.
BROTH. Judg. 6. 19; Isa. 65. 4.
BROTHER. Prov. 17. 17, *b.* born for adversity.
18. 9, slothful *b.* to waster.
19, *b.* offended harder to be won.
24, friend closer than *b.*
Eccl. 4. 8, neither child nor *b.*
Mat. 10. 21, *b.* shall deliver up *b.*
1 Cor. 6. 6, *b.* goeth to law with *b.*
2 Thess. 3. 15, admonish as *b.*
See Gen. 4. 9; Mat. 5. 23; 12. 50; Mat. 3. 35.
BROTHERLY. Rom. 12. 10; 1 Thess. 4. 9; Heb. 13. 1, *b.* love.
See Amos 1. 9; 2 Pet. 1. 7.
BROW. Isa. 48. 4; Lu. 4. 29.
BRUISE (*n.*). Isa. 1. 6; Jer. 30. 12; Nah. 3. 19.
BRUISE (*v.*). 2 Kings 18. 21, staff of this *b.* reed.
Isa. 42. 3; Mat. 12. 20, *b.* reed shall he not break.
53. 5, *b.* for our iniquities.
See Gen. 3. 15; Isa. 53. 10; Rom. 16. 20.
BRUIT. Jer. 10. 22; Nah. 3. 19.
BRUTISH. Ps. 92. 6, a *b.* man knoweth not.
Prov. 30. 2, I am more *b.* than any.
Jer. 10. 21, pastors are become *b.*
See Ps. 49. 10; Jer. 10. 8; Ezek. 21. 31.
BUCKET. Num. 24. 7; Isa. 40. 15.
BUCKLER. 2 Sam. 22. 31; Ps. 18. 2; 91. 4; Prov. 2. 7.
BUD. Num. 17. 8; Isa. 18. 5; 61. 11; Hos. 8. 7.
BUFFET. Mat. 26. 67; 1 Cor. 4. 11; 2 Cor. 12. 7; 1 Pet. 2. 20.
BUILD. Ps. 127. 1, labour in vain that *b.*
Eccl. 3. 3, a time to *b.* up.
Isa. 58. 12, *b.* old waste places.
Mat. 7. 24; Lu. 6. 48, wise man *b.* on rock.
Lu. 14. 30, began to *b.*, not able to finish.
Acts 20. 32, able to *b.* you up.
Rom. 15. 20, lest I *b.* on another.
1 Cor. 3. 12, if any *b.* on this foundation.
Eph. 2. 22, in whom ye are *b.* together.
See 1 Chron. 17. 12; 2 Chron. 6. 9; Eccl. 2. 4.
BUILDER. Ps. 118. 22; Mat. 21. 42; Mk. 12. 10; Lu. 20. 17; Acts 4. 11; 1 Pet. 2. 7, *b.* refused.
1 Cor. 3. 10, as a wise master-*b.*
Heb. 11. 10, whose *b.* and maker is God.
See 1 Kings 5. 18; Ezra 3. 10.
BUILDING. 1 Cor. 3. 9; 2 Cor. 5. 1; Eph. 2. 21; Col. 2. 7.
BULRUSH. Ex. 2. 3; Isa. 18. 2; 58. 5.
BULWARK. Isa. 26. 1, salvation for walls and *b.*
See Deut. 20. 20; Ps. 48. 13; Eccl. 9. 14.
BUNDLE. Gen. 42. 35; 1 Sam. 25. 29; Mat. 13. 30; Acts 28. 3.
BURDEN. Ps. 55. 22, cast thy *b.* on the Lord.

Eccl. 12. 5, grasshopper shall be a *b.*
Mat. 11. 30, my *b.* is light.
20. 12, borne *b.* and heat of day.
23. 4; Lu. 11. 46, bind heavy *b.*
Gal. 6. 2, 5, bear his own *b.*
See Num. 11. 11; Acts 15. 28; 2 Cor. 12. 16.
BURDENSOME. Zech. 12. 3; 2 Cor. 11. 9; 1 Thess. 2. 6.
BURIAL. Eccl. 6. 3; Jer. 22. 19; Mat. 26. 12; Acts 8. 2.
BURN. Ps. 39. 3, musing the fire *b.*
Prov. 26. 23, *b.* lips and wicked heart.
Isa. 9. 18, wickedness *b.* as fire.
33. 14, dwell with everlasting *b.*
Mal. 4. 1, day that shall *b.* as oven.
Mat. 13. 30, bind tares to *b.* them.
Lu. 3. 17, chaff *b.* with fire unquenchable.
12. 35, loins girded and lights *b.*
24. 32, did not our heart *b.*
John 5. 35, he was a *b.* and shining light.
1 Cor. 13. 3, give my body to be *b.*
Heb. 6. 8, whose end is to be *b.*
Rev. 4. 5, lamps *b.* before throne.
19. 20, into a lake *b.*
See Gen. 44. 18; Ex. 3. 2; 21. 25.
BURNT-OFFERING. Ps. 40. 6, *b.* thou hast not required.
Isa. 61. 8, I hate robbery for *b.*
Jer. 6. 20, your *b.* not acceptable.
Hos. 6. 6, knowledge more than *b.*
Mk. 12. 33, love neighbour more than *b.*
See Gen. 22. 7; Lev. 1. 4; 6. 9.
BURST. Job 32. 19; Prov. 3. 10; Mk. 2. 22; Lu. 5. 37.
BURY. Mat. 8. 21; Lu. 9. 59, suffer me to *b.* my father.
22; Lu. 9. 60, let dead *b.* dead.
John 19. 40, manner of the Jews is to *b.*
Rom. 6. 4; Col. 2. 12, *b.* with him by baptism.
1 Cor. 15. 4, he was *b.* and rose again.
See Gen. 23. 4; 47. 29; Mat. 14. 12.
BUSHEL. Mat. 5. 15; Mk. 4. 21; Lu. 11. 38.
BUSINESS. 1 Sam. 21. 8, king's *b.* requireth haste.
Ps. 107. 23, do *b.* in great waters.
Prov. 22. 29, diligent in *b.*
Lu. 2. 49, about my Father's *b.*
Rom. 12. 11, not slothful in *b.*
1 Thess. 4. 11, study to do your own *b.*
See Josh. 2. 14; Judg. 18. 7; Neh. 13. 30.
BUSYBODIES. 2 Thess. 3. 11, but are *b.*
1 Tim. 5. 13, tattlers also and *b.*
1 Pet. 4. 15, *b.* in other men's matters.
See Prov. 20. 3; 26. 17; 1 Thess. 4. 11.
BUTLER. Gen. 40. 1; 41. 9.
BUTTER. Isa. 7. 15, 22, *b.* and honey shall he eat.
See Judg. 5. 25; Job 29. 6; Ps. 55. 21; Prov. 30. 33.
BUY. Lev. 22. 11, *b.* any soul with money.
Prov. 23. 23, *b.* the truth.
Isa. 55. 1, *b.* and eat, *b.* wine and milk.
Mat. 25. 9, go to them that sell and *b.*
John 4. 8, disciples were gone to *b.* meat.
Jas. 4. 13, we will *b.* and sell and get gain.
Rev. 3. 18, *b.* of me gold tried.
13. 17, no man *b.* save he that had mark.
18. 11, no man *b.* her merchandise.
See Gen. 42. 2; 47. 19; Ruth 4. 4; Mat. 13. 44.
BUYER. Prov. 20. 14; Isa. 24. 2; Ezek. 7. 12.
BY-AND-BY. Mat. 13. 21; Mk. 6. 25; Lu. 17. 7; 21. 9.
BYWAYS. Judg. 5. 6.
BYWORD. Job 17. 6; 30. 9, a *b.* of the people.
Ps. 44. 14, a *b.* among the heathen.
See Deut. 28. 37; 1 Kings 9. 7; 2 Chron. 7. 20.

C

CABINS. Jer. 37. 16.
CAGE. Jer. 5. 27; Rev. 18. 2.
CAKE. 2 Sam. 6. 19, to every man a *c.* of bread.
1 Kings 17. 13, to make me a little *c.* first.
See Judg. 7. 13; Jer. 7. 18; 44. 19; Hos. 7. 8.
CALAMITY. Deut. 32. 35; 2 Sam. 22. 19; Ps. 18. 18, day of *c.*
Ps. 57. 1, until *c.* be overpast.
Prov. 1. 26, I will laugh at your *c.*
17. 5, he that is glad at *c.*
19. 13, foolish son *c.* of father.
27. 10, brother's house in day of *c.*
See Job 6. 2; Prov. 24. 22.
CALF. Ex. 32. 4; Isa. 11. 6; Lu. 15. 23.
CALKERS. Ezek. 27. 9, 27.
CALLING. Rom. 11. 29, *c.* of God without repentance.
1 Cor. 7. 20, abide in same *c.*
Eph. 1. 18, the hope of his *c.*
Phil. 3. 14, prize of high *c.*
2 Thess. 1. 11, worthy of this *c.*
2 Tim. 1. 9, called us with holy *c.*
Heb. 3. 1, partakers of heavenly *c.*
2 Pet. 1. 10, make *c.* and election sure.
See Acts 7. 59; 22. 16; 1 Cor. 1. 26.
CALM. Ps. 107. 29; Jon. 1. 11; Mat. 8. 26; Mk. 4. 39; Lu. 8. 24.
CALVES. 1 Kings 12. 28, made two *c.* of gold.
See Hos. 14. 2; Mal. 4. 2.
CAMEL'S HAIR. Mat. 3. 4, raiment of *c.*
CAMELS. Isa. 60. 6, the multitude of *c.* shall cover thee.
Mat. 19. 24, it is easier for a *c.*
23. 24, strain at a gnat, swallow a *c.*
See Gen. 24. 64; Ex. 9. 3; Lev. 11. 4; Deut. 14. 7; 1 Chron. 5. 21; Job 1. 3.
CAMP (*n.*). Ex. 14. 19, angel went before *c.*
16. 13, quails covered the *c.*
Num. 1. 52, every man by his own *c.*
Deut. 23. 14, Lord walketh in midst of *c.*
See 1 Sam. 4. 6, 7; Heb. 13. 13.
CAMP (*v.*). Isa. 29. 3; Jer. 50. 29; Nah. 3. 17.
CANDLE. Job 29. 3, when his *c.* shined upon my head.
Ps. 18. 28, thou wilt light my *c.*
Prov. 20. 27, spirit of man, *c.* of the Lord.
Zeph. 1. 12, search Jerusalem with *c.*
Mat. 5. 15; Mk. 4. 21; Lu. 8. 16; 11. 33, lighted a *c.*
Rev. 18. 23, *c.* shine no more in thee.
22. 5, need no *c.* nor light.
See Job 18. 6; 21. 17; Prov. 24. 20.
CANDLESTICK. 2 Kings 4. 10, let us set for him a *c.*
See Mk. 4. 21; Heb. 9. 2; Rev. 2. 5.
CANKERED. 2 Tim. 2. 17; Jas. 5. 3.
CAPTIVE. Ex. 12. 29, firstborn of *c.* in dungeon.
Isa. 51. 14, *c.* exile hasteneth.
52. 2, O *c.* daughter of Zion.
2 Tim. 2. 26, taken *c.* at his will.
3. 6, lead *c.* silly women.
See 2 Kings 5. 2; Isa. 14. 2; 61. 1; Lu. 4. 18.
CAPTIVITY. Rom. 7. 23, into *c.* to law of sin.
2 Cor. 10. 5, bringing into *c.* every thought.
See Job 42. 10; Ps. 14. 7; 85. 1; 126. 1.
CARCASE. Isa. 66. 24; Mat. 24. 28; Heb. 3. 17.
CARE (*n.*). Jer. 49. 31, nation that dwelleth without *c.*
Mat. 13. 22; Mk. 4. 19, *c.* of this world.
Lu. 8. 14; 21. 34, choked with *c.*
1 Cor. 9. 9, doth God take *c.* for oxen.
12. 25, have same *c.* one for another.
2 Cor. 11. 28, the *c.* of all the churches.
1 Pet. 5. 7, casting all your *c.* on him.
See 1 Sam. 10. 2; 2 Kings 4. 13; 2 Cor. 7. 12.
CARE (*v.*). Ps. 142. 4, no man *c.* for my soul.
John 12. 6, not that he *c.* for poor.
Acts 18. 17, Gallio *c.* for none of those things.
Phil. 2. 20, naturally *c.* for your state.
See 2 Sam. 18. 3; Lu. 10. 40.
CAREFUL. Jer. 17. 8, not be *c.* in year of drought.
Dan. 3. 16, we are not *c.* to answer.
Lu. 10. 41, thou art *c.* about many things.
Phil. 4. 6, be *c.* for nothing.
Heb. 12. 17, he sought it *c.* with tears.
See 2 Kings 4. 13; Phil. 4. 10; Tit. 3. 8.
CAREFULNESS. Ezek. 12. 18; 1 Cor. 7. 32; 2 Cor. 7. 11.
CARELESS. Judg. 18. 7; Isa. 32. 9; 47. 8; Ezek. 39. 6.

CARNAL. Rom. 7. 14, *c.*, sold under sin.
8. 7, *c.* mind is enmity.
1 Cor. 3. 1, not speak but as to *c.*
2 Cor. 10. 4, weapons of our warfare not *c.*
See 1 Cor. 9. 11; Col. 2. 18; Heb. 7. 16; 9. 10.
CARPENTER'S SON. Mat. 13. 55; Mk. 6. 3, is not this the *c.*?
CARPENTERS. 2 Sam. 5. 11, and cedar trees and *c.*
Zech. 1. 20, and the Lord shewed me four *c.*
CARRIAGE. Judg. 18. 21; Isa. 10. 28; 46. 1; Acts 21. 15.
CARRY. 1 Kings 18. 12, Spirit of the Lord shall *c.* thee.
Isa. 40. 11, *c.* lambs in his bosom.
53. 4, *c.* our sorrows.
63. 9, *c.* them all days of old.
Ezek. 22. 9, men *c.* tales to shed blood.
Mk. 6. 55, began to *c.* about in beds.
John 5. 10, not lawful to *c.* thy bed.
21. 18, and *c.* thee whither thou wouldest not.
Eph. 4. 14, *c.* about with every wind.
1 Tim. 6. 7, we can *c.* nothing out.
Heb. 13. 9, not *c.* about with divers.
2 Pet. 2. 17, clouds *c.* with a tempest.
Jude 12, clouds *c.* about of winds.
See Ex. 33. 15; Num. 11. 12; Deut. 14. 24.
CART. Isa. 5. 18, draw sin as with a *c.* rope.
Amos 2. 13, *c.* full of sheaves.
See 1 Sam. 6. 7; 2 Sam. 6. 3; 1 Chron. 13. 7; Isa. 28. 28.
CASE. Ps. 144. 15, happy people in such a *c.*
Mat. 5. 20, in no *c.* enter heaven.
John 5. 6, long time in that *c.*
See Ex. 5. 19; Deut. 19. 4; 24. 13.
CASSIA. Ex. 30. 24, of *c.* five hundred shekels.
Ps. 45. 8, thy garments smell of *c.*
CAST. Prov. 16. 33, lot is *c.* into lap.
Mat. 5. 29; Mk. 9. 45, whole body *c.* into hell.
Mk. 9. 38; Lu. 9. 49, one *c.* out devils.
Lu. 21. 1, *c.* gifts into treasury.
John 8. 7, first *c.* stone at her.
2 Cor. 10. 5, *c.* down imaginations.
1 Pet. 5. 7, *c.* all care upon him.
1 John 4. 18, love *c.* out fear.
See Ps. 76. 6; Prov. 26. 18; 3 John 10.
CASTAWAY. 1 Cor. 9. 27, lest I be a *c.*
CASTLE. Num. 31. 10; Prov. 18. 19; Acts 21. 34.
CATCH. Ps. 10. 9, to *c.* the poor.
Mat. 13. 19, devil *c.* away what was sown.
Lu. 5. 10, from henceforth thou shalt *c.* men.
John 10. 12, wolf *c.* and scattereth sheep.
See 2 Kings 7. 12; Ezek. 19. 3; Mk. 12. 13.
CATTLE. Gen. 46. 32, their trade to feed *c.*
Ex. 10. 26, our *c.* shall go with us.
Deut. 2. 35; 3. 7; Josh. 8. 2, the *c.* ye shall take for prey.
Ps. 50. 10, *c.* upon a thousand hills.
See Gen. 1. 25; 30. 43; Jon. 4. 11.
CAUGHT. Gen. 22. 13, ram *c.* by horns.
John 21. 3, that night they *c.* nothing.
2 Cor. 12. 2, *c.* up to third heaven.
16, I *c.* you with guile.
1 Thess. 4. 17, be *c.* up together with them.
See 2 Sam. 18. 9; Prov. 7. 13; Rev. 12. 5.
CAUSE (*n.*). Mat. 19. 5; Mk. 10. 7; Eph. 5. 31, for this *c.* shall a man leave.
1 Cor. 11. 30, for this *c.* many are sickly.
1 Tim. 1. 16, for this *c.* I obtained mercy.
See Prov. 18. 17; 2 Cor. 4. 16; 5. 13.
CAUSE (*v.*). Ezra 6. 12, God *c.* his name to dwell.
Ps. 67. 1; 80. 3, *c.* his face to shine.
Rom. 16. 17, them who *c.* divisions.
See Deut. 1. 38; 12. 11; Job 6. 24.
CAUSELESS. 1 Sam. 25. 31; Prov. 26. 2.
CAVES. 1 Kings 18. 4, Obadiah hid them by fifty in *c.*
19. 9, and he came thither into a *c.*
Isa. 2. 19, go into a *c.* for fear of the Lord.
See Gen. 19. 30; 23. 19; 49. 29; Josh. 10. 16; 1 Sam. 13. 6; 22. 1; 24. 10.
CEASE. Deut. 15. 11, poor never *c.* out of land.
Job 3. 17, the wicked *c.* from troubling.
Ps. 46. 9, he maketh wars to *c.*
Prov. 26. 20, strife *c.*
Eccl. 12. 3, grinders *c.* because few.
Acts 20. 31, I *c.* not to warn.
1 Cor. 13. 8, tongues they shall *c.*
1 Thess. 5. 17, pray without *c.*
1 Pet. 4. 1, hath *c.* from sin.
See Gen. 8. 22; Isa. 1. 16; 2. 22.
CEDAR. 1 Kings 5. 6, they hew me *c.* trees out of Lebanon.
6. 15, with boards of *c.*
Job 40. 17, he moveth his tail like a *c.*
Ps. 92. 12, grow like a *c.* in Lebanon.
CEDARS (of Lebanon). Judg. 9. 15, devour the *c.* of Lebanon.
Isa. 2. 13, upon all the *c.* of Lebanon.
See Ps. 104. 16; 148. 9; Cant. 5. 15; Ezek. 17. 3.
CELEBRATE. Lev. 23. 32; Isa. 38. 18.
CELESTIAL. 1 Cor. 15. 40.
CENSER. Ezek. 8. 11, every man his *c.*
Heb. 9. 4, holiest had the golden *c.*
Rev. 8. 3, angel having a golden *c.*
5, angel took the *c.* and filled.
See Lev. 10. 1; 16. 12; Num. 16. 36; 1 Kings 7. 30.
CEREMONIES. Num. 9. 3.
CERTAIN. Ex. 3. 12, *c.* I will be with thee.
1 Cor. 4. 11, no *c.* dwelling-place.
Heb. 10. 27, a *c.* looking for of judgment.
See Deut. 13. 14; 1 Kings 2. 37; Dan. 2. 45.
CERTIFY. 2 Sam. 15. 28; Gal. 1. 11.
CHAFF. Mat. 3. 12; Lu. 3. 17, burn up *c.* with fire.
See Jer. 23. 28; Hos. 13. 3; Zeph. 2. 2.
CHAIN. Mk. 5. 3, no, not with *c.*
Acts 12. 7, Peter's *c.* fell off.
2 Tim. 1. 16, not ashamed of my *c.*
2 Pet. 2. 4, into *c.* of darkness.
Jude 6, everlasting *c.* under darkness.
See Ps. 73. 6; Lam. 3. 7; Isa. 40. 19.
CHALCEDONY. Rev. 21. 19, the third, a *c.*
CHALLENGETH. Ex. 22. 9.
CHAMBER. 2 Kings 4. 10, little *c.* on wall.
Ps. 19. 5, as bridegroom coming out of *c.*
Isa. 26. 20, enter into thy *c.*
Ezek. 8. 12, *c.* of imagery.
Mat. 24. 26, in secret *c.*
Acts 9. 37; 20. 8, in upper *c.*
See Dan. 6. 10; Joel 2. 16; Prov. 7. 27.
CHAMPION. 1 Sam. 17. 4, 51.
CHANCE. 1 Sam. 6. 9; 2 Sam. 1. 6; Eccl. 9. 11; Lu. 10. 31.
CHANGE (*n.*). Job 14. 14, till my *c.* come.
Prov. 24. 21, meddle not with them given to *c.*
See Judg. 14. 12; Zech. 3. 4; Heb. 7. 12.
CHANGE (*v.*). Ps. 15. 4, sweareth and *c.* not.
102. 26, as vesture shalt thou *c.* them.
Lam. 4. 1, fine gold *c.*
Mal. 3. 6, I the Lord *c.* not.
Rom. 1. 23, *c.* glory of uncorruptible God.
1 Cor. 15. 51, we shall all be *c.*
2 Cor. 3. 18, *c.* from glory to glory.
See Job 17. 12; Jer. 2. 36; 13. 23.
CHANT. Amos 6. 5.
CHAPEL. Amos 7. 13, for it is the king's *c.*
CHAPMEN. 2 Chron. 9. 14.
CHAPT. Jer. 14. 4.
CHARGE. Job 1. 22, nor *c.* God foolishly.
4. 18, angels he *c.* with folly.
Mat. 9. 30; Mk. 5. 43; Lu. 9. 21, Jesus *c.* them.
Acts 7. 60; 2 Tim. 4. 16, lay not sin to their *c.*
Rom. 8. 33, who shall lay any thing to *c.*
1 Cor. 9. 18, gospel without *c.*
1 Tim. 1. 3, *c.* that they teach no other.
5. 21; 2 Tim. 4. 1, I *c.* thee before God.
6. 17, *c.* them that are rich.
See Ex. 6. 13; Ps. 35. 11; 91. 11; Mk. 9. 25.
CHARGEABLE. 2 Sam. 13. 25; 2 Cor. 11. 9; 1 Thess. 2. 9.
CHARIOT. 2 Kings 2. 11, there appeared a *c.* of fire.

CHARIOTS. Ex. 14. 6, he made ready his *c.*
1 Sam. 13. 5, Philistines gathered thirty thousand *c.*
2 Sam. 10. 18, David slew the men of seven hundred *c.*
Ps. 20. 7, some trust in *c.*
Nah. 3. 2, and of the jumping *c.*
See 2 Kings 6. 14, 17; Ps. 68. 17.
CHARITY. Rom. 14. 15, now walkest not *c.*
Col. 3. 14, put on *c.*
2 Thess. 1. 3, *c.* aboundeth.
1 Tim. 1. 5, end of commandment is *c.*
2 Tim. 2. 22, follow faith, *c.*, peace.
Tit. 2. 2, sound in faith, in *c.*
1 Pet. 4. 8, *c.* cover sins.
2 Pet. 1. 7, to brotherly kindness *c.*
Jude 12, spots in feasts of *c.*
See 1 Cor. 8. 1; 13. 1; 14. 1; 16. 14; Rev. 2. 19.
CHARMER. Deut. 18. 11; Ps. 58. 5; Jer. 8. 17.
CHASE. Lev. 26. 8, five *c.* hundred.
Deut. 32. 30; Josh. 23. 10, one *c.* thousand.
See Job 18. 18; Ps. 35. 5; Lam. 3. 52.
CHASTE. 2 Cor. 11. 2; Tit. 2. 5; 1 Pet. 3. 2.
CHASTEN. Deut. 8. 5, as a man *c.* son.
Ps. 6. 1; 38. 1, nor *c.* me in displeasure.
94. 12, blessed is the man whom thou *c.*
Prov. 19. 18, *c.* thy son while there is hope.
2 Cor. 6. 9, as *c.* and not killed.
Heb. 12. 6; Rev. 3. 19, whom the Lord loveth he *c.*
11, no *c.* seemeth to be joyous.
See Ps. 69. 10; 73. 14; 118. 18.
CHASTISEMENT. Deut. 11. 2; Job 34. 31; Isa. 53. 5.
CHATTER. Isa. 38. 14.
CHEEK. Mat. 5. 39; Lu. 6. 29, smiteth on right *c.*
See Job 16. 10; Isa. 50. 6; Lam. 3. 30.
CHEER. Prov. 15. 13, maketh a *c.* countenance.
Zech. 9. 17, corn make young men *c.*
John 16. 33, be of good *c.*, I have overcome.
Acts 23. 11; 27. 22, 25, be of good *c.*
Rom. 12. 8, he that showeth mercy with *c.*
2 Cor. 9. 7, God loveth a *c.* giver.
See Judg. 9. 13; Mat. 9. 2; 14. 27; Mk. 6. 50.
CHERISHETH. Eph. 5. 29; 1 Thess. 2. 7.
CHICKENS. Mat. 23. 37.
CHIDE. Ex. 17. 2; Judg. 8. 1; Ps. 103. 9.
CHIEFEST. Cant. 5. 10; Mk. 10. 44; 2 Cor. 11. 5.
CHILD. Gen. 42. 22, do not sin against the *c.*
Ps. 131. 2, quieted myself as a weaned *c.*
Prov. 20. 11, a *c.* is known by his doings.
22. 6, train up a *c.* in way.
15, foolishness in heart of *c.*
Isa. 9. 6, to us a *c.* is born.
65. 20, *c.* shall die an hundred years old.
Lu. 1. 66, what manner of *c.*
John 4. 49, come ere my *c.* die.
1 Cor. 13. 11, when I was a *c.*
2 Tim. 3. 15, from a *c.* hast known.
See Ex. 2. 2; Eccl. 4. 13; 10. 16; Heb. 11. 23.
CHILDREN. 1 Sam. 16. 11, are here all thy *c.*
Ps. 34. 11, come ye *c.* hearken to me.
45. 16, instead of fathers shall be *c.*
128. 3, thy *c.* like olive plants.
Isa. 8. 18; Heb. 2. 13, I and *c.* given me.
30. 9, lying *c.*, *c.* that will not hear.
63. 8, *c.* that will not lie.
Jer. 31. 15; Mat. 2. 18, Rachel weeping for her *c.*
Ezek. 18. 2, *c.* teeth on edge.
Mat. 15. 26; Mk. 7. 27; not take *c.* bread.
17. 26, then are the *c.* free.
19. 14; Mk. 10. 14; Lu. 18. 16, suffer little *c.*
Lu. 16. 8, *c.* of this world wiser than *c.* of light.
20. 36, *c.* of God and the resurrection.
John 12. 36; Eph. 5. 8; 1 Thess. 5. 5, *c.* of light.
Rom. 8. 16; Gal. 3. 26; 1 John 3. 10, witness that we are the *c.* of God.
Eph. 4. 14, be henceforth no more *c.*
5. 6; Col. 3. 6, *c.* of disobedience.
6. 1; Col. 3. 20, *c.* obey your parents.
1 Tim. 3. 4, having his *c.* in subjection.
See Num. 16. 27; Esth. 3. 13; Mat. 14. 21.

CHODE. Gen. 31. 36; Num. 20. 3.
CHOICE. 1 Sam. 9. 2, Saul a *c.* young man.
Acts 15. 7, God made *c.* among us.
See Gen. 23. 6; 2 Sam. 10. 9; Prov. 8. 10.
CHOKE. Mat. 13. 22; Mk. 4. 19; Lu. 8. 14.
CHOLER. Dan. 8. 7; 11. 11.
CHOSE. Ps. 33. 12, people *c.* for his inheritance.
89. 19, exalted one *c.* out of people.
Prov. 16. 16; 22. 1, rather to be *c.*
Jer. 8. 3, death *c.* rather than life.
Mat. 20. 16; 22. 14, many called, few *c.*
Lu. 10. 42, hath *c.* that good part.
14. 7, they *c.* the chief rooms.
John 15. 16, ye have not *c.* me.
Acts 9. 15, he is a *c.* vessel.
Rom. 16. 13, *c.* in the Lord.
1 Cor. 1. 27, 28, God hath *c.* foolish things.
Eph. 1. 4, according as he hath *c.* us.
1 Pet. 2. 4, *c.* of God and precious.
9, a *c.* generation.
See Ex. 18. 25; 2 Sam. 6. 21; 1 Chron. 16. 13.
CHRIST. Mat. 16. 16, thou art the *C.*
24. 5, many shall come, saying, I am *C.*
John 4. 25, the Messias which is called *C.*
29, is not this the *C.*?
6. 69, we are sure that thou art that *C.*
Phil. 1. 15, 16, some preach *C.* of contention.
1 Pet. 1. 11, the Spirit of *C.* did signify.
1 John 2. 22, denieth that Jesus is the *C.*?
5. 1, whoso believeth Jesus is the *C.*
Rev. 20. 4, they reigned with *C.* a thousand years.
6, priests of God and *C.*
See Mat. 1. 16; 2. 4; Lu. 2. 26.
CHRISTIAN. Acts 11. 26; 26. 28; 1 Pet. 4. 16.
CHRYSOLITE. Rev. 21. 20, the seventh *c.*
CHRYSOPRASUS. Rev. 21. 20, the tenth, a *c.*
CHURCH. Mat. 18. 17, tell it to the *c.*
Acts 2. 47, added to *c.* daily.
7. 38, the *c.* in the wilderness.
19. 37, neither robbers of *c.*
20. 28, feed the *c.* of God.
Rom. 16. 5; 1 Cor. 16. 19; Philem. 2, *c.* in house.
1 Cor. 14. 28, 34, keep silence in the *c.*
Eph. 5. 24, the *c.* is subject to Christ.
25, as Christ loved the *c.*
Col. 1. 18, 24, head of the body the *c.*
Heb. 12. 23, the *c.* of the firstborn.
See Mat. 16. 18; Rev. 1. 4; 2. 1; 22. 16.
CHURLISH. 1 Sam. 25. 3, but the man was *c.*
CIELED. 2 Chron. 3. 5; Jer. 22. 14; Hag. 1. 4.
CIRCLE. Isa. 40. 22.
CIRCUIT. 1 Sam. 7. 16; Job 22. 14; Ps. 19. 6; Eccl. 1. 6.
CIRCUMCISE. Rom. 4. 11, though not *c.*
Gal. 5. 2, if ye be *c.* Christ shall profit nothing.
Phil. 3. 5, *c.* the eighth day.
See Deut. 30. 6; John 7. 22; Acts 15. 1.
CIRCUMCISION. Rom. 3. 1, what profit is there of *c.*
15. 8, Jesus Christ minister of *c.*
Gal. 5. 6; 6. 15, in Christ neither *c.* availeth.
Phil. 3. 3, the *c.* which worship God.
Col. 2. 11, *c.* without hands.
3. 11, neither *c.* nor uncircumcision.
See Ex. 4. 26; John 7. 22; Acts 7. 8.
CIRCUMSPECT. Ex. 23. 13; Eph. 5. 15.
CISTERN. Eccl. 12. 6, the wheel broken at the *c.*
Jer. 2. 13, hewed out *c.*, broken *c.*
See 2 Kings 18. 31; Prov. 5. 15; Isa. 36. 16.
CITIZEN. Lu. 15. 15; 19. 14; Acts 21. 39; Eph. 2. 19.
CITY. Num. 35. 6; Josh. 15. 59, *c.* of refuge.
2 Sam. 19. 37, I may die in mine own *c.*
Ps. 46. 4, make glad the *c.* of God.
107. 4, found no *c.* to dwell in.
127. 1, except Lord build *c.*
Prov. 8. 3, wisdom crieth in *c.*
16. 32, than he that taketh a *c.*
Eccl. 9. 14, a little *c.* and few men.
Isa. 33. 20, *c.* of solemnities.
Zech. 8. 3, a *c.* of truth.

Mat. 5. 14, *c.* set on a hill.
21. 10, all the *c.* was moved.
Lu. 24. 49, tarry in the *c.*
Acts 8. 8, great joy in that *c.*
Heb. 11. 10, a *c.* that hath foundations.
12. 22, the *c.* of living God.
13. 14, no continuing *c.*
Rev. 16. 19, the *c.* of the nations fell.
20. 9, compassed the beloved *c.*
See Gen. 4. 17; 11. 4; Jon. 1. 2; Rev. 14. 8; 21. 10.
CLAD. 1 Kings 11. 29; Isa. 59. 17.
CLAMOUR. Prov. 9. 19; Eph. 4. 31.
CLAP. Ps. 47. 1, *c.* your hands all ye people.
98. 8, let the floods *c.* their hands.
Isa. 55. 12, the trees shall *c.* their hands.
Lam. 2. 15, all that pass by *c.* their hands.
See 2 Kings 11. 12; Job 27. 23; 34. 37.
CLAVE. Ruth 1. 14, Ruth *c.* to her mother-in-law.
2 Sam. 23. 10, his hand *c.* to the sword.
Neh. 10. 29, they *c.* to their brethren.
Acts 17. 34, certain men *c.* to Paul.
See Gen. 22. 3; Num. 16. 31; 1 Sam. 6. 14.
CLAWS. Deut. 14. 6; Dan. 4. 33; Zech. 11. 16.
CLAY. Job 10. 9, thou hast made me as *c.*
13. 12, bodies like to bodies of *c.*
33. 6, I also am formed out of *c.*
Ps. 40. 2, out of the miry *c.*
Dan. 2. 33, part of iron, part of *c.*
John 9. 6, made *c.* and anointed.
Rom. 9. 21, power over the *c.*
See Isa. 29. 16; 41. 25; 45. 9; 64. 8; Jer. 18. 4.
CLEAN. 2 Kings 5. 12, may I not wash and be *c.*
Job 14. 4, who can bring *c.* out of unclean.
15. 15, heavens not *c.* in his sight.
Ps. 24. 4, he that hath *c.* hands.
51. 10, create in me a *c.* heart.
77. 8, is his mercy *c.* gone for ever?
Prov. 16. 2, *c.* in his own eyes.
Isa. 1. 16, wash you, make you *c.*
52. 11, be *c.* that bear vessels of the Lord.
Ezek. 36. 25, then will I sprinkle *c.* water.
Mat. 8. 2; Mk. 1. 40; Lu. 5. 12, thou canst make me *c.*
23. 25; Lu. 11. 39, make *c.* the outside.
Lu. 11. 41, all things *c.* unto you.
John 13. 11, ye are not all *c.*
15. 3, *c.* through word I have spoken.
Acts 18. 6, I am *c.*
Rev. 19. 8, arrayed in fine linen *c.* and white.
See Lev. 23. 22; Josh. 3. 17; Prov. 14. 4.
CLEANNESS. 2 Sam. 22. 21; Ps. 18. 20; Amos 4. 6.
CLEANSE. Ps. 19. 12, *c.* me from secret faults.
73. 13, I have *c.* my heart in vain.
Prov. 20. 30, blueness of wound *c.* evil.
Mat. 8. 3, immediately his leprosy was *c.*
10. 8; 11. 5; Lu. 7. 22, *c.* lepers.
23. 26, *c.* first that which is within.
Lu. 4. 27, none was *c.* saving Naaman.
17. 17, were not ten *c.*
Acts 10. 15; 11. 9, what God hath *c.*
2 Cor. 7. 1, let us *c.* ourselves.
Jas. 4. 8, *c.* your hands, ye sinners.
1 John 1. 7, 9, *c.* us from all sin.
See Ezek. 36. 25; Mk. 1. 44.
CLEAR. Gen. 44. 16, how shall we *c.* ourselves?
Ex. 34. 7, by no means *c.* the guilty.
2 Sam. 23. 4, *c.* shining after rain.
Job 11. 17, age shall be *c.* than noonday.
Ps. 51. 4, be *c.* when thou judgest.
Mat. 7. 5; Lu. 6. 42, see *c.* to pull out mote.
Mk. 8. 25, saw every man *c.*
Rom. 1. 20, things from creation *c.* seen.
Rev. 21. 11; 22. 1, light *c.* as crystal.
See Gen. 24. 8; Cant. 6. 10; Zech. 14. 6.
CLEAVE. Josh. 23. 8, *c.* to the Lord your God.
2 Kings 5. 27, leprosy shall *c.* to thee.
Job 29. 10; Ps. 137. 6; Ezek. 3. 26, *c.* to roof of mouth.
Ps. 119. 25, my soul *c.* to dust.
Eccl. 10. 9, he that *c.* wood shall be endangered.
Acts 11. 23, with purpose of heart *c.*
Rom. 12. 9, *c.* to that which is good.
See Gen. 2. 24; Mat. 19. 5; Mk. 10. 7.
CLEFTS. Cant. 2. 14; Isa. 2. 21; Jer. 49. 16; Amos 6. 11; Obad. 3.
CLEMENCY. Acts 24. 4.
CLERK. Acts 19. 35.
CLIMB. John 10. 1, but *c.* up some other way.
See 1 Sam. 14. 13; Amos 9. 2; Lu. 19. 4.
CLODS. Job 21. 33, the *c.* of the valley shall be sweet.
See Job 7. 5; Isa. 28. 24; Hos. 10. 11; Joel 1. 17.
CLOKE. Mat. 5. 40; Lu. 6. 29, let him have thy *c.* also.
1 Thess. 2. 5, a *c.* of covetousness.
1 Pet. 2. 16, a *c.* of maliciousness.
CLOSE (*v.*). Gen. 2. 21; Isa. 29. 10; Mat. 13. 15.
CLOSE. Prov. 18. 24, sticketh *c.* than a brother.
Lu. 9. 36, they kept it *c.*
See Num. 5. 13; 1 Chron. 12. 1; Job 28. 21.
CLOSET. Mat. 6. 6; Lu. 12. 3.
CLOTH. 1 Sam. 19. 13; 21. 9; Mat. 9. 16; Mk. 2. 21.
CLOTHE. Ps. 65. 13, pastures *c.* with flocks.
109. 18, *c.* himself with cursing.
132. 9, *c.* with righteousness.
16, *c.* with salvation.
Prov. 23. 21, drowsiness shall *c.* a man.
31. 21, household *c.* with scarlet.
Isa. 50. 3, *c.* heavens with blackness.
61. 10, *c.* with garments of salvation.
Mat. 6. 30; Lu. 12. 28, *c.* grass of field.
31, wherewithal shall we be *c.*
11. 8; Lu. 7. 25, man *c.* in soft raiment.
25. 36, 43, naked and ye *c.* me.
Mk. 1. 6, *c.* with camel's hair.
5. 15; Lu. 8. 35, *c.* and in right mind.
15. 17, *c.* Jesus with purple.
Lu. 16. 19, *c.* in purple and fine linen.
2 Cor. 5. 2, desiring to be *c.* upon.
1 Pet. 5. 5, be *c.* with humility.
Rev. 3. 18, that thou mayest be *c.*
12. 1, woman *c.* with the sun.
19. 13, *c.* with a vesture dipped in blood.
See Gen. 3. 21; Ex. 40. 14; Esth. 4. 4.
CLOTHES. Deut. 29. 5; Neh. 9. 21, *c.* not waxen old.
Mk. 5. 28, if I touch but his *c.*
Lu. 2. 7, in swaddling *c.*
8. 27, a man that ware no *c.*
Lu. 19. 36, spread *c.* in the way.
24. 12; John 20. 5, linen *c.* laid.
John 11. 44, bound with grave-*c.*
Acts 7. 58, laid down *c.* at Saul's feet.
22. 23, cried out and cast off *c.*
See Gen. 49. 11; 1 Sam. 19. 24; Neh. 4. 23.
CLOTHING. Ps. 45. 13, her *c.* of wrought gold.
Prov. 27. 26, lambs are for thy *c.*
31. 22, her *c.* is silk and purple.
25, strength and honour are her *c.*
Isa. 3. 7, in my house is neither bread nor *c.*
23. 18, merchandise for durable *c.*
59. 17, garments of vengeance for *c.*
Mat. 7. 15, in sheep's *c.*
Mk. 12. 38, love to go in long *c.*
Acts 10. 30, a man in bright *c.*
Jas. 2. 3, to him that weareth gay *c.*
See Job 22. 6; 24. 7; 31. 19; Ps. 35. 13.
CLOUD. Ex. 13. 21; 14. 24; Neh. 9. 19, a pillar of *c.*
1 Kings 18. 44, 45, a little *c.*
Ps. 36. 5, faithfulness reacheth to *c.*
97. 2, *c.* and darkness round about him.
99. 7, spake in *c.* pillar.
Prov. 3. 20, *c.* dropped down dew.
Eccl. 11. 4, regardeth the *c.* not reap.
12. 2, nor *c.* return after rain.
Isa. 5. 6, command *c.* rain not.
44. 22, blotted out as thick *c.*
60. 8, fly as a *c.*
Dan. 7. 13; Lu. 21. 27, Son of man with *c.*

Hos. 6. 4; 13. 3, goodness as morning *c.*
Mat. 17. 5; Mk. 9. 7; Lu. 9. 34, *c.* overshadowed.
24. 30; 26. 64; Mk. 13. 26; 14. 62, in *c.* with power.
1 Cor. 10. 1, fathers under *c.*
1 Thess. 4. 17, caught up in *c.*
2 Pet. 2. 17, *c.* carried with tempest.
Jude 12, *c.* without water.
Rev. 1. 7, he cometh with *c.*
14. 14–16, white *c.*
See Gen. 9. 13; Ex. 24. 15; 40. 34.
CLOUT. Josh. 9. 5; Jer. 38. 11.
CLOVEN. Lev. 11. 3; Deut. 14. 7; Acts 2. 3.
CLUSTER. Isa. 65. 8, new wine in *c.*
See Num. 13. 23; Cant. 1. 14; Rev. 14. 18.
COAL. Prov. 6. 28, hot *c.* and not be burned.
25. 22; Rom. 12. 20, heap *c.* of fire.
John 18. 18; 21. 9, fire of *c.*
See Job 41. 21; Ps. 18. 8; Isa. 6. 6.
COAST. 1 Chron. 4. 10; Mat. 8. 34; Mk. 5. 17.
COAT. Mat. 5. 40, take away thy *c.*
10. 10; Mk. 6. 9, neither provide two *c.*
Lu. 6. 29, thy *c.* also.
John 19. 23, *c.* without seam.
21. 7, fisher's *c.*
Acts 9. 39, the *c.* which Dorcas made.
See Gen. 3. 21; 37. 3; 1 Sam. 2. 19.
COCK. Mat. 26. 34; Mk. 13. 35; 14. 30; Lu. 22. 34.
COCKATRICE. Isa. 11. 8; 14. 29; 59. 5.
COCKLE. Job 31. 40.
COFFER. 1 Sam. 6. 8, 11, 15.
COFFIN. Gen. 50. 26.
COGITATIONS. Dan. 7. 28.
COLD. Prov. 20. 4, by reason of *c.*
25. 13, *c.* of snow in harvest.
20, garment in *c.* weather.
25, *c.* waters to thirsty soul.
Mat. 10. 42, cup of *c.* water.
24. 12, love of many wax *c.*
2 Cor. 11. 27, in *c.* and nakedness.
Rev. 3. 15, neither *c.* nor hot.
See Gen. 8. 22; Job 24. 7; 37. 9; Ps. 147. 17.
COLLECTION. 2 Chron. 24. 6; Acts 11. 29; Rom. 15. 26; 1 Cor. 16. 1.
COLLEGE. 2 Kings 22. 14; 2 Chron. 34. 22.
COLOUR. Prov. 23. 31, *c.* in the cup.
Acts 27. 30, under *c.* as though.
See Gen. 37. 3; Ezek. 1. 4; Dan. 10. 6.
COMELY. Ps. 33. 1, praise is *c.*
1 Cor. 11. 13, is it *c.* that a woman.
See 1 Sam. 16. 18; Prov. 30. 29; Isa. 53. 2.
COMFORT (*n.*). Mat. 9. 22; Mk. 10. 49; Lu. 8. 48.
2 Cor. 13. 11, be of good *c.*
Acts 9. 31, *c.* of Holy Ghost.
Rom. 15. 4, patience and *c.* of scriptures.
2 Cor. 1. 3, God of all *c.*
7. 13, were comforted in your *c.*
Phil. 2. 1, if any *c.* of love.
See Job 10. 20; Ps. 94. 19; 119. 50; Isa. 57. 6.
COMFORT (*v.*). Gen. 37. 35; Ps. 77. 2; Jer. 31. 15, refused to be *c.*
Ps. 23. 4, rod and staff *c.*
Isa. 40. 1, *c.* ye, *c.* ye my people.
49. 13; 52. 9, God hath *c.* his people.
61. 2, *c.* all that mourn.
66. 13, as one whom his mother *c.*
Mat. 5. 4, they shall be *c.*
Lu. 16. 25, he is *c.*, and thou art tormented.
John 11. 19, to *c.* concerning their brother.
2 Cor. 1. 4, able to *c.* them.
1 Thess. 4. 18, *c.* one another with these words.
5. 11, wherefore *c.* yourselves together.
14, *c.* the feeble-minded.
See Gen. 5. 29; 18. 5; 37. 35.
COMFORTABLE. Isa. 40. 2; Hos. 2. 14; Zech. 1. 13.
COMFORTER. Job 16. 2, miserable *c.* are ye all.
Ps. 69. 20, looked for *c.* but I found none.
John 14. 16, give you another *C.*
15. 26, when the *C.* is come.
16. 7, *C.* will not come.
See 2 Sam. 10. 3; 1 Chron. 19. 3.
COMFORTLESS. John 14. 18.
COMMAND. Ps. 33. 9, he *c.* and it stood fast.
Lu. 8. 25, he *c.* even the winds.
9. 54, *c.* fire from heaven.
John 15. 14, if ye do what I *c.* you.
Acts 17. 30, *c.* all men everywhere.
See Gen. 18. 19; Deut. 28. 8.
COMMANDER. Isa. 55. 4.
COMMANDMENT. Ps. 119. 86, *c.* are faithful.
96, *c.* exceeding broad.
127, I love thy *c.*
143, thy *c.* are my delight.
Mat. 15. 9; Mk. 7. 7; Col. 2. 22, the *c.* of men.
Lu. 23. 56, rested according to *c.*
John 13. 34; 1 John 2. 7; 2 John 5, a new *c.*
Rom. 7. 12, *c.* is holy, just, and good.
1 Cor. 7. 6; 2 Cor. 8. 8, by permission, not by *c.*
Eph. 6. 2, first *c.* with promise.
1 Tim. 1. 5, end of the *c.* is charity.
See Esth. 3. 3.
COMMEND. Lu. 16. 8, *c.* unjust steward.
23. 46, into thy hands I *c.*
Rom. 3. 5, unrighteousness *c.* righteousness of God.
5. 8, God *c.* his love toward us.
1 Cor. 8. 8, meat *c.* us not.
2 Cor. 3. 1; 5. 12, *c.* ourselves.
4. 2, *c.* to every man's conscience.
10. 18, not he that *c.* himself is approved.
See Prov. 12. 8; Eccl. 8. 15; Acts 20. 32.
COMMISSION. Ezra 8. 36; Acts 26. 12.
COMMIT. Ps. 37. 5, *c.* thy way to the Lord.
Jer. 2. 13, have *c.* two evils.
John 2. 24, Jesus did not *c.* himself to them.
5. 22, hath *c.* judgment to Son.
Rom. 3. 2, were *c.* oracles of God.
2 Cor. 5. 19, had *c.* to us word of reconciliation.
1 Tim. 6. 20, keep what is *c.* to thee.
2 Tim. 2. 2, *c.* thou to faithful men.
1 Pet. 2. 23, *c.* himself to him that judgeth.
See Job 5. 8; Ps. 31. 5; 1 Cor. 9. 17.
COMMODIOUS. Acts 27. 12.
COMMON. Eccl. 6. 1, evil, and it is *c.* among men.
Mk. 12. 37, the *c.* people heard him gladly.
Acts 2. 44; 4. 32, all things *c.*
10. 14; 11. 8, never eaten any thing *c.*
15; 11. 9, call not thou *c.*
1 Cor. 10. 13, temptation *c.* to men.
Eph. 2. 12, aliens from *c.*-wealth.
See Lev. 4. 27; Num. 16. 29; 1 Sam. 21. 4.
COMMOTION. Jer. 10. 22; Lu. 21. 9.
COMMUNE. Job 4. 2, if we *c.* with thee.
Ps. 4. 4; 77. 6; Eccl. 1. 16, *c.* with own heart.
Zech. 1. 14, angel that *c.* with me.
See Ex. 25. 22; 1 Sam. 19. 3; Lu. 22. 4.
COMMUNICATE. Gal. 6. 6, let him that is taught *c.*
1 Tim. 6. 18, be willing to *c.*
Heb. 13. 16, do good and *c.*
See Gal. 2. 2; Phil. 4. 14, 15.
COMMUNICATION. Mat. 5. 37, let your *c.* be yea.
Lu. 24. 17, what manner of *c.*
1 Cor. 15. 33, evil *c.* corrupt good manners.
Eph. 4. 29, let no corrupt *c.* proceed.
See 2 Kings 9. 11; Philem. 6.
COMMUNION. 1 Cor. 10. 16; 2 Cor. 6. 14; 13. 14.
COMPACT. Ps. 122. 3; Eph. 4. 16.
COMPANY. 1 Sam. 10. 5; 19. 20, a *c.* of prophets.
Ps. 55. 14, walked to house of God in *c.*
68. 11, great was the *c.* of those.
Mk. 6. 39; Lu. 9. 14, sit down by *c.*
2 Thess. 3. 14, have no *c.* with him.
Heb. 12. 22, innumerable *c.* of angels.
See Num. 16. 6; Judg. 9. 37; 18. 23.
COMPANION. Job 30. 29, a *c.* to owls.
Ps. 119. 63, a *c.* to them that fear thee.
Prov. 13. 20, *c.* of fools shall be destroyed.
28. 7, *c.* of riotous men.

24, the *c.* of a destroyer.
Acts 19. 29, Paul's *c.* in travel.
Phil. 2. 25; Rev. 1. 9, brother and *c.* in labour.
See Ex. 32. 27; Judg. 11. 38; 14. 20.
COMPARE. Prov. 3. 15; 8. 11, not to be *c.* to wisdom.
Isa. 40. 18, what likeness will ye *c.* to him?
46. 5, to whom will ye *c.* me.
Lam. 4. 2, *c.* to fine gold.
Rom. 8. 18, not worthy to be *c.* with glory.
1 Cor. 2. 13, *c.* spiritual things with spiritual.
See Ps. 89. 6; 2 Cor. 10. 12.
COMPARISON. Judg. 8. 2; Hag. 2. 3; Mk. 4. 30.
COMPASS (*n.*). 2 Sam. 5. 23; 2 Kings 3. 9; Isa. 44. 13; Acts 28. 13.
COMPASS (*v.*). 2 Sam. 22. 5; Ps. 18. 4; 116. 3, waves of death *c.* me.
6; Ps. 18. 5, sorrows of hell *c.* me.
Ps. 5. 12, with favour *c.* as with a shield.
32. 7, *c.* with songs of deliverance.
10, mercy shall *c.* him about.
Isa. 50. 11, *c.* yourselves with sparks.
Mat. 23. 15, *c.* sea and land.
Lu. 21. 20, Jerusalem *c.* with armies.
Heb. 5. 2, he also is *c.* with infirmity.
12. 1, *c.* about with cloud of witnesses.
See Josh. 6. 3; Job 16. 13; Jer. 31. 22.
COMPASSION. Isa. 49. 15, that she should not have *c.*
Lam. 3. 22, his *c.* fail not.
32; Mic. 7. 19, yet will he have *c.*
Mat. 9. 36; 14. 14; Mk. 1. 41; 6. 34, Jesus moved with *c.*
18. 33, *c.* on thy fellowservant.
20. 34, had *c.* on them and touched.
Mk. 5. 19, the Lord hath had *c.*
9. 22, have *c.*, and help us.
Lu. 10. 33, the Samaritan had *c.*
15. 20, father had *c.*, and ran.
Rom. 9. 15, I will have *c.* on whom I will.
Heb. 5. 2, have *c.* on ignorant.
1 Pet. 3. 8, of one mind, having *c.*
1 John 3. 17, shutteth up bowels of *c.*
Jude 22, of some have *c.*, making a difference.
See Ps. 78. 38; 86. 15; 111. 4; 112. 4.
COMPEL. Mat. 5. 41, *c.* thee to go a mile.
27. 32; Mk. 15. 21, *c.* to bear cross.
Lu. 14. 23, *c.* to come in.
Acts 26. 11, I *c.* them to blaspheme.
See Lev. 25. 39; 2 Cor. 12. 11; Gal. 2. 3.
COMPLAIN. Ps. 144. 14, no *c.* in our streets.
Lam. 3. 39, wherefore doth a living man *c.*
Jude 16, these murmurers, *c.*
See Num. 11. 1; Judg. 21. 22; Job 7. 11.
COMPLAINT. Job 23. 2, to-day is my *c.* bitter.
Ps. 142. 2, I poured out my *c.* before him.
See 1 Sam. 1. 16; Job 7. 13; 9. 27; 10. 1.
COMPLETE. Lev. 23. 15; Col. 2. 10; 4. 12.
COMPREHEND. Job 37. 5; Isa. 40. 12; John 1. 5; Eph. 3. 18.
CONCEAL. Prov. 12. 23, prudent man *c.* knowledge.
25. 2, glory of God to *c.* a thing.
Jer. 50. 2, publish and *c.* not.
See Gen. 37. 26; Deut. 13. 8.
CONCEIT. Rom. 11. 25; 12. 16, wise in your own *c.*
CONCEIT (reproved). Prov. 3. 7; 12. 15; 18. 11; 20. 5; 28. 11; Isa. 5. 21.
CONCEIVE. Ps. 7. 14, *c.* mischief, brought forth falsehood.
Ps. 51. 5, in sin did my mother *c.* me.
Acts 5. 4, why hast thou *c.* this thing.
Jas. 1. 15, when lust *c.* it bringeth forth.
See Job 15. 35; Isa. 7. 14; 59. 4.
CONCERN. Lu. 24. 27, things *c.* himself.
Rom. 9. 5, as *c.* the flesh Christ came.
16. 19, simple *c.* evil.
Phil. 4. 15, *c.* giving and receiving.
1 Tim. 6. 21, have erred *c.* the faith.
1 Pet. 4. 12, *c.* fiery trial.
See Lev. 6. 3; Num. 10. 29; Ps. 90. 13; 135. 14.
CONCISION. Phil. 3. 2.
CONCLUDE. Rom. 3. 28; 11. 32; Gal. 3. 22.
CONCLUSION. Eccl. 12. 13.
CONCORD. 2 Cor. 6. 15.
CONCUPISCENCE. Col. 3. 5; 1 Thess. 4. 5, mortify evil *c.*
CONDEMN. Job 10. 2, I will say to God, do not *c.* me.
Amos 2. 8, drink wine of the *c.*
Mat. 12. 7, ye would not have *c.* the guiltless.
37, by thy words shalt be *c.*
42; Lu. 11. 31, rise in judgment and *c.*
20. 18, shall *c.* him to death.
27. 3, Judas when he saw he was *c.*
Mk. 14. 64, all *c.* him to be guilty.
Lu. 6. 37, *c.* not and ye shall not be *c.*
John 3. 17, God sent not his Son to *c.*
18, believe not is *c.*
8. 10, hath no man *c.* thee?
11, neither do I *c.* thee.
Rom. 2. 1, thou *c.* thyself.
8. 3, *c.* sin in the flesh.
34, who is he that *c.*?
14. 22, that *c.* not himself.
Tit. 2. 8, sound speech that cannot be *c.*
Jas. 5. 6, ye *c.* and killed the just.
9, grudge not lest ye be *c.*
1 John 3. 21, if our heart *c.* us not.
See Job 9. 20; 15. 6; Mat. 12. 41.
CONDEMNATION. John 3. 19, this is the *c.*, that light.
2 Cor. 3. 9, the ministration of *c.*
1 Tim. 3. 6, the *c.* of the devil.
Jas. 5. 12, lest ye fall into *c.*
Jude 4, of old ordained to this *c.*
See Lu. 23. 40; Rom. 5. 16; 8. 1.
CONDESCEND. Rom. 12. 16.
CONDITION. 1 Sam. 11. 2; Lu. 14. 32.
CONDUIT. 2 Kings 18. 17; 20. 20; Isa. 7. 3; 36. 2.
CONEY. Lev. 11. 5; Ps. 104. 18; Prov. 30. 26.
CONFECTION. Ex. 30. 35; 1 Sam. 8. 13.
CONFEDERATE. Gen. 14. 13; Isa. 7. 2; 8. 12; Obad. 7.
CONFERENCE. Gal. 2. 6.
CONFERRED. Gal. 1. 16.
CONFESS. Prov. 28. 13, whoso *c.* and forsaketh.
Mat. 10. 32; Lu. 12. 8, *c.* me before men.
John 9. 22, if any man did *c.*
12. 42, rulers did not *c.* him.
Acts 23. 8, Pharisees *c.* both.
Rom. 10. 9, shall *c.* with thy mouth.
14. 11; Phil. 2. 11, every tongue *c.*
Heb. 11. 13, *c.* they were strangers.
Jas. 5. 16, *c.* your faults one to another.
1 John 1. 9, if we *c.* our sins.
4. 2, every spirit that *c.* Christ.
15, whoso shall *c.* that Jesus is the Christ.
Rev. 3. 5, I will *c.* his name before my Father.
See Lev. 16. 21; 1 Kings 8. 33; 2 Chron. 6. 24.
CONFESSION. Rom. 10. 10; 1 Tim. 6. 13.
CONFIDENCE. Ps. 65. 5, the *c.* of all the ends of the earth.
118. 8, 9, than to put *c.* in man.
Prov. 3. 26, the Lord shall be thy *c.*
14. 26, in fear of the Lord is strong *c.*
Isa. 30. 15, in *c.* shall be your strength.
Jer. 2. 37, hath rejected thy *c.*
Eph. 3. 12, access with *c.* by the faith of him.
Phil. 3. 3, 4, no *c.* in flesh.
Heb. 3. 6, 14, hold fast *c.*
10. 35, cast not away *c.*
1 John 2. 28, we may have *c.*
3. 21, we have *c.* toward God.
5. 14, this is the *c.* we have in him.
See Job 4. 6; 18. 14; 31. 24; Prov. 25. 19.
CONFIDENT. Ps. 27. 3; Prov. 14. 16; 2 Cor. 5. 6; Phil. 1. 6.
CONFIRM. Isa. 35. 3, *c.* the feeble knees.
Mk. 16. 20, *c.* the word with signs.

Acts 14. 22, *c.* the souls of the disciples.
15. 32, 41, exhorted brethren, and *c.* them.
Rom. 15. 8, *c.* the promises made to fathers.
See 2 Kings 15. 19.
CONFIRMATION. Phil. 1. 7; Heb. 6. 16.
CONFISCATION. Ezra 7. 26.
CONFLICT. Phil. 1. 30; Col. 2. 1.
CONFORM. Rom. 8. 29; 12. 2; Phil. 3. 10.
CONFOUND. Ps. 22. 5, fathers trusted and were not *c.*
40. 14; 70. 2, ashamed and *c.*
Acts 2. 6, multitude were *c.*
9. 22, Saul *c.* the Jews.
See Gen. 11. 7; Ps. 71. 13; 129. 5.
CONFUSED. Isa. 9. 5; Acts 19. 32.
CONFUSION. Dan. 9. 7, to us belongeth *c.* of faces.
Acts 19. 29, city was filled with *c.*
1 Cor. 14. 33, God not author of *c.*
See Ps. 70. 2; 71. 1; 109. 29; Isa. 24. 10.
CONGEALED. Ex. 15. 8.
CONGRATULATE. 1 Chron. 18. 10.
CONGREGATION. Num. 14. 10, all the *c.* bade stone them.
Neh. 5. 13, all the *c.* said Amen.
Ps. 1. 5, nor sinners in the *c.* of the righteous.
26. 12, in the *c.* will I bless the Lord.
Prov. 21. 16, in the *c.* of the dead.
Joel 2. 16, sanctify the *c.*
Acts 13. 43, when the *c.* was broken up.
See Ex. 12. 6; 16. 2; 39. 32; Lev. 4. 13.
CONIES. Ps. 104. 18, the rocks for the *c.*
Prov. 30. 26, the *c.* are but a feeble folk.
See Lev. 11. 5; Deut. 14. 7.
CONQUERORS. Rom. 8. 37; Rev. 6. 2.
CONSCIENCE. Acts 24. 16, *c.* void of offence.
Rom. 2. 15; 9. 1; 2 Cor. 1. 12, *c.* bearing witness.
13. 5; 1 Cor. 10. 25, 27, 28, for *c.* sake.
1 Cor. 8. 10, 12, weak *c.*
1 Tim. 1. 5, 19; Heb. 13. 18; 1 Pet. 3. 16, a good *c.*
3. 9, mystery of faith in pure *c.*
4. 2, *c.* seared with hot iron.
Heb. 9. 14, purge *c.* from dead works.
10. 22, hearts sprinkled from evil *c.*
See John 8. 9; Acts 23. 1; 2 Cor. 4. 2.
CONSECRATE. 1 Chron. 29. 5, to *c.* his service to the Lord.
Mic. 4. 13, I will *c.*
Heb. 7. 28, who is *c.* for evermore.
10. 20, living way which he hath *c.*
See Ex. 28. 3; 29. 35; 32. 29; Lev. 7. 37.
CONSENT. Ps. 50. 18, a thief thou *c.* with him.
Prov. 1. 10, if sinners entice thee *c.* not.
Zeph. 3. 9, to serve with one *c.*
Lu. 14. 18, with one *c.* began to make excuse.
See Deut. 13. 8; Acts 8. 1; Rom. 7. 16.
CONSIDER. Ps. 8. 3, when I *c.* the heavens.
41. 1, blessed is he that *c.* the poor.
48. 13, *c.* her palaces.
50. 22, *c.* this, ye that forget God.
Prov. 6. 6, *c.* her ways and be wise.
23. 1, *c.* diligently what is before thee.
24. 12, doth not he *c.* it.?
28. 22, and *c.* not that poverty.
Eccl. 5. 1, they *c.* not that they do evil.
7. 14, in day of adversity *c.*
Isa. 1. 3, my people doth not *c.*
Jer. 23. 20; 30. 24, in latter days ye shall *c.*
Ezek. 12. 3, it may be they will *c.*
Hag. 1. 5, 7, *c.* your ways.
Mat. 6. 28; Lu. 12. 27, *c.* lilies of the field.
7. 3, *c.* not the beam.
Lu. 12. 24, *c.* the ravens.
Gal. 6. 1, *c.* thyself lest thou also be tempted.
Heb. 3. 1, *c.* the Apostle and High Priest.
7. 4, now *c.* how great this man was.
10. 21, *c.* one another to provoke.
12. 3, *c.* him that endured.
13. 7, *c.* the end of their conversation.
See Deut. 32. 29; Judg. 18. 14; 1 Sam. 12. 24.
CONSIST. Lu. 12. 15; Col. 1. 17.
CONSOLATION. Job 15. 11, are the *c.* of God small.
Lu. 6. 24, ye have received your *c.*
Rom. 15. 5, the God of *c.*
Phil. 2. 1, if there be any *c.* in Christ.
2 Thess. 2. 16, everlasting *c.*
Heb. 6. 18, strong *c.*
See Jer. 16. 7; Lu. 2. 25; Acts 4. 36.
CONSPIRACY. 2 Sam. 15. 2; Jer. 11. 9; Acts 23. 13.
CONSTANTLY. 1 Chron. 28. 7; Prov. 21. 28; Tit. 3. 8.
CONSTRAIN. Job 32. 18; Lu. 24. 29; 2 Cor. 5. 14; 1 Pet. 5. 2.
CONSULT. Ps. 83. 3; Mk. 15. 1; Lu. 14. 31; John 12. 10.
CONSUME. Ex. 3. 2, bush was not *c.*
Deut. 4. 24; 9. 3; Heb. 12. 29, a *c.* fire.
1 Kings 18. 38; 2 Chron. 7. 1, fire fell and *c.* the sacrifice.
Job 20. 26, fire not blown shall *c.* him.
Ps. 39. 11, *c.* away like a moth.
Mal. 3. 6, therefore ye are not *c.*
Lu. 9. 54, *c.* them as Elias did.
Gal. 5. 15, take heed ye be not *c.*
Jas. 4. 3, that ye may *c.* it on your lusts.
See Ex. 32. 10; 33. 3; Deut. 5. 25; Josh. 24. 20.
CONSUMMATION. Dan. 9. 27.
CONSUMPTION. Lev. 26. 16; Deut. 28. 22; Isa. 10. 22.
CONTAIN. 1 Kings 8. 27; 2 Chron. 2. 6; 6. 18; 1 Cor. 7. 9.
CONTEMN. Ps. 10. 13; 15. 4; 107. 11; Ezek. 21. 10.
CONTEMPT. Prov. 18. 3, wicked cometh, then cometh *c.*
Dan. 12. 2, awake to everlasting *c.*
See Esth. 1. 18; Job 31. 34; Ps. 119. 22.
CONTEMPTIBLE. Mal. 1. 7, 12; 2. 9; 2 Cor. 10. 10.
CONTEND. Isa. 49. 25, I will *c.* with him that *c.*
50. 8, who will *c.* with me.
Jer. 12. 5, how canst thou *c.* with horses.
See Job 10. 2; 13. 8; Eccl. 6. 10; Jude 3, 9.
CONTENT. Mk. 15. 15, willing to *c.* the people.
Lu. 3. 14, be *c.* with your wages.
Phil. 4. 11, I have learned to be *c.*
1 Tim. 6. 6, godliness with *c.* is great gain.
8, having food let us be *c.*
Heb. 13. 5, be *c.* with such things as ye have.
See Gen. 37. 27; Josh. 7. 7; Job 6. 28; Prov. 6. 35.
CONTENTION. Prov. 18. 18, the lot causeth *c.* to cease.
19. 13; 27. 15, *c.* of a wife.
23. 29, who hath *c.*
Acts 15. 39, the *c.* was sharp.
1 Cor. 1. 11, there are *c.* among you.
Phil. 1. 16, preach Christ of *c.*
1 Thess. 2. 2, to speak with much *c.*
Tit. 3. 9, avoid *c.* and strivings.
See Prov. 13. 10; 17. 14; 18. 6; 22. 10.
CONTENTIOUS. Prov. 21. 19; 26. 21; 27. 15; Rom. 2. 8; 1 Cor. 11. 16.
CONTINUAL. Ps. 34. 1; 71. 6, praise *c.* in my mouth.
40. 11, let thy truth *c.* preserve me.
73. 23, I am *c.* with thee.
Prov. 6. 21, bind them *c.* on thine heart.
15. 15, merry heart hath a *c.* feast.
Isa. 14. 6, smote with a *c.* stroke.
52. 5, my name is *c.* blasphemed.
Lu. 18. 5, lest by her *c.* coming.
24. 53, were *c.* in the temple.
Acts 6. 4, give ourselves *c.* to prayer.
Rom. 9. 2, I have *c.* sorrow in my heart.
Heb. 7. 3, abideth a priest *c.*
See Ex. 29. 42; Num. 4. 7; Job 1. 5.
CONTINUANCE. Deut. 28. 59; Ps. 139. 16; Isa. 64. 5; Rom. 2. 7.
CONTINUE. Job 14. 2, as a shadow and *c.* not.
Ps. 72. 17, name shall *c.* as long as the sun.

Isa. 5. 11, *c.* till wine inflame them.
Jer. 32. 14, evidences may *c.* many days.
Lu. 6. 12, he *c.* all night in prayer.
22. 28, that *c.* with me in my temptation.
John 8. 31, if ye *c.* in my word.
15. 9, *c.* ye in my love.
Acts 1. 14; 2. 46, *c.* with one accord.
12. 16, Peter *c.* knocking.
13. 43, to *c.* in grace of God.
14. 22, exhorting them to *c.* in faith.
26. 22, I *c.* unto this day.
Rom. 6. 1, shall we *c.* in sin?
12. 12; Col. 4. 2, *c.* in prayer.
Gal. 3. 10, that *c.* not in all things.
Col. 1. 23; 1 Tim. 2. 15, if ye *c.* in the faith.
1 Tim. 4. 16; 2 Tim. 3. 14, *c.* in them.
Heb. 7. 23, not suffered to *c.* by reason.
24, this man *c.* ever.
13. 1, let brotherly love *c.*
14, here have we no *c.* city.
Jas. 4. 13, and *c.* there a year.
2 Pet. 3. 4, all things *c.* as they were.
1 John 2. 19, no doubt have *c.* with us.
See 1 Sam. 12. 14; 13. 14; 2 Sam. 7. 29.
CONTRADICTION. Heb. 7. 7; 12. 3.
CONTRARIWISE. 2 Cor. 2. 7; Gal. 2. 7; 1 Pet. 3. 9.
CONTRARY. Acts 18. 13, *c.* to the law.
26. 9, many things *c.* to name of Jesus.
Gal. 5. 17, *c.* the one to the other.
1 Thess. 2. 15, *c.* to all men.
1 Tim. 1. 10, *c.* to sound doctrine.
Tit. 2. 8, he of the *c.* part may be ashamed.
See Lev. 26. 21; Esth. 9. 1; Mat. 14. 24; Acts 17. 7.
CONTRIBUTION. Rom. 15. 26.
CONTRITE. Ps. 34. 18; 51. 17; Isa. 57. 15; 66. 2.
CONTROVERSY. Jer. 25. 31, a *c.* with the nations.
Mic. 6. 2, hath a *c.* with his people.
1 Tim. 3. 16, without *c.* great is the mystery.
See Deut. 17. 8; 19. 17; 21. 5; 25. 1.
CONVENIENT. Prov. 30. 8, feed me with food *c.*
Acts 24. 25, when I have a *c.* season.
Rom. 1. 28, things which are not *c.*
Eph. 5. 4, talking, jesting, are not *c.*
See Jer. 40. 4; Mk. 6. 21; 1 Cor. 16. 12.
CONVERSANT. Josh. 8. 35; 1 Sam. 25. 15.
CONVERSATION. Ps. 37. 14, such as be of upright *c.*
50. 23, that ordereth his *c.* aright.
Phil. 1. 27, *c.* as becometh the gospel.
3. 20, our *c.* is in heaven.
1 Tim. 4. 12, an example in *c.*
Heb. 13. 5, *c.* without covetousness.
7, considering end of their *c.*
1 Pet. 1. 15; 2 Pet. 3. 11, holy *c.*
18, redeemed from vain *c.*
2. 12, your *c.* honest among Gentiles.
3. 1, won by *c.* of wives.
2 Pet. 2. 7, vexed with filthy *c.*
See Gal. 1. 13; Eph. 2. 3; 4. 22; Jas. 3. 13.
CONVERSION. Acts 15. 3.
CONVERT. Ps. 19. 7, perfect, *c.* the soul.
Isa. 6. 10; Mat. 13. 15; Mk. 4. 12; John 12. 40; Acts 28. 27, lest they *c.*
Mat. 18. 3, except ye be *c.*
Lu. 22. 32, when *c.* strengthen thy brethren.
Acts 3. 19, repent and be *c.*
Jas. 5. 19, 20, and one *c.* him.
See Ps. 51. 13; Isa. 1. 27; 60. 5.
CONVICTED. John 8. 9.
CONVINCE. John 8. 46, which of you *c.* me of sin.
Tit. 1. 9, able to *c.* gainsayers.
See Job 32. 12; Acts 18. 28; 1 Cor. 14. 24.
CONVOCATION. Ex. 12. 16; Lev. 23. 2; Num. 28. 26.
COOK. 1 Sam. 8. 13; 9. 23, 24.
COOL. Gen. 3. 8; Lu. 16. 24.
COPPER. Ezra 8. 27; 2 Tim. 4. 14.
COPY. Deut. 17. 18; Josh. 8. 32; Prov. 25. 1.
CORBAN. Mk. 7. 11, it is *c.*
CORD. Prov. 5. 22, holden with the *c.* of sins.
Eccl. 4. 12, a threefold *c.*
12. 6, silver *c.* loosed.
Isa. 5. 18, draw iniquity with *c.*
54. 2, lengthen *c.*
Hos. 11. 4, the *c.* of a man.
John 2. 15, scourge of small *c.*
See Judg. 15. 13; Ps. 2. 3; 118. 27; Jer. 38. 6.
CORN. Gen. 42. 2; Acts 7. 12, *c.* in Egypt.
Deut. 25. 4; 1 Cor. 9. 9; 1 Tim. 5. 18, ox treadeth *c.*
Judg. 15. 5, foxes into standing *c.*
Job 5. 26, like as a shock of *c.*
Ps. 4. 7, in time their *c.* increased.
65. 9, prepared them *c.*
13, valleys covered over with *c.*
72. 16, handful of *c.* in the earth.
Prov. 11. 26, he that withholdeth *c.*
Zech. 9. 17, *c.* shall make men cheerful.
Mat. 12. 1; Mk. 2. 23; Lu. 6. 1, pluck *c.*
Mk. 4. 28, full *c.* in the ear.
John 12. 24, a *c.* of wheat fall into ground.
See Gen. 27. 28; 41. 57; Deut. 33. 28; Isa. 36. 17.
CORNER. Ps. 118. 22; Eph. 2. 20, head stone of *c.*
144. 12, daughters as *c.* stones.
Isa. 28. 16; 1 Pet. 2. 6, a precious *c.* stone.
Mat. 6. 5, pray in *c.* of the streets.
Rev. 7. 1, on four *c.* of the earth.
See Job 1. 19; Prov. 7. 8; 21. 9.
CORNET. 2 Sam. 6. 5; 1 Chron. 15. 28; Dan. 3. 5.
CORPSE. 2 Kings 19. 35; Isa. 37. 36; Nah. 3. 3; Mk. 6. 29.
CORRECT. Prov. 3. 12, whom the Lord loveth he *c.*
29. 17, *c.* thy son.
19, servant will not be *c.* by words.
Jer. 10. 24, *c.* me, but with judgment.
30. 11; 46. 28, I will *c.* thee in measure.
Heb. 12. 9, we have had fathers which *c.* us.
See Job 5. 17; Ps. 39. 11; 94. 10.
CORRECTION. Prov. 22. 15, rod of *c.* shall drive it.
Jer. 2. 30; 5. 3; 7. 28; Zeph. 3. 2, receive *c.*
2 Tim. 3. 16, scripture profitable for *c.*
See Job 37. 13; Prov. 3. 11; 7. 22; 15. 10.
CORRUPT. Deut. 4. 16, take heed lest ye *c.*
31. 29, after my death ye will *c.*
Mat. 6. 19; Lu. 12. 33, moth *c.*
7. 17; 12. 33; Lu. 6. 43, a *c.* tree.
1 Cor. 15. 33, evil communications *c.*
2 Cor. 2. 17, not as many, which *c.* the word.
7. 2, we have *c.* no man.
11. 2, lest your minds be *c.*
Eph. 4. 22, put off old man which is *c.*
29, let no *c.* communication.
1 Tim. 6. 5; 2 Tim. 3. 8, men of *c.* minds.
Jas. 5. 1, your riches are *c.*
See Gen. 6. 11; Job 17. 1; Prov. 25. 26.
CORRUPTERS. Isa. 1. 4; Jer. 6. 28.
CORRUPTIBLE. Rom. 1. 23; 1 Cor. 9. 25; 15. 53; 1 Pet. 1. 18; 3. 4.
CORRUPTION. Ps. 16. 10; 49. 9; Acts 2. 27; 13. 35, not see *c.*
Jon. 2. 6, brought up life from *c.*
Rom. 8. 21, from bondage of *c.*
1 Cor. 15. 42, 50, sown in *c.*
Gal. 6. 8, of flesh reap *c.*
2 Pet. 1. 4, the *c.* that is in world.
2. 12, perish in their own *c.*
See Lev. 22. 25; Job 17. 14; Isa. 38. 17.
CORRUPTLY. 2 Chron. 27. 2; Neh. 1. 7.
COST. 2 Sam. 24. 24; 1 Chron. 21. 24, offer of that which *c.* nothing.
Lu. 14. 28, sitteth down and counteth *c.*
See 2 Sam. 19. 42; 1 Kings 5. 17; John 12. 3; 1 Tim. 2. 9.
COTTAGE. Isa. 1. 8; 24. 20; Zeph. 2. 6.
COUCH. Lu. 5. 19, let him down with *c.*

24, take up thy *c*.
Acts 5. 15, laid sick on *c*.
See Gen. 49. 11; Job 7. 13; 38. 40; Ps. 6. 6; Amos 6. 4.
COULD. Isa. 5. 4; Mk. 6. 19; 9. 18; 14. 8.
COULTER. 1 Sam. 13. 20, 21.
COUNCIL. Mat. 5. 22; 10. 17; Acts 5. 27; 6. 12.
COUNSEL. Neh. 4. 15, brought their *c*. to nought.
Job 38. 2; 42. 3, darkeneth *c*. by words.
Ps. 1. 1, *c*. of the ungodly.
33. 11; Prov. 19. 21, *c*. of Lord standeth.
55. 14, took sweet *c*. together.
73. 24, guide me with thy *c*.
Prov. 1. 25, 30, set at nought all my *c*.
11. 14, where no *c*. is, people fall.
15. 22, without *c*. purposes are disappointed.
21. 30, there is no *c*. against the Lord.
Eccl. 8. 2, I *c*. thee keep king's commandment.
Isa. 28. 29, wonderful in *c*.
30. 1, that take *c*., but not of me.
40. 14, with whom took he *c*.
46. 10, my *c*. shall stand.
Jer. 32. 19, great in *c*., mighty in working.
Hos. 10. 6, ashamed of his own *c*.
Mk. 3. 6; John 11. 53, took *c*. against Jesus.
Acts 2. 23, determinate *c*. of God.
4. 28, what thy *c*. determined before.
5. 38, if this *c*. be of men.
20. 27, declare all *c*. of God.
1 Cor. 4. 5, make manifest *c*. of the heart.
Eph. 1. 11, after the *c*. of his own will.
Heb. 6. 17, the immutability of his *c*.
Rev. 3. 18, I *c*. thee to buy gold tried in fire.
See Ex. 18. 19; Josh. 9. 14; 2 Sam. 15. 31.
COUNSELLOR. Prov. 11. 14; 15. 22; 24. 6, in multitude of *c*.
12. 20, to *c*. of peace is joy.
Mic. 4. 9, is thy *c*. perished?
Mk. 15. 43; Lu. 23. 50, an honourable *c*.
Rom. 11. 34, who hath been his *c*.
See 2 Chron. 22. 3; Job 3. 14; 12. 17.
COUNT. Gen. 15. 6; Ps. 106. 31; Rom. 4. 3; Gal. 3. 6, *c*. for righteousness.
Ps. 44. 22, *c*. as sheep for the slaughter.
Prov. 17. 28, even a fool is *c*. wise.
Isa. 32. 15, field be *c*. for a forest.
Mat. 14. 5; Mk. 11. 32, they *c*. him as a prophet.
Lu. 21. 36; Acts 5. 41; 2 Thess. 1. 5, 11; 1 Tim. 5. 17, *c*. worthy.
Acts 20. 24, neither *c*. I my life dear.
Phil. 3. 7, 8, I *c*. loss for Christ.
13, I *c*. not myself to have apprehended.
Heb. 10. 29, *c*. blood an unholy thing.
Jas. 1. 2, *c*. it all joy.
2 Pet. 3. 9, as some men *c*. slackness.
See Num. 23. 10; Job 31. 4; Ps. 139. 18, 22.
COUNTENANCE. 1 Sam. 16. 7, look not on his *c*. or stature.
12; 17. 42, David of beautiful *c*.
Neh. 2. 2, why is thy *c*. sad?
Job 14. 20, thou changest his *c*.
Ps. 4. 6; 44. 3; 89. 15; 90. 8, light of thy *c*.
Prov. 15. 13, merry heart maketh cheerful *c*.
27. 17, sharpeneth *c*. of his friend.
Eccl. 7. 3, by sadness of *c*. heart made better.
Isa. 3. 9, their *c*. doth witness against them.
Mat. 6. 16, hypocrites of a sad *c*.
28. 3; Lu. 9. 29, *c*. like lightning.
Rev. 1. 16, his *c*. as the sun shineth.
See Gen. 4. 5; Num. 6. 26; Judg. 13. 6.
COUNTRY. Prov. 25. 25, good news from a far *c*.
Mat. 13. 57; Mk. 6. 4; Lu. 4. 24; John 4. 44, in his own *c*.
21. 33; 25. 14; Mk. 12. 1, went to far *c*.
Lu. 4. 23, do also here in thy *c*.
Acts 12. 20, their *c*. nourished by king's *c*.
Heb. 11. 9, sojourned as in strange *c*.
16, desire a better *c*.
See Gen. 12. 1; 24. 4; Josh. 9. 6; Lu. 15. 13.
COUNTRYMEN. 2 Cor. 11. 26; 1 Thess. 2. 14.
COUPLED. 1 Pet. 3. 2.
COURAGE. Deut. 31. 6; 7. 23; Josh. 10. 25; Ps. 27. 14; Acts 28. 15, thanked God and took *c*.
See Num. 13. 20; Josh. 1. 7; 2. 11; 2 Sam. 13. 28.
COURSE. Acts 20. 24; 2 Tim. 4. 7, finished my *c*.
2 Thess. 3. 1, may have free *c*.
Jas. 3. 6, setteth on fire the *c*. of nature.
See Judg. 5. 20; Ps. 82. 5; Acts 13. 25.
COURT. Ex. 27. 9, thou shalt make the *c*. of the tabernacle.
38. 9, and he made the *c*.
Ps. 65. 4, that he may dwell in thy *c*.
84. 2, fainteth for the *c*. of the Lord.
92. 13, flourish in the *c*. of our God.
100. 4, enter into his *c*. with praise.
Isa. 1. 12, who required this to tread my *c*.?
Lu. 7. 25, live delicately are in kings' *c*.
See Isa. 34. 13; Jer. 19. 14; Ezek. 9. 7.
COURTEOUS. Acts 27. 3; 28. 7; 1 Pet. 3. 8.
COUSIN. Lu. 1. 36, 58.
COVENANT. Num. 18. 19; 2 Chron. 13. 5, *c*. of salt.
25. 12, my *c*. of peace.
Ps. 105. 8; 106. 45, he remembereth his *c*. for ever.
111. 5, ever mindful of his *c*.
Isa. 28. 18, your *c*. with death disannulled.
Mat. 26. 15; Lu. 22. 5, they *c*. with him.
Acts 3. 25, children of the *c*.
Rom. 9. 4, to whom pertaineth the *c*.
Eph. 2. 12, strangers from *c*. of promise.
Heb. 8. 6, mediator of a better *c*.
12. 24, mediator of the new *c*.
13. 20, blood of the everlasting *c*.
See Gen. 9. 15; Ex. 34. 28; Job 31. 1; Jer. 50. 5.
COVER. Ex. 15. 5, depths *c*. them, sank as stone.
33. 32, I will *c*. them.
1 Sam. 28. 14, an old man *c*. with a mantle.
Esth. 7. 8, they *c*. Haman's face.
Ps. 32. 1; Rom. 4. 7, blessed whose sin is *c*.
73. 6, violence *c*. them as a garment.
91. 4, he shall *c*. thee with his feathers.
Ps. 104. 6, thou *c*. it with the deep.
Prov. 10. 6, 11, violence *c*. mouth of the wicked.
12, love *c*. all sins.
12. 16, a prudent man *c*. shame.
17. 9, he that *c*. transgression seeketh love.
28. 13, he that *c*. sins shall not prosper.
Isa. 26. 21, earth no more *c*. her slain.
Mat. 8. 24, ship *c*. with waves.
10. 26; Lu. 12. 2, there is nothing *c*.
1 Cor. 11. 4, having his head *c*.
6, if women be not *c*.
7, a man ought not to *c*. his head.
1 Pet. 4. 8, charity shall *c*. multitude of sins.
See Gen. 7. 19; Ex. 8. 6; 21. 33; Lev. 16. 13.
COVERING. Job 22. 14, thick clouds are a *c*. to him.
24. 7, naked have no *c*. in the cold.
26. 6, destruction hath no *c*.
31. 19, if I have seen any poor without *c*.
Isa. 28. 20, *c*. narrower than he can wrap.
See Gen. 8. 13; Lev. 13. 45; 2 Sam. 17. 19.
COVERT. Ps. 61. 4; Isa. 4. 6; 16. 4; 32. 2.
COVET. Prov. 21. 26, he *c*. greedily all the day.
Hab. 2. 9, *c*. an evil covetousness.
Acts 20. 33, I have *c*. no man's silver.
1 Cor. 12. 31, *c*. earnestly the best gifts.
1 Tim. 6. 10, while some *c*. after, they erred.
See Ex. 20. 17; Deut. 5. 21; Rom. 7. 7; 13. 9.
COVETOUS. Prov. 28. 16, he that hateth *c*. shall prolong.
Ezek. 33. 31, their heart goeth after *c*.
Mk. 7. 22, out of heart proceedeth *c*.
Rom. 1. 29, filled with all *c*.
1 Cor. 6. 10; Eph. 5. 5, nor *c*. inherit kingdom.
Eph. 5. 3, but *c*., let it not be named.
2 Tim. 3. 2, men shall be *c*.
Heb. 13. 5, conversation without *c*.

2 Pet. 2. 3, through *c.* make merchandise.
14, exercised with *c.* practices.
See Ps. 10. 3; 119. 36; 1 Cor. 5. 10.
COW. Lev. 22. 28; Job 21. 10; Isa. 11. 7.
CRACKLING. Eccl. 7. 6.
CRAFT. Job 5. 13; 1 Cor. 3. 19, taketh wise in their *c.*
Lu. 20. 23, he perceived their *c.*
Acts 19. 25, by this *c.* we have our wealth.
27, our *c.* is in danger.
2 Cor. 4. 2, not walking in *c.*
12. 16, being *c.* I caught you.
Eph. 4. 14, carried away with cunning *c.*
See Dan. 8. 25; Acts 18. 3; Rev. 18. 22.
CRAG. Job 39. 28.
CRANE. Isa. 38. 14; Jer. 8. 7.
CRASHING. Zeph. 1. 10.
CRAVE. Prov. 16. 26; Mk. 15. 43.
CREATE. Isa. 40. 26, who hath *c.* these things?
43. 7, *c.* him for my glory.
65. 17, I *c.* new heavens and new earth.
Jer. 31. 22, the Lord hath *c.* a new thing.
Amos 4. 13, he that *c.* wind.
Mal. 2. 10, hath not one God *c.* us?
1 Cor. 11. 9, neither was man *c.* for woman.
Eph. 2. 10, *c.* in Christ Jesus.
4. 24, after God is *c.* in righteousness.
Col. 1. 16, by him were all things *c.*
1 Tim. 4. 3, which God *c.* to be received.
See Gen. 1. 1; 6. 7; Deut. 4. 32; Ps. 51. 10.
CREATION. Mk. 10. 6; 13. 19; Rom. 1. 20; 8. 22; 2 Pet. 3. 4.
CREATOR. Eccl. 12. 1; Isa. 40. 28; Rom. 1. 25; 1 Pet. 4. 19.
CREATURE. Mk. 16. 15; Col. 1. 23, preach to every *c.*
Rom. 8. 19, expectation of the *c.*
2 Cor. 5. 17; Gal. 6. 15, new *c.*
Col. 1. 15, firstborn of every *c.*
1 Tim. 4. 4, every *c.* of God is good.
See Gen. 1. 20; 2. 19; Isa. 13. 21; Ezek. 1. 20; Eph. 2. 10; 4. 24.
CREATURES. Ezek. 1. 5, came the likeness of four living *c.*
CREDITOR. Deut. 15. 2; 2 Kings 4. 1; Isa. 50. 1; Mat. 18. 23; Lu. 7. 41.
CREEK. Acts 27. 39.
CREEP. Ps. 104. 20, beasts of the forest *c.* forth.
25, in sea are *c.* things.
Ezek. 8. 10, form of *c.* things portrayed.
Acts 10. 12; 11. 6, Peter saw *c.* things.
2 Tim. 3. 6, they *c.* into houses.
Jude 4, certain men *c.* in unawares.
See Gen. 1. 25; 7. 8; Lev. 11. 41; Deut. 4. 18.
CREW. Mat. 26. 74; Mk. 14. 68; Lu. 22. 60.
CRIB. Job 39. 9; Prov. 14. 4; Isa. 1. 3.
CRIMSON. 2 Chron. 2. 7; Isa. 1. 18; Jer. 4. 30.
CRIPPLE. Acts 14. 8.
CROOKED. Eccl. 1. 15; 7. 13, *c.* cannot be made straight.
Isa. 40. 4; 42. 16; Lu. 3. 5, *c.* shall be made straight.
45. 2, make the *c.* places straight.
59. 8; Lam. 3. 9, *c.* paths.
Phil. 2. 15, in midst of a *c.* nation.
See Lev. 21. 20; Deut. 32. 5; Job 26. 13.
CROPS. Lev. 1. 16; Ezek. 17. 22.
CROSS. Mat. 16. 24; Mk. 8. 34; 10. 21; Lu. 9. 23, take up *c.*
27. 32; Mk. 15. 21; Lu. 23. 26, compelled to bear *c.*
40; Mk. 15. 30, come down from *c.*
John 19. 25, there stood by *c.*
1 Cor. 1. 17; Gal. 6. 12; Phil. 3. 18, *c.* of Christ.
18, preaching of the *c.*
Gal. 5. 11, offence of the *c.*
6. 14, glory save in the *c.*
Eph. 2. 16, reconcile both by the *c.*
Phil. 2. 8, the death of the *c.*
Col. 1. 20, peace through blood of the *c.*
2. 14, nailing it to his *c.*
Heb. 12. 2, for joy endured the *c.*
See Obad. 14; Mat. 10. 38; John 19. 17, 19.
CROUCH. 1 Sam. 2. 36; Ps. 10. 10.
CROWN. Job 19. 9, taken the *c.* from my head.
Ps. 8. 5; Heb. 2. 7, 9, *c.* with glory and honour.
65. 11, thou *c.* the year.
103. 4, *c.* thee with lovingkindness.
Prov. 4. 9, a *c.* of glory shall she deliver.
12. 4, virtuous woman is a *c.*
14. 18, prudent *c.* with knowledge.
16. 31, hoary head a *c.* of glory.
17. 6, children's children are the *c.* of old men.
Isa. 28. 1, woe to the *c.* of pride.
Mat. 27. 29; Mk. 15. 17; John 19. 2, a *c.* of thorns.
1 Cor. 9. 25, to obtain a corruptible *c.*
Phil. 4. 1, my joy and *c.*
1 Thess. 2. 19, a *c.* of rejoicing.
2 Tim. 2. 5, not *c.* except he strive.
4. 8, a *c.* of righteousness.
Jas. 1. 12; Rev. 2. 10, *c.* of life.
1 Pet. 5. 4, a *c.* of glory.
Rev. 3. 11, hold fast, that no man take thy *c.*
4. 10, cast *c.* before throne.
19. 12, on head were many *c.*
See Ex. 25. 25; 29. 6; Job 31. 36.
CRUCIFY. Mat. 27. 22, all said, let him be *c.*
Mk. 15. 13; Lu. 23. 21; John 19. 6, 15, *c.* him.
Acts 2. 23, by wicked hands ye have *c.*
Rom. 6. 6, old man is *c.* with him.
1 Cor. 1. 13, was Paul *c.* for you.
23, we preach Christ *c.*
2. 2, save Jesus Christ and him *c.*
2 Cor. 13. 4, though he was *c.* through weakness.
Gal. 2. 20, I am *c.* with Christ.
3. 1, Christ set forth *c.*
5. 24, have *c.* the flesh.
6. 14, the world is *c.* unto me.
Heb. 6. 6, *c.* to themselves afresh.
See Mat. 20. 19; 23. 34; 27. 31; Mk. 15. 20.
CRUEL. Ps. 25. 19, with *c.* hatred.
27. 12, breathe out *c.*
74. 20, full of the habitations of *c.*
Prov. 5. 9, give thy years to the *c.*
11. 17, *c.* troubleth his own flesh.
12. 10, tender mercies of the wicked are *c.*
27. 4, wrath is *c.*
Cant. 8. 6, jealousy is *c.*
Heb. 11. 36, trials of *c.* mockings.
See Gen. 49. 7; Ex. 6. 9; Deut. 32. 33.
CRUMBS. Mat. 15. 27; Mk. 7. 28; Lu. 16. 21.
CRUSE. 1 Sam. 26. 11; 1 Kings 14. 3; 17. 12; 19. 6.
CRUSH. Job 5. 4, children are *c.* in the gate.
39. 15, forgetteth that the foot may *c.* them.
See Lev. 22. 24; Num. 22. 25; Deut. 28. 33.
CRY (*n.*). 1 Sam. 5. 12, *c.* of the city went up to heaven.
Job 34. 28, he heareth the *c.* of the afflicted.
Ps. 9. 12, forgetteth not *c.* of the humble.
34. 15, ears are open to their *c.*
Prov. 21. 13, stoppeth his ears at the *c.* of the poor.
Mat. 25. 6, at midnight there was a *c.* made.
See Gen. 18. 20; Ex. 2. 23; Num. 16. 34.
CRY (*v.*). Ex. 14. 15, wherefore *c.* thou unto me?
Lev. 13. 45, cover his lip, and *c.* unclean.
Job 29. 12, I delivered poor that *c.*
Ps. 147. 9, food to young ravens which *c.*
Prov. 8. 1, doth not wisdom *c.*
Isa. 58. 1, *c.* aloud, spare not.
Mat. 12. 19, he shall not strive nor *c.*
20. 31; Mk. 10. 48; Lu. 18. 39, they *c.* the more.
Lu. 18. 7, elect who *c.* day and night.
John 7. 37, Jesus *c.*, if any man thirst.
Acts 19. 32; 21. 34, some *c.* one thing and some another.
See Ex. 5. 8; 32. 18; 2 Kings 8. 3.
CRYING. Prov. 19. 18; Isa. 65. 19; Heb. 5. 7; Rev. 21. 4.
CRYSTAL. Job 28. 17; Ezek. 1. 22; Rev. 4. 6; 21. 11; 22. 1.
CUBIT. Mat. 6. 27; Lu. 12. 25.
CUCUMBERS. Num. 11. 5; Isa. 1. 8,

CUMBER. Deut. 1. 12; Lu. 10. 40; 13. 7.
CUNNING. Ps. 137. 5, let my hand forget her *c.*
Jer. 9. 17, send for *c.* women.
Eph. 4. 14, carried about by *c.* craftiness.
2 Pet. 1. 16, not follow *c.* devised fables.
See Gen. 25. 27; Ex. 38. 23; 1 Sam. 16. 16; Dan. 1. 4.
CUP. Ps. 116. 13, take *c.* of salvation.
Mat. 10. 42; Mk. 9. 41, *c.* of cold water.
20. 22; Mk. 10. 39, drink of my *c.*
23. 25, make clean outside of *c.*
26. 27; Mk. 14. 23; Lu. 22. 17; 1 Cor. 11. 25, took *c.*
39; Mk. 14. 36; Lu. 22. 42, let this *c.* pass.
Lu. 22. 20; 1 Cor. 11. 25, this *c.* is new testament.
John 18. 11, *c.* which my father hath given.
1 Cor. 10. 16, *c.* of blessing we bless.
11. 26, as often as ye drink this *c.*
27, drink this *c.* unworthily.
See Gen. 40. 11; 44. 2; Prov. 23. 31.
CURDLED. Job 10. 10.
CURE. Lu. 7. 21, in that hour he *c.* many.
9. 1, power to *c.* diseases.
13. 32, I do *c.* to-day.
See Jer. 33. 6; 46. 11; Hos. 5. 13; Mat. 17. 16.
CURIOUS. Ex. 28. 8; Ps. 139. 15; Acts 19. 19.
CURRENT. Gen. 23. 16.
CURSE (*n.*). Deut. 11. 26, I set before you blessing and *c.*
23. 5, turned *c.* into blessing.
Mal. 3. 9, ye are cursed with a *c.*
Gal. 3. 10, are under the *c.*
Rev. 22. 3, no more *c.*
See Gen. 27. 12; Num. 5. 18.
CURSE (*v.*). Lev. 19. 14, not *c.* the deaf.
Num. 23. 8, how shall I *c.* whom God hath not.
Judg. 5. 23, *c.* ye Meroz, *c.* ye bitterly.
Job 2. 9, *c.* God, and die.
Ps. 62. 4, they bless, but *c.* inwardly.
Mal. 2. 2, I will *c.* your blessings.
Mat. 5. 44; Lu. 6. 28; Rom. 12. 14, bless them that *c.* you.
26. 74; Mk. 14. 71, he began to *c.*
Mk. 11. 21, fig tree thou *c.*
John 7. 49, knoweth not the law are *c.*
Gal. 3. 10, *c.* is every one that continueth not.
Jas. 3. 9, therewith *c.* we men.
See Gen. 8. 21; 12. 3; Num. 22. 6.
CURTAIN. Ex. 26. 36, the length of one *c.*
CUSTOM. Mat. 9. 9; Mk. 2. 14; Lu. 5. 27, receipt of *c.*
Mat. 17. 25, of whom do kings take *c.*
Lu. 4. 16, as his *c.* was, went into synagogue.
John 18. 39, ye have a *c.*
Acts 16. 21, teach *c.* which are not lawful.
Rom. 13. 7, *c.* to whom *c.*
1 Cor. 11. 16, we have no such *c.*
See Gen. 31. 35; Judg. 11. 39; Jer. 10. 3.
CUTTING. Ex. 31. 5; 35. 33; Isa. 38. 10; Mk. 5. 5.
CYMBAL. 1 Cor. 13. 1.
CYMBALS. 2 Sam. 6. 5, on cornets and on *c.*
1 Chron. 15. 16, harps and *c.*
16. 5, Asaph made a noise with *c.*
Ps. 150. 5, praise him upon the loud *c.*

D

DAGGER. Judg. 3. 16, 21, 22.
DAILY. Ps. 13. 2, sorrow in my heart *d.*
68. 19, *d.* loadeth us.
Prov. 8. 30, I was *d.* his delight.
Dan. 8. 11; 11. 31; 12. 11, *d.* sacrifice taken away.
Mat. 6. 11; Lu. 11. 3, our *d.* bread.
Lu. 9. 23, take up cross *d.*
Acts 2. 47, added to church *d.*
6. 1, the *d.* ministration.
16. 5, churches increased *d.*
17. 11, searched the scriptures ***d.***
1 Cor. 15. 31, I die *d.*
Jas. 2. 15, destitute of *d.* food.
See Num. 4. 16; 28. 24; Neh. 5. 18; Dan. 1. 5.
DAINTY. Ps. 141. 4, let me not eat of their *d.*
Prov. 23. 3, be not desirous of his *d.*
See Gen. 49. 20; Job 33. 20; Rev. 18. 14.
DALE. Gen. 14. 17; 2 Sam. 18. 18.
DAM. Ex. 22. 30; Lev. 22. 27; Deut. 22. 6.
DAMAGE. Prov. 26. 6, drinketh *d.*
Acts 27. 10, voyage will be with much *d.*
2 Cor. 7. 9, receive *d.* by us in nothing.
See Ezra 4. 22; Esth. 7. 4; Dan. 6. 2.
DAMNABLE. 2 Pet. 2. 1.
DAMNATION. Mat. 23. 33, can ye escape the *d.* of hell.
Mk. 3. 29, in danger of eternal *d.*
John 5. 29, the resurrection of *d.*
Rom. 13. 2, receive to themselves *d.*
1 Cor. 11. 29, eateth and drinketh *d.*
2 Pet. 2. 3, their *d.* slumbereth not.
See Mat. 23. 14; Mk. 12. 40; Lu. 20. 47; Rom. 3. 8.
DAMNED. Mk. 16. 16; Rom. 14. 23; 2 Thess. 2. 12.
DAMSEL. Ps. 68. 25, among them were the *d.* playing.
Mat. 14. 11; Mk. 6. 28, given to the *d.*
26. 69; John 18. 17, *d.* came to Peter.
Mk. 5. 39, the *d.* is not dead.
Acts 12. 13, a *d.* came to hearken.
16. 16, *d.* possessed with a spirit.
See Gen. 24. 55; 34. 3; Judg. 5. 30; Ruth 2. 5.
DANCE. Ex. 32. 19, he saw the calf, and *d.*
1 Sam. 18. 6, came out singing and *d.*
2 Sam. 6. 14, David *d.* before the Lord.
Job 21. 11, their children *d.*
Ps. 30. 11, turned my mourning into *d.*
149. 3; 150. 4, praise him in the *d.*
Eccl. 3. 4, a time to *d.*
Mat. 11. 17; Lu. 7. 32, piped, and ye have not *d.*
14. 6; Mk. 6. 22, daughter of Herodias *d.*
See Judg. 21. 23; Jer. 31. 13; Lam. 5. 15.
DANDLED. Isa. 66. 12.
DANGER. Mat. 5. 21; Mk. 3. 29; Acts 19. 27; 27. 9.
DARE. Rom. 5. 7, some would even *d.* to die.
See Job 41. 10; Rom. 15. 18; 1 Cor. 6. 1; 2 Cor. 10. 12.
DARK. Job 12. 25, they grope in the *d.*
22. 13, can he judge through *d.* cloud?
24. 16, in the *d.* they dig.
38. 2, that *d.* counsel by words.
Ps. 49. 4; Prov. 1. 6, *d.* sayings.
69. 23; Rom. 11. 10, let their eyes be ***d.***
88. 12, wonders be known in the *d.*
Eccl. 12. 2, stars be not *d.*
3, look out of windows be *d.*
Zech. 14. 6, shall not be clear nor *d.*
Mat. 24. 29; Mk. 13. 24, sun be *d.*
Lu. 23. 45, sun *d.* and vail rent.
John 20. 1, early, when it was yet *d.*
Rom. 1. 21, foolish heart was *d.*
Eph. 4. 18, understanding *d.*
See Gen. 15. 17; Ex. 10. 15; Num. 12. 8; Joel 2. 10.
DARKNESS. Deut. 5. 22, spake out of thick *d.*
28. 29, grope as the blind in *d.*
1 Sam. 2. 9, wicked shall be silent in *d.*
2 Sam. 22. 10; Ps. 18. 9, *d.* under his feet.
29; Ps. 18. 28, Lord will enlighten my *d.*
1 Kings 8. 12; 2 Chron. 6. 1, dwell in thick *d.*
Job 3. 5; Ps. 10. 10, *d.* and shadow of death.
10. 22, land where the light is as *d.*
30. 26, waited for light there came *d.*
Ps. 91. 6, pestilence that walketh in *d.*
97. 2, clouds and *d.* are round about him.
112. 4, to upright ariseth light in *d.*
139. 12, *d.* and light alike to thee.
Prov. 20. 20, lamp be put out in *d.*
Eccl. 2. 13, as far as light excelleth *d.*
14, fool walketh in *d.*
Isa. 58. 10, thy *d.* as noon day.
Isa. 60. 2, *d.* cover the earth, gross *d.*

Joel 2. 2, day of clouds and thick *d.*
Mat. 6. 23; Lu. 11. 34, body full of *d.*
8. 12; 22. 13; 25. 30, outer *d.*
10. 27; Lu. 12. 3, what I tell in *d.* speak.
Lu. 1. 79; Rom. 2. 19, light to them that sit in *d.*
22. 53; Col. 1. 13, the power of *d.*
23. 44, *d.* over all the earth.
John 1. 5, *d.* comprehended it not.
3. 19, loved *d.* rather than light.
12. 35, walk while ye have light, lest *d.*
Acts 26. 18, turn from *d.* to light.
Rom. 13. 12; Eph. 5. 11, works of *d.*
1 Cor. 4. 5, hidden things of *d.*
2 Cor. 4. 6, light to shine out of *d.*
6. 14, what communion hath light with *d.*?
Eph. 6. 12, rulers of the *d.* of this world.
1 Thess. 5. 5, not of the night nor of *d.*
Heb. 12. 18, to blackness and *d.*
1 Pet. 2. 9, out of *d.* into marvellous light.
2 Pet. 2. 4, into chains of *d.*
1 John 1. 5, in him is no *d.* at all.
6, and walk in *d.*, we lie.
2. 8, the *d.* is past.
9, hateth his brother, is in *d.*
11, *d.* hath blinded his eyes.
Rev. 16. 10, kingdom full of *d.*
See Gen. 1. 2; 15. 12; Ex. 10. 21; 20. 21.
DARLING. Ps. 22. 20; 35. 17.
DART. Job 41. 26; Prov. 7. 23; Eph. 6. 16.
DASH. Ps. 2. 9; Isa. 13. 16; Hos. 13. 16, *d.* in pieces.
91. 12; Mat. 4. 6; Lu. 4. 11, *d.* thy foot.
137. 9, that *d.* thy little ones.
See Ex. 15. 6; 2 Kings 8. 12; Jer. 13. 14.
DAUB. Ex. 2. 3; Ezek. 13. 10; 22. 28.
DAUGHTER. Gen. 24. 23, 47; Judg. 11. 34, whose *d.* art thou?
27. 46, weary of life because of *d.* of Heth.
Deut. 28. 53, eat flesh of sons and *d.*
2 Sam. 1. 20, lest *d.* of Philistines rejoice.
12. 3, lamb was unto him as a *d.*
Ps. 45. 9, kings' *d.* among honourable women.
144. 12, our *d.* as corner-stones.
Prov. 30. 15, horseleech hath two *d.*
31. 29, many *d.* have done virtuously.
Eccl. 12. 4, the *d.* of music.
Isa. 22. 4; Jer. 9. 1; Lam. 2. 11; 3. 48, spoiling of the *d.*
Jer. 6. 14, healed hurt of *d.* of my people.
8. 21, for hurt of *d.* am I hurt.
9. 1, weep for slain of *d.* of my people.
Mic. 7. 6; Mat. 10. 35; Lu. 12. 53, *d.* riseth against mother.
Mat. 15. 28, her *d.* was made whole.
Lu. 8. 42, one only *d.*, about twelve years of age.
13. 16, this woman *d.* of Abraham.
Heb. 11. 24, refused to be son of Pharaoh's *d.*
See Gen. 6. 1; Ex. 1. 16; 21. 7; Num. 27. 8.
DAWN. Ps. 119. 147, I prevented the *d.* of the morning.
2 Pet. 1. 19, till the day *d.*
See Josh. 6. 15; Judg. 19. 26; Job 3. 9; 7. 4.
DAY. Gen. 41. 9, I do remember my faults this *d.*
Deut. 4. 32, ask of the *d.* that are past.
1 Sam. 25. 8, come in a good *d.*
2 Kings 7. 9, this *d.* is a *d.* of good tidings.
1 Chron. 23. 1, 28; 2 Chron. 24. 15, full of *d.*
29. 15; Job 8. 9, our *d.* as a shadow.
Neh. 4. 2, will they make an end in a *d.*
Job 7. 1, *d.* like the *d.* of an hireling.
14. 6, till he accomplish his *d.*
19. 25, stand at latter *d.* upon the earth.
21. 30, reserved to *d.* of destruction.
32. 7, I said, *d.* should speak.
Ps. 2. 7; Acts 13. 33; Heb. 1. 5, this *d.* have I begotten thee.
19. 2, *d.* unto *d.* uttereth speech.
84. 10, a *d.* in thy courts.
Prov. 3. 2, 16, length of *d.*
4. 18, more and more to perfect *d.*
27. 1, what a *d.* may bring forth.
Eccl. 7. 1, *d.* of death better than *d.* of birth.
12. 1, while the evil *d.* come not.
Isa. 2. 12; 13. 6, 9; Joel 1. 15; 2. 1; Zeph. 1. 7; Zech. 14. 1, *d.* of the Lord.
10. 3, in the *d.* of visitation.
27. 3, the Lord will keep it night and *d.*
58. 5, acceptable *d.* to the Lord.
Isa. 65. 20, an infant of *d.*
Joel 2. 11, 31; Zeph. 1. 14; Mal. 4. 5; Acts 2. 20, great *d.* of the Lord.
Zech. 4. 10, despised *d.* of small things.
Mal. 3. 2, who may abide *d.* of his coming.
Mat. 7. 22, many will say in that *d.*
24. 36; Mk. 13. 32, that *d.* knoweth no man.
50; Lu. 12. 46, in a *d.* looked not for.
25. 13, ye know not the *d.* nor the hour.
Lu. 21. 34, that *d.* come unawares.
23. 43, to-*d.* shalt thou be with me.
John 6. 39, raise it again at last *d.*
8. 56, Abraham rejoiced to see my *d.*
9. 4, I must work while it is *d.*
Acts 17. 31, he hath appointed a *d.*
Rom. 2. 5, wrath against *d.* of wrath.
14. 5, esteemeth every *d.* alike.
2 Cor. 6. 2, the *d.* of salvation.
Phil. 1. 6, perform it until *d.* of Christ.
1 Thess. 5. 2; 2 Pet. 3. 10, *d.* cometh as a thief.
5, children of the *d.*
Heb. 13. 8, Jesus Christ same to-*d.* and for ever.
2 Pet. 3. 8, one *d.* as a thousand years.
See Gen. 1. 5; 27. 2; Job 1. 4; Ps. 77. 5; 118. 24; John 11. 24; 12. 48; 1 Cor. 3. 13; Rev. 6. 17; 16. 14; 20. 10.
DAYS (last). Isa. 2. 2, it shall come to pass in the last *d.*
See Mic. 4. 1; Acts 2. 17; 2 Tim. 3. 1; Heb. 1. 2; Jas. 5. 3; 2 Pet. 3. 3.
DAYSMAN. Job 9. 33.
DAYSPRING. Job 38. 12, *d.* to know his place.
Lu. 1. 78, *d.* from on high hath visited us.
DAYSTAR. 2 Pet. 1. 19, *d.* arise in your hearts.
DEAD. Lev. 19. 28, cuttings for the *d.*
Ruth 1. 8, as ye have dealt with *d.*
1 Sam. 24. 14; 2 Sam. 9. 8; 16. 9, *d.* dog.
Ps. 31. 12, forgotten as a *d.* man.
115. 17, *d.* praise not the Lord.
Prov. 9. 18, knoweth not that the *d.* are there.
Eccl. 4. 2, the *d.* which are already *d.*
9. 4, living dog better than *d.* lion.
5, *d.* know not any thing.
10. 1, *d.* flies cause ointment.
Isa. 26. 19, thy *d.* men shall live.
Jer. 22. 10, weep not for the *d.*
Mat. 8. 22, let the *d.* bury their *d.*
9. 24; Mk. 5. 39; Lu. 8. 52, not *d.*, but sleepeth.
11. 5; Lu. 7. 22, deaf hear, *d.* raised.
22. 32, not God of the *d.*
23. 27, full of *d.* men's bones.
Mk. 9. 10, rising from *d.* should mean.
Lu. 15. 24, 32; Rev. 1. 18, *d.* and is alive again.
16. 31, though one rose from the *d.*
John 5. 25, *d.* shall hear.
6. 49, did eat manna, and are *d.*
11. 25, though *d.*, yet shall he live.
44, he that was *d.* came forth.
Acts 10. 42; 2 Tim. 4. 1, judge of quick and *d.*
26. 23, first that should rise from *d.*
Rom. 6. 2, 11; 1 Pet. 2. 24, *d.* to sin.
7. 4; Gal. 2. 19, *d.* to the law.
14. 9, Lord both of *d.* and living.
1 Cor. 15. 15, if the *d.* rise not.
35, how are the *d.* raised.
2 Cor. 1. 9, trust in God who raiseth *d.*
5. 14, then were all *d.*
Eph. 2. 1; Col. 2, 13, *d.* in trespasses and sins.
5. 14, arise from the *d.*
Col. 1. 18, firstborn from the *d.*
2. 20; 2 Tim. 2. 11, *d.* with Christ.
1 Thess. 4. 16, *d.* in Christ shall rise first.
1 Tim. 5. 6, *d.* while she liveth.
Heb. 6. 1; 9. 14, from *d.* works.
11. 4, being *d.*, yet speaketh.

13. 20, brought again from the *d*.
Jas. 2. 17, 20, 26, faith *d*.
1 Pet. 4. 6, preached to them that are *d*.
Jude 12, twice *d*.
Rev. 1. 5, first-begotten of the *d*.
3. 1, a name that thou livest, and art *d*.
14. 13, blessed are the *d*.
20. 5, rest of *d*. lived not again.
12, the *d*. small and great.
13, sea gave up *d*.
See Gen. 23. 3; Ex. 12. 30; Mk. 9. 26; Rev. 1. 18.

DEADLY. Mk. 16. 18, drink any *d*. thing.
Jas. 3. 8, tongue full of *d*. poison.
See 1 Sam. 5. 11; Ps. 17. 9; Ezek. 30. 24.

DEAF. Ps. 58. 4, like *d*. adder that stoppeth.
Isa. 29. 18, shall the *d*. hear the words.
Mat. 11. 5; Lu. 7. 22, the *d*. hear.
Mk. 7. 37, he maketh the *d*. to hear.
9. 25, thou *d*. spirit, come out.
See Ex. 4. 11; Lev. 19. 14; Isa. 42. 18; 43. 8.

DEAL (a measure). Ex. 29. 40, with the one lamb, a tenth *d*. of flour.
Lev. 14. 10, three tenth *d*. of fine flour for a meat offering.

DEAL. Lev. 19. 11, nor *d*. falsely.
Job 42. 8, *d*. with you after folly.
Ps. 75. 4, *d*. not foolishly.
Prov. 12. 22, they that *d*. truly his delight.
Isa. 21. 2; 24. 16, treacherous dealer *d*. treacherously.
26. 10, in land of uprightness *d*. unjustly.
Jer. 6. 13; 8. 10, every one *d*. falsely.
Hos. 5. 7, have *d*. treacherously against the Lord.
Zech. 1. 6, as Lord thought, so hath he *d*.
Mk. 7. 36; 10. 48, the more a great *d*.
Lu. 2. 48, why hast thou thus *d*. with us?
Rom. 12. 3, according as God hath *d*.
See Gen. 32. 9; Ex. 1. 10; Deut. 7. 5; 2 Chron. 2. 3.

DEALING. 1 Sam. 2. 23; Ps. 7. 16; John 4. 9.

DEAR. Jer. 31. 20, is Ephraim my *d*. son.
Acts 20. 24, neither count I my life *d*.
Rom. 12. 19; 1 Cor. 10. 14; 2 Cor. 7. 1; 12. 19; Phil. 4. 1; 2 Tim. 1. 2; 1 Pet. 2. 11, *d*. beloved.
Eph. 5. 1, followers of God as *d*. children.
Col. 1. 13, into kingdom of his *d*. Son.
1 Thess. 2. 8, because ye were *d*. unto us.
See Jer. 12. 7; Lu. 7. 2; Philem. 1.

DEARTH. 2 Chron. 6. 28, if there be a *d*. in the land.
Neh. 5. 3, buy corn because of *d*.
Acts 11. 28, Agabus signified a great *d*.
See Gen. 41. 54; 2 Kings 4. 38; Jer. 14. 1; Acts 7. 11.

DEATH. Num. 16. 29, if these men die common *d*.
23. 10, let me die *d*. of righteous.
Judg. 5. 18, jeoparded lives to the *d*.
16. 16, soul was vexed to *d*.
30, which he slew at his *d*. were more.
Ruth 1. 17, if ought but *d*. part thee and me.
1 Sam. 15. 32, the bitterness of *d*. past.
20. 3, but a step between me and *d*.
2 Sam. 1. 23, in *d*. not divided.
22. 5; Ps. 18. 4; 116. 8, waves of *d*. compassed.
Job 3. 21, long for *d*., but it cometh not.
7. 15, my soul chooseth *d*.
30. 23, thou wilt bring me to *d*.
Ps. 6. 5, in *d*. no remembrance.
13. 3, lest I sleep the sleep of *d*.
23. 4, valley of shadow of *d*.
48. 14, our guide even unto *d*.
68. 20, the issues from *d*.
89. 48, what man shall not see *d*.
102. 20, loose those appointed to *d*.
107. 10, in darkness and shadow of *d*.
116. 15, precious is *d*. of his saints.
Prov. 7. 27, to chambers of *d*.
8. 36, that hate me love *d*.
14. 32, righteous hath hope in his *d*.
24. 11, deliver them drawn to *d*.
Cant. 8. 6, love is strong as *d*.
Isa. 9. 2; Jer. 2. 6, land of the shadow of *d*.
25. 8; 1 Cor. 15. 56, swallow up *d*. in victory.
38. 18, for *d*. cannot celebrate thee.
Jer. 8. 3, *d*. chosen rather than life.
9. 21, *d*. come up to our windows.
Ezek. 18. 32; 33. 11, no pleasure in *d*.
Hos. 13. 14, O *d*. I will be thy plagues.
Mat. 15. 4; Mk. 7. 10, let him die the *d*.
16. 28; Mk. 9. 1; Lu. 9. 27, not taste of *d*.
26. 38; Mk. 14. 34, my soul is sorrowful to *d*.
Mk. 5. 23; John 4. 47, lieth at point of *d*.
Lu. 2. 26, should not see *d*. before.
22. 33, will go to prison and *d*.
John 5. 24; 1 John 3. 14, passed from *d*. to life.
8. 51, 52, keep my saying, shall never see *d*.
11. 4, sickness not unto *d*.
12. 33; 18. 32; 21. 19, signifying what *d*.
Acts 2. 24, having loosed pains of *d*.
Rom. 1. 32, such things are worthy of *d*.
5. 10; Col. 1. 22, reconciled by the *d*.
12, *d*. by sin and so *d*. passed on all.
14, 17, *d*. reigned from Adam to Moses.
6. 5, planted in likeness of his *d*.
21, end of those things is *d*.
23, wages of sin is *d*.
8. 2, law of sin and *d*.
1 Cor. 3. 22, life or *d*. all are yours.
11. 26, show the Lord's *d*. till he come.
15. 21, by man came *d*.
55, 56, O *d*. where is thy sting?
2 Cor. 1. 9, sentence of *d*. in ourselves.
2. 16, savour of *d*. unto *d*.
4. 12, *d*. worketh in us.
11. 23, in *d*. oft.
Phil. 2. 8, *d*., even *d*. of the cross.
Heb. 2. 9, taste *d*. for every man.
15, through fear of *d*. were.
Jas. 1. 15, sin bringeth forth *d*.
1 John 5. 16, a sin unto *d*.
Rev. 1. 18, keys of hell and of *d*.
2. 10, be faithful unto *d*.
11; 6. 14, second *d*.
6. 8, his name that sat on him was *d*.
9. 6, seek *d*. and *d*. shall flee.
20. 13, *d*. and hell delivered up.
21. 4, no more *d*.
See Prov. 14. 12; 16. 25; John 18. 31; Jas. 5. 20.

DEBASE. Isa. 57. 9.

DEBATE. Prov. 25. 9; Isa. 58. 4; Rom. 1. 29; 2 Cor. 12. 20.

DEBT. 2 Kings 4. 7, go, pay thy *d*. and live.
Neh. 10. 31, leave the exaction of every *d*.
Prov. 22. 26, be not sureties for *d*.
Mat. 18. 27, forgave him the *d*.
See 1 Sam. 22. 2; Mat. 6. 12; Rom. 4. 4.

DEBTOR. Mat. 6. 12, as we forgive our *d*.
Lu. 7. 41, creditor which had two *d*.
Rom. 1. 14, I am *d*. to the Greeks.
8. 12, we are *d*., not to the flesh.
15. 27, their *d*. they are.
Gal. 5. 3, *d*. to do the whole law.
See Ezek. 18. 7; Mat. 18. 21; 23. 16; Lu. 16. 5.

DECAY. Lev. 25. 35; Neh. 4. 10; Heb. 8. 13.

DECEASE. Isa. 26. 14; Mat. 22. 25; Lu. 9. 31; 2 Pet. 1. 15.

DECEIT. Ps. 10. 7, mouth full of *d*. and fraud.
36. 3, words are iniquity and *d*.
55. 23, *d*. men shall not live half their days.
Prov. 12. 5, counsels of wicked are *d*.
20. 17, bread of *d*. is sweet.
27. 6, kisses of an enemy are *d*.
31. 30, favour is *d*. and beauty vain.
Jer. 14. 14; 23. 26, prophesy the *d*. of their heart.
17. 9, heart is *d*. above all things.
48. 10, that doeth work of the Lord *d*.
Hos. 11. 12, compasseth me with *d*.
Amos 8. 5, falsifying balances by *d*.
Zeph. 1. 9, fill their masters' houses with *d*.
Mat. 13. 22; Mk. 4. 19, the *d*. of riches.
Mk. 7. 22, out of heart proceed *d*.

Rom. 3. 13, they have used *d.*
2 Cor. 4. 2, handling word of God *d.*
11. 13, false apostles, *d.* workers.
Eph. 4. 22, according to *d.* lusts.
Col. 2. 8, vain *d.*, after tradition.
See Ps. 50. 19; Prov. 12. 20; Jer. 5. 27; Mic. 6. 11.
DECEIVE. Deut. 11. 16, take heed that your heart be not *d.*
2 Kings 19. 10; Isa. 37. 10, let not thy God *d.* thee.
Job 12. 16, the *d.* and the *d.* are his.
Jer. 20. 7, thou hast *d.* me and I was *d.*
37. 9, *d.* not yourselves.
Obad. 3, pride of heart hath *d.* thee.
Mat. 24. 24, if possible *d.* the very elect.
27. 63, remember that that *d.* said.
John 7. 12, nay, but he *d.* the people.
47, are ye also *d.*?
1 Cor. 6. 9; 15. 33; Gal. 6. 7, be not *d.*
2 Cor. 6. 8, as *d.*, and yet true.
Eph. 4. 14, whereby they lie in wait to *d.*
5. 6; 2 Thess. 2. 3; 1 John 3. 7, let no man *d.* you.
1 Tim. 2. 14, Adam was not *d.*
2 Tim. 3. 13, worse and worse, *d.* and being *d.*
1 John 1. 8, no sin, we *d.* ourselves.
2 John 7, many *d.* entered into world.
See Gen. 31. 7; Isa. 44. 20; Ezek. 14. 9; Rev. 12. 9; 19. 20.
DECENTLY. 1 Cor. 14. 40.
DECISION. Joel 3. 14.
DECK. Job 40. 10, *d.* thyself with majesty.
Isa. 61. 10, as a bridegroom *d.* himself.
Jer. 4. 30, though thou *d.* thee with ornaments.
10. 4, they *d.* it with silver.
See Prov. 7. 16; Ezek. 16. 11; Rev. 17. 4; 18. 16.
DECLARATION. Esth. 10. 2; Job 13. 17; Lu. 1. 1; 2 Cor. 8. 19.
DECLARE. 1 Chron. 16. 24; Ps. 96. 3, *d.* glory among heathen.
Job 21. 31, who shall *d.* his way to his face.
31. 37, I would *d.* number of my steps.
Ps. 2. 7, I will *d.* decree.
9. 11, *d.* among the people his doings.
19. 1, heavens *d.* glory of God.
30. 9, shall dust *d.* thy truth.
40. 10, I have *d.* thy faithfulness.
66. 16, I will *d.* what he hath done.
75. 9, I will *d.* for ever.
118. 17, live and *d.* the works of the Lord.
145. 4, one generation shall *d.* thy mighty acts.
Isa. 3. 9, they *d.* their sin as Sodom.
41. 26; 45. 21, who hath *d.* from beginning.
45. 19, I *d.* things that are right.
46. 10, *d.* end from the beginning.
53. 8; Acts 8. 33, who shall *d.* his generation.
66. 19, *d.* my glory among Gentiles.
John 17. 26, have *d.* thy name and will *d.* it.
Acts 13. 32, we *d.* to you glad tidings.
17. 23, him *d.* I unto you.
20. 27, *d.* the counsel of God.
Rom. 1. 4, *d.* to be Son of God with power.
1 Cor. 3. 13, day shall *d.* it.
See Josh. 20. 4; John 1. 18; Heb. 11. 14; 1 John 1. 3.
DECLINE. Deut. 17. 11, thou shalt not *d.* from sentence.
2 Chron. 34. 2, *d.* neither to right nor left.
Ps. 102. 11; 109. 23, days like a shadow that *d.*
119. 51, 157, not *d.* from thy law.
See Ex. 23. 2; Job 23. 11; Prov. 4. 5; 7. 25.
DECREASE. Gen. 8. 5; Ps. 107. 38; John 3. 30.
DECREE. Job 22. 28, thou shalt *d.* a thing and it shall be.
28. 26, made a *d.* for the rain.
Ps. 148, 6, a *d.* which shall not pass.
Prov. 8. 15, by me princes *d.* justice.
29, he gave to the sea his *d.*
Isa. 10. 1, that *d.* unrighteous *d.*
Acts 16. 4, delivered the *d.* to keep.
See Dan. 2. 9; 6. 8; Acts 17. 7; 1 Cor. 7. 37.
DEDICATE. Deut. 20. 5, lest he die and another *d.* it.
Judg. 17. 3, wholly *d.* silver to the Lord.
1 Chron. 26. 27, of spoil they did *d.*
Ezek. 44. 29, every *d.* thing shall be theirs.
See 1 Kings 7. 51; 8. 63; 15. 15; 1 Chron. 18. 11; Heb. 9. 18.
DEED. Ex. 9. 16; 1 Sam. 25. 34; 26. 4, in very *d.*
2 Sam. 12. 14, by this *d.* hast given occasion.
Ezra 9. 13, come upon us for our evil *d.*
Neh. 13. 14, wipe not out my good *d.*
Ps. 28. 4; Isa. 59. 18; Jer. 25. 14; Rom. 2. 6, according to their *d.*
Lu. 11. 48, ye allow the *d.* of your fathers.
23. 41, due reward of our *d.*
24. 19, a prophet mighty in *d.*
John 3. 19, because their *d.* were evil.
8. 41, ye do the *d.* of your father.
Acts 7. 22, Moses, mighty in word and *d.*
Rom. 3. 20, by *d.* of law, no flesh justified.
28, justified without *d.* of the law.
Col. 3. 9, put off old man with his *d.*
17, whatsoever ye do in word or *d.*
Jas. 1. 25, shall be blessed in his *d.*
1 John 3. 18, not love in word, but in *d.*
See Gen. 44. 15; Lu. 23. 51; Acts 19. 18.
DEEMED. Acts 27. 27.
DEEP. Gen. 7. 11; 8. 2, fountains of *d.*
Deut. 33. 13, the *d.* that coucheth beneath.
Job 38. 30, face of *d.* is frozen.
41. 31, maketh the *d.* boil like a pot.
Ps. 36. 6, thy judgments are a great *d.*
42. 7, *d.* calleth to *d.*
Ps. 95. 4, in his hand are the *d.* places.
107. 24, see his wonders in the *d.*
Prov. 22. 14; 23. 27, strange women *d.* pit.
Isa. 63. 13, led them through *d.*
Mat. 13. 5, no *d.* of earth.
Lu. 5. 4, launch into *d.*
6. 48, digged *d.* and laid foundations.
8. 31, command to go into the *d.*
John 4. 11, the well is *d.*
1 Cor. 2. 10, searcheth *d.* things of God.
See Job 4. 13; 33. 15; Prov. 19. 15; Rom. 10. 7.
DEER. Deut. 14. 5; 1 Kings 4. 23.
DEFAME. Jer. 20. 10; 1 Cor. 4. 13.
DEFEAT. 2 Sam. 15. 34; 17. 14.
DEFENCE. Job 22. 25, the Almighty shall be thy *d.*
Ps. 7. 10, my *d.* is of God.
59. 9, 17; 62. 2, for God is my *d.*
89. 18; 94. 22, Lord is *d.*
Eccl. 7. 12, wisdom a *d.* money a *d.*
Isa. 33. 16, place of *d.* munitions of rocks.
Phil. 1. 7, 17, in *d.* of the Gospel.
See Num. 14. 9; Acts 19. 33; 22. 1.
DEFEND. Ps. 5. 11, shout for joy, because thou *d.* them.
82. 3, *d.* the poor and fatherless.
Zech. 9. 15, Lord of hosts shall *d.* them.
Acts 7. 24, *d.* him and avenged the oppressed.
See Ps. 20. 1; 59. 1; Isa. 31. 5.
DEFILE. Ex. 31. 14, that *d.* sabbath be put to death.
Num. 35. 33, blood *d.* the land.
2 Kings 23. 13, high places did king *d.*
Neh. 13. 29, they have *d.* the priesthood.
Ps. 74. 7; 79. 1, *d.* dwelling-place of thy name.
106. 39, *d.* with their own works.
Isa. 59. 3, your hands are *d.* with blood.
Jer. 2. 7; 16. 18, ye *d.* my land.
Ezek. 4. 13, eat their *d.* bread.
23. 38, they have *d.* my sanctuary.
36. 17, they *d.* it by their own ways.
Dan. 1. 8, would not *d.* himself with meat.
Mat. 15. 11, 18, 20; Mk. 7. 15, 20, 23, *d.* a man.
John 18. 28, lest they should be *d.*
1 Cor. 3. 17, if any man *d.* temple of God.
8. 7, conscience being weak is *d.*
1 Tim. 1. 10, law for them that *d.* themselves.
Tit. 1. 15, to *d.* nothing pure, even conscience *d.*
Heb. 12. 15, thereby many be *d.*
Jude 8, filthy dreamers *d.* flesh.
Rev. 3. 4, few not *d.* their garments.
See Ex. 31. 41; Lev. 21. 4; Jas. 3. 6; Rev. 21. 27.

DEFRAUD. 1 Sam. 12. 3, 4, whom have I *d.*?
Mk. 10. 19; 1 Cor. 7. 5, *d.* not.
1 Cor. 6. 7, rather suffer to be *d.*
8, do wrong and *d.* your brethren.
2 Cor. 7. 2, we have *d.* no man.
See Lev. 19. 13; 1 Thess. 4. 6.
DEGENERATE. Jer. 2. 21.
DEGREE. Ps. 62. 9, men of low *d.*, high *d.*
1 Tim. 3. 13, purchase to themselves good *d.*
Jas. 1. 9, brother of low *d.* rejoice.
See 2 Kings 20. 9; 1 Chron. 17. 17; Isa. 38. 8; Lu. 1. 52.
DELAY. Mat. 24. 48; Lu. 12. 45, my lord *d.* his coming.
Acts 9. 38, that he would not *d.* to come.
See Ex. 22. 29; 32. 1; Acts 25. 17.
DELECTABLE. Isa. 44. 9.
DELICACY. Rev. 18. 3.
DELICATE. 1 Sam. 15. 32, Agag came to him *d.*
Prov. 29. 21, he that *d.* bringeth up servant.
Isa. 47. 1, no more called tender and *d.*
Lam. 4. 5, that did feed *d.* are desolate.
Lu. 7. 25, that live *d.* are in kings' courts.
See Deut. 28. 54, 56; Jer. 6. 2; Mic. 1. 16.
DELICIOUSLY. Rev. 18. 7.
DELIGHT (*n.*). Deut. 10. 15, Lord had a *d.* in thy fathers.
1 Sam. 15. 22, hath Lord as great *d.* in offerings.
2 Sam. 15. 26, I have no *d.* in thee.
Job 22. 26, shalt thou have *d.* in the Almighty.
Ps. 1. 2, his *d.* is in law of Lord.
16. 3, to excellent in whom is my *d.*
119. 24, testimonies my *d.* and counsel.
77, 92, 174, thy law is my *d.*
143, thy commandments are my *d.*
Prov. 8. 30, I was daily his *d.*
31, my *d.* were with sons of men.
Prov. 18. 2, fool hath no *d.* in understanding.
19. 10, *d.* not seemly for a fool.
Cant. 2. 3, under his shadow with great *d.*
Isa. 58. 13, call sabbath a *d.*
See Prov. 11. 1; 12. 22; 15. 8; 16. 13.
DELIGHT (*v.*) Job 27. 10, will he *d.* himself in the Almighty?
Ps. 37. 4, *d.* also in the Lord.
11, meek shall *d.* in abundance of peace.
51. 16, thou *d.* not in burnt offering.
94. 19, thy comforts *d.* my soul.
Isa. 42. 1, elect in whom my soul *d.*
55. 2, soul *d.* itself in fatness.
62. 4, the Lord *d.* in thee.
Mic. 7. 18, he *d.* in mercy.
Rom. 7. 22, I *d.* after the inward man.
See Num. 14. 8; Prov. 1. 22; 2. 14; Mal. 3. 1.
DELIGHTSOME. Mal. 3. 12.
DELIVER. Ex. 3. 8; Acts 7. 34, I am come down to *d.* them.
Num. 35. 25, congregation shall *d.* slayer.
Deut. 32. 39; Isa. 43. 13, any *d.* out of my hand.
2 Chron. 32. 13, were gods able to *d.* their lands.
Job 5. 19, shall *d.* thee in six troubles.
36. 18, great ransom cannot *d.*
Ps. 33. 17, nor *d.* any by great strength.
56. 13, *d.* my feet from falling.
144. 10, *d.* David from hurtful sword.
Prov. 24. 11, forbear to *d.* them.
Eccl. 9. 15, by wisdom *d.* city.
Isa. 50. 2, have I no power to d.?
Jer. 1. 8, I am with thee to *d.* thee.
39. 17, I will *d.* in that day.
Dan. 3. 17, for God is able to *d.*, and will *d.*
6. 14, king set heart on Daniel to *d.*
Amos 2. 14, neither shall mighty *d.*
9. 1, he that escapeth shall not be *d.*
Mal. 3. 15, they that tempt God are *d.*
Mat. 6. 13; Lu. 11. 4, *d.* us from evil.
11. 27; Lu. 10. 22, all things *d.* to me of my Father.
26. 15, I will *d.* him to you.
Acts 2. 23, being *d.* by the counsel of God.
Rom. 4. 25, was *d.* for our offences.
7. 6, we are *d.* from the law.
8. 21, creature shall be *d.*
2 Cor. 4. 11, *d.* to death for Jesus' sake.
2 Tim. 4. 18, *d.* me from every evil work.
Jude 3, faith once *d.* to saints.
See Rom. 8. 32; 2 Cor. 1. 10; Gal. 1. 4; 2 Pet. 2. 7.
DELIVERANCE. 2 Kings 5. 1, by him had given *d.* to Syria.
1 Chron. 11. 14, saved by great *d.*
Ps. 32. 7, compass me with songs of *d.*
Lu. 4. 18, preach *d.* to the captives.
Heb. 11. 35, not accepting *d.*
See Gen. 45. 7; Joel 2. 32; Obad. 17.
DELUSION. Isa. 66. 4; 2 Thess. 2. 11.
DEMAND. Dan. 4. 17; Mat. 2. 4; Lu. 3. 14.
DEMONSTRATION. 1 Cor. 2. 4.
DEN. Job 37. 8, then the beasts go into *d.*
Isa. 11. 8, put hand on cockatrice *d.*
Jer. 7. 11, is this house a *d.* of robbers.
Mat. 21. 13; Mk. 11. 17, a *d.* of thieves.
Heb. 11. 38, in deserts and in *d.*
See Judg. 6. 2; Dan. 6. 7; Amos 3. 4.
DENOUNCE. Deut. 30. 18.
DENY. Josh. 24. 27, lest ye *d.* your God.
Prov. 30. 9, lest I be full and *d.* thee.
Lu. 20. 27, which *d.* resurrection.
2 Tim. 2. 13, he cannot *d.* himself.
Tit. 1. 16, in works they *d.* him.
See 1 Tim. 5. 8; 2 Tim. 3. 5; Tit. 2. 12.
DEPART. Gen. 49. 10, sceptre shall not *d.* from Judah.
2 Sam. 22. 22; Ps. 18. 21, have not *d.* from my God.
Job 21. 14; 22. 17, they say to God, *d.*
28. 28, to *d.* from evil is understanding.
Ps. 6. 8; Mat. 7. 23; Lu. 13. 27, *d.* ye workers of iniquity.
34. 14; 37. 27, *d.* from evil, and do good.
105. 38, Egypt was glad when they *d.*
Prov. 15. 24, he may *d.* from hell beneath.
22. 6, when old he will not *d.* from it.
27. 22, yet will not foolishness *d.*
Mat. 14. 16, they need not *d.*
25. 41, *d.* from me, ye cursed.
Lu. 2. 29, lettest thou thy servant *d.* in peace.
Lu. 4. 13, devil *d.* for a season.
21. 21, let them in midst *d.*
John 13. 1, when Jesus knew he should *d.*
2 Cor. 12. 8, besought that it might *d.* from me.
Phil. 1. 23, desire to *d.*
1 Tim. 4. 1, some shall *d.* from the faith.
2 Tim. 2. 19, nameth Christ *d.* from iniquity.
See Isa. 54. 10; Mic. 2. 10; 2 Tim. 4. 6; Heb. 3. 12.
DEPOSED. Dan. 5. 20.
DEPRIVED. Gen. 27. 45; Job 39. 17; Isa. 38. 10.
DEPTH. Job 28. 14, *d.* saith, it is not in me.
Ps. 33. 7, he layeth up *d.* in storehouses.
77. 16, waters afraid, *d.* troubled.
106. 9, led through *d.* as through wilderness.
107. 26, they go down again to *d.*
Prov. 8. 24, when no *d.* I was brought forth.
25. 3, heaven for height, earth for *d.*
Mat. 18. 6, better drowned in *d.* of sea.
Mk. 4. 5, no *d.* of earth.
Rom. 11. 33, the *d.* of the riches.
See Isa. 7. 11; Mic. 7. 19; Rom. 8. 39.
DEPUTED. 2 Sam. 15. 3.
DEPUTY. 1 Kings 22. 47; Acts 13. 7; 18. 12; 19. 38.
DERIDE. Hab. 1. 10; Lu. 16. 14; 23. 35.
DERISION. Job 30. 1, younger than I have me in *d.*
Ps. 2. 4, the Lord shall have them in *d.*
44. 13; 79. 4, a *d.* to them round us.
Jer. 20. 7, 8, in *d.* daily.
Lam. 3. 14, I was a *d.* to my people.
See Ps. 119. 51; Ezek. 23. 32; 36. 4; Hos. 7. 16.
DESCEND. Ezek. 26. 20; 31. 16, with them that *d.* into pit.
Mat. 7. 25, 27, rain *d.* and floods came.
Mk. 1. 10; John 1. 32, 33, Spirit *d.*
15. 32, let Christ now *d.* from cross.

Rom. 10. 7, who shall *d.* into the deep?
Eph. 4. 10, he that *d.* is same that ascended.
Jas. 3. 15, this wisdom *d.* not.
Rev. 21. 10, great city *d.* out of heaven.
See Gen. 28. 12; Ps. 49. 17; 133. 3; Prov. 30. 4.
DESCENT. Lu. 19. 37; Heb. 7. 3, 6.
DESCRIBE. Josh. 18. 4; Judg. 8. 14; Rom. 4. 6; 10. 5.
DESCRY. Judg. 1. 23.
DESERT. Ps. 78. 40, oft did they grieve him in *d.*
102. 6, like an owl of the *d.*
Isa. 35. 1, the *d.* shall rejoice.
6; 43. 19, streams in the *d.*
40. 3, in *d.* a highway for our God.
Jer. 2. 6, led us through land of *d.*
17. 6, like the heath in the *d.*
25. 24, people that dwell in *d.* shall drink.
Mat. 24. 26, say, behold, he is in the *d.*
Lu. 1. 80, John in *d.* till his showing.
9. 10, aside privately into *d.* place.
John 6. 31, did eat manna in *d.*
See Ex. 5. 3; 19. 2; Isa. 51. 3; Mk. 6. 31.
DESERTS. Ps. 28. 4; Ezek. 7. 27.
DESERVE. Judg. 9. 16; Ezra 9. 13; Job 11. 6.
DESIRE (*n.*). 2 Chron. 15. 15, sought him with their whole *d.*
Job 34. 36, my *d.* is that Job may be tried.
Ps. 10. 3; 21. 2; Rom. 10. 1, heart's *d.*
37. 4, he shall give thee the *d.* of thine heart.
54. 7; 59. 10; 92. 11; 112. 8, *d.* on enemies.
92. 11; 112. 10; 140. 8, *d.* of the wicked.
145. 16, the *d.* of every living thing.
Prov. 10. 24; 11. 23, the *d.* of righteous.
13. 12, when *d.* cometh, it is a tree of life.
19. 22, the *d.* of a man is his kindness.
21. 25, the *d.* of slothful killeth him.
Eccl. 12. 5, *d.* shall fail.
Ezek. 24. 16, 21, 25, the *d.* of thine eyes.
Mic. 7. 3, great man uttereth mischievous *d.*
Hab. 2. 5, enlargeth *d.* as hell.
Hag. 2. 7, the *d.* of all nations.
Lu. 22. 15, with *d.* I have *d.* to eat.
Eph. 2. 3, fulfilling *d.* of flesh and mind.
Phil. 1. 23, having a *d.* to depart.
See Gen. 3. 16; Job 14. 15; 31. 16.
DESIRE (*v.*). Deut. 14. 26, bestow for whatsoever thy soul *d.*
1 Sam. 2. 16, take as much as thy soul *d.*
12. 13, behold the king whom ye *d.*
Neh. 1. 11, servants who *d.* to fear thy name.
Job 13. 3, I *d.* to reason with God.
Ps. 19. 10, more to be *d.* than gold.
27. 4, one thing I *d.* of the Lord.
34. 12, that *d.* life and loveth many days.
40. 6, sacrifice and offering thou didst not *d.*
45. 11, king greatly *d.* thy beauty.
73. 25, none on earth I *d.* beside thee.
107. 30, to their *d.* haven.
Prov. 3. 15; 8. 11, all thou canst *d.* not to be compared.
13. 4, soul of sluggard *d.*, and hath not.
Eccl. 2. 10, what my eyes *d.* I kept not.
Isa. 53. 2, no beauty that we should *d.*
Hos. 6. 6, I *d.* mercy and not sacrifice.
Mic. 7. 1, soul *d.* first-ripe fruit.
Zeph. 2. 1, gather together, O nation not *d.*
Mat. 12. 46; Lu. 8. 20, his brethren *d.*
13. 17, have *d.* to see those things.
20. 20, *d.* a certain thing of him.
Mk. 9. 35, if any *d.* to be first.
10. 35, do for us whatsoever we *d.*
11. 24, what things ye *d.* when ye pray.
15. 6; Lu. 23. 25, prisoner whom they *d.*
Lu. 9. 9, who is this, and he *d.* to see him.
10. 24, kings have *d.* to see.
16. 21, *d.* to be fed with crumbs.
20. 46, scribes *d.* to walk in long robes.
22. 15, have *d.* to eat this passover.
31, Satan hath *d.* to have you.
Acts 3. 14, *d.* a murderer to be granted.
1 Cor. 14. 1, and *d.* spiritual gifts.
2 Cor. 5. 2, *d.* to be clothed upon.
Gal. 4. 9, ye *d.* again to be in bondage.
21, ye that *d.* to be under the law.
6. 12, many *d.* to make show in the flesh.
Eph. 3. 13, I *d.* that ye faint not.
Phil. 4. 17, not because I *d.* a gift; I *d.* fruit.
1 Tim. 3. 1, he *d.* a good work.
Heb. 11. 16, they *d.* a better country.
Jas. 4. 2, ye *d.* to have, and cannot obtain.
1 Pet. 1. 12, the angels *d.* to look into.
2. 2, as babes *d.* sincere milk of word.
1 John 5. 15, we have petitions we *d.*
See Gen. 3. 6; Job 7. 2; Ps. 51. 6; Lu. 5. 39.
DESIRABLE. Ezek. 23. 6, 12, 23.
DESIROUS. Prov. 23. 3; Lu. 23. 8; John 16. 19; Gal. 5. 26.
DESOLATE. Ps. 25. 16, have mercy, for I am *d.*
40. 15, let them be *d.* for reward.
143. 4, my heart within me is *d.*
Isa. 54. 1; Gal. 4. 27, more are children of *d.*
62. 4, nor shall thy land any more be termed *d.*
Jer. 2. 12, be ye very *d.*, saith the Lord.
32. 43; 33. 12, *d.* without man or beast.
Ezek. 6. 6, your altars may be made *d.*
Dan. 11. 31; 12. 11, abomination that maketh *d.*
Mal. 1. 4, return and build the *d.* places.
Mat. 23. 38; Lu. 13. 35, house left to you *d.*
Acts 1. 20, let his habitation be *d.*
1 Tim. 5. 5, widow indeed, and *d.*
Rev. 18. 19, in one hour is she made *d.*
See Ps. 34. 22; Jer. 12. 10; Joel 2. 3; Zech. 7. 14.
DESOLATION. 2 Kings 22. 19, they should become a *d.* and a curse.
Ps. 46. 8, what *d.* he hath made in the earth.
74. 3; Jer. 25. 9; Ezek. 35. 9, perpetual *d.*
Prov. 1. 27, when your fear cometh as *d.*
3. 25, the *d.* of the wicked.
Isa. 61. 4, raise up former *d.*, the *d.* of many generations.
Dan. 9. 26, to end of war *d.* are determined.
Zeph. 1. 15, a day of wrath, wasting, and *d.*
Mat. 12. 25; Lu. 11. 17, house divided brought to *d.*
Lu. 21. 20, then know *d.* is nigh.
See Lev. 26. 31; Josh. 8. 28; Job 30. 14.
DESPAIR. 1 Sam. 27. 1; Eccl. 2. 20; 2 Cor. 4. 8.
DESPERATE. Job 6. 26; Isa. 17. 11; Jer. 17. 9.
DESPISE. Num. 11. 20, ye have *d.* the Lord.
15. 31; Prov. 13. 13; Isa. 5. 24; 30. 12, *d.* the word.
1 Sam. 2. 30, that *d.* me shall be lightly esteemed.
Neh. 4. 4, hear, O God, for we are *d.*
Esth. 1. 17, so that they *d.* their husbands.
Job 5. 17; Prov. 3. 11; Heb. 12. 5, *d.* not chastening.
19. 18, young children *d.* me.
36. 5, God is mighty and *d.* not any.
Ps. 51. 17, contrite heart thou wilt not *d.*
53. 5, put to shame, because God *d.* them.
Ps. 73. 20, thou shalt *d.* their image.
102. 17, he will not *d.* their prayer.
Prov. 1. 7, fools *d.* wisdom.
30; 5. 12, *d.* reproof.
6. 30, men do not *d.* a thief.
15. 5, fool *d.* father's instruction.
20, foolish man *d.* his mother.
32, refuseth instruction *d.* own soul.
19. 16, he that *d.* his ways shall die.
30. 17, *d.* to obey his mother, ravens shall.
Eccl. 9. 16, poor man's wisdom is *d.*
Isa. 33. 15, he that *d.* gain of oppressions.
49. 7, saith Lord to him whom man *d.*
Jer. 49. 15, I will make thee small and *d.*
Ezek. 20. 13, 16, they *d.* my judgments.
22. 8, thou hast *d.* holy things.
Amos 2. 4, they *d.* the law of the Lord.
Zech. 4. 10, who hath *d.* day of small things.
Mal. 1. 6, wherein have we *d.* thy name?
Mat. 6. 24; Lu. 16. 13, hold to one, *d.* the other.
18. 10, *d.* not one of these little ones.

Lu. 10. 16, *d.* you, *d.* me; *d.* him that sent me.
18. 9, righteous, and *d.* others.
Rom. 2. 4, *d.* thou the riches of his goodness.
1 Cor. 1. 28, things *d.* God hath chosen.
4. 10, ye are honourable, but we are *d.*
11. 22, *d.* ye the church of God.
16. 11, let no man therefore *d.* him.
1 Thess. 4. 8, *d.* not man, but God.
5. 20, *d.* not prophesyings.
1 Tim. 4. 12, let no man *d.* thy youth.
6. 2, not *d.* because brethren.
Tit. 2. 15, let no man *d.* thee.
Heb. 12. 2, endured cross, *d.* the shame.
Jas. 2. 6, ye have *d.* the poor.
See Gen. 16. 4; 25. 34; 2 Sam. 6. 16; Rom. 14. 3.
DESPISERS. Acts 13. 41; 2 Tim. 3. 3.
DESPITE. Ezek. 25. 6, 15; 36. 5; Rom. 1. 30; Heb. 10. 29.
DESPITEFULLY. Mat. 5. 44; Lu. 6. 28; Acts 14. 5.
DESTITUTE. Ps. 102. 17, will regard prayer of *d.*
Prov. 15. 21, folly is joy to him that is *d.* of wisdom.
1 Tim. 6. 5, *d.* of the truth.
Heb. 11. 37, being *d.*, afflicted, tormented.
See Gen. 24. 27; Ezek. 32. 15; Jas. 2. 15.
DESTROY. Gen. 18. 23, *d.* righteous with the wicked.
Ex. 22. 20, he shall be utterly *d.*
Deut. 9. 14, let me alone that I may *d.* them.
1 Sam. 15. 6, depart, lest I *d.* you with them.
2 Sam. 1. 14, *d.* Lord's anointed.
Job 2. 3, movedst me to *d.* without cause.
10. 8, made me, yet thou dost *d.* me.
19. 10, he hath *d.* me on every side.
26, though worms *d.* this body.
Ps. 40. 14; 63. 9, seek my soul to *d.* it.
145. 20, all the wicked will he *d.*
Prov. 1. 32, prosperity of fools shall *d.* them.
13. 23, is *d.* for want of judgment.
31. 3, that which *d.* kings.
Eccl. 9. 18, one sinner *d.* much good.
Isa. 10. 7, it is in his heart to *d.*
11. 9; 65. 25, *d.* in holy mountain.
19. 3, I will *d.* the counsel thereof.
28. 2, as a *d.* storm.
Jer. 13. 14, I will not spare but *d.* them.
17. 18, *d.* them with double destruction.
23. 1, woe to pastors that *d.* the sheep.
Ezek. 9. 1, with *d.* weapon in his hand.
22. 27, *d.* souls to get dishonest gain.
Dan. 8. 24, he shall *d.* wonderfully.
Hos. 13. 9, thou hast *d.* thyself.
Mat. 5. 17, not to *d.* but to fulfil.
10. 28, fear him that is able to *d.*
12. 14; Mk. 3. 6; 11. 18, they might *d.* him.
21. 41, he will miserably *d.* those.
22. 7, and *d.* those murderers.
27. 20, ask Barabbas and *d.* Jesus.
Mk. 1. 24; Lu. 4. 34, art thou come to *d.*
12. 9; Lu. 20. 16, *d.* the husbandmen.
14. 58, say, I will *d.* this temple.
15. 29, thou that *d.* the temple.
Lu. 6. 9, is it lawful to save life or *d.*
9. 56, is not come to *d.* men's lives.
17. 27, flood came and *d.* them all.
John 2. 19, Jesus said, *d.* this temple.
Rom. 14. 15, *d.* not him with thy meat.
1 Cor. 6. 13, God shall *d.* both it and them.
Gal. 1. 23, preacheth the faith he once *d.*
2. 18, if I build the things which I *d.*
2 Thess. 2. 8, *d.* with brightness of his coming.
Heb. 2. 14, *d.* him that had the power.
Jas. 4. 12, able to save and to *d.*
1 John 3. 8, *d.* the works of the devil.
See Gen. 6. 17; Isa. 65. 8; Rom. 6. 6; 2 Pet. 2. 12; Jude 5.
DESTROYER. Ex. 12. 23, not suffer *d.* to come.
Judg. 16. 24, delivered the *d.* of our country.
Job 15. 21, in prosperity the *d.* shall come.
Ps. 17. 4, kept from paths of the *d.*
Prov. 28. 24, the companion of a *d.*
See Job 33. 22; Isa. 49. 17; Jer. 22. 7; 50. 11.
DESTRUCTION. 2 Chron. 22. 4, his counsellors to his *d.*
26. 16, heart lifted up to *d.*
Esth. 8. 6, endure to see *d.* of my kindred.
Job 5. 21, neither be afraid of *d.*
21. 17, how oft cometh *d.*
26. 6, *d.* hath no covering.
31. 3, is not *d.* to the wicked.
Ps. 9. 6, *d.* are come to a perpetual end.
35. 8, into that very *d.* let him fall.
73. 18, thou castedst them down to *d.*
90. 3, turnest man to *d.*
91. 6, the *d.* that wasteth at noon day.
103. 4, redeemeth thy life from *d.*
Prov. 1. 27, your *d.* cometh as a whirlwind.
10. 14, mouth of foolish near *d.*
15, *d.* of poor is their poverty.
14. 28, want of people *d.* of the prince.
16. 18, pride goeth before *d.*
17. 19, exalteth gate seeketh *d.*
18. 7, fool's mouth is his *d.*
27. 20, hell and *d.* never full.
31. 8, such as are appointed to *d.*
Isa. 14. 23, the besom of *d.*
19. 18, the city of *d.*
59. 7, wasting and *d.* in their paths.
60. 18, *d.* be no more heard.
Jer. 17. 18, destroy with double *d.*
46. 20, *d.* cometh out of north.
50. 22, sound of great *d.* in the land.
Lam. 2. 11; 3. 48; 4. 10, *d.* of the daughter of my people.
Hos. 13. 14, O grave, I will be thy *d.*
Mat. 7. 13, broad way leadeth to *d.*
Rom. 3. 16, *d.* and misery in their ways.
9. 22, vessels fitted to *d.*
Phil. 3. 18, 19, many walk whose end is *d.*
1 Thess. 5. 3, then sudden *d.* cometh.
2 Thess. 1. 9, punished with everlasting *d.*
1 Tim. 6. 9, lusts drown men in *d.*
2 Pet. 2. 1, bring on themselves swift *d.*
3. 16, wrest to their own *d.*
See Job 21. 20; 31. 23; Prov. 10. 29; 21. 15.
DETAIN. Judg. 13. 15, 16; 1 Sam. 21. 7.
DETERMINATE. Acts 2. 23.
DETERMINATION. Zeph. 3. 8.
DETERMINE. Ex. 21. 22, pay as the judges *d.*
1 Sam. 20. 7, be sure evil is *d.* by him.
Job 14. 5, seeing his days are *d.*
Dan. 11. 36, that that is *d.* shall be done.
Lu. 22. 22, Son of man goeth as it was *d.*
Acts 3. 13, Pilate was *d.* to let him go.
17. 26, hath *d.* the times appointed.
1 Cor. 2. 2, I *d.* not to know anything.
See 2 Chron. 2. 1; 25. 16; Isa. 19. 17; Dan. 9. 24.
DETEST. Deut. 7. 26.
DETESTABLE. Jer. 16. 18; Ezek. 5. 11; 7. 20; 11. 18; 37. 23.
DEVICE. Esth. 9. 25, *d.* return on his own head.
Ps. 10. 2, let them be taken in the *d.*
33. 10, maketh *d.* of the people of none effect.
37. 7, bringeth wicked *d.* to pass.
Prov. 1. 31, be filled with their own *d.*
12. 2, man of wicked *d.* will he condemn.
19. 21, many *d.* in a man's heart.
Eccl. 9. 10, no work nor *d.* in grave.
Jer. 18. 12, will walk after our own *d.*
Dan. 11. 24, 25, he shall forecast *d.*
Acts 17. 29, like stone graven by man's *d.*
2 Cor. 2. 11, not ignorant of his *d.*
See 2 Chron. 2. 14; Esth. 8. 3; Job 5. 12.
DEVILISH. Jas. 3. 15.
DEVILS (sacrifices offered to). Lev. 17. 7, offer their sacrifices unto *d.*
See Deut. 32. 17; 2 Chron. 11. 15; Ps. 106. 37; 1 Cor. 10. 20; Rev. 9. 20.
DEVILS (confess Jesus to be Christ). Mat. 8. 29; Mk. 1. 24; 3. 11; 5. 7; Lu. 4. 34, 41; Acts 19. 15.
Jas. 2. 19, the *d.* also believe and tremble.

DEVISE. Ex. 31. 4; 35. 32, 35, *d.* works in gold.
Ps. 35. 4, to confusion that *d.* my hurt.
36. 4, he *d.* mischief on his bed.
41. 7, against me do they *d.* my hurt.
Prov. 3. 29, *d.* not evil against thy neighbour.
6. 14, he *d.* mischief continually.
18, a heart that *d.* wicked imaginations.
14. 22, err that *d.* evil, *d.* good.
16. 9, man's heart *d.* his way.
Isa. 32. 7, *d.* wicked devices to destroy poor.
8, the liberal *d.* liberal things.
2 Pet. 1. 16, cunningly *d.* fables.
See 2 Sam. 14. 14; Jer. 51. 12; Lam. 2. 17; Mic. 2. 1.
DEVOTE. Lev. 27. 21, 28; Num. 18. 14; Ps. 119. 38.
DEVOTIONS. Acts 17. 23.
DEVOUR. Gen. 37. 20, some evil beast hath *d.* him.
41. 7, 24, seven thin *d.* the seven rank.
Ex. 24. 17; Isa. 29. 6; 30. 27, 30; 33. 14, *d.* fire.
Lev. 10. 2, fire from Lord *d.* them.
Deut. 32. 24, *d.* with burning heat.
2 Sam. 11. 25, sword *d.* one as well as another.
18. 8, wood *d.* more than sword *d.*
22. 9; Ps. 18. 8, fire out of his mouth *d.*
Job 18. 13, death shall *d.* his strength.
Ps. 80. 13, beasts of field *d.* it.
Prov. 20. 25, man who *d.* that which is holy.
30. 14, jaw teeth as knives to *d.*
Isa. 1. 7, strangers *d.* it in your presence.
20, if ye rebel, be *d.* with sword.
Jer. 2. 30, your sword hath *d.* prophets.
3. 24, shame *d.* labour of our fathers.
30. 16, that *d.* thee shall be *d.*
Ezek. 15. 7, fire shall *d.* them.
23. 37, pass through fire to *d.* them.
Hos. 8. 14; Amos 1. 14; 2. 2, it shall *d.* palaces.
Joel 2. 3, a fire *d.* before them.
Amos 4. 9, fig trees, palmer-worm *d.* them.
Hab. 1. 13, wicked *d.* man that is more righteous.
Zeph. 1. 18; 3. 8, *d.* by fire of jealousy.
Mal. 3. 11, will rebuke the *d.* for your sakes.
Mat. 13. 4; Mk. 4. 4; Lu. 8. 5, fowls *d.* them.
23. 14; Mk. 12. 40; Lu. 20. 47, *d.* widows' houses.
Lu. 15. 30, thy son hath *d.* thy living.
2 Cor. 11. 20, if a man *d.* you.
Gal. 5. 15, ye bite and *d.* one another.
Heb. 10. 27, which shall *d.* adversaries.
1 Pet. 5. 8, seeking whom he may *d.*
See Gen. 31. 15; 2 Sam. 2. 26; Ps. 50. 3; 52. 4.
DEVOUT. Lu. 2. 25, Simeon was just and *d.*
Acts 2. 5; 8. 2, *d.* men.
See Acts 10. 2; 13. 50; 17. 4, 17; 22. 12.
DEW. Gen. 27. 28, God give thee the *d.* of heaven.
Deut. 32. 2, my speech shall distil as the *d.*
33. 13, for the *d.*, and for the deep.
Judg. 6. 37, if the *d.* be on the fleece only.
2 Sam. 1. 21, let there be no *d.*
17. 12, we will light on him as *d.* falleth.
1 Kings 17. 1, there shall not be *d.* nor rain.
Job 38, 28, who hath begotten drops of *d.*
Prov. 3. 20, clouds drop down *d.*
Isa. 18. 4, like *d.* in heat of harvest.
Dan. 4. 15, 23, 25, 33, wet with *d.* of heaven.
Hos. 6. 4; 13. 3, goodness as early *d.*
Hag. 1. 10, heaven is stayed from *d.*
See Ex. 16. 13; Num. 11. 9; Job 29. 19; Ps. 110. 3; 133. 3; Prov. 19. 12; Isa. 26. 19; Hos. 14. 5.
DIADEM. Job 29. 14; Isa. 28. 5; 62. 3; Ezek. 21. 26.
DIAL. 2 Kings 20. 11, it had gone down in the *d.* of Ahaz.
Isa. 38. 8, gone down in the sun *d.* of Ahaz.
DIAMOND (in high priest's breastplate). Ex. 28. 18; 39. 11.
See Jer. 17. 1; Ezek. 28. 13.
DID. Mat. 13. 58, he *d.* not many mighty works.
John 4. 29, all things that ever I *d.*
9. 26, what *d.* he to thee?
15. 24, works which none other man *d.*
See Gen. 6. 22; 1 Sam. 1. 7; Job 1. 5; 1 Pet. 2. 22.

DIE. Gen. 2. 17; 20. 7; 1 Sam. 14. 44; 22. 16; 1 Kings 2. 37, 42; Jer. 26. 8; Ezek. 3. 18; 33. 8, 14, surely *d.*
3. 3; Lev. 10. 6; Num. 18. 32, lest ye *d.*
27. 4; 45. 28; Prov. 30. 7, before I *d.*
Ex. 21. 12, smiteth a man that he *d.*
Lev. 7. 24; 22. 8; Deut. 14. 21; Ezek. 4. 14, that *d.* of itself.
Num. 16. 29, if these *d.* common death.
23. 10, let me *d.* death of righteous.
Deut. 31. 14, days approach that thou must *d.*
Ruth 1. 17, where thou *d.* will I *d.*
2 Sam. 3. 33, *d.* Abner as a fool *d.*?
2 Kings 20. 1; Isa. 38. 1, shalt *d.* and not live.
2 Chron. 25. 4; Jer. 31. 30, every man *d.* for own sin.
Job 2. 9, his wife said, Curse God and *d.*
3. 11, why *d.* I not from the womb?
12. 2, wisdom shall *d.* with you.
14. 14, if a man *d.*, shall he live again?
21. 23, one *d.* in full strength.
25, another *d.* in bitterness of soul.
29. 18, I shall *d.* in my nest.
Ps. 41. 5, when shall he *d.* and name perish?
49. 10, wise men *d.*, likewise the fool.
17, when he *d.* carry nothing away.
Prov. 5. 23, he shall *d.* without instruction.
10. 21, fools *d.* for want of wisdom.
11. 7, *d.* his expectation perish.
Eccl. 2. 16, how *d.* the wise man?
7. 17, why shouldest thou *d.* before thy time?
9. 5, living know they shall *d.*
Isa. 66. 24; Mk. 9. 44, worm shall not *d.*
Jer. 27. 13; Ezek. 18. 31; 33. 11, why will ye *d.*?
28. 16, this year thou shalt *d.*
34. 5, thou shalt *d.* in peace.
Ezek. 18. 4, 20, soul that sinneth shall *d.*
32, no pleasure in death of him that *d.*
33. 8, wicked man shall *d.* in iniquity.
Amos 6. 9, if ten men in house they shall *d.*
9. 10, sinners of my people shall *d.*
Jon. 4. 3, 8, it is better to *d.* than live.
Mat. 15. 4; Mk. 7. 10, let him *d.* the death.
22. 27; Mk. 12. 22; Lu. 20. 32, woman *d.* also.
26. 35; Mk. 14. 31, though I *d.* with thee.
Lu. 7. 2, servant was ready to *d.*
16. 22, beggar *d.*, rich man also *d.*
20. 36, nor can they *d.* any more.
John 4. 49, come down ere my child *d.*
11. 21, 32, my brother had not *d.*
37, that even this man should not have *d.*
50; 18. 14, that one man *d.* for people.
51, that Jesus should *d.* for nation.
12. 24, except a corn of wheat *d.*
19. 7, by our law he ought to *d.*
Acts 9. 37, Dorcas was sick and *d.*
21. 13, ready also to *d.* at Jerusalem.
25. 11, I refuse not to *d.*
Rom. 5. 7, for righteous man will one *d.*
7. 9, sin revived and I *d.*
8. 34, it is Christ that *d.*
14. 7, no man *d.* to himself.
9, Christ both *d.*, rose, and revived.
15; 1 Cor. 8. 11, for whom Christ *d.*
1 Cor. 15. 3, Christ *d.* for our sins.
22, as in Adam all *d.*
31, I *d.* daily.
36, not quickened except it *d.*
2 Cor. 5. 14, if one *d.* for all.
Phil. 1. 21, to *d.* is gain.
1 Thess. 4. 14, we believe that Jesus *d.*
5. 10, who *d.* for us that we should live.
Heb. 7. 8, here men that *d.* receive tithes.
9. 27, appointed unto men once to *d.*
11. 13, these all *d.* in faith.
Rev. 3. 2, things that are ready to *d.*
9. 6, men shall desire to *d.*
14. 13, the dead that *d.* in the Lord.
See Job 14. 10; Ps. 118. 17; Rom. 5. 6; 6. 10.
DIET. Jer. 52. 34.

DIFFER. Rom. 12. 6; 1 Cor. 4. 7; 15. 41; Gal. 4. 1.
DIFFERENCE. Lev. 10. 10; Ezek. 44. 23, a *d.* between holy and unholy.
11. 47; 20. 25, *d.* between clean and unclean.
Ezek. 22. 26, they have put no *d.* between.
Acts 15. 9, put no *d.* between us.
Rom. 3. 22; 10. 12, for there is no *d.*
See Ex. 11. 7; 1 Cor. 12. 5; Jude 22.
DIG. Ex. 21. 33, *d.* a pit and not cover it.
Deut. 6. 11; Neh. 9. 25, wells *d.* which thou *d.* not.
8. 9, out of hills mayest *d.* brass.
Job 6. 27, ye *d.* a pit for your friend.
24. 16, in the dark they *d.*
Ps. 7. 15; 57. 6, *d.* a pit and is fallen.
Isa. 51. 1, hole of pit whence ye are *d.*
Mat. 21. 33, and *d.* a winepress.
25. 18, *d.* in the earth and hid.
Lu. 13. 8, till I *d.* about it.
16. 3, I cannot *d.*, to beg I am ashamed.
See Job 3. 21; Ezek. 8. 8; 12. 5; Lu. 6. 48.
DIGNITY. Eccl. 10. 6, folly set in great *d.*
2 Pet. 2. 10; Jude 8, speak evil of *d.*
See Gen. 49. 3; Esth. 6. 3; Hab. 1. 7.
DILIGENCE. Prov. 4. 23; 2 Tim. 4. 9; Jude 3.
DILIGENT. Josh. 22. 5, take *d.* heed to commandment.
Ps. 64. 6, accomplish a *d.* search.
Lu. 15. 8, seek *d.* till she find it.
Acts 18. 25, taught *d.* the things of the Lord.
2 Tim. 1. 17, in Rome sought me *d.*
Heb. 12. 15, looking *d.* lest any man fail.
See Deut. 19. 18; Prov. 11. 27; 23. 1; Mat. 2. 7.
DIM. Deut. 34. 7, eye not *d.* nor force abated.
Job 17. 7, eye also *d.* by reason of sorrow.
Lam. 4. 1, gold become *d.*
See Gen. 27. 1; 48. 10; 1 Sam. 3. 2; Isa. 8. 22.
DIMINISH. Deut. 4. 2; 12. 32, nor *d.* ought from it.
Prov. 13. 11, gotten by vanity shall be *d.*
Rom. 11. 12, *d.* of them be riches of Gentiles.
See Ex. 5. 8; Lev. 25. 16; Jer. 26. 2; Ezek. 16. 27.
DINE. Gen. 43. 16; Lu. 11. 37; John 21. 12, 15.
DINNER. Prov. 15. 17; Mat. 22. 4; Lu. 11. 38; 14. 12.
DIP. Lev. 4. 6; 9. 9; 17. 14, priest shall *d.* his finger.
Ruth 2. 14, *d.* morsel in vinegar.
1 Sam. 14. 27, *d.* rod in honeycomb.
2 Kings 5. 14, Naaman *d.* in Jordan.
Mat. 26. 23; Mk. 14. 20, *d.* hand in dish.
John 13. 26, when he had *d.* the sop.
Rev. 19. 13, a vesture *d.* in blood.
See Gen. 37. 31; Josh. 3. 15; Lu. 16. 24.
DIRECT. Job 32. 14, he hath not *d.* his words.
37. 3, he *d.* it under the whole heaven.
Ps. 5. 3, in morning will I *d.* my prayer.
119. 5, O that my ways were *d.* to keep.
Prov. 3. 6, he shall *d.* thy paths.
11. 5, righteousness shall *d.* his way.
16. 9, the Lord *d.* his steps.
21. 29, as for upright he *d.* his way.
Eccl. 10. 10, wisdom profitable to *d.*
Isa. 40. 13, who hath *d.* Spirit of the Lord.
Jer. 10. 23, not in man to *d.* his steps.
2 Thess. 3. 5, *d.* your hearts into love of God.
See Gen. 46. 28; Isa. 45. 13; 61. 8; 1 Thess. 3. 11.
DIRECTION. Num. 21. 18.
DIRECTLY. Num. 19. 4; Ezek. 42. 12.
DIRT. Judg. 3. 22; Ps. 18. 42; Isa. 57. 20.
DISALLOWED. Num. 30. 5, 8, 11; 1 Pet. 2. 4, 7.
DISANNUL. Isa. 14. 27, Lord purposed, who shall *d.* it?
28. 18, your covenant with death shall be *d.*
Gal. 3. 15, 17, covenant no man *d.*
See Job 40. 8; Heb. 7. 18.
DISAPPOINT. Job 5. 12; Ps. 17. 13; Prov. 15. 22.
DISCERN. 2 Sam. 19. 35, can I *d.* between good and evil?
1 Kings 3. 9, that I may *d.* between good and bad.
1 King's 11, understanding to *d.* judgment.
Ezra 3. 13, could not *d.* noise of joy.
Job. 4. 16, could not *d.* form thereof.
6. 30, cannot my taste *d.* perverse things?
Prov. 7. 7, I *d.* among the youths.
Eccl. 8. 5, wise man's heart *d.* time.
Jon. 4. 11, cannot *d.* between right and left.
Mal. 3. 18, *d.* between righteous and wicked.
Mat. 16. 3; Lu. 12. 56, *d.* face of sky.
1 Cor. 2. 14, they are spiritually *d.*
11. 29, not *d.* the Lord's body.
12. 10, to another is given *d.* of spirits.
Heb. 4. 12, the word is a *d.* of the thoughts.
5. 14, exercised to *d.* good and evil.
See Gen. 27. 23; 31. 32; 38. 25; 2 Sam. 14. 17.
DISCHARGE. 1 Kings 5. 9; Eccl. 8. 8.
DISCIPLE. Isa. 8. 16, seal law among my *d.*
Mat. 10. 1; Lu. 6. 13, called his twelve *d.*
24; Lu. 6. 40, *d.* not above his master.
42, give cup of water in the name of a *d.*
12. 2, thy *d.* do that which is not lawful.
15. 2, why do *d.* transgress tradition.
17. 16, brought to thy *d.*, and they could not cure.
19. 13; Mk. 10. 13, the *d.* rebuked them.
20. 17, Jesus took *d.* apart.
22. 16, Pharisees sent their *d.*
26. 18; Mk. 14. 14; Lu. 22. 11, keep passover with *d.*
35, likewise also said the *d.*
56, all the *d.* forsook him and fled.
28. 7, tell his *d.* he is risen.
13, say ye, his *d.* came by night.
Mk. 2. 18; Lu. 5. 33, why do *d.* of John fast?
4. 34, he expounded all things to *d.*
7. 2, *d.* eat with unwashen hands.
5, why walk not *d.* according to tradition?
Lu. 5. 30, Pharisees murmured against *d.*
6. 20, lifted up eyes on *d.*
11. 1, as John taught his *d.*
14. 26, 27, 33, cannot be my *d.*
19. 37, *d.* began to rejoice and praise God.
39, Master, rebuke thy *d.*
John 2. 11, his *d.* believed on him.
4. 2, Jesus baptized not, but his *d.*
6. 22, his *d.* were gone away alone.
66, many of his *d.* went back.
7. 3, that thy *d.* may see works.
8. 31; 13. 35, then are ye my *d.* indeed.
9. 27, will ye also be his *d.*?
28, thou art his *d.*, we are Moses' *d.*
13. 5, began to wash *d.* feet.
15. 8, so shall ye be my *d.*
18. 15, 16, that *d.* was known.
17, 25, art not thou one of his *d.*?
19. 26; 20. 2; 21. 7, 20, *d.* whom Jesus loved.
38, a *d.* of Jesus, but secretly for fear.
20. 18, told *d.* she had seen the Lord.
21. 23, that that *d.* should not die.
24, this is the *d.* which testifieth.
Acts 9. 1, slaughter against *d.*
26, essayed to join himself to *d.*
11. 26, *d.* called Christians first.
20. 7, *d.* came together to break bread.
30, to draw away *d.* after them.
21. 16, an old *d.* with whom we should lodge.
See Mat. 11. 1; John 3. 25; 18. 1, 2; 20. 26.
DISCIPLINE. Job 36. 10.
DISCLOSE. Isa. 26. 21.
DISCOMFITED. Judg. 4. 15, Lord *d.* Sisera.
8. 12, Gideon *d.* all the host.
2 Sam. 22. 15; Ps. 18. 14, lightnings, and *d.* them.
Isa. 31. 8, his young men shall be *d.*
See Ex. 17. 13; Num. 14. 45; Josh. 10. 10.
DISCOMFITURE. 1 Sam 14. 20.
DISCONTENTED. 1 Sam. 22. 2.
DISCONTINUE. Jer. 17. 4.
DISCORD. Prov. 6. 14, 19.
DISCOURAGE. Num. 32. 7, wherefore *d.* the heart of the children of Israel.

Deut. 1. 21, fear not, nor be *d.*
28, our brethren have *d.* our heart.
Col. 3. 21, your children, lest they be *d.*
See Num. 21. 4; 32. 9; Isa. 42. 4.
DISCOVER. 1 Sam. 14. 8, 11, we will *d.* ourselves to them.
2 Sam. 22. 16; Ps. 18. 15, foundations of the world *d.*
Job 12. 22, he *d.* deep things.
41. 13, who can *d.* face of his garment?
Prov. 25. 9, *d.* not a secret to another.
Ezek. 21. 24, your transgressions are *d.*
See Ps. 29. 9; Hos. 7. 1; Hab. 3. 13; Acts 21. 3.
DISCREET. Gen. 41. 33, 39; Mk. 12. 34; Tit. 2. 5.
DISCRETION. Ps. 112. 5; Prov. 11. 22; Isa. 28. 26; Jer. 10. 12.
DISDAINED. 1 Sam. 17. 42; Job 30. 1.
DISEASE. Ex. 15. 26; Deut. 7. 15, none of these *d.* on you.
Deut. 28. 60, bring on thee all *d.* of Egypt.
2 Kings 1. 2; 8. 8, 9, recover of *d.*
2 Chron. 16. 12, in *d.* sought not the Lord.
Job 30. 18, by force of my *d.*
Ps. 103. 3, who healeth all thy *d.*
Eccl. 6. 2, vanity, and it is an evil *d.*
Ezek. 34. 4, *d.* have ye not strengthened.
21, have pushed *d.* with your horns.
See Mat. 4. 23; 14. 35; Lu. 9. 1; Acts 28. 9.
DISFIGURE. Mat. 6. 16.
DISGRACE. Jer. 14. 21.
DISGUISE. 1 Sam. 28. 8; 1 Kings 14. 2; 20. 38; 22. 30; 2 Chron. 18. 29; 35. 22; Job 24. 15.
DISH. Judg. 5. 25; 2 Kings 21. 13; Mat. 26. 23; Mk. 14. 20.
DISHONESTY. 2 Cor. 4. 2.
DISHONOUR. Ps. 35. 26; 71. 13, clothed with shame and *d.*
Prov. 6. 33, a wound and *d.* shall he get.
Mic. 7. 6, son *d.* father.
John 8. 49, I honour my Father, ye *d.* me.
Rom. 9. 21, one vessel to honour, another to *d.*
1 Cor. 15. 43, sown in *d.*
2 Cor. 6. 8, by honour and *d.*
2 Tim. 2. 20, some to honour, some to *d.*
See Ezra 4. 14; Rom. 1. 24; 2. 23; 1 Cor. 11. 4, 5.
DISINHERIT. Num. 14. 12.
DISMAYED. Deut. 31. 8; Josh. 1. 9; 8. 1; 10. 25; 1 Chron. 22. 13; 28. 20; 2 Chron. 20. 15, 17; 32. 7; Isa. 41. 10; Jer. 1. 17; 10. 2; 23. 4; 30. 10; 46. 27; Ezek. 2. 6; 3. 9, fear not nor be *d.*
Jer. 17. 18, let them be *d.*, let not me be *d.*
See 1 Sam. 17. 11; Jer. 8. 9; 46. 5; Obad. 9.
DISMISSED. 2 Chron. 23. 8; Acts 15. 30; 19. 41.
DISOBEDIENCE. Rom. 5. 19; Eph. 2. 2; 5. 6; Heb. 2. 2.
DISOBEDIENT. Lu. 1. 17, turn *d.* to wisdom of just.
Acts 26. 19, not *d.* to heavenly vision.
Rom. 1. 30; 2 Tim. 3. 2, *d.* to parents.
1 Tim. 1. 9, law for lawless and *d.*
Tit. 3. 3, we ourselves were sometimes *d.*
1 Pet. 2. 7, to them which be *d.*
3. 20, spirits, which sometime were *d.*
See 1 Kings 13. 26; Neh. 9. 26; Rom. 10. 21.
DISORDERLY. 1 Thess. 5. 14; 2 Thess. 3. 6, 7, 11.
DISPENSATION. 1 Cor. 9. 17, a *d.* of the gospel is committed me.
Eph. 1. 10, in the *d.* of the fulness of times.
3. 2, the *d.* of the grace of God.
Col. 1. 25, according to the *d.* of God.
DISPERSE. Prov. 15. 7, lips of wise *d.* knowledge.
See Ps. 112. 9; Jer. 25. 34; Ezek. 12. 15; 20. 23.
DISPERSED. Esth. 3. 8, and *d.* among the people.
Isa. 11. 12, the *d.* of Judah.
John 7. 35, go unto the *d.* among the Gentiles.
DISPERSED (prophecies concerning). Jer. 25. 24; Ezek. 36. 19; Zeph. 3. 10.
DISPLAYED. Ps. 60. 4.
DISPLEASE. Num. 11. 1, it *d.* the Lord.
22. 34, if it *d.* thee, I will get me back.
2 Sam. 11. 27, thing David had done *d.* the Lord.
1 Kings 1. 6, father had not *d.* him at any time.
Ps. 60. 1, thou hast been *d.*
Prov. 24. 18, lest the Lord see it, and it *d.* him.
Isa. 59. 15, it *d.* him there was no judgment.
Jon. 4. 1, it *d.* Jonah exceedingly.
Mat. 21. 15, scribes saw it, they were *d.*
Mk. 10. 14, Jesus was much *d.*
41, much *d.* with James and John.
See Gen. 48. 17; 1 Sam. 8. 6; 18. 8; Zech. 1. 2.
DISPLEASURE. Deut. 9. 19; Judg. 15. 3; Ps. 2. 5; 6. 1; 38. 1.
DISPOSE. Job 34. 13; 37. 15; Prov. 16. 33; 1 Cor. 10. 27.
DISPOSITION. Acts 7. 53.
DISPOSSESS. Num. 33. 53; Deut. 7. 17; Judg. 11. 23.
DISPUTATION. Acts 15. 2; Rom. 14. 1.
DISPUTE. Job 23. 7, the righteous might *d.* with him.
Mk. 9. 33, what was it ye *d.* of by the way?
1 Cor. 1. 20, where is the *d.* of this world?
Phil. 2. 14, do all things without *d.*
1 Tim. 6. 5, perverse *d.*
See Acts 9. 29; 15. 7; 17. 17; Jude 9.
DISQUIET. 1 Sam. 28. 15, why *d.* to bring me up?
Ps. 42. 5, 11; 43. 5, why art thou *d.* within me?
See Ps. 38. 8; 39. 6; Jer. 50. 34.
DISSEMBLE. Josh. 7. 11; Ps. 26. 4; Prov. 26. 24; Jer. 42. 20; Gal. 2. 13.
DISSENSION. Acts 15. 2; 23. 7, 10.
DISSIMULATION. Rom. 12. 9; Gal. 2. 13.
DISSOLVE. Isa. 34. 4, host of heaven shall be *d.*
Dan. 5. 16, thou canst *d.* doubts.
2 Cor. 5. 1, house of tabernacle *d.*
2 Pet. 3. 11, all these things shall be *d.*
12, heavens being on fire shall be *d.*
See Job 30. 22; Ps. 75. 3; Isa. 14. 31; 24. 19; Dan. 5. 12; Nah. 2. 6.
DISTAFF. Prov. 31. 19.
DISTIL. Deut. 32. 2; Job 36. 28.
DISTINCTION. 1 Cor. 14. 7.
DISTINCTLY. Neh. 8. 8.
DISTRACT. Ps. 88. 15; 1 Cor. 7. 35.
DISTRESS. Gen. 42. 21, therefore is this *d.* come upon us.
Judg. 11. 7, why are ye come when ye are in *d.*?
1 Sam. 22. 2, every one in *d.* came to David.
2 Sam. 22. 7; Ps. 18. 6; 118. 5; 120. 1, in *d.* I called.
1 Kings 1. 29, redeemed my soul out of all *d.*
2 Chron. 28. 22, in *d.* Ahaz trespassed more.
Neh. 2. 17, ye see the *d.* we are in.
Ps. 25. 17; 107. 6, 13, 19, 28, out of *d.*
Prov. 1. 27, mock when *d.* cometh.
Isa. 25. 4, a strength to needy in *d.*
Obad. 12, 14; Zeph. 1. 15, day of *d.*
Lu. 21. 23, shall be great *d.* in the land.
25, on earth *d.* of nations.
Rom. 8. 35, shall *d.* separate us?
1 Cor. 7. 26, good for present *d.*
2 Cor. 6. 4, approving ourselves in *d.*
12. 10, take pleasure in *d.*
See Gen. 35. 3; Neh. 9. 37; 2 Cor. 4. 8; 1 Thess. 3. 7.
DISTRIBUTE. Neh. 13. 13, office was to *d.* to brethren.
Job 21. 17, God *d.* sorrows in his anger.
Lu. 18. 22, sell and *d.* to poor.
John 6. 11, given thanks, he *d.*
Rom. 12. 13, *d.* to necessity of saints.
1 Cor. 7. 17, as God hath *d.* to every man.
2 Cor. 9. 13, your liberal *d.*
See Josh. 13. 32; Acts 4. 35; 2 Cor. 10. 13; 1 Tim. 6. 18.
DITCH. Ps. 7. 15, fallen into *d.* he made.
Mat. 15. 14; Lu. 6. 39, both fall into *d.*
See 2 Kings 3. 16; Job 9. 31; Prov. 23. 27; Isa. 22. 11.
DIVERS. Deut. 22. 9, sow vineyard with *d.* kinds.
11, garment of *d.* sorts.

Deut. 25. 13, not have in bag *d.* weights.
14, *d.* measures, great and small.
Prov. 20. 10, 23, *d.* weights and measures abomination.
Mat. 4. 24; Mk. 1. 34; Lu. 4. 40, *d.* diseases.
24. 7; Mk. 13. 8; Lu. 21. 11, in *d.* places.
Mk. 8. 3, for *d.* of them came from far.
1 Cor. 12. 10, to another *d.* kinds of tongues.
2 Tim. 3. 6; Tit. 3. 3, led away with *d.* lusts.
Jas. 1. 2, joy in *d.* temptations.
See Eccl. 5. 7; Heb. 1. 1; 2. 4; 9. 10; 13. 9.
DIVERSE. Esth. 3. 8, laws *d.* from all people.
1 Cor. 12. 6, *d.* of operations, but same God.
See Esth. 1. 7; 1 Cor. 12. 4, 28.
DIVIDE. Lev. 11. 4, 5, 6, 7, 26; Deut. 14. 7, not eat these of them that *d.* the hoof.
Josh. 19. 49, an end of *d.* the land.
1 Kings 3. 25, *d.* living child in two.
Job 27. 17, innocent shall *d.* silver.
Ps. 68. 12; Prov. 16. 19; Isa. 9. 3; 53. 12, *d.* spoil.
Amos 7. 17, thy land shall be *d.* by line.
Mat. 12. 25; Mk. 3. 24; Lu. 11. 17, kingdom or house *d.*
26; Mk. 3. 26; Lu. 11. 18, *d.* against himself.
Lu. 12. 13, that he *d.* inheritance with me.
14, who made me a *d.*?
52, five in one house *d.*
53, father *d.* against son.
15. 12, he *d.* unto them his living.
Acts 14. 4; 23. 7, multitude *d.*
1 Cor. 1. 13, is Christ *d.*?
12. 11, *d.* to every man severally as he will.
2 Tim. 2. 15, rightly *d.* word of truth.
Heb. 4. 12, piercing to *d.* asunder.
See Dan. 7. 25; Hos. 10. 2; Mat. 25. 32; Lu. 22. 17.
DIVINATION. Num. 23. 23, neither is any *d.* against Israel.
Acts 16. 16, damsel with a spirit of *d.*
See Deut. 18. 10; 2 Kings 17. 17; Ezek. 13. 23.
DIVINE (*v.*). Gen. 44. 15, wot ye not that I can *d.*?
1 Sam. 28. 8, *d.* unto me by the familiar spirit.
Ezek. 13. 9, prophets that *d.* lies.
21. 29, they *d.* lies unto thee.
Mic. 3. 11, prophets *d.* for money.
See Gen. 44. 5; Ezek. 22. 28; Mic. 3. 6.
DIVINE (*ad.*). Prov. 16. 10; Heb. 9. 1; 2 Pet. 1. 3, 4.
DIVINER. 1 Sam. 6. 2; Isa. 44. 25; Jer. 27. 9; 29. 8.
DIVISION. Ex. 8. 23, will put a *d.* between my people.
Judg. 5. 15, for *d.* of Reuben great thoughts of heart.
Lu. 12. 51, I tell you nay, but rather *d.*
John 7. 43; 9. 16; 10. 19, *d.* because of him.
Rom. 16. 17, mark them which cause *d.*
See 1 Cor. 1. 10; 3. 3; 11. 18.
DO. Ruth 3. 5, all thou sayest I will *d.*
Eccl. 3. 12, for a man to *d.* good.
Isa. 46. 11, I will also *d.* it.
Hos. 6. 4, what shall I *d.* unto thee?
Mat. 7. 12, men should *d.* to you, *d.* ye even so.
23. 3, they say, and *d.* not.
Lu. 10. 28, this *d.*, and thou shalt live.
22. 19; 1 Cor. 11. 24, this *d.* in remembrance.
John 15. 5, without me ye can *d.* nothing.
Rom. 7. 15, what I would, that *d.* I not.
2 Cor. 11. 12, what I *d.*, that I will *d.*
Gal. 5. 17, ye cannot *d.* the things ye would.
Phil. 4. 13, I can *d.* all things through Christ.
Heb. 4. 13, with whom we have to *d.*
Jas. 1. 23, a hearer, not a *d.* of the word.
See John 6. 38; 10. 37; Rev. 19. 10; 22. 9.
DOCTOR. Acts 5. 34, Gamaliel, a *d.* of the law.
Lu. 2. 46, sitting in the midst of the *d.*
5. 17, *d.* of the law sitting by.
DOCTRINE. Prov. 4. 2, I give you good *d.*
Isa. 28. 9, made to understand *d.*
Jer. 10. 8, the stock is a *d.* of vanities.
Mat. 15. 9; Mk. 7. 7, teaching for *d.* commandments of men.
16. 12, the *d.* of the Pharisees.
Mk. 1. 27; Acts 17. 19, what new *d.* is this?
John 7. 17, do his will shall know of the *d.*
Acts 2. 42, continued in apostles' *d.*
5. 28, filled Jerusalem with your *d.*
Rom. 6. 17, obeyed that form of *d.*
16. 17, contrary to the *d.*
1 Cor. 14. 26, every one hath a *d.*
Eph. 4. 14, every wind of *d.*
1 Tim. 1. 10, contrary to sound *d.*
4. 6, nourished in words of good *d.*
13, give attendance to *d.*
16, take heed to thyself and *d.*
2 Tim. 3. 10, hast fully known my *d.*
16, scripture profitable for *d.*
4. 2, exhort with all longsuffering and *d.*
Tit. 1. 9, by sound *d.* to exhort and convince.
2. 1, things which become sound *d.*
7, in *d.* showing uncorruptness.
10, adorn the *d.* of God our Saviour.
Heb. 6. 1, principles of the *d.*
2, the *d.* of baptisms.
13. 9, not carried about with strange *d.*
2 John 9, abideth in *d.* of Christ.
See Deut. 32. 2; Job 11. 4; John 7. 16; 1 Tim. 5. 17.
DOG. Ex. 11. 7, against Israel not a *d.* move.
Deut. 23. 18, not bring price of *d.* into house.
Judg. 7. 5, that lappeth as *d.* lappeth.
1 Sam. 17. 43; 24. 14; 2 Sam. 3. 8, am I a *d.*?
2 Sam. 9. 8, upon such a dead *d.* as I am.
2 Kings 8. 13, what, is thy servant a *d.*?
Job 30. 1, disdained to set with *d.*
Ps. 22. 20, darling from power of the *d.*
59. 6, they make noise like a *d.*
Prov. 26. 11; 2 Pet. 2. 22, as a *d.* returneth.
17, like one that taketh a *d.* by ears.
Eccl. 9. 4, living *d.* better than dead lion.
Isa. 56. 10, they are all dumb *d.*
66. 3, as if he cut off a *d.* neck.
Mat. 7. 6, give not that which is holy to *d.*
15. 27; Mk. 7. 28, the *d.* eat of crumbs.
Phil. 3. 2, beware of *d.*
Rev. 22. 15, without are *d.*
See Ex. 22. 31; 1 Kings 14. 11; 21. 23; 22. 28.
DOING. Ex. 15. 11, fearful in praises, *d.* wonders.
Judg. 2. 19, ceased not from their own *d.*
1 Sam. 25. 3, churlish and evil in his *d.*
1 Chron. 22. 16, arise, and be *d.*
Neh. 6. 3, I am *d.* a great work.
Ps. 9. 11; Isa. 12. 4, declare his *d.*
66. 5, terrible in *d.* toward children of men.
77. 12, I will talk of thy *d.*
118. 23; Mat. 21. 42; Mk. 12. 11, the Lord's *d.*
Mic. 2. 7, are these his *d.*?
Mat. 24. 46; Lu. 12. 43, shall find so *d.*
Acts 10. 38, went about *d.* good.
Rom. 2. 7, patient continuance in well *d.*
2 Cor. 8. 11, perform the *d.* of it.
Gal. 6. 9; 2 Thess. 3. 13, weary in well *d.*
Eph. 6. 6, *d.* will of God from heart.
1 Pet. 2. 15, with well *d.* put to silence.
3. 17, suffer for well *d.*
4. 19, commit souls in well *d.*
See Lev. 18. 3; Prov. 20. 11; Isa. 1. 16; Jer. 4. 4.
DOLEFUL. Isa. 13. 21; Mic. 2. 4.
DOMINION. Gen. 27. 40, when thou shalt have *d.*
37. 8, shalt thou have *d.* over us?
Num. 24. 19, come he that shall have *d.*
Job 25. 2, *d.* and fear are with him.
38. 33, canst thou set the *d.* thereof?
Ps. 8. 6, *d.* over works of thy hands.
19. 13; 119. 133, let them not have *d.* over me.
72. 8; Zech. 9. 10, *d.* from sea to sea.
Isa. 26. 13, other lords have had *d.* over us.
Dan. 4. 34; 7. 14, *d.* is an everlasting *d.*
Mat. 20. 25, princes of Gentiles exercise *d.*
Rom. 6. 9, death hath no more *d.*
14, sin shall not have *d.*
7. 1, law hath *d.* over a man.

2 Cor. 1. 24, not *d.* over your faith.
Eph. 1. 21, above all *d.*
Col. 1. 16, whether they be thrones or *d.*
See Dan. 6. 26; 1 Pet. 4. 11; Jude 25; Rev. 1. 6.
DOOR. Gen. 4. 7, sin lieth at the *d.*
Ex. 12. 7, strike blood on *d.* posts.
33. 8; Num. 11. 10, every man at tent *d.*
Judg. 16. 3, Samson took *d.* of the gate.
Job 31. 9, laid wait at neighbour's *d.*
32, I opened my *d.* to the travellers.
38. 17, the *d.* of the shadow of death.
41. 14, who can open *d.* of his face?
Ps. 24. 7, ye everlasting *d.*
78. 23, opened the *d.* of heaven.
84. 10, rather be *d.*-keeper.
141. 3, keep the *d.* of my lips.
Prov. 5. 8, come not nigh *d.* of her house.
8. 3, wisdom crieth at *d.*
26. 14, as *d.* turneth on hinges.
Eccl. 12. 4, *d.* shall be shut in the streets.
Isa. 6. 4, posts of the *d.* moved.
26. 20, enter, and shut thy *d.* about thee.
Hos. 2. 15, for a *d.* of hope.
Mal. 1. 10, who would shut the *d.* for nought?
Mat. 6. 6, when thou hast shut thy *d.*
24. 33; Mk. 13. 29, near, even at the *d.*
25. 10, and the *d.* was shut.
27. 60; 28. 2; Mk. 15. 46, *d.* of sepulchre.
Mk. 1. 33, city gathered at the *d.*
2. 2, not so much as about the *d.*
Lu. 13. 25, master hath shut to the *d.*
John 10. 1, 2, entereth not by *d.*
7. 9, I am the *d.*
18. 16, Peter stood at the *d.* without.
17, damsel that kept the *d.*
20. 19, 26, when *d.* were shut, Jesus came.
Acts 5. 9, feet at the *d.* to carry thee out.
14. 27, opened the *d.* of faith.
1 Cor. 16. 9, great *d.* and effectual.
2 Cor. 2. 12, *d.* opened to me of the Lord.
Col. 4. 3, open a *d.* of utterance.
Jas. 5. 9, judge standeth before the *d.*
Rev. 3. 8, set before thee an open *d.*
20, I stand at *d.* and knock.
4. 1, behold, a *d.* opened in heaven.
See Ex. 21. 6; Deut. 11. 20; Isa. 57. 8; Acts 5. 19; 16. 26.
DOTE. Jer. 50. 36; Ezek. 23. 5; 1 Tim. 6. 4.
DOUBLE. Gen. 43. 12, 15, take *d.* money in hand.
Ex. 22. 4, 7, 9, he shall restore *d.*
Deut. 15. 18, worth a *d.* hired servant.
2 Kings 2. 9, a *d.* portion of thy spirit.
1 Chron. 12. 33; Ps. 12. 2, a *d.* heart.
Isa. 40. 2, received *d.* for all her sins.
Jer. 16. 18, recompense their sin *d.*
1 Tim. 3. 8, deacons not *d.* tongued.
5. 17, worthy of *d.* honour.
Jas. 1. 8, a *d.* minded man unstable.
4. 8, purify your hearts, ye *d.* minded.
See Gen. 41. 32; Isa. 61. 7; Ezek. 21. 14; Rev. 18. 6.
DOUBT. Deut. 28. 66, thy life shall hang in *d.*
Job 12. 2, no *d.* ye are the people.
Ps. 126. 6, shall *d.* come again, rejoicing.
Dan. 5. 12, 16, dissolving of *d.*
Mat. 14. 31, wherefore didst thou *d.*?
21. 21, if ye have faith, and *d.* not.
Mk. 11. 23, shall not *d.* in his heart.
Lu. 11. 20, no *d.* kingdom of God is come.
John 10. 24, how long dost thou make us to *d.*?
Acts 5. 24, they *d.* whereunto this would grow.
28. 4, no *d.* this man is a murderer.
Rom. 14. 23, he that *d.* is damned if he eat.
Gal. 4. 20, I stand in *d.* of you.
1 Tim. 2. 8, pray without wrath and *d.*
1 John 2. 19, would no *d.* have continued.
See Lu. 12. 29; Acts 2. 12; Phil. 3. 8.
DOUGH. Num. 15. 20, a cake of the first of your *d.*
Neh. 10. 37, the firstfruits of our *d.*
Ezek. 44. 30, give unto the priest the first of your *d.*
DOVE. Ps. 55. 6, that I had wings like a *d.*
Isa. 59. 11, mourn sore like *d.*
60. 8, flee as *d.* to their windows.
Mat. 10. 16, be harmless as *d.*
21. 12; Mk. 11. 15; John 2. 14, them that sold *d.*
See Jer. 48. 28; Hos. 7. 11; Mat. 3. 16; Mk. 1. 10.
DOWN. 2 Sam. 3. 35, if I taste ought till sun be *d.*
2 Kings 19. 30; Isa. 37. 31, again take root *d.*
Ps. 59. 15, let them wander up and *d.*
109. 23, I am tossed up and *d.*
Eccl. 3. 21, spirit of the beast that goeth *d.*
Zech. 10. 12, walk up and *d.* in his name.
See Josh. 8. 29; Ps. 139. 2; Ezek. 38. 14.
DOWRY. Gen. 30. 20; 34. 12; Ex. 22. 17; 1 Sam. 18. 25.
DRAG. Hab. 1. 15, 16; John 21. 8.
DRAGON. Deut. 32. 33, their wine is the poison of *d.*
Neh. 2. 13, before the *d.* well.
Job 30. 29, I am a brother to *d.*
Ps. 91. 13, the *d.* shalt thou trample.
148. 7, praise the Lord, ye *d.*
Isa. 43. 20, the *d.* and owls shall honour me.
Jer. 9. 11, will make Jerusalem a den of *d.*
Rev. 20. 2, the *d.*, that old serpent.
See Rev. 12. 3; 13. 2, 11; 16. 13.
DRANK. 1 Sam. 30. 12, nor *d.* water three days and nights.
2 Sam. 12. 3, and *d.* of his own cup.
1 Kings 17. 6, and he *d.* of the brook.
Dan. 1. 5, appointed of the wine he *d.*
5. 4, they *d.* wine, and praised the gods.
Mk. 14. 23, and they all *d.* of it.
Lu. 17. 27, 28, they *d.*, they married.
John 4. 12, than our father, who *d.* thereof.
1 Cor. 10. 4, for they *d.* of that spiritual Rock.
See Gen. 9. 21; 24. 46; 27. 25; Num. 20. 11.
DRAUGHT. Mat. 15. 17; Mk. 7. 19; Lu. 5. 4, 9; 21. 6, 11.
DRAVE. Ex. 14. 25; Josh. 24. 12; Judg. 6. 9.
DRAW. Job 40. 23, trusteth he can *d.* up Jordan.
41. 1, canst thou *d.* out leviathan?
Ps. 28. 3, *d.* me not away with wicked.
37. 14, wicked have *d.* out sword.
55. 21, yet were they *d.* swords.
88. 3, my life *d.* nigh unto the grave.
Eccl. 12. 1, nor years *d.* nigh.
Cant. 1. 4, *d.* me, we will run after thee.
Isa. 5. 18, *d.* iniquity with cords.
12. 3, *d.* water from wells of salvation.
Jer. 31. 3, with lovingkindness have I *d.* thee.
Mat. 15. 8, people *d.* nigh me with their mouth.
Lu. 21. 8, the time *d.* near.
28, your redemption *d.* nigh.
John 4. 11, thou hast nothing to *d.* with.
15, thirst not, neither come hither to *d.*
John 6. 44, except the Father *d.* him.
12. 32, if lifted up, will *d.* all men.
Heb. 10. 22, *d.* near with true heart.
38, 39, if any *d.* back.
Jas. 4. 8, *d.* nigh to God, he will *d.*
See Acts 11. 10; 20. 30; Heb. 7. 19; Jas. 2. 6.
DRAWER. Deut. 29. 11; Josh. 9. 21.
DREAD. Gen. 28. 17, how *d.* is this place!
Deut. 2. 25; 11. 25, begin to put *d.* of thee.
Isa. 8. 13, let him be your *d.*
Mal. 4. 5, the great and *d.* day.
See Gen. 9. 2; Ex. 15. 16; Dan. 9. 4.
DREAM. Job 20. 8, shall fly away as a *d.*
33. 15, 16, in a *d.* he openeth the ears.
Ps. 73. 20, as a *d.* when one awaketh.
126. 1, we were like them that *d.*
Eccl. 5. 3, a *d.* cometh through much business.
Jer. 23. 28, prophet that hath a *d.*
Joel 2. 28; Acts 2. 17, old men *d. d.*
Jude 8, filthy *d.* defile the flesh.
See Job 7. 14; Isa. 29. 8; Jer. 27. 9.
DREGS. Ps. 75. 8; Isa. 51. 17.
DRESS. Gen. 2. 15, put man in garden to *d.* it.
Deut. 28. 39, plant vineyards and *d.* them.
2 Sam. 12. 4, poor man's lamb, and *d.* it.
See Ex. 30. 7; Lu. 13. 7; Heb. 6. 7.

DREW. Gen. 47. 29, time *d.* nigh that Israel must die.
Ex. 2. 10, because I *d.* him out of the water.
Josh. 8. 26, Joshua *d.* not his hand back.
1 Kings 22. 34; 2 Chron. 18. 33, man *d.* a bow.
2 Kings 9. 24, Jehu *d.* bow with full strength.
Hos. 11. 4, *d.* them with cords of a man.
Zeph. 3. 2, she *d.* not near to her God.
Mat. 21. 34, when time of fruit *d.* near.
Lu. 24. 15, Jesus himself *d.* near.
Acts 5. 37, and *d.* away much people.
See Esth. 5. 2; Lam. 3. 57; Acts 7. 17.
DRINK (*n.*). Lev. 10. 9, do not drink strong *d.* when ye go.
Num. 6. 3, separate himself from strong *d.*
Deut. 14. 26, bestow money for strong *d.*
29. 6, strong *d.* these forty years.
Prov. 20. 1, strong *d.* is raging.
31. 4, not for princes to drink strong *d.*
6, give strong *d.* to him that is ready to perish.
Isa. 24. 9, strong *d.* shall be bitter.
28. 7, erred through strong *d.*
Mic. 2. 11, prophesy of wine and strong *d.*
Hab. 2. 15, that giveth his neighbour *d.*
Hag. 1. 6, ye are not filled with *d.*
Mat. 25. 35, 37, 42, thirsty, and ye gave me *d.*
John 4. 9, a Jew, askest *d.* of me.
6. 55, my blood is *d.* indeed.
Rom. 12. 20, if thine enemy thirst, give him *d.*
14. 17, the kingdom of God is not meat and *d.*
1 Cor. 10. 4, same spiritual *d.*
Col. 2. 16, judge you in meat or in *d.*
See Gen. 21. 19; Isa. 5. 11, 22; 32. 6; 43. 20; Lu. 1. 15; 1 Tim. 5. 23.
DRINK (*v.*). Ex. 15. 24, what shall we *d.*?
17. 1, no water for people to *d.*
2 Sam. 23. 16; 1 Chron. 11. 18, David would not *d.*
Ps. 36. 8, *d.* of the river of thy pleasures.
60. 3, *d.* the wine of astonishment.
80. 5, gavest them tears to *d.*
110. 7, he shall *d.* of the brook in the way.
Prov. 5. 15, *d.* waters of thine own cistern.
31. 5, lest they *d.*, and forget the law.
7, let him *d.*, and forget his poverty.
Eccl. 9. 7, *d.* wine with merry heart.
Cant. 5. 1, *d.*, yea, *d.* abundantly.
Isa. 5. 22, mighty to *d.* wine.
65. 13, my servants shall *d.*, but ye.
Jer. 35. 2, give Rechabites wine to *d.*
6, we will *d.* no wine.
14, to this day they *d.* none.
Ezek. 4. 11, thou shalt *d.* water by measure.
Amos 2. 8, *d.* the wine of the condemned.
Zech. 9. 15, they shall *d.*, and make a noise.
Mat. 10. 42, whoso shall give to *d.*
20. 22; Mk. 10. 38, are ye able to *d.*?
26. 27, saying, *d.* ye all of it.
29; Mk. 14. 25; Lu. 22. 18, when I *d.* it new.
42, may not pass except I *d.*
Mk. 9. 41, shall give you cup of water to *d.*
16. 18, if they *d.* any deadly thing.
John 4. 10, give me to *d.*
7. 37, let him come to me, and *d.*
18. 11, cup given me, shall I not *d.* it?
Rom. 14. 21, not good to *d.* wine.
1 Cor. 10. 4, did all *d.* same spiritual drink.
11. 25, as oft as ye *d.* it.
12. 13, made to *d.* into one Spirit.
See Mk. 2. 16; Lu. 7. 33; 10. 7.
DRIVE. Gen. 4. 14, thou hast *d.* me out.
Ex. 23. 28, hornets shall *d.* out Hivite.
Deut. 4. 19, lest thou be *d.* to worship them.
Job 24. 3, they *d.* away ass of the fatherless.
30. 5, they were *d.* forth from among men.
Prov. 14. 32, wicked *d.* away in his wickedness.
22. 15, rod shall *d.* it away.
25. 23, north wind *d.* away rain.
Jer. 46. 15, stood not, because Lord did *d.* them.
Dan. 4. 25; 5. 21, they shall *d.* thee from men.
Hos. 13. 3, as chaff *d.* with whirlwind.
Lu. 8. 29, he was *d.* of the devil.
Jas. 1. 6, wave *d.* with the wind.
See 2 Kings 9. 20; Jer. 8. 3; Ezek. 31. 11.
DROMEDARIES. 1 Kings 4. 28, straw for the horses and *d.*
Esth. 8. 10, and young *d.*
Isa. 60. 6, the *d.* of Midian and Ephah.
Jer. 2. 23, thou art a swift *d.* traversing her ways.
DROP (*n.*). Job 36. 27, maketh small the *d.* of water.
Isa. 40. 15, as the *d.* of a bucket.
See Job 38. 28; Cant. 5. 2; Lu. 22. 44.
DROP (*v.*). Deut. 32. 2, doctrine shall *d.* as the rain.
Job 29. 22, my speech *d.* upon them.
Ps. 65. 11, paths *d.* fatness.
68. 8, heavens *d.* at presence of God.
Eccl. 10. 18, through idleness house *d.* through.
Isa. 45. 8, *d.* down, ye heavens.
Ezek. 20. 46, *d.* thy word toward the south.
See 2 Sam. 21. 10; Joel 3. 18; Amos 9. 13.
DROPSY. Lu. 14. 2, a man which had the *d.*
DROSS. Ps. 119. 119; Prov. 25. 4; 26. 23; Isa. 1. 22, 25; Ezek. 22. 18.
DROUGHT. Deut. 28. 24; 1 Kings 17; Isa. 58. 11; Jer. 17. 8; Hos. 13. 5; Hag. 1. 11.
DROVE. Gen. 3. 24; 15. 11; 32. 16; 33. 8; John 2. 15.
DROWN. Cant. 8. 7, neither can floods *d.* it.
1 Tim. 6. 9, that *d.* men in perdition.
See Ex. 15. 4; Mat. 18. 6; Heb. 11. 29.
DROWSINESS. Prov. 23. 21.
DRUNK. 2 Sam. 11. 13, David made Uriah *d.*
1 Kings 20. 16, was drinking himself *d.*
Job 12. 25; Ps. 107. 27, stagger like a *d.* man.
Jer. 23. 9, I am like a *d.* man.
Lam. 5. 4, we have *d.* water for money.
Hab. 2. 15, makest him *d.* also.
Mat. 24. 49; Lu. 12. 45, drink with the *d.*
Acts 2. 15, these are not *d.*
1 Cor. 11. 21, one is hungry, and another *d.*
1 Thess. 5. 7, they that be *d.* are *d.* in the night.
See Lu. 5. 39; John 2. 10; Eph. 5. 18; Rev. 17. 6.
DRUNKARD. Deut 21. 20, our son is a glutton and a *d.*
Prov. 23. 21, *d.* and glutton come to poverty.
26. 9, as a thorn goeth into hand of *d.*
1 Cor. 6. 10, nor *d.* shall inherit.
See Ps. 69. 12; Isa. 24. 20; Joel 1. 5; Nah. 1. 10.
DRUNKENNESS. Deut. 29. 19, to add *d.* to thirst.
Eccl. 10. 17, eat for strength, not for *d.*
Ezek. 23. 33, shalt be filled with *d.*
See Lu. 21. 34; Rom. 13. 13; Gal. 5. 21.
DRY. Prov. 17. 22, a broken spirit *d.* the bones.
Isa. 44. 3, pour floods on *d.* ground.
Mat. 12. 43; Lu. 11. 24, through *d.* places.
Mk. 5. 29, fountain of blood *d.* up.
See Ps. 107. 33, 35; Isa. 53. 2; Mk. 11. 20.
DUE. Lev. 10. 13, 14, it is thy *d.*, and thy sons' *d.*
26. 4; Deut. 11. 14, rain in *d.* season.
Ps. 104. 27; 145. 15; Mat. 24. 45; Lu. 14. 42, meat in *d.* season.
Prov. 15. 23, word spoken in *d.* season.
Mat. 18. 34, pay all that was *d.*
Lu. 23. 41, the *d.* reward of our deeds.
Rom. 5. 6, in *d.* time Christ died.
Gal. 6. 9, in *d.* season we shall reap.
See Prov. 3. 27; 1 Cor. 15. 8; Tit. 1. 3; 1 Pet. 5. 6.
DULL. Mat. 13. 15; Acts 28. 27; Heb. 5. 11.
DUMB. Ex. 4. 11, who maketh the *d.*?
Prov. 31. 8, open thy mouth for the *d.*
Isa. 35. 6, the tongue of the *d.* shall sing.
53. 7; Acts 8. 32, as sheep before shearers is *d.*
56. 10, they are all *d.* dogs.
Ezek. 3. 26, be *d.*, and shalt not be a reprover.
Hab. 2. 19, woe to him that saith to *d.* stone.
Mat. 9. 32; 12. 22; 15. 30; Mk. 7. 37; 9. 17; *d.* man.
See Ps. 39. 2; Dan. 10. 15; Lu. 1. 20; 11. 14; 2 Pet. 2. 16.
DUNG. 1 Sam. 2. 8; Ps. 113. 7, lifteth beggar from *d.*-hill.

Lu. 13. 8, till I dig about it, and *d.* it.
14. 35, neither fit for land nor *d.*-hill.
Phil. 3. 8, count all things but *d.*
See Neh. 2. 13; Lam. 4. 5; Mal. 2. 3.
DUNGEON. Gen. 40. 15; 41. 14; Ex. 12. 29; Jer. 38. 6; Lam. 3. 53.
DURABLE. Prov. 8. 18; Isa. 23. 18.
DURETH. Mat. 13. 21.
DURST. Mat. 22. 46; Mk. 12. 34; Lu. 20. 40, nor *d.* ask questions.
John 21. 12, none of disciples *d.* ask.
See Esth. 7. 5; Job 32. 6; Acts 5. 13; Jude 9.
DUST. Gen. 2. 7, Lord God formed man of *d.*
3. 14, *d.* shalt thou eat.
19, *d.* thou art.
18. 27, who am but *d.* and ashes.
Job 10. 9, wilt thou bring me into *d.* again?
22. 24; 27. 16, lay up gold as *d.*
34. 15, man shall turn again to *d.*
42. 6, I repent in *d.* and ashes.
Ps. 30. 9, shall the *d.* praise thee?
102. 14, servants favour *d.* thereof.
103. 14, remembereth that we are *d.*
104. 29, they die and return to their *d.*
Eccl. 3. 20, all are of the *d.*, and turn to *d.* again.
12. 7, then shall the *d.* return to the earth.
Isa. 40. 12, comprehended *d.* of the earth.
65. 25, *d.* shall be serpent's meat.
Lam. 3. 29, he putteth his mouth in the *d.*
Dan. 12. 2, many that sleep in *d.* shall awake.
Mic. 7. 17, lick the *d.* like a serpent.
Mat. 10. 14; Mk. 6. 11; Lu. 9. 5, shake off *d.* from feet.
Lu. 10. 11, even *d.* of your city.
Acts 22. 23, as they threw *d.* into the air.
See Ex. 8. 16; Num. 23. 10; Deut. 9. 21; Josh. 7. 6; Job 2. 12; 39. 14; Lam. 2. 10.
DUTY. Eccl. 12. 13, the whole *d.* of man.
Lu. 17. 10, that which was our *d.* to do.
Rom. 15. 27, their *d.* is to minister.
See Ex. 21. 10; Deut. 25. 5; 2 Chron. 8. 14; Ezra 3. 4.
DWELL. Deut. 12. 11, cause his name to *d.* there.
1 Sam. 4. 4; 2 Sam. 6. 2; 1 Chron. 13. 6, *d.* between the cherubims.
1 Kings 8. 30; 2 Chron. 6. 21, heaven thy *d.* place.
Ps. 23. 6, will *d.* in house of the Lord.
37. 3, so shalt thou *d.* in the land.
84. 10, than to *d.* in tents of wickedness.
132. 14, here will I *d.*
133. 1, good for brethren to *d.* together.
Isa. 33. 14, who shall *d.* with devouring fire?
16, he shall *d.* on high.
57. 15, I *d.* in the high and holy place.
John 6. 56, *d.* in me, and I in him.
14. 10, the Father that *d.* in me.
17, for he *d.* with you, and shall be in you.
Rom. 7. 17, sin that *d.* in me.
Col. 2. 9, in him *d.* fulness of Godhead.
3. 16, word of Christ *d.* in you richly.
1 Tim. 6. 16, *d.* in the light.
2 Pet. 3. 13, wherein *d.* righteousness.
1 John 3. 17, how *d.* the love of God in him?
4. 12, God *d.* in us.
See Rom. 8. 9; 2 Cor. 6. 16; Jas. 4. 5.
DYED. Ex. 25. 5; Isa. 63. 1; Ezek. 23. 15.
DYING. 2 Cor. 4. 10, the *d.* of Lord Jesus.
2 Cor. 6. 9, as *d.* and behold we live.
See Num. 17. 13; Lu. 8. 42; Heb. 11. 21.

E

EACH. Isa. 57. 2, *e.* one walking in his uprightness.
Ezek. 4. 6, *e.* day for a year.
Acts 2. 3, cloven tongues sat on *e.*
Phil. 2. 3, let *e.* esteem other.
See Ex. 18. 7; Ps. 85. 10; 2 Thess. 1. 3.
EAGLE. Ex. 19. 4, how I bare you on *e.* wings.
2 Sam. 1. 23, were swifter than *e.*
Job 9. 26, *e.* that hasteth to prey.
39. 27, doth the *e.* mount up?
Ps. 103. 5, youth renewed like *e.*
Isa. 40. 31, mount up with wings as *e.*
Ezek. 1. 10, they four also had the face of an *e.*
17. 3, a great *e.* with great wings.
Obad. 4, thou shalt exalt thyself as the *e.*
Mat. 24. 28; Lu. 17. 37, *e.* be gathered.
Rev. 4. 7, the fourth beast was like a flying *e.*
See Dan. 4. 33; Rev. 12. 14.
EAR (*n.*). Neh. 1. 6, let thine *e.* be attentive.
Job 12. 11; 34. 3, doth not *e.* try words?
29. 11, when the *e.* heard me, it blessed me.
42. 5, heard of thee by the hearing of the *e.*
Ps. 45. 10, and incline thine *e.*
58. 4, like the deaf adder that stoppeth her *e.*
78. 1, give *e.*, O my people.
94. 9, he that planted the *e.*, shall he not hear?
Prov. 15. 31, the *e.* that heareth the reproof.
17. 4, liar giveth *e.* to naughty tongue.
18. 15, *e.* of wise seeketh knowledge.
20. 12, hearing *e.*, seeing eye, Lord made.
22. 17, bow down thine *e.*
25. 12, wise reprover on obedient *e.*
Eccl. 1. 8, nor the *e.* filled with hearing.
Isa. 48. 8, from that time thine *e.* not opened.
50. 4, he wakeneth my *e.* to hear.
55. 3, incline your *e.*, and come unto me.
59. 1, nor his *e.* heavy, that it cannot.
Jer. 9. 20, let your *e.* receive word of the Lord.
Amos 3. 12, out of mouth of lion piece of an *e.*
1 Cor. 2. 9, nor *e.* heard.
12. 16, if *e.* say, because I am not the eye.
See Rev. 2. 7.
EAR (*v.*). Ex. 34. 21; Deut. 21. 4; 1 Sam. 8. 12.
EARLY. Ps. 46. 5, and that right *e.*
63. 1, *e.* will I seek thee.
90. 14, satisfy us *e.* with thy mercy.
Prov. 1. 28; 8. 17, seek me *e.* shall find me.
Cant. 7. 12, get up *e.* to vineyards.
Hos. 6. 4; 13. 3, as *e.* dew.
Jas. 5. 7, the *e.* and latter rain.
See Judg. 7. 3; Lu. 24. 22; John 20. 1.
EARNEST. Job 7. 2, as servant *e.* desireth shadow.
Jer. 31. 20, I do *e.* remember him still.
Mic. 7. 3, do evil with both hands *e.*
Lu. 22. 44, in agony he prayed more *e.*
Rom. 8. 19, the *e.* expectation of the creature.
1 Cor. 12. 31, covet *e.* best gifts.
2 Cor. 1. 22; 5. 5, the *e.* of the Spirit.
5. 2, *e.* desiring to be clothed.
Eph. 1. 14, the *e.* of our inheritance.
Phil. 1. 20, to my *e.* expectation and hope.
Jude 3, *e.* contend for the faith.
See Acts 3. 12; Heb. 2. 1; Jas. 5. 17.
EARNETH. Hag. 1. 6.
EARS. Ex. 10. 2, tell it in *e.* of thy son.
1 Sam. 3. 11; 2 Kings 21. 12; Jer. 19. 3, at which *e.* shall tingle.
2 Sam. 7. 22, we have heard with our *e.*
Job 15. 21, dreadful sound is in his *e.*
28. 22, heard fame with our *e.*
Ps. 18. 6, my cry came even into his *e.*
34. 15, his *e.* are open unto their cry.
115. 6; 135. 17, they have *e.*, but hear not.
Prov. 21. 13, stoppeth *e.* at cry of the poor.
23. 9, speak not in *e.* of a fool.
26. 17, one that taketh dog by the *e.*
Isa. 6. 10; Mat. 13. 15; Acts 28. 27, make *e.* heavy.
Mat. 10. 27, what ye hear in *e.*, preach.
13. 16, blessed are your *e.*
26. 51; Mk. 14. 47, smote off *e.*
Mk. 7. 33, put his fingers into *e.*
8. 18, having *e.*, hear ye not?
Acts 7. 51, uncircumcised in heart and *e.*
17. 20, strange things to our *e.*
2 Tim. 4. 3, having itching *e.*
Jas. 5. 4, entered into *e.* of the Lord.
1 Pet. 3. 12, his *e.* are open to prayer.
See Mat. 11. 15; Mk. 4. 9.
EARS (*of corn*). Deut. 23. 25; Mat. 12. 1.
EARTH. Gen. 8. 22, while *e.* remaineth.
10. 25, in his days was *e.* divided.

16. 6, though I forbear, what am I *e.*?
21. 23, dieth, being wholly at *e.*
Ps. 25. 13, his soul shall dwell at *e.*
Isa. 32. 9, 11, women that are at *e.*
Amos 6. 1, woe to them that are at *e.*
Mat. 9. 5; Mk. 2. 9; Lu. 5. 23, is *e.* to say.
19. 24; Mk. 10. 25; Lu. 18. 25, *e.* for camel.
1 Cor. 13. 5, not *e.* provoked.
Heb. 12. 1, sin which doth so *e.* beset.
See Jer. 46. 27; Zech. 1. 15; Lu. 12. 19.

EAST. Gen. 41. 6; 23. 27, blasted with *e.* wind.
Ex. 10. 13, Lord brought an *e.* wind.
Job 1. 3, greatest of all men of the *e.*
15. 2, fill his belly with *e.* wind.
27. 21, *e.* wind carrieth him away.
38. 24, scattereth *e.* wind on the earth.
Ps. 48. 7, breakest ships with *e.* wind.
75. 6, promotion cometh not from *e.*
103. 12, as far as *e.* from west.
Isa. 27. 8, stayeth rough wind in day of *e.* wind.
Ezek. 19. 12, the *e.* wind drieth up her fruit.
43. 2, glory of God of Israel came from way of *e.*
47. 1, house stood toward the *e.*
Hos. 12. 1, Ephraim followeth *e.* wind.
13. 15, though fruitful, an *e.* wind shall come.
See Jon. 4. 5, 8; Mat. 2. 1; 8. 11; 24. 27.

EASTER. Acts 12. 4, intending after *E.* to bring him forth.

EASY. Prov. 14. 6; Mat. 11. 30; 1 Cor. 14. 9; Jas. 3. 17.

EAT. Gen. 2. 17, in day thou *e.* thou shalt die.
9. 4; Lev. 19. 26; Deut. 12. 16, blood not *e.*
24. 33, not *e.* till I have told.
43. 32, Egyptians might not *e.* with Hebrews.
Ex. 12. 16, no work, save that which man must *e.*
23. 11, that the poor may *e.*
29. 34, shall not be *e.*, because holy.
Lev. 25. 20, what shall we *e.* seventh year?
Num. 13. 32, a land that *e.* up inhabitants.
Josh. 5. 11, 12, *e.* of old corn of the land.
1 Sam. 14. 30, if haply people had *e.* freely.
28. 20, had *e.* no bread all day.
22, *e.*, that thou mayest have strength.
2 Sam. 19. 42, have we *e.* at all of the king's cost?
1 Kings 19. 5; Acts 10. 13; 11. 7, angel said, Arise and *e.*
2 Kings 4. 43, 44, they shall *e.*, and leave thereof.
6. 28, give thy son, that we may *e.* him.
Neh. 5. 2, corn, that we may *e.*, and live.
Job 3. 24, my sighing cometh before I *e.*
5. 5, whose harvest the hungry *e.* up.
6. 6, *e.* without salt.
21. 25, another never *e.* with pleasure.
31. 17, have *e.* my morsel alone.
Ps. 22. 26, meek shall *e.* and be satisfied.
69. 9; John 2. 17, zeal hath *e.* me up.
102. 9, have *e.* ashes like bread.
Prov. 1. 31; Isa. 3. 10, *e.* fruit of their own way.
13. 25, *e.* to satisfying of soul.
18. 21, they that love it shall *e.* the fruit.
23. 1, sittest to *e.* with ruler.
24. 13, *e.* honey, because it is good.
25. 27, not good to *e.* much honey.
Eccl. 2. 25, who can *e.* more than I?
4. 5, fool *e.* his own flesh.
5. 11, goods increase, they increased that *e.*
12, sleep be sweet, whether he *e.* little or much.
17, all his days also he *e.* in darkness.
19; 6. 2, not power to *e.* thereof.
10. 16, thy princes *e.* in the morning.
17, blessed when princes *e.* in due season.
Isa. 4. 1, we will *e.* our own bread.
7. 15, 22, butter and honey shall he *e.*
11. 7; 65. 25, lion *e.* straw like ox.
29. 8, he *e.*, awaketh, and is hungry.
51. 8, worm shall *e.* them like wool.
55. 1, come ye, buy and *e.*
2, *e.* ye that which is good.
10, give bread to the *e.*
65. 13, my servants shall *e.*, but ye shall be.
Jer. 5. 17, they shall *e.* up thine harvest.
15. 16, words were found, and I did *e.* them.
24. 2; 29. 17, figs could not be *e.*
31. 29; Ezek. 18. 2, the fathers have *e.* sour grapes.
Ezek. 3. 1, 2, 3, *e.* this roll.
4. 10, *e.* by weight.
Dan. 4. 33, *e.* grass as oxen.
Hos. 4. 10; Mic. 6. 14; Hag. 1. 6, *e.*, and not have enough.
10. 13, have *e.* the fruit of lies.
Mic. 7. 1, there is no cluster to *e.*
Mat. 6. 25; Lu. 12. 22, what ye shall *e.*
9. 11; Mk. 2. 16; Lu. 15. 2, why *e.* with publicans?
12. 1, ears of corn, and *e.*
4, *e.* shewbread, which was not lawful to *e.*
14. 16; Mk. 6. 37; Lu. 9. 13, give ye them to *e.*
15. 20, to *e.* with unwashen hands.
Mat. 15. 27; Mk. 7. 28, dogs *e.* of crumbs.
32; Mk. 8. 1, multitude have nothing to *e.*
24. 49, to *e.* and drink with the drunken.
Mk. 2. 16, when they saw him *e.* with.
6. 31, no leisure so much as to *e.*
11. 14, no man *e.* fruit of thee.
Lu. 5. 33, but thy disciples *e.* and drink.
10. 8, *e.* such things as are set before you.
12. 19, take thine ease, *e.*, drink.
13. 26, we have *e.* and drunk in thy presence.
15. 23, let us *e.* and be merry.
22. 30, that ye may *e.* at my table.
24. 43, he took it, and did *e.* before them.
John 4. 31, Master, *e.*
32, meat to *e.* ye know not of.
6. 26, because ye did *e.* of loaves.
52, can this man give us his flesh to *e.*?
53, except ye *e.* the flesh.
Acts 2. 46, did *e.* their meat with gladness.
9. 9, Saul did neither *e.* nor drink.
11. 3, thou didst *e.* with them.
23. 14, will *e.* nothing until we have slain Paul.
Rom. 14. 2, one believeth he may *e.* all things; weak *e.* herbs.
6, *e.* to the Lord.
20, who *e.* with offence.
21, neither to *e.* flesh nor drink wine.
1 Cor. 5. 11, with such an one no not to *e.*
8. 7, *e.* it as a thing offered to idol.
8, neither if we *e.* are we better.
13, I will *e.* no flesh while world.
9. 4, have we not power to *e.*?
10. 3, all *e.* same spiritual meat.
27, *e.*, asking no question.
31, whether ye *e.* or drink.
11. 29, he that *e.* unworthily.
2 Thess. 3. 10, work not, neither should he *e.*
Heb. 13. 10, whereof they have no right to *e.*
Rev. 2. 7, *e.* of the tree of life.
17, will give to *e.* of hidden manna.
19. 18, *e.* flesh of kings.
See Judg. 14. 14; Prov. 31. 27; Isa. 1. 19; 65. 4.

EDGE. Prov. 5. 4; Heb. 4. 12; Eccl. 10. 10.

EDIFY. Rom. 14. 19, wherewith one may *e.*
15. 2, please his neighbour to *e.*
1 Cor. 8. 1, charity *e.*
14. 3, he that prophesieth speaketh to *e.*
4, *e.* himself, *e.* the church.
10. 23, all things lawful, but *e.* not.
Eph. 4. 12, for *e.* of the body of Christ.
See 2 Cor. 10. 8; 13. 10; 1 Tim. 1. 4.

EFFECT. Num. 30. 8, make vow of none *e.*
2 Chron. 7. 11, Solomon prosperously *e.* all.
Ps. 33. 10, devices of the people of none *e.*
Isa. 32. 17, the *e.* of righteousness quietness.
Mat. 15. 6; Mk. 7. 13, commandment of God of none *e.*
1 Cor. 1. 17, lest cross be of none *e.*
Gal. 5. 4, Christ is become of none *e.*
See Rom. 3. 3; 4. 14; 9. 6; Gal. 3. 17.

EFFECTUAL. 1 Cor. 16. 9, a great door and *e.* is opened.

Eph. 3. 7; 4. 16, the *e.* working.
Jas. 5. 16, *e.* prayer of righteous man.
See 2 Cor. 1. 6; Gal. 2. 8; 1 Thess. 2. 13.
EFFEMINATE. 1 Cor. 6. 9.
EGG. Job 6. 6, taste in the white of an *e.*
39. 14, ostrich leaveth *e.* in earth.
Lu. 11. 12, if he ask an *e.*
See Deut. 22. 6; Isa. 10. 14; 59. 5; Jer. 17. 11.
EITHER. Gen. 31. 24, speak not *e.* good or bad.
Eccl. 11. 6, prosper, *e.* this or that.
Mat. 6. 24; Lu. 16. 13, *e.* hate the one.
John 19. 18, on *e.* side one.
Rev. 22. 2, on *e.* side the river.
See Deut. 17. 3; 28. 51; Isa. 7. 11; Mat. 12. 33.
ELDER. 1 Sam. 15. 30, honour me before *e.* of people.
Job 15. 10, aged men, much *e.* than thy father.
32. 4, waited, because they were *e.* than he.
Prov. 31. 23, husband known among *e.*
Mat. 15. 2; Mk. 7. 3, tradition of the *e.*
1 Tim. 5. 17, let *e.* that rule be worthy.
Tit. 1. 5, ordain *e.* in every city.
Heb. 11. 2, the *e.* obtained good report.
Jas. 5. 14, call for *e.* of the church.
1 Pet. 5. 1, the *e.* I exhort, who am an *e.*
5, younger submit to the *e.*
See John 8. 9; 1 Tim. 5. 2; 2 John 1; 3 John 1.
ELECT. Isa. 42. 1, mine *e.*, in whom my soul delighteth.
45. 4, mine *e.* I have called by name.
65. 9, 22, mine *e.* shall inherit.
Mat. 24. 22; Mk. 13. 20, for *e.* sake days shortened.
24; Mk. 13. 22, deceive very *e.*
31; Mk. 13. 27, gather together his *e.*
Lu. 18. 7, avenge his own *e.*
Rom. 8. 33, to charge of God's *e.*
Col. 3. 12, put on as the *e.* of God.
1 Tim. 5. 21, charge thee before *e.* angels.
1 Pet. 1. 2, *e.* according to foreknowledge.
2. 6, corner stone, *e.*, precious.
See 2 Tim. 2. 10; Tit. 1. 1; 1 Pet. 5. 13; 2 John 1. 13.
ELECTION. Rom. 9. 11; 11. 5; 1 Thess. 1. 4; 2 Pet. 1. 10.
ELEMENTS. Gal. 4. 3, 9; 2 Pet. 3. 10.
ELEVEN. Gen. 32. 22, Jacob took his *e.* sons.
37. 9, and *e.* stars made obeisance.
Acts 1. 26, he was numbered with the *e.*
See Mat. 28. 16; Mk. 16. 14; Lu. 24. 9.
ELOQUENT. Ex. 4. 10; Isa. 3. 3; Acts 18. 24.
EMBALMED. Gen. 50. 2, the days of those which are *e.*
26, and they *e.* him.
See John 19. 39.
EMBOLDEN. Job 16. 3; 1 Cor. 8. 10.
EMBRACE. Job 24. 8, *e.* rock for want of shelter.
Eccl. 3. 5, a time to *e.*
Heb. 11. 13, seen and *e.* promises.
See Prov. 4. 8; 5. 20; Lam. 4. 5; Acts 20. 1.
EMBROIDER. Ex. 28. 39; 35. 35; 38. 23.
EMERALDS. Ex. 28. 18; 39. 11; Rev. 4. 3; 21. 19.
EMERODS. Deut. 28. 27, and with *e.*
1 Sam. 5. 6, and smote them with *e.*
EMINENT. Ezek. 16. 24, 31, 39; 17. 22.
EMPIRE. Esth. 1. 20.
EMPLOY. Deut. 20. 19; 1 Chron. 9. 3; Ezra. 10. 15; Ezek. 39. 14.
EMPTY. Gen. 31. 42; Mk. 12. 3; Lu. 1. 53; 20. 10, sent *e.* away.
Ex. 3. 21, ye shall not go *e.*
23. 15; 34. 20; Deut. 16. 16, appear before me *e.*
Deut. 15. 13, not let him go away *e.*
Job 22. 9, thou hast sent widows away *e.*
Eccl. 11. 3, clouds *e.* themselves on the earth.
Isa. 29. 8, awaketh, and his soul is *e.*
Jer. 48. 11, Moab *e.* from vessel to vessel.
Nah. 2. 2, the emptiers have *e.* them out.
Mat. 12. 44, come, he findeth it *e.*
See 2 Sam. 1. 22; 2 Kings 4. 3; Hos. 10. 1.
EMULATION. Rom. 11. 14; Gal. 5. 20.
ENABLED. 1 Tim. 1. 12.
ENCAMP. Ps. 27. 3, though host *e.* against me.
34. 7, angel of Lord *e.* round.
See Num. 10. 31; Job 19. 12; Ps. 53. 5.
ENCOUNTERED. Acts 17. 18.
ENCOURAGE. Deut. 1. 38; 3. 28; 2 Sam. 11. 25, *e.* him.
Ps. 64. 5, they *e.* themselves in an evil matter.
See 1 Sam. 30. 6; 2 Chron. 31. 4; 35. 2; Isa. 41. 7.
END. Gen. 6. 13, the *e.* of all flesh before me.
Ex. 23. 16; Deut. 11. 12, in the *e.* of the year.
Num. 23. 10, let my last *e.* be like his.
Deut. 8. 16, do thee good at thy latter *e.*
32. 29, consider their latter *e.*
Job 6. 11, what is mine *e.*, that I should prolong?
8. 7; 42. 12, thy latter *e.* shall increase.
16. 3, shall vain words have an *e.*?
26. 10, till day and night come to an *e.*
Ps. 7. 9, wickedness of wicked come to an *e.*
9. 6, destructions come to perpetual *e.*
37. 37, the *e.* of that man is peace.
39. 4, make me to know my *e.*
73. 17, then understood I their *e.*
102. 27, the same, thy years have no *e.*
107. 27, are at their wit's *e.*
119. 96, an *e.* of all perfection.
Prov. 14. 12, the *e.* thereof are ways of death.
17. 24, eyes of fool in *e.* of earth.
19. 20, be wise in thy latter *e.*
25. 8, lest thou know not what to do in *e.*
Eccl. 3. 11, find out from beginning to the *e.*
4. 8, no *e.* of all his labour.
16, no *e.* of all the people.
Eccl. 7. 2, that is the *e.* of all men.
8, better the *e.* of a thing.
10. 13, the *e.* of his talk is madness.
12. 12, of making books there is no *e.*
Isa. 9. 7, of his government shall be no *e.*
46. 10, declaring *e.* from beginning.
Jer. 5. 31, what will ye do in *e.* thereof?
8. 20, harvest past, summer *e.*
17. 11, at his *e.* shall be a fool.
29. 11, to give you an expected *e.*
31. 17, there is hope in thine *e.*
Lam. 1. 9, remembereth not her last *e.*
4. 18; Ezek. 7. 2, our *e.* is near, *e.* is come.
Ezek. 21. 25; 35. 5, iniquity shall have an *e.*
Dan. 8. 17, 19; 11. 27, at the time of *e.*
11. 45, he shall come to his *e.*, and none shall help him.
12. 8, what shall be the *e.*?
13, go thy way till the *e.* be.
Hab. 2. 3, at the *e.* it shall speak.
Mat. 10. 22; 24. 13; Mk. 13. 13, endureth to *e.*
13. 39, harvest is *e.* of the world.
24. 3, what sign of the *e.* of the world?
6; Mk. 13. 7; Lu. 21. 9, the *e.* is not yet.
14, then shall the *e.* come.
31, gather from one *e.* of heaven.
26. 58, Peter sat to see the *e.*
28. 20, I am with you, even unto the *e.*
Mk. 3. 26, cannot stand, but hath an *e.*
Lu. 1. 33, of his kingdom there shall be no *e.*
22. 37, things concerning me have an *e.*
John 13. 1, he loved them unto the *e.*
18. 37, to this *e.* was I born.
Rom. 6. 21, the *e.* of those things is death.
22, the *e.* everlasting life.
10. 4, the *e.* of the law for righteousness.
1 Cor. 10. 11, on whom *e.* of world are come.
Phil. 3. 19, whose *e.* is destruction.
1 Tim. 1. 5, the *e.* of the commandment.
Heb. 6. 8, whose *e.* is to be burned.
16, an oath an *e.* of strife.
7. 3, neither beginning nor *e.* of life.
9. 26, once in the *e.* hath he appeared.
13. 7, considering *e.* of their conversation.
Jas. 5. 11, ye have seen *e.* of the Lord.
1 Pet. 1. 9, receiving the *e.* of your faith.
13, be sober, and hope to the *e.*
4. 7, the *e.* of all things is at hand.

17, what shall the *e*. be of them that obey not?
Rev. 2. 26, keepeth my works unto *e*.
21. 6; 22. 13, the beginning and the *e*.
See Ps. 19. 6; 65. 5; Isa. 45. 22; 52. 10; Jer. 4. 27.
ENDAMAGE. Ezra 4. 13.
ENDANGER. Eccl. 10. 9; Dan. 1. 10.
ENDEAVOUR. Ps. 28. 4; Eph. 4. 3; 2 Pet. 1. 15.
ENDLESS. 1 Tim. 1. 4; Heb. 7. 16.
ENDUE. Gen. 30. 20; 2 Chron. 2. 12; Lu. 24. 49; Jas. 3. 13.
ENDURE. Gen. 33. 14, as the children be able to *e*.
Esth. 8. 6, how can I *e*. to see evil?
Job 8. 15, hold it fast, but it shall not *e*.
31. 23, I could not *e*.
Ps. 9. 7; 102. 12; 104. 31, Lord shall *e*. for ever.
30. 5, anger *e*. a moment, weeping *e*. for a night.
52. 1, goodness of God *e*. continually.
72. 5, as long as sun and moon *e*.
17, his name shall *e*. for ever.
100. 5, his truth *e*. to all generations.
106. 1; 107. 1; 118. 1; 136. 1; 138. 8; Jer. 33. 11, his mercy *e*. for ever.
111. 3; 112. 3, 9, his righteousness *e*. for ever.
119. 160, every one of thy judgments *e*.
135. 13, thy name, O Lord, *e*. for ever.
145. 13, thy dominion *e*.
Prov. 27. 24, doth *e*. to every generation.
Ezek. 22. 14, can thy heart *e*.?
Mat. 10. 22; 24. 13; Mk. 13. 13, *e*. to the end.
Mk. 4. 17, so *e*. but for a time.
John 6. 27, meat that *e*. unto life.
Rom. 9. 22, God *e*. with much longsuffering.
1 Cor. 13. 7, charity *e*. all things.
2 Tim. 2. 3, *e*. hardness as good soldier.
4. 3, they will not *e*. sound doctrine.
5, watch, *e*. afflictions.
Heb. 10. 34, in heaven a better and *e*. substance.
Heb. 12. 7, if ye *e*. chastening.
Jas. 1. 12, blessed is man that *e*. temptation.
5. 11, we count them happy which *e*.
1 Pet. 1. 25, the word of the Lord *e*. for ever.
2. 19, if a man for conscience *e*. grief.
See Heb. 10. 32; 11. 27; 12. 2, 3.
ENEMY. Ex. 23. 22, I will be *e*. to thine *e*.
Deut. 32. 31, our *e*. themselves being judges.
Josh. 7. 12, Israel turned backs before *e*.
Judg. 5. 31, so let all thy *e*. perish.
1 Sam. 24. 19, if man find *e*., will he let him go?
1 Kings 21. 20, hast thou found me, O mine *e*.?
Job 13. 24, wherefore holdest thou me for *e*.?
Ps. 8. 2, still the *e*. and avenger.
23. 5, in presence of mine *e*.
38. 19, mine *e*. are lively.
61. 3, a strong tower from the *e*.
72. 9, his *e*. shall lick the dust.
119. 98, wiser than mine *e*.
127. 5, speak with *e*. in the gate.
139. 22, I count them mine *e*.
Prov. 16. 7, maketh his *e*. at peace.
24. 17, rejoice not when *e*. falleth.
25. 21; Rom. 12. 20, if *e*. hunger, give bread.
27. 6, kisses of *e*. deceitful.
Isa. 9. 11, Lord shall join *e*. together.
59. 19, when *e*. shall come in like a flood.
63. 10, he was turned to be their *e*.
Jer. 15. 11, will cause *e*. to entreat thee well.
30. 14, wounded thee with wound of *e*.
Mic. 7. 6, man's *e*. men of his own house.
Mat. 5. 43, said, thou shalt hate thine *e*
44; Lu. 6. 27, 35, I say, love your *e*.
13. 25, 28, 39, his *e*. sowed tares.
Lu. 19. 43, thine *e*. shall cast a trench.
Acts 13. 10, thou *e*. of all righteousness.
Rom. 5. 10, if when *e*. we were reconciled.
11. 28, concerning the gospel they are *e*.
Gal. 4. 16, am I become your *e*.?
Phil. 3. 18, the *e*. of the cross.
Col. 1. 21, were *e*. in your mind.
2 Thess. 3. 15, count him not as an *e*.
Jas. 4. 4, friend of the world is the *e*. of God.
See Ps. 110. 1; Isa. 62. 8; Jer. 15. 14; Heb. 10. 13.
ENGAGED. Jer. 30. 21.
ENGINES. 2 Chron. 26. 15, and he made in Jerusalem *e*.
Ezek. 26. 9, and he shall set *e*. of war.
ENGRAFTED. Jas. 1. 21.
ENGRAVE. Ex. 28. 11; 35. 35; 38. 23; Zech. 3. 9; 2 Cor. 3. 7.
ENJOIN. Job 36. 23; Philem. 8; Heb. 9. 20.
ENJOY. Lev. 26. 34; 2 Chron. 36. 21, land shall *e*. her sabbaths.
Eccl. 2. 1, *e*. pleasure, this also is vanity.
24; 3. 13; 5. 18, soul *e*. good.
1 Tim. 6. 17, giveth us all things to *e*.
See Num. 36. 8; Isa. 65. 22; Heb. 11. 25.
ENLARGE. Deut. 12. 20, when the Lord shall *e*. thy border.
Ps. 4. 1, thou hast *e*. me in distress.
25. 17, troubles of heart *e*.
119. 32, when thou shalt *e*. my heart.
Isa. 5. 14, hell hath *e*. herself.
2 Cor. 6. 11, 13; 10. 15, our heart is *e*.
See Isa. 54. 2; Hab. 2. 5; Mat. 23. 5.
ENLIGHTEN. Ps. 19. 8; Eph. 1. 18; Heb. 6. 4.
ENMITY. Rom. 8. 7, carnal mind is *e*.
Eph. 2. 15, 16, having abolished the *e*.
Jas. 4. 4, friendship of world *e*. with God.
See Gen. 3. 15; Num. 35. 21; Lu. 23. 12.
ENOUGH. Gen. 33. 9, 11, I have *e*., my brother.
45. 28, it is *e*., Joseph is alive.
Ex. 36. 5, people bring more than *e*.
2 Sam. 24. 16; 1 Kings 19. 4; 1 Chron. 21. 15; Mk. 14. 41; Lu. 22. 38, it is *e*., stay thine hand.
Prov. 28. 19, shall have poverty *e*.
30. 15, four things say not, it is *e*.
16, fire saith not, it is *e*.
Isa. 56. 11, dogs which can never have *e*.
Jer. 49. 9, will destroy till they have *e*.
Hos. 4. 10, eat, and not have *e*.
Obad. 5, stolen till they had *e*.
Mal. 3. 10, room *e*. to receive it.
Mat. 10. 25, *e*. for disciple.
25. 9, lest there be not *e*.
See Deut. 1. 6; 2 Chron. 31. 10; Hag. 1. 6; Lu. 15. 17.
ENQUIRE. Ex. 18. 15, people come to me to *e*. of God.
2 Sam. 16. 23, as if a man had *e*. of oracle.
2 Kings 3. 11, is there not a prophet to *e*.?
Ps. 78. 34, returned and *e*. early after God.
Ezek. 14. 3, should I be *e*. of at all by them?
20. 3, 31, I will not be *e*.
36. 37, I will yet for this be *e*. of.
Zeph. 1. 6, those that have not *e*. for.
Mat. 10. 11, *e*. who in it is worthy.
1 Pet. 1. 10, of which salvation the prophets *e*.
See Deut. 12. 30; Isa. 21. 12; John 4. 52.
ENRICH. 1 Sam. 17. 25; Ps. 65. 9; Ezek. 27. 33; 1 Cor. 1. 5; 2 Cor. 9. 11.
ENSAMPLE. 1 Cor. 10. 11, happened to them for *e*.
Phil. 3. 17, as ye have us for an *e*.
2 Thess. 3. 9, to make ourselves an *e*.
See 1 Thess. 1. 7; 1 Pet. 5. 3; 2 Pet. 2. 6.
ENSIGN. Ps. 74. 4; Isa. 5. 26; 11. 10; 18. 3; 30. 17.
ENSNARED. Job 34. 30.
ENSUE. 1 Pet. 3. 11.
ENTANGLE. Ex. 14. 3; Mat. 22. 15; Gal. 5. 1.
ENTER. Ps. 100. 4, *e*. his gates with thanksgiving.
119. 130, the *e*. of thy word giveth light.
Isa. 26. 2, righteous nation may *e*. in.
20. *e*. thou into thy chambers.
Ezek. 44. 5, mark well *e*. in of the house.
Mat. 6. 6, prayest, *e*. into thy closet.
7. 13; Lu. 13. 24, *e*. in at strait gate.
10. 11; Lu. 10. 8, 10, what city ye *e*.
18. 8; Mk. 9. 43, better to *e*. into life.
19. 17, if thou wilt *e*. into life, keep.
25. 21, well done, *e*. into joy.
Mk. 5. 12; Lu. 8. 32, we may *e*. into swine.
14. 38; Lu. 22. 46, lest ye *e*. into temptation.

Lu. 9. 34, feared as they *e.* cloud.
13. 24, many will seek to *e.*
John 3. 4, can he *e.*?
4. 38, ye are *e.* into their labours.
10. 1, 2, *e.* not by the door.
Rom. 5. 12, sin *e.* into world.
1 Cor. 2. 9, neither have *e.* into heart of man.
Heb. 3. 11, 18, shall not *e.* into rest.
4. 10, he that is *e.* into rest.
6. 20, forerunner is for us *e.*
2 Pet. 1. 11, so an *e.* shall be ministered.
See Ps. 143. 2; Prov. 17. 10; Mat. 15. 17.
ENTICE. Judg. 14. 15; 16. 5, *e.* husband that he may declare.
2 Chron. 18. 19, Lord said, who shall *e.* Ahab?
Prov. 1. 10, if sinners *e.* thee.
1 Cor. 2. 4; Col. 2. 4, with *e.* words.
See Job 31. 27; Prov. 16. 29; Jas. 1. 14.
ENTIRE. Jas. 1. 4.
ENTREAT. Mat. 22. 6; Lu. 18. 32, *e.* them spitefully.
ENTRY. 1 Chron. 9. 19; Prov. 8. 3; Ezek. 8. 5; 40. 38.
ENVIRON. Josh. 7. 9.
ENVY. Job 5. 2, *e.* slayeth the silly one.
Ps. 73. 3, I was *e.* at the foolish.
Prov. 3. 31, *e.* not the oppressor.
14. 30, *e.* is rottenness of the bones.
23. 17, let not heart *e.* sinners.
24. 1, 19, be not *e.* against evil men.
27. 4, who is able to stand before *e.*?
Eccl. 4. 4, for this a man is *e.*
9. 6, their love, hatred, and *e.* is perished.
Mat. 27. 18; Mk. 15. 10, for *e.* they delivered.
Acts 7. 9, patriarchs moved with *e.*
13. 45; 17. 5, Jews filled with *e.*
Rom. 1. 29, full of *e.*, murder.
13. 13, walk honestly, not in *e.*
1 Cor. 3. 3, among you *e.* and strife.
13. 4, charity *e.* not.
2 Cor. 12. 20, I fear lest there be *e.*
Gal. 5. 21, works of flesh are *e.*, murders.
26, *e.* one another.
Phil. 1. 15, preach Christ even of *e.*
1 Tim. 6. 4, whereof cometh *e.*
Tit. 3. 3, living in malice and *e.*
Jas. 4. 5, spirit in us lusteth to *e.*
See Gen. 37. 11; Ps. 106. 16; Ezek. 31. 9; 35. 11.
EPHAH. Ex. 16. 36, now an omer is the tenth part of an *e.*
Lev. 19. 36, a just *e.* shall ye have.
Ezek. 45. 10, ye shall have just balances, and a just *e.*
Zech. 5. 6, this is an *e.* that goeth forth.
EPHOD. Ex. 28. 6, they shall make the *e.* of gold.
Ex. 39. 2, and he made the *e.* of gold.
Judg. 8. 27, and Gideon made an *e.* thereof.
17. 5, and made an *e.*
EPISTLE. 2 Cor. 3. 1, nor need *e.* of commendation.
2, ye are our *e.*
3, to be the *e.* of Christ.
2 Thess. 2. 15; 3. 14, by word or *e.*
2 Pet. 3. 16, as also in all his *e.*
See Acts 15. 30; 23. 33; 2 Cor. 7. 8; 2 Thess. 3. 17.
EQUAL. Ps. 17. 2, eyes behold things that are *e.*
55. 13, a man mine *e.*, my guide.
Prov. 26. 7, legs of lame not *e.*
Isa. 40. 25; 46. 5, to whom shall I be *e.*?
Ezek. 18. 25, 29; 33. 17, 20, is not my way *e.*?
Mat. 20. 12, hast made him *e.* to us.
Lu. 20. 36, are *e.* to angels.
John 5. 18; Phil. 2. 6, *e.* with God.
Col. 4. 1, give servants what is *e.*
See Ex. 36. 22; 2 Cor. 8. 14; Gal. 1. 14.
EQUITY. Ps. 98. 9, judge the people with *e.*
Prov 1. 3, receive instruction of *e.*
2. 9, understand judgment and *e.*
17. 26, not good to strike princes for *e.*
Eccl. 2. 21, a man whose labour is in *e.*
See Isa. 11. 4; 59. 14; Mic. 3. 9; Mal. 2. 6.

ERECTED. Gen. 33. 20.
ERR. Ps. 95. 10, people that do *e.* in their heart.
119. 21, do *e.* from thy commandments.
Isa. 3. 12; 9. 16, lead thee cause to *e.*
28. 7, they *e.* in vision.
35. 8, wayfaring men shall not *e.*
Mat. 22. 29; Mk. 12. 24, *e.*, not knowing scriptures.
1 Tim. 6. 10, have *e.* from the faith.
21, have *e.* concerning the faith.
Jas. 1. 16, do not *e.*, beloved brethren.
5. 19, if any do *e.* from truth.
See Isa. 28. 7; 29. 24; Ezek. 45. 20.
ERRAND. Gen. 24. 33; Judg. 3. 19; 2 Kings 9. 5.
ERROR. Ps. 19. 12, who can understand his *e.*?
Eccl. 5. 6, neither say thou, it was an *e.*
10. 5, evil which I have seen as an *e.*
Mat. 27. 64, last *e.* worse than first.
Jas. 5. 20, converteth sinner from *e.*
2 Pet. 3. 17, led away with *e.* of wicked.
1 John 4. 6, the spirit of *e.*
See Job 19. 4; Rom. 1. 27; Heb. 9. 7; Jude 11.
ESCAPE. Gen. 19. 17, *e.* for thy life, *e.* to mountain.
1 Kings 18. 40; 2 Kings 9. 15, let none of them *e.*
Esth. 4. 13, think not thou shalt *e.* in king's house.
Job 11. 20, wicked shall not *e.*
19. 20, *e.* with skin of my teeth.
Ps. 55. 8, I would hasten my *e.*
Prov. 19. 5, speaketh lies shall not *e.*
Eccl. 7. 26, whoso pleaseth God shall *e.*
Isa. 20. 6; Heb. 2. 3, how shall we *e.*?
Ezek. 33. 21, one that had *e.* came to me.
Amos 9. 1, he that *e.* shall not be delivered.
Mat. 23. 33, how can ye *e.* damnation?
Lu. 21. 36, worthy to *e.*
John 10. 39, he *e.* out of their hands.
Acts 27. 44, they *e.* all safe to land.
28. 4, he *e.* sea, yet vengeance.
Heb. 11. 34, through faith *e.* edge of sword.
12. 25, if they *e.* not who refused.
2 Pet. 1. 4, *e.* corruption in the world.
20, after they *e.* pollutions.
See Deut. 23. 15; Ps. 124. 7; 1 Cor. 10. 13.
ESCHEW. Job 1. 1; 2. 3; 1 Pet. 3. 11.
ESPECIALLY. Gal. 6. 10; 1 Tim. 4. 10; 5. 8; Philem. 16.
ESPOUSE. Cant. 3. 11; Jer. 2. 2; 2 Cor. 11. 2.
ESPY. Gen. 42. 27; Josh. 14. 7; Jer. 48. 19; Ezek. 20. 6.
ESTABLISH. Ps. 40. 2, and *e.* my goings.
90. 17, *e.* work of our hands.
Prov. 4. 26, let thy ways be *e.*
12. 19, lip of truth *e.* for ever.
16. 12, throne *e.* by righteousness.
20. 18, every purpose *e.* by counsel.
24. 3, by understanding is house *e.*
29. 4, king by judgment *e.* the land.
Isa. 7. 9, if ye will not believe, ye shall not be *e.*
16. 5, in mercy shall the throne be *e.*
Jer. 10. 12; 51. 15, he *e.* world by wisdom.
Mat. 18. 16, two witnesses every word *e.*
Rom. 3. 31, yea, we *e.* the law.
10. 3, to *e.* their own righteousness.
Heb. 13. 9, the heart be *e.* with grace.
2 Pet. 1. 12, be *e.* in the present truth.
See Amos 5. 15; Hab. 2. 12; Acts 16. 5.
ESTATE. Ps. 136. 23, remembered us in low *e.*
Eccl. 1. 16, lo, I am come to great *e.*
Mk. 6. 21, Herod made supper to chief *e.*
Rom. 12. 16, condescend to men of low *e.*
Jude 6, angels kept not first *e.*
See Ezek. 36. 11; Dan. 11. 7; Lu. 1. 48.
ESTEEM. Deut. 32. 15, lightly *e.* rock of salvation.
1 Sam. 2. 30, despise me shall be lightly *e.*
18. 23, I am a poor man, and lightly *e.*
Job 23. 12, I have *e.* the words of his mouth.
36. 19, will he *e.* thy riches?
41. 27, he *e.* iron as straw.
Ps. 119. 128, I *e.* all thy precepts.
Isa. 53. 4, did *e.* him smitten.

Lam. 4. 2, *e.* as earthen pitchers.
Lu. 16. 15, highly *e.* among men.
Rom. 14. 5, one man *e.* one day above another.
14, that *e.* any thing unclean.
Phil. 2. 3, let each *e.* other better.
1 Thess. 5. 13, *e.* highly for work's sake.
Heb. 11. 26, *e.* reproach greater riches.
See Prov. 17. 28; Isa. 29. 17; 1 Cor. 6. 4.
ESTIMATION. Lev. 27. 2–8, 13; Num. 18. 16.
ESTRANGED. Job 19. 13; Ps. 78. 30; Jer. 19. 4; Ezek. 14. 5.
ETERNAL. Deut. 33. 27, the *e.* God is thy refuge.
Isa. 60. 15, will make thee an *e.* excellency.
Mat. 19. 16; Mk. 10. 17; Lu. 10. 25; 18. 18, what shall I do that I may have *e.* life?
25. 46, righteous into life *e.*
Mk. 3. 29, is in danger of *e.* damnation.
10. 30, receive in world to come *e.* life.
John 3. 15, believeth in him have *e.* life.
4. 36, gathereth fruit unto life *e.*
5. 39, scriptures, in them *e.* life.
6. 54, drinketh my blood hath *e.* life.
68, thou hast words of *e.* life.
10. 28, give sheep *e.* life.
12. 25, hateth life, shall keep it to life *e.*
17. 2, give *e.* life to as many.
3, this is life *e.*, that they might know thee.
Acts 13. 48, many as were ordained to *e.* life.
Rom. 2. 7, who seek for glory, *e.* life.
5. 21, grace reign to *e.* life.
6. 23, gift of God is *e.* life.
2 Cor. 4. 17, an *e.* weight of glory.
18, things not seen are *e.*
5. 1, house *e.* in the heavens.
Eph. 3. 11, according to *e.* purpose.
1 Tim. 6. 12, 19, lay hold on *e.* life.
Tit. 1. 2; 3. 7, in hope of *e.* life.
Heb. 5. 9, author of *e.* salvation.
6. 2, doctrine of *e.* judgment.
9. 15, promise of *e.* inheritance.
1 Pet. 5. 10, called to *e.* glory by Christ.
1 John 1. 2, *e.* life, which was with the Father.
2. 25, this is the promise, even *e.* life.
3. 15, no murderer hath *e.* life.
5. 11, record, that God hath given to us *e.* life.
13, know that ye have *e.* life.
20, this is true God, and *e.* life.
Jude 7, vengeance of *e.* fire.
See Rom. 1. 20; 1 Tim. 1. 17; 2 Tim. 2. 10; Jude 21.
ETERNITY. Isa. 57. 15.
EUNUCHS. Isa. 56. 4, for thus saith the Lord to the *e.*
Mat. 19. 12, for there are some *e.*
Acts 8. 27, an *e.* of great authority.
See Isa. 56. 3.
EVANGELIST. Acts 21. 8; Eph. 4. 11; 2 Tim. 4. 5.
EVENING. 1 Sam. 14. 24, cursed that eateth till *e.*
1 Kings 17. 6, brought bread morning and *e.*
Ps. 90. 6, in *e.* cut down and withereth.
104. 23, goeth to his labour until the *e.*
141. 2, prayer as the *e.* sacrifice.
Eccl. 11. 6, in *e.* withhold not thine hand.
Jer. 6. 4, shadows of *e.* stretched out.
Hab. 1. 8; Zeph. 3. 3, *e.* wolves.
Zech. 14. 7, at *e.* time shall be light.
Mat. 14. 23, when *e.* was come, he was there alone.
Lu. 24. 29, abide, for it is toward *e.*
See Gen. 30. 16; Ps. 65. 8; Mat. 16. 2; Mk. 14. 17.
EVENT. Eccl. 2. 14; 9. 2, 3.
EVER. Gen. 3. 22, lest he eat, and live for *e.*
43. 9; 44. 32, let me bear blame for *e.*
Ex. 14. 13, ye shall see them no more for *e.*
Lev. 6. 13, fire *e.* burning on altar.
Deut. 5. 29; 12. 28, be well with them for *e.*
13. 16, a heap for *e.*
32. 40, lift up hand and say, I live for *e.*
Job 4. 7, who *e.* perished?
Ps. 9. 7, Lord shall endure for *e.*
12. 7, thou wilt preserve them for *e.*
22. 26, your heart shall live for *e.*
23. 6, dwell in house of the Lord for *e.*
29. 10, Lord sitteth king for *e.*
33. 11, counsel of Lord standeth for *e.*
37. 26, he is *e.* merciful, and lendeth.
48. 14, our God for *e.* and *e.*
49. 9, that he should still live for *e.*
51. 3, my sin is *e.* before me.
52. 8, trust in mercy of God for *e.* and *e.*
61. 4, will abide in tabernacle for *e.*
73. 26, my strength and portion for *e.*
74. 19, forget not congregation of poor for *e.*
81. 15, their time should have endured for *e.*
92. 7, they shall be destroyed for *e.*
93. 5, holiness becometh thine house for *e.*
102. 12, thou shalt endure for *e.*
103. 9, not keep his anger for *e.*
105. 8, remember his covenant for *e.*
119. 89, for *e.* thy word is settled.
132. 14, this is my rest for *e.*
146. 6, Lord keepeth truth for *e.*
10, Lord shall reign for *e.*
Prov. 27. 24, riches not for *e.*
Eccl. 3. 14, whatsoever God doeth shall be for *e.*
Isa. 26. 4, trust in Lord for *e.*
32. 17, assurance for *e.*
34. 10; Rev. 14. 11; 19. 3, smoke shall go up for *e.*
40. 8, word of God shall stand for *e.*
57. 16, will not contend for *e.*
Lam. 3. 31, Lord will not cast off for *e.*
Mat. 6. 13, thine is the glory for *e.*
21. 19; Mk. 11. 14, no fruit grow on thee for *e.*
John 8. 35, servant abideth not for *e.*
12. 34, heard that Christ abideth for *e.*
14. 16, Comforter abide for *e.*
Rom. 9. 5, God blessed for *e.*
1 Thess. 4. 17, so shall we *e.* be with the Lord.
5. 15, *e.* follow good.
2 Tim. 3. 7, *e.* learning.
Heb. 7. 25, he *e.* liveth to make.
13. 8, same yesterday, to day, and for *e.*
See Mat. 24. 21; Lu. 15. 31; John 10. 8.
EVERLASTING. Ex. 40. 15; Num. 25. 13, an *e.* priesthood.
Ps. 90. 2, from *e.* to *e.* thou art God.
139. 24, lead me in way *e.*
Prov. 8. 23, I was set up from *e.*
10. 25, righteous is an *e.* foundation.
Isa. 9. 6, called the *e.* Father.
26. 4, in the Lord is *e.* strength.
33. 14, with *e.* burnings.
35. 10; 51. 11; 61. 7, *e.* joy.
45. 17, with *e.* salvation.
54. 8, with *e.* kindness.
55. 13, for an *e.* sign.
56. 5; 63. 12, an *e.* name.
60. 19, 20, an *e.* light.
Jer. 31. 3, with an *e.* love.
Hab. 3. 6, the *e.* mountains.
Mat. 18. 8; 25. 41, into *e.* fire.
19. 29, inherit *e.* life.
25. 46, into *e.* punishment.
Lu. 16. 9, into *e.* habitations.
18. 30, in world to come *e.* life.
John 3. 16, 36, believeth shall have *e.* life.
4. 14, water springing up into *e.* life.
5. 24, heareth my word hath *e.* life.
6. 27, meat which endureth to *e.* life.
40, seeth Son may have *e.* life.
12. 50, his commandment is life *e.*
Acts 13. 46, unworthy of *e.* life.
Rom. 6. 22, free from sin, the end *e.* life.
Gal. 6. 8, of Spirit reap life *e.*
2 Thess. 1. 9, punished with *e.* destruction.
2. 16, given us *e.* consolation.
Jude 6, reserved in *e.* chains.
Rev. 14. 6, having the *e.* gospel.
See Dan. 4. 3; 7. 27; 2 Pet. 1. 11.
EVERMORE. Ps. 16. 11, pleasures for *e.*

37. 27, do good and dwell for *e*.
121. 8, preserve thy going out for *e*.
133. 3, the blessing, life for *e*.
John 6. 34, *e*. give us this bread.
1 Thess. 5. 16, rejoice *e*.
Heb. 7. 28, consecrated for *e*.
Rev. 1. 18, I am alive for *e*.
See 2 Kings 17. 37; Ps. 77. 8; 106. 31.

EVERY. Gen. 4. 14, *e*. one that findeth me shall slay me.
6. 5, *e*. imagination of heart evil.
Lev. 19. 10, neither shalt gather *e*. grape.
Deut. 4. 4, alive *e*. one of you this day.
2 Kings 18. 31, eat *e*. one of his fig tree.
2 Chron. 30. 18, pardon *e*. one.
Ps. 29. 9, *e*. one doth speak of glory.
32. 6, for this shall *e*. one that is godly.
68. 30, till *e*. one submit himself.
119. 101, refrained from *e*. evil way.
Prov. 2. 9, *e*. good path.
7. 12, in *e*. corner.
14. 15, simple believeth *e*. word.
20. 3, *e*. fool will be meddling.
30. 5, *e*. word of God is pure.
Eccl. 10. 3, saith to *e*. one he is a fool.
Jer. 51. 29, *e*. purpose of the Lord.
Mat. 4. 4, by *e*. word that proceedeth.
7. 8; Lu. 11. 10, *e*. one that asketh.
Mk. 1. 45, came from *e*. quarter.
Lu. 19. 26, to *e*. one which hath shall be given.
Rom. 14. 11, *e*. knee bow, *e*. tongue confess.
2 Cor. 10. 5, *e*. thought.
Eph. 1. 21; Phil. 2. 9, far above *e*. name.
1 Tim. 4. 4, *e*. creature of God.
2 Tim. 2. 19, *e*. one that nameth.
21, *e*. good work.
Heb. 12. 1, *e*. weight.
Jas. 1. 17, *e*. good and perfect gift.
1 Pet. 2. 13, *e*. ordinance of man.
1 John 4. 1, believe not *e*. spirit.
7, *e*. one that loveth.
Rev. 6. 11, robes given to *e*. one.
See Gen. 27. 29; Acts 2. 38; 17. 27; 20. 31.

EVIDENCE. Jer. 32. 10; Heb. 11. 1.

EVIDENT. Gal. 3. 1, Christ hath been *e*. set forth.
11, that no man is justified is *e*.
Phil. 1. 28, an *e*. token of perdition.
See Job 6. 28; Heb. 7. 14, 15.

EVIL. Gen. 6. 5; 8. 21, thoughts of heart only *e*.
47. 9, few and *e*. have the days.
Ex. 32. 14; 2 Sam. 24. 16; 1 Chron. 21. 15, repented of the *e*.
Deut. 28. 54, eye *e*. towards his brother.
56, her eye *e*. towards husband.
Job 2. 10, receive good, and not *e*.
30. 26, looked for good, then *e*. came.
Ps. 34. 14; 37. 27; Prov. 3. 7, depart from *e*.
35. 12; 109. 5, they rewarded me *e*.
40. 12, innumerable *e*. have compassed.
Prov. 14. 19, *e*. bow before the good.
15. 3, beholding the *e*. and good.
17. 13, whoso rewardeth *e*. for good.
Isa. 1. 4, a seed of *e*.-doers.
5. 20, that call *e*. good, and good *e*.
7. 15, 16, refuse the *e*. and choose the good.
Jer. 2. 13, have committed two *e*.
19, know it is an *e*. thing and bitter.
24. 3; 29. 17, *e*. figs, very *e*.
42. 6, whether good or *e*., we will obey.
Mat. 5. 45, rise on *e*. and good.
6. 34, sufficient unto the day is the *e*. thereof.
7. 11; Lu. 11. 13, if ye, being *e*.
18, good tree cannot bring forth *e*.
9. 4, wherefore think *e*. in your hearts?
Mk. 9. 39, lightly speak *e*. of me.
Lu. 6. 22, cast out your name as *e*.
35, he is kind to the *e*.
Lu. 6. 45, *e*. man bringeth forth *e*.
John 3. 20, doeth *e*. hateth light.
18. 23, if I have spoken *e*.
Acts 23. 5, not speak *e*. of ruler.
Rom. 7. 19, the *e*. I would not.
12. 9, abhor that which is *e*.
17, recompense to no man *e*. for *e*.
21, overcome *e*. with good.
1 Thess. 5. 22, appearance of *e*.
1 Tim. 6. 10, the root of all *e*.
2 Tim. 4. 18; Jas. 3. 16, every *e*. work.
Tit. 3. 2, speak *e*. of no man.
Jas. 3. 8, tongue an unruly *e*.
1 Pet. 3. 9, not rendering *e*. for *e*.
See Prov. 13. 21; Isa. 45. 7; Eccl. 12. 1; Eph. 5. 16; 6. 13.

EXACT. Deut. 15. 2, shall not *e*. it of neighbour.
Neh. 5. 7, 10, 11, you *e*. usury.
10. 31, leave the *e*. of every debt.
Job 11. 6, God *e*. of thee less.
Lu. 3. 13, *e*. no more than what is.
See Ps. 89. 22; Isa. 58. 3; 60. 17.

EXALT. 1 Chron. 29. 11, *e*. as head above all.
Ps. 12. 8, when vilest men are *e*.
34. 3, let us *e*. his name together.
92. 10, my horn shalt thou *e*.
97. 9, *e*. far above all gods.
Prov. 4. 8, *e*. her, and she shall promote thee.
11. 11, by blessing of upright the city is *e*.
14. 29, he that is hasty of spirit *e*. folly.
34, righteousness *e*. a nation.
17. 19, he that *e*. his gate.
Isa. 2. 2; Mic. 4. 1, mountain of Lord's house *e*.
40. 4, every valley shall be *e*.
Ezek. 21. 26, *e*. him that is low.
Mat. 11. 23; Lu. 10. 15, *e*. to heaven.
23. 12; Lu. 14. 11; 18. 14, *e*. himself shall be abased.
2 Cor. 11. 20, if a man *e*. himself.
12. 7, *e*. above measure.
Phil. 2. 9, God hath highly *e*. him.
2 Thess. 2. 4, *e*. himself above all that is called.
1 Pet. 5. 6, he may *e*. in due time.
See Ex. 15. 2; Job 24. 24; Lu. 1. 52; Jas. 1. 9.

EXAMINE. Ps. 26. 2, *e*. me, O Lord.
Acts 4. 9, if we this day be *e*.
22. 24, 29, *e*. by scourging.
1 Cor. 11. 28, let a man *e*. himself.
2 Cor. 13. 5, *e*. yourselves.
See Ezra 10. 16; Acts 24. 8; 25. 26; 1 Cor. 9. 3.

EXAMPLE. John 13. 15, I have given you an *e*.
1 Tim. 4. 12, be thou an *e*. of believers.
1 Pet. 2. 21, Christ suffered, leaving an *e*.
Jude 7, an *e*., suffering vengeance.
See Mat. 1. 19; 1 Cor. 10. 6; Heb. 4. 11; 8. 5.

EXCEED. Mat. 5. 20, except righteousness *e*.
2 Cor. 3. 9, ministration doth *e*. in glory.
See 1 Sam. 20. 41; 2 Chron. 9. 6; Job 36. 9.

EXCEEDING. Gen. 15. 1, thy *e*. great reward.
27. 34, an *e*. bitter cry.
Num. 14. 7, land is *e*. good.
1 Sam. 2. 3, so *e*. proud.
Ps. 21. 6, *e*. glad with thy countenance.
43. 4, God my *e*. joy.
119. 96, commandment *e*. broad.
Prov. 30. 24, four things *e*. wise.
Jon. 1. 16, men feared the Lord *e*.
4. 6, *e*. glad of the gourd.
Mat. 2. 10, with *e*. great joy.
4. 8, an *e*. high mountain.
5. 12, rejoice and be *e*. glad.
8. 28, possessed with devils, *e*. fierce.
17. 23; 26. 22, they were *e*. sorry.
19. 25, they were *e*. amazed.
26. 38; Mk. 14. 34, my soul is *e*. sorrowful.
Mk. 6. 26, king *e*. sorry.
9. 3, raiment *e*. white.
Lu. 23. 8, Herod was *e*. glad.
Acts 7. 20, Moses was *e*. fair.
26. 11, being *e*. mad against them.
Rom. 7. 13, sin might become *e*. sinful.
2 Cor. 4. 17, *e*. weight of glory.
7. 4, *e*. joyful in our tribulation.
Gal. 1. 14, *e*. zealous of traditions.

Eph. 1. 19, the *e.* greatness of his power.
Eph. 2. 7, the *e.* riches of his grace.
3. 20, able to do *e.* abundantly.
2 Thess. 1. 3, your faith groweth *e.*
2 Pet. 1. 4, *e.* great and precious promises.
Jude 24, present you faultless with *e.* joy.
See 1 Sam. 26. 21; Jonah 3. 3; Heb. 12. 21.
EXCEL. Gen. 49. 4, thou shalt not *e.*
Prov. 31. 29, thou *e.* them all.
Eccl. 2. 13, wisdom *e.* folly.
2 Cor. 3. 10, the glory that *e.*
See Ps. 103. 20; 1 Cor. 14. 12.
EXCELLENCY. Ex. 15. 7, the greatness of thine *e.*
Job 4. 21, doth not their *e.* go away?
13. 11, shall not his *e.* make you afraid?
Isa. 60. 15, will make thee an eternal *e.*
1 Cor. 2. 1, not with *e.* of speech.
2 Cor. 4. 7, that the *e.* of the power.
Phil. 3. 8, loss for the *e.* of Christ.
See Gen. 49. 3; Ex. 15. 7; Eccl. 7. 12; Ezek. 24. 21.
EXCELLENT. Job 37. 23, *e.* in power.
Ps. 8. 1, 9, how *e.* is thy name!
16. 3, to the *e.*, in whom is my delight.
36. 7, how *e.* thy lovingkindness!
Prov. 8. 6; 22. 20, I will speak of *e.* things.
12. 26, righteous more *e.* than neighbour.
17. 7, *e.* speech becometh not a fool.
27, of an *e.* spirit.
Isa. 12. 5, he hath done *e.* things.
28. 29, is *e.* in working.
Dan. 5. 12; 6. 3, *e.* spirit found in Daniel.
Rom. 2. 18; Phil. 1. 10, things more *e.*
1 Cor. 12. 31, a more *e.* way.
2 Pet. 1. 17, voice from the *e.* glory.
See Cant. 5. 15; Lu. 1. 3; Heb. 1. 4; 8. 6; 11. 4.
EXCEPT. Gen. 32. 26, *e.* thou bless me.
Deut. 32. 30, *e.* their Rock had sold them.
Ps. 127. 1, *e.* Lord build house.
Amos 3. 3, *e.* they be agreed.
Mat. 5. 20, *e.* your righteousness exceed.
18. 3, *e.* ye be converted.
24. 22; Mk. 13. 20, *e.* days be shortened.
Mk. 7. 3, Pharisees *e.* they wash oft.
Lu. 13. 3; Rev. 2. 5, 22, *e.* ye repent.
John 3. 2, *e.* God be with him.
5, *e.* man be born again.
4. 48, *e.* ye see signs and wonders.
20. 25, *e.* I see print of nails.
Acts 26. 29, *e.* these bonds.
Rom. 10. 15, how preach, *e.* they be sent?
1 Cor. 15. 36, *e.* it die.
2 Tim. 2. 5, *e.* he strive lawfully.
See Rom. 7. 7; 1 Cor. 14. 5; 15. 27; 2 Thess. 2. 3.
EXCESS. Mat. 23. 25; Eph. 5. 18; 1 Pet. 4. 3, 4.
EXCHANGE. Mat. 16. 26; Mk. 8. 37, in *e.* for his soul.
25. 27, put money to *e.*
See Gen. 47. 17; Lev. 27. 10; Ezek. 48. 14.
EXCLUDE. Rom. 3. 27; Gal. 4. 17.
EXCUSE. Lu. 14. 18; Rom. 1. 20; 2. 15; 2 Cor. 12. 19.
EXECRATION. Jer. 42. 18; 44. 12.
EXECUTE. Deut. 33. 21, he *e.* the justice of the Lord.
1 Chron. 6. 10; 24. 2; Lu. 1. 8, *e.* priest's office.
Ps. 9. 16, Lord known by the judgment he *e.*
103. 6, Lord *e.* righteousness and judgment.
Jer. 5. 1, if any *e.* judgment, I will pardon.
John 5. 27, authority to *e.* judgment.
Rom. 13. 4, minister of God to *e.* wrath.
See Hos. 11. 9; Mic. 5. 15; Joel. 2. 11.
EXERCISE. Ps. 131. 1, *e.* myself in things too high.
Jer. 9. 24, *e.* lovingkindness.
Mat. 20. 25; Mk. 10. 42; Lu. 22. 25, *e.* dominion.
Acts 24. 16, I *e.* myself to have a conscience.
1 Tim. 4. 7, *e.* thyself unto godliness.
Heb. 5. 14, *e.* to discern good and evil.
12. 11, to them which are *e.* thereby.
2 Pet. 2. 14, heart *e.* with covetous practices.
See Eccl. 1. 13; 3. 10; Ezek. 22. 29; Rev. 13. 12.
EXHORT. Lu. 3. 18, many things in his *e.*
Acts 13. 15, any words of *e.*
Rom. 12. 8, he that *e.*, on *e.*
1 Tim. 6. 2, these things *e.* and teach.
Tit. 1. 9, may be able to *e.*
2. 15, *e.* and rebuke with authority.
Heb. 3. 13; 10. 25, *e.* one another daily.
Heb. 13. 22, suffer word of *e.*
See Acts 11. 23; 2 Cor. 9. 5; Tit. 2. 6, 9.
EXILE. 2 Sam. 15. 19; Isa. 51. 14.
EXPECTATION. Ps. 9. 18, the *e.* of the poor.
62. 5, my *e.* is from him.
Prov. 10. 28; 11. 7, 23, *e.* of the wicked.
Isa. 20. 5, ashamed of their *e.*
6, such is our *e.*
Rom. 8. 19, the *e.* of the creature.
Phil. 1. 20, my earnest *e.* and hope.
See Jer. 29. 11; Acts 3. 5; Heb. 10. 13.
EXPEL. Josh. 23. 5; Judg. 11. 7; 2 Sam. 14. 14.
EXPENSES. Ezra 6. 4, 8.
EXPERIENCE. Gen. 30. 27; Eccl. 1. 16; Rom. 5. 4.
EXPLOITS. Dan. 11. 28, 32.
EXPOUND. Judg. 14. 14, 19, could not *e.* riddle.
Mk. 4. 34, when they were alone, he *e.* all things.
Lu. 24. 27, *e.* the scriptures.
See Acts 11. 4; 18. 26; 28. 23.
EXPRESS. Heb. 1. 3.
EXPRESSLY. 1 Sam. 20. 21; Ezek. 1. 3; 1 Tim. 4. 1.
EXTEND. Ps. 16. 2; 109. 12; Isa. 66. 12.
EXTINCT. Job 17. 1; Isa. 43. 17.
EXTOL. Ps. 30. 1; 145. 1, I will *e.* thee.
68. 4, *e.* him that rideth.
See Ps. 66. 17; Isa. 52. 13; Dan. 4. 37.
EXTORTION. Ezek. 22. 12; Mat. 23. 25.
EXTORTIONER. Ps. 109. 11, let *e.* catch all he hath.
Isa. 16. 4, the *e.* is at an end.
1 Cor. 5. 11, if any man be an *e.*
See Lu. 18. 11; 1 Cor. 5. 10; 6. 10.
EXTREME. Deut. 28. 22; Job 35. 15.
EYE. Gen. 3. 6, pleasant to the *e.*
7, *e.* of both were opened.
27. 1, his *e.* were dim.
49. 12, his *e.* shall be red with wine.
Num. 10. 31, be to us instead of *e.*
16. 14, wilt thou put out *e.*?
24. 3, 15, man whose *e.* are open said.
Deut. 3. 27, lift up *e.*, behold with thine *e.*
12. 8; Judg. 17. 6; 21. 25, right in own *e.*
16. 19, gift blind *e.* of wise.
28. 32, *e.* look, and fail with longing.
32. 10, kept him as apple of *e.*
34. 7, his *e.* was not dim.
1 Kings 1. 20, *e.* of all Israel upon thee.
8. 29, 52; 2 Chron. 6. 20, 40, *e.* open towards this house.
20. 6, whatsoever is pleasant in thine *e.*
2 Kings 6. 17, Lord opened *e.* of young man.
20, open the *e.* of these men.
2 Chron. 16. 9; Zech. 4. 10, *e.* of Lord run to and fro.
34. 28, nor thine *e.* see all the evil.
Job 7. 8; 20. 9, *e.* that hath seen me.
11. 20, the *e.* of wicked shall fail.
15. 12, what do thine *e.* wink at?
19. 27, mine *e.* shall behold, and not another.
28. 7, path vulture's *e.* hath not seen.
10, his *e.* seeth every precious thing.
29. 11, when the *e.* saw me.
15, I was *e.* to the blind.
31. 16, caused *e.* of widow to fail.
Ps. 11. 4, his *e.* try children of men.
15. 4, in whose *e.* a vile person.
19. 8, enlightening the *e.*
33. 18, *e.* of Lord on them that fear him.
34. 15; 1 Pet. 3. 12, *e.* of Lord on the righteous.
36. 1, no fear of God before his *e.*
69. 3; 119. 82, 123; Lam. 2. 11, mine *e.* fail.
77. 4, holdest mine *e.* waking.

Ps. 116. 8, delivered mine *e.* from tears.
119. 18, open mine *e.*
132. 4, not give sleep to mine *e.*
Prov. 10. 26, as smoke to the *e.*
20. 12, the seeing *e.*
22. 9, a bountiful *e.*
23. 29, redness of *e.*
27. 20, the *e.* of man never satisfied.
30. 17, the *e.* that mocketh.
Eccl. 1. 8, *e.* is not satisfied with seeing.
2. 14, wise man's *e.* are in his head.
6. 9, better sight of *e.* than wandering of desire.
11. 7, for the *e.* to behold the sun.
Isa. 1. 16, I will hide mine *e.* from you.
Isa. 29. 10, the Lord hath closed *e.*
33. 17, thine *e.* shall see the king in his beauty.
40. 26; Jer. 13. 20, lift up your *e.* on high.
Jer. 5. 21; Ezek. 12. 2, have *e.* and see not.
9. 1, mine *e.* a fountain of tears.
13. 17, mine *e.* shall weep sore.
14. 17, let mine *e.* run down with tears.
24. 6, set mine *e.* upon them for good.
Lam. 2. 18, let not apple of *e.* cease.
Ezek. 24. 16, 25, the desire of thine *e.*
Hab. 1. 13, of purer *e.* than to behold evil.
Mat. 5. 29, if right *e.* offend thee.
13. 16, blessed are your *e.*
18. 9; Mk. 9. 47, to enter with one *e.*
Mk. 8. 18, having *e.*, see ye not?
Lu. 1. 2, from beginning were *e.*-witnesses.
24. 16, their *e.* were holden.
John 11. 37, could not this man, which opened *e.*
Gal. 4. 15, have plucked out your *e.*
Eph. 1. 18, the *e.* of your understanding.
2 Pet. 2. 14, having *e.* full of adultery.
1 John 2. 16, the lust of the *e.*
See Deut. 11. 12; Ezra 5. 5; Ps. 32. 8; Prov. 3. 7; 12. 15; 15. 3; 16. 2; 21. 2; Mat. 20. 33; John 10. 21; 1 Pet. 3. 12.

EYESERVICE. Eph. 6. 6; Col. 3. 22, not with *e.* as menpleasers.

F

FABLES. 1 Tim. 1. 4; 4. 7; 2 Tim. 4. 4; Tit. 1. 14; 2 Pet. 1. 16.

FACE. Gen. 4. 14, from thy *f.* shall I be hid.
32. 30, I have seen God *f.* to *f.*
Ex. 33. 11, Lord spake to Moses *f.* to *f.*
34. 29, skin of *f.* shone.
33; 2 Cor. 3. 13, put vail on *f.*
Lev. 19. 32, shall honour the *f.* of the old man.
Deut. 25. 9, spit in *f.*, saying.
1 Sam. 5. 3, Dagon was fallen on his *f.*
2 Kings 4. 29, 31, lay staff on *f.* of child.
14. 8, let us look one another in *f.*
Ezra 9. 7; Dan. 9. 7, confusion of *f.*
Neh. 8. 6, worshipped with *f.* to ground.
Job 1. 11; 2. 5, curse thee to thy *f.*
4. 15, spirit passed before my *f.*
13. 24; Ps. 44. 24; 88. 14, wherefore hidest thou thy *f.*?
Ps. 13. 1, how long wilt thou hide thy *f.*?
27. 9; 69. 17; 102. 2; 143. 7, hide not thy *f.*
34. 5, *f.* not ashamed.
59. 2, sins have hid his *f.* from you.
84. 9, look upon *f.* of anointed.
Prov. 27. 19, in water *f.* answereth to *f.*
Eccl. 8. 1, wisdom maketh *f.* to shine.
Isa. 3. 15, ye grind *f.* of the poor.
25. 8, wipe tears from off all *f.*
50. 7, set my *f.* like flint.
Jer. 2. 27, turned their back, and not *f.*
5. 3, their *f.* harder than a rock.
30. 6, all *f.* turned into paleness.
Dan. 10. 6, *f.* as appearance of lightning.
Hos. 5. 5, testifieth to his *f.*
Mat. 6. 17, wash thy *f.*
11. 10; Mk. 1. 2; Lu. 7. 27, messenger before *f.*
16. 3; Lu. 12. 56, discern *f.* of sky.
17. 2, his *f.* did shine as sun.
18. 10, angels behold *f.* of my Father.
Lu. 2. 31, before *f.* of all people.
9. 51, 53, set his *f.* to Jerusalem.
22. 64, struck him on *f.*
1 Cor. 13. 12, then *f.* to *f.*
2 Cor. 3. 18, all, with open *f.*
Gal. 1. 22, I was unknown by *f.*
2. 11, withstood him to the *f.*
Jas. 1. 23, beholding *f.* in glass.
Rev. 20. 11, from whose *f.* earth fled away.
See 1 Kings 19. 13; Dan. 1. 10; Acts 6. 15; 20. 25.

FADE. Isa. 1. 30, whose leaf *f.*
24. 4, earth mourneth and *f.*, the world *f.*
40. 7, the flower *f.*
64. 6, all *f.* as a leaf.
Jer. 8. 13, and the leaf shall *f.*
Ezek. 47. 12, whose leaf shall not *f.*
1 Pet. 1. 4; 5. 4, inheritance that *f.* not away.
Jas. 1. 11, rich man shall *f.* away.
See 2 Sam. 22. 46; Ps. 18. 45; Isa. 28. 1.

FAIL. Gen. 47. 16, if money *f.*
Deut. 28. 32, thine eyes shall *f.* with longing.
Josh. 21. 45; 23. 14; 1 Kings 8. 56, there *f.* not any good thing.
1 Sam. 17. 32, let no man's heart *f.* him.
1 Kings 2. 4; 8. 25, shall not *f.* a man on throne.
17. 14, neither shall cruse of oil *f.*
Ezra 4. 22, take heed that ye *f.* not.
Job 14. 11, as waters *f.* from sea.
19. 14, my kinsfolk have *f.*
Ps. 12. 1, the faithful *f.* among men.
31. 10; 38. 10, my strength *f.* me.
77. 8, doth his promise *f.*
89. 33, nor suffer my faithfulness to *f.*
142. 4, refuge *f.* me.
Eccl. 10. 3, his wisdom *f.* him.
12. 5, desire shall *f.*
Isa. 15. 6, the grass *f.*
19. 5, waters shall *f.*
31. 3, they shall all *f.* together.
32. 6, cause drink of thirsty to *f.*
10, the vintage shall *f.*
34. 16, no one of these shall *f.*
38. 14, eyes *f.* with looking upward.
41. 17, tongue *f.* for thirst.
59. 15, truth *f.*
Jer. 14. 6, their eyes did *f.*
15. 18, as waters that *f.*
48. 33, I caused wine to *f.*
Lam. 3. 22, his compassions *f.* not.
4. 17, our eyes as yet *f.*
Ezek. 12. 22, every vision *f.*
Amos 8. 4, make poor of land to *f.*
Hab. 3. 17, labour of olive shall *f.*
Lu. 12. 33, treasure that *f.* not.
16. 9, when ye *f.* they may receive you.
17, one tittle of law *f.*
21. 26, hearts *f.* them for fear.
22. 32, that thy faith *f.* not.
1 Cor. 13. 8, charity never *f.*
Heb. 1. 12, thy years shall not *f.*
11. 32, time would *f.* me to tell.
12. 15, lest any man *f.* of grace of God.
See Deut. 31. 6; Ps. 40. 12; 143. 7; Isa. 44. 12.

FAIN. Job 27. 22; Lu. 15. 16.

FAINT. Gen. 25. 29, 30, came from field, and he was *f.*
45. 26, Jacob's heart *f.*
Judg. 8. 4, *f.* yet pursuing.
Job 4. 5, now it is come, and thou *f.*
Ps. 27. 13, I had *f.*, unless I had believed.
107. 5, their soul *f.* in them.
Prov. 24. 10, if thou *f.* in day of adversity.
Isa. 1. 5, whole heart *f.*
10. 18, as when a standardbearer *f.*
40. 28, Creator of earth *f.* not.
29, giveth power to the *f.*
30; Amos 8. 13, even youths shall *f.*
31, walk, and not *f.*
44. 12, he drinketh no water, and is *f.*
Jer. 8. 18; Lam. 1. 22; 5. 17, my heart is *f.*
Mat. 15. 32; Mk. 8. 3, lest they *f.* by the way.

Lu. 18. 1, pray, and not to *f*.
2 Cor. 4. 1, 16, as we have received mercy, we *f*. not.
Gal. 6. 9, reap, if we *f*. not.
Heb. 12. 3, wearied and *f*. in your minds.
5, nor *f*. when thou art rebuked.
See Deut. 20. 8; Ps. 84. 2; 119. 81; Mat. 9. 36.

FAIR. Job 37. 22, *f*. weather out of the north.
Ps. 45. 2, *f*. than children of men.
Prov. 11. 22, a *f*. woman without discretion.
26. 25, when he speaketh *f*., believe not.
Cant. 1. 8; 5. 9; 6. 1, thou *f*. among women.
6. 10, *f*. as the moon.
Isa. 5. 9, houses great and *f*.
Jer. 4. 30, in vain shalt thou make thyself *f*.
12. 6, though they speak *f*. words.
Dan. 1. 15, their countenances appeared *f*.
Mat. 16. 2, it will be *f*. weather.
Acts 7. 20, Moses was exceeding *f*.
Rom. 16. 18, by *f*. speeches deceive.
See Gen. 6. 2; Isa. 54. 11; Ezek. 27. 12.

FAITH. Deut. 32. 20, children in whom is no *f*.
Mat. 6. 30; 8. 26; 14. 31; 16. 8; Lu. 12. 28, ye of little *f*.
8. 10; Lu. 7. 9, so great *f*.
9. 2; Mk. 2. 5; Lu. 5. 20, seeing their *f*.
22; Mk. 5. 34; 10. 52; Lu. 8. 48; 17. 19, thy *f*. hath made thee whole.
29, according to your *f*.
15. 28, great is thy *f*.
17. 20, *f*. as a grain of mustard seed.
21. 21, if ye have *f*., ye shall not only do this.
23. 23, omitted judgment, mercy, and *f*.
Mk. 4. 40, how is it ye have no *f*.?
11. 22, have *f*. in God.
Lu. 7. 50, thy *f*. hath saved thee.
8. 25, where is your *f*.?
17. 5, increase our *f*.
18. 8, shall he find *f*. on the earth?
22. 32, that thy *f*. fail not.
Acts 3. 16, the *f*. which is by him.
6. 5; 11. 24, a man full of *f*.
14. 9, perceiving he had *f*. to be healed.
27. opened the door of *f*.
15. 9, purifying their hearts by *f*.
16. 5, established in the *f*.
26. 18, sanctified by *f*.
Rom. 1. 5, grace for obedience to *f*.
17, revealed from *f*. to *f*.
3. 27, boasting excluded by *f*.
28; 5. 1; Gal. 2. 16; 3. 24, justified by *f*.
4. 5, *f*. counted for righteousness.
16, it is of *f*., which is of the *f*. of Abraham.
19, 20, being not weak in *f*.
5. 2, we have access by *f*.
10. 8, the word of *f*., which we preach.
17, *f*. cometh by hearing.
12. 3, the measure of *f*.
6, prophesy according to proportion of *f*.
14. 1, weak in *f*. receive ye.
22, hast thou *f*.?
23, what is not of *f*. is sin.
1 Cor. 2. 5, your *f*. should not stand in wisdom.
13. 2, though I have all *f*.
13, now abideth *f*.
15. 14, and your *f*. is also vain.
16. 13, stand fast in the *f*.
2 Cor. 1. 24, not have dominion over *f*.
4. 13, same spirit of *f*.
5. 7, we walk by *f*.
13. 5, examine whether ye be in the *f*.
Gal. 2. 20, I live by the *f*. of Son of God.
3. 2, by the hearing of *f*.
12, law is not of *f*.
23, before *f*. came.
5. 6, *f*. which worketh by love.
6. 10, the household of *f*.
Eph. 3. 12, access by *f*. of him.
17, dwell in your hearts by *f*.
4. 5, one Lord, one *f*.
13, in the unity of the *f*.
Eph. 6. 16, the shield of *f*.
Phil. 1. 27, striving together for the *f*. of the gospel.
Col. 1. 23, if ye continue in the *f*.
2. 5, the stedfastness of your *f*.
1 Thess. 1. 3; 2 Thess. 1. 11, your work of *f*.
5. 8, the breastplate of *f*.
2 Thess. 3. 2, all men have not *f*.
1 Tim. 1. 2; Tit. 1. 4, my own son in the *f*.
5; 2 Tim. 1. 5, *f*. unfeigned.
2. 15, if they continue in *f*.
3. 13, great boldness in the *f*.
4. 1, shall depart from the *f*.
5. 8, he hath denied the *f*.
6. 10, 21, erred from the *f*.
12, fight the good fight of *f*.
2 Tim. 3. 8, reprobate concerning the *f*.
4. 7, I have kept the *f*.
Tit. 1. 1, the *f*. of God's elect.
Heb. 4. 2, not being mixed with *f*.
6. 1, not laying again the foundation of *f*.
12, through *f*. inherit the promises.
10. 22, in full assurance of *f*.
11. 1, *f*. is substance of things hoped for.
4, 5, 7, 8, 9, etc., by *f*. Abel, etc.
6, without *f*. it is impossible.
Heb. 11. 13, these all died in *f*.
33, through *f*. subdued kingdoms.
39, a good report through *f*.
12. 2, author and finisher of our *f*.
13. 7, whose *f*. follow.
Jas. 1. 3; 1 Pet. 1. 7, the trying of your *f*.
6, let them ask in *f*.
2. 1, I have not *f*. with respect of persons.
5, rich in *f*.
14, man say he hath *f*., can *f*. save him?
17, *f*. without works is dead.
18, thou hast *f*., and I have works.
22, *f*. wrought with his works
5. 15, the prayer of *f*. shall save.
1 Pet. 1. 9, the end of your *f*.
5. 9, resist stedfast in the *f*.
2 Pet. 1. 1, like precious *f*.
5, add to your *f*. virtue.
1 John 5. 4, overcometh the world, even our *f*.
Jude 3, earnestly contend for the *f*.
20, your most holy *f*.
Rev. 2. 13, hast not denied my *f*.
19, I know thy works and *f*.
13. 10, patience and *f*. of the saints.
14. 12, they that keep the *f*. of Jesus.
See Hab. 2. 4; Rom. 1. 12; 1 Tim. 4. 6.

FAITHFUL. 2 Sam. 20. 19, one of them that are *f*. in Israel.
Neh. 7. 2, a *f*. man, and feared God.
9. 8, his heart *f*. before thee.
13. 13, counted *f*. to distribute.
Ps. 12. 1, the *f*. fail among men.
89. 37, a *f*. witness in heaven.
101. 6, the *f*. of the land.
119. 86, commandments *f*.
138, testimonies *f*.
Prov. 11. 13, *f*. spirit concealeth.
13. 17, *f*. ambassador is health.
14. 5; Isa. 8. 2; Jer. 42. 5, a *f*. witness.
20. 6, a *f*. man who can find?
25. 13, as snow in harvest, so is a *f*. messenger.
27. 6, *f*. are wounds of a friend.
28. 20, *f*. man shall abound.
Isa. 1. 21, 26, *f*. city.
Mat. 24. 45; Lu. 12. 42, who is a *f*. and wise servant?
25. 21, good and *f*. servant.
23; Lu. 19. 17, *f*. in a few things.
Lu. 16. 10, *f*. in least *f*. in much.
Acts 16. 15, if ye have judged me *f*.
1 Cor. 4. 2, required in stewards that a man be *f*.
17, Timothy *f*. in the Lord.
Gal. 3. 9, blessed with *f*. Abraham.
Eph. 6. 21; Col. 1. 7; 4. 7, a *f*. minister.
1 Thess. 5. 24, *f*. is he that calleth you.

2 Thess. 3. 3, Lord is *f.*, who shall stablish you.
1 Tim. 1. 15; 4. 9; 2 Tim. 2. 11; Tit. 3. 8, a *f.* saying.
3. 11, wives *f.* in all things.
2 Tim. 2. 2, commit to *f.* men.
13, yet he abideth *f.*
Heb. 2. 17, a *f.* high priest.
3. 2, *f.* to him that appointed him.
10. 23; 11. 11, he is *f.* that promised.
1 Pet. 4. 19, as unto a *f.* Creator.
1 John 1. 9, he is *f.* and just to forgive.
Rev. 2. 10, be thou *f.* unto death.
13, my *f.* martyr.
17. 14, called, and chosen, and *f.*
21. 5; 22. 6, these words are true and *f.*
See Deut. 7. 9; Dan. 6. 4; Rev. 1. 5; 3. 14; 19. 11.
FAITHFULLY. 2 Chron. 19. 9; 34. 12; Jer. 23. 28; 3 John 5.
FAITHFULNESS. Ps. 5. 9, no *f.* in their mouths.
36. 5, thy *f.* reacheth unto the clouds.
40. 10; 88. 11, declared thy *f.*
89. 33, nor suffer my *f.* to fail.
92. 2, show forth thy *f.* every night.
Isa. 11. 5, *f.* the girdle of his reins.
Lam. 3. 23, great is thy *f.*
See 1 Sam. 26. 23; Ps. 119. 75; 143. 1.
FAITHLESS. Mat. 17. 17; Mk. 9. 19; Lu. 9. 41; John 20. 27.
FALL (*n.*). Prov. 16. 18, haughty spirit before a *f.*
Mat. 7. 27, great was the *f.* of it.
Lu. 2. 34, set for the rise and *f.* of many.
Rom. 11. 12, if the *f.* of them be the riches.
See Jer. 49. 21; Ezek. 26. 15; 31. 16; 32. 10.
FALL (*v.*). Gen. 45. 24, see ye *f.* not out by the way.
Lev. 25. 35, thy brother be *f.* in decay.
1 Sam. 3. 19, let none of his words *f.*
2 Sam. 1. 19, 25, 27, how are the mighty *f.*!
3. 38, great man *f.* this day.
24. 14; 1 Chron. 21. 13, *f.* into hands of God.
2 Kings 14. 10, why meddle that thou shouldest *f.*?
Job 4. 13; 33. 15, deep sleep *f.* on men.
Ps. 5. 10, let them *f.* by their own counsels.
7. 15, is *f.* into ditch.
16. 6, lines *f.* in pleasant places.
37. 24, though he *f.*, not utterly cast down.
56. 13; 116. 8, deliver my feet from *f.*
72. 11, kings shall *f.* down before him.
91. 7, a thousand shall *f.* at thy side.
Prov. 10. 8, 10, a prating fool shall *f.*
11. 14, where no counsel is, the people *f.*
28, he that trusteth in riches shall *f.*
13. 17; 17. 20; 24. 16, *f.* into mischief.
24. 16, just man *f.* seven times.
17, rejoice not when thine enemy *f.*
26. 27; Eccl. 10. 8, diggeth a pit shall *f.* therein.
Eccl. 4. 10, woe to him that is alone when he *f.*
11. 3, where the tree *f.*, there it shall be.
Isa. 14. 12, how art thou *f.*!
34. 4, as the leaf *f.* from the vine.
40. 30, the young men shall utterly *f.*
Jer. 49. 26; 50. 30, young men *f.* in her streets.
Ezek. 24. 6, let no lot *f.* on it.
Dan. 3. 5; 11. 26; Mat. 4. 9, *f.* down and worship.
Hos. 10. 8; Lu. 23. 30; Rev. 6. 16, say to hills, *f.* on us.
Mic. 7. 8, when I *f.*
Zech. 11. 2, the cedar is *f.*
Mat. 10. 29, sparrow *f.* on ground.
12. 11, *f.* into pit on sabbath day.
15. 14; Lu. 6. 39, both *f.* into the ditch.
21. 44; Lu. 20. 18, *f.* on this stone.
24. 29; Mk. 13. 25, stars *f.* from heaven.
Lu. 8. 13, in time of temptation *f.* away.
10. 18, Satan as lightning, *f.* from heaven.
Rom. 14. 4, to his master he standeth or *f.*
13, occasion to *f.*
1 Cor. 10. 12, take heed lest he *f.*
15. 6, 18, some are *f.* asleep.
Gal. 5. 4, ye are *f.* from grace.
1 Tim. 3. 6, *f.* into the condemnation.
7, lest he *f.* into reproach.
6. 9, rich *f.* into temptation.
Heb. 4. 11, lest any *f.* after same example.
6. 6, if they *f.* away.
10. 31, to *f.* into hands of living God.
Jas. 1. 2, joy when ye *f.* into temptation.
11; 1 Pet. 1. 24, flower thereof *f.*
5. 12, lest ye *f.* into condemnation.
2 Pet. 1. 10, ye shall never *f.*
3. 17, lest ye *f.* from stedfastness.
See Isa. 21. 9; Lam. 5. 16; Rev. 14. 8; 18. 2.
FALLING. Job 4. 4; 2 Thess. 2. 3; Jude 24.
FALLOW. Jer. 4. 3; Hos. 10. 12.
FALSE. Ex. 20. 16; Deut. 5. 20; Mat. 19. 18, shalt not bear *f.* witness.
23. 1, shalt not raise a *f.* report.
2 Kings 9. 12, it is *f.*, tell us now.
Ps. 119. 104, 128, I hate every *f.* way.
120. 3, thou *f.* tongue.
Prov. 6. 19; 12. 17; 14. 5; 19. 5; 21. 28; 25. 18, a *f.* witness.
11. 1; 20. 23, a *f.* balance.
Mat. 15. 19, out of heart proceed *f.* witness.
24. 24; Mk. 13. 22, *f.* Christs and *f.* prophets.
26. 59, 60; Mk. 14. 56, 57, *f.* witness against Christ.
Mk. 13. 22, *f.* prophets shall rise.
Lu. 19. 8, any thing by *f.* accusation.
1 Cor. 15. 15, found *f.* witnesses of God.
2 Cor. 11. 13, such are *f.* apostles.
11. 26, perils among *f.* brethren.
2 Tim. 3. 3; Tit. 2. 3, *f.* accusers.
See Gal. 2. 4; 2 Pet. 2. 1; 1 John 4. 1.
FALSEHOOD. Job 21. 34, in answers remaineth *f.*
Ps. 7. 14, hath brought forth *f.*
144. 8, 11, right hand of *f.*
Isa. 28. 15, under *f.* have we hid ourselves.
57. 4, a seed of *f.*
Isa. 59. 13, words of *f.*
Mic. 2. 11, walking in the spirit and *f.*
See 2 Sam. 18. 13; Jer. 13. 25; Hos. 7. 1.
FALSELY. Lev. 6. 3, 5; 19. 12; Jer. 5. 2; 7. 9; Zech. 5. 4, swear *f.*
Jer. 5. 31; 29. 9, prophets prophesy *f.*
Mat. 5. 11, evil *f.*, for my sake.
1 Tim. 6. 20, science *f.* so called.
See Jer. 43. 2; Lu. 3. 14; 1 Pet. 3. 16.
FAME. Josh. 9. 9, we heard the *f.* of God.
1 Kings 10. 1; 2 Chron. 9. 1, *f.* of Solomon.
Zeph. 3. 19, get them *f.* in every land.
Mat. 4. 24; Mk. 1. 28; Lu. 4. 14, 37; 5. 15, *f.* of Jesus.
9. 31, spread abroad his *f.*
14. 1, Herod heard of the *f.*
See Gen. 45. 16; Num. 14. 15; Job 28. 22; Isa. 66. 19.
FAMILIAR. Job 19. 14; Ps. 41. 9; Jer. 20. 10.
FAMILY. Gen. 12. 3; 28. 14, in thee all *f.* be blessed.
25. 10, return every man to his *f.*
Deut. 29. 18, lest a *f.* turn away from God.
1 Sam. 9. 21, my *f.* the least.
18. 18, what is my father's *f.*?
1 Chron. 4. 38, princes in their *f.*
Ps. 68. 6, setteth the solitary in *f.*
Jer. 3. 14, one of a city, and two of a *f.*
10. 25, on *f.* that call not.
31. 1, God of all the *f.* of Israel.
Zech. 12. 12, every *f.* apart.
Eph. 3. 15, whole *f.* in heaven and earth.
See Num. 27. 4; Judg. 1. 25; Amos 3. 2.
FAMINE. 2 Sam. 21. 1, a *f.* in days of David.
1 Kings 8. 37; 2 Chron. 20. 9, if there be *f.*
18. 2; 2 Kings 6. 25, sore *f.* in Samaria.
2 Kings 8. 1, the Lord hath called for a *f.*
Job 5. 20, in *f.* he shall redeem thee.
22, at *f.* thou shalt laugh.
Ps. 33. 19, to keep them alive in *f.*
37. 19, in the days of *f.* shall be satisfied.
Jer. 24. 10; 29. 17, will send *f.* among them.

Jer. 42. 16, *f.*, shall follow close.
Lam. 5. 10, black because of *f.*
Ezek. 5. 16, evil arrows of *f.*
36. 29, I will lay no *f.* upon you.
Amos 8. 11, a *f.*, not of bread.
Mat. 24. 7; Mk. 13. 8; Lu. 21. 11, *f.* in divers places.
See Gen. 12. 10; 41. 27; 47. 13; Lu. 15. 14; Rom. 8. 35.
FAMISH. Gen. 41. 55; Prov. 10. 3; Isa. 5. 13; Zeph. 2. 11.
FAMOUS. Ruth 4. 11, 14; 1 Chron. 5. 24; Ps. 74. 5; Ezek. 23. 10.
FAN. Isa. 30. 24; Jer. 15. 7; 51. 2; Mat. 3. 12.
FAR. Gen. 18. 25; 1 Sam. 20. 9, that be *f.* from thee.
Deut. 12. 21; 14. 24, if place too *f.* from thee.
Judg. 19. 11; Mk. 6. 35; Lu. 24. 29, day *f.* spent.
1 Sam. 2. 30; 22. 15; 2 Sam. 20. 20; 23. 17, be it *f.* from me.
Job 5. 4, children *f.* from safety.
11. 14; 22. 23, put iniquity *f.* away.
19. 13, put my brethren *f.* from me.
34. 10, *f.* be it from God to do wickedness.
Ps. 10. 5, thy judgments are *f.* out of sight.
22. 11; 35. 22; 38. 21; 71. 12, be not *f.* from me.
97. 9, *f.* above all gods.
103. 12, *f.* as east from west.
Prov. 31. 10, *f.* above rubies.
Isa. 43. 6; 60. 4, 9, sons from *f.*
46. 12, *f.* from righteousness.
57. 19, peace to him that is *f.* off.
Amos 6. 3, put *f.* away evil day.
Mat. 16. 22, be it *f.* from thee, Lord.
Mk. 12. 34, not *f.* from the kingdom.
13. 34, as a man taking a *f.* journey.
John 21. 8, they were not *f.* from land.
Acts 17. 27, not *f.* from every one of us.
Rom. 13. 12, the night is *f.* spent.
2 Cor. 4. 17, a *f.* more exceeding.
Eph. 1. 21, *f.* above all principality.
2. 13, *f.* off made nigh.
4. 10, *f.* above all heavens.
Phil. 1. 23, which is *f.* better.
Heb. 7. 15, it is yet *f.* more evident.
See Isa. 33. 17; Mat. 15. 8; Mk. 8. 3.
FARE. 1 Sam. 17. 18; Jon. 1. 3; Lu. 16. 19.
FAREWELL. Lu. 9. 61; Acts 18. 21; 2 Cor. 13. 11.
FARM. Mat. 22. 5.
FARTHING. Mat. 5. 26; 10. 29; Mk. 12. 42; Lu. 12. 6.
FASHION. Job 10. 8; Ps. 119. 73, thine hands have *f.* me.
31. 15, did not one *f.* us?
Ps. 33. 15, he *f.* hearts alike.
139. 16, in continuance were *f.*
Isa. 45. 9, say to him that *f.* it.
Mk. 2. 12, never saw it on this *f.*
Lu. 9. 29, the *f.* of his countenance.
1 Cor. 7. 31, the *f.* of this world passeth.
Phil. 2. 8, found in *f.* as a man.
See Gen. 6. 15; Ex. 32. 4; Ezek. 42. 11; Jas. 1. 11.
FAST. 2 Sam. 12. 23, he is dead, wherefore should I *f.*?
Ps. 33. 9, he commanded, and it stood *f.*
65. 6, setteth *f.* the mountains.
Isa. 58. 3, why have we *f.*, and thou seest not?
4, ye *f.* for strife.
5, wilt thou call this a *f.*?
6, is not this the *f.* that I have chosen?
Joel 1. 14, sanctify a *f.*?
Zech. 7. 5, did ye at all *f.* unto me?
Mat. 6. 16, when ye *f.*, be not.
18, appear not to *f.*
Mk. 2. 19, can children of bridechamber *f.*
Lu. 18. 12, I *f.* twice in the week.
See Jer. 14. 12; Mat. 4. 2; Acts 13. 2.
FASTEN. Eccl. 12. 11, as nails *f.* by the masters.
Isa. 22. 23, 25, I will *f.* him as a nail.
Lu. 4. 20, eyes of all were *f.* on him.
Acts 11. 6, when I had *f.* mine eyes.
See 1 Sam. 31. 10; Job 38. 6; Acts 3. 4; 28. 3.
FASTING. Ps. 35. 13, I humbled myself with *f.*
109. 24, knees weak through *f.*
Jer. 36. 6, upon the *f.* day.
Mk. 8. 3, send them away *f.*
1 Cor. 7. 5, give yourselves to *f.* and prayer.
2 Cor. 6. 5, in stripes, in *f.*
11. 27, in *f.* oft.
See Dan. 6. 18; 9. 3; Mat. 17. 21; Mk. 9. 29.
FAT. Gen. 45. 18, shall eat the *f.* of the land.
49. 20, his bread shall be *f.*
Deut. 32. 15, Jeshurun waxed *f.*, and kicked.
Neh. 8. 10, eat the *f.*, and drink the sweet.
9. 25, 35, took a *f.* land, and became *f.*
Ps. 17. 10, inclosed in their own *f.*
92. 14, shall be *f.* and flourishing.
119. 70, heart *f.* as grease.
Prov. 11. 25, liberal soul made *f.*
13. 4, soul of diligent made *f.*
15. 30, good report maketh the bones *f.*
Isa. 10. 16, among his *f.* ones leanness.
25. 6, feast of *f.* things.
Hab. 1. 16, by them their portion is *f.*
See Gen. 41. 2; Ex. 29. 13; Lev. 3. 3, 17; 7. 22; Num. 13. 20; Judg. 3. 17.
FATHER. Gen. 15. 15, go to thy *f.* in peace.
17. 4; Rom. 4. 17, a *f.* of nations.
Ex. 15. 2, he is my *f.* God, I will exalt him.
20. 5; Num. 14. 18, iniquity of *f.* upon children.
21. 15, he that smiteth his *f.*
17; Lev. 20. 9, he that curseth his *f.*
Judg. 17. 10; 18. 19, be to me a *f.* and a priest.
1 Sam. 10. 12, who is their *f.*?
2 Sam. 10. 2; 1 Chron. 19. 2, as his *f.* showed kindness.
1 Kings 19. 4, no better than my *f.*
2 Kings 2. 12; 13. 14, Elisha cried, my *f.*, my *f.*
6. 21, my *f.*, shall I smite them?
1 Chron. 28. 9, know thou the God of thy *f.*
2 Chron. 32. 13, what I and my *f.* have done.
Ezra 7. 27, blessed be the Lord God of our *f.*
Job 29. 16, I was a *f.* to the poor.
31. 18, brought up with me as with a *f.*
38. 28, hath the rain a *f.*?
Ps. 27. 10, when my *f.* and mother forsake me.
39. 12, as all my *f.* were.
68. 5, *f.* of fatherless.
95. 9; Heb. 3. 9, your *f.* tempted me.
103. 13, as a *f.* pitieth his children.
Prov. 4. 1, the instruction of a *f.*
3, I was my *f.* son.
10. 1; 15. 20, wise son maketh a glad *f.*
17. 21, the *f.* of a fool hath no joy.
25; 19. 13, foolish son grief to his *f.*
Isa. 9. 6, the everlasting *F.*
Isa. 49. 23, kings shall be thy nursing *f.*
63. 16; 64. 8, doubtless thou art our *f.*
Jer. 3. 4, wilt thou not cry, my *f.*?
31. 9, I am a *f.* to Israel.
29; Ezek. 18. 2, *f.* have eaten sour grapes.
Ezek. 18. 4, as the soul of the *f.*
22. 7, set light by *f.* and mother.
Mal. 1. 6, if I be a *f.*, where is mine honour?
2. 10, have we not all one *f.*?
Mat. 5. 16, 45, 48, your *F.* in heaven.
6. 8, 32; Lu. 12. 30, your *F.* knoweth.
9; Lu. 11. 2, our *F.* which art in heaven.
7. 21; 12. 50, the will of my *F.*
8. 21; Lu. 9. 59, to go and bury my *f.*
10. 21, *f.* deliver up the child.
37, he that loveth *f.* or mother.
18. 10, behold the face of my *F.*
14, not the will of your *F.*
23. 9, call no man *f.* on earth.
25. 34, ye blessed of my *F.*
Mk. 14. 36; Rom. 8. 15; Gal. 4. 6, Abba, *F.*
Lu. 2. 49, about my *F.* business.
6. 36, as your *F.* is merciful.
11. 11, of any that is a *f.*
12. 32, it is your *F.* good pleasure.
15. 21, *f.*, I have sinned.
16. 27, send him to my *f.* house.

Lu. 22. 42, *F.*, if thou be willing.
23. 34, *F.*, forgive them.
46, *F.*, into thy hands.
John 1. 14, as of the only begotten of the *F.*
5. 21, as the *F.* raiseth up the dead.
22, the *F.* judgeth no man.
23, even as they honour the *F.*
37; 8. 16; 12. 49; 14. 24, the *F.* which hath sent me.
6. 37, all the *F.* giveth me.
46; 14. 8, 9, hath seen the *F.*
8. 41, we have one *F.*, even God.
44, devil is a liar, and the *f.* of it.
49, I honour my *F.*
10. 15, as the *F.* knoweth me.
29, my *F.* is greater than all.
12. 27, *F.*, save me from this hour.
28, *F.*, glorify thy name.
13. 1, should depart unto the *F.*
14. 6, no man cometh to the *F.*, but by me.
16; 16. 26, I will pray the *F.*
28, I am come from the *F.*
15. 1, my *F.* is the husbandman.
16, whatsoever ye ask of the *F.*
16. 16, because I go to the *F.*
32, the *F.* is with me.
17. 1, *F.*, the hour is come.
20. 17, I ascend to my *F.* and your *F.*
Acts 24. 14, so worship I the God of my *f.*
Rom. 4. 11, the *f.* of all that believe.
1 Cor. 4. 15, yet have we not many *f.*
2 Cor. 1. 3, *F.* of mercies, God of all comfort.
Gal. 1. 14, zealous of the traditions of my *f.*
4. 2, the time appointed of the *f.*
Eph. 4. 6, one God and *F.* of all.
6. 4, *f.*, provoke not your children.
Phil. 2. 11, to the glory of the *F.*
22, as a son with the *f.*
Col. 1. 19, it pleased the *F.* that in him.
1 Tim. 5. 1, entreat him as a *f.*
Heb. 1. 5, I will be to him a *F.*
7. 3, without *f.*, without mother.
12. 9, the *F.* of spirits.
Jas. 1. 17, the *F.* of lights.
2 Pet. 3. 4, since the *f.* fell asleep.
1 John 1. 3, fellowship with the *F.*
2. 1, an advocate with the *F.*
13, I write unto you, *f.*
15, the love of the *F.* is not in him.
23, hath not the *F.*
3. 1, what manner of love the *F.* hath.
5. 7, the *F.*, the Word, and Holy Ghost.
See 1 Chron. 29. 10; Lu. 11. 2; John 5. 26; 20. 7; Acts 1. 4; 15. 10; Rom. 4. 16.

FATHERLESS. Ps. 10. 14, the helper of the *f.*
Prov. 23. 10, the fields of the *f.*
Isa. 1. 23, they judge not the *f.*
Isa. 10. 2, that they may rob the *f.*
Jer. 49. 11, leave thy *f.* children.
Hos. 14. 3, in thee the *f.* findeth mercy.
Mal. 3. 5, against those that oppress *f.*
Jas. 1. 27, to visit the *f.* and widows.
See Ex. 22. 22; Deut. 10. 18; 14. 29; 24. 17; Job 31. 17.

FATNESS. Ps. 36. 8, the *f.* of thine house.
63. 5, as with marrow and *f.*
65. 11, thy paths drop *f.*
73. 7, eyes stand out with *f.*
Isa. 55. 2, soul delight itself in *f.*
See Gen. 27. 28; Judg. 9. 9; Rom. 11. 17.

FAULT. Gen. 41. 9, I remember my *f.* this day.
Ps. 19. 12, cleanse me from secret *f.*
Dan. 6. 4, find none occasion nor *f.* in him.
Mat. 18. 15, tell him his *f.*
Lu. 23. 4; John 18. 38; 19. 4. 6, I find no *f.*
Rom. 9. 19, why doth he yet find *f.*?
Gal. 6. 1, overtaken in a *f.*
Jas. 5. 16, confess your *f.*
Rev. 14. 5, are without *f.* before throne.
See Deut. 25. 2; 1 Sam. 29. 3; 2 Sam. 3. 8.

FAULTLESS. Heb. 8. 7; Jude 24.

FAULTY. 2 Sam. 14. 13; Hos. 10. 2.

FAVOUR. Gen. 39. 21, *f.* in the sight of the keeper.
Ex. 3. 21; 11. 3; 12. 36, *f.* in sight of Egyptians.
Deut. 33. 23, satisfied with *f.*
Ps. 5. 12, with *f.* wilt thou compass him.
30. 5, his *f.* is life.
102. 13, the set time to *f.* her.
14, *f.* the dust thereof.
112. 5, a good man showeth *f.*
Prov. 13. 15, good understanding giveth *f.*
14. 35; 19. 12, the king's *f.*
18. 22, obtaineth *f.* of the Lord.
31. 30, *f.* is deceitful.
Lu. 2. 52, increased in *f.* with God and man.
Acts 2. 47, having *f.* with all people.
See Prov. 8. 35; 12. 2; Eccl. 9. 11; Dan. 1. 9.

FAVOURABLE. Judg. 21. 22; Job 33. 26; Ps. 77. 7; 85. 1.

FEAR (*n.*). Gen. 9. 2, the *f.* of you on every beast.
20. 11, *f.* of God not in this place.
Deut. 2. 25; 11. 25; 1 Chron. 14. 17, *f.* of thee on nations.
Job 4. 6, is not this thy *f.*?
15. 4, thou castest off *f.*
39. 22, he mocketh at *f.*
Ps. 5. 7, in thy *f.* will I worship.
14. 5, there were they in great *f.*
19. 9, *f.* of the Lord is clean.
34. 11, I will teach you the *f.* of the Lord.
36. 1; Rom. 3. 18, no *f.* of God before his eyes.
53. 5, in *f.*, where no *f.* was.
111. 10; Prov. 1. 7; 9. 10, *f.* beginning of wisdom.
Prov. 1. 26, 27, mock when your *f.* cometh.
3. 25, not afraid of sudden *f.*
10. 21, *f.* of Lord prolongeth days.
14. 26, in *f.* of Lord is strong confidence.
27, *f.* of Lord a fountain of life.
15. 16, better little with *f.* of Lord.
19. 23, *f.* of Lord tendeth to life.
29. 25, *f.* of man bringeth a snare.
Eccl. 12. 5, when *f.* shall be in the way.
Isa. 8. 12, neither fear ye their *f.*
14. 3, Lord give thee rest from *f.*
29. 13, *f.* toward me taught by men.
Jer. 30. 5, a voice of *f.*, not of peace.
32. 40, I will put my *f.* in their hearts.
Mal. 1. 6, where is my *f.*?
Mat. 14. 26, disciples cried for *f.*
Lu. 21. 26, hearts failing them for *f.*
John 7. 13; 19. 38; 20. 19, for *f.* of the Jews.
1 Cor. 2. 3, with you in weakness and *f.*
2 Cor. 7. 11, what *f.*, what desire.
Eph. 6. 5; Phil. 2. 12, with *f.* and trembling.
Heb. 2. 15, *f.* of death.
11. 7, Noah moved with *f.*
12. 28, with reverence and godly *f.*
Jude 12, feeding themselves without *f.*
23, others save with *f.*
See Ps. 2. 11; 2 Cor. 7. 5, 15; 1 Pet. 2. 18; 3. 2.

FEAR (*v.*). Gen. 22. 12, I know that thou *f.* God.
42. 18, this do, and live, for I *f.* God.
Ex. 1. 21, because they *f.* God.
Ex. 14. 13, *f.* not, stand still, and see.
18. 21, able men, such as *f.* God.
20. 20, *f.* not, God is come to prove.
Deut. 4. 10, that they may learn to *f.*
5. 29, O that they would *f.* me.
28. 58, *f.* this glorious name.
66, thou shalt *f.* day and night.
1 Chron. 16. 30; Ps. 96. 9, *f.* before him all earth.
Neh. 7. 2, he *f.* God above many.
Job 1. 9, doth Job *f.* God for nought?
11. 15, put iniquity away, thou shalt not *f.*
Ps. 27. 1, whom shall I *f.*?
3, my heart shall not *f.*
31. 19, laid up for them that *f.* thee.
34. 9, *f.* the Lord, ye his saints.
56. 4; 118. 6, will not *f.* what flesh can do.
66. 16, come all ye that *f.* God.
76. 7, thou art to be *f.*

Ps. 86. 11, unite my heart to *f.* thy name.
115. 11, ye that *f.* the Lord, trust.
119. 74, they that *f.* thee will be glad.
Prov. 3. 7; 24. 21, *f.* the Lord, and depart.
28. 14, happy is the man that *f.* always.
31. 30, woman that *f.* the Lord.
Eccl. 3. 14, that men should *f.* before him.
5. 7, but *f.* thou God.
9. 2, as he that *f.* an oath.
12. 13, *f.* God, and keep his commandments.
Isa. 8. 12, neither *f.* ye their fear.
35. 4, to them of fearful heart *f.* not.
41. 10; 43. 5, *f.* thou not, I am with thee.
14, *f.* not, thou worm Jacob.
Jer. 5. 24, neither say they, let us *f.* the Lord.
10. 7, who would not *f.* thee, King of nations?
33. 9, they shall *f.* and tremble.
Dan. 6. 26, that men *f.* before the God of Daniel.
Zeph. 3. 7, I said, surely thou wilt *f.* me.
Mal. 3. 16, they that *f.* the Lord spake.
4. 2, to you that *f.* my name.
Mat. 1. 20, *f.* not to take to thee.
10. 28; Lu. 12. 5, *f.* him who is able.
14. 5; 21. 46, Herod *f.* the multitude.
21. 26; Mk. 11. 32; Lu. 20. 19, we *f.* the people.
Mk. 4. 41, they *f.* exceedingly.
5. 33, woman *f.* and trembling came.
11. 18, scribes *f.* Jesus.
Lu. 9. 31, *f.* as they entered cloud.
12. 32, *f.* not, little flock.
18. 2, judge which *f.* not God.
19. 21, I *f.* thee, because thou art.
23. 40, dost not thou *f.* God?
John 9. 22, because they *f.* the Jews.
Acts 10. 22, just, and one that *f.* God.
35, he that *f.* is accepted.
13. 26, whosoever among you *f.* God.
Rom. 8. 15, bondage again to *f.*
11. 20, not highminded, but *f.*
2 Cor. 11. 3; 12. 20, I *f.* lest.
1 Tim. 5. 20, rebuke, that others may *f.*
Heb. 5. 7, heard in that he *f.*
13. 6, I will not *f.* what man.
1 John 4. 18, that *f.* not perfect in love.
See 1 Kings 18. 12; Col. 3. 22; Heb. 4. 1.
FEARFUL. Ex. 15. 11, *f.* in praises.
Ps. 139. 14, *f.* and wonderfully made.
Isa. 35. 4, to them of a *f.* heart.
Mat. 8. 26; Mk. 4. 40, why are ye *f.*?
Heb. 10. 27, *f.* looking for of judgment.
31, *f.* thing to fall into the hands.
See Deut. 20. 8; Judg. 7. 3; Lu. 21. 11; Rev. 21. 8.
FEARFULNESS. Ps. 55. 5; Isa. 21. 4; 33. 14.
FEAST. Job 1. 4, his sons went and *f.* in their houses.
Ps. 35. 16, hypocritical mockers in *f.*
Prov. 15. 15, merry heart continual *f.*
Eccl. 7. 2; Jer. 16. 8, the house of *f.*
10. 19, *f.* is made for laughter.
Isa. 1. 14, your appointed *f.* my soul hateth.
Amos 5. 21, I despise your *f.* days.
8. 10, turn your *f.* into mourning.
Mat. 23. 6; Mk. 12. 39; Lu. 20. 46, uppermost rooms at *f.*
26. 5; Mk. 14. 2, not on the *f.* day.
Lu. 2. 42, after the custom of the *f.*
14. 13, when thou makest a *f.*
John 7. 8, go ye up to this *f.*
14, about the midst of the *f.*
37, that great day of the *f.*
13. 29, buy what we need against the *f.*
Acts 18. 21, I must by all means keep this *f.*
1 Cor. 5. 8, let us keep the *f.*
10. 27, if any bid you to a *f.*
See Judg. 14. 10; Esth. 9. 17; Mal. 2. 3; Jude 12.
FEATHERS. Job 39. 13; Ps. 91. 4; Dan. 4. 33.
FED. Gen. 48. 15, who *f.* me all my life long.
Ps. 37. 3, verily thou shalt be *f.*
Ezek. 34. 8, shepherds *f.* themselves, not flock.
Mat. 25. 37, hungred, and *f.* thee.
1 Cor. 3. 2, I have *f.* you with milk.
See Deut. 8. 3; Ps. 78. 72; 81. 16; Lu. 16. 21.
FEEBLE. Neh. 4. 2, what do these *f.* Jews?
Job 4. 4; Isa. 35. 3; Heb. 12. 12, strengthened the *f.* knees.
Ps. 105. 37, not one *f.* person.
Prov. 30. 26, comes a *f.* folk.
Ezek. 7. 17; 21. 7, all hands shall be *f.*
1 Thess. 5. 14, comfort the *f.* minded.
See Gen. 30. 42; Jer. 47. 3; 1 Cor. 12. 22.
FEED. Gen. 46. 32, trade hath been to *f.* cattle.
1 Kings 17. 4, commanded ravens to *f.* thee.
22. 27, *f.* him with bread of affliction.
Ps. 28. 9, *f.* them, and lift them up for ever.
Prov. 15. 14, mouth *f.* on foolishness.
30. 8, *f.* me with food convenient.
Isa. 5. 17, lambs shall *f.* after their manner.
11. 7; 27. 10, cow and bear shall *f.*
44. 20, he *f.* on ashes.
61. 5, strangers shall *f.* your flocks.
65. 25, the wolf and lamb shall *f.*
Jer. 3. 15, pastors *f.* you with knowledge.
6. 3, *f.* every one in his place.
Hos. 12. 1, Ephraim *f.* on wind.
Zech. 11. 4, *f.* the flock of the slaughter.
Mat. 6. 26, your heavenly Father *f.* them.
Lu. 12. 24, sow not, yet God *f.* them.
John 21. 15, 16, 17, *f.* my lambs.
Rom. 12. 20, if enemy hunger, *f.* him.
1 Pet. 5. 2, *f.* the flock of God.
See Cant. 1. 7; Acts 20. 28; Rev. 7. 17.
FEEL. Gen. 27. 12, 21, my father will *f.* me.
Acts 17. 27, if haply they might *f.* after.
See Judg. 16. 26; Job 20. 20; Eccl. 8. 5.
FEELING. Eph. 4. 19, being past *f.*
Heb. 4. 15, touched with *f.* of infirmities.
FEET. Gen. 49. 10, lawgiver from between his *f.*
Deut. 2. 28, I will pass through on my *f.*
Josh. 3. 15, *f.* of priests dipped in Jordan.
14. 9, land whereon *f.* have trodden.
Ruth 3. 14, she lay at his *f.*
1 Sam. 2. 9, keep *f.* of his saints.
2 Sam. 22. 37; Ps. 18. 36, my *f.* did not slip.
2 Kings 6. 32, sound of his master's *f.*
13. 21, dead man stood on his *f.*
Neh. 9. 21, their *f.* swelled not.
Job 29. 15, *f.* was I to the lame.
Ps. 8. 6; 1 Cor. 15. 27; Eph. 1. 22, all things under his *f.*
22. 16, pierced my hands and my *f.*
31. 8, set my *f.* in a large room.
40. 2, my *f.* on a rock.
56. 13; 116. 8, deliver my *f.* from falling.
66. 9, suffered not our *f.* to be moved.
73. 2, my *f.* were almost gone.
115. 7, *f.* have they, but walk not.
119. 105, a lamp to my *f.*
122. 2, our *f.* shall stand within thy gates.
Prov. 1. 16; 6. 18; Isa. 59. 7, *f.* run to evil.
4. 26, ponder path of thy *f.*
5. 5, her *f.* go down to death.
6. 13, speaketh with his *f.*
28, and his *f.* not be burnt.
7. 11, her *f.* abide not in house.
19. 2, he that hasteth with his *f.*
Cant. 5. 3, washed my *f.*, how shall I defile?
7. 1; Isa. 52. 7, how beautiful are *f.*
Isa. 3. 16, tinkling with *f.*
6. 2, with twain he covered his *f.*
23. 7, her own *f.* shall carry her.
26. 6, the *f.* of the poor.
Isa. 49. 23; Mat. 10. 14; Mk. 6. 11; Lu. 9. 5; Acts 13. 51, dust of *f.*
52. 7; Nah. 1. 15, the *f.* of him that bringeth.
60. 13, place of my *f.* glorious.
Lam. 3. 34, crush under *f.* prisoners.
Ezek. 2. 1, 2; 3. 24, stand upon thy *f.*
24. 17, 23, shoes upon thy *f.*
25. 6, stamped with thy *f.*
32. 2, troublest waters with thy *f.*
34. 18, 19, foul residue with *f.*
Dan. 2. 33, 42, *f.* part iron and part clay.

Dan. 10. 6; Rev. 1. 15; 2. 18, *f.* like polished brass.
Nah. 1. 3, clouds are the dust of his *f.*
Zech. 14. 4, *f.* shall stand on Zion.
Mat. 7. 6, trample them under *f.*
18. 8, rather than having two *f.*
28. 9, they held him by the *f.*
Lu. 1. 79, guide our *f.* into way of peace.
7. 38, she kissed his *f.*, and anointed them.
8. 35, sitting at the *f.* of Jesus.
10. 39, Mary sat at Jesus' *f.*
24. 39, 40, behold my hands and my *f.*
John 11. 2; 12. 3, wiped *f.* with her hair.
12. 3, anointed the *f.* of Jesus.
13. 5, began to wash disciples' *f.*
6, dost thou wash my *f.*?
8, thou shalt never wash my *f.*
10, needeth not save to wash his *f.*
20. 12, one angel at head, other at *f.*
Acts 3. 7, his *f.* received strength.
4. 35, 37; 5. 2, laid at apostles' *f.*
5. 9, *f.* of them that buried thy husband.
14. 8, a man impotent in his *f.*
21. 11, Agabus bound his own hands and *f.*
22. 3, at *f.* of Gamaliel.
Rom. 3. 15, *f.* swift to shed blood.
10. 15, the *f.* of them that preach.
16. 20, bruise Satan under your *f.*
1 Cor. 12. 21, nor head to the *f.*, I have no need.
Eph. 6. 15, your *f.* shod with preparation.
Rev. 1. 17, I fell at his *f.* as dead.
13. 2, *f.* as *f.* of a bear.
19. 10; 22. 8, at his *f.* to worship.
See 2 Sam. 4. 4; 2 Kings 9. 35; 1 Tim. 5. 10.

FEIGN. 1 Sam. 21. 13, David *f.* himself mad.
Ps. 17. 1, prayer not out of *f.* lips.
Jer. 3. 10, turned to me *f.*
Lu. 20. 20, *f.* themselves just men.
See 2 Sam. 14. 2; 1 Kings 14. 5, 6; Neh. 6. 8.

FELL. Gen. 4. 5, his countenance *f.*
Josh. 6. 20, the wall *f.* flat.
1 Kings 18. 38, fire of Lord *f.*, and consumed.
2 Kings 6. 5, as one was *f.* a beam.
Dan. 4. 31, then *f.* a voice from heaven.
Jon. 1. 7, lot *f.* on Jonah.
Mat. 7. 25; Lu. 6. 49, house *f.* not.
Lu. 8. 23, Jesus *f.* asleep.
10. 30, 36, *f.* among thieves.
13. 4, upon whom tower *f.*
Acts 1. 25, from which Judas *f.*
26, lot *f.* on Matthias.
13. 36, *f.* on sleep.
2 Pet. 3. 4, since fathers *f.* asleep.
Rev. 16. 19, cities of the nations *f.*
See Mat. 13. 4; Acts 10. 44; 19. 35; 20. 9.

FELLOW. Ex. 2. 13, wherefore smitest thou thy *f.*?
1 Sam. 21. 15, this *f.* to play the madman.
2 Sam. 6. 20, as one of the vain *f.*
2 Kings 9. 11, wherefore came this mad *f.*?
Ps. 45. 7; Heb. 1. 9, oil of gladness above thy *f.*
Eccl. 4. 10, one shall lift up his *f.*
Zech. 13. 7, the man that is my *f.*
Mat. 11. 16, like children calling to their *f.*
24. 49, begin to smite his *f.*-servants.
26. 61, this *f.* said, I am able to destroy.
71; Lu. 22. 59, this *f.* was also with Jesus.
Lu. 23. 2, found this *f.* perverting.
John 9. 29, as for this *f.*
Acts 17. 5, lewd *f.* of the baser sort.
22. 22, away with such a *f.*
24. 5, this man a pestilent *f.*
Eph. 2. 19, *f.*-citizens with the saints.
3. 6, Gentiles *f.*-heirs.
Phil. 4. 3; 1 Thess. 3. 2; Philem. 24, *f.*-labourers.
3 John 8, *f.*-helpers to the truth.
See Col. 4. 11; Philem. 2; Rev. 19. 10; 22. 9.

FELLOWSHIP. Acts 2. 42, in doctrine and *f.*
1 Cor. 1. 9, called to the *f.* of his Son.
10. 20, not have *f.* with devils.
2 Cor. 6. 14, what *f.* hath righteousness?
Eph. 3. 9, the *f.* of mystery.
Eph. 5. 11, have no *f.* with.
Phil. 1. 5, your *f.* in the gospel.
2. 1, if any *f.* of the Spirit.
3. 10, the *f.* of his sufferings.
1 John 1. 3, our *f.* is with the Father.
7, we have *f.* one with another.
See Lev. 6. 2; Ps. 94. 20; 2 Cor. 8. 4, 13, 14; Gal. 2. 9.

FELT. Ex. 10. 21; Prov. 23. 35; Mk. 5. 29; Acts 28. 5.

FEMALE. Mat. 19. 4; Mk. 10. 6, made them male and *f.*
Gal. 3. 28, in Christ neither male nor *f.*
See Gen. 7. 16; Lev. 3. 1; 27. 4; Deut. 4. 16.

FENCE. Job 10. 11; 19. 8; Ps. 62. 3; Isa. 5. 2.

FERVENT. Acts 18. 25; Rom. 12. 11, *f.* in spirit.
Jas. 5. 16, *f.* prayer availeth much.
1 Pet. 1. 22, with a pure heart *f.*
2 Pet. 3. 10, 12, melt with *f.* heat.
See 2 Cor. 7. 7; Col. 4. 12; 1 Pet. 4. 8.

FETCH. Num. 20. 10, must we *f.* water?
Job 36. 3, I will *f.* my knowledge from far.
Isa. 56. 12, I will *f.* wine.
Acts 16. 37, come themselves and *f.* us out.
See Deut. 19. 5; 2 Sam. 14. 3; Acts 28. 13.

FETTERS. Judg. 16. 21; Ps. 105. 18; 149. 8; Mk. 5. 4; Lu. 8. 29.

FEVER. Deut. 28. 22, the Lord shall smite thee with a *f.*
Mat. 8. 14; Mk. 1. 30, Simon's wife's mother lay sick of a *f.*
John 4. 52, at the seventh hour the *f.* left him.

FEW. Gen. 29. 20, they seemed but a *f.* days.
47. 9, *f.* and evil have the days of my life.
1 Sam. 14. 6, to save by many or *f.*
17. 28, with whom left those *f.* sheep?
2 Kings 4. 3, borrow not a *f.*
Neh. 7. 4, city large, people *f.*
Job 14. 1, man is of *f.* days.
16. 22, when a *f.* years are come.
Eccl. 5. 2, let thy words be *f.*
Mat. 7. 14, *f.* there be that find it.
9. 37; Lu. 10. 2, the labourers are *f.*
15. 34; Mk. 8. 7, a *f.* little fishes.
20. 16; 22. 14, many called, *f.* chosen.
25. 21, faithful in a *f.* things.
Mk. 6. 5, laid hands on a *f.* sick folk.
Lu. 12. 48, beaten with *f.* stripes.
13. 23, are there *f.* that be saved?
Rev. 3. 4, a *f.* names even in Sardis.
See Deut. 7. 7; Ps. 109. 8; Heb. 12. 10.

FIDELITY. Tit. 2. 10, showing good *f.*

FIELD. Deut. 21. 1, if one be found slain in *f.*
1 Sam. 22. 7, will he give every one of you *f.*?
Prov. 24. 30, the *f.* of the slothful.
Isa. 5. 8, that lay *f.* to *f.*
Mat. 13. 38, the *f.* is the world.
44, treasure hid in a *f.*
John 4. 35, look on the *f.*
Jas. 5. 4, labourers which reaped your *f.*
See Mat. 6. 28; 27. 7; Acts 1. 19.

FIERCE. Gen. 49. 7, anger, for it was *f.*
Deut. 28. 50, a nation of a *f.* countenance.
Mat. 8. 28, exceeding *f.*
Lu. 23. 5, and they were more *f.*
2 Tim. 3. 3, men shall be incontinent, *f.*
Jas. 3. 4, driven of *f.* winds.
See 2 Sam. 19. 43; Isa. 33. 19; Dan. 8. 23.

FIERY. Deut. 33. 2, a *f.* law for them.
Dan. 3. 6, a *f.* furnace.
Eph. 6. 16, the *f.* darts of the wicked.
Heb. 10. 27, judgment and *f.* indignation.
1 Pet. 4. 12, concerning the *f.* trial.
See Num. 21. 6; Deut. 8. 15; Isa. 14. 29.

FIG. 1 Kings 4. 25; Mic. 4. 4, dwelt under his *f.* tree.
2 Kings 18. 31; Isa. 36. 16, eat every one of his *f.* tree.
20. 7, Isaiah said, Take a lump of *f.*
Isa. 38. 21, let them take a lump of *f.*
Jer. 24. 1, two baskets of *f.* were set before the temple.

Hab. 3. 17, although *f.* tree shall not blossom.
Mat. 7. 16; Lu. 6. 44, do men gather *f.* of thistles?
Lu. 21. 29, behold the *f.* tree.
Jas. 3. 12, can the *f.* tree bear olive berries?
Rev. 6. 13, casteth untimely *f.*
See Judg. 9. 10; Jer. 8. 13; Lu. 13. 6; John 1. 48.
FIGHT. Ex. 14. 14; Deut. 1. 30; 3. 22; 20. 4, Lord *f.* for you.
Josh. 23. 10, he it is that *f.* for you.
1 Sam. 25. 28, *f.* the battles of the Lord.
2 Kings 10. 3, *f.* for your master's house.
Neh. 4. 14, *f.* for your brethren, sons, and wives.
Ps. 144. 1, teacheth my fingers to *f.*
John 18. 36, then would my servants *f.*
Acts 5. 39; 23. 9, *f.* against God.
1 Cor. 9. 26, so *f.* I.
2 Cor. 7. 5, without were *f.*
1 Tim. 6. 12; 2 Tim. 4. 7, the good *f.*
Heb. 10. 32, great *f.* of afflictions.
11. 34, valiant in *f.*
Jas. 4. 1, wars and *f.* among you.
2, ye *f.* and war.
See Zech. 10. 5; 14. 14; Rev. 2. 16.
FIG-TREE. Mat. 21. 19, presently the *f.* withered away.
Mk. 11. 13, seeing a *f.* afar off.
FIG-TREE (parable of). Mat. 24. 32; Lu. 21. 29.
FIGURE. Deut. 4. 16; Rom. 5. 14; 1 Cor. 4. 6; Heb. 9. 9; 1 Pet. 3. 21.
FILL. Num. 14. 21; Ps. 72. 19; Hab. 2. 14, earth *f.* with glory.
Job 23. 4, *f.* my mouth with arguments.
Ps. 81. 10, open mouth, I will *f.* it.
104. 28, they are *f.* with good.
Prov. 3. 10, barns *f.* with plenty.
14. 14, *f.* with his own ways.
30. 22, a fool when *f.* with meat.
Isa. 65. 20, who hath not *f.* his days.
Mat. 5. 6; Lu. 6. 21, they shall be *f.*
Mk. 7. 27, let the children first be *f.*
Lu. 1. 15; Acts 4. 8; 9. 17; 13. 9, *f.* with Holy Ghost.
14. 23, that my house may be *f.*
John 16. 6, sorrow hath *f.* your heart.
Acts 5. 28, ye have *f.* Jerusalem with your doctrine.
14. 17, *f.* our hearts with food and gladness.
Rom. 1. 29, *f.* with all unrighteousness.
15. 14, *f.* with all knowledge.
Eph. 1. 23, him that *f.* all in all.
3. 19, *f.* with fulness of God.
5. 18, be *f.* with the Spirit.
Phil. 1. 11, *f.* with fruits of righteousness.
Col. 1. 24, *f.* up what is behind.
Jas. 2. 16, be ye warned and *f.*
Rev. 15. 1, in them is *f.* up wrath of God.
See Dan. 2. 35; Lu. 2. 40; 15. 16; John 2. 7.
FILTH. Isa. 4. 4, washed away the *f.* of Zion.
1 Cor. 4. 13, as the *f.* of the world.
FILTHINESS. 2 Cor. 7. 1, cleanse from all *f.* of flesh.
Eph. 5. 4, nor let *f.* be named.
Jas. 1. 21, lay apart all *f.*
See Ezek. 22. 15; 36. 25.
FILTHY. Job 15. 16, how much more *f.* is man?
Ps. 14. 3; 53. 3, altogether become *f.*
Isa. 64. 6, as *f.* rags.
Zech. 3. 3, clothed with *f.* garments.
Col. 3. 8, put off *f.* communication.
1 Tim. 3. 3; Tit. 1. 7; 1 Pet. 5. 2, *f.* lucre.
2 Pet. 2. 7, vexed with *f.* conversation.
Jude 8, *f.* dreamers.
Rev. 22. 11, he that is *f.*, let him be *f.*
FINALLY. 2 Cor. 13. 11; Eph. 6. 10; Phil. 3. 1; 4. 8; 2 Thess. 3. 1; 1 Pet. 3. 8.
FIND. Num. 32. 23, be sure your sin will *f.* you out.
Job 9. 10; Rom. 11. 33, things past *f.* out.
23. 3, where I might *f.* him.
Prov. 4. 22, life to those that *f.* them.
8. 17; Jer. 29. 13, seek me early shall *f.* me.
35, whoso *f.* me, *f.* life.
Prov. 18. 22, *f.* a wife, *f.* a good thing.
Eccl. 9. 10, thy hand *f.* to do, do it.
11. 1, *f.* it after many days.
Isa. 58. 13, *f.* thine own pleasure.
Jer. 6. 16; Mat. 11. 29, *f.* rest to your souls.
Mat. 7. 7; Lu. 11. 9, seek, and ye shall *f.*
Mat. 7. 14, few there be that *f.* it.
10. 39, loseth his life shall *f.* it.
22. 9, as many as ye shall *f.*
Mk. 11. 13, he might *f.* any thing thereon.
13. 36, he *f.* you sleeping.
Lu. 15. 4, 8, till he *f.* it.
18. 8, shall he *f.* faith on earth?
John 1. 41, first *f.* his brother.
Rom. 7. 21, I *f.* a law that when I would.
Heb. 4. 16, *f.* grace to help.
See John 7. 34; 2 Tim. 1. 18; Rev. 9. 6.
FINE. Ps. 19. 10, more to be desired than *f.* gold.
81. 16; 147. 14, the *f.* of the wheat.
Prov. 25. 12, as an ornament of *f.* gold.
Lam. 4. 1, how is the *f.* gold changed!
Mk. 15. 46, Joseph brought *f.* linen.
See Job 28. 1, 17; Lu. 16. 19; Rev. 18. 12; 19. 8.
FINGER. Ex. 8. 19, this is the *f.* of God.
31. 18; Deut. 9. 10, written with the *f.* of God.
1 Kings 12. 10; 2 Chron. 10. 10, little *f.* thicker.
Prov. 7. 3, bind them on thy *f.*
Isa. 58. 9, the putting forth of the *f.*
Dan. 5. 5, the *f.* of a man's hand.
Mat. 23. 4; Lu. 11. 46, not move with *f.*
Lu. 16. 24, the tip of his *f.*
John 8. 6, with his *f.* wrote on ground.
20. 25, put my *f.* into print of nails.
27, reach hither thy *f.*
See Ps. 8. 3; Prov. 6. 13; Isa. 2. 8; 59. 3; Lu. 11. 20.
FINISH. 1 Chron. 28. 20, till thou hast *f.*
Neh. 6. 15, so the wall was *f.*
Lu. 14. 28, 29, 30, whether sufficient to *f.*
John 4. 34, to do his will, and *f.* his work.
5. 36, which the Father hath given me to *f.*
17. 4, have *f.* the work.
19. 30, it is *f.*
Acts 20. 24; 2 Tim. 4. 7, that I might *f.* my course.
2 Cor. 8. 6, *f.* in you the same grace.
Heb. 12. 2, Jesus, author and *f.* of our faith.
Jas. 1. 15, sin, when it is *f.*
See Dan. 9. 24; Rev. 19. 7; 11. 7; 20. 5.
FIRE. Gen. 22. 7, behold the *f.* and the wood.
Ex. 3. 2, bush burned with *f.*
22. 6, he that kindled *f.* shall make restitution.
Lev. 10. 2, *f.* from the Lord.
18. 21; Deut. 18. 10; 2 Kings 17. 17; 23. 10, pass through *f.*
Judg. 15. 5, brands on *f.*, and burnt corn.
1 Kings 18. 24, that answereth by *f.*
19. 12, the Lord was not in the *f.*
1 Chron. 21. 26, Lord answered him by *f.*
Ps. 39. 3, musing, the *f.* burned.
74. 7, they have cast *f.* into thy sanctuary.
Prov. 6. 27, can a man take *f.*?
26. 18, mad man who casteth *f.*-brands.
20, no wood, the *f.* goeth out.
21, as wood is to *f.*, so is a contentious man.
Isa. 9. 19, as the fuel of the *f.*
24. 15, glorify the Lord in the *f.*
43. 2, walkest through *f.* not be burned.
44. 16, I have seen the *f.*
64. 2, the melting *f.* burneth.
66. 15, the Lord will come with *f.*
16, by *f.* will the Lord plead.
24; Mk. 9. 44, neither their *f.* quenched.
Jer. 20. 9, word as a *f.* in my bones.
Ezek. 36. 5, in the *f.* of my jealousy.
Dan. 3. 27, the *f.* had no power.
Amos 4. 11, as a *f.*-brand plucked out.
Nah. 1. 6, fury poured out like *f.*
Zech. 2. 5, a wall of *f.* round about.
3. 2, a brand plucked out of the *f.*
Mal. 3. 2, like a refiner's *f.*

Mat. 3. 10; 7. 19; Lu. 3. 9; John 15. 6, tree cast into *f.*
11; Lu. 3. 16, baptize with *f.*
13. 42, cast them into furnace of *f.*
18. 8; 25. 41; Mk. 9. 43, 46, everlasting *f.*
Lu. 9. 54, wilt thou that we command *f.*?
12. 49, come to send *f.* on earth.
17. 29, same day it rained *f.* and brimstone.
Acts 2. 3, cloven tongues like as of *f.*
1 Cor. 3. 13, revealed by *f.* and the *f.* shall try.
15, saved, yet so as by *f.*
2 Thess. 1. 8, in flaming *f.* taking vengeance.
Heb. 1. 7, his ministers a flame of *f.*
11. 34, quenched violence of *f.*
Jas. 3. 5, a little *f.* kindleth.
6, the tongue is a *f.*
1 Pet. 1. 7, gold tried with *f.*
2 Pet. 3. 7, reserved unto *f.*
12, heavens being on *f.*
Jude 7, vengeance of eternal *f.*
23, pulling them out of the *f.*
Rev. 3. 18, buy gold tried in the *f.*
20. 9, *f.* came down from God.
10, devil cast into lake of *f.*
14, death and hell cast into *f.*
21. 8, the lake that burneth with *f.*
See Isa. 33. 14; Jer. 23. 29; Heb. 12. 29.

FIRM. Josh. 3. 17; Job 41. 24; Ps. 73. 4; Heb. 3. 6.

FIRMAMENT. Gen. 1. 6, let there be a *f.*
Ps. 19. 1, the *f.* sheweth his handywork.
Ezek. 1. 22, the likeness of the *f.*
Dan. 12. 3, shine as the brightness of the *f.*

FIRST. 1 Kings 17. 13, make a little cake *f.*
Ezra 3. 12; Hag. 2. 3, the glory of the *f.* house.
Job 15. 7, art thou the *f.* man born?
Prov. 3. 9, honour the Lord with *f.*-fruits.
18. 17, *f.* in his own cause.
Isa. 43. 27, thy *f.* father hath sinned.
Mat. 5. 24, *f.* be reconciled.
6. 33, seek ye *f.* the kingdom.
7. 5, *f.* cast out the beam.
12. 29; Mk. 3. 27, except he *f.* bind strong man.
45, last state of that man worse than *f.*
17. 10, 11; Mk. 9. 12, Elias must *f.* come.
20. 10, when the *f.* came, they supposed.
22. 38; Mk. 12. 28, 29, 30, the *f.* commandment.
Mk. 4. 28, *f.* the blade.
9. 35, if any desire to be *f.*, same shall be last.
13. 10, gospel must *f.* be published.
Lu. 14. 28, sitteth not down *f.*
17. 25, but *f.* must he suffer many things.
John 1. 41, *f.* findeth his brother Simon.
5. 4, whosoever *f.* stepped in.
8. 7, let him *f.* cast a stone.
Acts 11. 26, called Christians *f.* at Antioch.
Rom. 2. 9, 10, of the Jew *f.*
8. 23, the *f.*-fruits of the Spirit.
29, *f.*-born among many brethren.
11. 16, if the *f.*-fruit be holy.
1 Cor. 12. 28, *f.* apostles, secondarily prophets.
14. 30, let the *f.* hold peace.
15. 20, 23, Christ the *f.*-fruits.
45, the *f.* man was made a living soul.
46, not *f.* which is spiritual.
47, *f.* man is of the earth.
2 Cor. 8. 5, *f.* gave their own selves.
12, if there be *f.* a willing mind.
Eph. 6. 2, the *f.* commandment with promise.
Col. 1. 15, 18, the *f.*-born of every creature.
1 Thess. 4. 16, dead in Christ shall rise *f.*
2 Thess. 2. 3, a falling away *f.*
1 Tim. 1. 16, that in me *f.*
2. 13, Adam was *f.* formed.
3. 10, let these *f.* be proved.
5. 4, learn *f.* to show piety at home.
12, cast off their *f.* faith.
2 Tim. 4. 16, at my *f.* answer no man.
Tit. 3. 10, after *f.* and second admonition.
Heb. 5. 12, which be the *f.* principles.
Heb. 7. 27, *f.* for his own sins.
10. 9, taketh away the *f.*
Jas. 3. 17, *f.* pure, then peaceable.
1 Pet. 4. 17, if judgment *f.* begin at us.
1 John 4. 19, because he *f.* loved us.
Jude 6, kept not their *f.* estate.
Rev. 2. 4, left thy *f.* love.
5, do thy *f.* works.
20. 5, this is the *f.* resurrection.
21. 1, *f.* heaven and *f.* earth passed away.
See Ex. 4. 8; Num. 18. 13; John 12. 16.

FIR TREE. Isa. 41. 19, I will set in the desert the *f.*
55. 13, instead of the thorn shall come up the *f.*
60. 13, the *f.*
Hos. 14. 8, I am like a green *f.*

FISH. Eccl. 9. 12, *f.* taken in an evil net.
Hab. 1. 14, men as the *f.* of the sea.
Mat. 7. 10, if he ask a *f.*
14. 17; Mk. 6. 38; Lu. 9. 13, five loaves and two *f.*
John 21. 3, Peter saith, I go a *f.*
1 Cor. 15. 39, one flesh of beasts, another of *f.*
See Jer. 16. 16; Mat. 4. 19; Mk. 1. 17; Lu. 24. 42.

FISHERS. Mat. 4. 18; Mk. 1. 16, for they were *f.*
John 21. 7, he girt his *f.* coat unto him.
See Lu. 5. 2.

FIT. Job 34. 18, is it *f.* to say to a king?
Lu. 9. 62, is *f.* for the kingdom.
14. 35, it is not *f.* for the dunghill.
Col. 3. 18, submit, as it is *f.* in the Lord.
See Lev. 16. 21; Prov. 24. 27; Ezek. 15. 5; Rom. 9. 22.

FITLY. Prov. 25. 11; Eph. 2. 21; 4. 16.

FIXED. Ps. 57. 7; 108. 1; 112. 7; Lu. 16. 26.

FLAME. Gen. 3. 24, at garden of Eden a *f.* sword.
Judg. 13. 20, angel ascended in *f.*
Isa. 5. 24, as the *f.* consumeth chaff.
29. 6, a *f.* of devouring fire.
43. 2, neither shall *f.* kindle.
66. 15, rebuke with *f.* of fire.
Ezek. 20. 47, the *f.* *f.* shall not be quenched.
Lu. 16. 24, tormented in this *f.*
See Ps. 29. 7; Heb. 1. 7; Rev. 1. 14; 2. 18.

FLATTER. Job 17. 5, he speaketh *f.* to his friends.
32. 21, 22, give *f.* titles to man.
Ps. 5. 9, they *f.* with their tongue.
12. 2, *f.* lips and double heart.
Prov. 20. 19, meddle not with him that *f.*
26. 28, a *f.* mouth worketh ruin.
1 Thess. 2. 5, neither used we *f.* words.
See Prov. 28. 23; 29. 5; Dan. 11. 21, 32, 34.

FLATTERY. Ps. 78. 36; Prov. 2. 16; 24. 24.

FLEE. Lev. 26. 17, 36, ye shall *f.* when none pursueth.
Num. 10. 35, them that hate thee *f.* before thee.
Neh. 6. 11, should such a man as I *f.*?
Job 14. 2, he *f.* as a shadow.
Ps. 139. 7, whither shall I *f.*?
Prov. 28. 1, the wicked *f.* when no man pursueth.
17, he shall *f.* to the pit.
Cant. 2. 17; 4. 6, till shadows *f.* away.
Isa. 35. 10; 51. 11, sighing shall *f.* away.
Mat. 3. 7; Lu. 3. 7, to *f.* from wrath to come.
10. 23, in one city, *f.* to another.
24. 16; Mk. 13. 14; Lu. 21. 21, *f.* to mountains.
26. 56; Mk. 14. 50, forsook him and *f.*
John 10. 5, not follow, but will *f.* from him.
13, the hireling *f.*
1 Tim. 6. 11, *f.* these things.
2 Tim. 2. 22, *f.* youthful lusts.
Jas. 4. 7, he will *f.* from you.
See 1 Cor. 6. 18; 10. 14; Rev. 12. 6, 14.

FLEECE. Judg. 6. 37, I will put a *f.* of wool in the floor.

FLESH. Gen. 2. 24; Mat. 19. 5; Mk. 10. 8; 1 Cor. 6. 16; Eph. 5. 31, one *f.*
6. 12, all *f.* had corrupted his way.
13, end of all *f.* is come.
7. 21, all *f.* died.

Ex. 16. 3, when we sat by the *f.* pots.
Lev. 17. 14, the life of all *f.* is the blood.
19. 28, cuttings in your *f.*
Num. 11. 33, while *f.* was between their teeth.
16. 22; 27. 16, God of spirits of all *f.*
1 Kings 17. 6, bread and *f.* in morning and evening.
2 Chron. 32. 8, with him is an arm of *f.*
Neh. 5. 5, our *f.* is as the *f.* of our brethren.
Job 19. 26, in my *f.* shall I see God.
33. 21, his *f.* is consumed away.
Ps. 16. 9; Acts 2. 26, my *f.* shall rest in hope.
65. 2, to thee shall all *f.* come.
78. 20, can he provide *f.*?
Prov. 5. 11, mourn, when *f.* consumed.
11. 17, the cruel troubleth his own *f.*
23. 20, among riotous eaters of *f.*
Eccl. 4. 5, the fool eateth his own *f.*
12. 12, weariness of the *f.*
Isa. 40. 5, all *f.* shall see it.
6; 1 Pet. 1. 24, all *f.* is grass.
Ezek. 11. 19; 36. 26, a heart of *f.*
Joel 2. 28; Acts 2. 17, pour Spirit on all *f.*
Mat. 16. 17, *f.* and blood hath not revealed it.
24. 22; Mk. 13. 20, there should no *f.* be saved.
Mat. 26. 41; Mk. 14. 38, spirit willing, *f.* weak.
Lu. 24. 39, spirit hath not *f.* and bones.
John 1. 14, Word made *f.*, and dwelt.
6. 51, 54, 55, bread I give is my *f.*
52, can this man give us his *f.*?
63, the *f.* profiteth nothing.
8. 15, ye judge after the *f.*
17. 2, power over all *f.*
Rom. 6. 19, because of the infirmity of your *f.*
8. 3, condemned sin in the *f.*
8, they that are in *f.* cannot please God.
9, not in the *f.*, but the Spirit.
12, 13, to live after the *f.*
9. 3, kinsmen according to the *f.*
5, of whom as concerning the *f.*
13. 14, make not provision for the *f.*
1 Cor. 1. 29, that no *f.* should glory.
15. 39, all *f.* not the same *f.*
50, *f.* and blood cannot inherit.
2 Cor. 12. 7, a thorn in the *f.*
Gal. 1. 16, I conferred not with *f.* and blood.
2. 20, life I now live in the *f.*
5. 17, *f.* lusteth against the Spirit.
Eph. 2. 3, lusts of *f.*, desires of *f.*
Phil. 3. 3, 4, no confidence in the *f.*
1 Tim. 3. 16, manifest in the *f.*
1 Pet. 3. 18, Christ put to death in *f.*
1 John 4. 2; 2 John 7, denieth that Christ is come in *f.*
Jude 8, dreamers defile the *f.*
23, hating garment spotted by *f.*
See John 1. 13; 3. 6; Gal. 5. 19; Heb. 2. 14.

FLESHLY. 2 Cor. 1. 12; 3. 3; Col. 2. 18; 1 Pet. 2. 11.

FLIES. Ex. 8. 21, 31, I will send swarms of *f.* upon thee.
Ps. 78. 45, he sent divers sorts of *f.* among them.
105. 31, he spake, and there came divers sorts of *f.*

FLIGHT. Isa. 52. 12; Amos 2. 14; Mat. 24. 20; Heb. 11. 34.

FLINT. Num. 20. 11; Deut. 8. 15; 32. 13; Ps. 114. 8; Isa. 5. 28; 50. 7; Ezek. 3. 9; 1 Cor. 10. 4.

FLOCK. Jer. 13. 20, where is the *f.*, thy beautiful *f.*?
Ezek. 34. 31, the *f.* of my pasture are men.
Zech. 11. 7, the poor of the *f.*
Lu. 12. 32, fear not, little *f.*
Acts 20. 28, take heed to the *f.*
29, not sparing the *f.*
1 Pet. 5. 2, feed the *f.* of God.
3, being ensamples to the *f.*
See Ezek. 36. 37; Mal. 1. 14; Mat. 26. 31.

FLOOD. Josh. 24. 2, on other side of the *f.*
Job 28. 11, he bindeth *f.* from overflowing.
Ps. 32. 6, in *f.* of great waters.
Cant. 8. 7, neither can *f.* drown love.
Isa. 44. 3, *f.* upon the dry ground.
59. 19, enemy come in like a *f.*
Mat. 7. 25, the *f.* came, and the winds blew.
24. 38, in days before the *f.*
39; Lu. 17. 27, knew not till *f.* came.
See Gen. 6. 17; 7. 11; 8; 9. 11; Ps. 90. 5; 2 Pet. 2. 5; Rev. 12. 15.

FLOOR. 1 Sam. 23. 1, they rob the threshing-*f.*
2 Sam. 24. 21, to buy the threshing-*f.* of thee.
Hos. 9. 1, loved a reward on every corn-*f.*
Mic. 4. 12, gather as sheaves into the *f.*
Mat. 3. 12; Lu. 3. 17, purge his *f.*
See Deut. 15. 14; Dan. 2. 35; Joel 2. 24.

FLOUR. Ex. 29. 2, of wheaten *f.* shalt thou make them.
Lev. 2. 2, take thereout his handful of the *f.*

FLOURISH. Ps. 72. 7, in his days shall the righteous *f.*
90. 6, in the morning it *f.*
92. 12, righteous shall *f.* like a palm tree.
103. 15, as flower so he *f.*
Prov. 11. 28, righteous shall *f.* as branch.
14. 11, tabernacle of upright *f.*
Eccl. 12. 5, when the almond tree shall *f.*
Cant. 6. 11; 7. 12, whether the vine *f.*
Ezek. 17. 24, have made dry tree to *f.*
Phil. 4. 10, your care of me hath *f.*
See Ps. 92. 14; Dan. 4. 4.

FLOW. Ps. 147. 18, wind to blow, and waters *f.*
Cant. 4. 16, that the spices may *f.* out.
Isa. 2. 2, all nations shall *f.* unto it.
64. 1, 3, mountains *f.* at thy presence.
Jer. 31. 12, shall *f.* to the goodness of the Lord.
John 7. 38, shall *f.* living water.
See Job 20. 28; Isa. 60. 5; Joel 3. 18; Mic. 4. 1.

FLOWER. 1 Sam. 2. 33, shall die in *f.* of age.
Job 14. 2, cometh forth as a *f.*
Cant. 2. 12, the *f.* appear on earth.
Isa. 28. 1, 4, glorious beauty is a fading *f.*
40. 6, as the *f.* of the field.
7; Nah. 1. 4; Jas. 1. 10; 1 Pet. 1. 24, *f.* fadeth.
See Job 15. 33; Isa. 18. 5; 1 Cor. 7. 36.

FLY. Job 5. 7, as sparks *f.* upward.
Ps. 55. 6, then would I *f.* away.
90. 10, and we *f.* away.
Prov. 23. 5, riches *f.* away.
Isa. 60. 8, that *f.* as a cloud.
See Dan. 9. 21; Rev. 14. 6; 19. 17.

FOAM. Hos. 10. 7; Mk. 9. 18; Lu. 9. 39; Jude 13.

FOES. Ps. 27. 2; 30. 1; 89. 23; Mat. 10. 36; Acts 2. 35.

FOLD. Prov. 6. 10; 24. 33, *f.* of the hands to sleep.
Eccl. 4. 5, fool *f.* his hands and eateth.
Hab. 3. 17, flock cut off from the *f.*
John 10. 16, one *f.*, and one shepherd.
See Isa. 13. 20; 65. 10; Nah. 1. 10.

FOLK. Prov. 30. 26; Jer. 51. 58; Mk. 6. 5; John 5. 3.

FOLLOW. Num. 14. 24, Caleb hath *f.* me fully.
1 Kings 18. 21, God, *f.* him.
Ps. 23. 6, goodness and mercy shall *f.* me.
63. 8, my soul *f.* hard after thee.
68. 25, the players *f.* after.
Prov. 12. 11; 28. 19, that *f.* vain persons.
Isa. 5. 11, that they may *f.* strong drink.
Hos. 6. 3, if we *f.* on to know the Lord.
Amos 7. 15, took me as I *f.* the flock.
Mat. 4. 19; 8. 22; 9. 9; 16. 24; 19. 21; Mk. 2. 14; 8. 34; 10. 21; Lu. 5. 27; 9. 23, 59; John 1. 43; 21. 22, Jesus said, *f.* me.
8. 19; Lu. 9. 57, 61, Master, I will *f.* thee.
Mk. 10. 28; Lu. 18. 28, we left all, and *f.* thee.
32, as they *f.*, they were afraid.
Lu. 22. 54, Peter *f.* afar off.
John 10. 27, my sheep hear my voice, and *f.* me.
13. 36, thou canst not *f.* me now.
Rom. 14. 19, *f.* things that make for peace.
1 Cor. 10. 4, the rock that *f.* them.

1 Cor. 14. 1, *f.* after charity.
Phil. 3. 12, I *f.* after.
1 Thess. 5. 15, ever *f.* that which is good.
1 Tim. 5. 24, some men they *f.* after.
6. 11; 2 Tim. 2. 22, *f.* righteousness.
Heb. 12. 14, *f.* peace with all men.
13. 7, whose faith *f.*
1 Pet. 1. 11, the glory that should *f.*
2. 21, that ye should *f.* his steps.
2 Pet. 2. 15, *f.* the way of Balaam.
Rev. 14. 4, they that *f.* the Lamb.
13, their works do *f.* them.
See Mk. 9. 38; 1 Pet. 3. 13; 2 Pet. 1. 16; Rev. 6. 8.

FOLLOWER. Eph. 5. 1, *f.* of God, as dear children.
Heb. 6. 12, *f.* of them who through faith.

FOLLY. 1 Sam. 25. 25, and *f.* is with him.
Job 4. 18, his angels he charged with *f.*
24. 12, yet God layeth not *f.* to them.
42. 8, lest I deal with you after your *f.*
Ps. 49. 13, this their way is their *f.*
85. 8, let them not turn again to *f.*
Prov. 13. 16, a fool layeth open his *f.*
14. 8, the *f.* of fools is deceit.
18, the simple inherit *f.*
16. 22, instruction of fools is *f.*
17. 12, rather than a fool in his *f.*
26. 4, answer not a fool according to his *f.*
5, answer fool according to his *f.*
Eccl. 1. 17, to know wisdom and *f.*
2. 13, wisdom excelleth *f.*
7. 25, the wickedness of *f.*
10. 6, *f.* is set in great dignity.
2 Cor. 11. 1, bear with me a little in my *f.*
2 Tim. 3. 9, their *f.* shall be manifest.
See Josh. 7. 15; Prov. 14. 24; Isa. 9. 17.

FOOD. Gen. 3. 6, tree good for *f.*
Ex. 21. 10, her *f.* shall not be diminished.
Deut. 10. 18, in giving him *f.* and raiment.
Job 23. 12, more than my necessary *f.*
24. 5, wilderness yieldeth *f.*
Ps. 78. 25, did eat angels' *f.*
104. 14, bring forth *f.* out of the earth.
136. 25, giveth *f.* to all flesh.
Prov. 6. 8, gathereth her *f.* in harvest.
13. 23, much *f.* in tillage of poor.
30. 8, with *f.* convenient for me.
31. 14, she bringeth her *f.* from far.
2 Cor. 9. 10, minister bread for your *f.*
1 Tim. 6. 8, having *f.* and raiment.
Jas. 2. 15, destitute of daily *f.*
See Gen. 1. 29; 2. 9; 6. 21; 9. 3; 41. 35; Lev. 22. 7; Ps. 145. 16; 147. 9.

FOOL. 2 Sam. 3. 33, died Abner as a *f.* dieth?
Ps. 14. 1; 53. 1, *f.* said in his heart.
75. 4, to *f.*, deal not foolishly.
Prov. 1. 7, *f.* despise wisdom.
3. 35, shame the promotion of *f.*
10. 8, 10, a prating *f.* shall fall.
21, *f.* die for want of wisdom.
23, sport to a *f.* to do mischief.
11. 29, the *f.* shall be servant to the wise.
12. 15, way of *f.* right in own eyes.
16, *f.* wrath presently known.
13. 16, *f.* layeth open his folly.
20, companion of *f.* shall be destroyed.
14. 8, folly of *f.* is deceit.
9, *f.* make a mock at sin.
16, the *f.* rageth, and is confident.
15. 2, mouth of *f.* poureth out foolishness.
5, a *f.* despiseth his father's instruction.
16. 22, the instruction of *f.* is folly.
17. 28, a *f.*, when he holdeth his peace, counted wise.
20. 3, every *f.* will be meddling.
29. 11, a *f.* uttereth all his mind.
Eccl. 2. 14, *f.* walketh in darkness.
16, how dieth wise man? as the *f.*
19, who knoweth whether wise or a *f.*?
5. 3, a *f.* voice is known by multitude of words.
10. 14, a *f.* is full of words.
Isa. 35. 8, wayfaring men, though *f.*
Jer. 17. 11, at his end he shall be a *f.*
Hos. 9. 7, the prophet is a *f.*
Mat. 5. 22, shall say, thou *f.*
23. 17, ye *f.* and blind.
Lu. 12. 20, thou *f.*, this night.
24. 25, O *f.*, and slow of heart.
1 Cor. 3. 18, let him become a *f.*
2 Cor. 11. 16, let no man think me a *f.*
12. 11, I am a *f.* in glorying.
Eph. 5. 15, walk not as *f.*, but as wise.
See Prov. 10. 18; 19. 1; 28. 26; Eccl. 10. 3.

FOOLISH. Deut. 32. 6, O *f.* people.
2 Sam. 24. 10; 1 Chron. 21. 8, I have done very *f.*
Job 2. 10, as one of the *f.* women.
Ps. 73. 3, I was envious at the *f.*
Prov. 9. 6, forsake the *f.*, and live.
13, a *f.* woman is clamorous.
14. 1, the *f.* plucketh it down.
17. 25; 19. 13, a *f.* son is grief.
Eccl. 7. 17, neither be thou *f.*
Jer. 4. 22, my people are *f.*
Mat. 7. 26, unto a *f.* man.
Rom. 1. 21, their *f.* heart was darkened.
1 Cor. 1. 20, hath not God made *f.*
Gal. 3. 1, O *f.* Galatians.
3. 3, are ye so *f.*?
Eph. 5. 4, nor *f.* talking.
1 Tim. 6. 9, rich fall into *f.* lusts.
2 Tim. 2. 23; Tit. 3. 9, *f.* questions avoid.
Tit. 3. 3, we were sometimes *f.*
1 Pet. 2. 15, ignorance of *f.* men.
See Job 5. 3; Lam. 2. 14; Ezek. 13. 3.

FOOLISHNESS. Ps. 69. 5, thou knowest my *f.*
Prov. 22. 15, *f.* is bound in heart of child.
24. 9, thought of *f.* is sin.
1 Cor. 1. 18, to them that perish *f.*
21, by the *f.* of preaching.
23, Christ crucified, to Greeks *f.*
25, the *f.* of God is wiser than men.
2. 14, things of Spirit are *f.* to him.
3. 19, wisdom of world *f.* with God.
See 2 Sam. 15. 31; Prov. 27. 22.

FOOT. Gen. 41. 44, without thee no man lift *f.*
Deut. 2. 5, not so much as *f.* breadth.
11. 10, wateredst it with thy *f.*
Ps. 38. 16, when my *f.* slippeth.
91. 12; Mat. 4. 6; Lu. 4. 11, dash *f.* against stone.
94. 18, my *f.* slippeth, thy mercy.
121. 3, not suffer *f.* to be moved.
Prov. 3. 23, thy *f.* shall not stumble.
25. 17, withdraw *f.* from neighbour's house.
Eccl. 5. 1, keep thy *f.* when thou goest.
Isa. 1. 6, from sole of *f.* to head no soundness.
Mat. 14. 13, people followed on *f.*
18. 8; Mk. 9. 45, if thy *f.* offend thee.
1 Cor. 12. 15, if the *f.* say, because I am not.
Heb. 10. 29, trodden under *f.* the Son of God.
See Jer. 12. 5; Mat. 5. 35; Jas. 2. 3.

FORBADE. Mat. 3. 14; Mk. 9. 38; Lu. 9. 49.

FORBEAR. Ex. 23. 5, wouldest *f.* to help.
2 Chron. 35. 21, *f.* from meddling with God.
Neh. 9. 30, many years didst thou *f.* them.
Ezek. 2. 5; 3. 11, whether hear or *f.*
1 Cor. 9. 6, power to *f.* working.
Eph. 4. 2; Col. 3. 13, *f.* one another in love.
6. 9, *f.* threatening.
See Prov. 24. 11; Ezek. 3. 27; Zech. 11. 12.

FORBID. Num. 11. 28, Joshua said, *f.* them.
Mk. 9. 39; Lu. 9. 50, *f.* him not.
10. 14; Lu. 18. 16, children, *f.* them not.
Lu. 6. 29, *f.* not to take coat.
23. 2, *f.* to give tribute.
Acts 10. 47, can any *f.* water?
1 Cor. 14. 39, *f.* not to speak with tongues.
1 Tim. 4. 3, *f.* to marry.
See Acts 16. 6; 28. 31; 1 Thess. 2. 16.

FORCE. Deut. 34. 7, nor natural *f.* abated.
Ezra 4. 23, made them cease by *f.*

Mat. 11. 12, violent take it by *f.*
John 6. 15, perceived they would take him by *f.*
Heb. 9. 17, a testament is of *f.* after.
See Deut. 20. 19; Prov. 30. 33; Amos 2. 14.
FORCIBLE. Job 6. 25.
FOREFATHERS. Jer. 11. 10; 2 Tim. 1. 3.
FOREHEAD. Ex. 28. 38, it shall always be on his *f.*
1 Sam. 17. 49, smote Philistine in his *f.*
Ezek. 3. 8, made thy *f.* strong.
9. 4, set a mark on *f.* of them that sigh.
Rev. 7. 3; 9. 4, sealed in their *f.*
22. 4, his name shall be in their *f.*
See Rev. 13. 16; 14. 1; 17. 5; 20. 4.
FOREIGNER. Ex. 12. 45; Deut. 15. 3; Eph. 2. 19.
FOREKNOW. Rom. 8. 29; 11. 2; 1 Pet. 1. 2.
FOREKNOWLEDGE. Acts 2. 23, delivered by *f.* of God.
FOREMOST. Gen. 32. 17; 33. 2; 2 Sam. 18. 27.
FOREORDAINED. 1 Pet. 1. 20.
FORERUNNER. Heb. 6. 20.
FORESEE. Prov. 22. 3; 27. 12; Gal. 3. 8.
FOREST. Ps. 50. 10, every beast of *f.* is mine.
Isa. 29. 17; 32. 15, field esteemed as *f.*
Jer. 5. 6, lion out of *f.* shall slay them.
26. 18; Mic. 3. 12, high places of the *f.*
46. 23, they shall cut down her *f.*
Amos 3. 4, will lion roar in the *f.*?
See Ezek. 15. 6; 20. 46; Hos. 2. 12.
FORETELL. Mk. 13. 23; Acts 3. 24; 2 Cor. 13. 2.
FOREWARN. Lu. 12. 5; 1 Thess. 4. 6.
FORGAT. Judg. 3. 7, they *f.* the Lord.
Ps. 78. 11, they *f.* his works.
106. 13, soon *f.* his works.
Lam. 3. 17, I *f.* prosperity.
See Gen. 40. 23; Hos. 2. 13.
FORGAVE. Mat. 18. 27, 32, and *f.* him the debt.
Lu. 7. 42, he frankly *f.* them both.
43, he to whom he *f.* most.
2 Cor. 2. 10, if I *f.* any thing.
Col. 3. 13, even as Christ *f.* you.
See Ps. 32. 5; 78. 38; 99. 8.
FORGE. Job 13. 4; Ps. 119. 69.
FORGET. Deut. 4. 9, lest thou *f.* things thine eyes have seen.
23, lest ye *f.* the covenant.
6. 12; 8. 11, beware lest thou *f.* the Lord.
Job 8. 13, so are the paths of all that *f.* God.
Ps. 9. 17, all nations that *f.* God.
10. 12, *f.* not the humble.
45. 10, *f.* thine own people.
Ps. 50. 22, consider, ye that *f.* God.
78. 7, that they might not *f.* works of God.
88. 12, in the land of *f.*
102. 4, I *f.* to eat my bread.
103. 2, *f.* not all his benefits.
119. 16, I will not *f.* thy word.
137. 5, if I *f.* thee, O Jerusalem.
Prov. 2. 17, *f.* the covenant of her God.
3. 1, *f.* not my law.
31. 5, lest they drink and *f.*
7, let him drink, and *f.* his poverty.
Isa. 49. 15, can a woman *f.*?
51. 13, and *f.* the Lord thy Maker.
65. 11, *f.* my holy mountain.
Jer. 2. 32, maid *f.* her ornaments.
23. 27, cause my people to *f.* my name.
Amos 8. 7, I will never *f.* their works.
Phil. 3. 13, *f.* those things which are behind.
Heb. 6. 10, not unrighteous to *f.*
13. 2, not *f.* to entertain.
16, to communicate *f.* not.
Jas. 1. 24, *f.* what manner of man.
See Gen. 41. 51; Lam. 5. 20; Hos. 4. 6.
FORGIVE. Ex. 32. 32, if thou wilt *f.* their sin.
34. 7; Num. 14. 18, *f.* iniquity, transgression.
1 Kings 8. 30, 39; 2 Chron. 6. 21, 30, hearest, *f.*
2 Chron. 7. 14, then will I hear and *f.*
Ps. 32. 1; Rom. 4. 7, whose transgression is *f.*
86. 5, good, and ready to *f.*
103. 3, who *f.* all thine iniquities.
Mat. 6. 12; Lu. 11. 4, *f.* us, as we *f.*
14, if ye *f.*
15, if ye *f.* not.
9. 6; Mk. 2. 10; Lu. 5. 24, power to *f.* sin.
18. 21, how oft, and I *f.* him?
35, if ye from your hearts *f.*
Mk. 2. 7, who can *f.* sins?
11. 25, *f.* that your Father may *f.*
26, not *f.*, Father will not *f.*
Lu. 6. 37, *f.*, and ye shall be *f.*
7. 47, her sins, which are many, are *f.*
49, who is this *f.* sins also?
17. 3, 4, if brother repent, *f.* him.
23. 34, Father *f.* them, they know not.
Acts 8. 22, thought of thine heart may be *f.*
2 Cor. 2. 7, ye ought rather to *f.*
10, to whom ye *f.*, I *f.* also.
12. 13, *f.* me this wrong.
Eph. 4. 32, as God for Christ's sake hath *f.*
Col. 2. 13, quickened, having *f.*
1 John 1. 9, faithful and just to *f.*
See Mat. 9. 2; 12. 31; Mk. 3. 28; Lu. 12. 10.
FORGIVENESS. Ps. 130. 4, *f.* with thee, that thou mayest be feared.
Mk. 3. 29, hath never *f.*
Acts 5. 31, exalted to give *f.*
Eph. 1. 7; Col. 1. 14, in whom we have *f.*
See Dan. 9. 9; Acts 13. 38; 26. 18.
FORGOTTEN. Deut. 24. 19, and hast *f.* a sheaf.
32. 18, *f.* God that formed thee.
Ps. 9. 18, needy not always *f.*
10. 11, said, God hath *f.*
31. 12, *f.* as a dead man.
42. 9, why hast thou *f.* me?
44. 20, if we have *f.* name of our God.
77. 9, hath God *f.* to be gracious?
Eccl. 2. 16, in days to come all *f.*
8. 10, wicked were *f.* in city.
9. 5, the memory of them is *f.*
Isa. 17. 10, *f.* the God of thy salvation.
44. 21, thou shalt not be *f.* of me.
49. 14, my Lord hath *f.* me.
65. 16, former troubles are *f.*
Jer. 2. 32; 13. 25; 18. 15, my people have *f.*
3. 21, *f.* the Lord their God.
44. 9, *f.* the wickedness of your fathers.
50. 6, *f.* their restingplace.
Ezek. 22. 12; 23. 35, thou hast *f.* me.
Mat. 16. 5; Mk. 8. 14, *f.* to take bread.
Lu. 12. 6, not one *f.* before God.
2 Pet. 1. 9, *f.* that he was purged.
See Lam. 2. 6; Hos. 4. 6; 8. 14; 13. 6.
FORM (*n.*). Gen. 1. 2; Jer. 4. 23, without *f.*, and void.
Job 4. 16, could not discern the *f.*
Isa. 52. 14, *f.* more than sons of men.
Ezek. 10. 8, the *f.* of a man's hand.
Dan. 3. 19, *f.* of visage changed.
25, *f.* of fourth like Son of God.
Mk. 16. 12, appeared in another *f.*
Rom. 2. 20, hast *f.* of knowledge and truth.
Phil. 2. 6, being in the *f.* of God.
7, the *f.* of a servant.
2 Tim. 1. 13, *f.* of sound words.
3. 5, having *f.* of godliness.
See 1 Sam. 28. 14; Ezek. 43. 11; Rom. 6. 17.
FORM (*v.*). Deut. 32. 18, forgotten God that *f.* thee.
2 Kings 19. 25; Isa. 37. 26, that I have *f.* it.
Job 26. 5, dead things are *f.*
13, hath *f.* crooked serpent.
33. 6, I also am *f.* of clay.
Ps. 90. 2, or ever thou hadst *f.*
94. 9, he that *f.* the eye.
Prov. 26. 10, great God that *f.* all things.
Isa. 43. 1, he that *f.* thee, O Israel.
7; 44. 21, I have *f.* him.
10, before me was no God *f.*
21, people have I *f.* for myself.
44. 10, who hath *f.* a god?
54. 17, no weapon *f.* against thee.
Amos 7. 1, he *f.* grasshoppers.

Rom. 9. 20, shall thing *f.* say.
Gal. 4. 19, till Christ be *f.* in you.
See Gen. 2. 7, 19; Ps. 95. 5; Jer. 1. 5.

FORMER. Ruth 4. 7, manner in *f.* time.
Job 8. 8, enquire of the *f.* age.
Ps. 89. 49, where are thy *f.* lovingkindnesses?
Eccl. 1. 11, no remembrance of *f.* things.
7. 10, *f.* days better than these.
Isa. 43. 18, remember not the *f.* things.
46. 9, remember the *f.* things of old.
48. 3, declared *f.* things from beginning.
65. 7, measure their *f.* work.
16, *f.* troubles are forgotten.
Jer. 5. 24; Hos. 6. 3; Joel 2. 23, *f.* and latter rain.
10. 16; 51. 19, the *f.* of all things.
Hag. 2. 9, glory of *f.* house.
Zech. 1. 4; 7. 7, 12, *f.* prophets have cried.
8. 11, I will not be as in *f.* days.
14. 8, half of them toward *f.* sea.
Mal. 3. 4, pleasant as in *f.* years.
Eph. 4. 22, concerning the *f.* conversation.
Rev. 21. 4, for the *f.* things are passed away.
See Gen. 40. 13; Dan. 11. 13; Acts 1. 1.

FORSAKE. Deut. 4. 31; 31. 6; 1 Chron. 28. 20, he will not *f.*
12. 19, *f.* not the Levite.
32. 15, he *f.* God which made him.
Josh. 1. 5; Heb. 13. 5, I will not fail nor *f.*
Judg. 9. 11, *f.* my sweetness and fruit.
1 Chron. 28. 9, if thou *f.* him, he will cast thee off.
2 Chron. 15. 2, if ye *f.* him, he will *f.* you.
Neh. 10. 39, we will not *f.* house of our God.
13. 11, why is house of God *f.*?
Job 6. 14, he *f.* the fear of the Almighty.
20. 19, oppressed and *f.* the poor.
Ps. 22. 1; Mat. 27. 46; Mk. 15. 34, why hast thou *f.* me?
37. 25, yet have I not seen the righteous *f.*
28, the Lord *f.* not his saints.
119. 8, *f.* me not utterly.
138. 8, *f.* not work of thine own hands.
Prov. 1. 8; 6. 20, *f.* not law of thy mother.
2. 17, *f.* the guide of her youth.
4. 6, *f.* her not, and she shall preserve thee.
27. 10, thy friend, and father's friend, *f.* not.
Isa. 6. 12, a great *f.* in the land.
17. 9, as a *f.* bough.
32. 14; Jer. 4. 29; Ezek. 36. 4, a *f.* city.
54. 6, as a woman *f.*
7, for a small moment *f.*
62. 4, no more be termed *f.*
12, a city not *f.*
Jer. 2. 13; 17. 13, *f.* fountain of living waters.
Mat. 19. 27; Lu. 5. 11, we have *f.* all.
29, that hath *f.* houses.
26. 56; Mk. 14. 50, disciples *f.* him, and fled.
Mk. 1. 18, they *f.* their nets.
Lu. 14. 33, whosoever *f.* not all.
2 Cor. 4. 9, persecuted, but not *f.*
2 Tim. 4. 10, Demas hath *f.* me.
16, all men *f.* me.
Heb. 10. 25, not *f.* assembling of ourselves.
11. 27, by faith Moses *f.* Egypt.
See Ps. 71. 11; Isa. 49. 14; Jer. 5. 7; 22. 9; Ezek. 8. 12.

FORSWEAR. Mat. 5. 33.

FORTRESS. 2 Sam. 22. 2; Ps. 18. 2; Jer. 16. 19, Lord is my *f.*

FORTY STRIPES. Deut. 25. 3, *f. s.* he may give him.
2 Cor. 11. 24, of the Jews five times received I *f. s.* save one.

FORTY YEARS. Ex. 16. 35, Israel did eat manna *f. y.*
Num. 14. 33, your children shall wander in the wilderness *f. y.*
Ps. 95. 10, *f. y.* long was I grieved.
See Judg. 3. 11; 5. 31; 8. 28.

FORWARD. Jer. 7. 24, backward, and not *f.*
Zech. 1. 15, helped *f.* the affliction.
See 2 Cor. 8. 8; 9. 2; 3 John 6.

FOUL. Job 16. 16; Mat. 16. 3; Mk. 9. 25; Rev. 18. 2.

FOUND. Gen. 27. 20, *f.* it so quickly.
37. 32, this have we *f.*
44. 16, hath *f.* out iniquity.
1 Kings 20. 36, a lion *f.* him.
21. 20, hast thou *f.* me?
2 Kings 22. 8, I *f.* book of the law.
2 Chron. 19. 3, good things *f.* in thee.
Job 28. 12, 13, where shall wisdom be *f.*?
33. 24, I have *f.* a ransom.
Ps. 32. 6, when thou mayest be *f.*
36. 2, iniquity *f.* to be hateful.
84. 3, sparrow hath *f.* an house.
Prov. 25. 16, hast thou *f.* honey?
Eccl. 7. 28, one among a thousand have I *f.*
29, this only have I *f.*
Cant. 3. 4, but I *f.* him whom my soul loveth.
Isa. 65. 1; Rom. 10. 20, *f.* of them that sought me not.
Jer. 2. 26, thief ashamed when he is *f.*
34, in thy skirts is *f.*
41. 8, ten men were *f.*
Ezek. 22. 30, I sought for a man, but *f.* none.
Dan. 5. 27, weighed, and *f.* wanting.
Mal. 2. 6, iniquity not *f.* in his lips.
Mat. 7. 25; Lu. 6. 48, it was *f.* on a rock.
8. 10; Lu. 7. 9, have not *f.* so great faith.
13. 46, *f.* one pearl of great price.
20. 6, *f.* others standing idle.
21. 19; Mk. 14. 40; Lu. 22. 45, *f.* nothing thereon.
Mk. 7. 2, they *f.* fault.
30, she *f.* the devil gone out.
Lu. 2. 46, they *f.* him in the temple.
8. 35, they *f.* the man clothed.
15. 5, 6, *f.* the sheep.
9, *f.* the piece of money.
24, 32, was lost, and is *f.*
23. 14, I have *f.* no fault.
24. 2, *f.* the stone rolled away.
3, 23 *f.* not the body.
John 1. 41, 45, we have *f.* the Messias.
Acts 7. 11, our fathers *f.* no sustenance.
9. 2, if he *f.* any of this way.
17. 23, I *f.* an altar.
Rom. 7. 10, I *f.* to be unto death.
Gal. 2. 17, we ourselves also are *f.* sinners.
Phil. 2. 8, *f.* in fashion as a man.
Heb. 11. 5, Enoch was not *f.*
12. 17, he *f.* no place of repentance.
Rev. 3. 2, not *f.* thy works perfect.
12. 8, nor was their place *f.* any more.
16. 20, mountains were not *f.*
See Gen. 6. 8; 2 Chron. 15. 4; 2 Cor. 5. 3; Phil. 3. 9.

FOUNDATION. Josh. 6. 26; 1 Kings 16. 34, lay the *f.* in his firstborn.
Job 4. 19, them whose *f.* is in dust.
Ps. 11. 3, if *f.* be destroyed.
82. 5, all the *f.* of earth out of course.
102. 25, of old laid *f.* of earth.
137. 7, rase it even to the *f.*
Prov. 10. 25, righteous an everlasting *f.*
Isa. 28. 16, I lay in Zion a *f.*
Isa. 58. 12, the *f.* of many generations.
Lu. 6. 48, laid the *f.* on a rock.
49, without a *f.*
Rom. 15. 20, on another man's *f.*
1 Cor. 3. 10, I laid the *f.*
11, other *f.* can no man lay.
12, if any man build on this *f.*
Eph. 2. 20, on the *f.* of the apostles and prophets.
1 Tim. 6. 19, laying up for themselves a good *f.*
2 Tim. 2. 19, the *f.* of God standeth sure.
Heb. 6. 1, not laying the *f.* of repentance.
11. 10, a city that hath *f.*
Rev. 21. 14, the wall had twelve *f.*
See Mat. 13. 35; John 17. 24; Acts 16. 26.

FOUNTAIN. Gen. 7. 11; 8. 2, *f.* of great deep.

Deut. 8. 7, a land of *f*.
2 Chron. 32. 3, took counsel to stop *f*. of water.
Ps. 36. 9, the *f*. of life.
Prov. 5. 16, let thy *f*. be dispersed.
8. 24, no *f*. abounding with water.
13. 14, law of the wise a *f*. of life.
14. 27, fear of the Lord a *f*. of life.
25. 26, a troubled *f*. and corrupt spring.
Eccl. 12. 6, pitcher broken at the *f*.
Cant. 4. 12, a *f*. sealed.
15, a *f*. of gardens.
Jer. 2. 13; 17. 13, forsaken *f*. of living waters.
9. 1, eyes a *f*. of tears.
Hos. 13. 15, his *f*. shall be dried up.
Zech. 13. 1, in that day shall be a *f*. opened.
Jas. 3. 11, 12, doth a *f*. send forth.
Rev. 7. 17, lead them to living *f*.
14. 7, worship him that made *f*. of waters.
21. 6, of the *f*. of life freely.
See Isa. 12. 3; 44. 3; 55. 1; Jer. 6. 7; Joel 3. 18; Mk. 5. 29; John 4. 10.

FOWLS. Gen. 1. 20, and *f*. that may fly above the earth.
7. 3, of *f*. also of the air by sevens.
Ps. 104. 12, the *f*. of heaven have their habitation.
148. 10, creeping things, and flying *f*.

FOXES. Cant. 2. 15, take us the *f*., the little *f*.
Lam. 5. 18, the *f*. walk upon it.
Mat. 8. 20, the *f*. have holes.
Lu. 13. 32, go ye, and tell that *f*.
See Judg. 15. 4.

FRAGMENTS. John 6. 12, 13, gather up *f*. that remain.
See Mat. 14. 20; Mk. 6. 43; 8. 19; Lu. 9. 17.

FRAIL. Ps. 39. 4.

FRAME. Judg. 12. 6, he could not *f*. to pronounce.
Ps. 94. 20, *f*. mischief by a law.
103. 14, he knoweth our *f*.
Isa. 29. 16, shall thing *f*. say of him that *f*. it?
Eph. 2. 21, building fitly *f*. together.
See Ezek. 40. 2; Hos. 5. 4; Heb. 11. 3.

FRANKLY. Lu. 7. 42.

FRAUD. Ps. 10. 7; Jas. 5. 4.

FRAY. Deut. 28. 26; Jer. 7. 33; Zech. 1. 21.

FREE. Gen. 2. 16, of every tree thou mayest *f*. eat.
Deut. 24. 5, shall be *f*. at home one year.
John. 9. 23, there shall none of you be *f*.
1 Sam. 14. 30, if people had eaten *f*.
2 Chron. 29. 31, of *f*. heart offered.
Ezra 2. 68, chief fathers offered *f*.
7. 15, king and counsellors offered *f*. to God.
Ps. 51. 12, with thy *f*. spirit.
88. 5, *f*. among the dead.
Isa. 58. 6, let the oppressed go *f*.
Hos. 14. 4, I will love them *f*.
Mat. 10. 8, *f*. ye have received, *f*. give.
17. 26, then are the children *f*.
Mk. 7. 11, if a man say Corban, he shall be *f*.
John 8. 32, the truth shall make you *f*.
33, how sayest thou, ye shall be *f*.?
36, Son make you *f*., ye shall be *f*. indeed.
Acts 22. 28, I was *f*. born.
Rom. 3. 24, justified *f*. by his grace.
5. 15, the *f*. gift.
6. 18, 22, being made *f*. from sin.
20, servants of sin, *f*. from righteousness.
8. 2, *f*. from the law of sin and death.
32, with him *f*. give us all things.
1 Cor. 9. 1, am I not *f*.?
19, though *f*. from all men.
12. 13; Eph. 6. 8, whether bond or *f*.
Gal. 3. 28; Col. 3. 11, there is neither bond nor *f*.
5. 1, wherewith Christ hath made us *f*.
2 Thess. 3. 1, word have *f*. course.
1 Pet. 2. 16, as *f*., and not using liberty.
Rev. 21. 6, give of fountain of life *f*.
22. 17, let him take water of life *f*.
See Ex. 21. 2; Deut. 15. 13; Jer. 34. 9; Gal. 4. 22.

FREEWILL. Lev. 22. 18, and for all his *f*. offerings.
Num. 15. 3, or in a *f*. offering.
Deut. 16. 10, a tribute of a *f*. offering.
See Ezra 3. 5.

FREEWOMAN. Gal. 4. 22.

FRESH. Num. 11. 8; Job 29. 20; 33. 25; Jas. 3. 12.

FRET. Ps. 37. 1, 7, 8; Prov. 24. 19, *f*. not thyself.
Prov. 19. 3, his heart *f*. against the Lord.
See 1 Sam. 1. 6; Isa. 8. 21; Ezek. 16. 43.

FRIEND. Ex. 33. 11, as a man to his *f*.
2 Sam. 19. 6, lovest thine enemies, and hatest *f*.
2 Chron. 20. 7, Abraham thy *f*. for ever.
Job 6. 27, ye dig a pit for your *f*.
42. 10, when he prayed for his *f*.
Ps. 35. 14, as though he had been my *f*.
41. 9, my familiar *f*. hath lifted.
88. 18, lover and *f*. hast thou put far from me.
Prov. 6. 1, if thou be surety for thy *f*.
3, make sure thy *f*.
14. 20, the rich hath many *f*.
16. 28; 17. 9, whisperer separateth chief *f*.
17. 17, *f*. loveth at all times.
18. 24, a *f*. that sticketh closer than a brother.
19. 4, wealth maketh many *f*.
27. 6, faithful are wounds of a *f*.
10, thine own *f*. and father's *f*. forsake not.
17, man sharpeneth countenance of his *f*.
Cant. 5. 16, this is my *f*.
Isa. 41. 8, seed of Abraham my *f*.
Jer. 20. 4, a terror to thy *f*.
Mic. 7. 5, trust not in a *f*.
Zech. 13. 6, wounded in house of my *f*.
Mat. 11. 19; Lu. 7. 34, a *f*. of publicans.
20. 13, *f*., I do thee no wrong.
22. 12, *f*., how camest thou hither?
26. 50, *f*., wherefore art thou come?
Mk. 5. 19, go home to thy *f*.
Lu. 11. 5, which of you shall have a *f*.
8, though he give not because he is his *f*.
14. 12, call not thy *f*.
15. 6, 9, calleth his *f*. and neighbours.
16. 9, *f*. of the mammon.
John 11. 11, our *f*. Lazarus sleepeth.
15. 13, lay down his life for his *f*.
14, ye are my *f*., if ye do whatsoever I command.
15, not servants, but *f*.
19. 12, thou art not Cæsar's *f*.
Jas. 2. 23, Abraham was called the *f*. of God.
4. 4, a *f*. of the world.
See Prov. 22. 24; Lu. 14. 10; 3 John 14.

FRINGES. Num. 15. 37, that they make them *f*.
Deut. 22. 12, thou shalt make thee *f*.
See Mat. 23. 5.

FROWARD. Deut. 32. 20, a very *f*. generation.
Prov. 2. 12, man that speaketh *f*. things.
3. 32, the *f*. is abomination.
4. 24, put away *f*. mouth.
11. 20; 17. 20, of a *f*. heart.
16. 28, a *f*. man soweth strife.
21. 8, the way of man is *f*.
22. 5, snares are in way of the *f*.
See Prov. 10. 32; Isa. 57. 17; 1 Pet. 2. 18.

FRUIT. Num. 13. 26, showed them the *f*. of the land.
Deut. 26. 2, take the first of all *f*.
33. 14, precious *f*. brought forth.
Ps. 107. 37, yield *f*. of increase.
127. 3, the *f*. of the womb is his reward.
Prov. 8. 19, my *f*. is better than gold.
11. 30, *f*. of the righteous a tree of life.
12. 14; 18. 20, satisfied by the *f*. of his mouth.
Cant. 2. 3, his *f*. was sweet to my taste.
4. 13, 16, orchard with pleasant *f*.
Isa. 3. 10; Mic. 7. 13, the *f*. of their doings.
27. 6, fill face of the world with *f*.
28. 4, the hasty *f*. before summer.
57. 19, I create the *f*. of the lips.
Jer. 17. 10; 21. 14; 32. 19, according to *f*. of doings.
Hos. 10. 13, eaten the *f*. of lies.
Amos 8. 1, basket of summer *f*.
Mic. 6. 7, *f*. of body for sin of soul.
Hab. 3. 17, neither shall *f*. be in vines.

Hag. 1. 10, earth is stayed from her *f.*
Mat. 3. 8; Lu. 3. 8, *f.* meet for repentance.
7. 16, 20, by their *f.* ye shall know them.
12. 33, make tree good, and his *f.* good.
13. 23, is he who beareth *f.*
21. 19, let no *f.* grow on thee.
34, when time of *f.* drew near.
26. 29; Mk. 14. 25, drink of *f.* of vine.
Mk. 4. 28, earth bringeth forth *f.* of herself.
12. 2, receive the *f.* of the vineyard.
Lu. 13. 6, he sought *f.* thereon.
7, I come seeking *f.* on this fig tree.
9, if it bear *f.*, well.
John 4. 36, *f.* to life eternal.
15. 2, branch that beareth *f.*
4, branch cannot bear *f.* of itself.
8, that ye bear much *f.*
16, ordained that ye should bring forth *f.*
Rom. 1. 13, have some *f.* among you.
6. 21, what *f.* had ye then.
7. 4, bring forth *f.* unto God.
2 Cor. 9. 10; Phil. 1. 11, the *f.* of righteousness.
Gal. 5. 22; Eph. 5. 9, the *f.* of the Spirit.
Phil. 1. 22, this is the *f.* of my labour.
4. 17, I desire *f.* that may abound.
Col. 1. 6, the gospel bringeth forth *f.* in you.
2 Tim. 2. 6, first partaker of the *f.*
Heb. 12. 11, peaceable *f.* of righteousness.
13. 15, the *f.* of our lips.
Jas. 3. 17, wisdom full of good *f.*
5. 7, waiteth for the precious *f.*
Jude 12, trees whose *f.* withereth, without *f.*
Rev. 22. 2, yielded her *f.* every month.
See Gen. 30. 2; Ps. 92. 14; Jer. 12. 2; Col. 1. 10.
FROGS. Ex. 8. 6; Ps. 78. 45; 105. 30; Rev. 16. 13.
FRONTLETS. Ex. 13. 16; Deut. 6. 8, for *f.* between thine eyes.
FRUSTRATE. Ezra 4. 5; Isa. 44. 25; Gal. 2. 21.
FUEL. Isa. 9. 5; Ezek. 15. 4; 21. 32.
FULFIL. Ps. 20. 4, the Lord *f.* all thy counsel.
5, *f.* all thy petitions.
145. 19, he will *f.* the desire of them.
Mat. 3. 15, to *f.* all righteousness.
5. 17, not to destroy, but to *f.*
18; 24. 34, till all be *f.*
Mk. 13. 4, what the sign when these shall be *f.*?
Lu. 1. 20, my words shall be *f.* in season.
21. 24, times of the Gentiles be *f.*
22. 16, till it be *f.* in kingdom of God.
John 3. 29; 17. 13, this my joy is *f.*
Acts 13. 25, and as John *f.* his course.
33, God hath *f.* the same unto us.
Rom. 13. 10, love is the *f.* of the law.
Gal. 5. 14, all the law is *f.* in one word.
6. 2, so *f.* the law of Christ.
Eph. 2. 3, *f.* the desires of the flesh.
Phil. 2. 2, *f.* ye my joy.
Col. 4. 17, take heed thou *f.* the ministry.
2 Thess. 1. 11, *f.* good pleasure of his will.
Jas. 2. 8, if ye *f.* the royal law.
See Ex. 5. 13; 23. 26; Gal. 5. 16; Rev. 17. 17.
FULL. Lev. 19. 29, land became *f.* of wickedness.
Deut. 6. 11, houses *f.* of good things.
34. 9, Joshua was *f.* of spirit of wisdom.
Ruth 1. 21, I went out *f.*
2 Kings 6. 17, mountain was *f.* of horses.
1 Chron. 21. 22, 24, for the *f.* price.
Job 5. 26, come to grave in *f.* age.
11. 2, a man *f.* of talk.
14. 1, *f.* of trouble.
20. 11, *f.* of the sins of youth.
21. 23, dieth in his *f.* strength.
32. 18, I am *f.* of matter.
Ps. 10. 7; Rom. 3. 14, mouth *f.* of cursing.
65. 9, which is *f.* of water.
74. 20, *f.* of habitations of cruelty.
88. 3, soul *f.* of troubles.
119. 64, earth is *f.* of thy mercy.
127. 5, happy the man that hath his quiver *f.*
Prov. 27. 7, the *f.* soul loatheth an honeycomb.
20, hell and destruction are never *f.*
Prov. 30. 9, lest I be *f.*, and deny thee.
Eccl. 1. 7, yet the sea is not *f.*
Hab. 3. 3, earth *f.* of his praise.
Zech. 8. 5, streets *f.* of boys and girls.
Mat. 6. 22; Lu. 11. 36, *f.* of light.
Lu. 6. 25, woe unto you that are *f.*!
11. 39, *f.* of ravening.
John 1. 14, *f.* of grace and truth.
15. 11; 16. 24, that your joy may be *f.*
Acts 6. 3; 7. 55; 11. 24, men *f.* of the Holy Ghost.
9. 36, *f.* of good works.
Rom. 15. 14, ye also are *f.* of goodness.
1 Cor. 4. 8, now ye are *f.*
Phil. 4. 12, I am instructed to be *f.*
18, I am *f.*
2 Tim. 4. 5, make *f.* proof of thy ministry.
Heb. 5. 14, meat to them of *f.* age.
1 Pet. 1. 8, with joy unspeakable and *f.* of glory.
Rev. 15. 7, *f.* of the wrath of God.
See Lev. 2. 14; 2 Kings 4. 6; 10. 21; Amos 2. 13.
FULLY. Num. 14. 24, Caleb hath followed me *f.*
Eccl. 8. 11, heart is *f.* set to do evil.
Rom. 14. 5, let every man be *f.* persuaded.
15. 19, I have *f.* preached the gospel.
Rev. 14. 18, her grapes are *f.* ripe.
See 1 Kings 11. 6; Acts 2. 1; Rom. 4. 21.
FULNESS. Ps. 16. 11, *f.* of joy.
John 1. 16, of his *f.* have we received.
Rom. 11. 25, the *f.* of the Gentiles.
Eph. 1. 23, the *f.* of him that filleth all in all.
3. 19, filled with the *f.* of God.
4. 13, the stature of the *f.* of Christ.
Col. 1. 19, in him should all *f.* dwell.
2. 9, the *f.* of the Godhead bodily.
See Num. 18. 27; Ps. 96. 11; Rom. 11. 12.
FURIOUS. Prov. 22. 24, with a *f.* man thou shalt not go.
29. 22, a *f.* man aboundeth in transgression.
Nah. 1. 2, the Lord is *f.*
See 2 Kings 9. 20; Ezek. 5. 15; 23. 25.
FURNACE. Deut. 4. 20, Lord hath taken you out of *f.*
Ps. 12. 6, as silver tried in a *f.*
Isa. 48. 10, in the *f.* of affliction.
Mat. 13. 42, into a *f.* of fire.
See Gen. 15. 17; 19. 28; 1 Kings 8. 51; Dan. 3. 6, 11, 15, etc.; Ezek. 22. 18.
FURNISH. Ps. 78. 19; Mat. 22. 10; 2 Tim. 3. 17.
FURROWS. Ps. 65. 10; 129. 3; Hos. 10. 4; 12. 11.
FURTHER. Ezra 8. 36, they *f.* the people.
Job 38. 11, hitherto shalt thou come, but no *f.*
Lu. 24. 28, as though he would have gone *f.*
Acts 4. 17, that it spread no *f.*
2 Tim. 3. 9, they shall proceed no *f.*
See Mk. 5. 35; Phil. 1. 12, 25.
FURY. Gen. 27. 44, till thy brother's *f.* turn.
Isa. 27. 4, *f.* is not in me.
63. 5, my *f.* uphold me.
Jer. 21. 5, I will fight against thee in *f.*
25. 15, the wine cup of this *f.*
Ezek. 21. 17, I will cause my *f.* to rest.
See Dan. 3. 13, 19; 8. 6; 9. 16; 11. 44.

G

GAIN. Job 22. 3, is it *g.* to him that thou makest thy ways perfect?
Prov. 1. 19; 15. 27; Ezek. 22. 12, greedy of *g.*
3. 14, the *g.* thereof better than gold.
28. 8, by usury and unjust *g.*
Ezek. 22. 13, 27, at thy dishonest *g.*
Dan. 11. 39, he shall divide the land for *g.*
Mic. 4. 13, consecrate their *g.* to the Lord.
Mat. 16. 26; Mk. 8. 36; Lu. 9. 25, if he *g.* the world.
18. 15, thou hast *g.* thy brother.
25. 17, 22, had also *g.* other two.
Lu. 19. 15, 16, 18, had *g.* by trading.
Acts 16. 19, hope of their *g.* was gone.
19. 24, no small *g.* to the craftsmen.
1 Cor. 9. 19, that I might *g.* the more.
20, that I might *g.* the Jews.

2 Cor. 12. 17, 18, did I make a *g.* of you?
Phil. 1. 21, to die is *g.*
3. 7, *g.* to me, I counted loss.
1 Tim. 6. 5, supposing that *g.* is godliness.
6, godliness with contentment is great *g.*
See Judg. 5. 19; Job 27. 8; Jas. 4. 13.
GAINSAY. Lu. 21. 15; Tit. 1. 9; Jude 11.
GALL. Ps. 69. 21; Lam. 3. 19; Mat. 27. 34; Acts 8. 23.
GALLOWS. Esth. 7. 10, they hanged Haman on the *g.*
GAP. Ezek. 13. 5; 22. 30.
GARDEN. Gen. 2. 8, God planted a *g.* eastward in Eden.
13. 10, as the *g.* of the Lord.
Deut. 11. 10; 1 Kings 21. 2, as a *g.* of herbs.
Cant. 4. 12, a *g.* enclosed.
16, blow upon my *g.*
5. 1, I am come into my *g.*
6. 2, 11, gone down into his *g.*
Isa. 1. 8, as a lodge in a *g.*
30, as a *g.* that hath no water.
51. 3, her desert like the *g.* of the Lord.
58. 11; Jer. 31. 12, like a watered *g.*
61. 11, as the *g.* causeth things sown to spring forth.
Jer. 29. 5, plant *g.*, and eat the fruit.
Ezek. 28. 13, in Eden the *g.* of God.
31. 8, 9, cedars in *g.* of God.
36. 35, is become like the *g.* of Eden.
Joel 2. 3, land as the *g.* of Eden before them.
John 18. 1, where was a *g.*
26, did not I see thee in the *g.*?
19. 41, there was a *g.*, and in the *g.*
See Gen. 2. 15; Amos 4. 9; 9. 14; John 20. 15.
GARMENT. Gen. 39. 12, he left his *g.*, and fled.
49. 11, washed his *g.* in wine.
Josh. 7. 21, a goodly Babylonish *g.*
9. 5, Gibeonites took old *g.*
2 Kings 5. 26, is it a time to receive *g.*?
7. 15, all the way was full of *g.*
Job 37. 17, how thy *g.* are warm.
Ps. 22. 18, they part my *g.* among them.
102. 26; Isa. 50. 9; 51. 6; Heb. 1. 11, wax old as a *g.*
104. 2, with light as with a *g.*
6, coveredst it with the deep as with a *g.*
109. 18, clothed himself with cursing as with his *g.*
Prov. 20. 16, take his *g.* that is surety.
25. 20, a *g.* in cold weather.
30. 4, who hath bound the waters in a *g.*?
Eccl. 9. 8, let thy *g.* be always white.
Isa. 52. 1, put on thy beautiful *g.*
61. 3, *g.* of praise for spirit of heaviness.
10, the *g.* of salvation.
Joel 2. 13, rend your heart and not your *g.*
Zech. 13. 4, a rough *g.* to deceive.
Mat. 9. 16; Mk. 2. 21; Lu. 5. 36, new cloth, old *g.*
20. 14, 36; Mk. 5. 27; Lu. 8. 44, hem of *g.*
21. 8; Mk. 11. 8, spread *g.* in way.
22. 11, 12, wedding *g.*
23. 5, enlarge borders of *g.*
27. 35; Mk. 15. 24, parted *g.*, casting lots.
Mk. 11. 7; Lu. 19. 35, cast *g.* on colt.
13. 16, not turn back again to take *g.*
Lu. 22. 36, let him sell his *g.*
24. 4, in shining *g.*
Acts 9. 39, showing the coats and *g.*
Jas. 5. 2, your *g.* are motheaten.
Jude 23, the *g.* spotted by the flesh.
Rev. 3. 4, not defiled their *g.*
16. 15, that watcheth, and keepeth his *g.*
GARNER. Ps. 144. 13; Joel 1. 17; Mat. 3. 12.
GARNISH. Job 26. 13; Mat. 12. 44; 23. 29.
GATE. Gen. 28. 17, the *g.* of heaven.
Deut. 6. 9; 11. 20, write them on thy *g.*
Ps. 9. 13, the *g.* of death.
118. 19, the *g.* of righteousness.
Prov. 17. 19, exalteth *g.* seeketh destruction.
31. 23, her husband known in the *g.*
Isa. 26. 2, open the *g.*, that righteous may enter.
38. 10, the *g.* of the grave.
45. 1, open the two-leaved *g.*
60. 11, thy *g.* shall be open continually.
18, walls Salvation, and *g.* Praise.
Mat. 7. 13; Lu. 13. 24, strait *g.*, wide *g.*
16. 18, *g.* of hell shall not prevail.
Heb. 13. 12, also suffered without the *g.*
Rev. 21. 25, *g.* not shut at all by day.
See Ps. 24. 7; Isa. 28. 6; Nah. 2. 6.
GATHER. Gen. 41. 35, let them *g.* all the food.
49. 10, to him shall *g.* of the people be.
Ex. 16. 17, *g.*, some more, some less.
Deut. 28. 38, carry much out, and *g.* little in.
30. 3; Ezek. 36. 24, will *g.* thee from all nations.
2 Sam. 14. 14, spilt, which cannot be *g.* up.
Job 11. 10, if he *g.* together, who can hinder?
Ps. 26. 9, *g.* not my soul with sinners.
39. 6, knoweth not who shall *g.* them.
Prov. 6. 8, the ant *g.* her food.
10. 5, he that *g.* in summer.
13. 11, he that *g.* by labour shall increase.
Isa. 27. 12, ye shall be *g.* one by one.
40. 11, he shall *g.* the lambs.
56. 8, yet will I *g.* others.
62. 10, *g.* out the stones.
Mat. 3. 12; Lu. 3. 17, *g.* wheat into garner.
6. 26, nor *g.* into barns.
7. 16; Lu. 6. 44, do men *g.* grapes of thorns?
12. 30; Lu. 11. 23, he that *g.* not scattereth.
13. 28, wilt thou that we *g.* them up?
29, lest while ye *g.* up the tares.
41, shall *g.* out of his kingdom.
25. 32, before him shall be *g.* all nations.
John 6. 12, *g.* up fragments.
15. 6, men *g.* them, and cast.
1 Cor. 16. 2, that there be no *g.* when I come.
2 Thess. 2. 1, by our *g.* together unto him.
See Mat. 23. 37; John 4. 36; 11. 52.
GAVE. Gen. 3. 12, the woman *g.* me.
Josh. 21. 44; 2 Chron. 15. 15; 20. 30, Lord *g.* them rest.
1 Sam. 10. 9, *g.* to Saul another heart.
Neh. 8. 8., they read, and *g.* the sense.
Job 1. 21, the Lord *g.*
Ps. 21. 4, he asked life, and thou *g.* it.
68. 11, the Lord *g.* the word.
Eccl. 12. 7, to God who *g.* it.
Amos. 2. 12, ye *g.* the Nazarites wine.
Mat. 21. 23; Mk. 11. 28; Lu. 20. 2, who *g.* thee this authority?
25. 35, 42, ye *g.* me meat.
Lu. 15. 16, no man *g.* unto him.
John 10. 29, my Father, who *g.* them.
Acts 2. 4, as the Spirit *g.* them utterance.
26. 10, I *g.* my voice against them.
Rom. 1. 28, God *g.* them over.
1 Cor. 3. 6, God *g.* the increase.
Eph. 4. 8, *g.* gifts unto men.
11, he *g.* some apostles.
See 2 Cor. 8. 5; Gal. 1. 4; Tit. 2. 14.
GAY. Jas. 2. 3.
GAZE. Ex. 19. 21; Nah. 3. 6; Acts 1. 11; Heb. 10. 33.
GENERATION. Deut. 1. 35, not one of this evil *g.*
32. 5, 20, a perverse and crooked *g.*
Ps. 14. 5, God is in the *g.* of the righteous.
22. 30, it shall be accounted for a *g.*
102. 18, written for the *g.* to come.
145. 4, one *g.* shall praise thy works.
Prov. 27. 24, crown endure to every *g.*
30. 11, there is a *g.* that curseth.
Eccl. 1. 4, one *g.* passeth away.
Isa. 34. 10, from *g.* to *g.* it shall lie waste.
Joel 1. 3, children tell another *g.*
Mat. 3. 7; 12. 34; 23. 33; Lu. 3. 7, *g.* of vipers.
12. 41, in judgment with this *g.*
17. 17; Mk. 9. 19; Lu. 9. 41, perverse *g.*
23. 36, shall come on this *g.*
24. 34; Mk. 13. 30; Lu. 21. 32, this *g.* shall not pass.
Lu. 16. 8, are in their *g.* wiser.

Lu. 17. 25, rejected of this *g.*
1 Pet. 2. 9, a chosen *g.*
See Isa. 53. 8; Dan. 4. 3; Mat. 1. 1; Lu. 11. 30.
GENTILES. Mat. 10. 5, go not in way of the *G.*
John 7. 35, to the dispersed among *G.*
Acts 9. 15, bear my name before the *G.*
13. 42, *G.* besought that these words.
46, we turn to the *G.*
15. 3, declaring conversion of the *G.*
18. 6, from henceforth I will go to the *G.*
Rom. 3. 29, is he not also of the *G.*?
11. 11, salvation is come to the *G.*
11. 13, as the apostle of the *G.*
1 Cor. 5. 1, not so much as named among *G.*
Eph. 4. 17, walk not as other *G.*
2 Tim. 1. 11, I am ordained a teacher of *G.*
3 John 7, taking nothing of the *G.*
See Rom. 2. 9; 1 Pet. 2. 12; Rev. 11. 2.
GENTLE. 1 Thess. 2. 7, we were *g.* among you.
2 Tim. 2. 24, servant of Lord be *g.*
Tit. 3. 2, *g.*, showing all meekness.
Jas. 3. 17, wisdom is pure and *g.*
1 Pet. 2. 18, not only to the good and *g.*
See 2 Sam. 18. 5; 22. 36; Gal. 5. 22.
GETTETH. Prov. 3. 13; 4. 7; 19. 8; Jer. 17. 11.
GIFT. Ex. 23. 8; Deut. 16. 19, a *g.* blindeth.
2 Sam. 19. 42, hath he given us any *g.*?
2 Chron. 19. 7, with the Lord no taking of *g.*
Ps. 68. 18; Eph. 4. 8, *g.* unto men.
72. 10, kings of Sheba and Seba offer *g.*
Prov. 6. 35, not content, though many *g.*
15. 27, he that hateth *g.* shall live.
17. 8, a *g.* is as a precious stone.
18. 16, man's *g.* maketh room for him.
21. 14, a *g.* in secret pacifieth anger.
Eccl. 3. 13; 5. 19, enjoy good, it is God's *g.*
7. 7, a *g.* destroyeth the heart.
Isa. 1. 23, every one loveth *g.*
Mat. 5. 23, bring thy *g.* to the altar.
24, leave thy *g.* before the altar.
7. 11; Lu. 11. 13, know how to give good *g.*
Lu. 21. 1, casting *g.* into treasury.
John 4. 10, if thou knewest the *g.* of God.
Acts 8. 20, thought the *g.* of God may be purchased.
Rom. 1. 11, some spiritual *g.*
5. 15, free *g.*, *g.* by grace.
6. 23, the *g.* of God is eternal life.
11. 29, *g.* of God without repentance.
12. 6, *g.* differing according to grace.
1 Cor. 7. 7, his proper *g.* of God.
12. 4, diversities of *g.*
31, covet best *g.*
14. 1, 12, desire spiritual *g.*
2 Cor. 9. 15, unspeakable *g.*
Eph. 2. 8, faith the *g.* of God.
Phil. 4. 17, not because I desire a *g.*
1 Tim. 4. 14, neglect not the *g.*
2 Tim. 1. 6, stir up the *g.*
Jas. 1. 17, good and perfect *g.*
See Num. 18. 29; Mat. 15. 5; Acts 2. 38; 10. 45; 1 Cor. 13. 2.
GIRD. 2 Sam. 22. 40; Ps. 18. 39, hast *g.* me with strength.
Isa. 45. 5, I *g.* thee, though thou hast not.
Joel 1. 13, *g.* yourselves, and lament.
Eph. 6. 14, having your loins *g.*
See Prov. 31. 17; John 13. 4; 21. 18; Rev. 15. 6.
GIRDLE. Ex. 28. 4, and a *g.*
Jer. 13. 1, go and get thee a linen *g.*
See Isa. 11. 5; Mat. 3. 4; Mk. 1. 6.
GIRL. Joel 3. 3; Zech. 8. 5.
GIVE. Gen. 28. 22, I will *g.* the tenth.
Ex. 30. 15, rich shall not *g.* more, poor not *g.* less.
Deut. 15. 10, thou shalt *g.* him thine heart.
16. 17; Ezek. 46. 5, *g.* as he is able.
1 Chron. 29. 14, of thine own have we *g.* thee.
Ezra 9. 9, to *g.* us a reviving.
Ps. 2. 8, I shall *g.* thee the heathen.
6. 5, in the grave who shall *g.* thanks?
Ps. 29. 11, Lord will *g.* strength.
37. 4, *g.* thee the desires of thy heart.
21, the righteous showeth mercy, and *g.*
84. 11, Lord will *g.* grace and glory.
109. 4, I *g.* myself unto prayer.
Prov. 23. 26, *g.* me thine heart.
Isa. 55. 10, *g.* seed to the sower.
Mat. 5. 42, *g.* to him that asketh.
6. 11; Lu. 11. 3, *g.* daily bread.
7. 9, will he *g.* him a stone?
10. 8, freely *g.*
13. 11; Mk. 4. 11, it is *g.* to you to know.
16. 26; Mk. 8. 37, *g.* in exchange.
19. 21; Mk. 10. 21, go sell, and *g.* to the poor.
20. 23; Mk. 10. 40, not mine to *g.*
26. 9; Mk. 14. 5, sold, and *g.* to the poor.
Lu. 6. 38, *g.* and it shall be *g.*
John 4. 7, 10, *g.* me to drink.
6. 37, all that the Father *g.* me.
65, no man can come, except it were *g.* him.
10. 28, I *g.* to them eternal life.
13. 29, that he should *g.* something to poor.
14. 27, not as the world *g.*, *g.* I.
Acts 3. 6, such as I have *g.* I thee.
6. 4, we will *g.* ourselves to prayer.
20. 35, more blessed to *g.*
Rom. 12. 8, he that *g.*, let him do it.
19, rather *g.* place unto wrath.
1 Cor. 3. 7, God *g.* the increase.
2 Cor. 9. 7, *g.* not grudgingly, a cheerful *g.*
Phil. 4. 15, concerning *g.* and receiving.
1 Tim. 4. 13, *g.* attendance to reading.
15, *g.* thyself wholly to them.
6. 17, who *g.* us richly.
Jas. 1. 5, that *g.* to all men liberally.
4. 6, *g.* more grace, *g.* grace to humble.
2 Pet. 1. 5, *g.* all diligence.
See Mk. 12. 15; Lu. 12. 48; John 3. 34.
GLAD. Ex. 4. 14, he will be *g.* in heart.
Job 3. 22, *g.* when they can find the grave.
Ps. 16. 9, therefore my heart is *g.*
34. 2; 69. 32, humble shall hear, and be *g.*
46. 4, make *g.* the city of God.
101. 15, maketh *g.* the heart of man.
122. 1, I was *g.* when they said.
126. 3, whereof we are *g.*
Prov. 10. 1; 15. 20, wise son maketh a *g.* father.
24. 17, let not thine heart be *g.*
Lam. 1. 21, they are *g.* that thou hast done it.
Lu. 15. 32, make merry, and be *g.*
John 8. 56, saw my day, and was *g.*
11. 15, I am *g.* for your sakes.
Acts 11. 23, when he had seen grace of God, was *g.*
See Mk. 6. 20; 12. 37; Lu. 1. 19; 8. 1.
GLADNESS. Num. 10. 10, in day of your *g.*
Deut. 28. 47, servedst not with *g.* of heart.
Neh. 8. 17, there was very great *g.*
Ps. 4. 7, thou hast put *g.* in my heart.
45. 7; Heb. 1. 9, the oil of *g.*
97. 11, *g.* is sown for the upright.
Isa. 35. 10; 51. 11, they shall obtain joy, and *g.*
Acts 2. 46, did eat with *g.* of heart.
12. 14, opened not for *g.*
14. 17, filling our hearts with food and *g.*
See Ps. 100. 2; Prov. 10. 28; Isa. 51. 3.
GLASS. 1 Cor. 13. 12, we see through a *g.* darkly.
2 Cor. 3. 18, beholding as in a *g.* the glory of the Lord.
Rev. 4. 6; 15. 2, a sea of *g.*, like unto crystal.
GLEAN. Lev. 19. 10; Jer. 6. 9; 49. 9.
GLISTERING. 1 Chron. 29. 2; Lu. 9. 29.
GLITTERING. Deut. 32. 41; Job 20. 25; 39. 23; Nah. 3. 3.
GLOOMINESS. Joel 2. 2; Zeph. 1. 15.
GLORIFY. Lev. 10. 3, before all people I will be *g.*
Ps. 50. 23, whoso offereth praise *g.* me.
86. 9, all nations shall *g.* thy name.
12, I will *g.* thy name for evermore.
Isa. 24. 15, *g.* the Lord in the fires.

Isa. 60. 7, I will *g.* house of my glory.
Ezek. 28. 22, I will be *g.* in midst of thee.
Dan. 5. 23, God hast thou not *g.*
Mat. 5. 16, *g.* your Father in heaven.
15. 31, they *g.* God of Israel.
Lu. 4. 15, being *g.* of all.
John 7. 39, because Jesus was not yet *g.*
11. 4, that the Son of God might be *g.*
12. 16, but when Jesus was *g.*, they remembered.
28, Father, *g.* thy name: I have both *g.*
13. 32, God shall also *g.* him.
15. 8, herein is my Father *g.*
17. 1, *g.* thy Son.
4, I have *g.* thee on earth.
21. 19, by what death he should *g.* God.
Rom. 1. 21, they *g.* him not as God.
8. 17, suffer with him, that we may be *g.*
30, them he also *g.*
1 Cor. 6. 20, *g.* God in body and spirit.
Gal. 1. 24, they *g.* God in me.
2 Thess. 1. 10, to be *g.* in his saints.
Heb. 5. 5., so Christ *g.* not himself.
See Isa. 25. 5; Mat. 9. 8; 15. 31; Lu. 7. 16.

GLORIOUS. Ex. 15. 11, *g.* in holiness.
Deut. 28. 58; 1 Chron. 29. 13, this *g.* name.
Ps. 45. 13, all *g.* within.
66. 2, make his praise *g.*
72. 19, blessed be his *g.* name.
87. 3, *g.* things are spoken.
Isa. 11. 10, his rest shall be *g.*
28. 1, whose *g.* beauty is a fading flower.
60. 13, place of my feet *g.*
63. 1, *g.* in his apparel.
14, to make thyself a *g.* name.
Jer. 17. 12, a *g.* high throne.
Dan. 11. 16, 41, stand in the *g.* land.
45, in the *g.* holy mountain.
Lu. 13. 17, rejoiced for *g.* things done.
Rom. 8. 21, *g.* liberty of children of God.
2 Cor. 3. 7, 8, ministration *g.*
4. 4, light of *g.* gospel.
Eph. 5. 27, a *g.* church.
Phil. 3. 21, like to his *g.* body.
1 Tim. 1. 11, the *g.* gospel of the blessed God.
Tit. 2. 13, the *g.* appearing of the great God.
See Ex. 15. 1; 2 Sam. 6. 20; Isa. 24. 23.

GLORY. Ex. 33. 18, show me thy *g.*
Num. 14. 21; Ps. 72. 19; Isa. 6. 3, earth filled with *g.*
Ps. 8. 1, thy *g.* above the heavens.
16. 9, my *g.* rejoiceth.
24. 7, 10, the King of *g.*
73. 24, afterward receive me to *g.*
84. 11, will give grace and *g.*
108. 1, will give praise with my *g.*
145. 11, the *g.* of thy kingdom.
Prov. 3. 35, the wise shall inherit *g.*.
17. 6, the *g.* of children are their fathers.
20. 29, the *g.* of young men is their strength.
25. 2, *g.* of God to conceal.
27, for men to search their own *g.* is not *g.*
Isa. 10. 2, where will ye leave your *g.*?
24. 16, even *g.* to the righteous.
42. 8, my *g.* will I not give to another.
43. 7, have created him for my *g.*
60. 7, will glorify house of my *g.*
Jer. 2. 11, my people have changed their *g.*
Ezek. 20. 6, 15, the *g.* of all lands.
31. 18, to whom art thou thus like in *g.*?
Dan. 2. 37; 7. 14, God hath given power and *g.*
Hos. 4. 7, change *g.* into shame.
Hag. 2. 7, I will fill this house with *g.*
Mat. 6. 2, that ye may have *g.* of men.
29; Lu. 12. 27, Solomon in all his *g.*
16. 27; Mk. 8. 38, in *g.* of his Father.
19. 28; Lu. 9. 26, Son of man sit in his *g.*
24. 30; Mk. 13. 26; Lu. 21. 27, power and great *g.*
Lu. 2. 14; 19. 38, *g.* to God in the highest.
9. 31, appeared in *g.*, and spake of his decease.
Lu. 9, 32, they saw his *g.*
24. 26, to enter into his *g.*
John 1. 14, we beheld his *g.*
2. 11, thus did Jesus, and manifested his *g.*
8. 50, I seek not mine own *g.*
17. 5, the *g.* I had with thee.
24, that they may behold my *g.*
Acts 12. 23, he gave not God the *g.*
Rom. 3. 23, come short of *g.* of God.
8. 18, not worthy to be compared with *g.*
11. 36; Gal. 1. 5; 2 Tim. 4. 18; Heb. 13. 21; 1 Pet. 5. 11, to whom be *g.*
1 Cor. 2. 8, crucified the Lord of *g.*
10. 31, do all to *g.* of God.
11. 7, woman is the *g.* of the man.
15, long hair, it is a *g.* to her.
15. 40, *g.* of celestial, *g.* of terrestrial.
43, raised in *g.*
2 Cor. 3. 18, beholding as in a glass the *g.*
4. 17, eternal weight of *g.*
Eph. 1. 17, the Father of *g.*
3. 21, to him be *g.* in the church.
Phil. 3. 19, whose *g.* is in their shame.
4. 19, according to his riches in *g.*
Col. 1. 27, Christ in you, the hope of *g.*
3. 4, appear with him in *g.*
2 Thess. 1. 9, the *g.* of his power.
1 Tim. 3. 16, received up into *g.*
Heb. 1. 3, the brightness of his *g.*
2. 10, in bringing many sons to *g.*
3. 3, this man was counted worthy of more *g.*
1 Pet. 1. 8, joy unspeakable and full of *g.*
11, the *g.* that should follow.
24, the *g.* of man as flower of grass.
4. 14, the spirit of *g.* and of God.
5. 10, called to eternal *g.*
2 Pet. 1. 17, voice from the excellent *g.*
Rev. 4. 11; 5. 12, worthy to receive *g.*
7. 12, blessing, and *g.*, and wisdom.
18. 1, earth lightened with his *g.*
21. 23, *g.* of God did lighten it.
See Lu. 17. 18; 2 Cor. 3. 18; Jas. 2. 1; Jude 25.

GLORYING. 1 Cor. 5. 6; 9. 15; 2 Cor. 7. 4; 12. 11.

GNASH. Mat. 8. 12; 13. 42; 22. 13; 24. 51; 25. 30; Lu. 13. 28, *g.* of teeth.
Mk. 9. 18, he foameth, and *g.* with his teeth.
See Job 16. 9; Ps. 35. 16; Acts 7. 54.

GNAT. Mat. 23. 24.

GO. Gen. 32. 26, let me *g.*, for the day breaketh.
Ex. 14. 15; Job 23. 8, *g.* forward.
23. 23; 32. 34, angel shall *g.* before thee.
33. 15, presence *g.* not with me.
Ruth 1. 16, whither thou *g.*, I will *g.*
Ps. 139. 7, whither shall I *g.*?
Prov. 22. 6, the way he should *g.*
30. 29, three things which *g.* well.
Mat. 5. 41, to *g.* a mile, *g.* twain.
21. 30, I *g.* sir, and went not.
Lu. 10. 37, *g.* and do likewise.
John 14. 12, I *g.* to the Father.
See Mat. 8. 9; Lu. 7. 8; 1 Cor. 9. 7; Rev. 14. 4.

GOATS. Job 39. 1, the wild *g.* of the rock.

GOD. Gen. 5. 22; 6. 9, walked with *G.*
16. 13, thou *G.* seest me.
32. 28, hath power with *G.*
48. 21, I die, but *G.* shall be with you.
Num. 23. 19, *G.* is not a man, that he should lie.
23, what hath *G.* wrought?
Deut. 3. 24, what *G.* is there that can do.
33. 27, the eternal *G.* is thy refuge.
1 Sam. 17. 46, may know there is a *G.* in Israel.
1 Kings 18. 21, if the Lord be *G.*, follow him.
39, he is the *G.*, he is the *G.*
Job 22. 13; Ps. 73. 11, how doth *G.* know?
Ps. 14. 1; 53. 1, hath said, there is no *G.*
22. 1; Mat. 27. 46, my *G.*, my *G.*, why hast.
56. 9, this I know, for *G.* is for me.
86. 10; Isa. 37. 16, thou art *G.* alone.
Eccl. 5. 2, *G.* is in heaven.

Isa. 44. 8, is there a *G.* beside me?
45. 22; 46. 9, I am *G.*, there is none else.
Hos. 11. 9, I am *G.*, and not man.
Amos 5. 27, whose name is the *G.* of hosts.
Jon. 1. 6, arise, call upon thy *G.*
Mic. 6. 8, walk humbly with thy *G.*
Mat. 1. 23, *G.* with us.
22. 32, *G.* is not *G.* of dead.
Mk. 12. 32, one *G.*, and none other.
John 3. 33, that *G.* is true.
4. 24, *G.* is a spirit.
13. 3, come from *G.*, and went to *G.*
20. 17, ascend to my *G.* and your *G.*
Rom. 3. 4, let *G.* be true.
8. 31, if *G.* be for us.
1 Cor. 1. 9; 19. 13, *G.* is faithful.
14. 25, that *G.* is in you.
33, *G.* is not author of confusion.
Gal. 3. 20, but *G.* is none.
6. 7, *G.* is not mocked.
2 Thess. 2. 4, above all that is called *G.*
1 Tim. 3. 16, *G.* manifest in the flesh.
Heb. 8. 10, I will be to them a *G.*
11. 16, not ashamed to be called their *G.*
12. 23, but ye are come to *G.*
1 John 1. 5, *G.* is light.
4. 8, 16, *G.* is love.
12, no man hath seen *G.*
5. 19, we know that we are of *G.*
Rev. 21. 3, *G.* himself shall be with them.
4, *G.* shall wipe away all tears.
7, I will be his *G.*
See Job 33. 12; 36. 5; Ps. 10. 4; 33. 12.

GOD (*an idol*). Gen. 31. 30, stolen my *g.*
Ex. 32. 1, make us *g.*, which shall go before us.
4, these be thy *g.*
Judg. 5. 8, they chose new *g.*
6. 31, if he be a *g.*, let him plead.
10. 14, go and cry to the *g.* ye have chosen.
17. 5, Micah had a house of *g.*
18. 24, ye have taken away my *g.*
2 Kings 17. 29, every nation made *g.*
33, they feared the Lord, and served own *g.*
Isa. 44. 15, maketh a *g.* and worshippeth it.
45. 20, pray to a *g.* that cannot save.
Jon. 1. 5, cried every man to his *g.*
Acts 12. 22, the voice of a *g.*, not a man.
14. 11, the *g.* are come down.
1 Cor. 8. 5, there be *g.* many.
See Ex. 12. 12; 20. 23; Jer. 2. 11; Dan. 3. 28.

GODDESS. 1 Kings 11. 5; Acts 19. 27, 35, 37.

GODHEAD. Acts 17. 29; Rom. 1. 20; Col. 2. 9.

GODLINESS. 1 Tim. 3. 16, the mystery of *g.*
4. 7, exercise thyself to *g.*
8, *g.* is profitable.
6. 3, doctrine according to *g.*
5, supposing that gain is *g.*
2 Tim. 3. 5, a form of *g.*
Tit. 1. 1, the truth which is after *g.*
2 Pet. 1. 3, pertain to life and *g.*
6, and to patience *g.*
3. 11, in all holy conversation, and *g.*
See 1 Tim. 2. 2, 10; 6. 6, 11.

GODLY. Ps. 12. 1, the *g.* man ceaseth.
Mal. 2. 15, seek a *g.* seed.
2 Cor. 1. 12, in *g.* sincerity.
7. 9, 10, *g.* sorrow worketh repentance.
2 Tim. 3. 12, all that will live *g.* in Christ.
Tit. 2. 12, live *g.* in this world.
Heb. 12. 28, reverence and *g.* fear.
2 Pet. 2. 9, how to deliver the *g.*
3 John 6, bring forward after a *g.* sort.
See Ps. 4. 3; 32. 6; 2 Cor. 7. 9; 11. 2.

GOD SAVE THE KING. 2 Sam. 16. 16, Hushai said unto Absalom, *G.*

GOING. Josh. 23. 14, I am *g.* the way of all the earth.
2 Sam. 5. 24; 1 Chron. 14. 15, sound of *g.* in trees.
Job 33. 24, 28, from *g.* down to pit.
Ps. 17. 5, hold up my *g.*
Ps. 40. 2, establish my *g.*
Prov. 5. 21, pondereth all his *g.*
20. 24, man's *g.* are of the Lord.
Dan. 6. 14, laboured till *g.* down of the sun.
Mic. 5. 2, whose *g.* forth have been from of old.
Mat. 26. 46, rise, let us be *g.*
Rom. 10. 3, *g.* about to establish.
1 Tim. 5. 24, *g.* before to judgment.
See Prov. 7. 27; 14. 15; Isa. 59. 8; Hos. 6. 3.

GOLD. Num. 31. 22, only *g.*, etc., that may abide fire.
Deut. 8. 13, when thy *g.* is multiplied.
17. 17, nor shall he greatly multiply *g.*
1 Kings 20. 3, silver and *g.* is mine.
Job 22. 24, then shalt thou lay up *g.* as dust.
28. 1, a vein for silver, a place for *g.*
19, wisdom not valued with *g.*
31. 24, if I made *g.* my hope.
Ps. 19. 10, more to be desired than *g.*
21. 3, thou settest a crown of pure *g.* upon his head.
Prov. 25. 11, like apples of *g.*
Isa. 46. 6, they lavish *g.* out of the bag.
60. 17, for brass I will bring *g.*
Hag. 2. 8, the silver is mine, and the *g.* is mine.
Zech. 4. 2, behold, a candlestick all of *g.*
13. 9, try them as *g.* is tried.
Mal. 10. 9, provide neither *g.* nor silver.
Acts 3. 6, silver and *g.* have I none.
17. 29, not think Godhead like to *g.*
20. 33, coveted no man's *g.*
2 Tim. 2. 20, in great house not only vessels of *g.*
Jas. 2. 2, man with a *g.* ring.
5. 3, your *g.* is cankered.
1 Pet. 1. 7, trial more precious than of *g.*
18, not redeemed with *g.*
Rev. 3. 18, buy of me *g.* tried in the fire.
21. 18, city was pure *g.*
See Gen. 2. 11; Eccl. 12. 6; Isa. 13. 12.

GONE. Deut. 23. 23, that which is *g.* out of thy lips.
1 Kings 20. 40, busy here and there, he was *g.*
Ps. 42. 4, I had *g.* with the multitude.
73. 2, my feet were almost *g.*
77. 8, mercy clean *g.* for ever.
103. 16, wind passeth, and it is *g.*
109. 23, I am *g.* like the shadow.
119. 176; Isa. 53. 6, *g.* astray like sheep.
Eccl. 8. 10, come and *g.* from place of the holy.
Jer. 15. 9, sun *g.* down while yet day.
Mat. 12. 43; Lu. 11. 24, spirit *g.* out.
25. 8, lamps are *g.* out.
Mk. 5. 30; Lu. 8. 46, virtue had *g.* out of him.
John 12. 19, the world is *g.* after him.
Acts 16. 19, hope of their gains *g.*
Rom. 3. 12, they are all *g.* out of the way.
Jude 11, *g.* in the way of Cain.
See Ps. 89. 34; Cant. 2. 11; Isa. 45. 23.

GOOD (*n.*). Gen. 14. 21, take the *g.* to thyself.
24. 10, the *g.* of his master in his hand.
50. 20, God meant it unto *g.*
Neh. 5. 19; 13. 31, think upon me for *g.*
Job 2. 10, shall we receive *g.*
22. 21, thereby *g.* shall come.
Ps. 4. 6, who will show us any *g.*?
14. 1; 53. 1; Rom. 3. 12, none doeth *g.*
34. 12, loveth days that he may see *g.*
39. 2, held my peace even from *g.*
86. 17, a token for *g.*
Prov. 3. 27, withhold not *g.*
Eccl. 3. 12, I know there is no *g.* in them.
5. 11, when *g.* increase.
9. 18, destroyeth much *g.*
Mat. 12. 29; Mk. 3. 27, spoil his *g.*
24. 27, ruler over all his *g.*
26. 24, been *g.* for that man.
Lu. 6. 30, of him that taketh away thy *g.*
12. 19, much *g.* laid up.
15. 12, the portion of *g.*
16. 1, accused that he had wasted his *g.*
19. 8, half of my *g.* I give.

Acts 10. 38, went about doing *g.*
Rom. 8. 28, work together for *g.*
13. 4, minister of God for *g.*
1 Cor. 13. 3, bestow all my *g.* to feed.
Heb. 10. 34, joyfully the spoiling of your *g.*
1 John 3. 17, this world's *g.*
Rev. 3. 17, rich and increased with *g.*
See Job 5. 27; 7. 7; Prov. 11. 17; 13. 21.
GOOD (*adj.*). Gen. 1. 4, 10, 12, 18, 21, 25, 31, God saw it was *g.*
2. 18, not *g.* that man should be alone.
27. 46, what *g.* shall my life do me?
Deut. 2. 4; Josh. 23. 11, take *g.* heed.
1 Sam. 2. 24, no *g.* report I hear.
12. 23, I will teach you the *g.* way.
25. 15, men were very *g.* to us.
Ezra 7. 9; Neh. 2. 8, the *g.* hand of God on him.
Neh. 9. 20, thy *g.* spirit to instruct.
Ps. 34. 8, taste and see that the Lord is *g.*
45. 1, my heart is inditing a *g.* matter.
112. 5, a *g.* man showeth favour.
119. 68, thou art *g.*, and doest *g.*
145. 9, the Lord is *g.* to all.
Prov. 12. 25, a *g.* word maketh the heart glad.
15. 23, in season, how *g.* is it!
20. 18, with *g.* advice make war.
22. 1, a *g.* name rather to be chosen.
25. 25, *g.* news from a far country.
Eccl. 6. 12, who knoweth what is *g.*?
Isa. 55. 2, eat ye that which is *g.*
Lam. 3. 26, it is *g.* that a man hope.
27, *g.* that a man bear yoke.
Zech. 1. 13, answered with *g.* words.
Mat. 5. 13, it is *g.* for nothing.
7. 11; Lu. 11. 13, how to give *g.* gifts.
9. 22; Lu. 8. 48, be of *g.* comfort.
19. 16, what *g.* thing shall I do?
17; Lu. 18. 19, none *g.*, save one.
20. 15, is thine eye evil because I am *g.*?
25. 21, *g.* and faithful servant.
Mk. 9. 50; Lu. 14. 34, salt is *g.*, but.
Lu. 1. 53, filled the hungry with *g.* things.
6. 38, *g.* measure, pressed down.
10. 42, chosen that *g.* part.
12. 32, your Father's *g.* pleasure.
16. 25, thou in thy lifetime receivedst *g.* things.
23. 50, Joseph was a *g.* man, and a just.
John 1. 46, can any *g.* thing come out of Nazareth?
2. 10, kept *g.* wine until now.
7. 12, some said, he is a *g.* man.
10. 11, I am the *g.* shepherd.
33, for a *g.* work we stone thee not.
Rom. 7. 12, the commandment holy, just, and *g.*
18, in my flesh dwelleth no *g.* thing.
12. 2, that *g.* and perfect will of God.
14. 21, it is *g.* neither to eat.
1 Cor. 7. 26, this is *g.* for the present.
15. 33, corrupt *g.* manners.
2 Cor. 9. 8, abound in every *g.* work.
Gal. 6. 6, communicate in all *g.* things.
Phil. 1. 6, hath begun a *g.* work.
Col. 1. 10, fruitful in every *g.* work.
1 Thess. 5. 15; 3 John 11, follow that which is *g.*
21, hold fast that which is *g.*
1 Tim. 1. 8, the law is *g.*
3. 1, desireth a *g.* work.
4. 4, every creature of God is *g.*
2 Tim. 3. 3, despisers of *g.*
Tit. 2. 7, a pattern in *g.* works.
14, zealous of *g.* works.
Heb. 6. 5, tasted the *g.* work of God.
13. 9, *g.* thing that the heart be established.
Jas. 1. 17, every *g.* gift.
See 2 Thess. 2. 17; Tit. 1. 16; 3. 8.
GOODLINESS. Isa. 40. 6.
GOODLY. Gen. 49. 21, giveth *g.* words.
Ex. 2. 2, a *g.* child.
Deut. 8. 12, when thou hast built *g.* houses.
1 Sam. 9. 2, a choice young man, and a *g.*
16. 12, ruddy, and *g.* to look to.
Ps. 16. 6; Jer. 3. 19, a *g.* heritage.
Zech. 11. 13, a *g.* price I was prized at.
Mat. 13. 45, *g.* pearls.
Jas. 2. 2, a man in *g.* apparel.
See 1 Sam. 8. 16; 1 Kings 20. 3; Lu. 21. 5.
GOODNESS. Ex. 33. 19, make all my *g.* pass.
34. 6, abundant in *g.* and truth.
Ps. 16. 2, my *g.* extendeth not to thee.
23. 6, *g.* and mercy shall follow.
27. 13, believed to see the *g.* of the Lord.
31. 19; Zech. 9. 17, how great is thy *g.*
33. 5, earth full of thy *g.*
65. 11, crownest the year with thy *g.*
145. 7, the memory of thy *g.*
Prov. 20. 6, proclaim every one his own *g.*
Hos. 6. 4, your *g.* is as a morning cloud.
Rom. 2. 4, the riches of his *g.*
11. 22, the *g.* and severity of God.
See Neh. 9. 25; Isa. 63. 7; Gal. 5. 22; Eph. 5. 9.
GOSPEL. Rom. 2. 16, according to my *g.*
2 Cor. 4. 3, if our *g.* be hid.
Gal. 1. 8, 9, any other *g.*
2. 7, the *g.* of uncircumcision, *g.* of circumcision.
Col. 1. 23, the hope of the *g.*
1 Tim. 1. 11, *g.* of the blessed God.
Rev. 14. 6, everlasting *g.*
See Mat. 4. 23; Mk. 16. 15; Acts 20. 24.
GOURD. Jon. 4. 6, and the Lord God prepared a *g.*
See Jon. 4. 7, 9, 10.
GOVERNMENT. Isa. 9. 6; 1 Cor. 12. 28; 2 Pet. 2. 10.
GRACE. Ps. 45. 2, *g.* is poured into thy lips.
Prov. 1. 9, an ornament of *g.*
3. 22, life to thy soul, and *g.* to thy neck.
34; Jas. 4. 6, giveth *g.* to the lowly.
Zech. 4. 7, crying, *g.*, *g.* unto it.
12. 10, spirit of *g.* and supplications.
John 1. 14, full of *g.* and truth.
16, all received, and *g.* for *g.*
17, *g.* and truth came by Jesus Christ.
Acts 4. 33, great *g.* was upon them all.
11. 23, when he had seen the *g.*
14. 3, the word of his *g.*
Rom. 1. 7; 1 Cor. 1. 3; 2 Cor. 1. 2; Gal. 1. 3; Eph. 1. 2; Phil. 1. 2; Col. 1. 2; 1 Thess. 1. 1; 2 Thess. 1. 2; Philem. 3; 1 Pet. 1. 2; 2 Pet. 1. 2; Rev. 1. 4, *g.* and peace.
3. 24, justified freely by his *g.*
4. 4, not reckoned of *g.*, but of debt.
5. 2, access into this *g.*
17, abundance of *g.*
20, where sin abounded, *g.* did much more abound.
6. 14, 15, under *g.*
11. 5, the election of *g.*
2 Cor. 8. 9, know the *g.* of our Lord.
9. 8, able to make all *g.* abound.
12. 9, my *g.* is sufficient.
Gal. 1. 6, 15, who called you by his *g.*
5. 4, ye are fallen from *g.*
Eph. 2. 5, 8, by *g.* ye are saved.
3. 8, to me is this *g.* given.
4. 29, minister *g.* to hearers.
6. 24, *g.* be with all that love our Lord.
Col. 4. 6, let your speech be alway with *g.*
2 Thess. 2. 16, good hope through *g.*
1 Tim. 1. 2; 2 Tim. 1. 2; Tit. 1. 4; 2 John 3, *g.*, mercy, and peace.
Heb. 4. 16, the throne of *g.*
10. 29, despite to the Spirit of *g.*
12. 28, *g.* to serve God acceptably.
13. 9, heart established with *g.*
Jas. 1. 11, the *g.* of the fashion of it.
4. 6, he giveth more *g.*
1 Pet. 3. 7, heirs of *g.*
5. 5, giveth *g.* to the humble.
2 Pet. 3. 18, grow in *g.*
Jude 4, turning *g.* of God into lasciviousness.
See Acts 20. 24; 2 Cor. 6. 1; Gal. 2. 21.
GRACIOUS. Gen. 43. 29, God be *g.* to thee.
Ex. 22. 27, I will hear, for I am *g.*
33. 19, I will be *g.* to whom I will be *g.*

Neh. 9. 17, 31, ready to pardon, *g.*, merciful.
Ps. 77. 9, hath God forgotten to be *g.*?
Prov. 11. 16, a *g.* woman retaineth honour.
Isa. 30. 18, wait, that he may be *g.*
Amos 5. 15, may be the Lord will be *g.*
Jon. 4. 2, I know thou art a *g.* God.
Lu. 4. 22, wondered at the *g.* words.
1 Pet. 2. 3, tasted that the Lord is *g.*
See Ex. 34. 6; 2 Chron. 30. 9; Hos. 14. 2.
GRAFT. Rom. 11. 17, 19, 23, 24.
GRAIN. Mat. 13. 31; 17. 20; Mk. 4. 31; Lu. 13. 19; 17. 6, *g.* of mustard seed.
See Amos 9. 9; 1 Cor. 15. 37.
GRANT. Ruth 1. 9, *g.* that you may find rest.
1 Chron. 4. 10, God *g.* him that which he requested.
Job 6. 8, *g.* the thing I long for.
Mat. 20. 21; Mk. 10. 37, *g.* that my two sons.
Rev. 3. 21, will I *g.* to sit with me.
See Ps. 20. 4; 85. 7; Acts 4. 29.
GRAPE. Gen. 49. 11, washed clothes in the blood of *g.*
Num. 6. 3, nor eat moist *g.*, or dried.
Deut. 23. 24, then thou mayest eat *g.* thy fill.
24. 21, when thou gatherest the *g.* of thy vineyard.
32. 14, drink the blood of the *g.*
Cant. 2. 13, 15, vines with tender *g.*
Isa. 5. 2, looked it should bring forth *g.*
17. 6; 24. 13, yet gleaning *g.*
Jer. 8. 13, there shall be no *g.*
31. 29, 30; Ezek. 18. 2, have eaten a sour *g.*
Amos 9. 13, treader of *g.* shall overtake.
See Lev. 19. 10; 25. 5; Lu. 6. 44; Rev. 14. 18.
GRASS. Deut. 32. 2, as showers upon the *g.*
2 Kings 19. 26; Ps. 129. 6, as *g.* on housetops.
Ps. 72. 6, like rain upon mown *g.*
90. 5, like *g.* which groweth up.
102. 4, 11, withered like *g.*
103. 15, days are as *g.*
Isa. 40. 6; 1 Pet. 1. 24, all flesh is *g.*
Mat. 6. 30; Lu. 12. 28, if God so clothe the *g.*
See Prov. 27. 25; John 6. 10; Rev. 8. 7; 9. 4.
GRASSHOPPERS. Amos 7. 1, and, behold, he formed *g.*
GRAVE (*n.*). Gen. 42. 38; 44. 31, with sorrow to the *g.*
Ex. 14. 11, no *g.* in Egypt.
Num. 19. 16, or a *g.*
Job 5. 26, come to *g.* in full age.
7. 9, he that goeth to the *g.*
14. 13, hide me in the *g.*
17. 1, the *g.* are ready for me.
13, if I wait, the *g.* is mine house.
33. 22, his soul draweth near to the *g.*
Ps. 6. 5, in the *g.* who shall give thee thanks?
31. 17, let wicked be silent in the *g.*
49. 14, like sheep laid in the *g.*
15; Hos. 13. 14, the power of the *g.*
Eccl. 9. 10, no wisdom in the *g.*
Isa. 38. 18, the *g.* cannot praise thee.
53. 9, made his *g.* with the wicked.
Hos. 13. 14, O *g.*, I will be thy destruction.
John 5. 28, all in the *g.* shall hear.
11. 31, she goeth to the *g.*
1 Cor. 15. 55, O *g.*, where is thy victory?
See Mat. 27. 52; Lu. 11. 44; Rev. 11. 9; 20. 13.
GRAVE (*v.*). Isa. 49. 16, I have *g.* thee upon the palms.
Hab. 2. 18, that the maker hath *g.* it.
See Ex. 28. 9; 2 Chron. 2. 7; 3. 7.
GRAVE (*adj.*). 1 Tim. 3. 8; Tit. 2. 2.
GRAVEL. Prov. 20. 17; Isa. 48. 19; Lam. 3. 16.
GRAVITY. 1 Tim. 3. 4; Tit. 2. 7.
GRAY. Ps. 71. 18; Prov. 20. 29; Hos. 7. 9.
GREAT. Gen. 12. 2; 18. 18; 46. 3, make a *g.* nation.
48. 19, he also shall be *g.*
Deut. 29. 24, the heat of his *g.* anger.
1 Sam. 12. 24, consider how *g.* things.
2 Kings 5. 13, bid thee do some *g.* thing.
2 Chron. 2. 5, the house is *g.*, for *g.* is our God.
Neh. 6. 3, I am doing a *g.* work.
Job 32. 9, *g.* men not always wise.
36. 18, a *g.* ransom.
Ps. 14. 5; 53. 5, there were they in *g.* fear.
19. 11, there is *g.* reward.
31. 19, how *g.* is thy goodness!
92. 5, how *g.* are thy works!
139. 17, how *g.* is the sum of them!
Prov. 18. 16, gift bringeth before *g.* men.
25. 6, stand not in place of *g.* men.
Mat. 5. 12, *g.* is your reward.
19, called *g.* in kingdom of heaven.
13. 46, pearl of *g.* price.
15. 28, *g.* is thy faith.
20. 26, whosoever will be *g.* among you.
22. 36, 38, the *g.* commandment.
Lu. 10. 2, the harvest is *g.*
16. 26, a *g.* gulf fixed.
Acts 8. 9, giving out he was some *g.* one.
19. 28, 34, *g.* is Diana.
1 Tim. 3. 16, *g.* is the mystery.
Heb. 2. 3, so *g.* salvation.
12. 1, so *g.* a cloud of witnesses.
Jas. 3. 5, how *g.* a matter a little fire kindleth!
See Deut. 9. 2; Eccl. 2. 9; Rev. 7. 9.
GREATER. Gen. 4. 13, punishment *g.* than I can bear.
1 Chron. 11. 9; Esth. 9. 4, waxed *g.* and *g.*
Hag. 2. 9, glory of latter house *g.*
Mat. 11. 11; Lu. 7. 28, *g.* than he.
12. 6, one *g.* than the temple.
Mk. 12. 31, no commandment *g.* than these.
John 1. 50; 5. 20; 14. 12, shalt see *g.* things.
4. 12; 8. 53, art thou *g.* than our father?
10. 29; 14. 28, my Father is *g.* than all.
13. 16; 15. 20, servant not *g.* than his lord.
15. 13, *g.* love hath no man.
1 Cor. 15. 6, the *g.* part remain.
Heb. 6. 13, he could swear by no *g.*
1 John 3. 20, God is *g.* than our hearts.
4. 4, *g.* is he in you than he in world.
3 John 4, no *g.* joy.
See Gen. 41. 40; 48. 19; Heb. 9. 11.
GREATEST. Mat. 13. 32, it is *g.* among herbs.
18. 1, 4, who is *g.* in kingdom?
Mk. 9. 34; Lu. 9. 46, disputed who should be *g.*
1 Cor. 13. 13, the *g.* of these is charity.
See Job 1. 3; Jer. 31. 34; Lu. 22. 24.
GREATLY. 2 Sam. 24. 10; 1 Chron. 21. 8, I have sinned *g.*
1 Kings 18. 3, Obadiah feared the Lord *g.*
Ps. 28. 7, my heart *g.* rejoiceth.
47. 9, God is *g.* exalted.
89. 7, *g.* to be feared in the assembly.
116. 10, I was *g.* afflicted.
Dan. 9. 23; 10. 11, thou art *g.* beloved.
Obad. 2, thou art *g.* despised.
Mk. 12. 27, ye do *g.* err.
See Ps. 62. 2; Mk. 9. 15; Acts 3. 11; 6. 7.
GREATNESS. 1 Chron. 29. 11, thine is the *g.*, power, and glory.
Ps. 145. 3, his *g.* is unsearchable.
Prov. 5. 23, in the *g.* of his folly.
Isa. 63. 1, travelling in *g.* of strength.
Eph. 1. 19, the exceeding *g.* of his power.
See 2 Chron. 9. 6; Ps. 66. 3; 79. 11; 150. 2.
GREEDILY. Prov. 21. 26; Ezek. 22. 12.
GREEDINESS. Eph. 4. 19.
GREEDY. Prov. 1. 19; 15. 27, *g.* of gain.
Isa. 56. 11, they are *g.* dogs.
See Ps. 17. 12; 1 Tim. 3. 3.
GREEN. Lev. 23. 14; Judg. 16. 7; Lu. 23. 31.
GRIEF. 2 Chron. 6. 29, every one shall know his own *g.*
Job 6. 2, Oh that my *g.* were weighed!
Ps. 31. 10, life spent with *g.*
Eccl. 1. 18, in much wisdom is much *g.*
Isa. 53. 3, acquainted with *g.*
Jer. 10. 19, this is a *g.*, and I must bear it.
See Jon. 4. 6; Heb. 13. 17; 1 Pet. 2. 19.
GRIEVE. Gen. 6. 6, it *g.* him at his heart.
45. 5, be not *g.* that ye sold me.

1 Sam. 2. 33, the man shall be to *g.* thine heart.
Ps. 78. 40, they *g.* him in the desert.
95. 10, forty years was I *g.*
Lam. 3. 33, doth not willingly *g.*
Mk. 3. 5, being *g.* for the hardness.
10. 22, he went away *g.*
John 21. 17, Peter was *g.*
Rom. 14. 15, brother *g.* with meat.
Eph. 4. 30, *g.* not the holy Spirit of God.
See Neh. 2. 10; 13. 8; Ps. 119. 158; 139. 21.
GRIEVOUS. Gen. 21. 11, thing was *g.* in Abraham's sight.
50. 11, a *g.* mourning.
Ps. 10. 5, his ways are always *g.*
Prov. 15. 1, *g.* words stir up anger.
Isa. 15. 4, his life shall be *g.*
Jer. 30. 12; Nah. 3. 19, thy wound is *g.*
Mat. 23. 4; Lu. 11. 46, burdens *g.* to be borne.
Phil. 3. 1, to me is not *g.*
Heb. 12. 11, chastening *g.*
1 John 5. 3, commandments not *g.*
See Eccl. 2. 17; Jer. 16. 4; Acts 20. 29.
GRIND. Isa. 3. 15, *g.* faces of the poor.
Lam. 5. 13, took young men to *g.*
Mat. 21. 44; Lu. 20. 18, it will *g.* him to powder.
See Eccl. 12. 3; Mat. 24. 41; Lu. 17. 35.
GROAN. Ex. 2. 24, God heard their *g.*
Job 24. 12, men *g.* from out the city.
Joel 1. 18, how do the beasts *g.*!
Rom. 8. 23, we ourselves *g.*
2 Cor. 5. 2, 4, in this we *g.*
See Job 23. 2; Ps. 6. 6; John 11. 33, 38.
GROPE. Deut. 28. 29; Job 5. 14; 12. 25; Isa. 59. 10.
GROSS. Isa. 60. 2; Jer. 13. 16; Mat. 13. 15; Acts 28. 27.
GROUND. Ex. 3. 5; Acts 7. 33, holy *g.*
Job 5. 6, nor trouble spring out of the *g.*
Isa. 35. 7, parched *g.* become a pool.
Jer. 4. 3; Hos. 10. 12, break up fallow *g.*
Mat. 13. 8; Lu. 8. 8, good *g.*
Mk. 4. 16, stony *g.*
Lu. 13. 7, why cumbereth it the *g.*?
14. 18, bought a piece of *g.*
19. 44, lay thee even with the *g.*
John 8. 6, he wrote on the *g.*
See Zech. 8. 12; Mal. 3. 11; John 12. 24.
GROUNDED. Eph. 3. 17; Col. 1. 23.
GROW. Gen. 48. 16, let them *g.* into a multitude.
2 Sam. 23. 5, though he make it not to *g.*
Ps. 92. 12, *g.* like a cedar.
Isa. 53. 2, he shall *g.* up before him.
Hos. 14. 5, he shall *g.* as the lily.
Mal. 4. 2, *g.* up as calves of the stall.
Mat. 13. 30, let both *g.* together.
Mk. 4. 27, seed should *g.* up, he knoweth not.
Acts 5. 24, whereunto this would *g.*
Eph. 2. 21, *g.* unto an holy temple.
4. 15, may *g.* up into him.
2 Thess. 1. 3, your faith *g.* exceedingly.
1 Pet. 2. 2, that ye may *g.* thereby.
2 Pet. 3. 18, *g.* in grace.
See 2 Kings 19. 26; Jer. 12. 2; Zech. 6. 12.
GRUDGE. Lev. 19. 18; 2 Cor. 9. 7; Jas. 5. 9; 1 Pet. 4. 9.
GUESTS. Zeph. 1. 7; Mat. 22. 10; Lu. 19. 7.
GUIDE. Ps. 25. 9, meek will he *g.* in judgment.
32. 8, I will *g.* thee with mine eye.
48. 14, our *g.* even unto death.
73. 24, *g.* me with thy counsel.
Prov. 6. 7, having no *g.*, overseer, or ruler.
Isa. 58. 11, the Lord shall *g.* thee.
Jer. 3. 4, the *g.* of my youth.
Mat. 23. 16, 24, ye blind *g.*
Lu. 1. 79, *g.* our feet into the way of peace.
John 16. 13, *g.* you into all truth.
See Gen. 48. 14; Prov. 11. 3; 23. 19.
GUILE. Ps. 32. 2, in whose spirit is no *g.*
34. 13; 1 Pet. 3. 10, keep lips from speaking *g.*
John 1. 47, in whom is no *g.*
2 Cor. 12. 16, I caught you with *g.*
1 Pet. 2. 1, laying aside *g.*
1 Pet. 22, nor was *g.* found in his mouth.
3. 10, and his lips that they speak no *g.*
See Ex. 21. 14; 1 Thess. 2. 3; Rev. 14. 5.
GUILTLESS. Ex. 20. 7; Deut. 5. 11, will not hold him *g.*
Josh. 2. 19, we will be *g.*
2 Sam. 3. 28, are *g.* of blood.
Mat. 12. 7, ye would not have condemned the *g.*
See Num. 5. 31; 1 Sam. 26. 9; 1 Kings 2. 9.
GUILTY. Gen. 42. 21, verily *g.* concerning our brother.
Ex. 34. 7; Num. 14. 18, by no means clear the *g.*
Lev. 5. 3, when he knoweth of it, he shall be *g.*
Rom. 3. 19, all the world *g.* before God.
1 Cor. 11. 27, *g.* of the body and blood.
Jas. 2. 10 he is *g.* of all.
See Num. 35. 27; Prov. 30. 10; Mat. 26. 66.
GULF. Lu. 16. 26.
GUSH. 1 Kings 18. 28; Ps. 78. 20; 105. 41; Jer. 9. 18.

H

HABITATION. Ex. 15. 13, guided them to thy holy *h.*
2 Chron. 6. 2, have built an house of *h.*
Ps. 26. 8, have loved the *h.*
33. 14, from the place of his *h.*
69. 25, let their *h.* be desolate.
74. 20, full of *h.* of cruelty.
89. 14, justice and judgment the *h.* of thy throne.
107. 7, 36, a city of *h.*
132. 13, the Lord desired it for his *h.*
Prov. 3. 33, he blesseth the *h.* of the just.
Isa. 32. 18, dwell in a peaceable *h.*
Jer. 21. 13, who shall enter into our *h.*
25. 37, the peaceable *h.* are cut down.
Lu. 16. 9, into everlasting *h.*
Eph. 2. 22, an *h.* of God through the Spirit.
Jude 6, angels which left their own *h.*
See Prov. 8. 31; Acts 1. 20; 17. 26 Rev. 18. 2.
HAIL. Job 38. 22, the treasures of the *h.*
Isa. 28. 17, *h.* sweep away refuge of lies.
See Ex. 9. 18; Josh. 10. 11; Rev. 8. 7; 11. 19; 16. 21.
HAIR. Gen. 42. 38; 44. 29, bring down gray *h.* with sorrow.
Judg. 20. 16, sling stones at *h.* breadth.
Job 4. 15, the *h.* of my flesh stood up.
Ps. 40. 12, more than the *h.* of my head.
Mat. 3. 4; Mk. 1. 6, raiment of camel's *h.*
5. 36, make one *h.* white or black.
10. 30, *h.* of head numbered.
1 Cor. 11. 14, 15, long *h.*, it is a shame.
1 Tim. 2. 9, broided *h.*
1 Pet. 3. 3, plaiting the *h.*
See 2 Sam. 14. 26; Hos. 7. 9; John 11. 2; Rev. 1. 14.
HALE. Lu. 12. 58; Acts 8. 3.
HALL. John 18. 28, then led they Jesus from Caiaphas unto the *h.* of judgment.
33; 19. 9, then Pilate entered into the judgment *h.*
See Acts 25. 23.
HALLOW. Lev. 22. 32, I am the Lord which *h.* you.
25. 10, shall *h.* the fiftieth year.
Num. 5. 10, every man's *h.* things.
1 Kings 9. 3, I have *h.* this house.
Jer. 17. 22; 24. 27, but *h.* ye the sabbath day.
Ezek. 20. 20; 44. 24, and *h.* my sabbaths.
Mat. 6. 9; Lu. 11. 2, *h.* be thy name.
HALT. 1 Kings 18. 21, how long *h.* ye?
Ps. 38. 17, I am ready to *h.*
Jer. 20. 10, my familiars watched for my *h.*
See Gen. 32. 31; Mic. 4. 6; Zeph. 3. 19.
HAND. Gen. 16. 12, *h.* against every man.
24. 2; 47. 29, put thy *h.* under my thigh.
27. 22, the *h.* are the *h.* of Esau.
31. 29, in the power of my *h.* to do you hurt.
Ex. 21. 24; Deut. 19. 21, *h.* for *h.*, foot for foot.
33. 22, cover with my *h.* while I pass.
Num. 11. 23; Isa. 59. 1, Lord's *h.* waxed short.

Num. 22. 29, would there were sword in mine *h.*
Deut. 8. 17, my *h.* hath gotten this wealth.
33. 2, from right *h.* went fiery law.
Judg. 7. 2, saying, my own *h.* hath saved me.
1 Sam. 5. 11, *h.* of God was heavy.
6. 9, not his *h.* that smote us, but a chance.
12. 3, of whose *h.* have I received any bribe?
19. 5; 28. 21, put his life in his *h.*
23. 16, Jonathan strengthened his *h.* in God.
26. 18, what evil is in mine *h.*?
2 Sam. 14. 19, is not *h.* of Joab in this?
24. 14; 1 Chron. 21. 13, let us fall into *h.* of Lord.
1 Kings 18. 44, cloud like a man's *h.*
2 Kings 5. 11, strike his *h.* over the place.
1 Chron. 12. 2, could use right *h.* and left.
Ezra 7. 9; 8. 18; Neh. 2. 8, good *h.* of God.
10. 19, they gave their *h.* that they would.
Neh. 2. 18, strengthened their *h.* for work.
6. 5, with open letter in his *h.*
Job 12. 10, in whose *h.* is the soul.
19. 21, the *h.* of God hath touched me.
40. 14, that thine own *h.* can save.
Ps. 16. 11, at right *h.* pleasures for evermore.
24. 4, clean *h.* and pure heart.
68. 31, stretch out her *h.* unto God.
90. 17, establish thou the work of our *h.*
137. 5, let my right *h.* forget her cunning.
Prov. 3. 16, in left *h.* riches and honour.
6. 10; 24. 33, folding of *h.* to sleep.
10. 4, that dealeth with slack *h.*
11. 21; 16. 5, though *h.* join *h.*
12. 24, *h.* of diligent shall bear rule.
19. 24; 26. 15, slothful man hideth his *h.*
22. 26, be not of them that strike *h.*
Eccl. 2. 24, this I saw was from *h.* of God.
9. 10, whatsoever thy *h.* findeth.
11. 6, in evening withhold not thine *h.*
Isa. 1. 12, who hath required this at your *h.*?
5. 25; 9. 12; 10. 4; 14. 27, his *h.* stretched out still.
14. 26, this is the *h.* that is stretched out.
40. 12, measured waters in hollow of *h.*
44. 5, subscribe with his *h.* to the Lord.
53. 10, pleasure of Lord shall prosper in his *h.*
56. 2, keepeth his *h.* from evil.
Jer. 23. 14, strengthen *h.* of evil doers.
33. 13, shall pass under *h.* of him that telleth.
Lam. 2. 4, with his right *h.* as adversary.
4. 10, *h.* of pitiful women have sodden.
Ezek. 7. 17; 21. 7, all *h.* shall be feeble.
10. 2, fill *h.* with coals of fire.
17. 18, lo, he had given his *h.*
Dan. 4. 35, none can stay his *h.*
Hos. 7. 5, stretched out *h.* with scorners.
Mic. 7. 3, do evil with both *h.* earnestly.
Zeph. 3. 16, let not thine *h.* be slack.
Zech. 13. 6, what are these wounds in thine *h.*?
Mat. 3. 2; 4. 17; 10. 7, kingdom of heaven at *h.*
12; Lu. 3. 17, whose fan is in his *h.*
6. 3, let not left *h.* know.
18. 8; Mk. 9. 43, if thy *h.* or foot offend.
26. 18, my time is at *h.*
46; Mk. 14. 42, he is at *h.* that doth betray.
Mk. 14. 62, sitting on right *h.* of power.
16. 19, sat on right *h.* of God.
Lu. 9. 44, delivered into *h.* of men.
John 10. 28, nor pluck out of my *h.*
29, my Father's *h.*
20. 27, reach hither thy *h.*
Acts 20. 34, these *h.* have ministered.
2 Cor. 5. 1, house not made with *h.*
Phil. 4. 5, moderation be known, the Lord is at *h.*
1 Thess. 4. 11, work with your own *h.*
2 Thess. 2. 2, the day of Christ is at *h.*
1 Tim. 2. 8, lifting up holy *h.*
Heb. 10. 31, the *h.* of living God.
Jas. 4. 8, cleanse your *h.*
1 Pet. 4. 7, end of all things is at *h.*
1 John 1. 1, our *h.* have handled of the Word.
See Isa. 49. 16; Lu. 9. 62; John 18. 22; Col. 2. 14.

HANDLE. Judg. 5. 14, that *h.* pen of the writer.
Ps. 115. 7, hands, but they *h.* not.
Prov. 16. 20, that *h.* a matter wisely.
Jer. 2. 8, they that *h.* the law.
Mk. 12. 4, sent away shamefully *h.*
Lu. 24. 39, *h.* me, and see.
2 Cor. 4. 2, not *h.* word deceitfully.
Col. 2. 21, taste not, *h.* not.
1 John 1. 1, have *h.* of Word of life.
See Gen. 4. 21; 1 Chron. 12. 8; Ezek. 27. 29.

HANDMAID. Ps. 86. 16; 116. 16; Prov. 30. 23; Lu. 1. 38.

HANG. Deut. 21. 23; Gal. 3. 13, he that is *h.* is accursed.
Job 26. 7, *h.* the earth on nothing.
Ps. 137. 2, we *h.* our harps upon the willows.
Mat. 18. 6; Mk. 9. 42; Lu. 17. 2, millstone *h.* about neck.
22. 40, on these *h.* the law and the prophets.
27. 5, went and *h.* himself.
Heb. 12. 12, lift up the hands which *h.* down.
See Gen. 40. 22; Esth. 7. 10; Lu. 23. 39.

HAPLY. 1 Sam. 14. 30; Mk. 11. 13; Acts 5. 39; 17. 27.

HAPPEN. 1 Sam. 6. 9, it was a chance that *h.*
Prov. 12. 21, there shall no evil *h.* to the just.
Isa. 41. 22, let them show us what shall *h.*
Jer. 44. 23, therefore this evil is *h.*
Mk. 10. 32, to tell what should *h.*
Lu. 24. 14, talked of things that had *h.*
Rom. 11. 25, blindness is *h.* to Israel.
1 Cor. 10. 11, things *h.* for ensamples.
Phil. 1. 12, things which *h.* to me.
1 Pet. 4. 12, as though some strange thing *h.*
2 Pet. 2. 22, it is *h.* according to proverb.
See Eccl. 2. 14; 8. 14; 9. 11; Acts 3. 10.

HAPPY. Gen. 30. 13, *h.* am I.
Deut. 33. 29, *h.* art thou.
Job 5. 17, *h.* is the man whom God correcteth.
Ps. 127. 5, *h.* is the man that hath quiver full.
128. 2, *h.* shalt thou be.
144. 15, *h.* is that people.
Prov. 3. 13, 18, *h.* that findeth wisdom.
14. 21, he that hath mercy, *h.* is he.
28. 14, *h.* is the man that feareth alway.
Jer. 12. 1, why are they *h.* that deal treacherously?
Mal. 3. 15, now we call proud *h.*
John 13. 17, if ye know, *h.* if ye do them.
Rom. 14. 22, *h.* is he that condemneth not.
Jas. 5. 11, we count them *h.* that endure.
1 Pet. 3. 14; 4. 14, *h.* are ye.
See Ps. 146. 5; Prov. 29. 18; 1 Cor. 7. 40.

HARD. Gen. 18. 14, is any thing too *h.* for the Lord?
Deut. 1. 17; 17. 8, cause that is too *h.*
15. 18, it shall not seem *h.* to thee.
1 Kings 10. 1; 2 Chron. 9. 1, prove with *h.* questions.
Job 41. 24, *h.* as piece of nether millstone.
Prov. 13. 15, the way of transgressors is *h.*
18. 19, brother offended *h.* to be won.
Jer. 32. 17, 27, there is nothing too *h.* for thee.
Ezek. 3. 5, 6, to a people of *h.* language.
Mat. 25. 24, thou art an *h.* man.
John 6. 60, this is an *h.* saying.
Acts 9. 5; 26. 14, *h.* to kick against the pricks.
Heb. 5. 11, many things *h.* to be uttered.
2 Pet. 3. 16, things *h.* to be understood.
See Deut. 15. 18; 2 Kings 2. 10; Mk. 10. 24.

HARDEN. Ex. 4. 21; 7. 3; 14. 4, I will *h.* Pharaoh's heart.
14. 17, *h.* hearts of Egyptians.
Job 6. 10, I would *h.* myself in sorrow.
9. 4, who hath *h.* himself against him?
Prov. 21. 29, a wicked man *h.* his face.
28. 14, he that *h.* his heart.
29. 1, he that being often reproved *h.* his neck.
Isa. 63. 17, why hast thou *h.* our heart?
Mk. 6. 52; 8. 17, their heart was *h.*
John 12. 40, he hath *h.* their heart.

Acts 19. 9, when divers were *h.*
Rom. 9. 18, whom he will he *h.*
Heb. 3. 13, lest any of you be *h.*
See Deut. 15. 7; 2 Kings 17. 14; Job 39. 16.
HARDLY. Gen. 16. 6; Mat. 19. 23; Mk. 10. 23; Lu. 18. 24.
HARDNESS. Mk. 3. 5, grieved for *h.* of their hearts.
116. 14, upbraided them for *h.* of heart.
2 Tim. 2. 3, endure *h.*, as good soldier.
See Job 38. 38; Mat. 19. 8; Mk. 10. 5; Rom. 2. 5.
HARM. Lev. 5. 16, make amends for *h.*
Num. 35. 23, nor sought his *h.*
1 Sam. 26. 21, I will no more do thee *h.*
2 Kings 4. 41, no *h.* in the pot.
1 Chron. 16. 22; Ps. 105. 15, do prophets no *h.*
Prov. 3. 30, if he have done thee no *h.*
Acts 16. 28, do thyself no *h.*
28. 5, he felt no *h.*
1 Pet. 3. 13, who will *h.* you?
See Gen. 31. 52; Jer. 39. 12; Acts 27. 21.
HARMLESS. Mat. 10. 16; Phil. 2. 15; Heb. 7. 26.
HARP. 1 Sam. 16. 16, cunning player on an *h.*
Ps. 49. 4, dark sayings on the *h.*
137. 2, hanged *h.* on the willows.
Isa. 5. 12, *h.* and viol are in their feasts.
24. 8, joy of the *h.* ceaseth.
1 Cor. 14. 7, what is piped or *h.*, except they give.
Rev. 14. 2, harping with their *h.*
See Gen. 4. 21; Ezek. 26. 13; Dan. 3. 5.
HARROW. 2 Sam. 12. 31; 1 Chron. 20. 3; Job 39. 10.
HART. Deut. 12. 15, and as of the *h.*
1 Kings 4. 23, besides *h.* and roebucks.
See Ps. 42. 1; Isa. 35. 6.
HARVEST. Gen. 8. 22, *h.* shall not cease.
Ex. 23. 16; 34. 22, the feast of *h.*
Lev. 19. 19; 23. 10; Deut. 24. 19, when ye reap *h.*
1 Sam. 12. 17, is it not wheat *h.* to-day?
Job 5. 5, whose *h.* the hungry eateth up.
Prov. 6. 8, the ant gathereth food in *h.*
10. 5, he that sleepeth in *h.*
25. 13, cold of snow in time of *h.*
26. 1, as rain in *h.*
Isa. 9. 3, according to joy in *h.*
16. 9, thy *h.* is fallen.
18. 4, dew in heat of *h.*
Jer. 5. 17, they shall eat up thine *h.*
24, appointed weeks of *h.*
8. 20, the *h.* is past, the summer ended.
51. 33, the time of her *h.* shall come.
Joel 3. 13; Rev. 14. 15, the *h.* is ripe.
Mat. 9. 37, the *h.* is plenteous.
38; Lu. 10. 2, the Lord of the *h.*
13. 30, in the time of *h.* I will say.
Mk. 4. 29, putteth in sickle, because *h.* is come.
Lu. 10. 2, the *h.* truly is great.
John 4. 35, the fields are white to *h.*
See Josh. 3. 15; Isa. 23. 3; Mat. 13. 39.
HASTE. Ex. 12. 11, shall eat it in *h.*
1 Sam. 21. 8, king's business required *h.*
Ps. 31. 22; 116. 11, I said in my *h.*
Prov. 19. 2, he that *h.* with feet sinneth.
28. 22, he that *h.* to be rich.
Isa. 51. 14, captive exile *h.*
60. 22, will *h.* it in his time.
Jer. 1. 12, I will *h.* my word.
Zeph. 1. 14, day of the Lord *h.* greatly.
See 2 Kings 7. 15; Ps. 16. 4; 55. 8; Eccl. 1. 5.
HASTILY. Prov. 20. 21; 25. 8.
HASTY. Prov. 14. 29; 21. 5; 29. 20; Eccl. 5. 2; 7. 9.
HATE. Gen. 37. 4, 5, 8, *h.* Joseph yet the more.
Lev. 19. 17, shall not *h.* thy brother.
1 Kings 22. 8; 2 Chron. 18. 7, one man, but I *h.* him.
2 Chron. 19. 2, and love them that *h.* the Lord.
Ps. 34. 21, they that *h.* righteous shall be desolate.
97. 10, ye that love the Lord, *h.* evil.
139. 21, do not I *h.* them that *h.* thee?
Prov. 1. 22, how long will ye *h.* knowledge?
Prov. 13. 24, he that spareth his rod *h.* his son.
14. 20, the poor is *h.* of his neighbour.
15. 10, he that *h.* reproof shall die.
27, he that *h.* gifts shall live.
Eccl. 2. 17, I *h.* life.
3. 8, a time to *h.*
Isa. 1. 14, your feasts my soul *h.*
61. 8, I *h.* robbery for burnt offering.
Amos 5. 15, *h.* the evil, and love the good.
Mic. 3. 2, who *h.* the good, and love the evil.
Zech. 8. 17, these are things that I *h.*
Mal. 1. 3; Rom. 9. 13, I loved Jacob, and *h.* Esau.
Mat. 5. 44; Lu. 6. 27, do good to them that *h.* you.
6. 24, either he will *h.* the one.
10. 22; Mk. 13. 13; Lu. 21. 17, ye shall be *h.*
24. 10, and shall *h.* one another.
Lu. 6. 22, blessed are ye when men shall *h.* you.
14. 26, and *h.* not his father.
John 3. 20, *h.* the light.
7. 7, the world cannot *h.* you.
12. 25, he that *h.* his life.
15. 18; 1 John 3. 13, marvel not if world *h.* you.
24, they have both seen and *h.*
Eph. 5. 29, no man ever yet *h.* his own flesh.
1 John 2. 9, 11; 3. 15; 4. 20, *h.* his brother.
See Gen. 27. 41; Deut. 1. 27; Prov. 6. 16; Rev. 2. 6.
HATEFUL. Ps. 36. 2; Ezek. 23. 29; Tit. 3. 3.
HATERS. Ps. 81. 15; Rom. 1. 30.
HAUGHTY. 2 Sam. 22. 28, thine eyes are upon the *h.*
Ps. 131. 1, my heart is not *h.*
Prov. 16. 18, a *h.* spirit before a fall.
21. 24, proud and *h.* scorner.
Isa. 10. 33, the *h.* shall be humbled.
Zeph. 3. 11, no more be *h.* because.
See Isa. 2. 11; 13. 11; 24. 4; Ezek. 16. 50.
HAWK. Lev. 11. 16, and the *h.* after his kind.
Job 39. 26, doth the *h.* fly by wisdom?
HEAD. Gen. 3. 15, it shall bruise thy *h.*
Josh. 2. 19, blood be on his *h.*
Judg. 11. 9, shall I be your *h.*?
2 Kings 2. 3, take thy master from thy *h.* to-day.
4. 19, he said, My *h.*, my *h.*
Ps. 24. 7, 9, lift up your *h.*
66. 12, caused men to ride over our *h.*
110. 7, therefore shall he lift up the *h.*
141. 5, oil, which shall not break my *h.*
Prov. 10. 6, blessings on *h.* of the just.
11. 26, on *h.* of him that selleth corn.
25. 22; Rom. 12. 20, coals of fire on his *h.*
Eccl. 2. 14, a wise man's eyes are in his *h.*
Isa. 1. 5, the whole *h.* is sick.
35. 10; 51. 11, everlasting joy upon their *h.*
58. 5, to bow down *h.* as bulrush.
59. 17; Eph. 6. 17, helmet of salvation on *h.*
Jer. 9. 1, Oh that my *h.* were waters.
14. 3, 4, ashamed, and covered their *h.*
Dan. 2. 38, thou art this *h.* of gold.
Amos 2. 7, that pant after dust on *h.*
9. 1, cut them in the *h.*
Zech. 1. 21, no man did lift up his *h.*
4. 7, the *h.*-stone with shoutings.
Mat. 5. 36, neither swear by *h.*
27. 39; Mk. 15. 29, reviled, wagging their *h.*
Lu. 7. 46, my *h.* thou didst not anoint.
21. 18, not hair of *h.* perish.
28, then look up, and lift up your *h.*
John 13. 9, also my hands and my *h.*
1 Cor. 11. 3, the *h.* of every man is Christ.
4, dishonoureth his *h.*
10, woman to have power on her *h.*
Eph. 1. 22; 4. 15; Col. 1. 18, the *h.* of the church.
5. 23, husband is *h.* of the wife.
Col. 2. 19, not holding the *h.*
See Num. 6. 5; Josh. 7. 6; Acts 18. 6; Rev. 13. 1.
HEAL. Ex. 15. 26, I am the Lord that *h.* thee.
Deut. 32. 39, I wound, I *h.*
2 Kings 2. 22, waters were *h.*

2 Kings 20. 5, 8, I will *h.* thee.
Ps. 6. 2, O Lord, *h.* me.
41. 4, *h.* my soul, for I have sinned.
103. 3, who *h.* all thy diseases.
107. 20, sent his word, and *h.* them.
Isa. 6. 10, lest they convert and be *h.*
53. 5, with his stripes we are *h.*
Jer. 6. 14; 8. 11, they have *h.* the hurt slightly.
15. 18, wound refuseth to be *h.*
17. 14, *h.* me, and I shall be *h.*
Lam. 2. 13, who can *h.* thee?
Hos. 5. 13, yet could he not *h.* thee.
6. 1, he hath torn, and he will *h.* us.
14. 4, I will *h.* their backslidings.
Mat. 8. 7, I will come and *h.* him.
8. 8, speak, and my servant shall be *h.*
10. 1, to *h.* all manner of sickness.
8; Lu. 9. 2; 10. 9, *h.* the sick.
12. 10; Lu. 14. 3, is it lawful to *h.* on sabbath?
Mk. 3. 2; Lu. 6. 7, whether he would *h.* on the sabbath day.
Lu. 4. 18, to *h.* broken-hearted.
23, physician, *h.* thyself.
5. 17, power of the Lord present to *h.*
John 5. 47, that he would come and *h.*
5. 13, he that was *h.* wist not.
Acts 4. 14, beholding the man which was *h.*
5. 16, they were *h.* every one.
14. 9, he had faith to be *h.*
Heb. 12. 13, let it rather be *h.*
Jas. 5. 16, pray that ye may be *h.*
1 Pet. 2. 24, by whose stripes ye were *h.*
Rev. 13. 3, his deadly wound was *h.*
See Eccl. 3. 3; Isa. 3. 7; Mat. 4. 21; 14. 14.
HEALING. Jer. 14. 19, there is no *h.* for us.
Nah. 3. 19, no *h.* of thy bruise.
Mal. 4. 2, with *h.* in his wings.
Mat. 4. 23, went about *h.* all.
Lu. 9. 11, that had need of *h.*
1 Cor. 12. 9, 28, 30, the gift of *h.*
Rev. 22. 2, for the *h.* of the nations.
See Jer. 30. 13; Lu. 9. 6; Acts 4. 22; 10. 38.
HEALTH. 2 Sam. 20. 9, art thou in *h.*, my brother?
Ps. 42. 11; 43. 5, the *h.* of my countenance.
67. 2, thy saving *h.*
Prov. 3. 8, *h.* to thy navel.
4. 22, they are *h.* to all their flesh.
16. 24, *h.* to the bones.
Isa. 58. 8, thy *h.* shall spring forth.
Jer. 8. 15, looked for a time of *h.*
22, why is not *h.* recovered?
3 John 2, mayest be in *h.*
See Gen. 43. 28; Jer. 30. 17; Acts 27. 34.
HEAP. Deut. 32. 23, *h.* mischiefs upon them.
Job 16. 4, I could *h.* up words.
27. 16, though he *h.* up silver.
Ps. 39. 6, he *h.* up riches.
Prov. 25. 22; Rom. 12. 20, *h.* coals of fire.
Ezek. 24. 10, *h.* on wood.
Hab. 1. 10, they shall *h.* dust.
Mic. 3. 12, Jerusalem shall become *h.*
2 Tim. 4. 3, *h.* to themselves teachers.
Jas. 5. 3, ye have *h.* treasure for last days.
See Judg. 15. 16; Neh. 4. 2; Eccl. 2. 26.
HEAR. Ex. 6. 12, how shall Pharaoh *h.* me?
1 Sam. 15. 14, lowing of oxen which I *h.*
1 Kings 8. 42, they shall *h.* of thy great name.
18. 26, O Baal, *h.* us.
2 Kings 18. 28; Isa. 36. 13, *h.* words of the great king.
1 Chron. 14. 15, when thou *h.* a sound of going.
Neh. 8. 2, all that could *h.* with understanding.
Job 31. 35, Oh that one would *h.* me!
Ps. 4. 1; 39. 12; 54. 2; 84. 8; 102. 1; 143. 1; Dan. 9. 17, *h.* my prayer.
3; 17. 6; Zech. 10. 6, the Lord will *h.*
10. 17, cause thine ear to *h.*
49. 1, *h.* this, all ye people.
59. 7, who, say they, doth *h.*?
66. 18, if I regard iniquity, the Lord will not *h.* me.
Ps. 85. 8, I will *h.* what God the Lord will speak.
102. 20, *h.* groaning of the prisoner.
Prov. 13. 8, the poor *h.* not rebuke.
18. 13, answereth a matter before he *h.*
22. 17, *h.* the words of the wise.
Eccl. 5. 1, more ready to *h.* than give.
7. 5, better to *h.* rebuke of wise.
12. 13, *h.* conclusion of the whole matter.
Isa. 1. 2, *h.*, O heavens, and give ear.
15; Jer. 7. 16; 11. 14; 14. 12; Ezek. 8. 18, make many prayers, I will not *h.*
6. 9; Mk. 4. 12, *h.* but understand not.
29. 18, shall deaf *h.* words of the book.
33. 13, *h.*, ye that are afar off.
34. 1, let the earth *h.*
42. 20, opening ears, but he *h.* not.
55. 3; John 5. 25, *h.*, and your soul shall live.
Ezek. 3. 27, he that *h.*, let him *h.*
33. 31, they *h.* words, but will not do them.
Mat. 7. 24; Lu. 6. 47, whoso *h.* these sayings.
11. 4, show things ye do *h.* and see.
5; Mk. 7. 37; Lu. 7. 22, the deaf *h.*
13. 17; Lu. 10. 24, those things which ye *h.*
17. 5; Mk. 9. 7, my beloved Son, *h.* him.
18. 16, if he will not *h.* thee.
Mk. 4. 24; Lu. 8. 18, take heed what ye *h.*
Lu. 9. 9, of whom I *h.* such things.
10. 16, he that *h.* you, *h.* me.
John 5. 25, dead shall *h.* voice of Son of God.
30, as I *h.*, I judge.
6. 60, who can *h.* it?
8. 47, he that is of God *h.* God's words.
9. 31, God *h.* not sinners.
11. 42, I know thou *h.* me always.
12. 47, if any man *h.* my words.
14. 24, the word ye *h.* is not mine.
Acts 2. 8, how *h.* we every man?
13. 44, whole city came to *h.*
Rom. 10. 14, *h.* without a preacher.
1 Cor. 11. 18, I *h.* there be divisions.
1 Tim. 4. 16, save thyself, and them that *h.*
Jas. 1. 19, swift to *h.*
1 John 4. 5, the world *h.* them.
6, he that knoweth God *h.* us.
5. 15, we know that he *h.* us.
Rev. 2. 7; 3. 6, 13, 22, let him *h.*
3. 20, if any man *h.* my voice.
See Deut. 30. 17; 2 Kings 19. 16; 2 Chron. 6. 21.
HEARD. Gen. 3. 8, they *h.* voice of the Lord.
21. 17, God *h.* voice of the lad.
45. 2, Joseph wept, and the Egyptians *h.*
Ex. 3. 7, I have *h.* their cry.
Num. 11. 1; 12. 2, the Lord *h.* it.
Deut. 4. 12, only he *h.* a voice.
1 Kings 6. 7, nor any tool of iron *h.*
10. 7; 2 Chron. 9. 6, exceedeth the fame I *h.*
2 Kings 19. 25; Isa. 37. 26, hast thou not *h.* long ago?
Ezra 3. 13; Neh. 12. 43, the noise was *h.* afar off.
Job 15. 8, hast thou *h.* the secret of God?
16. 2, I have *h.* many such things.
19. 7, but I am not *h.*
26. 14, how little a portion is *h.*?
29. 11, when the ear *h.* me, it blessed me.
Ps. 6. 9, the Lord hath *h.* my supplication.
10. 17, hast *h.* the desire of the humble.
34. 4, I sought the Lord, and he *h.*
38. 13, I, as a deaf man, *h.* not.
61. 5, thou hast *h.* my vows.
81. 5, I *h.* language I understood not.
116. 1, I love the Lord, because he hath *h.*
Cant. 2. 12, voice of turtle is *h.*
Isa. 40. 21, 28, have ye not *h.*?
64. 4, not *h.* what he hath prepared.
65. 19, weeping no more be *h.*
66. 8, who hath *h.* such a thing?
Jer. 7. 13, rising early, but ye *h.* not.
8. 6, I *h.*, but they spake not aright.
51. 46; Obad. 1, a rumour that shall be *h.*
Dan. 12. 8, I *h.*, but understood not.
Zech. 8. 23, we have *h.* God is with you.

Mal. 3. 16, the Lord hearkened, and *h.* it.
Mat. 6. 7, *h.* for much speaking.
26. 65; Mk. 14. 64, ye have *h.* the blasphemy.
Lu. 12. 3, shall be *h.* in the light.
John 4. 42, we have *h.* him ourselves.
8. 36, as though he *h.* them not.
11. 41, I thank thee thou hast *h.* me.
Acts 4. 4, many which *h.* believed.
20, cannot but speak things we have *h.*
16. 25, the prisoners *h.* them.
22. 15, witness of what thou hast seen and *h.*
Rom. 10. 14, of whom they have not *h.*
18, have they not *h.*?
1 Cor. 2. 9, eye hath not seen, nor ear *h.*
2 Cor. 12. 4, *h.* unspeakable words.
Eph. 4. 21, if so be ye have *h.* him.
Phil. 4. 9, things ye have *h.* and seen in me.
2 Tim. 2. 2, things thou hast *h.* of me.
Heb. 2. 3, confirmed by them that *h.*
4. 2, with faith in them that *h.*
5. 7, was *h.* in that he feared.
1 John 1. 1, 3, that which we have *h.* and seen.
Rev. 3. 3, remember how thou hast *h.*
10. 4; 14. 2; 18. 4, *h.* a voice from heaven.
See Jer. 31. 18; John 5. 37; Rev. 19. 6; 22. 8.

HEARER. Rom. 2. 13; Eph. 4. 29; Jas. 1. 23.

HEARING. Deut. 31. 11, read this law in their *h.*
2 Kings 4. 31, neither voice nor *h.*
Job 42. 5, by the *h.* of the ear.
Prov. 20. 12, the *h.* ear.
Eccl. 1. 8, nor ear filled with *h.*
Amos 8. 11, a famine of *h.* the word.
Mat. 13. 13, *h.*, they hear not.
Acts 9. 7, *h.* a voice, but seeing no man.
Rom. 10. 17, faith cometh by *h.*
1 Cor. 12. 17, where were the *h.*?
Heb. 5. 11, ye are dull of *h.*
See Acts 28. 27; Gal. 3. 2; 2 Pet. 2. 8.

HEARKEN. Deut. 18. 15, unto him ye shall *h.*
Josh. 1. 17, so will we *h.* unto thee.
1 Sam. 15. 22, to *h.* than the fat of rams.
Prov. 29. 12, if a ruler *h.* to lies.
Isa. 55. 2, *h.* diligently unto me.
Dan. 9. 19, O Lord, *h.* and do.
Mk. 7. 14, *h.* to me, every one of you.
See Ps. 103. 20; Prov. 1. 33; 12. 15; Acts 4. 19.

HEART. Ex. 23. 9, ye know the *h.* of a stranger.
Deut. 11. 13; Josh. 22. 5; 1 Sam. 12. 20, 24, serve him with all your *h.*
13. 3; 30. 6; Mat. 22. 37; Mk. 12. 30, 33; Lu. 10. 27, love the Lord with all your *h.*
Judg. 5. 16, great searchings of *h.*
1 Sam. 10. 9, God gave him another *h.*
16. 7, the Lord looketh on the *h.*
1 Kings 3. 9, 12, give an understanding *h.*
4. 29, gave Solomon largeness of *h.*
8. 17; 2 Chron. 6. 7, it was in the *h.* of David.
11. 4, not perfect, as was *h.* of David.
14. 8, followed me with all his *h.*
1 Chron. 12. 33, not of double *h.*
29. 17; Jer. 11. 20, I know thou triest the *h.*
2 Chron. 31. 21, he did it with all his *h.*
32. 25, his *h.* was lifted up.
Neh. 2. 2, nothing else but sorrow of *h.*
Job 23. 16, maketh my *h.* soft.
29. 13, caused the widow's *h.* to sing.
Ps. 10. 6; 11. 13; 14. 1; 53. 1, said in his *h.*
19. 8, rejoicing the *h.*
27. 3, my *h.* shall not fear.
28. 7, my *h.* trusted in him.
64. 6, the *h.* is deep.
73. 7, more than *h.* could wish.
78. 37, their *h.* was not right.
97. 11, gladness sown for upright in *h.*
119. 11, thy word have I hid in my *h.*
80, let my *h.* be sound.
139. 23, search me and know my *h.*
Prov. 4. 23, keep thy *h.* with all diligence.
14. 10, the *h.* knoweth his own bitterness.
21. 1, king's *h.* is in the hand of the Lord.
23. 7, as he thinketh in his *h.*, so is he.
Prov. 25. 3, king's *h.* is unsearchable.
20, songs to a heavy *h.*
31. 11, *h.* of her husband doth trust.
Eccl. 8. 5, wise man's *h.* discerneth.
Isa. 35. 4, say to them of fearful *h.*
44. 20, a deceived *h.*
57. 1; Jer. 12. 11, no man layeth it to *h.*
15, revive *h.* of contrite.
65. 14, sing for joy of *h.*
Jer. 11. 20; 20. 12, thou triest the *h.*
17. 9, the *h.* is deceitful above all things.
20. 9, in mine *h.* as a burning fire.
24. 7, I will give them a *h.* to know me.
30. 21, that engaged his *h.* to approach.
49. 16; Obad. 3, pride of *h.* deceived thee.
Ezek. 11. 19, take stony *h.*
18. 31, make you a new *h.*
36. 26, will give you a *h.* of flesh.
44. 7; Acts 7. 51, uncircumcised in *h.*
Dan. 1. 8, Daniel purposed in his *h.*
Joel 2. 13, rend your *h.*
Zech. 7. 12, made *h.* as adamant.
Mal. 2. 2, if ye will not lay it to *h.*
4. 6, turn *h.* of fathers to children.
Mat. 5. 8, blessed are the pure in *h.*
6. 21; Lu. 12. 34, there will your *h.* be also.
11. 29, meek and lowly in *h.*
12. 34; Lu. 6. 45, out of abundance of the *h.*
15. 19, out of the *h.* proceed evil thoughts.
18. 35, if ye from your *h.* forgive not.
Mk. 2. 8, why reason ye in your *h.*?
8. 17, have ye your *h.* yet hardened?
10. 5; 16. 14, hardness of *h.*
Lu. 2. 19, 51, kept them in her *h.*
21. 14, settle it in your *h.*
24. 25, slow of *h.* to believe.
32, did not our *h.* burn within us?
John 14. 1, 27, let not your *h.* be troubled.
Acts 5. 23; 7. 54, were cut to the *h.*
11. 23, with purpose of *h.*
Rom. 10. 10, with the *h.* man believeth.
1 Cor. 2. 9, neither have entered into *h.*
2 Cor. 3. 3, in fleshy tables of the *h.*
5. 12, glory in appearance, not in *h.*
Eph. 3. 17, that Christ dwell in your *h.* by faith.
5. 19, singing and making melody in your *h.*
6. 6, doing will of God from the *h.*
Phil. 4. 7, keep your *h.* and minds.
Col. 3. 22, in singleness of *h.*
2 Thess. 3. 5, direct your *h.* into love of God.
Heb. 4. 12, discerner of intents of the *h.*
10. 22, draw near with true *h.*
13. 9, good that the *h.* be established.
Jas. 3. 14, if ye have strife in your *h.*
4. 8, purify your *h.*
1 Pet. 3. 4, the hidden man of the *h.*
15, sanctify the Lord in your *h.*
See Ps. 57. 7; 108. 1; Col. 3. 15; 2 Pet. 1. 19.

HEARTH. Gen. 18. 6; Ps. 102. 3; Isa. 30. 14; Jer. 36. 22.

HEARTILY. Col. 3. 23.

HEAT. Deut. 29. 24, the *h.* of this great anger.
Ps. 19. 6, nothing hid from *h.* thereof.
Eccl. 4. 11, two together, then they have *h.*
Isa. 4. 6; 25. 4, a shadow from the *h.*
18. 4, *h.* upon herbs, dew in *h.* of harvest.
49. 10, neither shall *h.* smite them.
Hos. 7. 4, as oven *h.* by the baker.
Mat. 20. 12, burden and *h.* of the day.
Jas. 1. 11, sun no sooner risen with burning *h.*
2 Pet. 3. 10, melt with fervent *h.*
See Dan. 3. 19; Lu. 12. 55; Acts 28. 3.

HEATH. Jer. 17. 6; 48. 6.

HEATHEN. Ps. 2. 1; Acts 4. 25, why do the *h.* rage?
8, give *h.* for inheritance.
102. 15, the *h.* shall fear name of the Lord.
Ezek. 36. 24, I will take you from among *h.*
Zech. 8. 13, ye were a curse among the *h.*
Mat. 6. 7, repetitions, as the *h.*
18. 17, let him be as *h.* man.

See Lev. 25. 44; Deut. 4. 27; Neh. 5. 8.
HEAVEN. Gen. 28. 17, the gate of *h.*
Ex. 20. 22, have talked with you from *h.*
Lev. 26. 19, make your *h.* as iron.
Deut. 10. 14; 1 Kings 8. 27; Ps. 115. 16, the *h.* and *h.* of heavens.
33. 13, the precious things of *h.*
2 Kings 7. 2, if the Lord make windows in *h.*
Job 15. 15, the *h.* are not clean in his sight.
22. 12, is not God in the height of *h.*?
Ps. 8. 3, when I consider thy *h.*
14. 2; 53. 2, had looked down from *h.*
73. 25, whom have I in *h.*?
89. 6, who in *h.* can be compared to the Lord?
119. 89, thy word is settled in *h.*
Prov. 8. 27, when he prepared the *h.* I was there.
25. 3, the *h.* for height.
Eccl. 5. 2, for God is in *h.*
Isa. 13. 13; Hag. 2. 6, will shake the *h.*
40. 12, meted out *h.* with the span.
65. 17; Rev. 21. 1, new *h.* and new earth.
Jer. 7. 18, make cakes to queen of *h.*
23. 24, do not I fill *h.* and earth?
31. 37, if *h.* can be measured.
Ezek. 1. 1; Mat. 3. 16; Mk. 1. 10, the *h.* were opened.
32. 7, I will cover the *h.*
Dan. 7. 13, with clouds of *h.*
Hag. 1. 10, *h.* over you is stayed from dew.
Mal. 3. 10, if I will not open windows of *h.*
Mat. 5. 18, till *h.* and earth pass.
11. 23, exalted to *h.*
24. 29; Mk. 13. 25, the powers of *h.*
Mk. 13. 32, no, not the angels in *h.*
Lu. 15. 18, I have sinned against *h.*
John 1. 51, ye shall see *h.* open.
6. 31, 32, bread from *h.*
Acts 4. 12, none other name under *h.*
Rom. 1. 18, wrath of God revealed from *h.*
2 Cor. 5. 1, eternal in the *h.*
2, our house that is from *h.*
Gal. 1. 8, though an angel from *h.* preach.
Eph. 1. 10, gather in one, things in *h.*
3. 15, whole family in *h.*
6. 9; Col. 4. 1, your master is in *h.*
Phil. 3. 20, our conversation is in *h.*
Heb. 12. 23, written in *h.*
1 John 5. 7, three that bear record in *h.*
Rev. 4. 1, door opened in *h.*
2, throne set in *h.*
8. 1, silence in *h.*
12. 1, 3, a great wonder in *h.*
See 2 Cor. 12. 2; 1 Thess. 4. 16; 2 Thess. 1. 7.
HEAVENLY. Lu. 2. 13, multitude of the *h.* host.
John 3. 12, I tell you of *h.* things.
Acts 26. 19, the *h.* vision.
1 Cor. 15. 48, as is the *h.*, such are they.
Eph. 1. 3; 2. 6; 3. 10, in *h.* places.
Heb. 3. 1, partakers of the *h.* calling.
8. 5; 9. 23, shadow of *h.* things.
11. 16, an *h.* country.
See 2 Tim. 4. 18; Heb. 6. 4; 12. 22.
HEAVENLY FATHER. Mat. 6. 14, your *h. f.* also will forgive you.
Lu. 11. 13, how much more shall your *h. f.* give the Holy Spirit to them that ask him?
HEAVINESS. Ps. 69. 20, I am full of *h.*
Prov. 12. 25, *h.* in the heart maketh it stoop.
14. 13, the end of that mirth is *h.*
Isa. 61. 3, garment of praise for spirit of *h.*
Jas. 4. 9, let your joy be turned to *h.*
See Ezra 9. 5; Prov. 10. 1; Rom. 9. 2.
HEAVY. Ex. 17. 12, Moses' hands were *h.*
1 Kings 14. 6, sent with *h.* tidings.
Neh. 5. 18, the bondage was *h.*
Job 33. 7; Ps. 32. 4, hand *h.*
Prov. 25. 20, songs to a *h.* heart.
31. 6, wine to those of *h.* hearts.
Isa. 58. 6, to undo the *h.* burdens.
Mat. 11. 28, all ye that are *h.* laden.
23. 4, they bind *h.* burdens.
Mat. 26. 37, he began to be very *h.*
43; Mk. 14. 33, their eyes were *h.*
See Prov. 27. 3; Isa. 59. 1; Lu. 9. 32.
HEDGE. Job 3. 23, whom God hath *h.* in.
Prov. 15. 19, way of slothful an *h.* of thorns.
Eccl. 10. 8, whoso breaketh an *h.*
Lam. 3. 7, he hath *h.* me about.
Hos. 2. 6, I will *h.* up thy way.
Mk. 12. 1, he set a *h.* about it.
Lu. 14. 23, the highways and *h.*
See Isa. 5. 5; Ezek. 13. 5; 22. 30; Nah. 3. 17.
HEED. 2 Sam. 20. 10, took no *h.* to the sword.
Ps. 119. 9, by taking *h.* thereto.
Eccl. 12. 9, preacher gave good *h.*
Isa. 21. 7, hearkened diligently with much *h.*
Jer. 18. 18, let us not give *h.*
1 Tim. 1. 4; Tit. 1. 14, neither give *h.* to fables.
4. 1, giving *h.* to seducing spirits.
Heb. 2. 1, give more earnest *h.*
See Prov. 17. 4; Acts 3. 5; 8. 6.
HEEL. Gen. 3. 15, thou shalt bruise his *h.*
Ps. 49. 5, when the iniquity of my *h.* shall compass me about.
HEIGHT. Ps. 102. 19, from *h.* of his sanctuary.
Prov. 25. 3, the heaven for *h.*
Isa. 7. 11, ask it either in the depth, or in the *h.* above.
Eph. 3. 18, 19, the *h.* of the love of Christ.
See Job 22. 12; Ps. 148. 1; Amos 2. 9.
HEIR. 2 Sam. 14. 7, we will destroy the *h.*
Prov. 30. 23, handmaid that is *h.* to her mistress.
Mat. 21. 38; Mk. 12. 7; Lu. 20. 14, this is the *h.*
Rom. 8. 17, *h.* of God, joint-*h.* with Christ.
Gal. 3. 29, *h.* according to the promise.
4. 7, an *h.* of God through Christ.
Eph. 3. 6, Gentiles fellow-*h.*
Tit. 3. 7, *h.* according to hope of eternal life.
Heb. 1. 14, who shall be *h.* of salvation.
6. 17, the *h.* of promise.
11. 7, *h.* of the righteousness.
Jas. 2. 5, *h.* of the kingdom.
1 Pet. 3. 7, as *h.* together of the grace.
See Jer. 49. 1; Mic. 1. 15; Rom. 4. 13.
HELL. Deut. 32. 22, fire shall burn to lowest *h.*
2 Sam. 22. 6; Ps. 18. 5, sorrows of *h.* compassed me.
Job 11. 8, deeper than *h.*
26. 6, *h.* is naked before him.
Ps. 9. 17, wicked turned into *h.*
16. 10; Acts 2. 27, not leave soul in *h.*
55. 15, let them go down quick into *h.*
139. 8, if I make my bed in *h.*
Prov. 5. 5, her steps take hold on *h.*
7. 27, house is the way to *h.*
9. 18, her guests are in the depths of *h.*
15. 11, *h.* and destruction before the Lord.
24, that he may depart from *h.* beneath.
23. 14, deliver his soul from *h.*
27. 20, *h.* and destruction are never full.
Isa. 14. 9, *h.* from beneath is moved.
28. 15, 18, with *h.* are we at agreement.
Ezek. 31. 16, when I cast him down to *h.*
32. 21, shall speak out of the midst of *h.*
Amos 9. 2, though they dig into *h.*
Jon. 2. 2, out of the belly of *h.*
Hab. 2. 5, enlargeth his desire as *h.*
Mat. 5. 22, in danger of *h.* fire.
29, 30, whole body cast into *h.*
10. 28; Lu. 12. 5, destroy soul and body in *h.*
11. 23; Lu. 10. 15, brought down to *h.*
16. 18, gates of *h.* shall not prevail.
18. 9; Mk. 9. 47, having two eyes to be cast into *h.*
23. 15, more the child of *h.*
33, now can ye escape the damnation of *h.*?
Lu. 16. 23, in *h.* he lift up.
Acts 2. 31, soul not left in *h.*
Jas. 3. 6, tongue set on fire of *h.*
2 Pet. 2. 4, cast angels down to *h.*
See Isa. 5. 14; Rev. 1. 18; 6. 8; 20. 13.
HELP. Gen. 2. 18, 20, an *h.* meet for him.
Deut. 33. 29, the shield of thy *h.*

2 Chron. 26. 15, he was marvellously *h.*
Job 6. 13, is not my *h.* in me?
Ps. 22. 11, for there is none to *h.*
33. 20, he is our *h.* and our shield.
42. 5, the *h.* of his countenance.
46. 1, a very present *h.* in trouble.
60. 11; 108. 12, vain is the *h.* of man.
89. 19, laid *h.* on one that is mighty.
121. 1, the hills from whence cometh my *h.*
124. 8, our *h.* is in the name of the Lord.
Isa. 10. 3, to whom will ye flee for *h.*?
41. 6, they *h.* every one his neighbour.
Hos. 13. 9, in me is thine *h.*
Mat. 15. 25, Lord, *h.* me.
Mk. 9. 24, *h.* thou mine unbelief.
Acts 21. 28, men of Israel, *h.*
26. 22, having obtained *h.* of God.
Heb. 4. 16, grace to *h.* in time of need.
See Isa. 31. 3; Rom. 8. 26; 2 Cor. 1. 24.
HELPER. Heb. 13. 6.
HEM. Mat. 9. 20, touched the *h.* of his garment.
14. 36, might only touch the *h.* of his garment.
See Num. 15. 38, 39; Mat. 23. 5.
HEMLOCK. Hos. 10. 4, judgment springeth up as *h.*
Amos 6. 12, the fruit of righteousness into *h.*
HEN. Mat. 23. 37; Lu. 13. 34.
HENCEFORTH. 2 Cor. 5. 15; Gal. 6. 17; 2 Tim. 4. 8.
HERITAGE. Job 20. 29, *h.* appointed by God.
Ps. 16. 6; Jer. 3. 19, a goodly *h.*
61. 5, the *h.* of those that fear.
127. 3, children are an *h.* of the Lord.
Isa. 54. 17, this is the *h.* of the servants.
Mic. 7. 14, feed flock of thine *h.*
1 Pet. 5. 3, lords over God's *h.*
See Joel 2. 17; 3. 2; Mal. 1. 3.
HID. 2 Kings 4. 27, the Lord hath *h.* it from me.
Job 3. 21, more than for *h.* treasures.
Ps. 32. 5, mine iniquity have I not *h.*
69. 5, my sins are not *h.*
119. 11, thy word have I *h.* in mine heart.
Zeph. 2. 3, it may be ye shall be *h.*
Mat. 10. 26; Mk. 4. 22, there is nothing *h.*
Lu. 19. 42, now they are *h.* from thine eyes.
1 Cor. 2. 7, even the *h.* wisdom.
2 Cor. 4. 3, if our gospel be *h.*
Col. 3. 3, your life is *h.* with Christ.
1 Pet. 3. 4, the *h.* man of the heart.
Rev. 2. 17, to eat of the *h.* manna.
See Gen. 3. 8; Mat. 5. 14; Mk. 7. 24.
HIDE. Gen. 18. 17, shall I *h.* from Abraham.
Job 14. 13, *h.* me in the grave.
34. 29, when he *h.* his face.
Ps. 10. 11, he *h.* his face.
17. 8, *h.* me under the shadow of thy wings.
27. 5, *h.* me in pavilion.
31. 20, *h.* them in secret of thy presence.
89. 46, how long wilt thou *h.* thyself?
139. 12, darkness *h.* not from thee.
Isa. 1. 15, I will *h.* mine eyes from you.
3. 9, they *h.* not their sin.
26. 20, *h.* thyself for a little moment.
32. 2, a man shall be as an *h.* place.
45. 15, thou art a God that *h.* thyself.
Ezek. 28. 3, no secret they can *h.* from thee.
Jas. 5. 20, *h.* a multitude of sins.
Rev. 6. 16, *h.* us from the face of him.
See Job 13. 24; Prov. 28. 28; Amos 9. 3.
HIGH. Job 11. 8, it is as *h.* as heaven.
22. 12, behold stars, how *h.* they are!
41. 34, he beholdeth all *h.* things.
Ps. 62. 9, men of *h.* degree are a lie.
68. 18, thou hast ascended on *h.*
103. 11, as the heaven is *h.* above the earth.
131. 1, in things too *h.* for me.
138. 6, though the Lord be *h.*
139. 6, it is *h.*, I cannot attain unto it.
Eccl. 12. 5, afraid of that which is *h.*
Isa. 32. 15, spirit poured on us from on *h.*
33. 16, he shall dwell on *h.*
Isa. 35. 8, an *h.*-way shall be there.
62. 10, cast up the *h.*-way.
Jer. 49. 16, though thou make thy nest *h.*
Mat. 22. 9; Lu. 14. 23, go into the *h.*-ways.
Lu. 1. 78, dayspring from on *h.*
24. 49, power from on *h.*
Rom. 12. 16, mind not *h.* things.
13. 11, it is *h.* time.
Phil. 3. 14, for prize of the *h.* calling.
See Isa. 57. 15; 2 Cor. 10. 5.
HIGHER. Isa. 55. 9, heavens *h.* than the earth.
Lu. 14. 10, friend, go up *h.*
Heb. 7. 26, made *h.* than the heavens.
HILL. Gen. 49. 26, the everlasting *h.*
Deut. 11. 11, a land of *h.* and valleys.
Ps. 2. 6, set my king on holy *h.*
15. 1, who shall dwell in thy holy *h.*?
24. 3, who shall ascend the *h.* of the Lord?
43. 3, bring me to thy holy *h.*
50. 10, cattle on a thousand *h.*
95. 4, strength of the *h.* is his.
121. 1, I will lift up mine eyes to the *h.*
Prov. 8. 25, before the *h.* was I brought forth.
Isa. 40. 12, weighed the *h.* in balance.
Jer. 3. 23, salvation hoped for from the *h.*
Hos. 10. 8; Lu. 23. 30, to the *h.*, fall on us.
Mat. 5. 14, city set on an *h.*
See Lu. 4. 29; 9. 37; Acts 17. 22.
HINDER. Gen. 24. 56, *h.* me not.
Job 9. 12; 11. 10, who can *h.* him?
Lu. 11. 52, them that were entering ye *h.*
Acts 8. 36, what doth *h.* me to be baptized?
1 Cor. 9. 12, lest we *h.* the gospel.
Gal. 5. 7, who did *h.* you?
1 Thess. 2. 18, but Satan *h.* us.
1 Pet. 3. 7, that your prayers be not *h.*
See Num. 22. 16; Neh. 4. 8; Isa. 14. 6.
HIRE. Deut. 24. 15, thou shalt give him his *h.*
Mic. 3. 11, priests teach for *h.*
Mat. 20. 7, no man hath *h.* us.
8, give them their *h.*
Mk. 1. 20, in ship with *h.* servants.
Lu. 10. 7, labourer worthy of his *h.*
15. 17, how many *h.* servants.
Jas. 5. 4, *h.* of labourers which is kept back.
See Ex. 12. 45; Lev. 25. 40; Deut. 15. 18.
HIRELING. Job 7. 1, like the days of an *h.*
2, as *h.* looketh for reward.
14. 6, accomplish, as an *h.*, his day.
Mal. 3. 5, that oppress the *h.*
See Isa. 16. 14; 21. 16; John 10. 12.
HITHERTO. Josh. 17. 14, the Lord hath blessed me *h.*
1 Sam. 7. 12, *h.* hath the Lord helped us.
Job 38. 11, *h.* shalt thou come.
John 5. 17, my Father worketh *h.*
16. 24, *h.* have ye asked nothing in my name.
1 Cor. 3. 2, *h.* ye were not able to bear it.
See Judg. 16. 13; 2 Sam. 15. 34; Isa. 18. 2.
HOARY. Job 41. 32.
HOLD. Gen. 21. 18, *h.* him in thine hand.
Ex. 20. 7; Deut. 5. 11, will not *h.* him guiltless.
2 Kings 7. 9, good tidings, and we *h.* our peace.
Esth. 4. 14, if thou altogether *h.* thy peace.
Job 36. 8, *h.* in cords of affliction.
Ps. 18. 35, thy right hand hath *h.* me up.
71. 6, by thee have I been *h.*
73. 23, thou hast *h.* me by my right hand.
119. 117, *h.* me up, and I shall be safe.
Prov. 11. 12, man of understanding *h.* his peace.
17. 28, a fool, when he *h.* his peace.
Isa. 41. 13, the Lord will *h.* thy hand.
62. 1, for Zion's sake will I not *h.* my peace.
Jer. 4. 19, I cannot *h.* my peace.
Amos 6. 10, *h.* thy tongue.
Mat. 6. 14; Lu. 16. 13, he will *h.* to the one.
Mk. 1. 25; Lu. 4. 35, *h.* thy peace, come out.
Rom. 1. 18, *h.* the truth in unrighteousness.
1 Cor. 14. 30, let the first *h.* his peace.
Phil. 2. 16, *h.* forth the word of life.
29, *h.* such in reputation.

Col. 2. 19, not *h.* the Head.
1 Thess. 5. 21, *h.* fast that which is good.
1 Tim. 1. 19, *h.* faith and good conscience.
3. 9, *h.* the mystery of faith.
2 Tim. 1. 13, *h.* fast form of sound words.
Tit. 1. 9, *h.* fast the faithful word.
Heb. 3. 14, *h.* beginning of confidence.
4. 14; 10. 23, *h.* fast our profession.
Rev. 2. 13, thou *h.* fast my name.
25, *h.* fast till I come.
3. 3, *h.* fast, and repent.
11, *h.* that fast which thou hast.
See Job 2. 3; Jer. 2. 13; 51. 30; Ezek. 19. 9.
HOLE. Isa. 11. 8, child shall play on *h.* of the asp.
51. 1, *h.* of pit whence ye are digged.
Jer. 13. 4, hide in a *h.* of the rock.
Ezek. 8. 7, a *h.* in the wall.
Hag. 1. 6, a bag with *h.*
Mat. 8. 20; Lu. 9. 58, foxes have *h.*
See Cant. 5. 4; Mic. 7. 17; Nah. 2. 12.
HOLIER. Isa. 65. 5.
HOLIEST. Heb. 9. 3; 10. 19.
HOLILY. 1 Thess. 2. 10.
HOLINESS. Ex. 15. 11, glorious in *h.*
28. 36; 39. 30; Zech. 14. 20, *h.* to the Lord.
1 Chron. 16. 29; 2 Chron. 20. 21; Ps. 29. 2; 96. 9; 110. 3, beauty of *h.*
Ps. 30. 4; 97. 12, at remembrance of his *h.*
47. 8, the throne of his *h.*
60. 6; 108. 7, God hath spoken in his *h.*
93. 5, *h.* becometh thine house.
Isa. 35. 8, the way of *h.*
63. 15, habitation of thy *h.*
Jer. 23. 9, the words of his *h.*
Obad. 17, upon mount Zion there shall be *h.*
Lu. 1. 75, might serve him in *h.*
Acts 3. 12, as though by our *h.*
Rom. 1. 4, according to the spirit of *h.*
6. 22, fruit unto *h.*
2 Cor. 7. 1, perfecting *h.* in fear of God.
Eph. 4. 24, created in righteousness and *h.*
1 Thess. 3. 13, unblameable in *h.*
4. 7, not called to uncleanness, but *h.*
1 Tim. 2. 15, continue in faith and *h.*
Tit. 2. 3, in behaviour as becometh *h.*
Heb. 12. 10, partakes of his *h.*
14, *h.*, without which no man.
See Ps. 89. 35; Isa. 23. 18; Jer. 2. 3.
HOLLOW. Gen. 32. 25; Judg. 15. 19; Isa. 40. 12.
HOLPEN. Ps. 86. 17; Isa. 31. 3; Dan. 11. 34; Lu. 1. 54.
HOLY. Ex. 3. 5; Josh. 5. 15, is *h.* ground.
19. 6; 1 Pet. 2. 9, an *h.* nation.
20. 8; 31. 14, sabbath day, to keep it *h.*
Lev. 10. 10, difference between *h.* and unholy.
20. 7, be ye *h.*
Num. 16. 5, Lord will show who is *h.*
2 Kings 4. 9, this is an *h.* man of God.
Ezra 9. 2; Isa. 6. 13, the *h.* seed.
Ps. 20. 6, hear from his *h.* heaven.
22. 3, thou art *h.* that inhabitest.
86. 2, preserve my soul, for I am *h.*
98. 1, his *h.* arm hath gotten victory.
99. 9, worship at his *h.* hill.
145. 17, the Lord is *h.* in all his works.
Prov. 20. 25, who devoureth that which is *h.*
Isa. 6. 3; Rev. 4. 8, *h.*, *h.*, *h.*, is the Lord.
52. 10, make bare his *h.* arm.
64. 10, thy *h.* cities are a wilderness.
11, our *h.* and beautiful house.
Ezek. 22. 26, put no difference between *h.* and profane.
Mat. 1. 18, 20, with child of the *H.* Ghost.
3. 11; Mk. 1. 8; Lu. 3. 16; John 1. 33; Acts 1. 5, baptize with *H.* Ghost.
7. 6, give not that which is *h.*
12. 31; Mk. 3. 29, blasphemy against *H.* Ghost.
Mk. 13. 11, not ye that speak, but *H.* Ghost.
Lu. 1. 15, shall be filled with the *H.* Ghost.
35, that *h.* thing which shall be born of thee.
3. 22, *H.* Ghost descended in bodily shape.
Lu. 4. 1, Jesus being full of the *H.* Ghost.
12. 12, *H.* Ghost shall teach you.
John 7. 39, the *H.* Ghost was not yet given.
14. 26, the Comforter, which is the *H.* Ghost.
17. 11, *h.* Father, keep those.
20. 22, receive ye the *H.* Ghost.
Acts 1. 8, after the *H.* Ghost is come.
2. 4; 4. 31, all filled with *H.* Ghost.
4. 27, 30, against thy *h.* child Jesus.
5. 3, to lie to the *H.* Ghost.
6. 3, look out men full of the *H.* Ghost.
7. 51, ye do always resist the *H.* Ghost.
8. 15, prayed that they might receive *H.* Ghost.
9. 31, in comfort of the *H.* Ghost.
10. 44, *H.* Ghost fell on all which heard.
47, received *H.* Ghost as well as we.
15. 8, giving them *H.* Ghost, as he did unto us.
28, seemed good to the *H.* Ghost.
16. 6, forbidden of the *H.* Ghost.
19. 2, have ye received the *H.* Ghost?
20. 28, *H.* Ghost hath made you overseers.
Rom. 1. 2, promised in the *h.* scriptures.
7. 12, commandment is *h.*, just, and good.
9. 1, bearing witness in *H.* Ghost.
11. 16, if firstfruit be *h.*, if root be *h.*
12. 1, a living sacrifice, *h.*, acceptable to God.
14. 17, joy in the *H.* Ghost.
16. 16; 1 Cor. 16. 20; 2 Cor. 13. 12; 1 Thess. 5. 26; 1 Pet. 5. 14, with a *h.* kiss.
1 Cor. 2. 13, words which the *H.* Ghost teacheth.
3. 17, the temple of God is *h.*
7. 14, now are they *h.*
2 Cor. 13. 14, communion of the *H.* Ghost.
Eph. 1. 4; 5. 27, be *h.* and without blame.
2. 21, groweth to an *h.* temple in the Lord.
Col. 1. 22, present you *h.* and unblameable.
3. 12, elect of God, *h.* and beloved.
1 Thess. 5. 27, all the *h.* brethren.
1 Tim. 2. 8, lifting up *h.* hands.
2 Tim. 1. 9, called us with an *h.* calling.
Tit. 1. 8, bishop must be *h.*
3. 5, the renewing of the *H.* Ghost.
Heb. 3. 1, *h.* brethren, partakers.
1 Pet. 1. 12, *H.* Ghost sent down from heaven.
15; 2 Pet. 3. 11, *h.* in all conversation.
2. 5, an *h.* priesthood.
3. 5, the *h.* women, who trusted.
2 Pet. 1. 18, with him in the *h.* mount.
21, *h.* men moved by *H.* Ghost.
Rev. 3. 7, saith he that is *h.*
6. 10, O Lord, *h.* and true.
20. 6, *h.* is he that hath part.
21. 10, the *h.* Jerusalem.
22. 11, he that is *h.*, let him be *h.*
See 2 Tim. 3. 15; Heb. 2. 4; 1 Pet. 1. 16; 2 Pet. 3. 2; Jude 20.
HOME. Ex. 9. 19, and shall not be brought *h.*
Lev. 18. 9, whether born at *h.* or abroad.
Deut. 24. 5, free at *h.* one year.
Ruth 1. 21, the Lord hath brought me *h.* empty.
2 Sam. 14. 13, fetch *h.* his banished.
1 Kings 13. 7, come *h.* with me.
2 Kings 14. 10; 2 Chron. 25. 19, tarry at *h.*
1 Chron. 13. 12, bring ark of God *h.*
Job 39. 12, he will bring *h.* thy seed.
Ps. 68. 12, she that tarried at *h.*
Eccl. 12. 5, man goeth to his long *h.*
Lam. 1. 20, at *h.* there is as death.
Hag. 1. 9, when ye brought it *h.*
Mk. 5. 19, go *h.* to thy friends.
John 19. 27, took her to his own *h.*
20. 10, went away to their own *h.*
1 Cor. 11. 34, let him eat at *h.*
14. 35, ask their husbands at *h.*
2 Cor. 5. 6, at *h.* in the body.
1 Tim. 5. 4, show piety at *h.*
Tit. 2. 5, keepers at *h.*
See Jer. 2. 14; Lu. 9. 61; 15. 6.
HONEST. Lu. 8. 15, an *h.* and good heart.
Acts 6. 3, men of *h.* report.
Rom. 12. 17; 2 Cor. 8. 21, provide things *h.*

Rom. 13. 13, let us walk *h.*, as in the day.
Phil. 4. 8, whatsoever things are *h.*
1 Pet. 2. 12, conversation *h.* among Gentiles.
See 1 Thess. 4. 12; 1 Tim. 2. 2; Heb. 13. 18.
HONOUR (*n.*). Num. 22. 17, I will promote thee to *h.*
24. 11, hath kept thee back from *h.*
2 Sam. 6. 22, of them shall I be had in *h.*
1 Kings 3. 13, also given thee riches and *h.*
1 Chron. 29. 28, died full of riches and *h.*
2 Chron. 1. 11, 12, thou hast not asked *h.*
26. 18, neither shall it be for thy *h.*
Esth. 1. 20, the wives shall give their husbands *h.*
Job 14. 21, his sons come to *h.*
Ps. 7. 5, lay mine *h.* in the dust.
8. 5; Heb. 2. 7, crowned him with *h.*
26. 8, place where thine *h.* dwelleth.
49. 12, man being in *h.* abideth not.
96. 6, *h.* and majesty are before him.
149. 9, this *h.* have all his saints.
Prov. 3. 16, in left hand riches and *h.*
4. 8, she shall bring thee to *h.*
5. 9, lest thou give their *h.* to others.
14. 28, in multitude of people is king's *h.*
20. 3, an *h.* to cease from strife.
25. 2, the *h.* of kings to search out.
26. 1, 8, *h.* is not seemly for a fool.
31. 25, strength and *h.* are her clothing.
Eccl. 6. 2, to whom God hath given *h.*
Mal. 1. 6, where is mine *h.*?
Mat. 13. 57; Mk. 6. 4; John 4. 44, not without *h.*
John 5. 41, I receive not *h.* from men.
44, who receive *h.* one of another.
Rom. 2. 7, in well doing seek for *h.*
10, *h.* to every man that worketh good.
12. 10, in *h.* preferring one another.
13. 7, *h.* to whom *h.*
2 Cor. 6. 8, by *h.* and dishonour.
Col. 2. 23, not in any *h.* to satisfying.
1 Thess. 4. 4, possess his vessel in *h.*
1 Tim. 5. 17, elders worthy of double *h.*
6. 1, count masters worthy of *h.*
16, to whom be *h.* and power everlasting.
2 Tim. 2. 20, 21, some to *h.*, some to dishonour.
Heb. 3. 3, more *h.* than the house.
5. 4, no man taketh this *h.* unto himself.
1 Pet. 3. 7, giving *h.* to the wife.
Rev. 4. 11; 5. 12, thou art worthy to receive *h.*
See Rev. 5. 13; 7. 12; 19. 1; 21. 24.
HONOUR (*v.*). Ex. 14. 4, I will be *h.* upon Pharaoh.
Ex. 20. 12; Deut. 5. 16; Mat. 15. 4; 19. 19; Mk. 7. 10; 10. 19; Lu. 18. 20; Eph. 6. 2, *h.* thy father and mother.
Lev. 19. 32, thou shalt *h.* the face of the old man.
1 Sam. 2. 30, them that *h.* me I will *h.*
15. 30, *h.* me now before elders.
Esth. 6. 6, the king delighteth to *h.*
Ps. 15. 4, he *h.* them that fear the Lord.
Prov. 3. 9, *h.* the Lord with thy substance.
12. 9, better than he that *h.* himself.
Mal. 1. 6, a son *h.* his father.
Mat. 15. 8; Mk. 7. 6, *h.* me with their lips.
John 5. 23, *h.* the Son as they *h.* the Father.
1 Tim. 5. 3, *h.* widows that are widows indeed.
1 Pet. 2. 17, *h.* all men, *h.* the king.
See Isa. 29. 13; 58. 13; Acts 28. 10.
HONOURABLE. Ps. 45. 9, among thy *h.* women.
Isa. 3. 3, take away the *h.* man.
9. 15, ancient and *h.*, he is the head.
42. 21, magnify the law, and make it *h.*
See Lu. 14. 8; 1 Cor. 4. 10; 12. 23; Heb. 13. 4.
HOPE (*n.*). Job 7. 6, my days are spent without *h.*
8. 13, the hypocrite's *h.* shall perish.
17. 15, where is now my *h.*?
19. 10, my *h.* hath he removed.
Ps. 16. 9; Acts 2. 26, my flesh also shall rest in *h.*
39. 7, my *h.* is in thee.
119. 116, let me not be ashamed of my *h.*
Prov. 13. 12, *h.* deferred maketh the heart sick.
Prov. 14. 32, hath *h.* in his death.
26. 12; 29. 20, more *h.* of a fool.
Eccl. 9. 4, to all the living there is *h.*
Jer. 17. 7, the man whose *h.* the Lord is.
31. 17, there is *h.* in thine end.
Hos. 2. 15, for a door of *h.*
Zech. 9. 12, ye prisoners of *h.*
Acts 28. 20, for the *h.* of Israel I am bound.
Rom. 4. 18, who against *h.* believed in *h.*
8. 24, we are saved by *h.*
12. 12, rejoicing in *h.*
1 Cor. 13. 13, faith, *h.*, charity.
15. 19, if in this life only we have *h.*
Eph. 1. 18, the *h.* of his calling.
2. 12, having no *h.*, and without God.
Col. 1. 27, Christ in you, the *h.* of glory.
1 Thess. 4. 13, even as others who have no *h.*
5. 8, for an helmet, the *h.* of salvation.
2 Thess. 2. 16, good *h.* through grace.
Tit. 3. 7, the *h.* of eternal life.
Heb. 6. 18, lay hold on *h.* set before us.
19, *h.* as an anchor of the soul.
1 Pet. 1. 3, begotten to a lively *h.*
3. 15, a reason of the *h.* that is in you.
See Lam. 3. 18; Col. 1. 5; 1 John 3. 3.
HOPE (*v.*). Ps. 22. 9, thou didst make me *h.*
31. 24, all ye that *h.* in the Lord.
42. 5, 11; 43. 5, *h.* thou in God.
71. 14, I will *h.* continually.
Lam. 3. 26, good that a man both *h.* and wait.
Rom. 8. 25, if we *h.* for that we see not.
1 Pet. 1. 13, *h.* to the end.
See Jer. 3. 23; Acts 24. 26; Heb. 11. 1.
HORRIBLE. Ps. 11. 6; 40. 2; Jer. 2. 12; Ezek. 32. 10.
HOSPITALITY. Rom. 12. 13; 1 Tim. 3. 2; Tit. 1. 8; 1 Pet. 4. 9.
HOT. Ps. 39. 3; Prov. 6. 28; 1 Tim. 4. 2; Rev. 3. 15.
HOUR. Mat. 10. 19; Lu. 12. 12, shall be given you in that same *h.*
20. 12, have wrought but one *h.*
24. 36; Mk. 13. 32, that *h.* knoweth no man.
26. 40; Mk. 14. 37, could ye not watch one *h.*?
Lu. 12. 39, what *h.* the thief would come.
22. 53, but this is your *h.*
John 5. 25; 16. 32, the *h.* is coming, and now is.
11. 9, are there not twelve *h.* in the day?
12. 27, save me from this *h.*
Acts 3. 1, at the *h.* of prayer.
Gal. 2. 5, give place, no, not for an *h.*
Rev. 3. 10, the *h.* of temptation.
See Acts 2. 15; 1 Cor. 4. 11; 15. 30; Rev. 3. 3.
HOUSE. Gen. 28. 17, none other but the *h.* of God.
Deut. 8. 12, when thou hast built goodly *h.*
2 Kings 20. 1; Isa. 38. 1, set thine *h.* in order.
20. 15, what have they seen in thine *h.*?
Neh. 13. 11, why is the *h.* of God forsaken?
Job 30. 23, *h.* appointed for all living.
Ps. 26. 8, have loved the habitation of thy *h.*
65. 4, satisfied with goodness of thy *h.*
69. 9; John 2. 17, the zeal of thine *h.*
84. 3, the sparrow hath found an *h.*
92. 13, planted in the *h.* of the Lord.
118. 26, blessed you out of the *h.* of the Lord.
Prov. 2. 18, her *h.* inclineth to death.
9. 1, wisdom hath builded her *h.*
12. 7, *h.* of the righteous shall stand.
19. 14, *h.* and riches are inheritance.
Eccl. 7. 2, *h.* of mourning, *h.* of feasting.
12. 3, when keepers of the *h.* shall tremble.
Isa. 3. 14, spoil of poor in your *h.*
5. 8, woe unto them that join *h.* to *h.*
64. 11, our holy and beautiful *h.* is burned.
Hos. 9. 15, I will drive them out of mine *h.*
Hag. 1. 4, and this *h.* lie waste.
9, because of mine *h.* that is waste.
Mal. 3. 10, that there may be meat in mine *h.*
Mat. 7. 25; Lu. 6. 48, beat upon that *h.*
10. 12, when ye come into an *h.*
12. 25; Mk. 3. 25, *h.* divided cannot stand.
23. 38, your *h.* is left desolate.

Mat. 24. 17; Mk. 13. 15, to take anything out of *h*.
Lu. 10. 7, go not from *h*. to *h*.
14. 23, that my *h*. may be filled.
18. 14, went down to his *h*. justified.
John 12. 3, *h*. filled with odour.
14. 2, in my Father's *h*. are many mansions.
Acts 2. 46, breaking bread from *h*. to *h*.
5. 42, in every *h*. ceased not to preach.
10. 2; 16. 34; 18. 8, with all his *h*.
20. 20, I taught you from *h*. to *h*.
1 Cor. 11. 22, have ye not *h*. to eat in?
2 Cor. 5. 1, *h*. not made with hands.
Col. 4. 15, church in his *h*.
1 Tim. 3. 4, 5, 12, ruleth well his own *h*.
5. 8, especially for those of his own *h*.
2 Tim. 3. 6, which creep into *h*.
Tit. 1. 11, subvert whole *h*.
See Mat. 9. 6; Lu. 7. 44; 19. 5; Acts 4. 34.
HOUSEHOLD. Gen. 18. 19, command his *h*. after him.
1 Sam. 27. 3; 2 Sam. 2. 3, every man with his *h*.
2 Sam. 6. 20, returned to bless his *h*.
Prov. 31. 27, looketh well to her *h*.
Mat. 10. 36, a man's foes shall be of his own *h*.
Gal. 6. 10, the *h*. of faith.
Eph. 2. 19, of the *h*. of God.
See Gen. 31. 37; 47. 12; 2 Sam. 17. 23.
HUMBLE. Deut. 8. 2, to *h*. thee and prove thee.
2 Chron. 33. 12, *h*. himself greatly.
Ps. 9. 12; 10. 12, forgetteth not cry of the *h*.
34. 2, the *h*. shall hear thereof.
35. 13, I *h*. my soul with fasting.
113. 6, *h*. himself to behold things in heaven.
Prov. 16. 19, better be of *h*. spirit.
Isa. 57. 15, of contrite and *h*. spirit.
Mat. 18. 4; 23. 12; Lu. 14. 11; 18. 14, *h*. himself.
Phil. 2. 8, he *h*. himself.
Jas. 4. 6; 1 Pet. 5. 5, God giveth grace to the *h*.
1 Pet. 5. 6, *h*. yourselves under mighty hand of God.
See Isa. 2. 11; 5. 15; Lam. 3. 20.
HUMBLY. 2 Sam. 16. 4; Mic. 6. 8.
HUMILITY. Prov. 15. 33; 18. 12, before honour is *h*.
22. 4, by *h*. are riches.
See Acts 20. 19; Col. 2. 18, 23; 1 Pet. 5. 5.
HUNGER. Deut. 8. 3, he suffered thee to *h*.
Job 18. 12, his strength shall be *h*.-bitten.
Ps. 34. 10, young lions do lack, and suffer *h*.
Prov. 19. 15, an idle soul shall suffer *h*.
Isa. 49. 10, shall not *h*. nor thirst.
Jer. 38. 9, he is like to die for *h*.
Mat. 5. 6; Lu. 6. 21, blessed are ye that *h*.
Lu. 6. 25, woe unto ye that are full! for ye shall *h*.
John 6. 35, he that cometh to me shall never *h*.
Rom. 12. 20, if thine enemy *h*.
1 Cor. 4. 11, we both *h*. and thirst.
11. 34, if any man *h*., let him eat at home.
Rev. 7. 16, they shall *h*. no more.
See Mat. 4. 2; 12. 1; 25. 35; Lu. 15. 17.
HUNGRY. Job 22. 7, withholden bread from *h*.
24. 10, they take away the sheaf from the *h*.
Ps. 50. 12, if I were *h*., I would not tell thee.
107. 5, *h*. and thirsty, their soul fainted in them.
9, he filled the *h*. soul with goodness.
146. 7, which giveth food to the *h*.
Prov. 25. 21, if thine enemy be *h*., give him bread to eat.
27. 7, to the *h*. every bitter thing is sweet.
Isa. 29. 8, when a *h*. man dreameth.
58. 7, is it not to deal thy bread to the *h*.?
65. 13, my servants eat, but ye shall be *h*.
Ezek. 18. 7, given his bread to the *h*.
Lu. 1. 53, he hath filled the *h*. with good things.
Acts 10. 10, and he became very *h*.
1 Cor. 11. 21, one is *h*., and another drunken.
Phil. 4. 12, instructed both to be full and to be *h*.
See Prov. 6. 30; Isa. 8. 21; 9. 20; Mk. 11. 12.
HUNT. 1 Sam. 26. 20, as when one doth *h*. a partridge.
Jer. 16. 16, *h*. them from every mountain.
Ezek. 13. 18, *h*. souls of my people.
Mic. 7. 2, they *h*. every man his brother.
See Gen. 10. 9; 27. 5; 1 Sam. 24. 11.
HUNTING. Prov. 12. 27.
HURL. Num. 35. 20; 1 Chron. 12. 2; Job 27. 21.
HURT. Ps. 15. 4, that sweareth to his own *h*.
Eccl. 8. 9, ruleth over another to his own *h*.
Isa. 11. 9, shall not *h*. nor destroy.
Jer. 6. 14; 8. 11, have healed *h*. slightly.
8. 21, for the *h*. of my people.
25. 6, provoke not, I will do no *h*.
Dan. 3. 25, they have no *h*.
6. 23, no manner of *h*. found upon him.
Mk. 16. 18, deadly thing, it shall not *h*.
Lu. 10. 19, nothing shall by any means *h*. you.
Acts 18. 10, no man set on thee to *h*. thee.
Rev. 6. 6, *h*. not the oil and the wine.
See Rev. 7. 2; 9. 4; 11. 5.
HURTFUL. Ezra 4. 15; Ps. 144. 10; 1 Tim. 6. 9.
HUSBAND. Ex. 4. 25, a bloody *h*. art thou.
Prov. 12. 4, virtuous wife a crown to her *h*.
31. 11, 23, 28, her *h*. doth safely trust.
Isa. 54. 5, thy Maker is thy *h*.
John 4. 16, go, call thy *h*.
1 Cor. 7. 16, whether thou shalt save thy *h*.
14. 35, let them ask their *h*. at home.
Eph. 5. 22, submit yourselves to your *h*.
25; Col. 3. 19, *h*., love your wives.
1 Tim. 3. 12, the *h*. of one wife.
Tit. 2. 4, teach young women to love their *h*.
5, obedient to their own *h*.
1 Pet. 3. 1, be in subjection to your *h*.
7, ye *h*., dwell with them.
See Gen. 3. 6; Ruth 1. 11; Esth. 1. 17, 20.
HYMN. Mat. 26. 30; Mk. 14. 26; Eph. 5. 19; Col. 3. 16.
HYPOCRISY. Mat. 23. 28, within ye are full of *h*.
Mk. 12. 15, he, knowing their *h*.
Lu. 12. 1, leaven of Pharisees, which is *h*.
Jas. 3. 17, wisdom is pure, and without *h*.
See Isa. 32. 6; 1 Tim. 4. 2.
HYPOCRITE. Job 8. 13, the *h*. hope shall perish.
20. 5, the joy of the *h*. but for a moment.
36. 13, the *h*. in heart.
Isa. 9. 17, every one is an *h*.
Mat. 6. 2, 5, 16, as the *h*. do.
7. 5; Lu. 6. 42; 13. 15, thou *h*.
15. 7; 16. 3; 22. 18; Mk. 7. 6; Lu. 12. 56, ye *h*.
23. 13; Lu. 11. 44, woe unto you, *h*.
24. 51, appoint his portion with the *h*.
See Job 13. 16; 27. 8; Prov. 11. 9.
HYPOCRITICAL. Ps. 35. 16; Isa. 10. 6.

I

IDLE. Ex. 5. 8, 17, they be *i*.
Prov. 19. 15, an *i*. soul shall hunger.
31. 27, she eateth not bread of *i*.
Mat. 12. 36, every *i*. word men speak.
20. 3, 6, others standing *i*.
See Eccl. 10. 18; Ezek. 16. 49; 1 Tim. 5. 13.
IDOL. 1 Chron. 16. 26; Ps. 96. 5, all gods of the people are *i*.
Isa. 66. 3, as if he blessed an *i*.
Jer. 50. 38, they are mad upon their *i*.
Hos. 4. 17, Ephraim is joined to *i*.
Acts 15. 20, abstain from pollutions of *i*.
1 Cor. 8. 4, we know an *i*. is nothing.
7, with conscience of the *i*.
1 Thess. 1. 9, ye turned to God from *i*.
1 John 5. 21, keep yourselves from *i*.
See Acts 17. 16; Gal. 5. 20; Col. 3. 5.
IGNORANCE. Acts 3. 17, through *i*. ye did it.
17. 30, the times of *i*. God winked at.
Eph. 4. 18, alienated through *i*.
1 Pet. 2. 15, put to silence *i*. of foolish men.
See Lev. 4. 2, 13, 22, 27; 5. 15; Num. 15. 24.
IGNORANT. Ps. 73. 22, so foolish was I and *i*.
Isa. 63. 16, though Abraham be *i*. of us.
Acts 4. 13, perceived they were *i*. men.
Rom. 10. 3, being *i*. of God's righteousness.
1 Cor. 14. 38, if any man be *i*., let him be *i*.

2 Cor. 2. 11, not *i.* of his devices.
Heb. 5. 2, can have compassion on the *i.*
2 Pet. 3. 5, they willingly are *i.*
See Num. 15. 28; Acts 17. 23; 1 Tim. 1. 13.
IMAGINATION. Gen. 6. 5; 8. 21, *i.* of heart evil.
Deut. 29. 19; Jer. 23. 17, walk in *i.* of heart.
1 Chron. 28. 9, understandeth all the *i.* of thoughts.
Rom. 1. 21, vain in their *i.*
2 Cor. 10. 5, casting down *i.*
See Deut. 31. 21; Prov. 6. 18; Lam. 3. 60.
IMAGINE. Ps. 62. 3, how long will ye *i.* mischief?
Nah. 1. 9, what do ye *i.* against the Lord?
11, there is one that *i.* evil.
Zech. 7. 10; 8. 17, let none *i.* evil.
See Job 21. 27; Ps. 10. 2; 21. 11; Acts 4. 25.
IMMORTAL. 1 Tim. 1. 17.
IMMORTALITY. Rom. 2. 7; 1 Cor. 15. 53; 1 Tim. 6. 16; 2 Tim. 1. 10.
IMPART. Job 39. 17; Lu. 3. 11; Rom. 1. 11; 1 Thess. 2. 8.
IMPEDIMENT. Mk. 7. 32.
IMPENITENT. Rom. 2. 5.
IMPLACABLE. Rom. 1. 31.
IMPOSE. Ezra 7. 24; Heb. 9. 10.
IMPOSSIBLE. Mat. 19. 26; Mk. 10. 27; Lu. 18. 27, with men it is *i.*
Lu. 1. 37; 18. 27, with God nothing *i.*
See Mat. 17. 20; Lu. 17. 1; Heb. 6. 4, 18; 11. 6.
IMPOTENT. John 5. 3; Acts 4. 9; 14. 8.
IMPOVERISH. Judg. 6. 6; Isa. 40. 20; Jer. 5. 17.
IMPRISONMENT. Ezra 7. 26; 2 Cor. 6. 5; Heb. 11. 36.
IMPUDENT. Prov. 7. 13; Ezek. 2. 4; 3. 7.
IMPUTE. Lev. 17. 4, blood shall be *i.* to that man.
Ps. 32. 2; Rom. 4. 8, to whom the Lord *i.* not iniquity.
Hab. 1. 11, *i.* his power to his god.
Rom. 5. 13, sin is not *i.* when there is no law.
See 1 Sam. 22. 15; 2 Sam. 19. 19; 2 Cor. 5. 19.
INCLINE. Josh. 24. 23, *i.* your hearts to the Lord.
1 Kings 8. 58, that he may *i.* hearts to keep law.
Ps. 40. 1; 116. 2, he *i.* unto me, and heard my cry.
119. 36, *i.* my heart to thy testimonies.
Jer. 7. 24; 11. 8; 17. 23; 34. 14, nor *i.* ear.
See Prov. 2. 18; Jer. 25. 4; 44. 5.
INCLOSED. Ps. 17. 10; 22. 16; Lu. 5. 6.
INCONTINENT. 1 Cor. 7. 5; 2 Tim. 3. 3.
INCORRUPTIBLE. 1 Cor. 9. 25, an *i.* crown.
1 Pet. 1. 4, inheritance *i.*
23, born of *i.* seed.
See Rom. 1. 23; 1 Cor. 15. 42, 50, 52, 53, 54.
INCREASE (*n.*). Lev. 25. 36, take no usury or *i.*
26. 4, the land shall yield her *i.*
Deut. 14. 22, 28, tithe all *i.*
Ps. 67. 6; Ezek. 34. 27, earth shall yield her *i.*
Prov. 18. 20, with the *i.* of his lips.
Eccl. 5. 10, not satisfied with *i.*
Isa. 9. 7, *i.* of his government.
1 Cor. 3. 6, 7, God gave the *i.*
See Jer. 2. 3; Eph. 4. 16; Col. 2. 19.
INCREASE (*v.*). Job 8. 7, thy latter end shall greatly *i.*
Ps. 4. 7, that their corn and wine *i.*
62. 10, if riches *i.*, set not your heart upon them.
115. 14, Lord shall *i.* you more and more.
Prov. 1. 5; 9. 9, a wise man will *i.* learning.
11. 24, there is that scattereth, and yet *i.*
Eccl. 1. 18, he that *i.* knowledge *i.* sorrow.
Isa. 9. 3, multiplied the nation, and not *i.* the joy.
40. 29, he *i.* strength.
Ezek. 36. 37, *i.* them with men like a flock.
Dan. 12. 4, knowledge shall be *i.*
Hos. 12. 1, he daily *i.* lies.
Hab. 2. 6, that *i.* that which is not his.
Lu. 2. 52, Jesus *i.* in wisdom.
Acts 6. 7, word of God *i.*
16. 5, churches *i.* daily.
Rev. 3. 17, I am rich, and *i.* with goods.
See Eccl. 2. 9; 5. 11; Mk. 4. 8; Col. 2. 19.
INCREDIBLE. Acts 26. 8.
INCURABLE. 2 Chron. 21. 18; Jer. 15. 18; Mic. 1. 9.
INDEED. 1 Kings 8. 27; 2 Chron. 6. 18, will God *i.* dwell on the earth?
1 Chron. 4. 10, bless me *i.*
Mk. 11. 32, a prophet *i.*
Lu. 24. 34, the Lord is risen *i.*
John 1. 47, an Israelite *i.*
6. 55, my flesh is meat *i.*, and my blood is drink *i.*
8. 36, ye shall be free *i.*
1 Tim. 5. 3, that are widows *i.*
See Gen. 37. 8; Isa. 6. 9; Rom. 8. 7.
INDIGNATION. Ps. 78. 49, wrath, *i.*, and trouble.
Isa. 26. 20, till the *i.* be overpast.
Nah. 1. 6, who can stand before his *i.*?
Mat. 20. 24, moved with *i.*
26. 8, they had *i.*
2 Cor. 7. 11, yea, what *i.*
Heb. 10. 27, fearful looking for of fiery *i.*
Rev. 14. 10, the cup of his *i.*
See Zech. 1. 12; Acts 5. 17; Rom. 2. 8.
INDITING. Ps. 45. 1.
INDUSTRIOUS. 1 Kings 11. 28.
INEXCUSABLE. Rom. 2. 1.
INFANT. Job 3. 16; Isa. 65. 20; Lu. 18. 15.
INFIDEL. 2 Cor. 6. 15; 1 Tim. 5. 8.
INFIRMITY. Ps. 77. 10, this is mine *i.*
Prov. 18. 14, spirit of man will sustain his *i.*
Mat. 8. 17, himself took our *i.*
Rom. 6. 19, the *i.* of your flesh.
8. 26, the Spirit helpeth our *i.*
15. 1, bear the *i.* of the weak.
2 Cor. 12. 5, 10, glory in mine *i.*
1 Tim. 5. 23, wine for thine often *i.*
Heb. 4. 15, touched with the feeling of our *i.*
See Lu. 5. 15; 7. 21; John 5. 5; Heb. 5. 2.
INFLAME. Isa. 5. 11; 57. 5.
INFLICTED. 2 Cor. 2. 6.
INFLUENCES. Job 38. 31.
INGRAFTED. Jas. 1. 21.
INHABIT. Isa. 57. 15; 65. 21; Amos 9. 14.
INHABITANT. Num. 13. 32, land eateth up *i.*
Judg. 5. 23, curse bitterly the *i.*
Isa. 6. 11, cities wasted without *i.*
33. 24, *i.* shall not say, I am sick.
40. 22, the *i.* thereof are as grasshoppers.
Jer. 44. 22, land without an *i.*
See Jer. 2. 15; 4. 7; Zech. 8. 21.
INHERIT. Ex. 32. 13, they shall *i.* it for ever.
Ps. 25. 13, shall *i.* the earth.
37. 11, the meek shall *i.* the earth.
Prov. 14. 18, the simple *i.* folly.
Mat. 19. 29, shall *i.* everlasting life.
25. 34, *i.* kingdom prepared.
Mk. 10. 17; Lu. 10. 25; 18. 18, *i.* eternal life.
1 Cor. 6. 9; 15. 50; Gal. 5. 21, not *i.* the kingdom.
Heb. 12. 17, when he would have *i.* the blessing.
See Heb. 6. 12; 1 Pet. 3. 9; Rev. 21. 7.
INHERITANCE. Ps. 16. 5, Lord is portion of mine *i.*
47. 4, shall choose our *i.* for us.
Prov. 20. 21, an *i.* may be gotten hastily.
Eccl. 7. 11, wisdom good with an *i.*
Mk. 12. 7; Lu. 20. 14, the *i.* shall be ours.
Lu. 12. 13, that he divide the *i.* with me.
Acts 20. 32; 26. 18, an *i.* among the sanctified.
Eph. 1. 14, earnest of our *i.*
Heb. 9. 15, promise of eternal *i.*
See Eph. 5. 5; Col. 1. 12; Heb. 1. 4.
INIQUITY. Ex. 20. 5; 34. 7; Num. 14. 18; Deut. 5. 9, visiting the *i.* of the fathers.
34. 7; Num. 14. 18, forgiving *i.* and transgression.
Job 4. 8, they that plow *i.* reap the same.
13. 26, to possess the *i.* of my youth.
34. 32, if I have done *i.*, I will do no more.
Ps. 25. 11, pardon mine *i.*, for it is great.
32. 5, mine *i.* have I not hid.

39. 11, when thou dost correct man for *i*.
51. 5, I was shapen in *i*.
66. 18, if I regard *i*. in my heart.
69. 27, add *i*. to their *i*.
79. 8, remember not former *i*.
90. 8, thou hast set our *i*.
103. 3, who forgiveth all thine *i*.
10, not rewarded according to *i*.
107. 17, fools, because of *i*., are afflicted.
119. 3, they also do no *i*.
130. 3, if thou shouldest mark *i*.
Prov. 22. 8, he that soweth *i*. shall reap vanity.
Isa. 1. 4, a people laden with *i*.
6. 7, thine *i*. is taken away.
40. 2, her *i*. is pardoned.
53. 5, he was bruised for our *i*.
59. 2, your *i*. separated between you and God.
Jer. 5. 25, your *i*. turned away these things.
Ezek. 18. 30, repent, so *i*. shall not be your ruin.
Hab. 1. 13, canst not look on *i*.
Mat. 24. 12, because *i*. shall abound.
Acts 1. 18, purchased with reward of *i*.
8. 23, in the bond of *i*.
Rom. 6. 19, servants to *i*. unto *i*.
2 Thess. 2. 7, the mystery of *i*.
2 Tim. 2. 19, depart from *i*.
Jas. 3. 6, a world of *i*.
See Ps. 36. 2; Jer. 31. 30; Ezek. 3. 18; 18. 26.
INJURIOUS. 1 Tim. 1. 13.
INK. Jer. 36. 18; 2 Cor. 3. 3; 2 John 12; 3 John 13.
INN. Gen. 42. 27; Ex. 4. 24; Lu. 2. 7; 10. 34.
INNOCENT. Job 4. 7, who ever perished, being *i*.?
9. 23, laugh at trial of *i*.
27. 17, the *i*. shall divide the silver.
Ps. 19. 13, *i*. from the great transgression.
Prov. 28. 20, he that maketh haste to be rich shall not be *i*.
Jer. 2. 34; 19. 4, blood of the *i*.
See Gen. 20. 5; Ex. 23. 7; Mat. 27. 24.
INNUMERABLE. Job 21. 33; Ps. 40. 12; Heb. 12. 22.
INORDINATE. Ezek. 23. 11; Col. 3. 5.
INQUISITION. Deut. 19. 18; Esth. 2. 23; Ps. 9. 12.
INSCRIPTION. Acts 17. 23.
INSPIRATION. Job 32. 8; 2 Tim. 3. 16.
INSTANT. Rom. 12. 12; 2 Tim. 4. 2.
INSTRUCT. Neh. 9. 20, thy good spirit to *i*. them.
Ps. 16. 7, my reins *i*. me in night season.
32. 8, I will *i*. thee and teach thee.
Isa. 40. 14, who *i*. him?
Mat. 13. 52, every scribe *i*. unto the kingdom.
Phil. 4. 12, in all things I am *i*.
See Prov. 21. 11; Acts 18. 25; 2 Tim. 2. 25.
INSTRUCTION. Ps. 50. 17, thou hatest *i*.
Prov. 1. 7; 15. 5, fools despise *i*.
4. 13, take fast hold of *i*.
8. 33, hear *i*., and be wise.
12. 1, whoso loveth *i*. loveth knowledge.
16. 22, the *i*. of fools is folly.
24. 32, I looked upon it, and received *i*.
2 Tim. 3. 16, profitable for *i*.
See Jer. 17. 23; 35. 15; Zeph. 3. 7.
INSTRUMENT. Ps. 7. 13, hath prepared *i*. of death.
Isa. 41. 15, a new sharp threshing *i*.
Ezek. 33. 32, of one that can play on an *i*.
Rom. 6. 13, members *i*. of unrighteousness.
See Num. 35. 16; Ps. 68. 25; 150. 4.
INTEGRITY. Job 2. 3, he holdeth fast his *i*.
31. 6, that God may know my *i*.
Ps. 25. 21, let *i*. preserve me.
26. 1, I walked in *i*.
Prov. 11. 3, the *i*. of the upright.
19. 1; 20. 7, that walketh in his *i*.
See Gen. 20. 5; Ps. 7. 8; 41. 12; 78. 72.
INTENTS. Jer. 30. 24; Heb. 4. 12.
INTERCESSION. Isa. 53. 12, make *i*. for transgressors.
Rom. 8. 26, the Spirit itself maketh *i*.
Heb. 7. 25, ever liveth to make *i*.
See Jer. 7. 16; 27. 18; 1 Tim. 2. 1.
INTERCESSOR. Isa. 59. 16.
INTERMEDDLE. Prov. 14. 10; 18. 1.
INTREAT. Ruth 1. 16, *i*. me not to leave thee.
1 Sam. 2. 25, if a man sin, who shall *i*. for him?
Ps. 119. 58, I *i*. thy favour.
Isa. 19. 22, he shall be *i*. of them.
1 Tim. 5. 1, but *i*. him as a father.
Jas. 3. 17, wisdom is easy to be *i*.
See Prov. 18. 23; Lu. 15. 28.
INTRUDING. Col. 2. 18.
INVENTIONS. Ps. 106. 29; Prov. 8. 12; Eccl. 7. 29.
INVISIBLE. Col. 1. 15; 1 Tim. 1. 17; Heb. 11. 27.
INWARD. Job 38. 36, wisdom in the *i*. parts.
Ps. 51. 6, truth in the *i*. parts.
64. 6, *i*. thought of every one is deep.
Jer. 31. 33, I will put my law in their *i*. parts.
Rom. 7. 22, delight in law of God after the *i*. man.
2 Cor. 4. 16, the *i*. man is renewed.
See Ps. 62. 4; Mat. 7. 15; Rom. 2. 29.
ISSUES. Ps. 68. 20; Prov. 4. 23.
ITCHING. 2 Tim. 4. 3.

J

JACINTH. Rev. 9. 17; 21. 20.
JANGLING. 1 Tim. 1. 6.
JASPER. Ex. 28. 20; Ezek. 28. 13, and a *j*.
Rev. 4. 3, he that sat was to look upon like a *j*.
21. 11, even like a *j*. stone.
18, the building of the wall of it was of *j*.
19, the first foundation was *j*.
JAVELIN. Num. 25. 7, took a *j*. in his hand.
1 Sam. 18. 10, and there was a *j*. in Saul's hand.
19. 10, even to the wall with a *j*.
JEALOUS. Ex. 20. 5; 34. 14; Deut. 4. 24; 5. 9; 6. 15; Josh. 24. 19, I am a *j*. God.
1 Kings 19. 10, 14, I have been *j*. for the Lord.
Ezek. 39. 25, will be *j*. for my holy name.
2 Cor. 11. 2, I am *j*. over you.
See Num. 5. 14; Joel 2. 18; Zech. 1. 14; 8. 2.
JEALOUSY. Deut. 32. 16; 1 Kings 14. 22, they provoked him to *j*.
Prov. 6. 34, *j*. is the rage of a man.
Cant. 8. 6, *j*. is cruel as the grave.
Ezek. 36. 5, in fire of *j*. have I spoken.
1 Cor. 10. 22, do we provoke the Lord to *j*.?
See Ps. 78. 58; 79. 5; Isa. 42. 13.
JESTING. Eph. 5. 4.
JEWELS. Isa. 61. 10; Mal. 3. 17.
JOIN. Prov. 11. 21; 16. 5, hand *j*. in hand.
Eccl. 9. 4, to him *j*. to living there is hope.
Isa. 5. 8, that *j*. house to house.
Jer. 50. 5, let us *j*. ourselves to the Lord.
Hos. 4. 17, Ephraim is *j*. to idols.
Mat. 19. 6; Mk. 10. 9, what God hath *j*.
Acts 5. 13, durst no man *j*. himself.
1 Cor. 1. 10, perfectly *j*. in same mind.
6. 17, *j*. to the Lord.
Eph. 4. 16, whole body *j*. together.
See Acts 8. 29; 9. 26; 18. 7; Eph. 5. 31.
JOINT. Gen. 32. 25; Ps. 22. 14; Prov. 25. 19, out of *j*.
Eph. 4. 16, which every *j*. supplieth.
Heb. 4. 12, dividing asunder of *j*. and marrow.
See 1 Kings 22. 34; Rom. 8. 17; Col. 2. 19.
JOURNEY (*n*.). 1 Kings 18. 27, or he is in a *j*.
Neh. 2. 6, for how long shall thy *j*. be?
Mat. 10. 10; Mk. 6. 8; Lu. 9. 3, nor scrip for your *j*.
John 4. 6, Jesus wearied with his *j*.
JOURNEY (*v*.). Num. 10. 29, we are *j*. to the place.
See Gen. 12. 9; 13. 11.
JOURNEYINGS. Num. 10. 28, thus were the *j*.
2 Cor. 11. 26, in *j*. often.
JOY. Ezra 3. 13, not discern noise of *j*.
Neh. 8. 10, *j*. of the Lord is your strength.
Job 20. 5, the *j*. of the hypocrite is but a moment.

Job 29. 13, widow's heart sing for *j.*
33. 26, he will see his face with *j.*
41. 22, sorrow is turned into *j.*
Ps. 16. 11, fulness of *j.*
30. 5, *j.* cometh in the morning.
48. 2, the *j.* of the whole earth.
51. 12, restore the *j.* of thy salvation.
126. 5, they that sow in tears shall reap in *j.*
137. 6, prefer Jerusalem above my chief *j.*
Prov. 14. 10, not intermeddle with his *j.*
21. 15, it is *j.* to the just to do judgment.
Eccl. 2. 10, I withheld not my heart from *j.*
9. 7, eat thy bread with *j.*
Isa. 9. 3, not increased the *j.*
12. 3, with *j.* draw water.
24. 8, *j.* of the harp ceaseth.
29. 19, meek shall increase their *j.*
35. 10; 51. 11, and everlasting *j.*
65. 14, my servants sing for *j.* of heart.
Jer. 15. 16, thy word was the *j.* of my heart.
31. 13, will turn their mourning into *j.*
49. 25, the city of my *j.*
Lam. 2. 15, the *j.* of the whole earth.
Mat. 13. 20; Lu. 8. 13, with *j.* receiveth it.
44, for *j.* goeth and selleth.
25. 21, 23, the *j.* of thy Lord.
Lu. 15. 7, *j.* in heaven over one sinner.
10, there is *j.* in presence of angels.
24. 41, they believed not for *j.*
John 3. 29, this my *j.* is fulfilled.
15. 11; 16. 24, that your *j.* may be full.
Acts 8. 8, great *j.* in that city.
20. 24, finish my course with *j.*
2 Cor. 1. 24, helpers of your *j.*
Phil. 2. 2, fulfil ye my *j.*
Heb. 12. 2, for the *j.* that was set before him.
Jas. 1. 2, count it all *j.* when ye fall.
1 Pet. 1. 8, with *j.* unspeakable.
4. 13, glad also with exceeding *j.*
2 John 12, that our *j.* may be full.
Jude 24, faultless, with exceeding *j.*
See Rom. 14. 17; Gal. 5. 22; Phil. 1. 4.

JOYFUL. Ps. 35. 9, my soul shall be *j.* in the Lord.
63. 5, praise thee with *j.* lips.
66. 1; 81. 1; 95. 1; 98. 6, make a *j.* noise.
Eccl. 7. 14, in day of prosperity be *j.*
Isa. 56. 7, *j.* in my house of prayer.
See 2 Cor. 7. 4; Col. 1. 11; Heb. 10. 34.

JUDGE (*n.*). Gen. 18. 25; Ps. 94. 2, the *j.* of all the earth.
Ps. 50. 6, God is *j.* himself.
68. 5, a *j.* of the widows.
Mic. 7. 3, the *j.* asketh a reward.
Lu. 12. 14, who made me a *j.* over you?
18. 6, the unjust *j.*
Acts 10. 42, the *J.* of quick and dead.
2 Tim. 4. 8, the Lord, the righteous *j.*
Heb. 12. 23, to God the *J.* of all.
Jas. 5. 9, the *j.* standeth before the door.
See 2 Sam. 15. 4; Mat. 5. 25; Jas. 4. 11.

JUDGE (*v.*). Gen. 16. 5, Lord *j.* between me and thee.
Deut. 32. 36; Ps. 7. 8, Lord *j.* the people.
Ps. 58. 11, he is a God that *j.* in the earth.
Isa. 1. 17, *j.* the fatherless.
Mat. 7. 1, *j.* not, that ye be not *j.*
Lu. 7. 43, thou hast rightly *j.*
John 7. 24, *j.* righteous judgment.
Rom. 14. 4, who art thou that *j.*?
See John 16. 11; Rom. 2. 16; 3. 6; 2 Tim. 4. 1.

JUDGMENT. Deut. 1. 17, the *j.* is God's.
Ps. 1. 5, shall not stand in the *j.*
101. 1, I will sing of mercy and *j.*
Prov. 29. 26, *j.* cometh from the Lord.
Eccl. 11. 9; 12. 14, God will bring into *j.*
Isa. 28. 17, *j.* will I lay to the line.
53. 8, taken from prison and from *j.*
Jer. 5. 1, if there be any that executeth *j.*
10. 24, correct with *j.*, not in anger.
Hos. 12. 6, keep mercy and *j.*
Mat. 5. 21, in danger of the *j.*
John 5. 22, Father committed all *j.* to the Son.
9. 39, for *j.* I am come.
16. 8, reprove the world of *j.*
Acts 24. 25, reasoned of *j.* to come.
Rom. 14. 10, we shall all stand before the *j.* seat.
Heb. 9. 27, after this the *j.*
1 Pet. 4. 17, *j.* must begin at house of God.
See Mat. 12. 41; Heb. 10. 27; Jas. 2. 13.

JUST. Job 9. 2, how should man be *j.* with God?
Prov. 3. 33, God blesseth the habitation of the *j.*
4. 18, path of *j.* as shining light.
10. 7, memory of *j.* is blessed.
Isa. 26. 7, way of the *j.* is uprightness.
Hab. 2. 4; Rom. 1. 17; Gal. 3. 11; Heb. 10. 38, the *j.* shall live by faith.
Mat. 5. 45, sendeth rain on *j.* and unjust.
Lu. 14. 14, recompensed at resurrection of *j.*
15. 7, ninety and nine *j.* persons.
Acts 24. 15, resurrection both of *j.* and unjust.
Rom. 3. 26, that he might be *j.*
Phil. 4. 8, whatsoever things are *j.*
Heb. 2. 2, a *j.* recompence of reward.
12. 23, spirits of *j.* men made perfect.
1 Pet. 3. 18, the *j.* for the unjust.
See Job 34. 17; Acts 3. 14; Col. 4. 1.

JUSTICE. 2 Sam. 15. 4, I would do *j.*
Ps. 89. 14, *j.* and judgment are the habitation.
Prov. 8. 15, by me princes decree *j.*
Isa. 59. 4, none calleth for *j.*
Jer. 23. 5, execute judgment and *j.* in the earth.
50. 7, the habitation of *j.*
See Job 8. 3; 36. 17; Isa. 9. 7; 56. 1.

JUSTIFICATION. Rom. 4. 25; 5. 16, 18.

JUSTIFY. Job 11. 2, should a man full of talk be *j.*?
25. 4, how then can man be *j.* with God?
Ps. 51. 4, be *j.* when thou speakest.
143. 2, in thy sight shall no man living be *j.*
Isa. 5. 23, which *j.* the wicked for reward.
Mat. 11. 19; Lu. 7. 35, wisdom is *j.* of her children.
12. 37, by thy words thou shalt be *j.*
Lu. 10. 29, willing to *j.* himself.
18. 14, *j.* rather than the other.
Acts 13. 39, all that believe are *j.*
Rom. 3. 24; Tit. 3. 7, *j.* freely by his grace.
5. 1, being *j.* by faith.
9, being now *j.* by his blood.
Gal. 2. 16, man is not *j.* by works of the law.
1 Tim. 3. 16, *j.* in the Spirit.
See Isa. 50. 8; Rom. 4. 5; 8. 33.

JUSTLY. Mic. 6. 8; Lu. 23. 41; 1 Thess. 2. 10.

K

KEEP. Gen. 18. 19, they shall *k.* the way of the Lord.
Num. 6. 24, the Lord bless thee, and *k.* thee.
1 Sam. 2. 9, he will *k.* the feet of his saints.
25. 34, the Lord God hath *k.* me back from hurting thee.
Ps. 17. 8, *k.* me as the apple of the eye.
34. 13, *k.* thy tongue from evil.
91. 11, angels charge to *k.* thee in all thy ways.
121. 3, he that *k.* thee will not slumber.
127. 1, except the Lord *k.* the city.
141. 3, *k.* the door of my lips.
Prov. 4. 6, love wisdom, she shall *k.* thee.
21, *k.* my sayings in midst of thine heart.
23, *k.* thy heart with all diligence.
6. 20, my son, *k.* thy father's commandment.
Eccl. 3. 6, a time to *k.*
5. 1, *k.* thy foot when thou goest.
12. 13, fear God, and *k.* his commandments.
Isa. 26. 3, thou wilt *k.* him in perfect peace.
27. 3, I the Lord do *k.* it, I will *k.* it.
Jer. 3. 5, 12, will he *k.* his anger?
Hab. 2. 20, let the earth *k.* silence.
Mal. 3. 14, what profit that we have *k.*
Mat. 19. 17, if thou wilt enter life, *k.* the commandments.
Lu. 11. 28, blessed are they that *k.*
19. 43, enemies shall *k.* thee in on every side.

John 8. 51, 52, *k.* my sayings.
12. 25, he that hateth his life shall *k.* it.
14. 23, if a man love me, he will *k.* my words.
17. 11, holy Father, *k.* through thine own name.
15, that thou shouldest *k.* them from the evil.
Acts 16. 4, delivered the decrees to *k.*
21. 25, *k.* from things offered to idols.
1 Cor. 5. 8, let us *k.* the feast.
9. 27, I *k.* under my body.
Eph. 4. 3, *k.* the unity of the Spirit.
Phil. 4. 7, the peace of God shall *k.* your hearts.
1 Tim. 5. 22, *k.* thyself pure.
6. 20, *k.* that which is committed.
Jas. 1. 27, *k.* himself unspotted.
1 John 5. 21, *k.* yourselves from idols.
Jude 21, *k.* yourselves in the love of God.
24, him that is able to *k.* you from falling.
Rev. 3. 10, I will *k.* thee from hour of temptation.
22. 9, which *k.* the sayings of this book.
See 1 Pet. 1. 5; 4. 19; Jude 6; Rev. 3. 8.

KEEPER. Ps. 121. 5, the Lord is thy *k.*
Eccl. 12. 3, when the *k.* of the house shall tremble.
Cant. 1. 6, they made me *k.* of the vineyards.
Tit. 2. 5, chaste, *k.* at home.
See Gen. 4. 2, 9; Mat. 28. 4; Acts 5. 23; 16. 27.

KEY. Mat. 16. 19, the *k.* of kingdom of heaven.
Lu. 11. 52, ye have taken away *k.* of knowledge.
Rev. 1. 18, the *k.* of hell and of death.
See Isa. 22. 22; Rev. 3. 7; 9. 1.

KICK. Deut. 32. 15; 1 Sam. 2. 29; Acts 9. 5.

KILL. Num. 16. 13, to *k.* us in the wilderness.
2 Kings 5. 7, am I a God to *k.*?
7. 4, if they *k.* us, we shall but die.
Eccl. 3. 3, a time to *k.*
Mat. 10. 28; Lu. 12. 4, fear not them that *k.* the body.
Mk. 3. 4, is it lawful to save life, or to *k.*?
John 5. 18, the Jews sought the more to *k.* him.
7. 19, why go ye about to *k.* me?
8. 22, will he *k.* himself?
Rom. 8. 36, for thy sake we are *k.* all the day.
2 Cor. 3. 6, the letter *k.*
6. 9, chastened, and not *k.*
Jas. 4. 2, ye *k.*, and desire to have.
5. 6, ye condemned and *k.* the just.
See Mat. 23. 37; Mk. 12. 5; Lu. 22. 2.

KIND. 2 Chron. 10. 7, if thou be *k.* to this people.
Mat. 17. 21; Mk. 9. 29, this *k.* goeth not out.
Lu. 6. 35, *k.* to unthankful and evil.
1 Cor. 13. 4, charity suffereth long, and is *k.*
See Mat. 13. 47; Eph. 4. 32; Jas. 3. 7.

KINDLE. Ps. 2. 12, his wrath is *k.* but a little.
Prov. 26. 21, a contentious man to *k.* strife.
Isa. 50. 11, walk in sparks that ye have *k.*
Hos. 11. 8, my repentings are *k.* together.
Lu. 12. 49, what will I, if it be already *k.*?
Jas. 3. 5, how great a matter a little fire *k.*
See Job 19. 11; 32. 2; Ezek. 20. 48.

KINDLY. Gen. 24. 49; 50. 21; Ruth 1. 8; Rom. 12. 10.

KINDNESS. Ruth 3. 10, thou hast showed more *k.*
2 Sam. 2. 6, I will requite you this *k.*
9. 1, 7, show him *k.* for Jonathan's sake.
Ps. 17. 7; 92. 2, thy marvellous loving-*k.*
36. 7, how excellent is thy loving-*k.*!
63. 3, thy loving-*k.* is better than life.
117. 2; 119. 76, his merciful *k.*
141. 5, righteous smite me, it shall be a *k.*
Prov. 31. 26, in her tongue is the law of *k.*
Isa. 54. 8, with everlasting *k.*
Jer. 2. 2, I remember the *k.* of thy youth.
31. 3, with loving-*k.* have I drawn thee.
Col. 3. 12, put on *k.*, meekness.
2 Pet. 1. 7, to godliness, brotherly *k.*
See Josh. 2. 12; Neh. 9. 17; Joel 2. 13; Jon. 4. 2.

KINDRED. Acts 3. 25; Rev. 1. 7; 5. 9; 7. 9.

KING. Num. 23. 21, the shout of a *k.* is among them.
Judg. 9. 8, the trees went forth to anoint a *k.*
Judg. 17. 6, no *k.* in Israel.
1 Sam. 8. 5, now make us a *k.*
19, we will have a *k.*
10. 24; 2 Sam. 16. 16, God save the *k.*
Job 18. 14, bring him to the *k.* of terrors.
34. 18, is it fit to say to a *k.*?
Ps. 5. 2; 84. 3, my *K.* and my God.
10. 16, the Lord is *K.* for ever.
20. 9, let the *k.* hear us when we call.
74. 12, God is my *K.* of old.
102. 15, the *k.* of the earth shall fear.
Prov. 8. 15, by me *k.* reign.
22. 29, the diligent shall stand before *k.*
31. 3, that which destroyeth *k.*
4, it is not for *k.* to drink wine.
Eccl. 2. 12, what can the man do that cometh after the *k.*?
10. 16, woe to thee when thy *k.* is a child!
20, curse not the *k.*
Isa. 32. 1, a *k.* shall reign in righteousness.
33. 17, thine eyes shall see the *k.* in his beauty.
49. 23, *k.* shall be thy nursing fathers.
Jer. 10. 10, the Lord is an everlasting *k.*
Mat. 22. 11, when the *k.* came in to see the guests.
Lu. 19. 38, blessed be the *K.* that cometh.
23. 2, saying that he himself is Christ a *k.*
John 6. 15, by force, to make him a *k.*
19. 14, behold your *K.*!
15, we have no *k.* but Cæsar.
1 Tim. 1. 17, now unto the *K.* eternal.
6. 15, the *K.* of *k.* and Lord of lords.
Rev. 1. 6; 5. 10, made us *k.* and priests unto God.
15. 3, thou *K.* of saints.
See Lu. 10. 24; 1 Tim. 2. 2; 1 Pet. 2. 17.

KINGDOM. Ex. 19. 6, a *k.* of priests.
1 Chron. 29. 11; Mat. 6. 13, thine is the *k.*
Ps. 22. 28, the *k.* is the Lord's.
103. 19, his *k.* ruleth over all.
145. 12, the glorious majesty of his *k.*
Isa. 14. 16, is this the man that did shake *k.*?
Dan. 4. 3, his *k.* is an everlasting *k.*
Mat. 4. 23; 9. 35; 24. 14, gospel of the *k.*
8. 12, children of the *k.* cast out.
12. 25; Mk. 3. 24; Lu. 11. 17, *k.* divided against itself.
13. 38, good seed are children of the *k.*
25. 34, inherit the *k.*
Lu. 12. 32, Father's good pleasure to give you the *k.*
22. 29, I appoint unto you a *k.*
John 18. 36, my *k.* is not of this world.
Acts 1. 6, wilt thou restore the *k.* to Israel?
1 Cor. 15. 24, when he shall have delivered up the *k.*
Col. 1. 13, into the *k.* of his dear Son.
2 Tim. 4. 18, to his heavenly *k.*
Jas. 2. 5, heirs of the *k.* he hath promised.
2 Pet. 1. 11, entrance into everlasting *k.*
See Rev. 1. 9; 11. 15; 16. 10; 17. 17.

KISS. Ps. 85. 10; Prov. 27. 6; Lu. 7. 38; Rom. 16. 16.

KNEW. Gen. 28. 16, the Lord is in this place, and I *k.* it not.
Jer. 1. 5, before I formed thee I *k.* thee.
Mat. 7. 23, I never *k.* you, depart.
John 4. 10, if thou *k.* the gift of God.
2 Cor. 5. 21, who *k.* no sin.
See Gen. 3. 7; Deut. 34. 10; John 1. 10; Rom. 1. 21.

KNOW. 1 Sam. 3. 7, Samuel did not yet *k.* the Lord.
1 Chron. 28. 9, *k.* thou the God of thy father.
Job 5. 27, *k.* thou it for thy good.
8. 9, we are but of yesterday, and *k.* nothing.
13. 23, make me to *k.* my transgression.
19. 25, I *k.* that my redeemer liveth.
Job 22. 13; Ps. 73. 11, how doth God *k.*?
Ps. 39. 4, make me to *k.* mine end.
46. 10, be still, and *k.* that I am God.
56. 9, this I *k.*, for God is for me.

Ps. 103. 14, he *k.* our frame.
139. 23, *k.* my heart.
Eccl. 9. 5, the living *k.* they shall die.
11. 9, *k.* that for all these things.
Isa. 1. 3, the ox *k.* his owner.
Jer. 17. 9, the heart is deceitful, who can *k.* it?
31. 34; Heb. 8. 11, *k.* the Lord, for all shall *k.* me.
Ezek. 2. 5; 33. 33, *k.* there hath been a prophet.
Hos. 2. 20, thou shalt *k.* the Lord.
7. 9, yet he *k.* it not.
Mat. 6. 3, let not thy left hand *k.*
13. 11; Mk. 4. 11; Lu. 8. 10, given to you to *k.*
25. 12, I *k.* you not.
Mk. 1. 24; Lu. 4. 34, I *k.* thee, who thou art.
Lu. 19. 42, if thou hadst *k.*
22. 57. 60, I *k.* him not.
John 7. 17, he shall *k.* of the doctrine.
10. 14, I *k.* my sheep, and am *k.* of mine.
13. 7, *k.* not now, but shalt *k.* hereafter.
17, if ye *k.* these things.
35, by this shall all men *k.* ye are my disciples.
Acts 1. 7, it is not for you to *k.*
Rom. 8. 28, we *k.* that all things work.
1 Cor. 2. 14, neither can he *k.* them.
13. 9, 12, we *k.* in part.
Eph. 3. 19, and to *k.* the love of Christ.
2 Tim. 1. 12, I *k.* whom I have believed.
3. 15, thou hast *k.* the scriptures.
1 John 2. 4, he that saith, I *k.* him.
3. 2, we *k.* that when he shall appear.
Rev. 2. 2, 9, 13, 19; 3. 1, 8, I *k.* thy works.
See Mat. 6. 8; 2 Tim. 2. 19; 2 Pet. 2. 9; Rev. 2. 17.

KNOWLEDGE. 2 Chron. 1. 10, 11, 12, give me *k.*
Job 21. 14, we desire not *k.* of thy ways.
Ps. 94. 10, he that teacheth man *k.*
139. 6, such *k.* is too wonderful.
144. 3, that thou takest *k.* of him.
Prov. 10. 14, wise men lay up *k.*
14. 6, *k.* is easy to him that understandeth.
17. 27, he that hath *k.* spareth words.
24. 5, a man of *k.* increaseth strength.
30. 3, nor have the *k.* of the holy.
Eccl. 1. 18, increaseth *k.* increaseth sorrow.
9. 10, nor *k.* in the grave.
Isa. 11. 2, the spirit of *k.*
40. 14, who taught him *k.*?
53. 11, by his *k.* justify many.
Dan. 1. 17, God gave them *k.*
12. 4, *k.* shall be increased.
Hos. 4. 6, destroyed for lack of *k.*
Hab. 2. 14, earth shall be filled with the *k.*
Lu. 11. 52, taken away key of *k.*
Acts 4. 13, took *k.* of them.
24. 22, more perfect *k.* of that way.
Rom. 10. 2, zeal of God, but not according to *k.*
1 Cor. 8. 1, *k.* puffeth up.
13. 8, *k.* shall vanish away.
15. 34, some have not the *k.* of God.
Eph. 3. 19, love of Christ, which passeth *k.*
Phil. 3. 8, but loss for the *k.* of Christ.
Col. 2. 3, treasures of wisdom and *k.*
1 Tim. 2. 4; 2 Tim. 3. 7, the *k.* of the truth.
Heb. 10. 26, sin after we have received *k.*
2 Pet. 1. 5, 6, to virtue *k.* and to *k.* temperance.
3. 18, grow in grace and *k.*
See Gen. 2. 9; 1 Sam. 2. 3; Prov. 19. 2; Hos. 4. 1.

L

LABOUR (*n.*). Ps. 90. 10, yet is their strength *l.* and sorrow.
104. 23, goeth to his *l.* till evening.
Prov. 13. 11, he that gathereth by *l.* shall increase.
14. 23, in all *l.* there is profit.
Eccl. 1. 8, all things are full of *l.*
2. 22, what hath man of all his *l.*?
6. 7, all the *l.* of man is for his mouth.
John 4. 38, are entered into their *l.*
1 Cor. 15. 58, your *l.* is not in vain.
1 Thess. 1. 3; Heb. 6. 10, your *l.* of love.
Rev. 2. 2, I know thy *l.* and patience.
14. 13, rest from their *l.*
See Gen. 31. 42; Isa. 58. 3; 2 Cor. 6. 5; 11. 23.

LABOUR (*v.*). Ex. 20. 9; Deut. 5. 13, six days shalt thou *l.*
Neh. 4. 21, so we *l.* in the work.
Ps. 127. 1, they *l.* in vain.
144. 14, our oxen may be strong to *l.*
Prov. 16. 26, he that *l. l.* for himself.
23. 4, *l.* not to be rich.
Eccl. 4. 8, for whom do I *l.*?
5. 12, the sleep of a *l.* man is sweet.
Mat. 11. 28, all ye that *l.*
John 6. 27, *l.* not for the meat which perisheth.
1 Cor. 3. 9, we are *l.* together with God.
Eph. 4. 28, but rather *l.*, working with his hands.
1 Thess. 5. 12, which *l.* among you.
1 Tim. 5. 17, they who *l.* in word and doctrine.
See Mat. 9. 37; 20. 1; Lu. 10. 2.

LACK. Mat. 19. 20; Lu. 22. 35; Acts 4. 34.

LADEN. Isa. 1. 4; Mat. 11. 28; 2 Tim. 3. 6.

LAMB. Isa. 5. 17, the *l.* feed after their manner.
11. 6, the wolf shall dwell with the *l.*
53. 7; Jer. 11. 19, as *l.* to the slaughter.
John 1. 29, 36, behold the *L.* of God.
1 Pet. 1. 19, as of a *l.* without blemish.
Rev. 5. 6; 13. 8, stood a *L.* slain.
12. 11, by the blood of the *L.*
22. 1, the throne of God and of the *L.*
See Isa. 40. 11; Lu. 10. 3; John 21. 15.

LAME. Job 29. 15; Prov. 26. 7; Isa. 35. 6; Heb. 12. 13.

LAMENT. Mat. 11. 17; John 16. 20; Acts 8. 2.

LAMP. Ps. 119. 105; Prov. 13. 9; Isa. 62. 1; Mat. 25. 1.

LAP. Judg. 7. 6; Prov. 16. 33.

LAST. Num. 23. 10, let my *l.* end be like his.
Prov. 23. 32, at the *l.* it biteth like a serpent.
Mat. 12. 45; Lu. 11. 26, *l.* state of that man.
19. 30; 20. 16; Mk. 10. 31; Lu. 13. 30, first shall be *l.*
John 6. 39; 11. 24; 12. 48, the *l.* day.
See Lam. 1. 9; 2 Tim. 3. 1; 1 Pet. 1. 5; 1 John 2. 18.

LATTER. Job 19. 25; Prov. 19. 20; Hag. 2. 9.

LAUGH. Prov. 1. 26; Eccl. 3. 4; Lu. 6. 21; Jas. 4. 9.

LAW. Josh. 8. 34, all the words of the *l.*
Ps. 37. 31, the *l.* of his God is in his heart.
40. 8, thy *l.* is within my heart.
119. 70, 77, 92, 174, I delight in thy *l.*
97. 113, 163, 165, how I love thy *l.*
Prov. 13. 14, the *l.* of the wise is a fountain of life.
Isa. 8. 20, to the *l.* and to the testimony.
Mal. 2. 6, the *l.* of truth was in his mouth.
Mat. 5. 17, not come to destroy the *l.*
23. 23, the weightier matters of the *l.*
John 7. 51, doth our *l.* judge any man.
19. 7, we have a *l.*, and by our *l.*
Rom. 2. 14, are a *l.* unto themselves.
3. 20, by the deeds of the *l.*
7. 12, the *l.* is holy.
14, the *l.* is spiritual.
16; 1 Tim. 1. 8, the *l.* is good.
8. 3, what the *l.* could not do.
Gal. 3. 24, the *l.* was our schoolmaster.
5. 14, all the *l.* is fulfilled in one word.
23, against such there is no *l.*
6. 2, so fulfil the *l.* of Christ.
1 Tim. 1. 9, the *l.* is not made for a righteous man.
Heb. 7. 16, the *l.* of a carnal commandment.
Jas. 1. 25; 2. 12, perfect *l.* of liberty.
2. 8, the royal *l.*
See Ps. 1. 2; 19. 7; Mat. 7. 12; Rom. 10. 4.

LAWFUL. Mat. 12. 2; John 5. 10; 1 Cor. 6. 12.

LAWLESS. 1 Tim. 1. 9.

LEAD. Deut. 4. 27; 28. 37, whither the Lord shall *l.* you.
Ps. 23. 2, he *l.* me beside still waters.
27. 11, *l.* me in a plain path.
31. 3, *l.* me, and guide me.
61. 2, *l.* me to the rock that is higher than I.

Ps. 139. 10, there shall thy hand *l.* me.
24, *l.* me in the way everlasting.
Prov. 6. 22, when thou goest, it shall *l.* thee.
Isa. 11. 6, a little child shall *l.* them.
42. 16, I will *l.* them in paths not known.
48. 17, I am the Lord which *l.* thee.
Mat. 6. 13; Lu. 11. 4, *l.* us not into temptation.
15. 14; Lu. 6. 39, if the blind *l.* the blind.
Acts 13. 11, seeking some to *l.* him.
1 Tim. 2. 2, we may *l.* a quiet life.
See John 10. 3; 1 Cor. 9. 5; 2 Tim. 3. 6; Rev. 7. 17.

LEAF. Lev. 26. 36; Ps. 1. 3; Isa. 64. 6; Mat. 21. 19.

LEAN. Prov. 3. 5; Amos 5. 19; Mic. 3. 11; John 13. 23; 21. 20.

LEARN. Deut. 31. 13, *l.* to fear the Lord.
Prov. 1. 5; 9. 9; 16. 21, will increase *l.*
22. 25, lest thou *l.* his ways.
Isa. 1. 17, *l.* to do well.
2. 4; Mic. 4. 3, neither shall they *l.* war.
29. 11, 12, deliver to one that is *l.*
John 6. 45, every one that hath *l.* of the Father.
7. 15, having never *l.*
Acts 7. 22, *l.* in all the wisdom of the Egyptians.
26. 24, much *l.* doth make thee mad.
Rom. 15. 4, written for our *l.*
Eph. 4. 20, ye have not so *l.* Christ.
2 Tim. 3. 14, in the things thou hast *l.*
Heb. 5. 8, though a Son, yet *l.* he obedience.
See Mat. 9. 13; 11. 29; Phil. 4. 11; Rev. 14. 3.

LEAST. Mat. 5. 19, one of these *l.* commandments.
11. 11; Lu. 7. 28, he that is *l.* in kingdom of heaven.
25. 40, 45, done it to the *l.* of these.
Lu. 12. 26, not able to do that which is *l.*
16. 10, faithful in that which is *l.*
Eph. 3. 8, less than the *l.* of all saints.
See Gen. 32. 10; Jer. 31. 34; 1 Cor. 6. 4.

LEAVE. Gen. 2. 24; Mat. 19. 5; Mk. 10. 7; Eph. 5. 31, *l.* father and mother, and shall cleave.
Ps. 16. 10; Acts 2. 27, not *l.* my soul in hell.
27. 9; 119. 121, *l.* me not.
Mat. 23. 23, and not to *l.* the other undone.
John 14. 27, peace I *l.* with you.
Heb. 13. 5, I will never *l.* thee.
See Ruth 1. 16; Mat. 5. 24; John 16. 28.

LEES. Isa. 25. 6; Jer. 48. 11; Zeph. 1. 12.

LEND. Deut. 15. 6, thou shalt *l.* to many nations.
Ps. 37. 26; 112. 5, ever merciful, and *l.*
Prov. 19. 17, he that hath pity on poor *l.* to the Lord.
22. 7, the borrower is servant to the *l.*
Lu. 6. 34, if ye *l.* to them of whom.
See 1 Sam. 1. 28; Isa. 24. 2; Lu. 11. 5.

LESS. Ex. 30. 15; Job 11. 6; Isa. 40. 17.

LIARS. Ps. 116. 11; John 8. 44; Tit. 1. 12; Rev. 2. 2; 21. 8.

LIBERAL. Prov. 11. 25; Isa. 32. 5, 8; Jas. 1. 5.

LIBERTY. Ps. 119. 45, I will walk at *l.*
Isa. 61. 1; Jer. 34. 8; Lu. 4. 18, to proclaim *l.*
Rom. 8. 21, the glorious *l.* of the children of God.
1 Cor. 8. 9, take heed lest this *l.* of yours.
2 Cor. 3. 17, where the Spirit is, there is *l.*
Gal. 5. 1, stand fast in the *l.*
Jas. 1. 25; 2. 12, the law of *l.*
See Lev. 25. 10; Gal. 5. 13; 1 Pet. 2. 16.

LIFE. Gen. 2. 7; 6. 17; 7. 22, the breath of *l.*
9; 3. 24; Rev. 2. 7, the tree of *l.*
Deut. 30. 15; Jer. 21. 8, I have set before thee *l.*
Josh. 2. 14, our *l.* for yours.
1 Sam. 25. 29, bound in the bundle of *l.*
Ps. 16. 11, show me the path of *l.*
17. 14; Eccl. 9. 9, their portion in this *l.*
26. 9, gather not my *l.* with bloody men.
27. 1, the strength of my *l.*
30. 5, in his favour is *l.*
34. 12, what man is he that desireth *l.*?
36. 9, the fountain of *l.*
91. 16, with long *l.* will I satisfy him.
Ps. 133. 3, even *l.* for evermore.
Prov. 3. 22, so shall they be *l.* to thy soul.
8. 35, whoso findeth me findeth *l.*
15. 24, the way of *l.* is above to the wise.
Mat. 6. 25; Lu. 12. 22, take no thought for your *l.*
18. 8; 19. 17; Mk. 9. 43, to enter into *l.*
Lu. 12. 15, a man's *l.* consisteth not.
23, the *l.* is more than meat.
John 1. 4, in him was *l.*
5. 24; 1 John 3. 14, passed from death to *l.*
26, as the Father hath *l.* in himself.
40; 10. 10, will not come that ye might have *l.*
6. 33, 47, 48, 54, the bread of *l.*
10. 15, 17; 13. 37, I lay down my *l.*
11. 25; 14. 6, the resurrection and the *l.*
Rom. 6. 4, in newness of *l.*
11. 15, *l.* from the dead.
2 Cor. 2. 16, the savour of *l.* unto *l.*
Gal. 2. 20, the *l.* that I now live.
Eph. 4. 18, alienated from the *l.* of God.
Col. 3. 3, your *l.* is hid.
1 Tim. 4. 8; 2 Tim. 1. 1, the promise of the *l.*
2 Tim. 1. 10, brought *l.* to light by gospel.
Jas. 4. 14, what is your *l.*?
1 John 1. 2, the *l.* was manifested.
2. 16, the pride of *l.*
5. 11, this *l.* is in his Son.
Rev. 22. 1, 17, river of water of *l.*
See Mat. 10. 39; 20. 28; Acts 5. 20.

LIGHT. Ex. 10. 23, Israel had *l.* in their dwellings.
Job 18. 5, the *l.* of the wicked.
37. 21, men see not bright *l.* in clouds.
Ps. 4. 6; 90. 8, the *l.* of thy countenance.
27. 1, the Lord is my *l.*
36. 9, in thy *l.* shall we see *l.*
97. 11, *l.* is sown for the righteous.
119. 105, a *l.* to my path.
Eccl. 11. 7, the *l.* is sweet.
Isa. 5. 20, darkness for *l.*, and *l.* for darkness.
30. 26, the *l.* of the moon as *l.* of sun.
59. 9, we wait for *l.*
60. 1, arise, shine, for thy *l.* is come.
Zech. 14. 6, the *l.* shall not be clear.
Mat. 5. 14; John 8. 12; 9. 5, the *l.* of the world.
16. let your *l.* so shine.
6. 22, the *l.* of the body is the eye.
Lu. 12. 35, your loins girded, and *l.* burning.
16. 8, wiser than children of *l.*
John 1. 9, that was the true *L.*
3. 19, *l.* is come into the world.
20, hateth the *l.*
5. 35, burning and shining *l.*
12. 35, yet a little while is the *l.* with you.
36, while ye have *l.*, believe in the *l.*
Acts 26. 18, turn from darkness to *l.*
1 Cor. 4. 5, bring to *l.* hidden things.
2 Cor. 4. 4, *l.* of the gospel.
6, commanded *l.* to shine out of darkness.
11. 14, an angel of *l.*
Eph. 5. 8, now are ye *l.*, walk as children of *l.*
14, Christ shall give thee *l.*
1 Tim. 6. 16, in *l.* which no man can approach.
2 Pet. 1. 19, a *l.* shining in a dark place.
1 John 1. 5, God is *l.*
7, walk in the *l.*, as he is in the *l.*
Rev. 22. 5, they need no candle, neither *l.* of the sun.
See 2 Tim. 1. 10; Rev. 7. 16; 18. 23; 21. 23.

LIGHTNING. Ex. 19. 16; Mat. 24. 27; Lu. 10. 18.

LIKENESS. Ps. 17. 15, when I awake, with thy *l.*
Isa. 40. 18, what *l.* will ye compare?
Acts 14. 11, gods are come down in *l.* of men.
Rom. 6. 5, *l.* of his death, *l.* of his resurrection.
8. 3, in the *l.* of sinful flesh.
Phil. 2. 7, was made in the *l.* of men.
See Gen. 1. 26; 5. 1; Ex. 20. 4; Deut. 4. 16.

LIMIT. Ps. 78. 41; Ezek. 43. 12; Heb. 4. 7.

LINE. Ps. 16. 6; Isa. 28. 10, 17; 34. 11; 2 Cor. 10. 16.

LINGER. Gen. 19. 16; 43. 10; 2 Pet. 2. 3.

LIP. 1 Sam. 1. 13, only her *l.* moved.
Job 27. 4, my *l.* shall not speak wickedness.

Ezek. 37. 11, our hope is *l.*
Mat. 10. 6; 15. 24, go to *l.* sheep of Israel.
18. 11; Lu. 19. 10, to save that which was *l.*
John 6. 12, that nothing be *l.*
17. 12, none of them is *l.*
18. 9, have I *l.* none.
See Lev. 6. 3; Deut. 22. 3; 2 Cor. 4. 3.
LOT. Ps. 16. 5, thou maintainest my *l.*
125. 3, not rest on the *l.* of the righteous.
Prov. 1. 14, cast in thy *l.* among us.
16. 33, *l.* is cast into the lap.
18. 18, *l.* causeth contention to cease.
Dan. 12. 13, stand in thy *l.*
Acts 8. 21, neither part nor *l.* in this matter.
See Num. 26. 55; Mat. 27. 35; Acts 1. 26.
LOUD. Ezra 3. 13; Prov. 7. 11; 27. 14; Lu. 23. 23.
LOVE (*n.*). 2 Sam. 1. 26, wonderful, passing the *l.* of women.
Prov. 10. 12, *l.* covereth all sins.
15. 17, better a dinner of herbs where *l.* is.
Cant. 2. 4, his banner over me was *l.*
8. 6, *l.* is strong as death.
Jer. 31. 3, loved thee with everlasting *l.*
Hos. 11. 4, the bands of *l.*
Mat. 24. 12, *l.* of many shall wax cold.
John 5. 42, ye have not the *l.* of God in you.
13. 35, if ye have *l.* one to another.
15. 13, greater *l.* hath no man than this.
Rom. 13. 10, *l.* worketh no ill.
2 Cor. 5. 14, the *l.* of Christ constraineth us.
13. 11, the God of *l.* shall be with you.
Eph. 3. 19, the *l.* of Christ, which passeth.
1 Tim. 6. 10, *l.* of money is the root of all evil.
Heb. 13. 1, let brotherly *l.* continue.
1 John 4. 7, *l.* is of God.
8, 16, God is *l.*
10, herein is *l.*, not that we loved God.
18, no fear in *l.*
Rev. 2. 4, thou hast left thy first *l.*
See Gen. 29. 20; Gal. 5. 22; 1 Thess. 1. 3.
LOVE (*v.*). Lev. 19. 18; Mat. 19. 19; 22. 39; Mk. 12. 31, thou shalt *l.* thy neighbour.
Deut. 6. 5; 10. 12; 11. 1; 19. 9; 30. 6; Mat. 22. 37; Mk. 12. 30; Lu. 10. 27, *l.* the Lord thy God.
Ps. 18. 1, I will *l.* thee, O Lord, my strength.
26. 8, I have *l.* the habitation of thy house.
34. 12, what man is he that *l.* many days?
69. 36, they that *l.* his name.
97. 10, ye that *l.* the Lord.
109. 17, as he *l.* cursing.
122. 6, they shall prosper that *l.* thee.
Prov. 8. 17, I *l.* them that *l.* me.
17. 17, a friend *l.* at all times.
Eccl. 3. 8, a time to *l.*
Jer. 5. 31, my people *l.* to have it so.
31. 3, I have *l.* thee with an everlasting *l.*
Hos. 14. 4, I will *l.* them freely.
Amos 5. 15, hate the evil, and *l.* the good.
Mic. 6. 8, but to *l.* mercy, and walk humbly.
Mat. 5. 44; Lu. 6. 27, I say, *l.* your enemies.
46, if ye *l.* them which *l.* you.
Lu. 7. 42, which will *l.* him most?
John 11. 3, he whom thou *l.* is sick.
15. 12, 17, that ye *l.* one another.
21. 15, 16, 17, *l.* thou me?
Rom. 13. 8, owe no man any thing, but to *l.*
Eph. 6. 24, grace be with all them that *l.* our Lord.
1 Pet. 1. 8, whom having not seen, ye *l.*
2. 17, *l.* the brotherhood.
1 John 4. 19, we *l.* him, because he first *l.* us.
Rev. 3. 19, as many as I *l.* I rebuke.
See Gen. 22. 2; John 14. 31; 1 John 4. 20. 21.
LOVELY. 2 Sam. 1. 23; Cant. 5. 16; Ezek. 33. 32; Phil. 4. 8.
LOVER. 1 Kings 5. 1; Ps. 88. 18; 2 Tim. 3. 4; Tit. 1. 8.
LOW. Ps. 136. 23; Rom. 12. 16; Jas. 1. 9, 10.
LOWER. Ps. 8. 5; 63. 9; Eph. 4. 9; Heb. 2. 7.
LOWEST. Deut. 32. 22; Ps. 86. 13; Lu. 14. 9.
LOWLINESS. Eph. 4. 2; Phil. 2. 3.
LOWLY. Prov. 11. 2, with the *l.* is wisdom.
Mat. 11. 29, I am meek and *l.*
See Ps. 138. 6; Prov. 3. 34; 16. 19; Zech. 9. 9.
LUST. Deut. 12. 15, 20, 21; 14. 26, whatsoever thy soul *l.* after.
Ps. 81. 12, gave them up to their own *l.*
Rom. 7. 7, I had not known *l.*
Gal. 5. 24, Christ's have crucified flesh with *l.*
1 Tim. 6. 9, rich fall into hurtful *l.*
Tit. 2. 12, denying worldly *l.*
Jas. 1. 14, when he is drawn of his own *l.*
1 Pet. 2. 11, abstain from fleshly *l.*
1 John 2. 16, the *l.* of the flesh.
17, the world passeth away, and the *l.* thereof.
Jude 16, 18, walking after *l.*
See Mat. 5. 28; 1 Cor. 10. 6; Rev. 18. 14.
LYING. Ps. 31. 18, let the *l.* lips be put to silence.
119. 163, I abhor *l.*, but thy law I love.
Prov. 6. 17, the Lord hateth a *l.* tongue.
12. 19, a *l.* tongue is but for a moment.
Jer. 7. 4, trust not in *l.* words.
Eph. 4. 25, putting away *l.*
See 1 Kings 22. 22; 2 Chron. 18. 21; Dan. 2. 9.

M

MAD. John 10. 20; Acts 26. 11, 24; 1 Cor. 14. 23.
MADE. Ex. 2. 14, who *m.* thee a prince over us?
Ps. 118. 24, this is the day the Lord hath *m.*
Prov. 16. 4, the Lord *m.* all things for himself.
Eccl. 3. 11, he hath *m.* every thing beautiful.
7. 29, God hath *m.* man upright.
Isa. 66. 2, all these things hath mine hand *m.*
John 1. 3, all things were *m.* by him.
5. 6, wilt thou be *m.* whole?
2 Cor. 5. 21, he hath *m.* him to be sin for us.
Eph. 2. 13, *m.* nigh by the blood of Christ.
3. 7; Col. 1. 23, I was *m.* a minister.
Col. 1. 20, having *m.* peace.
Heb. 2. 17, to be *m.* like his brethren.
See Ps. 95. 5; 149. 2; John 19. 7; Acts 17. 24.
MAGNIFY. Josh 3. 7, this day will I begin to *m.* thee.
Job 7. 17, what is man, that thou shouldest *m.* him?
Ps. 34. 3; 40. 16; Lu. 1. 46, *m.* the Lord.
35. 26; 38. 16, that *m.* themselves.
138. 2, thou hast *m.* thy word above all.
Isa. 42. 21, *m.* the law.
Acts 19. 17, the name of Jesus was *m.*
Rom. 11. 13, I *m.* mine office.
See Dan. 8. 25; 11. 36; Acts 5. 13; Phil. 1. 20.
MAIDSERVANTS. Ex. 20. 10, nor thy *m.*
21. 7, if a man sell his daughter to be a *m.*
Deut. 15. 17, unto thy *m.* thou shalt do likewise.
MAIL. 1 Sam. 17. 5.
MAINTAIN. 1 Kings 8. 45; 49. 59; 2 Chron. 35. 39, *m.* their cause.
Ps. 16. 5, thou *m.* my lot.
Tit. 3. 8, 14, careful to *m.* good works.
See Job 13. 15; Ps. 9. 4; 140. 12.
MAINTENANCE. Ezra 4. 14; Prov. 27. 27.
MAKER. Job 4. 17, shall a man be more pure than his *m.*?
32. 22, my *m.* would soon take me away.
35. 10, none saith, where is God my *m.*?
36. 3, ascribe righteousness to my *m.*
Ps. 95. 6, kneel before the Lord our *m.*
Prov. 14. 31; 17. 5, reproacheth his *m.*
22. 2, the Lord is *m.* of them all.
Isa. 45. 9, that striveth with his *m.*
51. 13, forgettest the Lord thy *m.*
54. 5, thy *m.* is thine husband.
Heb. 11. 10, whose builder and *m.* is God.
See Isa. 1. 31; 17. 7; 22. 11; Hab. 2. 18.
MALICIOUSNESS. Rom. 1. 29; 1 Pet. 2. 16.
MAN. Gen. 3. 22, the *m.* is become as one of us.
8. 21, for *m.* sake.
Num. 23. 19, God is not a *m.*
Neh. 6. 11, should such a *m.* as I flee?
Job 5. 7, *m.* is born to trouble.
10. 4, seest thou as *m.* seeth?
11. 12, vain *m.* would be wise.
14. 1, *m.* that is born of a woman.

Job 15. 7, art thou the first *m.* that was born?
25. 6, *m.* that is a worm.
33. 12, God is greater than *m.*
Ps. 10. 18, the *m.* of earth.
49. 12, *m.* being in honour abideth not.
89. 48, what *m.* is he that liveth?
90. 3, thou turnest *m.* to destruction.
104. 23, *m.* goeth forth to his labour.
118. 6, I will not fear, what can *m.* do?
Prov. 12. 2, a good *m.* obtaineth favour.
Eccl. 6. 12, who knoweth what is good for *m.*?
Isa. 2. 22, cease ye from *m.*
Jer. 10. 23, it is not in *m.* to direct his steps.
Lam. 3. 1, I am the *m.* that hath seen affliction.
Hos. 11. 9, I am God, and not *m.*
Mat. 6. 24; Lu. 16. 13, no *m.* can serve.
8. 4; Mk. 8. 26, 30; Lu. 5. 14; 9. 21, tell no *m.*
17. 8, they saw no *m.*
John 1. 18; 1 John 4. 12, no *m.* hath seen God.
19. 5, behold the *m.*!
1 Cor. 2. 11, what *m.* knoweth things of a *m.*?
11. 8, *m.* is not of the woman.
2 Cor. 4. 16, though our outward *m.* perish.
Phil. 2. 8, in fashion as a *m.*
1 Tim. 2. 5, the *m.* Christ Jesus.
See John 7. 46; 1 Cor. 15. 47; Eph. 4. 24.

MANDRAKES. Gen. 30. 14, found *m.* in the field.
Cant. 7. 13, the *m.* give a smell.

MANEH. Ezek. 45. 12.

MANGER. Lu. 2. 7.

MANIFEST. Mk. 4. 22, nothing hid that shall not be *m.*
John 2. 11, and *m.* forth his glory.
14. 22, how is it thou wilt *m.* thyself?
1 Cor. 4. 5, who will make *m.* the counsels of the hearts.
2 Cor. 2. 14, maketh *m.* savour of knowledge.
Gal. 5. 19, the works of the flesh are *m.*
2 Thess. 1. 5, a *m.* token of righteous judgment.
1 Tim. 3. 16, God was *m.* in the flesh.
5. 25, good works of some are *m.* beforehand.
Heb. 4. 13, no creature that is not *m.*
1 John 1. 2, the life was *m.*
3. 5, he was *m.* to take away our sins.
4. 9, in this was *m.* the love of God.
See Rom. 8. 19; John 17. 6; 1 John 3. 10.

MANIFOLD. Ps. 104. 24, how *m.* are thy works!
Eph. 3. 10, the *m.* wisdom of God.
1 Pet. 1. 6, through *m.* temptations.
4. 10, stewards of the *m.* grace of God.
See Neh. 9. 19, 27; Amos 5. 12; Lu. 18. 30.

MANNER. 2 Sam. 7. 19, is this the *m.* of man?
Ps. 144. 13, all *m.* of store.
Isa. 5. 17, lambs shall feed after their *m.*
Mat. 8. 27; Mk. 4. 41; Lu. 8. 25, what *m.* of man is this!
12. 31, all *m.* of sin shall be forgiven.
Acts 26. 4, my *m.* of life from my youth.
1 Cor. 15. 33, evil communications corrupt good *m.*
Heb. 10. 25, as the *m.* of some is.
Jas. 1. 24, forgetteth what *m.* of man.
1 Pet. 1. 15, holy in all *m.* of conversation.
2 Pet. 3. 11, what *m.* of persons ought ye to be?
See Mat. 4. 23; 5. 11; Lu. 9. 55; Rev. 22. 2.

MANTLE. 2 Kings 2. 8; Job 1. 20; Ps. 109. 29.

MAR. Lev. 19. 27, nor *m.* the corners of thy beard.
1 Sam. 6. 5, images of your mice that *m.* the land.
Job 30. 13, they *m.* my path.
Isa. 52. 14, visage *m.* more than any man.
Mk. 2. 22, wine spilled, and bottles *m.*
See Ruth 4. 6; 2 Kings 3. 19; Jer. 13. 7; 18. 4.

MARBLE. 1 Chron. 29. 2, and *m.* stones in abundance.
Cant. 5. 15, his legs are as pillars of *m.*

MARK. Gen. 4. 15, the Lord set a *m.* on Cain.
Job 22. 15, hast thou *m.* the old way?
Ps. 37. 37, *m.* the perfect man.
48. 13, *m.* well her bulwarks.
130. 3, if thou shouldest *m.* iniquities.
Jer. 2. 22, thine iniquity is *m.* before me.
Jer. 23. 18, who hath *m.* his word?
Phil. 3. 14, I press toward the *m.* for the prize.
17, *m.* them which walk so.
See Lu. 14. 7; Rom. 16. 17; Rev. 13. 16; 20. 4.

MARROW. Job 21. 24; Ps. 63. 5; Prov. 3. 8; Heb. 4. 12.

MARVEL. Mat. 8. 10; Mk. 6. 6; Lu. 7. 9, Jesus *m.*
Mk. 5. 20, all men did *m.*
John 3. 7; 5. 28; 1 John 3. 13, *m.* not.
See Eccl. 5. 8; John 7. 21; Gal. 1. 6.

MARVELLOUS. Job 5. 9, *m.* things without number.
Ps. 17. 7, *m.* lovingkindness.
118. 23; Mat. 21. 42; Mk. 12. 11, *m.* in our eyes.
John 9. 30, herein is a *m.* thing.
1 Pet. 2. 9, into his *m.* light.
See Ps. 105. 5; 139. 14; Dan. 11. 36; Mic. 7. 15.

MASTER. 2 Kings 6. 32, sound of his *m.* feet behind him.
Mal. 1. 6, if I be a *m.*, where is my fear?
2. 12, the Lord will cut off the *m.* and the scholar.
Mat. 6. 24; Lu. 16. 13, no man can serve two *m.*
10. 24; Lu. 6. 40, disciple not above his *m.*
25, enough for the disciple that he be as his *m.*
17. 24, doth not your *m.* pay tribute?
23. 8, 10, one is your *M.*, even Christ.
26. 25, *M.*, is it I?
Mk. 5. 35; Lu. 8. 49, why troublest thou the *M.*?
9. 5; Lu. 9. 33, *M.*, it is good for us to be here.
10. 17; Lu. 10. 25, good *M.*, what shall I do?
Lu. 13. 25, when once the *m.* of the house is risen.
John 3. 10, art thou a *m.* of Israel?
11. 28, the *M.* is come, and calleth.
13. 13, ye call me *M.*, and ye say well.
Rom. 14. 4, to his own *m.* he standeth or falleth.
1 Cor. 3. 10, as a wise *m.*-builder.
Eph. 6. 5; Col. 3. 22; Tit. 2. 9; 1 Pet. 2. 18, be obedient to *m.*
9; Col. 4. 1, *m.*, do the same things to them.
1 Tim. 6. 1, count their *m.* worthy of honour.
2, that have believing *m.*
Jas. 3. 1, be not many *m.*
See Gen. 24. 12; 39. 8; Prov. 25. 13; Eccl. 12. 11.

MASTERY. Ex. 32. 18; 1 Cor. 9. 25; 2 Tim. 2. 5.

MATTER. Ezra 10. 4, arise, for this *m.* belongeth to thee.
Job 19. 28, the root of the *m.* is found in me.
32. 18, I am full of *m.*
Ps. 45. 1, my heart is inditing a good *m.*
Prov. 16. 20, handleth a *m.* wisely.
18. 13, answereth a *m.* before he heareth it.
Eccl. 10. 20, that which hath wings shall tell the *m.*
12. 13, conclusion of the whole *m.*
Mat. 23. 23, the weightier *m.*
Acts 18. 14, if it were a *m.* of wrong.
1 Cor. 6. 2, to judge the smallest *m.*
2 Cor. 9. 5, as a *m.* of bounty.
Jas. 3. 5, how great a *m.* a little fire kindleth!
See Gen. 30. 15; Dan. 3. 16; Acts 8. 21; 17. 32.

MAY. Mat. 9. 21; 26. 42; Acts 8. 37.

MEAN. Ex. 12. 26; Josh. 4. 6, what *m.* ye by this service?
Deut. 6. 20, what *m.* the testimonies?
Prov. 22. 29, not stand before *m.* men.
Isa. 2. 9; 5. 15; 31. 8, the *m.* man.
Ezek. 17. 12, know ye not what these things *m.*?
Mk. 9. 10, what the rising from the dead should *m.*
Acts 21. 39, citizen of no *m.* city.
See Acts 10. 17; 17. 20; 21. 13.

MEANS. Ex. 34. 7; Num. 14. 18, by no *m.* clear guilty.
Ps. 49. 7, none can by any *m.* redeem.
Mal. 1. 9, this hath been by your *m.*
Mat. 5. 26, shalt by no *m.* come out.
Lu. 10. 19, nothing shall by any *m.* hurt you.
John 9. 21, by what *m.* he now seeth.
1 Cor. 8. 9, lest by any *m.* this liberty.
9. 22, that I might by all *m.* save some.
Phil. 3. 11, by any *m.* attain.
2 Thess. 3. 16, give you peace always by all *m.*

See Jer. 5. 31; 1 Cor. 9. 27; Gal. 2. 2.
MEASURE (*n.*). Deut. 25. 14; Prov. 20. 10, thou shalt not have divers *m.*
Job 11. 9, the *m.* is longer than the earth.
28. 25, he weigheth the waters by *m.*
Ps. 39. 4, the *m.* of my days.
Isa. 40. 12, the dust of the earth in a *m.*
Jer. 30. 11; 46. 28, I will correct thee in *m.*
Ezek. 4. 11, thou shalt drink water by *m.*
Mat. 7. 2; Mk. 4. 24; Lu. 6. 38, with what *m.* ye mete.
13. 33; Lu. 13. 21, three *m.* of meal.
23. 32, fill up *m.* of your fathers.
Lu. 6. 38, good *m.*, pressed down.
John 3. 34, giveth not the Spirit by *m.*
Rom. 12. 3, to every man the *m.* of faith.
2 Cor. 12. 7, exalted above *m.*
Eph. 4. 7, the *m.* of the gift of Christ.
13, to the *m.* of the stature.
16, in the *m.* of every part.
Rev. 6. 6, a *m.* of wheat for a penny.
21. 17, according to the *m.* of a man.
See Ps. 80. 5; Isa. 5. 14; Mic. 6. 10.
MEASURE (*v.*). Isa. 40. 12, who hath *m.* the waters?
65. 7, I will *m.* former work into bosom.
Jer. 31. 37, if heaven can be *m.*
33. 22; Hos. 1. 10, as the sand cannot be *m.*
2 Cor. 10. 12, *m.* themselves by themselves.
See Ezek. 40. 3; 42. 15; Zech. 2. 1.
MEAT. Gen. 27. 4, make me savoury *m.*
1 Kings 19. 8, went in strength of that *m.*
Ps. 59. 15, wander up and down for *m.*
69. 21, they gave me also gall for my *m.*
78. 25, he sent them *m.* to the full.
145. 15, *m.* in due season.
Prov. 23. 3, dainties, for they are deceitful *m.*
30. 22, a fool when filled with *m.*
31. 15, she giveth *m.* to her household.
Isa. 65. 25, dust shall be the serpent's *m.*
Ezek. 4. 10, thy *m.* shall be by weight.
47. 12, fruit for *m.*
Dan. 1. 8, not defile himself with king's *m.*
Hab. 1. 16, because their *m.* is plenteous.
3. 17, fields yield no *m.*
Mal. 3. 10, bring tithes, that there may be *m.*
Mat. 6. 25; Lu. 12. 23, life more than *m.*?
10. 10, workman worthy of his *m.*
15. 37; Mk. 8. 8, of broken *m.*
25. 35, ye gave me *m.*
Lu. 3. 11, he that hath *m.* let him do likewise.
24. 41; John 21. 5, have ye any *m.*?
John 4. 32, I have *m.* to eat.
34, my *m.* is to do the will of him that sent me.
6. 27, labour not for the *m.* that perisheth.
Acts 2. 46, did eat *m.* with gladness.
15. 29, abstain from *m.* offered to idols.
Rom. 14. 15, destroy not him with thy *m.*
17, kingdom of God is not *m.* and drink.
20, for *m.* destroy not the work of God.
1 Cor. 6. 13, *m.* for the belly.
8. 13, if *m.* make my brother to offend.
10. 3, the same spiritual *m.*
1 Tim. 4. 3, to abstain from *m.*
Heb. 5. 12, 14, not of strong *m.*
12. 16, who for one morsel of *m.*
See Gen. 1. 29; 9. 3; Mat. 3. 4; Col. 2. 16.
MEDDLE. 2 Kings 14. 10; 2 Chron. 25. 19, why *m.* to thy hurt?
Prov. 20. 3, every fool will be *m.*
19, *m.* not with him that flattereth.
26. 17, that *m.* with strife.
See 2 Chron. 35. 21; Prov. 17. 14; 24. 21.
MEDITATE. Gen. 24. 63, Isaac went out to *m.*
Josh. 1. 8, thou shalt *m.* therein.
Ps. 1. 2, in his law doth he *m.*
63. 6; 119. 148, *m.* in the night watches.
77. 12; 143. 5, I will *m.* of thy works.
Isa. 33. 18, thine heart shall *m.* terror.
Lu. 21. 14, not to *m.* before.
1 Tim. 4. 15, *m.* upon these things.

See Ps. 19. 14; 104. 34; 119. 97, 99.
MEEK. Num. 12. 3, Moses was very *m.*
Ps. 22. 26, the *m.* shall eat and be satisfied.
25. 9, the *m.* will he guide.
37. 11; Mat. 5. 5, the *m.* shall inherit the earth.
149. 4, will beautify the *m.*
Isa. 29. 19, the *m.* shall increase their joy.
61. 1, good tidings to the *m.*
Mat. 11. 29, for I am *m.*
1 Pet. 3. 4, a *m.* and quiet spirit.
See Ps. 76. 9; 147. 6; Isa. 11. 4; Mat. 21. 5.
MEEKNESS. 2 Cor. 10. 1, by the *m.* of Christ.
Gal. 6. 1, restore in the spirit of *m.*
1 Tim. 6. 11, follow after *m.*
2 Tim. 2. 25, in *m.* instructing.
Tit. 3. 2, showing *m.* to all men.
1 Pet. 3. 15, give reason of hope in you with *m.*
See Zeph. 2. 3; Gal. 5. 23; Eph. 4. 2.
MEET. Prov. 11. 24, withholdeth more than is *m.*
Mat. 15. 26, not *m.* to take children's bread.
25. 1, 6, to *m.* the bridegroom.
1 Cor. 15. 9, not *m.* to be called an apostle.
1 Thess. 4. 17, to *m.* the Lord in the air.
See Prov. 22. 2; Amos 4. 12; Mat. 8. 34.
MELODY. Isa. 23. 16; 51. 3; Amos 5. 23; Eph. 5. 19.
MELT. Ps. 46. 6, the earth *m.*
97. 5, the hills *m.*
107. 26, their soul *m.*
147. 18, he sendeth his word, and *m.* them.
Isa. 13. 7, every man's heart shall *m.*
64. 2, as when the *m.* fire burneth.
See Ex. 15. 15; Josh. 14. 8; Jer. 9. 7.
MEMBER. Ps. 139. 16, all my *m.* were written.
Rom. 6. 13, 19, neither yield your *m.*
12. 4, as we have many *m.*
1 Cor. 6. 15, bodies *m.* of Christ.
Jas. 3. 5, the tongue is a little *m.*
4. 1, lusts which war in your *m.*
See Job 17. 7; Mat. 5. 29; Eph. 4. 25; 5. 30.
MEMORY. Ps. 109. 15; 145. 7; Prov. 10. 7; Eccl. 9. 5.
MEN. 2 Chron. 6. 18, will God dwell with *m.*?
1 Sam. 4. 9; 1 Cor. 16. 13, quit yourselves like *m.*
Ps. 9. 20, know themselves to be but *m.*
82. 7, but ye shall die like *m.*
Eccl. 12. 3, strong *m.* shall bow themselves.
Isa. 31. 3, the Egyptians are *m.*, and not God.
46. 8, show yourselves *m.*
Gal. 1. 10, do I now persuade *m.*?
1 Thess. 2. 4, not as pleasing *m.*, but God.
See Ps. 116. 11; 1 Tim. 2. 4; 1 Pet. 2. 17.
MEND. 2 Chron. 24. 12; 34. 10; Mat. 4. 21; Mk. 1. 19.
MENTION. Gen. 40. 14, make *m.* of me to Pharaoh.
Ps. 71. 16, I will make *m.* of thy righteousness.
Isa. 12. 4, make *m.* that his name is exalted.
63. 7, I will *m.* the lovingkindnesses of the Lord.
Rom. 1. 9; Eph. 1. 16; 1 Thess. 1. 2, *m.* of you in my prayers.
See Isa. 62. 6; Ezek. 18. 22; 33. 16.
MERCHANDISE. Prov. 3. 14, *m.* of it better than *m.* of silver.
Isa. 23. 18, *m.* shall be holiness to the Lord.
Mat. 22. 5, one to his farm, another to his *m.*
John 2. 16, my father's house an house of *m.*
2 Pet. 2. 3, make *m.* of you.
See Deut. 21. 14; 24. 7; Ezek. 26. 12; Rev. 18. 11.
MERCHANT. Gen. 23. 16, current money with the *m.*
Isa. 23. 8, whose *m.* are princes.
47. 15, even thy *m.* shall wander.
Rev. 18. 3, 11, the *m.* of the earth.
23, thy *m.* were great men of the earth.
See Prov. 31. 24; Isa. 23. 11; Mat. 13. 45.
MERCIFUL. Ps. 37. 26, ever *m.*, and lendeth.
67. 1, God be *m.* to us, and bless us.
Prov. 11. 17, the *m.* doeth good to his own soul.
Isa. 57. 1, *m.* men are taken away.

Jer. 3. 12, return, for I am *m.*
Mat. 5. 7, blessed are the *m.*
Lu. 6. 36, be ye *m.*, as your Father is *m.*
18. 13, God be *m.* to me a sinner.
Heb. 2. 17, a *m.* High Priest.
See Ex. 34. 6; 2 Sam. 22. 26; 1 Kings 20. 31.
MERCY. Gen. 32. 10, not worthy the least of the *m.*
Ex. 33. 19, will show *m.* on whom I will show *m.*
34. 7; Dan. 9. 4, keeping *m.* for thousands.
Num. 14. 18; Ps. 103. 11; 145. 8, longsuffering and of great *m.*
1 Chron. 16. 34, 41; 2 Chron. 5. 13; 7. 3, 6; Ezra 3. 11; Ps. 106. 1; 107. 1; 118. 1; 136. 1; Jer. 33. 11, his *m.* endureth for ever.
Ps. 23. 6, surely goodness and *m.* shall follow.
25. 7, according to thy *m.* remember me.
33. 22, let thy *m.* be upon us.
52. 8, I trust in the *m.* of God.
59. 10, the God of my *m.*
66. 20, not turned his *m.* from me.
77. 8, is his *m.* clean gone for ever?
85. 10, *m.* and truth are met together.
89. 2, *m.* shall be built up for ever.
90. 14, satisfy us early with thy *m.*
101. 1, I will sing of *m.*
108. 4, thy *m.* is great above the heavens.
115. 1, for thy *m.*, and for thy truth's sake.
119. 64, the earth is full of thy *m.*
130. 7, with the Lord there is *m.*
Prov. 3. 3, let not *m.* and truth forsake thee.
14. 21, 31, he that hath *m.* on the poor.
16. 6; 20. 28, *m.* and truth.
Isa. 54. 7, with great *m.* will I gather thee.
Jer. 6. 23, they are cruel, and have no *m.*
Lam. 3. 22, it is of the Lord's *m.*
Hos. 4. 1, because there is no *m.* in the land.
6. 6; Mat. 9. 13, I desired *m.*, and not sacrifice.
10. 12, sow in righteousness, reap in *m.*
14. 3, in thee the fatherless find *m.*
Mic. 6. 8, but to do justly, and love *m.*
7. 18, he delighteth in *m.*
Hab. 3. 2, in wrath remember *m.*
Mat. 5. 7, the merciful shall obtain *m.*
9. 27; 15. 22; 20. 30; Mk. 10. 47, 48; 18. 38, 39, thou son of David have *m.* on me.
Lu. 10. 37, he that showed *m.*
Rom. 9. 15, 18, *m.* on whom I will have *m.*
16, of God that showeth *m.*
12. 1, beseech you by the *m.* of God.
8, he that showeth *m.*, with cheerfulness.
2 Cor. 1. 3, the Father of *m.*
Eph. 2. 4, God, who is rich in *m.*
1 Tim. 1. 13, 16, I obtained *m.*, because.
2 Tim. 1. 18, that he may find *m.* in that day.
Heb. 4. 16, obtain *m.*, and find grace.
Jas. 2. 13, without *m.*, that showed no *m.*
1 Pet. 1. 3, according to his abundant *m.*
See Prov. 12. 10; Dan. 4. 27; 1 Tim. 1. 2.
MERRY. Gen. 43. 34, were *m.* with him.
Judg. 16. 25, their hearts were *m.*
Prov. 15. 13, *m.* heart maketh cheerful countenance.
15, *m.* heart hath a continual feast.
17. 22, *m.* heart doeth good like a medicine.
Eccl. 8. 15, nothing better than to eat and be *m.*
9. 7, drink thy wine with a *m.* heart.
10. 19, wine maketh *m.*
Jas. 5. 13, is any *m.*?
See Lu. 12. 19; 15. 23; Rev. 11. 10.
MESSENGER. Job 33. 23; Prov. 25. 13; Isa. 42. 19.
METE. Isa. 40. 12; Mat. 7. 2; Mk. 4. 24; Lu. 6. 38.
MIDDLE. Ezek. 1. 16; Eph. 2. 14.
MIDST. Ps. 102. 24, in the *m.* of my days.
Prov. 23. 34, lieth down in *m.* of the sea.
Dan. 9. 27, in the *m.* of the week.
Mat. 18. 2; Mk. 9. 36, a little child in the *m.*
20, there am I in the *m.*
Lu. 24. 36; John 20. 19, Jesus himself in the *m.*
Phil. 2. 15, in the *m.* of a crooked nation.
Rev. 2. 7, in the *m.* of the Paradise of God.
4. 6; 5. 6; 7. 17, in the *m.* of the throne.
See Gen. 2. 9; Isa. 12. 6; Hos. 11. 9.
MIGHT. Deut. 6. 5, love God with all thy *m.*
8. 17, the *m.* of mine hand hath gotten.
2 Sam. 6. 14, David danced with all his *m.*
Eccl. 9. 10, do it with thy *m.*
Isa. 40. 29, to them that have no *m.*
Jer. 9. 23, mighty man glory in his *m.*
51. 30, their *m.* hath failed.
Zech. 4. 6, not by *m.*, nor by power.
Eph. 3. 16; Col. 1. 11, strengthened with *m.*
See Eph. 6. 10; 2 Pet. 2. 11; Rev. 7. 12.
MIGHTILY. Jon. 3. 8; Acts 18. 28; 19. 20; Col. 1. 29.
MIGHTY. Gen. 10. 9, he was a *m.* hunter.
Judg. 5. 23, to the help of the Lord against the *m.*
2 Sam. 1. 19, 25, how are the *m.* fallen!
23. 8, these be the names of the *m.* men whom David had.
1 Chron. 11. 10, the chief of the *m.* men.
Job 9. 4, wise in heart and *m.* in strength.
Ps. 24. 8, strong and *m.*, *m.* in battle.
89. 13, thou hast a *m.* arm.
19, help upon one that is *m.*
93. 4, the *m.* waves of the sea.
Isa. 1. 24; 30. 29; 49. 26; 60. 16, the *m.* One of Israel.
5. 15, *m.* to drink wine.
63. 1, *m.* to save.
Jer. 32. 19, *m.* in work.
Amos 2. 14, neither shall *m.* deliver himself.
Mat. 11. 20; 13. 54; 14. 2; Mk. 6. 2, *m.* works.
Lu. 9. 43, the *m.* power of God.
24. 19, prophet *m.* in deed and word.
Acts 18. 24, *m.* in the scriptures.
1 Cor. 1. 26, not many *m.*
2 Cor. 10. 4, weapons *m.* through God.
Eph. 1. 19, the working of his *m.* power.
See Num. 14. 12; Eccl. 6. 10; Mat. 3. 11.
MILK. Gen. 49. 12, teeth white with *m.*
Prov. 30. 33, churning of *m.*
Isa. 55. 1, buy wine and *m.*
Lam. 4. 7, Nazarites were whiter than *m.*
Ezek. 25. 4, shall eat thy fruit and drink thy *m.*
Heb. 5. 12, 13, such as have need of *m.*
1 Pet. 2. 2, the sincere *m.* of the word.
See Judg. 4. 19; 5. 25; Job 21. 24; Joel 3. 18.
MIND (*n.*). Neh. 4. 6, the people had a *m.* to work.
Job 23. 13, he is in one *m.*, who can turn him?
34. 33, should it be according to thy *m.*?
Ps. 31. 12, as a dead man out of *m.*
Prov. 29. 11, a fool uttereth all his *m.*
Isa. 26. 3, whose *m.* is stayed on thee.
Mk. 5. 15; Lu. 8. 35, sitting, in his right *m.*
Lu. 12. 29, neither be of doubtful *m.*
Rom. 8. 7, the carnal *m.* is enmity against God.
12. 16, be of the same *m.*
14. 5, fully persuaded in his own *m.*
2 Cor. 8. 12, if there be first a willing *m.*
13. 11; Phil. 1. 27; 2. 2, be of one *m.*
Phil. 2. 3, in lowliness of *m.*
5, let this *m.* be in you.
4. 7, peace of God keep your *m.*
1 Tim. 6. 5; 2 Tim. 3. 8, men of corrupt *m.*
2 Tim. 1. 7, spirit of sound *m.*
Tit. 3. 1, put them in *m.* to be subject.
1 Pet. 1. 13, the loins of your *m.*
2 Pet. 3. 1, stir up your pure *m.*
See Rom. 8. 6; 11. 20; 1 Thess. 5. 14; Jas. 1. 8.
MIND (*v.*). Rom. 8. 5; 12. 16; Phil. 3. 16, 19.
MINDFUL. Ps. 8. 4; 111. 5; Isa. 17. 10; 2 Pet. 3. 2.
MINGLE. Lev. 19. 19; Isa. 5. 22; Mat. 27. 34; Lu. 13. 1.
MINISTER (*n.*). Ps. 103. 21, ye *m.* of his.
104. 4; Heb. 1. 7, his *m.* a flame of fire.
Isa. 61. 6, men shall call you the *m.* of God.
Joel 1. 9, the Lord's *m.* mourn.
Mat. 20. 26; Mk. 10. 43, let him be your *m.*
Rom. 13. 4, he is the *m.* of God to thee.
2 Cor. 3. 6, able *m.* of new testament.
Gal. 2. 17, is Christ the *m.* of sin?
Eph. 3. 7; Col. 1. 23, whereof I was made a *m.*

Eph. 6. 21; Col. 1. 7; 4. 7, a faithful *m.*
1 Tim. 4. 6, a good *m.*
See 2 Cor. 6. 4; 11. 23; 1 Thess. 3. 2.
MINISTER (*v.*). 1 Sam. 2. 11, the child did *m.* unto the Lord.
1 Chron. 15. 2, chosen to *m.* for ever.
Dan. 7. 10, thousand thousands *m.* to him.
Mat. 4. 11; Mk. 1. 13, angels *m.* to him.
20. 28; Mk. 10. 45, not to be *m.* unto, but to *m.*
Lu. 8. 3, which *m.* of their substance.
Acts 20. 34, these hands have *m.*
See 2 Cor. 9. 10; Heb. 1. 14; 2 Pet. 1. 11.
MINISTRATION. Lu. 1. 23; Acts 6. 1; 2 Cor. 3. 7; 9. 13.
MINISTRY. Acts 6. 4, give ourselves to the *m.*
2 Cor. 4. 1, seeing we have this *m.*
5. 18, the *m.* of reconciliation.
6. 3, that the *m.* be not blamed.
Eph. 4. 12, for the work of the *m.*
Col. 4. 17, take heed to the *m.*
2 Tim. 4. 5, make full proof of thy *m.*
See Acts 1. 17; 12. 25; Rom. 12. 7; Heb. 8. 6.
MINSTREL. 2 Kings 3. 15; Mat. 9. 23.
MIRACLE. Judg. 6. 13, where be all his *m.*?
Mk. 9. 39, no man which shall do a *m.* in my name.
Lu. 23. 8, hoped to have seen some *m.*
John 2. 11, beginning of *m.*
4. 54, this is the second *m.*
10. 41, said, John did no *m.*
Acts 2. 22, approved of God by *m.* and signs.
1 Cor. 12. 10, to another, the working of *m.*
See Gal. 3. 5; Heb. 2. 4; Rev. 13. 14; 16. 14; 19. 20.
MIRTH. Ps. 137. 3; Prov. 14. 13; Eccl. 2. 1; 7. 4; 8. 15.
MIRY. Ps. 40. 2; Ezek. 47. 11; Dan. 2. 41.
MISCHIEF. Job 15. 35; Ps. 7. 14; Isa. 59. 4, they conceive *m.*
Ps. 28. 3, *m.* is in their hearts.
94. 20, frameth *m.* by a law.
Prov. 10. 23, it is as sport to a fool to do *m.*
11. 27, he that seeketh *m.*
24. 2, lips talk of *m.*
Ezek. 7. 26, *m.* shall come upon *m.*
Acts 13. 10, O full of all subtilty and all *m.*
See Prov. 24. 8; Eccl. 10. 13; Mic. 7. 3.
MISERABLE. Job 16. 2; Mat. 21. 41; 1 Cor. 15. 19; Rev. 3. 17.
MISERY. Prov. 31. 7, drink, and remember his *m.* no more.
Eccl. 8. 6, the *m.* of man is great upon him.
Lam. 1. 7, remembered in days of her *m.*
Jas. 5. 1, howl for your *m.* that shall come.
See Judg. 10. 16; Job 3. 20; 11. 16; Rom. 3. 16.
MIXED. Prov. 23. 30, they seek *m.* wine.
Isa. 1. 22, thy wine *m.* with water.
Heb. 4. 2, not being *m.* with faith.
See Ex. 12. 38; Num. 11. 4; Neh. 13. 3.
MOCK. Gen. 19. 14, he seemed as one that *m.*
Num. 22. 29; Judg. 16. 10, 13, 15, thou hast *m.* me.
1 Kings 18. 27, at noon Elijah *m.* them.
2 Chron. 36. 16, they *m.* the messengers of God.
Prov. 1. 26, I will *m.* when your fear cometh.
17. 5, whoso *m.* the poor.
30. 17, the eye that *m.* at his father.
Gal. 6. 7, God is not *m.*
See 2 Kings 2. 23; Mat. 2. 16; 27. 29; Mk. 15. 20.
MOCKER. Ps. 35. 16; Prov. 20. 1; Isa. 28. 22; Jude 18.
MODERATION. Phil. 4. 5.
MOISTURE. Ps. 32. 4; Lu. 8. 6.
MOLLIFIED. Isa. 1. 16.
MOMENT. Num. 16. 21, 45, consume them in a *m.*
Job 7. 18, try him every *m.*
21. 13, and in a *m.* they go down.
Ps. 30. 5, his anger endureth but a *m.*
Isa. 26. 20, hide thyself as it were a *m.*
27. 3, I will water it every *m.*
54. 7, for a small *m.* have I forsaken thee.
1 Cor. 15. 51, 52, we shall all be changed in a *m.*
2 Cor. 4. 17, affliction, which is but for a *m.*
See Ex. 33. 5; Ezek. 26. 16; 32. 10; Lu. 4. 5.
MONEY. 2 Kings 5. 26, is it a time to receive *m.*?
Eccl. 7. 12, *m.* is a defence.
10. 19, *m.* answereth all things.
Isa. 52. 3, redeemed without *m.*
55. 1, he that hath no *m.*
2, wherefore do ye spend *m.*
Mat. 17. 24; 22. 19, the tribute *m.*
25. 18, hid his lord's *m.*
Acts 8. 20, thy *m.* perish with thee.
1 Tim. 6. 10, the love of *m.*
See Gen. 23. 9; Mk. 6. 8; Lu. 9. 3; Acts 4. 37.
MORROW. Prov. 27. 1, boast not thyself of to-*m.*
Isa. 22. 13; 1 Cor. 15. 32, for to-*m.* we die.
56. 12, to-*m.* shall be as this day.
Mat. 6. 34, take no thought for the *m.*
Jas. 4. 14, ye know not what shall be on the *m.*
See Josh. 5. 12; 2 Kings 7. 1; Prov. 3. 28.
MORSEL. Job 31. 17; Ps. 147. 17; Prov. 17. 1; Heb. 12. 16.
MORTAL. Job 4. 17, shall *m.* man be more just?
Rom. 6. 12; 8. 11, in your *m.* body.
1 Cor. 15. 53, 54, this *m.* must put on immortality.
See Deut. 19. 11; 2 Cor. 4. 11; 5. 4.
MORTAR. Prov. 27. 22; Ezek. 13. 11, 22, 28.
MORTIFY. Rom. 8. 13; Col. 3. 5.
MOTE. Mat. 7. 3; Lu. 6. 41.
MOTH. Job 27. 18, he buildeth his house as a *m.*
Ps. 39. 11, consume away like a *m.*
Isa. 50. 9, the *m.* shall eat them up.
Hos. 5. 12, unto Ephraim as a *m.*
Mat. 6. 19, where *m.* and rust doth corrupt.
MOTHER. Judg. 5. 7; 2 Sam. 20. 19, a *m.* in Israel.
1 Kings 22. 52, Ahaziah walked in the way of his *m.*
2 Chron. 22. 3, his *m.* was his counsellor.
Job 17. 14, to the worm, thou art my *m.*
Ps. 113. 9, a joyful *m.* of children.
Isa. 66. 13, as one whom his *m.* comforteth.
Ezek. 16. 44, as is the *m.*, so is her daughter.
Mat. 12. 48; Mk. 3. 33, who is my *m.*?
John 2. 1; Acts 1. 14, the *m.* of Jesus.
See Gen. 3. 20; 17. 16; Gal. 4. 26; 1 Tim. 1. 9; 5. 2.
MOULDY. Josh 9. 5, 12.
MOUNT. Ex. 18. 5, the *m.* of God.
Ps. 107. 26, they *m.* up to heaven.
Isa. 40. 31, *m.* with wings, as eagles.
See Job 20. 6; 39. 27; Isa. 27. 13.
MOURN. Gen. 37. 35, down to the grave *m.*
Prov. 5. 11, and thou *m.* at the last.
Isa. 61. 2, to comfort all that *m.*
Jer. 31. 13, I will turn their *m.* into joy.
Mat. 5. 4, blessed are they that *m.*
24. 30, then shall all the tribes of the earth *m.*
Lu. 6. 25, woe to you that laugh, for ye shall *m.*
See Neh. 8. 9; Zech. 7. 5; Jas. 4. 9.
MOURNER. 2 Sam. 14. 2; Eccl. 12. 5; Hos. 9. 4.
MOURNFULLY. Mal. 3. 14.
MOUTH. Job 9. 20, mine own *m.* shall condemn me.
40. 4, I will lay my hand on my *m.*
Ps. 8. 2; Mat. 21. 16, out of the *m.* of babes.
39. 1, I will keep my *m.* with a bridle.
49. 3, my *m.* shall speak of wisdom.
55. 21, words of his *m.* smoother than butter.
81. 10, open thy *m.* wide.
Prov. 10. 14; 14. 3; 15. 2, the *m.* of the foolish.
13. 2, good by the fruit of his *m.*
3; 21. 23, he that keepeth his *m.*
Eccl. 6. 7, all the labour of a man is for his *m.*
Isa. 29. 13; Mat. 15. 8, this people draw near with *m.*
Ezek. 33. 31, with their *m.* they show much love.
Mal. 2. 6, the law of truth was in his *m.*
Mat. 12. 34; Lu. 6. 45, the *m.* speaketh.
13. 35, I will open my *m.* in parables.
Lu. 21. 15, I will give you a *m.* and wisdom.
Rom. 10. 10, with the *m.* confession is made.
Tit. 1. 11, whose *m.* must be stopped.
Jas. 3. 10, out of the same *m.* proceedeth.

See Lam. 3. 29; John 19. 29; 1 Pet. 2. 22.
MOVE. Ps. 10. 6; 16. 8; 30. 6; 62. 2, I shall not be *m.*
Mat. 21. 10; Acts 21. 30, all the city was *m.*
John 5. 3, waiting for the *m.* of the water.
Acts 17. 28, in him we live, and *m.*
20. 24, none of these things *m.* me.
See Prov. 23. 31; Isa. 7. 2; 2 Pet. 1. 21.
MUCH. Ex. 16. 18; 2 Cor. 8. 15, he that gathered *m.*
Num. 16. 3, ye take too *m.* upon you.
Lu. 7. 47, for she loved *m.*
12. 48, to whom *m.* is given.
16. 10, faithful in *m.*
See Prov. 25. 16; Eccl. 5. 12; Jer. 2. 22.
MULTIPLY. Isa. 9. 3, thou hast *m.* the nation, and not increased the joy.
Jer. 3. 16, when ye be *m.* they shall say.
Dan. 4. 1; 6. 25; 1 Pet. 1. 2; 2 Pet. 1. 2; Jude 2, peace be *m.*
Nah. 3. 16, thou hast *m.* thy merchants.
See Acts 6. 1; 7. 17; 9. 31; 12. 24.
MULTITUDE. Ex. 23. 2, a *m.* to do evil.
Job 32. 7, *m.* of years should teach wisdom.
Ps. 5. 7; 51. 1; 69. 13; 106. 7, in the *m.* of thy mercy.
33. 16, no king saved by the *m.* of an host.
94. 19, in the *m.* of my thoughts.
Prov. 10. 19, in *m.* of words there wanteth not sin.
11. 14; 15. 22; 24. 6, in the *m.* of counsellors.
Eccl. 5. 3, through the *m.* of business.
Jas. 5. 20; 1 Pet. 4. 8, hide a *m.* of sins.
See Deut. 1. 10; Josh. 11. 4; Lu. 2. 13.
MURMURINGS. Ex. 16. 7; Num. 14. 27; Phil. 2. 14.
MUSE. Ps. 39. 3; 143. 5; Lu. 3. 15.
MUTTER. Isa. 8. 19; 59. 3.
MUTUAL. Rom. 1. 12.
MYSTERY. Mat. 13. 11; 1 Cor. 2. 7; 15. 51; Eph. 5. 32.

N

NAIL. Ezra 9. 8, give us a *n.* in his holy place.
Isa. 22. 23, fasten as a *n.* in sure place.
John 20. 25, put finger into print of *n.*
Col. 2. 14, *n.* it to his cross.
See Judg. 4. 21; Eccl. 12. 11; Dan. 4. 33.
NAKED. Ex. 32. 25, made *n.* to their shame.
Job 1. 21, *n.* came I out, and *n.* shall I return.
Mat. 25. 36, *n.*, and ye clothed me.
1 Cor. 4. 11, to this present hour we are *n.*
2 Cor. 5. 3, we shall not be found *n.*
Heb. 4. 13, all things are *n.* to eyes of him.
See John 21. 7; Jas. 2. 15; Rev. 3. 17; 16. 15.
NAKEDNESS. Rom. 8. 35; 2 Cor. 11. 27; Rev. 3. 18.
NAME (*n.*). Gen. 32. 29; Judg. 13. 18, wherefore dost thou ask after my *n.*?
Ex. 3. 15, this is my *n.* for ever.
23. 21, my *n.* is in him.
Josh. 7. 9, what wilt thou do to thy great *n.*?
2 Chron. 14. 11, in thy *n.* we go.
Neh. 9. 10, so didst thou get thee a *n.*
Job 18. 17, he shall have no *n.* in the street.
Ps. 20. 1, the *n.* of God defend thee.
5, in the *n.* of God set up banners.
22. 22; Heb. 2. 12, I will declare thy *n.*
48. 10, according to thy *n.* so is thy praise.
69. 36, they that love his *n.*
111. 9, holy and reverend is his *n.*
115. 1, unto thy *n.* give glory.
138. 2, thy word above all thy *n.*
Prov. 10. 7, the *n.* of the wicked shall rot.
18. 10, the *n.* of the Lord a strong tower.
22. 1; Eccl. 7. 1, good *n.* rather to be chosen.
Cant. 1. 3, thy *n.* is as ointment poured forth.
Isa. 42. 8, I am the Lord, that is my *n.*
55. 13, it shall be to the Lord for a *n.*
56. 5; 63. 12, an everlasting *n.*
57. 15, whose *n.* is Holy.
62. 2, called by a new *n.*
64. 7, there is none that calleth on thy *n.*
Jer. 10. 6, thou art great, and thy *n.* is great.
14. 14; 23. 25; 27. 15, prophesy lies in my *n.*
44. 26, sworn by my great *n.*
Zech. 10. 12, walk up and down in his *n.*
14. 9, one Lord, and his *n.* one.
Mal. 1. 6, wherein have we despised thy *n.*?
4. 2, to you that fear my *n.*
Mat. 6. 9; Lu. 11. 2, hallowed be thy *n.*
10. 22; 19. 29; Mk. 13. 13; Lu. 21. 12; John 15. 21; Acts 9. 16, for my *n.* sake.
12. 21, in his *n.* shall the Gentiles trust.
18. 5; Mk. 9. 37; Lu. 9. 48, receive in my *n.*
20, gathered together in my *n.*
24. 5; Mk. 13. 6; Lu. 21. 8, many shall come in my *n.*
Mk. 5. 9; Lu. 8. 30, what is thy *n.*?
9. 39, do a miracle in my *n.*
Lu. 10. 20, *n.* written in heaven.
John 5. 43, if another shall come in his own *n.*
14. 13; 15. 16; 16. 23, 24, 26, whatsoever ye ask in my *n.*
Acts 3. 16. his *n.* through faith in his *n.*
4. 12, none other *n.* under heaven.
5. 28, that ye should not teach in this *n.*
41, worthy to suffer for his *n.*
Eph. 1. 21, far above every *n.*
Phil. 2. 9, 10, a *n.* above every *n.*
4. 3, whose *n.* are in the book of life.
Col. 3. 17, do all in the *n.* of the Lord Jesus.
Heb. 1. 4, obtained a more excellent *n.*
Jas. 2. 7, that worthy *n.*
Rev. 2. 13, holdest fast my *n.*
17, a *n.* written, which no man knoweth.
3. 1, thou hast a *n.* that thou livest.
4, a few *n.* in Sardis.
13. 1, the *n.* of blasphemy.
14. 1; 22. 4, Father's *n.* in their foreheads.
See Gen. 2. 20; Ex. 28. 9; Isa. 45. 3; John 10. 3.
NAME (*v.*). Eccl. 6. 10, that which hath been is *n.* already.
Isa. 61. 6, ye shall be *n.* Priests of the Lord.
Rom. 15. 20, not where Christ was *n.*
2 Tim. 2. 19, every one that *n.* the name of Christ.
See 1 Sam. 16. 3; Isa. 62. 2; Lu. 2. 21; 6. 13.
NARROW. Isa. 28. 20; 49. 19; Mat. 7. 14.
NATION. Gen. 10. 32, by these were the *n.* divided.
20. 4, wilt thou slay a righteous *n.*?
Num. 14. 12; Deut. 9. 14, I will make thee a greater *n.*
2 Sam. 7. 23; 1 Chron. 17. 21, what *n.* like thy people?
Ps. 33. 12, blessed is the *n.* whose God is the Lord.
147. 20, he hath not dealt so with any *n.*
Prov. 14. 34, righteousness exalteth a *n.*
Isa. 2. 4; Mic. 4. 3, *n.* shall not lift sword against *n.*
18. 2, a. *n.* scattered and peeled.
26. 2, that the righteous *n.* may enter in.
34. 1, come near, ye *n.*, to hear.
52. 15, so shall he sprinkle many *n.*
Jer. 10. 7, O King of *n.*
Zech. 2. 11, many *n.* shall be joined to the Lord.
8. 22, strong *n.* shall seek the Lord.
Mat. 24. 7; Mk. 13. 8; Lu. 21. 10, *n.* against *n.*
Lu. 7. 5, he loveth our *n.*
21. 25, distress of *n.*
John 11. 50, that the whole *n.* perish not.
Acts 2. 5, devout men of every *n.*
10. 35, in every *n.* he that feareth.
Phil. 2. 15, crooked and perverse *n.*
Rev. 5. 9, redeemed out of every *n.*
See Deut. 4. 27; 15. 6; Jer. 2. 11; 4. 2; 31. 10.
NATIVITY. Gen. 11. 28; Jer. 46. 16; Ezek. 21. 30; 23. 15.
NATURAL. Deut. 34. 7, nor his *n.* force abated.
Rom. 1. 31; 2 Tim. 3. 3, without *n.* affection.
1 Cor. 2. 14, the *n.* man receiveth not.
See 1 Cor. 15. 44; Phil. 2. 20; Jas. 1. 23.
NATURE. 1 Cor. 11. 14, doth not even *n.* itself teach?

Eph. 2. 3, by *n.* children of wrath.
Heb. 2. 16, the *n.* of angels.
2 Pet. 1. 4, partakers of the divine *n.*
See Rom. 1. 26; 2. 14, 27; Gal. 2. 15; 4. 8.

NAUGHT. Prov. 20. 14, it is *n.*, saith the buyer.
Isa. 49. 4, spent strength for *n.*
52. 3, ye have sold yourselves for *n.*
Mal. 1. 10, shut the doors for *n.*
Acts 5. 38, if of men, it will come to *n.*
See Deut. 15. 9; Job 1. 9; Rom. 14. 10; 1 Cor. 1. 28.

NAUGHTINESS. 1 Sam. 17. 28; Prov. 11. 6; Jas. 1. 21.

NAUGHTY. Prov. 6. 12; 17. 4; Jer. 24. 2.

NAY. Mat. 5. 37; 2 Cor. 1. 17, 18, 19; Jas. 5. 12.

NEAR. Judg. 20. 34, knew not evil was *n.*
Ps. 22. 11, trouble is *n.*
148. 14, a people *n.* to him.
Prov. 27. 10, better a neighbour that is *n.*
Isa. 50. 8, he is *n.* that justifieth.
55. 6, call upon the Lord while he is *n.*
Obad. 15; Zeph. 1. 14, the day of the Lord is *n.*
Mat. 24. 33, it is *n.*, even at the doors.
Mk. 13. 28, ye know that summer is *n.*
See Ezek. 11. 3; 22. 5; Rom. 13. 11.

NECESSARY. Job 23. 12; Acts 15. 28; 28. 10; Tit. 3. 14.

NECESSITIES. 2 Cor. 6. 4, as the ministers of God, in *n.*

NECESSITY. Rom. 12. 13, distributing to the *n.* of saints.
1 Cor. 9. 16, *n.* is laid upon me.
2 Cor. 9. 7; Philem. 14, give, not grudgingly, or of *n.*
See Acts 20. 34; 2 Cor. 12. 10; Phil. 4. 16.

NECK. Prov. 3. 3; 6. 21, bind them about thy *n.*
Mat. 18. 6; Mk. 9. 42; Lu. 17. 2, millstone about his *n.*
Lu. 15. 20; Acts 20. 37, fell on his *n.*
Acts 15. 10, yoke on the *n.* of disciples.
See Neh. 9. 29; Isa. 3. 16; Lam. 5. 5; Rom. 16. 4.

NEED. 2 Chron. 20. 17, ye shall not *n.* to fight.
Prov. 31. 11, he shall have no *n.* of spoil.
Mat. 6. 8; Lu. 12. 30, what things ye have *n.* of.
9. 12; Mk. 2. 17; Lu. 5. 31, *n.* not a physician.
14. 16, they *n.* not depart.
21. 3; Mk. 11. 3; Lu. 19. 31, 34, the Lord hath *n.* of them.
Lu. 11. 8, as many as he *n.*
Acts 2. 45; 4. 35, as every man had *n.*
1 Cor. 12. 21, cannot say, I have no *n.* of thee.
Phil. 4. 12, to abound and to suffer *n.*
19, God shall supply all your *n.*
2 Tim. 2. 15, that *n.* not to be ashamed.
Heb. 4. 16, grace to help in time of *n.*
5. 1, ye have *n.* that one teach you.
1 John 3. 17, seeth his brother have *n.*
Rev. 3. 17, rich, and have *n.* of nothing.
21. 23; 22. 5, city had no *n.* of the sun.
See Deut. 15. 8; Lu. 9. 11; John 2. 25; Acts 17. 25.

NEEDFUL. Lu. 10. 42; Phil. 1. 24; Jas. 2. 16.

NEEDY. Deut. 15. 11, thou shalt open thine hand to thy *n.*
Job 24. 4, they turn the *n.* out of the way.
Ps. 9. 18, the *n.* shall not alway be forgotten.
40. 17; 70. 5; 86. 1; 109. 22, I am poor and *n.*
74. 21, let the poor and *n.* praise thy name.
Prov. 31. 9, plead the cause of the poor and *n.*
Isa. 41. 17, when the *n.* seek water.
See Ezek. 16. 49; 18. 12; 22. 29; Amos 8. 4, 6.

NEGLECT. Mat. 18. 17; Acts 6. 1; 1 Tim. 4. 14; Heb. 2. 3.

NEGLIGENT. 2 Chron. 29. 11; 2 Pet. 1. 12.

NEIGHBOUR. Prov. 3. 28, say not to thy *n.*, go and come again.
14. 20, the poor is hated even of his *n.*
21. 10, his *n.* findeth no favour.
Eccl. 4. 4, envied of his *n.*
Jer. 22. 13, that useth his *n.* service without wages.
Hab. 2. 15, that giveth his *n.* drink.
Zech. 8. 16; Eph. 4. 25, speak every man truth to his *n.*
Lu. 10. 29, who is my *n.*?
14. 12, call not thy rich *n.*
See Ex. 20. 16; Lev. 19. 13; Mat. 5. 43; Rom. 13. 10.

NEST. Num. 24. 21, thou puttest thy *n.* in a rock.
Deut. 32. 11, as an eagle stirreth up her *n.*
Job 29. 18, I shall die in my *n.*
Ps. 84. 3, the swallow hath found a *n.*
Mat. 8. 20; Lu. 9. 58, birds of the air have *n.*
See Prov. 27. 8; Isa. 16. 2; Jer. 49. 16; Obad. 4; Hab. 2. 9.

NET. Ps. 141. 10, let the wicked fall into their own *n.*
Prov. 1. 17, in vain the *n.* is spread.
Eccl. 9. 12, as fishes taken in an evil *n.*
Hab. 1. 16, they sacrifice unto their *n.*
Mat. 13. 47, kingdom of heaven like a *n.*
Mk. 1. 18, they forsook their *n.*
Lu. 5. 5, at thy word I will let down the *n.*
See Mat. 4. 21; Mk. 1. 16; John 21. 6.

NETHER. Deut. 24. 6; Job 41. 24.

NEVER. Lev. 6. 13, the fire shall *n.* go out.
Job 3. 16, as infants which *n.* saw light.
Ps. 10. 11, he will *n.* see it.
15. 5; 30. 6, shall *n.* be moved.
Prov. 27. 20; 30. 15, *n.* satisfied.
Isa. 56. 11, which can *n.* have enough.
Mat. 7. 23, I *n.* knew you.
9. 33, it was *n.* so seen in Israel.
26. 33, yet will I *n.* be offended.
Mk. 2. 12, we *n.* saw it on this fashion.
3. 29, hath *n.* forgiveness.
14. 21, if he had *n.* been born.
John 4. 14; 6. 35, shall *n.* thirst.
7. 46, *n.* man spake like this man.
8. 51; 10. 28; 11. 26, shall *n.* see death.
1 Cor. 13. 8, charity *n.* faileth.
Heb. 13. 5, I will *n.* leave thee.
2 Pet. 1. 10, ye shall *n.* fall.
See Judg. 2. 1; Ps. 58. 5; Jer. 33. 17; Dan. 2. 44.

NEW. Num. 16. 30, if the Lord make a *n.* thing.
Ps. 33. 3; 40. 3; 96. 1; 98. 1; 144. 9; 149. 1; Isa. 42. 10; Rev. 5. 9; 14. 3, a *n.* song.
Eccl. 1. 9, no *n.* thing under the sun.
Isa. 65. 17; 66. 22; Rev. 21. 1, *n.* heavens and *n.* earth.
Lam. 3. 23, *n.* every morning.
Mat. 9. 16; Mk. 2. 21; Lu. 5. 36, *n.* cloth to old garment.
13. 52, things *n.* and old.
Mk. 1. 27; Acts 17. 19, what *n.* doctrine is this?
John 13. 34; 1 John 2. 7, 8, a *n.* commandment.
Acts 17. 21, to tell or hear some *n.* thing.
2 Cor. 5. 17; Gal. 6. 15, a *n.* creature.
Eph. 2. 15; 4. 24; Col. 3. 10, *n.* man.
Heb. 10. 20, *n.* and living way.
Rev. 2. 17; 3. 12, a *n.* name.
21. 5, I make all things *n.*
See Isa. 24. 7; 43. 19; 65. 8; Acts 2. 13.

NEWLY. Deut. 32. 17; Judg. 7. 19.

NEWNESS. Rom. 6. 4; 7. 6.

NEWS. Prov. 25. 25.

NIGH. Num. 24. 17, but not *n.*
Deut. 30. 14; Rom. 10. 8, the word is *n.* unto thee.
Ps. 34. 18, *n.* to them of broken heart.
145. 18, *n.* to all that call upon him.
Eph. 2. 13, made *n.* by the blood of Christ.
See Joel 2. 1; Lu. 21. 20; Heb. 6. 8.

NIGHT. Ex. 12. 42, a *n.* to be much observed.
Job 7. 4, when shall I arise, and the *n.* be gone?
35. 10; Ps. 77. 6, songs in the *n.*
Ps. 30. 5, weeping may endure for a *n.*
91. 5, the terror by *n.*
136. 9; Jer. 31. 35, moon and stars to rule by *n.*
139. 11, the *n.* shall be light about me.
Isa. 21. 4, the *n.* of my pleasure.
11, watchman, what of the *n.*?
Lu. 6. 12, he continued all *n.* in prayer.
John 9. 4, the *n.* cometh, when no man can work.

John 11. 10, walk in the *n.*, he stumbleth.
Rom. 13. 12, the *n.* is far spent.
1 Thess. 5. 2; 2 Pet. 3. 10, cometh as a thief in the *n.*
Rev. 21. 25; 22. 5, no *n.* there.
See Job 7. 3; Ps. 121. 6; Mat. 27. 64; John 3. 2.
NOBLE. Neh. 3. 5, the *n.* put not their neck.
Job 29. 10, the *n.* held their peace.
Jer. 2. 21, planted thee a *n.* vine.
14. 3, their *n.* sent their little ones to the waters.
Acts 17. 11, Bereans were more *n.*
1 Cor. 1. 26, not many *n.*
See Num. 21. 18; Ps. 149. 8; Eccl. 10. 17.
NOISE. Ezra 3. 13, not discern *n.* of joy.
Ps. 66. 1; 81. 1; 95. 1; 98. 4; 100. 1, joyful *n.*
Ezek. 1. 24; 43. 2, *n.* of great waters.
2 Pet. 3. 10, pass away with great *n.*
See Josh. 6. 27; Mat. 9. 23; Mk. 2. 1; Acts 2. 6.
NOISOME. Ps. 91. 3; Ezek. 14. 21; Rev. 16. 2.
NOTHING. Deut. 2. 7; Neh. 9. 21, thou hast lacked *n.*
2 Sam. 24. 24, neither offer of that which doth cost *n.*
2 Chron. 14. 11, it is *n.* with thee to help.
Neh. 8. 10, portions to them for whom *n.* is prepared.
Job 8. 9, but of yesterday, and know *n.*
Ps. 49. 17, he shall carry *n.* away.
119. 165, *n.* shall offend them.
Prov. 13. 4, the sluggard desireth, and hath *n.*
7, there is that maketh himself rich, yet hath *n.*
Lam. 1. 12, is it *n.* to you?
Mat. 17. 20; Lu. 1. 37, *n.* shall be impossible.
21. 19; Mk. 11. 13, *n.* but leaves.
Lu. 6. 35, hoping for *n.* again.
7. 42, they had *n.* to pay.
John 15. 5, without me ye can do *n.*
1 Cor. 4. 4, I know *n.* by myself.
2 Cor. 6. 10, as having *n.*
13. 8, we can do *n.* against the truth.
1 Tim. 4. 4, *n.* to be refused.
6. 7, brought *n.* into this world, can carry *n.* out.
See Phil. 4. 6; Jas. 1. 4; 3 John 7.
NOURISH. Isa. 1. 2, I have *n.* and brought up children.
1 Tim. 4. 6, *n.* in words of faith.
Jas. 5. 5, have *n.* your hearts.
See Gen. 45. 11; 50. 21; Acts 12. 20; Col. 2. 19.
NOW. Job 4. 5, *n.* it is come upon thee.
Ps. 119. 67, but *n.* have I kept thy word.
Hos. 2. 7, then was it better than *n.*
Lu. 14. 17, all things are *n.* ready.
John 13. 7, thou knowest not *n.*
16. 12, ye cannot bear them *n.*
1 Cor. 13. 12, *n.* I know in part.
Gal. 2. 20, the life I *n.* live.
1 Tim. 4. 8, the life that *n.* is.
1 Pet. 1. 8, though *n.* ye see him not.
1 John 3. 2, *n.* are we sons of God.
See Rom. 6. 22; Gal. 3. 3; Heb. 2. 8.
NUMBER (*n.*). Job 5. 9; 9. 10, marvellous things without *n.*
25. 3, is there any *n.* of his armies?
Ps. 139. 18, more in *n.* than the sand.
147. 4, he telleth the *n.* of the stars.
Acts 11. 21, a great *n.* believed.
16. 5, the churches increased in *n.* daily.
Rev. 13. 17, 18, the *n.* of his name.
See Deut. 7. 7; Hos. 1. 10; Rom. 9. 27.
NUMBER (*v.*). Gen. 41. 49, gathered corn till he left *n.*
2 Sam. 24. 2; 1 Chron. 21. 2, *n.* the people.
Ps. 90. 12, so teach us to *n.* our days.
Eccl. 1. 15, that which is wanting cannot be *n.*
Isa. 53. 12; Mk. 15. 28, he was *n.* with transgressors.
Mat. 10. 30; Lu. 12. 7, hairs are all *n.*
Rev. 7. 9, multitude which no man could *n.*
See Ex. 30. 12; Job 14. 16; Ps. 40. 5; Acts 1. 17.
NURSE. Gen. 35. 8, Deborah Rebekah's *n.* died.
2 Sam. 4. 4, and his *n.* took him up and fled.
1 Thess. 2. 7, even as a *n.* cherisheth her children.
See Ex. 2. 7, 9; Isa. 60. 4.
NURSING. Isa. 49. 23, kings shall be thy *n.* fathers, and their queens thy *n.* mothers.
NURTURE. Eph. 6. 4.

O

OBEDIENCE. Rom. 5. 19, by the *o.* of one.
16. 26, the *o.* of faith.
Heb. 5. 8, yet learned he *o.*
See Rom. 16. 19; 2 Cor. 10. 5; 1 Pet. 1. 2.
OBEDIENT. Ex. 24. 7, all will we do, and be *o.*
Prov. 25. 12, wise reprover upon an *o.* ear.
Isa. 1. 19, if *o.* ye shall eat.
2 Cor. 2. 9, *o.* in all things.
Eph. 6. 5; Tit. 2. 9, be *o.* to your masters.
Phil. 2. 8, *o.* unto death.
1 Pet. 1. 14, as *o.* children.
See Num. 27. 20; 2 Sam. 22. 45; Tit. 2. 5.
OBEISANCE. Gen. 37. 7; 43. 28; 2 Sam. 15. 5.
OBEY. Deut. 11. 27, a blessing if ye *o.*
Josh. 24. 24, his voice will we *o.*
1 Sam. 15. 22, to *o.* is better than sacrifice.
Jer. 7. 23, *o* my voice, and I will be your God.
Acts 5. 29, we ought to *o.* God rather than men.
Rom. 6. 16, his servants ye are to whom ye *o.*
Eph. 6. 1; Col. 3. 20, *o.* your parents in the Lord.
2 Thess. 1. 8; 1 Pet. 4. 17, that *o.* not the gospel.
Heb. 13. 17, *o.* them that have rule over you.
1 Pet. 1. 22, purified your souls in *o.* the truth.
See Ex. 5. 2; 23. 21; Dan. 9. 10; Mat. 8. 27.
OBJECT. Acts 24. 19.
OBSCURE. Prov. 20. 20.
OBSCURITY. Isa. 29. 18; 58. 10; 59. 9.
OBSERVATION. Lu. 17. 20.
OBSERVE. Gen. 37. 11, his father *o.* the saying.
Ps. 107. 43, whoso is wise, and will *o.* these things.
Prov. 23. 26, let thine eyes *o.* my ways.
Eccl. 11. 4, he that *o.* the wind.
Jon. 2. 8, that *o.* lying vanities.
Mat. 28. 20, teaching them to *o.* all things.
Mk. 6. 20, Herod feared John, and *o.* him.
10. 20, all these have I *o.*
See Ex. 12. 42; 31. 16; Ezek. 20. 18; Gal. 4. 10.
OBSERVER. Deut. 18. 10.
OBSTINATE. Deut. 2. 30; Isa. 48. 4.
OBTAIN. Prov. 8. 35, shall *o.* favour of the Lord.
Isa. 35. 10; 51. 11, shall *o.* joy and gladness.
Lu. 20. 35, worthy to *o.* that world.
Acts 26. 22, having *o.* help of God.
1 Cor. 9. 24, so run that ye may *o.*
1 Thess. 5. 9; 2 Tim. 2. 10, to *o.* salvation.
1 Tim. 1. 13, I *o.* mercy.
Heb. 4. 16, *o.* mercy, and find grace to help.
9. 12, having *o.* eternal redemption.
1 Pet. 2. 10, which had not *o.* mercy, but now have *o.*
2 Pet. 1. 1, *o.* like precious faith.
See Dan. 11. 21; Hos. 2. 23; Acts 1. 17; 22. 28.
OCCASION. 2 Sam. 12. 14, great *o.* to enemies to blaspheme.
Dan. 6. 4, sought to find *o.*
Rom. 7. 8, sin, taking *o.* by the commandment.
14. 13, an *o.* to fall in his brother's way.
1 Tim. 5. 14, give none *o.* to the adversary.
See Gen. 43. 18; Ezra 7. 20; Ezek. 18. 3.
OCCUPATION. Gen. 46. 33; Jon. 1. 8; Acts 18. 3; 19. 25.
OCCUPY. Ezek. 27. 9; Lu. 19. 13.
ODOUR. John 12. 3; Phil. 4. 18; Rev. 5. 8.
OFFENCE. Eccl. 10. 4, yielding pacifieth great *o.*
Isa. 8. 14; Rom. 9. 33; 1 Pet. 2. 8, a rock of *o.*
Mat. 16. 23, thou art an *o.* to me.
18. 7; Lu. 17. 1, woe to the world because of *o.*!
Acts 24. 16, conscience void of *o.*
Rom. 14. 20, that man who eateth with *o.*
1 Cor. 10. 32; 2 Cor. 6. 3, give none *o.*
Phil. 1. 10, without *o.* till the day of Christ.
See 1 Sam. 25. 31; Rom. 5. 15; 16. 17; Gal. 5. 11.
OFFEND. Job 34. 31, I will not *o.* any more.

Ps. 119. 165, nothing shall *o.* them.
Prov. 18. 19, brother *o.* is harder to be won.
Mat. 5. 29; 18. 9; Mk. 9. 47, if thine eye *o.* thee.
13. 41, gather all things that *o.*
57; Mk. 6. 3, they were *o.* in him.
26. 33, though all shall be *o.*, yet will I never be.
Rom. 14. 21, whereby thy brother is *o.*
Jas. 2. 10, yet *o.* in one point.
See Gen. 20. 9; Jer. 37. 18; 2 Cor. 11. 29.
OFFENDER. 1 Kings 1. 21; Isa. 29. 21; Acts 25. 11.
OFFER. Judg. 5. 2, people willingly *o.* themselves.
Ps. 50. 23, whoso *o.* praise.
Mat. 5. 24, then come and *o.* thy gift.
Lu. 6. 29, one cheek, *o.* also the other.
1 Cor. 8. 1, 4, 7; 10. 19, things *o.* to idols.
Phil. 2. 17, *o.* in the service of your faith.
2 Tim. 4. 6, now ready to be *o.*
Heb. 9. 28, Christ once *o.* to bear the sins of many.
See 2 Chron. 17. 16; Ezra 1. 6; 2. 68; Mal. 1. 8.
OFFICE. 1 Sam. 2. 36, put me into one of the priests' *o.*
Rom. 11. 13, I magnify mine *o.*
1 Tim. 3. 1, the *o.* of a bishop.
Heb. 7. 5, the *o.* of the priesthood.
See Gen. 41. 13; Ps. 109. 8; Rom. 12. 4.
OFFSCOURING. Lam. 3. 45; 1 Cor. 4. 13.
OFFSPRING. Job 27. 14; Acts 17. 28; Rev. 22. 16.
OFTEN. Prov. 29. 1, being *o.* reproved.
Mal. 3. 16, spake *o.* one to another.
Mat. 23. 37; Lu. 13. 34, how *o.* would I have gathered.
1 Cor. 11. 26, as *o.* as ye eat.
1 Tim. 5. 23, thine *o.* infirmities.
See 2 Cor. 11. 26; Heb. 9. 25; 10. 11.
OIL. Ps. 45. 7; Heb. 1. 9, with *o.* of gladness.
92. 10, be anointed with fresh *o.*
104. 15, *o.* to make his face to shine.
Isa. 61. 3, *o.* of joy for mourning.
Mat. 25. 3, took no *o.* with them.
Lu. 10. 34, pouring in *o.* and wine.
See Ex. 27. 20; Mic. 6. 7; Lu. 7. 46.
OLD. Deut. 8. 4; 29. 5; Neh. 9. 21, waxed not *o.*
Josh. 5. 11, did eat of the *o.* corn.
Ps. 37. 25, I have been young, and now am *o.*
71. 18, when I am *o.* forsake me not.
Prov. 22. 6, when he is *o.* he will not.
Isa. 58. 12, build the *o.* waste places.
Jer. 6. 16, ask for the *o.* paths.
Lu. 5. 39, he saith, the *o.* is better.
2 Cor. 5. 17, *o.* things are passed away.
2 Pet. 2. 5, God spared not the *o.* world.
1 John 2. 7, the *o.* commandment is the word.
Rev. 12. 9; 20. 2, that *o.* serpent.
See Job 22. 15; Ps. 77. 5; Mat. 5. 21; Rom. 7. 6.
OMITTED. Mat. 23. 23.
ONCE. Gen. 18. 32, yet but this *o.*
Num. 13. 30, let us go up at *o.*
Job 33. 14; Ps. 62. 11, speaketh *o.*, yea twice.
Isa. 66. 8, shall a nation be born at *o.*?
Heb. 6. 4, *o.* enlightened.
9. 27, *o.* to die.
See Rom. 6. 10; Heb. 10. 10; 1 Pet. 3. 18.
ONE. Job 9. 3, *o.* of a thousand.
Eccl. 7. 27; Isa. 27. 12, *o.* by *o.*
Mk. 10. 21; Lu. 18. 22, *o.* thing thou lackest.
Lu. 10. 42, *o.* thing is needful.
John 9. 25, *o.* thing I know.
17. 11, 21, 22, that they may be *o.*
Gal. 3. 28, all *o.* in Christ.
Eph. 4. 5, *o.* Lord, *o.* faith, *o.* baptism.
See Deut. 6. 4; Mk. 12. 32; 1 Tim. 2. 5.
ONYX. Ex. 28. 20; 39. 13, and an *o.*
OPEN. Num. 16. 30, if the earth *o.* her mouth.
Ps. 49. 4, I will *o.* my dark saying.
51. 15, *o.* thou my lips.
81. 10, *o.* thy mouth wide.
104. 28; 145. 16, thou *o.* thine hand.
119. 18, *o.* thou mine eyes.
Prov. 31. 8, *o.* thy mouth for the dumb.
Isa. 22. 22, he shall *o.*, and none shall shut.
42. 7, to *o.* the blind eyes.
60. 11, thy gates shall be *o.* continually.
Ezek. 16. 63, never *o.* thy mouth.
Mal. 3. 10, *o.* windows of heaven.
Mat. 25. 11; Lu. 13. 25, Lord *o.* to us.
27. 52, graves were *o.*
Mk. 7. 34, that is, be *o.*
Lu. 24. 32, while he *o.* to us the scriptures.
45, then *o.* he their understanding.
Acts 26. 18, to *o.* their eyes, and turn them.
1 Cor. 16. 9, great door and effectual is *o.*
Col. 4. 3, *o.* to us a door of utterance.
See Acts 16. 14; 2 Cor. 2. 12; Heb. 4. 13; Rev. 5. 2.
OPERATION. Ps. 28. 5; Isa. 5. 12; 1 Cor. 12. 6; Col. 2. 12.
OPINION. 1 Kings 18. 21; Job 32. 6.
OPPORTUNITY. Gal. 6. 10; Phil. 4. 10; Heb. 11. 15.
OPPOSE. Job 30. 21; 2 Thess. 2. 4; 2 Tim. 2. 25.
OPPOSITIONS. 1 Tim. 6. 20.
OPPRESS. Ex. 22. 21; 23. 9, *o.* a stranger.
Lev. 25. 14, 17, ye shall not *o.* one another.
1 Sam. 12. 3, whom have I *o.*?
Ps. 10. 18, that the man of earth may no more *o.*
Prov. 14. 31; 22. 16, he that *o.* the poor.
28. 3, a poor man that *o.* the poor.
Jer. 7. 6, if ye *o.* not the stranger.
Hos. 12. 7, he loveth to *o.*
Zech. 7. 10, *o.* not the widow.
See Mal. 3. 5; Acts 7. 24; 10. 38; Jas. 2. 6.
OPPRESSION. Deut. 26. 7, the Lord looked on our *o.*
Ps. 62. 10, trust not in *o.*
119. 134, deliver me from the *o.* of man.
Eccl. 4. 1, I considered the *o.*
7. 7, *o.* maketh a wise man mad.
Isa. 30. 12, ye trust in *o.*
See Isa. 33. 15; Zech. 9. 8; 10. 4.
ORATOR. Isa. 3. 3; Acts 24. 1.
ORDAIN. 1 Chron. 17. 9, I will *o.* a place for my people.
Ps. 8. 2, hast thou *o.* strength.
81. 5, this he *o.* in Joseph.
132. 17, I have *o.* a lamp for mine anointed.
Isa. 26. 12, thou wilt *o.* peace for us.
30. 33, Tophet is *o.* of old.
Jer. 1. 5, I *o.* thee a prophet.
Mk. 3. 14, Jesus *o.* twelve.
John 15. 16, have *o.* you, that ye should bring forth.
Acts 1. 22, one be *o.* to be a witness.
10. 42, *o.* of God to be the Judge.
13. 48, *o.* to eternal life.
14. 23; Tit. 1. 5, *o.* elders.
16. 4, decrees that were *o.*
17. 31, by that man whom he hath *o.*
Rom. 13. 1, the powers that be are *o.* of God.
Gal. 3. 19, the law was *o.* by angels.
Eph. 2. 10, good works which God hath before *o.*
Jude 4, of old *o.* to this condemnation.
See 1 Cor. 2. 7; 9. 14; 1 Tim. 2. 7; Heb. 5. 1.
ORDER. Judg. 13. 12, how shall we *o.* the child?
2 Kings 20. 1; Isa. 38. 1, set thine house in *o.*
Job 10. 22, land without any *o.*
23. 4, I would *o.* my cause.
37. 19, we cannot *o.* our speech.
Ps. 40. 5, they cannot be reckoned in *o.*
50. 21, I will set them in *o.*
23, to him that *o.* his conversation aright.
110. 4; Heb. 5. 6; 6. 20; 7. 11, the *o.* of Melchisedec.
1 Cor. 14. 40, decently and in *o.*
Tit. 1. 5, that thou shouldest set in *o.*
See Ps. 37. 23; Acts 21. 24; 1 Cor. 15. 23.
ORDINANCE. Isa. 58. 2; Rom. 13. 2, the *o.* of their God.
Mal. 3. 14, what profit that we have kept *o.*?
Eph. 2. 15, commandments contained in *o.*
Col. 2. 14, handwriting of *o.*
Heb. 9. 10, in carnal *o.*

See Jer. 31. 36; Luke 1. 6; 1 Pet. 2. 13.
ORPHANS. Lam. 5. 3.
OSTRICH. Job 39. 13, or wings and feathers unto the *o*.
Lam. 4. 3, like the *o*. in the wilderness.
OUGHT. 1 Chron. 12. 32, to know what Israel *o*. to do.
Mat. 23. 23; Lu. 11. 42, these *o*. ye to have done.
Lu. 24. 26, *o*. not Christ to have suffered?
John 4. 20, the place where men *o*. to worship.
Acts 5. 29, we *o*. to obey God.
Rom. 8. 26, what we should pray for as we *o*.
Heb. 5. 12, when ye *o*. to be teachers.
Jas. 3. 10, these things *o*. not so to be.
Pet. 3. 11, what manner of persons *o*. ye to be?
See Rom. 12. 3; 15. 1; 1 Tim. 3. 15.
OURS. Mk. 12. 7; Lu. 20. 14; 1 Cor. 1. 2; 2 Cor. 1. 14.
OUT. Num. 32. 23, be sure your sin will find you *o*.
Ps. 82. 5, are *o*. of course.
Prov. 4. 23, *o*. of it are the issues of life.
Mat. 12. 34; 15. 19, *o*. of abundance of heart the mouth speaketh.
2 Tim. 3. 11, *o*. of them all the Lord delivered me.
4. 2, instant in season, *o*. of season.
See Gen. 2. 9, 23; 3. 19; John 15. 19; Acts 2. 5.
OUTCAST. Ps. 147. 2; Isa. 11. 12; 27. 13; Jer. 30. 17.
OUTGOINGS. Josh. 17. 18; Ps. 65. 8.
OUTRAGEOUS. Prov. 27. 4.
OUTRUN. John 20. 4.
OUTSIDE. Judg. 7. 11; Mat. 23. 25; Lu. 11. 39.
OUTSTRETCHED. Deut. 26. 8; Jer. 21. 5; 27. 5.
OUTWARD. 1 Sam. 16. 7, looketh on *o*. appearance.
Mat. 23. 27, appear beautiful *o*.
Rom. 2. 28, not a Jew, which is one *o*.
2 Cor. 4. 16, though our *o*. man perish.
See Mat. 23. 28; Rom. 2. 28; 1 Pet. 3. 3.
OVERCHARGE. Lu. 21. 34; 2 Cor. 2. 5.
OVERCOME. Gen. 49. 19, he shall *o*. at last.
Jer. 23. 9, like a man whom wine hath *o*.
John 16. 33, I have *o*. the world.
Rom. 12. 21, be not *o*. of evil, but *o*. evil.
1 John 5. 4, 5, victory that *o*. the world.
Rev. 2. 7, 17, 26; 3. 12, 21, to him that *o*.
See Cant. 6. 5; 2 Pet. 2. 19; Rev. 12. 11.
OVERMUCH. Eccl. 7. 16; 2 Cor. 2. 7.
OVERPAST. Ps. 57. 1; Isa. 26. 20.
OVERPLUS. Lev. 25. 27.
OVERSEER. Gen. 41. 34; Prov. 6. 7; Acts 20. 28.
OVERSHADOW. Mat. 17. 5; Mk. 9. 7; Lu. 1. 35; Acts 5. 15.
OVERSIGHT. Gen. 43. 12; Neh. 11. 16; 1 Pet. 5. 2.
OVERSPREAD. Gen. 9. 19; Dan. 9. 27.
OVERTAKE. Amos. 9. 13, plowman shall *o*. the reaper.
Gal. 6. 1, if a man be *o*. in a fault.
1 Thess. 5. 4, day should *o*. you as a thief.
See Deut. 19. 6; Isa. 59. 9; Jer. 42. 16.
OVERTHROW. Ex. 23. 24, utterly *o*. them.
Job 19. 6, God hath *o*. me.
Ps. 140. 4, purposed to *o*. my goings.
Prov. 13. 6, wickedness *o*. the sinner.
Jon. 3. 4, yet forty days, and Nineveh shall be *o*.
Acts 5. 39, if it be of God, ye cannot *o*. it.
See Gen. 19. 21; Prov. 29. 4; 2 Tim. 2. 18.
OVERTURN. Job 9. 5; 12. 15; 28. 9; Ezek. 21. 27.
OVERWHELM. Job 6. 27, ye *o*. the fatherless.
Ps. 61. 2, when my heart is *o*.
77. 3; 142. 3; 143. 4, my spirit was *o*.
See Ps. 55. 5; 78. 53; 124. 4.
OVERWISE. Eccl. 7. 16.
OWE. Lu. 16. 5, 7, how much *o*. thou?
Rom. 13. 8, *o*. no man any thing.
See Mat. 18. 24, 28; Lu. 7. 41; Philem. 18.
OWN. Num. 32. 42, called if after his *o*. name.
1 Chron. 29. 14, of thine *o*. have we given thee.
Ps. 12. 4, our lips are our *o*.
Ps. 67. 6, even our *o*. God shall bless us.
Mat. 20. 15, do what I will with mine *o*.
John 1. 11, to his *o*., and his *o*. received him not.
13. 1, having loved his *o*.
1 Cor. 6. 19, ye are not your *o*.
See Acts 5. 4; Phil. 3. 9; 1 Tim. 5. 8; Rev. 1. 5.
OWNER. Ex. 21. 28; 22. 11; Eccl. 5. 13; Isa. 1. 3.

P

PACIFY. Prov. 16. 14; 21. 14; Eccl. 10. 4; Ezek. 16. 63.
PAIN. Ps. 55. 4, my heart is sore *p*.
116. 3, the *p*. of hell gat hold upon me.
Acts 2. 24, having loosed the *p*. of death.
Rom. 8. 22, creation travaileth in *p*.
Rev. 21. 4, neither shall there be any more *p*.
See Ps. 73. 16; Jer. 4. 19; 2 Cor. 11. 27.
PAINTED. 2 Kings 9. 30; Jer. 4. 30; 22. 14; Ezek. 23. 40.
PALACE. Ps. 48. 13, consider her *p*.
122. 7, prosperity within thy *p*.
144. 12, the similitude of a *p*.
Jer. 9. 21, death is entered into our *p*.
Lu. 11. 21, a strong man keepeth his *p*.
Phil. 1. 13, manifest in all the *p*.
See 1 Chron. 29. 1; Neh. 1. 1; 2. 8; Isa. 25. 2.
PALE. Isa. 29. 22; Jer. 30. 6; Rev. 6. 8.
PALM. Isa. 49. 16; Mat. 26. 67; Mk. 14. 65; Rev. 7.
PANT. Ps. 38. 10; 42. 1; 119. 131; Amos 2. 7.
PARCHMENTS. 2 Tim. 4. 13, but especially the *p*.
PARDON. Ex. 23. 21, he will not *p*.
2 Kings 5. 18, the Lord *p*. thy servant.
2 Chron. 30. 18, the good Lord *p*. every one.
Neh. 9. 17, a God ready to *p*.
Isa. 55. 7, he will abundantly *p*.
See Jer. 33. 8; 50. 20; Lam. 3. 42; Mic. 7. 18.
PARENTS. Mat. 10. 21; Mk. 13. 12, children rise up against *p*.
Lu. 18. 29, no man that hath left *p*.
21. 16, ye shall be betrayed by *p*.
John 9. 2, who did sin, this man, or his *p*.?
Rom. 1. 30; 2 Tim. 3. 2, disobedient to *p*.
2 Cor. 12. 14, not to lay up for *p*., but *p*. for children.
Eph. 6. 1; Col. 3. 20, children, obey your *p*.
See Lu. 2. 27; 8. 56; 1 Tim. 5. 4; Heb. 11. 23.
PART (*n*.). Josh 22. 25, 27, ye have no *p*. in the Lord.
Ps. 5. 9, their inward *p*. is very wickedness.
51. 6, in hidden *p*. make me to know.
118. 7, the Lord taketh my *p*.
139. 9, dwell in the uttermost *p*.
Mk. 9. 40, he that is not against us is on our *p*.
Lu. 10. 42, that good *p*.
John 13. 8, thou hast no *p*. with me.
Acts 8. 21, neither *p*. nor lot.
2 Cor. 6. 15, what *p*. hath he that believeth?
See Tit. 2. 8; Rev. 20. 6; 21. 8; 22. 19.
PART (*v*.). Ruth 1. 17, if ought but death *p*. thee and me.
2 Sam. 14. 6, there was none to *p*. them.
Ps. 22. 18, they *p*. my garments.
Lu. 24. 51, while he blessed them he was *p*.
Acts 2. 45, *p*. them to all men.
See Mat. 27. 35; Mk. 15. 24; Lu. 23. 34; John 19. 24.
PARTAKE. Ps. 50. 18, hast been *p*. with adulterers.
Rom. 15. 27, *p*. of their spiritual things.
1 Cor. 9. 10, *p*. of his hope.
13; 10. 18, *p*. with the altar.
10. 17, *p*. of that one bread.
21, *p*. of the Lord's table.
1 Tim. 5. 22, neither be *p*. of other men's sins.
Heb. 3. 1, *p*. of the heavenly calling.
1 Pet. 4. 13, *p*. of Christ's sufferings.
5. 1, a *p*. of the glory.
2 Pet. 1. 4, *p*. of the divine nature.
See Eph. 3. 6; Phil. 1. 7; Col. 1. 12; Rev. 18. 4.
PARTIAL. Mal. 2. 9; 1 Tim. 5. 21; Jas. 2. 4; 3. 17.

PARTICULAR. 1 Cor. 12. 27; Eph. 5. 33.
PARTITION. 1 Kings 6. 21; Eph. 2. 14.
PARTNER. Prov. 29. 24; Lu. 5. 7; 2 Cor. 8. 23.
PASS. Ex. 12. 13, when I see the blood I will *p.* over.
Isa. 43. 2, when thou *p.* through waters.
Mat. 26. 39; Mk. 14. 36, let this cup *p.*
Lu. 16. 26, neither can they *p.* to us.
1 Cor. 7. 31; 1 John 2. 17, fashion of this world *p.*
Eph. 3. 19, love of Christ, which *p.* knowledge.
Phil. 4. 7, which *p.* all understanding.
See Jer. 2. 6; Lu. 18. 37; Rom. 5. 12; Rev. 21. 1.
PASSION. Acts 1. 3; 14. 15; Jas. 5. 17.
PAST. Job 29. 2, as in months *p.*
Eccl. 3. 15, God requireth that which is *p.*
Cant. 2. 11, the winter is *p.*
Jer. 8. 20, the harvest is *p.*
Rom. 3. 25, of sins that are *p.*
11. 33, ways *p.* finding out.
2 Cor. 5. 17, old things *p.* away.
Eph. 4. 19, being *p.* feeling.
See Eph. 2. 2; 2 Tim. 2. 18; 1 Pet. 2. 10.
PASTOR. Jer. 3. 15; 17. 16; 23. 1; Eph. 4. 11.
PASTURE. Ps. 95. 7; 100. 3; Ezek. 34. 14; John 10. 9.
PATE. Ps. 7. 16.
PATH. Job 28. 7, there is a *p.* which no fowl knoweth.
Ps. 16. 11, show me the *p.* of life.
27. 11, lead me in a plain *p.*
65. 11, thy *p.* drop fatness.
77. 19, thy *p.* is in the great waters.
119. 105, a light to my *p.*
Prov. 4. 18, the *p.* of the just.
Isa. 2. 3; Mic. 4. 2, we will walk in his *p.*
42. 16, in *p.* they have not known.
58. 12, restorer of *p.* to dwell in.
Jer. 6. 16, ask for the old *p.*
Mat. 3. 3; Mk. 1. 3; Lu. 3. 4, make his *p.* straight.
See Ps. 139. 3; Prov. 3. 17; Lam. 3. 9; Heb. 12. 13.
PATIENCE. Mat. 18. 26, 29, have *p.* with me.
Lu. 8. 15, bring forth fruit with *p.*
21. 19, in your *p.* possess ye your souls.
Rom. 5. 3, tribulation worketh *p.*
8. 25, with *p.* wait for it.
15. 4, through *p.* and comfort.
5, the God of *p.*
2 Cor. 6. 4, as ministers of God in much *p.*
Col. 1. 11, strengthened with all might to all *p.*
1 Thess. 1. 3, your *p.* of hope.
2 Thess. 1. 4, glory in you for your *p.*
1 Tim. 6. 11, follow after *p.*
Tit. 2. 2, sound in faith, charity, *p.*
Heb. 10. 36, ye have need of *p.*
12. 1, run with *p.*
Jas. 1. 3, trying of your faith worketh *p.*
4, let *p.* have her perfect work.
5. 7, the husbandman hath long *p.*
10, for an example of *p.*
11, ye have heard of the *p.* of Job.
2 Pet. 1. 6, add to temperance *p.*
Rev. 2. 2, 19, I know thy *p.*
3. 10, thou hast kept word of *p.*
13. 10; 14. 12, here is the *p.* of saints.
See Eccl. 7. 8; Rom. 12. 12; 1 Thess. 5. 14.
PATIENTLY. Ps. 37. 7; 40. 1; Heb. 6. 15; 1 Pet. 2. 20.
PATTERN. 1 Tim. 1. 16; Tit. 2. 7; Heb. 8. 5; 9. 23.
PAVILION. 2 Sam. 22. 12, and he made darkness *p.*
See Ps. 18. 11; 27. 5; 31. 20; Jer. 43. 10.
PAY. Ex. 22. 7, let him *p.* double.
Num. 20. 19, water, I will *p.* for it.
2 Kings 4. 7, sell the oil, and *p.* thy debt.
Ps. 22. 25; 66. 13; 116. 14, will *p.* my vows.
Prov. 22. 27, if thou hast nothing to *p.*
Eccl. 5. 4, defer not to *p.* it.
Mat. 18. 26, I will *p.* thee all.
18. 28, *p.* that thou owest.
23. 23, ye *p.* tithe of mint.
See Ex. 21. 19; Mat. 17. 24; Rom. 13. 6; Heb. 7. 9.
PEACE. Gen. 41. 16, an answer of *p.*
Num. 6. 26, the Lord give thee *p.*
25. 12, my covenant of *p.*
Deut. 20. 10, proclaim *p.* to it.
23. 6, thou shalt not seek their *p.*
1 Sam. 25. 6; Lu. 10. 5, *p.* be to this house.
2 Kings 9. 19, what hast thou to do with *p.*?
31, had Zimri *p.*, who slew his master?
Job 5. 23, beasts shall be at *p.* with thee.
22. 21, acquaint thyself with him, and be at *p.*
Ps. 4. 8, I will lay me down in *p.*
29. 11, the Lord will bless his people with *p.*
34. 14; 1 Pet. 3. 11, seek *p.*, and pursue it.
37. 37, the end of that man is *p.*
85. 8, will speak *p.* to his people.
122. 6, pray for *p.* of Jerusalem.
Eccl. 3. 8, a time of *p.*
Isa. 26. 3, keep him in perfect *p.*
32. 17, work of righteousness shall be *p.*
45. 7, I make *p.*, and create evil.
48. 18, thy *p.* as a river.
22; 57. 21, no *p.* to the wicked.
52. 7; Nah. 1. 15, that publisheth *p.*
59. 8; Rom. 3. 17, the way of *p.* they know not.
Jer. 6. 14; 8. 11, saying *p.*, *p.*, when there is no *p.*
8. 15; 14. 19, we looked for *p.*
34. 5, thou shalt die in *p.*
Ezek. 7. 25, they shall seek *p.*
Dan. 4. 1; 6. 25; 1 Pet. 1. 2; 2 Pet. 1. 2; Jude 2, *p.* be multiplied.
Hag. 2. 9, in this place will I give *p.*
Mat. 10. 13, let your *p.* come upon it.
34; Lu. 12. 51, to send *p.* on earth.
Mk. 9. 50, have *p.* one with another.
Lu. 1. 79, to guide our feet into way of *p.*
2. 14, on earth *p.*
19. 42, things which belong to thy *p.*
John 14. 27, *p.* I leave, my *p.* I give you.
16. 33, that in me ye might have *p.*
Rom. 1. 7; 1 Cor. 1. 3; 2 Cor. 1. 2; Gal. 1. 3; Eph. 1. 2; Phil. 1. 2, *p.* from God our Father.
5. 1, we have *p.* with God.
10. 15; Eph. 6. 15, the gospel of *p.*
14. 19, follow after the things which make for *p.*
15. 33; 16. 20; 2 Cor. 13. 11; Phil. 4. 9; 1 Thess. 5. 23; Heb. 13. 20, the God of *p.*
1 Cor. 14. 33, author of *p.*
2 Cor. 13. 11, live in *p.*
Eph. 2. 14, he is our *p.*
17, *p.* to you which were afar off.
4. 3, in the bond of *p.*
Phil. 4. 7, *p.* of God which passeth all understanding.
Col. 1. 2; 1 Thess. 1. 1; 2 Thess. 1. 2; 1 Tim. 1. 2; 2 Tim. 1. 2; Tit. 1. 4; Philem. 3; 2 John 3, grace and *p.* from God.
3. 15, let the *p.* of God rule in your hearts.
1 Thess. 5. 13, be at *p.* among yourselves.
2 Thess. 3. 16, Lord of *p.* give you *p.* always.
2 Tim. 2. 22; Heb. 12. 14, follow *p.* with all men.
Heb. 7. 2, king of *p.*
Jas. 2. 16, depart in *p.*
3. 18, fruit of righteousness is sown in *p.*
2 Pet. 3. 14, found of him in *p.*
See Mat. 5. 9; Lu. 24. 36; John 20. 19; Gal. 6. 16.
PEACEABLE. Isa. 32. 18; 1 Tim. 2. 2; Heb. 12. 11; Jas. 3. 17.
PEACEABLY. Gen. 37. 4; 1 Sam. 16. 4; Jer. 9. 8; Rom. 12. 18.
PEACOCKS. 2 Chron. 9. 21, the ships of Tarshish bringing *p.*
Job 39. 13, gavest thou the goodly wings unto the *p.*
PEELED. Isa. 18. 2; Ezek. 29. 18.
PEEP. Isa. 8. 19; 10. 14.
PELICAN. Lev. 11. 18, and the swan, and the *p.*
Deut. 14. 17, the *p.*, and the gier eagle.
Ps. 102. 6, I am like a *p.* of the wilderness.
PEN. Judg. 5. 14, they that handle the *p.*
Job 19. 24, graven with an iron *p.*

Ps. 45. 1, my tongue is the *p.* of a ready writer.
Isa. 8. 1, write in it with a man's *p.*
Jer. 8. 8, the *p.* of the scribes is in vain.
17. 1, is written with a *p.* of iron.
3 John 13, I will not with ink and *p.* write.
PENCE. Mat. 18. 28; Mk. 14. 5; Lu. 7. 41; 10. 35.
PENNY. Mat. 20. 13, didst not thou agree with me for a *p.*?
22. 19, they brought him a *p.*
Mk. 12. 15, bring me a *p.*
Rev. 6. 6, a measure of wheat for a *p.*
PENURY. Prov. 14. 23; Lu. 21. 4.
PEOPLE. Ex. 6. 7; Deut. 4. 20; 2 Sam. 7. 24; Jer. 13. 11, I will take you to me for a *p.*
Lev. 20. 24, 26, separated from other *p.*
Deut. 4. 33, did ever *p.* hear voice of God and live?
33. 29, O *p.* saved by the Lord.
2 Sam. 22. 44; Ps. 18. 43, a *p.* I knew not.
Ps. 81. 11, my *p.* would not hearken.
144. 15, happy is that *p.*
Prov. 30. 25, the ants are a *p.* not strong.
Isa. 1. 4, a *p.* laden with iniquity.
27. 11, a *p.* of no understanding.
43. 4, I will give *p.* for thy life.
8, blind *p.* that have eyes.
Jer. 6. 22; 50. 41, a *p.* cometh from the north.
Jon. 1. 8, of what *p.* art thou?
Lu. 1. 17, a *p.* prepared for the Lord.
Tit. 2. 14, purify unto himself a peculiar *p.*
See Mat. 1. 21; Rom. 11. 2; Heb. 11. 25.
PERCEIVE. Deut. 29. 4, a heart to *p.*
Josh. 22. 31, we *p.* the Lord is among us.
Job 9. 11, I *p.* him not.
23. 8, I cannot *p.* him.
Isa. 6. 9, see indeed, but *p.* not.
33. 19, deeper speech than thou canst *p.*
64. 4, nor *p.* by the ear what God hath.
Mat. 22. 18, Jesus *p.* their wickedness.
Mk. 8. 17, *p.* ye not yet?
Lu. 8. 46, I *p.* that virtue is gone out.
John 4. 19, I *p.* thou art a prophet.
Acts 10. 34, I *p.* God is no respecter of persons.
1 John 3. 16, hereby *p.* we the love of God.
See 1 Sam. 3. 8; Neh. 6. 12; Job 33. 14; Mk. 12. 28.
PERFECT. Gen. 6. 9, Noah was *p.*
17. 1, walk before me, and be thou *p.*
Deut. 18. 13, thou shalt be *p.* with the Lord.
32. 4, his work is *p.*
2 Sam. 22. 31; Ps. 18. 30, his way is *p.*
Ps. 19. 7, law of the Lord is *p.*
37. 37, mark the *p.* man.
Prov. 4. 18, more and more to *p.* day.
Ezek. 28. 15, thou wast *p.* in thy ways.
Mat. 5. 48; 2 Cor. 13. 11, be ye *p.*
19. 21, if thou wilt be *p.*
John 17. 23, be made *p.* in one.
Rom. 12. 2, that *p.* will of God.
1 Cor. 2. 6, wisdom among them that are *p.*
2 Cor. 12. 9, strength made *p.* in weakness.
Eph. 4. 13, unto a *p.* man.
Phil. 3. 12, not as though I were already *p.*
15, let us, as many as be *p.*
Col. 1. 28, present every man *p.*
4. 12, may stand *p.* and complete.
2 Tim. 3. 17, that the man of God may be *p.*
Heb. 2. 10, make *p.* through suffering.
11. 40, without us should not be made *p.*
12. 23, spirits of just men made *p.*
13. 21, make you *p.* in every good work.
Jas. 1. 4, patience have her *p.* work.
17, every good and *p.* gift.
25, *p.* law of liberty.
3. 2, the same is a *p.* man.
1 John 4. 18, *p.* love casteth out fear.
See 2 Chron. 8. 16; Lu. 6. 40; 2 Cor. 7. 1; Eph. 4. 12.
PERFECTION. Job 11. 7; Ps. 119. 96; 2 Cor. 13. 9; Heb. 6. 1.
PERFECTLY. Jer. 23. 20; Acts 18. 26; 1 Cor. 1. 10.
PERFECTNESS. Col. 3. 14.
PERFORM. Ex. 18. 18, not able to *p.* it thyself alone.
Esth. 5. 6; 7. 2, to half of kingdom it shall be *p.*
Job 5. 12, cannot *p.* their enterprise.
Ps. 65. 1, unto thee shall the vow be *p.*
119. 106, I have sworn, and I will *p.* it.
Isa. 9. 7, zeal of the Lord will *p.* this.
44. 28, shall *p.* all my pleasure.
Jer. 29. 10; 33. 14, I will *p.* my good word.
Rom. 4. 21, able also to *p.*
7. 18, how to *p.* that which is good I find not.
Phil. 1. 6, *p.* it until day of Christ.
See Job 23. 14; Ps. 57. 2; Jer. 35. 14; Mat. 5. 33.
PERFORMANCE. Lu. 1. 45; 2 Cor. 8. 11.
PERIL. Lam. 5. 9; Rom. 8. 35; 2 Cor. 11. 26.
PERILOUS. 2 Tim. 3. 1.
PERISH. Num. 17. 12, we die, we *p.*, we all *p.*
Deut. 26. 5, a Syrian ready to *p.*
Job 4. 7, who ever *p.*, being innocent?
29. 13, blessing of him that was ready to *p.*
34. 15, all flesh shall *p.* together.
Ps. 1. 6, way of ungodly shall *p.*
37. 20, the wicked shall *p.*
49. 12, like the beasts that *p.*
80. 16, they *p.* at rebuke of thy countenance.
102. 26, they shall *p.*, but thou shalt endure.
Prov. 11. 10; 28. 28, when the wicked *p.*
29. 18, no vision, the people *p.*
31. 6, strong drink to him that is ready to *p.*
Isa. 27. 13, they shall come that were ready to *p.*
Jer. 7. 28, truth is *p.*
Jon. 1. 6; 3. 9, God will think on us, that we *p.* not.
14, let us not *p.* for this man's life.
Mat. 8. 25; Lu. 8. 24, save us, we *p.*
18. 14, that one of these little ones should *p.*
26. 52, shall *p.* with the sword.
Mk. 4. 38, carest thou not that we *p.*?
Lu. 13. 3, 5, ye shall all likewise *p.*
15. 17, I *p.* with hunger.
21. 18, there shall not an hair of your head *p.*
John 6. 27, labour not for the meat which *p.*
Acts 8. 20, thy money *p.* with thee.
Col. 2. 22, which are to *p.* with the using.
2 Pet. 3. 9, not willing that any should *p.*
See Ps. 2. 12; Jer. 6. 21; John 10. 28; Rom. 2. 12.
PERMISSION. 1 Cor. 7. 6.
PERMIT. 1 Cor. 14. 34; 16. 7; Heb. 6. 3.
PERNICIOUS. 2 Pet. 2. 2.
PERPETUAL. Ex. 31. 16, sabbath for a *p.* covenant.
Lev. 25. 34, their *p.* possession.
Ps. 9. 6, destructions are come to a *p.* end.
74. 3; Jer. 25. 9; Ezek. 35. 9, the *p.* desolations.
Jer. 8. 5, a *p.* backsliding.
15. 18, why is my pain *p.*?
Hab. 3. 6, the *p.* hills.
See Gen. 9. 12; Jer. 5. 22; 50. 5; 51. 39; Ezek. 46. 14.
PERPETUALLY. 1 Kings 9. 3; 2 Chron. 7. 16; Amos 1. 11.
PERPLEXED. Lu. 9. 7; 24. 4; 2 Cor. 4. 8.
PERPLEXITY. Isa. 22. 5; Mic. 7. 4; Lu. 21. 25.
PERSECUTE. Job 19. 22, why do ye *p.* me?
Ps. 7. 1, save me from them that *p.* me.
10. 2, the wicked doth *p.* the poor.
71. 11, *p.* and take him, there is none to deliver.
143. 3, the enemy hath *p.* my soul.
Mat. 5. 11, 12, blessed are ye when men *p.* you.
44, pray for them that *p.* you.
John 15. 20, if they have *p.* me.
Acts 9. 4; 22. 7; 26. 14, why *p.* thou me?
22. 4, I *p.* this way unto death.
26. 11, I *p.* them even to strange cities.
1 Cor. 4. 12, being *p.*, we suffer it.
15. 9; Gal. 1. 13, I *p.* the church of God.
2 Cor. 4. 9, *p.* but not forsaken.
Phil. 3. 6, concerning zeal, *p.* the church.
See John 5. 16; Acts 7. 52; Rom. 12. 14; Gal. 1. 23; 4. 29.
PERSECUTION. Mat. 13. 21; Mk. 4. 17, when *p.* ariseth.
2 Cor. 12. 10, take pleasure in *p.*

2 Tim. 3. 12, all that will live godly shall suffer *p*.
See Lam. 5. 5; Acts 8. 1; Gal. 6. 12; 1 Tim. 1. 13.
PERSEVERANCE. Eph. 6. 18.
PERSON. Deut. 10. 17; 2 Sam. 14. 14, God, which regardeth not *p*.
2 Sam. 17. 11, go to battle in thine own *p*.
Ps. 15. 4; Isa. 32. 5, 6, vile *p*.
26. 4; Prov. 12. 11; 28. 19, with vain *p*.
105. 37, not one feeble *p*.
Mat. 22. 16; Mk. 12. 14, regardest not *p*. of men.
2 Cor. 2. 10, forgave I it in the *p*. of Christ.
Heb. 1. 3, the express image of his *p*.
2 Pet. 3. 11, what manner of *p*. ought ye to be?
See Mal. 1. 8; Lu. 15. 7; Heb. 12. 16; Jude 16.
PERSUADE. 1 Kings 22. 20, who shall *p*. Ahab?
Prov. 25. 15, by long forbearing is a prince *p*.
Mat. 28. 14, we will *p*. him, and secure you.
Acts 26. 28, almost thou *p*. me.
Rom. 14. 5, let every man be fully *p*.
2 Cor. 5. 11, we *p*. men.
Gal. 1. 10, do I now *p*. men or God?
Heb. 6. 9, we are *p*. better things of you.
See 2 Kings 18. 32; 2 Chron. 18. 2; 2 Tim. 1. 12.
PERTAIN. Rom. 15. 17; 1 Cor. 6. 3; 2 Pet. 1. 3.
PERVERSE. Deut. 32. 5, a *p*. and crooked generation.
Job 6. 30, cannot my taste discern *p*. things?
Prov. 4. 24, *p*. lips put far from thee.
12. 8, *p*. heart shall be despised.
17. 20, *p*. tongue falleth into mischief.
23. 33, thine heart shall utter *p*. things.
Phil. 2. 15, in the midst of a *p*. nation.
See Num. 23. 21; Isa. 30. 12; 1 Tim. 6. 5.
PERVERT. Deut. 16. 19, a gift doth *p*. words.
Job 8. 3, doth God *p*. judgment?
Prov. 10. 9, he that *p*. his ways shall be known.
19. 3, the foolishness of man *p*. his way.
Jer. 3. 21, they have *p*. their way.
23. 36, ye have *p*. the words of God.
Acts 13. 10, wilt thou not cease to *p*. right ways?
Gal. 1. 7, would *p*. the gospel.
See Eccl. 5. 8; Mic. 3. 9; Lu. 23. 2.
PESTILENCE. Ex. 5. 3; 9. 15; Jer. 42. 17; 44. 13.
PESTILENT. Acts 24. 5.
PETITION. 1 Sam. 1. 17, God of Israel grant thee thy *p*.
1 Kings 2. 20, one small *p*.
Esth. 5. 6; 7. 2; 9. 12, what is thy *p*.?
Dan. 6. 7, whosoever shall ask a *p*.
13, maketh his *p*. three times a day.
See Esth. 7. 3; Ps. 20. 5; 1 John 5. 15.
PHILOSOPHERS. Acts 17. 18, then certain *p*. of the Epicureans.
PHILOSOPHY. Col. 2. 8.
PHYLACTERIES. Mat. 23. 5, they make broad their *p*.
See Ex. 13. 9, 16; Num. 15. 38.
PHYSICIAN. Mat. 9. 12; Mk. 2. 17; Lu. 5. 31, they that be whole need not a *p*.
Lu. 4. 23, *p*., heal thyself.
See Jer. 8. 22.
PICK. Prov. 30. 17.
PICTURES. Num. 33. 52; Prov. 25. 11; Isa. 2. 16.
PIECE. 1 Sam. 2. 36; Prov. 6. 26; 28. 21, a *p*. of bread.
15. 33, Samuel hewed Agag in *p*.
Ps. 7. 2, rending in *p*. while none to deliver.
50. 22, consider, lest I tear you in *p*.
Jer. 23. 29, hammer that breaketh rock in *p*.
Amos 4. 7, one *p*. was rained upon.
Zech. 11. 12, weighed for my price thirty *p*.
13; Mat. 27. 6, 9, took thirty *p*. of silver.
See Lu. 14. 18; Acts 19. 19; 23. 10; 27. 44.
PIERCE. 2 Kings 18. 21; Isa. 36. 6, into his hand and *p*. it.
Zech. 12. 10; John 19. 37, they shall look on me whom they have *p*.
1 Tim. 6. 10, *p*. themselves with many sorrows.
See Isa. 27. 1; Lu. 2. 35; Heb. 4. 12; Rev. 1. 7.
PIETY. 1 Tim. 5. 4, let them learn first to show *p*. at home.
PILE. Isa. 30. 33; Ezek. 24. 9.
PILLAR. Gen. 19. 26, a *p*. of salt.
Job 9. 6; 26. 11, the *p*. thereof tremble.
Prov. 9. 1, she hath hewn out her seven *p*.
Gal. 2. 9, Cephas and John, who seemed to be *p*.
1 Tim. 3. 15, the *p*. and ground of the truth.
Rev. 3. 12, him that overcometh will I make a *p*.
See Isa. 19. 19; Jer. 1. 18; Joel 2. 30; Lu. 17. 32; Rev. 10. 1.
PILLOW. Gen. 28. 11; 1 Sam. 19. 13; Ezek. 13. 18; Mk. 4. 38.
PILOTS. Ezek. 27. 8.
PIN. Judg. 16. 14; Ezek. 15. 3.
PINE. Lev. 26. 39; Lam. 4. 9; Isa. 38. 12; Ezek. 24. 23.
PINE TREE. Isa. 41. 19; 60. 13, and the *p. t.*
PIPE. Isa. 5. 12, the harp and *p*. are in their feasts.
Mat. 11. 17; Lu. 7. 32, we have *p*. unto you.
1 Cor. 14. 7, how shall it be known what is *p*.?
Rev. 18. 22, voice of *p*. shall be heard no more.
See 1 Sam. 10. 5; 1 Kings 1. 40; Isa. 30. 29.
PIT. Gen. 37. 20, cast him into some *p*.
Ex. 21. 33, 34, if a man dig a *p*.
Num. 16. 30, 33, go down quick into the *p*.
Job 33. 24, deliver him from going down to the *p*.
Ps. 28. 1; 143. 7, like them that go down into the *p*.
40. 2, out of an horrible *p*.
Prov. 22. 14; 23. 27, a deep *p*.
28. 10, shall fall into his own *p*.
Isa. 38. 17, the *p*. of corruption.
Mat. 12. 11; Lu. 14. 5, fall into a *p*. on sabbath.
PITCHER. Gen. 24. 14, let down thy *p*.
Judg. 7. 16, lamps within the *p*.
Eccl. 12. 6, or the *p*. be broken.
Lam. 4. 2, esteemed as earthen *p*.
Mk. 14. 13; Lu. 22. 10, a man bearing a *p*. of water.
PITIFUL. Lam. 4. 10; Jas. 5. 11; 1 Pet. 3. 8.
PITY. Deut. 7. 16; 13. 8; 19. 13, thine eye shall have no *p*.
2 Sam. 12. 6, because he had no *p*.
Job 19. 21, have *p*. on me, my friends.
Ps. 69. 20, I looked for some to take *p*.
Prov. 19. 17, that hath *p*. on the poor lendeth.
28. 8, gather for him that will *p*. the poor.
Isa. 13. 18, they shall have no *p*. on fruit.
63. 9, in his *p*. he redeemed them.
Jer. 13. 14, I will not *p*. nor spare.
Ezek. 16. 5, none eye *p*. thee.
24. 21, I will profane what your soul *p*.
Joel 2. 18, the Lord will *p*. his people.
Zech. 11. 5, their own shepherds *p*. them not.
Mat. 18. 33, as I had *p*. on thee.
See Ps. 103. 13; Jer. 15. 5; Lam. 2. 2; Jon. 4. 10.
PLACE. Ex. 3. 5; Josh. 5. 15, *p*. whereon thou standest is holy.
Judg. 18. 10, a *p*. where there is no want.
2 Kings 5. 11, strike his hand over the *p*.
6. 1; Isa. 49. 20, the *p*. is too strait for us.
Ps. 26. 8, the *p*. where thine honour dwelleth.
32. 7; 119. 114, thou art my hiding *p*.
37. 10, thou shalt diligently consider his *p*.
74. 20, the dark *p*. of the earth.
90. 1, our dwelling *p*.
Prov. 14. 26, his children have a *p*. of refuge.
15. 3, the eyes of the Lord in every *p*.
Eccl. 3. 20, all go to one *p*.
Isa. 5. 8, lay field to field, till there be no *p*.
60. 13, the *p*. of my feet.
66. 1, where is the *p*. of my rest?
Jer. 6. 3, they shall feed every one in his *p*.
Mic. 1. 3, the Lord cometh out of his *p*.
Zech. 10. 10, *p*. shall not be found for them.
Mal. 1. 11, in every *p*. incense shall be offered.
Mat. 28. 6; Mk. 16. 6, see the *p*. where the Lord lay.
Lu. 10. 1, two and two into every *p*.
14. 9, give this man *p*.
John 8. 37, my word hath no *p*. in you.
18. 2, Judas knew the *p*.

Acts 2. 1, with one accord in one *p*.
4. 31, the *p*. was shaken.
Rom. 12. 19, rather give *p*. to wrath.
Eph. 4. 27, neither give *p*. to the devil.
Heb. 12. 17, found no *p*. of repentance.
Rev. 20. 11, there was found no *p*. for them.
See Ps. 16. 6; Isa. 40. 4; Eph. 1. 3; 2. 6; 3. 10.
PLAGUE. Lev. 26. 21, I will bring seven times more *p*.
Deut. 28. 59, will make thy *p*. wonderful.
29. 22, when they see the *p*. of that land.
1 Kings 8. 38, every man the *p*. of his own heart.
Ps. 73. 5, nor are they *p*. like other men.
91. 10, nor any *p*. come nigh thy dwelling.
Hos. 13. 14, O death, I will be thy *p*.
Rev. 18. 4, that ye receive not of her *p*.
22. 18, shall add to him the *p*. written.
See Lev. 14. 35; Num. 8. 19; 16. 46; Mk. 3. 10.
PLAIN. Gen. 25. 27, Jacob was a *p*. man.
Ps. 27. 11, lead me in a *p*. path.
Prov. 8. 9, they are *p*. to him that understandeth.
15. 19, the way of the righteous is made *p*.
Isa. 40. 4, rough places *p*.
Hab. 2. 2, write the vision, make it *p*.
See Gen. 13. 10; 19. 17; Isa. 28. 25; Mk. 7. 35.
PLAINLY. Deut. 27. 8, write the words very *p*.
Isa. 32. 4, stammerers shall speak *p*.
John 10. 24, tell us *p*.
16. 25, I shall show you *p*. of the Father.
29, now speakest thou *p*.
See Ex. 21. 5; Ezra 4. 18; John 11. 14; 2 Cor. 3. 12.
PLAITING. 1 Pet. 3. 3.
PLANES. Isa. 44. 13.
PLANT (*n*.). Job 14. 9, bring forth boughs like a *p*.
Ps. 128. 3, children like olive *p*.
144. 12, sons as *p*. grown up.
Isa. 5. 7; 17. 10, his pleasant *p*.
16. 8, broken down principal *p*.
53. 2, as a tender *p*.
Ezek. 34. 29, a *p*. of renown.
Mat. 15. 13, every *p*. my Father hath not planted.
See Gen. 2. 5; 1 Chron. 4. 23; Jer. 48. 32.
PLANT (*v*.). Num. 24. 6, as trees which the Lord hath *p*.
2 Sam. 7. 10; 1 Chron. 17. 9, I will *p*. them.
Ps. 1. 3; Jer. 17. 8, like a tree *p*.
80. 15, the vineyard thy right hand hath *p*.
92. 13, *p*. in the house of the Lord.
94. 9, he that *p*. the ear.
Jer. 2. 21, I had *p*. thee a noble vine.
Ezek. 17. 10, being *p*. shall it prosper?
Lu. 17. 6, be thou *p*. in the sea.
Rom. 6. 5, if we have been *p*. together.
1 Cor. 3. 6, I have *p*.
See Mat. 21. 33; Mk. 12. 1; Lu. 20. 9.
PLATE. Ex. 28. 36; 39. 30; Jer. 10. 9.
PLATTED. Mat. 27. 29; Mk. 15. 17; John 19. 2.
PLATTER. Mat. 23. 25; Lu. 11. 39.
PLAY. Ex. 32. 6; 1 Cor. 10. 7, people rose up to *p*.
1 Sam. 16. 17, a man that can *p*. well.
2 Sam. 6. 21, I will *p*. before the Lord.
10. 12, let us *p*. the men.
Job 41. 5, wilt thou *p*. with him?
Ps. 33. 3, *p*. skilfully with a loud noise.
Isa. 11. 8, the sucking child shall *p*.
Ezek. 33. 32, can *p*. well on an instrument.
See 2 Sam. 2. 14; 1 Chron. 15. 29; Ps. 68. 25; Zech. 8. 5.
PLEA. Deut. 17. 8.
PLEAD. Judg. 6. 31, 32, will ye *p*. for Baal?
Job 9. 19, who shall set me a time to *p*.?
13. 19, who will *p*. with me?
16. 21, that one might *p*. for a man.
23. 6, will he *p*. against me with his great power?
Isa. 1. 17, *p*. for the widow.
3. 13, the Lord standeth up to *p*.
43. 26, let us *p*. together.
59. 4, none *p*. for truth.
Jer. 2. 9, I will yet *p*. with you.
Lam. 3. 58, thou hast *p*. the causes of my soul.
Joel 3. 2, I will *p*. with them for my people.
See 1 Sam. 25. 39; Job 13. 6; Isa. 66. 16; Hos. 2. 2.
PLEASANT. Gen. 3. 6, *p*. to the eyes.
2 Sam. 1. 23, were *p*. in their lives.
26, very *p*. hast thou been to me.
Ps. 16. 6, lines fallen in *p*. places.
106. 24, they despised the *p*. land.
133. 1, how *p*. for brethren to dwell together.
Prov. 2. 10, knowledge is *p*. to thy soul.
15. 26, the words of the pure are *p*. words.
16. 24, *p*. words are as honeycomb.
Eccl. 11. 7, it is *p*. to behold the sun.
Cant. 4. 13, 16; 7. 13, with *p*. fruits.
Isa. 64. 11, our *p*. things are laid waste.
Jer. 31. 20, is Ephraim a *p*. child?
Ezek. 33. 32, of one that hath a *p*. voice.
Dan. 10. 3, I ate no *p*. bread.
See Amos 5. 11; Mic. 2. 9; Nah. 2. 9; Zech. 7. 14.
PLEASANTNESS. Prov. 3. 17.
PLEASE. 1 Kings 3. 10, the speech *p*. the Lord.
Ps. 51. 19, then shalt thou be *p*. with sacrifices.
115. 3; 135. 6; Jon. 1. 14, he hath done whatsoever he *p*.
Prov. 16. 7, when a man's ways *p*. the Lord.
Isa. 2. 6, they *p*. themselves in children of strangers.
53. 10, it *p*. the Lord to bruise him.
55. 11, accomplish that which I *p*.
Mic. 6. 7, will the Lord be *p*. with rams?
Mal. 1. 8, offer it, will he be *p*. with thee?
John 8. 29, I do always those things that *p*. him.
Rom. 8. 8, in the flesh cannot *p*. God.
15. 1, to bear, and not to *p*. ourselves.
3, even Christ *p*. not himself.
1 Cor. 1. 21, it *p*. God by the foolishness of preaching.
10. 33, as I *p*. men in all things.
Gal. 1. 10, do I seek to *p*. men?
Eph. 6. 6; Col. 3. 22, as men-*p*.
Heb. 11. 6, without faith it is impossible to *p*. God.
See 1 Cor. 7. 32; Col. 1. 19; 1 Thess. 2. 4; 1 John 3. 22.
PLEASURE. 1 Chron. 29. 17, hast *p*. in uprightness.
Esth. 1. 8, do according to every man's *p*.
Job 21. 21, what *p*. hath he in his house?
25, another never eateth with *p*.
22. 3, is it any *p*. to the Almighty?
Ps. 16. 11, *p*. for evermore.
35. 27, hath *p*. in the prosperity of his servants.
51. 18, do good in thy good *p*.
102. 14, thy servants take *p*. in her stones.
103. 21, ye ministers of his that do his *p*.
111. 2, of all them that have *p*. therein.
147. 11, taketh *p*. in them that fear him.
149. 4, the Lord taketh *p*. in his people.
Prov. 21. 17, he that loveth *p*. shall be poor.
Eccl. 5. 4, he hath no *p*. in fools.
12. 1, I have no *p*. in them.
Isa. 44. 28, Cyrus shall perform all my *p*.
53. 10, the *p*. of the Lord shall prosper.
58. 3, in the day of your fast ye find *p*.
13, doing thy *p*. on my holy day.
Jer. 22. 28; 48. 38; Hos. 8. 8, a vessel wherein is no *p*.
Ezek. 18. 23; 33. 11, have I any *p*.?
Mal. 1. 10, I have no *p*. in you, saith the Lord.
Lu. 8. 14, choked with *p*. of this life.
12. 32, Father's good *p*.
Eph. 1. 5, the good *p*. of his will.
Phil. 2. 13, to will and to do of his good *p*.
1 Tim. 5. 6, she that liveth in *p*.
2 Tim. 3. 4, lovers of *p*.
Heb. 10. 38, my soul shall have no *p*. in him.
11. 25, the *p*. of sin for a season.
12. 10, chastened us after their own *p*.
Jas. 5. 5, ye have lived in *p*. on earth.
Rev. 4. 11, for thy *p*. they were created.
See Gen. 18. 12; Ps. 5. 4; Eccl. 2. 1; Tit. 3. 3; 2 Pet. 2. 13.

PLENTEOUS. Ps. 86. 5; 103. 8, *p.* in mercy.
130. 7, *p.* redemption.
Hab. 1. 16, portion fat and meat *p.*
Mat. 9. 37, the harvest truly is *p.*
See Gen. 41. 34; Deut. 28. 11; 30. 9; Prov. 21. 5; Isa. 30. 23.
PLENTIFUL. Ps. 31. 23; 68. 9; Jer. 2. 7; 48. 33; Lu. 12. 16.
PLENTY. Gen. 27. 28, *p.* of corn and wine.
Job 22. 25, *p.* of silver.
37. 23, *p.* of justice.
Prov. 3. 10, barns filled with *p.*
See 2 Chron. 31. 10; Prov. 28. 19; Jer. 44. 17; Joel 2. 26.
PLOW. Job 4. 8, that *p.* iniquity shall reap.
Prov. 20. 4, not *p.* by reason of cold.
21. 4, the *p.* of the wicked is sin.
Isa. 2. 4; Mic. 4. 3, beat swords into *p.*-shares.
28. 24, doth plowman *p.* all day to sow?
Joel 3. 10, beat your *p.*-shares into swords.
Amos 9. 13, the *p.*-man overtake the reaper.
See Deut. 22. 10; 1 Sam. 14. 14; Job 1. 14; 1 Cor. 9. 10.
PLUCK. Deut. 23. 25, mayest *p.* the ears with thy hand.
2 Chron. 7. 20, then will I *p.* them up.
Job 24. 9, they *p.* the fatherless from the breast.
Ps. 25. 15, he shall *p.* my feet out of the net.
74. 11, *p.* it out of thy bosom.
Prov. 14. 1, foolish *p.* it down with her hands.
Eccl. 3. 2, a time to *p.* up.
Isa. 50. 6, my cheeks to them that *p.*
Jer. 22. 24, yet I would *p.* thee thence.
Amos 4. 11; Zech. 3. 2, a firebrand *p.* out.
Mat. 5. 29; 18. 9; Mk. 9. 47, offend thee, *p.* it out.
12. 1; Mk. 2. 23; Lu. 6. 1, began to *p.* ears.
John 10. 28, nor shall any *p.* out of my hand.
See Gen. 8. 11; Lu. 17. 6; Gal. 4. 15; Jude 12.
POINT. Jer. 17. 1, written with the *p.* of a diamond.
Heb. 4. 15, in all *p.* tempted.
Jas. 2. 10, yet offend in one *p.*
See Gen. 25. 32; Eccl. 5. 16; Mk. 5. 23; John 4. 47.
POLE. Num. 21. 8.
POLICY. Dan. 8. 25.
POLISHED. Ps. 144. 12; Isa. 49. 2; Lam. 4. 7; Dan. 10. 6.
POLL. 2 Sam. 14. 26; Ezek. 44. 20; Mic. 1. 16.
POMP. Isa. 5. 14; 14. 11; Ezek. 7. 24; 30. 18; Acts 25. 23.
PONDER. Prov. 4. 26, *p.* the path of thy feet.
5. 6, lest thou shouldest *p.*
21, the Lord *p.* all his goings.
See Prov. 21. 2; 24. 12; Lu. 2. 19.
POOL. Ps. 84. 6; Isa. 35. 7; 41. 18; John 5. 2; 9. 7.
POOR. Ex. 30. 15, the *p.* shall not give less.
Deut. 15. 11, the *p.* shall never cease.
2 Kings 24. 14, none remained, save *p.* sort.
Job 24. 4, the *p.* of the earth hide.
29. 16, I was a father to the *p.*
Ps. 10. 14, the *p.* committeth himself to thee.
34. 6, this *p.* man cried.
40. 17; 69. 29; 70. 5; 86. 1; 109. 22, I am *p.*
49. 2, rich and *p.* together.
Prov. 10. 4, becometh *p.* that dealeth with slack hand.
13. 23, food in the tillage of the *p.*
18. 23, the *p.* useth entreaties.
22. 2, rich and *p.* meet together.
30. 9, lest I be *p.* and steal.
Isa. 41. 17, when *p.* and needy seek water.
Amos 2. 6, they sold the *p.*
Zech. 11. 7, 11, I will feed even you, O *p.* of the flock.
Mat. 5. 3, blessed are the *p.* in spirit.
2 Cor. 6. 10, as *p.*, yet making many rich.
8. 9, for your sakes he became *p.*
See Lev. 27. 8; Jas. 2. 2; Rev. 3. 17; 13. 16.
POPULOUS. Deut. 26. 5; Nah. 3. 8.
PORTION. Gen. 31. 14, is there yet any *p.* for us?
48. 22, one *p.* above thy brethren.
Deut. 32. 9, the Lord's *p.* is his people.
2 Kings 2. 9, a double *p.* of thy spirit.
Neh. 8. 10; Esth. 9. 19, send *p.* to them.
Job 20. 29, this is the *p.* of a wicked man.
24. 18, their *p.* is cursed.
26. 14; 27. 13, how little a *p.* is heard of him?
31. 2, what *p.* of God is there from above?
Ps. 11. 6, this shall be the *p.* of their cup.
16. 5, Lord is the *p.* of mine inheritance.
17. 14, have their *p.* in this life.
73. 26, God is my *p.*
119. 57; 142. 5, thou art my *p.*, O Lord.
Prov. 31. 15, giveth a *p.* to her maidens.
Eccl. 2. 10, this was my *p.* of all my labour.
3. 22; 5. 18; 9. 9, rejoice, for that is his *p.*
5. 19, God hath given power to take *p.*
9. 6, nor have they any more *p.* for ever.
11. 2, give a *p.* to seven.
Isa. 53. 12, divide a *p.* with the great.
61. 7, they shall rejoice in their *p.*
Jer. 10. 16; 51. 19, *p.* of Jacob not like them.
12. 10, my pleasant *p.* a wilderness.
52. 34, every day a *p.*
Dan. 1. 8, with *p.* of king's meat.
Mic. 2. 4, he hath changed the *p.* of my people.
Mat. 24. 51, appoint him *p.* with hypocrites.
Lu. 12. 42, their *p.* in due season.
46, his *p.* with unbelievers.
15. 12, the *p.* of goods that falleth.
See Gen. 47. 22; Josh. 17. 14; Dan. 4. 15; 11. 26.
POSSESS. Gen. 22. 17; 24. 60, thy seed shall *p.* the gate.
Job 7. 3, made to *p.* months of vanity.
13. 26, *p.* iniquities of my youth.
Prov. 8. 22, the Lord *p.* me in beginning.
Lu. 18. 12, I give tithes of all I *p.*
21. 19, in patience *p.* your souls.
See Lu. 12. 15; Acts 4. 32; 1 Cor. 7. 30; 2 Cor. 6. 10.
POSSESSION. Gen. 17. 8; 48. 4, an everlasting *p.*
Prov. 28. 10, good things in *p.*
Eccl. 2. 7; Mat. 19. 22; Mk. 10. 22, great *p.*
Acts 2. 45, and sold their *p.*
Eph. 1. 14, redemption of purchased *p.*
See Lev. 25. 10; 27. 16; 1 Kings 21. 15.
POSSIBLE. Mat. 19. 26; Mk. 10. 27, with God all things are *p.*
24. 24; Mk. 13. 22, if *p.* deceive elect.
26. 39; Mk. 14. 35, 36, if *p.* let this cup.
Mk. 9. 23, all things are *p.* to him that believeth.
14. 36; Lu. 18. 27, all things are *p.* to thee.
Rom. 12. 18, if *p.* live peaceably.
See Acts 2. 24; 20. 16; Gal. 4. 15; Heb. 10. 4.
POST. Deut. 6. 9; Job 9. 25; Jer. 51. 31; Amos 9. 1.
POSTERITY. Gen. 45. 7; Ps. 49. 13; 109. 13; Dan. 11. 4.
POT. 2 Kings 4. 2, not anything save a *p.* of oil.
40, there is death in the *p.*
Job 41. 31, maketh the deep boil like a *p.*
Zech. 14. 21, every *p.* shall be holiness.
Mk. 7. 4, the washing of cups and *p.*
John 2. 6, six water-*p.*
See Ex. 16. 33; Jer. 1. 13; John 4. 28; Heb. 9. 4.
POTENTATE. 1 Tim. 6. 15.
POUND. Lu. 19. 13; John 12. 13.
POUR. Job 10. 10, hast thou not *p.* me out as milk.
29. 6, rock *p.* out rivers of oil.
30. 16, my soul is *p.* out upon me.
Ps. 45. 2, grace is *p.* into thy lips.
62. 8, *p.* out your heart before him.
Prov. 1. 23; Isa. 44. 3; Joel 2. 28, 29; Acts 2. 17, 18, I will *p.* out my Spirit.
Cant. 1. 3, as ointment *p.* forth.
Isa. 26. 16, *p.* out prayer when chastening.
32. 15, till the spirit be *p.* on us.
44. 3, I will *p.* water on thirsty.
53. 12, *p.* out his soul unto death.
Jer. 7. 20; 42. 18, my fury shall be *p.* out.
Lam. 2. 19, *p.* out thine heart like water.
Nah. 1. 6, fury is *p.* out like fire.
Mal. 3. 10, if I will not *p.* out a blessing.

Mat. 26. 7; Mk. 14. 3, *p.* ointment on his head.
John 2. 15, he *p.* out the changers' money.
See 2 Sam. 23. 16; 2 Kings 3. 11; Rev. 14. 10; 16. 1.

POURTRAY. Ezek. 4. 1; 8. 10; 23. 14.

POVERTY. Gen. 45. 11; Prov. 20. 13, lest thou come to *p.*
Prov. 6. 11; 24. 34, thy *p.* come as one that travelleth.
10. 15, destruction of poor is *p.*
11. 24, it tendeth to *p.*
13. 18, *p.* to him that refuseth instruction.
28. 19, shall have *p.* enough.
30. 8, give me neither *p.* nor riches.
31. 7, drink and forget his *p.*
See Prov. 23. 21; 2 Cor. 8. 2; Rev. 2. 9.

POWDER. Ex. 32. 20; 2 Kings 23. 6; Mat. 21. 44.

POWER. Gen. 32. 28; Hos. 12. 3, hast thou *p.* with God.
Ex. 15. 6, glorious in *p.*
Lev. 26. 19, the pride of your *p.*
Deut. 8. 18, he giveth thee *p.* to get wealth.
2 Sam. 22. 33, God is my strength and *p.*
1 Chron. 29. 11; Mat. 6. 13, thine is the *p.* and glory.
2 Chron. 25. 8, God hath *p.* to help.
Job 26. 2, him that is without *p.*
Ps. 49. 15, from the *p.* of the grave.
65. 6, being girded with *p.*
90. 11, who knoweth *p.* of thine anger.
Prov. 3. 27, when it is in *p.* to do it.
18. 21, in the *p.* of the tongue.
Eccl. 5. 19; 6. 2, *p.* to eat thereof.
8. 4, where word of king is, there is *p.*
Isa. 40. 29, he giveth *p.* to the faint.
Mic. 3. 8, full of *p.* by the spirit.
Hab. 3. 4, the hiding of his *p.*
Zech. 4. 6, not by might, nor by *p.*
Mat. 9. 6; Mk. 2. 10; Lu. 5. 24, *p.* on earth to forgive.
8, who had given such *p.* to men.
24. 30; Lu. 21. 27, coming in clouds with *p.*
28. 18, all *p.* is given to me.
Lu. 1. 35, the *p.* of the Highest.
4. 6, all this *p.* will I give thee.
14, Jesus returned in the *p.* of the Spirit.
32, his word was with *p.*
5. 17, the *p.* of the Lord was present.
9. 43, amazed at the mighty *p.* of God.
12. 5, that hath *p.* to cast into hell.
11, bring you unto magistrates and *p.*
22. 53, your hour and the *p.* of darkness.
24. 49, with *p.* from on high.
John 1. 12, *p.* to become sons of God.
10. 18, I have *p.* to lay it down.
17. 2, *p.* over all flesh.
19. 10, I have *p.* to crucify thee.
Acts 1. 8, *p.* after the Holy Ghost is come.
3. 12, as though by our own *p.*
5. 4, was it not in thine own *p.*
8. 10, this man is the great *p.* of God.
19, give me also this *p.*
26. 18, from the *p.* of Satan unto God.
Rom. 1. 20, his eternal *p.* and Godhead.
9. 17, that I might show my *p.* in thee.
13. 2, whosoever resisteth the *p.*
1 Cor. 15. 43, it is raised in *p.*
Eph. 2. 2, prince of the *p.* of the air.
3. 7, the effectual working of his *p.*
Phil. 3. 10, the *p.* of his resurrection.
2 Thess. 1. 9, from the glory of his *p.*
2 Tim. 1. 7, spirit of *p.* and love.
3. 5, form of godliness, but denying the *p.*
Heb. 2. 14, him that had *p.* of death.
6. 5, the *p.* of the world to come.
7. 16, the *p.* of an endless life.
Rev. 2. 26, to him will I give *p.*
4. 11, worthy to receive *p.*
See Mat. 22. 29; Lu. 22. 69; Rom. 1. 16.

POWERFUL. Ps. 29. 4; 2 Cor. 10. 10; Heb. 4. 12.

PRAISE (*n.*). Ex. 15. 11, fearful in *p.*
Deut. 10. 21, he is thy *p.* and thy God.
Judg. 5. 3; Ps. 7. 17; 9. 2; 57. 7; 61. 8; 104. 33, I will sing *p.*
Neh. 9. 5, above all blessing and *p.*
Ps. 22. 3, that inhabitest the *p.* of Israel.
25, my *p.* shall be of thee.
33. 1; 147. 1, *p.* is comely for the upright.
34. 1, his *p.* continually be in my mouth.
50. 23, whoso offereth *p.* glorifieth me.
65. 1, *p.* waiteth for thee.
66. 2, make his *p.* glorious.
109. 1, O God of my *p.*
148. 14, the *p.* of all his saints.
Prov. 27. 21, so is a man to his *p.*
Isa. 60. 18, call thy gates *P.*
61. 3, garment of *p.*
62. 7, a *p.* in the earth.
Jer. 13. 11, that they might be to me for a *p.*
49. 25, how is the city of *p.*
Hab. 3. 3, earth was full of his *p.*
Zeph. 3. 30, a *p.* among all people.
John 9. 24, give God the *p.*
12. 43, the *p.* of men.
Rom. 2. 29, whose *p.* is not of men.
13. 3, thou shalt have *p.*
1 Cor. 4. 5, every man have *p.* of God.
2 Cor. 8. 18, whose *p.* is in the gospel.
Eph. 1. 6, 12, *p.* of glory of his grace.
Phil. 4. 8, if there be any *p.*
Heb. 13. 15, offer sacrifice of *p.*
1 Pet. 2. 14, *p.* of them that do well.
4. 11, to whom be *p.* and dominion.
See 2 Chron. 29. 30; Acts 16. 25; 1 Pet. 2. 9.

PRAISE (*v.*). Gen. 49. 8, whom thy brethren shall *p.*
2 Sam. 14. 25, none to be so much *p.*
Ps. 30. 9, shall the dust *p.* thee?
42. 5, 11; 43. 5, I shall yet *p.* him.
45. 17, therefore shall the people *p.* thee.
49. 18, men will *p.* thee when thou doest well.
63. 3, my lips shall *p.* thee.
67. 3, 5, let the people *p.* thee.
71. 14, I will yet *p.* thee more and more.
72. 15, daily shall he be *p.*
76. 10, the wrath of man shall *p.* thee.
88. 10, shall the dead arise and *p.* thee?
107. 32, *p.* him in the assembly.
115. 17, the dead *p.* not.
119. 164, seven times a day do I *p.* thee.
145. 4, one generation shall *p.* thy works.
10, all thy works shall *p.* thee.
Prov. 27. 2, let another *p.* thee.
31. 31, her own works *p.* her in the gates.
Isa. 38. 19, the living shall *p.* thee.
See Lu. 2. 13; 24. 53; Acts 2. 47; 3. 8.

PRANCING. Judg. 5. 22; Nah. 3. 2.

PRATING. Prov. 10. 8; 3 John 10.

PRAY. Gen. 20. 7, a prophet and shall *p.* for thee.
1 Sam. 7. 5, I will *p.* for you to the Lord.
12. 23, sin in ceasing to *p.* for you.
2 Chron. 7. 14, if my people shall *p.*
Ezra 6. 10, *p.* for the life of the king.
Job 21. 15, what profit if we *p.* to him.
Ps. 5. 2, to thee will I *p.*
55. 17, evening, morning, and at noon will I *p.*
122. 6, *p.* for the peace of Jerusalem.
Isa. 45. 20, *p.* to a god that cannot save.
Jer. 7. 16; 11. 14; 14. 11, *p.* not for this people.
37. 3; 42. 2, 20, *p.* now to the Lord for us.
Zech. 7. 2, they sent men to *p.*
Mat. 5. 44, and *p.* for them which despitefully use you.
6. 5, they love to *p.* standing.
14. 23; Mk. 6. 46; Lu. 6. 12; 9. 28, apart to *p.*
26. 36; Mk. 14. 32, while I *p.* yonder.
Mk. 11. 25, and when ye stand *p.*, forgive.
Lu. 11. 1, Lord, teach us to *p.*
18. 1, men ought always to *p.*
John 14. 16; 16. 26, I will *p.* the Father.
17. 9, I *p.* for them, I *p.* not for the world.
20, neither *p.* I for these alone.
Acts 9. 11, behold he *p.*

Rom. 8. 26, know not what we should *p.* for.
1 Cor. 14. 15, I will *p.* with the spirit, and *p.* with understanding also.
Eph. 6. 18, *p.* always with all prayer.
1 Thess. 5. 17, *p.* without ceasing.
1 Tim. 2. 8, that men *p.* everywhere.
Jas. 5. 13, is any afflicted? let him *p.*
16, *p.* one for another.
1 John 5. 16, I do not say he shall *p.* for it.
See Lu. 9. 29; 1 Cor. 11. 4; 14. 14; 1 Thess. 5. 25.
PRAYER. 2 Chron. 7. 15, ears shall be attent to the *p.*
Job 15. 4, thou restrainest *p.*
16. 17; Ps. 4. 1; 5. 3; 6. 9; 17. 1; 35. 13; 39. 12; 66. 19; Lam. 3. 8, my *p.*
Ps. 65. 2, thou that hearest *p.*
72. 15, *p.* shall be made continually.
109. 4, I give myself to *p.*
Prov. 15. 8, the *p.* of the upright.
Isa. 1. 15, when ye make many *p.*
56. 7; Mat. 21. 13; Mk. 11. 17; Lu. 19. 46, house of *p.*
Mat. 21. 22, whatever ye ask in *p.*, believing.
23. 14; Mk. 12. 40; Lu. 20. 47, long *p.*
Lu. 6. 12, all night in *p.* to God.
Acts 3. 1, the hour of *p.*
6. 4, give ourselves continually to *p.*
12. 5, *p.* was made without ceasing.
16. 13, where *p.* was wont to be made.
Phil. 4. 6, in everything by *p.*
Jas. 5. 15, *p.* of faith shall save the sick.
16, effectual fervent *p.* of a righteous man.
1 Pet. 4. 7, watch unto *p.*
Rev. 5. 8; 8. 3, the *p.* of the saints.
See Ps. 72. 20; Dan. 9. 21; Rom. 12. 12; Col. 4. 2.
PREACH. Neh. 6. 7, appointed prophets to *p.* of thee.
Isa. 61. 1, to *p.* good tidings.
Jon. 3. 2, *p.* the preaching I bid thee.
Mat. 4. 17; 10. 7, Jesus began to *p.*
11. 1, to *p.* in their cities.
5, the poor have the gospel *p.*
Mk. 2. 2, he *p.* the word to them.
16. 20, and *p.* everywhere.
Lu. 9. 60, go thou and *p.* kingdom of God.
Acts 8. 5, and *p.* Christ unto them.
10. 36, *p.* peace by Jesus Christ.
13. 38, through this man is *p.* forgiveness.
17. 18, he *p.* Jesus and the resurrection.
Rom. 2. 21, thou that *p.* a man should not steal.
10. 15, how shall they *p.* except.
1 Cor. 1. 18, the *p.* of the cross is foolishness.
21, by the foolishness of *p.*
23, but we *p.* Christ crucified.
9. 27, lest when I have *p.* to others.
15. 11, so we *p.* and so ye believed.
14, then is our *p.* vain.
2 Cor. 4. 5, we *p.* not ourselves.
Phil. 1. 15, some *p.* Christ of envy and strife.
2 Tim. 4. 2, *p.* the word; be instant.
Heb. 4. 2, word *p.* did not profit.
1 Pet. 3. 19, *p.* to spirits in prison.
See Ps. 40. 9; 2 Cor. 11. 4; Gal. 1. 8; Eph. 2. 17.
PREACHER. Rom. 10. 14, how shall they hear without a *p.*?
1 Tim. 2. 7, whereunto I am ordained a *p.*
2 Pet. 2. 5, Noah, a *p.* of righteousness.
See Eccl. 1. 1; 7. 27; 12. 8; 2 Tim. 1. 11.
PRECEPT. Neh. 9. 14, commandedst them *p.*
Isa. 28. 10, 13, *p.* must be upon *p.*
29. 13, taught by *p.* of men.
Jer. 35. 18, ye have kept Jonadab's *p.*
See Ps. 119. 4, etc.; Dan. 9. 5; Mk. 10. 5; Heb. 9. 19.
PRECIOUS. Deut. 33. 13, 14, 15, 16, *p.* things.
1 Sam. 3. 1, the word was *p.* in those days.
26. 21, my soul was *p.* in thine eyes.
2 Kings 1. 13, let my life be *p.*
Ezra 8. 27, fine copper, *p.* as gold.
Ps. 49. 8, the redemption of their soul is *p.*
72. 14, *p.* shall their blood be in his sight.
Ps. 116. 15, *p.* in sight of the Lord is death of saints.
126. 6, bearing *p.* seed.
133. 2, like *p.* ointment upon the head.
139. 17, how *p.* are thy thoughts.
Prov. 3. 15, wisdom more *p.* than rubies.
Eccl. 7. 1, good name better than *p.* ointment.
Isa. 13. 12, I will make a man more *p.*
28. 16; 1 Pet. 2. 6, a *p.* corner stone.
43. 4, since thou wast *p.* in my sight.
Jer. 15. 19, take the *p.* from the vile.
Lam. 4. 2, the *p.* sons of Zion.
1 Pet. 1. 7, trial of faith more *p.* than gold.
19, the *p.* blood of Christ.
2. 7, to you which believe he is *p.*
2 Pet. 1. 1, like *p.* faith.
4, great and *p.* promises.
See Mat. 26. 7; Mk. 14. 3; Jas. 5. 7; Rev. 21. 11.
PREEMINENCE. Eccl. 3. 19; Col. 1. 18; 3 John 9.
PREFER. Ps. 137. 6; John 1. 15; Rom. 12. 10; 1 Tim. 5. 21.
PREMEDITATE. Mk. 13. 11.
PREPARATION. Prov. 16. 1, *p.* of the heart.
Eph. 6. 15, feet shod with *p.* of gospel.
See Mat. 27. 62; Mk. 15. 42; Lu. 23. 54; John 19. 14.
PREPARE. 1 Sam. 7. 3, *p.* your hearts unto the Lord.
2 Chron. 20. 33, as yet the people had not *p.*
Ps. 68. 10, thou hast *p.* of thy goodness.
107. 36, that they may *p.* a city.
Prov. 8. 27, when he *p.* the heavens I was there.
Isa. 40. 3; Mal. 3. 1; Mat. 3. 3; Mk. 1. 2; Lu. 1. 76, *p.* way of the Lord.
62. 10, *p.* the way of the people.
Amos 4. 12, *p.* to meet thy God.
Jon. 1. 17, Lord had *p.* a great fish.
Mat. 20. 23; Mk. 10. 40, to them for whom *p.*
John 14. 2, I go to *p.* a place for you.
Rom. 9. 23, afore *p.* to glory.
1 Cor. 2. 9, things God hath *p.*
Heb. 10. 5, a body hast thou *p.* me.
See 1 Chron. 22. 5; Ps. 23. 5; Rev. 21. 2.
PRESCRIBE. Ezra 7. 22; Isa. 10. 1.
PRESENCE. Gen. 4. 16, Cain went out from the *p.* of the Lord.
47. 15, why should we die in thy *p.*
Ex. 33. 15, if thy *p.* go not with me.
Job 23. 15, I am troubled at his *p.*
Ps. 16. 11, in thy *p.* is fulness of joy.
17. 2, my sentence come forth from thy *p.*
31. 20, in the secret of thy *p.*
51. 11, cast me not away from thy *p.*
139. 7, whither shall I flee from thy *p.*?
Prov. 14. 7, go from *p.* of a foolish man.
Isa. 63. 9, angel of his *p.* saved them.
Jer. 23. 39; 52. 3, I will cast you out of my *p.*
Jon. 1. 3, to flee from *p.* of the Lord.
Zeph. 1. 7, hold thy peace at *p.* of the Lord.
Lu. 13. 26, we have eaten and drunk in thy *p.*
Acts 3. 19, times of refreshing from the *p.*
2 Cor. 10. 1, 10, who in *p.* am base.
2 Thess. 1. 9, destruction from the *p.* of the Lord.
See Gen. 16. 12; Ps. 23. 5; Prov. 25. 6; Lu. 15. 10.
PRESENT. 1 Sam. 10. 27, they brought him no *p.*
Ps. 46. 1, a very *p.* help in trouble.
John 14. 25, being yet *p.* with you.
Acts 10. 33, all here *p.* before God.
Rom. 7. 18, to will is *p.* with me.
21, evil is *p.* with me.
8. 18, sufferings of this *p.* time.
12. 1, *p.* your bodies a living sacrifice.
1 Cor. 7. 26, good for the *p.* distress.
2 Cor. 5. 8, to be *p.* with the Lord.
9, whether *p.* or absent.
Gal. 1. 4, deliver us from this *p.* world.
Col. 1. 28, *p.* every man perfect.
2 Tim. 4. 10, having loved this *p.* world.
Tit. 2. 12, live godly in this *p.* world.
Heb. 12. 11, no chastening for *p.* seemeth joyous.
2 Pet. 1. 12, established in the *p.* truth.

Jude 24, able to *p.* you faultless.
See Ps. 72. 10; Mat. 2. 11; Lu. 2. 22.
PRESENTLY. Prov. 12. 16; Mat. 21. 19; 26. 53.
PRESERVE. Gen. 32. 30, I have seen God, and my life is *p.*
45. 5, did send me before you to *p.* life.
Job 29. 2, as in days when God *p.* me.
Ps. 36. 6, thou *p.* man and beast.
121. 7, the Lord *p.* thee from evil.
8, *p.* thy going out and coming in.
Prov. 2. 8, he *p.* the way of his saints.
11, discretion shall *p.* thee.
20. 28, mercy and truth *p.* the king.
Jer. 49. 11, I will *p.* them alive.
Lu. 17. 33, lose his life shall *p.* it.
See Neh. 9. 6; Isa. 49. 6; Hos. 12. 13; Jude 1.
PRESS. Prov. 3. 10, *p.* burst with new wine.
Amos 2. 13, I am *p.* under you as a cart is *p.*
Mk. 3. 10, they *p.* on him to touch him.
Lu. 6. 38, good measure, *p.* down.
16. 16, every man *p.* into it.
Phil. 3. 14, I *p.* toward the mark.
See Mk. 2. 4; 5. 27; Lu. 8. 19; 19. 3.
PRESUME. Deut. 18. 20; Esth. 7. 5.
PRESUMPTUOUS. Num. 15. 30; Ps. 19. 13; 2 Pet. 2. 10.
PRETENCE. Mat. 23. 14; Mk. 12. 40; Phil. 1. 18.
PREVAIL. Gen. 32. 28; Hos. 12. 4, power with God, and hast *p.*
Ex. 17. 11, Moses held up hand, Israel *p.*
1 Sam. 2. 9, by strength shall no man *p.*
Ps. 9. 19, let not man *p.*
65. 3, iniquities *p.* against me.
Eccl. 4. 12, if one *p.* against him.
Mat. 16. 18, gates of hell shall not *p.*
Acts 19. 20, grew word of God and *p.*
See Job 14. 20; Jer. 20. 7; Lam. 1. 16; John 12. 19.
PREVENT. 2 Sam. 22. 6; Ps. 18. 5, snares of death *p.* me.
Ps. 88. 13, in the morning shall my prayer *p.* thee.
119. 147, I *p.* the dawning of the morning.
See Ps. 21. 3; 79. 8; Isa. 21. 14; 1 Thess. 4. 15.
PREY. Isa. 49. 24, shall the *p.* be taken from the mighty?
Jer. 21. 9; 38. 2; 39. 18; 45. 5, his life shall be for a *p.*
Ezek. 34. 22, my flock shall no more be a *p.*
See Gen. 49. 9; Num. 14. 3; Neh. 4. 4; Amos 3. 4.
PRICE. Lev. 25. 52, the *p.* of his redemption.
2 Sam. 24. 24; 1 Chron. 21. 22, I will buy it at a *p.*
Acts 5. 2, kept back part of the *p.*
1 Cor. 6. 20; 7. 23, bought with a *p.*
1 Pet. 3. 4, meek spirit of great *p.*
See Deut. 23. 18; Prov. 31. 10; Zech. 11. 12.
PRICKS. Num. 33. 55; Acts 9. 5; 26. 14.
PRIDE. Ps. 31. 20, hide them from *p.* of man.
Prov. 8. 13, *p.* do I hate.
14. 3, in mouth of foolish is rod of *p.*
Isa. 28. 1, woe to the crown of *p.*
Jer. 49. 16, *p.* of thine heart hath deceived thee.
See Mk. 7. 22; 1 Tim. 3. 6; 1 John 2. 16.
PRIEST. Gen. 14. 18; Heb. 7. 1, *p.* of most high God.
Ex. 19. 6, a kingdom of *p.*
1 Sam. 2. 35, I will raise up a faithful *p.*
2 Chron. 6. 41; Ps. 132. 16, *p.* clothed with salvation.
13. 9, *p.* of them that are no gods.
15. 3, without a teaching *p.*
Isa. 24. 2, as with the people, so with the *p.*
28. 7, *p.* and prophet have erred.
61. 6, shall be named the *p.* of the Lord.
Jer. 13. 13, will fill *p.* with drunkenness.
Mic. 3. 11, the *p.* teach for hire.
Mal. 2. 7, the *p.* lips should keep knowledge.
Lu. 17. 14, show yourselves to the *p.*
Acts 6. 7, *p.* were obedient to the faith.
Rev. 1. 6; 5. 10; 20. 6, kings and *p.* to God.
See Heb. 2. 17; 3. 1; 4. 15; 7. 26.
PRIESTHOOD. Ex. 40. 15; Num. 25. 13, an everlasting *p.*
Num. 16. 10, seek ye the *p.* also.
Heb. 7. 24, an unchangeable *p.*
1 Pet. 2. 5, an holy *p.*
9, ye are a royal *p.*
See Num. 18. 1; Josh. 18. 7; Neh. 13. 29.
PRINCE. Gen. 32. 28, as a *p.* hast thou power.
Ex. 2. 14; Num. 16. 13, who made thee a *p.* over us?
1 Sam. 2. 8; Ps. 113. 8, to set them among *p.*
2 Sam. 3. 38, a *p.* fallen in Israel.
Job 12. 21; Ps. 107. 40, poureth contempt on *p.*
21. 28, where is the house of the *p.*?
31. 37, as a *p.* would I go near him.
Ps. 45. 16, make *p.* in all the earth.
118. 9, than to put confidence in *p.*
146. 3, put not your trust in *p.*
Prov. 8. 15, by me *p.* decree justice.
31. 4, nor for *p.* strong drink.
Eccl. 10. 7, *p.* walking as servants.
16, when thy *p.* eat in the morning.
17, blessed when *p.* eat in due season.
Isa. 34. 12; 40. 23, all her *p.* shall be nothing.
Hos. 3. 4, abide many days without a *p.*
Mat. 9. 34; 12. 24; Mk. 3. 22, by *p.* of devils.
John 12. 31; 14. 30; 16. 11, the *p.* of this world.
Acts 3. 15, and killed the *P.* of life.
5. 31, exalted to be a *P.* and Saviour.
1 Cor. 2. 6, wisdom of the *p.* of this world.
8, which none of *p.* of this world knew.
Eph. 2. 2, the *p.* of the power of the air.
See Isa. 3. 4; Hos. 7. 5; Mat. 20. 25.
PRINCIPAL. Prov. 4. 7; Isa. 28. 25; Acts 25. 23.
PRINCIPALITY. Eph. 6. 12, we wrestle against *p.* and powers.
Tit. 3. 1, to be subject to *p.*
See Rom. 8. 38; Eph. 1. 21; 3. 10; Col. 1. 16.
PRINCIPLES. Heb. 5. 12; 6. 1.
PRINT. Lev. 19. 28; Job 13. 27; 19. 23; John 20. 25.
PRISON. Ps. 142. 7, bring my soul out of *p.*
Eccl. 4. 14, out of *p.* he cometh to reign.
Isa. 53. 8, taken from *p.* and from judgment.
61. 1, opening of the *p.*
Mat. 5. 25; Lu. 12. 58, thou be cast into *p.*
11. 2, John heard in the *p.*
25. 36, 39, in *p.* that ye came unto me.
Lu. 22. 33, to go with thee to *p.* and to death.
2 Cor. 11. 23, in *p.* more frequent.
1 Pet. 3. 19, spirits in *p.*
See Jer. 32. 2; 39. 14; Lu. 3. 20; Acts 5. 18.
PRISONER. Ps. 79. 11; Zech. 9. 12; Mat. 27. 16; Eph. 3. 1.
PRIVATE. 2 Pet. 1. 20.
PRIVATELY. Mat. 24. 3; Mk. 9. 28; Lu. 10. 23; Gal. 2. 2.
PRIVILY. Mat. 1. 19; 2. 7; Acts 16. 37; Gal. 2. 4; 2 Pet. 2. 1.
PRIZE. 1 Cor. 9. 24; Phil. 3. 14.
PROCEED. Gen. 24. 50, the thing *p.* from the Lord.
Deut. 8. 3; Mat. 4. 4, that *p.* out of mouth of God.
Job 40. 5, I will *p.* no further.
Isa. 29. 14, I will *p.* to do a marvellous work.
51. 4, a law shall *p.* from me.
Jer. 9. 3, they *p.* from evil to evil.
Mat. 15. 18; Mk. 7. 21, *p.* out of the mouth.
John 8. 42, I *p.* forth from God.
Jas. 3. 10, *p.* blessing and cursing.
See Lu. 4. 22; John 15. 26; Eph. 4. 29; Rev. 22. 1.
PROCLAIM. Ex. 33. 19; 34. 5, I will *p.* the name of the Lord.
Isa. 61. 1, to *p.* liberty to captives.
2, to *p.* acceptable year.
62. 11, Lord hath *p.*, thy salvation cometh.
Jer. 34. 15, in *p.* liberty every man to his neighbour.
Lu. 12. 3, *p.* upon the housetops.
See Deut. 20. 10; Prov. 20. 6; Jer. 3. 12; Joel 3. 9.

PROCURE. Prov. 11. 27; Jer. 2. 17; 4. 18; 26. 19; 33. 9.
PRODUCE. Isa. 41. 21.
PROFANE. Lev. 18. 21; 19. 12; 20. 3; 21. 6; 22. 2, *p.* name of God.
Jer. 23. 11, prophet and priest are *p.*
Ezek. 22. 26, no difference between holy and *p.*
Mat. 12. 5, priests in temple *p.* sabbath.
Acts 24. 6, hath gone about to *p.* temple.
1 Tim. 1. 9, law for unholy and *p.*
4. 7, refuse *p.* and old wives' fables.
6. 20; 2 Tim. 2. 16, avoiding *p.* babblings.
Heb. 12. 16, any *p.* person.
See Ps. 89. 39; Jer. 23. 15; Mal. 1. 12; 2. 10.
PROFESS. Rom. 1. 22; 2 Cor. 9. 13; 1 Tim. 2. 10; 6. 12.
PROFIT (*n.*). Gen. 25. 32, what *p.* shall birthright do me?
37. 26, what *p.* if we slay?
Job 21. 15, what *p.* if we pray?
Prov. 14. 23, in all labour there is *p.*
Eccl. 1. 3; 3. 9; 5. 16, what *p.* of labour?
2. 11, there was no *p.* under the sun.
5. 9, *p.* of the earth for all.
7. 11, by wisdom there is *p.*
Jer. 16. 19, things wherein is no *p.*
Mal. 3. 14, what *p.* that we have kept.
1 Cor. 10. 33, not seeking own *p.*, but *p.* of many.
2 Tim. 2. 14, about words to no *p.*
Heb. 12. 10, he chasteneth us for our *p.*
See Esth. 3. 8; Ps. 30. 9; Isa. 30. 5; 1 Tim. 4. 15.
PROFIT (*v.*). 1 Sam. 12. 21, vain things which cannot *p.*
Job 33. 27, I have sinned, and it *p.* not.
34. 9, *p.* nothing to delight in God.
Prov. 10. 2, treasures of wickedness *p.* nothing.
11. 4, riches *p.* not in the day of wrath.
Isa. 30. 5, 6, people that could not *p.*
48. 17, the Lord which teacheth thee to *p.*
Jer. 2. 11, changed for that which doth not *p.*
23. 32, they shall not *p.* this people.
Mat. 16. 26; Mk. 8. 36, what is a man *p.*?
1 Cor. 12. 7, to every man to *p.* withal.
Gal. 5. 2, Christ shall *p.* you nothing.
1 Tim. 4. 8, bodily exercise *p.* little.
Heb. 4. 2, the word preached did not *p.*
See Mat. 15. 5; Rom. 2. 25; 1 Cor. 13. 3; Jas. 2. 14.
PROFITABLE. Job 22. 2, can a man be *p.* to God?
Eccl. 10. 10, wisdom is *p.* to direct.
Acts 20. 20, I kept back nothing *p.*
1 Tim. 4. 8, godliness is *p.* to all things.
2 Tim. 3. 16, scripture is *p.* for doctrine.
See Mat. 5. 29; 2 Tim. 4. 11; Tit. 3. 8; Philem. 11.
PROLONG. Deut. 4. 26; 30. 18, ye shall not *p.* your days.
Job 6. 11, what is mine end that I should *p.* my life?
Prov. 10. 27, fear of the Lord *p.* days.
Eccl. 8. 12, though a sinner's days be *p.*
See Ps. 61. 6; Prov. 28. 2; Isa. 13. 22; 53. 10.
PROMISE (*n.*). Num. 14. 34, ye shall know my breach of *p.*
1 Kings 8. 56, hath not failed one word of *p.*
Ps. 77. 8, doth his *p.* fail?
Lu. 24. 49; Acts 1. 4, *p.* of Father.
Acts 2. 39, the *p.* is to you and your children.
26. 6, for hope of the *p.*
Rom. 4. 14, the *p.* made of none effect.
20, staggered not at the *p.*
9. 4, to whom pertain the *p.*
8; Gal. 4. 28, the children of the *p.*
2 Cor. 1. 20, *p.* are yea and Amen.
Gal. 3. 21, is the law against the *p.* of God?
1 Tim. 4. 8; 2 Tim. 1. 1, *p.* of the life that now is.
Heb. 6. 12, through faith and patience inherit the *p.*
9. 15; 10. 36, the *p.* of eternal inheritance.
11. 13, died, not having received *p.*
2 Pet. 1. 4, great and precious *p.*
3. 4, where is the *p.* of his coming?
2 Pet. 3. 9, not slack concerning his *p.*
See Eph. 1. 13; 2. 12; 6. 2; Heb. 4. 1; 11. 9.
PROMISE (*v.*). Ex. 12. 25, will give you as he hath *p.*
Num. 14. 40, will go to place the Lord *p.*
Deut. 1. 11; 15. 6, the Lord bless you as he hath *p.*
9. 28, not able to bring into land *p.*
19. 8; 27. 3, give the land he *p.* to give.
Josh. 23. 15, all good things which the Lord *p.*
2 Kings 8. 19; 2 Chron. 21. 7, he *p.* to give him a light.
Mk. 14. 11, they *p.* to give him money.
Rom. 4. 21, what he *p.* he was able to perform.
Heb. 10. 23; 11. 11, he is faithful that *p.*
1 John 2. 25, he hath *p.* eternal life.
See 1 Kings 8. 24; Neh. 9. 15; Ezek. 13. 22.
PROMOTE. Num. 22. 17; 24. 11; Prov. 4. 8.
PROMOTION. Ps. 75. 6; Prov. 3. 35.
PRONOUNCE. Judg. 12. 6; Jer. 34. 5.
PROOF. 2 Cor. 2. 9; 8. 24; 13. 3; Phil. 2. 22; 2 Tim. 4. 5.
PROPER. 1 Chron. 29. 3; 1 Cor. 7. 7; Heb. 11. 23.
PROPHECY. 1 Cor. 13. 8, whether *p.*, shall fail.
2 Pet. 1. 19, sure word of *p.*
21, *p.* came not in old time.
Rev. 1. 3; 22. 7, the words of this *p.*
See Neh. 6. 12; Prov. 31. 1; 1 Tim. 4. 14.
PROPHESY. Num. 11. 25, they *p.* and did not cease.
2 Chron. 18. 7, he never *p.* good to me.
Isa. 30. 10, *p.* not to us right things.
Jer. 5. 31, prophets *p.* falsely.
14. 14; 23. 25, prophets *p.* lies.
28. 9, the prophet which *p.* of peace.
Ezek. 37. 9, *p.* to the wind.
Joel 2. 28; Acts 2. 17, your sons shall *p.*
Amos 3. 8, who can but *p.*
7. 13, *p.* not again any more.
Mic. 2. 11, I will *p.* of wine.
Mat. 26. 68; Mk. 14. 65; Lu. 22. 64, *p.*, thou Christ.
Rom. 12. 6, let us *p.* according to the proportion.
1 Cor. 13. 9, we *p.* in part.
14. 39, covet to *p.*
1 Thess. 5. 20, despise not *p.*
See Amos. 2. 12; 1 Cor. 11. 5; Rev. 10. 11; 11. 3.
PROPHET. Ex. 7. 1, Aaron shall be thy *p.*
Num. 11. 29, would all Lord's people were *p.*
12. 6, if there be a *p.* among you.
Deut. 13. 1, if there arise a *p.* or dreamer.
18. 15; Acts 3. 22; 7. 37, the Lord will raise up a *P.*
34. 10, there arose not a *p.* like Moses.
1 Sam. 10. 12; 19. 24, is Saul among *p.*?
1 Kings 13. 11, there dwelt an old *p.* in Beth-el.
18. 22, I only remain a *p.*
22. 7; 2 Kings 3. 11, is there not a *p.* besides?
2 Kings 5. 8, he shall know there is a *p.*
1 Chron. 16. 22; Ps. 105. 15, do my *p.* no harm.
2 Chron. 20. 20, believe his *p.*, so shall ye prosper.
Ps. 74. 9, there is no more any *p.*
Isa. 3. 2, the Lord taketh away the *p.*
Jer. 29. 26, mad, and maketh himself a *p.*
37. 19, where are now your *p.*?
Ezek. 2. 5; 33. 33, there hath been a *p.* among them.
Hos. 9. 7, the *p.* is a fool.
Amos 7. 14, I was no *p.*, nor *p.* son.
Zech. 1. 5, the *p.*, do they live for ever?
Mat. 7. 15, beware of false *p.*
10. 41, that receiveth a *p.* in name of a *p.*
13. 57; Mk. 6. 4; Lu. 4. 24; John 4. 44, a *p.* not without honour.
23. 29; Lu. 11. 47, ye build the tombs of the *p.*
Lu. 1. 76, be called the *p.* of the Highest.
7. 16, a great *p.* is risen.
28, not a greater *p.* than John.
39, if he were a *p.* would have known.

Lu. 13. 33, it cannot be that a *p*. perish out of.
24. 19, Jesus, who was a *p*. mighty.
John 4. 19, I perceive thou art a *p*.
7. 40, of a truth this is the *P*.
52. out of Galilee ariseth no *p*.
Acts 26. 27, believest thou the *p*.?
1 Cor. 12. 29, are all *p*.?
14. 37, if any man think himself a *p*.
Eph. 2. 20, built on foundation of *p*.
4. 11, he gave some *p*.
1 Pet. 1. 10, of which salvation the *p*. enquired.
Rev. 22. 9, I am of thy brethren the *p*.
See 1 Kings 20. 35; Neh. 6. 14; 1 Cor. 14. 32.

PROPORTION. 1 Kings 7. 36; Job 41. 12; Rom. 12. 6.

PROSPER. Gen. 24. 56, the Lord hath *p*. my way.
39. 3, the Lord made all Joseph did to *p*.
Num. 14. 41, transgress, but it shall not *p*.
Deut. 28. 29, thou shalt not *p*. in thy ways.
1 Chron. 22. 11, *p*. thou, and build.
2 Chron. 20. 20, believe, so shall ye *p*.
26. 5, God made him to *p*.
Ezra 5. 8, this work *p*. in their hands.
Neh. 2. 20, the God of heaven will *p*. us.
Job 9. 4, who hardened himself and *p*.
Ps. 1. 3, whatsoever he doeth shall *p*.
37. 7, fret not because of him who *p*.
73. 12, the ungodly who *p*. in the world.
122. 6, they shall *p*. that love thee.
Prov. 28. 13, he that covereth sins shall not *p*.
Eccl. 11. 6, knowest not whether shall *p*.
Isa. 53. 10, pleasure of the Lord shall *p*.
54. 17, no weapon against thee shall *p*.
55. 11, it shall *p*. in the thing.
Jer. 2. 37, thou shalt not *p*. in them.
12. 1, wherefore doth way of wicked *p*.?
22. 30, no man of his seed shall *p*.
Ezek. 17. 9, 10, shall it *p*.?
15, shall he *p*., shall he escape?
1 Cor. 16. 2, lay by as God hath *p*. him.
3 John 2, in health, even as thy soul *p*.
See Prov. 17. 8; Dan. 6. 28; 8. 12.

PROSPERITY. Deut. 23. 6, thou shalt not seek their *p*.
1 Sam. 25. 6, say to him that liveth in *p*.
Job 15. 21, in *p*. the destroyer shall come.
Ps. 30. 6, in my *p*. I said, I shall never.
73. 3, when I saw the *p*. of the wicked.
Prov. 1. 32, *p*. of fools shall destroy them.
Eccl. 7. 14, in day of *p*. be joyful.
Jer. 22. 21, I spake to thee in thy *p*.
See 1 Kings 10. 7; Job 36. 11; Ps. 35. 17; 122. 7.

PROSPEROUS. Gen. 39. 2, he was a *p*. man.
Josh. 1. 8, then thou shalt make thy way *p*.
Job 8. 6, make habitation of thy righteousness *p*.
Zech. 8. 12, the seed shall be *p*.
See Gen. 24. 21; Judg. 18. 5; 2 Chron. 7. 11; Rom. 1. 10.

PROTECTION. Deut. 32. 38.

PROTEST. Gen. 43. 3; Jer. 11. 7; Zech. 3. 6; 1 Cor. 15. 31.

PROUD. Job 38. 11, here shall thy *p*. waves be stayed.
40. 11, every one that is *p*., and abase him.
Ps. 31. 23, rewardeth the *p*. doer.
40. 4, man that respecteth not the *p*.
94. 2, render a reward to the *p*.
101. 5, him that hath a *p*. heart will not I suffer.
123. 4, soul filled with contempt of the *p*.
138. 6, the *p*. he knoweth afar off.
Prov. 6. 17, the Lord hateth a *p*. look.
15. 25, the Lord will destroy house of the *p*.
16. 5, *p*. in heart is abomination.
21. 4, a *p*. heart is sin.
Eccl. 7. 8, patient better than *p*. in spirit.
Hab. 2. 5, he is a *p*. man.
Mal. 3. 15, we call the *p*. happy.
Lu. 1. 51, scattered the *p*.
1 Tim. 6. 4, he is *p*., knowing nothing.
Jas. 4. 6; 1 Pet. 5. 5, God resisteth the *p*.
See Job 9. 13; 26. 12; Rom. 1. 30; 2 Tim. 3. 2.

PROUDLY. Ex. 18. 11; 1 Sam. 2. 3; Neh. 9. 10; Isa. 3. 5; Obad. 12.

PROVE. Ex. 15. 25, there he *p*. them.
Judg. 6. 39, let me *p*. thee but this once.
1 Sam. 17. 39, I have not *p*. them.
1 Kings 10. 1; 2 Chron. 9. 1, she came to *p*. Solomon.
Ps. 17. 3, thou hast *p*. mine heart.
81. 7, I *p*. thee at the waters.
95. 9; Heb. 3. 9, when your fathers *p*. me.
Mal. 3. 10, *p*. me now herewith.
Lu. 14. 19, I go to *p*. them.
2 Cor. 8. 22, whom we have often *p*. diligent.
13. 5, *p*. your own selves.
1 Thess. 5. 21, *p*. all things.
See Eccl. 2. 1; 7. 23; Dan. 1. 14; John 6. 6.

PROVERB. Deut. 28. 37, a *p*. and a byword.
Ps. 69. 11, I became a *p*. to them.
Eccl. 12. 9, set in order many *p*.
Ezek. 16. 44, every one that useth *p*.
Lu. 4. 23, will surely say this *p*.
John 16. 29, speakest plainly, and no *p*.
See Num. 21. 27; 1 Sam. 10. 12; Prov. 1. 6.

PROVIDE. Gen. 22. 8, God will *p*. himself a lamb.
30. 30, when shall I *p*. for mine own house?
Ps. 78. 20, can he *p*. flesh?
Mat. 10. 9, *p*. neither gold nor silver.
Lu. 12. 20, whose shall those things be thou hast *p*.?
33, *p*. bags that wax not old.
Rom. 12. 17; 2 Cor. 8. 21, *p*. things honest.
1 Tim. 5. 8, if any *p*. not for his own.
Heb. 11. 40, having *p*. better thing for us.
See Job 38. 41; Prov. 6. 8; Acts 23. 24.

PROVIDENCE. Acts 24. 2.

PROVISION. Gen. 42. 25; 45. 21, *p*. for the way.
Ps. 132. 15, I will abundantly bless her *p*.
Rom. 13. 14, make not *p*. for the flesh.
See Josh. 9. 5; 1 Kings 4. 7; 2 Kings 6. 23.

PROVOCATION. Job 17. 2; Ps. 95. 8; Ezek. 20. 28.

PROVOKE. Ex. 23. 21, obey his voice and *p*. him not.
Num. 14. 11, how long will this people *p*. me?
Deut. 31. 20, *p*. me and break my covenant.
Job 12. 6, they that *p*. God are secure.
Ps. 106. 7, they *p*. him at the sea.
29, they *p*. him with their inventions.
Lu. 11. 53, began to urge and *p*. him to speak.
Rom. 10. 19; 11. 11, I will *p*. to jealousy.
1 Cor. 13. 5, is not easily *p*.
Gal. 5. 26, *p*. one another.
Eph. 6. 4, *p*. not your children to wrath.
Heb. 10. 24, to *p*. to love and good works.
See Prov. 20. 2; Isa. 65. 3; Jer. 7. 19; 44. 8.

PRUDENCE. 2 Chron. 2. 12; Prov. 8. 12; Eph. 1. 8.

PRUDENT. Prov. 12. 16, a *p*. man covereth shame.
23, a *p*. man concealeth knowledge.
14. 15, the *p*. looketh well to his going.
16. 21, wise in heart called *p*.
19. 14, *p*. wife is from the Lord.
22. 3; 27. 12, *p*. man foreseeth evil.
Isa. 5. 21, woe unto them that are *p*. in their own sight.
Jer. 49. 7, counsel perished from *p*.
Hos. 14. 9, who is *p*.?
Mat. 11. 25; Lu. 10. 21, hast hid things from *p*.
See Isa. 52. 13; Amos 5. 13; Acts 13.

PRUNE. Lev. 25. 3; Isa. 2. 4; Joel 3. 10; Mic. 4. 3.

PSALTERY. Dan. 3. 5, the sound of the cornet, flute, *p*., etc.
See 2 Sam. 6. 5; 2 Chron. 9. 11.

PUBLIC. Mat. 1. 19; Acts 18. 28; 20. 20.

PUBLISH. Deut. 32. 3, I will *p*. the name of the Lord.

2 Sam. 1. 20, *p.* it not in Askelon.
Ps. 68. 11, great was the company that *p.* it.
Isa. 52. 7; Nah. 1. 15, that *p.* peace.
Mk. 1. 45; 5. 20, he began to *p.* it much.
Lu. 8. 39, *p.* throughout the whole city.
See Esth. 1. 20; 3. 14; Jon. 3. 7; Mk. 13. 10.
PUFFED. 1 Cor. 4. 6; 5. 2; 13. 4; Col. 2. 18.
PUFFETH. Ps. 10. 5; 12. 5; 1 Cor. 8. 1.
PULL. Lam. 3. 11, *p.* me in pieces.
Amos 9. 15, shall no more be *p.* up.
Zech. 7. 11, they *p.* away the shoulder.
Mat. 7. 4; Lu. 6. 42, *p.* mote out of thine eye.
Lu. 12. 18, will *p.* down barns.
14. 5, will not *p.* him out on sabbath.
2 Cor. 10. 4, to the *p.* down of strong holds.
Jude 23, *p.* them out of the fire.
See Gen. 8. 9; Ezra 6. 11; Ps. 31. 4; Isa. 22. 19.
PULPIT. Neh. 8. 4.
PULSE. 2 Sam. 17. 28; Dan. 1. 12.
PUNISH. Ezra 9. 13, *p.* less than iniquities deserve.
Prov. 17. 26, to *p.* the just is not good.
Isa. 13. 11, I will *p.* the world for their evil.
26. 21, Lord cometh to *p.* inhabitants.
Jer. 13. 21, what wilt thou say when he *p.*
Acts 26. 11, I *p.* them in every synagogue.
2 Thess. 1. 9, *p.* with everlasting destruction.
2 Pet. 2. 9, to day of judgment to be *p.*
See Lev. 26. 18; Prov. 21. 11; 22. 3; 27. 12.
PUNISHMENT. Gen. 4. 13, my *p.* is greater than I can bear.
Lev. 26. 41, accept the *p.* of their iniquity.
1 Sam. 28. 10, no *p.* shall happen to thee.
Lam. 3. 39, a man for the *p.* of his sins.
4. 6, *p.* greater than *p.* of Sodom.
22, the *p.* is accomplished.
Ezek. 14. 10, shall bear *p.* of their iniquity.
Mat. 25. 46, everlasting *p.*
Heb. 10. 29, of how much sorer *p.*
1 Pet. 2. 14, the *p.* of evildoers.
See Prov. 19. 19; Amos 1. 3; 2. 1; 2 Cor. 2. 6.
PURCHASE. Ruth 4. 10, have I *p.* to be my wife.
Ps. 74. 2, congregation thou hast *p.*
Acts 1. 18, *p.* a field with reward of iniquity.
8. 20, gift of God *p.* by money.
20. 28, he hath *p.* with his own blood.
Eph. 1. 14, redemption of *p.* possession.
1 Tim. 3. 13, *p.* to themselves a good degree.
See Gen. 49. 32; Ex. 15. 16; Lev. 25. 33; Jer. 32. 11.
PURE. Deut. 32. 14, the *p.* blood of the grape.
2 Sam. 22. 27; Ps. 18. 26, with *p.* show thyself *p.*
Job 4. 17, shall man be more *p.*?
8. 6, if thou wert *p.* and upright.
11. 4, my doctrine is *p.*
16. 17, my prayer is *p.*
25. 5, stars are not *p.* in his sight.
Ps. 12. 6, the words of the Lord are *p.*
19. 8, commandment of the Lord is *p.*
119. 140, thy word is very *p.*
Prov. 15. 26, words of the *p.* are pleasant.
20. 9, who can say, I am *p.*?
Mic. 6. 11, shall I count them *p.*?
Zeph. 3. 9, turn to the people a *p.* language.
Acts 20. 26, *p.* from blood of all men.
Rom. 14. 20, all things indeed are *p.*
Phil. 4. 8, whatsoever things are *p.*
1 Tim. 3. 9; 2 Tim. 1. 3, in a *p.* conscience.
5. 22, keep thyself *p.*
Tit. 1. 15, to the *p.* all things are *p.*
Jas. 1. 27, *p.* religion.
3. 17, first *p.*, then peaceable.
2 Pet. 3. 1, stir up your *p.* minds.
1 John 3. 3, even as he is *p.*
Rev. 22. 1, a *p.* river of water of life.
See Ex. 27. 20; Ezra 6. 20; Mal. 1. 11.
PURELY. Isa. 1. 25.
PURENESS. Job 22. 30; Prov. 22. 11; 2 Cor. 6. 6.
PURER. Lam. 4. 7; Hab. 1. 13.
PURGE. 2 Chron. 34. 8, when he had *p.* the land.
Ps. 51. 7, *p.* me with hyssop.
Ps. 65. 3, transgressions, thou shalt *p.* them.
Isa. 1. 25, and purely *p.* away thy dross.
6. 7, thy sin is *p.*
22. 14, this iniquity shall not be *p.*
Ezek. 24. 13, I have *p.* thee and thou wast not *p.*
Mal. 3. 3, *p.* them as gold.
Mat. 3. 12; Lu. 3. 17, *p.* his floor.
John 15. 2, he *p.* it, that it may bring forth.
1 Cor. 5. 7, *p.* out the old leaven.
2 Tim. 2. 21, if a man *p.* himself from these.
Heb. 9. 14, *p.* your conscience.
22, all things are *p.* with blood.
See Prov. 16. 6; Heb. 1. 3; 10. 2; 2 Pet. 1. 9.
PURIFY. Tit. 2. 14; Jas. 4. 8; 1 Pet. 1. 22.
PURITY. 1 Tim. 4. 12; 5. 2.
PURLOINING. Tit. 2. 10.
PURPOSE. Job 17. 11, my *p.* are broken off.
Prov. 20. 18, every *p.* established by counsel.
Isa. 14. 27, the Lord hath *p.*, who shall disannul?
46. 11, I have *p.*, I will also do it.
Mat. 26. 8, to what *p.* is this waste?
Acts 11. 23, with *p.* of heart.
Rom. 8. 28, called according to his *p.*
9. 11, that the *p.* of God might stand.
Eph. 1. 11, according to the *p.*
3. 11, eternal *p.* in Christ.
See 2 Cor. 1. 17; 2 Tim. 1. 9; 1 John 3. 8.
PURSE. Prov. 1. 14; Mat. 10. 9; Mk. 6. 8; Lu. 10. 4.
PURSUE. Lev. 26. 17; Prov. 28. 1, shall flee when none *p.*
Deut. 19. 6; Josh. 20. 5, lest avenger *p.*
Job 13. 25, wilt thou *p.* the stubble?
30. 15, terrors *p.* my soul.
Ps. 34. 14, seek peace and *p.* it.
Prov. 11. 19, he that *p.* evil *p.* it to death.
13. 21, evil *p.* sinners.
Jer. 48. 2, the sword shall *p.* thee.
See Ex. 15. 9; 2 Sam. 24. 13; 1 Kings 18. 27.
PUSH. Ex. 21. 29; 1 Kings 22. 11; Job 30. 12.
PUT. Ex. 23. 1, *p.* not thine hand with the wicked.
Lev. 26. 8; Deut. 32. 30, *p.* ten thousand to flight.
Judg. 12. 3; 1 Sam. 28. 21, I *p.* my life in my hands.
1 Sam. 2. 36, *p.* me into one of priests' offices.
1 Kings 9. 3; 14. 21, to *p.* my name there.
Eccl. 10. 10, must he *p.* to more strength.
Isa. 43. 26, *p.* me in remembrance.
Mat. 19. 6; Mk. 10. 9, let not man *p.* asunder.
Mk. 10. 16, *p.* his hands on them and blessed.
Philem. 18, *p.* that on mine account.
2 Pet. 1. 14, I must *p.* off this tabernacle.
See Lu. 9. 62; John 13. 2; 1 Thess. 5. 8.
PUTRIFYING. Isa. 1. 6.

Q

QUAKE. Joel 2. 10; Nah. 1. 5; Mat. 27. 51; Heb. 12. 21.
QUANTITY. Isa. 22. 24.
QUARREL. Lev. 26. 25; 2 Kings 5. 7; Mk. 6. 19; Col. 3. 13.
QUARTER. Ex. 13. 7; Mk. 1. 45; Rev. 20. 8.
QUATERNIONS. Acts 12. 4, delivered him to four *q.*
QUEEN. Jer. 44. 17, 25, burn incense unto the *q.*
QUENCH. Num. 11. 2, the fire was *q.*
2 Sam. 21. 17, *q.* not light of Israel.
Cant. 8. 7, many waters cannot *q.* love.
Isa. 34. 10, shall not be *q.* night nor day.
42. 3; Mat. 12. 20, smoking flax not *q.*
66. 24, neither shall their fire be *q.*
Mk. 9. 43, 48, fire that never shall be *q.*
Eph. 6. 16, able to *q.* fiery darts.
1 Thess. 5. 19, *q.* not the Spirit.
Heb. 11. 34, *q.* violence of fire.
See Ps. 104. 11; 118. 12; Ezek. 20. 47; Amos 5. 6.
QUESTION. 1 Kings 10. 1; 2 Chron. 9. 1, to prove him with *q.*
Mat. 22. 46, neither durst ask him *q.*
Mk. 9. 16, what *q.* ye with them?
11. 29, I will ask you one *q.*

1 Cor. 10. 25, asking no *q*. for conscience.
1 Tim. 1. 4, which minister *q*. rather.
6. 4, doting about *q*.
2 Tim. 2. 23; Tit. 3. 9, unlearned *q*. avoid.
See Mk. 1. 27; 9. 10; Acts 18. 15; 19. 40.
QUICK. Num. 16. 30; Ps. 55. 15, go down *q*.
Isa. 11. 3, of *q*. understanding.
Acts 10. 42; 2 Tim. 4. 1; 1 Pet. 4. 5, Judge of *q*. and dead.
Heb. 4. 12, the word is *q*. and powerful.
See Lev. 13. 10, 24; Ps. 124. 3.
QUICKEN. Ps. 71. 20, thou shalt *q*. me again.
80. 18, *q*. us and we will call.
119. 25, *q*. me according to thy word.
37, *q*. me in thy way.
50, thy word hath *q*. me.
Rom. 8. 11, shall also *q*. your bodies.
1 Cor. 15. 36, that thou sowest is not *q*.
Eph. 2. 1, you hath he *q*.
5; Col. 2. 13, *q*. us together with Christ.
1 Pet. 3. 18, to death in flesh, *q*. by Spirit.
See John 5. 21; 6. 63; Rom. 4. 17; 1 Tim. 6. 13.
QUICKLY. Ex. 32. 8; Deut. 9. 12, have turned aside *q*.
Num. 16. 46, go *q*. to congregation.
Josh. 10. 6, come *q*. and save us.
Eccl. 4. 12, threefold cord not *q*. broken.
Mat. 5. 25, agree with adversary *q*.
Lu. 14. 21, go *q*. into streets and lanes.
John 13. 27, that thou doest, do *q*.
Rev. 2. 5, 16, repent, else I will come *q*.
3. 11; 22. 7, 12, I come *q*.
22. 20, surely I come *q*.
See Gen. 18. 6; 27. 20; Lu. 16. 6; Acts 22. 18.
QUICKSANDS. Acts 27. 17, fearing lest they should fall into the *q*.
QUIET. Ps. 107. 30, then are they glad because *q*.
131. 2, I have *q*. myself as a child.
Eccl. 9. 17, words of wise are heard in *q*.
Isa. 7. 4, be *q*., fear not.
14. 7, earth is at rest and *q*.
32. 18, in *q*. resting places.
33. 20, a *q*. habitation.
Jer. 49. 23, sorrow on the sea, it cannot be *q*.
Ezek. 16. 42, I will be *q*.
Acts 19. 36, ye ought to be *q*.
1 Thess. 4. 11, study to be *q*.
1 Tim. 2. 2, a *q*. and peaceable life.
1 Pet. 3. 4, ornament of a meek and *q*. spirit.
See 2 Kings 11. 20; 2 Chron. 14. 1; Job 3. 13; 21. 23.
QUIETLY. 2 Sam. 3. 27; Lam. 3. 26.
QUIETNESS. Job 34. 29, when he giveth *q*.
Prov. 17. 1, better a dry morsel and *q*.
Eccl. 4. 6, better handful with *q*. than both.
Isa. 30. 15, in *q*. and confidence strength.
32. 17, effect of righteousness *q*.
See Judg. 8. 28; 1 Chron. 22. 9; 2 Thess. 3. 12.
QUIT. Ex. 21. 19; Josh. 2. 20; 1 Sam. 4. 9; 1 Cor. 16. 13.
QUITE. Gen. 31. 15; Job 6. 13; Hab. 3. 9.
QUIVER. Ps. 127. 5; Jer. 5. 16; Lam. 3. 13.

R

RACE. Ps. 19. 5; Eccl. 9. 11; 1 Cor. 9. 24; Heb. 12. 1.
RAGE. 2 Kings 5. 12, turned away in a *r*.
Ps. 2. 1; Acts 4. 25, why do the heathen *r*.
Prov. 14. 16, the fool *r*. and is confident.
See Prov. 6. 34; 29. 9; Dan. 3. 13; Hos. 7. 16.
RAGGED. Isa. 2. 21.
RAGING. Ps. 89. 9; Prov. 20. 1; Lu. 8. 24; Jude 13.
RAGS. Prov. 23. 21; Isa. 64. 6; Jer. 38. 11.
RAIMENT. Gen. 28. 20, if the Lord will give me *r*.
Deut. 8. 4, thy *r*. waxed not old.
24. 13, that he may sleep in his *r*.
17, nor take a widow's *r*. to pledge.
Job 27. 16, though he prepare *r*. as the clay.
Isa. 63. 3, I will stain all my *r*.
Zech. 3. 4, I will clothe thee with *r*.
Mat. 6. 25; Lu. 12. 23, the body more than *r*.
Mat. 6. 28, why take thought for *r*.
11. 8; Lu. 7. 25, man clothed in soft *r*.
17. 2; Mk. 9. 3; Lu. 9. 29, his *r*. was white as light.
1 Tim. 6. 8, having food and *r*., be content.
Jas. 2. 2, poor man in vile *r*.
Rev. 3. 18, buy white *r*.
See Mat. 3. 4; Lu. 10. 30; 23. 34; Acts 22. 20.
RAIN (*n*.). Lev. 26. 4; Deut. 11. 14; 28. 12, *r*. in due season.
Deut. 11. 11, drinketh water of the *r*. of heaven.
32. 2, my doctrine shall drop as the *r*.
2 Sam. 23. 4, clear shining after *r*.
1 Kings 18. 41, sound of abundance of *r*.
Ezra 10. 13, a time of much *r*.
Job 5. 10, who giveth *r*. on earth.
37. 6, to small *r*. and to great *r*.
38. 28, hath the *r*. a father.
Ps. 72. 6, like *r*. on mown grass.
Prov. 25. 14, like clouds and wind without *r*.
23, north wind driveth away *r*.
26. 1, as *r*. in harvest.
28. 3, that oppresseth poor is like sweeping *r*.
Eccl. 11. 3, if clouds be full of *r*.
12. 2, nor clouds return after *r*.
Cant. 2. 11, the *r*. is over and gone.
Isa. 4. 6, covert from storm and *r*.
55. 10, as the *r*. cometh down.
Ezek. 38. 22, I will *r*. an overflowing *r*.
Hos. 6. 3, he shall come unto us as the *r*.
Mat. 5. 45, *r*. on just and unjust.
7. 25, the *r*. descended and floods came.
See Jer. 5. 24; Acts 14. 17; 28. 2; Heb. 6. 7.
RAIN (*v*.). Ex. 16. 4, I will *r*. bread from heaven.
Job 20. 23, God shall *r*. his fury on him.
Ps. 11. 6, on wicked he shall *r*. snares.
78. 24. 27, and *r*. down manna.
Ezek. 22. 24, thou art the land not *r*. upon.
Hos. 10. 12, till he come and *r*. righteousness.
See Gen. 2. 5; 7. 4; Amos 4. 7; Rev. 11. 6.
RAINY. Prov. 27. 15.
RAISE. Deut. 18. 15; Acts 3. 22, will *r*. up a Prophet.
Judg. 2. 16, 18, the Lord *r*. up judges.
1 Sam. 2. 8; Ps. 113. 7, he *r*. poor out of dust.
Job 41. 25, when he *r*. himself, mighty are.
Ps. 145. 14; 146. 8, he *r*. those that be bowed down.
Isa. 45. 13, I have *r*. him in righteousness.
Hos. 6. 2, in third day he will *r*. us up.
Mat. 10. 8; 11. 5; Lu. 7. 22, *r*. the dead.
16. 21; 17. 23; Lu. 9. 22, be *r*. the third day.
John 2. 19, in three days I will *r*. it up.
6. 39, 40, 44, 54, I will *r*. him up at last day.
Acts 2. 24, 32; 3. 15; 4. 10; 5. 30; 10. 40; 13. 30, 33, 34; 17. 31; Rom. 10. 9; 1 Cor. 6. 14; 2 Cor. 4. 14; Gal. 1. 1; Eph. 1. 20, whom God hath *r*. up.
26. 8, why incredible that God should *r*. the dead?
Rom. 4. 25, *r*. again for our justification.
6. 4, like as Christ was *r*. from the dead.
8. 11, Spirit of him that *r*. up Jesus.
1 Cor. 6. 14, and will also *r*. up us by his power.
15. 15, *r*. up Christ, whom he *r*. not up.
16, then is not Christ *r*.
17, if Christ be not *r*.
35, how are the dead *r*.
43, it is *r*. in glory, it is *r*. in power.
2 Cor. 1. 9, trust in God which *r*. the dead.
4. 14, he shall *r*. up us also.
Eph. 2. 6, and hath *r*. us up together.
Heb. 11. 19, accounting God was able to *r*. him.
35, women received dead *r*. to life.
Jas. 5. 15, and the Lord shall *r*. him up.
See Lu. 20. 37; John 5. 21; 2 Tim. 2. 8.
RAN. Ex. 9. 23; Num. 16. 47; Jer. 23. 21.
RANG. 1 Sam. 4. 5; 1 Kings 1. 45.
RANKS. 1 Kings 7. 4; Joel 2. 7; Mk. 6. 40.
RANSOM. Ex. 21. 30, give for the *r*. of his life.
30. 12, every man a *r*. for his soul.

Job 33. 24, I have found a *r.*
36. 18, a great *r.* cannot deliver.
Ps. 49. 7, nor give a *r.* for him.
Prov. 13. 8, the *r.* of a man's life are his riches.
Isa. 35. 10, the *r.* of the Lord shall return.
43. 3, I gave Egypt for thy *r.*
Hos. 13. 14, I will *r.* them from the grave.
Mat. 20. 28; Mk. 10. 45, to give his life a *r.*
1 Tim. 2. 6, gave himself a *r.* for all.
See Prov. 6. 35; Isa. 51. 10; Jer. 31. 11.
RARE. Dan. 2. 11.
RASE. Ps. 137. 7.
RASH. Eccl. 5. 2; Acts 19. 36.
RATHER. Job 7. 15; Jer. 8. 3, death *r.* than life.
Ps. 84. 10, *r.* be a doorkeeper.
Mat. 10. 6, go *r.* to lost sheep.
28, *r.* fear him that is able.
25. 9, go *r.* to them that sell.
Mk. 5. 26, but *r.* grew worse.
Lu. 18. 14, justified *r.* than the other.
John 3. 19, loved darkness *r.* than light.
Acts 5. 29, obey God *r.* than men.
Rom. 8. 34, that died, yea *r.*, that is risen.
12. 19, *r.* give place to wrath.
1 Cor. 6. 7, why do ye not *r.* take wrong.
Heb. 11. 25, choosing *r.* to suffer.
12. 13, let it *r.* be healed.
See Josh. 22. 24; 2 Kings 5. 13; Phil. 1. 12.
RAVENING. Ps. 22. 13; Ezek. 22. 25; Mat. 7. 15.
RAVENOUS. Isa. 35. 9; 46. 11; Ezek. 39. 4.
REACH. Gen. 11. 4; John 20. 27; 2 Cor. 10. 13.
READ. Deut. 17. 19, king shall *r.* all his life.
Isa. 34. 16, seek out of book of Lord and *r.*
Mat. 12. 3; 19. 4; 21. 16; 22. 31; Mk. 2. 25; 12. 10; Lu. 6. 3, have ye not *r.*
Lu. 4. 16, Jesus stood up to *r.*
2 Cor. 3. 2, epistle known and *r.* of all men.
1 Tim. 4. 13, give attendance to *r.*
See Hab. 2. 2; 2 Cor. 3. 14; Rev. 1. 3; 5. 4.
READINESS. Acts 17. 11; 2 Cor. 8. 11; 10. 6.
READY. Num. 32. 17, we will go *r.* armed.
Deut. 26. 5, a Syrian *r.* to perish.
2 Sam. 18. 22, wherefore run, no tidings *r.*
Neh. 9. 17, thou art a God *r.* to pardon.
Job 12. 5, *r.* to slip with his feet.
17. 1, the graves are *r.* for me.
29. 13, blessing of him *r.* to perish.
Ps. 38. 17, I am *r.* to halt.
45. 1, pen of a *r.* writer.
86. 5, good and *r.* to forgive.
88. 15, *r.* to die from my youth.
Prov. 24. 11, deliver those *r.* to be slain.
31. 6, give strong drink to *r.* to perish.
Eccl. 5. 1, be more *r.* to hear.
Isa. 27. 13, shall come that were *r.* to perish.
32. 4, stammerers *r.* to speak plainly.
38. 20, the Lord was *r.* to save me.
Dan. 3. 15, if ye be *r.* to fall down.
Mat. 22. 4; Lu. 14. 17, all things are *r.*
8, the wedding is *r.*
24. 44; Lu. 12. 40, be ye also *r.*
25. 10, they that were *r.* went in.
Mk. 14. 38, the spirit is *r.*
Lu. 22. 33, I am *r.* to go with thee.
John 7. 6, your time is alway *r.*
Acts 21. 13, *r.* not to be bound only, but.
Rom. 1. 15, I am *r.* to preach at Rome.
2 Cor. 8. 19, declaration of your *r.* mind.
9. 2, Achaia was *r.* a year ago.
1 Tim. 6. 18, *r.* to distribute.
2 Tim. 4. 6, *r.* to be offered.
Tit. 3. 1, *r.* to every good work.
1 Pet. 1. 5, *r.* to be revealed.
3. 15, *r.* always to give an answer.
5. 2, but of a *r.* mind.
Rev. 3. 2, things that are *r.* to die.
See Ex. 17. 4; 19. 11; Ezra 7. 6; Job 15. 23.
REAP. Lev. 25. 11, in jubilee neither sow nor *r.*
Eccl. 11. 4, regardeth clouds shall not *r.*
Jer. 12. 13, sown wheat, but shall *r.* thorns.
Hos. 8. 7, shall *r.* the whirlwind.
Hos. 10. 12, sow in righteousness, *r.* in mercy.
Mic. 6. 15, shalt sow, but not *r.*
Mat. 6. 26; Lu. 12. 24, sow not, neither *r.*
25. 26; Lu. 19. 21, *r.* where I sowed not.
John 4. 38, *r.* whereon ye bestowed no labour.
1 Cor. 9. 11, if we shall *r.* your carnal things.
2 Cor. 9. 6, shall *r.* sparingly.
Gal. 6. 7, that shall he also *r.*
Jas. 5. 4, cried of them which *r.*
See Isa. 17. 5; John 4. 36, 37; Rev. 14. 15.
REASON (*n.*). Job 32. 11, I gave ear to your *r.*
Prov. 26. 16, seven men that can render a *r.*
Eccl. 7. 25, to search out the *r.* of things.
Isa. 41. 21, bring forth your strong *r.*
1 Pet. 3. 15, a *r.* of the hope in you.
See 1 Kings 9. 15; Dan. 4. 36; Acts 6. 2.
REASON (*v.*). Job 9. 14, choose words to *r.* with you.
13. 3, I desire to *r.* with God.
15. 3, should he *r.* with unprofitable talk.
Isa. 1. 18, let us *r.* together.
Mat. 16. 7; 21. 25; Mk. 8. 16; 11. 31; Lu. 20. 5, they *r.* among themselves.
Lu. 5. 22, what *r.* ye in your hearts.
24. 15, while they *r.* Jesus drew near.
Acts 24. 25, as he *r.* of righteousness.
See 1 Sam. 12. 7; Mk. 2. 6; 12. 28; Acts 28. 29.
REASONABLE. Rom. 12. 1.
REBEL. Num. 14. 9, only *r.* not against the Lord.
Josh. 1. 18, whosoever doth *r.* he shall die.
Neh. 2. 19, will ye *r.* against the king.
Job 24. 13, that *r.* against the light.
Ps. 105. 28, they *r.* not against his word.
Isa. 1. 2, have nourished children and they *r.*
63. 10, they *r.* and vexed his holy Spirit.
Lam. 3. 42, we have *r.*, thou hast not pardoned.
Dan. 9. 9, though we have *r.* against him.
See 1 Sam. 12. 14; Ezek. 2. 3; Hos. 7. 14; 13. 16.
REBELLION. 1 Sam. 15. 23, *r.* is as the sin of witchcraft.
Job 34. 37, he addeth *r.* to his sin.
Prov. 17. 11, an evil man seeketh *r.*
Jer. 28. 16, thou hast taught *r.*
See Deut. 31. 27; Ezra 4. 19; Neh. 9. 17.
REBELLIOUS. Deut. 21. 18, 20, a stubborn and *r.* son.
1 Sam. 20. 30, son of perverse *r.* woman.
Ps. 66. 7, let not the *r.* exalt themselves.
68. 6, the *r.* dwell in a dry land.
Isa. 1. 23, *r.*, companions of thieves.
Jer. 5. 23, this people hath a *r.* heart.
See Ezek. 2. 3; 3. 9; 12. 2; 17. 12; 24. 3.
REBELS. Num. 17. 10; 20. 10; Ezek. 20. 38.
REBUKE (*n.*). 2 Kings 19. 3; Isa. 37. 3, this is a day of *r.*
Ps. 39. 11, when thou with *r.* dost correct.
80. 16, perish at *r.* of thy countenance.
104. 7, at thy *r.* they fled.
Prov. 13. 8, the poor heareth not *r.*
27. 5, open *r.* is better than secret love.
Eccl. 7. 5, better to hear *r.* of wise.
Isa. 30. 17, thousand flee at *r.* of one.
Jer. 15. 15, for thy sake I suffered *r.*
Phil. 2. 15, without *r.*
See Deut. 28. 20; Isa. 25. 8; 50. 2.
REBUKE (*v.*). Ps. 6. 1; 38. 1, *r.* me not in anger.
Prov. 9. 7, he that *r.* a wicked man getteth a blot.
8, *r.* a wise man, and he will love thee.
28. 23, he that *r.* a man shall find favour.
Isa. 2. 4; Mic. 4. 3, he shall *r.* many nations.
Zech. 3. 2; Jude 9, the Lord *r.* thee.
Mal. 3. 11, I will *r.* the devourer for your sakes.
Mat. 8. 26; Mk. 4. 39; Lu. 8. 24, he *r.* wind.
16. 22; Mk. 8. 32, Peter began to *r.* him.
Lu. 4. 39, he *r.* the fever.
17. 3, if thy brother trespass, *r.* him.
19. 39, Master, *r.* thy disciples.
1 Tim. 5. 1, *r.* not an elder.
20, them that sin, *r.* before all.
2 Tim. 4. 2, *r.*, exhort, with longsuffering.
Tit. 1. 13; 2. 15, *r.* them sharply.
Heb. 12. 5, nor faint when thou art *r.*

See Ruth 2. 16; Neh. 5. 7; Amos 5. 10.
RECALL. Lam. 3. 21.
RECEIPT. Mat. 9. 9; Mk. 2. 14; Lu. 5. 27.
RECEIVE. 2 Kings 5. 26, is it a time to *r.* money.
Job 4. 12, mine ear *r.* a little.
22. 22, *r.* law from his mouth.
Ps. 6. 9, the Lord will *r.* my prayer.
49. 15, he shall *r.* me.
68. 18, hast *r.* gifts for men.
73. 24, afterwards *r.* me to glory.
Prov. 2. 1, if thou wilt *r.* my words.
Isa. 40. 2, she hath *r.* double.
Jer. 2. 30, your children *r.* no correction.
Hos. 10. 6, Ephraim shall *r.* shame.
14. 2, *r.* us graciously.
Mat. 11. 5, the blind *r.* their sight.
14, if ye will *r.* it, this is Elias.
18. 5, whoso shall *r.* one such little child.
19. 12, he that is able let him *r.* it.
21. 22, ask, believing ye shall *r.*
Mk. 15. 23, but he *r.* it not.
16. 19; Acts 1. 9, he was *r.* up into heaven.
Lu. 16. 9, *r.* you into everlasting habitations.
18. 42; Acts 22. 13, *r.* thy sight.
John 1. 11, his own *r.* him not.
12, to as many as *r.* him.
3. 27, can *r.* nothing, except.
5. 43, in his own name, him ye will *r.*
44, which *r.* honour one of another.
16. 24, ask, and ye shall *r.*
20. 22, *r.* ye the Holy Ghost.
Acts 7. 59, *r.* my spirit.
8. 17, they *r.* the Holy Ghost.
10. 43, shall *r.* remission of sins.
19. 2, have ye *r.* the Holy Ghost.
20. 24, which I have *r.* of the Lord.
Rom. 5. 11, by whom we *r.* atonement.
14. 3, for God hath *r.* him.
15. 7, *r.* ye one another.
1 Cor. 3. 8, every man shall *r.* his own reward.
11. 23, I *r.* of the Lord that which also I delivered.
2 Cor. 4. 1, as we have *r.* mercy we faint not.
5. 10, every one may *r.* things done.
7. 2, *r.* us; we have wronged no man.
Phil. 2. 29, *r.* him in the Lord.
4. 15, as concerning giving and *r.*
Col. 2. 6, as ye have *r.* Christ.
1 Tim. 3. 16, *r.* up into glory.
4. 4, if it be *r.* with thanksgiving.
1 John 3. 22, whatsoever we ask we *r.*
See Ezek. 3. 10; Acts 20. 35; Jas. 4. 3.
RECKON. Lev. 25. 50, he shall *r.* with him that bought him.
Ps. 40. 5, thy thoughts cannot be *r.* up.
Mat. 18. 24, when he had begun to *r.*
25. 19, lord of servants *r.* with them.
Rom. 4. 4, reward is not *r.* of grace.
6. 11, *r.* yourselves dead to sin.
8. 18, I *r.* the sufferings of this present time.
See 2 Kings 22. 7; Isa. 38. 13; Lu. 22. 37.
RECOMMENDED. Acts 14. 26; 15. 40.
RECOMPENCE. Deut. 32. 35, to me belongeth *r.*
Job 15. 31, vanity shall be his *r.*
Isa. 35. 4, God will come with a *r.*
Hos. 9. 7, days of *r.* are come.
Joel 3. 4, will ye render me a *r.*?
Lu. 14. 12, and a *r.* be made thee.
2 Cor. 6. 13, for a *r.*, be ye also enlarged.
Heb. 2. 2; 10. 35; 11. 26, just *r.* of reward.
See Prov. 12. 14; Isa. 34. 8; Jer. 51. 56.
RECOMPENSE. Num. 5. 7, he shall *r.* his trespass.
Ruth 2. 12, the Lord *r.* thy work.
2 Sam. 19. 36, why should the king *r.* me?
Job 34. 33, he will *r.* it, whether.
Prov. 20. 22, say not, I will *r.* evil.
Isa. 65. 6, but will *r.*, even *r.* into their bosom.
Jer. 25. 14; Hos. 12. 2, will *r.* according to deeds.
Lu. 14. 14, for they cannot *r.* thee.
Rom. 12. 17, *r.* to no man evil for evil.
Rom. 11. 35, it shall be *r.* to him again.
See 2 Chron. 6. 23; Jer. 32. 18; Heb. 10. 30.
RECONCILE. 1 Sam. 29. 4, wherewith should he *r.* himself.
Ezek. 45. 20, so shall ye *r.* the house.
Mat. 5. 24, first be *r.* to thy brother.
Rom. 5. 10, if when enemies we were *r.*
Eph. 2. 16, that he might *r.* both.
See Lev. 16. 20; Rom. 11. 15; 2 Cor. 5. 19.
RECORD. Ex. 20. 24, in places where I *r.* my name.
Deut. 30. 19; 31. 28, I call heaven to *r.*
Job 16. 19, my *r.* is on high.
John 8. 13, thou bearest *r.* of thyself.
Rom. 10. 2, I bare them *r.*
Phil. 1. 8, God is my *r.* how greatly I long.
1 John 5. 7, three that bare *r.*
10, he believeth not the *r.*
11, this is the *r.*, that God hath given.
3 John 12, we bare *r.*, and our *r.* is true.
See Acts 20. 26; John 1. 19; Rev. 1. 2.
RECOUNT. Nah. 2. 5, *r.* his worthies.
RECOVER. 2 Kings 5. 3, the prophet would *r.* him.
Ps. 39. 13, that I may *r.* strength.
Isa. 11. 11, to *r.* remnant of his people.
Hos. 2. 9, and I will *r.* my wool and flax.
Mk. 16. 18, lay hands on sick, and they shall *r.*
Lu. 4. 18, preach *r.* of sight to blind.
See Isa. 38. 16; Jer. 8. 22; 41. 16; 2 Tim. 2. 16.
RED. Gen. 25. 30, *r.* pottage.
49. 12, eyes *r.* with wine.
2 Kings 3. 22, water *r.* as blood.
Ps. 75. 8, wine is *r.*, full of mixture.
Prov. 23. 31, look not on wine when *r.*
Isa. 1. 18, though your sins be *r.* like crimson.
27. 2, a vineyard of *r.* wine.
63. 2, *r.* in thine apparel.
Mat. 16. 2, fair weather, for the sky is *r.*
See Lev. 13. 19; Num. 19. 2; Nah. 2. 3; Rev. 6. 4.
REDEEM. Gen. 48. 16, angel which *r.* me.
Ex. 6. 6, I will *r.* you.
15. 13, people whom thou hast *r.*
Lev. 27. 28, no devoted thing, shall be *r.*
2 Sam. 4. 9, the Lord hath *r.* my soul.
Neh. 5. 5, nor is it in our power to *r.* them.
8, after our ability have *r.* Jews.
Job 5. 20, in famine he shall *r.* thee.
6. 23, to *r.* me from hand of mighty.
Ps. 25. 22, *r.* Israel out of all his troubles.
34. 22, the Lord *r.* the soul of his servants.
44. 26, *r.* us for thy mercies' sake.
49. 7, none can *r.* his brother.
15, God will *r.* my soul from the grave.
72. 14, he shall *r.* their soul from deceit.
107. 2, let the *r.* of the Lord say so.
130. 8, he shall *r.* Israel.
Isa. 1. 27, Zion shall be *r.* with judgment.
35. 9, the *r.* shall walk there.
44. 22, return, for I have *r.* thee.
50. 2, is my hand shortened, that it cannot *r.*
51. 11, the *r.* of the Lord shall return.
52. 3, *r.* without money.
63. 4, the year of my *r.* is come.
Hos. 7. 13, though I *r.* them, they have spoken lies.
13. 14, I will *r.* them from death.
Lu. 1. 68, hath visited, and *r.* his people.
24. 21, he who should have *r.* Israel.
Gal. 3. 13, *r.* us from curse of the law.
4. 5, *r.* them that were under the law.
Tit. 2. 14, that he might *r.* us from iniquity.
1 Pet. 1. 18, not *r.* with corruptible things.
Rev. 5. 9, thou hast *r.* us by thy blood.
See Num. 18. 15; 2 Sam. 7. 23; Eph. 5. 16; Col. 4. 5.
REDEEMER. Job 19. 25, I know that my *r.* liveth.
Ps. 19. 14, O Lord, my strength and my *r.*
78. 35, God was their *r.*
Prov. 23. 11, their *r.* is mighty.
Isa. 47. 4, as for our *r.*, the Lord of hosts is his name.

Isa. 49. 26; 60. 16, know that I am thy *R*.
59. 20, the *R*. shall come to Zion.
63. 16, thou art our *r*.
See Isa. 41. 14; 44. 6; 48. 17; 54. 5; Jer. 50. 34.
REDEMPTION. Lev. 25. 24, grant a *r*. for the land.
Ps. 49. 8, the *r*. of their soul is precious.
111. 9, he sent *r*. to his people.
130. 7, plenteous *r*.
Jer. 32. 7, the right of *r*. is thine.
Lu. 2. 38, that looked for *r*. in Jerusalem.
21. 28, your *r*. draweth nigh.
Rom. 8. 23, the *r*. of our body.
Eph. 4. 30, sealed unto the day of *r*.
See Num. 3. 49; Rom. 3. 24; 1 Cor. 1. 30; Heb. 9. 12.
REDOUND. 2 Cor. 4. 15, grace might *r*.
REFORMATION. Heb. 9. 10, time of *r*.
REFORMED. Lev. 26. 23, if ye will not be *r*.
REFRAIN. Gen. 45. 1, Joseph could not *r*. himself.
Job 7. 11, I will not *r*. my mouth.
29. 9, princes *r*. talking.
Ps. 40. 9, I have not *r*. my lips.
119. 101, *r*. my feet from every evil way.
Prov. 1. 15, *r*. thy foot from their path.
10. 19, he that *r*. his lips is wise.
Acts 5. 38, *r*. from these men.
See Gen. 43. 31; Isa. 64. 12; Jer. 31. 16; 1 Pet. 3. 10.
REFRESH. Ex. 31. 17, he rested and was *r*.
Job 32. 20, I will speak that I may be *r*.
Prov. 25. 13, he *r*. the soul of his masters.
Acts 3. 19, times of *r*. shall come.
1 Cor. 16. 18, they *r*. my spirit.
See 1 Kings 13. 7; Isa. 28. 12; Rom. 15. 32; 2 Cor. 7. 13.
REFUSE(*n*.). 1 Sam. 15. 9; Lam. 3. 45; Amos 8. 6.
REFUSE (*v*.). Gen. 37. 35, Jacob *r*. to be comforted.
Num. 22. 13, the Lord *r*. to give me leave.
1 Sam. 16. 7, look not on him, for I have *r*. him.
Job 6. 7, things my soul *r*. to touch.
Ps. 77. 2, my soul *r*. to be comforted.
78. 10, they *r*. to walk in his law.
118. 22, stone the builders *r*.
Prov. 1. 24, I have called and ye *r*.
8. 33, be wise and *r*. it not.
10. 17, he that *r*. reproof.
13. 18, shame to him that *r*. instruction.
15. 32, he that *r*. instruction despiseth his soul.
21. 25, his hands *r*. to labour.
Isa. 7. 15, 16, may know to *r*. the evil.
Jer. 8. 5, they *r*. to return.
9. 6, they *r*. to know me.
15. 18, my wound *r*. to be healed.
25. 28, if they *r*. to take the cup.
38. 21, if thou *r*. to go forth.
Zech. 7. 11, they *r*. to hearken.
Acts 7. 35, this Moses whom they *r*.
1 Tim. 4. 4, nothing to be *r*.
7, *r*. profane and old wives' fables.
5. 11, the younger widows *r*.
Heb. 11. 24, Moses *r*. to be called.
12. 25, *r*. not him that speaketh.
See Ex. 4. 23; 10. 3; 1 Kings 20. 35; 2 Kings 5. 16.
REGARD. Gen. 45. 20, *r*. not your stuff.
Ex. 5. 9, let them not *r*. vain words.
Deut. 10. 17, that *r*. not persons.
1 Kings 18. 29, neither voice, nor any that *r*.
Job 4. 20, they perish without any *r*. it.
34. 19, nor *r*. rich more than poor.
39. 7, neither *r*. crying of the driver.
Ps. 28. 5; Isa. 5. 12, they *r*. not works of the Lord.
66. 18, if I *r*. iniquity in my heart.
102. 17, he will *r*. prayer of the destitute.
106. 44, he *r*. their affliction.
Prov. 1. 24, and no man *r*.
5. 2, that thou mayest *r*. discretion.
6. 35, he will not *r*. any ransom.
12. 10, *r*. the life of his beast.
Prov. 13. 18; 15. 5, he that *r*. reproof.
Eccl. 11. 4, he that *r*. the clouds.
Lam. 4. 16, the Lord will no more *r*. them.
Dan. 11. 37, *r*. God of his fathers, nor *r*. any god.
Mal. 1. 9, will he *r*. your persons.
Mat. 22. 16; Mk. 12. 14, *r*. not the person of men.
Lu. 18. 2, neither *r*. man.
Rom. 14. 6, he that *r*. the day, *r*. it to the Lord.
See Deut. 28. 50; 2 Kings 3. 14; Amos 5. 22; Phil. 2. 30.
REGENERATION. Mat. 19. 28, in the *r*.
Tit. 3. 5, by the washing of *r*.
See John 1. 13; 3. 3.
REGISTER. Ezra 2. 62; Neh. 7. 5, 64.
REHEARSE. Judg. 5. 11, *r*. the righteous acts.
Acts 14. 27, they *r*. all God had done.
See Ex. 17. 14; 1 Sam. 8. 21; 17. 31; Acts 11. 4.
REIGN. Gen. 37. 8, shalt thou *r*. over us?
Ex. 15. 18; Ps. 146. 10, Lord shall *r*. for ever.
Lev. 26. 17, that hate you shall *r*. over you.
Deut. 15. 6, thou shalt *r*. over many nations.
Judg. 9. 8, the trees said, *r*. thou over us?
1 Sam. 11. 12, shall Saul *r*. over us.
12. 12, nay, but a king shall *r*. over us.
2 Sam. 16. 8, in whose stead thou hast *r*.
Job 34. 30, that the hypocrite *r*. not.
Ps. 47. 8, God *r*. over the heathen.
93. 1; 96. 10; 97. 1; 99. 1, the Lord *r*.
Prov. 8. 15, by me kings *r*.
30. 22, for a servant when he *r*.
Eccl. 4. 14, out of prison he cometh to *r*.
Isa. 32. 1, a king shall *r*. in righteousness.
52. 7, that saith unto Zion, thy God *r*.
Jer. 22. 15, shalt thou *r*. because thou closest?
23. 5, a king shall *r*. and prosper.
Mic. 4. 7, the Lord shall *r*. over them.
Lu. 19. 14, not have this man to *r*. over us.
27, that would not I should *r*.
Rom. 5. 14, death *r*. from Adam to Moses.
17, death *r*. by one.
21, as sin hath *r*., so might grace *r*.
6. 12, let not sin *r*. in your bodies.
1 Cor. 4. 8, ye have *r*. as kings without us.
15. 25, for he must *r*.
2 Tim. 2. 12, if we suffer we shall also *r*. with him.
Rev. 5. 10, we also shall *r*. on the earth.
11. 15, he shall *r*. for ever and ever.
19. 6, the Lord God omnipotent *r*.
See Isa. 24. 23; Luke 1. 33; Rev. 20. 4; 22. 5.
REINS. Job 16. 13, he cleaveth my *r*. asunder.
19. 27, though my *r*. be consumed.
Ps. 7. 9, God trieth the *r*.
16. 7, my *r*. instruct me.
26. 2, examine me, try my *r*.
73. 21, thus I was pricked in my *r*.
139. 13, thou hast possessed my *r*.
Prov. 23. 16, my *r*. shall rejoice.
Isa. 11. 5, faithfulness the girdle of his *r*.
Rev. 2. 23, I am he who searcheth the *r*.
See Jer. 11. 20; 12. 2; 17. 10; 20. 12; Lam. 3. 13.
REJECT. 1 Sam. 8. 7, they have not *r*. thee, but they have *r*. me.
10. 19, ye have *r*. God who saved you.
15. 23, because thou hast *r*. the word of the Lord.
16. 1, I have *r*. him from being king.
Isa. 53. 3, despised and *r*. of men.
Jer. 2. 37, the Lord hath *r*. thy confidence.
7. 29, the Lord hath *r*. the generation.
8. 9, they have *r*. the word of the Lord.
14. 19, thou hast utterly *r*. Judah.
Lam. 5. 22, thou hast utterly *r*. us.
Hos. 4. 6, because thou hast *r*. knowledge, I will *r*. thee.
Mat. 21. 42; Mk. 12. 10; Lu. 20. 17, the stone which builders *r*.
Mk. 7. 9, full well ye *r*. the commandment.
Lu. 7. 30, lawyers *r*. the counsel of God.
17. 25, must first be *r*. of this generation.
Tit. 3. 10, after admonition *r*.
Heb. 12. 17, when he would have inherited was *r*.

See Jer. 6. 19; Mk. 6. 26; 8. 31; Lu. 9. 22; John 12. 48.
REJOICE. Deut. 12. 7, shall *r.* in all ye put your hand to.
16. 14, thou shalt *r.* in thy feast.
26. 11, thou shalt *r.* in every good thing.
28. 63; 30. 9, the Lord will *r.* over you.
30. 9, *r.* for good as he *r.* over thy fathers.
1 Sam. 2. 1, because I *r.* in thy salvation.
1 Chron. 16. 10, let the heart of them *r.* that seek the Lord.
2 Chron. 6. 41, let thy saints *r.* in goodness.
Job 21. 12, they *r.* at sound of the organ.
31. 25, if I *r.* because my wealth was great.
29, if I *r.* at destruction of him that.
39. 21, the horse *r.* in his strength.
Ps. 2. 11, *r.* with trembling.
5. 11, let all that trust in thee *r.*
9. 14, I will *r.* in thy salvation.
19. 5, *r.* as a strong man to run a race.
33. 21, our heart shall *r.* in him.
35. 15, in mine adversity they *r.*
26, let them be ashamed that *r.* at my hurt.
38. 16, hear me, lest they should *r.* over me.
51. 8, bones thou hast broken may *r.*
58. 10, righteous shall *r.* when he seeth.
63. 7, in shadow of thy wings will I *r.*
68. 3, let righteous *r.*, yea, exceedingly *r.*
85. 6, that thy people may *r.* in thee.
89. 16, in thy name shall they *r.* all the day.
96. 11, let the heavens *r.*
97. 11, the Lord reigneth, let the earth *r.*
104. 31, the Lord shall *r.* in his works.
107. 42, the righteous shall see it and *r.*
109. 28, let thy servant *r.*
149. 2, let Israel *r.* in him that made him.
Prov. 2. 14, who *r.* to do evil.
5. 18, *r.* with the wife of thy youth.
23. 15, if thine heart be wise, mine shall *r.*
24, father of the righteous shall greatly *r.*
25, she that bare thee shall *r.*
24. 17, *r.* not when thine enemy falleth.
29. 2, when righteous are in authority people *r.*
31. 25, she shall *r.* in time to come.
Eccl. 2. 10, my heart *r.* in all my labour.
3. 12, for a man to *r.* and do good.
22; 5. 19, that a man should *r.* in his works.
11. 9, *r.* O young man in thy youth.
Isa. 9. 3, as men *r.* when they divide the spoil.
24. 8, noise of them that *r.* endeth.
29. 19, poor among men shall *r.*
35. 1, the desert shall *r.*
62. 5, as the bridegroom *r.* over the bride.
64. 5, him that *r.* and worketh righteousness.
65. 13, my servants shall *r.*, but ye.
66. 14, when ye see this, your heart shall *r.*
Jer. 11. 15, when thou doest evil, then thou *r.*
32. 41, I will *r.* over them to do them good.
51. 39, that they may *r.* and sleep.
Ezek. 7. 12, let not buyer *r.*
Amos 6. 13, which *r.* in a thing of nought.
Mic. 7. 8, *r.* not against me.
Hab. 3. 18, yet I will *r.* in the Lord.
Mat. 18. 13, he *r.* more of that sheep.
Lu. 1. 14, many shall *r.* at his birth.
6. 23, *r.* ye in that day, and leap for joy.
10. 20, in this *r.* not, but rather *r.* because.
21, in that hour Jesus *r.* in spirit.
15. 6, 9, *r.* with me.
John 5. 35, willing for a season to *r.* in his light.
8. 56, Abraham *r.* to see my day.
14. 28, if ye loved me, ye would *r.*
16. 20, ye shall weep, but the world shall *r.*
22, I will see you again, and your heart shall *r.*
Rom. 5. 2, and *r.* in hope.
12. 15, *r.* with them that do *r.*
1 Cor. 7. 30, they that *r.* as though they *r.* not.
13. 6, *r.* not in iniquity, but *r.* in the truth.
Phil. 1. 18, I therein do *r.* and will *r.*
2. 16, that I may *r.* in the day of Christ.
3. 1, finally, *r.* in the Lord.
Phil. 4. 4, *r.* in the Lord alway, and again I say *r.*
1 Thess. 5. 16, *r.* evermore.
Jas. 1. 9, let the brother of low degree *r.*
2. 13, mercy *r.* against judgment.
1 Pet. 1. 8, *r.* with joy unspeakable.
See 1 Kings 1. 40; 5. 7; 2 Kings 11. 14; 1 Chron. 29. 9.
REJOICING. Job 8. 21, till he fill thy lips with *r.*
Ps. 107. 22, declare his works with *r.*
118. 15, voice of *r.* is in tabernacles of the righteous.
119. 111, they are the *r.* of my heart.
126. 6, shall doubtless come again *r.*
Prov. 8. 31, *r.* in the habitable part of his earth.
Isa. 65. 18, I create Jerusalem a *r.*
Jer. 15. 16, thy word was to me the *r.* of my heart.
Zeph. 2. 15, this is the *r.* city.
Acts 5. 41, *r.* that they were counted worthy.
Rom. 12. 12, *r.* in hope.
2 Cor. 6. 10, as sorrowful, yet alway *r.*
1 Thess. 2. 19, what is our crown of *r.*
See Hab. 3. 14; Acts 8. 39; Gal. 6. 4; Jas. 4. 16.
RELEASE. Esth. 2. 18; Mat. 27. 17; Mk. 15. 11; John 19. 10.
RELIEVE. Lev. 25. 35, then thou shalt *r.* him.
Ps. 146. 9, he *r.* the fatherless and widow.
Isa. 1. 17, *r.* the oppressed.
Lam. 1. 16, comforter that should *r.* my soul is far from me.
See Acts 11. 29; 1 Tim. 5. 10, 16.
RELIGION. Acts 26. 5; Gal. 1. 13; Jas. 1. 26, 27.
RELIGIOUS. Acts 13. 43; Jas. 1. 26.
RELY. 2 Chron. 13. 18; 16. 7, 8.
REMAIN. Gen. 8. 22, while earth *r.*
14. 10, they that *r.* fled to the mountain.
Ex. 12. 10, let nothing of it *r.* until morning.
Josh. 13. 1, there *r.* yet much land to be possessed.
1 Kings 18. 22, I only *r.* a prophet.
Job 21. 32, yet shall he *r.* in the tomb.
Prov. 2. 21, the perfect shall *r.* in the land.
Eccl. 2. 9, my wisdom *r.* with me.
Jer. 17. 25, this city shall *r.* for ever.
37. 10, there *r.* but wounded men.
Lam. 2. 22, in day of anger none *r.*
Mat. 11. 23, would have *r.* until this day.
John 6. 12, gather up the fragments that *r.*
9. 41, ye say, we see, therefore your sin *r.*
Acts 5. 4, whiles it *r.*, was it not thine own?
1 Cor. 15. 6, the greater part *r.* to this present.
1 Thess. 4. 15, we which are alive and *r.* unto coming of the Lord.
Heb. 4. 9, there *r.* a rest to the people of God.
10. 26, there *r.* no more sacrifice for sins.
Rev. 3. 2, things which *r.* ready to die.
See Ps. 76. 10; Lam. 5. 19; John 1. 33; 1 John 3. 9.
REMEDY. 2 Chron. 36. 16; Prov. 6. 15; 29. 1.
REMEMBER. Gen. 40. 23, yet did not the butler *r.*
41. 9, I do *r.* my faults this day.
Ex. 13. 3, *r.* this day ye came out of Egypt.
20. 8, *r.* the sabbath day.
Num. 15. 39, *r.* all the commandments.
Deut. 5. 15; 15. 15; 16. 12; 24. 18, 22, *r.* thou wast a servant.
8. 2, *r.* all the way the Lord led thee.
32. 7, *r.* the days of old.
1 Chron. 16. 12, *r.* his marvellous works.
Neh. 13. 14, *r.* me, O God, concerning this.
Job 7. 7, O *r.* my life is wind.
11. 16, *r.* it as waters that pass away.
14. 13, appoint me a set time and *r.* me.
24. 20, the sinner shall be no more *r.*
Ps. 9. 12, when he maketh inquisition he *r.*
20. 7, he will *r.* the name of the Lord.
25. 6, *r.* thy mercies, they have been ever of old.
7, *r.* not sins of my youth, by mercy *r.* me.
63. 6, when I *r.* thee upon my bed.
77. 3, I *r.* God and was troubled.
78. 39, he *r.* that they were but flesh.

Ps. 79. 8, *r.* not against us former iniquities.
89. 47, *r.* how short my time is.
105. 8, he hath *r.* his covenant for ever.
119. 55, I have *r.* thy name in the night.
136. 23, who *r.* us in our low estate.
137. 1, we wept when we *r.* Zion.
Prov. 31. 7, drink and *r.* his misery no more.
Eccl. 5. 20, not much *r.* the days of his life.
11. 8, let him *r.* the days of darkness.
12. 1, *r.* now thy Creator.
Cant. 1. 4, we will *r.* thy love.
Isa. 23. 16, sing songs that thou mayest be *r.*
43. 18; 46. 9, *r.* ye not the former things.
57. 11, thou hast not *r.* me.
65. 17, the former heavens shall not be *r.*
Jer. 31. 20, I do earnestly *r.* him still.
51. 50, ye that have escaped *r.* the Lord.
Lam. 1. 9, she *r.* not her last end.
Ezek. 16. 61; 20. 43; 36. 31, then shalt thou *r.* thy ways.
Amos 1. 9, and *r.* not the brotherly covenant.
Hab. 3. 2, in wrath *r.* mercy.
Zech. 10. 9, they shall *r.* me in far countries.
Mat. 26. 75, Peter *r.* the word of Jesus.
Lu. 16. 25, son, *r.* that thou in thy lifetime.
17. 32, *r.* Lot's wife.
23. 42, Lord *r.* me when thou comest.
24. 8, and they *r.* his words.
John 2. 22, when he was risen, they *r.*
15. 20, *r.* the word I said unto you.
Acts 11. 16, then *r.* I the word of the Lord.
20. 35, *r.* the words of the Lord Jesus.
Gal. 2. 10, that we should *r.* the poor.
Col. 4. 18, *r.* my bonds.
1 Thess. 1. 3, *r.* your work of faith.
Heb. 13. 3, *r.* them that are in bonds.
7, *r.* them that have the rule over you.
Rev. 2. 5, *r.* from whence thou art fallen.
3. 3, *r.* how thou hast received.
See Ps. 88. 5; 103. 14; Mat. 5. 23; John 16. 21.

REMEMBRANCE. Num. 5. 15, bringing iniquity to *r.*
2 Sam. 18. 18, no son to keep my name in *r.*
1 Kings 17. 18, art thou come to call my sin to *r.*
Job 18. 17, his *r.* shall perish.
Ps. 6. 5, in death there is no *r.* of thee.
30. 4; 97. 12, give thanks at *r.* of his holiness.
77. 6, I call to *r.* my song in the night.
112. 6, righteous shall be in everlasting *r.*
Eccl. 1. 11, there is no *r.* of former things.
2. 16, no *r.* of wise more than the fool.
Isa. 43. 26, put me in *r.*
57. 8, behind doors hast thou set up thy *r.*
Lam. 3. 20, my soul hath them still in *r.*
Ezek. 23. 19, calling to *r.* days of youth.
Mal. 3. 16, a book of *r.*
Lu. 22. 19; 1 Cor. 11. 24, this do in *r.* of me.
John 14. 26, bring all things to your *r.*
Acts 10. 31, thine alms are had in *r.*
2 Tim. 1. 3, I have *r.* of thee in my prayers.
2. 14, of these things put them in *r.*
See Heb. 10. 3; 2 Pet. 1. 12; 3. 1; Jude 5; Rev. 16. 19.

REMIT. John 20. 23, whose soever sins ye *r.*, are *r.*

REMNANT. Lev. 5. 13, the *r.* shall be the priest's.
2 Kings 19. 4; Isa. 37. 4, lift up prayer for the *r.*
Ezra 9. 8, grace shewed to leave us a *r.*
Isa. 1. 9, unless the Lord had left a *r.*
11. 11, to recover the *r.* of his people.
16. 14, the *r.* shall be very small and feeble.
Jer. 44. 28, *r.* shall know whose words shall stand.
Ezek. 6. 8, yet will I leave a *r.*
Joel 2. 32, the *r.* whom the Lord shall call.
See Mic. 2. 12; Hag. 1. 12; Rom. 11. 5; Rev. 11. 13.

REMOVE. Deut. 19. 14, shall not *r.* landmark.
Job 9. 5, *r.* the mountains and they know not.
14. 18, the rock is *r.* out of his place.
Ps. 36. 11, let not hand of wicked *r.* me.
39. 10, *r.* thy stroke away from me.
Ps. 46. 2, not fear though the earth be *r.*
81. 6, I *r.* his shoulder from burden.
103. 12, so far hath he *r.* our transgressions.
119. 22, *r.* from me reproach.
125. 1, as mount Zion, which cannot be *r.*
Prov. 4. 27, *r.* thy foot from evil.
10. 30, the righteous shall never be *r.*
Eccl. 11. 10, *r.* sorrow from thy heart.
Isa. 13. 13, earth shall *r.* out of her place.
24. 20, earth shall be *r.* like a cottage.
29. 13, have *r.* their heart far from me.
54. 10, the hills shall be *r.*
Jer. 4. 1, return unto me, then shalt thou not *r.*
Lam. 3. 17, thou hast *r.* my soul from peace.
Mat. 17. 20, ye shall say, *r.* hence, and it shall *r.*
Lu. 22. 42, *r.* this cup from me.
Gal. 1. 6, I marvel ye are so soon *r.*
Rev. 2. 5, or else I will *r.* thy candlestick.
See Job 19. 10; Eccl. 10. 9; Ezek. 12. 3; Heb. 12. 27.

REND. 1 Kings 11. 11, I will *r.* the kingdom.
Isa. 64. 1, that thou wouldest *r.* the heavens.
Hos. 13. 8, I will *r.* the caul of their heart.
Joel 2. 13, *r.* your heart.
Mat. 7. 6, lest they turn again and *r.* you.
See Ps. 7. 2; Eccl. 3. 7; Jer. 4. 30; John 19. 24.

RENDER. Deut. 32. 41, *r.* vengeance.
1 Sam. 26. 23, *r.* to every man his faithfulness.
Job 33. 26, he will *r.* to man his righteousness.
34. 11, the work of a man shall be *r.* to him.
Ps. 28. 4, *r.* to them their desert.
38. 20, they that *r.* evil for good.
79. 12, and *r.* to our neighbour sevenfold.
94. 2, *r.* a reward to the proud.
116. 12, what shall I *r.* to the Lord.
Prov. 24. 12; Rom. 2. 6, *r.* to every man according.
26. 16, wiser than seven men who can *r.* a reason.
Hos. 14. 2, so will we *r.* the calves of our lips.
Joel 3. 4, will ye *r.* me a recompence.
Zech. 9. 12, I will *r.* double.
Mat. 21. 41, *r.* fruits in their seasons.
22. 21; Mk. 12. 17; Lu. 20. 25, *r.* unto Cæsar.
Rom. 13. 7, *r.* to all their dues.
1 Thess. 3. 9, what thanks can we *r.*
5. 15, see that none *r.* evil for evil.
1 Pet. 3. 9, not *r.* evil for evil, or railing.
See Num. 18. 9; Judg. 9. 56; Ps. 62. 12; Isa. 66. 6.

RENEW. Job 10. 17, thou *r.* thy witnesses.
29. 20, my bow was *r.* in my hand.
Ps. 51. 10, and *r.* a right spirit within me.
103. 5, thy youth is *r.* like the eagle's.
104. 30, thou *r.* the face of the earth.
Isa. 40. 31, wait on Lord shall *r.* strength.
41. 1, let the people *r.* their strength.
Lam. 5. 21, *r.* our days as of old.
2 Cor. 4. 16, the inward man is *r.* day by day.
Eph. 4. 23, be *r.* in spirit of your mind.
Col. 3. 10, new man which is *r.* in knowledge.
Heb. 6. 6, if they fall away, to *r.* them again.
See 2 Chron. 15. 8; Rom. 12. 2; Tit. 3. 5.

RENOUNCED. 2 Cor. 4. 2, have *r.* hidden things.

RENOWN. Gen. 6. 4; Num. 16. 2, men of *r.*
Num. 1. 16, the *r.* of the congregation.
Isa. 14. 20, evil doers shall never be *r.*
Ezek. 16. 14, thy *r.* went forth among the heathen.
34. 29, a plant of *r.*
See Ezek. 23. 23; 26. 17; 39. 13; Dan. 9. 15.

RENT. Gen. 37. 33, Joseph is *r.* in pieces.
Josh. 9. 4, bottles old and *r.*
Judg. 14. 5, 6, *r.* lion as he would have *r.* a kid.
1 Kings 13. 3, the altar shall be *r.*
Job 26. 8, the cloud is not *r.* under them.
Mat. 9. 16; Mk. 2. 21, the *r.* is made worse.
27. 51; Mk. 15. 38; Lu. 23. 45, veil was *r.* in twain.
See 1 Sam. 15. 27; Job 1. 20; 2. 12; Jer. 36. 24.

REPAID. Prov. 13. 21, to righteous good shall be *r.*

REPAIR. 2 Chron. 24. 5, gather money to *r.* the house.

Isa. 61. 4, they shall *r.* the waste cities.
See 2 Kings 12. 5; Ezra 9. 9; Neh. 3. 4; Isa. 58. 12.
REPAY. Deut. 7. 10, he will *r.* to his face.
Lu. 10. 35, when I come I will *r.* thee.
Rom. 12. 19, vengeance is mine, I will *r.*
Philem. 19, I have written it, I will *r.* it.
See Job 21. 31; 41. 11; Isa. 59. 18.
REPEATETH. Prov. 17. 9, he that *r.* a matter.
REPENT. Gen. 6. 6, it *r.* the Lord.
Ex. 13. 17, lest the people *r.*
32. 14; 2 Sam. 24. 16; 1 Chron. 21. 15; Jer. 26. 19, Lord *r.* of evil he thought to do.
Num. 23. 19, neither son of man that he should *r.*
Deut. 32. 36, Lord shall *r.* for his servants.
1 Sam. 15. 29, will not *r.*, for he is not a man that he should *r.*
Job 42. 6, I *r.* in dust and ashes.
Ps. 90. 13, let it *r.* thee concerning thy servants.
106. 45, Lord *r.* according to his mercies.
110. 4; Heb. 7. 21, Lord hath sworn and will not *r.*
Jer. 8. 6, no man *r.* of his wickedness.
18. 8; 26. 13, if that nation turn I will *r.*
31. 19, after that I was turned I *r.*
Joel 2. 13, he is slow to anger and *r.* him.
Mat. 12. 41; Lu. 11. 32, they *r.* at the preaching.
21. 29, afterward he *r.* and went.
27. 3, Judas *r.* himself.
Lu. 13. 3, except ye *r.*
15. 7, joy over one sinner that *r.*
17. 3, if thy brother *r.*, forgive him.
Acts 8. 22, *r.* of this thy wickedness.
Rev. 2. 21, space to *r.*, and she *r.* not.
See Acts 2. 38; 17. 30; Rev. 2. 5; 3. 3; 16. 9.
REPENTANCE. Hos. 13. 14, *r.* shall be hid.
Mat. 3. 8; Lu. 3. 8; Acts 26. 2, fruits meet for *r.*
Rom. 2. 4, goodness of God leadeth thee to *r.*
11. 29, gifts of God are without *r.*
2 Cor. 7. 10, *r.* not to be repented of.
Heb. 6. 1, not laying again the foundation of *r.*
6, to renew them again to *r.*
12. 17, no place of *r.*, though he sought it.
See Lu. 15. 7; Acts 20. 21; 2 Tim. 2. 25; 2 Pet. 3. 9.
REPLENISH. Gen. 1. 28; 9. 1; Jer. 31. 25; Ezek. 26. 2.
REPLIEST. Rom. 9. 20, that *r.* against God.
REPORT (*n.*). Gen. 37. 2, their evil *r.*
Ex. 23. 1, thou shalt not *r.* a false *r.*
Num. 13. 32, an evil *r.* of the land.
1 Sam. 2. 24, it is no good *r.* I hear.
1 Kings 10. 6; 2 Chron. 9. 5, it was a true *r.* I heard.
Prov. 15. 30, a good *r.* maketh the bones fat.
Isa. 28. 19, a vexation only to understand *r.*
53. 1, who hath believed our *r.*
Acts 6. 3, men of honest *r.*
10. 22, of good *r.* among the Jews.
2 Cor. 6. 8, by evil *r.* and good *r.*
Phil. 4. 8, whatsoever things are of good *r.*
1 Tim. 3. 7, a bishop must have a good *r.*
See Deut. 2. 25; Heb. 11. 2, 39; 3 John 12.
REPORT (*v.*). Neh. 6. 6, it is *r.* among heathen.
Jer. 20. 10, *r.*, say they, and we will *r.* it.
Mat. 28. 15, saying is commonly *r.*
Acts 16. 2, well *r.* of by the brethren.
1 Cor. 14. 25, he will *r.* that God is in you.
See Ezek. 9. 11; Rom. 3. 8; 1 Tim. 5. 10; 1 Pet. 1. 12.
REPROACH (*n.*). Gen. 30. 23, hath taken away my *r.*
34. 14, that were a *r.* to us.
1 Sam. 11. 2, lay it for a *r.* upon all Israel.
Neh. 2. 17, build that we be no more a *r.*
Ps. 15. 3, that taketh not up a *r.*
22. 6, a *r.* of men.
31. 11, I was a *r.* among mine enemies.
44. 13; 79. 4; 89. 41, a *r.* to our neighbours.
69. 9; Rom. 15. 3, the *r.* of them that reproached thee.
Ps. 78. 66, put them to a perpetual *r.*
Prov. 6. 33, his *r.* shall not be wiped away.
14. 34, sin is a *r.* to any people.
18. 3, with ignominy cometh *r.*
Isa. 43. 28, I have given Israel to *r.*
51. 7, fear not the *r.* of men.
Jer. 23. 40, I will bring an everlasting *r.*
31. 19, I did bear the *r.* of my youth.
Lam. 3. 30, he is filled full with *r.*
Ezek. 5. 14, I will make thee a *r.* among nations.
15, Jerusalem shall be a *r.* and a taunt.
Mic. 6. 16, ye shall bear the *r.* of my people.
2 Cor. 11. 21, I speak as concerning *r.*
12. 10, pleasure in *r.* for Christ's sake.
1 Tim. 3. 7, good report lest he fall into *r.*
4. 10, we labour and suffer *r.*
Heb. 11. 26, the *r.* of Christ greater riches.
13. 13, without the camp bearing his *r.*
See Ps. 69. 10; 119. 39; Jer. 6. 10; 20. 8; 24. 9.
REPROACH (*v.*). Num. 15. 30, *r.* the Lord.
Ruth 2. 15, *r.* her not.
2 Kings 19. 22; Isa. 37. 23, whom hast thou *r.*
Job 19. 3, these ten times have ye *r.* me.
27. 6, my heart shall not *r.* me.
Ps. 42. 10, as with a sword mine enemies *r.* me.
44. 16, the voice of him that *r.*
74. 22, how the foolish man *r.* thee.
119. 42; Prov. 27. 11, to answer him that *r.* me.
Prov. 14. 31; 17. 5, oppresseth poor *r.* his Maker.
Lu. 6. 22, men shall *r.* you for my sake.
1 Pet. 4. 14, if ye be *r.* for Christ's sake.
See Ps. 55. 12; 74. 18; 79. 12; 89. 51; Zeph. 2. 8.
REPROACHFULLY. Job 16. 10; 1 Tim. 5. 14.
REPROVE. 1 Chron. 16. 21, *r.* kings for their sakes.
Job 6. 25, what doth your arguing *r.*
13. 10, he will *r.* you if ye accept.
22. 4, will he *r.* thee for fear.
40. 2, he that *r.* God let him answer it.
Ps. 50. 8, I will not *r.* thee for burnt offerings.
141. 5, let him *r.* me, it shall be excellent oil.
Prov. 9. 8, *r.* not a scorner lest he hate thee.
15. 12, a scorner loveth not one that *r.*
19. 25, *r.* one that hath understanding.
29. 1, he that being often *r.*
30. 6, lest he *r.* thee and thou be found.
Isa. 11. 4, *r.* with equity for the meek.
Jer. 2. 19, thy backslidings shall *r.* thee.
John 3. 20, lest his deeds should be *r.*
16. 8, he will *r.* the world of sin.
See Lu. 3. 19; Eph. 5. 11, 13; 2 Tim. 4. 2.
REPROVER. Prov. 25. 12; Ezek. 3. 26.
REPUTATION. Eccl. 10. 1, him that is in *r.* for wisdom.
Acts 5. 34, had in *r.* among the people.
Phil. 2. 7, made himself of no *r.*
29, hold such in *r.*
See Job 18. 3; Dan. 4. 35; Gal. 2. 2.
REQUEST. Judg. 8. 24, I would desire a *r.* of thee.
Ezra 7. 6, the king granted all his *r.*
Job 6. 8, Oh that I might have my *r.*
Ps. 21. 2, hast not withholden *r.* of his lips.
106. 15, he gave them their *r.*
Phil. 1. 4, in every prayer making *r.* with joy.
4. 6, let your *r.* be made known.
See 2 Sam. 14. 15; Neh. 2. 4; Esth. 4. 8; 5. 3.
REQUESTED. 1 Kings 19. 4, Elijah *r.* that he might die.
REQUIRE. Gen. 9. 5, blood of your lives will I *r.*
31. 39, of my hand didst thou *r.* it.
Deut. 10. 12; Mic. 6. 8, what doth the Lord *r.*
Josh. 22. 23; 1 Sam. 20. 16, let the Lord himself *r.* it.
Ruth 3. 11, I will do all thou *r.*
1 Sam. 21. 8, the king's business *r.* haste.
2 Sam. 3. 13, one thing I *r.* of thee.
19. 38, whatsoever thou shalt *r.* I will do.
2 Chron. 24. 22, the Lord look on it and *r.* it.
Neh. 5. 12, we will restore and *r.* nothing of them.
Ps. 10. 13, he hath said thou wilt not *r.* it.

Ps. 40. 6, sin offering hast thou not *r.*
137. 3, they that wasted us *r.* of us mirth.
Prov. 30. 7, two things have I *r.* of thee.
Eccl. 3. 15, God *r.* that which is past.
Isa. 1. 12, who hath *r.* this at your hand?
Ezek. 3. 18; 33. 6, his blood will I *r.* at thine hand.
34. 10, I will *r.* my flock at their hand.
Lu. 11. 50, may be *r.* of this generation.
12. 20, this night thy soul shall be *r.*
48, of him shall much be *r.*
19. 23, I might have *r.* mine own with usury.
1 Cor. 1. 22, the Jews *r.* a sign.
4. 2, it is *r.* in stewards.
See 2 Chron. 8. 14; Ezra 3. 4; Neh. 5. 18; Esth. 2. 15.

REQUITE. Gen. 50. 15, Joseph will certainly *r.* us.
Deut. 32. 6, do ye thus *r.* the Lord.
Judg. 1. 7, as I have done so God hath *r.* me.
2 Sam. 2. 6, I also will *r.* you this kindness.
16. 12, it may be the Lord will *r.* good for this.
1 Tim. 5. 4, learn to *r.* their parents.
See Ps. 10. 14; 41. 10; Jer. 51. 56.

REREWARD. Josh. 6. 9; Isa. 52. 12; 58. 8.

RESCUE. Ps. 35. 17, *r.* my soul.
Hos. 5. 14, none shall *r.* him.
See Deut. 28. 31; 1 Sam. 14. 45; Dan. 6. 27; Acts 23. 27.

RESEMBLANCE. Zech. 5. 6, this is their *r.*

RESEMBLE. Judg. 8. 18; Lu. 13. 18.

RESERVE. Gen. 27. 36, hast thou not *r.* a blessing.
Ruth 2. 18, gave her mother in law that she had *r.*
Job 21. 30, the wicked is *r.* to day of destruction.
38. 23, which I have *r.* against time of trouble.
Jer. 3. 5, will he *r.* anger for ever.
5. 24, he *r.* the weeks of harvest.
50. 20, I will pardon them whom I *r.*
Nah. 1. 2, the Lord *r.* wrath for his enemies.
1 Pet. 1. 4, an inheritance *r.* in heaven.
2 Pet. 2. 4, to be *r.* to judgment.
3. 7, the heavens and earth are *r.* unto fire.
See Num. 18. 9; Rom. 11. 4; 2 Pet. 2. 9; Jude 6. 13.

RESIDUE. Ex. 10. 5, locusts shall eat the *r.*
Isa. 38. 10, I am deprived of the *r.* of my years.
Jer. 15. 9, *r.* of them will I deliver to the sword.
Ezek. 9. 8, wilt thou destroy all the *r.*
Zech. 8. 11, I will not be to the *r.* as in former days.
Mal. 2. 15, yet had he the *r.* of the Spirit.
Acts 15. 17, that the *r.* might seek the Lord.
See Neh. 11. 20; Jer. 8. 3; 29. 1; 39. 3.

RESIST. Zech. 3. 1, at his right hand to *r.*
Mat. 5. 39, *r.* not evil.
Lu. 21. 15, adversaries shall not be able to *r.*
Rom. 9. 19, who hath *r.* his will.
13. 2, whoso *r.* power, *r.* ordinance of God.
Jas. 4. 6; 1 Pet. 5. 5, God *r.* the proud.
7, *r.* the devil, and he will flee.
1 Pet. 5. 9, whom *r.* stedfast in the faith.
See Acts 6. 10; 7. 51; 2 Tim. 3. 8; Heb. 12. 4.

RESORT. Neh. 4. 20, *r.* hither to us.
Ps. 71. 3, whereunto I may continually *r.*
John 18. 2, Jesus ofttimes *r.* thither.
See Mk. 2. 13; 10. 1; John 18. 20; Acts 16. 13.

RESPECT (*n.*). Gen. 4. 4, Lord had *r.* to Abel.
Ex. 2. 25, God had *r.* unto them.
1 Kings 8. 28; 2 Chron. 6. 19, have *r.* unto their prayer.
2 Chron. 19. 7; Rom. 2. 11; Eph. 6. 9; Col. 3. 25, there is no *r.* of persons with God.
Ps. 74. 20, have *r.* unto thy covenant.
119. 15, I will have *r.* unto thy ways.
138. 6, yet hath he *r.* to the lowly.
Prov. 24. 23; 28. 31, not good to have *r.* of persons.
Isa. 17. 7, his eyes shall have *r.* to Holy One.
22. 11, nor had *r.* to him that fashioned it.
Phil. 4. 11, not that I speak in *r.* of want.
See Heb. 11. 26; Jas. 2. 1, 3, 9; 1 Pet. 1. 17.

RESPECT (*v.*). Lev. 19. 15, shalt not *r.* person of poor.
Deut. 1. 17, ye shall not *r.* persons in judgment.
Job 37. 24, he *r.* not any that are wise of heart.
See Num. 16. 15; 2 Sam. 14. 14; Ps. 40. 4; Lam. 4. 16.

RESPITE. Ex. 8. 15; 1 Sam. 11. 3.

REST (*n.*). Gen. 49. 15, Issachar saw that *r.* was good.
Ex. 31. 15; 35. 2; Lev. 16. 31; 23. 3, 32; 25. 4, the sabbath of *r.*
33. 14, my presence shall go with thee, and I will give thee *r.*
Lev. 25. 5, a year of *r.* to the land.
Deut. 12. 10, when he giveth you *r.* from your enemies.
Judg. 3. 30, the land had *r.* fourscore years.
Ruth 3. 1, shall not I seek *r.* for thee.
1 Chron. 22. 9, a man of *r.*, and I will give him *r.*
18, hath he not given you *r.* on every side.
28. 2, to build a house of *r.*
Neh. 9. 28, after they had *r.* they did evil.
Esth. 9. 16, the Jews had *r.* from their enemies.
Job 3. 17, there the weary be at *r.*
11. 18, thou shalt take thy *r.* in safety.
17. 16, when our *r.* together is in the dust.
Ps. 55. 6, then would I fly away and be at *r.*
95. 11; Heb. 3. 11, not enter into my *r.*
116. 7, return to thy *r.*, O my soul.
132. 8, arise into thy *r.*
14, this is my *r.* for ever.
Eccl. 2. 23, his heart taketh not *r.* in the night.
Isa. 11. 10, his *r.* shall be glorious.
14. 7; Zech. 1. 11, earth is at *r.* and quiet.
18. 4, I will take my *r.*
30. 15, in returning and *r.* shall ye be saved.
66. 1, where is the place of my *r.*?
Jer. 6. 16, ye shall find *r.* for your souls.
Ezek. 38. 11, I will go to them that are at *r.*
Mic. 2. 10, depart, this is not your *r.*
Mat. 11. 28, I will give you *r.*
29, ye shall find *r.* to your souls.
12. 43; Lu. 11. 24, seeking *r.* and finding none.
26. 45; Mk. 14. 41, sleep on and take your *r.*
John 11. 13, of taking *r.* in sleep.
Acts 9. 31, then had the churches *r.*
See Prov. 29. 17; Eccl. 6. 5; Dan. 4. 4; 2 Thess. 1. 7.

REST (*v.*). Gen. 2. 2, he *r.* on seventh day.
Num. 11. 25, when the Spirit *r.* upon them.
2 Chron. 32. 8, people *r.* on the words.
Job 3. 18, there the prisoners *r.* together.
Ps. 16. 9; Acts 2. 26, my flesh shall *r.* in hope.
37. 7, *r.* in the Lord.
Eccl. 7. 9, anger *r.* in bosom of fools.
Isa. 11. 2, the spirit of the Lord shall *r.* upon him.
28. 12, ye may cause the weary to *r.*
57. 20, like the sea when it cannot *r.*
62. 1, for Jerusalem's sake I will not *r.*
63. 14, Spirit of the Lord caused him to *r.*
Jer. 47. 6, *r.* and be still.
Dan. 12. 13, thou shalt *r.* and stand in thy lot.
Mk. 6. 31, come and *r.* awhile.
2 Cor. 12. 9, power of Christ may *r.* on me.
Rev. 4. 8, they *r.* not day and night.
6. 11, *r.* yet for a little season.
14. 13, that they may *r.* from their labours.
See Prov. 14. 33; Cant. 1. 7; Isa. 32. 18; Lu. 10. 6.

RESTORE. Ex. 22. 4, he shall *r.* double.
Lev. 6. 4, he shall *r.* that he took away.
Deut. 22. 2, things strayed thou shalt *r.* again.
Ps. 23. 3, he *r.* my soul.
51. 12, *r.* to me the joy of thy salvation.
69. 4, I *r.* that which I took not away.
Isa. 1. 26, I will *r.* thy judges as at the first.
Jer. 27. 22, I will *r.* them to this place.
30. 17, I will *r.* health to thee.
Ezek. 33. 15, if wicked *r.* pledge.
Mat. 17. 11; Mk. 9. 12, Elias shall *r.* all things.
Lu. 19. 8, I *r.* him fourfold.
Acts 1. 6, wilt thou at this time *r.* the kingdom.
Gal. 6. 1, *r.* such an one in meekness.

See Ruth 4. 15; Isa. 58. 12; Joel 2. 25; Mk. 8. 25.
RESTRAIN. Gen. 11. 6, nothing will be *r.*
Ex. 36. 6, people were *r.* from bringing.
1 Sam. 3. 13, his sons made themselves vile, and he *r.* them not.
Job 15. 4, thou *r.* prayer before God.
8, dost thou *r.* wisdom to thyself.
Ps. 76. 10, remainder of wrath shalt thou *r.*
See Gen. 8. 2; Isa. 63. 15; Ezek. 31. 15; Acts 14. 18.
RETAIN. Job 2. 9, dost thou still *r.* integrity.
Prov. 3. 18, happy is every one that *r.* her.
4. 4, let thine heart *r.* my words.
11. 16, a gracious woman *r.* honour.
Eccl. 8. 8, no man hath power to *r.* the spirit.
John 20. 23, whose soever sins ye *r.* they are *r.*
See Mic. 7. 18; Rom. 1. 28; Philem. 13.
RETIRE. Judg. 20. 39; 2 Sam. 11. 15; Jer. 4. 6.
RETURN. Gen. 3. 19, to dust shalt thou *r.*
Ex. 14. 27, the sea *r.* to his strength.
Judg. 7. 3, whosoever is fearful, let him *r.*
Ruth 1. 16, entreat me not to leave thee or *r.*
2 Sam. 12. 23, he shall not *r.* to me.
2 Kings 20. 10, let the shadow *r.* backward.
Job 1. 21, naked shall I *r.* thither.
7. 10, he shall *r.* no more.
10. 21; 16. 22, I go whence I shall not *r.*
15. 22, he believeth not he shall *r.* out of darkness.
33. 25, he shall *r.* to the days of his youth.
Ps. 35. 13, my prayer *r.* into mine own bosom.
73. 10, his people *r.* hither.
90. 3, thou sayest, *r.*, ye children of men.
104. 29, they die and *r.* to their dust.
116. 7, *r.* to thy rest, O my soul.
Prov. 2. 19, none that go to her *r.* again.
26. 11, as a dog *r.* to his vomit.
27, he that rolleth a stone, it will *r.*
Eccl. 1. 7, whence rivers come, thither they *r.* again.
5. 15, naked shall he *r.* to go as he came.
12. 2, nor the clouds *r.* after the rain.
7, dust *r.* to earth and spirit *r.* to God.
Isa. 21. 12, if ye will enquire, enquire ye; *r.*, come.
35. 10; 51. 11, the ransomed of the Lord shall *r.*
44. 22, *r.* unto me, for I have redeemed thee.
45. 23, word is gone out and shall not *r.*
55. 11, it shall not *r.* to me void.
Jer. 4. 1, if thou wilt *r.*, saith the Lord, *r.* unto me.
15. 19, let them *r.* unto thee, but *r.* not thou.
24. 7, they shall *r.* with whole heart.
31. 8, a great company shall *r.* thither.
36. 3, *r.* every man from his evil way.
Ezek. 46. 9, he shall not *r.* by the way he came.
Hos. 2. 7, I will *r.* to my first husband.
5. 15, I will *r.* to my place.
7. 16, they *r.*, but not to the most High.
14. 7, they that dwell under his shadow shall *r.*
Amos 4. 6, yet have ye not *r.* to me.
Joel 2. 14, who knoweth if he will *r.* and repent.
Zech. 1. 16, I am *r.* to Jerusalem with mercies.
8. 3, I am *r.* to Zion and will dwell.
Mal. 3. 7, *r.* to me and I will *r.* to you.
18, then shall ye *r.* and discern.
Mat. 12. 44; Lu. 11. 24, I will *r.* into my house.
24. 18, neither let him in the field *r.* back.
Lu. 9. 10, apostles *r.* and told him all.
10. 17, the seventy *r.* with joy.
12. 36, when he will *r.* from wedding.
17. 18, not found that *r.* to give glory.
Acts 13. 34, now no more to *r.* to corruption.
Heb. 11. 15, might have had opportunity to *r.*
1 Pet. 2. 25, now *r.* to the Shepherd of your souls.
See Gen. 31. 3; Ex. 4. 18; Lev. 25. 10; Isa. 55. 7.
REVEAL. Deut. 29. 29, things *r.* belong unto us and to our children.
1 Sam. 3. 7, nor was word of Lord *r.* to him.
Job 20. 27, the heaven shall *r.* his iniquity.
Prov. 11. 13; 20. 19, a talebearer *r.* secrets.
Isa. 22. 14, it was *r.* in mine ears.
40. 5, glory of the Lord shall be *r.*
53. 1; John 12. 38, to whom is arm of Lord *r.*
Isa. 56. 1, my righteousness is near to be *r.*
Jer. 11. 20, unto thee have I *r.* my cause.
33. 6, I will *r.* abundance of peace.
Dan. 2. 22, he *r.* deep and secret things.
28, there is a God that *r.* secrets.
Amos 3. 7, he *r.* his secrets to the prophets.
Mat. 10. 26; Lu. 12. 2, nothing covered that shall not be *r.*
11. 25, hast *r.* them unto babes.
16. 17, flesh and blood hath not *r.* it.
Lu. 2. 35, that thoughts of many hearts may be *r.*
17. 30, in day when Son of man is *r.*
Rom. 1. 17, righteousness of God *r.*
18, wrath of God is *r.* from heaven.
8. 18, glory which shall be *r.* in us.
1 Cor. 2. 10, God hath *r.* them by his Spirit.
3. 13, it shall be *r.* by fire.
14. 30, if anything be *r.* to another.
Gal. 1. 16, to *r.* his Son in me.
2 Thess. 1. 7, when Lord Jesus shall be *r.*
2. 3, man of sin be *r.*
8, that wicked one be *r.*
1 Pet. 1. 5, ready to be *r.* in last time.
4. 13, when his glory shall be *r.*
5. 1, partaker of glory that shall be *r.*
See Eph. 3. 5; Phil. 3. 15; 2 Thess. 2. 6.
REVELATION. Rom. 2. 5, *r.* of righteous judgment.
16. 25, *r.* of the mystery.
1 Cor. 14. 26, every one hath a *r.*
2 Cor. 12. 1, to visions and *r.*
See Gal. 2. 2; Eph. 1. 17; 3. 3; 1 Pet. 1. 13; Rev. 1. 1.
REVELLINGS. Gal. 5. 21; 1 Pet. 4. 3.
REVENGE. Jer. 15. 15, O Lord, *r.* me.
20. 10, we shall take our *r.* on him.
Nah. 1. 2, the Lord *r.* and is furious.
2 Cor. 7. 11, what *r.* it wrought in you.
10. 6, in readiness to *r.*
See Ps. 79. 10; Ezek. 25. 12; Rom. 13. 4.
REVENUE. Prov. 8. 19, my *r.* better than silver.
16. 8, better than great *r.* without right.
Jer. 12. 13, ashamed of your *r.*
See Ezra 4. 13; Prov. 15. 6; Isa. 23. 3; Jer. 12. 13.
REVERENCE. Ps. 89. 7; Mat. 21. 37; Mk. 12. 6; Heb. 12. 9.
REVEREND. Ps. 111. 9, holy and *r.* is his name.
REVERSE. Num. 23. 20; Esth. 8. 5, 8.
REVILE. Isa. 51. 7, neither be afraid of *r.*
Mat. 27. 39, they that passed by *r.* him.
Mk. 15. 32, they that were crucified *r.* him.
1 Cor. 4. 12, being *r.* we bless.
1 Pet. 2. 23, when he was *r.*, *r.* not again.
See Ex. 22. 28; Mat. 5. 11; John 9. 28; Acts 23. 4.
REVIVE. Neh. 4. 2, will they *r.* the stones.
Ps. 85. 6, wilt thou not *r.* us.
138. 7, thou wilt *r.* me.
Isa. 57. 15, to *r.* spirit of the humble.
Hos. 6. 2, after two days will he *r.* us.
14. 7, they shall *r.* as corn.
Hab. 3. 2, *r.* thy work in midst of years.
Rom. 7. 9, when commandment came sin *r.*
14. 9, Christ both died, rose, and *r.*
See Gen. 45. 27; 2 Kings 13. 21; Ezra 9. 8.
REVOLT. Isa. 1. 5; 31. 6; 59. 13; Jer. 5. 23.
REWARD (*n.*). Gen. 15. 1, thy exceeding great *r.*
Num. 22. 7, *r.* of divination in their hand.
Deut. 10. 17, God who taketh not *r.*
Ruth 2. 12, full *r.* be given thee of the Lord.
2 Sam. 4. 10, thought I would have given *r.*
Job 6. 22, did I say, give a *r.*
7. 2, as an hireling looketh for *r.*
Ps. 19. 11, in keeping them there is great *r.*
58. 11, there is a *r.* for the righteous.
91. 8, thou shalt see the *r.* of the wicked.
127. 3, fruit of womb is his *r.*
Prov. 11. 18, soweth righteousness a sure *r.*
21. 14, a *r.* in the bosom.
24. 20, no *r.* to the evil man.
Eccl. 4. 9, they have a good *r.* for labour.

Eccl. 9. 5, neither have they any more a *r*.
Isa. 1. 23, every one followeth after *r*.
5. 23, justify wicked for *r*.
40. 10; 62. 11, his *r*. is with him.
Ezek. 16. 34, thou givest *r*., and no *r*. is given thee.
Dan. 5. 17, give thy *r*. to another.
Hos. 9. 1, thou hast loved a *r*.
Mic. 3. 11, the heads thereof judge for *r*.
7. 3, judge asketh for a *r*.
Mat. 5. 12; Lu. 6. 23, great is your *r*. in heaven.
46, what *r*. have ye.
6. 1, ye have no *r*. of your father.
2, 5, 16, they have their *r*.
10. 41, a prophet's *r*., a righteous man's *r*.
42; Mk. 9. 41, in no wise lose *r*.
Lu. 6. 35, do good and your *r*. shall be great.
23. 41, we receive due *r*. of our deeds.
Acts 1. 18, purchased with *r*. of iniquity.
Rom. 4. 4, the *r*. is not reckoned.
1 Cor. 3. 8, every man shall receive his own *r*.
9. 18, what is my *r*. then.
Col. 2. 18, let no man beguile you of your *r*.
3. 24, the *r*. of the inheritance.
1 Tim. 5. 18, labourer worthy of his *r*.
Heb. 2. 2; 10. 35; 11. 26, recompence of *r*.
2 Pet. 2. 13, the *r*. of unrighteousness.
See 2 John 8; Jude 11; Rev. 11. 18; 22. 12.
REWARD (*v*.). Gen. 44. 4, wherefore have ye *r*.
Deut. 32. 41, I will *r*. them that hate me.
1 Sam. 24. 17, thou hast *r*. me good.
2 Chron. 15. 7, be strong, and your work shall be *r*.
20. 11, behold how they *r*. us.
Job 21. 19, he *r*. him and he shall know it.
Ps. 31. 23, plentifully *r*. the proud doer.
35. 12; 109. 5, they *r*. me evil for good.
103. 10, nor *r*. us according to our iniquities.
137. 8, happy is he that *r*. thee.
Prov. 17. 13, whoso *r*. evil, evil shall not depart.
25. 22, heap coals, and the Lord shall *r*. thee.
26. 10, both *r*. the fool and *r*. transgressors.
Jer. 31. 16, thy work shall be *r*.
See 2 Sam. 22. 21; Mat. 6. 4; 16. 27; 2 Tim. 4. 14.
RICH. Gen. 13. 2, Abram was very *r*.
14. 23, lest thou shouldest say, I have made Abram *r*.
Ex. 30. 15, the *r*. shall not give more.
Josh. 22. 8, return with much *r*. to your tents.
Ruth 3. 10, followedst not poor or *r*.
1 Sam. 2. 7, the Lord maketh poor and *r*.
1 Kings 3. 11; 2 Chron. 1. 11, neither hast asked *r*.
13, I have given thee both *r*. and honour.
10. 23; 2 Chron. 9. 22, Solomon exceeded all for *r*.
1 Chron. 29. 12, both *r*. and honour come of thee.
Job 15. 29, he shall not be *r*.
20. 15, he swallowed down *r*.
27. 19, *r*. man shall lie down, but shall not be gathered.
36. 19, will he esteem thy *r*.
Ps. 37. 16, better than *r*. of many wicked.
39. 6, he heapeth up *r*.
45. 12, the *r*. shall entreat thy favour.
49. 16, be not afraid when one is made *r*.
52. 7, trusted in abundance of *r*.
62. 10, if *r*. increase set not your heart.
73. 12, the ungodly increase in *r*.
104. 24, the earth is full of thy *r*.
112. 3, wealth and *r*. shall be in his house.
Prov. 3. 16, in left hand *r*. and honour.
8. 18, *r*. and honour are with me.
10. 4, hand of diligent maketh *r*.
22, blessing of the Lord maketh *r*.
11. 4, *r*. profit not in day of wrath.
13. 7, poor yet hath great *r*.
18. 23, the *r*. answereth roughly.
21. 17, he that loveth wine shall not be *r*.
23. 5, *r*. make themselves wings.
28. 11, *r*. man is wise in his own conceit.
30. 8, give me neither poverty nor *r*.
Eccl. 5. 13, *r*. kept for owners to their hurt.
10. 20, curse not *r*. in thy bedchamber.
Isa. 45. 3, I will give thee hidden *r*.
53. 9, with the *r*. in his death.
Jer. 9. 23, let not *r*. man glory in his *r*.
17. 11, getteth *r*. and not by right.
Ezek. 28. 5, heart lifted up because of *r*.
Hos. 12. 8, Ephraim said, I am become *r*.
Zech. 11. 5, blessed be the Lord, for I am *r*.
Mat. 13. 22; Mk. 4. 19; Lu. 8. 14, deceitfulness of *r*.
Mk. 10. 23, hardly shall they that have *r*.
12. 41, *r*. cast in much.
Lu. 1. 53, *r*. he hath sent empty away.
6. 24, woe to you *r*. for ye have received.
12. 21, not *r*. toward God.
14. 12, call not thy *r*. neighbours.
18. 23, sorrowful, for he was very *r*.
Rom. 2. 4, the *r*. of his goodness.
9. 23, make known the *r*. of his glory.
10. 12, the Lord is *r*. to all that call.
11. 12, fall of them the *r*. of the world.
33, the depth of the *r*. of the wisdom.
1 Cor. 4. 8, now ye are full, now ye are *r*.
2 Cor. 6. 10, poor, yet making many *r*.
8. 9, *r*., yet for your sakes.
Eph. 1. 7, redemption according to the *r*. of grace.
2. 4, God, who is *r*. in mercy.
7, that he might show the exceeding *r*. of grace.
3. 8, unsearchable *r*. of Christ.
Phil. 4. 19, according to his *r*. in glory by Christ.
Col. 1. 27, *r*. of the glory of this mystery.
2. 2, the *r*. of the full assurance.
1 Tim. 6. 9, they that will be *r*. fall into temptation.
17, nor trust in uncertain *r*.
18, do good and be *r*. in good works.
Heb. 11. 26, reproach of Christ greater *r*.
Jas. 1. 10, let *r*. rejoice that he is made low.
2. 5, hath not God chosen the poor, *r*. in faith.
5. 2, your *r*. are corrupted.
Rev. 2. 9, but thou art *r*.
3. 17, because thou sayest, I am *r*.
18, buy of me gold that thou mayest be *r*.
5. 12, worthy is the Lamb to receive *r*.
See Lev. 25. 47; Jas. 1. 11; 2. 6; 5. 1; Rev. 6. 15.
RICHLY. Col. 3. 16; 1 Tim. 6. 17.
RIDDANCE. Lev. 23. 22; Zeph. 1. 18.
RIDDLE. Judg. 14. 12; Ezek. 17. 2.
RIDE. Deut. 32. 13, *r*. on high places of the earth.
33. 26, who *r*. upon the heaven.
Judg. 5. 10, ye that *r*. on white asses.
2 Kings 4. 24, slack not thy *r*. for me.
Job 30. 22, causest me to *r*. upon the wind.
Ps. 45. 4, in thy majesty *r*. prosperously.
66. 12, hast caused men to *r*. over our heads.
68. 4, 33, extol him that *r*. on the heavens.
Isa. 19. 1, the Lord *r*. on a swift cloud.
See Hos. 14. 3; Amos 2. 15; Hab. 3. 8; Hag. 2. 22.
RIDER. Gen. 49. 17; Ex. 15. 1; Job 39. 18; Zech. 10. 5.
RIDGES. Ps. 65. 10, waterest the *r*. thereof.
RIGHT (*n*.). Gen. 18. 25, shall not Judge of all do *r*.?
Deut. 6. 18; 12. 25; 21. 9, shalt do that is *r*.
21. 17, the *r*. of the firstborn is his.
2 Sam. 19. 28, what *r*. have I to cry to the king.
Neh. 2. 20, ye have no *r*. in Jerusalem.
Job 34. 6, should I lie against my *r*.
36. 6, he giveth *r*. to the poor.
Ps. 9. 4, thou maintainest my *r*.
17. 1, hear the *r*., O Lord.
140. 12, Lord will maintain *r*. of the poor.
Prov. 16. 8, great revenues without *r*.
Jer. 17. 11, that getteth riches and not by *r*.
Ezek. 21. 27, till he come whose *r*. it is.
See Amos 5. 12; Mal. 3. 5; Heb. 13. 10.
RIGHT (*adj*.). Gen. 24. 48, the Lord led me in *r*. way.
Deut. 32. 4, God of truth, just and *r*. is he.
1 Sam. 12. 23, I will teach you the good and *r*. way.

2 Sam. 15. 3, thy matters are good and *r.*
Neh. 9. 13, thou gavest them *r.* judgments.
Job 6. 25, how forcible are *r.* words.
34. 23, he will not lay on man more than *r.*
Ps. 19. 8, the statutes of the Lord are *r.*
45. 6, sceptre is a *r.* sceptre.
51. 10, renew a *r.* spirit within me.
107. 7, he led them forth by the *r.* way.
119. 75, thy judgments are *r.*
Prov. 4. 11, I have led thee in *r.* paths.
8. 6, opening of my lips shall be *r.* things.
12. 5, thoughts of the righteous are *r.*
15, way of a fool is *r.* in his own eyes.
14. 12; 16. 25, there is a way that seemeth *r.*
21. 2, every way of man is *r.* in his own eyes.
24. 26, kiss his lips that giveth a *r.* answer.
Isa. 30. 10, prophesy not *r.* things.
Jer. 2. 21, planted wholly a *r.* seed.
Ezek. 18. 5, if a man do that which is *r.*
19; 21. 27; 33. 14, that which is lawful and *r.*
Hos. 14. 9, the ways of the Lord are *r.*
Amos 3. 10, they know not how to do *r.*
Mat. 20. 4, whatsoever is *r.* I will give you.
Mk. 5. 15; Lu. 8. 35, in his *r.* mind.
Lu. 10. 28, thou hast answered *r.*
Eph. 6. 1, obey your parents, this is *r.*
See Judg. 17. 6; Lu. 12. 57; Acts 8. 21; 2 Pet. 2. 15.

RIGHTEOUS. Gen. 7. 1, thee have I seen *r.* before me.
18. 23, wilt thou destroy *r.* with wicked.
20. 4, wilt thou slay also a *r.* nation?
38. 26, she hath been more *r.* than I.
Ex. 23. 8, gift perverteth words of the *r.*
Num. 23. 10, let me die the death of the *r.*
Deut. 25. 1; 2 Chron. 6. 23, they shall justify the *r.*
1 Sam. 24. 17, thou art more *r.* than I.
1 Kings 2. 32, two men more *r.* than he.
Job 4. 7, where were the *r.* cut off.
9. 15, though I were *r.* yet would I not answer.
15. 14, what is man that he should be *r.*
17. 9, *r.* shall hold on his way.
22. 3, is it any pleasure that thou art *r.*
23. 7, there the *r.* might dispute with him.
34. 5, Job hath said, I am *r.*
Ps. 1. 5, the congregation of the *r.*
6, the Lord knoweth the way of the *r.*
7. 9, the *r.* God trieth the hearts.
11. 3, what can the *r.* do.
34. 17, the *r.* cry, and the Lord heareth them.
19, many are the afflictions of the *r.*
37. 16, a little that a *r.* man hath.
21, the *r.* showeth mercy and giveth.
25, have not seen the *r.* forsaken.
29, the *r.* shall inherit the land.
30, mouth of *r.* speaketh wisdom.
39, salvation of *r.* is of the Lord.
55. 22, never suffer the *r.* to be moved.
58. 11, there is a reward for the *r.*
69. 28, let them not be written with the *r.*
92. 12, the *r.* shall flourish like palm tree.
97. 11, light is sown for the *r.*
112. 6, *r.* shall be in everlasting remembrance.
125. 3, rod shall not rest on lot of *r.*
140. 13, the *r.* shall give thanks.
141. 5, let the *r.* smite me.
146. 8, the Lord loveth the *r.*
Prov. 2. 7, he layeth up wisdom for the *r.*
3. 32, his secret is with the *r.*
10. 3, the Lord will not suffer *r.* to famish.
11, the mouth of *r.* is a well of life.
16, labour of *r.* tendeth to life.
21, lips of *r.* feed many.
24, desire of the *r.* shall be granted.
25, the *r.* is an everlasting foundation.
28, hope of the *r.* shall be gladness.
30, the *r.* shall never be removed.
11. 8, the *r.* is delivered out of trouble.
10, when it goeth well with the *r.*
21, seed of the *r.* shall be delivered.
12. 3, the root of the *r.* shall not be moved.
Prov. 5, thoughts of the *r.* are right.
7, house of the *r.* shall stand.
10, *r.* man regardeth the life of his beast.
26, the *r.* is more excellent than his neighbour.
13. 9, the light of the *r.* rejoiceth.
21, to the *r.* good shall be repaid.
25, *r.* eateth to the satisfying of his soul.
14. 9, among the *r.* there is favour.
32, the *r.* hath hope in his death.
15. 6, in the house of the *r.* is much treasure.
19, the way of the *r.* is made plain.
28, the heart of the *r.* studieth to answer.
29, he heareth the prayer of the *r.*
16. 13, *r.* lips are delight of kings.
18. 10, *r.* runneth into it and is safe.
28. 1, the *r.* are bold as a lion.
29. 2, when the *r.* are in authority, people rejoice.
Eccl. 7. 16, be not *r.* overmuch.
9. 1, the *r.* and the wise are in the hand of God.
2, one event to *r.* and wicked.
Isa. 3. 10, say to *r.* it shall be well.
24. 16, songs, even glory to the *r.*
26. 2, that the *r.* nation may enter.
41. 2, raised up a *r.* man from the east.
53. 11, shall my *r.* servant justify.
57. 1, *r.* perisheth, and no man layeth it.
60. 21, thy people shall be all *r.*
Jer. 23. 5, raise to David a *r.* branch.
Ezek. 13. 22, with lies ye have made *r.* sad.
16. 52, thy sisters are more *r.* than thou.
33. 12, the righteousness of the *r.* shall not.
Amos 2. 6, they sold the *r.* for silver.
Mal. 3. 18, discern between the *r.* and wicked.
Mat. 9. 13; Mk. 2. 17; Lu. 5. 32, not come to call *r.*
13. 17, many *r.* men have desired.
43, then shall the *r.* shine forth.
23. 28, outwardly appear *r.* to men.
29, garnish sepulchres of the *r.*
25. 46, the *r.* unto life eternal.
Lu. 1. 6, they were both *r.* before God.
18. 9, trusted they were *r.* and despised others.
23. 47, certainly this was a *r.* man.
John 7. 24, judge *r.* judgment.
Rom. 3. 10, there is none *r.*, no not one.
5. 7, scarcely for a *r.* man will one die.
19, many be made *r.*
2 Thess. 1. 6, it is a *r.* thing with God.
2 Tim. 4. 8, the Lord, the *r.* Judge.
Heb. 11. 4, obtained witness that he was *r.*
1 Pet. 3. 12, eyes of the Lord are over the *r.*
4. 18, if the *r.* scarcely be saved.
2 Pet. 2. 8, Lot vexed his *r.* soul.
1 John 2. 1, Jesus Christ the *r.*
3. 7, *r.* as he is *r.*
Rev. 22. 11, he that is *r.* let him be *r.* still.
See Ezek. 3. 20; Mat. 10. 41; 1 Tim. 1. 9; Jas. 5. 16.

RIGHTEOUSLY. Deut. 1. 16; Prov. 31. 9, judge *r.*
Ps. 67. 4; 96. 10, thou shalt judge the people *r.*
Isa. 33. 15, he that walketh *r.* shall dwell on high.
See Jer. 11. 20; Tit. 2. 12; 1 Pet. 2. 23.

RIGHTEOUSNESS. Gen. 30. 33, so shall my *r.* answer for me.
Deut. 33. 19, offer sacrifices of *r.*
1 Sam. 26. 23; Job 33. 26, render to every man his *r.*
Job 6. 29, return again, my *r.* is in it.
27. 6, my *r.* I hold fast.
29. 14, I put on *r.* and it clothed me.
35. 2, thou saidst, My *r.* is more than God's?
36. 3, I will ascribe *r.* to my Maker.
Ps. 4. 1, hear me, O God of my *r.*
5, offer the sacrifice of *r.*
9. 8, he shall judge the world in *r.*
15. 2, he that worketh *r.* shall never be moved.
17. 15, as for me, I will behold thy face in *r.*
23. 3, leadeth me in paths of *r.*
24. 5, and *r.* from the God of his salvation.

Ps. 40. 9, I have preached *r*.
45. 7; Heb. 1. 9, thou lovest *r*.
50. 6; 97. 6, heavens shall declare his *r*.
72. 2, he shall judge thy people with *r*.
85. 10, *r*. and peace have kissed each other.
94. 15, judgment shall return unto *r*.
97. 2, *r*. is the habitation of his throne.
111. 3; 112. 3, 9, his *r*. endureth for ever.
118. 19, open to me the gates of *r*.
132. 9, let thy priests be clothed with *r*.
Prov. 8. 18, durable riches and *r*. are with me.
10. 2; 11. 4, but *r*. delivereth from death.
11. 5, *r*. of the perfect shall direct his way.
6, *r*. of the upright shall deliver.
19, *r*. tendeth to life.
12. 28, in the way of *r*. is life.
14. 34, *r*. exalteth a nation.
16. 8, better is a little with *r*.
12, the throne is established by *r*.
31, crown of glory if found in way of *r*.
Eccl. 7. 15, a just man that perisheth in his *r*.
Isa. 11. 5, *r*. the girdle of his loins.
26. 10, yet will he not learn *r*.
32. 1, a king shall reign in *r*.
17, the work of *r*. peace, and the effect of *r*.
41. 10, uphold thee with right hand of my *r*.
46. 12, ye that are far from *r*.
58. 8, thy *r*. shall go before thee.
59. 16, his *r*. sustained him.
62. 2, the Gentiles shall see thy *r*.
64. 6, our *r*. are as filthy rags.
Jer. 23. 6; 33. 16, this is his name, The Lord our *r*.
33. 15, cause the branch of *r*. to grow.
51. 10, the Lord hath brought forth our *r*.
Ezek. 3. 20; 18. 24, righteous man turn from *r*.
14. 14, deliver but their own souls by *r*.
18. 20, the *r*. of the righteous shall be upon him.
33. 13, if he trust to his own *r*.
Dan. 4. 27, break off thy sins by *r*.
9. 7, *r*. belongeth to thee.
24, to bring in everlasting *r*.
12. 3, they that turn many to *r*.
Hos. 10. 12, till he rain *r*. upon you.
Amos 5. 24, let *r*. run down as a stream.
6. 12, turned fruit of *r*. into hemlock.
Zeph. 2. 3, ye meek of the earth, seek *r*.
Mal. 4. 2, shall the Sun of *r*. arise.
Mat. 3. 15, to fulfil all *r*.
5. 6, hunger and thirst after *r*.
10, persecuted for *r*. sake.
20, except your *r*. exceed the *r*.
21. 32, John came to you in the way of *r*.
Lu. 1. 75, in *r*. before him.
John 16. 8, reprove the world of *r*.
Acts 10. 35, he that worketh *r*.
13. 10, thou enemy of all *r*.
24. 25, as he reasoned of *r*.
Rom. 1. 17; 3. 5; 10. 3, the *r*. of God.
4. 6, to whom God imputeth *r*.
11, seal of the *r*. of faith.
5. 17, which receive the gift of *r*.
18, by the *r*. of one.
21, so might grace reign through *r*.
6. 13, yield your members as instruments of *r*.
20, ye were free from *r*.
8. 10, the Spirit is life, because of *r*.
9. 30, the *r*. which is of faith.
10. 3, going about to establish their own *r*.
4, Christ is the end of the law for *r*.
10, with the heart man believeth unto *r*.
14. 17, kingdom of God not meat and drink, but *r*.
1 Cor. 1. 30, Christ is made unto us *r*.
15. 34, awake to *r*.
2 Cor. 5. 21, that we might be made the *r*.
6. 7, the armour of *r*.
14, what fellowship hath *r*.
Gal. 2. 21, if *r*. come by the law.
5. 5, we wait for the hope of *r*.
Eph. 6. 14, the breastplate of *r*.
Phil. 1. 11, filled with the fruits of *r*.
3. 6, touching the *r*. in the law, blameless.
9, not having mine own *r*., but the *r*. of God.
1 Tim. 6. 11, follow after *r*.
2 Tim. 3. 16, for instruction in *r*.
4. 8, laid up for me a crown of *r*.
Tit. 3. 5, not by works of *r*.
Heb. 1. 8, a sceptre of *r*.
5. 13, unskilful in the word of *r*.
7. 2, by interpretation, King of *r*.
11. 7, heir of the *r*. which is by faith.
33, through faith wrought *r*.
12. 11, the peaceable fruit of *r*.
Jas. 1. 20, wrath of man worketh not *r*. of God.
3. 18, the fruit of *r*. is sown in peace.
1 Pet. 2. 24, dead to sins should live unto *r*.
2 Pet. 2. 5, a preacher of *r*.
21, better not to have known way of *r*.
3. 13, new earth, wherein dwelleth *r*.
1 John 2. 29, every one that doeth *r*.
See Isa. 54. 14; 63. 1; Zech. 8. 8; Rev. 19. 8.
RIGHTLY. Gen. 27. 36; Lu. 7. 43; 20. 21; 2 Tim. 2. 15.
RIGOUR. Ex. 1. 13, 14; Lev. 25. 43, 46, 53.
RINGLEADER. Acts 24. 5, a *r*. of the sect of the Nazarenes.
RIOT. Rom. 13. 13; Tit. 1. 6; 1 Pet. 4. 4; 2 Pet. 2. 13.
RIPE. Gen. 40. 10, brought forth *r*. grapes.
Ex. 22. 29, offer the first of thy *r*. fruits.
Num. 18. 13, whatsoever is first *r*. be thine.
Joel 3. 13, put in sickle, for the harvest is *r*.
Mic. 7. 1, my soul desired the first-*r*. fruit.
Rev. 14. 5, time to reap, for harvest of earth is *r*.
See Num. 13. 20; Jer. 24. 2; Hos. 9. 10; Nah. 3. 12.
RISE. Gen. 19. 2, ye shall *r*. up early.
23, the sun was *r*. when Lot entered Zoar.
Num. 24. 17, a sceptre shall *r*. out of Israel.
32. 14, ye are *r*. up in your fathers' stead.
Job 9. 7, commandeth the sun and it *r*. not.
14. 12, man lieth down and *r*. not.
24. 22, he *r*. up, and no man is sure of life.
31. 14, what shall I do when God *r*. up.
Ps. 27. 3, though war should *r*. against me.
119. 62, at midnight I will *r*. to give thanks.
127. 2, it is vain to *r*. up early.
Prov. 31. 15, she *r*. up while it is yet night.
28, her children *r*. up and call her blessed.
Eccl. 12. 4, he shall *r*. at the voice of the bird.
Isa. 33. 10, now will I *r*., saith the Lord.
58. 10, then shall thy light *r*. in obscurity.
60. 1, the glory of the Lord is *r*. upon thee.
Jer. 7. 13; 25. 3; 35. 14, I spake unto you, *r*. up early.
25; 25. 4; 26. 5; 29. 19; 35. 15; 44. 4, I sent my servants, *r*. early.
11. 7, *r*. early and protesting.
25. 27, fall and *r*. no more.
Lam. 3. 63, sitting down and *r*. up, I am their music.
Mat. 5. 45, maketh sun to *r*. on evil and good.
17. 9; Mk. 9. 9, until Son of man be *r*.
20. 19; Mk. 9. 31; 10. 34; Lu. 18. 33; 24. 7, the third day he shall *r*. again.
26. 32; Mk. 14. 28, after I am *r*. I will go before you.
46, *r*., let us be going.
Mk. 4. 27, should sleep, and *r*. night and day.
9. 10, what the *r*. from dead should mean.
10. 49, *r*., he calleth thee.
Lu. 2. 34, this child is set for the fall and *r*.
11. 7, I cannot *r*. and give thee.
22. 46, why sleep ye, *r*. and pray.
24. 34, the Lord is *r*. indeed.
John 11. 23, thy brother shall *r*. again.
Acts 10. 13, *r*., Peter, kill and eat.
26. 16, *r*., and stand upon thy feet.
23, the first that should *r*. from the dead.
Rom. 8. 34, that died, yea rather that is *r*.
1 Cor. 15. 15, if so be the dead *r*. not.
20, but now is Christ *r*.

Col. 3. 1, if ye then be *r.* with Christ.
1 Thess. 4. 16, the dead in Christ shall *r.* first.
See Prov. 30. 31; Isa. 60. 3; Mk. 16. 2; Col. 2. 12.
RITES. Num. 9. 3, according to all the *r.* of it.
RIVER. Ex. 7. 19; 8. 5, stretch out hand on *r.*
2 Sam. 17. 13, that city, and we will draw it into the *r.*
2 Kings 5. 12, are the *r.* of Damascus better.
Job 20. 17, ye shall not see the *r.* of honey.
28. 10, he cutteth out *r.* among the rocks.
29. 6, the rock poured out *r.* of oil.
40. 23, he drinketh up a *r.*, and hasteth not.
Ps. 1. 3, tree planted by the *r.*
36. 8, the *r.* of thy pleasures.
46. 4, *r.*, the streams whereof make glad.
65. 9, enrichest it with *r.* of God.
107. 33, turneth *r.* into a wilderness.
119. 136, *r.* of waters run down mine eyes.
137. 1, by the *r.* of Babylon we sat.
Eccl. 1. 7, all the *r.* run into the sea.
Isa. 32. 2, shall be as *r.* of water in a dry place.
43. 2, through the *r.*, they shall not overflow.
19, I will make *r.* in the desert.
48. 18, then had thy peace been as a *r.*
66. 12, I will extend peace like a *r.*
Lam. 2. 18, let tears run down like *r.*
Mic. 6. 7, be pleased with *r.* of oil.
John 7. 38, shall flow *r.* of living water.
Rev. 22. 1, a pure *r.* of water of life.
See Gen. 41. 1; Ex. 1. 22; Ezek. 47. 9; Mk. 1. 5.
ROAD. 1 Sam. 27. 10, whither have ye made a *r.*
ROAR. 1 Chron. 16. 32; Ps. 96. 11; 98. 7, let the sea *r.*
Job 3. 24, my *r.* are poured out.
Ps. 46. 3, will not fear, though waters *r.*
104. 21, young lions *r.* after their prey.
Prov. 19. 12; 20. 2, king's wrath as the *r.* of a lion.
Isa. 59. 11, we *r.* like bears.
Jer. 6. 23, their voice *r.* like the sea.
25. 30, the Lord shall *r.* from on high.
Hos. 11. 10, he shall *r.* like a lion.
Joel 3. 16; Amos 1. 2, the Lord shall *r.* out of Zion.
Amos 3. 4, will a lion *r.* when he hath no prey?
See Ps. 22. 1; 32. 3; Zech. 11. 3; Rev. 10. 3.
ROARING. Prov. 28. 15, as a *r.* lion, is a wicked ruler.
Lu. 21. 25, distress, the sea and waves *r.*
1 Pet. 5. 8, the devil as a *r.* lion.
See Ps. 22. 13; Isa. 31. 4; Ezek. 22. 25; Zeph. 3. 3.
ROAST. Ex. 12. 9, not raw, but *r.* with fire.
Prov. 12. 27, slothful man *r.* not that he took.
Isa. 44. 16, he *r. r.*, and is satisfied.
See Deut. 16. 7; 1 Sam. 2. 15; 2 Chron. 35. 13.
ROB. Prov. 22. 22, *r.* not the poor.
Isa. 10. 2, that they may *r.* the fatherless.
13, I have *r.* their treasures.
42. 22, this is a people *r.* and spoiled.
Ezek. 33. 15, if he give again that he had *r.*
Mal. 3. 8, ye have *r.* me.
2 Cor. 11. 8, I *r.* other churches.
See Judg. 9. 25; 2 Sam. 17. 8; Ps. 119. 61; Prov. 17. 12.
ROBBER. Job 12. 6, tabernacles of *r.* prosper.
Isa. 42. 24, who gave Israel to the *r.*
Jer. 7. 11, is this house become a den of *r.*
John 10. 1, the same is a thief and a *r.*
8, all that came before me are *r.*
Acts 19. 37, these men are not *r.* of churches.
2 Cor. 11. 26, in perils of *r.*
See Ezek. 7. 22; 18. 10; Dan. 11. 14; Hos. 6. 9.
ROBBERY. Phil. 2. 6, thought it not *r.* to be equal.
ROBE. 1 Sam. 24. 4, cut off skirt of Saul's *r.*
Job 29. 14, my judgment was as a *r.*
Isa. 61. 10, covered me with *r.* of righteousness.
Lu. 15. 22, bring forth the best *r.*
20. 46, desire to walk in long *r.*
See Ex. 28. 4; Mic. 2. 8; Mat. 27. 28; Rev. 6. 11.
ROCK. Ex. 33. 22, I will put thee in a clift of *r.*
Num. 20. 8, speak to the *r.* before their eyes.
10, must we fetch you water out of this *r.*
23. 9, from the top of the *r.* I see him.
24. 21, thou puttest thy nest in a *r.*
Deut. 8. 15, who brought thee water out of the *r.*
32. 4, he is the *R.*
15, lightly esteemed the *R.* of his salvation.
18, of the *R.* that begat thee.
30, except their *R.* had sold them.
31, their *r.* is not as our *R.*
37, where is their *r.* in whom they trusted?
1 Sam. 2. 2, neither is there any *r.* like our God.
2 Sam. 22. 2; Ps. 18. 2; 92. 15, the Lord is my *r.*
3, the God of my *r.*
32; Ps. 18. 31, who is a *r.*, save our God?
23. 3, the *R.* of Israel spake.
1 Kings 19. 11, strong wind brake in pieces the *r.*
Job 14. 18, the *r.* is removed out of his place.
19. 24, graven in the *r.* for ever.
24. 8, embrace the *r.* for want of shelter.
Ps. 27. 5; 40. 2, shall set me up upon a *r.*
31. 3; 71. 3, thou art my *r.* and my fortress.
61. 2, lead me to the *r.* that is higher than I.
81. 16, with honey out of the *r.*
Prov. 30. 26, yet make their houses in the *r.*
Cant. 2. 14, that art in the clefts of the *r.*
Isa. 8. 14, for a *r.* of offence.
17. 10, not mindful of the *r.* of thy strength.
32. 2, as the shadow of a great *r.*
33. 16, defence shall be munitions of *r.*
Jer. 5. 3, they made their faces harder than *r.*
23. 29, hammer that breaketh the *r.* in pieces.
Nah. 1. 6, the *r.* are thrown down by him.
Mat. 7. 25; Lu. 6. 48, it was founded upon a *r.*
16. 18, upon this *r.* I will build my church.
27. 51, and the *r.* rent.
Lu. 8. 6, some fell upon a *r.*
Rom. 9. 33; 1 Pet. 2. 8, I lay a *r.* of offence.
1 Cor. 10. 4, spiritual *R.*, and that *R.* was Christ.
Rev. 6. 16, said to the *r.*, fall on us.
See Judg. 6. 20; 13. 19; 1 Sam. 14. 4; Prov. 30. 19.
ROD. Job 9. 34, let him take his *r.* from me.
21. 9, neither is the *r.* of God upon them.
Ps. 2. 9, break them with a *r.* of iron.
23. 4, thy *r.* and thy staff comfort me.
Prov. 10. 13; 26. 3, *r.* for the back of fools.
13. 24, he that spareth his *r.*
22. 8, the *r.* of his anger shall fail.
23. 13, thou shalt beat him with thy *r.*
29. 15, the *r.* and reproof give wisdom.
Isa. 10. 15, as if the *r.* should shake itself.
11. 1, shall come forth a *r.*
Jer. 48. 17, how is the beautiful *r.* broken.
Ezek. 20. 37, cause you to pass under the *r.*
Mic. 6. 9, hear ye the *r.*, and who hath appointed it.
2 Cor. 11. 25, thrice was I beaten with *r.*
See Gen. 30. 37; 1 Sam. 14. 27; Rev. 2. 27; 11. 1.
RODE. 2 Sam. 18. 9; 2 Kings 9. 25; Neh. 2. 12; Ps. 18. 10.
ROLL. Josh. 5. 9, I have *r.* away reproach.
Job 30. 14, they *r.* themselves on me.
Isa. 9. 5, with garments *r.* in blood.
34. 4; Rev. 6. 14, the heavens shall be *r.* together.
Mk. 16. 3, who shall *r.* us away the stone?
Lu. 24. 2, they found the stone *r.* away.
See Gen. 29. 8; Prov. 26. 27; Isa. 17. 13; Mat. 27. 60.
ROOF. Gen. 19. 8, under the shadow of my *r.*
Deut. 22. 8, make a battlement for thy *r.*
Job 29. 10; Ps. 137. 6; Lam. 4. 4; Ezek. 3. 26, tongue cleaveth to *r.* of mouth.
Mat. 8. 8; Lu. 7. 6, I am not worthy that thou shouldest come under my *r.*
Mk. 2. 4, they uncovered the *r.*
See Josh. 2. 6; Judg. 16. 27; 2 Sam. 11. 2; Jer. 19. 13.
ROOM. Gen. 24. 23, is there *r.* for us.
26. 22, the Lord hath made *r.* for us.
Ps. 31. 8, set my feet in a large *r.*

Ps. 80. 9, thou preparedst *r.* before it.
Prov. 18. 16, a man's gift maketh *r.* for him.
Mal. 3. 10, there shall not be *r.* enough.
Mat. 23. 6; Mk. 12. 39; Lu. 20. 46, love uppermost *r.*
Mk. 2. 2, there was no *r.* to receive them.
Lu. 2. 7, no *r.* for them in the inn.
12. 17, no *r.* to bestow my goods.
14. 7, how they chose out the chief *r.*
9, begin with shame to take the lowest *r.*
22, it is done, and yet there is *r.*
See Gen. 6. 14; 1 Kings 8. 20; 19. 16; Mk. 14. 15.
ROOT (*n.*). Deut. 29. 18, a *r.* that beareth gall.
2 Kings 19. 30, shall again take *r.* downward.
Job 5. 3, I have seen the foolish taking *r.*
8. 17, his *r.* are wrapped about the heap.
14. 8, the *r.* thereof wax old in the earth.
18. 16, his *r.* shall be dried up.
19. 28, the *r.* of the matter.
29. 19, my *r.* was spread out by the waters.
Prov. 12. 3, *r.* of righteous shall not be moved.
12, *r.* of righteous yieldeth fruit.
Isa. 5. 24, their *r.* shall be rottenness.
11. 1, a Branch shall grow out of his *r.*
10; Rom. 15. 12, there shall be a *r.* of Jesse.
27. 6; 37. 31, them that come of Jacob to take *r.*
53. 2, as a *r.* out of a dry ground.
Ezek. 31. 7, his *r.* was by great waters.
Hos. 14. 5, cast forth his *r.* as Lebanon.
Mal. 4. 1, leave them neither *r.* nor branch.
Mat. 3. 10; Lu. 3. 9, axe laid to *r.* of trees.
13. 6; Mk. 4. 6; Lu. 8. 13, because they had no *r.*
Mk. 11. 20, fig tree dried up from the *r.*
Rom. 11. 16, if the *r.* be holy.
1 Tim. 6. 10, love of money the *r.* of all evil.
Heb. 12. 15, lest any *r.* of bitterness.
Jude 12, twice dead, plucked up by the *r.*
Rev. 22. 16, *r.* and offspring of David.
See 2 Chron. 7. 20; Dan. 4. 15; 7. 8; 11. 7.
ROOT (*v.*). Deut. 29. 28, Lord *r.* them out.
1 Kings 14. 15, he shall *r.* up Israel.
Job 18. 14, confidence shall be *r.* out.
31. 8, let my offspring be *r.* out.
12, *r.* out all mine increase.
Ps. 52. 5, *r.* thee out of land of the living.
Mat. 13. 29, lest ye *r.* up also the wheat.
15. 13, hath not planted shall be *r.* up.
Eph. 3. 17, being *r.* and grounded in love.
Col. 2. 7, *r.* and built up in him.
See Prov. 2. 22; Jer. 1. 10; Zeph. 2. 4.
ROSE (*n.*). Cant. 2. 1; Isa. 35. 1.
ROSE (*v.*). Gen. 32. 31, the sun *r.* upon him as he passed.
Josh. 3. 16, waters *r.* up on an heap.
Lu. 16. 31, though one *r.* from the dead.
Rom. 14. 9, to this end Christ both died and *r.*
1 Cor. 15. 4, buried, and *r.* the third day.
2 Cor. 5. 15, live to him who died and *r.*
See Lu. 24. 33; Acts 10. 41; 1 Thess. 4. 14; Rev. 19. 3.
ROT. Num. 5. 21; Prov. 10. 7; Isa. 40. 20.
ROTTEN. Job 41. 27; Jer. 38. 11; Joel 1. 17.
ROTTENNESS. Prov. 12. 4; 14. 30; Isa. 5. 24.
ROUGH. Isa. 27. 8, stayeth his *r.* wind.
40. 4; Lu. 3. 5, *r.* places made plain.
Zech. 13. 4, wear a *r.* garment to deceive.
See Deut. 21. 4; Jer. 51. 27; Dan. 8. 21.
ROUGHLY. Gen. 42. 7, Joseph spake *r.*
Prov. 18. 23, the rich answereth *r.*
See 1 Sam. 20. 10; 1 Kings 12. 13; 2 Chron. 10. 13.
ROUND. Ex. 16. 14; Isa. 3. 18; Lu. 19. 43.
ROWED. Jonah 1. 13; Mk. 6. 48; John 6. 19.
ROYAL. Gen. 49. 20, yield *r.* dainties.
Esth. 1. 7, *r.* wine in abundance.
5. 1; 6. 8; 8. 15; Acts 12. 21, *r.* apparel.
Jas. 2. 8, fulfil the *r.* law.
1 Pet. 2. 9, a *r.* priesthood.
See 1 Chron. 29. 25; Isa. 62. 3; Jer. 43. 10.
RUBIES. Job 28. 18; Prov. 8. 11; 31. 10.
RUDDY. 1 Sam. 16. 12; Cant. 5. 10; Lam. 4. 7.
RUDE. 2 Cor. 11. 6, *r.* in speech.
RUDIMENTS. Col. 2. 8, 20, *r.* of the world.
RUIN. 2 Chron. 28. 23, they were the *r.* of him.
Ps. 89. 40, hast brought his strong holds to *r.*
Prov. 24. 22, who knoweth the *r.* of both.
26. 28, a flattering mouth worketh *r.*
Ezek. 18. 30, so iniquity shall not be your *r.*
21. 15, that their *r.* may be multiplied.
Lu. 6. 49, the *r.* of that house was great.
See Isa. 3. 8; Ezek. 36. 35; Amos 9. 11; Acts 15. 16.
RULE (*n.*). Esth. 9. 1, Jews had *r.* over them.
Prov. 17. 2, a wise servant shall have *r.*
19. 10, servant to have *r.* over princes.
25. 28, no *r.* over his own spirit.
Isa. 63. 19, thou never barest *r.* over them.
1 Cor. 15. 24, when he shall put down all *r.*
Gal. 6. 16, as many as walk according to this *r.*
Heb. 13. 7, 17, them that have the *r.* over you.
See Eccl. 2. 19; Isa. 44. 13; 2 Cor. 10. 13.
RULE (*v.*). Gen. 1. 16, to *r.* the day.
3. 16, thy husband shall *r.* over thee.
Judg. 8. 23, I will not *r.* over you.
2 Sam. 23. 3, that *r.* over men must be just.
Ps. 66. 7, he *r.* by his power for ever.
89. 9, thou *r.* the raging of the sea.
103. 19, his kingdom *r.* over all.
Prov. 16. 32, that *r.* his spirit.
22. 7, rich *r.* over the poor.
Eccl. 9. 17, him that *r.* among fools.
Isa. 3. 4, babes *r.* over them.
32. 1, princes shall *r.* in judgment.
40. 10, his arm shall *r.* for him.
Ezek. 29. 15, shall no more *r.* over nations.
Rom. 12. 8, he that *r.* with diligence.
Col. 3. 15, peace of God *r.* in your hearts.
1 Tim. 3. 4, one that *r.* well his own house.
5. 17, elders that *r.* well.
See Dan. 5. 21; Zech. 6. 13; Rev. 2. 27; 12. 5.
RULER. Num. 13. 2, every one a *r.* among them.
Prov. 6. 7, ant, having no guide, overseer, or *r.*
23. 1, when thou sittest to eat with a *r.*
28. 16, a wicked *r.* over the poor.
Isa. 3. 6, be thou our *r.*
Mic. 5. 2, out of thee shall come *r.*
Mat. 25. 21, I will make thee *r.*
John 7. 26, do the *r.* know that this is Christ?
48, have any of the *r.* believed.
Rom. 13. 3, *r.* not a terror to good works.
See Gen. 41. 43; Neh. 5. 7; Ps. 2. 2; Isa. 1. 10.
RUMOUR. Jer. 49. 14, I have heard a *r.*
Ezek. 7. 26, *r.* shall be upon *r.*
Mat. 24. 6; Mk. 13. 7, wars and *r.* of wars.
See 2 Kings 19. 7; Obad. 1; Lu. 7. 17.
RUN. 2 Sam. 18. 27, the *r.* of the foremost is like.
2 Chron. 16. 9, eyes of Lord *r.* to and fro.
Ps. 19. 5, as a strong man to *r.* a race.
23. 5, my cup *r.* over.
147. 15, his word *r.* very swiftly.
Cant. 1. 4, draw me, we will *r.* after thee.
Isa. 40. 31, they shall *r.* and not be weary.
55. 5, nations shall *r.* to thee.
Jer. 12. 5, if thou hast *r.* with the footmen.
51. 31, one post shall *r.* to meet another.
Dan. 12. 4, many shall *r.* to and fro.
Hab. 2. 2, that he may *r.* that readeth.
Zech. 2. 4, *r.*, speak to this young man.
Lu. 6. 38, good measure *r.* over.
Rom. 9. 16, nor of him that *r.*
1 Cor. 9. 24, they which *r.* in a race *r.* all.
26, I therefore so *r.*
Gal. 2. 2, lest I should *r.* or had *r.* in vain.
5. 7, ye did *r.* well.
Heb. 12. 1, let us *r.* with patience.
1 Pet. 4. 4, that ye *r.* not to same excess.
See Prov. 4. 12; Jer. 5. 1; Lam. 2. 18; Amos 8. 12.
RUSH (*n.*). Job 8. 11; Isa. 9. 14; 19. 15; 35. 7.
RUSH (*v.*). Isa. 17. 13; Jer. 8. 6; Ezek. 3. 12; Acts 2. 2.
RUST. Mat. 6. 19, 20; Jas. 5. 3.

S

SABBATH. Lev. 25. 8, number seven *s.* of years.
2 Kings 4. 23, it is neither new moon nor *s.*
2 Chron. 36. 21, as long as desolate she kept *s.*
Ezek. 46. 1, on the *s.* it shall be opened.
Amos 8. 5, when will the *s.* be gone.
Mk. 2. 27, the *s.* was made for man.
28; Lu. 6. 5, the Son of man is Lord of the *s.*
Lu. 13. 15, doth not each on *s.* loose.
See Isa. 1. 13; Lam. 1. 7; 2. 6; Mat. 28. 1; John 5. 18.
SACK. Gen. 42. 25; 43. 21; 44. 1, 11, 12; Josh. 9. 4.
SACKCLOTH. 2 Sam. 3. 31, gird you with *s.*
1 Kings 20. 32, they girded *s.* on their loins.
Neh. 9. 1, assembled with fasting and *s.*
Esth. 4. 1, put on *s.* with ashes.
Ps. 30. 11, thou hast put off my *s.*
35. 13, my clothing was *s.*
Jonah 3. 5, and put on *s.*
SACRIFICE (*n.*). Gen. 31. 54, Jacob offered *s.*
Ex. 5. 17, let us go and do *s.* to the Lord.
Num. 25. 2, called people to the *s.* of their gods.
1 Sam. 2. 29, wherefore kick ye at my *s.*
9. 13, he doth bless the *s.*
15. 22, to obey is better than *s.*
Ps. 4. 5, offer the *s.* of righteousness.
27. 6, will I offer *s.* of joy.
40. 6; 51. 16, *s.* thou didst not desire.
51. 17, the *s.* of God are a broken spirit.
118. 27, bind the *s.* with cords.
Prov. 15. 8, *s.* of wicked an abomination.
17. 1, than a house full of *s.* with strife.
21. 3, to do justice is more acceptable than *s.*
Eccl. 5. 1, the *s.* of fools.
Isa. 1. 11, to what purpose is multitude of *s.*
Jer. 6. 20, nor are your *s.* sweet unto me.
33. 18, nor want a man to do *s.*
Dan. 8. 11; 9. 27; 11. 31; daily *s.* taken away.
Hos. 3. 4, many days without a *s.*
6. 6; Mat. 9. 13; 12. 7, I desired mercy and not *s.*
Amos 4. 4, bring your *s.* every morning.
Zeph. 1. 7, the Lord hath prepared a *s.*
Mal. 1. 8, ye offer the blind for *s.*
Mk. 9. 49, every *s.* shall be salted.
12. 33, to love the Lord is more than *s.*
Lu. 13. 1, blood Pilate mingled with *s.*
Acts 7. 42, have ye offered *s.* forty years.
14. 13, and would have done *s.*
Rom. 12. 1, present your bodies a living *s.*
1 Cor. 8. 4; 10. 19, 28, offered in *s.* to idols.
Eph. 5. 2, a *s.* to God for sweet-smelling savour.
Phil. 2. 17, upon the *s.* of your faith.
4. 18, a *s.* acceptable, well pleasing.
Heb. 9. 26, put away sin by *s.* of himself.
10. 12, offered one *s.* for sins.
10. 26, there remaineth no more *s.* for sin.
11. 4, a more excellent *s.*
13. 15, let us offer the *s.* of praise.
16, with such *s.* God is well pleased.
1 Pet. 2. 5, to offer up spiritual *s.*
See 2 Chron. 7. 1; Ezra 6. 10; Neh. 12. 43; Jonah 1. 16.
SACRIFICE (*v.*). Ex. 22. 20, he that *s.* to any god.
Ezra 4. 2, we seek your God, and do *s.* to him.
Neh. 4. 2, will they *s.*
Ps. 54. 6, I will freely *s.* to thee.
106. 37, they *s.* their sons to devils.
107. 22, let them *s.* sacrifices of thanksgiving.
Eccl. 9. 2, to him that *s.* and that *s.* not.
Isa. 65. 3, people that *s.* in gardens.
Hos. 8. 13, they *s.*, but the Lord accepteth not.
Hab. 1. 16, they *s.* unto their net.
1 Cor. 5. 7, Christ our passover is *s.* for us.
10. 20, things Gentiles *s.*, they *s.* to devils.
See Ex. 8. 26; Deut. 15. 21; 1 Sam. 1. 3; 15. 15.
SACRILEGE. Rom. 2. 22, dost thou commit *s.*
SAD. 1 Kings 21. 5, why is thy spirit so *s.*
Eccl. 7. 3, by *s.* of countenance the heart is made better.
Mat. 6. 16, be not of a *s.* countenance.
Mk. 10. 22, he was *s.* at that saying.
Lu. 24. 17, as ye walk and are *s.*
See Gen. 40. 6; 1 Sam. 1. 18; Neh. 2. 1; Ezek. 13. 22.
SADDLE. 1 Sam. 19. 26; 1 Kings 13. 13.
SAFE. 2 Sam. 18. 29, is the young man *s.*
Job 21. 9, their houses are *s.* from fear.
Ps. 119. 117, hold me up and I shall be *s.*
Prov. 18. 10, righteous run and are *s.*
29. 25, whoso trusteth in the Lord shall be *s.*
Ezek. 34. 27, they shall be *s.* in their land.
Acts 27. 44, so they escaped all *s.*
See 1 Sam. 12. 11; Isa. 5. 29; Lu. 15. 27; Phil. 3. 1.
SAFEGUARD. 1 Sam. 22. 23, with me thou shalt be in *s.*
SAFELY. Ps. 78. 53, he led them on *s.*
Prov. 1. 33, shall dwell *s.*
3. 23, shalt thou walk *s.*
31. 11, doth *s.* trust in her.
Hos. 2. 18, I will make them to lie down *s.*
See Isa. 41. 3; Zech. 14. 11; Mk. 14. 44; Acts 16. 23.
SAFETY. Job 3. 26, I was not in *s.*
5. 4, his children are far from *s.*
11. 18, thou shalt take thy rest in *s.*
Prov. 11. 14; 24. 6, in the multitude of counsellors is *s.*
21. 31, *s.* is of the Lord.
1 Thess. 5. 3, when they say peace and *s.*
See Job 24. 23; Ps. 12. 5; 33. 17; Isa. 14. 30.
SAIL. Isa. 33. 23; Ezek. 27. 7; Lu. 8. 23; Acts 27. 9.
SAINTS. 1 Sam. 2. 9, he will keep feet of *s.*
Job 5. 1, to which of the *s.* wilt thou turn.
15. 15, he putteth no trust in his *s.*
Ps. 16. 3, but to the *s.* that are in the earth.
30. 4, sing to the Lord, O ye *s.* of his.
37. 28, the Lord forsaketh not his *s.*
50. 5, gather my *s.* together.
89. 5, the congregation of the *s.*
7, to be feared in assembly of *s.*
97. 10, preserveth the souls of his *s.*
116. 15, precious is the death of his *s.*
132. 9, let thy *s.* shout for joy.
149. 9, this honour have all his *s.*
Dan. 7. 18, but the *s.* shall take the kingdom.
8. 13, then I heard one *s.* speaking.
Mat. 27. 52, many bodies of *s.* arose.
Acts 9. 13, evil he hath done to thy *s.*
Rom. 1. 7; 1 Cor. 1. 2, called to be *s.*
8. 27, he maketh intercession for the *s.*
12. 13, distributing to the necessity of *s.*
16. 2, receive her as becometh *s.*
1 Cor. 6. 1, dare any go to law, and not before *s.*
2, the *s.* shall judge the world.
16. 1, concerning collection for *s.*
16. 15, the ministry of *s.*
Eph. 1. 18, his inheritance in the *s.*
2. 19, fellowcitizens with the *s.*
3. 8, less than least of all *s.*
4. 12, perfecting of the *s.*
5. 3, not named among you, as becometh *s.*
Col. 1. 12, the *s.* in light.
1 Thess. 3. 13, at coming of our Lord with *s.*
2 Thess. 1. 10, to be glorified in his *s.*
1 Tim. 5. 10, if she have washed the *s.* feet.
Jude 3, faith once delivered to *s.*
Rev. 5. 8; 8. 3, 4, the prayers of *s.*
See Phil. 4. 21; Rev. 11. 18; 13. 7; 14. 12; 15. 3.
SAKE. Gen. 3. 17, cursed for thy *s.*
8. 21, not curse ground for man's *s.*
12. 13, be well with me for thy *s.*
18. 26, I will spare for their *s.*
30. 27, the Lord hath blessed me for thy *s.*
Num. 11. 29, enviest thou for my *s.*
Deut. 1. 37; 3. 26; 4. 21, angry with me for your *s.*
2 Sam. 9. 1, shew kindness for Jonathan's *s.*
18. 5, deal gently for my *s.*
Neh. 9. 31, for thy great mercies' *s.*
Ps. 6. 4; 31. 16, save me for thy mercies' *s.*
23. 3, he leadeth me for his name's *s.*

Ps. 44. 22, for thy *s.* are we killed.
106. 8, he saved them for his name's *s.*
Mat. 5. 10, persecuted for righteousness' *s.*
10. 18; Mk. 13. 9; Lu. 21. 12, for my *s.*
24. 22; Mk. 13. 20, for the elect's *s.*
John 11. 15, I am glad for your *s.*
13. 38, wilt thou lay down thy life for my *s.*
Rom. 13. 5; 1 Cor. 10. 25, for conscience *s.*
Col. 1. 24, for his body's *s.* which is the church.
1 Thess. 5. 13, for their work's *s.*
1 Tim. 5. 23, for thy stomach's *s.*
Tit. 1. 11, for lucre's *s.*
2 John 2, for the truth's *s.*
See Rom. 11. 28; 2 Cor. 8. 9; 1 Thess. 3. 9.
SALUTATION. Mk. 12. 38; Lu. 1. 29; Col. 4. 18; 2 Thess. 3. 17.
SALUTE. 1 Sam. 10. 4; 2 Kings 4. 29; Mk. 15. 18.
SALVATION. Gen. 49. 18, I have waited for thy *s.*
Ex. 14. 13; 2 Chron. 20. 17, see the *s.* of the Lord.
15. 2, he is become my *s.*
Deut. 32. 15, lightly esteemed the rock of his *s.*
1 Sam. 11. 13; 19. 5, the Lord wrought *s.* in Israel.
14. 45, Jonathan, who hath wrought this *s.*
2 Sam. 22. 51, he is the tower of *s.* for his king.
1 Chron. 16. 23, show forth from day to day his *s.*
2 Chron. 6. 41, let thy priests be clothed with *s.*
Ps. 3. 8, *s.* belongeth to the Lord.
9. 14, I will rejoice in thy *s.*
14. 7, O that the *s.* of Israel were come.
25. 5, thou art the God of my *s.*
27. 1; 62. 6; Isa. 12. 2, my light and my *s.*
35. 3, say unto my soul, I am thy *s*
37. 39, the *s.* of the righteous is of the Lord.
40. 10, I have declared thy faithfulness and *s.*
50. 23, to him will I show the *s.* of God.
51. 12; 70. 4, restore the joy of thy *s.*
68. 20, he that is our God, is the God of *s.*
69. 13, hear me in the truth of thy *s.*
29, let thy *s.* set me up on high.
71. 15, my mouth shall show forth thy *s.*
74. 12, working *s.* in the midst of the earth.
78. 22, they trusted not in his *s.*
85. 9, his *s.* is nigh them that fear him.
91. 16, will satisfy him and show him my *s.*
96. 2, show forth his *s.* from day to day.
98. 3, ends of the earth have seen the *s.*
116. 13, the cup of *s.*
118. 14; Isa. 12. 2, the Lord is become my *s.*
119. 41, let thy *s.* come.
81, my soul fainteth for thy *s.*
123, mine eyes fail for thy *s.*
155, *s.* is far from the wicked.
174, I have longed for thy *s.*
132. 16, I will clothe her priests with *s.*
144. 10, that giveth *s.* unto kings.
149. 4, beautify the meek with *s.*
Isa. 12. 3, the wells of *s.*
26. 1, *s.* will God appoint for walls.
33. 2, be thou our *s.* in time of trouble.
45. 8, earth open and let them bring forth *s.*
17, saved with an everlasting *s.*
49. 8, in a day of *s.* have I helped thee.
51. 5, my *s.* is gone forth.
52. 7, feet of him that publisheth *s.*
10, ends of the earth shall see *s.*
56. 1, my *s.* is near to come.
59. 11, we look for *s.*, but it is far off.
16, his arm brought *s.*
17, an helmet of *s.* on his head.
60. 18, call thy walls *S.*
61. 10, the garments of *s.*
62. 1, the *s.* thereof as a lamp.
63. 5, mine own arm brought *s.*
Jer. 3. 23, in vain is *s.* hoped for.
Lam. 3. 26, wait for the *s.* of the Lord.
Jonah 2. 9, *s.* is of the Lord.
Hab. 3. 8, ride on thy chariots of *s.*
18, I will joy in the God of my *s.*
Zech. 9. 9, thy King, just, and having *s.*
Lu. 1. 69, an horn of *s.* for us.
Lu. 1. 77, give knowledge of *s.* to his people.
2. 30, mine eyes have seen thy *s.*
3. 6, all flesh shall see the *s.* of God.
19. 9, this day is *s.* come to this house.
John 4. 22, *s.* is of the Jews.
Acts 4. 12, neither is there *s.* in any other.
13. 26, to you is the word of *s.* sent.
16. 17, these men show to us the way of *s.*
Rom. 1. 16, the power of God to *s.*
10. 10, confession is made to *s.*
13. 11, now is our *s.* nearer.
2 Cor. 1. 6, comforted, it is for your *s.*
6. 2, the day of *s.*
7. 10, sorrow worketh repentance to *s.*
Eph. 1. 13, the Gospel of your *s.*
6. 17; 1 Thess. 5. 8, the helmet of *s.* and sword.
Phil. 1. 19, this shall turn to my *s.*
28, an evident token of *s.*
2. 12, work out your own *s.*
1 Thess. 5. 9, hath appointed us to obtain *s.*
2 Thess. 2. 13, God hath chosen you to *s.*
2 Tim. 3. 15, wise unto *s.*
Tit. 2. 11, grace of God that bringeth *s.*
Heb. 1. 14, for them who shall be heirs of *s.*
2. 3, if we neglect so great *s.*
10, the captain of their *s.*
5. 9, author of eternal *s.*
6. 9, things that accompany *s.*
9. 28, without sin unto *s.*
1 Pet. 1. 5, kept through faith unto *s.*
9, end of faith, *s.* of your souls.
10, of which *s.* the prophets enquired.
2 Pet. 3. 15, longsuffering of the Lord is *s.*
Jude 3, of the common *s.*
Rev. 7. 10, saying, *s.* to our God.
See Job 13. 16; 1 Sam. 2. 1; 2 Sam. 22. 36.
SAME. Job 4. 8, sow wickedness, reap the *s.*
Ps. 102. 27; Heb. 1. 12, thou art the *s.*
Mat. 5. 46, do not the publicans the *s.*
Acts 1. 11, this *s.* Jesus shall come.
Rom. 10. 12, the *s.* Lord over all.
12. 16; 1 Cor. 1. 10; Phil. 4. 2, be of *s.* mind.
Heb. 13. 8, *s.* yesterday, to-day, and for ever.
See 1 Cor. 10. 3; 12. 4; 15. 39; Eph. 4. 10.
SANCTIFY. Lev. 11. 44; 20. 7; Num. 11. 18; Josh. 3. 5; 7. 13; 1 Sam. 16. 5, *s.* yourselves.
Isa. 5. 16, God shall be *s.* in righteousness.
13. 3, I have commanded my *s.* ones.
29. 23, they shall *s.* the Holy One.
66. 17, *s.* themselves in gardens.
Jer. 1. 5, I *s.* and ordained thee a prophet.
Ezek. 20. 41; 36. 23, I will be *s.* in you.
28. 25; 39. 27, *s.* in them in sight of heathen.
Joel 1. 14; 2. 15, *s.* ye a fast.
John 10. 36, him whom the Father *s.*
17. 17, *s.* them through thy truth.
19, for their sakes I *s.* myself.
Acts 20. 32; 26. 18, inheritance among them that are *s.*
Rom. 15. 16, being *s.* by the Holy Ghost.
1 Cor. 1. 2, to them that are *s.*
6. 11, but now ye are *s.*
7. 14, husband is *s.* by the wife, and the wife is *s.*
Eph. 5. 26, *s.* and cleanse the church.
1 Thess. 5. 23, the very God of peace *s.* you.
1 Tim. 4. 5, it is *s.* by the word of God.
2 Tim. 2. 21, a vessel *s.* for the Master's use.
Heb. 2. 11, he that *s.* and they who are *s.*
10. 10, by the which will we are *s.*
14, perfected for ever them that are *s.*
13. 12, that he might *s.* the people.
1 Pet. 3. 15, *s.* the Lord God in your hearts.
Jude 1, to them that are *s.* by God the Father.
See Gen. 2. 3; Ex. 13. 2; Job 1. 5; Mat. 23. 17.
SANCTUARY. Ex. 15. 17, plant them in the *s.*
25. 8, let them make me a *s.*
36. 1; 3. 4, work for the *s.*
Num. 7. 9, service of *s.* belongeth to them.
Neh. 10. 39, where are the vessels of the *s.*
Ps. 74. 7, they have cast fire into thy *s.*
Isa. 60. 13, beautify the place of my *s.*

Lam. 2. 7, the Lord hath abhorred his *s.*
See Dan. 8. 11; 9. 17; Heb. 8. 2; 9. 1.
SAND. Gen. 22. 17, as the *s.* which is upon the sea shore.
Hos. 1. 10; Rev. 20. 8, as the *s.* of the sea.
Heb. 11. 12, the *s.* which is by the sea.
See Job 6. 3; Prov. 27. 3; Mat. 7. 26.
SANDALS. Mk. 6. 9, be shod with *s.*
Acts 12. 8, bind on thy *s.*
SANG. Ex. 15. 1; Neh. 12. 42; Job 38. 7.
SANK. Ex. 15. 5, they *s.* into the bottom.
SAP. Ps. 104. 16, trees full of *s.*
SAPPHIRE. Ex. 24. 10, a paved work of a *s.* stone.
28. 18; Ezek. 28. 13; Rev. 21. 19, and a *s.*
Ezek. 1. 26, as the appearance of a *s.* stone.
10. 1, as it were a *s.* stone.
SARDINE. Rev. 4. 3, like a jasper and *s.* stone.
SARDIUS. Ex. 28. 17, the first row shall be a *s.*
Ezek. 28. 13; Rev. 21. 20, *s.* etc.
SARDONYX. Rev. 21. 20, the fifth *s.*
SAT. Judg. 20. 26, they *s.* before the Lord.
Job 29. 25, I *s.* chief.
Ps. 26. 4, have not *s.* with vain persons.
Jer. 15. 17, I *s.* alone because of thy hand.
Ezek. 3. 15, I *s.* where they *s.*
Mat. 4. 16, the people who *s.* in darkness.
Mk. 16. 19, he *s.* on the right hand of God.
Lu. 7. 15, he that was dead *s.* up.
10. 39, Mary *s.* at Jesus' feet.
John 4. 6, *s.* thus on the well.
Acts 2. 3, cloven tongues *s.* upon each.
See Ezra 10. 16; Neh. 1. 4; Ps. 137. 1; Rev. 4. 3.
SATAN. 1 Chron. 21. 1, *S.* provoked David.
Ps. 109. 6, let *S.* stand at his right hand.
Mat. 12. 26; Mk. 3. 23; Lu. 11. 18, if *S.* cast out *S.*
16. 23; Mk. 8. 33; Lu. 4. 8, get behind me, *S.*
Lu. 10. 18, I beheld *S.* as lightning fall.
Acts 5. 3, why hath *S.* filled thine heart.
26. 18, turn them from power of *S.*
2 Cor. 12. 7, messenger of *S.* to buffet me.
2 Thess. 2. 9, after the working of *S.*
1 Tim. 1. 20, whom I have delivered unto *S.*
5. 15, already turned aside after *S.*
See Rom. 16. 20; 1 Cor. 5. 5; 2 Cor. 2. 11; 11. 14.
SATIATE. Jer. 31. 14, 25; 46. 10.
SATISFY. Job 38. 27, to *s.* the desolate.
Ps. 17. 15, I shall be *s.* when I awake.
22. 26, the meek shall eat and be *s.*
36. 8, they shall be *s.* with fatness.
37. 19, in days of famine be *s.*
59. 15, and grudge if they be not *s.*
63. 5, my soul shall be *s.*
81. 16, with honey should I have *s.* thee.
90. 14, *s.* us early with thy mercy.
91. 16, with long life will I *s.* him.
103. 5, who *s.* thy mouth with good.
104. 13, the earth is *s.*
105. 40, he *s.* them with bread from heaven.
107. 9, he *s.* the longing soul.
132. 15, I will *s.* her poor with bread.
Prov. 6. 30, if he steal to *s.* his soul.
12. 11, he that tilleth his land shall be *s.*
14. 14, a good man shall be *s.* from himself.
19. 23, he that hath it shall abide *s.*
20. 13, open thine eyes and thou shalt be *s.*
30. 15, three things never *s.*
Eccl. 1. 8, the eye is not *s.* with seeing.
4. 8, neither is his eye *s.* with riches.
5. 10, shall not be *s.* with silver.
Isa. 9. 20; Mic. 6. 14, shall eat and not be *s.*
53. 11, travail of his soul and be *s.*
58. 10, if thou *s.* the afflicted soul.
11, the Lord shall *s.* thy soul in drought.
Jer. 31. 14, shall be *s.* with my goodness.
Ezek. 16. 28, yet thou couldest not be *s.*
Amos 4. 8, wandered to drink, but were not *s.*
Hab. 2. 5, as death and cannot be *s.*
See Ex. 15. 9; Deut. 14. 29; Job 19. 22; 27. 14.
SAVE. Gen. 45. 7, to *s.* your lives.
47. 25, thou hast *s.* our lives.
Deut. 28. 29, spoiled and no man shall *s.* thee.
33. 29, O people, *s.* by the Lord.
Josh. 10. 6, come up quickly and *s.* us.
Judg. 6. 15, wherewith shall I *s.* Israel?
1 Sam. 4. 3, the ark may *s.* us.
10. 27, how shall this man *s.* us?
11. 3, if there be no man to *s.* us we will come.
14. 6, no restraint to *s.* by many or by few.
2 Sam. 19. 9, the king *s.* us, and now he is fled.
2 Kings 6. 10, *s.* himself there, not once nor twice.
Job 2. 6, in thine hand, but *s.* his life.
22. 29, he shall *s.* the humble.
26. 2, how *s.* thou.
Ps. 7. 10, God who *s.* the upright.
20. 6, the Lord *s.* his anointed.
34. 18, he *s.* such as be of a contrite spirit.
44. 3, neither did their own arm *s.* them.
60. 5, *s.* with thy right hand.
72. 4, he shall *s.* the children of the needy.
80. 3; Prov. 28. 18; Jer. 17. 14; Mat. 10. 22; 24. 13; Mk. 13. 13; 16. 16; John 10. 9; Acts 2. 21; 16. 31; Rom. 5. 9; 9. 27; 10. 9; 11. 26, shall be *s.*
86. 2, *s.* thy servant that trusteth.
109. 31, *s.* him from those that condemn.
118. 25, *s.*, I beseech thee, send prosperity.
119. 94, *s.* me, for I have sought.
146, *s.* me, and I shall keep thy testimonies.
138. 7, thy right hand shall *s.*
Prov. 20. 22, wait on Lord and he shall *s.* thee.
Isa. 35. 4, your God will come and *s.* you.
43. 12, I have declared and have *s.*
45. 20, pray to a god that cannot *s.*
22, look unto me and be ye *s.*
47. 15, they shall wander, none shall *s.*
49. 25, I will *s.* thy children.
59. 1, Lord's hand not shortened, that it cannot *s.*
63. 1, mighty to *s.*
Jer. 2. 28, let them arise if they can *s.*
8. 20, summer is ended, and we are not *s.*
11. 12, but they shall not *s.*
14. 9, as a mighty man that cannot *s.*
15. 20; 30. 11; 42. 11; 46. 27, I am with thee to *s.* thee.
17. 14, *s.* me and I shall be *s.*
30. 10, I will *s.* thee from afar.
48. 6, flee, *s.* your lives.
Lam. 4. 17, a nation that could not *s.* us.
Ezek. 3. 18, to warn wicked, to *s.* his life.
34. 22, therefore will I *s.* my flock.
Hos. 1. 7, I will *s.* them by the Lord.
13. 10, is there any other that may *s.* thee.
Hab. 1. 2, cry to thee and thou wilt not *s.*
Zeph. 3. 17, he will *s.*
Mat. 1. 21, *s.* his people from their sins.
16. 25; Mk. 8. 35; Lu. 9. 24, will *s.* his life.
18. 11; Lu. 19. 10, to seek and to *s.* that which was lost.
19. 25; Mk. 10. 26; Lu. 18. 26, who then can be *s.*?
27. 40; Mk. 15. 30, *s.* thyself.
42; Mk. 15. 31, he *s.* others, himself he cannot *s.*
Mk. 3. 4; Lu. 6. 9, is it lawful to *s.*
Lu. 7. 50; 18. 42, thy faith hath *s.* thee.
8. 12, lest they should believe and be *s.*
9. 56, not to destroy but to *s.*
13. 23, are there few that be *s.*?
23. 35, let him *s.* himself.
39, if thou be Christ, *s.* thyself and us.
John 3. 17, that the world might be *s.*
5. 34, these things I say that ye might be *s.*
12. 47, not to judge but to *s.*
Acts 2. 47, such as should be *s.*
4. 12, no other name whereby we must be *s.*
15. 1, except ye be circumcised ye cannot be *s.*
16. 30, what must I do to be *s.*?
27. 43, the centurion willing to *s.* Paul.
Rom. 8. 24, we are *s.* by hope.
10. 1 my prayer is that they might be *s.*

Rom. 11. 14; 1 Cor. 9. 22, if I might *s.* some.
1 Cor. 1. 18, to us who are *s.*
21, by foolishness of preaching to *s.* some.
3. 15, *s.* yet so as by fire.
5. 5, that the spirit may be *s.*
7. 16, shalt *s.* thy husband.
2 Cor. 2. 15, savour in them that are *s.*
Eph. 2. 5, 8, by grace ye are *s.*
1 Tim. 1. 15, came to *s.* sinners.
2. 4, who will have all men to be *s.*
4. 16, thou shalt *s.* thyself and them.
Heb. 5. 7, able to *s.* him from death.
7. 25, able to *s.* to the uttermost.
10. 39, believe to *s.* of soul.
11. 7, an ark to the *s.* of his house.
Jas. 1. 21, word which is able to *s.* your souls.
2. 14, can faith *s.* him?
4. 12, able to *s.* and destroy.
5. 15, prayer of faith shall *s.* sick.
20, shall *s.* a soul from death.
1 Pet. 3. 20, souls were *s.* by water.
4. 18, righteous scarcely be *s.*
Jude 23, others *s.* with fear.
See Mat. 14. 30; John 12. 27; 1 Pet. 3. 21.
SAVE (*except*). 2 Sam. 22. 32, who is God, *s.* the Lord?
Mat. 11. 27, nor knoweth any *s.* the Son.
13. 57, *s.* in his own country.
17. 8; Mk. 9. 8, *s.* Jesus only.
Lu. 17. 18, *s.* this stranger.
18. 19, none good *s.* one.
2 Cor. 11. 24, forty stripes *s.* one.
Gal. 6. 14, glory *s.* in the cross.
See Mk. 5. 37; Lu. 4. 26; Rev. 2. 17; 13. 17.
SAVIOUR. 2 Sam. 22. 3, my refuge, my *s.*
2 Kings 13. 5, the Lord gave Israel a *s.*
Ps. 106. 21, they forgat God their *s.*
Isa. 19. 20, he shall send them a *s.*
45. 21, a just God and a *S.*
49. 26, all shall know I am thy *S.*
63. 8, so he was their *S.*
Eph. 5. 23, Christ is the *s.* of the body.
1 Tim. 4. 10, who is the *S.* of all men.
Tit. 2. 10, adorn doctrine of God our *S.*
13, glorious appearing of our *S.*
Jude 25, the only wise God our *S.*
See Neh. 9. 27; Obad. 21; John 4. 42; Acts 5. 31.
SAVOUR. Gen. 8. 21, Lord smelled a sweet *s.*
Ex. 5. 21, have made our *s.* to be abhorred.
Cant. 1. 3, *s.* of thy good ointment.
Joel 2. 20, his ill *s.* shall come up.
Mat. 5. 13; Lu. 14. 34, if salt have lost his *s.*
See Eccl. 10. 1; Ezek. 6. 13; 20. 41; Eph. 5. 2.
SAVOUREST. Mat. 16. 23; Mk. 8. 33.
SAVOURY. Gen. 27. 4, 7, 14, 31.
SAW. Gen. 22. 4, Abraham *s.* the place.
26. 28, we *s.* the Lord was with thee.
Ex. 10. 23, they *s.* not one another.
24. 10, they *s.* the God of Israel.
2 Chron. 25. 21, they *s.* one another in the face.
Job 29. 11, when the eye *s.* me.
Ps. 77. 16, the waters *s.* thee.
Eccl. 2. 24, this I *s.*, it was from hand of God.
Cant. 3. 3, *s.* ye him whom my soul loveth.
Mat. 12. 22, both spake and *s.*
17. 8, they *s.* no man.
Mk. 8. 23, if he *s.* ought.
John 1. 48, under the fig-tree I *s.* thee.
8. 56, Abraham *s.* my day.
20. 20, glad when they *s.* the Lord.
See 1 Sam. 19. 5; Ps. 50. 18; Isa. 59. 16.
SAY. Ex. 3. 13, what shall I *s.* unto them?
4. 12, teach thee what thou shalt *s.*
Num. 22. 19, know what the Lord will *s.*
Judg. 18. 24, what is this ye *s.* to me?
Ezra 9. 10, what shall we *s.* after this?
Mat. 3. 9, think not to *s.* within yourselves.
7. 22, many will *s.* in that day.
16. 13; Mk. 8. 27, whom do men *s.* that I am?
23. 3, they *s.* and do not.
Lu. 7. 40, I have somewhat to *s.* to thee.
1 Cor. 12. 3, no man can *s.* that Jesus.
See Lu. 7. 7; John 4. 20; 8. 26; 16. 12.
SAYING. Deut. 1. 23, the *s.* pleased me well.
1 Kings 2. 38, the *s.* is good.
Ps. 49. 4, my dark *s.* upon the harp.
78. 2, utter dark *s.* of old.
Prov. 1. 6, the dark *s.* of the wise.
Mat. 28. 15, this *s.* is commonly reported.
Lu. 2. 51, kept all these *s.* in her heart.
John 4. 37, herein is that *s.* true.
6. 60, an hard *s.*, who can hear it?
See John 21. 23; Rom. 13. 9; 1 Tim. 1. 15.
SCAB. Lev. 13. 2, a *s.* or bright spot.
Deut. 28. 27, and with the *s.*
Isa. 3. 17, the Lord will smite with a *s.*
SCANT. Mic. 6. 10, *s.* measure.
SCARCE. Gen. 27. 30; Acts 14. 18.
SCARCELY. Rom. 5. 7; 1 Pet. 4. 18.
SCARCENESS. Deut. 8. 9, bread without *s.*
SCAREST. Job 7. 14, thou *s.* me with dreams.
SCATTER. Gen. 11. 4, lest we be *s.* abroad.
Lev. 26. 33, I will *s.* you among the heathen.
Num. 10. 35; Ps. 68. 1, let thine enemies be *s.*
Job 18. 15, brimstone shall be *s.* on his habitation.
37. 11, he *s.* his bright cloud.
38. 24, which *s.* the east wind.
Ps. 68. 30, *s.* thou the people that delight in war.
92. 9, the workers of iniquity shall be *s.*
147. 16, he *s.* the hoar frost.
Prov. 11. 24, there is that *s.* and yet increaseth.
20. 8, a king *s.* evil with his eyes.
26, a wise king *s.* the wicked.
Jer. 10. 21, all their flocks shall be *s.*
23. 1, woe to pastors that *s.* the sheep.
50. 17, Israel is a *s.* sheep.
Zech. 13. 7; Mat. 26. 31; Mk. 14. 27, sheep shall be *s.*
Mat. 9. 36, *s.* as sheep having no shepherd.
12. 30; Lu. 11. 23, he that gathereth not with me *s.*
See John 11. 52; 16. 32; Acts 8. 1; Jas. 1. 1.
SCENT. Job 14. 9; Jer. 48. 11; Hos. 14. 7.
SCHOLAR. 1 Chron. 25. 8; Mal. 2. 12.
SCHOOLMASTER. Gal. 3. 24, the law was our *s.*
SCIENCE. Dan. 1. 4; 1 Tim. 6. 20.
SCOFF. Hab. 1. 10; 2 Pet. 3. 3.
SCORCH. Mat. 13. 6; Mk. 4. 6; Rev. 16. 8.
SCORN. Esth. 3. 6; Job 16. 20; Ps. 44. 13; 79. 4.
SCORNER. Prov. 9. 8, reprove not a *s.*
13. 1, a *s.* heareth not rebuke.
19. 25, smite a *s.*
28, an ungodly witness *s.* judgment.
29, judgments are prepared for *s.*
21. 11, when *s.* is punished simple is made wise.
24. 9, the *s.* is an abomination.
Isa. 29. 20, the *s.* is consumed.
Hos. 7. 5, stretched out hands with *s.*
See Ps. 1. 1; Prov. 1. 22; 3. 34; 9. 12.
SCORPIONS. Deut. 8. 15, fiery serpents and *s.*
Lu. 10. 19, power to tread on *s.*
Rev. 9. 3, as the *s.* of the earth.
SCOURGE. Job 5. 21, the *s.* of the tongue.
9. 23, if the *s.* slay suddenly.
Isa. 28. 15, the overflowing *s.*
Mat. 10. 17; 23. 34, they will *s.* you.
John 2. 15, a *s.* of small cords.
Acts 22. 25, is it lawful to *s.* a Roman.
Heb. 12. 6, the Lord *s.* every son.
See Josh. 23. 13; Isa. 10. 26; Mat. 27. 26; John 19. 1.
SCRAPE. Lev. 14. 41; Job 2. 8; Ezek. 26. 4.
SCRIBE. 1 Chron. 27. 32, a wise man and a *s.*
Isa. 33. 18, where is the *s.*?
Jer. 8. 8, the pen of the *s.* is in vain.
Mat. 5. 20, exceed righteousness of the *s.*
7. 29, authority, and not as the *s.*
13. 52, every *s.* instructed unto kingdom.
Mk. 12. 38; Lu. 20. 46, beware of the *s.*
See Ezra 4. 8; 7. 6; Neh. 8. 4; Mat. 8. 19.

SCRIP. 1 Sam. 17. 40; Mat. 10. 10; Lu. 10. 4; 22. 35.
SEARCH (*n.*). Ps. 64. 6; 77. 6; Jer. 2. 34.
SEARCH (*v.*). Num. 13. 2, that they may *s.* the land.
1 Chron. 28. 9, the Lord *s.* all hearts.
Job 11. 7, canst thou by *s.* find out God?
13. 9, is it good that he should *s.* you out?
28. 27, he prepared it and *s.* it out.
29. 16, the cause I knew not I *s.* out.
32. 11, I waited whilst ye *s.* out what to say.
36. 26, can number of his years be *s.* out.
Ps. 44. 21, shall not God *s.* this out?
139. 1, thou hast *s.* me and known me.
23, *s.* me and know my heart.
Prov. 25. 2, honour of kings to *s.* out a matter.
27, for men to *s.* out their own glory.
Eccl. 1. 13; 7. 25, I gave my heart to *s.* wisdom.
Isa. 40. 28, no *s.* of his understanding.
Jer. 17. 10, I the Lord *s.* the heart.
29. 13, when ye shall *s.* for me with all.
31. 37, foundations of the earth *s.* out.
Lam. 3. 40, let us *s.* our ways, and turn.
Ezek. 34. 6, none did *s.* or seek after them.
8, neither did my shepherds *s.* for my flock.
11, I will *s.* my sheep.
Amos 9. 3, I will *s.* and take them out thence.
Zeph. 1. 12, I will *s.* Jerusalem with candles.
John 5. 39; Acts 17. 11, *s.* the scriptures.
Rom. 8. 27, that *s.* hearts knoweth mind.
1 Cor. 2. 10, the Spirit *s.* all things.
1 Pet. 1. 10, which salvation prophets *s.* diligently.
See Job 10. 6; 28. 3; Prov. 2. 4; 1 Pet. 1. 11.
SEARED. 1 Tim. 4. 2, conscience *s.*
SEASON. Gen. 1. 14, for signs, and *s.*, and days.
Deut. 28. 12, give rain in his *s.*
2 Chron. 15. 3, for long *s.* without true God.
Job 5. 26, as a shock of corn in his *s.*
Ps. 1. 3, that bringeth forth fruit in his *s.*
22. 2, I cry in the night *s.*
104. 19, appointed the moon for *s.*
Prov. 15. 23, word spoken in due *s.*
Eccl. 3. 1, to everything there is a *s.* and a time.
Isa. 50. 4, know how to speak a word in *s.*
Jer. 5. 24, former and latter rain in his *s.*
33. 20, day and night in their *s.*
Ezek. 34. 26, cause shower to come down in *s.*
Dan. 2. 21, changeth the times and *s.*
7. 12, lives prolonged for a *s.*
Hos. 2. 9, take away my wine in *s.*
Mat. 21. 41, render the fruits in their *s.*
Lu. 1. 20, my words shall be fulfilled in *s.*
20. 10, at the *s.* he sent servant.
23. 8, desirous to see him of a long *s.*
John 5. 4, angel went down at certain *s.*
35, willing for a *s.* to rejoice.
Acts 1. 7, not for you to know times and *s.*
13. 11, not seeing the sun for a *s.*
24. 25, a convenient *s.*
2 Tim. 4. 2, be instant in *s.*
Heb. 11. 25, pleasure of sin for a *s.*
See 1 Thess. 5. 1; 1 Pet. 1. 6; Rev. 6. 11; 20. 3.
SEAT. 1 Sam. 20. 18, thy *s.* will be empty.
Job 23. 3, that I might come even to his *s.*
29. 7, when I prepared my *s.* in the street.
Ps. 1. 1, the *s.* of the scornful.
Amos 6. 3, cause *s.* of violence to come near.
Mat. 21. 12, *s.* of them that sold doves.
23. 2, scribes sit in Moses' *s.*
6; Mk. 12. 39, chief *s.* in synagogues.
See Ezek. 8. 3; 28. 2; Lu. 1. 52; Rev. 2. 13; 4. 4.
SECRET (*n.*). Gen. 49. 6, come not into their *s.*
Job 11. 6, the *s.* of wisdom.
15. 8, hast thou heard the *s.* of God?
29. 4, the *s.* of God was upon my tabernacle.
Ps. 25. 14, *s.* of Lord is with them that fear.
27. 5, in *s.* of his tabernacle will he hide.
139. 15, when I was made in *s.*
Prov. 3. 32, his *s.* is with the righteous.
9. 17, bread eaten in *s.*
21. 14, a gift in *s.* pacifieth anger.
Isa. 45. 19; 48. 16, I have not spoken in *s.*
Mat. 6. 4, thy Father who seeth in *s.*
6, pray to thy Father which is in *s.*
24. 26, he is in the *s.* chambers.
John 18. 20, in *s.* have I said nothing.
See Prov. 11. 13; 20. 19; Dan. 2. 18; 4. 9.
SECRET (*adj.*). Deut. 29. 29, *s.* things belong to God.
Judg. 3. 19, I have a *s.* errand.
13. 18, my name, seeing it is *s.*
Ps. 19. 12, cleanse thou me from *s.* faults.
90. 8, our *s.* sins.
Prov. 27. 5, open rebuke better than *s.* love.
See Cant. 2. 14; Isa. 45. 3; Jer. 13. 17.
SECRETLY. Gen. 31. 27, flee away *s.*
Deut. 13. 6, entice thee *s.*, saying.
1 Sam. 18. 22, commune with David *s.*
23. 9, Saul *s.* practised mischief.
2 Sam. 12. 12, for thou didst it *s.*
Job 4. 12, a thing was *s.* brought to me.
13. 10, if you *s.* accept persons.
31. 27, my heart hath been *s.* enticed.
Ps. 10. 9, he lieth in wait *s.*
31. 20, keep them *s.* from the strife.
John 11. 28, she called her sister *s.*
19. 38, *s.* for fear of the Jews.
See Deut. 27. 24; Lev. 28. 57; 2 Kings 17. 9.
SECT. Acts 5. 17; 15. 5; 24. 5; 26. 5; 28. 22.
SECURE. Job 11. 18; 12. 6; Mat. 28. 14.
SECURELY. Prov. 3. 29; Mic. 2. 8.
SEDUCE. Mk. 13. 22, show signs to *s.*
1 John 2. 26, concerning them that *s.* you.
Rev. 2. 20, to *s.* my servants.
See Prov. 12. 26; 1 Tim. 4. 1; 2 Tim. 3. 13.
SEE. Gen. 11. 5, came down to *s.* the city.
44. 23, you shall *s.* my face no more.
45. 28, I will go and *s.* him before I die.
Ex. 12. 13, when I *s.* the blood.
14. 13, *s.* the salvation of the Lord.
33. 20, there shall no man *s.* me and live.
Deut. 3. 25, let me *s.* the good land.
34. 4, I have caused thee to *s.* it.
2 Kings 6. 17, open his eyes, that he may *s.*
10. 16, *s.* my zeal for the Lord.
Job 7. 7, mine eye shall no more *s.* good.
19. 26, yet in my flesh shall I *s.* God.
Ps. 27. 13, believed to *s.* the goodness.
66. 5, come and *s.* the works of God.
94. 9, shall he not *s.*
Isa. 6. 10, lest they *s.* with their eyes.
32. 3, eyes of them that *s.* shall not be dim.
33. 17, shall *s.* the king in his beauty.
40. 5, all flesh shall *s.* it together.
52. 8, they shall *s.* eye to eye.
Jer. 5. 21; Ezek. 12. 12, eyes and *s.* not.
Mat. 5. 8, they shall *s.* God.
12. 38, we would *s.* a sign.
13. 14; Mk. 4. 12; Acts 28. 26, *s.* ye shall *s.*
27. 4, *s.* thou to that.
28. 6, *s.* the place where the Lord lay.
Mk. 8. 18, having eyes *s.* ye not.
Lu. 17. 23, *s.* here or *s.* there.
John 1. 39; 11. 34; Rev. 6. 1, come and *s.*
50, thou shalt *s.* greater things.
9. 25, I was blind, now I *s.*
39, that they who *s.* not might *s.*
Heb. 2. 9, but we *s.* Jesus.
1 Pet. 1. 8, though now we *s.* him not.
1 John 3. 2, we shall *s.* him as he is.
See Mat. 27. 24; John 1. 51.
SEED. Gen. 3. 15, enmity between thy *s.*
47. 19, give us *s.*
Ex. 16. 31, manna like coriander *s.*
Lev. 19. 19, thou shalt not sow mingled *s.*
26. 16, ye shall sow your *s.* in vain.
Num. 20. 5, it is no place of *s.*
Deut. 1. 8, to give it to their *s.* after them.
11. 10, not as Egypt where thou sowedst *s.*
14. 22, tithe all the increase of your *s.*
28. 38, thou shalt carry much *s.* into field.
Ps. 126. 6, bearing precious *s.*

Eccl. 11. 6, in the morning sow thy *s.*
Isa. 5. 10, the *s.* of an homer shall yield.
17. 11, in morning make thy *s.* to flourish.
55. 10, give *s.* to the sower.
61. 9, the *s.* which the Lord hath blessed.
Jer. 2. 21, I had planted thee wholly a right *s.*
Joel 1. 17, the *s.* is rotten.
Amos 9. 13, overtake him that soweth *s.*
Hag. 2. 19, is the *s.* yet in the barn?
Zech. 8. 12, the *s.* shall be prosperous.
Mal. 2. 15, that he might seek a godly *s.*
See Mat. 13. 19; Lu. 8. 5; 1 Cor. 15. 38; 1 Pet. 1. 23.

SEEK. Gen. 37. 15, what *s.* thou?
Num. 15. 39, that ye *s.* not after your own heart.
16. 10, *s.* ye the priesthood also.
Deut. 4. 29, if thou *s.* him with all thy heart.
12. 5, even to his habitation shall ye *s.* and come.
23. 6; Ezra 9. 12, thou shalt not *s.* their peace.
Ruth 3. 1, shall I not *s.* rest for thee.
1 Chron. 28. 9; 2 Chron. 15. 2, if thou *s.* him, he will be found.
2 Chron. 19. 3, hast prepared thine heart to *s.* God.
34. 3, Josiah began to *s.* after God.
Ezra 4. 2, we *s.* your God as ye do.
Neh. 2. 10, to *s.* the welfare of Israel.
Job 5. 8, I would *s.* unto God.
8. 5, *s.* unto God betimes.
20. 10, children shall *s.* to please the poor.
39. 29, from thence she *s.* the prey.
Ps. 9. 10, hast not forsaken them that *s.* thee.
10. 4, the wicked will not *s.* after God.
15, *s.* out his wickedness till thou find none.
14. 2; 53. 2, if there were any that did *s.* God.
24. 6, generation of them that *s.* him.
27. 4, desired, that will I *s.* after.
8, *s.* ye my face, thy face will I *s.*
34. 14; 1 Pet. 3. 11, *s.* peace and pursue it.
63. 1, early will I *s.* thee.
69. 32, your heart shall live that *s.* God.
83. 16, that they may *s.* thy name.
122. 9, I will *s.* thy good.
Prov. 1. 28, they shall *s.* me, but not find.
8. 17, those that *s.* me early shall find me.
11. 27, that diligently *s.* good.
21. 6, of them that *s.* death.
23. 30, they that go to *s.* mixed wine.
35, I will *s.* it yet again.
Eccl. 1. 13; 7. 25, gave my heart to *s.* wisdom.
Cant. 3. 2, I will *s.* him whom my soul loveth.
Isa. 1. 17, learn to do well, *s.* judgment.
8. 19, should not a people *s.* unto their God.
19. 3, they shall *s.* to charmers.
34. 16, *s.* ye out of the book of the Lord.
41. 17, when the needy *s.* water.
45. 19, I said not, *s.* ye my face in vain.
Jer. 5. 1, any that *s.* the truth.
29. 13, ye shall *s.* me and find when ye search.
30. 17, Zion whom no man *s.* after.
38. 4, this man *s.* not welfare of people.
Lam. 3. 25, the Lord is good to the soul that *s.* him.
Ezek. 7. 25, they shall *s.* peace.
34. 16, I will *s.* that which was lost.
Dan. 9. 3, I set my face to *s.* by prayer.
Amos 5. 4, *s.* me and ye shall live.
Zeph. 2. 3, *s.* ye the Lord, all ye meek.
Mal. 2. 7, they should *s.* the law at his mouth.
Mat. 6. 32, after these things do Gentiles *s.*
33; Lu. 12. 31, *s.* first the kingdom of God.
7. 7; Lu. 11. 9, *s.* and ye shall find.
12. 39; 16. 4, adulterous generation *s.* a sign.
28. 5; Mk. 16. 6, I know that ye *s.* Jesus.
Mk. 1. 37, all men *s.* for thee.
8. 11, *s.* of him a sign from heaven.
Lu. 13. 7, I come *s.* fruit.
24, many will *s.* to enter in.
15. 8, doth she not *s.* diligently.
19. 10, is come to *s.* and to save.
24. 5, why *s.* ye the living among the dead?
John 1. 38, what *s.* ye?
John 4. 23, the Father *s.* such to worship him.
7. 25, is not this he whom they *s.* to kill?
34, ye shall *s.* me and shall not find me.
18. 8, if ye *s.* me, let these go their way.
20. 15, woman, whom *s.* thou?
Rom. 3. 11, there is none that *s.* after God.
1 Cor. 1. 22, the Greeks *s.* after wisdom.
10. 24, let no man *s.* his own.
13. 5, charity *s.* not her own.
2 Cor. 12. 14, I *s.* not yours, but you.
Phil. 2. 21, all *s.* their own things.
Col. 3. 1, *s.* those things which are above.
Heb. 11. 6, a rewarder of them that *s.* him.
14, declare plainly that they *s.* a country.
13. 14, but we *s.* one to come.
1 Pet. 5. 8, *s.* whom he may devour.
Rev. 9. 6, in those days shall men *s.* death.
See Jer. 45. 5; Mat. 13. 45; John 6. 24; 1 Cor. 10. 33.

SEEM. Gen. 19. 14, he *s.* as one that mocked.
29. 20, they *s.* to him but a few days.
Num. 16. 9, *s.* it but a small thing.
Prov. 14. 12, there is a way that *s.* right.
Lu. 8. 18, taken away that he *s.* to have.
24. 11, words *s.* as idle tales.
1 Cor. 3. 18, if any *s.* to be wise.
11. 16, if any man *s.* to be contentious.
Heb. 4. 1, lest any *s.* to come short.
12. 11, now no chastening *s.* to be joyous.
See Gen. 27. 12; Eccl. 9. 13; Acts 17. 18; Gal. 2. 6.

SEEMLY. Prov. 19. 10; 26. 1.

SEEN. Gen. 32. 30, I have *s.* God face to face.
Ex. 14. 13, Egyptians whom ye have *s.* to-day.
Judg. 6. 22, because I have *s.* an angel.
2 Kings 20. 15, what have they *s.*
Job 13. 1, mine eye hath *s.* all this.
28. 7, a path the vulture's eye hath not *s.*
Ps. 37. 25, have I not *s.* righteous forsaken.
90. 15, years wherein we have *s.* evil.
Eccl. 6. 5, he hath not *s.* the sun.
Isa. 9. 2, have *s.* a great light.
64. 4; 1 Cor. 2. 9, neither hath eye *s.*
66. 8, who hath *s.* such things.
Mat. 6. 1; 23. 5, to be *s.* of men.
9. 33, never so *s.* in Israel.
Mk. 9. 1, till they have *s.* the kingdom of God.
Lu. 5. 26, we have *s.* strange things to-day.
John 1. 18, no man hath *s.* God.
8. 57, hast thou *s.* Abraham?
14. 9, he that hath *s.* me hath *s.* the Father.
Acts 11. 23, when he had *s.* the grace of God.
1 Cor. 9. 1, have I not *s.* Jesus Christ.
1 Tim. 6. 16, whom no man hath *s.*, nor can see.
Heb. 11. 1, evidence of things not *s.*
1 Pet. 1. 8, whom having not *s.*, ye love.
See John 5. 37; 9. 37; 15. 24; 20. 29; Rom. 1. 20.

SEER. 1 Sam. 9. 9, a prophet was beforetime called a *s.*
2 Sam. 24. 11, the prophet Gad, David's *s.*

SEETHE. Ex. 23. 19; 2 Kings 4. 38; Ezek. 24. 5.

SEIZE. Job 3. 6; Ps. 55. 15; Jer. 49. 24; Mat. 21. 38.

SELF. Tit. 1. 7; 2 Pet. 2. 10.

SELL. Gen. 25. 31, *s.* me thy birthright.
37. 27, come, let us *s.* him.
1 Kings 21. 25, Ahab did *s.* himself to work.
Neh. 5. 8, will ye even *s.* your brethren.
Prov. 23. 23, buy the truth, and *s.* it not.
Joel 3. 8, I will *s.* your sons and daughters.
Amos 8. 5, that we may *s.* corn.
6, and *s.* the refuse of the wheat.
Mat. 19. 21; Mk. 10. 21; Lu. 12. 33; 18. 22, *s.* that thou hast.
Lu. 22. 36, let him *s.* his garment.
Jas. 4. 13, we will buy and *s.*, and get gain.
See Ps. 44. 12; Prov. 11. 26; 31. 24; Mat. 13. 44.

SELLER. Isa. 24. 2; Ezek. 7. 12, 13; Acts 16. 14.

SEND. Gen. 24. 7, God shall *s.* his angel.
12, *s.* me good speed this day.
Ex. 4. 13, *s.* by hand of him whom thou wilt *s.*
2 Chron. 7. 13; Ezek. 14. 9, if I *s.* pestilence.
Ps. 20. 2, *s.* thee help from the sanctuary.

Ps. 43. 3, *s.* out thy light and truth.
118. 25, *s.* now prosperity.
Isa. 6. 8, whom shall I *s.*? *s.* me.
Mat. 9. 38; Lu. 10. 2, *s.* labourers.
12. 20, till he *s.* forth judgment.
15. 23, *s.* her away, for she crieth after us.
Mk. 3. 14, that he might *s.* them to preach.
John 14. 26, whom the Father will *s.* in my name.
17. 8, believed that thou didst *s.* me.
Rom. 8. 3, God *s.* his Son in likeness.
See Lu. 10. 3; 24. 49; John 20. 21; 2 Thess. 2. 11.
SENSUAL. Jas. 3. 15; Jude 19.
SENT. Gen. 45. 5, God *s.* me.
Judg. 6. 14, have not I *s.* thee.
Ps. 77. 17, the skies *s.* out a sound.
106. 15, he *s.* leanness into their soul.
107. 20, he *s.* his word and healed them.
Jer. 23. 21, I have not *s.* these prophets.
Mat. 15. 24, I am not *s.* but to lost sheep.
John 4. 34, the will of him that *s.* me.
9. 4, work the works of him that *s.* me.
17. 3, life eternal to know him whom thou hast *s.*
Acts 10. 29, as soon as I was *s.* for.
Rom. 10. 15, preach, except they be *s.*
See Isa. 61. 1; John 1. 6; 3. 28; 1 Pet. 1. 12.
SENTENCE. Ps. 17. 2, let my *s.* come forth.
Prov. 16. 10, a divine *s.* in the lips of the king.
Eccl. 8. 11, because *s.* is not executed speedily.
2 Cor. 1. 9, *s.* of death in ourselves.
See Deut. 17. 9; Jer. 4. 12; Dan. 5. 12; 8. 23.
SEPARATE. Gen. 13. 9, *s.* thyself from me.
Deut. 19. 2, thou shalt *s.* three cities.
Prov. 16. 28; 17. 9, whisperer *s.* chief friends.
19. 4, the poor is *s.* from his neighbour.
Mat. 25. 32, he shall *s.* them.
Rom. 8. 35, who shall *s.* us from love of God?
2 Cor. 6. 17, be ye *s.*
Heb. 7. 26, *s.* from sinners.
See Num. 6. 2; Ezra 10. 11; Isa. 56. 3; 59. 2.
SEPARATION. Num. 6. 8; 19. 9; 31. 23; Ezek. 42. 20.
SERPENT. Gen. 3. 1, the *s.* was more subtil.
49. 17, Dan shall be a *s.* by the way.
Job 26. 13, his hand formed the crooked *s.*
Ps. 58. 4, like the poison of a *s.*
140. 3, sharpened their tongues like a *s.*
Prov. 23. 32, at last it biteth like a *s.*
Eccl. 10. 8, breaketh a hedge, a *s.* shall bite him.
11, *s.* will bite without enchantment.
Isa. 27. 1, the Lord shall punish the *s.*
65. 25, dust shall be the *s.* meat.
Jer. 8. 17, I will send *s.* among you.
Amos 9. 3, I will command the *s.*
Mic. 7. 17, they shall lick dust like a *s.*
Mat. 7. 10; Lu. 11. 11, will he give him a *s.*?
10. 16, be ye wise as *s.*
23. 33, ye *s.*, how can ye escape.
Mk. 16. 18, they shall take up *s.*
John 3. 14, as Moses lifted up the *s.*
Rev. 12. 9; 20. 2, that old *s.* called the Devil.
See Ex. 4. 3; Num. 21. 8; 2 Kings 18. 4; Jas. 3. 7.
SERVANT. Gen. 9. 25, a *s.* of *s.* shall he be.
Job 3. 19, the *s.* is free.
7. 2, as a *s.* desireth the shadow.
Ps. 116. 16; 119. 125; 143. 12, I am thy *s.*
Prov. 22. 7, the borrower is *s.* to the lender.
29. 19, a *s.* will not be corrected with words.
Isa. 24. 2, as with *s.* so with master.
Mat. 10. 25, enough for *s.* to be as his lord.
25. 21, good and faithful *s.*
Lu. 12. 47, that *s.* which knew his lord's will.
17. 10, unprofitable *s.*
John 8. 35, *s.* abideth not in house for ever.
15. 15, *s.* knoweth not what his lord doeth.
1 Cor. 7. 21, art thou called, being a *s.*
23, be not ye the *s.* of men.
Eph. 6. 5; Col. 3. 22; Tit. 2. 9; 1 Pet. 2. 18, *s.* be obedient.
See Rom. 6. 16; Col. 4. 1; 1 Tim. 6. 1; Rev. 22. 3.
SERVE. Gen. 25. 23, elder shall *s.* the younger.
Deut. 6. 13; 10. 12, 20; 11. 13; 13. 4; Josh. 22. 5; 24. 14; 1 Sam. 7. 3; 12. 14, thou shalt fear the Lord and *s.* him.
Josh. 24. 15, choose ye whom ye will *s.*
1 Chron. 28. 9, *s.* him with a perfect heart.
Job 21. 15, what is the Almighty, that we should *s.* him?
Ps. 22. 30, a seed shall *s.* him.
72. 11, all nations shall *s.* him.
Isa. 43. 23, I have not caused thee to *s.*
24, thou hast made me to *s.* with thy sins.
Jer. 5. 19, so shall ye *s.* strangers.
Dan. 6. 16, thy God whom thou *s.* will deliver.
Zeph. 3. 9, to *s.* him with one consent.
Mal. 3. 17, spareth his son that *s.* him.
18, between him that *s.* God and him that.
Mat. 6. 24; Lu. 16. 13, no man can *s.* two masters.
Lu. 10. 40, hath left me to *s.* alone.
15. 29, these many years do I *s.* thee.
John 12. 26, if any man *s.* me, let him.
Acts 6. 2, leave word of God and *s.* tables.
Rom. 6. 6, henceforth we should not *s.* sin.
Gal. 5. 13, by love *s.* one another.
Col. 3. 24, for ye *s.* the Lord Christ.
1 Thess. 1. 9, from idols to *s.* living God.
Rev. 7. 15, they *s.* him day and night.
See Lu. 22. 27; Acts 13. 36; Heb. 9. 14; 12. 28.
SERVICE. Ex. 12. 26, what mean ye by this *s.*?
1 Chron. 29. 5, who is willing to consecrate his *s.*
John 16. 2, will think he doeth God *s.*
Rom. 12. 1, your reasonable *s.*
Eph. 6. 7, doing *s.* as to the Lord.
Phil. 2. 30, to supply your lack of *s.*
See Ezra 6. 18; Ps. 104. 14; Jer. 22. 13.
SET. Gen. 4. 15, the Lord *s.* a mark on Cain.
9. 13, I do *s.* my bow in the cloud.
Deut. 1. 8, I have *s.* the land before thee.
Job 33. 5, *s.* thy words in order.
Ps. 16. 8, I have *s.* the Lord before me.
20. 5, we will *s.* up our banners.
91. 14, he hath *s.* his love upon me.
Eccl. 7. 14, hath *s.* the one against the other.
Cant. 8. 6, *s.* me as a seal upon thine heart.
Mat. 5. 14, a city *s.* on a hill.
Acts 18. 10, no man shall *s.* on thee.
Heb. 6. 18, the hope *s.* before us.
See Ps. 75. 7; 107. 41; Eph. 1. 20; Col. 3. 2.
SETTLE. Zeph. 1. 12; Lu. 21. 14; Col. 1. 23.
SEVER. Lev. 20. 26; Ezek. 39. 14; Mat. 13. 49.
SEW. Gen. 3. 7; Job 14. 17; Eccl. 3. 7; Mk. 2. 21.
SHADE. Ps. 121. 5, the Lord is thy *s.*
SHADOW. Gen. 19. 8, the *s.* of my roof.
Job 7. 2, as servant earnestly desireth the *s.*
14. 2, he fleeth as a *s.* and continueth not.
17. 7, all my members are as a *s.*
Ps. 91. 1, under the *s.* of the Almighty.
102. 11, my days are like a *s.*
144. 4; Eccl. 8. 13, his days are as a *s.*
Eccl. 6. 12, life which he spendeth as a *s.*
Cant. 2. 3, under his *s.* with great delight.
17; 4. 6, till the *s.* flee away.
Isa. 4. 6, for a *s.* in the daytime.
25. 4, a *s.* from the heat.
32. 2, as the *s.* of a great rock.
49. 2; 51. 16, in the *s.* of his hand.
Jer. 6. 4, the *s.* of evening are stretched out.
Lam. 4. 20, under his *s.* we shall live.
Hos. 14. 7, they that dwell under his *s.* shall return.
Acts 5. 15, the *s.* of Peter might overshadow.
Jas. 1. 17, with whom is no *s.* of turning.
See Judg. 9. 15, 36; Isa. 38. 8; Jonah 4. 5.
SHAFT. Ex. 25. 31; 37. 17; Isa. 49. 2.
SHAKE. Judg. 16. 20, I will *s.* myself.
Ps. 29. 8, voice of Lord *s.* wilderness.
72. 16, fruit thereof shall *s.* like Lebanon.
Isa. 2. 19, when he ariseth to *s.* the earth.
13. 13; Joel 3. 16; Hag. 2. 6, 21, I will *s.* the heavens.
52. 2, *s.* thyself from the dust

Hag. 2. 7, I will *s.* all nations.
Mat. 11. 7; Lu. 7. 24, a reed *s.* with the wind.
Lu. 6. 38, good measure, *s.* together.
2 Thess. 2. 2, be not soon *s.* in mind.
Heb. 12. 26, I *s.* not earth only.
27, things which cannot be *s.*
See Job 9. 6; Ezek. 37. 7; Mat. 24. 29.
SHAME. Ps. 4. 2, turn my glory into *s.*
40. 14; 83. 17, let them be put to *s.*
Prov. 10. 5; 17. 2, a son that causeth *s.*
Isa. 61. 7, for your *s.* ye shall have double.
Jer. 51. 51, *s.* hath covered our faces.
Ezek. 16. 52, bear thine own *s.*
Dan. 12. 2, awake, some to *s.*
Zeph. 3. 5, the unjust knoweth no *s.*
Lu. 14. 9, with *s.* to take lowest room.
Acts 5. 41, worthy to suffer *s.*
1 Cor. 6. 5; 15. 34, I speak this to your *s.*
Eph. 5. 12, a *s.* to speak of those things.
Phil. 3. 19, whose glory is in their *s.*
Heb. 6. 6, put him to an open *s.*
12. 2, despising the *s.*
See 1 Cor. 11. 6; 14. 35; 1 Thess. 2. 2; 1 Tim. 2. 9.
SHAPE. Lu. 3. 22; John 5. 37; Rev. 9. 7.
SHARP. 1 Sam. 13. 20, to *s.* every man his share.
21, a file to *s.* the goads.
Ps. 52. 2, tongue like a *s.* razor.
140. 3, they *s.* their tongues like a serpent.
Prov. 25. 18, false witness is *s.* arrow.
27. 17, iron *s.* iron, so a man *s.* his friend.
Isa. 41. 15, a *s.* threshing instrument.
Acts 15. 39, the contention was so *s.*
Heb. 4. 12, *s.* than any two-edged sword.
See Mic. 7. 4; 2 Cor. 13. 10; Rev. 1. 16; 14. 14.
SHEAF. Deut. 24. 19; Ruth 2. 7; Ps. 126. 6; 129. 7.
SHEARERS. Gen. 38. 12; 1 Sam. 25. 7; Isa. 53. 7.
SHEATH. 1 Sam. 17. 51; 1 Chron. 21. 27; Ezek. 21. 3.
SHED. Gen. 9. 6, shall his blood be *s.*
Mat. 26. 28, *s.* for many for remission of sins.
Rom. 5. 5, love of God *s.* in our hearts.
Tit. 3. 6, which he *s.* on us abundantly.
Heb. 9. 22, without *s.* of blood is no remission.
See Ezek. 18. 10; 22. 3; Acts 2. 33.
SHEEP. Gen. 4. 2, Abel was a keeper of *s.*
Num. 27. 17; 1 Kings 22. 17; 2 Chron. 18. 16; Mat. 9. 36; Mk. 6. 34, as *s.* which have no shepherd.
1 Sam. 15. 14, what meaneth this bleating of *s.*
Ps. 49. 14, like *s.* are laid in the grave.
95. 7; 100. 3, we are the *s.* of his hand.
Isa. 53. 6, all we like *s.* have gone astray.
Jer. 12. 3, pull them out like *s.* for slaughter.
Ezek. 34. 6, my *s.* wandered.
Mat. 7. 15, false prophets in *s.* clothing.
10. 6, go rather to lost *s.*
12. 12, how much is a man better than a *s.*
John 10. 2, that entereth by door is shepherd of *s.*
11, good shepherd giveth his life for the *s.*
21. 16, feed my *s.*
See Mat. 10. 16; 12. 11; 18. 12; 25. 32; Heb. 13. 20.
SHEET. Judg. 14. 12; Acts 10. 11; 11. 5.
SHELTER. Job 24. 8; Ps. 61. 3.
SHEPHERD. Gen. 46. 34, *s.* abomination to Egyptians.
Ps. 23. 1, the Lord is my *s.*
Isa. 13. 20, nor shall *s.* make their fold there.
40. 11, he shall feed his flock like a *s.*
56. 11, they are *s.* that cannot understand.
Jer. 23. 4, I will set *s.* over them who shall feed.
50. 6, their *s.* have caused them to go astray.
Amos 3. 12, as the *s.* taketh out of the mouth.
Zech. 11. 17, woe to the idol *s.*
John 10. 14, I am the good *s.*
See Zech. 11. 3; Lu. 2. 8; 1 Pet. 2. 25; 5. 4.
SHIELD. Judg. 5. 8, was there a *s.* seen.
Ps. 5. 12, compass him as with a *s.*
33. 20; 59. 11; 84. 9, the Lord is our *s.*
84. 11, a sun and *s.*
Ps. 91. 4, truth shall be thy *s.*
Isa. 21. 5, anoint the *s.*
Eph. 6. 16, taking the *s.* of faith.
See Prov. 30. 5; Jer. 51. 11; Ezek. 23. 24; 39. 9.
SHINE. Job 22. 28, the light shall *s.* upon thy ways.
29. 3, when his candle *s.* upon my head.
Ps. 104. 15, oil to make his face *s.*
139. 12, the night *s.* as the day.
Prov. 4. 18, light that *s.* more and more.
Isa. 9. 2, upon them hath the light *s.*
60. 1, arise, *s.*, for thy light is come.
Dan. 12. 3, wise shall *s.* as the brightness.
Mat. 5. 16, let your light so *s.*
13. 43, the righteous *s.* as the sun.
2 Cor. 4. 6, God who commanded the light to *s.*
See John 1. 5; 2 Pet. 1. 19; 1 John 2. 8; Rev. 1. 16.
SHOCK. Judg. 15. 5; Job 5. 26.
SHOD. Mk. 6. 9; Eph. 6. 15.
SHOOT. Ps. 22. 7, they *s.* out the lip.
64. 3, to *s.* their arrows, even bitter words.
144. 6, *s.* out thine arrows and destroy them.
See 1 Chron. 12. 2; Mk. 4. 32; Lu. 21. 30.
SHORT. Job 17. 12, the light is *s.*
20. 5, triumphing of wicked is *s.*
Ps. 89. 47, remember how *s.* my time is.
Rom. 3. 23, come *s.* of the glory of God.
1 Cor. 7. 29, the time is *s.*
See Num. 11. 23; Isa. 50. 2; 59. 1; Mat. 24. 22.
SHORTER. Isa. 28. 20, the bed is *s.*
SHORTLY. Gen. 41. 32; Ezek. 7. 8; Rom. 16. 20.
SHOUT. Ps. 47. 5, God is gone up with a *s.*
Lam. 3. 8, when I *s.* he shutteth out my prayer.
1 Thess. 4. 16, shall descend with a *s.*
See Num. 23. 21; 1 Sam. 4. 5; Isa. 12. 6.
SHOWER. Ps. 65. 10, makest it soft with *s.*
72. 6, like *s.* that water the earth.
Ezek. 34. 26, will cause *s.* to come in season.
See Deut. 32. 2; Job 24. 8; Jer. 3. 3; 14. 22.
SHUN. Acts 20. 27; 2 Tim. 2. 16.
SHUT. Gen. 7. 16, the Lord *s.* him in.
Isa. 22. 22, he shall open and none shall *s.*
60. 11, gates shall not be *s.* day nor night.
Jer. 36. 5, I am *s.* up, I cannot go to the house of the Lord.
Lam. 3. 8, he *s.* out my prayer.
See Gal. 3. 23; 1 John 3. 17; Rev. 3. 7; 20. 3.
SICK. Prov. 13. 12, maketh the heart *s.*
23. 35, stricken me and I was not *s.*
Cant. 2. 5, I am *s.* of love.
Isa. 1. 5, the whole head is *s.*
Hos. 7. 5, made him *s.* with bottles of wine.
Mat. 8. 14, wife's mother *s.*
Jas. 5. 14, is any *s.*? call elders of the church.
15, prayer of faith shall save the *s.*
SICKNESS. Ps. 41. 3; Eccl. 5. 17; Mat. 8. 17.
SIFT. Isa. 30. 28; Amos 9. 9; Lu. 22. 31.
SIGHT. Ex. 3. 3, this great *s.*
Deut. 28. 34, for *s.* of thine eyes.
Eccl. 6. 9, better is *s.* of eyes.
Mat. 11. 5; 20. 34; Lu. 7. 21, blind receive *s.*
26; Lu. 10. 21, it seemed good in thy *s.*
Lu. 18. 42; Acts 22. 13, receive thy *s.*
21. 11, fearful *s.* and signs from heaven.
Rom. 12. 17, things honest in *s.* of all men.
2 Cor. 5. 7, walk by faith, not by *s.*
See Eccl. 11. 9; Isa. 43. 4; Dan. 4. 11; Heb. 4. 13.
SIGN. Isa. 7. 11, ask thee a *s.* of the Lord.
55. 13, for an everlasting *s.*
Ezek. 12. 6, I have set thee for a *s.*
Dan. 4. 3, how great are his *s.*
Mat. 16. 3, *s.* of the times.
Mk. 16. 20, with *s.* following.
Lu. 2. 34, for a *s.* which shall be spoken against.
John 4. 48, except ye see *s.*
Acts 2. 22, man approved of God by *s.*
4. 30, that *s.* may be done by the name.
See Rom. 4. 11; 15. 19; 1 Cor. 1. 22; Rev. 15. 1.
SIGNIFY. John 12. 33; Heb. 9. 8; 1 Pet. 1. 11.
SILENCE. Mat. 22. 34; 1 Tim. 2. 11; 1 Pet. 2. 15.
SILENT. 1 Sam. 2. 9, *s.* in darkness.
Ps. 28. 1, be not *s.* to me.

Ps. 31. 17, let the wicked be *s.* in the grave.
Zech. 2. 13, be *s.*, all flesh, before the Lord.
See Ps. 22. 2; 30. 12; Isa. 47. 5; Jer. 8. 14.
SILK. Prov. 31. 22, her clothing is *s.* and purple.
Ezek. 16. 10, I covered thee with *s.*
SILLY. Job 5. 2; Hos. 7. 11; 2 Tim. 3. 6.
SILVER. 1 Kings 10. 27, king made *s.* as stones.
Job 22. 25, thou shalt have plenty of *s.*
Ps. 12. 6; 66. 10, as *s.* is tried.
Prov. 8. 10, receive instruction and not *s.*
Eccl. 5. 10, he that loveth *s.* shall not be satisfied.
Isa. 1. 22, thy *s.* is become dross.
Jer. 6. 30, reprobate *s.* shall men call them.
Mal. 3. 3, sit as a refiner and purifier of *s.*
See Gen. 44. 2; Eccl. 12. 6; Mat. 27. 6; Acts 19. 24.
SIMILITUDE. Num. 12. 8, the *s.* of the Lord.
Deut. 4. 12, saw no *s.*
Ps. 144. 12, after the *s.* of a palace.
Rom. 5. 14, after the *s.* of Adam's transgression.
Jas. 3. 9, made after the *s.* of God.
See Hos. 12. 10; Dan. 10. 16; Heb. 7. 15.
SIMPLE (foolish). Ps. 19. 7, making wise the *s.*
116. 6, the Lord preserveth the *s.*
119. 130, it giveth understanding to the *s.*
Prov. 1. 22, how long, ye *s.* ones?
32, the turning away of the *s.*
7. 7, and behold among the *s.*
8. 5, O ye *s.* understand wisdom.
9. 4, whoso is *s.*
14. 15, the *s.* believeth every word.
19. 25, and the *s.* will beware.
22. 3; 27. 12, the *s.* pass on, and are punished.
Rom. 16. 18, deceive the hearts of the *s.*
SIMPLICITY. 2 Cor. 1. 12, that in *s.* and godly sincerity.
11. 3, from the *s.* that is in Christ.
SIN (*n.*). Gen. 4. 7, *s.* lieth at the door.
Num. 27. 3, died in his own *s.*
Deut. 24. 16; 2 Kings 14. 6; 2 Chron. 25. 4, put to death for his own *s.*
Job 10. 6, thou searchest after my *s.*
Ps. 19. 13, from presumptuous *s.*
25. 7, remember not *s.* of my youth.
32. 1, blessed is he whose *s.* is covered.
38. 18, I will be sorry for my *s.*
51. 3, my *s.* is ever before me.
90. 8, our secret *s.*
103. 10, hath not dealt with us according to our *s.*
Prov. 5. 22, holden with cords of *s.*
10. 19, in multitude of words wanteth not *s.*
14. 9, fools make a mock at *s.*
34, *s.* is a reproach to any people.
Isa. 30. 1, to add *s.* to *s.*
43. 25; 44. 22, not remember *s.*
53. 10, offering for *s.*
12, bare the *s.* of many.
Jer. 51. 5, land filled with *s.*
Ezek. 33. 16, none of his *s.* shall be mentioned.
Hos. 4. 8, they eat up *s.* of my people.
Mic. 6. 7, fruit of my body for *s.* of my soul.
Mat. 12. 31, all manner of *s.* shall be forgiven.
John 1. 29, the *s.* of the world.
8. 7, he that is without *s.*
16. 8, will reprove the world of *s.*
19. 11, hath the greater *s.*
Acts 7. 60, lay not this *s.* to their charge.
22. 16, wash away thy *s.*
Rom. 5. 20, where *s.* abounded.
6. 1, shall we continue in *s.*
7. 7, I had not known *s.*
14. 23, whatsoever is not of faith is *s.*
2 Cor. 5. 21, made him to be *s.* for us.
2 Thess. 2. 3, that man of *s.*
1 Pet. 2. 24, his own self bare our *s.*
See 1 John 1. 8; 3. 4; 4. 10; 5. 16; Rev. 1. 5.
SIN (*v.*). Gen. 42. 22, do not *s.* against the child.
Ex. 9. 27; 10. 16; Num. 22. 34; Josh. 7. 20; 1 Sam. 15. 24; 26. 21; 2 Sam. 12. 13; Job 7. 20; Ps. 41. 4; Mat. 27. 4; Lu. 15. 18, I have *s.*
Job 10. 14, if I *s.*, thou markest me.
Ps. 4. 4, stand in awe and *s.* not.
39. 1, that I *s.* not with my tongue.
Prov. 8. 36, he that *s.* against me.
Isa. 43. 27, thy first father hath *s.*
Ezek. 18. 4, the soul that *s.* it shall die.
Hos. 13. 2, now they *s.* more and more.
Mat. 18. 21, how oft shall my brother *s.*
John 5. 14; 8. 11, *s.* no more.
Rom. 6. 15, shall we *s.* because.
1 Cor. 15. 34, awake to righteousness and *s.* not.
Eph. 4. 26, be ye angry, and *s.* not.
1 John 3. 9, he cannot *s.* because born of God.
See Num. 15. 28; Job 1. 5, 22; Rom. 3. 23.
SINCERE. Phil. 1. 10; 1 Pet. 2. 2.
SINCERITY. Josh. 24. 14; 1 Cor. 5. 8; Eph. 6. 24.
SINFUL. Lu. 5. 8; 24. 7; Rom. 7. 13; 8. 3.
SINGING. Ps. 100. 2; 126. 2; Cant. 2. 12; Eph. 5. 19.
SINGLE. Mat. 6. 22; Lu. 11. 34.
SINGLENESS. Acts 2. 46; Eph. 6. 5; Col. 3. 22.
SINNER. Gen. 13. 13, men of Sodom *s.* exceedingly.
Ps. 1. 1, standeth not in way of *s.*
25. 8, teach *s.* in the way.
26. 9, gather not my soul with *s.*
51. 13, *s.* shall be converted.
Prov. 1. 10, if *s.* entice thee.
13. 21, evil pursueth *s.*
Eccl. 9. 18, one *s.* destroyeth much good.
Isa. 33. 14, the *s.* in Zion are afraid.
Mat. 9. 11; Mk. 2. 16; Lu. 5. 30; 15. 2, eat with *s.*
13; Mk. 2. 17; Lu. 5. 32, call *s.* to repentance.
11. 19; Lu. 7. 34, a friend of *s.*
Lu. 7. 37, woman who was a *s.*
13. 2, suppose ye these were *s.* above all?
15. 7, 10, joy over one *s.*
18. 13, be merciful to me a *s.*
John 9. 16, how can a man that is a *s.* do such miracles?
25, whether he be a *s.* I know not.
Rom. 5. 8, while we were yet *s.*
19, many were made *s.*
Heb. 7. 26, separate from *s.*
See Jas. 4. 8; 5. 20; 1 Pet. 4. 18; Jude 15.
SISTER. Job 17. 14; Prov. 7. 4; Mat. 12. 50; 1 Tim. 5. 2.
SIT. 2 Kings 7. 3, why *s.* we here until we die?
Ps. 69. 12, they that *s.* in the gate.
107. 10, such as *s.* in darkness.
Isa. 30. 7, their strength is to *s.* still.
Jer. 8. 14, why do we *s.* still?
Ezek. 33. 31, they *s.* before thee as thy people.
Mic. 4. 4, they *s.* every man under his vine.
Mal. 3. 3, he shall *s.* as a refiner.
Mat. 20. 23; Mk. 10. 37, to *s.* on my right hand.
See Prov. 23. 1; Lam. 3. 63; Acts 2. 2.
SITUATION. 2 Kings 2. 19; Ps. 48. 2.
SKILFUL. 1 Chron. 28. 21; Ps. 33. 3; Ezek. 21. 31; Dan. 1. 4.
SKILL. 2 Chron. 2. 7; Eccl. 9. 11; Dan. 1. 17; 9. 22.
SKIN. Ex. 34. 29, wist not that *s.* of his face shone.
Job 2. 4, *s.* for *s.*
10. 11, thou hast clothed me with *s.* and flesh.
19. 26, though after my *s.* worms destroy.
Jer. 13. 23, can the Ethiopian change his *s.*
Ezek. 37. 6, I will cover you with *s.*
Heb. 11. 37, wandered in sheep-*s.*
See Gen. 3. 21; 27. 16; Ps. 102. 5; Mic. 3. 2; Mk. 1. 6.
SKIP. Ps. 29. 6; 114. 4; Jer. 48. 27.
SKIRT. Ps. 133. 2; Jer. 2. 34; Zech. 8. 23.
SLACK. Deut. 7. 10; Prov. 10. 4; Zeph. 3. 16; 2 Pet. 3. 9.
SLAIN. Gen. 4. 23, I have *s.* a man.
Prov. 7. 26, strong men have been *s.* by her.
22. 13, the slothful man saith, I shall be *s.*
24. 11, deliver those ready to be *s.*
Isa. 22. 2, thy *s.* men are not *s.* with the sword.

Isa. 26. 21, earth shall no more cover her *s.*
66. 16, the *s.* of the Lord shall be many.
Jer. 9. 1, weep for the *s.* of my people.
Lam. 4. 9, *s.* with sword better than *s.* with hunger.
Ezek. 37. 9, breathe upon these *s.*
Eph. 2. 16, having *s.* the enmity.
Rev. 5. 6, a Lamb as it had been *s.*
See 1 Sam. 18. 7; 22. 21; Lu. 9. 22; Heb. 11. 37.
SLANDEROUSLY. Rom. 3. 8, as we be *s.* reported.
SLAUGHTER. Ps. 44. 22, as sheep for the *s.*
Isa. 53. 7; Jer. 11. 19, brought as a lamb to the *s.*
Jer. 7. 32; 19. 6, valley of *s.*
Ezek. 9. 2, every man a *s.* weapon.
See Hos. 5. 2; Zech. 11. 4; Acts 9. 1; Jas. 5. 5.
SLAVE. Jer. 2. 14; Rev. 18. 13.
SLAY. Gen. 18. 25, far from thee to *s.* the righteous.
Job 9. 23, if scourge *s.* suddenly.
13. 15, though he *s.* me.
See Gen. 4. 15; Ex. 21. 14; Neh. 4. 11; Lu. 11. 49; 19. 27.
SLEEP (*n.*). 1 Sam. 26. 12, deep *s.* from God.
Job 4. 13; 33. 15, when deep *s.* falleth.
Ps. 13. 3, lest I sleep the *s.* of death.
127. 2, giveth his beloved *s.*
Prov. 3. 24, thy *s.* shall be sweet.
6. 10; 24. 33, yet a little *s.*
20. 13, love not *s.*, lest.
Eccl. 5. 12, the *s.* of a labouring man.
Jer. 51. 39, sleep a perpetual *s.*
Lu. 9. 32, heavy with *s.*
John 11. 13, of taking rest in *s.*
Rom. 13. 11, high time to awake out of *s.*
See Dan. 2. 1; 6. 18; 8. 18; Acts 16. 27; 20. 9.
SLEEP (*v.*). Ex. 22. 27, raiment, wherein shall he *s.*
Job 7. 21, now shall I *s.* in the dust.
Ps. 4. 8, I will lay me down and *s.*
121. 4, shall neither slumber nor *s.*
Prov. 4. 16, they *s.* not, except they have done.
6. 22, when thou *s.* it shall keep thee.
10. 5, he that *s.* in harvest is a son that causeth shame.
Cant. 5. 2, I *s.*, but my heart waketh.
Dan. 12. 2, many that *s.* in the dust.
Mat. 9. 24; Mk. 5. 39; Lu. 8. 52, not dead but *s.*
13. 25, while men *s.* the enemy sowed.
26. 45; Mk. 14. 41, *s.* on now.
Mk. 13. 36, coming suddenly he find you *s.*
Lu. 22. 46, why *s.* ye? rise and pray.
John 11. 11, our friend Lazarus *s.*
1 Cor. 11. 30, for this cause many *s.*
15. 51, we shall not all *s.*
Eph. 5. 14, awake thou that *s.*
1 Thess. 4. 14, them which *s.* in Jesus.
5. 6, let us not *s.* as do others.
7, they that *s. s.* in the night.
10, that whether we wake or *s.*
See Gen. 28. 11; 1 Kings 18. 27; Acts 12. 6; 1 Cor. 15. 20.
SLEIGHT. Eph. 4. 14, the *s.* of men.
SLEW. Judg. 9. 54, a woman *s.* him.
1 Sam. 17. 36, *s.* both the lion and the bear.
29. 5, Saul *s.* his thousands.
2 Kings 10. 9, who *s.* all these?
Ps. 78. 34, when he *s.* them, then they sought him.
Isa. 66. 3, killeth an ox is as if he *s.* a man.
Dan. 5. 19, whom he would he *s.*
Mat. 23. 35, whom ye *s.* between temple and altar.
Acts 5. 30; 10. 39, whom ye *s.* and hanged on a tree.
22. 20, kept raiment of them that *s.* him.
Rom. 7. 11, sin by the commandment *s.* me.
See Gen. 4. 8; Ex. 2. 12; 13. 15; Neh. 9. 26; Lam. 2. 4.
SLIDE. Deut. 32. 35; Ps. 26. 1; 37. 31; Hos. 4. 16.
SLIGHTLY. Jer. 6. 14; 8. 11, healed hurt *s.*
SLIME. Gen. 11. 3; 14. 10; Ex. 2. 3.
SLIP. 2 Sam. 22. 37; Ps. 18. 36, feet did not *s.*
Job 12. 5, he that is ready to *s.*
Ps. 17. 5, that my footsteps *s.* not.
38. 16, when my foot *s.* they magnify.
73. 2, my steps had well nigh *s.*
Heb. 2. 1, lest we should let them *s.*
See Deut. 19. 5; 1 Sam. 19. 10; Ps. 94. 18.
SLIPPERY. Ps. 35. 6; 73. 18; Jer. 23. 12.
SLOTHFUL. Judg. 18. 9, be not *s.* to possess.
Mat. 25. 26, thou *s.* servant.
Rom. 12. 11, not *s.* in business.
Heb. 6. 12, that ye be not *s.*
See Prov. 18. 9; 19. 24; 24. 30; Eccl. 10. 18.
SLOW. Ex. 4. 10, I am *s.* of speech.
Neh. 9. 17, a God *s.* to anger.
Prov. 14. 29, *s.* to wrath is of great understanding.
Lu. 24. 25, *s.* of heart.
See Acts 27. 7; Tit. 1. 12; Jas. 1. 19.
SLUGGARD. Prov. 6. 6, go to the ant, thou *s.*
10. 26, so is the *s.* to them that send him.
13. 4, the soul of the *s.* desireth.
20. 4, the *s.* will not plow.
26. 16, the *s.* is wiser in his own conceit.
SLUMBER. Ps. 121. 3, that keepeth thee will not *s.*
Prov. 6. 4, give not *s.* to thine eyelids.
10; 24. 33, a little more *s.*
Isa. 5. 27, none shall *s.* among them.
56. 10, loving to *s.*
Nah. 3. 18, thy shepherds *s.*
Rom. 11. 8, hath given them the spirit of *s.*
See Job 33. 15; Mat. 25. 5; 2 Pet. 2. 3.
SMALL. Ex. 16. 14, *s.* round thing, *s.* as hoar frost.
18. 22, every *s.* matter they shall judge.
Num. 16. 9, a *s.* thing that God hath separated.
13, a *s.* thing that thou hast brought us.
Deut. 9. 21, I ground the calf *s.*, even as *s.* as dust.
32. 2, doctrine distil as *s.* rain.
2 Sam. 7. 19; 1 Chron. 17. 17, yet a *s.* thing in thy sight.
1 Kings 2. 20, one *s.* petition of thee.
2 Kings 19. 26, inhabitants of *s.* power.
Job 8. 7, thy beginning was *s.*
15. 11, are consolations of God *s.*?
36. 27, he maketh *s.* the drops of water.
Ps. 119. 141, I am *s.*
Prov. 24. 10, thy strength is *s.*
Isa. 7. 13, is it a *s.* thing to weary men?
16. 14, remnant very *s.* and feeble.
40. 15, nations as the *s.* dust.
54. 7, for a *s.* moment.
60. 22, a *s.* one shall become a strong nation.
Jer. 49. 15, I will make thee *s.* among heathen.
Dan. 11. 23, strong with a *s.* people.
Amos 7. 2, by whom shall Jacob arise? for he is *s.*
Zech. 4. 10, the day of *s.* things.
Mk. 8. 7; John 6. 9, a few *s.* fishes.
Acts 12. 18; 19. 23, no *s.* stir.
15. 2, had no *s.* dissension.
Jas. 3. 4, turned with very *s.* helm.
See Jer. 44. 28; Ezek. 34. 18; 1 Cor. 6. 2.
SMART. Prov. 11. 15, shall *s.* for it.
SMELL. Gen. 27. 27, as *s.* of field which the Lord hath blessed.
Deut 4. 28, gods that neither see nor *s.*
Job 39. 25, he *s.* the battle.
Ps. 45. 8, thy garments *s.* of myrrh.
115. 6, noses have they, but they *s.* not.
Isa. 3. 24, instead of sweet *s.*
Dan. 3. 27, nor the *s.* of fire.
1 Cor. 12. 17, hearing, where were the *s.*?
Eph. 5. 2, sacrifice for sweet-*s.* savour.
Phil. 4. 18, an odour of a sweet *s.*
See Cant. 1. 12; 2. 13; 4. 10; 7. 8; Amos 5. 21.
SMITE. Ex. 2. 13, wherefore *s.* thou?
21. 12, he that *s.* a man.
1 Sam. 26. 8, I will not *s.* him the second time.
2 Kings 6. 18, *s.* this people with blindness.
21, shall I *s.* them?

Ps. 121. 6, the sun shall not *s.* thee by day.
141. 5, let the righteous *s.* me.
Prov. 19. 25, *s.* a scorner.
Isa. 10. 24, he shall *s.* thee with a rod.
49. 10, neither shall heat *s.* thee.
50. 6, gave my back to the *s.*
58. 4, to *s.* with the fist of wickedness.
Jer. 18. 18, let us *s.* him with the tongue.
Lam. 3. 30, giveth his cheek to him that *s.*
Ezek. 7. 9, know that I am the Lord that *s.*
21. 14, prophesy, and *s.* thine hands together.
Nah. 2. 10, the knees *s.* together.
Zech. 13. 7, awake, O sword, and *s.* the shepherd.
Mal. 4. 6, lest I *s.* the earth with a curse.
Mat. 5. 39, *s.* thee on the right cheek.
24. 49, shall begin to *s.* his fellow servants.
Lu. 22. 49, shall we *s.* with sword?
John 18. 23, why *s.* thou me?
See Lu. 6. 29; Acts 23. 2; 2 Cor. 11. 20; Rev. 11. 6.
SMITH. 1 Sam. 13. 19; Isa. 44. 12; Jer. 24. 1.
SMITTEN. Num. 22. 28, that thou hast *s.*
Deut. 28. 25, cause thee to be *s.*
1 Sam. 4. 3, wherefore hath the Lord *s.* us?
2 Kings 13. 19, thou shouldest have *s.* five or six times.
Ps. 3. 7, thou hast *s.* all mine enemies.
102. 4, my heart is *s.*
Isa. 24. 12, the gate is *s.* with destruction.
53. 4, *s.* of God.
Jer. 2. 30, in vain have I *s.* your children.
Hos. 6. 1, he hath *s.* and he will bind.
Amos 4. 9, I have *s.* you.
See Job 16. 10; Ezek. 22. 13; Acts 23. 3.
SMOKE. Gen. 19. 28, as the *s.* of a furnace.
Deut. 29. 20, the anger of the Lord shall *s.*
Ps. 37. 20, wicked consume into *s.*
68. 2, as *s.* is driven away.
74. 1, why doth thy anger *s.*?
102. 3, my days are consumed like *s.*
104. 32; 144. 5, he toucheth the hills, and they *s.*
119. 83, like a bottle in the *s.*
Prov. 10. 26, as *s.* to the eyes.
Isa. 6. 4, the house was filled with *s.*
34. 10, the *s.* thereof shall go up for ever.
51. 6, the heavens shall vanish like *s.*
65. 5, these are a *s.* in my nose.
Hos. 13. 3, as the *s.* out of a chimney.
See Rev. 9. 2; 14. 11; 15. 8; 18. 9; 19. 3.
SMOKING. Gen. 15. 17; Ex. 20. 18; Isa. 42. 3; Mat. 12. 20.
SMOOTH. Gen. 27. 11, I am a *s.* man.
1 Sam. 17. 40; Isa. 57. 6, five *s.* stones.
Isa. 30. 10, speak unto us *s.* things.
Lu. 3. 5, rough ways shall be made *s.*
See Ps. 55. 21; Prov. 5. 3; Isa. 41. 7.
SMOTE. Num. 20. 11, Moses *s.* the rock twice.
Judg. 15. 8, Samson *s.* them hip and thigh.
1 Sam. 24. 5, David's heart *s.* him.
Isa. 60. 10, in my wrath I *s.* thee.
Jer. 31. 19, I *s.* upon my thigh.
Hag. 2. 17, I *s.* you with blasting and mildew.
Mat. 26. 68; Lu. 22. 64, who is he that *s.* thee?
Lu. 18. 13, *s.* upon his breast.
Acts 12. 23, immediately angel *s.* him.
See 2 Sam. 14. 7; Dan. 2. 34; Mat. 27. 30.
SNARE. Ex. 10. 7, this man be a *s.* unto us.
Deut. 7. 25, nor take silver of idols, lest thou be *s.*
12. 30, take heed that thou be not *s.* by them.
Josh. 23. 13, they shall be *s.* unto you.
Judg. 8. 27, which thing became a *s.* to Gideon.
1 Sam. 18. 21, that she may be a *s.*
28. 9, wherefore layest thou a *s.* for my life?
2 Sam. 22. 6; Ps. 18. 5, *s.* of death prevented me.
Job 18. 8, he walketh on a *s.*
22. 10, *s.* are round about thee.
Ps. 11. 6, upon the wicked he shall rain *s.*
38. 12, they lay *s.* for me.
64. 5, commune of laying *s.* privily.
69. 22, let their table become a *s.*
91. 3, deliver thee from *s.* of fowler.
Ps. 124. 7, the *s.* is broken.
Prov. 6. 2; 12. 13, *s.* with words of thy mouth.
7. 23, as a bird hasteth to the *s.*
13. 14; 14. 27, the *s.* of death.
18. 7, a fool's lips are the *s.* of his soul.
22. 25, learn his ways, and get a *s.* to thy soul.
29. 8, bring city into *s.*
25, fear of man bringeth a *s.*
Eccl. 9. 12, *s.* in an evil time.
Isa. 24. 17; Jer. 48. 43, the *s.* are upon thee.
Lam. 3. 47, fear and a *s.* is come upon us.
Ezek. 12. 13, he shall be taken in my *s.*
Hos. 9. 8, the prophet is a *s.*
Amos 3. 5, can a bird fall in a *s.*?
Lu. 21. 35, as a *s.* shall it come.
1 Tim. 3. 7, lest he fall into the *s.*
6. 9, they that will be rich fall into a *s.*
2 Tim. 2. 26, recover out of the *s.* of the devil.
See Ex. 23. 33; Deut. 7. 16; Judg. 2. 3; Eccl. 7. 26.
SNATCH. Isa. 9. 20, shall *s.* and be hungry.
SNOW. Ex. 4. 6; Num. 12. 10; 2 Kings 5. 27, leprous as *s.*
2 Sam. 23. 20, slew lion in time of *s.*
Job 6. 16, wherein the *s.* is hid.
9. 30, wash myself in *s.* water.
24. 19, drought and heat consume *s.* waters.
37. 6, saith to *s.*, be thou on the earth.
38. 22, the treasures of the *s.*
Ps. 51. 7, I shall be whiter than *s.*
147. 16, he giveth *s.* like wool.
Prov. 25. 13, cold of *s.* in harvest.
26. 1, as *s.* in summer.
31. 21, she is not afraid of the *s.*
Isa. 1. 18, your sins shall be white as *s.*
55. 10, as the *s.* from heaven returneth not.
Jer. 18. 14, will a man leave the *s.* of Lebanon?
Lam. 4. 7, Nazarites purer than *s.*
Dan. 7. 9; Mat. 28. 3; Mk. 9. 3, garment white as *s.*
See Ps. 68. 14; 148. 8; Rev. 1. 14.
SNUFFED. Jer. 14. 6; Mal. 1. 13.
SOAKED. Isa. 34. 7, land *s.* with blood.
SOAP. Jer. 2. 22; Mal. 3. 2.
SOBER. 2 Cor. 5. 13, *s.* for your cause.
1 Thess. 5. 6, let us watch and be *s.*
1 Tim. 3. 2; Tit. 1. 8, a bishop must be *s.*
Tit. 2. 2, aged men be *s.*
4, teach young women to be *s.*
1 Pet. 4. 7, be ye therefore *s.*, and watch.
See Acts 26. 25; Rom. 12. 3; Tit. 2. 6.
SODDEN. Ex. 12. 9; 1 Sam. 2. 15; Lam. 4. 10.
SOFT. Job 23. 16, God maketh my heart *s.*
41. 3, will he speak *s.* words?
Ps. 65. 10, thou makest it *s.* with showers.
Prov. 15. 1, a *s.* answer turneth away wrath.
25. 15, a *s.* tongue breaketh the bone.
See Ps. 55. 21; Mat. 11. 8; Lu. 7. 25.
SOFTLY. Gen. 33. 14; Judg. 4. 21; 1 Kings 21. 27; Isa. 38. 15.
SOIL. Ezek. 17. 8, planted in a good *s.*
SOJOURN. Gen. 19. 9, this fellow came in to *s.*
26. 3, *s.* in this land, and I will be with thee.
47. 4, to *s.* in the land are we come.
Deut. 26. 5, *s.* with a few, and became a nation.
Judg. 17. 9, I go to *s.* where I may find place.
2 Kings 8. 1, *s.* wheresoever thou canst *s.*
Ps. 120. 5, woe is me, that I *s.*
Isa. 23. 7, feet carry her afar off to *s.*
Jer. 42. 22, die in place whither ye desire to *s.*
Lam. 4. 15, they shall no more *s.* there.
Heb. 11. 9, by faith he *s.* in land of promise.
1 Pet. 1. 17, pass time of your *s.* here in fear.
SOJOURNER. Gen. 23. 4; Ps. 39. 12.
SOLD. Gen. 31. 15, our father hath *s.* us.
45. 4, whom ye *s.* into Egypt.
Lev. 25. 23, the land shall not be *s.* for ever.
42, shall not be *s.* as bondmen.
27. 28, no devoted thing shall be *s.*
Deut. 15. 12, if thy brother be *s.* unto thee.
32. 30, except their Rock had *s.* them.
1 Kings 21. 20, thou hast *s.* thyself to work evil.
Neh. 5. 8, or shall they be *s.* unto us?

Esth. 7. 4, for we are *s.* to be slain.
Isa. 50. 1, have ye *s.* yourselves?
52. 3, ye have *s.* yourselves for nought.
Lam. 5. 4, our wood is *s.* unto us.
Joel 3. 3, they have *s.* a girl for wine.
Amos 2. 6, they *s.* the righteous for silver.
Mat. 10. 29, are not two sparrows *s.* for a farthing?
13. 46, went and *s.* all that he had.
18. 25, his lord commanded him to be *s.*
21. 12; Mk. 11. 15, cast out them that *s.*
26. 9; Mk. 14. 5, might have been *s.* for much.
Lu. 17. 28, they bought, they *s.*, they planted.
Acts 2. 45, and *s.* their possessions.
Rom. 7. 14, *s.* under sin.
1 Cor. 10. 25, whatsoever is *s.* in the shambles.
See Lu. 19. 45; John 12. 5; Acts 5. 1; Heb. 12. 16.

SOLDIER. Ezra 8. 22, ashamed to require *s.*
Mat. 8. 9; Lu. 7. 8, having *s.* under me.
Lu. 3. 14, *s.* demanded, what shall we do?
Acts 10. 7, a devout *s.*
2 Tim. 2. 3, as a good *s.* of Jesus Christ.
See 2 Chron. 25. 13; Isa. 15. 4; Acts 27. 31.

SOLE. Gen. 8. 9, dove found no rest for *s.* of her foot.
2 Sam. 14. 25; Isa. 1. 6, from *s.* of foot to crown.
See Deut. 28. 35, 56, 65; Josh. 1. 3; Job 2. 7.

SOLEMN. Ps. 92. 3, sing praise with a *s.* sound.
See Num. 10. 10; Isa. 1. 13; Lam. 2. 22; Hos. 9. 5.

SOLEMNITY. Isa. 30. 29, when a holy *s.* is kept.
See Deut. 31. 10; Isa. 33. 20; Ezek. 45. 17; 46. 11.

SOLEMNLY. Gen. 43. 3; 1 Sam. 8. 9.

SOLITARY. Ps. 68. 6, God setteth the *s.* in families.
107. 4, wandered in a *s.* way.
Isa. 35. 1, the wilderness and *s.* place shall be glad.
See Job 3. 7; 30. 3; Lam. 1. 1; Mic. 7. 14; Mk. 1. 35.

SOME. Gen. 37. 20, *s.* evil beast.
Ex. 16. 17, gathered, *s.* more, *s.* less.
1 Kings 14. 13, found *s.* good thing.
Ps. 20. 7, *s.* trust in chariots.
69. 20, I looked for *s.* to take pity.
Dan. 12. 2, *s.* to life, and *s.* to shame.
Mat. 16. 14; Mk. 8. 28; Lu. 9. 19, *s.* say thou art John the Baptist.
28. 17, *s.* doubted.
John 6. 64, *s.* of you that believe not.
Acts 19. 32; 21. 34, *s.* cried one thing, *s.* another.
Rom. 3. 3, what if *s.* did not believe?
5. 7, *s.* would even dare to die.
1 Cor. 6. 11, such were *s.* of you.
15. 34, *s.* have not knowledge.
Eph. 4. 11, *s.* prophets, *s.* evangelists.
1 Tim. 5. 24, *s.* men's sins are open.
Heb. 10. 25, as the manner of *s.* is.
2 Pet. 3. 9, as *s.* men count slackness.
See 1 Tim. 1. 19; 2 Tim. 2. 18; Jude 22.

SOMEBODY. Lu. 8. 46; Acts 5. 36.

SOMETIMES. Eph. 2. 13, *s.* far off.
5. 8, ye were *s.* darkness.
Col. 1. 21, *s.* alienated.
See Col. 3. 7; Tit. 3. 3; 1 Pet. 3. 20.

SOMEWHAT. 1 Kings 2. 14; Gal. 2. 6; Rev. 2. 4.

SON. Gen. 6. 2; Job 1. 6; 2. 1; 38. 7; John 1. 12; Phil. 2. 15; 1 John 3. 1, *s.* of God.
Job 14. 21, his *s.* come to honour.
Ps. 2. 12, kiss the *S.*, lest he be angry.
86. 16, save *s.* of thine handmaid.
116. 16, I am the *s.* of thine handmaid.
Prov. 10. 1; 13. 1; 15. 20; 17. 2; 19. 26, a wise *s.*
17. 25; 19. 13, a foolish *s.*
31. 2, *s.* of my womb, *s.* of my vows.
Isa. 9. 6, unto us a *s.* is given.
14. 12, *s.* of the morning.
Jer. 35. 5, *s.* of the Rechabites.
Ezek. 20. 31; 23. 37, *s.* pass through fire.
Hos. 1. 10, the *s.* of the living God.
Mal. 3. 17, as a man spareth his *s.*
Mat. 11. 27, no man knoweth the *S.*
13. 55; Mk. 6. 3; Lu. 4. 22, the carpenter's *s.*
17. 5, this is my beloved *S.*
22. 42, Christ, whose *s.* is he?
Lu. 7. 12, only *s.* of his mother.
10. 6, if the *s.* of peace.
19. 9, he also is a *s.* of Abraham.
John 1. 18; 3. 18, only begotten *S.*
5. 21, the *S.* quickeneth whom he will.
8. 35, the *S.* abideth ever.
36, if the *S.* make you free.
17. 12; 2 Thess. 2. 3, the *s.* of perdition.
Acts 4. 36, *s.* of consolation.
Rom. 1. 9, serve in the gospel of his *S.*
8. 3, God sending his own *S.*
29, conformed to the image of his *S.*
32, spared not his own *S.*
1 Cor. 4. 14, as my beloved *s.* I warn you.
Gal. 4. 5, the adoption of *s.*
7, if a *s.*, then an heir.
Col. 1. 13, the kingdom of his dear *S.*
Heb. 2. 10, bringing many *s.* to glory.
5. 8, though a *S.*, yet learned he obedience.
11. 24, refused to be called *s.*
12. 6, scourgeth every *s.*
1 John 2. 22, antichrist denieth the *s.*
5. 12, he that hath the *S.* hath life.
See 1 John 1. 7; 4. 9; 5. 10, 11; Rev. 21. 7.

SONGS. Job 30. 9, now am I their *s.*
35. 10; Ps. 77. 6, who giveth *s.* in the night.
Ps. 32. 7, with *s.* of deliverance.
33. 3; Isa. 42. 10, sing unto him a new *s.*
40. 3, he hath put a new *s.* in my mouth.
69. 12, I was the *s.* of drunkards.
119. 54, my *s.* in house of my pilgrimage.
137. 4, the Lord's *s.* in a strange land.
Prov. 25. 20, that singeth *s.* to an heavy heart.
Isa. 23. 16, sing many *s.*
35. 10, the ransomed shall come with *s.*
Ezek. 33. 32, as a very lovely *s.*
Amos 8. 3, *s.* of the temple.
Eph. 5. 19; Col. 3. 16, in psalms and spiritual *s.*
See Cant. 1. 1; Rev. 5. 9; 14. 3; 15. 3.

SOON. Ex. 2. 18, how is it ye are come so *s.*?
Job 32. 22, my Maker would *s.* take me away.
Ps. 37. 2, shall *s.* be cut down.
58. 3, go astray as *s.* as born.
68. 31, Ethiopia shall *s.* stretch out her hands.
90. 10, it is *s.* cut off.
106. 13, they *s.* forgat his works.
Prov. 14. 17, he that is *s.* angry.
See Mat. 21. 20; Gal. 1. 6; 2 Thess. 2. 2; Tit. 1. 7.

SORE. 2 Chron. 6. 29; Isa. 1. 6; Lu. 16. 20.

SORROW. Gen. 3. 16, multiply thy *s.*
42. 38, with *s.* to the grave.
Job 6. 10, I would harden myself in *s.*
21. 17, God distributeth *s.* in his anger.
41. 22, *s.* is turned into joy.
Ps. 13. 2, having *s.* in my heart daily.
90. 10, yet is their strength labour and *s.*
116. 3, I found trouble and *s.*
127. 2, to eat the bread of *s.*
Prov. 10. 22, maketh rich, addeth no *s.*
23. 29, who hath *s.*?
Eccl. 2. 23, all his days are *s.*
7. 3, *s.* is better than laughter.
11. 10, remove *s.* from thy heart.
Isa. 17. 11, day of desperate *s.*
35. 10; 51. 11, *s.* and sighing shall flee away.
53. 3, a man of *s.*
Jer. 30. 15, thy *s.* is incurable.
49. 23, there is *s.* on the sea.
Lam. 1. 12, any *s.* like unto my *s.*
Mat. 24. 8; Mk. 13. 8, beginning of *s.*
Lu. 22. 45, sleeping for *s.*
John 16. 6, *s.* hath filled your heart.
2 Cor. 2. 7, with overmuch *s.*
7. 10, godly *s.* worketh repentance.
1 Thess. 4. 13, *s.* not as others.
1 Tim. 6. 10, pierced with many *s.*
See Prov. 15. 13; Hos. 8. 10; Rev. 21. 4.

SORROWFUL. 1 Sam. 1. 15, woman of a *s.* spirit.
Ps. 69. 29, I am poor and *s.*
Prov. 14. 13, even in laughter the heart is *s.*
Jer. 31. 25, replenished every *s.* soul.
Zeph. 3. 18, I will gather them that are *s.*
Mat. 19. 22; Lu. 18. 23, went away *s.*
26. 37, he began to be *s.*
38; Mk. 14. 34, my soul is exceeding *s.*
John 16. 20, ye shall be *s.*
See Job 6. 7; 2 Cor. 6. 10; Phil. 2. 28.
SORRY. Ps. 38. 18, I will be *s.* for my sin.
Isa. 51. 19, who shall be *s.* for thee?
See 1 Sam. 22. 8; Neh. 8. 10; Mat. 14. 9.
SORT. Gen. 6. 19, two of every *s.*
1 Chron. 29. 14, to offer after this *s.*
Dan. 3. 29, deliver after this *s.*
Acts 17. 5, fellows of the baser *s.*
2 Cor. 7. 11; 3 John 6, after a godly *s.*
2 Tim. 3. 6, of this *s.* are they.
See Deut. 22. 11; Eccl. 2. 8; Ezek. 27. 24; 38. 4.
SOTTISH. Jer. 4. 22, they are *s.* children.
SOUGHT. Gen. 43. 30, he *s.* where to weep.
Ex. 4. 24, the Lord *s.* to kill him.
1 Sam. 13. 14, the Lord hath *s.* him a man.
1 Chron. 15. 13, we *s.* him not after due order.
2 Chron. 15. 4, when they *s.* him he was found.
15, they *s.* him with their whole desire.
16. 12, in his disease he *s.* not the Lord.
26. 5, as long as he *s.* the Lord.
Ps. 34. 4; 77. 2, I *s.* the Lord, and he heard me.
111. 2, *s.* out of all that have pleasure.
Eccl. 7. 29, *s.* out many inventions.
12. 10, the preacher *s.* to find acceptable words.
Isa. 62. 12, shalt be called, *S.* out.
65. 1, *s.* of them that asked not.
Jer. 10. 21, pastors have not *s.* the Lord.
Lam. 1. 19, they *s.* meat to relieve their souls.
Ezek. 22. 30, I *s.* for a man among them.
34. 4, neither have ye *s.* that which was lost.
Lu. 11. 16, *s.* of him a sign.
13. 6, he *s.* fruit thereon.
19. 3, *s.* to see Jesus.
Rom. 9. 32, *s.* it not by faith.
Heb. 12. 17, though he *s.* it carefully with tears.
See Cant. 3. 1; Lu. 2. 44; 1 Thess. 2. 6.
SOUL. Gen. 2. 7, a living *s.*
Ex. 30. 12, a ransom for his *s.*
Deut. 11. 13, serve him with all your *s.*
13. 6, thy friend, which is as thine own *s.*
30. 2; Mat. 22. 37, obey with all thy *s.*
Judg. 10. 16, his *s.* was grieved.
1 Sam. 18. 1; 20. 17, loved him as his own *s.*
1 Kings 8. 48, return with all their *s.*
1 Chron. 22. 19, set your *s.* to seek the Lord.
Job 3. 20, life unto the bitter in *s.*
12. 10, in whose hand is the *s.*
16. 4, if your *s.* were in my *s.* stead.
23. 13, what his *s.* desireth, even that he doeth.
31. 30, wishing a curse to his *s.*
33. 22, his *s.* draweth near to the grave.
Ps. 33 19, to deliver their *s.* from death.
34. 22, redeemeth the *s.* of his servants.
49. 8, the redemption of their *s.* is precious.
62. 1, my *s.* waiteth upon God.
63. 1, my *s.* thirsteth for thee.
74. 19, the *s.* of thy turtledove.
103. 1; 104. 1, bless the Lord, O my *s.*
116. 7, return to thy rest, O my *s.*
8, thou hast delivered my *s.* from death.
119. 175, let my *s.* live.
142. 4, no man cared for my *s.*
Prov. 11. 25, the liberal *s.* shall be made fat.
19. 2, *s.* without knowledge.
25. 25, cold waters to thirsty *s.*
Isa. 55. 3, hear, and your *s.* shall live.
58. 10, if thou wilt satisfy the afflicted *s.*
Jer. 20. 13, hath delivered the *s.* of the poor.
31. 12, their *s.* shall be as a watered garden.
Ezek. 18. 4, all *s.* are mine.
22. 25, they have devoured *s.*
Hab. 2. 10, thou hast sinned against thy *s.*
Mat. 10. 28, to destroy both *s.* and body.
16. 26; Mk. 8. 36, lose his own *s.*
26. 38; Mk. 14. 34, my *s.* is exceeding sorrowful.
Lu. 21. 19, in your patience possess ye your *s.*
Acts 4. 32, of one heart and *s.*
Rom. 13. 1, let every *s.* be subject.
1 Thess. 5. 23, that your *s.* and body be preserved.
Heb. 6. 19, an anchor of the *s.*
13. 17, they watch for your *s.*
Jas. 5. 20, shall save a *s.* from death.
1 Pet. 2. 11, which war against the *s.*
4. 19, commit keeping of *s.* to him.
2 Pet. 2. 14, beguiling unstable *s.*
3 John 2, even as thy *s.* prospereth.
See Prov. 3. 22; Ezek. 3. 19; Acts 15. 24.
SOUND (*n.*). Lev. 26. 36, the *s.* of a shaken leaf.
1 Kings 18. 41, *s.* of abundance of rain.
Job 15. 21, a dreadful *s.* is in his ears.
Ps. 89. 15, that know the joyful *s.*
92. 3, harp with a solemn *s.*
Eccl. 12. 4, *s.* of grinding is low.
Jer. 50. 22, *s.* of battle in the land.
51. 54, *s.* of a cry cometh.
Ezek. 33. 5, he heard *s.*, and took not warning.
John 3. 8, thou hearest the *s.*, but canst not tell.
Acts 2. 2, suddenly a *s.* from heaven.
Rom. 10. 18, *s.* went into all the earth.
1 Cor. 14. 8, an uncertain *s.*
See 2 Kings 6. 32; Rev. 1. 15; 9. 9; 18. 22.
SOUND (*adj.*). Prov. 2. 7; 3. 21; 8. 14, *s.* wisdom.
Prov. 14. 30, a *s.* heart is life of the flesh.
1 Tim. 1. 10; 2 Tim. 4. 3; Tit. 1. 9; 2. 1, *s.* doctrine.
2 Tim. 1. 7, spirit of a *s.* mind.
13, form of *s.* words.
See Ps. 119. 80; Lu. 15. 27; Tit. 2. 2, 8.
SOUND (*v.*). Ex. 19. 19, the trumpet *s.* long.
Joel 2. 1, *s.* an alarm in holy mountain.
Mat. 6. 2, do not *s.* a trumpet before thee.
1 Thess. 1. 8, from you *s.* out word of the Lord.
See Neh. 4. 18; 1 Cor. 13. 1; 15. 52; Rev. 8. 7.
SOUR. Isa. 18. 5; Jer. 31. 29; Ezek. 18. 2; Hos. 4. 18.
SOW. Job 4. 8, they that *s.* wickedness.
Ps. 97. 11, light is *s.* for the righteous.
126. 5, *s.* in tears.
Prov. 6. 16, he that *s.* discord.
Eccl. 11. 4, he that observeth the wind shall not *s.*
6, in morning *s.* thy seed.
Isa. 32. 20, that *s.* beside all waters.
Jer. 4. 3, *s.* not among thorns.
12. 13, they have *s.* wheat, but shall reap thorns.
Hos. 10. 12, *s.* in righteousness, reap in mercy.
Nah. 1. 14, that no more of thy name be *s.*
Hag. 1. 6, ye have *s.* much, and bring in little.
Mat. 6. 26, they *s.* not.
37, he that *s.* good seed.
John 4. 36, both he that *s.* and he that reapeth.
1 Cor. 15. 36, that which thou *s.* is not quickened.
2 Cor. 9. 6, he which *s.* sparingly.
Gal. 6. 7, whatsoever a man *s.*, that shall he reap.
See Lev. 26. 5; Deut. 11. 10; Jer. 2. 2; Jas. 3. 18.
SOWER. Isa. 55. 10; Jer. 50. 16; Mat. 13. 3; Mk. 4. 3; Lu. 8. 5; 2 Cor. 9. 10.
SPAKE. Ps. 39. 3, then *s.* I with my tongue.
106. 33, he *s.* unadvisedly with his lips.
Mal. 3. 16, *s.* often one to another.
John 7. 46, never man *s.* like this man.
1 Cor. 13. 11, I *s.* as a child.
Heb. 12. 25, refused him that *s.* on earth.
2 Pet. 1. 21, holy men *s.* as they were moved.
See Gen. 35. 15; John 9. 29; Heb. 1. 1.
SPAN. Ex. 28. 16; Isa. 40. 12; 48. 13; Lam. 2. 20.
SPARE. Gen. 18. 26, I will *s.* for their sakes.
Neh. 13. 22, *s.* me according to thy mercy.
Ps. 39. 13, *s.* me, that I may recover strength.
Prov. 13. 24, he that *s.* the rod.
19. 18, let not thy soul *s.* for his crying.
Joel 2. 17, *s.* thy people.
Mal. 3. 17, I will *s.* them as a man *s.*

Lu. 15. 17, bread enough and to *s*.
Rom. 8. 32, *s*. not his own Son.
11. 21, if God *s*. not the natural branches.
2 Pet. 2. 4, if God *s*. not the angels.
See Prov. 17. 27; 21. 26; Isa. 54. 2; 58. 1.
SPARK. Job 5. 7; 18. 5; Isa. 1. 31; 50. 11.
SPEAK. Gen. 18. 37, to *s*. to God.
Ex. 4. 14, I know he can *s*. well.
33. 11, spake to Moses as a man *s*. to his friend.
Num. 20. 8, *s*. to the rock.
1 Sam. 25. 17, a man cannot *s*. to him.
Job 11. 5, oh that God would *s*. against thee.
13. 7, will ye *s*. wickedly for God?
32. 7, days should *s*.
33. 14, God *s*. once, yea, twice.
37. 20, if a man *s*. he shall be swallowed up.
Ps. 85. 8, I will hear what the Lord will *s*.
Prov. 23. 9, *s*. not in the ears of a fool.
Cant. 7. 9, causing lips of those asleep to *s*.
Isa. 19. 18, shall *s*. language of Canaan.
63. 1, I that *s*. in righteousness.
65. 24, while they are yet *s*., I will hear.
Jer. 20. 9, I will not *s*. any more in his name.
Hab. 2. 3, at the end it shall *s*.
Zech. 8. 16; Eph. 4. 25, *s*. every man the truth.
Mat. 8. 8, *s*. the word only, and my servant.
10. 19; Mk. 13. 11, how or what ye shall *s*.
12. 34; Lu. 6. 45, of abundance of heart mouth *s*.
36, every idle word that men shall *s*.
Mk. 9. 39, can lightly *s*. evil of me.
Lu. 6. 26, when all men *s*. well of you.
John 3. 11, we *s*. that we do know.
Acts 4. 17, that they *s*. to no man in this name.
20, we cannot but *s*.
26. 25, I *s*. words of truth and soberness.
1 Cor. 1. 10, that ye all *s*. the same thing.
14. 28, let him *s*. to himself and to God.
2 Cor. 4. 13, we believe and therefore *s*.
Eph. 4. 15, *s*. the truth in love.
Heb. 11. 4, he being dead yet *s*.
12. 24, that *s*. better things than that of Abel.
Jas. 1. 19, slow to *s*.
See 1 Cor. 14. 2; 1 Pet. 2. 1; 2 Pet. 2. 12.
SPEAR. Josh. 8. 18, stretch out the *s*.
Judg. 5. 8, was there a shield or *s*. seen?
1 Sam. 13. 22, nor *s*. with any but Saul.
17. 7, the staff of his *s*.
45, thou comest to me with a *s*.
Ps. 46. 9, he cutteth the *s*. in sunder.
Isa. 2. 4; Mic. 4. 3, beat *s*. into pruninghooks.
See Job 41. 29; Jer. 6. 23; Hab. 3. 11; John 19. 34.
SPECIAL. Deut. 7. 6; Acts 19. 11.
SPECTACLE. 1 Cor. 4. 9, made a *s*. to the world.
SPEECH. Gen. 11. 1, earth was of one *s*.
Ex. 4. 10, I am slow of *s*.
Num. 12. 8, not in dark *s*.
Deut. 32. 2, my *s*. shall distil as dew.
1 Kings 3. 10, Solomon's *s*. pleased the Lord.
Job 6. 26, the *s*. of one that is desperate.
15. 3, or with *s*. wherewith he can do no good.
Ps. 19. 2, day unto day uttereth *s*.
3, there is no *s*. where their voice is not heard.
Prov. 17. 7, excellent *s*. becometh not a fool.
Cant. 4. 3, thy *s*. is comely.
Isa. 33. 19, of deeper *s*. than thou canst perceive.
Mat. 26. 73, thy *s*. bewrayeth thee.
1 Cor. 2. 1, not with excellency of *s*.
4. 19, not the *s*., but the power.
2 Cor. 3. 12, we use great plainness of *s*.
10. 10, his *s*. is contemptible.
Col. 4, 6, let your *s*. be alway with grace.
Tit. 2. 8, sound *s*., that cannot be condemned.
See Ezek. 3. 5; Rom. 16. 18; 2 Cor. 11. 6.
SPEECHLESS. Mat. 22. 12; Lu. 1. 22; Acts 9. 7.
SPEED. Gen. 24. 12, send me good *s*.
2 John 10, receive him not, neither bid him God *s*.
See Ezra 6. 12.; Isa. 5. 26; Acts 17. 15.
SPEEDILY. Ps. 31. 2, deliver me *s*.
63. 17; 143. 7, hear me *s*.

Ps. 79. 8, let thy mercies *s*. prevent us.
102. 2, when I call, answer me *s*.
Eccl. 8. 11, because sentence is not executed *s*.
Isa. 58. 8, thy health shall spring forth *s*.
Zech. 8. 21, let us go *s*. to pray.
Lu. 18. 8, he will avenge them *s*.
See 1 Sam. 27. 1; Ezra 6. 13; 7. 17; Joel 3. 4.
SPEND. Job 21. 13, they *s*. their days in wealth.
36. 11, they *s*. their days in prosperity.
Ps. 90. 9, we *s*. our years as a tale that is told.
Isa. 55. 2, why *s*. money for that which is not bread?
2 Cor. 12. 15, very gladly *s*. and be spent for you.
See Prov. 21. 20; Eccl. 6. 12; Lu. 10. 35.
SPENT. Gen. 21. 15, water was *s*. in the bottle.
Job 7. 6, days *s*. without hope.
Ps. 31. 10, my life is *s*. with grief.
Isa. 49. 4, I have *s*. my strength for nought.
Acts 17. 21, *s*. their time to tell some new thing.
See Mk. 6. 35; Lu. 15. 14; 24. 29; Rom. 13. 12.
SPILT. 2 Sam. 14. 14, as water *s*.
SPIN. Ex. 35. 25; Mat. 6. 28; Lu. 12. 27.
SPIRIT. Gen. 6. 3, my *s*. shall not always strive.
Ex. 35. 21, every one whom his *s*. made willing.
Num. 11. 17, take of the *s*. that is on thee.
14. 24, he had another *s*. with him.
16. 22; 27. 16, the God of the *s*. of all flesh.
27. 18, a man in whom is the *s*.
Josh. 5. 1, nor was there any more *s*. in them.
1 Kings 22. 21; 2 Chron. 18. 20, there came forth a *s*.
2 Kings 2. 9, let a double portion of thy *s*.
Neh. 9. 20, thou gavest thy good *s*. to instruct.
Job 4. 15, a *s*. passed before my face.
15. 13, thou turnest thy *s*. against God.
26. 4, whose *s*. came from thee?
32. 8, there is a *s*. in man.
Ps. 31. 5; Lu. 23. 46, into thine hand I commit my *s*.
32. 2, in whose *s*. there is no guile.
51. 10, renew a right *s*. within me.
78. 8, whose *s*. was not stedfast.
104. 4; Heb. 1. 7, who maketh his angels *s*.
106. 33, they provoked his *s*.
139. 7, whither shall I go from thy *s*.?
Prov. 16. 2, the Lord weigheth the *s*.
18, an haughty *s*. goeth before a fall.
19; 29. 23; Isa. 57. 15, an humble *s*.
32, he that ruleth his *s*. better than he.
Eccl. 3. 21, who knoweth *s*. of man, and *s*. of beast?
7. 8, the patient in *s*. better than the proud.
8. 8, no man hath power over *s*. to retain *s*.
11. 5, the way of the *s*.
12. 7, the *s*. shall return to God.
Isa. 4. 4; 28. 6, *s*. of judgment.
11. 2; Eph. 1. 17, the *s*. of wisdom.
34. 16, his *s*. it hath gathered them.
42. 1, I have put my *s*. upon him.
57. 16, the *s*. should fail before me.
61. 1; Lu. 4. 18, the *S*. of the Lord is upon me.
Ezek. 3. 14; 8. 3; 11. 1, I went in the heat of my *s*.
11. 19; 18. 31; 36. 26, a new *s*.
Mic. 2. 11, a man walking in the *s*. and falsehood.
Mat. 14. 26; Mk. 6. 49, it is a *s*.
26. 41; Mk. 14. 38, the *s*. is willing.
Mk. 1. 10; John 1. 32, the *S*. descending on him.
8. 12, sighed deeply in his *s*.
Lu. 1. 17, go before him in *s*. and power of Elias.
2. 27, came by the *S*. into the temple.
8. 55, her *s*. came again.
9. 55, ye know not what manner of *s*.
10. 21, Jesus rejoiced in *s*.
24. 39, a *s*. hath not flesh and bones.
John 3. 34, God giveth not the *S*. by measure.
4. 24, God is a *S*., worship him in *s*. and in truth.
6. 63, it is the *s*. that quickeneth.
14. 17; 15. 26; 16. 13; 1 John 4. 6, *S*. of truth.
Acts 2. 4, begin to speak as the *S*. gave utterance.
6. 10, not able to resist the wisdom and *s*.
17. 16, his *s*. was stirred within him.

Acts 23. 8, say that there is neither angel nor *s.*
Rom. 8. 1, walk not after the flesh, but after the *S.*
2, the law of the *S.* of life.
11, the *S.* of him that raised up Jesus.
16, the *S.* itself beareth witness.
26, the *S.* maketh intercession.
12. 11, fervent in *s.*
1 Cor. 2. 4, in demonstration of the *S.*
10, the *S.* searcheth all things.
4. 21; Gal. 6. 1, in the *s.* of meekness.
6. 17, he that is joined to the Lord is one *s.*
20, glorify God in body and *s.*
12. 4, diversities of gifts, but the same *S.*
10, to another discerning of *s.*
14. 2, in the *s.* he speaketh mysteries.
15. 45, the last Adam made a quickening *s.*
2 Cor. 3. 6, the letter killeth, but the *s.* giveth life.
17, where the *S.* of the Lord is, there is liberty.
Gal. 3. 3, having begun in the *S.*
5. 16, walk in the *S.*
22; Eph. 5. 9, the fruit of the *S.*
25, if we live in the *S.*, let us walk in the *S.*
6. 8, he that soweth to the *S.* shall of the *S.* reap.
Eph. 2. 2, the *s.* that worketh in children of disobedience.
18, access by one *S.*
22, habitation of God through the *S.*
3. 16, strengthened by his *S.* in inner man.
4. 3, the unity of the *S.*
4, one body and one *S.*
23, renewed in *s.* of your mind.
30, grieve not the holy *S.* of God.
5. 18, be filled with the *S.*
6. 17, take sword of the *S.*
Phil. 1. 27, stand fast in one *s.*
2. 1, if any fellowship of the *S.*
Col. 1. 8, your love in the *s.*
2. 5, absent in flesh, yet with you in the *s.*
1 Thess. 5. 19, quench not the *S.*
2 Thess. 2. 13, chosen through sanctification of the *S.*
1 Tim. 3. 16, justified in the *S.*
4. 1, giving heed to seducing *s.*
12, be thou an example in *s.*
2 Tim. 4. 22, the Lord Jesus be with thy *s.*
Heb. 1. 14, ministering *s.*
4. 12, dividing asunder of soul and *s.*
9. 14, who through the eternal *S.*
12. 9, in subjection to the Father of *s.*
23, to *s.* of just men made perfect.
Jas. 2. 26, the body without the *s.* is dead.
4. 5, the *s.* lusteth to envy.
1 Pet. 1. 2, through sanctification of the *S.*
3. 4, ornament of a meek and quiet *s.*
18, but quickened by the *S.*
19, preached to *s.* in prison.
4. 6, live according to God in the *s.*
1 John 3. 24, by the *S.* he hath given us.
4. 1, believe not every *s.*, but try the *s.*
2, hereby know ye the *S.* of God.
3, every *s.* that confesseth not.
5. 6, it is the *S.* that beareth witness.
8, the *s.*, the water, and the blood.
Jude 19, sensual, having not the *S.*
Rev. 1. 10, I was in the *S.* on the Lord's day.
2. 7, 11, 17, 29; 3. 6, 13, 22, hear what the *S.* saith.
4. 2, I was in the *s.*, and, behold.
11. 11, the *S.* of life from God entered.
14. 13, blessed are the dead: Yea, saith the *S.*
22. 17, the *S.* and the bride say, Come.
See Mat. 8. 16; John 3. 5; Acts 7. 59; Rom. 7. 6.

SPIRITUAL. Hos. 9. 7, the *s.* man is mad.
Rom. 1. 11, impart some *s.* gift.
7. 14, the law is *s.*
15. 27, partakers of their *s.* things.
1 Cor. 2. 13, comparing *s.* things with *s.*
15, he that is *s.* judgeth all things.
3. 1, not speak unto you as unto *s.*
10. 3, all eat the same *s.* meat.
1 Cor. 12. 1; 14. 1, concerning *s.* gifts.
15. 44, it is raised a *s.* body.
46, that was not first which is *s.*
Gal. 6. 1, ye which are *s.*, restore such an one.
Eph. 5. 19, in psalms and hymns and *s.* songs.
6. 12, *s.* wickedness in high places.
1 Pet. 2. 5, a *s.* house, to offer up *s.* sacrifices
See 1 Cor. 9. 11; Col. 1. 9; 3. 16.

SPIRITUALLY. Rom. 8. 6; 1 Cor. 2. 14; Rev. 11. 8.

SPITE. Ps. 10. 14, thou beholdest mischief and *s.*

SPOIL (*n.*). Judg. 5. 30, necks of them that take *s.*
1 Sam. 14. 32, people flew upon the *s.*
2 Chron. 15. 11, offered to the Lord of the *s.*
20. 25, three days gathering the *s.*
28. 15, with the *s.* they clothed the naked.
Esth. 3. 13; 8. 11, take the *s.* of them for a prey.
9. 10, on the *s.* laid they not their hand.
Job 29. 17, I plucked the *s.* out of his teeth.
Ps. 119. 162, rejoice as one that findeth great *s.*
Prov. 16. 19, than to divide *s.* with the proud.
31. 11, he shall have no need of *s.*
Isa. 3. 14, the *s.* of the poor is in your houses.
42. 24, who gave Jacob for a *s.*?
53. 12, divide the *s.* with the strong.
See Isa. 9. 3; Ezek. 7. 21; 38. 13; Nah. 2. 9; Zech. 14. 1.

SPOIL (*v.*). Ex. 3. 22, ye shall *s.* the Egyptians.
Ps. 78. 5, the stouthearted are *s.*
Cant. 2. 15, the little foxes that *s.* the vines.
Isa. 33. 1, woe to thee that *s.*, and thou wast not *s.*!
42. 22, this is a people robbed and *s.*
Jer. 4. 30, when *s.*, what wilt thou do?
Hab. 2. 8, thou hast *s.* many nations.
Zech. 11. 2, howl because the mighty are *s.*
Col. 2. 15, having *s.* principalities.
See Ps. 35. 10; Isa. 22. 4; Col. 2. 8; Heb. 10. 34.

SPOKEN. Num. 23. 19, hath he *s.*, and shall he not make it good?
1 Sam. 1. 16, out of my grief have I *s.*
1 Kings 18. 24, the people said, it is well *s.*
2 Kings 4. 13, wouldest thou be *s.* for to the king?
Ps. 62. 11, God hath *s.* once.
66. 14, my mouth hath *s.* when in trouble.
87. 3, glorious things are *s.* of thee.
Prov. 15. 23, a word *s.* in due season.
25. 11, a word fitly *s.* is like.
Eccl. 7. 21, take no heed to all words *s.*
Isa. 48. 15, I, even I, have *s.*
Mal. 3. 13, what have we *s.* so much against?
Mk. 14. 9, shall be *s.* of for a memorial.
Lu. 2. 34, for a sign which shall be *s.* against.
Acts 19. 36, these things cannot be *s.* against.
Rom. 1. 8, your faith is *s.* of.
14. 16, let not your good be evil *s.* of.
Heb. 2. 2, the word *s.* by angels.
See Heb. 13. 7; 1 Pet. 4. 14; 2 Pet. 3. 2.

SPOKESMAN. Ex. 4. 16, he shall be thy *s.*

SPORT. Gen. 26. 8; Isa. 57. 4; 2 Pet. 2. 13.

SPOT. Num. 28. 3; 9. 11; 29. 17, lambs without *s.*
Deut. 32. 5, their *s.* is not the *s.* of his children.
Job 11. 15, lift up thy face without *s.*
Jer. 13. 23, or the leopard his *s.*
Eph. 5. 27, glorious church, not having *s.*
1 Tim. 6. 14, commandment without *s.*
Heb. 9. 14, offered himself without *s.*
1 Pet. 1. 19, lamb without blemish or *s.*
2 Pet. 3. 14, that ye may be found without *s.*
Jude 12, these are *s.* in your feasts.
See Cant. 4. 7; 2 Pet. 2. 13; Jude 23.

SPOUSE. Cant. 4. 8; 5. 1; Hos. 4. 13.

SPRANG. Mk. 4. 8; Acts 16. 29; Heb. 7. 14; 11. 12.

SPREAD. Deut. 32. 11, eagle *s.* abroad her wings.
2 Kings 19. 14; Isa. 37. 14, *s.* letter before the Lord.
Job 9. 8, God who alone *s.* out the heavens.
26. 9, he *s.* his cloud upon it.
29. 19, my root was *s.* out by waters.
36. 30, he *s.* his light upon it.

Job 37. 18, hast thou with him *s.* out the sky?
Ps. 105. 39, he *s.* a cloud for a covering.
140. 5, they have *s.* a net by the wayside.
Isa. 1. 15, when ye *s.* forth your hands I will hide.
33. 23, they could not *s.* the sail.
65. 2, *s.* out hands to a rebellious people.
Jer. 8. 2, they shall *s.* them before the sun.
Ezek. 26. 14, a place to *s.* nets upon.
Mat. 21. 8; Mk. 11. 8; Lu. 19. 36, *s.* garments.
Acts 4. 17, but that it *s.* no further.
See Judg. 8. 25; 1 Kings 8. 54; Ezra 9. 5.
SPRIGS. Isa. 18. 5; Ezek. 17. 6.
SPRING. Num. 21. 17, *s.* up, O well.
1 Sam. 9. 26, about the *s.* of the day.
Job 5. 6, neither doth trouble *s.* out of the ground.
38. 16, hast thou entered into the *s.* of the sea?
Ps. 87. 7, all my *s.* are in thee.
104. 10, he sendeth the *s.* into valleys.
107. 33, he turneth water-*s.* into dry ground.
35, turneth dry ground into water-*s.*
Prov. 25. 26, a troubled fountain, and a corrupt *s.*
Isa. 42. 9, before they *s.* forth I tell you.
43. 19, a new thing, now it shall *s.* forth.
45. 8, let righteousness *s.* up together.
58. 8, thine health shall *s.* forth.
11, shall be like a *s.* of water.
Mk. 4. 27, seed should *s.* he knoweth not how.
See Joel 2. 22; John 4. 14; Heb. 12. 15.
SPRINKLE. Job 2. 12; Isa. 52. 15; Ezek. 36. 25.
SPROUT. Job 14. 7, a tree will *s.* again.
SPUNGE. Mat. 27. 48; Mk. 15. 36; John 19. 29.
SPY. Num. 13. 16; Josh. 2. 1; Gal. 2. 4.
STABILITY. Isa. 33. 6, the *s.* of thy times.
STABLE. 1 Chron. 16. 30; Ezek. 25. 5.
STAFF. Gen. 32. 10, with my *s.* I passed over.
Ex. 12. 11, eat it with *s.* in hand.
Num. 13. 23, bare grapes between two on a *s.*
Judg. 6. 21, the angel put forth end of his *s.*
2 Sam. 3. 29, not fail one that leaneth on a *s.*
2 Kings 4. 29, lay my *s.* on face of the child.
18. 21; Isa. 36. 6, thou trustest on *s.*
Ps. 23. 4, thy rod and *s.* comfort me.
Isa. 3. 1, the stay and *s.*, the whole stay of bread.
9. 4, thou hast broken the *s.* of his shoulder.
10. 5, the *s.* in their hand is mine indignation.
15, as if the *s.* should lift up itself.
14. 5, the Lord hath broken the *s.* of the wicked.
Jer. 48. 17, how is the strong *s.* broken?
Zech. 11. 10, took my *s.*, even Beauty.
Mk. 6. 8, take nothing, save *s.* only.
Heb. 11. 21, leaning on the top of his *s.*
See Ex. 21. 19; Num. 22. 27; Isa. 28. 27.
STAGGER. Job 12. 25; Ps. 107. 27, *s.* like a drunken man.
Isa. 29. 9, they *s.*, but not with strong drink.
See Isa. 19. 14; Rom. 4. 20.
STAIN. Job 3. 5; Isa. 23. 9; 63. 3.
STAIRS. 1 Kings 6. 8; Neh. 9. 4; Cant. 2. 14.
STAKES. Isa. 33. 20; 54. 2.
STALK. Gen. 41. 5; Josh. 2. 6; Hos. 8. 7.
STALL. Prov. 15. 17; Hab. 3. 17; Mal. 4. 2.
STAMMERING. Isa. 28. 11; 32. 4; 33. 19.
STAMP. Deut. 9. 21; 2 Sam. 22. 43; Jer. 47. 3.
STAND. Ex. 14. 13; 2 Chron. 20. 17, *s.* still, and see.
Deut. 29. 10, ye *s.* this day all of you before the Lord.
1 Sam. 9. 27, *s.* thou still a while.
1 Kings 8. 11; 2 Chron. 5. 14, priests could not *s.* to minister.
17. 1; 18. 15; 2 Kings 3. 14; 5. 16, the Lord before whom I *s.*
2 Kings 10. 4, two kings stood not, how shall we *s.*?
2 Chron. 34. 32, caused all present to *s.* to it.
Esth. 8. 11, to *s.* for their life.
Job 8. 15, shall lean on his house, but it shall not *s.*
19. 25, he shall *s.* at the latter day.
Ps. 1. 1, nor *s.* in the way of sinners.
5, the ungodly shall not *s.* in judgment.
4. 4, *s.* in awe, and sin not.
Ps. 10. 1, why *s.* thou afar off?
24. 3, who shall *s.* in his holy place?
33. 11, the counsel of the Lord *s.* for ever.
35. 2, *s.* up for my help.
76. 7, who may *s.* in thy sight?
94. 16, who will *s.* up for me?
109. 31, shall *s.* at right hand of the poor.
122. 2, our feet shall *s.* within thy gates.
130. 3, if thou, Lord, mark iniquities, who shall *s.*?
147. 17, who can *s.* before his cold?
Prov. 22. 29, shall *s.* before kings.
27. 4, who is able to *s.* before envy?
Eccl. 8. 3, *s.* not in an evil thing.
Isa. 7. 7; 8. 10, thus saith the Lord, it shall not *s.*
21. 8, I *s.* continually on watchtower.
28. 18, your agreement with hell shall not *s.*
40. 8, the word of God shall *s.* for ever.
65. 5, *s.* by thyself, I am holier than thou.
Jer. 6. 16, *s.* ye in the ways, ask for the old paths.
35. 19, shall not want a man to *s.* before me.
Dan. 11. 16, he shall *s.* in the glorious land.
12. 13, and shall *s.* in thy lot.
Mic. 5. 4, he shall *s.* and feed in strength.
Nah. 2. 8, *s.*, *s.*, shall they cry.
Zech. 3. 1, Satan *s.* at his right hand.
Mal. 3. 2, who shall *s.* when he appeareth?
Mat. 12. 25; Mk. 3. 24, 25; Lu. 11. 18, house divided shall not *s.*
16. 28; Lu. 9. 27, there be some *s.* here.
20. 3, others *s.* idle in the marketplace.
Rom. 5. 2, this grace wherein we *s.*
14. 4, God is able to make him *s.*
1 Cor. 2. 5, faith should not *s.* in wisdom.
16. 13, *s.* fast in the faith.
Gal. 4. 20, I *s.* in doubt of you.
5. 1, *s.* fast in the liberty.
Eph. 6. 13, having done all, to *s.*
Phil. 1. 27, *s.* fast in one spirit.
4. 1; 1 Thess. 3. 8, *s.* fast in the Lord.
1 Thess. 3. 8, we live, if ye *s.* fast.
2 Tim. 2. 19, the foundation of God *s.* sure.
Jas. 5. 9, the judge *s.* before the door.
Rev. 3. 20, I *s.* at the door, and knock.
6. 17, is come, and who shall be able to *s.*?
20. 12, the dead, small and great, *s.* before God.
See Rom. 14. 4; 1 Cor. 10. 12; Rev. 15. 2.
STANDARD. Isa. 10. 18, as when *s.*-bearer fainteth.
49. 22, I will set up my *s.* to the people.
59. 19, Spirit of the Lord shall lift up *s.* against.
62. 10, go through, lift up a *s.*
Jer. 4. 6; 50. 2; 51. 12, set up a *s.*
See Num. 1. 52; 2. 3; 10. 14.
STATE. Ps. 39. 5; Mat. 12. 45; Lu. 11. 26.
STATURE. Num. 13. 32, men of great *s.*
1 Sam. 16. 7, look not on height of his *s.*
Isa. 10. 33, high ones of *s.* hewn down.
45. 14, men of *s.* shall come.
Mat. 6. 27; Lu. 12. 25, not add to *s.*
Lu. 2. 52, Jesus increased in *s.*
19. 3, little of *s.*
Eph. 4. 13, *s.* of the fulness of Christ.
See 2 Sam. 21. 20; Cant. 7. 7; Ezek. 17. 6; 31. 3.
STATUTE. Ex. 18. 16, the *s.* of God.
Lev. 3. 17; 16. 34; 24. 9, a perpetual *s.*
2 Kings 17. 8, *s.* of the heathen.
Neh. 9. 14, *s.* and laws.
Ps. 19. 8, the *s.* of the Lord are right.
50. 16, to declare my *s.*
Ezek. 5. 6, hath changed my *s.*
20. 25, *s.* that were not good.
33. 15, walk in the *s.* of life.
Zech. 1. 6, my *s.*, did they not take hold?
See Ps. 18. 22; 105. 45; 119. 12, etc.; Ezek. 18. 19.
STAVES. Num. 21. 18, nobles digged with *s.*
1 Sam. 17. 43, am I a dog, that thou comest with *s.*?
Hab. 3. 14, strike through with his *s.*
Zech. 11. 7, took unto me two *s.*
Mat. 10. 10; Lu. 9. 3, neither two coats, nor *s.*

See Mat. 26. 47; Mk. 14. 43; Lu. 22. 52.
STAY (*n.*). 2 Sam. 22. 19; Ps. 18. 18, the Lord was my *s.*
Isa. 3. 1, take away the *s.* and staff.
See Lev. 13. 5; 1 Kings 10. 19; Isa. 19. 13.
STAY (*v.*). Gen. 19. 17, neither *s.* in plain.
Ex. 9. 28, ye shall *s.* no longer.
Num. 16. 48; 25. 8; 2 Sam. 24. 25; 1 Chron. 21. 22; Ps. 106. 30, the plague was *s.*
2 Sam. 24. 16; 1 Chron. 21. 15, *s.* now thine hand.
Job 37. 4, he will not *s.* them.
38. 11, here shall thy proud waves be *s.*
37, who can *s.* the bottles of heaven?
Prov. 28. 17, let no man *s.* him.
Isa. 26. 3, whose mind is *s.* on thee.
27. 8, he *s.* his rough wind.
29. 9, *s.* yourselves, and wonder.
30. 12, ye trust in oppression, and *s.* thereon.
50. 10, trust in name of the Lord, and *s.* on his God.
Dan. 4. 35, none can *s.* his hand.
Hag. 1. 10, heaven is *s.*, earth is *s.*
See Josh. 10. 13; 1 Sam. 24. 7; Jer. 4. 6; 20. 9.
STEAD. Ex. 4. 16, be to him in *s.* of God.
Num. 10. 31, be to us in *s.* of eyes.
32. 14, risen in your fathers' *s.*
Job 16. 4, if your soul were in my soul's *s.*
31. 40, thistles grow in *s.* of wheat.
34. 24, he shall set others in their *s.*
Ps. 45. 16, in *s.* of fathers shall be children.
Prov. 11. 8, the wicked cometh in his *s.*
Isa. 3. 24, in *s.* of girdle a rent.
55. 13, in *s.* of the thorn shall come up the fir tree.
2 Cor. 5. 20, we pray you in Christ's *s.*
See Gen. 30. 2; 2 Kings 17. 24; 1 Chron. 5. 22.
STEADY. Ex. 17. 12, Moses' hands were *s.*
STEAL. Gen. 31. 27, wherefore didst thou *s.* away?
44. 8, how then should we *s.* silver or gold?
Prov. 6. 30, if he *s.* to satisfy his soul.
30. 9, lest I be poor, and *s.*
Jer. 23. 30, prophets that *s.* my words.
Mat. 6. 19, thieves break through and *s.*
John 10. 10, thief cometh not, but to *s.*
See Hos. 4. 2; Mat. 27. 64; Rom. 2. 21.
STEALTH. 2 Sam. 19. 3, by *s.* into city.
STEDFAST. Ps. 78. 8, not *s.* with God.
Dan. 6. 26, living God, and *s.* for ever.
Heb. 2. 2, word spoken by angels was *s.*
3. 14, hold our confidence *s.* to end.
6. 19, hope as anchor, sure and *s.*
1 Pet. 5. 9, resist *s.* in the faith.
See Acts 2. 42; Col. 2. 5; 2 Pet. 3. 17.
STEEL. 2 Sam. 22. 35; Job 20. 24; Jer. 15. 12.
STEEP. Ezek. 38. 20; Mic. 1. 4; Mat. 8. 32.
STEP. 1 Sam. 20. 3, but a *s.* between me and death.
Job 14. 16, thou numberest my *s.*
23. 11, my foot hath held his *s.*
29. 6, I washed my *s.* with butter.
31. 4, doth not he count my *s.*?
7, if my *s.* hath turned out of the way.
Ps. 37. 23, the *s.* of a good man are ordered.
31, none of his *s.* shall slide.
44. 18, nor have our *s.* declined.
56. 6, they mark my *s.*
73. 2, my *s.* had well nigh slipped.
85. 13, set us in the way of his *s.*
119. 133, order my *s.* in thy word.
Prov. 4. 12, thy *s.* shall not be straitened.
5. 5, her *s.* take hold on hell.
16. 9, the Lord directeth his *s.*
Isa. 26. 6, the *s.* of the needy shall tread it down.
Jer. 10. 23, not in man to direct his *s.*
Rom. 4. 12, walk in *s.* of that faith.
2 Cor. 12. 18, walked we not in same *s.*?
1 Pet. 2. 21, that ye should follow his *s.*
See Ex. 20. 26; 2 Sam. 22. 37; Lam. 4. 18; Ezek. 40. 22.
STEWARD. 1 Kings 16. 9, drunk in house of his *s.*
Lu. 12. 42, that faithful and wise *s.*
See Gen. 15. 2; Lu. 8. 3; 1 Cor. 4. 1; 1 Pet. 4. 10.
STICK. Num. 15. 32, gathered *s.* on sabbath.
1 Kings 17. 12, I am gathering two *s.*
Job 33. 21, his bones *s.* out.
Ps. 38. 2, thine arrows *s.* fast in me.
Prov. 18. 24, a friend that *s.* closer than a brother.
Ezek. 37. 16, take *s.*, and write on it.
See 2 Kings 6. 6; Lam. 4. 8; Ezek. 29. 4.
STIFF. Ex. 32. 9; 33. 3; 34. 9; Deut. 9. 6, 13; 10. 16, *s.*-necked people.
Ps. 75. 5, speak not with *s.* neck.
Jer. 17. 23, obeyed not, but made their neck *s.*
Ezek. 2. 4, impudent and *s.*-hearted.
Acts 7. 51, ye *s.*-necked, ye do always resist.
See Deut. 31. 27; 2 Chron. 30. 8; 36. 13.
STILL. Ex. 15. 16, as *s.* as a stone.
Num. 14. 38, Joshua and Caleb lived *s.*
Josh. 24. 10, Balaam blessed you *s.*
Judg. 18. 9, the land is good, and are ye *s.*?
2 Sam. 14. 32, good to have been there *s.*
2 Kings 7. 4, if we sit *s.* here, we die also.
2 Chron. 22. 9, no power to keep *s.* the kingdom.
Job 2. 9, dost thou *s.* retain thine integrity?
Ps. 4. 4, commune with thine heart, and be *s.*
8. 2, *s.* the enemy and avenger.
23. 2, beside the *s.* waters.
46. 10, be *s.*, and know that I am God.
76. 8, earth feared, and was *s.*
83. 1, hold not thy peace, and be not *s.*, O God.
84. 4, they will be *s.* praising thee.
107. 29, so that the waves thereof are *s.*
139. 18, when I awake, I am *s.* with thee.
Eccl. 12. 9, he *s.* taught knowledge.
Isa. 5. 25; 9. 12; 10. 4, his hand is stretched out *s.*
30. 7, their strength is to sit *s.*
42. 14, I have been *s.*, and refrained.
Jer. 8. 14, why do we sit *s.*?
31. 20, I do earnestly remember him *s.*
Zech. 11. 16, nor feed that that standeth *s.*
Mk. 4. 39, arose, and said, peace, be *s.*
Rev. 22. 11, unjust *s.*, filthy *s.*, holy *s.*
See Num. 13. 30; Ps. 65. 7; 89. 9; 92. 14.
STING. Prov. 23. 32; 1 Cor. 15. 55; Rev. 9. 10.
STIR. Num. 24. 9, who shall *s.* him up?
Deut. 32. 11, as an eagle *s.* up her nest.
1 Sam. 22. 8, my son hath *s.* up my servant.
26. 19, if the Lord have *s.* thee up.
1 Kings 11. 14, the Lord *s.* up an adversary.
1 Chron. 5. 26; 2 Chron. 36. 22; Hag. 1. 14, God *s.* up the spirit.
Job 17. 8, the innocent shall *s.* up himself.
41. 10, none dare *s.* him up.
Ps. 35. 23, *s.* up thyself.
39. 2, my sorrow was *s.*
Prov. 10. 12, hatred *s.* up strifes.
15. 18; 29. 22, a wrathful man *s.* up strife.
Isa. 10. 26, the Lord shall *s.* up a scourge.
14. 9, hell from beneath *s.* up the dead.
64. 7, none *s.* up himself to take hold.
Lu. 23. 5, he *s.* up the people.
Acts 17. 16, his spirit was *s.* in him.
19. 23, no small *s.* about that way.
2 Tim. 1. 6, *s.* up gift of God in thee.
2 Pet. 1. 13, I think it meet to *s.* you up.
See Cant. 2. 7; 3. 5; 8. 4; Isa. 22. 2; Acts 12. 18.
STOCK. Job 14. 8, though the *s.* thereof die.
Isa. 40. 24, their *s.* shall not take root.
44. 19, shall I fall down to the *s.* of a tree?
Hos. 4. 12, my people ask counsel at their *s.*
Nah. 3. 6; Heb. 10. 33, a gazing-*s.*
Acts 13. 26, children of the *s.* of Abraham.
See Jer. 2. 27; 10. 8; 20. 2; Phil. 3. 5.
STOLE. 2 Sam. 15. 6, Absalom *s.* the hearts.
Eph. 4. 28, let him that *s.* steal no more.
See Gen. 31. 20; 2 Kings 11. 2; 2 Chron. 22. 11; Mat. 28. 13.
STOLEN. Josh. 7. 11, they have *s.*, and dissembled.

2 Sam. 21. 12, men had *s.* the bones of Saul.
Prov. 9. 17, *s.* waters are sweet.
Obad. 5, *s.* till they had enough.
See Gen. 30. 33; 31. 19; Ex. 22. 7; 2 Sam. 19. 41.
STOMACH. 1 Tim. 5. 23, for thy *s.* sake.
STONE. Gen. 11. 3, they had brick for *s.*
28. 18, 22; 31. 45; 35. 14, set up a *s.* for a pillar.
Deut. 8. 9, a land whose *s.* are iron.
Josh. 24. 27, this *s.* shall be a witness.
2 Sam. 17. 13, till there be not one small *s.* found there.
2 Kings 3. 25, cast every man his *s.*
Job 5. 23, in league with *s.* of the field.
6. 12, is my strength the strength of *s.*?
14. 19, the waters wear the *s.*
28. 3, he searcheth out the *s.* of darkness.
41. 24, his heart is as firm as a *s.*
Ps. 91. 12; Mk. 4. 6; Lu. 4. 11, lest thou dash thy foot against a *s.*
118. 22; Mat. 21. 42; Mk. 12. 10, the *s.* which the builders refused is become the head *s.*
Prov. 27. 3, a *s.* is heavy, a fool's wrath heavier.
Isa. 54. 11, I will lay thy *s.* with fair colours.
60. 17, bring for *s.* iron.
62. 10, gather out the *s.*
Jer. 2. 27, and to a *s.*, thou hast brought me forth.
Dan. 2. 34, a *s.* was cut out of the mountain.
Hab. 2. 11, the *s.* shall cry out of the wall.
19, that saith to the dumb *s.*, arise.
Hag. 2. 15, before *s.* was laid upon *s.*
Zech. 3. 9, upon one *s.* shall be seven eyes.
4. 7, bring forth the head-*s.* thereof.
7. 12, they made their hearts as *s.*
Mat. 7. 9; Lu. 11. 11, will he give him a *s.*?
21. 44; Lu. 20. 18, whosoever shall fall on this *s.*
24. 2; Mk. 13. 2; Lu. 19. 44; 21. 6, not one *s.* upon another.
Mk. 13. 1, see what manner of *s.* are here!
16. 4; Lu. 24. 2, found *s.* rolled away.
Lu. 4. 3, command this *s.* that it be made bread.
John 1. 42, Cephas, by interpretation a *s.*
8. 7, first cast a *s.*
11. 39, take ye away the *s.*
Acts 17. 29, that the Godhead is like to *s.*
1 Pet. 2. 5, as lively *s.*, are built up.
See 1 Sam. 30. 6; 1 Cor. 3. 12; 2 Cor. 3. 3; Rev. 2. 17.
STONY. Ps. 141. 6; Ezek. 11. 19; 36. 26; Mat. 13. 5.
STOOD. Gen. 18. 22, *s.* yet before the Lord.
Num. 14. 19, *s.* behind them.
Josh. 3. 16, waters *s.* up on an heap.
2 Kings 23. 3, all the people *s.* to the covenant.
Esth. 9. 16, Jews *s.* for their lives.
Ps. 33. 9, he commanded, and it *s.* fast.
Lu. 24. 36, Jesus himself *s.* in the midst.
2 Tim. 4. 16, no man *s.* with me.
See Gen. 23. 3; Job 29. 8; Ezek. 37. 10; Rev. 7. 11.
STOOP. Gen. 49. 9, Judah *s.* down.
Prov. 12. 25, heaviness maketh the heart *s.*
John 8. 6, *s.* down, and wrote on the ground.
See 2 Chron. 36. 17; Job 9. 13; Mk. 1. 7; John 20. 11.
STOP. Gen. 8. 2, windows of heaven were *s.*
1 Kings 18. 44, that the rain *s.* thee not.
Ps. 107. 42, iniquity shall *s.* her mouth.
Zech. 7. 11, refused, and *s.* their ears.
Acts 7. 57, *s.* their ears, and ran upon him.
Rom. 3. 19, that every mouth may be *s.*
Tit. 1. 11, whose mouths must be *s.*
Heb. 11. 33, through faith *s.* mouths of lions.
See Gen. 26. 15; Job 5. 16; Ps. 58. 4; Prov. 21. 13.
STORE. Lev. 25. 22; 26. 10, eat of the old *s.*
Deut. 28. 5, blessed be thy basket and *s.*
2 Kings 20. 17, thy fathers have laid up in *s.*
Ps. 144. 13, affording all manner of *s.*
Nah. 2. 9, none end of the *s.* and glory.
Mal. 3. 10, bring tithes into *s.*-house.
Lu. 12. 24, neither have *s.*-house nor barn.
1 Cor. 16. 2, every one lay by him in *s.*
1 Tim. 6. 19, laying up in *s.* a good foundation.
2 Pet. 3. 7, by same word are kept in *s.*
See 1 Kings 10. 10; 1 Chron. 29. 16; Ps. 33. 7.
STORK. Ps. 104. 17, as for the *s.*, the fir trees are her house.
Jer. 8. 7, yea, the *s.* in the heaven.
Zech. 5. 9, like the wings of a *s.*
STORM. Ps. 55. 8, escape from windy *s.*
83. 15, make them afraid with thy *s.*
107. 29, he maketh the *s.* a calm.
Isa. 4. 6; 25. 4, a covert from *s.*
28. 2, as a destroying *s.*
Ezek. 38. 9, shalt ascend and come like a *s.*
Nah. 1. 3, the Lord hath his way in the *s.*
See Job 21. 18; 27. 21; Mk. 4. 37; Lu. 8. 23.
STORMY. Ps. 107. 25; 148. 8; Ezek. 13. 11.
STORY. 2 Chron. 13. 22; 24. 27.
STOUT. Dan. 7. 20, whose look was more *s.*
Mal. 3. 13, words have been *s.* against me.
See Ps. 76. 5; Isa. 9. 9; 10. 12; 46. 12.
STRAIGHT. Ps. 5. 8, make thy way *s.*
Prov. 4. 25, let eyelids look *s.* before thee.
Eccl. 1. 15; 7. 13, crooked cannot be made *s.*
Isa. 40. 3, make *s.* a highway.
4; 42. 16; 45. 2; Lu. 3. 5, crooked shall be made *s.*
Jer. 31. 9, cause them to walk in a *s.* way.
Mat. 3. 3; Mk. 1. 3; Lu. 3. 4; John 1. 23, make his paths *s.*
Lu. 13. 13, she was made *s.*
Acts 9. 11, street which is called *S.*
Heb. 12. 13, make *s.* paths for your feet.
See Josh. 6. 5; 1 Sam. 6. 12; Ezek. 1. 7; 10. 22.
STRAIGHTWAY. Prov. 7. 22, he goeth after her *s.*
Mat. 4. 20; Mk. 1. 18, they *s.* left their nets.
Jas. 1. 24, *s.* forgetteth what manner of man.
See Lu. 14. 5; John 13. 32; Acts 9. 20; 16. 33.
STRAIN. Mat. 23. 24, *s.* at a gnat.
STRAIT. 2 Sam. 24. 14, I am in a great *s.*
Job 20. 22, he shall be in *s.*
Isa. 49. 20, the place is too *s.* for me, give place.
Mic. 2. 7, is spirit of the Lord *s.*?
Mat. 7. 13; Lu. 13. 24, enter in at the *s.* gate.
Lu. 12. 50, how am I *s.* till it be accomplished!
2 Cor. 6. 12, ye are not *s.* in us.
Phil. 1. 23, I am in a *s.* betwixt two.
See 2 Kings 6. 1; Job 18. 7; 37. 10; Jer. 19. 9.
STRAITLY. Gen. 43. 7; Josh. 6. 1; Acts 4. 17.
STRAITNESS. Deut. 28. 53; Job 36. 16.
STRANGE. Gen. 42. 7, Joseph made himself *s.*
Ex. 2. 22; 18. 3; Ps. 137. 4, in a *s.* land.
Lev. 10. 1; Num. 3. 4; 26. 61, offered *s.* fire.
1 Kings 11. 1, Solomon loved many *s.* women
Job 19. 17, my breath is *s.* to my wife.
31. 3, a *s.* punishment to workers.
Prov. 2. 16, to deliver thee from the *s.* woman.
5. 3, 20, for the lips of a *s.* woman.
21. 8, the way of man is froward and *s.*
23. 27, a *s.* woman is a narrow pit.
Isa. 28. 21, his *s.* work, his *s.* act.
Ezek. 3. 5, not sent to people of a *s.* speech.
Zeph. 1. 8, clothed with *s.* apparel.
Lu. 5. 26, we have seen *s.* things to-day.
Acts 17. 20, thou bringest *s.* things to our ears.
26. 11, persecuted them even to *s.* cities.
Heb. 13. 9, carried about with *s.* doctrines.
1 Pet. 4. 4, they think it *s.* ye run not.
12, not *s.* concerning the fiery trial.
See Judg. 11. 2; Ezra 10. 2; Prov. 2. 16; Jer. 8. 19.
STRANGER. Gen. 23. 4; Ps. 39. 12, I am a *s.* with you.
Ex. 23. 9, ye know the heart of a *s.*
1 Chron. 29. 15, we are *s.*, as were all our fathers.
Job 15. 19, no *s.* passed among them.
31. 32, the *s.* did not lodge in the street.
Ps. 54. 3, for *s.* are risen up against me.
109. 11, let the *s.* spoil his labour.
146. 9, the Lord preserveth the *s.*
Prov. 2. 16, to deliver thee even from the *s.*
5. 10, lest *s.* be filled with thy wealth.

Prov. 17, let them be thine own, not s. with thee.
6. 1, stricken thy hand with a s.
7. 5, from the s. which flattereth.
11. 15, he that is surety for a s. shall smart.
14. 10, a s. doth not intermeddle.
20. 16; 27. 13, garment that is surety for a s.
27. 2, let a s. praise thee.
Isa. 1. 7, your land, s. devour it.
2. 6, please themselves in children of s.
14. 1, the s. shall be joined with them.
56. 3, neither let the son of the s. speak.
Jer. 14. 8, why be as a s. in the land?
Ezek. 28. 10, thou shalt die by the hand of s.
Hos. 7. 9, s. have devoured his strength.
Mat. 25. 35, I was a s., and ye took me in.
Lu. 17. 18, that returned, save this s.
Eph. 2. 12, s. from the covenant.
19, no more s., but fellowcitizens.
Heb. 11. 13, confessed they were s.
13. 2, be not forgetful to entertain s.
See Mat. 17. 25; John 10. 5; 1 Pet. 2. 11.

STRANGLED. Nah. 2. 12; Acts 15. 20; 21. 25.

STREAM. Ps. 124. 4; Isa. 35. 6; 66. 12; Amos 5. 24.

STREET. Prov. 1. 20; Lu. 14. 21; Rev. 21. 21; 22. 2.

STRENGTH. Ex. 15. 2; 2 Sam. 22. 33; Ps. 18. 2; 28. 7; 118. 14; Isa. 12. 2, the Lord is my s.
Judg. 5. 21, thou hast trodden down s.
1 Sam. 2. 9, by s. shall no man prevail.
5. 29, the S. of Israel will not lie.
Job 9. 19, if I speak of s., lo, he is strong.
12. 13, with him is wisdom and s.
Ps. 18. 32, girded me with s.
27. 1, the Lord is the s. of my life.
29. 11, the Lord will give s. to his people.
33. 16, mighty not delivered by much s.
39. 13, spare me, that I may recover s.
46. 1; 81. 1, God is our refuge and s.
68. 34, ascribe s. to God, his s. is in the clouds.
35, God giveth s. and power.
73. 26, God is the s. of my heart.
84. 5, the man whose s. is in thee.
7, they go from s. to s.
96. 6, s. and beauty are in his sanctuary.
138. 3, strengthenedst me with s. in my soul.
Prov. 10. 29, the way of the Lord is s.
Eccl. 9. 16, wisdom is better than s.
10. 17, princes eat for s.
Isa. 25. 4, a s. to the poor, a s. to the needy.
40. 29, he increaseth s.
51. 9, awake, put on s.
Hag. 2. 22, I will destroy the s. of the kingdoms.
Lu. 1. 51, he hath showed s. with his arm.
Rom. 5. 6, when ye were without s.
1 Cor. 15. 56, the s. of sin is the law.
Rev. 3. 8, thou hast a little s.
See Job 21. 23; Prov. 20. 29; 2 Cor. 12. 9.

STRENGTHEN. Job 15. 25, he s. himself against.
Ps. 20. 2, s. thee out of Zion.
104. 15, bread which s. man's heart.
Eccl. 7. 19, wisdom s. the wise.
Isa. 35. 3, s. ye the weak hands.
Lu. 22. 32, when converted, s. thy brethren.
Eph. 3. 16; Col. 1. 11, to be s. with might.
Phil. 4. 13, all things through Christ who s. me.
See Lu. 22. 43; 1 Pet. 5. 10; Rev. 3. 2.

STRETCH. Ps. 68. 31, s. out her hands to God.
Isa. 28. 20, shorter than a man can s. himself.
Jer. 10. 12; 51. 15, he s. out the heavens.
Ezek. 16. 27, I have s. out my hand over thee.
Mat. 12. 13, s. forth thine hand.
See Ps. 104. 2; Prov. 1. 24; Rom. 10. 21; 2 Cor. 10. 14.

STRIKE. Job 17. 3; Prov. 22. 26, s. hands.
Ps. 110. 5, shall s. through kings.
Prov. 7. 23, till a dart s. through his liver.
See Prov. 23. 35; Isa. 1. 5; 1 Tim. 3. 3; Tit. 1. 7.

STRIPES. Deut. 25. 3, forty s. he may give.
2 Cor. 11. 24, five times received I forty s.

STRIVE. Gen. 6. 3, shall not always s.
Prov. 3. 30, s. not without cause.
Lu. 13. 24, s. to enter in at strait gate.
2 Tim. 2. 5, if a man s. for mastery.
24, the servant of the Lord must not s.
See Isa. 45. 9; Jer. 50. 24; Mat. 12. 19; Heb. 12. 4.

STRONG. 1 Sam. 4. 9; 1 Kings 2. 2; 2 Chron. 15. 7; Isa. 35. 4; Dan. 10. 19, be s.
Job 9. 19, if I speak of strength, lo, he is s.
Ps. 19. 5, as a s. man to run a race.
24. 8, the Lord is s.
31. 2, be thou my s. rock.
71. 7, thou art my s. refuge.
Prov. 10. 15, the rich man's wealth is his s. city.
18. 10, the name of the Lord is a s. tower.
Eccl. 9. 11, the battle is not to the s.
Isa. 40. 26, for that he is s. in power.
Mat. 12. 29, first bind the s. man.
Rom. 4. 20, s. in faith.
1 Cor. 4. 10, we are weak, ye are s.
2 Thess. 2. 11, s. delusion.
Heb. 5. 12, of milk, and not of s. meat.
6. 18, we have a s. consolation.
See Prov. 14. 26; Joel 3. 10; Rom. 15. 1; Rev. 5. 2.

STUBBLE. Ps. 83. 13, make them as s.
Isa. 33. 11, conceive chaff, bring forth s.
41. 2, as driven s.
Jer. 13. 24, I will scatter them as s.
See Joel 2. 5; Nah. 1. 10; Mal. 4. 1; 1 Cor. 3. 12.

STUDY. Eccl. 12. 12, much s. is a weariness of the flesh.
See 1 Thess. 4. 11; 2 Tim. 2. 15.

STUMBLE. Prov. 4. 19, know not at what they s.
Isa. 28. 7, they s. in judgment.
59. 10, we s. at noonday.
Jer. 46. 6; Dan. 11. 19, s. and fall.
Mal. 2. 8, have caused many to s.
1 Pet. 2. 8, that s. at the word.
See John 11. 9; Rom. 9. 32; 11. 11; 14. 21.

SUBDUE. Ps. 47. 3, he shall s. the people.
Mic. 7. 19, he will s. our iniquities.
Phil. 3. 21, able to s. all things.
Heb. 11. 33, through faith s. kingdoms.
See Dan. 2. 40; Zech. 9. 15; 1 Cor. 15. 28.

SUBJECT. Lu. 10. 17, devils are s. unto us.
Rom. 8. 7, not s. to law of God.
20, creature s. to vanity.
13. 1, s. to the higher powers.
1 Cor. 14. 32, spirits of prophets s. to prophets.
15. 28, then shall the Son also be s. to him.
Eph. 5. 24, as the church is s. to Christ.
Heb. 2. 15, all their lifetime s. to bondage.
Jas. 5. 17, a man s. to like passions.
1 Pet. 2. 18, servants, be s. to your masters.
3. 22, angels and powers s. to him.
5. 5, all of you be s. one to another.
See Lu. 2. 51; Col. 2. 20; Tit. 3. 1.

SUBMIT. 2 Sam. 22. 45, s. themselves.
Ps. 68. 30, till every one s. himself.
Eph. 5. 22, wives s. yourselves.
Jas. 4. 7, s. yourselves to God.
1 Pet. 2. 13, s. yourselves to every ordinance of man.
See Rom. 10. 3; Eph. 5. 21; Heb. 13. 17.

SUBSCRIBE. Isa. 44. 5; Jer. 32. 44.

SUBSTANCE. Gen. 13. 6, their s. was great.
Deut. 33. 11, bless his s.
Job 30. 22, thou dissolvest my s.
Ps. 17. 14, they leave their s. to babes.
139. 15, my s. was not hid from thee.
Prov. 3. 9, honour the Lord with thy s.
28. 8, he that by usury increaseth his s.
Cant. 8. 7, give all his s. for love.
Jer. 15. 13; 17. 3, thy s. will I give to spoil.
Hos. 12. 8, I have found me out s.
Mic. 4. 13, I will consecrate their s.
Lu. 8. 3, ministered to him of their s.
15. 13, wasted his s.
Heb. 10. 34, a better s.

Heb. 11. 1, the *s.* of things hoped for.
See Prov. 1. 13; 6. 31; 8. 21; 12. 27; 29. 3.
SUBTIL. Gen. 3. 1; 2 Sam. 13. 3; Prov. 7. 10.
SUBTILTY. Gen. 27. 35; Mat. 26. 4; Acts 13. 10.
SUBVERT. Lam. 3. 36; 2 Tim. 2. 14; Tit. 1. 11; 3. 11.
SUCCESS. Josh. 1. 8, have good *s.*
SUCK. Deut. 32. 13, *s.* honey out of rock.
33. 19, *s.* abundance of the seas.
Job 20. 16, *s.* poison of asps.
Isa. 60. 16, *s.* the milk of the Gentiles.
See Mat. 24. 19; Mk. 13. 17; Lu. 21. 23; 23. 29.
SUDDEN. Job 22. 10; Prov. 3. 25; 1 Thess. 5. 3.
SUDDENLY. Prov. 29. 1, be *s.* destroyed.
Eccl. 9. 12, when it falleth *s.*
Mal. 3. 1, shall *s.* come to his temple.
Mk. 13. 36, lest coming *s.* he find you sleeping.
1 Tim. 5. 22, lay hands *s.* on no man.
SUFFER. Job 21. 3, *s.* me that I may speak.
Ps. 55. 22, never *s.* righteous to be moved.
89. 33, nor *s.* my faithfulness to fail.
Prov. 19. 15, the idle soul shall *s.* hunger.
Eccl. 5. 12, not *s.* him to sleep.
Mat. 3. 15, *s.* it to be so now.
8. 21; Lu. 9. 59, *s.* me first to bury my father.
16. 21; 17. 12; Mk. 8. 31; Lu. 9. 22, *s.* many things.
19. 14; Mk. 10. 14; Lu. 18. 16, *s.* little children.
23. 13, neither *s.* ye them that are entering to go in.
Lu. 24. 46; Acts 3. 18, behoved Christ to *s.*
Rom. 8. 17, if we *s.* with him.
1 Cor. 3. 15, he shall *s.* loss.
10. 13, will not *s.* you to be tempted.
12. 26, whether one member *s.*, all *s.* with it.
Gal. 6. 12, lest they should *s.* persecution.
2 Tim. 2. 12, if we *s.*, we shall also reign.
3. 12, shall *s.* persecution.
Heb. 13. 3, remember them who *s.*
1 Pet. 2. 21, *s.* for us, leaving an example.
4. 1, he that hath *s.* in the flesh.
See Gal. 3. 4; Phil. 3. 8; Heb. 2. 18; 5. 8.
SUFFICIENCY. Job 20. 22; 2 Cor. 3. 5; 9. 8.
SUFFICIENT. Isa. 40. 16, not *s.* to burn.
Mat. 6. 34, *s.* for the day is the evil.
2 Cor. 2. 16, who is *s.* for these things?
See Deut. 15. 8; John 6. 7; 2 Cor. 3. 5; 12. 9.
SUM. Ps. 139. 17; Acts 22. 28; Heb. 8. 1.
SUMMER. Gen. 8. 22; Ps. 74. 17, *s.* and winter.
Prov. 6. 8; 30. 25, provideth meat in *s.*
10. 5, he that gathereth in *s.* is a wise son.
26. 1, as snow in *s.*
Jer. 8. 20, the *s.* is ended.
Mat. 24. 32; Mk. 13. 28, ye know *s.* is nigh.
See Dan. 2. 35; Zech. 14. 8; Lu. 21. 30.
SUMPTUOUSLY. Lu. 16. 19, fared *s.* every day.
SUN. Josh. 10. 12, *s.*, stand thou still.
Judg. 5. 31, as the *s.* in his might.
Job 8. 16, hypocrite is green before the *s.*
Ps. 58. 8, that they may not see the *s.*
84. 11, a *s.* and shield.
121. 6, the *s.* shall not smite thee.
Eccl. 1. 9, no new thing under the *s.*
11. 7, a pleasant thing it is to behold the *s.*
12. 2, while the *s.* or stars be not darkened.
Cant. 1. 6, because the *s.* hath looked upon me.
6. 10, clear as the *s.*
Jer. 15. 9, her *s.* is gone down while yet day.
Joel 2. 10; 3. 15, the *s.* be darkened.
Mal. 4. 2, the *S.* of righteousness.
Mat. 5. 45, maketh his *s.* to rise on evil.
13. 43, then shall righteous shine as *s.*
Eph. 4. 26, let not *s.* go down on your wrath.
See 1 Cor. 15. 41; Jas. 1. 11; Rev. 7. 16; 21. 23.
SUPERFLUITY. Jas. 1. 21, *s.* of naughtiness.
SUPPLICATION. 1 Kings 9. 3, I have heard thy *s.*
Job 9. 15, I would make *s.* to my judge.
Ps. 6. 9, the Lord hath heard my *s.*
Dan. 9. 3, to seek by prayer and *s.*
Zech. 12. 10, spirit of grace and *s.*
Eph. 6. 18, with all prayer and *s.*
1 Tim. 2. 1, that *s.* be made for all men.
See Ps. 28. 6; 31. 22; Phil. 4. 6; Heb. 5. 7.
SUPPLY. Phil. 1. 19; 2. 30; 4. 19.
SUPPORT. Acts 20. 35; 1 Thess. 5. 14.
SUPREME. 1 Pet. 2. 13, to the king as *s.*
SURE. Num. 32. 23, be *s.* your sin will find you out.
Job 24. 22, no man is *s.* of life.
Prov. 6. 3, make *s.* thy friend.
Isa. 55. 3; Acts 13. 34, the *s.* mercies of David.
2 Tim. 2. 19, the foundation of God standeth *s.*
See Isa. 33. 16; Heb. 6. 19; 2 Pet. 1. 10, 19.
SURFEITING. Lu. 21. 34, overcharged with *s.*
SURPRISED. Isa. 33. 14; Jer. 48. 41; 51. 41.
SUSTAIN. Ps. 3. 5; 55. 22; Prov. 18. 14; Isa. 59. 16.
SWALLOW. Ps. 84. 3, the *s.* a nest for her young.
Prov. 26. 2, as the *s.* by flying.
Isa. 38. 14, like a crane or a *s.*
Jer. 8. 7, the *s.* observe the time.
SWAN. Lev. 11. 8; Deut. 14. 16, and the *s.*
SWEAR. Ps. 15. 4, that *s.* to his hurt.
Eccl. 9. 2, he that *s.*, as he that feareth an oath.
Isa. 45. 23, to me every tongue shall *s.*
65. 16, shall *s.* by the God of truth.
Jer. 4. 2, *s.*, the Lord liveth, in truth.
23. 10, because of *s.* the land mourneth.
Hos. 4. 2, by *s.*, and lying, they break out.
10. 4, *s.* falsely in making a covenant.
Zech. 5. 3, every one that *s.* shall be cut off.
Mal. 3. 5, a witness against false *s.*
See Zeph. 1. 5; Mat. 26. 74; Heb. 6. 13.
SWEAT. Gen. 3. 19; Ezek. 44. 18; Lu. 22. 44.
SWEET. Job 20. 12, though wickedness be *s.*
Ps. 55. 14, we took *s.* counsel together.
104. 34, my meditation shall be *s.*
Prov. 3. 24, thy sleep shall be *s.*
9. 17, stolen waters are *s.*
13. 19, desire accomplished is *s.*
16. 24, pleasant words are *s.*
27. 7, to the hungry every bitter thing is *s.*
Eccl. 5. 12, sleep of labouring man is *s.*
11. 7, truly the light is *s.*
Cant. 2. 3, his fruit was *s.* to my taste.
Isa. 5. 20, put bitter for *s.*, and *s.* for bitter.
23. 16, make *s.* melody.
Jas. 3. 11, at same place *s.* water and bitter.
See Judg. 14. 18; Mic. 6. 15; Mk. 16. 1.
SWELLING. Jer. 12. 5; 2 Pet. 2. 18; Jude 16.
SWIFT. Eccl. 9. 11, the race is not to the *s.*
Amos 2. 15, the *s.* of foot shall not deliver.
Rom. 3. 15, feet *s.* to shed blood.
See Job 7. 6; 9. 25; Jer. 46. 6; Mal. 3. 5.
SWIM. 2 Kings 6. 6, iron did *s.*
Ezek. 47. 5, waters to *s.* in.
See Ps. 6. 6; Isa. 25. 11; Ezek. 32. 6; Acts 27. 42.
SWOLLEN. Acts 28. 6, when he should have *s.*
SWOON. Lam. 2. 11, children *s.* in the streets.
SWORD. Ps. 57. 4, their tongue a sharp *s.*
Isa. 2. 4, nation shall not lift up *s.*
Ezek. 7. 15, the *s.* is without, pestilence within.
Mat. 10. 34, not to send peace, but a *s.*
Lu. 2. 35, a *s.* shall pierce thy own soul.
Rom. 13. 4, he beareth not the *s.* in vain.
Eph. 6. 17, the *s.* of the Spirit.
Heb. 4. 12, sharper than twoedged *s.*
Rev. 1. 16; 19. 15, out of his mouth a sharp *s.*
13. 10, that killeth with *s.* must be killed with *s.*
See Isa. 2. 4; Joel 3. 10; Mic. 4. 3; Lu. 22. 38.

T

TABERNACLE. Ps. 15. 1, abide in thy *t.*
27. 5, in secret of his *t.* shall he hide me.
84. 1, how amiable are thy *t.*!
Isa. 33. 20, a *t.* that shall not be taken down.
See Job 5. 24; Prov. 14. 11; 2 Cor. 5. 1.
TABLE. Ps. 23. 5, thou preparest a *t.*
69. 22, let their *t.* become a snare.
78. 19, can God furnish a *t.* in the wilderness?
128. 3, like olive plants about thy *t.*

Prov. 9. 2, wisdom hath furnished her *t.*
Mat. 15. 27; Mk. 7. 28, from their masters' *t.*
Acts 6. 2, leave word of God, and serve *t.*
2 Cor. 3. 3, fleshy *t.* of the heart.
See Prov. 3. 3; Jer. 17. 1; Mal. 1. 7; 1 Cor. 10. 21.
TABRET. Gen. 31. 27; 1 Sam. 18. 6; Isa. 5. 12, the *t.*
TAKE. Ex. 6. 7, I will *t.* you to me for a people.
34. 9, *t.* us for thine inheritance.
Judg. 19. 30, *t.* advice, and speak your minds.
2 Kings 19. 30; Isa. 37. 31, shall yet *t.* root.
Job 23. 10, he knoweth the way that I *t.*
Ps. 51. 11, *t.* not thy holy spirit from me.
116. 13, I will *t.* the cup of salvation.
Cant. 2. 15, *t.* us the foxes, the little foxes.
Isa. 33. 23, the lame *t.* the prey.
Hos. 14. 2, *t.* with you words.
Amos 9. 2, thence shall mine hand *t.* them.
Mat. 6. 25, 28, 31, 34; 10. 19; Mk. 13. 11; Lu. 12. 11, 22, 26, *t.* no thought.
11. 29, *t.* my yoke.
16. 5; Mk. 8. 14, forgotten to *t.* bread.
18. 16, then *t.* with thee one or two more.
20. 14, *t.* that thine is, and go thy way.
26. 26; Mk. 14. 22; 1 Cor. 11. 24, *t.*, eat; this is my body.
Lu. 6. 29, forbid him not to *t.* thy coat also.
12. 19, soul, *t.* thine ease.
John 16. 15, he shall *t.* of mine.
1 Cor. 6. 7, why do ye not rather *t.* wrong?
1 Tim. 3. 5, how shall he *t.* care of the church?
1 Pet. 2. 20, if ye *t.* it patiently.
Rev. 3. 11, that no man *t.* thy crown.
See John 1. 29; 10. 18; 1 Cor. 10. 13; Rev. 22. 19.
TALE. Ps. 90. 9; Lu. 24. 11.
TALK. Deut. 5. 24, God doth *t.* with man.
6. 7, *t.* of them when thou sittest.
Job 11. 2, a man full of *t.*
13. 7, will ye *t.* deceitfully for him?
15. 3, reason with unprofitable *t.*
Ps. 71. 24, *t.* of thy righteousness.
145. 11, *t.* of thy power.
Prov. 6. 22, it shall *t.* with thee.
Jer. 12. 1, let me *t.* with thee of thy judgments.
Ezek. 3. 22, arise, and I will *t.* with thee there.
Mat. 22. 15, they might entangle him in his *t.*
Lu. 24. 32, while he *t.* with us by the way.
John 9. 37, it is he that *t.* with thee.
See Prov. 14. 23; John 14. 30; Eph. 5. 4.
TALL. Deut. 1. 28; 2. 10; 2 Kings 19. 23.
TAME. Mk. 5. 4; Jas. 3. 7, 8.
TARE. 2 Sam. 13. 31; 2 Kings 2. 24; Mk. 9. 20.
TARRY. Gen. 27. 44, and *t.* a few days.
Ex. 12. 39, were thrust out, and could not *t.*
2 Kings 7. 9, if we *t.* till morning light.
9. 3, flee, and *t.* not.
Ps. 68. 12, she that *t.* at home divided the spoil.
101. 7, he that telleth lies shall not *t.* in my sight.
Prov. 23. 30, they that *t.* long at the wine.
Isa. 46. 13, my salvation shall not *t.*
Jer. 14. 8, that turneth aside to *t.* for a night.
Hab. 2. 3, though it *t.*, wait for it.
Mat. 25. 5, while the bridegroom *t.*
26. 38; Mk. 14. 34, *t.* here and watch.
Lu. 24. 29, he went in to *t.* with them.
49, *t.* ye in city of Jerusalem until endued.
John 21. 22, if I will that he *t.*
Acts 22. 16, why *t.* thou, arise, and be baptized.
1 Cor. 11. 33, *t.* one for another.
Heb. 10. 37, will come, and will not *t.*
See 1 Sam. 30. 24; Mic. 5. 7; John 3. 22.
TASKMASTERS. Ex. 1. 11, they did set over them *t.*
5. 6, the *t.* of the people.
TASTE. Num. 11. 8, the *t.* of it as *t.* of fresh oil.
Job 6. 6, is any *t.* in white of egg?
12. 11, doth not the mouth *t.* his meat?
34. 3, trieth words as mouth *t.* meat.
Ps. 34. 8, *t.* and see that the Lord is good.
119. 103, how sweet are thy words to my *t.*!
Jer. 48. 11, his *t.* remained in him.
Mat. 16. 28; Mk. 9. 1; Lu. 9. 27, some, which shall not *t.* death.
Lu. 14. 24, none bidden shall *t.* of my supper.
John 8. 52, keep my saying, shall never *t.* of death.
Col. 2. 21, touch not, *t.* not.
Heb. 2. 9, *t.* death for every man.
6. 4, and have *t.* of the heavenly gift.
1 Pet. 2. 3, have *t.* that the Lord is gracious.
See 1 Sam. 14. 43; 2 Sam. 19. 35; Mat. 27. 34.
TATTLERS. 1 Tim. 5. 13, *t.* and busybodies.
TAUGHT. Judg. 8. 16, he *t.* the men of Succoth.
2 Chron. 6. 27, thou hast *t.* them the good way.
23. 13, such as *t.* to sing praise.
Ps. 71. 17; 119. 102, thou hast *t.* me.
Prov. 4. 4, he *t.* me also, and said.
11, I have *t.* thee in way of wisdom.
Eccl. 12. 9, he still *t.* the people knowledge.
Isa. 29. 13, their fear is *t.* by precept of men.
54. 13, all thy children shall be *t.* of God.
Jer. 12. 16, as they *t.* my people to swear by Baal.
32. 33, *t.* them, rising up early.
Zech. 13. 5, *t.* me to keep cattle.
Mat. 7. 29; Mk. 1. 22, *t.* as one having authority.
28. 15, and did as they were *t.*
Lu. 13. 26, thou hast *t.* in our streets.
John 6. 45, they shall be all *t.* of God.
8. 28, as my Father hath *t.* me.
Gal. 1. 12, nor was I *t.* it, except by revelation.
6. 6, let him that is *t.* in the word.
Eph. 4. 21, if so be ye have been *t.* by him.
2 Thess. 2. 15, the traditions ye have been *t.*
See Col. 2. 7; 1 Thess. 4. 9; Tit. 1. 9; 1 John 2. 27.
TAUNT. Jer. 24. 9; Ezek. 5. 15; Hab. 2. 6.
TEACH. Ex. 4. 15, I will *t.* you.
Deut. 4. 10, that they may *t.* their children.
6. 7; 11. 19, *t.* them diligently.
Judg. 13. 8, *t.* us what we shall do to the child.
1 Sam. 12. 23, I will *t.* you the good way.
2 Sam. 1. 18, bade them *t.* the use of the bow.
2 Chron. 15. 3, without a *t.* priest.
Job 6. 24, *t.* me, and I will hold my tongue.
8. 10, thy fathers, shall not they *t.* thee?
12. 7, ask the beasts, and they shall *t.* thee.
34. 32, that which I see not *t.* thou me.
36. 22, God exalteth, who *t.* like him?
Ps. 25. 4, *t.* me thy paths.
8, he will *t.* sinners in the way.
27. 11; 86. 11, *t.* me thy way, and lead me.
34. 11, I will *t.* you the fear of the Lord.
51. 13, then will I *t.* transgressors.
90. 12, so *t.* us to number our days.
94. 12, blessed is the man whom thou *t.*
Prov. 6. 13, the wicked man *t.* with his finger.
Isa. 2. 3; Mic. 4. 2, he will *t.* us of his ways.
28. 9, whom shall he *t.* knowledge?
26, God doth *t.* him discretion.
48. 17, I am thy God which *t.* thee to profit.
Jer. 9. 20, and *t.* your daughters wailing.
Ezek. 44. 23, *t.* my people the difference.
Mic. 3. 11, priests *t.* for hire.
Mat. 28. 19, *t.* all nations.
Lu. 11. 1, *t.* us to pray.
12. 12, the Holy Ghost shall *t.* you.
John 9. 34, dost thou *t.* us?
14. 26, shall *t.* you all things.
Acts 5. 42, they ceased not to *t.* and preach.
Rom. 12. 7, he that *t.*, on *t.*
1 Cor. 4. 17, as I *t.* every where.
11. 14, doth not even nature *t.* you?
14. 19, that by my voice I might *t.* others.
Col. 1. 28, *t.* every man in all wisdom.
3. 16, *t.* and admonishing one another.
1 Tim. 1. 3, charge some that they *t.* no other.
2. 12, I suffer not a woman to *t.*
3. 2; 2 Tim. 2. 24, apt to *t.*
4. 11, these things command and *t.*
6. 2, these things *t.* and exhort.
2 Tim. 2. 2, faithful men, able to *t.*
Tit. 1. 11, *t.* things they ought not.

Tit. 2. 4, *t.* young women to be sober.
12, *t.* us, that denying ungodliness.
Heb. 5. 12, ye have need that one *t.* you again.
See Mat. 22. 16; Mk. 6. 34; 12. 14; Rev. 2. 20.
TEACHER. 1 Chron. 25. 8, as well *t.* as scholar.
Ps. 119. 99, more understanding than all my *t.*
Prov. 5. 13, have not obeyed the voice of my *t.*
Isa. 30. 20, thine eyes shall see thy *t.*
Hab. 2. 18, a *t.* of lies.
John 3. 2, a *t.* come from God.
Rom. 2. 20, thou art a *t.* of babes.
1 Cor. 12. 29, are all *t.*?
Eph. 4. 11, evangelists, pastors, and *t.*
1 Tim. 1. 7, desiring to be *t.* of the law.
Tit. 2. 3, aged women, *t.* of good things.
See 1 Tim. 2. 7; 2 Tim. 1. 11; Heb. 5. 12; 2 Pet. 2. 1.
TEAR. Job 16. 9, he *t.* me in his wrath.
18. 4, he *t.* himself in his anger.
Ps. 7. 2, lest he *t.* my soul.
35. 15, they did *t.* me, and ceased not.
50. 22, lest I *t.* you in pieces.
Hos. 5. 14, I will *t.* and go away.
See Mic. 5. 8; Zech. 11. 16; Mk. 9. 18; Lu. 9. 39.
TEARS. 2 Kings 20. 5; Isa. 38. 5, I have seen thy *t.*
Job 16. 20, mine eye poureth out *t.*
Ps. 6. 6, I water my couch with *t.*
39. 12, hold not thy peace at my *t.*
42. 3, *t.* have been my meat.
56. 8, put thou my *t.* into thy bottle.
80. 5, the bread of *t.*, and *t.* to drink.
116. 8, thou hast delivered mine eyes from *t.*
126. 5, they that sow in *t.*
Isa. 16. 9, I will water thee with my *t.*
25. 8, will wipe away *t.*
Jer. 9. 1, oh that mine eyes were a fountain of *t.*!
13. 17; 14. 17, mine eyes run down with *t.*
31. 16, refrain thine eyes from *t.*
Lam. 1. 2, her *t.* are on her cheeks.
2. 11, mine eyes do fail with *t.*
Ezek. 24. 16, neither shall thy *t.* run down.
Mal. 2. 13, covering the altar with *t.*
Lu. 7. 38, to wash his feet with her *t.*
Acts 20. 19, serving the Lord with many *t.*
31, ceased not to warn with *t.*
2 Tim. 1. 4, being mindful of thy *t.*
See 2 Cor. 2. 4; Heb. 5. 7; 12. 17; Rev. 7. 17.
TEDIOUS. Acts 24. 4, that I be not further *t.*
TEETH. Gen. 49. 12, *t.* white with milk.
Num. 11. 33, flesh yet between their *t.*
Job 19. 20, escaped with the skin of my *t.*
Prov. 10. 26, as vinegar to the *t.*
Isa. 41. 15, an instrument having *t.*
Jer. 31. 29; Ezek. 18. 2, *t.* set on edge.
Amos 4. 6, cleanness of *t.*
See Mic. 3. 5; Zech. 9. 7; Mat. 27. 44; Rev. 9. 8.
TELL. Gen. 15. 5, *t.* the stars.
32. 29, *t.* me thy name.
2 Sam. 1. 20, *t.* it not in Gath.
Ps. 48. 12, *t.* the towers thereof.
50. 12, if I were hungry, I would not *t.* thee.
Eccl. 6. 12; 10. 14, who can *t.* what shall be after?
10. 20, that which hath wings shall *t.*
Jonah 3. 9, who can *t.* if God will turn?
Mat. 18. 15, *t.* him his fault.
17, *t.* it unto the church.
21. 27; Mk. 11. 33; Lu. 20. 8, neither *t.* I you.
Mk. 5. 19, *t.* how great things.
11. 33; Lu. 20. 7, we cannot *t.*
Lu. 13. 32, *t.* that fox.
John 3. 8, canst not *t.* whence.
12, if I *t.* you of heavenly things.
4. 25, he will *t.* us all things.
18. 34, did others *t.* it thee of me?
Acts 17. 21, either to *t.* or hear some new thing.
See Ps. 56. 8; Isa. 19. 12; Mat. 28. 7; 2 Cor. 12. 2.
TEMPER. Ex. 29. 2; 30. 35; Ezek. 46. 14; 1 Cor. 12. 24.
TEMPEST. Job 9. 17, breaketh me with a *t.*
Ps. 11. 6, on wicked he shall rain a *t.*
55. 8, hasten from windy storm and *t.*
Isa. 32. 2, a covert from the *t.*
Heb. 12. 18, not come to darkness and *t.*
2 Pet. 2. 17, clouds carried with a *t.*
TEMPESTUOUS. Ps. 50. 3; Jonah 1. 11; Acts 27. 14.
TEMPLE. 2 Sam. 22. 7, hear my voice out of his *t.*
Neh. 6. 10, meet together in the *t.*
Ps. 27. 4, to enquire in his *t.*
29. 9, in his *t.* doth every one speak of his glory.
Isa. 6. 1, his train filled the *t.*
Amos 8. 3, songs of the *t.* shall be howlings.
Mal. 3. 1, the Lord shall suddenly come to his *t.*
Mat. 12. 6, one greater than the *t.*
John 2. 19, destroy this *t.*
1 Cor. 3. 16; 6. 19; 2 Cor. 6. 16, ye are the *t.* of God.
See Hos. 8. 14; Rev. 7. 15; 11. 19; 21. 22.
TEMPORAL. 2 Cor. 4. 18, things seen are *t.*
TEMPT. Gen. 22. 1, God did *t.* Abraham.
Ex. 17. 2, wherefore do ye *t.* the Lord?
Num. 14. 22, have *t.* me these ten times.
Deut. 6. 16; Mat. 4. 7; Lu. 4. 12, ye shall not *t.* the Lord your God.
Ps. 78. 18, they *t.* God in their heart.
Isa. 7. 12, I will not ask, neither *t.* the Lord.
Mal. 3. 15, they that *t.* God are delivered.
Mat. 22. 18; Mk. 12. 15; Lu. 20. 23, why *t.* ye me?
Lu. 10. 25, a lawyer, *t.* him.
Acts 5. 9, agreed together to *t.* the Spirit.
15. 10, why *t.* ye God to put a yoke?
1 Cor. 10. 13, will not suffer you to be *t.*
Gal. 6. 1, considering thyself, lest thou be *t.*
Heb. 2. 18, hath suffered, being *t.*
4. 15, in all points *t.* like as we are.
Jas. 1. 13, cannot be *t.*, neither *t.* he any man.
See Mat. 4. 1; Mk. 1. 13; Lu. 4. 2; John 8. 6.
TEMPTATION. Mat. 6. 13, lead us not into *t.*
26. 41; Mk. 14. 38; Lu. 22. 46, lest ye enter into *t.*
Lu. 8. 13, in time of *t.* fall away.
1 Cor. 10. 13, there hath no *t.* taken you.
Gal. 4. 14, my *t.* in flesh ye despised not.
1 Tim. 6. 9, they that will be rich fall into *t.*
Jas. 1. 2, when ye fall into divers *t.*
2 Pet. 2. 9, how to deliver out of *t.*
See Lu. 11. 4; Acts 20. 19; 1 Pet. 1. 6; Rev. 3. 10.
TEMPTER. Mat. 4. 3, and when the *t.* came to him.
1 Thess. 3. 5, the *t.* have tempted you.
TEND. Prov. 11. 19; 14. 23; 19. 23; 21. 5.
TENDER. Deut. 28. 54, man that is *t.*
32. 2, distil as small rain on *t.* herb.
2 Kings 22. 19; 2 Chron. 34. 27, thy heart was *t.*
Job 14. 7, the *t.* branch will not cease.
Prov. 4. 3, *t.* in sight of my mother.
Cant. 2. 13, 15; 7. 12, vines with *t.* grapes.
Isa. 47. 1, no more be called *t.*
53. 2, grow up before him as a *t.* plant.
Dan. 1. 9, God brought Daniel into *t.* love.
Lu. 1. 78, through the *t.* mercy of our God.
Eph. 4. 32, be kind and *t.*-hearted.
Jas. 5. 11, the Lord is pitiful, and of *t.* mercy.
See 1 Chron. 22. 5; Ezek. 17. 22; Mk. 13. 28.
TENOR. Gen. 43. 7; Ex. 34. 27.
TENT. Gen. 9. 21, was uncovered within his *t.*
27, he shall dwell in the *t.* of Shem.
12. 8, and pitched his *t.*
25. 27, a plain man, dwelling in *t.*
Num. 24. 5, how goodly are thy *t.*!
1 Sam. 4. 10; 2 Sam. 18. 17, fled every man to his *t.*
1 Kings 12. 16, to your *t.*, O Israel.
Ps. 84. 10, than to dwell in *t.* of wickedness.
Isa. 38. 12, removed as a shepherd's *t.*
54. 2, enlarge the place of thy *t.*
Jer. 10. 20, there is none to stretch forth my *t.*
Acts 18. 3, by occupation they were *t.*-makers.
See Isa. 40. 22; Jer. 4. 20; 35. 7; Zech. 12. 7; Heb. 11. 9.

TENTH. Gen. 28. 22; Lev. 27. 32; Isa. 6. 13.
TERRIBLE. Ex. 34. 10, a *t.* thing I will do.
Deut. 1. 19; 8. 15, that *t.* wilderness.
7. 21; 10. 17; Neh. 1. 5; 4. 14; 9. 32, a mighty God and *t.*
10. 21, hath done for thee *t.* things.
Judg. 13. 6, like an angel of God, very *t.*
Job 37. 22, with God is *t.* majesty.
39. 20, the glory of his nostrils is *t.*
Ps. 45. 4, thy right hand shall teach thee *t.* things.
65. 5, by *t.* things in righteousness.
66. 3, say unto God, how *t.* art thou!
5, *t.* in his doing.
68. 35, *t.* out of thy holy places.
76. 12, he is *t.* to the kings of the earth.
99. 3, thy great and *t.* name.
145. 6, the might of thy *t.* acts.
Cant. 6. 4, *t.* as an army with banners.
Isa. 25. 4, blast of the *t.* ones.
64. 3, when thou didst *t.* things.
Jer. 15. 21, redeem thee out of hand of the *t.*
Joel 2. 11, the day of the Lord is very *t.*
Heb. 12. 21, so *t.* was the sight.
See Lam. 5. 10; Ezek. 1. 22; 28. 7; Dan. 7. 7.
TERRIBLENESS. Deut. 26. 8; 1 Chron. 17. 21; Jer. 49. 16.
TERRIBLY. Isa. 2. 19, 21; Nah. 2. 3.
TERRIFY. Job 9. 34, let not his fear *t.*
Lu. 21. 9, when ye hear of wars, be not *t.*
24. 37, they were *t.* and affrighted.
Phil. 1. 28, in nothing *t.* by adversaries.
See Job 7. 14; 2 Cor. 10. 9.
TERROR. Gen. 35. 5; Job 6. 4, the *t.* of God.
Deut. 32. 25, the sword without and *t.* within.
Josh. 2. 9, your *t.* is fallen upon us.
Job 18. 11, *t.* shall make him afraid.
24. 17, in the *t.* of the shadow of death.
31. 23, destruction was a *t.* to me.
33. 7, my *t.* shall not make thee afraid.
Ps. 55. 4, the *t.* of death are fallen upon me.
73. 19, utterly consumed with *t.*
91. 5, afraid for the *t.* by night.
Jer. 17. 17, be not a *t.* to me.
20. 4, a *t.* to thyself.
Ezek. 26. 21; 27. 36; 28. 19, I will make thee a *t.*
Rom. 13. 3, rulers are not *t.* to good works.
2 Cor. 5. 11, knowing the *t.* of the Lord.
See Jer. 15. 8; Lam. 2. 22; Ezek. 21. 12; 1 Pet. 3. 14.
TESTIFY. Num. 35. 30, one witness shall not *t.*
Deut. 31. 21, this song shall *t.* against them.
Ruth 1. 21, seeing the Lord hath *t.* against me.
2 Sam. 1. 16, thy mouth hath *t.* against thee.
Neh. 9. 30, *t.* against them by thy spirit.
Job 15. 6, thine own lips *t.* against thee.
Isa. 59. 12, our sins *t.* against us.
Hos. 5. 5; 7. 10, the pride of Israel doth *t.*
Mic. 6. 3, what have I done? *t.* against me.
Lu. 16. 28, send Lazarus, that he may *t.*
John 2. 25, needed not that any should *t.*
3. 32, seen and heard, that he *t.*
5. 39, they *t.* of me.
7. 7, because I *t.* of it.
15. 26, he shall *t.* of me.
21. 24, the disciple which *t.* of these things.
Acts 23. 11, as thou hast *t.* in Jerusalem.
1 Tim. 2. 6, gave himself to be *t.* in due time.
1 Pet. 1. 11, it *t.* beforehand the sufferings.
1 John 4. 14, we have seen and do *t.*
See 1 Cor. 15. 15; 1 Thess. 4. 6; Rev. 22. 16.
TESTIMONY. 2 Kings 17. 15, rejected his *t.*
Ps. 93. 5, thy *t.* are sure.
119. 22, I have kept thy *t.*
24, thy *t.* are my delight.
46, I will speak of thy *t.*
59, I turned my feet to thy *t.*
119, I love thy *t.*
129, thy *t.* are wonderful.
Isa. 8. 16, bind up the *t.*
20, to the law and to the *t.*
Mat. 10. 18; Mk. 13. 9, for a *t.* against them.
Lu. 21. 13, it shall turn to you for a *t.*
John 3. 32, no man receiveth his *t.*
21. 24, we know that his *t.* is true.
Acts 14. 3, *t.* to the word of his grace.
1 Cor. 2. 1, declaring the *t.* of God.
2 Cor. 1. 12, the *t.* of our conscience.
2 Tim. 1. 8, be not ashamed of the *t.*
Heb. 11. 5, Enoch had this *t.*
See Rev. 1. 2; 6. 9; 11. 7; 12. 11; 19. 10.
THANK. Mat. 11. 25; Lu. 10. 21; 18. 11; John 11. 41, I *t.* thee.
Acts 28. 15, *t.* God, and took courage.
1 Cor. 1. 4, I *t.* God on your behalf.
2 Thess. 1. 3, we are bound to *t.* God.
1 Tim. 1. 12, I *t.* Jesus Christ.
See 1 Chron. 23. 30; Dan. 2. 23; Rom. 6. 17.
THANKS. Neh. 12. 31, companies that gave *t.*
Mat. 26. 27; Lu. 22. 17, took the cup, and gave *t.*
Lu. 2. 38, Anna gave *t.* to the Lord.
Rom. 14. 6, eateth to the Lord, for he giveth *t.*
1 Cor. 15. 57, *t.* be to God, who giveth us the victory.
Eph. 5. 20, giving *t.* always for all things.
1 Thess. 3. 9, what *t.* can we render?
Rev. 4. 9, give *t.* to him that sat on the throne.
See 2 Cor. 1. 11; 2. 14; 8. 16; 9. 15; Heb. 13. 15.
THANKSGIVING. Ps. 26. 7, the voice of *t.*
95. 2, come before his face with *t.*
Isa. 51. 3, *t.* and melody shall be found therein.
Amos 4. 5, offer a sacrifice of *t.*
Phil. 4. 6, with *t.* let your requests be made.
Col. 4. 2, watch in the same with *t.*
1 Tim. 4. 3, to be received with *t.*
See Neh. 11. 17; 12. 8; 2 Cor. 4. 15; 9. 11.
THAT. Gen. 18. 25, *t.* be far from thee.
Num. 24. 13; 1 Kings 22. 14, *t.* will I speak.
Job 23. 13, even *t.* he doeth.
Ps. 27. 4, *t.* will I seek after.
Zech. 11. 9, *t. t.* dieth, let it die.
Mat. 10. 15; Mk. 6. 11, than for *t.* city.
13. 12; 25. 29; Mk. 4. 25, *t.* he hath.
John 1. 8, he was not *t.* light.
5. 12, what man is *t.* which said?
13. 27, *t.* thou doest, do quickly.
21. 22, what is *t.* to thee?
Rom. 7. 19, the evil which I would not, *t.* I do.
Jas. 4. 15, we shall live, and do this or *t.*
See Mk. 13. 11; 1 Cor. 11. 23; 2 Cor. 8. 12; Philem. 18.
THEN. Gen. 4. 26, *t.* began men to call.
Josh. 14. 12, if the Lord be with me, *t.* I shall be able.
Ps. 27. 10, *t.* the Lord will take me up.
55. 12, *t.* I could have borne it.
Isa. 58. 8, *t.* shall thy light break forth.
Ezek. 39. 28, *t.* shall they know.
Mat. 5. 24, *t.* come and offer thy gift.
19. 25; Mk. 10. 26, who *t.* can be saved?
24. 14, *t.* shall the end come.
2 Cor. 12. 10, *t.* am I strong.
See 1 Cor. 4. 5; 13. 12; 1 Thess. 5. 3; 2 Thess. 2. 8.
THESE. Ex. 32. 4, *t.* be thy gods, O Israel.
Eccl. 7. 10, former days better than *t.*
Isa. 60. 8, who are *t.* that fly?
Mat. 5. 37, whatsoever is more than *t.*
23, 23, *t.* ought ye to have done.
25. 40, one of the least of *t.*
John 17. 20, neither pray I for *t.* alone.
21. 15, lovest thou me more than *t.*?
See Job 26. 14; Ps. 73. 12; Jer. 7. 4.
THICK. Deut. 32. 15, thou art grown *t.*
2 Sam. 18. 9, the mule went under the *t.* boughs.
Ps. 74. 5, lifted up axes on the *t.* trees.
Ezek. 31. 3, top was among *t.* boughs.
Hab. 2. 6, ladeth himself with *t.* clay.
See 1 Kings 12. 10; 2 Chron. 10. 10; Neh. 8. 15; Job 15. 26.
THICKET. Gen. 22. 13; Isa. 9. 18; Jer. 4. 7, 29.
THIEF. Ps. 50. 18, when thou sawest a *t.*

Jer. 2. 26, as the *t.* is ashamed.
Joel 2. 9, enter at windows like a *t.*
Lu. 12. 33, where no *t.* approacheth.
John 10. 1, the same is a *t.* and a robber.
1 Pet. 4. 15, let none suffer as a *t.*
See Prov. 6. 30; 29. 24; Mat. 24. 43.
THIEVES. Isa. 1. 23; Lu. 10. 30; John 10. 8; 1 Cor. 6. 10.
THIGH. Gen. 24. 2; 47. 29, put hand under *t.*
32. 25, touched hollow of Jacob's *t.*
Judg. 15. 8, smote them hip and *t.*
Cant. 3. 8, every man hath sword on his *t.*
See Ps. 45. 3; Jer. 31. 19; Ezek. 21. 12; Rev. 19. 16.
THINE. Gen. 31. 32, discern what is *t.*
1 Sam. 15. 28, to a neighbour of *t.*
1 Kings 20. 4, I am *t.*, and all I have.
1 Chron. 29. 11, *t.* is the greatness.
Ps. 74. 16, the day is *t.*, the night also is *t.*
119. 94, I am *t.*, save me.
Isa. 63. 19, we are *t.*
Mat. 20. 14, take that is *t.*
Lu. 4. 7, worship me, all shall be *t.*
22. 42, not my will, but *t.* be done.
John 17. 6, *t.* they were, and thou gavest them me.
10, all mine are *t.*, and *t.* are mine.
See Gen. 14. 23; Josh. 17. 18; 1 Chron. 12. 18; Lu. 15. 31.
THING. Gen. 21. 11, the *t.* was very grievous.
Ex. 18. 17, the *t.* thou doest is not good.
2 Sam. 13. 33, let not my lord take the *t.* to heart.
2 Kings 2. 10, thou hast asked a hard *t.*
Eccl. 1. 9, the *t.* that hath been.
Isa. 7. 13, is it a small *t.* to weary?
41. 12, as a *t.* of nought.
43. 19; Jer. 31. 22, a new *t.*
Mk. 1. 27, what *t.* is this?
John 5. 14, lest a worse *t.* come unto thee.
Phil. 3. 16, let us mind the same *t.*
See Heb. 10. 29; 1 Pet. 4. 12; 1 John 2. 8.
THINK. Gen. 40. 14, but *t.* on me when it shall be well.
Neh. 5. 19, *t.* on me, O my God, for good.
Ps. 40. 17, I am poor, yet the Lord *t.* on me.
Prov. 23. 7, as he *t.* in his heart, so is he.
Isa. 10. 7, nor doth his heart *t.* so.
Jonah 1. 6, if God will *t.* upon us.
Mat. 3. 9, *t.* not to say within yourselves.
6. 7, *t.* they shall be heard.
9. 4, why *t.* ye evil in your hearts?
17. 25; 22. 17, what *t.* thou?
22. 42; 26. 66; Mk. 14. 64, what *t.* ye of Christ?
Rom. 12. 3, more highly than he ought to *t.*
1 Cor. 10. 12, that *t.* he standeth.
2 Cor. 3. 5, to *t.* any thing as of ourselves.
Gal. 6. 3, if a man *t.* himself to be something.
Eph. 3. 20, able to do above all we ask or *t.*
Phil. 4. 8, *t.* on these things.
Jas. 1. 7, let not that man *t.* he shall receive.
1 Pet. 4. 12, *t.* it not strange.
See Job 35. 2; Jer. 29. 11; Ezek. 38. 10; Lu. 10. 36.
THIRST (*n.*). Ex. 17. 3, to kill us with *t.*
Deut. 29. 19, to add drunkenness to *t.*
Judg. 15. 18, now I shall die for *t.*
2 Chron. 32. 11, doth persuade you to die by *t.*
Ps. 69. 21, in my *t.* they gave me vinegar.
Isa. 41. 17, when their tongue faileth for *t.*
Amos 8. 11, not a *t.* for water, but of hearing.
2 Cor. 11. 27, in hunger and *t.* often.
See Deut. 28. 48; Job 24. 11; Ps. 104. 11.
THIRST (*v.*). Ps. 42. 2; 63. 1; 143. 6, my soul *t.* for God.
Isa. 49. 10; Rev. 7. 16, shall not hunger nor *t.*
55. 1, every one that *t.*
Mat. 5. 6, *t.* after righteousness.
John 4. 14; 6. 35, shall never *t.*
7. 37, if any man *t.*, let him come unto me.
19. 28, I *t.*
See Ex. 17. 3; Isa. 48. 21; Rom. 12. 20; 1 Cor. 4. 11.
THIRSTY. Ps. 63. 1; 143. 6, in a *t.* land.
Ps. 107. 5, hungry and *t.*, their soul fainted.
Prov. 25. 25, as cold waters to a *t.* soul.
Isa. 21. 14, brought water to him that was *t.*
29. 8, as when a *t.* man dreameth.
44. 3, pour water on him that is *t.*
65. 13, but ye shall be *t.*
See Judg. 4. 19; Isa. 32. 6; Ezek. 19. 13; Mat. 25. 35.
THISTLE. Gen. 3. 18, thorns and *t.* shall it bring forth.
Job 31. 40, let *t.* grow instead of wheat.
Mat. 7. 16, do men gather figs of *t.*?
See 2 Kings 14. 9; 2 Chron. 25. 18; Hos. 10. 8.
THORN. Num. 33. 55; Judg. 2. 3, *t.* in your sides.
Ps. 118. 12, quenched as the fire of *t.*
Prov. 15. 19, way of slothful man is as an hedge of *t.*
24. 31, it was all grown over with *t.*
26. 9, as a *t.* goeth into hand of drunkard.
Eccl. 7. 6, crackling of *t.* under a pot.
Cant. 2. 2, as the lily among *t.*
Isa. 33. 12, as *t.* cut up shall they be burned.
34. 13, and *t.* shall come up in her palaces.
55. 13, instead of the *t.* shall come up the fir tree.
Jer. 4. 3, sow not among *t.*
12. 13, but shall reap *t.*
Hos. 2. 6, I will hedge up thy way with *t.*
9. 6, *t.* shall be in their tabernacles.
10. 8, the *t.* shall come up on their altars.
Mic. 7. 4, most upright is sharper than *t.* hedge.
2 Cor. 12. 7, a *t.* in the flesh.
See Mat. 13. 7; 27. 29; Mk. 15. 17; John 19. 2.
THOUGHT (*n.*). 1 Chron. 28. 9, the Lord understandeth the *t.*
Job 4. 13, in *t.* from the visions of the night.
12. 5, despised in *t.* of him that is at ease.
42. 2, no *t.* can be withholden from thee.
Ps. 10. 4, God is not in all his *t.*
40. 5, thy *t.* cannot be reckoned.
92. 5, thy *t.* are very deep.
94. 11, the Lord knoweth the *t.* of man.
19, in the multitude of my *t.*
139. 2, thou understandest my *t.* afar off.
17, how precious are thy *t.* to me!
23, try me, and know my *t.*
Prov. 12. 5, the *t.* of the righteous are right.
16. 3, thy *t.* shall be established.
24. 9, the *t.* of foolishness is sin.
Isa. 55. 7, and the unrighteous man his *t.*
8, my *t.* are not your *t.*
9, so are my *t.* higher than your *t.*
Mic. 4. 12, they know not the *t.* of the Lord.
Mat. 6. 25, 31, 34; 10. 19; Mk. 13. 11; Lu. 12. 11, 22, take no *t.*
9. 4; 12. 25; Lu. 5. 22; 6. 8; 9. 47; 11. 17, Jesus knowing their *t.*
15. 19; Mk. 7. 21, out of the heart proceed evil *t.*
Lu. 2. 35, the *t.* of many hearts may be revealed.
24. 38, why do *t.* arise in your hearts?
Acts 8. 22, if the *t.* of thine heart may be forgiven.
1 Cor. 3. 20, the Lord knoweth the *t.* of the wise.
2 Cor. 10. 5, bringing into captivity every *t.*
Heb. 4. 12, the word of God is a discerner of the *t.*
Jas. 2. 4, ye are become judges of evil *t.*
See Gen. 6. 5; Jer. 4. 14; 23. 20; Amos 4. 13.
THOUGHT (*v.*). Gen. 48. 11, I had not *t.* to see thy face.
Num. 24. 11, I *t.* to promote thee.
Deut. 19. 19, do to him as he *t.* to have done.
2 Kings 5. 11, I *t.*, he will surely come out.
Neh. 6. 2, they *t.* to do me mischief.
Ps. 48. 9, we have *t.* of thy lovingkindness.
50. 21, thou *t.* I was such an one as thyself.
73. 16, when I *t.* to know this.
119. 59, I *t.* on my ways.
Prov. 30. 32, if thou hast *t.* evil.
Isa. 14. 24, as I have *t.*, so shall it come.

Jer. 18. 8, I will repent of the evil I *t.* to do.
Zech. 8. 14, as I *t.* to punish you.
15, I *t.* to do well.
Mal. 3. 16, for them that *t.* on his name.
Mat. 1. 20, but while he *t.* on these things.
Mk. 14. 72, when he *t.* thereon, he wept.
Lu. 12. 17, he *t.* within himself, what shall I do?
19. 11, *t.* the kingdom of God should appear.
John 11. 13, they *t.* he had spoken of taking of rest.
Acts 10. 19, while Peter *t.* on the vision.
26. 8, why should it be *t.* a thing incredible?
1 Cor. 13. 11, I *t.* as a child.
Phil. 2. 6, *t.* it not robbery to be equal with God.
See Gen. 20. 11; 50. 20; 1 Sam. 1. 13; Heb. 10. 29.
THREAD. Gen. 14. 23; Josh. 2. 18; Judg. 16. 9.
THREATEN. Acts 4. 17; 9. 1; Eph. 6. 9; 1 Pet. 2. 23.
THREEFOLD. Eccl. 4. 12, a *t.* cord.
THRESH. Isa. 41. 15, thou shalt *t.* the mountains.
Jer. 51. 33, it is time to *t.* her.
Mic. 4. 13, arise and *t.*
Hab. 3. 12, thou didst *t.* the heathen.
1 Cor. 9. 10, *t.* in hope.
See Lev. 26. 5; 1 Chron. 21. 20; Isa. 21. 10; 28. 28.
THREW. 2 Kings 9. 33; Mk. 12. 42; Lu. 9. 42; Acts 22. 23.
THROAT. Ps. 5. 9; 115. 7; Prov. 23. 2; Mat. 18. 28.
THRONE. Ps. 11. 4, the Lord's *t.* is in heaven.
94. 20, shall *t.* of iniquity have fellowship with thee?
122. 5, there are set *t.* of judgment.
Prov. 20. 28, his *t.* is upholden by mercy.
Isa. 66. 1; Acts 7. 49, heaven is my *t.*
Jer. 17. 12, a glorious high *t.* from the beginning.
Dan. 7. 9, his *t.* was like the fiery flame.
Mat. 19. 28; 25. 31, the Son of man shall sit in the *t.*
Col. 1. 16, whether they be *t.*
Heb. 4. 16, the *t.* of grace.
Rev. 3. 21, to him will I grant to sit on my *t.*
4. 2, a *t.* was set in heaven.
See Rev. 6. 16; 7. 9; 14. 3; 19. 4; 20. 11; 22. 1.
THRONG. Mk. 3. 9; 5. 31; Lu. 8. 42, 45.
THROW. Mic. 5. 11; Mal. 1. 4; Mat. 24. 2.
THRUST. Job 32. 13, God *t.* him down, not man.
Joel 2. 8, neither shall one *t.* another.
Lu. 10. 15, shall be *t.* down to hell.
13. 28, and you yourselves *t.* out.
John 20. 25, and *t.* my hand into his side.
Rev. 14. 15, *t.* in thy sickle.
See Ex. 11. 1; 1 Sam. 31. 4; Ezek. 34. 21.
TIDINGS. Ps. 112. 7, afraid of evil *t.*
Jer. 20. 15, cursed be the man who brought *t.*
Dan. 11. 44, *t.* out of the east.
Lu. 1. 19; 2. 10; 8. 1; Acts 13. 32; Rom. 10. 15, glad *t.*
See Ex. 33. 4; 1 Kings 14. 6; Jer. 49. 23.
TILL. Gen. 2. 5; Prov. 12. 11; 28. 19; Ezek. 36. 9.
TILLAGE. 1 Chron. 27. 26; Neh. 10. 37; Prov. 13. 23.
TIME. Gen. 47. 29, the *t.* drew nigh.
Job 22. 16, cut down out of *t.*
38. 23, reserved against the *t.* of trouble.
Ps. 32. 6, in a *t.* when thou mayest be found.
37. 19, not ashamed in the evil *t.*
41. 1, deliver him in *t.* of trouble.
56. 3, what *t.* I am afraid.
69. 13; Isa. 49. 8; 2 Cor. 6. 2, acceptable *t.*
89. 47, remember how short my *t.* is.
Eccl. 3. 1, there is a *t.* to every purpose.
9. 11, *t.* and chance happeneth to all.
Isa. 60. 22, I will hasten it in his *t.*
Jer. 46. 21, the *t.* of their visitation.
Ezek. 16. 8, thy *t.* was the *t.* of love.
Dan. 7. 25, a *t.* and *t.* and the dividing of *t.*
Hos. 10. 12, it is *t.* to seek the Lord.
Mal. 3. 11, neither shall vine cast fruit before the *t.*
Mat. 16. 3, the signs of the *t.*
Lu. 19. 44, the *t.* of thy visitation.
Acts 3. 19, the *t.* of refreshing.
21, the *t.* of restitution.
Rom. 13. 11, it is high *t.* to awake.
1 Cor. 7. 29, the *t.* is short.
Eph. 5. 16; Col. 4. 5, redeeming the *t.*
Heb. 4. 16, help in *t.* of need.
1 Pet. 1. 11, what manner of *t.*
Rev. 1. 3, the *t.* is at hand.
10. 6, *t.* no longer.
See Prov. 17. 17; Eph. 1. 10; 1 Tim. 4. 1.
TINGLE. 1 Sam. 3. 11; 2 Kings 21. 12; Jer. 19. 3.
TINKLING. Isa. 3. 16, 18; 1 Cor. 13. 1.
TOGETHER. Prov. 22. 2, meet *t.*
Amos 3. 3, can two walk *t.*?
Mat. 18. 20, where two or three are gathered *t.*
Rom. 8. 28, work *t.* for good.
1 Thess. 4. 17, caught up *t.*
See Mat. 19. 6; Eph. 2. 21; 2 Thess. 2. 1.
TOIL. Gen. 5. 29; 41. 51; Mat. 6. 28; Lu. 12. 27.
TOLERABLE. Mat. 10. 15; 11. 24; Mk. 6. 11; Lu. 10. 12.
TONGUE. Job 5. 21, hid from scourge of the *t.*
20. 12, hide wickedness under his *t.*
Ps. 34. 13; 1 Pet. 3. 10, keep thy *t.* from evil.
Prov. 10. 20, *t.* of the just as choice silver.
12. 18; 31. 26, *t.* of the wise is health.
19, the lying *t.* is but for a moment.
15. 4, a wholesome *t.* is a tree of life.
18. 21, death and life are in the power of the *t.*
21. 23, whoso keepeth his *t.* keepeth his soul.
25. 15, a soft *t.* breaketh the bone.
Isa. 30. 27, his *t.* as a devouring fire.
50. 4, hath given me the *t.* of the learned.
Jer. 9. 5, taught their *t.* to speak lies.
18. 18, let us smite him with the *t.*
Mk. 7. 35, his *t.* was loosed.
Jas. 1. 26, and bridleth not his *t.*
3. 5, the *t.* is a little member.
6, the *t.* is a fire.
8, the *t.* can no man tame.
1 John 3. 18, not love in word, neither in *t.*
See Ps. 45. 1; Lu. 16. 24; Rom. 14. 11; Phil. 2. 11.
TOOL. Ex. 20. 25; 32. 4; Deut. 27. 5; 1 Kings 6. 7.
TOOTH. Ex. 21. 24; Prov. 25. 19; Mat. 5. 38.
TOPAZ. Ex. 28. 17; Rev. 21. 20.
TORCHES. Nah. 2. 3; Zech. 12. 6; John 18. 3.
TORMENT. Mat. 8. 29, to *t.* before the time.
Lu. 16. 23, being in *t.*
Heb. 11. 37, destitute, afflicted, *t.*
1 John 4. 18, fear hath *t.*
Rev. 9. 5, *t.* as *t.* of a scorpion.
14. 11, the smoke of their *t.*
See Mat. 4. 24; Mk. 5. 7; Lu. 8. 28.
TORN. Gen. 44. 28, surely he is *t.* in pieces.
Ezek. 4. 14, have not eaten of that which is *t.*
Hos. 6. 1, he hath *t.*, and he will heal us.
See Isa. 5. 25; Mal. 1. 13; Mk. 1. 26.
TORTOISE. Lev. 11. 29, and the *t.* after his kind.
TOSS. Ps. 109. 23, I am *t.* up and down.
Isa. 22. 18, he will *t.* thee like a ball.
54. 11, afflicted, *t.* with tempest.
Eph. 4. 14, no more children, *t.* to and fro.
See Mat. 14. 24; Acts 27. 18; Jas. 1. 6.
TOUCH. Gen. 3. 3, nor *t.* it, lest ye die.
1 Sam. 10. 26, a band whose hearts God had *t.*
1 Chron. 16. 22; Ps. 105. 15, *t.* not mine anointed.
Job 5. 19, there shall no evil *t.* thee.
6. 7, things my soul refused to *t.*
Isa. 6. 7, lo, this hath *t.* thy lips.
Jer. 1. 9, the Lord *t.* my mouth.
Zech. 2. 8, he that *t.* you, *t.* the apple of his eye.
Mat. 9. 21; Mk. 5. 28, if I may but *t.* his garment.
Mk. 10. 13; Lu. 18. 15, children, that he should *t.* them.
John 20. 17, *t.* me not.
2 Cor. 6. 17, *t.* not the unclean thing.
Col. 2. 21, *t.* not, taste not.
See Job 19. 21; Lu. 7. 14; 11. 46; 1 Cor. 7. 1.

TOWER. 2 Sam. 22. 3; Ps. 18. 2; 144. 2, my high *t.*
Ps. 61. 3, a strong *t.* from the enemy.
Prov. 18. 10, the name of the Lord is a strong *t.*
Isa. 33. 18, where is he that counted the *t.*?
See Isa. 2. 15; 5. 2; Mic. 4. 8; Mat. 21. 33.
TRADITION. Mat. 15. 2; Mk. 7. 3, thy disciples transgress the *t.*
Gal. 1. 14, zealous of the *t.* of my fathers.
Col. 2. 8, after the *t.* of men.
1 Pet. 1. 18, received by *t.* from your fathers.
TRAFFICK. Gen. 42. 34; 1 Kings 10. 15; Ezek. 17. 4.
TRAIN. 1 Kings 10. 2; Prov. 22. 6; Isa. 6. 1.
TRAITOR. Lu. 6. 16; 2 Tim. 3. 4.
TRAMPLE. Ps. 91. 13; Isa. 63. 3; Mat. 7. 6.
TRANQUILLITY. Dan. 4. 27, lengthening of thy *t.*
TRANSFORM. Rom. 12. 2; 2 Cor. 11. 13, 14, 15.
TRANSGRESS. Num. 14. 41, wherefore do ye *t.*?
1 Sam. 2. 24, make the Lord's people to *t.*
Neh. 1. 8, if ye *t.*, I will scatter you abroad.
Ps. 17. 3, my mouth shall not *t.*
Prov. 28. 21, for a piece of bread that man will *t.*
Jer. 2. 8, the pastors *t.*
3. 13, only acknowledge that thou hast *t.*
Hab. 2. 5, he *t.* by wine.
See Mat. 15. 2; Rom. 2. 27; 1 John 3. 4; 2 John 9.
TRANSGRESSION. Ex. 34. 7; Num. 14. 18, forgiving *t.*
1 Chron. 10. 13, Saul died for his *t.*
Ezra 10. 6, he mourned because of their *t.*
Job 7. 21, why dost thou not pardon my *t.*?
13. 23, make me to know my *t.*
14. 17, my *t.* is sealed up.
31. 33, if I covered my *t.*
Ps. 19. 13, innocent from the great *t.*
25. 7, remember not my *t.*
32. 1, blessed is he whose *t.* is forgiven.
51. 1, blot out all my *t.*
65. 3, as for our *t.*, thou shalt purge them.
107. 17, fools because of their *t.* are afflicted.
Prov. 17. 9, he that covereth a *t.*
Isa. 43. 25; 44. 22, blotteth out thy *t.*
53. 5, he was wounded for our *t.*
8, for the *t.* of my people was he smitten.
58. 1, show my people their *t.*
Ezek. 18. 22, his *t.* shall not be mentioned.
Mic. 1. 5, what is the *t.* of Jacob?
See Rom. 4. 15; 5. 14; 1 Tim. 2. 14; Heb. 2. 2.
TRANSGRESSOR. Ps. 51. 13, teach *t.* thy ways.
59. 5, be not merciful to any wicked *t.*
Prov. 13. 15, the way of *t.* is hard.
21. 18, the *t.* shall be ransom for the upright.
Isa. 48. 8, thou wast called a *t.* from the womb.
53. 12; Mk. 15. 28; Lu. 22. 37, numbered with the *t.*
See Dan. 8. 23; Hos. 14. 9; Gal. 2. 18.
TRANSLATE. 2 Sam. 3. 10; Col. 1. 13; Heb. 11. 5.
TRAP. Job 18. 10; Ps. 69. 22; Jer. 5. 26; Rom. 11. 9.
TRAVAIL. Ps. 7. 14, he *t.* with iniquity.
Isa. 23. 4, I *t.* not.
53. 11, the *t.* of his soul.
Rom. 8. 22, the whole creation *t.* in pain.
Gal. 4. 19, my children, of whom I *t.*
See Job 15. 20; Isa. 13. 8; Mic. 5. 3; Rev. 12. 2.
TRAVEL. Eccl. 1. 13; 2. 23; 1 Thess. 2. 9; 2 Thess. 3. 8.
TRAVELLER. Judg. 5. 6; 2 Sam. 12. 4; Job 31. 32.
TREACHEROUS. Isa. 21. 2; Jer. 9. 2; Zeph. 3. 4.
TREACHEROUSLY. Isa. 33. 1, thou dealest *t.*
Jer 12. 1, why are they happy that deal *t.*?
Lam. 1. 2, her friends have dealt *t.* with her.
See Hos. 5. 7; 6. 7; Mal. 2. 10, 15.
TREAD. Deut. 11. 24, whereon soles of feet *t.*
Deut. 25. 4; 1 Cor. 9. 9; 1 Tim. 5. 18, not muzzle the ox when he *t.*
Ps. 7. 5, let him *t.* down my life.
44. 5, through thy name will we *t.* them under.
60. 12; 108. 13, shall *t.* down our enemies.
91. 13, thou shalt *t.* upon lion and adder.
Isa. 10. 6, to *t.* them down like mire.
16. 10, shall *t.* out no wine.
63. 3, I will *t.* them in mine anger.
Jer. 48. 33, none shall *t.* with shouting.
Ezek. 34. 18, but ye must *t.* the residue.
Hos. 10. 11, loveth to *t.* out corn.
Mal. 4. 3, ye shall *t.* down the wicked.
See Job 9. 8; Isa. 41. 25; 63. 2; Rev. 19. 15.
TREASURE. Gen. 43. 23, God hath given you *t.*
Ex. 19. 5; Ps. 135. 4, a peculiar *t.* to me.
Deut. 28. 12, open to thee his good *t.*
Job 3. 21; Ps. 17. 14; Prov. 2. 4, for hid *t.*
38. 22, the *t.* of the snow.
Prov. 8. 21, I will fill *t.* of those that love me.
10. 2, *t.* of wickedness profiteth nothing.
15. 16, than great *t.* and trouble therewith.
21. 20, there is a *t.* to be desired.
Eccl. 2. 8, I gathered the peculiar *t.* of kings.
Isa. 2. 7, neither is there any end of their *t.*
45. 3, I will give thee the *t.* of darkness.
Jer. 41. 8, slay us not, for we have *t.*
51. 13, waters abundant in *t.*
Dan. 11. 43, power over the *t.* of gold.
Mic. 6. 10, the *t.* of wickedness.
Mat. 6. 21; Lu. 12. 34, where your *t.* is.
12. 35, out of the good *t.* of the heart.
13. 44, like unto *t.* hid in a field.
52. out of his *t.* things new and old.
19. 21; Mk. 10. 21; Lu. 18. 22, thou shalt have *t.* in heaven.
Lu. 12. 21, that layeth up *t.* for himself.
Col. 2. 3, in whom are hid *t.* of wisdom.
2 Cor. 4. 7, we have this *t.* in earthen vessels.
Heb. 11. 26, greater riches than the *t.* in Egypt.
Jas. 5. 3, ye have heaped *t.*
See Deut. 32. 34; 33. 19; Isa. 33. 6; Mat. 2. 11.
TREASURER. Neh. 13. 13; Isa. 22. 15; Dan. 3. 2.
TREASURY. Mk. 12. 41, the people cast money into the *t.*
Lu. 21. 1, rich men casting their gifts into the *t.*
See Josh. 6. 19; Jer. 38. 11; Mat. 27. 6.
TREE. Deut. 20. 19, the *t.* is man's life.
Job 14. 7, there is hope of a *t.*
24. 20, wickedness shall be broken as a *t.*
Ps. 1. 3; Jer. 17. 8, like a *t.* planted.
104. 16, the *t.* of the Lord are full of sap.
Eccl. 11. 3, where the *t.* falleth.
Isa. 56. 3, I am a dry *t.*
61. 3, called *t.* of righteousness.
Ezek. 15. 2. what is the vine *t.* more than any *t.*?
31. 9, all the *t.* of Eden envied him.
See Mk. 8. 24; Lu. 21. 29; Jude 12; Rev. 7. 3.
TREMBLE. Deut. 2. 25, the nations shall *t.*
Judg. 5. 4; 2 Sam. 22. 8; Ps. 18. 7; 77. 18; 97. 4, the earth *t.*
Ezra 9. 4, then assembled to me every one that *t.*
Job 9. 6, the pillars thereof *t.*
26. 11, the pillars of heaven *t.*
Ps. 2. 11, rejoice with *t.*
60. 2, thou hast made earth to *t.*
99. 1, the Lord reigneth, let the people *t.*
104. 32, he looketh on the earth, and it *t.*
Eccl. 12. 3, the keepers of the house shall *t.*
Isa. 14. 16, is this the man that made earth *t.*?
64. 2, that the nations may *t.* at thy presence.
66. 5, ye that *t.* at his word.
Jer. 5. 22, will ye not *t.* at my presence?
33. 9, they shall *t.* for all the goodness.
Amos 8. 8, shall not the land *t.* for this?
Acts 24. 25, Felix *t.*
Jas. 2. 19, devils also believe, and *t.*
See Acts 9. 6; 16. 29; 1 Cor. 2. 3; Eph. 6. 5; Phil. 2. 12.
TRENCH. 1 Sam. 17. 20; 26. 5; 1 Kings 18. 32; Lu. 19. 43.

TRESPASS. Gen. 31. 36, what is my *t.*?
50. 17, we pray thee forgive the *t.*
Ezra 9. 2, rulers have been chief in this *t.*
Ps. 68. 21, goeth on still in his *t.*
Mat. 6. 14, if ye forgive men their *t.*
18. 15, if thy brother *t.*, tell him his fault.
Lu. 17. 3, if thy brother *t.* against thee.
2 Cor. 5. 19, not imputing their *t.*
Eph. 2. 1, dead in *t.* and sins.
Col. 2. 13, having forgiven you all *t.*
See Num. 5. 6; 1 Kings 8. 31; Ezek. 17. 20; 18. 24.
TRIAL. Job 9. 23, the *t.* of the innocent.
2 Cor. 8. 2, a great *t.* of affliction.
See Ezek. 21. 13; Heb. 11. 36; 1 Pet. 1. 7; 4. 12.
TRIBES. Ps. 105. 37, not one feeble person among their *t.*
122. 4, whither the *t.* go up.
Isa. 19. 13, they that are the stay of the *t.*
49. 6, my servant to raise up the *t.*
Hab. 3. 9, according to oaths of the *t.*
Mat. 24. 30, then shall all *t.* of the earth mourn.
See Num. 24. 2; Deut. 1. 13; 12. 5; 18. 5.
TRIBULATION. Deut. 4. 30, when thou art in *t.*
Judg. 10. 14, let them deliver you in *t.*
Mat. 13. 21, when *t.* ariseth.
24. 21, then shall be great *t.*
John 16. 33, in the world ye shall have *t.*
Acts 14. 22, through much *t.*
Rom. 5. 3, we glory in *t.* also.
12. 12, patient in *t.*
See 2 Cor. 1. 4; 7. 4; Eph. 3. 13; Rev. 7. 14.
TRIBUTARY. Deut. 20. 11; Judg. 1. 30; Lam. 1. 1.
TRIBUTE. Gen. 49. 15, a servant to *t.*
Num. 31. 37, the Lord's *t.*
Deut. 16. 10, *t.* of freewill offering.
Ezra 7. 24, not lawful to impose *t.*
Neh. 5. 4, borrowed money for king's *t.*
Prov. 12. 24, the slothful shall be under *t.*
See Mat. 17. 24; 22. 17; Lu. 23. 2.
TRIM. 2 Sam. 19. 24; Jer. 2. 33; Mat. 25. 7.
TRIUMPH. Ex. 15. 1, he hath *t.* gloriously.
Ps. 25. 2, let not mine enemies *t.*
92. 4, I will *t.* in the works of thy hands.
2 Cor. 2. 14, which always causeth us to *t.*
Col. 2. 15, a show of them openly, *t.* over them.
See 2 Sam. 20; Job 20. 5; Ps. 47. 1.
TRODDEN. Job 22. 15, the old way which wicked men have *t.*
Ps. 119. 118, thou hast *t.* down all that err.
Isa. 5. 5, the vineyard shall be *t.* down.
63. 3, I have *t.* the winepress alone.
Mic. 7. 10, now shall she be *t.* as mire.
Mat. 5. 13, salt to be *t.* under foot.
Lu. 21. 24, Jerusalem shall be *t.* down.
Heb. 10. 29, hath *t.* under foot the Son of God.
See Deut. 1. 36; Judg. 5. 21; Isa. 18. 2.
TRODE. 2 Kings 14. 9; 2 Chron. 25. 18; Lu. 12. 1.
TROOP. 2 Sam. 22. 30; Ps. 18. 29; Hos. 7. 1.
TROUBLE (*n.*). Deut. 31. 17, many *t.* shall befall.
1 Chron. 22. 14, in my *t.* I prepared for the house.
Neh. 9. 32, let not the *t.* seem little.
Job 3. 26, yet *t.* came.
5. 6, neither doth *t.* spring out of the ground.
7, man is born to *t.*
19, shall deliver thee in six *t.*
14. 1, of few days, and full of *t.*
30. 25, weep for him that was in *t.*
34. 29, he giveth quietness, who can make *t.*?
38. 23, I have reserved against the time of *t.*
Ps. 9. 9, a refuge in time of *t.*
22. 11, for *t.* is near.
25. 17, the *t.* of mine heart are enlarged.
22, redeem Israel out of all his *t.*
27. 5, in time of *t.* he shall hide me.
46. 1, a very present help in *t.*
73. 5, they are not in *t.* as other men.
88. 3, my soul is full of *t.*
Ps. 119. 143, *t.* and anguish have taken hold on me.
138. 7, though I walk in the midst of *t.*
Isa. 17. 14, at eveningtide *t.*
30. 6, into the land of *t.* they will carry riches.
65. 16, because former *t.* are forgotten.
23, they shall not bring forth for *t.*
Jer. 2. 27, in time of *t.* they will say, save us.
8. 15, we looked for health, and behold *t.*
1 Cor. 7. 28, such shall have *t.* in the flesh.
2 Cor. 1. 4, able to comfort them in *t.*
See Prov. 15. 6; 25. 19; Jer. 11. 12; 30. 7; Lam. 1. 21.
TROUBLE (*v.*). Josh 7. 25, why hast thou *t.* us?
1 Kings 18. 17, art thou he that *t.* Israel?
18, I have not *t.* Israel, but thou.
Job 4. 5, now it toucheth thee, and thou art *t.*
Ps. 3. 1, how are they increased that *t.* me!
77. 4, I am so *t.* that I cannot speak.
Prov. 25. 26, is as a *t.* fountain.
Isa. 57. 20, the wicked are like the *t.* sea.
Dan. 5. 10, let not thy thoughts *t.* thee.
11. 44, tidings out of the north shall *t.* him.
Mat. 24. 6, see that ye be not *t.*
26. 10; Mk. 14. 6, why *t.* ye the woman?
John 5. 4, an angel *t.* the water.
11. 33; 12. 27; 13. 21, Jesus groaned, and was *t.*
2 Cor. 4. 8; 7. 5, we are *t.* on every side.
Gal. 1. 7, there be some that *t.* you.
6. 17, let no man *t.* me.
See 2 Thess. 1. 7; 2. 2; Heb. 12. 15; 1 Pet. 3. 14.
TROUBLING. Job 3. 17; John 5. 4.
TRUCE. 2 Tim. 3. 3, men shall be *t.*-breakers.
TRUE. Gen. 42. 11, we are *t.* men.
1 Kings 22. 16, tell me nothing but that which is *t.*
2 Chron. 15. 3, Israel hath been without the *t.* God.
Neh. 9. 13, thou gavest them *t.* laws.
Ps. 119. 160, thy word is *t.* from the beginning.
Prov. 14. 25, a *t.* witness delivereth souls.
Jer. 10. 10, the Lord is the *t.* God.
Mat. 22. 16; Mk. 12. 14, we know that thou art *t.*
Lu. 16. 11, the *t.* riches.
John 1. 9, that was the *t.* light.
4. 23, when the *t.* worshippers.
5. 31, if I bear witness of myself, my witness is not *t.*
6. 32, the *t.* bread.
10. 41, all things that John spake were *t.*
15. 1, I am the *t.* vine.
17. 3; 1 John 5. 20, to know thee the only *t.* God.
2 Cor. 6. 8, as deceivers, and yet *t.*
Eph. 4. 24, created in *t.* holiness.
Phil. 4. 8, whatsoever things are *t.*
Heb. 10. 22, draw near with a *t.* heart.
See Rev. 3. 7; 6. 10; 15. 3; 16. 7; 19. 9, 11; 21. 5.
TRUST. Job 13. 15, though he slay me, yet will I *t.*
39. 11, wilt thou *t.* him, because his strength is great?
Ps. 25. 2; 31. 6; 55. 23; 56. 3; 143. 8, I *t.* in thee.
37. 3; 40. 3; 62. 8; 115. 9; Prov. 3. 5; Isa. 26. 4, *t.* in the Lord.
118. 8, better to *t.* in the Lord.
144. 2, he in whom I *t.*
Prov. 28. 26, he that *t.* in his own heart is a fool.
Isa. 50. 10, let him *t.* in the name of the Lord.
Jer 49. 11, let thy widows *t.* in me.
Mic. 7. 5, *t.* ye not in a friend.
Nah. 1. 7, the Lord knoweth them that *t.* in him.
Mat. 27. 43, he *t.* in God, let him deliver him.
Lu. 18. 9, certain which *t.* in themselves.
See Jer. 17. 5; 2 Cor. 1. 9; 1 Tim. 4. 10.
TRUTH. Deut. 32. 4, a God of *t.*
Ps. 15. 2, speaketh the *t.* in his heart.
51. 6, desirest *t.* in inward parts.
91. 4, his *t.* shall be thy shield.
117. 2, his *t.* endureth for ever.
119. 30, I have chosen the way of *t.*

Prov. 23. 23, buy the *t*.
Isa. 59. 14, *t*. is fallen in the streets.
Jer. 9. 3, they are not valiant for the *t*.
Zech. 8. 16, speak every man *t*. to his neighbour.
Mal. 2. 6, the law of *t*. was in his mouth.
John 1. 14, full of grace and *t*.
8. 32, know the *t*., and the *t*. shall make you free.
14. 6, I am the way, the *t*., and the life.
16. 13, Spirit of *t*. will guide you into all *t*.
18. 38, what is *t*.?
Rom. 1. 18, who hold the *t*. in unrighteousness.
1 Cor. 5. 8, unleavened bread of sincerity and *t*.
2 Cor. 13. 8, can do nothing against *t*., but for the *t*.
Eph. 4. 15, speaking the *t*. in love.
1 Tim. 3. 15, the pillar and ground of *t*.
2 Tim. 2. 15, rightly dividing the word of *t*.
Jas. 5. 19. if any err from the *t*.
See 1 Cor. 13. 6; 2 Tim. 3. 7; 1 John 3. 19; 5. 6.
TRY. 2 Chron. 32. 31, God left him, to *t*. him.
Job 23. 10, when he hath *t*. me.
Ps. 26. 2, *t*. my reins and my heart.
Jer. 9. 7; Zech. 13. 9, I will melt them and *t*. them.
1 Cor. 3. 13, shall *t*. every man's work.
Jas. 1. 12, when *t*. he shall receive the crown.
1 John 4. 1, *t*. the spirits.
See Prov. 17. 3; Isa. 28. 16; 1 Pet. 4. 12; Rev. 3. 18.
TURN. Job 23. 13, who can *t*. him.
Ps. 7. 12, if he *t*. not, he will whet his sword.
Prov. 1. 23, *t*. at my reproof.
Jer. 31. 18; Lam. 5. 21, *t*. thou me, and I shall be *t*.
Ezek. 14. 6; 18. 30; 33. 9; Hos. 12. 6; Joel 2. 12, repent, and *t*.
Zech. 9. 12, *t*. you to the strong hold, ye prisoners.
Mat. 5. 39, *t*. the other also.
Acts 26. 18, to *t*. them from darkness to light.
2 Tim. 3. 5, from such *t*. away.
See Prov. 21. 1; 26. 14; Hos. 7. 8; Lu. 22. 61; Jas. 1. 17.
TWAIN. Isa. 6. 2; Mat. 5. 41; 19. 5; Eph. 2. 15.
TWICE. Job 33. 14; Mk. 14. 30; Lu. 18. 12; Jude 12.
TWINKLING. 1 Cor. 15. 52, in the *t*. of an eye.

U

UNADVISEDLY. Ps. 106. 33, he spake *u*.
UNAWARES. Lu. 21. 34; Gal. 2. 4; Heb. 13. 2; Jude 4.
UNBELIEF. Mk. 9. 24, help thou mine *u*.
Rom. 3. 3, shall *u*. make faith without effect?
11. 32, concluded all in *u*.
Heb. 3. 12, evil heart of *u*.
See Mat. 13. 58; Mk. 6. 6; 1 Tim. 1. 13; Heb. 4. 11.
UNBLAMEABLE. Col. 1. 22; 1 Thess. 3. 13.
UNCERTAIN. 1 Cor. 9. 26; 14. 8; 1 Tim. 6. 17.
UNCLEAN. Acts 10. 28; Rom. 14. 14; 2 Cor. 6. 17.
UNCLOTHED. 2 Cor. 5. 4, not that we would be *u*.
UNCORRUPTNESS. Tit. 2. 7, in doctrine showing *u*.
UNCTION. 1 John 2. 20, an *u*. from the Holy One.
UNDEFILED. Ps. 119. 1, blessed are the *u*.
Jas. 1. 27, pure religion and *u*.
1 Pet. 1. 4, an inheritance *u*.
See Cant. 5. 2; 6. 9; Heb. 7. 26; 13. 4.
UNDER. Rom. 3. 9; 1 Cor. 9. 27; Gal. 3. 10.
UNDERSTAND. Ps. 19. 12, who can *u*. his errors?
73. 17, then *u*. I their end.
119. 100, I *u*. more than the ancients.
139. 2, thou *u*. my thought afar off.
Prov. 8. 9, all plain to him that *u*.
20. 24, how can a man *u*. his own way?
29. 19, though he *u*. he will not answer.
Isa. 6. 9, hear ye indeed, but *u*. not.
28. 19, a vexation only to *u*. the report.
Jer. 9. 24, let him glory in this, that he *u*. me.
Dan. 10. 12, thou didst set thine heart to *u*.
12. 10, wicked shall not *u*., the wise shall *u*.
Hos. 14. 9, who is wise, and he shall *u*. these things?
Mat. 13. 51, have ye *u*. all these things?
24. 15, whoso readeth, let him *u*.
Lu. 24. 45, that they might *u*. the scriptures.
John 8. 43, why do ye not *u*. my speech?
Rom. 3. 11, there is none that *u*.
15. 21, they that have not heard shall *u*.
1 Cor. 13. 2, though I *u*. all mysteries.
11, I *u*. as a child.
See 1 Cor. 14. 2; Heb. 11. 3; 2 Pet. 2. 12; 3. 16.
UNDERSTANDING. Ex. 31. 3; Deut. 4. 6, wisdom and *u*.
1 Kings 3. 11, hast asked for thyself *u*.
4. 29, gave Solomon wisdom and *u*.
7. 14, filled with wisdom and *u*.
1 Chron. 12. 32, men that had *u*. of the times.
2 Chron. 26. 5, had *u*. in visions.
Job 12. 13, he hath counsel and *u*.
20, he taketh away the *u*. of the aged.
17. 4, thou hast hid their heart from *u*.
28. 12, where is the place of *u*.?
32. 8, the Almighty giveth them *u*.
38. 36, who hath given *u*. to the heart?
39. 17, neither imparted to her *u*.
Ps. 47. 7, sing ye praises with *u*.
49. 3, the meditation of my heart shall be of *u*.
119. 34, 73, 125, 144, 169, give me *u*.
99, I have more *u*. than my teachers.
104, through thy precepts I get *u*.
147. 5, his *u*. is infinite.
Prov. 2. 2, apply thine heart to *u*.
11, *u*. shall keep thee.
3. 5, lean not to thine own *u*.
19, by *u*. hath he established the heavens.
4. 5, 7, get wisdom, get *u*.
8. 1, doth not *u*. put forth her voice?
9. 6, go in the way of *u*.
10, the knowledge of the holy is *u*.
14. 29, he that is slow to wrath is of great *u*.
16. 22, *u*. is a wellspring of life.
17. 24, wisdom is before him that hath *u*.
19. 8, he that keepeth *u*. shall find good.
21. 30, there is no *u*. against the Lord.
24. 3, by *u*. an house is established.
30. 2, have not the *u*. of a man.
Eccl. 9. 11, nor yet riches to men of *u*.
Isa. 11. 2, the spirit of *u*. shall rest on him.
27. 11, it is a people of no *u*.
29. 14, the *u*. of prudent men shall be hid.
40. 14, who showed him the way of *u*.?
28, there is no searching of his *u*.
Jer. 3. 15, pastors shall feed you with *u*.
Ezek. 28. 4, with thy *u*. thou hast gotten riches.
Dan. 4. 34, mine *u*. returned.
Mat. 15. 16; Mk. 7. 18, are ye also without *u*.?
Mk. 12. 33, to love him with all the *u*.
Lu. 2. 47, astonished at his *u*.
24. 45, then opened he their *u*.
1 Cor. 1. 19, bring to nothing *u*. of prudent.
14. 15, I will pray with the *u*. also.
20, be not children in *u*.
Eph. 4. 18, having the *u*. darkened.
Phil. 4. 7, peace of God, which passeth all *u*.
See Col. 1. 9; 2. 2; 2 Tim. 2. 7; 1 John 5. 20.
UNDERTAKE. Isa. 38. 14, *u*. for me.
UNDONE. Josh. 11. 15; Isa. 6. 5; Mat. 23. 23; Lu. 11. 42.
UNEQUAL. Ezek. 18. 25, 29; 2 Cor. 6. 14.
UNFAITHFUL. Ps. 78. 57; Prov. 25. 19.
UNFEIGNED. 2 Cor. 6. 6; 1 Tim. 1. 5; 2 Tim. 1. 5; 1 Pet. 1. 22.
UNFRUITFUL. Mat. 13. 22; Eph. 5. 11; Tit. 3. 14; 2 Pet. 1. 8.
UNGODLINESS. Rom. 1. 18; 11. 26; 2 Tim. 2. 16; Tit. 2. 12.
UNGODLY. 2 Chron. 19. 2, shouldest thou help the *u*.?

Job 16. 11, God hath delivered me to the *u.*
Ps. 1. 1, counsel of *u.*
6, the way of the *u.* shall perish.
43. 1, plead my cause against an *u.* nation.
Prov. 16. 27, an *u.* man diggeth up evil.
Rom. 5. 6, Christ died for the *u.*
1 Pet. 4. 18, where shall the *u.* appear?
2 Pet. 3. 7, perdition of *u.* men.
See Rom. 4. 5; 1 Tim. 1. 9; 2 Pet. 2. 5; Jude 15.
UNHOLY. Lev. 10. 10; 1 Tim. 1. 9; 2 Tim. 3. 2; Heb. 10. 29.
UNICORN. Num. 23. 22, he hath as it were the strength of an *u.*
Deut. 33. 17, his horns are like the horns of an *u.*
Job 39. 9. will the *u.* be willing to serve thee?
Isa. 34. 7, the *u.* shall come down with them.
UNITE. Gen. 49. 6; Ps. 86. 11.
UNITY. Ps. 133. 1; Eph. 4. 3, 13.
UNJUST. Ps. 43. 1; Prov. 11. 7; 29. 27, *u.* man.
Prov. 28. 8, he that by *u.* gain.
Zeph. 3. 5, the *u.* knoweth no shame.
Mat. 5. 44, he sendeth rain on the just and *u.*
Lu. 18. 6, hear what the *u.* judge saith.
11, not as other men, *u.*
Acts 24. 15, a resurrection both of the just and *u.*
1 Cor. 6. 1, go to law before the *u.*
1 Pet. 3. 18, suffered, the just for the *u.*
Rev. 22. 11, he that is *u.*, let him be *u.* still.
See Ps. 82. 2; Isa. 26. 10; Lu. 16. 8; 2 Pet. 2. 9.
UNKNOWN. Acts 17. 23; 1 Cor. 14. 2; 2 Cor. 6. 9; Gal. 1. 22.
UNLAWFUL. Acts 10. 28; 2 Pet. 2. 8.
UNLEARNED. Acts 4. 13; 1 Cor. 14. 16; 2 Tim. 2. 23; 2 Pet. 3. 16.
UNMINDFUL. Deut. 32. 18, thou art *u.*
UNMOVEABLE. Acts 27. 41; 1 Cor. 15. 58.
UNPERFECT. Ps. 139. 16, yet being *u.*
UNPREPARED. 2 Cor. 9. 4, find you *u.*
UNPROFITABLE. Job 15. 3, *u.* talk.
Mat. 25. 30; Lu. 17. 10, *u.* servant.
See Rom. 3. 12; Tit. 3. 9; Philem. 11; Heb. 7. 18; 13. 17.
UNPUNISHED. Prov. 11. 21; 16. 5; 17. 5; 19. 5; Jer. 25. 29; 49. 12, shall not be *u.*
See Jer. 30. 11; 46. 28.
UNQUENCHABLE. Mat. 3. 12; Lu. 3. 17.
UNREASONABLE. Acts 25. 27; 2 Thess. 3. 2.
UNREPROVEABLE. Col. 1. 22, *u.* in his sight.
UNRIGHTEOUS. Ex. 23. 1, an *u.* witness.
Isa. 10. 1, decree *u.* decrees.
55. 7, let the *u.* man forsake his thoughts.
Rom. 3. 5, is God *u.*?
Heb. 6. 10, God is not *u.* to forget your work.
See Deut. 25. 16; Ps. 71. 4; Lu. 16. 11; 1 Cor. 6. 9.
UNRIGHTEOUSNESS. Lu. 16. 9, mammon of *u.*
Rom. 1. 18, hold the truth in *u.*
2. 8, to them that obey *u.*
3. 5, if our *u.* commend righteousness.
6. 13, instruments of *u.*
9. 14, is there *u.* with God?
2 Cor. 6. 14, what fellowship with *u.*?
2 Thess. 2. 12, had pleasure in *u.*
2 Pet. 2. 13, receive the reward of *u.*
1 John 1. 9, cleanse us from all *u.*
5. 17, all *u.* is sin.
See Lev. 19. 15; Ps. 92. 15; Jer. 22. 13; John 7. 18.
UNRULY. 1 Thess. 5. 14; Tit. 1. 6; Jas. 3. 8.
UNSAVOURY. Job 6. 6, can that which is *u.* be eaten?
UNSEARCHABLE. Job 5. 9; Ps. 145. 3; Rom. 11. 33; Eph. 3. 8.
UNSEEMLY. Rom. 1. 27; 1 Cor. 13. 5.
UNSKILFUL. Heb. 5. 13, is *u.* in the word.
UNSPEAKABLE. 2 Cor. 9. 15; 12. 4; 1 Pet. 1. 8.
UNSPOTTED. Jas. 1. 27, *u.* from the world.
UNSTABLE. Gen. 49. 4; Jas. 1. 8; 2 Pet. 2. 14.
UNTHANKFUL. Lu. 6. 35; 2 Tim. 3. 2.
UNWASHEN. Mat. 15. 20; Mk. 7. 2, 5.
UNWISE. Deut. 32. 6; Hos. 13. 13; Rom. 1. 14; Eph. 5. 17.
UNWORTHY. Acts 13. 46; 1 Cor. 6. 2; 11. 27.
UPBRAID. Mat. 11. 20; Mk. 16. 14; Jas. 1. 5.
UPHOLD. Ps. 51. 12, *u.* me with thy free spirit.
54. 4, with them that *u.* my soul.
119. 116, *u.* me according to thy word.
145. 14, the Lord *u.* all that fall.
Isa. 41. 10, I will *u.* thee with right hand.
42. 1, my servant, whom I *u.*
63. 5, wondered there was none to *u.*
Heb. 1. 3, *u.* all things by the word of his power.
See Ps. 37. 17; 41. 12; 63. 8; Prov. 20. 28.
UPPERMOST. Mat. 23. 6; Mk. 12. 39; Lu. 11. 43.
UPRIGHT. Job 12. 4, the *u.* man is laughed to scorn.
17. 8, *u.* men shall be astonied.
Ps. 19. 13, then shall I be *u.*
25. 8; 92. 15, good and *u.* is the Lord.
37. 14, such as be of *u.* conversation.
49. 14, the *u.* shall have dominion.
111. 1, the assembly of the *u.*
112. 4, to the *u.* ariseth light.
125. 4, that are *u.* in their hearts.
Prov. 2. 21, the *u.* shall dwell in the land.
11. 3, the integrity of the *u.*
20, such as are *u.* in their way.
14. 11, the tabernacle of the *u.*
15. 8, the prayer of the *u.* is his delight.
28. 10, the *u.* shall have good things.
Eccl. 7. 29, God hath made man *u.*
Cant. 1. 4, the *u.* love thee.
See Isa. 26. 7; Jer. 10. 5; Mic. 7. 2; Hab. 2. 4.
UPRIGHTLY. Ps. 58. 1; 75. 2, do ye judge *u.*?
84. 11, withhold no good from them that walk *u.*
Prov. 10. 9; 15. 21; 28. 18, he that walketh *u.*
Isa. 33. 15, he that speaketh *u.*
See Ps. 15. 2; Amos 5. 10; Mic. 2. 7; Gal. 2. 14.
UPRIGHTNESS. 1 Kings 3. 6, in *u.* of heart.
1 Chron. 29. 17, thou hast pleasure in *u.*
Job 4. 6, the *u.* of thy ways.
33. 23, to show unto man his *u.*
Ps. 25. 21, let *u.* preserve me.
143. 10, lead me into the land of *u.*
Prov. 2. 13, who leave the paths of *u.*
See Ps. 111. 8; Prov. 14. 2; 28. 6; Isa. 26. 7, 10.
UPROAR. Mat. 26. 5; Mk. 14. 2; Acts 17. 5; 21. 31.
UPWARD. Job 5. 7; Eccl. 3. 21; Isa. 38. 14.
URGE. Gen. 33. 11; 2 Kings 2. 17; Lu. 11. 53.
URGENT. Ex. 12. 33; Dan. 3. 22.
USE. Mat. 6. 7, *u.* not vain repetitions.
1 Cor. 7. 31, they that *u.* this world.
Gal. 5. 13, *u.* not liberty for an occasion.
1 Tim. 1. 8, if a man *u.* it lawfully.
See Ps. 119. 132; 1 Cor. 9. 12; 1 Tim. 5. 23.
USURP. 1 Tim. 2. 12, I suffer not a woman to *u.*
USURY. Ex. 22. 25, neither shalt thou lay upon him *u.*
Lev. 25. 36, take thou no *u.* of him.
Deut. 23. 20, thou mayest lend upon *u.*
Neh. 5. 7, ye exact *u.*
Ezek. 18. 8, not given forth upon *u.*
13, hath given forth upon *u.*
17, that hath not received *u.*
22. 12, thou hast taken *u.*
UTTER. Ps. 78. 2, I will *u.* dark sayings.
106. 2, who can *u.* the mighty acts?
119. 171, my lips shall *u.* praise.
Prov. 1. 20, wisdom *u.* her voice.
23. 33, thine heart shall *u.* perverse things.
29. 11, a fool *u.* all his mind.
Eccl. 5. 2, let not thine heart be hasty to *u.*
Rom. 8. 26, which cannot be *u.*
2 Cor. 12. 4, not lawful for a man to *u.*
Heb. 5. 11, many things hard to be *u.*
See Job 33. 3; Isa. 48. 20; Joel 2. 11; Mat. 13. 35.
UTTERANCE. Acts 2. 4, as the Spirit gave *u.*
See 1 Cor. 1. 5; 2 Cor. 8. 7; Eph. 6. 19; Col. 4. 3.
UTTERLY. Ps. 119. 8, forsake me not *u.*
Jer. 23. 39, I will *u.* forget you.
Zeph. 1. 2, I will *u.* consume all things.
2 Pet. 2. 12, these shall *u.* perish.

See Deut. 7. 2; Neh. 9. 31; Isa. 40. 30; Rev. 18. 8.
UTTERMOST. Mat. 5. 26; 1 Thess. 2. 16; Heb. 7. 25.

V

VAGABOND. Gen. 4. 12, a *v.* shalt thou be in the earth.
See Ps. 109. 10; Acts 19. 13.
VAIL. Mat. 27. 51; 2 Cor. 3. 14; Heb. 6. 19.
VAIN. Ex. 5. 9, not regard *v.* words.
20. 7; Deut. 5. 11, shalt not take name of the Lord in *v.*
Deut. 32. 47, it is not a *v.* thing for you.
2 Sam. 6. 20, as one of the *v.* fellows.
2 Kings 18. 20; Isa. 36. 5, they are but *v.* words.
Job 11. 12, *v.* man would be wise.
16. 3, shall *v.* words have an end?
21. 34, how then comfort ye me in *v.*?
Ps. 2. 1; Acts 4. 25, the people imagine a *v.* thing.
26. 4, I have not sat with *v.* persons.
33. 17, an horse is a *v.* thing for safety.
39. 6, every man walketh in a *v.* show.
60. 11; 108. 12. *v.* is the help of man.
89. 47, wherefore hast thou made men in *v.*?
127. 1, labour in *v.*, watchman waketh in *v.*
Prov. 12. 11; 28. 19, followeth *v.* persons.
31. 30, beauty is *v.*
Eccl. 6. 12, all the days of his *v.* life.
Isa. 1. 13, bring no more *v.* oblations.
45. 18, he created it not in *v.*
19, I said not, seek ye me in *v.*
49. 4; 65. 23, laboured in *v.*
Jer. 3. 23, in *v.* is salvation hoped for.
10. 3, the customs of the people are *v.*
46. 11, in *v.* shalt thou use medicines.
Mal. 3. 14, ye have said, it is *v.* to serve God.
Mat. 6. 7, use not *v.* repetitions.
15. 9; Mk. 7. 7, in *v.* do they worship me.
Rom. 13. 4, he beareth not the sword in *v.*
1 Cor. 15. 2, unless ye have believed in *v.*
2 Cor. 6. 1, receive not the grace of God in *v.*
Gal. 2. 2, lest I should run in *v.*
Tit. 1. 10, unruly and *v.* talkers.
Jas. 1. 26, this man's religion is *v.*
1 Pet. 1. 18, redeemed from *v.* conversation.
See Prov. 1. 17; Rom. 1. 21; Gal. 5. 26; Phil. 2. 3.
VALIANT. 1 Sam. 18. 17, be *v.* for me.
1 Kings 1. 42, for thou art a *v.* man.
Isa. 10. 13, put down inhabitants like a *v.* man.
Jer. 9. 3, they are not *v.* for truth.
Heb. 11. 34, waxed *v.* in fight.
See Ps. 60. 12; 118. 15; Isa. 33. 7; Nah. 2. 3.
VALUE. Job 13. 4, physicians of no *v.*
Mat. 10. 31; Lu. 12. 7, of more *v.*
See Lev. 27. 16; Job 28. 16; Mat. 27. 9.
VANISH. Isa. 51. 6; 1 Cor. 13. 8; Heb. 8. 13.
VANITY. Job 7. 3, to possess months of *v.*
15. 31, *v.* shall be his recompence.
35. 13, God will not hear *v.*
Ps. 12. 2, speak *v.* every one with his neighbour.
39. 5, every man at his best state is *v.*
62. 9, are *v.*, lighter than *v.*
144. 4, man is like to *v.*
Prov. 13. 11, wealth gotten by *v.*
30. 8, remove from me *v.*
Eccl. 6. 11, many things increase *v.*
11. 10, childhood and youth are *v.*
Isa. 30. 28, with the sieve of *v.*
Jer. 18. 15, they have burned incense to *v.*
Hab. 2. 13, people shall weary themselves for *v.*
Rom. 8. 20, the creature was made subject to *v.*
Eph. 4. 17, walk in *v.* of mind.
2 Pet. 2. 18, great swelling words of *v.*
See Eccl. 1. 2; Jer. 10. 8; 14. 22; Acts 14. 15.
VAPOURS. Job 36. 27, according to the *v.* thereof.
Ps. 135. 7; Jer. 10. 13, he causeth the *v.* to ascend, 148. 8, snow and *v.*
VARIABLENESS. Jas. 1. 17, with whom is no *v.*
VARIANCE. Mat. 10. 35; Gal. 5. 20.
VAUNT. Judg. 7. 2; 1 Cor. 13. 4.
VEHEMENT. Cant. 8. 6; Mk. 14. 31; 2 Cor. 7. 11.
VENGEANCE. Deut. 32. 35, to me belongeth *v.*
Prov. 6. 34; Isa. 34. 8; 61. 2; Jer. 51. 6, the day of *v.*
Isa. 59. 17, garments of *v.* for clothing.
Acts 28. 4, whom *v.* suffereth not to live.
Jude 7, the *v.* of eternal fire.
See Mic. 5. 15; Nah. 1. 2; Lu. 21. 22; Rom. 12. 19.
VENISON. Gen. 25. 28, he did eat of his *v.*
27. 3, take me some *v.*
VERILY. Gen. 42. 21; Ps. 58. 11; 73. 13; Mk. 9. 12.
VERITY. Ps. 111. 7; 1 Tim. 2. 7.
VESSEL. 2 Kings 4. 6, there is not a *v.* more.
Ps. 31. 12, I am like a potter's *v.*
Isa. 66. 20, bring an offering in a clean *v.*
Jer. 22. 28, a *v.* wherein is no pleasure.
25. 34, fall like a pleasant *v.*
Mat. 13. 48, gathered the good into *v.*
25. 4, the wise took oil in their *v.*
Acts 9. 15, he is a chosen *v.* unto me.
Rom. 9. 22, the *v.* of wrath.
23, the *v.* of mercy.
1 Thess. 4. 4, to possess his *v.* in sanctification.
2 Tim. 2. 21, he shall be a *v.* to honour.
1 Pet. 3. 7, giving honour to the wife as to weaker *v.*
See Isa. 52. 11; 65. 4; Jer. 14. 3; Mk. 11. 16.
VESTRY. 2 Kings 10. 22, him that was over the *v.*
VESTURE. Gen. 41. 42; Ps. 22. 18; 102. 26; Mat. 27. 35; Heb. 1. 12; Rev. 19. 13.
VEX. Ex. 22. 21; Lev. 19. 33, not *v.* a stranger.
Num. 33. 55, those ye let remain shall *v.* you.
2 Sam. 12. 18, how will he *v.* himself?
Job 19. 2, how long will ye *v.* my soul?
Isa. 11. 13, Judah shall not *v.* Ephraim.
Ezek. 32. 9, I will *v.* the hearts of many.
Mat. 15. 22, my daughter is grievously *v.*
2 Pet. 2. 8, *v.* his righteous soul.
See Lev. 18. 18; Judg. 16. 16; Isa. 63. 10; Hab. 2. 7.
VEXATION. Eccl. 1. 14; 2. 22; Isa. 9. 1; 28. 19; 65. 14.
VICTORY. 2 Sam. 19. 2, *v.* was turned to mourning.
1 Chron. 29. 11, thine is the *v.*
Ps. 98. 1, hath gotten him the *v.*
Mat. 12. 20, send forth judgment unto *v.*
1 John 5. 4, this is the *v.*, even our faith.
See Isa. 25. 8; 1 Cor. 15. 54, 55, 57.
VICTUALS. Ex. 12. 39, neither had they prepared *v.*
Josh. 9. 14, the men took of their *v.*
Neh. 10. 31, bring *v.* on the sabbath.
13. 15, in the day wherein they sold *v.*
Mat. 14. 15; Lu. 9. 12, into villages to buy *v.*
See Gen. 14. 11; Judg. 17. 10; 1 Sam. 22. 10.
VIEW. Josh. 2. 7; 7. 2; 2 Kings 2. 7; Neh. 2. 13.
VIGILANT. 1 Tim. 3. 2; 1 Pet. 5. 8.
VILE. 1 Sam. 3. 13, made themselves *v.*
Job 18. 3, wherefore are we reputed *v.*?
40. 4, I am *v.*, what shall I answer thee?
Ps. 15. 4; Isa. 32. 5; Dan. 11. 21, a *v.* person.
Jer. 15. 19, take the precious from the *v.*
Lam. 1. 11, see, O Lord, for I am become *v.*
Nah. 3. 6, I will make thee *v.*
Rom. 1. 26, gave them up to *v.* affections.
Phil. 3. 21, shall change our *v.* body.
Jas. 2. 2, a poor man in *v.* raiment.
See 2 Sam. 1. 21; Job 30. 8; Ps. 12. 8; Nah. 1. 14.
VILLANY. Isa. 32. 6; Jer. 29. 23.
VINE. Deut. 32. 32, their *v.* is of the *v.* of Sodom.
Judg. 13. 14, may not eat any thing that cometh of the *v.*
1 Kings 4. 25, dwelt every man under his *v.*
2 Kings 18. 31; Isa. 36. 16, eat every man of his own *v.*

Ps. 80. 8, a *v.* out of Egypt.
128. 3, thy wife as a fruitful *v.*
Isa. 24. 7, the new wine mourneth, the *v.* languisheth.
Hos. 10. 1, Israel is an empty *v.*
Mic. 4. 4, they shall sit every man under his *v.*
Mat. 26. 29; Mk. 14. 25; Lu. 22. 18, this fruit of the *v.*
John 15. 1, I am the true *v.*
See Deut. 8. 8; Cant. 2. 15; Joel 1. 7; Hab. 3. 17.
VINTAGE. Job 24. 6; Isa. 16. 10; 32. 10; Mic. 7. 1.
VIOL. Isa. 5. 12; 14. 11; Amos 5. 23; 6. 5.
VIOLENCE. Gen. 6. 11, earth was filled with *v.*
Ps. 11. 5, him that loveth *v.*
55. 9, I have seen *v.* in the city.
58. 2, weigh the *v.* of your hands.
72. 14, redeem their soul from *v.*
73. 6, *v.* covereth them as a garment.
Prov. 4. 17, they drink the wine of *v.*
10. 6, *v.* covereth the mouth of the wicked.
Isa. 53. 9, because he had done no *v.*
60. 18, *v.* shall no more be heard.
Ezek. 8. 17; 28. 16, they have filled the land with *v.*
Amos 3. 10, store up *v.* in their palaces.
Hab. 1. 3, *v.* is before me.
Mal. 2. 16, one covereth *v.* with his garment.
Mat. 11. 12, kingdom of heaven suffereth *v.*
Lu. 3. 14, do *v.* to no man.
See Mic. 2. 2; 6. 12; Zeph. 1. 9; Heb. 11. 34.
VIOLENT. Ps. 7. 16, his *v.* dealing.
18. 48; 140. 1; Prov. 16. 29, the *v.* man.
See 2 Sam. 22. 49; Eccl. 5. 8; Mat. 11. 12.
VIOLENTLY. Isa. 22. 18; Mat. 8. 32; Mk. 5. 13.
VIRGIN. Isa. 23. 12; 47. 1; 62. 5; Jer. 14. 17.
VIRTUE. Mk. 5. 30; Lu. 6. 19; 8. 46; Phil. 4. 8; 2 Pet. 1. 5.
VIRTUOUS. Ruth 3. 11; Prov. 12. 4; 31. 10, 29.
VISAGE. Isa. 52. 14; Lam. 4. 8; Dan. 3. 19.
VISION. Job 20. 8, as a *v.* of the night.
Prov. 29. 18, where there is no *v.*, people perish.
Isa. 22. 1, the valley of *v.*
28. 7, they err in *v.*
Lam. 2. 9, prophets find no *v.* from the Lord.
Hos. 12. 10, I have multiplied *v.*
Joel 2. 28; Acts 2. 17, young men shall see *v.*
Zech. 13. 4, ashamed every one of his *v.*
Mat. 17. 9, tell the *v.* to no man.
Lu. 24. 23, had seen a *v.* of angels.
Acts 26. 19, not disobedient to heavenly *v.*
See Job 4. 13; Ezek. 1. 1; 8. 3; Mic. 3. 6.
VISIT. Gen. 50. 24; Ex. 13. 19, God will *v.* you.
Ex. 20. 5; 34. 7; Num. 14. 18; Deut. 5. 9, *v.* the iniquity of the fathers.
32. 34, when I *v.*, I will *v.* their sin upon them.
Ruth 1. 6, how the Lord had *v.* his people.
Job 5. 24, thou shalt *v.* thy habitation.
7. 18, shouldest *v.* him every morning.
Ps. 8. 4; Heb. 2. 6, the son of man, that thou *v.* him.
106. 4, *v.* me with thy salvation.
Jer. 5. 9; 9. 9, shall I not *v.* for these things?
29. 10, I will *v.*, and perform my good word.
Ezek. 38. 8, after many days thou shalt be *v.*
Mat. 25. 36, I was sick, and ye *v.* me.
Acts 15. 14, how God did *v.* the Gentiles.
Jas. 1. 27, to *v.* the fatherless and widows.
See Job 31. 14; Lu. 1. 68, 78; 7. 16.
VISITATION. Job 10. 12, thy *v.* hath preserved.
Isa. 10. 3; 1 Pet. 2. 12, in the day of *v.*
Jer. 8. 12; 10. 15; 46. 21; 50. 27; Lu. 19. 44, in the time of *v.*
See Num. 16. 29; Jer. 11. 23; Hos. 9. 7.
VOCATION. Eph. 4. 1, worthy of the *v.*
VOICE. Gen. 4. 10, *v.* of thy brother's blood.
27. 22, the *v.* is Jacob's *v.*
Ex. 23. 21, obey his *v.*, provoke him not.
24. 3, all the people answered with one *v.*
32. 18, it is not the *v.* of them that shout.
Deut. 4. 33, did ever people hear *v.* of God and live?
Josh. 6. 10, nor make any noise with thy *v.*
1 Sam. 24. 16; 26. 17, is this thy *v.*?
1 Kings 19. 12, after the fire, a still small *v.*
2 Kings 4. 31, there was neither *v.* nor hearing.
Job 3. 7, let no joyful *v.* come therein.
30. 31, my organ into the *v.* of them that weep.
37. 4, a *v.* roareth.
40. 9, canst thou thunder with a *v.* like him?
Ps. 5. 3, my *v.* shalt thou hear in the morning.
31. 22; 86. 6, the *v.* of my supplications.
42. 4, with the *v.* of joy.
95. 7, to day, if ye will hear his *v.*
103. 20, the *v.* of his word.
Prov. 1. 20, wisdom uttereth her *v.* in the streets.
5. 13, not obeyed the *v.* of my teachers.
8. 1, doth not understanding put forth her *v.*?
4, my *v.* is to the sons of man.
Eccl. 5. 3, a fool's *v.* is known.
12. 4, rise up at the *v.* of the bird.
Cant. 2. 8; 5. 2, the *v.* of my beloved.
12, the *v.* of the turtle is heard.
14, sweet is thy *v.*
Isa. 13. 2, exalt the *v.* unto them.
40. 3; Mat. 3. 3; Mk. 1. 3; Lu. 3. 4, *v.* of him that crieth.
6, the *v.* said, cry.
48. 20, with a *v.* of singing.
52. 8, with the *v.* together shall they sing.
65. 19, the *v.* of weeping shall be no more heard.
66. 6, a *v.* of noise, a *v.* from the temple.
Jer. 7. 34, the *v.* of mirth, and the *v.* of gladness.
30. 19, the *v.* of them that make merry.
48. 3, a *v.* of crying shall be.
Ezek. 23. 42, a *v.* of a multitude at ease.
33. 32, one that hath a pleasant *v.*
43. 2, *v.* like a noise of many waters.
Nah. 2. 7, lead her as with the *v.* of doves.
Mat. 12. 19, neither shall any man hear his *v.*
Lu. 23. 23, the *v.* of them and of the chief priests prevailed.
John 5. 25, the dead shall hear the *v.* of Son of God.
10. 4, the sheep follow, for they know his *v.*
5, they know not the *v.* of strangers.
12. 30, this *v.* came not because of me.
18. 37, every one that is of the truth heareth my *v.*
Acts 12. 14, and when she knew Peter's *v.*
26. 10, I gave my *v.* against them.
1 Cor. 14. 10, there are so many *v.* in the world.
19, that by my *v.* I might teach others.
Gal. 4. 20, I desire now to change my *v.*
1 Thess. 4. 16, descend with *v.* of archangel.
2 Pet. 2. 16, the dumb ass speaking with man's *v.*
Rev. 3. 20, if any man hear my *v.*
4. 5, out of the throne proceeded *v.*
See Gen. 3. 17; Ps. 58. 5; John 3. 29; Acts 12. 22.
VOID. Gen. 1. 2; Jer. 4. 23, without form, and *v.*
Deut. 32. 28, a people *v.* of counsel.
Ps. 89. 39, made *v.* the covenant.
119. 126, they have made *v.* thy law.
Prov. 11. 12, *v.* of wisdom.
Isa. 55. 11, my word shall not return to me *v.*
Jer. 19. 7, make *v.* the counsel of Judah.
Nah. 2. 10, empty, *v.*, and waste.
Acts 24. 16, a conscience *v.* of offence.
See Num. 30. 12; Rom. 3. 31; 4. 14.
VOLUME. Ps. 40. 7; Heb. 10. 7.
VOLUNTARY. Lev. 1. 3; 7. 16; Ezek. 46. 12; Col. 2. 18.
VOMIT. Job 20. 15; Prov. 26. 11; 2 Pet. 2. 22.
VOW (*n.*). Gen. 28. 20; 31. 13, Jacob vowed a *v.*
Num. 29. 39, these ye shall do beside your *v.*
Deut. 12. 6, thither bring your *v.*
Judg. 11. 30, Jephthah vowed a *v.*, and said.
39, her father did with her according to his *v.*
1 Sam. 1. 21, Elkanah went up to offer his *v.*
Job 22. 27, thou shalt pay thy *v.*
Ps. 22. 25; 66. 13; 116. 14, I will pay my *v.*
50. 14, pay thy *v.* unto the most High.

Ps. 56. 12, thy *v.* are upon me, O God.
61. 5, for thou hast heard my *v.*
8, that I may daily perform my *v.*
65. 1, to thee shall the *v.* be performed.
Prov. 7. 14, this day have I paid my *v.*
20. 25, after *v.* to make enquiry.
31. 2, the son of my *v.*
Eccl. 5. 4, when thou vowest a *v.*, defer not to pay.
Isa. 19. 21, they shall vow a *v.* unto the Lord.
Jonah 1. 16, feared the Lord, and made *v.*
Acts 18. 18, shorn his head, for he had a *v.*
21. 23, four men which have a *v.* on them.
See 2 Sam. 15. 7; Jer. 44. 25; Nah. 1. 15.
VOW (*v.*). Deut. 23. 22, if forbear to *v.*, no sin.
Ps. 76. 11, *v.*, and pay to the Lord your God.
132. 2, and *v.* to the mighty God.
See Num. 21. 2; Eccl. 5. 5; Jonah 2. 9.
VULTURE. Lev. 11. 14; Deut. 14. 13, and the *v.* after his kind.
Job 28. 7, which the *v.* eye hath not seen.
Isa. 34. 15, there shall the *v.* be.

W

WAG. Jer. 18. 16; Lam. 2. 15; Zeph. 2. 15.
WAGES. Gen. 29. 15, what shall thy *w.* be?
Gen. 30. 28, appoint me thy *w.*
31. 7, changed my *w.* ten times.
Ex. 2. 9, nurse this child, I will give *w.*
Jer. 22. 13, useth neighbour's service without *w.*
Hag. 1. 6, earneth *w.* to put in bag with holes.
Lu. 3. 14, be content with your *w.*
John 4. 36, he that reapeth receiveth *w.*
Rom. 6. 23, the *w.* of sin is death.
2 Pet. 2. 15, the *w.* of unrighteousness.
See Ezek. 29. 18; Mal. 3. 5; 2 Cor. 11. 8.
WAGONS. Gen. 45. 19; Num. 7. 7; Ezek. 23. 24.
WAIL. Ezek. 32. 18, *w.* for the multitude.
Amos 5. 16, *w.* shall be in all streets.
Mic. 1. 8, therefore I will *w.* and howl.
Mat. 13. 42, there shall be *w.* and gnashing.
Mk. 5. 38, he seeth them that *w.* greatly.
Rev. 1. 7, all kindreds of the earth shall *w.*
18. 15, the merchants shall stand afar off *w.*
See Esth. 4. 3; Jer. 9. 10, 19, 20; Ezek. 7. 11.
WAIT. Gen. 49. 18, I have *w.* for thy salvation.
Num. 35. 20; Jer. 9. 8, by laying of *w.*
2 Kings 6. 33, should I *w.* for the Lord any longer?
Job 14. 14, I will *w.* till my change come.
15. 22, he is *w.* for of the sword.
17. 13, if I *w.*, the grave is my house.
29. 21, to me men *w.*, and kept silence.
23, they *w.* for me as for rain.
30. 26, when I *w.* for light, darkness came.
Ps. 25. 3; 69. 6, let none that *w.* be ashamed.
27. 14; 37. 34; Prov. 20. 22, *w.* on the Lord.
33. 20, our soul *w.* for the Lord.
37. 7, *w.* patiently.
52. 9, I will *w.* on thy name.
62. 1; 130. 6, my soul *w.* upon God.
5, *w.* only on God.
65. 1, praise *w.* for thee in Zion.
69. 3, mine eyes fail while I *w.* for God.
104. 27, these all *w.* upon thee.
106. 13, they *w.* not for counsel.
123. 2, so our eyes *w.* on the Lord.
Prov. 27. 18, he that *w.* on his master.
Isa. 30. 18, the Lord *w.* to be gracious.
40. 31, they that *w.* on the Lord shall renew.
42. 4, the isles shall *w.* for his law.
59. 9, we *w.* for light.
64. 4, prepared for him that *w.* for him.
Lam. 3. 26, good that a man hope and quietly *w.*
Dan. 12. 12, blessed is he that *w.*, and cometh to the days.
Hab. 2. 3, though the vision tarry, *w.* for it.
Zech. 11. 11, poor of the flock that *w.* upon me.
Mk. 15. 43, who also *w.* for the kingdom of God.
Lu. 2. 25, *w.* for the consolation of Israel.
12. 36, like unto men that *w.* for their lord.
Acts 1. 4, but *w.* for promise of the Father.
Rom. 8. 23, groan, *w.* for the adoption.
25, then do we with patience *w.* for it.
12. 7, let us *w.* on our ministering.
1 Cor. 9. 13, they which *w.* at the altar are partakers.
Gal. 5. 5, we *w.* for the hope.
1 Thess. 1. 10, to *w.* for his Son from heaven.
See Num. 3. 10; Neh. 12. 44; Isa. 8. 17.
WAKE. Ps. 139. 18, when I *w.* I am still with thee.
Jer. 51. 39, sleep a perpetual sleep, and not *w.*
Joel 3. 9, prepare war, *w.* up the mighty men.
Zech. 4. 1, the angel came again, and *w.* me.
1 Thess. 5. 10, whether we *w.* or sleep.
See Ps. 77. 4; 127. 1; Cant. 5. 2; Isa. 50. 4.
WALK. Gen. 17. 1, *w.* before me, and be perfect.
24. 40, the Lord before whom I *w.*
48. 15, before whom my fathers did *w.*
Ex. 16. 4, whether they will *w.* in my law.
18. 20, the way wherein they must *w.*
Lev. 26. 12, I will *w.* among you.
Deut. 23. 14, God *w.* in midst of the camp.
Judg. 5. 10, speak, ye that *w.* by the way.
2 Sam. 2. 29, Abner and his men *w.* all that night.
Job 18. 8, he *w.* on a snare.
22. 14, he *w.* in the circuit of heaven.
29. 3, when by his light I *w.* through darkness.
Ps. 23. 4, though I *w.* through the valley of the shadow of death.
26. 11, as for me, I will *w.* in mine integrity.
48. 12, *w.* about Zion, and go round about her.
55. 14, we *w.* to house of God in company.
56. 13, that I may *w.* before God in the light of the living.
84. 11, from them that *w.* uprightly.
91. 6, the pestilence that *w.* in darkness.
104. 3, who *w.* upon wings of the wind.
116. 9, I will *w.* before the Lord.
119. 45, I will *w.* at liberty.
138. 7, though I *w.* in the midst of trouble.
Prov. 10. 9; 28. 18, he that *w.* uprightly *w.* surely.
13. 20, he that *w.* with wise men shall be wise.
19. 1; 28. 6, better is the poor that *w.* in integrity.
28. 26, whoso *w.* wisely shall be delivered.
Eccl. 2. 14, the fool *w.* in darkness.
Isa. 2. 5, let us *w.* in the light of the Lord.
9. 2, the people that *w.* in darkness.
20. 3, as my servant hath *w.* naked and barefoot.
30. 21, a voice saying, this is the way, *w.* in it.
35. 9, the redeemed shall *w.* there.
50. 10, that *w.* in darkness, and hath no light.
11, *w.* in the light of your fire.
Jer. 6. 16, ask where is the good way, and *w.* therein.
10. 23, it is not in man that *w.* to direct his steps.
Ezek. 28. 14, hast *w.* in midst of stones of fire.
Dan. 4. 37, those that *w.* in pride.
Hos. 14. 9, the just shall *w.* in them.
Amos 3. 3, can two *w.* together?
Mic. 6. 8, to *w.* humbly with thy God.
Nah. 2. 11, where the lion *w.*
Zech. 1. 11, we have *w.* to and fro through the earth.
Mal. 3. 14, what profit that we have *w.* mournfully?
Mat. 9. 5; Mk. 2. 9; Lu. 5. 23; John 5. 8, 11, 12; Acts 3. 6, arise, and *w.*
12. 43; Lu. 11. 24, *w.* through dry places.
14. 29, he *w.* on the water.
Mk. 16. 12, he appeared to two of them, as they *w.*
Lu. 13. 33, I must *w.* to day and to morrow.
John 8. 12, shall not *w.* in darkness.
11. 9, if any man *w.* in the day.
Rom. 4. 12, who *w.* in steps of that faith.
6. 4, *w.* in newness of life.
8. 1, who *w.* not after the flesh, but after the Spirit.

2 Cor. 5. 7, we *w.* by faith.
Gal. 6. 16, as many as *w.* according to this rule.
Eph. 2. 2; Col. 3. 7, in time past ye *w.*
10, ordained that we should *w.* in them.
4. 1, *w.* worthy of the vocation.
17, that ye *w.* not as other Gentiles.
5. 15, *w.* circumspectly.
Phil. 3. 17, mark them which *w.*
18, many *w.*, of whom I told you.
Col. 1. 10; 1 Thess. 2. 12, that ye might *w.* worthy of the Lord.
1 Thess. 4. 1, how ye ought to *w.*
12, ye may *w.* honestly.
2 Thess. 3. 6, from every brother that *w.* disorderly.
1 Pet. 4. 3, when we *w.* in lasciviousness.
5. 8, *w.* about, seeking whom he may devour.
1 John 1. 7, if we *w.* in the light.
2. 6, to *w.*, even as he *w.*
See Gal. 5. 16; Eph. 5. 2; Phil. 3. 16.

WALKING. Deut. 2. 7, the Lord knoweth thy *w.*
Job 31. 26, the moon *w.* in brightness.
Dan. 3. 25, four men loose, *w.* in the fire.
Mat. 14. 25, Jesus went to them, *w.* on the sea.
Mk. 8. 24, I see men as trees, *w.*
Acts 9. 31, *w.* in the fear of the Lord.
See Isa. 3. 16; 2 Cor. 4. 2; 2 Pet. 3. 3; Jude 16.

WALL. Gen. 49. 22, branches run over the *w.*
Ex. 14. 22, the waters were a *w.* to them.
Num. 22. 24, a *w.* being on this side, a *w.* on that.
2 Sam. 22. 30; Ps. 18. 29, have I leaped over a *w.*
2 Kings 20. 2; Isa. 36. 11, turned his face to the *w.*
Ezra 5. 3, who commanded you to make this *w.*?
Neh. 4. 6, so built we the *w.*
Ps. 62. 3, a bowing *w.* shall ye be.
122. 7, peace be within thy *w.*
Prov. 24. 31, the *w.* thereof was broken down.
25. 28, like a city without *w.*
Isa. 26. 1, salvation will God appoint for *w.*
59. 10, we grope for the *w.*
60. 18, thou shalt call thy *w.* Salvation.
Ezek. 8. 7, a hole in the *w.*
Dan. 5. 5, fingers wrote on the *w.*
Amos 5. 19, leaned hand on *w.*, and serpent bit him.
Hab. 2. 11, the stone shall cry out of the *w.*
Acts 23. 3, thou whited *w.*
Eph. 2. 14, the middle *w.* of partition.
See Ezek. 38. 11; Zech. 2. 4; Acts 9. 25; Rev. 21. 14.

WALLOW. Jer. 6. 26; 25. 34, *w.* in ashes.
2 Pet. 2. 22, washed, to her *w.* in the mire.
See 2 Sam. 20. 12; Ezek. 27. 30.

WANDER. Num. 14. 33, your children shall *w.*
Deut. 27. 18, cursed be he that maketh blind to *w.*
Job 12. 24, he causeth them to *w.*
15. 23, he *w.* abroad for bread.
38. 41, young ravens *w.* for lack of meat.
Ps. 55. 7, then would I *w.* far off.
59. 15, let them *w.* up and down.
119. 10, let me not *w.* from thy commandments.
Prov. 27. 8, as a bird that *w.* from nest.
Isa. 16. 3, bewray not him that *w.*
47. 15, *w.* every one to his quarter.
Jer. 14. 10, thus have they loved to *w.*
Lam. 4. 14, they have *w.* as blind men.
Ezek. 34. 6, my sheep *w.* through mountains.
Amos 4. 8, two cities *w.* to one city to drink.
See Hos. 9. 17; 1 Tim. 5. 13; Heb. 11. 37; Jude 13.

WANT (*n.*). Deut. 28. 48, thou shalt serve in *w.*
Judg. 18. 10, a place where there is no *w.*
19. 20, let all thy *w.* lie on me.
Job 24. 8, they embrace the rock for *w.*
31. 19, if I have seen any perish for *w.*
Ps. 34. 9, there is no *w.* to them that fear him.
Amos 4. 6, I have given you *w.* of bread.
Mk. 12. 44, she of her *w.* cast in all.
Lu. 15. 14, he began to be in *w.*
Phil. 2. 25, that ministered to my *w.*
See Prov. 6. 11; Lam. 4. 9; 2 Cor. 8. 14; Phil. 4. 11.

WANT (*v.*). Ps. 23. 1, I shall not *w.*
34. 10, shall not *w.* any good thing.
Prov. 9. 4, for him that *w.* understanding.
10. 19, in multitude of words there *w.* not sin.
13. 25, the belly of the wicked shall *w.*
Eccl. 6. 2, he *w.* nothing for his soul.
Isa. 34. 16, none shall *w.* her mate.
Jer. 44. 18, we have *w.* all things.
Ezek. 4. 17, that they may *w.* bread and water.
John 2. 3, when they *w.* wine.
2 Cor. 11. 9, when I *w.*, I was chargeable to no man.
See Eccl. 1. 15; Dan. 5. 27; Tit. 1. 5; Jas. 1. 4.

WANTON. Isa. 3. 16; Rom. 13. 13; 1 Tim. 5. 11; Jas. 5. 5.

WAR (*n.*). Ex. 32. 17, there is a noise of *w.*
Num. 32. 6, shall your brethren go to *w.*, and shall ye sit here?
Deut. 24. 5, taken a wife, he shall not go out to *w.*
Judg. 5. 8, then was *w.* in the gates.
1 Chron. 5. 22, many slain, because the *w.* was of God.
Job 10. 17, changes and *w.* are against me.
38. 23, reserved against the day of *w.*
Ps. 27. 3, though *w.* should rise against me.
46. 9, he maketh *w.* to cease.
55. 21, *w.* was in his heart.
68. 30, scatter the people that delight in *w.*
Prov. 20. 18, with good advice make *w.*
Eccl. 3. 8, a time of *w.*
8. 8, no discharge in that *w.*
Isa. 2. 4; Mic. 4. 3, nor learn *w.* any more.
Jer. 42. 14, to Egypt, where we shall see no *w.*
Mic. 2. 8, as men averse from *w.*
Mat. 24. 6; Mk. 13. 7; Lu. 21. 9, *w.* and rumours of *w.*
Lu. 14. 31, what king, going to make *w.*?
Jas. 4. 1, from whence come *w.*?
Rev. 12. 7, there was *w.* in heaven.
See Eccl. 9. 18; Ezek. 32. 27; Dan. 7. 21; 9. 26.

WAR (*v.*). 2 Sam. 22. 35; Ps. 18. 34; 144. 1, teacheth my hands to *w.*
2 Chron. 6. 34, if thy people go to *w.*
Isa. 41. 12, they that *w.* against thee.
2 Cor. 10. 3, we do not *w.* after the flesh.
1 Tim. 1. 18, *w.* a good warfare.
2 Tim. 2. 4, no man that *w.* entangleth himself.
Jas. 4. 1, lusts that *w.* in your members.
2, ye fight and *w.*, yet ye have not.
1 Pet. 2. 11, from lusts which *w.* against the soul.
See 1 Kings 14. 19; Isa. 37. 8; Rom. 7. 23.

WARDROBE. 2 Kings 22. 14; 2 Chron. 34. 22

WARE. Mat. 24. 50; Lu. 8. 27; 2 Tim. 4. 15.

WARFARE. Isa. 40. 2, that her *w.* is accomplished.
2 Cor. 10. 4, weapons of our *w.* are not carnal.
See 1 Sam. 28. 1; 1 Cor. 9. 7; 1 Tim. 1. 18.

WARM. Eccl. 4. 11, how can one be *w.* alone?
Isa. 47. 14, there shall not be a coal to *w.* at.
Hag. 1. 6, ye clothe you, but there is none *w.*
Mk. 14. 54; John 18. 18, Peter *w.* himself.
Jas. 2. 16, be ye *w.* and filled.
See 2 Kings 4. 34; Job 37. 17; 39. 14; Isa. 44. 15.

WARN. Ezek. 3. 18; Acts 20. 31; 1 Thess. 5. 14.

WASH. 2 Kings 5. 10, go, *w.* in Jordan.
12, may I not *w.* in them, and be clean?
Job 9. 30, if I *w.* myself with snow water.
14. 19, thou *w.* away things which grow.
29. 6, when I *w.* my steps with butter.
Ps. 26. 6; 73. 13, I will *w.* my hands in innocency.
51. 2, *w.* me throughly from mine iniquity.
7, *w.* me, and I shall be whiter than snow.
Prov. 30. 12, a generation not *w.*
Cant. 5. 12, his eyes are *w.* with milk.
Isa. 1. 16, *w.* you, make you clean.

Jer. 2. 22, though thou *w.* thee with nitre.
4. 14, *w.* thy heart.
Ezek. 16. 4, nor wast *w.* in water to supple thee.
Mat. 6. 17, when thou fastest, *w.* thy face.
27. 24, took water, and *w.* his hands.
Mk. 7. 3, except they *w.* oft, eat not.
Lu. 7. 38, began to *w.* his feet with tears.
44, she hath *w.* my feet with her tears.
John 9. 7, go, *w.* in the pool of Siloam.
Acts 16. 33, he *w.* their stripes.
22. 16, *w.* away thy sins.
1 Cor. 6. 11, but ye are *w.*
Heb. 10. 22, having our bodies *w.* with pure water.
2 Pet. 2. 22, the sow that was *w.*
Rev. 1. 5, that *w.* us from our sins.
7. 14, have *w.* their robes.
See Neh. 4. 23; Eph. 5. 26; Tit. 3. 5; Heb. 9. 10.
WASTE. Deut. 32. 10; Job 30. 3, in *w.* wilderness.
1 Kings 17. 14, the barrel of meal shall not *w.*
Ps. 80. 13, the boar out of the wood doth *w.* it.
91. 6, nor for the destruction that *w.* at noonday.
Isa. 24. 1, the Lord maketh the earth *w.*
61. 4, they shall build the old *w.*
Joel 1. 10, the field is *w.*, the corn is *w.*
See Prov. 18. 9; Isa. 59. 7; Mat. 26. 8; Mk. 14. 4.
WATCH (*n.*). Ps. 90. 4, as a *w.* in the night.
119. 148, mine eyes prevent the night *w.*
Jer. 51. 12, make the *w.* strong.
Hab. 2. 1, I will stand upon my *w.*
See Mat. 14. 25; 24. 43; 27. 65; Lu. 2. 8.
WATCH (*v.*). Gen. 31. 49, the Lord *w.* between me and thee.
Job 14. 16, dost thou not *w.* over my sin?
Ps. 37. 32, the wicked *w.* the righteous.
102. 7, I *w.*, and am as a sparrow.
130. 6, more than they that *w.* for morning.
Isa. 29. 20, all that *w.* for iniquity are cut off.
Jer. 20. 10, my familiars *w.* for my halting.
31. 28, so will I *w.* over them, to build.
44. 27, I will *w.* over them for evil.
Ezek. 7. 6, the end is come, it *w.* for thee.
Hab. 2. 1, I will *w.* to see what he will say.
Mat. 24. 42; 25. 13; Mk. 13. 35; Lu. 21. 36; Acts 20. 31, *w.* therefore.
26. 41; Mk. 13. 33; 14. 38, *w.* and pray.
1 Thess. 5. 6; 1 Pet. 4. 7, let us *w.* and be sober.
Heb. 13. 17, for they *w.* for your souls.
See 1 Cor. 16. 13; 2 Tim. 4. 5; Rev. 3. 2; 16. 15.
WATCH TOWER. 2 Chron. 20. 24; Judah came toward the *w.*
Isa. 21. 5, watch in the *w.*
WATER (*n.*). Gen. 26. 20, the *w.* is ours.
49. 4, unstable as *w.*
Deut. 8. 7, a land of brooks of *w.*
11. 11, the land drinketh *w.* of rain of heaven.
Josh. 7. 5 their hearts melted, and became as *w.*
2 Sam. 14. 14, as *w.* spilt on the ground.
1 Kings 13. 22, eat no bread, and drink no *w.*
22. 27; 2 Chron. 18. 26, *w.* of affliction.
2 Kings 3. 11, who poured *w.* on Elijah's hands.
20. 20, brought *w.* into the city.
Neh. 9. 11, threwest as a stone into mighty *w.*
Job 8. 11, can the flag grow without *w.*?
14. 9, through the scent of *w.* it will bud.
19, the *w.* wear the stones.
15. 16, who drinketh iniquity like *w.*
22. 7, thou hast not given *w.* to weary to drink.
26. 8, he bindeth up the *w.* in his thick clouds.
38. 30, the *w.* are hid as with a stone.
Ps. 22. 14, I am poured out like *w.*
23. 2, beside the still *w.*
33. 7, he gathereth the *w.* of the sea.
46. 3, though the *w.* roar and be troubled.
63. 1, a dry and thirsty land, where no *w.* is.
73. 10, *w.* of a full cup are wrung out to them.
77. 16, the *w.* saw thee.
79. 3, their blood have they shed like *w.*
124. 4, then the *w.* had overwhelmed us.
148. 4, praise him, ye *w.* above the heavens.
Prov. 5. 15, drink *w.* out of thine own cistern.
9. 17, stolen *w.* are sweet.
20. 5, counsel is like deep *w.*
25. 25, as cold *w.* to a thirsty soul.
27. 19, as in *w.* face answereth to face.
30. 4, who hath bound the *w.* in a garment?
Eccl. 11. 1, cast thy bread upon the *w.*
Cant. 4. 15; John 7. 38, well of living *w.*
8. 7, many *w.* cannot quench love.
Isa. 1. 22, thy wine is mixed with *w.*
3. 1, take away the whole stay of *w.*
11. 9; Hab. 2. 14, as the *w.* cover the seas.
19. 5, the *w.* shall fail from the sea.
28. 17, *w.* shall overflow the hiding place.
32. 20, blessed are ye that sow beside all *w.*
33. 16, his *w.* shall be sure.
35. 6, in the wilderness shall *w.* break out.
41. 17, when the poor seek *w.*
43. 2, when thou passest through the *w.*
16, a path in the mighty *w.*
20, I give *w.* in the wilderness.
44. 3, I will pour *w.* on him that is thirsty.
55. 1, come ye to the *w.*
57. 20, whose *w.* cast up mire and dirt.
Jer. 2. 13; 17. 13, the fountain of living *w.*
9. 1, Oh that my head were *w.*!
14. 3, their nobles sent little ones to the *w.*
47. 2, behold, *w.* rise up out of the north.
Ezek. 4. 17, that they may want bread and *w.*
7. 17; 21. 7, be weak as *w.*
31. 4, the *w.* made him great.
36. 25, then will I sprinkle clean *w.* upon you.
Amos 8. 11, not famine of bread nor thirst for *w.*
Mat. 3. 11; Mk. 1. 8; Lu. 3. 16; John 1. 26; Acts 1. 5; 11. 16, baptize you with *w.*
10. 42; Mk. 9. 41, whoso giveth a cup of cold *w.*
14. 28, bid me come to thee on the *w.*
27. 24, Pilate took *w.*, and washed.
Lu. 8. 23, ship filled with *w.*
24, and rebuked the raging of the *w.*
16. 24, dip the tip of his finger in *w.*
John 3. 5, except a man be born of *w.*
23, there was much *w.* there.
4. 15, give me this *w.*
5. 3, waiting for moving of the *w.*
19. 34, forthwith came out blood and *w.*
Acts 10. 47, can any forbid *w.*?
2 Cor. 11. 26, in perils of *w.*
Eph. 5. 26, cleanse it with washing of *w.*
1 Pet. 3. 20, eight souls were saved by *w.*
2 Pet. 2. 17, wells without *w.*
1 John 5. 6, this is he that came by *w.*
Rev. 22. 17, let him take the *w.* of life freely.
See Ps. 29. 3; Jer. 51. 13; Ezek. 32. 2; 47. 1.
WATER (*v.*). Gen. 2. 6, mist that *w.* face of ground.
13. 10, the plain was well *w.*
Deut. 11. 10, *w.* it with thy foot, as a garden.
Ps. 6. 6, I *w.* my couch with tears.
72. 6, as showers that *w.* the earth.
104. 13, he *w.* the hills from his chambers.
Prov. 11. 25, he that *w.*, shall be *w.*
Isa. 16. 9, I will *w.* thee with my tears.
27. 3, I will *w.* it every moment.
55. 10, returneth not, but *w.* the earth.
58. 11; Jer. 31. 12, thou shalt be like a *w.* garden.
Ezek. 32. 6, I will also *w.* with thy blood.
1 Cor. 3. 6, Apollos *w.*, but God gave the increase.
See Ps. 65. 9; Ezek. 17. 7; Joel 3. 18.
WAVERING. Heb. 10. 23, the profession of our faith without *w.*
Jas. 1. 5, ask in faith, nothing *w.*
WAVES. Ps. 42. 7, all thy *w.* are gone over me.
65. 7; 89. 9; 107. 29, stilleth noise of *w.*
93. 4, the Lord is mightier than mighty *w.*
Isa. 48. 18, thy righteousness as the *w.* of the sea.
Jer. 5. 22, though the *w.* toss.
Zech. 10. 11, shall smite the *w.* in the sea.
Jude 13, raging *w.* of the sea.

See Mat. 8. 24; 14. 24; Mk. 4. 37; Acts 27. 41.
WAX (*n.*). Ps. 22. 14; 68. 2; 97. 5; Mic. 1. 4.
WAX (*v.*). Ex. 22. 24; 32. 10, my wrath shall *w.* hot.
Num. 11. 23, is the Lord's hand *w.* short?
Deut. 8. 4; 29. 5; Neh. 9. 21, raiment *w.* not old.
32. 15, Jeshurun *w.* fat, and kicked.
Ps. 102. 26; Isa. 50. 9; 51. 6; Heb. 1. 11, shall *w.* old as doth a garment.
Mat. 24. 12, the love of many shall *w.* cold.
Lu. 12. 33, bags which *w.* not old.
See Mat. 13. 15; 1 Tim. 5. 11; 2 Tim. 3. 13.
WAY. Gen. 6. 12, all flesh had corrupted his *w.*
24. 20, if God will keep me in this *w.*
56, seeing the Lord hath prospered my *w.*
Num. 22. 32, thy *w.* is perverse.
Deut. 8. 6; 26. 17; 28. 9; 30. 16; 1 Kings 2. 3; Ps. 119. 3; 128. 1; Isa. 42. 24, walk in his *w.*
Josh. 23. 14; 1 Kings 2. 2, the *w.* of all the earth.
1 Sam. 12. 23, teach you the good and right *w.*
2 Sam. 22. 31; Ps. 18. 30, as for God, his *w.* is perfect.
2 Kings 7. 15, all the *w.* was full of garments.
2 Chron. 6. 27, when thou hast taught them the good *w.*
Ezra 8. 21, to seek of him a right *w.*
Job 3. 23, to a man whose *w.* is hid.
12. 24; Ps. 107. 40, to wander where there is no *w.*
16. 22, I go the *w.* whence I shall not return.
19. 8, fenced up my *w.*
22. 15, hast thou marked the old *w.*?
23. 10, he knoweth the *w.* that I take.
24. 13, they know not the *w.* of the light.
31. 4, doth not he see my *w.*?
38. 19, where is the *w.* where light dwelleth?
Ps. 1. 6, the Lord knoweth the *w.* of righteous.
2. 12, lest ye perish from the *w.*
25. 9, the meek will he teach his *w.*
27. 11; 86. 11, teach me thy *w.*
36. 4, in a *w.* that is not good.
37. 5, commit thy *w.* unto the Lord.
39. 1, I will take heed to my *w.*
49. 13, this their *w.* is their folly.
67. 2, that thy *w.* may be known.
78. 50, he made a *w.* to his anger.
95. 10; Heb. 3. 10, they have not known my *w.*
101. 2, behave wisely in a perfect *w.*
119. 5, O that my *w.* were directed.
30, I have chosen the *w.* of truth.
59, I thought on my *w.*
168, all my *w.* are before thee.
139. 24, lead me in the *w.* everlasting.
Prov. 2. 8, he preserveth the *w.* of his saints.
3. 6, in all thy *w.* acknowledge him.
17, her *w.* are *w.* of pleasantness.
5. 21, the *w.* of man are before the Lord.
6. 6, consider her *w.*, and be wise.
23; 15. 24; Jer. 21. 8, the *w.* of life.
12. 15, the *w.* of a fool is right in his own eyes.
15. 19, the *w.* of the slothful man.
16. 7, when a man's *w.* please the Lord.
22. 6, train up a child in the *w.*
23. 19, guide thy heart in the *w.*
26, let thine eyes observe my *w.*
26. 13, there is a lion in the *w.*
Eccl. 11. 5, the *w.* of the spirit.
12. 5, fears shall be in the *w.*
Isa. 2. 3; Mic. 4. 2, he will teach us of his *w.*
30. 21, this is the *w.*, walk ye in it.
35. 8, and a *w.*, called the *w.* of holiness.
40. 27, my *w.* is hid from the Lord.
42. 16, the blind by a *w.* they knew not.
24, they would not walk in his *w.*
45. 13, I will direct all his *w.*
55. 8, neither are your *w.* my *w.*
58. 2, they delight to know my *w.*
Jer. 6. 16, where is the good *w.*?
17. 10; 32. 19, every man according to his *w.*
18. 11, make your *w.* and doings good.
Jer. 32. 39, I will give them one heart and one *w.*
50. 5, they shall ask the *w.* to Zion.
Ezek. 3. 18, to warn the wicked from his *w.*
18. 29, are not my *w.* equal? are not your *w.* unequal?
Joel 2. 7, march every one on his *w.*
Nah. 1. 3, the Lord hath his *w.* in the whirlwind.
Hag. 1. 5, consider your *w.*
Mal. 3. 1, he shall prepare the *w.* before me.
Mat. 7. 13, broad is the *w.* that leadeth.
10. 5, go not into *w.* of Gentiles.
22. 16; Mk. 12. 14; Lu. 20. 21, teachest the *w.* of God.
Mk. 8. 3, they will faint by the *w.*
11. 8; Mat. 21. 8; Lu. 19. 36, spread garments in the *w.*
Lu. 15. 20, when he was yet a great *w.* off.
19. 4, he was to pass that *w.*
John 10. 1, but climbeth up some other *w.*
14. 4, and the *w.* ye know.
6, I am the *w.*, the truth, and the life.
Acts 9. 2, if he found any of this *w.*
27, how he had seen the Lord in the *w.*
16. 17, which show unto us the *w.* of salvation.
18. 26, expounded the *w.* of God more perfectly.
19. 23, no small stir about that *w.*
24. 14, after the *w.* which they call heresy.
Rom. 3. 12, they are all gone out of the *w.*
11. 33, his *w.* are past finding out.
1 Cor. 10. 13, will make a *w.* to escape.
12. 31, a more excellent *w.*
Col. 2. 14, took handwriting of ordinances out of the *w.*
Heb. 5. 2, compassion on them out of the *w.*
9. 8, the *w.* into the holiest.
10. 20, by a new and living *w.*
Jas. 1. 8, unstable in all his *w.*
5. 20, the sinner from error of his *w.*
2 Pet. 2. 2, many shall follow their pernicious *w.*
15, which have forsaken the right *w.*
21, better not to have known *w.* of righteousness.
Jude 11, they have gone in the *w.* of Cain.
See Hos. 2. 6; Lu. 10. 31; Rev. 15. 3.
WEAK. Judg. 16. 7, *w.* as other men.
2 Sam. 3. 1, Saul's house waxed *w.* and *w.*
2 Chron. 15. 7, let not your hands be *w.*
Job 4. 3, thou hast strengthened the *w.* hands.
Ps. 6. 2, I am *w.*
Isa. 14. 10, art thou also become *w.* as we?
35. 3, strengthen ye the *w.* hands.
Ezek. 7. 17; 21. 7, shall be *w.* as water.
16. 30, how *w.* is thy heart!
Joel 3. 10, let the *w.* say, I am strong.
Mat. 26. 41; Mk. 14. 38, but the flesh is *w.*
Acts 20. 35, ye ought to support the *w.*
Rom. 4. 19, being not *w.* in faith.
8. 3, for the law was *w.*
1 Cor. 1. 27, *w.* things to confound the mighty.
11. 30, for this cause many are *w.*
2 Cor. 10. 10, his bodily presence is *w.*
11. 29, who is *w.*, and I am not *w.*?
12. 10, when I am *w.*, then am I strong.
Gal. 4. 9, turn again to *w.* elements.
1 Pet. 3. 7, giving honour to the wife, as *w.* vessel.
See Job 12. 21; Jer. 38. 4; Rom. 15. 1; 1 Thess. 5. 14.
WEAKNESS. 1 Cor. 1. 25, the *w.* of God.
2. 3, I was with you in *w.*
15. 43, it is sown in *w.*, raised in power.
See 2 Cor. 12. 9; 13. 4; Heb. 7. 18; 11. 34.
WEALTH. Deut. 8. 18, Lord giveth power to get *w.*
1 Sam. 2. 32, thou shalt see an enemy in all the *w.*
2 Chron. 1. 11, thou hast not asked *w.*
Esth. 10. 3, seeking the *w.* of his people.
Job 21. 13, they spend their days in *w.*
31. 25, if I rejoiced because my *w.* was great.

Ps. 44. 12, dost not increase *w.* by price.
49. 6, they that trust in *w.*
49. 10, wise men die, and leave *w.* to others.
112. 3, *w.* and riches shall be in his house.
Prov. 5. 10, lest strangers be filled with thy *w.*
10. 15; 18. 11, the rich man's *w.* is his strong city.
13. 11, *w.* gotten by vanity.
19. 4, *w.* maketh many friends.
Acts 19. 25, by this craft we have our *w.*
1 Cor. 10. 24, seek every man another's *w.*
See Deut. 8. 17; Ruth 2. 1; Ezra 9. 12; Zech. 14. 14.
WEALTHY. Ps. 66. 12; Jer. 49. 31.
WEANED. 1 Sam. 1. 22; Ps. 131. 2; Isa. 11. 8; 28. 9.
WEAPON. Neh. 4. 17, with the other hand held a *w.*
Isa. 13. 5; Jer. 50. 25, the *w.* of his indignation.
54. 17, no *w.* formed against thee shall prosper.
Jer. 22. 7, every one with his *w.*
Ezek. 9. 1, with destroying *w.* in his hand.
2 Cor. 10. 4, the *w.* of our warfare.
See Job 20. 24; Ezek. 39. 9; John 18. 3.
WEAR. Job 14. 19, the waters *w.* the stones.
Isa. 4. 1, we will *w.* our own apparel.
Zech. 13. 4, nor shall they *w.* a rough garment.
Mat. 11. 8, that *w.* soft clothing.
See Deut. 22. 5; Esth. 6. 8; Lu. 9. 12; 1 Pet. 3. 3.
WEARINESS. Eccl. 12. 12; Mal. 1. 13; 2 Cor. 11. 27.
WEARY. Gen. 27. 46, I am *w.* of my life.
2 Sam. 23. 10, he smote till his hand was *w.*
Job 3. 17, and the *w.* be at rest.
10. 1, my soul is *w.*
16. 7, now he hath made me *w.*
22. 7, thou hast not given water to the *w.*
Ps. 6. 6, I am *w.* with groaning.
Prov. 3. 11, be not *w.* of the Lord's correction.
25. 17, lest he be *w.* of thee.
Isa. 5. 27, none shall be *w.* among them.
7. 13, will ye *w.* my God also?
28. 12, cause the *w.* to rest.
32. 2, as the shadow of a great rock in *w.* land.
40. 28, God fainteth not, neither is *w.*
31, they shall run, and not be *w.*
43. 22, thou hast been *w.* of me.
46. 1, a burden to the *w.* beast.
50. 4, a word in season to him that is *w.*
Jer. 6. 11, I am *w.* with holding in.
15. 6, I am *w.* with repenting.
20. 9, I was *w.* with forbearing.
31. 25, I have satiated the *w.* soul.
Lu. 18. 5, lest she *w.* me.
Gal. 6. 9; 2 Thess. 3. 13, be not *w.* in well doing.
See Judg. 4. 21; Ps. 68. 9; 69. 3; Hab. 2. 13.
WEARY (*v.*). Isa. 43. 24, thou hast *w.* me.
47. 13, *w.* in the multitude of counsels.
57. 10, *w.* in the greatness of thy way.
Jer. 12. 5, with footmen, and they *w.* thee.
Ezek. 24. 12, she hath *w.* herself with lies.
Mic. 6. 3, wherein have I *w.* thee?
John 4. 6, being *w.*, sat thus on the well.
Heb. 12. 3, lest ye be *w.* and faint.
See Eccl. 10. 15; Jer. 4. 31; Mal. 2. 17.
WEASEL. Lev. 11. 29.
WEATHER. Job 37. 22; Prov. 25. 20; Mat. 16. 2.
WEB. Judg. 16. 13; Job 8. 14; Isa. 59. 5.
WEDGE. Josh. 7. 21; Isa. 13. 12.
WEEK. Gen. 29. 27, fulfil her *w.*
Jer. 5. 24, the appointed *w.* of harvest.
Dan. 9. 27, in the midst of the *w.*
Mat. 28. 1; Mk. 16. 2, 9; Lu. 24. 1; John 20. 1, 19; Acts 20. 7; 1 Cor. 16. 2, the first day of the *w.*
See Num. 28. 26; Dan. 10. 2; Lu. 18. 12.
WEEP. Gen. 43. 30, he sought where to *w.*
1 Sam. 1. 8; John 20. 13, why *w.* thou?
11. 5, what aileth the people that they *w.*?
30. 4, no more power to *w.*
Neh. 8. 9, mourn not, nor *w.*
Job 27. 15, his widows shall not *w.*
30. 25, did not I *w.* for him that was in trouble?
Eccl. 3. 4, a time to *w.*
Isa. 15. 2, he is gone up to *w.*
22. 4, I will *w.* bitterly.
30. 19, thou shalt *w.* no more.
Jer. 9. 1, that I might *w.* day and night.
22. 10, *w.* ye not for the dead.
Joel 1. 5, awake, ye drunkards, and *w.*
Mk. 5. 39, why make ye this ado, and *w.*?
Lu. 6. 21, blessed are ye that *w.* now.
7. 13; 8. 52; Rev. 5. 5, *w.* not.
23. 28, *w.* not for me, but *w.* for yourselves.
John 11. 31, she goeth to the grave to *w.* there.
Acts 21. 13, what mean ye to *w.*?
Rom. 12. 15, and *w.* with them that *w.*
See John 16. 20; 1 Cor. 7. 30; Jas. 4. 9; 5. 1.
WEEPING. 2 Sam. 15. 30, *w.* as they went.
Ezra 3. 13, could not discern noise of joy from *w.*
Job 16. 16, my face is foul with *w.*
Ps. 6. 8, the Lord hath heard the voice of my *w.*
30. 5, *w.* may endure for a night.
102. 9, I have mingled my drink with *w.*
Isa. 65. 19, the voice of *w.* be no more heard.
Jer. 31. 16, refrain thy voice from *w.*
48. 5, continual *w.* shall go up.
Joel 2. 12, turn to me with fasting and *w.*
Mat. 8. 12; 22. 13; 24. 51; 25. 30; Lu. 13. 28, *w.* and gnashing of teeth.
Lu. 7. 38, stood at his feet behind him *w.*
John 11. 33, when Jesus saw her *w.*
20. 11, Mary stood without at sepulchre *w.*
Phil. 3. 18, now tell you even *w.*
See Num. 25. 6; Jer. 31. 15; Mal. 2. 13; Mat. 2. 18; Acts 9. 39.
WEIGH. 2 Sam. 14. 26, *w.* the hair of his head.
Job 6. 2, oh that my grief were *w.*!
31. 6, let me be *w.* in an even balance.
Isa. 26. 7, thou dost *w.* the path of the just.
40. 12, who hath *w.* the mountains?
Dan. 5. 27, thou art *w.* in the balances.
See Job 28. 25; Prov. 16. 2; Zech. 11. 12.
WEIGHT. Lev. 26. 26, deliver your bread by *w.*
Job 28. 25, to make the *w.* for the winds.
Ezek. 4. 10, thy meat shall be by *w.*
16, they shall eat bread by *w.*
2 Cor. 4. 17, a more exceeding *w.* of glory.
Heb. 12. 1, lay aside every *w.*
See Deut. 25. 13; Prov. 16. 11; Mic. 6. 11.
WEIGHTY. Prov. 27. 3; Mat. 23. 23; 2 Cor. 10. 10.
WELFARE. Neh. 2. 10, to seek *w.* of Israel.
Job 30. 15, my *w.* passeth away.
Ps. 69. 22, which should have been for their *w.*
Jer. 38. 4, seeketh not the *w.* of this people.
See Gen. 43. 27; Ex. 18. 7; 1 Chron. 18. 10.
WELL (*n.*). Num. 21. 17, spring up, O *w.*
Deut. 6. 11, and *w.* which thou diggedst not.
2 Sam. 23. 15; 1 Chron. 11. 17, water of the *w.* of Bethlehem.
Ps. 84. 6, through valley of Baca make it a *w.*
Prov. 5. 15, waters out of thine own *w.*
10. 11, a *w.* of life.
Cant. 4. 15; John 4. 14, *w.* of living waters.
Isa. 12. 3, the *w.* of salvation.
John 4. 6, sat thus on the *w.*
2 Pet. 2. 17, *w.* without water.
See Gen. 21. 19; 49. 22; 2 Sam. 17. 18.
WELL (*adv.*). Gen. 4. 7, if thou doest *w.*
12. 13, *w.* with me for thy sake.
29. 6, is he *w.*? and they said, he is *w.*
40. 14, think on me when it shall be *w.* with thee.
Ex. 4. 14, I know he can speak *w.*
Num. 11. 18, it was *w.* with us in Egypt.
Deut. 4. 40; 5. 16; 6. 3; 12. 25; 19. 13; 22. 7; Ruth 3. 1; Eph. 6. 3, that it may go *w.* with thee.
1 Sam. 20. 7, if he say thus, it is *w.*
2 Kings 4. 26, is it *w.* with thee, is it *w.*?

2 Chron. 12. 12, in Judah things went *w.*
Ps. 49. 18, when thou doest *w.* to thyself.
Prov. 11. 10, when it goeth *w.* with the righteous.
14. 15, looketh *w.* with the righteous.
30. 29, three things which go *w.*
Eccl. 8. 12, it shall be *w.* with them that fear God.
Isa. 3. 10, say to the righteous, it shall be *w.*
Ezek. 33. 32, one that can play *w.*
Jonah 4. 4, doest thou *w.* to be angry?
Mat. 25. 21; Lu. 19. 17, *w.* done.
Mk. 7. 37, he hath done all things *w.*
Lu. 6. 26, when all men speak *w.* of you.
Gal. 5. 7, ye did run *w.*
See Phil. 4. 14; 1 Tim. 3. 5; 5. 17; Tit. 2. 9.
WENT. Gen. 4. 16, Cain *w.* out from the presence.
Deut. 1. 31, in all the way ye *w.*
2 Kings 5. 26, *w.* not my heart with thee?
Ps. 42. 4, I *w.* with them to the house of God.
106. 32, it *w.* ill with Moses.
Mat. 21. 30, I go, sir, and *w.* not.
Lu. 17. 14, as they *w.* they were cleansed.
18. 10, two men *w.* up into the temple to pray.
See Mat. 11. 7; 20. 1; Lu. 6. 19; John 8. 9.
WEPT. 2 Kings 8. 11, the man of God *w.*
Ezra 10. 1; Neh. 8. 9, the people *w.* very sore.
Neh. 1. 4, I *w.* before God.
Lu. 7. 32, we mourned, and ye have not *w.*
19. 41, beheld the city, and *w.* over it.
John 11. 35, Jesus *w.*
1 Cor. 7. 30, that weep as though they *w.* not.
See 2 Sam. 12. 22; Ps. 69. 10; 137. 1; Rev. 5. 4.
WET. Job 24. 8; Dan. 4. 15; 5. 21.
WHAT. Ex. 16. 15, they wist not *w.* it was.
2 Sam. 16. 10, *w.* have I to do with you?
Ezra 9. 10, *w.* shall we say after this?
Job 7. 17; 15. 14; Ps. 8. 4; 144. 3, *w.* is man?
Isa. 38. 15; John 12. 27, *w.* shall I say?
Hos. 6. 4, *w.* shall I do unto thee?
Mat. 5. 47, *w.* do ye more than others?
Mk. 14. 36, not *w.* I will, but *w.* thou wilt.
John 21. 22, *w.* is that to thee?
See Acts 9. 6; 10. 4; 16. 30; 1 Pet. 1. 11.
WHATSOEVER. Ps. 1. 3, *w.* he doeth shall prosper.
Eccl. 3. 14, *w.* God doeth shall be for ever.
Mat. 5. 37, *w.* is more than these cometh of evil.
7. 12, *w.* ye would that men should do to you.
20. 4, *w.* is right I will give you.
Phil. 4. 8, *w.* things are true.
See John 15. 16; Rom. 14. 23; 1 Cor. 10. 31.
WHEAT. 1 Sam. 12. 17, is it not *w.* harvest to-day?
Job 31. 40, let thistles grow instead of *w.*
Ps. 81. 16; 147. 14, the finest of the *w.*
Jer. 12. 13, they have sown *w.*, but reap thorns.
23. 28, what is the chaff to the *w.*?
Mat. 3. 12, gather his *w.* into the garner.
Lu. 22. 31, that he may sift you as *w.*
See John 12. 24; Acts 27. 38; 1 Cor. 15. 37.
WHEEL. Ex. 14. 25, took off their chariot *w.*
Judg. 5. 28, why tarry the *w.*?
Ps. 83. 13, make them like a *w.*
Prov. 20. 26, a wise king bringeth the *w.* over them.
Eccl. 12. 6, or the *w.* broken at the cistern.
Isa. 28. 28, nor break it with the *w.* of his cart.
Nah. 3. 2, the noise of the rattling of the *w.*
See Isa. 5. 28; Jer. 18. 3; 47. 3; Ezek. 1. 16.
WHELP. 2 Sam. 17. 8; Prov. 17. 12; Hos. 13. 8.
WHEN. 1 Sam. 3. 12, *w.* I begin, I will also.
1 Kings 8. 30, *w.* thou hearest, forgive.
Ps. 94. 8, *w.* will ye be wise?
Eccl. 8. 7, who can tell him *w.* it shall be?
Mat. 24. 3; Mk. 13. 4; Lu. 21. 7, *w.* shall these things be?
See Deut. 6. 7; John 4. 25; 16. 8; 1 John 2. 28.
WHENCE. Gen. 42. 7; Josh. 9. 8, *w.* come ye?
Job 10. 21, *w.* I shall not return.
Isa. 51. 1, the rock *w.* ye are hewn.
Jas. 4. 1, from *w.* come wars?
Rev. 7. 13, *w.* came they?
See Mat. 13. 54; John 1. 48; 7. 28; 9. 29.
WHERE. Gen. 3. 9, *w.* art thou?
Ex. 2. 20; 2 Sam. 9. 4; Job 14. 10, *w.* is he?
Job 9. 24, if not, *w.*, and who is he?
Ps. 42. 3, *w.* is thy God?
Jer. 2. 6, *w.* is the Lord?
Zech. 1. 5, your fathers, *w.* are they?
See Isa. 49. 21; Hos. 1. 10; Lu. 17. 37.
WHEREBY. Lu. 1. 18, *w.* shall I know this?
Acts 4. 12, none other name *w.* we must be saved.
Rom. 8. 15, the spirit of adoption, *w.* we cry.
See Jer. 33. 8; Ezek. 18. 31; 39. 26; Eph. 4. 30.
WHEREFORE. 2 Sam. 12. 23, *w.* should I fast?
Mat. 14. 31, *w.* didst thou doubt?
26. 50, *w.* art thou come?
See 2 Sam. 16. 10; Mal. 2. 15; Acts 10. 21.
WHERETO. Isa. 55. 11; Phil. 3. 16.
WHEREWITH. Judg. 6. 5, *w.* shall I save Israel?
Ps. 119. 42, so shall I have *w.* to answer.
Mic. 6. 6, *w.* shall I come before the Lord?
See Mat. 5. 13; Mk. 9. 5; John 17. 26; Eph. 2. 4.
WHET. Deut. 32. 41; Ps. 7. 12; 64. 3; Eccl. 10. 10.
WHETHER. Mat. 21. 31, *w.* of them did the will.
Mat. 23. 17, *w.* is greater, the gold or the temple?
Rom. 14. 8, *w.* we live or die.
2 Cor. 12. 2, *w.* in the body, or out of the body.
See 1 Kings 20. 18; Ezek. 2. 5; 3. 11; 1 John 4. 1.
WHILE. 2 Chron. 15. 2, with you, *w.* ye be with him.
Ps. 49. 18, *w.* he lived he blessed his soul.
Isa. 55. 6, *w.* he may be found.
Jer. 15. 9, her sun is gone down *w.* it was yet day.
Lu. 18. 4, he would not for a *w.*
24. 44, *w.* I was yet with you.
John 9. 4, work *w.* it is day.
1 Tim. 5. 6, she is dead *w.* she liveth.
See 1 Sam. 9. 27; 2 Sam. 7. 19; Acts 20. 11.
WHIP. 1 Kings 12. 11; Prov. 26. 3; Nah. 3. 2.
WHIT. 1 Sam. 3. 18; John 7. 23; 13. 10; 2 Cor. 11. 5.
WHITE. Gen. 49. 12, his teeth shall be *w.* with milk.
Num. 12. 10, leprous, *w.* as snow.
Job 6. 6, is any taste in the *w.* of an egg?
Eccl. 9. 8, let thy garments be always *w.*
Cant. 5. 10, my beloved is *w.* and ruddy.
Isa. 1. 18, they shall be *w.* as snow.
Mat. 5. 36, thou canst not make one hair *w.* or black.
John 4. 35, *w.* already to harvest.
Rev. 2. 17, a *w.* stone.
3. 4, walk with me in *w.*
See Dan. 11. 35; 12. 10; Mat. 17. 2; 28. 3.
WHITED. Mat. 23. 27; Acts 23. 3.
WHITER. Ps. 51. 7; Lam. 4. 7.
WHITHER. 2 Kings 5. 25; Cant. 6. 1; Heb. 11. 8.
WHOLE. 2 Sam. 1. 9, my life is yet *w.* in me.
Eccl. 12. 13, this is the *w.* duty of man.
Jer. 19. 11, a vessel that cannot be made *w.*
Ezek. 15. 5, when *w.* it was meet for no work.
Mat. 5. 29, not that thy *w.* body be cast into hell.
9. 12; Mk. 2. 17, the *w.* need not a physician.
13. 33; Lu. 13. 21, till the *w.* was leavened.
16. 26; Mk. 8. 36; Lu. 9. 25, gain the *w.* world.
John 11. 50, expedient that the *w.* nation perish not.
1 Cor. 12. 17, if the *w.* body were an eye.
1 Thess. 5. 23, I pray God your *w.* spirit.
Jas. 2. 10, keep the *w.* law.
1 John 2. 2, for the sins of the *w.* world.
5. 19, the *w.* world lieth in wickedness.
See Mat. 15. 31; John 5. 6; 7. 23; Acts 9. 34.
WHOLESOME. Prov. 15. 4; 1 Tim. 6. 3.
WHOLLY. Job 21. 23, dieth, being *w.* at ease.
Jer. 2. 21, planted thee *w.* a right seed.
46. 28, not *w.* unpunished.
Acts 17. 16, the city *w.* given to idolatry.

1 Thess. 5. 23, sanctify you *w.*
1 Tim. 4. 15, give thyself *w.* to them.
See Lev. 19. 9; Deut. 1. 36; Josh. 14. 8.
WHOMSOEVER. Dan. 4. 17, 25, 32, to *w.* he will.
Mat. 11. 27, to *w.* the Son will reveal him.
21. 44; Lu. 20. 18, on *w.* it shall fall.
Lu. 4. 6, to *w.* I will, I give it.
12. 48, to *w.* much is given.
See Gen. 31. 32; Judg. 11. 24; Acts 8. 19.
WHOSE. Gen. 32. 17, *w.* art thou, *w.* are these?
Jer. 44. 28, shall know *w.* words shall stand.
Mat. 22. 20; Mk. 12. 16; Lu. 20. 24, *w.* is this image?
Lu. 12. 20, then *w.* shall these things be?
Acts 27. 23, *w.* I am, and whom I serve.
See 1 Sam. 12. 3; Dan. 5. 23; John 20. 23.
WHOSOEVER. 1 Cor. 11. 27, *w.* shall eat this bread.
Gal. 5. 10, bear his judgment, *w.* he be.
Rev. 22. 17, *w.* will, let him take.
See Mat. 11. 6; 13. 12; Lu. 8. 18; Rom. 2. 1.
WHY. 1 Sam. 2. 23, *w.* do ye such things?
Jer. 8. 14, *w.* do we sit still?
27. 13; Ezek. 18. 31; 33. 11, *w.* will ye die?
Mat. 21. 25; Mk. 11. 31; Lu. 20. 5, *w.* did ye not believe?
Mk. 5. 39, *w.* make ye this ado?
Acts 9. 4; 22. 7; 26. 14, *w.* persecutest thou me?
Rom. 9. 19, *w.* doth he yet find fault?
20, *w.* hast thou made me thus?
See 2 Chron. 25. 16; Lu. 2. 48; John 7. 45; 10. 20.
WICKED. Gen. 18. 23, destroy righteous with *w.*
Deut. 15. 9, a thought in thy *w.* heart.
1 Sam. 2. 9, the *w.* shall be silent.
Job 3. 17, there the *w.* cease from troubling.
8. 22, dwelling place of the *w.* shall come to nought.
9. 29; 10. 15, if I be *w.*, why labour I in vain?
Job 21. 7, wherefore do the *w.* live?
30, the *w.* is reserved to destruction.
Ps. 7. 9, let the wickedness of the *w.* come to an end.
11, God is angry with the *w.*
9. 17, the *w.* shall be turned into hell.
10. 4, the *w.* will not seek God.
11. 2, the *w.* bend their bow.
6, upon the *w.* he shall rain snares.
12. 8, the *w.* walk on every side.
26. 5, I will not sit with the *w.*
34. 21, evil shall slay the *w.*
37. 21, the *w.* borroweth, and payeth not.
32, the *w.* watcheth the righteous.
35, I have seen the *w.* in great power.
58. 3, the *w.* are estranged from the womb.
68. 2, so let the *w.* perish.
94. 3, how long shall the *w.* triumph?
139. 24, see if there be any *w.* way in me.
145. 20, all the *w.* will he destroy.
Prov. 11. 5, the *w.* shall fall by his own wickedness.
14. 32, the *w.* is driven away.
28. 1, the *w.* flee when no man pursueth.
Eccl. 7. 17, be not overmuch *w.*
8. 10, I saw the *w.* buried.
Isa. 13. 11, I will punish the *w.*
53. 9, he made his grave with the *w.*
55. 7, let the *w.* forsake his way.
57. 20, the *w.* are like the troubled sea.
Jer. 17. 9, the heart is desperately *w.*
Ezek. 3. 18; 33. 8, to warn the *w.*
11. 2, these men give *w.* counsel.
18. 23, have I any pleasure that the *w.* should die?
33. 15, if the *w.* restore the pledge.
Dan. 12. 10, the *w.* shall do wickedly.
Mic. 6. 11, with *w.* balances.
Nah. 1. 3, the Lord will not at all acquit the *w.*
Mat. 12. 45; Lu. 11. 26, more *w.* than himself.
13. 49, sever the *w.* from the just.
18. 32; 25. 26; Lu. 19. 22, thou *w.* servant.
Acts 2. 23, and by *w.* hands have crucified and slain.
1 Cor. 5. 13, put away that *w.* person.
Eph. 6. 16, the fiery darts of the *w.*
Col. 1. 21, enemies in your mind by *w.* works.
2 Thess. 2. 8, then shall that *W.* be revealed.
See Eccl. 9. 2; Isa. 48. 22; 2 Pet. 2. 7; 3. 17.
WICKEDLY. Job 13. 7, will you speak *w.* for God?
34. 12, God will not do *w.*
Ps. 73. 8; 139. 20, they speak *w.*
Dan. 12. 10, the wicked shall do *w.*
Mal. 4. 1, all that do *w.*
See 2 Chron. 6. 37; 22. 3; Neh. 9. 33; Ps. 106. 6.
WICKEDNESS. Gen. 39. 9, this great *w.*
Judg. 20. 3, how was this *w.*?
1 Sam. 24. 13, *w.* proceedeth from the wicked.
1 Kings 21. 25, sold himself to work *w.*
Job 4. 8, they that sow *w.*, reap the same.
22. 5, is not thy *w.* great?
35. 8, thy *w.* may hurt a man.
Ps. 7. 9, let the *w.* of the wicked come to an end.
55. 11, *w.* is in the midst thereof.
15, *w.* is in their dwellings.
58. 2, in heart ye work *w.*
84. 10, the tents of *w.*
Prov. 4. 17, they eat the bread of *w.*
8. 7, *w.* is an abomination to my lips.
11. 5, the wicked shall fall by his own *w.*
13. 6, *w.* overthroweth the sinner.
26. 26, his *w.* shall be shewed.
Eccl. 7. 25, the *w.* of folly.
Isa. 9. 18, *w.* burneth as the fire.
47. 10, thou hast trusted in thy *w.*
Jer. 2. 19, thine own *w.* shall correct thee.
6. 7, she casteth out her *w.*
8. 6, no man repented of his *w.*
44. 9, have you forgot the *w.* of your kings?
Ezek. 3. 19, if he turn not from his *w.*
7. 11, violence is risen up into a rod of *w.*
31. 11, I have driven him out for his *w.*
33. 12, in the day he turneth from his *w.*
Hos. 9. 15, for the *w.* of their doings.
10. 13, ye have ploughed *w.*
Mic. 6. 10, are treasures of *w.* in house.
Zech. 5. 8, he said, this is *w.*
Mal. 1. 4, the border of *w.*
3. 15, they that work *w.* are set up.
Mk. 7. 21, out of the heart proceed *w.*
Lu. 11. 39, your inward part is full of *w.*
Rom. 1. 29, being filled with all *w.*
1 Cor. 5. 8, nor with the leaven of *w.*
Eph. 6. 12, spiritual *w.* in high places.
1 John 5. 19, the whole world lieth in *w.*
See Gen. 6. 5; Ps. 94. 23; Prov. 21. 12; Jer. 23. 11.
WIDE. Ps. 35. 21, they opened their mouth *w.*
104. 25, this great and *w.* sea.
Prov. 21. 9; 25. 24; Jer. 22. 14, a *w.* house.
Mat. 7. 13, *w.* is the gate that leadeth to destruction.
See Deut. 15. 8; Ps. 81. 10; Nah. 3. 13.
WIFE. Prov. 5. 18; Eccl. 9. 9, the *w.* of thy youth.
18. 22, whoso findeth a *w.* findeth a good thing.
19. 14, a prudent *w.* is from the Lord.
Lu. 14. 20, I have married a *w.*
17. 32, remember Lot's *w.*
1 Cor. 7. 14, the unbelieving *w.* is sanctified.
Eph. 5. 23, the husband is the head of the *w.*
Rev. 21. 9, the bride, the Lamb's *w.*
See 1 Tim. 3. 2; 5. 9; Tit. 1. 6; 1 Pet. 3. 7.
WILES. Num. 25. 18; Eph. 6. 11.
WILFULLY. Heb. 10. 26, if we sin *w.*
WILL. Mat. 8. 3; Mk. 1. 41; Lu. 5. 13, I *w.*, be thou clean.
18. 14, not the *w.* of your Father.
26. 39, not as I *w.*, but as thou wilt.
Mk. 3. 35, whosoever shall do the *w.* of God.
John 1. 13, born not of the *w.* of the flesh.
4. 34, to do the *w.* of him that sent me.
Acts 21. 14, the *w.* of the Lord be done.
Rom. 7. 18, to *w.* is present with me.

Phil. 2. 13, both to *w.* and to do.
1 Tim. 2. 8, I *w.* that men pray every where.
Rev. 22. 17, whosoever *w.*, let him take.
See Rom. 9. 16; Eph. 1. 11; Heb. 2. 4; Jas. 1. 18.
WILLING. Ex. 35. 5, a *w.* heart.
1 Chron. 28. 9, serve God with a *w.* mind.
29. 5, who is *w.* to consecrate his service?
Ps. 110. 3, *w.* in the day of thy power.
Mat. 26. 41, the spirit is *w.*
2 Cor. 5. 8, *w.* rather to be absent.
8. 12, if there be first a *w.* mind.
1 Tim. 6. 18, *w.* to communicate.
2 Pet. 3. 9, not *w.* that any should perish.
See Lu. 22. 42; John 5. 35; Philem. 14; 1 Pet. 5. 2.
WIN. 2 Chron. 32. 1; Prov. 11. 30; Phil. 3. 8.
WIND. Job 6. 26, reprove speeches which are as *w.*
7. 7, remember that my life is *w.*
Prov. 11. 29, he shall inherit *w.*
25. 23, the north *w.* driveth away rain.
30. 4, gathereth the *w.* in his fists.
Eccl. 11. 4, he that observeth the *w.*
Isa. 26. 18, we have brought forth *w.*
27. 8, he stayeth his rough *w.*
Ezek. 37. 9, prophesy to the *w.*
Hos. 8. 7, they have sown *w.*
Amos 4. 13, he that createth the *w.*
Mat. 11. 7, a reed shaken with the *w.*
John 3. 8, the *w.* bloweth where it listeth.
Eph. 4. 14, carried about with every *w.* of doctrine.
See Acts 2. 2; Jas. 1. 6; Jude 12.
WINDOWS. Gen. 7. 11; Eccl. 12. 3; Jer. 9. 21; Mal. 3. 10.
WINGS. Ps. 17. 8; 36. 7; 57. 1; 61. 4; 68. 13;
91. 4, the shadow of thy *w.*
18. 10; 104. 3, on the *w.* of the wind.
55. 6, Oh that I had *w.* like a dove!
139. 9, the *w.* of the morning.
Prov. 23. 5, riches make themselves *w.*
Mal. 4. 2, with healing in his *w.*
See Ezek. 1. 6; Zech. 5. 9; Mat. 23. 37; Lu. 13. 34.
WINK. Job 15. 12; Ps. 35. 19; Prov. 6. 13; 10. 10; Acts 17. 30.
WINTER. Gen. 8. 22; Cant. 2. 11; Mat. 24. 20; Mk. 13. 18.
WIPE. 2 Kings 21. 13; Isa. 25. 8; Lu. 7. 38; John 13. 5.
WISDOM. Job 4. 21, they die without *w.*
12. 2, *w.* shall die with you.
Prov. 4. 7, *w.* is the principal thing.
16. 16, better to get *w.* than gold.
19. 8, he that getteth *w.* loveth his own soul.
23. 4, cease from thine own *w.*
Eccl. 1. 18, in much *w.* is much grief.
Isa. 10. 13, by my *w.* I have done it.
29. 14, the *w.* of their wise men shall perish.
Jer. 8. 9, they have rejected the word of the Lord; and what *w.* is in them?
Mic. 6. 9, the man of *w.* shall see thy name.
Mat. 11. 19, *w.* is justified of her children.
1 Cor. 1. 17, not with *w.* of words.
24, Christ the *w.* of God.
30, who of God is made unto us *w.*
2. 6, we speak *w.* among them that are perfect.
3. 19, the *w.* of this world is foolishness with God.
2 Cor. 1. 12, not with fleshly *w.*
Col. 1. 9, that ye might be filled with all *w.*
4. 5, walk in *w.* toward them.
Jas. 1. 5, if any lack *w.*
3. 17, the *w.* from above is pure.
Rev. 5. 12, worthy is the Lamb to receive *w.*
13. 18, here is *w.*
See Eccl. 1. 16; Rom. 11. 33; Col. 2. 3; 3. 16.
WISE. Gen. 3. 6, to make one *w.*
Ex. 23. 8, the gift blindeth the *w.*
Deut. 4. 6, this nation is a *w.* people.
32. 29, O that they were *w.*!
1 Kings 3. 12, I have given thee a *w.* heart.
Job 9. 4, he is *w.* in heart.
11. 12, vain man would be *w.*
22. 2, he that is *w.* may be profitable.
32. 9, great men are not always *w.*
Ps. 2. 10, be *w.* now, O ye kings.
19. 7, making *w.* the simple.
36. 3, he hath left off to be *w.*
94. 8, when will ye be *w.*?
107. 43, whoso is *w.*, and will observe.
Prov. 1. 5, a *w.* man shall attain *w.* counsels.
3. 7, be not *w.* in thine own eyes.
6. 6; 8. 33; 23. 19; 27. 11, be *w.*
9. 12, thou shalt be *w.* for thyself.
11. 30, he that winneth souls is *w.*
16. 21, the *w.* in heart shall be called prudent.
20. 26, a *w.* king scattereth the wicked.
Eccl. 7. 23, I said, I will be *w.*
9. 1, the *w.* are in the hands of God.
12. 11, the words of the *w.* are as goads.
Isa. 19. 11, I am the son of the *w.*
Dan. 12. 3, they that be *w.* shall shine.
Mat. 10. 16, be *w.* as serpents.
11. 25, hid these things from the *w.*
Rom. 1. 14, I am debtor to the *w.*
12. 16, be not *w.* in your own conceits.
1 Cor. 1. 20, where is the *w.*?
4. 10, ye are *w.* in Christ.
2 Tim. 3. 15, *w.* unto salvation.
See Isa. 5. 21; Jer. 4. 22; Mat. 25. 2.
WISELY. Ps. 58. 5, charmers, charming never so *w.*
101. 2, I will behave myself *w.*
Prov. 16. 20, that handleth a matter *w.*
See Prov. 21. 12; 28. 26; Eccl. 7. 10; Lu. 16. 8.
WISER. 1 Kings 4. 31; Lu. 16. 8; 1 Cor. 1. 25.
WISH. Ps. 73. 7, more than heart could *w.*
Rom. 9. 3, I could *w.* myself accursed.
3 John 2, I *w.* above all things.
See Job 33. 6; Jonah 4. 8; 2 Cor. 13. 9.
WITCH. Ex. 22. 18, thou shalt not suffer a *w.* to live.
Deut. 18. 10, or a *w.*
WITHDRAW. Job 9. 13; Prov. 25. 17; 2 Thess. 3. 6.
WITHER. Ps. 1. 3, his leaf shall not *w.*
37. 2, they shall *w.* as the green herb.
129. 6; Isa. 40. 7; 1 Pet. 1. 24, the grass *w.*
Mat. 21. 19; Mk. 11. 21, the fig tree *w.* away.
Jude 12, trees whose fruit *w.*
See Joel 1. 12; John 15. 6; Jas. 1. 11.
WITHHOLD. Ps. 40. 11, *w.* not thy mercies.
84 11, no good thing will he *w.*
Prov. 3. 27, *w.* not good from them to whom it is due.
23. 13, *w.* not correction.
Eccl. 11. 6, *w.* not thy hand.
Jer. 5. 25, your sins have *w.* good things.
See Job 22. 7; 42. 2; Ezek. 18. 16; Joel 1. 13.
WITHIN. Mat. 23. 26, cleanse first what is *w.*
Mk. 7. 21, from *w.* proceed evil thoughts.
2 Cor. 7. 5, *w.* were fears.
See Ps. 45. 13; Mat. 3. 9; Lu. 12. 17; 16. 3.
WITHOUT. Gen. 24. 31, wherefore standest thou *w.*?
2 Chron. 15. 3, for a long season *w.* the true God.
Prov. 1. 20, wisdom crieth *w.*
Isa. 52. 3; 55. 1, *w.* money.
Jer. 33. 10, *w.* man, *w.* beast, *w.* inhabitant.
Hos. 3. 4, Israel *w.* king, *w.* prince, *w.* sacrifice.
Eph. 2. 12, *w.* God in the world.
Col. 4. 5; 1 Thess. 4. 12; 1 Tim. 3. 7, them that are *w.*
Heb. 13. 12, Jesus suffered *w.* the gate.
Rev. 22. 15, for *w.* are dogs.
See Prov. 22. 12; Mat. 10. 29; Lu. 11. 40.
WITHSTAND. Eccl. 4. 12, two shall *w.* him.
Acts 11. 17, what was I that I could *w.* God?
Eph. 6. 13, able to *w.* in evil day.
See Num. 22. 32; 2 Chron. 20. 6; Esth. 9. 2.
WITNESS (*n.*). Gen. 31. 50, God is *w.* betwixt.
Josh. 24. 27, this stone shall be a *w.*

Job 16. 19, my *w.* is in heaven.
Ps. 89. 37, as a faithful *w.* in heaven.
Prov. 14. 5, a faithful *w.* will not lie.
Isa. 55. 4, I have given him for a *w.* to the people.
Jer. 42. 5, the Lord be a true and faithful *w.*
Mat. 24. 14, for a *w.* unto all nations.
John 1. 7, the same came for a *w.*
3. 11, ye receive not our *w.*
5. 36, I have greater *w.* than that of John.
Acts 14. 17, he left not himself without *w.*
Rom. 2. 15, conscience also bearing them *w.*
1 John 5. 9, the *w.* of God is greater.
10, hath the *w.* in himself.
See Isa. 43. 10; Lu. 24. 48; Acts 1. 8; 13. 31.
WITNESS (*v.*). Deut. 4. 26, heaven and earth to *w.*
Isa. 3. 9, countenance doth *w.* against them.
Acts 20. 23, the Holy Ghost *w.* in every city.
Rom. 3. 21, being *w.* by the law and prophets.
1 Tim. 6. 13, before Pilate *w.* a good confession.
See 1 Sam. 12. 3; Mat. 26. 62; 27. 13; Mk. 14. 60.
WITS. Ps. 107. 27, are at their *w.* end.
WITTY. Prov. 8. 12, knowledge of *w.* inventions.
WIZARD. Lev. 20. 27, or that is a *w.*
WOEFUL. Jer. 17. 16, the *w.* day.
WOMAN. Judg. 9. 54, a *w.* slew him.
Ps. 48. 6; Isa. 13. 8; 21. 3; 26. 17; Jer. 4. 31; 6. 24; 13. 21, 22, 23; 30. 6; 31. 8; 48. 41; 49. 22, 24; 50. 43, pain as of a *w.* in travail.
Prov. 6. 24, to keep thee from the evil *w.*
9. 13, a foolish *w.* is clamorous.
12. 4; 31. 10, a virtuous *w.*
14. 1, every wise *w.* buildeth her house.
21. 9, with a brawling *w.* in wide house.
Eccl. 7. 28, a *w.* among all those have I not found.
Isa. 54. 6, as a *w.* forsaken.
Jer. 31. 22, a *w.* shall compass a man.
Mat. 5. 28, whoso looketh on a *w.*
15. 28, O *w.*, great is thy faith.
22. 27; Mk. 12. 22; Lu. 20. 32, the *w.* died also.
26. 10, why trouble ye the *w.*?
13, shall this, that this *w.* hath done, be told.
John 2. 4, *w.*, what have I to do with thee?
8. 3, a *w.* taken in adultery.
19. 26, *w.*, behold thy son.
Acts 9. 36, this *w.* was full of good works.
Rom. 1. 27, the natural use of the *w.*
1 Cor. 7. 1, it is good for a man not to touch a *w.*
11. 7, the *w.* is the glory of the man.
Gal. 4. 4, God sent forth his Son, made of a *w.*
1 Tim. 2. 12, I suffer not a *w.* to teach.
14, the *w.* being deceived.
See Isa. 49. 15; Lu. 7. 39; 13. 16; Rev. 12. 1.
WOMB. Gen. 49. 25, blessings of the *w.*
1 Sam. 1. 5, the Lord had shut up her *w.*
Ps. 22. 9, took me out of the *w.*
10, cast upon thee from the *w.*
127. 3, the fruit of the *w.* is his reward.
139. 13, thou hast covered me in my mother's *w.*
Eccl. 11. 5, how bones grow in the *w.*
Isa. 44. 2; 49. 5, the Lord formed thee from the *w.*
48. 8, a transgressor from the *w.*
49. 15, compassion on son of her *w.*
Hos. 9. 14, give them miscarrying *w.*
Lu. 1. 42, blessed is the fruit of thy *w.*
11. 27, blessed is the *w.* that bare thee.
23. 29, blessed are the *w.* that never bare.
See Job 3. 11; 24. 20; 31. 15; Prov. 30. 16.
WOMEN. Judg. 5. 24, blessed above *w.*
1 Sam. 18. 7, the *w.* answered one another.
2 Sam. 1. 26, passing the love of *w.*
Ps. 45. 9, among thy honourable *w.*
Prov. 31. 3, give not thy strength to *w.*
Lam. 4. 10, the pitiful *w.* have sodden their children.
Mat. 11. 11; Lu. 7. 28, among them that are born of *w.*
24. 41; Lu. 17. 35, two *w.* grinding at the mill.
Lu. 1. 28, blessed art thou among *w.*
1 Cor. 14. 34, let your *w.* keep silence.
1 Tim. 2. 9, *w.* adorn themselves.
11, let the *w.* learn in silence.
5. 14, that the younger *w.* marry.
2 Tim. 3. 6, lead captive silly *w.*
Tit. 2. 3, the aged *w.* in behaviour as becometh holiness.
Heb. 11. 35, *w.* received their dead.
See Acts 16. 13; 17. 4; Phil. 4. 3; 1 Pet. 3. 5.
WONDER (*n.*). Ps. 71. 7, as *w.* unto many.
77. 14, thou art the God that doest *w.*
88. 12, shall thy *w.* be known in the dark?
96. 3, declare his *w.* among all people.
107. 24, his *w.* in the deep.
Isa. 20. 3, walked barefoot for a sign and a *w.*
29. 14, I will do a marvellous work and a *w.*
Joel 2. 30; Acts 2. 19, I will show *w.* in heaven.
John 4. 48, except ye see signs and *w.*
Acts 4. 30, that *w.* may be done by the name.
See Rom. 15. 19; 2 Cor. 12. 12; 2 Thess. 2. 9.
WONDER (*v.*). Isa. 29. 9, stay yourselves, and *w.*
59. 16, he *w.* there was no intercessor.
63. 5, I *w.* there was none to uphold.
Hab. 1. 5, regard, and *w.* marvellously.
Zech. 3. 8, they are men *w.* at.
Lu. 4. 22, all *w.* at the gracious words.
See Acts 3. 11; 8. 13; 13. 41; Rev. 13. 3; 17. 6.
WONDERFUL. 2 Sam. 1. 26, thy love was *w.*
Job 42. 3, things too *w.* for me.
Ps. 139. 6, such knowledge is too *w.* for me.
Isa. 9. 6, his name shall be called *W.*
28. 29, who is *w.* in counsel.
See Deut. 28. 59; Jer. 5. 30; Mat. 21. 15.
WONDERFULLY. Ps. 139. 14; Lam. 1. 9; Dan. 8. 24.
WONDROUS. 1 Chron. 16. 9; Job 37. 14; Ps. 26. 7; 75. 1; 78. 32; 105. 2; 106. 22; 119. 27; 145. 5; Jer. 21. 2, *w.* works.
Ps. 72. 18; 86. 10; 119. 18, *w.* things.
WONT. Ex. 21. 29, if the ox were *w.* to push.
Mat. 27. 15, the governor was *w.* to release.
Mk. 10. 1, as he was *w.*, he taught them.
Lu. 22. 39, he went, as he was *w.*
Acts 16. 13, where prayer was *w.* to be made.
See Num. 22. 30; 2 Sam. 20. 18; Dan. 3. 19.
WOOD. Gen. 22. 7, behold the fire and the *w.*
Deut. 29. 11; Josh. 9. 21; Jer. 46. 22, hewer of *w.*
2 Sam. 18. 8, the *w.* devoured more people.
Ps. 141. 7, as one cleaveth *w.*
Prov. 26. 20, where no *w.* is, the fire goeth out.
See Jer. 7. 18; Hag. 1. 8; 1 Cor. 3. 12.
WOOL. Ps. 147. 16, he giveth snow like *w.*
Isa. 1. 18, your sins shall be as *w.*
Dan. 7. 9; Rev. 1. 14, hair like *w.*
See Prov. 31. 13; Ezek. 34. 3; 44. 17; Hos. 9. 1.
WORD. Deut. 8. 3; Mat. 4. 4, every *w.* of God.
30. 14; Rom. 10. 8, the *w.* is very nigh.
Job 12. 11, doth not the ear try *w.*?
35. 16, he multiplieth *w.*
38. 2, by *w.* without knowledge.
Ps. 19. 14, let the *w.* of my mouth be acceptable.
68. 11, the Lord gave the *w.*
119. 43; 2 Cor. 6. 7; Eph. 1. 13; Col. 1. 5; 2 Tim. 2. 15; Jas. 1. 18, the *w.* of truth.
Prov. 15. 23, a *w.* spoken in due season.
25. 11, a *w.* fitly spoken.
Isa. 29. 21, an offender for a *w.*
30. 21, thine ears shall hear a *w.* behind thee.
50. 4, how to speak a *w.* in season.
Jer. 5. 13, the *w.* is not in them.
18. 18, nor shall the *w.* perish.
44. 28, know whose *w.* shall stand.
Hos. 14. 2, take with you *w.*
Mat. 8. 8, speak the *w.* only.
12. 36, every idle *w.* that men shall speak.
18. 16, that every *w.* may be established.
24. 35, my *w.* shall not pass away.
Mk. 4. 14, the sower soweth the *w.*
8. 38; Lu. 9. 26, ashamed of my *w.*

Lu. 4. 22, gracious *w.* which proceeded.
36, amazed, saying, what a *w.* is this!
24. 19, a prophet mighty in deed and *w.*
John 6. 63, the *w.* I speak are life.
68, thou hast the *w.* of eternal life.
12. 48, the *w.* I have spoken shall judge him.
14. 24, the *w.* ye hear is not mine.
17. 8, I have given them the *w.* thou gavest me.
Acts 13. 15, any *w.* of exhortation.
20. 35, remember the *w.* of the Lord Jesus.
26. 25, the *w.* of truth and soberness.
1 Cor. 1. 17, not with wisdom of *w.*
4. 20, not in *w.*, but in power.
14. 9, except ye utter *w.* easy to be understood.
2 Cor. 1. 18, our *w.* was not yea and nay.
5. 19, the *w.* of reconciliation.
Gal. 5. 14, all the law is fulfilled in one *w.*
6. 6, him that is taught in the *w.*
Eph. 5. 6, deceive you with vain *w.*
Phil. 2. 16, holding forth the *w.* of life.
Col. 3. 16, let the *w.* of Christ dwell in you.
1 Thess. 1. 5, the gospel came not in *w.* only.
4. 18, comfort one another with these *w.*
1 Tim. 4. 6, nourished in *w.* of faith.
5. 17, labour in the *w.* and doctrine.
2 Tim. 2. 14, strive not about *w.*
4. 2, preach the *w.*
Tit. 1. 3, in due times manifested his *w.*
9, holding fast the faithful *w.*
Heb. 1. 3, by the *w.* of his power.
2. 2, if the *w.* spoken by angels was stedfast.
4. 2, the *w.* preached did not profit.
12, the *w.* of God is quick and powerful.
5. 13, is unskilful in the *w.*
6. 5, and have tasted the good *w.* of God.
7. 28, the *w.* of the oath.
11. 3, the worlds were framed by the *w.* of God.
13. 7, who have spoken to you the *w.*
Jas. 1. 21, the engrafted *w.*
22, be ye doers of the *w.*
23, if any be a hearer of the *w.*
3. 2, if any man offend not in *w.*
1 Pet. 1. 23, being born again by the *w.*
25, this is the *w.* which is preached.
2. 2, the sincere milk of the *w.*
8, them that stumble at the *w.*
3. 1, if any obey not the *w.*, they also may without the *w.*
2 Pet. 1. 19, a more sure *w.* of prophecy.
3. 2, the *w.* spoken by the prophets.
5, by the *w.* of God the heavens were of old.
7, the heavens by the same *w.* are kept in store.
1 John 1. 1, hands have handled, of *W.* of life.
2. 5, whoso keepeth his *w.*, in him is the love.
3. 18, let us not love in *w.*
Rev. 3. 8, thou hast kept my *w.*
10, the *w.* of my patience.
6. 9, that were slain for the *w.*
22. 19, take away from the *w.* of this prophecy.
See Isa. 8. 20; Jer. 20. 9; Mic. 2. 7; Rev. 21. 5.

WORK (*n.*). Gen. 2. 2, God ended his *w.*
5. 29, shall comfort us concerning our *w.*
Ex. 20. 9; 23. 12; Deut. 5. 13, six days thou shalt do all thy *w.*
35. 2, six days shall *w.* be done.
Deut. 3. 24, what God can do according to thy *w.*?
4. 28; 27. 15; 2 Kings 19. 18; 2 Chron. 32. 19; Ps. 115. 4; 135. 15, the *w.* of men's hands.
1 Chron. 16. 37, as every day's *w.* required.
2 Chron. 31. 21, in every *w.* he began he did it.
34. 12, the men did the *w.* faithfully.
Ezra 5. 8, this *w.* goeth fast on.
6. 7, let the *w.* alone.
Neh. 3. 5, their nobles put not their necks to the *w.*
6. 3, why should the *w.* cease?
16, they perceived this *w.* was of God.
Job 1. 10, thou hast blessed the *w.* of his hands.
10. 3; 14. 15; Ps. 143. 5, the *w.* of thine hands.
34. 11, the *w.* of a man shall he render unto him.
Ps. 8. 3, the *w.* of thy fingers.
19. 1, his handy-*w.*
33. 4, all his *w.* are done in truth.
40. 5; 78. 4; 107. 8; 111. 4; Mat. 7. 22; Acts 2. 11, wonderful *w.*
90. 17, establish thou the *w.* of our hands.
101. 3, I hate the *w.* of them that turn aside.
104. 23, man goeth forth to his *w.*
111. 2, the *w.* of the Lord are great.
141. 4, to practise wicked *w.*
Prov. 16. 3, commit thy *w.* unto the Lord.
20. 11, whether his *w.* be pure.
24. 12; Mat. 16. 27; 2 Tim. 4. 14, to every man according to his *w.*
31. 31, let her own *w.* praise her.
Eccl. 1. 14, I have seen all the *w.* that are done.
3. 17, there is a time for every *w.*
5. 6, wherefore should God destroy the *w.*?
8. 9, I applied my heart to every *w.*
9. 1, their *w.* are in the hand of God.
7, God now accepteth thy *w.*
10, there is no *w.* in the grave.
12. 14, God shall bring every *w.* into judgment.
Isa. 2. 8; 37. 19; Jer. 1. 16; 10. 3, 9, 15; 51. 18, they worship the *w.* of their own hands.
5. 19, let him hasten his *w.*
10. 12, when the Lord hath performed his whole *w.*
26. 12, thou hast wrought all our *w.* in us.
28. 21, do his *w.*, his strange *w.*
29. 15, their *w.* are in the dark.
49. 4, my *w.* is with my God.
66. 18, I know their *w.* and their thoughts.
Jer. 32. 19, great in counsel, and mighty in *w.*
48. 7, thou hast trusted in thy *w.*
Amos 8. 7, I will never forget any of their *w.*
Hab. 1. 5, I will work a *w.* in your days.
Mat. 23. 3, do not ye after their *w.*
5, all their *w.* they do to be seen of men.
Mk. 6. 5, he could there do no mighty *w.*
John 5. 20, greater *w.* than these.
6. 28, that we might work the *w.* of God.
29, this is the *w.* of God, that ye believe.
7. 21, I have done one *w.*, and ye all marvel.
9. 3, that the *w.* of God should be made manifest.
10. 25, the *w.* I do in my Father's name.
32, for which of those *w.* do ye stone me?
14. 12, the *w.* I do shall he do, and greater *w.*
17. 4, I have finished the *w.*
Acts 5. 38, if this *w.* be of men, it will come to nought.
15. 38, who went not with them to the *w.*
Rom. 3. 27, by what law? of *w.*?
4. 6, imputeth righteousness without *w.*
9. 11, not of *w.*, but of him that calleth.
11. 6, grace, otherwise *w.* is no more *w.*
13. 12, let us therefore cast off the *w.* of darkness.
14. 20, for meat destroy not the *w.* of God.
1 Cor. 3. 13, every man's *w.* shall be made manifest.
9. 1, are not ye my *w.* in the Lord?
Gal. 2. 16, by *w.* of law shall no flesh be justified.
6. 4, let every man prove his own *w.*
Eph. 2. 9, not of *w.*, lest any man should boast.
4. 12, the *w.* of the ministry.
5. 11, the unfruitful *w.* of darkness.
Col. 1. 21, enemies in your mind by wicked *w.*
1 Thess. 5. 13, esteem them in love for their *w.* sake.
2 Thess. 2. 17, in every good word and *w.*
2 Tim. 1. 9; Tit. 3. 5, saved us, not according to our *w.*
4. 5, do the *w.* of an evangelist.
Tit. 1. 16, in *w.* they deny him.
Heb. 6. 1; 9. 14, from dead *w.*
Jas. 1. 4, let patience have her perfect *w.*
2. 14, if he have not *w.*, can faith save him?
17, faith, if it hath not *w.*, is dead, being alone.
18, shew me thy faith without thy *w.*

Jas. 21, was not Abraham justified by *w.*?
22, by *w.* was faith made perfect.
2 Pet. 3. 10, earth and *w.* therein shall be burnt up.
1 John 3. 8, destroy the *w.* of the devil.
Rev. 2. 2, 9, 13, 19; 3. 1, 8, 15, I know thy *w.*
26, he that keepeth my *w.* to the end.
3. 2, I have not found thy *w.* perfect.
14. 13, and their *w.* do follow them.
See Gal. 5. 19; 2 Thess. 1. 11; Rev. 18. 6; 20. 12.
WORK (*v.*). 1 Sam. 14. 6, the Lord will *w.* for us.
1 Kings 21. 20, sold thyself to *w.* evil.
Neh. 4. 6, the people had a mind to the *w.*
Job 23. 9, on the left hand, where he doth *w.*
33. 29, all these things *w.* God with man.
Ps. 58. 2, in heart ye *w.* wickedness.
101. 7, he that *w.* deceit.
119. 126, it is time for thee to *w.*
Isa. 43. 13, I will *w.*, and who shall let it?
Mic. 2. 1, woe to them that *w.* evil.
Hag. 2. 4, *w.*, for I am with you.
Mal. 3. 15, they that *w.* wickedness are set up.
Mat. 21. 28, son, go *w.* to day in my vineyard.
Mk. 16. 20, the Lord *w.* with them.
John 5. 17, my Father *w.* hitherto, and I *w.*
6. 28, that we might *w.* the works of God.
30, what dost thou *w.*?
9. 4, the night cometh, when no man can *w.*
Acts 10. 35, he that *w.* righteousness is accepted.
Rom. 4. 15, the law *w.* wrath.
5. 3, tribulation *w.* patience.
8. 28, all things *w.* together for good.
1 Cor. 4. 12, and labour, *w.* with our own hands.
12. 6, it is the same God which *w.* all in all.
2 Cor. 4. 12, death *w.* in us.
17, *w.* for us a far more exceeding weight of glory.
Gal. 5. 6, faith which *w.* by love.
Eph. 1. 11, who *w.* all things after the counsel.
2. 2, the spirit that now *w.*
3. 20, the power that *w.* in us.
4. 28, *w.* with his hands the thing that is good.
Phil. 2. 12, *w.* out your own salvation.
1 Thess. 4. 11, *w.* with your own hands.
2 Thess. 2. 7, the mystery of iniquity doth *w.*
3. 10, if any would not *w.*, neither should he eat.
Jas. 1. 3, the trying of your faith *w.* patience.
See Ezek. 46. 1; Prov. 11. 18; 31. 13; Eccl. 3. 9.
WORKMAN. Hos. 8. 6; Eph. 2. 10; 2 Tim. 2. 15.
WORLD. Job 18. 18, chased out of the *w.*
34. 13, who hath disposed the whole *w.*?
37. 12, on the face of the *w.*
Ps. 17. 14, from men of the *w.*
50. 12, the *w.* is mine.
73. 12, the ungodly, who prosper in the *w.*
77. 18; 97. 4, lightnings lightened the *w.*
93. 1, the *w.* also is stablished.
Eccl. 3. 11, he hath set the *w.* in their heart.
Isa. 14. 21, nor fill the face of the *w.* with cities.
24. 4, the *w.* languisheth.
34. 1, let the *w.* hear.
Mat. 4. 8; Lu. 4. 5, all the kingdoms of the *w.*
5. 14, the light of the *w.*
13. 22; Mk. 4. 19, the cares of this *w.* choke.
38, the field is the *w.*
40, in the end of the *w.*
16. 26; Mk. 8. 36; Lu. 9. 25, gain the whole *w.*
18. 7, woe to the *w.* because of offences.
Mk. 10. 30; Lu. 18. 30; Heb. 2. 5; 6. 5, in the *w.* to come.
Lu. 1. 70; Acts 3. 21, since the *w.* began.
2. 1, all the *w.* should be taxed.
16. 8; 20. 34, children of this *w.*
20. 35, worthy to obtain that *w.*
John 1. 10, he was in the *w.*
29, which taketh away the sin of the *w.*
3. 16, God so loved the *w.*
4. 42; 1 John 4. 14, the Saviour of the *w.*
6. 33, he that giveth life unto the *w.*
7. 4, shew thyself to the *w.*
7, the *w.* cannot hate you.
John 8. 12; 9. 5, I am the light of the *w.*
12. 19, the whole *w.* is gone after him.
31, now is the judgment of this *w.*
47, not to judge the *w.*, but to save the *w.*
13. 1, depart out of this *w.*
14. 17, whom the *w.* cannot receive.
22, manifest thyself unto us, and not unto the *w.*
27, not as the *w.* giveth, give I unto you.
30, the prince of this *w.* cometh.
15. 18; 1 John 3. 13, if the *w.* hate you.
19, the *w.* would love his own.
16. 33, in the *w.* ye shall have tribulation.
17. 9, I pray not for the *w.*
16, they are not of the *w.*
21, that the *w.* may believe.
21. 25, the *w.* could not contain the books.
Acts 17. 6, turned the *w.* upside down.
Rom. 3. 19, that all the *w.* may become guilty.
12. 2, be not conformed to this *w.*
1 Cor. 1. 20, where is the disputer of this *w.*?
2. 6, the wisdom of this *w.*
7. 31, they that use this *w.* as not abusing it.
2 Cor. 4. 4, the god of this *w.* hath blinded.
Gal. 1. 4, this present evil *w.*
6. 14, the *w.* is crucified unto me.
Eph. 2. 2, according to the course of this *w.*
12, without God in the *w.*
1 Tim. 6. 7, we brought nothing into this *w.*
17, them that are rich in this *w.*
2 Tim. 4. 10, having loved this present *w.*
Heb. 11. 38, of whom the *w.* was not worthy.
Jas. 1. 27, unspotted from the *w.*
3. 6, the tongue is a *w.* of iniquity.
4. 4, the friendship of the *w.*
2 Pet. 2. 5, God spared not the old *w.*
3. 6, the *w.* that then was.
1 John 2. 15, love not the *w.*
3. 1, the *w.* knoweth us not.
5. 19, the whole *w.* lieth in wickedness.
See 2 Sam. 22. 16; 1 Chron. 16. 30; Prov. 8. 26.
WORLDLY. Tit. 2. 12; Heb. 9. 1.
WORM. Job 7. 5, my flesh is clothed with *w.*
17. 14, I said to the *w.*, thou art my mother.
19. 26, though *w.* destroy this body.
21. 26, shall lie down, and *w.* shall cover them.
24. 20, the *w.* shall feed sweetly on him.
25, 6, man, that is a *w.*, etc.
Ps. 22. 6, I am a *w.*, and no man.
Isa. 14. 11, the *w.* is spread under thee.
41. 14, fear not, thou *w.* Jacob.
66. 24; Mk. 9. 44, 46, 48, their *w.* shall not die.
Mic. 7. 17, like *w.* of the earth.
See Jonah 4. 7; Acts 12. 23.
WORMWOOD. Jer. 9. 15; 23. 15; Amos 5. 7.
WORSE. Mat. 9. 16; Mk. 2. 21, the rent is made *w.*
12. 45; 27. 64; Lu. 11. 26, last state *w.* than the first.
Mk. 5. 26, nothing bettered, but grew *w.*
John 5. 14, lest a *w.* thing come unto thee.
1 Cor. 11. 17, not for the better, but for the *w.*
1 Tim. 5. 8, he is *w.* than an infidel.
2 Tim. 3. 13, shall wax *w.* and *w.*
2 Pet. 2. 20, the latter end is *w.* with them.
See Jer. 7. 26; 16. 12; Dan. 1. 10; John 2. 10.
WORSHIP. Ps. 95. 6, let us *w.* and bow down.
97. 7, *w.* him, all ye gods.
99. 5, *w.* at his footstool.
Isa. 27. 13, shall *w.* the Lord in the holy mount.
Jer. 44. 19, did we *w.* her without our men?
Zeph. 1. 5, them that *w.* the host of heaven.
Mat. 4. 9; Lu. 4. 7, fall down and *w.* me.
15. 9, in vain they do *w.* me.
John 4. 20, our fathers *w.* in this mountain.
22, ye *w.* ye know not what.
12. 20, Greeks came to *w.*
Acts 17. 23, whom ye ignorantly *w.*
24. 14, so *w.* I the God of my fathers.
Rom. 1. 25, *w.* the creature more than the Creator.
1 Cor. 14. 25, so falling down he will *w.* God.
See Col. 2. 18; Heb. 1. 6; Rev. 4. 10; 9. 20.

WORTH. Job 24. 25; Prov. 10. 20; Ezek. 30. 2.
WORTHY. Gen. 32. 10, I am not *w.* of the least.
1 Sam. 26. 16, ye are *w.* to die.
1 Kings 1. 52, if he shew himself a *w.* man.
Mat. 3. 11, whose shoes I am not *w.* to bear.
8. 8; Lu. 7. 6, I am not *w.* that thou shouldest come.
10. 10, the workman is *w.* of his meat.
37, loveth father or mother more than me is not *w.* of me.
22. 8, they which were bidden were not *w.*
Mk. 1. 7; Lu. 3. 16; John 1. 27, not *w.* to unloose.
Lu. 3. 8, fruits *w.* of repentance.
7. 4, that he was *w.* for whom he should do this.
10. 7; 1 Tim. 5. 18, the labourer is *w.* of his hire.
12. 48, things *w.* of stripes.
15. 19, no more *w.* to be called thy son.
20. 35, *w.* to obtain that world.
Acts 24. 2, very *w.* deeds are done.
Rom. 8. 18, not *w.* to be compared with the glory.
Eph. 4. 1; Col. 1. 10; 1 Thess. 2. 12, walk *w.*
Heb. 11. 38, of whom the world was not *w.*
Jas. 2. 7, that *w.* name.
Rev. 3. 4, for they are *w.*
See Nah. 2. 5; Rev. 4. 11; 5. 2; 16. 6.
WOULD. Num. 22. 29, I *w.* there were a sword.
Ps. 81. 11, Israel *w.* none of me.
Prov. 1. 25, ye *w.* none of my reproof.
30, they *w.* none of my counsel.
Dan. 5. 19, whom he *w.* he slew.
Mat. 7. 12; Lu. 6. 31, whatsoever ye *w.* that men.
Mk. 3. 13, and calleth unto him whom he *w.*
Rom. 7. 15, what I *w.*, that do I not.
1 Cor. 7. 7, I *w.* that all men were even as I.
Rev. 3. 15, I *w.* thou wert cold or hot.
See Num. 11. 29; Acts 26. 29; Gal. 5. 17.
WOUND (*n.*). Ex. 21. 25, give *w.* for *w.*
Job 34. 6, my *w.* is incurable.
Ps. 147. 3, he bindeth up their *w.*
Prov. 23. 29, who hath *w.* without cause?
27. 6, faithful are the *w.* of a friend.
Isa. 1. 6, but *w.* and bruises.
Jer. 15. 18, why is my *w.* incurable?
30. 17, I will heal thee of thy *w.*
Zech. 13. 6, what are these *w.* in thy hands?
Lu. 10. 34, bound up his *w.*
See Prov. 6. 33; 20. 30; Hos. 5. 13; Rev. 13. 3.
WOUND (*v.*). Deut. 32. 39, I *w.*, and I heal.
1 Kings 22. 34; 2 Chron. 18. 33, carry me out, for I am *w.*
Job 5. 18, he *w.*, and his hands make whole.
Ps. 64. 7, suddenly shall they be *w.*
109. 22, my heart is *w.* within me.
Prov. 7. 26, she hath cast down many *w.*
18. 14, a *w.* spirit who can bear?
Isa. 53. 5, he was *w.* for our transgressions.
Jer. 37. 10, there remained but *w.* men.
See Gen. 4. 23; Mk. 12. 4; Lu. 10. 30; Acts 19. 16.
WRAP. Isa. 28. 20; Mic. 7. 3; John 20. 7.
WRATH. Gen. 49. 7, cursed be their *w.*
Deut. 32. 27, were it not I feared the *w.* of the enemy.
Job 21. 30; Prov. 11. 4; Zeph. 1. 15; Rom. 2. 5; Rev. 6. 17, the day of *w.*
36. 18, because there is *w.*, beware.
Ps. 76. 10, the *w.* of man shall praise thee.
90. 7, by thy *w.* are we troubled.
Prov. 16. 14, *w.* of a king is as messengers of death.
19. 19, a man of great *w.* shall suffer.
27. 3, a fool's *w.* is heavier.
4, *w.* is cruel, and anger outrageous.
Eccl. 5. 17, much *w.* with his sickness.
Isa. 13. 9, the day of the Lord cometh with *w.*
54. 8, in a little *w.* I hid my face.
Nah. 1. 2, he reserveth *w.* for his enemies.
Hab 3. 2, in *w.* remember mercy.
Mat. 3. 7; Lu. 3. 7, from the *w.* to come.
Rom. 2. 5, *w.* against the day of *w.*
Eph. 6. 4, provoke not your children to *w.*
1 Thess. 5. 9, God hath not appointed us to *w.*
1 Tim. 2. 8, lifting up holy hands, without *w.*
See Jas. 1. 19; Rev. 6. 16; 12. 12; 14. 8.
WRATHFUL. Ps. 69. 24; Prov. 15. 18.
WREST. Ex. 23. 2; Deut. 16. 19; Ps. 56. 5; 2 Pet. 3. 16.
WRESTLE. Gen. 32. 24; Eph. 6. 12.
WRETCHED. Num. 11. 15; Rom. 7. 24; Rev. 3. 17.
WRING. Judg. 6. 38; Ps. 75. 8; Prov. 30. 33.
WRINKLE. Job 16. 8; Eph. 5. 27.
WRITE. Prov. 3. 3; 7. 3, *w.* on table of thy heart.
Isa. 10. 1, *w.* grievousness which they have prescribed.
19, few, that a child may *w.* them.
Jer. 22. 30, *w.* ye this man childless.
31. 33; Heb. 8. 10, I will *w.* it in their hearts.
Hab. 2. 2, *w.* the vision, make it plain.
See Job 13. 26; Ps. 87. 6; Rev. 3. 12.
WRITING. Ex. 32. 16; John 5. 47; Col. 2. 14.
WRITTEN. Job 19. 23, Oh that my words were *w.*
Ps. 69. 28, let them not be *w.* with the righteous.
Ezek. 2. 10, roll was *w.* within and without.
Lu. 10. 20, because your names are *w.* in heaven.
John 19. 22, what I have *w.* I have *w.*
1 Cor. 10. 11, *w.* for our admonition.
2 Cor. 3. 2, ye are our epistle *w.* in our hearts.
See Isa. 4. 3; Jer. 17. 1; Rev. 2. 17; 13. 8.
WRONG. Ex. 2. 13, to him that did the *w.*
1 Chron. 12. 17, there is no *w.* in mine hands.
Job 19. 7, I cry out of *w.*, but am not heard.
Jer. 22. 3, do no *w.*
Mat. 20. 13, friend, I do thee no *w.*
1 Cor. 6. 7, why do ye not rather take *w.*?
2 Cor. 12. 13, forgive me this *w.*
Col. 3. 25, he that doeth *w.* shall receive.
Philem. 18, if he hath *w.* thee.
See Prov. 8. 36; Acts 25. 10; 2 Cor. 7. 2.
WRONGFULLY. Job 21. 27; Ezek. 22. 29; 1 Pet. 2. 19.
WROTE. Dan. 5. 5; John 8. 6; 19. 19; 2 John 5.
WROTH. Gen. 4. 6, why art thou *w.*?
Deut. 1. 34; 3. 26; 9. 19; 2 Sam. 22. 8; 2 Chron. 28. 9; Ps. 18. 7; 78. 21, heard your words, and was *w.*
2 Kings 5. 11, but Naaman was *w.*, and went away.
Ps. 89. 38, thou hast been *w.* with thine anointed.
Isa. 47. 6, I was *w.* with my people.
54. 9, I have sworn I would not be *w.*
57. 16, neither will I be always *w.*
64. 9, be not *w.* very sore.
Mat. 18. 34, his lord was *w.*, and delivered.
See Num. 16. 22; Isa. 28. 21; Mat. 2. 16.
WROUGHT. Num. 23. 23, what hath God *w.*!
1 Sam. 6. 6, when God had *w.* wonderfully.
14. 45, Jonathan hath *w.* with God this day.
Neh. 4. 17, with one of his hands *w.* in the work.
6. 16, this work was *w.* of our God.
Job 12. 9, the hand of the Lord hath *w.* this.
36. 23, who can say, thou hast *w.* iniquity?
Ps. 31. 19, hast *w.* for them that trust in thee.
68. 28, strengthen that which thou hast *w.* for us.
139. 15, curiously *w.* in lowest parts of the earth.
Eccl. 2. 11, I looked on all my hands had *w.*
Isa. 26. 12, thou also hast *w.* all our works in us.
41. 4, who hath *w.* and done it?
Jer. 18. 3, he *w.* a work on the wheels.
Ezek. 20. 9, I *w.* for my name's sake.
Dan. 4. 2, the wonders God hath *w.* toward me.
Mat. 20. 12, these last have *w.* but one hour.
26. 10; Mk. 14. 6, she hath *w.* a good work on me.

John 3. 21, manifest that they are *w.* in God.
Acts 15. 12, what wonders God had *w.*
18. 3, he abode with them, and *w.*
19. 11, *w.* special miracles by hands of Paul.
Rom. 7. 8, *w.* in me all manner of concupiscence.
15. 18, things which Christ hath not *w.*
2 Cor. 5. 5, he that hath *w.* us for the selfsame thing.
7. 11, what carefulness it *w.* in you.
12. 12, the signs of an apostle were *w.*
Gal. 2. 8, he that *w.* effectually in Peter.
Eph. 1. 20, which he *w.* in Christ.
2 Thess. 3. 8, but we *w.* with labour.
Heb. 11. 33, through faith *w.* righteousness.
Jas. 2. 22, faith *w.* with his works.
1 Pet. 4. 3, to have *w.* the will of the Gentiles.
2 John 8, lose not those things which we have *w.*
Rev. 19. 20, the false prophet that *w.* miracles.
See Ex. 36. 4; 2 Sam. 18. 13; 1 Kings 16. 25.
WRUNG. Lev. 1. 15; Ps. 73. 10; Isa. 51. 17.

Y

YARN. 1 Kings 10. 28; 2 Chron. 1. 16.
YE. 1 Cor. 6. 11; 2 Cor. 3. 2; Gal. 6. 1.
YEA. Mat. 5. 37; Jas. 5. 12, let your communication be *y.*, *y.*
2 Cor. 1. 17, there should be *y.*, *y.*, and nay, nay.
See 2 Cor. 1. 18; Phil. 3. 8; 2 Tim. 3. 12.
YEAR. Gen. 1. 14, for seasons, days, and *y.*
47. 9, few and evil have the *y.* of my life been.
Ex. 13. 10, keep this ordinance from *y.* to *y.*
23. 29, I will not drive them out in one *y.*
Lev. 16. 34, make atonement once a *y.*
25. 5, it is a *y.* of rest.
Num. 14. 31, each day for a *y.* shall ye bear.
Deut. 14. 22, thou shalt tithe the increase *y.* by *y.*
15. 9, the *y.* of release is at hand.
26. 12, the third *y.*, which is the *y.* of tithing.
32. 7, consider the *y.* of many generations.
Judg. 11. 40, to lament four days in a *y.*
1 Sam. 2. 19, brought a coat from *y.* to *y.*
7. 16, went from *y.* to *y.* in circuit.
2 Sam. 14. 26, every *y.* he polled it.
1 Kings 17. 1, there shall not be dew nor rain these *y.*
2 Chron. 14. 6, the land had rest, no war in those *y.*
Job 10. 5, are thy *y.* as man's days?
15. 20, the number of *y.* is hidden.
16. 22, when a few *y.* are come.
32. 7, multitude of *y.* should teach wisdom.
36. 11, they shall spend their *y.* in pleasures.
26, nor can the number of his *y.* be searched out.
Ps. 31. 10, my *y.* are spent with sighing.
61. 6, prolong his *y.* as many generations.
65. 11, thou crownest the *y.* with thy goodness.
77. 5, the *y.* of ancient times.
10, I will remember the *y.* of the right hand.
78. 33, their *y.* did he consume in trouble.
90. 4, a thousand *y.* in thy sight.
9, we spend our *y.* as a tale that is told.
10, the days of our *y.* are threescore and ten.
102. 24, thy *y.* are throughout all generations.
27, thy *y.* shall have no end.
Prov. 4. 10, the *y.* of thy life shall be many.
5. 9, lest thou give thy *y.* to the cruel.
10. 27, the *y.* of the wicked shall be shortened.
Eccl. 12. 1, nor the *y.* draw nigh.
Isa. 21. 16, according to the *y.* of an hireling.
29. 1, add ye *y.* to *y.*
38. 15, go softly all my *y.*
61. 2; Lu. 4. 19, the acceptable *y.* of the Lord.
63. 4, the *y.* of my redeemed is come.
Jer. 11. 23; 23. 12; 48. 44, the *y.* of their visitation.
17. 8, shall not be careful in *y.* of drought.
28. 16, this *y.* thou shalt die.
51. 46, a rumour shall come in one *y.*
Ezek. 4. 5, I have laid on thee the *y.* of their iniquity.
Ezek. 22. 4, thou art come even unto thy *y.*
38. 8, in latter *y.* thou shalt come.
46. 17, it shall be his to the *y.* of liberty.
Dan. 11. 6, in the end of *y.* they shall join.
Joel 2. 2, to the *y.* of many generations.
Mic. 6. 6, shall I come with calves of a *y.* old?
Hab. 3. 2, revive thy work in the midst of the *y.*
Mal. 3. 4, the offering be pleasant, as in former *y.*
Lu. 13. 8, let it alone this *y.* also.
Gal. 4. 10, ye observe days and *y.*
Rev. 20. 2, Satan bound for a thousand *y.*
See Zech. 14. 16; Jas. 4. 13; Rev. 9. 15.
YEARLY. 1 Sam. 1. 3; 20. 6; Esth. 9. 21.
YEARN. Gen. 43. 30; 1 Kings 3. 26.
YELL. Jer. 2. 15; 51. 38.
YESTERDAY. Job 8. 9; Ps. 90. 4; Heb. 13. 8.
YET. Gen. 40. 23, *y.* did not the butler remember.
Ex. 10. 7, knowest thou not *y.*?
Deut. 9. 29, *y.* they are thy people.
12. 9, ye are not as *y.* come.
Judg. 7. 4, the people are *y.* too many.
1 Kings 19. 18, *y.* I have left me.
2 Kings 13. 23, nor cast them from his presence as *y.*
Ezra 3. 6, the foundation was not *y.* laid.
Job 1. 16, while he was *y.* speaking.
13. 15, though he slay me, *y.* will I trust in him.
29. 5, when the Almighty was *y.* with me.
Ps. 2. 6, *y.* have I set my king.
Eccl. 4. 3, he which hath not *y.* been.
Isa. 28. 4, while it is *y.* in his hand.
49. 15, *y.* will I not forget.
Jer. 2. 9, I will *y.* plead with you.
23. 21, *y.* they ran.
Ezek. 11. 16, *y.* will I be to them.
36. 37, I will *y.* for this be enquired of.
Dan. 11. 35, it is *y.* for a time appointed.
Hos. 7. 9, *y.* he knoweth not.
Amos 6. 10, is there *y.* any with thee?
Jonah 3. 4, *y.* forty days.
Hab. 3. 18, *y.* I will rejoice.
Mat. 15. 17, do not ye *y.* understand?
19. 20, what lack I *y.*?
24. 6; Mk. 13. 7, the end is not *y.*
Mk. 11. 13, the time of figs was not *y.*
Lu. 24. 44, while I was *y.* with you.
John 2. 4; 7. 6; 8. 20, hour is not *y.* come.
11. 25, though dead, *y.* shall he live.
Rom. 5. 6, *y.* without strength.
8. 24, why doth he *y.* hope for?
1 Cor. 3. 15, *y.* so as by fire.
15. 17, ye are *y.* in your sins.
Gal. 2. 20, *y.* not I, but Christ.
Heb. 4. 15, *y.* without sin.
1 John 3. 2, it doth not *y.* appear.
See Acts 8. 16; Rom. 9. 19; 1 Cor. 3. 3.
YIELD. Gen. 4. 12, not henceforth *y.* strength.
Lev. 19. 25, that it may *y.* the increase.
26. 4, the land shall *y.* her increase.
Num. 17. 8, the rod *y.* almonds.
2 Chron. 30. 8, *y.* yourselves to the Lord.
Neh. 9. 37, it *y.* much increase to the kings.
Ps. 67. 6, the earth *y.* her increase.
107. 37, plant vineyards, which may *y.* fruits.
Prov. 7. 21, she caused him to *y.*
Eccl. 10. 4, *y.* pacifieth great offences.
Hos. 8. 7, if it *y.*, the strangers shall swallow it up.
Joel 2. 22, the fig tree and vine do *y.* their strength.
Hab. 3. 17, though fields shall *y.* no meat.
Mat. 27. 50, cried again, and *y.* up the ghost.
Acts 23. 21, do not thou *y.* to them.
Rom. 6. 13, neither *y.* ye your members, but *y.* yourselves to God.
16, to whom ye *y.* yourselves servants.
Heb. 12. 11, *y.* the peaceable fruits of righteousness.
See Gen. 1. 29; Isa. 5. 10; Dan. 3. 28.
YOKE. Gen. 27. 40, thou shalt break his *y.*

Lev. 26. 13, I have broken the bands of your y.
Num. 19. 2; 1 Sam. 6. 7, on which never came y.
Deut. 28. 48, he shall put a y. on thy neck.
1 Kings 12. 4, thy father made our y. grievous.
Isa. 9. 4; 10. 27; 14. 25, thou hast broken the y. of his burden.
58. 6, that ye break every y.
Jer. 2. 20, of old time I have broken thy y.
27. 2; 28. 13, make thee bonds and y.
31. 18, as a bullock unaccustomed to the y.
Lam. 3. 27, it is good to bear the y. in youth.
Mat. 11. 29, take my y. upon you.
30, for my y. is easy.
Acts 15. 10, to put a y. upon the neck of the disciples.
2 Cor. 6. 14, not unequally y. with unbelievers.
Gal. 5. 1, entangled with the y. of bondage.
Phil. 4. 3, I entreat thee also, true y.-fellow.
1 Tim. 6. 1, as many servants as are under the y.
See Job 1. 3; 42. 12; Lam. 1. 14; Lu. 14. 19.

YONDER. Gen. 22. 5; Num. 23. 15; Mat. 17. 20.

YOU. Gen. 48. 21, God shall be with y.
Ruth 2. 4, the Lord be with y.
1 Chron. 22. 18, is not the Lord with y.?
2 Chron. 15. 2, the Lord is with y., while ye be with him.
Jer. 18. 6, cannot I do with y.
42. 11; Hag. 1. 13; 2. 4, for I am with y.
Zech. 8. 23, we will go with y., God is with y.
Mat. 7. 12; Lu. 6. 21, that men should do to y.
28. 20, I am with y. alway.
Lu. 10. 16, he that heareth y. heareth me.
13. 28, and y. yourselves thrust out.
Acts 13. 46, seeing ye put it from y.
Rom. 16. 20; 1 Cor. 16. 23; Phil. 4. 23; Col. 4. 18; 1 Thess. 5. 28; 2 Thess. 3. 18; 2 Tim. 4. 15; Tit. 3. 15; Heb. 13. 25; 2 John 3; Rev. 22. 21, grace be with y.
1 Cor. 6. 11, such were some of y.
2 Cor. 12. 14, I seek not yours, but y.
Eph. 2. 1; Col. 2. 13, y. hath he quickened.
Col. 1. 27, Christ in y.
4. 9, a brother, who is one of y.
1 Thess. 5. 12, know them that are over y.
1 John 4. 4, greater is he that is in y.
See Hag. 1. 4; Mal. 2. 1; 2 Cor. 8. 13; Phil. 3. 1; 1 Pet. 2. 7.

YOUNG. Ex. 23. 26, there shall nothing cast their y.
Lev. 22. 28, ye shall not kill it and her y. in one day.
Deut. 22. 6, thou shalt not take the dam with the y.
28. 50, which will not show favour to the y.
57, her eyes shall be evil toward her y. one.
32. 11, as an eagle fluttereth over her y.
1 Chron. 22. 5; 29. 1, Solomon my son is y.
2 Chron. 13. 7, when Rehoboam was y. and tender.
34. 3, while he was yet y., he began to seek God.
Job 38. 41, when his y. ones cry to God, they wander.
39. 16, the ostrich is hardened against her y.
Ps. 37. 25, I have been y., and now am old.
78. 71, from following ewes great with y.
84. 3, a nest where she may lay her y.
147. 9, he giveth food to the y. ravens which cry.
Prov. 30. 17, the y. eagles shall eat it.
Cant. 2. 9; 8. 14, my beloved is like a y. hart.
Isa. 11. 7, their y. shall lie down together.
40. 11, and gently lead those that are with y.
Jer. 31. 12, flow together for y. of the flock.
Ezek. 17. 4, cropped off his y. twigs.
John 21. 18, when y. thou girdedst thyself.
Tit. 2. 4, teach the y. women to be sober.
See Gen. 33. 13; Isa. 30. 6; Mk. 7. 25; John 12. 14.

YOUNGER. Gen. 25. 23, the elder shall serve the y.
Job 30. 1, they that are y. have me in derision.
Lu. 22. 26, he that is greatest, let him be as the y.
1 Tim. 5. 1, intreat the y. men as brethren.
1 Pet. 5. 5, ye y., submit yourselves to the elder.
See Gen. 29. 18; Lu. 15. 12; 1 Tim. 5. 2, 11.

YOUNGEST. Gen. 42. 13; Josh. 6. 26; 1 Kings 16. 34.

YOURS. 2 Chron. 20. 15; Lu. 6. 20; 1 Cor. 3. 21.

YOUTH. Gen. 8. 21, imagination is evil from y.
46. 34, about cattle from our y. till now.
1 Sam. 17. 33, he a man of war from his y.
55, whose son is this y.?
2 Sam. 19. 7, evil that befell thee from thy y.
1 Kings 18. 12, I fear the Lord from my y.
Job 13. 26, to possess the iniquities of my y.
20. 11, his bones are full of the sin of his y.
29. 4, as in days of my y.
30. 12, on my right hand rise the y.
33. 25, he shall return to the days of his y.
36. 14, hypocrites die in y.
Ps. 25. 7, remember not the sins of my y.
71. 5, thou art my trust from my y.
17, thou hast taught me from my y.
88. 15, ready to die from my y. up.
89. 45, the days of his y. hast thou shortened.
103. 5, thy y. is renewed like the eagle's.
110. 3, the dew of thy y.
127. 4, the children of thy y.
129. 1, they have afflicted me from my y.
144. 12, as plants grown up in y.
Prov. 2. 17, forsaketh the guide of her y.
5. 18, rejoice with the wife of thy y.
Eccl. 11. 9, rejoice, young man, in thy y.
10, childhood and y. are vanity.
12. 1, remember now thy Creator in days of y.
Isa. 47. 12, wherein thou hast laboured from thy y.
54. 4, forget the shame of thy y.
Jer. 2. 2, the kindness of thy y.
3. 4, thou art the guide of my y.
22. 21, this hath been thy manner from thy y.
31. 19, bear the reproach of my y.
32. 30, have done evil before me from their y.
48. 11, hath been at ease from his y.
Lam. 3. 27, it is good that he bear the yoke in his y.
Ezek. 4. 14, soul not polluted from y.
16. 22, thou hast not remembered the days of thy y.
Hos. 2. 15, she shall sing as in the days of her y.
Joel 1. 8, lament for husband of her y.
Zech. 13. 5, man taught me to keep cattle from my y.
Mat. 19. 20; Mk. 10. 20; Lu. 18. 21, have kept from my y.
Acts 26. 4, my manner of life from my y.
1 Tim. 4. 12, let no man despise thy y.
See Prov. 7. 7; Isa. 40. 30; Jer. 3. 24, 25.

YOUTHFUL. 2 Tim. 2. 22, flee y. lusts.

Z

ZEAL. 2 Sam. 21. 2, sought to slay them in his z.
2 Kings 10. 16, come and see my z. for the Lord.
Ps. 69. 9; John 2. 17, the z. of thine house.
119. 139, my z. hath consumed me.
Isa. 9. 7, the z. of the Lord will perform this.
59. 17, clad with z. as a cloak.
63. 15, where is thy z.?
Ezek. 5. 13, I have spoken it in my z.
Rom. 10. 2, they have a z. of God.
2 Cor. 9. 2, your z. hath provoked many.
Phil. 3. 6, concerning z. persecuting the church.
Col. 4. 13, he hath a great z. for you.
See 2 Kings 19. 31; Isa. 37. 32; 2 Cor. 7. 11.

ZEALOUS. Num. 25. 11, he was z. for my sake.
Acts 21. 20, they are all z. of the law.
1 Cor. 14. 12, as ye are z. of spiritual gifts.
Tit. 2. 14, z. of good works.
Rev. 3. 19, be z. therefore, and repent.
See Num. 25. 13; Acts 22. 3; Gal. 1. 14.

ZEALOUSLY. Gal. 4. 18, z. affected.

THE NEW OXFORD

BIBLE MAPS

LIST OF MAPS

Prepared by the Cartographic Department
of the Clarendon Press, Oxford
and based on the Oxford Bible Atlas

MAPS PRINTED BY
THE CARTOGRAPHIC PRESS, MITCHAM

INDEX TO MAPS

Printed in Great Britain
at the University Press, Oxford
by Vivian Ridler
Printer to the University

MAP I
The Background of the Exodus
THE GREAT SEA
EGYPT
GOSHEN
SINAI
EDOM
MOAB
MIDIAN
Menzaleh
Mons Casius
Pelusium (Sin)
Raamses (Zoan, Tanis, Avaris)
Baal-zephon
Pi-beseth
Pithom
Succoth
Lake Timsah
Great Bitter Lake
Little Bitter Lake
Heliopolis (On)
Memphis (Noph)
River Nile
The Way to the Land of the Philistines
Brook of Egypt
Wilderness of Shur
The Way to Shur
Gerar
Beer-sheba
Hormah
Arad
Kir-hareseth
The Negeb
Wilderness of Zin
Bene-jaakan (Beeroth)
Azmon
Hazar-addar
Oboth
Punon
Bozrah
Mt. Sinai? (Jebel Helal)
Kadesh-barnea (Meribah)
The Arabah
Sela
Teman
The King's Highway
Line of border fortresses
Wilderness of Paran
Ezion-geber
(Gulf of Aqaba)
(Gulf of Suez)
Wilderness of Sin?
Dophkah (Serabit el Khadim)
Mt. Sinai? (Mt. Horeb)
0 20 40 Miles
0 20 40 Kilometres

MAP 2
E
3
4
5
E
G
Gordion
Gomer
(Gimarrai)
Meshech
(Mushki)
R. Halys
LYDIA
R. Hermus
Sardis
(Sepharad)
R. Maeander
Usiana
Tubal (Tabal)
KUMUK
Musri
JAVAN
CILICIA
(KHILAKKU)
Kue
Amanus Mts.
R. Orontes
HATTINA
Rhodes
Crete
(Caphtor)
Cyprus
(Iadanna)
Arvad
Gebal (Byblos)
Berytus
Lebanon
Helbon
Sidon
Tyre
Ushu
Acco
Hauran
ISRAEL
Samaria
AMMON
Jerusalem
JUDAH
MOAB
Gaza
Raphia
The Great Sea
(The Upper Sea, the Western Sea)
Libya
Sais
Zoan
(Tanis)
Migdol
Pelusium
Tahpanhes
Athribis
Heliopolis
(On)
Memphis
(Noph)
EDOM
Sela
Ezion-geber
(Elath)
Sinai
EGYPT
R. Nile
Hermopolis
Lycopolis
(Siut)
Red Sea
Thebes
ETHIOPIA
25°
30°
35°

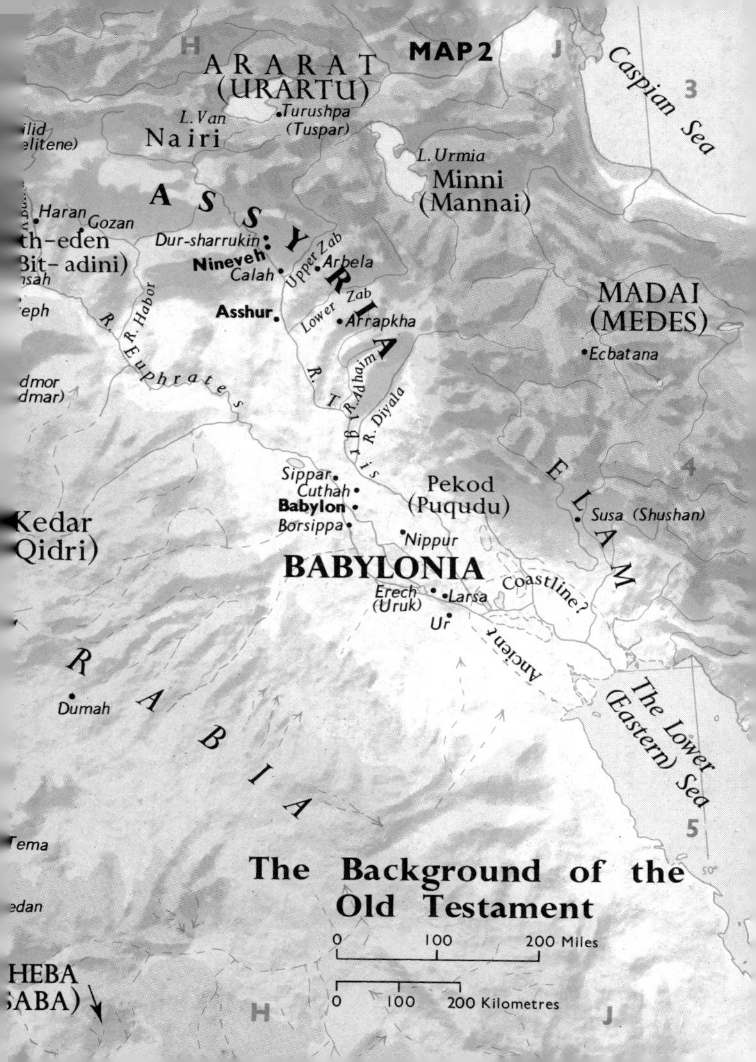
MAP 2
The Background of the Old Testament
ARARAT
(URARTU)
L. Van
Turushpa
(Tuspar)
Nairi
L. Urmia
Minni
(Mannai)
Caspian Sea
ASSYRIA
Haran
Gozan
Dur-sharrukin
Nineveh
Calah
Arbela
Upper Zab
Lower Zab
Asshur
Arrapkha
R. Habor
R. Euphrates
R. Adhaim
R. Tigris
R. Diyala
MADAI
(MEDES)
Ecbatana
ELAM
Susa (Shushan)
Sippar
Cuthah
Babylon
Borsippa
Nippur
Pekod
(Puqudu)
BABYLONIA
Erech
(Uruk)
Larsa
Ur
Coastline?
Ancient
The Lower
(Eastern) Sea
ARABIA
Dumah
Kedar
Qidri)
Tema
H
J
3
4
5
0 100 200 Miles
0 100 200 Kilometres

MAP 3
Palestine in Old Testament times
ISRAEL, JUDAH Hebrew Kingdoms
ASHER, etc. Israelite tribes
SYRIA, etc. Non-Israelite peoples
0 10 20 Miles
0 10 20 Kilometres
SIDONIANS
SYRIA (ARAM)
BETH-REHOB
MAACAH
BASHAN
ARGOB
GESHUR
HAVVOTH-JAIR
ASHER
NAPHTALI
ZEBULUN
ISSACHAR
THE GREAT SEA
Sidon
Zarephath
Tyre
Damascus
Mt. Lebanon
Mt. Hermon
Baal-gad
Abel-beth-maacah
Dan
Beth-rehob
Lake Huleh
Hazor
Merom
R. Jordan
Acco
Cabul
Aphek (Aphik)
Sea of Chinnereth
Aphek
Karnaim
Ashtaroth
Golan
Helam
Mt. Carmel
Jokneam (Jokmeam)
R. Kishon
Dor
Megiddo
Jezreel
V. of Jezreel
Taanach
Mt. Gilboa
Beth-shean
Lo-debar
Rogelim
Edrei
Tob
Ramoth-gilead

MAP 3
Plain of
Hepher
Socoh
Samaria
MANASSE
Thebez
Tirzah
Mt. Ebal
Shechem
Mt. Gerizim
Pirathon
River Jordan
Jabesh-gilead
The Arabah
Zarethan
Succoth
Penuel (Peniel)
R. Jabbok
Mahanaim
GIL
AMMON
Aphek
Gath-rimmon
Joppa
Bene-berak
Beth-dagon
EPHRAIM
Zeredah
Shiloh
Gilgal
Timnath-serah (Timnath)
Baal-hazor
Ephraim
Jazer
Rabbah (Rabbath-ammon)
Bethel
Beth-hanan
Lower Beth-horon
Upper Beth-horon
Beeroth
Gilgal
Jericho
Jabneel
Gezer
Shaalbim
Gibeon
Geba
Baalath
Makaz
Elon
Kiriath-jearim
Gibeah
BENJAMIN
Anathoth
High Place
Jerusalem
Beth-haram
Heshbon
Bezer (Bozrah?)
Mt. Pisgah
Nebo
Medeba
Ekron
Sorek
Beth-shemesh
Ashdod
PHILISTINES
Ashkelon
Libnah
City of Salt
Bethlehem
Netophah
Tekoa
Moresheth-gath
Gath
Adullam
Giloh
(Shephelah)
JUDAH
Salt Sea
R. Nahaliel
Ataroth
Kiriathaim
Dibon
Aroer
Kerioth
R. Arnon
Eglon
Hebron
Gaza
The Lowland
Debir
Carmel
Wilderness of Judah
En-gedi
(Sea of the Arabah)
MOAB
Gerar
Ziklag
4
5
6
W
X
Z
150
100
250

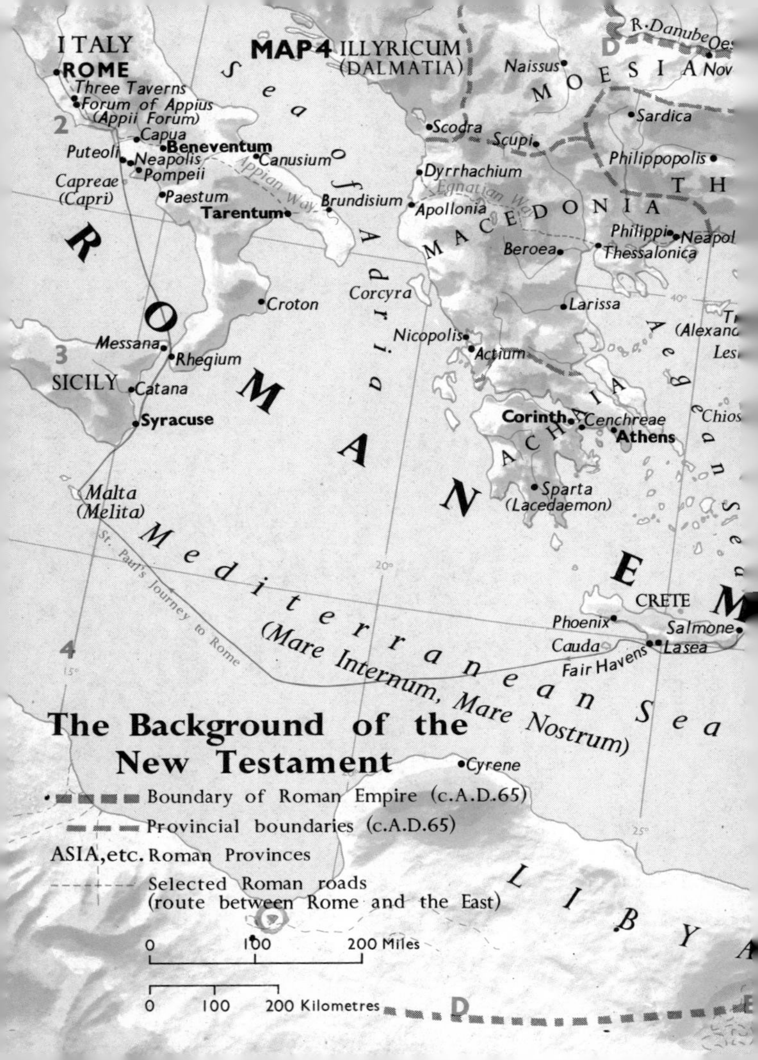
MAP 4
ITALY
ROME
Three Taverns
Forum of Appius
(Appii Forum)
Capua
Beneventum
Puteoli
Neapolis
Canusium
Pompeii
Capreae
(Capri)
Paestum
Tarentum
Brundisium
Appian Way
ILLYRICUM
(DALMATIA)
Sea of Adria
Scodra
Dyrrhachium
Apollonia
Egnatian Way
R. Danube
Naissus
MOESIA
Sardica
Scupi
Philippopolis
MACEDONIA
Philippi
Neapol
Beroea
Thessalonica
Croton
Corcyra
Larissa
Nicopolis
Actium
(Alexanc
Les
Aegean Sea
Chios
Messana
Rhegium
SICILY
Catana
Syracuse
Corinth
Cenchreae
Athens
ACHAIA
Sparta
(Lacedaemon)
Malta
(Melita)
ROMAN EM
St. Paul's Journey to Rome
Mediterranean Sea
(Mare Internum, Mare Nostrum)
CRETE
Phoenix
Salmone
Cauda
Lasea
Fair Havens
Cyrene
LIBYA
2
3
4
D
The Background of the New Testament
Boundary of Roman Empire (c.A.D.65)
Provincial boundaries (c.A.D.65)
ASIA, etc. Roman Provinces
Selected Roman roads
(route between Rome and the East)
0 100 200 Miles
0 100 200 Kilometres

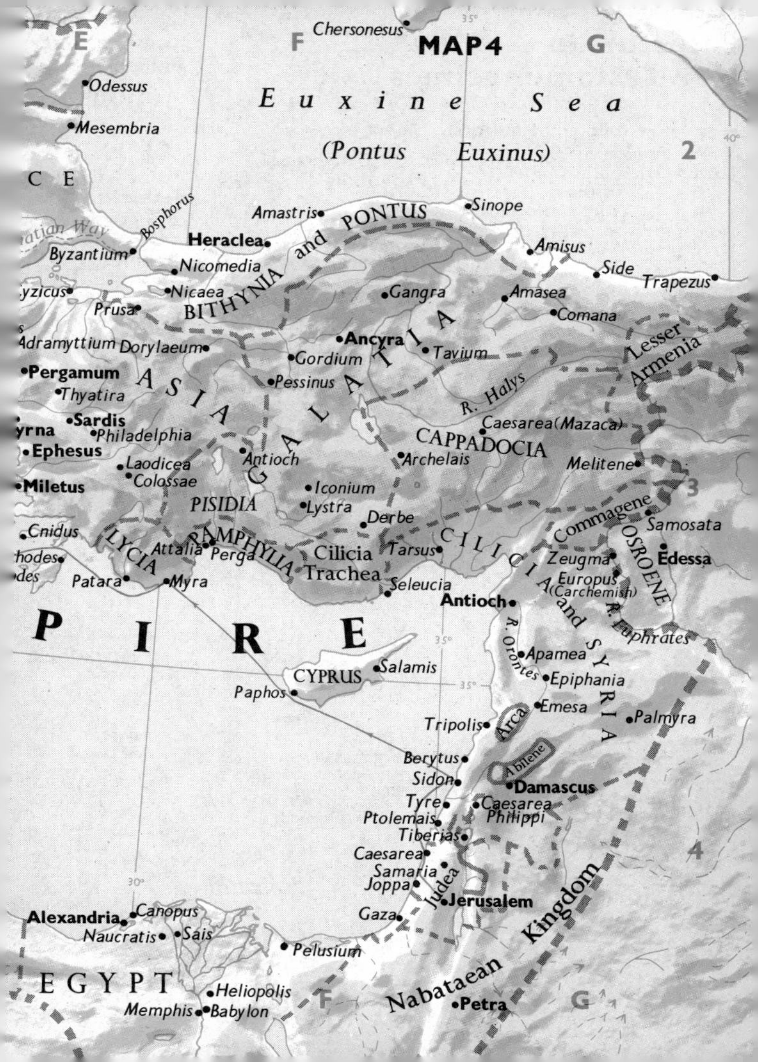
MAP 4
Euxine Sea
(Pontus Euxinus)
Chersonesus
Odessus
Mesembria
Bosphorus
Byzantium
Heraclea
Amastris
Sinope
Amisus
Side
Trapezus
Nicomedia
Nicaea
Prusa
BITHYNIA and PONTUS
Gangra
Amasea
Comana
Adramyttium
Dorylaeum
Ancyra
Tavium
Gordium
Lesser Armenia
Pergamum
Thyatira
Sardis
Philadelphia
Ephesus
Miletus
ASIA
GALATIA
Pessinus
R. Halys
Caesarea (Mazaca)
CAPPADOCIA
Archelais
Melitene
Antioch
Laodicea
Colossae
Iconium
Lystra
Derbe
PISIDIA
Commagene
Samosata
Cnidus
LYCIA
Attalia
Perga
PAMPHYLIA
Cilicia Trachea
Tarsus
CILICIA and SYRIA
OSROENE
Edessa
Zeugma
Europus (Carchemish)
Patara
Myra
Seleucia
Antioch
R. Euphrates
R. Orontes
CYPRUS
Salamis
Paphos
Apamea
Epiphania
Emesa
Arca
Tripolis
Palmyra
Berytus
Abilene
Sidon
Damascus
Tyre
Caesarea Philippi
Ptolemais
Tiberias
Caesarea
Samaria
Joppa
Judea
Jerusalem
Gaza
Alexandria
Canopus
Naucratis
Sais
Pelusium
EGYPT
Heliopolis
Memphis
Babylon
Nabataean Kingdom
Petra
E
F
G
2
3
4

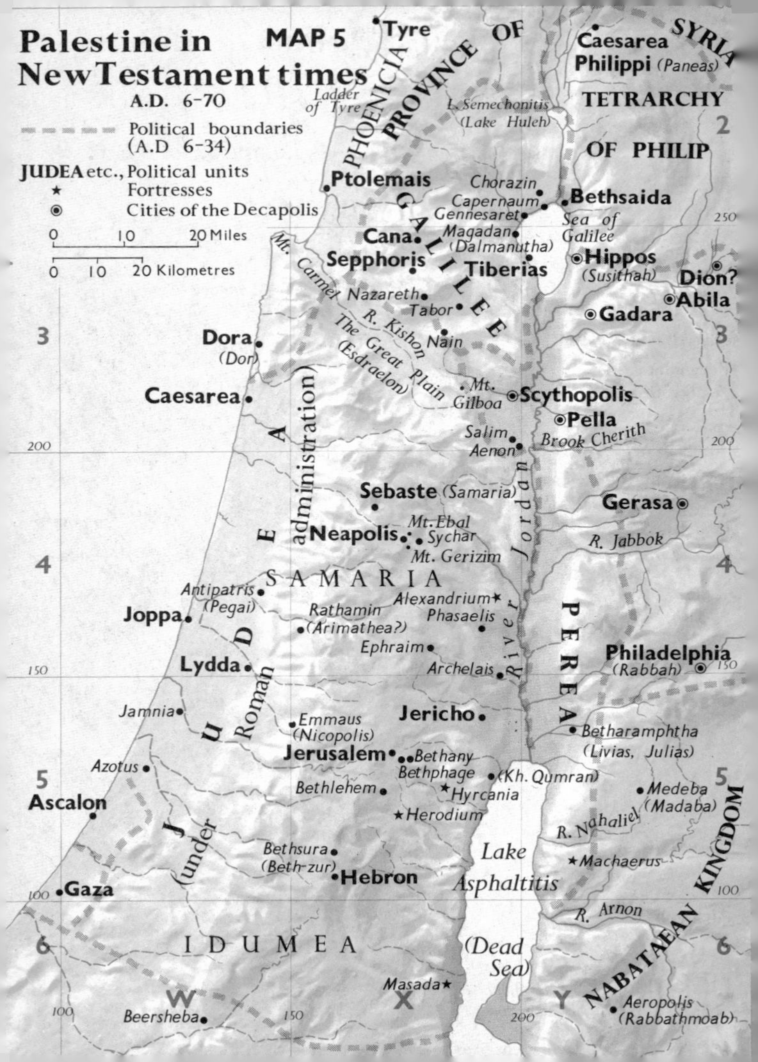
Palestine in New Testament times
MAP 5
A.D. 6-70
Political boundaries (A.D 6-34)
JUDEA etc., Political units
Fortresses
Cities of the Decapolis
0 10 20 Miles
0 10 20 Kilometres
Tyre
PHOENICIA
PROVINCE OF SYRIA
Ladder of Tyre
Caesarea Philippi (Paneas)
TETRARCHY OF PHILIP
L. Semechonitis (Lake Huleh)
Ptolemais
Chorazin
Capernaum
Bethsaida
Gennesaret
Sea of Galilee
Magadan (Dalmanutha)
Cana
Sepphoris
Tiberias
GALILEE
Hippos (Susithah)
Dion?
Abila
Gadara
Mt. Carmel
Nazareth
Tabor
R. Kishon
The Great Plain (Esdraelon)
Nain
Dora (Dor)
Caesarea
Mt. Gilboa
Scythopolis
Pella
Salim
Aenon
Brook Cherith
JUDEA (under Roman administration)
Sebaste (Samaria)
Gerasa
Neapolis
Mt. Ebal
Sychar
Mt. Gerizim
R. Jabbok
River Jordan
SAMARIA
Antipatris (Pegai)
Alexandrium
Joppa
Rathamin (Arimathea?)
Phasaelis
PEREA
Ephraim
Philadelphia (Rabbah)
Lydda
Archelais
Jamnia
Jericho
Emmaus (Nicopolis)
Betharamphtha (Livias, Julias)
Jerusalem
Bethany
Bethphage
Azotus
(Kh. Qumran)
Bethlehem
Hyrcania
Medeba (Madaba)
Ascalon
Herodium
R. Nahaliel
Lake Asphaltitis
Machaerus
Bethsura (Beth-zur)
Hebron
Gaza
R. Arnon
NABATAEAN KINGDOM
IDUMEA
(Dead Sea)
Masada
Beersheba
Aeropolis (Rabbathmoab)
W
X
Y
2
3
4
5
6
100
150
200
250